SEVENTH EDITION

ATLANTIC CRUISING CLUB

GUIDE TO

CHESAPEAKE BAY MARINAS

Powered by Datastract™

Elizabeth Adams Smith

Richard Y. Smith, Editor

Jerawyn Publishing Inc.

www.AtlanticCruisingClub.com

Atlantic Cruising Club's Guide to Chesapeake Bay Marinas

SEVENTH EDITION

ISBN 0-966-4028-5-5
ISBN 978-0-9664028-5-8
Library of Congress Catalog Number: 2003101655

Front Cover Photo by James Kirkikis
Back Cover Photos by Beth Adams Smith & Richard Y. Smith

Front Cover: Annapolis, MD
Back Cover: Rock Hall Harbor, MD; Carter Creek, VA; St. Michaels Harbor, MD; Hampton, VA

Senior Editor and Researcher — Irina Adams
Managing Editor — Ellen McEvily
Associate Editor — Alice Picon
Communications Manager — Catherine Rose
Executed Cover Designs — Jessica Williams, Spark Design
Initial Cover Design — Rob Johnson
Book Design — Spark Design
Photo Retouching — Gunshe Ramchandani, FotoCafe Studios
Cartography — Amy Rock
Research Assistant — Sarah Newgaard
Printed by Walsworth Publishing Company

Bulk purchase discounts are available to yacht clubs, rendezvous organizers, boat manufacturers and other nautical groups for any of the Atlantic Cruising Club's Guides to Marinas. Please contact Guide@AtlanticCruisingClub.com or call 888-967-0994.

Atlantic Cruising Club's Guide to Chesapeake Bay Marinas
is written, compiled, edited and published by the Atlantic Cruising Club, an imprint of:

Jerawyn Publishing Inc.
PO Box 978; Rye, New York 10580

www.AtlanticCruisingClub.com

Table of Contents

INTRODUCTION 3

GEOGRAPHIC COVERAGE — LIST OF MARINAS 15

GUIDE TO CHESAPEAKE BAY MARINAS — THE MARINA REPORTS 23

ADDENDA 299

INDEX ET AL. 319

To ensure objectivity, ACC neither solicits nor accepts marina advertising and there is absolutely no charge to marinas or boating facilities for their inclusion in the *Atlantic Cruising Club's Guides to Marinas*. ACC reviewers have personally visited every marina included in this Guide — most two or three times.

Preface

The romance of the Chesapeake is a powerful streak that runs through Richard's and my personal history. When this NY-suburban girl was taken home to meet her DC-suburban boyfriend's family — it wasn't to Washington — it was to "The Beach" — aka Scientists' Cliffs in Calvert County, MD. It was the Smith's annual Labor Day Crab Feast, and it was a water shed week-end on many levels.

It turned out that this do-not-miss event was something of an annual pilgrimage for multiple generations of Washington friends. As they took turns tutoring the neophyte in the fine art of crab-picking, I met a panorama of friends and family. More important, I met the sweet, funny 10-year-old boy in this now-worldly, impeccably educated man. The moment the engine stopped, his shoes came off. Tales and reminisces circled the late-night bonfires on the beach — biking to Parker's Creek, learning to water ski behind a 10 hp motor, searching the beach and the cliffs for coveted sharks'teeth, lazy days drifting in the boat, dangling chicken necks over the side awaiting the telltale nibble of a blue crab.

I was smitten — with this many-faceted boy-man, with his family and friends, and also with his "Bay." It must have gone well on his side, too — we were engaged a month later. In our early years, the "Beach" and the Bay became a second home. Our children became champion crab-pickers, carried their personal bottle of Adolph's for nettle stings and eschewed shoes as soon as they could smell the Bay in the air.

In later years, as we moved up to "big boats" from one-designs, the Chesapeake became a prized destination. We headed down through the C & D, stopped at Schaefer's, watched Chesapeake City literally re-invent itself, and learned that you could really swim in the less salty, nettle-free water of the Upper Bay. We also discovered the rivers of the Eastern Shore and Virginia. Our bible was William Shellenberger's "Cruising the Chesapeake," and we explored many of the anchorages and harbors in the book. One memorable night, we were all alone, snugged into a peaceful little 3-star cove far up the Wye East River's Skipton Creek — across from a small fleet of miniature black sheep munching Wye Heights' lawn. Darkness fell as we set the anchor; it was an absolutely perfect setting. But, at 0500, we were startled awake by dozens of little runabouts laying out strings of personal crab pots and trot lines. We put the coffee on, dug out our own pots, and joined the party.

We also had a little fun while researching Chesapeake marinas. One of our fondest memories was picking up a beer-box of perfectly steamed large crabs from Buck's, just up the road from Hartge's in Galesville. The day was glorious, a big race had just ended, and we were bucking the traffic as we threaded our way across the Bay to St. Michael's — all the while picking those perfect crustaceans. We left the boat in Baltimore's Anchorage Marina several times, and, with all the back and forths, we really had a chance to get to know Charm City and all her waterfront neighborhoods. And, like most boaters, we really fell in love with her neighbor to the south, Annapolis. We also learned that everyone you ever met while cruising anywhere will inevitably be at the October Annapolis Boat Shows.

We "discovered" placid Swan Creek at Rock Hall — we'd get on our bikes and head over to Waterman's deck for steamed crabs. Next stop was always St. Michaels — Higgins was also a good "leave the boat" place. Followed by charming Oxford — crab cakes at the Robert Morris Inn a must. When we recently returned to Smith and Tangier Islands, outposts of fiercely independent watermen communities, we were struck by how much had managed to stay the same — despite the incursion of commercialism on the mainland and the natives' unique take on managing the tourism market.

The Chesapeake helped us hone the basics of what we call "achievable cruising" — cruise a week or two, leave the boat, go home for a month or so, come back and keep going. A few seasons later, we took those useful skills and headed farther afield — Bermuda (from Hampton, VA with Steve Black's Cruising Rally) and ports further north and south.

On those many trips back and forth to Hampton, we had a chance to explore the Virginia shore — by land and water. We were fascinated by the mother menhaden ships and baby purse boats up Cockrell Creek, loved Reedville, tucked into sweet Onancock, and found out that the Bay can get really, really nasty in a blow. We also learned to really appreciate why the FFVs (First Families of Virginia) — and lots of regular folk — summer on "The Rivah." We toured the Rappahannock — became enamored with little, but growing, Urbanna and had a taste of true elegance docking at The Tides — right next to the 125 foot "Miss Ann."

We return often to the Bay — lately the focus has been research, research, research — and every few years we make the JCD August reunion (that's the Junior Cliff Dwellers at Scientists' Cliffs). We sit around those same bonfires that marked the beginning of our new life, share our stories, marvel at how sleepy little Solomon's morphed into one of the boating capitals of the Bay, pick crabs (of course there's a crab feast), and, as if we hadn't had enough, usually head to Stoney's on Broome Island for a golf-ball size crab cake sandwich.

Researching this book was a true gift — with every harbor was another piece of nostalgia, a funny story or a sense of home-coming. Real estate prices have sky rocketed, development is rampant — but somehow the Bay always feels the same. In a remarkable number of areas it has clung to its roots and so many people — on its shores and on its waters — are fighting to slow the change. As frequent visitors, we are always grateful for their successes.

Beth Adams Smith

Rye, New York
November 2005

ACC's Guide to Chesapeake Bay Marinas' Sixteen Sub-Regions

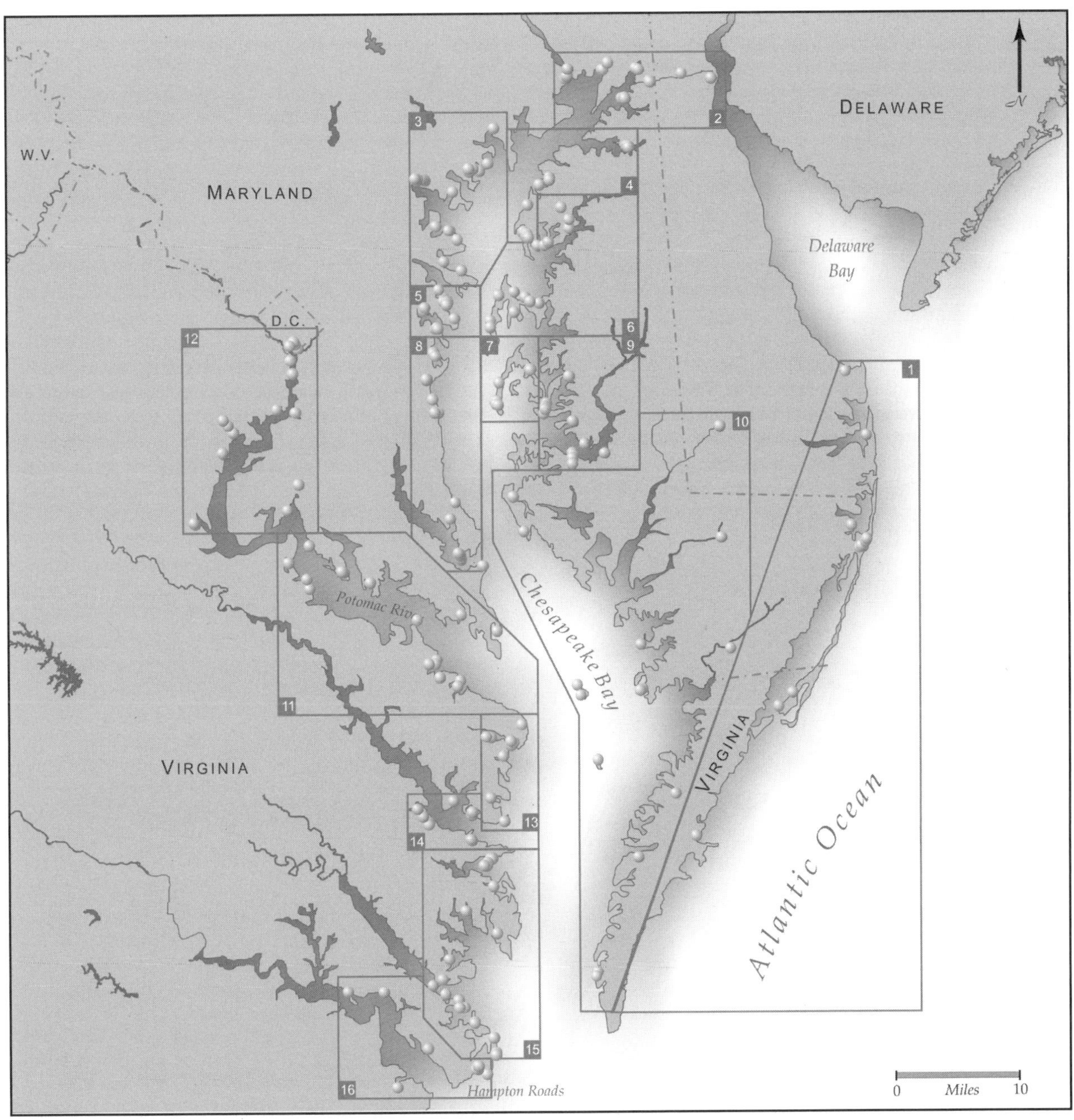

Atlantic Cruising Club's Ratings

The Bell Ratings generally reflect the services and amenities available for the captain and crew rather than the services available for the boat. By their nature, ratings are subjective and may also reflect certain biases of the writers, editors and other reviewers. It is important to note that a five-bell marina will not always be a boater's best choice. There tends to be a correlation between higher bell ratings and higher overnight transient rates. Many of the resort-type amenities available at four- and five-bell marinas may be of little interest to boaters arriving late in the day and planning an early start the next morning. Similarly, a facility which has a one- or two-bell rating, good security, convenient transportation and a service-oriented staff, may be the best place to "leave the boat" for a period of time between legs of a longer cruise.

The Boatyard Ratings, on the other hand, are less subjective. They simply indicate the extent of the boatyard services and the size of yachts that the facility can manage. To receive a boatyard rating at all (one-travelift), a facility must have a haul-out mechanism — a travelift or marine railway (or, in some cases, a heavy-duty crane or forklift) plus, at a minimum, a standard array of basic boatyard services. To receive a two-travelift rating, a facility will generally have haul-out capacity in excess of 70 tons and a full complement of all possible boatyard services. Facilities that are primarily dry-stack storage operations are not given boatyard designations.

The Sunset Rating is the most subjective rating of all. This symbol indicates remarkable places with special appeal — like a pristine, untouched mooring field with no other facilities in sight, a marina that is, itself, so exquisitely turned out that it is truly beautiful, a view from the docks of a skyline or distant vista that is simply breathtaking, above and beyond services or amenities that are more than the basic rating would suggest, or a marina that offers the possibility of a unique experience. A Sunset means that, in our view, there is more here than the first two ratings can convey — and only you can determine if the additional notation is valid for you and your crew. We'd be very interested in hearing your collective views.

The Bell Ratings

Outlined below are some of the facilities and amenities one might generally find at a marina or boating facility within a given Bell-Rating category. Please note that some marinas within a particular category may not have all of the facilities listed here and some may have more. (The word "Marina" is used generically here, and throughout the *Guide*, to denote all types of marine facilities.)

One Bell: The marina comfortably accommodates vessels over thirty feet in length, accepts overnight transients at docks or on moorings, and generally has heads. These are the "basic requirements" for ACC inclusion. Most facilities that are strictly mooring fields with a dinghy dock or basic docks with limited or no power pedestals or other services fall into this category, as do boatyards with docks.

Two Bells: In addition to meeting the basic ACC requirements, the marina generally has docks with power pedestals or a mooring field served by a launch (or a "dinghy loaner"). It has a dedicated marina staff, offers docking assistance, monitors the VHF radio, holds mail, and has an available fax machine. There are heads, showers, and, perhaps, a laundry. It likely has dock carts, a picnic area and grills.

Three Bells: With attractive and convenient facilities, the marina significantly exceeds basic requirements in many physical and operational categories. In addition to the two-bell services described above, the docks will usually have finger piers, and there will usually be a restaurant onsite or adjacent. A pool, beach, or major recreational amenity (i.e. a sport fishing center, a museum or sightseeing venue, a nature preserve, a significant "downtown") may also be nearby. The marina usually offers docking assistance and other customer-oriented services, a ships' store, cable TV, some kind of internet access, and, hopefully, a pump-out facility.

Four Bells: Worth changing course to visit, the marina significantly exceeds requirements in most physical and operational categories and offers above average service in well-appointed, appealing, and thoughtfully turned-out facilities. In addition to the three-bell services described above, it will have a restaurant onsite, as well as a pool or beach and other desirable amenities like tennis courts, sport fishing charter, or historic or scenic sites. The marina will generally offer concierge services and have a particularly inviting environment.

Five Bells: A renowned, "destination" facility, the marina is worth a special trip. It has truly superior facilities, services and atmosphere. A five-bell marina is located in a luxurious, impeccably maintained environment and provides absolutely everything a cruising boater might reasonably expect, including room service to the boat. It offers all that is promised in a four-bell marina, plus outstanding quality in every respect.

Bell ratings reflect both subjective judgment and objective criteria. The ratings are intended to reflect the overall boater experience and are significantly impacted by a marina's setting and general ambiance. An ACC bias is discovering interesting and distinctive waterfront destinations which may not have all the standard marina services, but which provide a unique experience. These may be given ratings higher than their facilities would suggest. Similarly, maritime museums, which most boaters find particularly compelling, are usually given a "Sunset" to indicate that they offer maritime buffs more than just services. Ratings are also geographically specific and reflect the general level of available services in a given region. In other words, a five-bell marina in Florida (with a year-round season) will usually offer significantly more services and facilities than a five-bell marina in Maine (with a three month season).

A Tour of a Marina Report

Photos: *One for each marina in the printed Marina Report, up to 17 in full-color on the enclosed CD-ROM and on the website. Most were taken by ACC personnel during periodic visits. They are intended to provide a non-commercial, visual sense of each facility.*

Ratings: *Bells (1 - 5) reflect the quality of onsite marina facilities plus location, recreation, dining, lodgings, etc. Travelifts (1 - 2) indicate the extent of the boatyard services. A Sunset notes a particularly beautiful, special, unique, or interesting place.*

Top Section: *Facts, facts and more facts, including VHF channels, phone numbers, e-mail/ website addresses, number of slips, moorings, power options (rates for all), and much more. The format of this section is identical for every Marina Report for easy reference and comparison.*

Bowleys Marina

3. WS - BALTIMORE REGION

Navigational Information

Lat: 39°18.150' **Long:** 076°26.200' **Tide:** 1 ft. **Current:** 1 kt. **Chart:** 12273
Rep. Depths (*MLW*): Entry 8 ft. **Fuel Dock** 8 ft. **Max Slip/Moor** 8 ft./-
Access: Chesapeake Bay to the mouth of Middle River

Marina Facilities *(In Season/Off Season)*

Fuel: Gasoline, Diesel
Slips: 505 Total, 20 Transient **Max LOA:** 60 ft. **Max Beam:** n/a
Rate *(per ft.)*: **Day** $1.75/Inq. **Week** $8 **Month** $10
Power: 30 amp $5, **50 amp** $10, **100 amp** n/a, **200 amp** n/a
Cable TV: No **Dockside Phone:** No
Dock Type: Fixed, Wood
Moorings: 0 Total, 0 Transient **Launch:** n/a, Dinghy Dock
Rate: Day n/a **Week** n/a **Month** n/a
Heads: 14 Toilet(s), 8 Shower(s) *(with dressing rooms)*
Laundry: 2 Washer(s), 2 Dryer(s), Book Exchange **Pay Phones:** Yes, 1
Pump-Out: OnSite, Full Service **Fee:** $10 **Closed Heads:** Yes

Marina Operations

Owner/Manager: Rich Yarborough **Dockmaster:** Same
In-Season: Year-Round, 8am-5pm* **Off-Season:** n/a
After-Hours Arrival: Call ahead
Reservations: Yes **Credit Cards:** Visa/MC, Amex
Discounts: None
Pets: Welcome **Handicap Access:** No

Bowleys Marina

1700 Bowleys Quarters Road; Middle River, MD 21220

Tel: (410) 335-3553 **VHF: Monitor** 9 **Talk** 9
Fax: (410) 335-5478 **Alternate Tel:** n/a
Email: mary@bowleysmarina.com **Web:** www.bowleysmarina.com
Nearest Town: Baltimore *(9 mi.)* **Tourist Info:** (410) 686-2233

Marina Services and Boat Supplies

Services - Docking Assistance, Boaters' Lounge, Security *(24 hrs., gate)*, Trash Pick-Up, Dock Carts **Communication -** FedEx, DHL, UPS, Express Mail **Supplies - OnSite:** Ice *(Block, Cube, Shaved)*, Ships' Store *(ice-cream and gifts)* **1-3 mi:** West Marine *(335-7896)*, Marine Discount Store **3+ mi:** Boat/US *(918-9344, 8 mi.)*, Bait/Tackle *(Bowleys Bait & Tackle 687-2107, 4 mi.)*, Propane *(Hodges True Value 686-1389, 7 mi.)*

Boatyard Services

OnSite: Travelift *(35T)*, Forklift, Launching Ramp, Engine mechanic *(gas, diesel)*, Bottom Cleaning, Compound, Wash & Wax **Yard Rates:** $35/hr., Haul & Launch $8-12/ft. *(blocking $150)*, Bottom Paint $9.50/ft.

Restaurants and Accommodations

OnSite: Lite Fare *(Bowley's Snack Bar L $2-6, D $2-6, hamburgers, hot dogs, pizza at the rec room - Fri 6pm-1am, Sat 9am-1am, Sun 9am-3pm)* **OnCall:** Pizzeria *(Domino's 682-5315)* **1-3 mi:** Restaurant *(Caroll Island Diner 335-2004, L $6-13, D $6-13)*, *(Bruno's Italian Quarter 344-1506)*, *(Wild Duck Café 335-2121, L $5-10, D $14-28)*, *(China Town Express 335-7800)*, *(Legendary's Classic 344-9183)*, Lite Fare *(Mama Maria's Carry-out 335-7430)* **3+ mi:** Restaurant *(The Mariner's Landing 477-1261, L $5-15, D $15-30, 6 mi.)*, Seafood Shack *(Als Seafood Restaurant 687-3264, 8 mi.)*, Motel *(Super 8 780-0030, $65-83, 7 mi.)*, *(Star Motel 687-3169, 7 mi.)*, *(Blue Star 335-6653, 9 mi.)*, *(Colony Motel 335-6577, $36-75, 6 mi.)*

Recreation and Entertainment

OnSite: Pool, Picnic Area, Grills, Playground *(and horseshoes)*, Volleyball

Near: Park **1-3 mi:** Fitness Center *(Middle River Gym 682-4044)*, Video Rental *(Blockbuster 335-2807)* **3+ mi:** Golf Course *(Rocky Point 887-4653, 11 mi.)*, Bowling *(AMF Bowling Centers 686-2556, 8 mi.)*, Museum *(Glenn L Martin Aviation Museum 682-6122, 11am-3pm Wed-Sat, Free, 6 mi.)*

Provisioning and General Services

Under 1 mi: Green Grocer *(Howell's Blue Farm)* **1-3 mi:** Convenience Store *(uner 1 mi: Green Grocer, Howell's Blue Farm/1-3 mi: 7-Eleven 335-7932; Royal Farm 335-7567)*, Supermarket *(Safeway 335-3668)*, Wine/Beer, Liquor Store *(Island Spirits 335-7200)*, Fishmonger *(Carolina Gardens 335-7775)*, Bank/ATM, Post Office, Catholic Church, Protestant Church, Beauty Salon, Dry Cleaners *(Magic Professional 1 hr. 335-3232)*, Laundry *(Sudsville 433-9620)*, Pharmacy *(Rite Aid 335-2323)*, Florist, Department Store *(Wal-Mart 335-5669)* **3+ mi:** Hardware Store *(Carroll Island 335-5434, 6 mi.)*, Copies Etc. *(Cogar Printing 391-8888, 6 mi.)*

Transportation

OnCall: Rental Car *(Enterprise 931-7455; Alamo 661-6900, 3 mi.)*, Taxi *(Reliable Sedan 686-2180)*, Airport Limo *(Baltimore Limo 335-1160)*
Airport: Baltimore/Washington International *(20 mi.)*

Medical Services

911 Service **OnCall:** Ambulance **1-3 mi:** Doctor **3+ mi:** Dentist *(Hepner 335-9661, 6 mi.)*, Chiropractor *(Eastern Chiropractic 686-1117, 6 mi.)*, Veterinarian *(Essex Dog & Cat Hospital 687-1111, 6.5 mi.)* **Hospital:** Franklin Square 443-777-7000 *(9 mi.)*

Setting -- Just inside the mouth of Middle River, Bowley's is a destination family resort marina and a self-contained kids' paradise. The recreational facilities surround a renovated 1887 two-story manor house once home to Baltimore sea-captain Daniel Bowley . Trees punctuate the grassy expanses and willows weep over the bulkhead. Gazebos and benches are scattered about; picnic areas poke out over the bulkhead. An extensive network of docks hosts over 500 vessels, protected from wakes and the Bay by a wave fence. Signature blue & white striped awnings annotate the buildings and step up the atmosphere.

Marina Notes -- *Nov-Mar, Sat & Sun 10am-3pm. MCM. Service oriented staff: just ask - if it can be done it will be. Member-owned slips are managed by Coastal Properties (transient fees are shared with owners). Private club atmosphere. Five main piers flanked by slips: the two end piers with slips on one side, all renovated with new power pedestals courtesy of Isabel. The fuel dock is at the end of "D" dock. The small ships' store also has T-shirts and ice cream. Lovely climate controlled bathhouses have tiled floors, fiberglass shower stalls with glass doors & dressing rooms; sinks set in well-lighted Corian vanities.

Notable -- As close as it is to the bay, that's how far it is from everything on land. Come fully provisioned to kick back and enjoy the resort - that is how it was designed. There's lots to do right here and there's really no place to walk or ride your bike. There's a big pool with a cement surround and lots of chaises on the grass patio, plus volleyball, horseshoes, playground, picnic-tables, grills, a clubhouse and covered pavilions. The big rec hall has a bar that serves hot dogs, hamburgers and pizza -- kids welcome -- karaoke twice a month. Club or group cruises are graciously accommodated.

PHOTOS ON CD-ROM:

MIDDLE RIVER | 59

Marina Name: *253 marinas and marine facilities are included in the Chesapeake Bay volume.*

Sub-Regions: *The Chesapeake Bay volume includes 16 sub-regions. For quick reference, these sub-region tabs are visible on the outside page edges. In each sub-region, Marina Reports are ordered North to South.*

Middle Section: *What's available, where and how to find it. Marine Services & Boat Supplies, Boatyard Services (including rates), Restaurants and Accommodations, Recreation and Entertainment, Provisioning and General Services, Transportation and Medical Services, all classified by distance — OnSite, Nearby, Within 1 mile, 1-3 miles or beyond. Names, phone numbers, price ranges and more.*

Photos on CD: *Indicates the number of full-color photos of this facility that are on the CD-ROM.*

Bottom Section: The *"Setting" commentary portrays a sense of the marina's surroundings and location. "Marina Notes" provides important and interesting facts about the marina and its operations that may not have been covered in either of the earlier sections. "Notable" addresses anything the writers/reviewers feel is noteworthy about this facility, from special events or services to interesting side trips and/or local lore.*

Harbor: *Harbor or major body of water on which the marina resides.*

The Marina Reports

In the book, individual Marina Reports are presented in a one page, easy-reference format to make the Guide as user-friendly as possible. On the CD-ROM, as well as on the website, second and third pages contain up to sixteen additional full-color photos.

Each Report provides over 300 items of information, grouped into the following sections and categories:

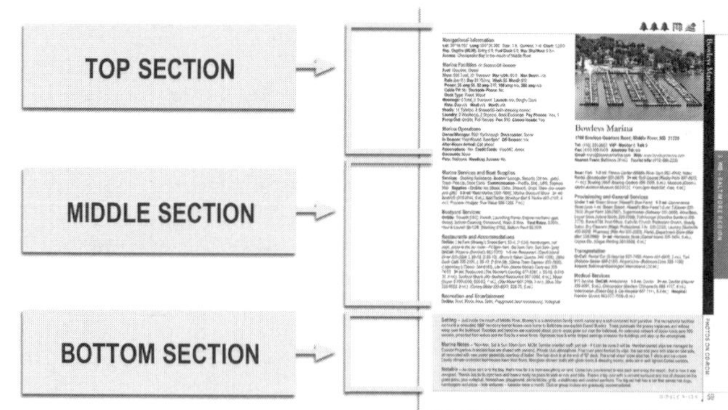

TOP SECTION

Name
Address

Primary & Toll-Free Phone numbers
Alternate Phone — after-hours
Fax number

VHF channels — Talk & Monitor
E-mail address
Web URL

Nearest Town (distance)
Tourist Office Phone

Navigational Information

Harbor (*bottom of page*)
Latitude/Longitude

Tidal Range & Maximum Current
Chart Number

Access — General Directions
MLW Depths *(Reported by the marinas)*

Entry & Fuel Dock Depths
Deepest Slip/Mooring

Marina Facilities (In Season/Off Season)

Fuel: Availability and Brand
- Diesel or Gasoline
- Slip-Side or OnCall Fueling
- High-Speed Pumps

Maximum Boat LOA & Beam
Slips: Number of Total/Transient
- Rates: Daily, Weekly, Monthly

Power (Availability & Rates):
- 30amp, 50 amp, 100 amp, 200 amp
- Cable TV: Availability, Terms, Rates
- Dockside Phone: Terms, Rates

Dock Type
- Fixed or Floating
- Alongside
- Short or Long Fingers, Pilings

Dock Material
- Wood, Concrete, Vinyl,
- Aluminum or Composite

Moorings: Total/Transient
- Rates: Daily, Weekly, Monthly
- Launch Service — Terms and Fees
- Dinghy Dock — Terms and Fees

Heads:
- Number of Toilets
- Number of Showers
- Dressing Rooms
- Hair Dryers & Other Amenities

Laundry:
- Number of Washers & Dryers
- Irons and Ironing Boards
- Book Exchange
- Pay Phones

Services to Anchored Boats

Pump-out Availability & Fees
- OnSite or OnCall
- Full Service or Self Service
- Number of Central Stations
- Number of Portable Stations
- In-Slip Dedicated Units
- Pump-Out Boats

Closed Head Requirements

The number of transient slips or moorings does not necessarily mean dedicated transient slips or moorings. Many facilities rent open slips and moorings to transient cruisers when their seasonal tenants are not in port. The number of Transient Slips/Moorings indicated is the facility's guesstimate, based on past experience, of the number generally available at any given time. In-Season and Off-Season rates are listed as $2.50/1.75. The parameters of those seasons are outlined in "Marina Operations" — Dates and Hours. If rates are complicated, which is becoming the norm, then the daily rate for a 40-foot boat is selected, followed by an asterisk, and a complete explanation of the rate structure is given in the "Marina Notes" section. The availability of 300 amp, European Voltage and 3-Phase is listed under "Marina Services and Boat Supplies." If there is alongside dockage, rather than individual slips, then the total number of alongside feet is divided by an average boat length of 40 feet and that number is displayed next to the Total/Transient Slips heading — followed by another asterisk. Dock Type is then listed as "Alongside" and the specifics are explained in "Marina Notes." The lack of finger piers — long or short — may signal a "Stern-To, Med-Mooring" approach. Since this can be a critical factor in choosing a marina, this will be highlighted in "Marina Notes." Since Book Exchanges or Lending Libraries, along with Pay Phones, are traditionally in the laundry room, these are itemized in the Laundry section. If there is Launch Service, the hours are usually included in Marina Notes, too.

A discussion of Designated Clean Marinas, Pump-Out Facilities and the current Federal and State Regulations pertaining to Delaware, Maryland and Virginia can be found in the Addendum on pages 307 – 309.

Marina Operations

Marina Owner/Manager
Harbormaster
Dockmaster
Dates & Hours of Operation

After Hours Arrival Procedure
Reservation Policies
Pets: Welcome?
Dog Walk Area, Kennel

Discount Programs
- Boat-US, Nautical Miles, Safe/Sea
- Dockage Fuel & Repair Discounts

Handicap Accessibility

Credit Cards Accepted:
- Visa, MasterCard, Discover,
- Diners Club, American Express

For municipal facilities the Harbormaster is listed under "Marina Owner/Manager" with the designation "(Harbormaster)" following his/her name. Dates and Hours for both in-season and off-season are provided and indicate the requisite time frames for the In-season and Off-season rates. In-season precedes off-season, separated by a (/) slash.

MIDDLE SECTION

Most of the information in this section is classified by "Proximity" — the distance from the marina to the service or facility, as follows:

OnSite — at the marina
OnCall — pick-up, delivery or slipside service
Nearby — up to approximately 4/10 of a mile — a very easy walking distance
Within 1 mile — a reasonable, though more strenuous, walking distance
1 – 3 miles — a comfortable biking distance, a major hike or a cab ride
3+ miles — a taxi, courtesy car or rental car distance — generally included is the approximate distance from the marina

(FYI: In this section, telephone area codes are included only if they are different from the area codes in the marina's contact information.)

Marina Services and Boat Supplies

General Services:
Docking Assistance
Dock Carts
Trash Pick-up
Security — Type & Hours
Concierge Services
Room Service to the Boat

Megayacht Facilities:
Additional Power Options:
300 Amps
Three-Phase
European Voltage
Crew Lounge

Communications:
Mail and Package Hold
Courier Services
FedEx. Airborne, UPS
Express Mail, Saturday Delivery
Phone Messages
Fax In and Out — Fees
Internet Access/Data Ports
Type, Location & Fees

Supplies: (Listed by Proximity)
Ice — Block, Cubes, Shaved
Ships' Stores — Local Chandlery
West Marine, Boat-U.S.,
Boaters World,
Other Marine Discount Stores
Bait & Tackle
Live Bait
Propane & CNG

Under Services are additional power options beyond the basic amperage covered in the "Marina Facilities" section. Communications covers Internet access, specifying the presence of Wi-Fi as well as the locations of broadband or dial-up dataports — plus the fees. Additional information is in "Marina Notes." (A discussion of Wi-Fi systems can be found on page 306 in the Addendum.) Communications also lists couriers that service the marina's area; this does not imply that the marina will manage the process (unless concierge services are offered). Assume that dealing with couriers will be up to the individual boater. The notation Megayacht Facilities means a marina accommodates at least 100 feet LOA with 100 or higher amperage service. Listed here, too, are additional power options, beyond the 30, 50, 100 & 200 amp services covered in the "Marina Facilities" section. Under Supplies are, among many other items, resources for galley fuel. As those who rely on CNG know, it is becoming harder and harder to find. (Please share any sources you discover with your fellow boaters.) Note, too, that West Marine now owns the Boat/US stores, but continues to operate them under the Boat/US name — so they are listed separately.

Boatyard Services

Nearest Boatyard (If not onsite):
Travelift (including tonnage)
Railway
Forklift
Crane
Hydraulic Trailer
Launching Ramp
Engine Mechanics — Gas & Diesel
Electrical Repairs
Electronic Sales
Electronic Repairs
Propeller Repairs

Air Conditioning
Refrigeration
Rigger
Sail Loft
Canvas Work
Upholstery
Yacht Interiors
Brightwork
Painting
Awlgrip (or similar finish)
Woodworking
Hull repairs

Metal Fabrication
Divers
Bottom Cleaning
Compound, Wash & Wax
Inflatable Repairs
Life Raft Service
Interior Cleaning
Yacht Design
Yacht Building
Total Refits
Yacht Broker
Dealer For: (Boats, Engines, Parts)

Yard Rates:
General Hourly Rate
Haul & Launch (Blocking included)
Power Wash
Bottom Paint (Paint included?)
Boat Storage Rates:
On Land (Inside/Outside)
In the Water
Memberships & Certifications:
ABBRA — No. of Cert. Techs.
ABYC — No. of Cert. Techs.
Other Certifications

If the facility does not have a boatyard onsite, then the name and telephone number of the nearest boatyard is provided. In most cases, the services listed as "Nearby" or "Within 1 mile" will be found at that facility. "Dealer For" lists the manufacturers that the Boatyard services and its Authorized Dealerships. "Memberships and Certifications" refers to the two maritime trade organizations (ABBRA — American Boat Builders & Repairers Association & ABYC — American Boat and Yacht Council) which have programs that train and certify boatyard craftspeople and technicians. Several of the other professional maritime organizations and many manufacturers also offer rigorous training and certification on their particular product lines. These are included under "Other Certifications." A brief description of ABBRA and ABYC, and their certification programs, as well as the other major marine industry organizations is provided in the Addenda section on page 310.

Restaurants and Accommodations

Restaurants
Seafood Shacks
Raw Bars

Snack Bars
Coffee Shops
Lite Fare

Fast Food
Pizzeria
Hotels

Motels
Inns/B&Bs
Cottages/Condos

Since food is a major component of cruising, considerable attention has been given to both restaurants and provisioning resources. Eateries of all kinds are included (with phone numbers); full-service restaurants are listed simply as Restaurants. If delivery is available it is either noted or the establishment is listed as "OnCall." An attempt has been made to provide a variety of dining options and, whenever possible, to include the meals served Breakfast, Lunch, Dinner, Sunday Brunch (B, L, and/or D) plus the price range for entrées at each meal. If the menu is Prix Fixe (table d'hôte or one-price for 3-4 courses), this is indicated in the commentary. On rare occasion, if a restaurant has received very high marks from a variety of reviewers, that will be noted, too. If we are aware of a children's menu, the listing will indicate "Kids' Menu." Often the hours of onsite restaurants are included in "Marina Notes" or "Notable."

Price ranges have been gathered from menus, websites, site visits, marina notes and phone calls. Although these change over time, the range should give you an idea of the general price point. In large cities, the list generally consists of a handful of the closest restaurants — we expect that you will supplement this with a local restaurant guide. In small towns, the list provided may be "exhaustive" — these may be all there are and they may not be close.

Frequently, the need for local off-boat overnight accommodations arises — either for guests, crew changes, or just because it's time for a real shower or a few more amenities or a bed that doesn't rock. We have attempted to list a variety of local lodgings and, whenever possible, have included the room rate, too. The rates listed generally cover a 12-month range. So, if you are cruising in high season, expect the high end of the range. If the lodgings are part of the marina, then there is often a "package deal" of some sort for marina guests wishing to come ashore. We have asked the question about "package deals" and included the answers in "Marina Notes."

Recreation and Entertainment

Pools (heated or not)
Beach
Picnic Areas & Grills
Children's Playground
Dive Shop
Volleyball

Tennis Courts
Golf Course
Fitness Center
Jogging Paths
Horseback Riding
Roller Blade & Bicycle Paths

Bowling
Sport Fishing Charter
Group Fishing Boat
Movie Theater
Video Rentals
Video Arcade

Park
Museum
Galleries
Cultural Attractions
Sightseeing
Special Events

What there is to do, once you're tied up and cleaned up, is often a driving force in choosing a harbor or a particular marina. If you are choosing a facility to spend a lay-day or escape foul weather, the potential land-based activities become even more important. We have created a list of the possible major types of recreation and entertainment activities and have organized them, again, by proximity; if they are more easily reached by dinghy we note that, too.

A public golf course is almost always listed unless it is farther than 25 miles. Boat Rentals include kayaks, canoes and small sailboats. Group Fishing Boats are sometimes known as "head boats." Museums cover the gamut from art and maritime to historic houses and districts to anthropological and environmental. Cultural Attractions can range from local craft ateliers to aquaria to live theaters to all manner of musical concerts. Sightseeing can range from whale watching to historical walking tours. Special Events usually covers the major once-a-year local tourist extravaganzas — and almost all require significant advance planning (often these also appear in the "Notable" section). Galleries, both fine art and crafts, are listed under Entertainment rather than General Services since we view them more as opportunities for enlightenment than the shops that they really are. Admission prices are provided for both Adults and Children, when available, and are listed with the Adult price first, followed by the Children's price, i.e. $15/7. Occasionally, there is a family package price, which is also listed. Most entertainment and recreation facilities also offer Student and Senior Citizen pricing and other discounts; unfortunately, we don't have space to note them, but we do provide a phone number, so call and ask.

Provisioning and General Services

Complete Provisioning Service
Convenience Store
Supermarket — usually major chain
Market — smaller, local store
Gourmet Shop
Delicatessen
Health Food Store
Wine/Beer Purveyor
Liquor/Package Store

Bakery
Farmers' Markets
Green Grocer
Fishmonger
Lobster Pound
Meat Market
Bank/ATMs
Post Office
Library

Houses Of Worship
- Catholic Church
- Protestant Church
- Synagogue
- Mosque

Beauty Salon
Barber Shop
Dry Cleaners
Laundry

Bookstore
Pharmacy
Newsstand
Hardware Store
Florist
Retail Shops
Department Store
Copy Shops
Buying Club

As noted previously, we think that most boaters travel on their stomachs, so knowing how to find local provisioning resources is very important. In addition, there is a fairly constant need for all kinds of services and supplies. When delivery is available for any of the provisioning resources or services, we've either noted that in the commentary or listed it as "OnCall."

For major provisioning runs, we have tried to identify the closest outlet for a regional supermarket chain. If a smaller, but fairly well supplied, market is close by, we include it as well as the more distant chain supermarket. Most people, we've discovered, really prefer to find interesting, local purveyors, so the presence of a Farmers' Market is notable. Usually these are a one or two-day-a-week events, so the exact days, times and locations are included. To differentiate Farmers' Markets from produce markets and farm stands, the latter are listed as Green Grocers. We've also tried to locate full Provisioning Services that will "do it all" and deliver dockside. And Fishmonger is just another name for fish sellers — these could be regular fish markets or directly "off-the-boat."

In the "General Services" category, we've included the nearest libraries because they can be wonderful sources of all kinds of "local knowledge," and can provide a welcome port on a foul weather day. They also usually have children's programs during the "season" and, with growing frequency, offer data ports or public Internet access on their own PCs. The Laundry in this section should not to be confused with the washers and dryers at the marina. Laundries are usually combination "do it for you" drop-off and self-service operations — and are frequently near restaurants or recreation or entertainment venues.

Transportation

Courtesy Car or Van
Bikes
Water Taxi

Rental Car — Local and Nat'l
Taxi
Local Bus

Intercity Bus
Rail — Amtrak & Commuter
Ferry Service

Airport Limo
Airport — Regional & Nat'l

Once most cruisers hit land, they are on foot (except for those fortunate souls with sufficient on-board storage to travel with folding bikes). So transportation, in all its guises, becomes a very important consideration. We've divided transportation into two categories — getting around while in port and the longer-range issue of getting to and from the boat. If the marina or boatyard provides some form of courtesy car or van service, it's noted first. These services can include unlimited use of a car (very rare), scheduled use of a car (often 2 hours), an on-demand "chauffeured" van service, a scheduled van service, or a marina manager or employee willing to drive you to "town" at a mutually convenient time. The guests' use of this service is sometimes completely unrestricted; other times, it is reserved exclusively for provisioning or restaurant trips. If the details of this arrangement are simple, they are explained in the commentary; if complicated, they are explained in the "Marina Notes." Courtesy cars and/or vans are one of the most volatile of the marina services so, if this is important to you, call ahead to confirm that it's still available and to ask about the terms.

The Airport Limo services are either individual car services or vans. Rail covers Amtrak as well as commuter services that connect to a city, an Amtrak stop, or an airport. Local Buses also include the seasonal Trolleys that are becoming more common (and extraordinarily useful) in more tourist-oriented ports. Local, regional and inter-city ferry services are listed. Rates, when included, are usually for both Adults and Children, and indicate if one-way or round-trip; they are listed with the Adult price first, followed by the Children's price, i.e. $25/17RT. Note that there are usually Senior Citizen and Student prices but space has precluded their inclusion. Don't forget to ask.

For those of us cruising the coast less than full time, the logistics of going back and forth to the boat is often the stuff of nightmares. Rental cars have a variety of uses — local touring or long distance (back to where you left your car, to the airport or back home). We list local rental car agencies (for day rents), and regional ones (like Enterprise). We tend not to list the national ones (where pick-up and drop-off may be restricted to airports or downtown locations) because these are obvious and often very difficult to get to. Because Enterprise delivers and picks up — remembering that you have to return the driver to his/her office — we always include the nearest Enterprise office, if one exists, as "OnCall." (If another agency advertises pick-up/delivery, that information is included as "OnCall", too).

Note that some franchise auto rentals, because the outlets are locally or regionally owned, seem to have a wide range of "drop-off" policies. Sometimes, if the region is large enough, it is possible to pick the car up at the current marina and drive to the marina where you left your own car, and leave the rental right there. When available, this service is just great. Call and check. The Airport listing often includes both the nearest regional and the nearest international. Because, as noted, long-distance, one-way car rentals are often based at airport locations, a marina's distance from an airport takes on a larger meaning than just catching a plane.

Medical Services

911 Service	Dentist	Holistic Service	Ambulance	Optician
Doctor	Chiropractor	Veterinarian	Hospital	

The data in this section is provided for informational purposes only and does not imply any recommendation. ACC is simply listing the nearest practitioner in each category. The first listing is the availability of 911 service; this service is surprisingly not ubiquitous — so it is important to know if dialing 911 will "work" in a given area. In the listings for Doctors, preference is given to walk-in clinics, then group practices and then general practitioners or internists. Dentists, Chiropractors, Veterinarians, and Holistic Services are also chosen in a similar fashion. A single practitioner is listed only if a "group" is not nearby. Holistic services will generally list massage therapists, but may also include acupuncturists, energy healers, and yoga classes when we find them. Hospital is usually the nearest major facility; if this is very far away and we are aware of a satellite, that will be noted — especially if there are no physicians nearby.

BOTTOM SECTION

Setting

This section provides a description of the location, environment and ambiance of each marina, boatyard or mooring field, including its views both landside and waterside, and any easily identifiable landmarks.

Marina Notes

Marina-specific information not included in the middle and top sections is detailed here. The source for this data includes interviews with marina staff, marina literature, marina comments provided to ACC, and surveyor/reviewer observations during site visits. If the rate structure is too complicated to detail in the "Facilities" section, a thorough explanation will be included here, preceded by an asterisk. Anything that is noteworthy or interesting about the facility is described in this paragraph. This includes history, background, recent changes, damage, renovations, new facilities, new management, comments on heads and showers (if they are, for instance, below par for the rating or particularly nice) and general marina atmosphere. If there is a restaurant or some form of lodging on-site, it is noted here, including any special deals for marina guests. If the marine services are part of a resort or a private yacht club with extensive recreation facilities, the level of access to those facilities is also detailed here or in "Notable." The facilities and services available to the visiting cruiser are also reflected in the rating. Designated Clean Marinas are indicated by DCM (see pages 307 – 309 for a complete explanation).

Notable

This section focuses on what is special or unique about this facility — additional items of interest related to the marina itself or the surrounding area. Details on special events, nearby attractions, the local community, ways of "getting around", the best beaches, special things to do, or other noteworthy facilities and/or services are listed here. Occasionally, there's also an elaboration on the onsite or nearby restaurants, amenities or accommodations. Or, perhaps this marina is near an airport, in a secure basin, the owner lives onsite, or the rates are low — any or all of which might make this a good place to leave the boat for while.

For a complete explanation of the Data Gathering and Review Process, please see page 322.

The Atlantic Cruising Club Website and Boaters' Comments

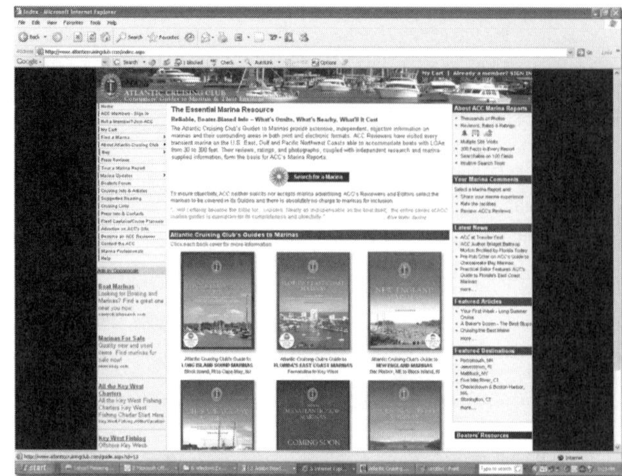

Marina Search — Find A Marina: The ACC WebSite houses the complete 2,000 marina database which underlies the *Atlantic Cruising Club's* regional *Guides to Marinas*. There are two ways for boaters to use the website to find the *right* marina:

- **The Map/Chart or Geographic Interface —** Beginning with a map of North America, a boater can "drill down" through increasingly more detailed maps — 1. Choose a specific region; 2. Choose a specific geographic area; then 3. Choose a marina. It's all point & click simple. Pass the cursor over the numbered button and the marina name appears; click and the complete full-color Marina Report is displayed — with up to 17 photos.
- **The Marina Search Screen Interface —** The same tabbed Marina Search screen that's on the CD-ROM is also on the WebSite. Select up to 100 different search criteria – either singly or in any combination – and the program will display all the marinas that meet those criteria. Or simply choose a harbor to see all the facilities located there; or just type in the name of a marina. The complete full-color Marina Report — with all of its photos — will display.

Boaters' Comments – A new section has been added to each on-line Marina Report allowing boaters to share their experiences. At the top of each on-line Marina Report are the words "Add a Comment/Read Others' Comments." Please share your experiences.

Please Rate the Following on a Scale of 1 (basic) to 5 (world class)

- **Facilities & Services** (Fuel, Reservations, Concierge Services and General Helpfulness):
- **Amenities** (Pool, Beach, Internet Access, including Wi-Fi, Picnic/Grill area, Boaters' Lounge):
- **Setting** (Views, Design, Landscaping, Maintenance, Ship-Shapeness, Overall Ambiance):
- **Convenience** (Access (including delivery services) to Supermarkets, other provisioning sources, Shops, Services. Attractions, Entertainment, Sightseeing, Recreation, including Golf and Sport Fishing & Medical Services):
- **Restaurants/Eateries/Lodgings** (Availability of Fine Dining, Snack Bars, Lite Fare, On Call food service, and Lodgings ashore):
- **Transportation** (Courtesy Car/Vans, Buses, Water Taxis, Bikes, Taxis, Rental Cars, Airports, Amtrak, Commuter Trains):
- **Please Add Any Additional comments** *(such as ... "Good place to leave the boat unattended for a week/month." "Accommodates catamarans with no up-charge." "Snug spot in a storm." "Excellent fuel prices." "Caters to Sport fish/sailboats/trawlers, etc." "Boats over 50 ft. LOA/beam may find tight maneuvering" "Many Liveaboards", "Megayacht haven" "Hurricane damage still not repaired." "Terrific spot for kids." "Excellent mechanics/electricians/carpenters/varnishers" "Watch out for alligators.")*

Marina Updates: The Reports in the *Atlantic Cruising Club's Guide to Chesapeak Bay Marinas – Book & CD-ROM* are current when published, but marinas are in a fairly constant state of evolution. ACC updates the Marina Reports as facts change, as new information is received from the facilities, or as new site visits by ACC Reviewers provide added insights. These updates are posted on the ACC Website. Reports for new marinas are posted after data has been gathered and confirmed.

Boaters' Forum: This serves as an information exchange among Atlantic Cruising Club members. Topics range from cruising and boating experiences to queries to the ACC membership for opinions on a host of water-related topics.

Cruising Info and Articles: ACC writers and reviewers share their experiences in articles on destinations, harbors, cruise itineraries, vacations for boaters (on and off boats), provisioning, cruising lifestyles, etc.

Suggested Reading: For every region, there is an extensive reference list of books that cruisers might find interesting. This is an expanded version of the Suggested Reading section in this *Guide* – with photos of the covers, pricing, and direct links for purchases. Additional recommendations are always welcome.

Cruising Links: These are hot URLs to resources on the web that ACC Reviewers, Writers and Editors have found particularly useful. Recommendations are welcome.

Fleet Captains/Cruise Planners: A discussion board just for those planning group events, along with articles and cruise suggestions.

The Digital Guide on CD-ROM

The enclosed CD-ROM contains the *Atlantic Cruising Club's Digital Guide to Chesapeake Bay Marinas*; it includes all of the data and Marina Reports that are in this print version, but in full color, with more than 2900 color photographs, all searchable on over 100 datafields.

- **Installation**
  Simply insert the enclosed CD-ROM into the CD drive of your computer. The installation program starts automatically. If it doesn't, click Start/ Run and enter "d:\setup.exe" (assuming "d:" is the address of your computer's CD drive). During the installation process, you are asked to choose which of the three ACC Digital Guide components you wish to copy to your hard drive — this affects the amount hard disk space the program uses: Program (2.5 mb), Database (55 mb), and Photos file (650 mb). If you have the hard disk capacity, it is best to install all three components. The program will run somewhat faster, and you will not need to have the CD always at hand.

- **The Digital Guide is built around four screens:**

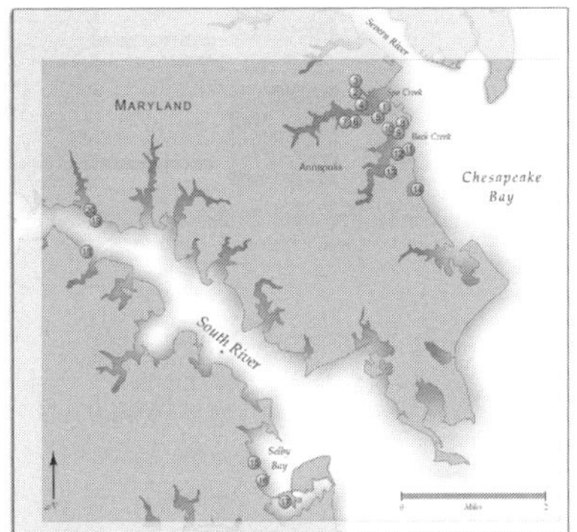

Region and Sub-Region Charts — Click on the "Charts" button to view a chart of the Chesapeake Bay Region with each of the 16 sub-regions outlined. Click on one of the outlines to access the chart for that particular Sub-Region. The locations of each of the marinas in that geographic area are displayed on the map. The location "points" and the marina names are "hot." Click on them to display the Marina Report for that marina. If you would prefer to add additional criteria to a marina search (or to skip the graphics interface entirely) the "search" button on the Chesapeake Bay Regional chart screen and on each of the Sub-Region chart screens, takes you directly to the Marina Search screen.

Marina Search Settings — This screen permits the user to enter up to 100 different search criteria — either singly or in combination. You may search for a particular marina by name (or part of name), for all of the marinas in a particular geographic region, city, or body of water, for marinas able to accommodate your vessel's LOA and draft, etc., etc., etc. If you arrived at this screen from one of the Sub-Region charts, then that Sub-Region is already entered in the "Location Search" box. You may add more sub-regions using the "Select Sub-Region" button. Once you have set the criteria for your search, click the "Find Marinas" button at the bottom of the screen (or the "Find" button in the toolbar). The search result (the number of marinas meeting your criteria) is indicated in the "Marinas Found" field. At this point, either refine your search to generate more or fewer marina choices or click the "Show Marinas" button to proceed to the next screen.

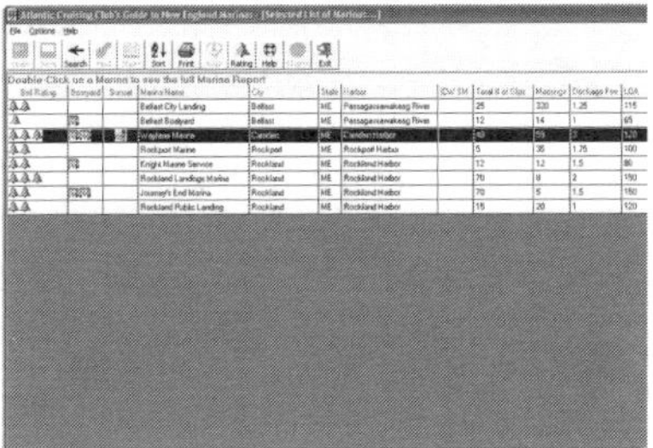

List of Selected Marinas — All of the marinas that meet your criteria are displayed on this screen. Next to each Marina Name are several items of information, including: bell, boatyard, and sunset ratings, city, state, and harbor. If, during the search, you set a criterion for "Slips," "Moorings," "LOA" or "Dockage Fee," a column for each selection also appears in the "List of Selected Marinas." The List may be sorted either geographically (default) or alphabetically. To view a full Marina Report for any of the marinas on the List, simply double-click on its name.

Marina Report — The Marina Reports in *ACC's Digital Guide* are identical to the Marina Reports in this printed version of the *Guide* but with some enhancements: The Reports are in color and each contains from 6 to 16 additional full-color marina photos. The Marina Reports Screen also lists the names of the other marinas that met your most recent search criteria. Clicking on one of those marina names displays its Marina Report. Finally, there is a box in the lower left hand corner of the Marina Report for you to enter your comments and observations about a given marina. This data is stored within the program and becomes part of the record for that marina. You can also print Marina Reports (and your comments, if you wish) using the Print command.

Note: ***For proper operation of the digital Guide, Internet Explorer 6.0 (or higher) must be installed on your computer. Each regional volume of the ACC Guides will automatically install into a separate, clearly labeled folder. They will operate independently.***

Acknowledgments

The author, editors and publishers would like to express their deep appreciation to a number of people who have contributed to the compilation and production of past and present editions of the Atlantic Cruising Club's Guides to Marinas:

Senior Editor: Irina Adams for her tenacity and impeccable research and editorial skills. **Managing Editor:** Ellen McEvily for her superb graphic sense and oversight of this complex process. **Associate Editor:** Alice Picon for her early initiatives in structuring the Chesapeake Guide. **Communications Manager:** Catherine Rose, for her dogged insistence on "getting it right." **Book & Page Design, Cover Execution, Back Cover Design & Execution:** Jessica Williams & Rupert Edson at Spark Design for an elegant volume and CD-ROM that has stood the test of many volumes; they were truly the midwives of the 7th Edition. **Icon Design:** Jennifer Grassmeyer for the pitch perfect new icons. **Maps:** Cartographer Amy Rock for her technical skills and graphic interpretations of the GPS data. **Research:** Next Meridian for locating and mapping all the "what's nearby" and Sarah Newgaard for following up with enthusiasm, commitment and excellent technical skills. **Photo Retouching:** Gunshe Ramchandani at FotoCafe Studios for 253 crisp B&W images and 2,500 sharp and colorful CD-ROM and Web images. **Transcriptions:** Nikki Weir for her perfect translations of onsite dictations. **Proofreading:** Claudia Volkman for being our last line of defense.

And our very special thanks to:

Rick and Mary Ellen Adams, for discovering the original Atlantic Cruising Club. We often cruised together and Rick, then captain of "Elixir," a Wilbur 38, was, and is, physically challenged — so we really learned a lot about marinas, their accessibility and their services.

The author and editors owe an extraordinary debt of gratitude to Connie Yingling from the Maryland Office of Tourism Development and Richard Lewis and Martha Steger from the Virginia Tourism Corporation — their assistance was invaluable throughout the entire research process; they took an overwhelming task and made it manageable and possible. And, just as important, they also connected us with their exceptionally helpful local tourism offices which provided assistance at every step. They not only assisted in planning our final trips, gave us great "on the ground" local insights and provided us with mountains of very useful literature, but they also reviewed each of the Marina Reports in their regions for accuracy. A very sincere thank you to: Julie Widdowson, Somerset County Office of Tourism; Jody Dix, Robie Marsh & Rose Rulon, Eastern Shore of Virginia Tourism; Martha Clements, Ocean City Department of Tourism; Suzanne Taylor, Chincoteague Chamber of Commerce; Jane Haseldine, Delaware Tourism Office; Joanne Roland, Charles County Office of Tourism; Susan Steckman, Annapolis & Anne Arundel County Conference & Visitors Bureau; Herman E. Schieke, Jr., Calvert County Department of Economic Development; Carolyn Laray, St. Mary's County Department of Economic Development; Debbi Dodson, Talbot County Office of Tourism; Mary Calloway, Dorchester County Tourism; Carol Steele, Gloucester County Parks, Recreation and Tourism; Sallye Grant DiVenuti, Hampton Convention & Visitor Bureau; Harla Sherwood, Middle Peninsula Convention & Visitors Bureau; Bobbi McElroy, Mathews County Visitor & Information Center; Cheryl Morales, Newport News Tourism Development Office; Kristi Olsen, York County Tourism and Events; Matthew Neitzey, Prince George's County Convention & Visitor Bureau; Winifred J. Roche, The Havre de Grace Office of Tourism & Visitor Center; Sandy Turner, Cecil County DMO; Margot Amelia and Kristin Zissel, Baltimore Area Convention & Visitors Association; Bernadette VanPelt, Kent County DMO; Barbara Siegert, Queen Anne's County DMO; Mary Fugere, Hampton Convention & Visitors Bureau; Patty Long, Northern Neck Convention & Visitor Bureau; Priscilla Caldwell, Williamsburg Area Convention & Visitors Bureau; and Laura Overstreet, Alexandria Convention & Visitors' Association. They know their areas very well land are always happy to help, so if you need more information than what's in the Marina Report, the appropriate tourism office's phone number is listed right under the marina's contact information.

Also our deep appreciation and heartfelt thanks to: Jan & Ruth Cort of Peninsula House in Annapolis, MD; Henry Kotoriy, Jr, Sandy Walker & Gayle Hansen of Chesapeake Beach Resort & Spa, Chesapeake Beach, MD; John Simpson of Holiday Inn Select Solomons Conference Center, Solomons, MD; Sleep Inn, California, MD; Mary and Al Ioppolo of the Inn At The Canal, South Chesapeake City, MD; Bruce & Jerren Wetterau of The Granary Restaurant, Georgetown, MD; Franz Portmann of Bayard House, South Chesapeake City, MD; Jonathan Wright of The Inn at Osprey Point, Rock Hall, MD; Kent Island Holiday Inn Express, Grasonville, MD; Mark Julan of Knapp's Narrows Inn, Tilghman Island, MD; Holiday Inn Express, Cambridge, MD; John Harper of the Hyatt Regency Chesapeake Bay Resort, Cambridge, MD; Snappers Waterfront Café, Cambridge, MD; Jerry Prewitt and Andrew "A.D." Dawson of 1848 Island Manor House, Chincoteague, VA; Sharryl Lindberg & LeRoy Friesen, Inn at Silent Music, Tylerton, MD; Glenna Crockett at Chesapeake House, Tangier Island, VA; Captains Larry & Terry Laird of the "Captain Jason," Crisfield, MD; Wallace & Mindy Thomas, Tangier Island Cruises; Phyllis Tyndall of Chesapeake Charm B & B, Cape Charles, VA; Hampton Marriott Courtyard, Hampton, VA; Hampton Radisson, Hampton, VA; Paul Brown of The Tides, Irvington, VA; Marguerite Slaughter of Fleeton Fields Bed & Breakfast, Reedville, VA; Anne Bolin of The Bell House Bed & Breakfast, Colonial Beach, VA ; Phyllis Garber Hall of Atherston Hall Bed & Breakfast, Urbanna, VA; Alexandria Mariott, Alexandria, VA; Wes Robison of the Inn at Henderson's Wharf, Baltimore, MD; Larry Metz of The Wellwood, Charlestown, MD and Richard & Judy Price of Charlestown, MD.

We also want to thank original ACC Founder John Curry, and Editors Nancy Schilling and Jennifer Wise, for their impressive initial ground work. Jason C. Smith of Outsource Technology Group for his invaluable ongoing technical support and for his vision in taking the JPI/ACC digital publishing house to the next step; he reorganized and up-scaled the technological end of the publishing process, increasing everyone's productivity and reducing stress at every turn. Christopher Adams of Next Meridian for re-charting and confirming all of the latitudes & longitudes to be sure we got that right. The members of the Atlantic Cruising Club for their notes and emails describing their marina experiences. And, most important, the facilities owners, managers and dockmasters who provided enormous quantities of detailed information on their marina and boatyard operations, along with aerial and ancillary photos (and reviewed ACC's interpretation at each step along the way), despite their discomfort with their inability to control the final Marina Report.

Thank you all!!
The Author, Editors and Publishers

ATLANTIC CRUISING CLUB'S

GUIDE TO
CHESAPEAKE BAY MARINAS

THE
MARINA REPORTS

Geographical Listing of Marinas

Continued on the next page

Boaters' Notes

Add Your Ratings and Reviews at www.AtlanticCruisingClub.com

AtlanticCruisingClub.com provides updated Marina Reports, Destination and Harbor Articles, a Boaters' Forum and much more — including an option within each on-line Marina Report for Boaters to add their ratings and comments regarding that facility. Please log on frequently to share your experiences — and to read other boaters' comments.

On the website, boaters may rate marinas on one or more of the following categories — on a scale of 1 (basic) to 5 (world class) — and also enter additional commentary.

- **Facilities & Services** (Fuel, Reservations, Concierge Services and General Helpfulness):
- **Amenities** (Pool, Beach, Internet Access, including Wi-Fi, Picnic/Grill area, Boaters' Lounge):
- **Setting** (Views, Design, Landscaping, Maintenance, Ship-Shapeness, Overall Ambiance):
- **Convenience** (Access — including delivery services — to Supermarkets, other provisioning sources, Shops, Services. Attractions, Entertainment, Sightseeing, Recreation, including Golf and Sport Fishing & Medical Services):
- **Restaurants/Eateries/Lodgings** (Availability of Fine Dining, Snack Bars, Lite Fare, On Call food service, and Lodgings ashore):
- **Transportation** (Courtesy Car/Vans, Buses, Water Taxis, Bikes, Taxis, Rental Cars, Airports, Amtrak, Commuter Trains):
- **Please Add Any Additional Comments**

1. Atlantic Coast: Delmarva

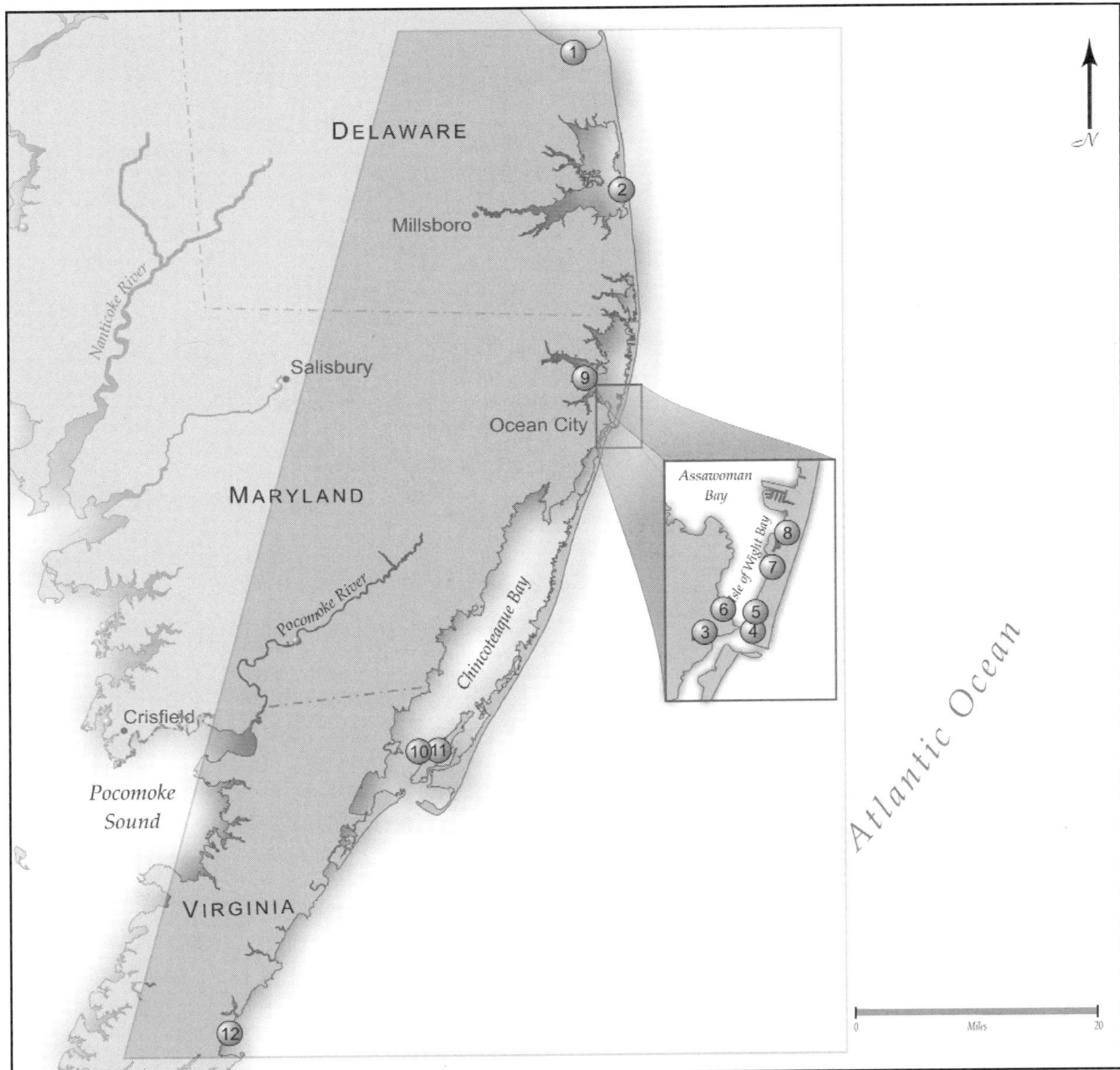

MAP	MARINA	HARBOR	PAGE
1	**City of Lewes Docks**	*Lewes-Rehoboth Canal*	24
2	**Indian River Inlet Marina**	*Indian River Inlet*	25
3	**Sunset Marina**	*Isle of Wight Bay*	26
4	**White Marlin Marina**	*Isle of Wight Bay*	27
5	**Angler Marina — Ocean City**	*Isle of Wight Bay*	28
6	**Ocean City Fishing Center**	*Isle of Wight Bay*	29
7	**Harbor Island Marina**	*Isle of Wight Bay*	30
8	**Bahia Marina**	*Isle of Wight Bay*	31
9	**Ocean Pines Marina**	*Assawoman Bay/Martin River*	32
10	**Chincoteague Inn & Marina**	*Chincoteague Inlet*	33
11	**Chincoteague's Rob't N. Reed Park**	*Chincoteague Inlet*	34
12	**Captain Zed's Marina**	*Wachapreague Inlet*	35

- **A "DCM" symbol in Marina Notes means Designated Clean Marina** — This is a coveted state-level award given to marinas that meet stringent, environmentally supportive requirements (see page 307). *For a list of DCM's & pump-out facilities, see page 308.*
- **Ratings & Reviews** — An explanation of the Atlantic Cruising Club's rating system, and a detailed explanation of what is in each section of the Marina Report is on pages 6 – 11. *The Data-Gathering Process is detailed on page 322.*
- **Marina Report Updates** — Updates to Marina Reports (from readers, ACC reviewers, and marinas) are posted regularly on *www.AtlanticCruisingClub.com.*

City of Lewes Docks

211 Front Street; Lewes, DE 19958

Tel: (302) 645-7777 **VHF: Monitor** n/a **Talk** n/a
Fax: (302) 645-6560 **Alternate Tel:** n/a
Email: canalpark@verizon.net **Web:** www.lewescanalfrontpark.org
Nearest Town: Lewes **Tourist Info:** (302) 645-8073

Navigational Information

Lat: 38°46.566' **Long:** 075°08.380' **Tide:** n/a **Current:** 0 **Chart:** 12216
Rep. Depths (*MLW*): Entry 5 ft. **Fuel Dock** n/a **Max Slip/Moor** 5 ft./-
Access: Roosevelt Inlet to Lewes-Rehoboth Canal

Marina Facilities *(In Season/Off Season)*

Fuel: No
Slips: 4 Total, 4 Transient **Max LOA:** 200 ft. **Max Beam:** n/a
Rate *(per ft.)*: **Day** $2.00* **Week** n/a **Month** n/a
Power: 30 amp Incl., **50 amp** Incl., **100 amp** n/a, **200 amp** n/a
Cable TV: No **Dockside Phone:** No
Dock Type: Floating, Alongside, Wood
Moorings: 0 Total, 0 Transient **Launch:** n/a
Rate: Day n/a **Week** n/a **Month** n/a
Heads: 6 Toilet(s)
Laundry: None **Pay Phones:** No
Pump-Out: OnSite **Fee:** n/a **Closed Heads:** Yes

Marina Operations

Owner/Manager: City of Lewes **Dockmaster:** Bill Massey
In-Season: Year-Round, 9am-5pm **Off-Season:** n/a
After-Hours Arrival: after Jul '06 call in advance
Reservations: **after Jul '06 **Credit Cards:** Cash
Discounts: None
Pets: Welcome **Handicap Access:** Yes, Heads, Docks

Marina Services and Boat Supplies

Communication - FedEx, UPS, Express Mail **Supplies - Near:** Ice *(Cube)*, Ships' Store, Bait/Tackle *(Old Hookers 645-8866)*, Live Bait, Propane, CNG **3+ mi:** West Marine *(644-9424, 4 mi.)*

Boatyard Services

Near: Travelift, Launching Ramp, Engine mechanic *(gas, diesel)*, Bottom Cleaning, Propeller Repairs. **Under 1 mi:** Compound, Wash & Wax.

Restaurants and Accommodations

Near: Restaurant *(The Lighthouse 645-6271, B $4-7, L $6-12, D $8-24)*, *(Gilligan's Waterfront 644-7230, L $6-14, D $22-28, 11-3pm & 5-8pm - at the Inn at Canal Square)*, *(Café Azafran 644-4446, wine-n-dine on Sun)*, *(Irish Eyes 645-6888)*, *(Striper Bites Bistro 645-4657, L $7-10, D $16-23)*, *(Buttery 645-7755, L $7-10, D $19-34)*, *(Jerry's Seafood 645-6611)*, Coffee Shop *(Notting Hill Coffee Roastery 645-0733)*, Lite Fare *(King's Ice Cream)*, Motel *(Vesuvio 645-2224, $65-125)*, Inn/B&B *(Zwaandael Inn 645-6466, $45-260)*, *(Inn at Canal Square 644-3377, $100-270, rates include a European style breakfast)* **Under 1 mi:** Motel *(Cape Henlopen 645-2828)*

Recreation and Entertainment

Near: Picnic Area, Fishing Charter, Museum *(Zwaandael Museum 645-1148 Tue-Sat, 10am-4:30pm, Sun 1:30-4:30pm, Free; Indian River Lifesaving Museum 227-0478 - 1.5 mi.)*, Cultural Attract *(Cannonball House & Maritime Museum 645-7670 In-Season Mon-Fri 10am-4pm, Sat 10am-1pm, $6/under 12 free)*, Galleries **Under 1 mi:** Beach *(Cape Henlopen - 2 beaches, life guards, bathhouse, food concession, umbrellas, bike paths)*, Golf Course, Boat Rentals *(Hook, Line & Sinker at CHSP 644-2291- Kayaks 9am-6pm, 7 days)*, Park *(Cape Henlopen State Park 645-8983)* **1-3 mi:** Movie Theater *(Movies at Midway 645-0200)*, Video Rental

Provisioning and General Services

Near: Delicatessen, Health Food, Wine/Beer, Liquor Store *(R&L 645-9183)*, Bakery *(Rocky Mountain Chocolate Factory 645-5528)*, Bank/ATM, Post Office, Protestant Church *(St. Peter's; Lewes Presbyterian, built 1832)*, Library *(Lewes PL 645-4633)*, Beauty Salon *(Ocean Retreat Day Spa 645-6868)*, Barber Shop, Dry Cleaners, Bookstore *(Books by the Bay 645-2304)*, Newsstand, Florist *(Flowers by Majumi 644-4468)*, Retail Shops *(boutiques)* **Under 1 mi:** Fishmonger, Market *(Lloyd's Food Rite 645-6589)*, Laundry *(Quick Wash 645-8542)*, Pharmacy *(Rite Aid 645-6243)*, Copies Etc. **1-3 mi:** Supermarket *(Food Lion 645-6933)*, Hardware Store *(Millman's 645-8419)*, Clothing Store *(2 Tanger Outlet Centers - LL Bean, Ralph Lauren, Ann Taylor, Liz Claiborne - bus available)*, Department Store *(Wal-Mart 644-8014)*

Transportation

OnCall: Taxi *(Seaport Taxi 645-6800)*, Airport Limo *(Surfside Limo 945-7175)* **Under 1 mi:** Bikes *(Lewes Cycle 645-4544)*, Ferry Service *(to Cape May 644-6030)* **3+ mi:** Rental Car *(Enterprise 645-5005, 14 mi.)*
Airport: Ocean City *(35 mi.)*

Medical Services

911 Service **OnCall:** Ambulance, Veterinarian *(Visiting Vet 945-2767)*
Under 1 mi: Doctor, Holistic Services *(Cape Henlopen Massage 645-2552)*
1-3 mi: Dentist *(Tetzner 645-7203)*, Chiropractor *(Foster 644-1595)*
Hospital: Beebe Medical Center 645-3300 *(1 mi.)*

Setting -- About 3 miles from Roosevelt Inlet, just before the 35-foot Rt. 9 bridge and turning basin, is the City of Lewes Dock's 200-foot floating pier with 4 pedestals. It parallels a small park displaying a half-dozen cannons from the War of 1812. Just steps away is the delightful village of Lewes. The opening of the new Canalfront Park in mid '06 will add 22 new slips, making Lewes a convenient, protected stop on either the outside route or inside via the C&D Canal.

Marina Notes -- *1st 6 hrs. free, 7-day max. **No reservations currently; with the addition of the new docks (about 16 dedicated transients), the city intends to accept reservations. New slips will parallel the shore anchored by a boardwalk. The Canalfront Park will gradually incorporate 4 acres and will feature a locked boaters' bathhouse incorporated into an "overlook" structure, a well-landscaped upland with shade arbors, foot paths, and onsite boaters' services. Originally authorized in 1912, the Lewes-Rehoboth Canal was finally completed in 1927 as a vehicle by which farmers and mills delivered products to market.

Notable -- Across Front Street next to the Post Office, the Lewes Historical Society's Cannonball House bears the scars of the War of 1812. Next to the docks, the original Maritime Exchange Building hosts the Maritime Yacht Club and antique shops. Wander west along the Canal to Gilligan's at the Inn at Canal Square for inside or outside dining overlooking the water. Inviting shops are tucked in here and there along the way. Heading inland a block to Second Street, another charming four-block lane is lined with boutiques, an intriguing assortment of restaurants, two ice cream shops, and the Zwaandael Inn and Galleries. The surrounding streets are dotted with restored nineteenth-century houses; St. Peter's Episcopal Church (c.1681) anchors the far end of town.

PHOTOS ON CD-ROM: 13

Indian River Inlet Marina

39415 Inlet Road; Rehoboth Beach, DE 19971

Tel: (302) 227-3071 **VHF: Monitor** 16 **Talk** 16
Fax: (302) 227-7400 **Alternate Tel:** n/a
Email: n/a **Web:** www.destateparks.com
Nearest Town: Dewey Beach *(3 mi.)* **Tourist Info:** (302) 645-8073

Navigational Information

Lat: 38°36.766' **Long:** 075°04.283' **Tide:** n/a **Current:** n/a **Chart:** 12216
Rep. Depths (*MLW*): Entry 6 ft. **Fuel Dock** n/a **Max Slip/Moor** 6 ft./-
Access: Indian River Inlet to north shore

Marina Facilities *(In Season/Off Season)*

Fuel: *89 Octane Gas, Biodiesel* - Gasoline, Diesel
Slips: 258 Total, 25 Transient **Max LOA:** 120 ft. **Max Beam:** 19 ft.
Rate *(per ft.)*: **Day** $2.50 **Week** n/a **Month** n/a
Power: 30 amp 1.75/Kwh, **50 amp** 1.75/Kwh, **100 amp** n/a, **200 amp** n/a
Cable TV: No **Dockside Phone:** No
Dock Type: Floating, Long Fingers, Composition
Moorings: 0 Total, 0 Transient **Launch:** yes, Dinghy Dock
Rate: Day n/a **Week** n/a **Month** n/a
Heads: 20 Toilet(s), 12 Shower(s) *(with dressing rooms)*
Laundry: None **Pay Phones:** Yes
Pump-Out: OnSite **Fee:** n/a **Closed Heads:** Yes

Marina Operations

Owner/Manager: Gary King **Dockmaster:** Same
In-Season: Apr-Oct, 7am-4:30pm **Off-Season:** Nov-Mar, 7am-4pm
After-Hours Arrival: Check-in with night watch
Reservations: Required **Credit Cards:** Visa/MC, Dscvr
Discounts: Boat/US **Dockage:** 25% **Fuel:** $0.10/gal **Repair:** n/a
Pets: Welcome **Handicap Access:** Yes, Heads, Docks

Marina Services and Boat Supplies

Services - Docking Assistance, Security *(24 hrs.)*, Dock Carts **Communication -** Mail & Package Hold, Phone Messages, Fax in/out *(Inq.)*, UPS, Express Mail **Supplies - OnSite:** Ice *(Block, Cube)*, Ships' Store, Bait/Tackle **3+ mi:** Propane *(Suburban 227-2504, 9 mi.)*

Boatyard Services

OnSite: Travelift *(50T)*, Launching Ramp **Yard Rates:** Flat Rates, Haul & Launch $8.20-9.20/ft. *(blocking $2/ft.)*, Power Wash $2/ft. **Storage:** On-Land $10.10/ft.

Restaurants and Accommodations

OnSite: Seafood Shack *(Hook 'Em & Cook 'Em 226-8220, steamed fish, lobsters, shrimp, crabs)*, Snack Bar *(B $2-4, L $2-6)*, Condo/Cottage *(Indian River Inlet Cottages 877-987-2757, $150-265, 2 bedrooms, loft, porch, full kitchen, satellite TV, VCR, DVD - 2 day weekend min. in season)*
1-3 mi: Hotel *(Marina Suites 226-2012, $49-249)*, *(Atlantic Inn and Suites 866-820-4430, $64-165)* **3+ mi:** Restaurant *(Baja Beach House Grill 537-9993, B $6, L $5-10, D $5-10, 6 mi., Mexican; carryout)*, *(Blue Crab 537-4700, 6 mi.)*, *(Mango Mike's 537-6621, 6 mi.)*, *(Mickey's Family Crabhouse 539-5384, 6 mi., year-round, carryout - jumbo lump crabcakes, crabs, fish, steaks)*, *(Dewey Beach Club 227-0669, 4 mi.)*, Pizzeria *(Papa John's 541-8081, 6 mi.)*, Motel *(Best Western 226-1800, 4 mi.)*

Recreation and Entertainment

OnSite: Picnic Area, Grills, Boat Rentals *(G-Dock Boats)*, Fishing Charter *(Amethyst 934-8119, Karen Sue 539-1359, Spectacle 732-9533, Sport Fishing Bass 945-7023, Number One Hooker 732-1274, Reel Escape 218-2984, On Delivery 443-463-7849, HH Charter 684-3302, Fish Buster 354-3224. Black Magic 841-5955, Razor Back 656-9559, Half Moon 227-2879)*, Group Fishing Boat *(Judy V. & Captain Bob 226-8220)*, Special Events *(Rocktober Fishing Tournament & Festival - 3rd week in Oct $25,000 in prizes)* **Near:** Park *(Delaware Seashore State Park)*
Under 1 mi: Beach *(0.5 mi across the dunes)* **3+ mi:** Golf Course *(Old Landing 227-3131, 9 mi.)*

Provisioning and General Services

OnSite: Convenience Store **1-3 mi:** Gourmet Shop, Farmers' Market, Fishmonger **3+ mi:** Supermarket *(Shore Stop 539-8806/Food Lion 227-5756, 9 mi.)*, Delicatessen *(Difebo's 539-4914, 6 mi.)*, Health Food *(Wholesome Habits 537-0567, 6 mi.)*, Liquor Store *(Total Wine & Spirits 541-4200, 6 mi.)*, Bakery *(Bethany Bakery 539-4432, 6 mi.)*, Bank/ATM *(6 mi.)*, Post Office *(539-9874, 6 mi.)*, Catholic Church *(6 mi.)*, Protestant Church *(6 mi.)*, Library *(South Coastal 539-5231, 6 mi.)*, Dry Cleaners *(Bethany Beach Laundry & Dry Cleaners 537-1646, 6 mi.)*, Bookstore *(Bethany Beach Books 359-2522, 6 mi.)*, Pharmacy *(Happy Harry's 537-3700, 8 mi.)*, Hardware Store *(True Value 227-2533, 8 mi.)*

Transportation

OnCall: Rental Car *(Enterprise 732-3534)*, Taxi *(A-Ocean 541-8294)*, Airport Limo *(Coastal 537-2324)* **Airport:** Ocean City *(19 mi.)*

Medical Services

911 Service **OnCall:** Ambulance **3+ mi:** Doctor *(6 mi.)*, Dentist *(Wright 226-3398, 6 mi.)*, Chiropractor *(Schierl 645-6681, 7 mi.)*
Hospital: Beebe 645-3300 *(14 mi.)*

Setting -- Right off the Inlet, this state marina is part of the 2825-acre Delaware Seashore State Park. Peach cement buildings with teal trim dot the upland. The views from the slips are of shimmering, unspoiled marsh. Smaller boats anchor or drift outboard of the docks hinting at the inshore angling possibilities.

Marina Notes -- DCM. The State has embarked on a $15 million renovation plan. In the 2005 season, dredging was completed with all new IPE floating docks (vinyl edging, full-length fingers and high-end pedestals) in the north half of the basin ("C", "D", "E" & "G"), plus dry stack storage, charter boat dockage, and a new fuel dock. '06 brings new boater-dedicated heads and showers, new ships' store, convenience store and new offices - at present the main office has a sun deck on the 2nd floor and small breakfast & lunch concession on the first. Haul-out managed by the state; all other BY services are private concessions. Self-serve yard, dripless oil change cart and used oil collections available. Current heads are nicely done cinderblock with Corian sinks.

Notable -- Lovely new 900-sq. ft. shingled 2-bedroom rental cottages offer a landside break. The Inlet Bridge is being rebuilt - new height will be 45 feet with a 1,000-foot span ('05-'08). Indian River is home to many private sportfish boats, two party boats, a plethora of sportfish charter boats (a 169- b. bluefin tuna came in during one visit) plus a few commercial fishing vessels offl-oad here as well. A special access pier at the inlet allows the physically challenged to join in the fun. Buzz & Judy Adams at on-site Hook 'Em & Cook 'Em offer a small food concession, fish cleaning station, and a variety of fresh seafood, which they'll also steam. Also will clean angler's catch: $0.15/lb. for rockfish to $0.75/lb. for flounder. A beautiful stretch of ocean beach is a short half-mile walk.

PHOTOS ON CD-ROM: 14

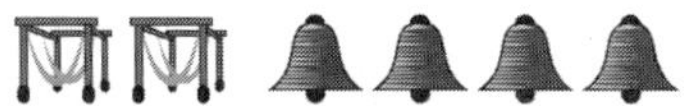

Sunset Marina

12911 Sunset Avenue; Ocean City, MD 21842

Tel: (410) 213-9600; (877) 514-3474 **VHF: Monitor** 16 **Talk** 74
Fax: (410) 213-9666 **Alternate Tel:** n/a
Email: office@ocsunsetmarina.com **Web:** www.ocsunsetmarina.com
Nearest Town: Ocean City *(2 mi.)* **Tourist Info:** (800) 626-2326

Navigational Information

Lat: 38°19.718' **Long:** 075°06.227' **Tide:** 3 ft. **Current:** 0 kt. **Chart:** 12211
Rep. Depths (*MLW*): Entry 12 ft. **Fuel Dock** 8 ft. **Max Slip/Moor** 8 ft./-
Access: Marina entrance 1/8 mile west of Marker 12

Marina Facilities *(In Season/Off Season)*

Fuel: Slip-Side Fueling, Gasoline, Diesel, High-Speed Pumps
Slips: 204 Total, 20 Transient **Max LOA:** 110 ft. **Max Beam:** 25 ft.
Rate *(per ft.)*: **Day** $2.00* **Week** n/a **Month** $20
Power: 30 amp $5, **50 amp** $10, **100 amp** $20, **200 amp** n/a
Cable TV: Yes, $4 **Dockside Phone:** No
Dock Type: Fixed, Long Fingers, Pilings, Wood
Moorings: 0 Total, 0 Transient **Launch:** n/a
Rate: Day n/a **Week** n/a **Month** n/a
Heads: 20 Toilet(s), 12 Shower(s)
Laundry: 6 Washer(s), 6 Dryer(s), Book Exchange **Pay Phones:** Yes
Pump-Out: OnSite, 1 Central **Fee:** $5 **Closed Heads:** Yes

Marina Operations

Owner/Manager: Brian G. Tinkler **Dockmaster:** Same
In-Season: May-Oct, 5am-11pm **Off-Season:** Nov-Apr, 8am-5pm
After-Hours Arrival: Call in advance
Reservations: Preferred **Credit Cards:** Visa/MC, Dscvr, Amex
Discounts: None
Pets: Welcome, Dog Walk Area **Handicap Access:** Yes, Heads, Docks

Marina Services and Boat Supplies

Services - Docking Assistance, Boaters' Lounge, Trash Pick-Up, Dock Carts, Megayacht Facilities **Communication -** Mail & Package Hold, Phone Messages, Fax in/out *($1)*, Data Ports *(Office)*, FedEx, DHL, UPS, Express Mail *(Sat Del)* **Supplies - OnSite:** Ice *(Block, Cube)*, Ships' Store, Bait/Tackle *(4:30am-11pm)*, Live Bait

Boatyard Services

OnSite: Travelift *(88T)*, Forklift, Bottom Cleaning, Divers **OnCall:** Engine mechanic *(gas, diesel)*, Electrical Repairs, Electronics Repairs, Hull Repairs, Brightwork, Air Conditioning, Refrigeration, Compound, Wash & Wax, Interior Cleaning, Propeller Repairs, Woodworking, Inflatable Repairs, Life Raft Service, Upholstery, Yacht Interiors, Metal Fabrication, Painting, Awlgrip **Near:** Launching Ramp, Canvas Work. **Yard Rates:** Haul & Launch $8/ft. *(blocking $2/ft.)*, Power Wash $2/ft. **Storage:** On-Land $0.50/ft.

Restaurants and Accommodations

OnSite: Restaurant *(Teasers L $6-10, D $6-10, entertainment on weekends)*, *(Sunset Grill 213-8110, L $7-10, D $7-25, kids' menu $3-5, indoor, outdoor & porch)*, Coffee Shop *(Sunset Provisions)* **Near:** Restaurant *(Captain's Galley II 213-2525)*, *(Crab Alley 213-7800)*, *(Harborside 213-1846)*, Pizzeria *(Miones 213-2231, L $7-11, D $7-11, nightly Italian D special)* **Under 1 mi:** Restaurant *(Sneaky Pete's 213-4771)*, Motel *(Comfort Suites 213-7171)*, *(Rambler 213-8030, $75)* **1-3 mi:** Motel *(Castle in the Sand 289-6846, $59-295)*, *(Francis Scott Key 213-0088, $40-85)*

Recreation and Entertainment

OnSite: Heated Pool, Picnic Area, Grills *(charcoal)*, Fishing Charter *(877-514-3474 - 21 boats 35-61 ft., $550-1800/day or $250/pp)* **Near:** Playground, Dive Shop, Fitness Center, Jogging Paths, Boat Rentals, Video Arcade, Park, Museum **Under 1 mi:** Beach, Video Rental *(Blockbuster 213-7967)*, Cultural Attract, Sightseeing, Galleries **1-3 mi:** Golf Course *(Eagle's Landing 213-7277)*, Movie Theater *(Fox Theatres 213-1505)* **3+ mi:** Tennis Courts *(OC Tennis Center 524-8337 $10-14/hr., 5 mi.)*

Provisioning and General Services

OnSite: Convenience Store *(Sunset Provisions)*, Liquor Store, Bank/ATM, Newsstand **Near:** Delicatessen *(Oliveros Dockside 213-7067)*, Crabs/Waterman, Shrimper, Beauty Salon **Under 1 mi:** Bakery, Green Grocer, Meat Market, Market *(Marlin 213-7577)*, Post Office, Florist **1-3 mi:** Supermarket *(Super Fresh 213-0410)*, Catholic Church, Protestant Church, Synagogue, Library *(289-7297)*, Dry Cleaners *(Wilgus 289-0009)*, Laundry, Bookstore *(Joseph's by the Sea 289-7025)*, Pharmacy *(Rite Aid 213-2536, CVS 213-1526)*, Hardware Store *(A Plus 289-4500)*, Copies Etc. *(Staples 213-1168)* **3+ mi:** Department Store *(Wal-Mart 221-0292, 5 mi.)*

Transportation

OnSite: Water Taxi *($5)* **OnCall:** Rental Car *(Enterprise 213-0886)*, Taxi *(Dave's 24 hr. 250-2400)*, Airport Limo *(Coast To Coast 723-5466)* **Near:** Local Bus *(The Whale $2/24 hr. pass)* **1-3 mi:** Bikes *(Jo's 289-5298)* **Airport:** Ocean City/Salisbury *(3 mi./20 mi.)*

Medical Services

911 Service **OnCall:** Ambulance **Under 1 mi:** Chiropractor *(OC Chiropractic Clinic 213-1233)*, Veterinarian *(OC Animal Hospital 213-1170)* **1-3 mi:** Doctor, Dentist **Hospital:** Atlantic General 641-9450 *(6 mi.)*

Setting -- In a protected basin off the Inlet, pale-blue clapboard edifices with French-blue metal roofs, Key West-style cupolas and white picket fences set the tone for this elegant marina. Impeccable docks are surrounded by a community of pricey homes that match the many private sportfish yachts in the slips.

Marina Notes -- *$60 min. DCM. Sunset Marina is service-oriented - witness the hours (5am-11pm). A staffed fish-cleaning station next to the weigh station. The furthest outboard docks have generous, full-length finger piers (half-length on closer-in docks). Very beamy berths, designed for large sportfish boats, also serve catamarans. 90 ft. fairways. In-slip fueling in 80 berths. Pedestals have cable, phone, etc. A large, very well equipped store offers snack food, drinks, beer, wine, all kinds of B&T, some boat supplies and tubs of live bait. Boatyard hauls, launches and blocks - everything else is subcontracted. Large dry-stack storage operation. Same managment as OC Fishing Center. Bathhouse is adequate, but not up to standard of the rest of the facility.

Notable -- The slips are well protected in a 20-acre surge-free basin and the resort atmosphere is well conceived and impressively executed. Upscale Sunset Grill serves until 10pm - indoors, on the porch, and outdoors on the deck - all with expansive views of the docks. Adjacent Teasers has an outdoor bar, a casual menu (food until 1am) and entertainment - reggae on Fri and a variety on Sat - country, rock, blues, etc. Both 11am-2am. Charcoal grills are poked in here and there, and seating areas abound along the shoreline. The impeccably furnished pool is nicely screened from the restaurants, but still has great views across the docks. The commercial docks host the working fleet; reportedly, fish, scallops, etc. can be purchased directly from the boats.

PHOTOS ON CD-ROM: 15

White Marlin Marina

PO Box 1139; 205 Somerset Street; Ocean City, MD 21843

Tel: (410) 289-6470 **VHF: Monitor** 16 **Talk** 68
Fax: (410) 213-0385 **Alternate Tel:** (410) 289-6470
Email: n/a **Web:** www.whitemarlinmarina.com
Nearest Town: Ocean City **Tourist Info:** (800) 626-2326

Navigational Information

Lat: 38°19.810' **Long:** 075°05.390' **Tide:** 3 ft. **Current:** 3 kt. **Chart:** 12211
Rep. Depths (*MLW*): Entry 18 ft. **Fuel Dock** 12 ft. **Max Slip/Moor** 12 ft./-
Access: Isle of Wight Bay, 1/4 mile North of Ocean City Inlet

Marina Facilities *(In Season/Off Season)*

Fuel: *Shell* - Slip-Side Fueling, Gasoline, Diesel
Slips: 53 Total, 53 Transient **Max LOA:** 130 ft. **Max Beam:** 25 ft.
Rate *(per ft.)*: **Day** $1.75/Inq. **Week** Inq. **Month** Inq.
Power: 30 amp Incl., **50 amp** Incl., **100 amp** n/a, **200 amp** n/a
Cable TV: Yes, Incl. **Dockside Phone:** No
Dock Type: Fixed, Short Fingers, Pilings, Wood
Moorings: 0 Total, 0 Transient **Launch:** n/a
Rate: Day n/a **Week** n/a **Month** n/a
Heads: 2 Toilet(s), 2 Shower(s)
Laundry: 1 Washer(s), 1 Dryer(s) **Pay Phones:** No
Pump-Out: No **Fee:** n/a **Closed Heads:** Yes

Marina Operations

Owner/Manager: Tom Terry **Dockmaster:** Same
In-Season: Apr-Nov, 5am-9pm **Off-Season:** Dec-Mar, On call
After-Hours Arrival: Directions listed at Dock Office - Pager Information
Reservations: Yes, Preferred **Credit Cards:** Visa/MC, Dscvr, Amex, Tex
Discounts: None
Pets: Welcome **Handicap Access:** No

Marina Services and Boat Supplies

Services - Docking Assistance, Trash Pick-Up, Dock Carts **Communication -** Mail & Package Hold, Phone Messages, FedEx, DHL, UPS, Express Mail **Supplies - OnSite:** Ice *(Block, Cube)* **OnCall:** Ships' Store **Near:** Bait/Tackle *(Skip's 289-8555)*, CNG

Boatyard Services

OnCall: Engine mechanic *(gas, diesel)*, Electrical Repairs, Electronics Repairs, Hull Repairs, Canvas Work, Bottom Cleaning, Brightwork, Air Conditioning, Refrigeration, Divers, Compound, Wash & Wax, Interior Cleaning, Propeller Repairs, Woodworking, Upholstery, Yacht Interiors, Metal Fabrication, Painting, Awlgrip **Under 1 mi:** Travelift *(70T)*, Launching Ramp, Inflatable Repairs. **Nearest Yard:** O.C. Travelift (410) 213-7575

Restaurants and Accommodations

OnSite: Seafood Shack *(Bahama Mama's 289-0291, L $4-11, D $4-27, entrees mostly in teens, kids' menu $3-5, Noon-11pm; famous steamed-crabs, all-you-can-eat)* **Near:** Restaurant *(Angler 289-7424, B $3-12, L $6-13, D $6-24)*, *(Marina Deck 289-4411, B $3-10, L $5-12, D $12-26, kids' menu, Mar-Nov 11am-11pm)*, Seafood Shack *(Phillips North Seafood 250-1200, D $9-23)*, Snack Bar *(Sorianos B $4, L $4, D $5)*, Lite Fare *(M. R. Duck's Dockside Grille 289-3503)*, Inn/B&B *(Talbot Inn 289-9125, $32-139)* **Under 1 mi:** Inn/B&B *(Atlantic House 289-2333)* **1-3 mi:** Motel *(Francis Scott Key 213-0088)*, *(Castle in the Sand 289-6846, $80-389)*

Recreation and Entertainment

OnSite: Pool, Picnic Area, Grills, Boat Rentals, Fishing Charter *(7 vessels, 289-6470, 31-58 ft., e.g. in shore tuna fishing $800-1000)* **Near:** Beach *(Volleyball too)*, Playground, Tennis Courts *(3rd St. Bayside)*, Fitness Center *(Mussell 289-5656)*, Roller Blade/Bike Paths *(Skateboard Park)*, Movie Theater *(Fox Theatre at White Marlin Mall 213-1505)*, Video Arcade, Park *(Assateague Island)*, Museum *(Life Saving Station 289-4991, 11am-10pm, $3/1)*, Cultural Attract *(historic Trimper's Amusements 289-8617)*, Galleries *(Ocean Gallery 289-5300)* **1-3 mi:** Golf Course *(Eagle's Landing 213-7277)*, Video Rental *(Blockbuster 213-7967)*

Provisioning and General Services

OnSite: Wine/Beer **Near:** Supermarket *(Mitchell's 289-9136)*, Delicatessen *(Fat Daddy's 289-4040)*, Health Food *(OC Organics 213-9818)*, Liquor Store *(Bearded Clam 289-4498)*, Bakery, Fishmonger *(Martin's)*, Market *(Mitchell's 289-9136)*, Bank/ATM, Catholic Church, Beauty Salon *(Marion 289-6351)*, Bookstore *(Atlantic Books 289-8383)*, Hardware Store *(Elliott's 289-6123)*, Florist, Copies Etc. **Under 1 mi:** Post Office, Protestant Church, Library *(OC 289-7297)*, Dry Cleaners, Laundry, Pharmacy *(CVS 289-6513)*

Transportation

OnSite: Local Bus *(Whale $2/24 hr. pass)* **OnCall:** Water Taxi *(Buzz Boat 561-512-ASAP, Ch.72, $10)*, Airport Limo *(Limo Masters 250-7400)* **Near:** Bikes *(Dandy Don's 289-2289)*, Rental Car *(Enterprise 213-0886)*, Taxi *(Dave's 250-2400)* **Airport:** Ocean City/Salisbury *(3 mi./30 mi.)*

Medical Services

911 Service **OnCall:** Ambulance **Near:** Chiropractor *(Family Chiro 213-0900)*, Holistic Services *(Touch of Energy 723-5533)* **Under 1 mi:** Doctor *(10th St. 289-6241)*, Dentist *(43rd St. 289-8828)* **1-3 mi:** Veterinarian *(OC Animal 213-1170)* **Hospital:** Atlantic General 641-0430 *(7 mi.)*

Setting -- The first facility on the starboard side, well-appointed White Marlin is in the heart of Ocean City's "Old Towne." A five-story, gray shingled condominium complex with brick-red metal roofs backs the docks and acts as a locator beacon to the marina. Picnic tables, a few grills, benches and an occasional flower-bedecked gazebo dot the grassy strip along the slips. A small, inviting pool overlooks the docks - a welcome relief from Ocean City summers.

Marina Notes -- White Marlin is a stone's throw from the hustle and bustle of O.C. It offers wide, generous stationary docks with standard pedestals, short, tapered finger piers, and attractive, traditional lighting. Easy access to a nice, long fuel dock for gas and diesel. The pool belongs to the condo association, but is available to transient boaters. The marina's basin has been catering to sport fishermen since the early '30s. Helpful staff will offer directions to Island Park, less than 1 mile by dinghy.

Notable -- Walking distance to almost everything, while affording some privacy and quiet. Three blocks to the boardwalk, ocean beach, and Trimper's Family Amusement Center. Good public transportation goes everywhere else. Adjacent to the south, Bahama Mama's Big Crab House has an Islands theme and grass-thatch roofed tiki huts overlooking the water - seating inside and out, open from Noon to 11pm, 7 days in season (shorter hours off-season). Directly north is the Marina Deck Restaurant and all the activities at Old Town Marina. Just beyond that is M.R. Duck and Angler. Walk down to the pier next to the Lifesaving Station, and watch the sportfish boats enter the inlet at full throttle, sometimes two or more abreast, or dinghy over to the tip of 37-mile Assateague Island.

PHOTOS ON CD-ROM: 11

Angler Restaurant & Dock

312 Talbot Street; Ocean City, MD 21842

Tel: (410) 289-7424 **VHF: Monitor** n/a **Talk** n/a
Fax: (410) 289-7236 **Alternate Tel:** n/a
Email: angler@beachin.net **Web:** www.theangleroc.com
Nearest Town: Ocean City **Tourist Info:** (800) 626-2326

Navigational Information

Lat: 38°19.883' **Long:** 075°05.390' **Tide:** 3 ft. **Current:** 3 kt. **Chart:** 12211
Rep. Depths (*MLW*): Entry 12 ft. **Fuel Dock** n/a **Max Slip/Moor** 5 ft./-
Access: Follow channel to just south of the Route 50 bridge

Marina Facilities *(In Season/Off Season)*

Fuel: Gasoline, Diesel
Slips: 7 Total, 3 Transient **Max LOA:** 50 ft. **Max Beam:** 10 ft.
Rate *(per ft.)*: **Day** $1.50 **Week** n/a **Month** n/a
Power: 30 amp Incl., **50 amp** n/a, **100 amp** n/a, **200 amp** n/a
Cable TV: No **Dockside Phone:** No
Dock Type: Fixed, Short Fingers, Alongside, Wood
Moorings: 0 Total, 0 Transient **Launch:** n/a
Rate: Day n/a **Week** n/a **Month** n/a
Heads: 4 Toilet(s)
Laundry: None **Pay Phones:** Yes
Pump-Out: No **Fee:** n/a **Closed Heads:** Yes

Marina Operations

Owner/Manager: Julie Smith **Dockmaster:** Joyce Bunting
In-Season: May-Oct, 6am-8pm **Off-Season:** Nov-Apr, 7am-5pm
After-Hours Arrival: Call in advance
Reservations: Preferred **Credit Cards:** Visa/MC, Dscvr, Amex
Discounts: None
Pets: Welcome **Handicap Access:** Yes, Docks

Marina Services and Boat Supplies

Communication - FedEx, DHL, UPS, Express Mail **Supplies - Near:** Bait/Tackle *(Joe's 213-9378)* **Under 1 mi:** Ships' Store *(General Marine Supply 213-8123)* **3+ mi:** Propane *(Eastern Shore Gas 524-7060, 5 mi.)*

Boatyard Services

Nearest Yard: Sunset Marina (410) 213-9600

Restaurants and Accommodations

OnSite: Restaurant *(Angler 289-7424, B $3-12, L $6-13, D $6-24, features local fish, kids' $4-8; happy hour daily 3-6pm)*, Motel *(Talbot St. Inn 289-9125, $32-125, bay front rooms)* **Near:** Restaurant *(Bahama Mama's 289-0291, L $4-11, D $4-27, kids' $3-5)*, *(Marine Deck 289-4411, L $7-10, D $8-30)*, *(BJ's on the Water 289-7555)*, Lite Fare *(M.R. Ducks Dockside Grille 289-3503, L $4-10, D $4-10, kids' $3.50-5; outdoor bar)*, Pizzeria *(Captain's 289-8900)*, Motel *(Castle in the Sand 284-6846, $70-300)*, *(Madison Beach 289-6282)*, Hotel *(Park Place 289-6440, $89-259)*, Inn/B&B *(Atlantic House B&B 289-2333)*

Recreation and Entertainment

OnSite: Boat Rentals *(pontoon boats, Wave Runners)*, Fishing Charter *(M.R. Ducks 289-9125; The Lisa 213-0080)*, Group Fishing Boat *(65 ft. Angler 289-7424 $20-40; 35 ft. Arno 726-1833;)*, Sightseeing *(Angler Native Cruise, Ocean City Rocket, Pirate Ventures)* **Near:** Beach *(few blocks to boardwalk and a 10-mi. ocean beach)*, Playground, Tennis Courts *(3rd St. Bayside)*, Fitness Center *(Mussell & Fitness 289-5656)*, Roller Blade/Bike Paths *(Skateboard Park - 3rd Ave)*, Volleyball *(at the beach)*, Movie Theater *(White Marlin 213-1505)*, Park, Museum *(Ocean City Life-Saving 289-4991 $3/1)*, Special Events *(Sunfest - late Sep 250-0125)* **1-3 mi:** Golf Course *(Eagle's Landing 213-7277)*, Video Rental *(Blockbuster 213-7967)*

Provisioning and General Services

OnCall: Florist *(Flowers by Allison)* **Near:** Convenience Store *(7-Eleven)*, Supermarket *(SuperFresh 213-0410)*, Delicatessen *(Fat Daddy's 289-4040)*, Health Food *(Oganics 213-9818)*, Wine/Beer *(The Wharf 250-1013)*, Liquor Store *(Bearded Clam 289-4498)*, Fishmonger *(Martin's)*, Bank/ATM, Post Office *(drop-off at marina)*, Catholic Church *(St. Mary's by the Sea)*, Laundry, Bookstore *(Atlantic Books 289-8383)*, Hardware Store *(Elliott's 289-6123)*, Clothing Store *(outlets)*, Copies Etc. **Under 1 mi:** Library *(OC 289-7297)*, Pharmacy *(CVS 289-6512)* **1-3 mi:** Gourmet Shop *(Connoisseurs 213-0620)*, Beauty Salon *(Avery)* **3+ mi:** Department Store *(Wal-Mart 221-0292, 5 mi.)*

Transportation

OnCall: Water Taxi *(Buzz Boat 561-512-ASAP, Ch.72, $10)*, Rental Car *(Enterprise 213-0886)* **Near:** Bikes *(Bike World 289-2587)*, Taxi *(Dave's 250-2400, White's 250-8249)*, Local Bus *(Boardwalk Tram $2.50/pp 10am-Mid; OC Muni $2/day - up & down the island 24 hrs.)*, InterCity Bus *(The Whale $2/24 hr. pass)*, Airport Limo *(Limo Masters 250-7400)*
Airport: Ocean City/Salisbury *(3 mi./30 mi.)*

Medical Services

911 Service **OnCall:** Ambulance **Near:** Chiropractor *(Family Chiro 213-0900)*, Holistic Services *(A Touch of Energy 723-5533)* **Under 1 mi:** Doctor *(10th St Medical 289-6241)*, Dentist *(Golden 289-8828)* **1-3 mi:** Veterinarian *(OC Animal Hospital 213-1170)* **Hospital:** Atlantic General 641-0430 *(7 mi.)*

Setting -- Angler Restaurant and Dock is smack in the middle of the busiest stretch of waterfront in Ocean City's Old Towne - just before the Kelley Memorial Bridge. A plethora of of waterborne rides and activities are based here, so if you like to be at action central, snag one of the few transients slips and be part of the scene. The main focus is the large casual restaurant and the activity kiosks here and in front of adjacent Talbot Street Pier - really an extension of Angler.

Marina Notes -- Established in 1938, this is an O.C. fixture. Restaurant heads only and no showers. Transients might be right in front of Angler, on adjacent Talbot St. Pier, on a northern dock where the rental boats are kept, or where the charter fish boats live - wherever there's space.

Notable -- Capt. Bill Bunting's Angler serves three meals a day (starting at 6am-11pm, in the bar 'til 2am) in spacious nautically inspired casual dining spaces - inside in air conditioning or outside on the large waterfront deck. The resident 65 ft. Angler party boat departs daily at 7:30am (back at 1:30pm) for deep sea fishing. Afternoons it does offshore nature cruises - dolphin & whale-watch - and at night it offers free harbor cruises with dinner. Directly on the other side of Talbot Street Pier is M.R. Ducks, which has a very, very popular outdoor bar that sits on pilings - literally out on the water. Ocean City Parasail offers sails from 400, 600, and 800-feet for $50, $60 & $70 respectively (tandem, too) 289-BEST, 10am-6pm. Turtle Bay Runners rents a variety of vessels: the Gray Cat X-Treme Bandit, WaveRunners, and pontoon boats. The agressively painted bright yellow OC Rocket ocean speedboat ($12/6 kids/$8 60+) is based here as well. Assateague Adventure makes the nearby island very accessible - explore the national seashore and watch wild ponies ($14.50/$8; $12 60+ seniors).

PHOTOS ON CD-ROM: 9

Navigational Information
Lat: 38°20.025' **Long:** 075°05.807' **Tide:** 3 ft. **Current:** n/a **Chart:** 12211
Rep. Depths (*MLW*): Entry 7 ft. **Fuel Dock** 8 ft. **Max Slip/Moor** 8 ft./-
Access: Right at G11 to entrance buoys, turn to port before construction

Marina Facilities *(In Season/Off Season)*
Fuel: *Shell* - Slip-Side Fueling, Gasoline, Diesel, High-Speed Pumps
Slips: 170 Total, 10 Transient **Max LOA:** 65 ft. **Max Beam:** 19 ft.
Rate *(per ft.)*: **Day** $1.75/1.00 **Week** n/a **Month** Inq.
Power: 30 amp Incl., **50 amp** Incl., **100 amp** n/a, **200 amp** n/a
Cable TV: Yes, Free **Dockside Phone:** No
Dock Type: Fixed, Short Fingers, Pilings, Alongside, Wood
Moorings: 0 Total, 0 Transient **Launch:** n/a
Rate: Day n/a **Week** n/a **Month** n/a
Heads: 10 Toilet(s), 10 Shower(s) *(with dressing rooms)*
Laundry: 3 Washer(s), 4 Dryer(s) **Pay Phones:** Yes, 2
Pump-Out: OnSite, Full Service **Fee:** $5 **Closed Heads:** Yes

Marina Operations
Owner/Manager: Rolfe Gudelsky **Dockmaster:** Same
In-Season: Apr-Oct, 5am-9pm **Off-Season:** Nov-Mar, 8:30am-5pm
After-Hours Arrival: Tie up on T-head, Check in am
Reservations: Required **Credit Cards:** Visa/MC, Dscvr, Amex, Shell
Discounts: None
Pets: Welcome, Dog Walk Area **Handicap Access:** Yes, Heads, Docks

Ocean City Fishing Center

12940 Inlet Isle Lane; Ocean City, MD 21842

Tel: (410) 213-1121; (800) 322-3065 **VHF: Monitor** 16 **Talk** 71
Fax: (410) 213-0693 **Alternate Tel:** (410) 213-1121
Email: ocfc@ocfishing.com **Web:** www.ocfishing.com
Nearest Town: Ocean City *(0.5 mi.)* **Tourist Info:** (800) 626-2326

Marina Services and Boat Supplies
Services - Docking Assistance, Security *(24 hrs.)*, Trash Pick-Up, Dock Carts **Communication -** Mail & Package Hold, Phone Messages, Fax in/out *($1)*, FedEx, UPS, Express Mail *(Sat Del)* **Supplies - OnSite:** Ice *(Cube, Shaved)*, Ships' Store, Bait/Tackle, Live Bait **OnCall:** Boat/US

Boatyard Services
OnSite: Travelift *(35T)*, Bottom Cleaning, Yacht Broker **OnCall:** Engine mechanic *(gas, diesel)*, Electrical Repairs, Hull Repairs, Brightwork, Air Conditioning, Refrigeration, Divers, Compound, Wash & Wax, Interior Cleaning, Propeller Repairs, Woodworking, Upholstery, Yacht Interiors, Painting, Awlgrip **Near:** Forklift, Hydraulic Trailer, Launching Ramp, Electronics Repairs.

Restaurants and Accommodations
OnSite: Restaurant *(Mickey Finn's 213-9559, B $3-7, L $3-15, D $9-20, raw bar)* **Near:** Restaurant *(Sunset Grille 213-8110, L $7-10, D $7-25)*, *(Harborside 213-1846)*, *(Papa Vito's 213-7211)*, *(Buddy's Bistro 213-7211)*, *(Hooper's Crab House 213-1771, L $10-25, D $10-30)*, *(Crab Alley 213-7800)*, *(Outback Steakhouse 213-2595)*, *(Applebee's 213-7395)*, Lite Fare *(OC Jerky Outlet 213-1830, L & D $5-13, Polish and Italian Sausage for $4.99 lb.)*, Pizzeria *(Mione's 213-2231)* **Under 1 mi:** Motel *(Comfort Suites 213-7171)*, *(Rambler 213-8030, $75)*, Hotel *(Castle In the Sand 284-6846, $70-300)*

Recreation and Entertainment
OnSite: Heated Pool, Fishing Charter *(35 vessels 26-51 ft., $600-1800/day or $225/pp. 800-322-3065)*, Group Fishing Boat *(The Bay-Bee $20/14 half day, $5 rods)*, Special Events *(Arts on the Dock on Wed, OC Shark Tournament - Jun, OC Tuna Tournament - Jul)* **Near:** Beach, Picnic Area, Fitness Center, Video Arcade, Park, Sightseeing **Under 1 mi:** Roller Blade/Bike Paths, Bowling, Movie Theater *(Fox 213-1509)*, Video Rental *(Blockbuster 213-7967)*, Museum *(OC LifeSaving Museum)*, Galleries **1-3 mi:** Playground, Golf Course *(Eagle's Landing 213-7277)*, Boat Rentals, Volleyball **3+ mi:** Tennis Courts *(OC Tennis 524-8337 $10-14/hr., 5 mi.)*

Provisioning and General Services
OnSite: Bank/ATM **Near:** Provisioning Service, Convenience Store *(Royal Farms)*, Supermarket *(SuperFresh 213-0410)*, Gourmet Shop *(Harry & David 213-8182)*, Delicatessen, Health Food *(GNC 213-9523)*, Wine/Beer, Liquor Store, Bakery, Fishmonger, Lobster Pound, Meat Market, Market, Post Office, Catholic Church, Library, Beauty Salon, Barber Shop, Dry Cleaners, Laundry, Bookstore *(Book Warehouse 213-1226)*, Pharmacy, Newsstand, Hardware Store, Florist, Clothing Store, Retail Shops *(OC Factory Outlets 213-7898)*, Department Store, Copies Etc. **1-3 mi:** Crabs/Waterman

Transportation
OnSite: InterCity Bus *(OC Bus $2/24hrs.)* **OnCall:** Water Taxi *(Buzz Boat 561-512-ASAP, Ch.72, $10)*, Rental Car *(Enterprise 213-0886)*, Taxi *(Daves Taxi 24 hr. 250-2400)* **Near:** Local Bus *(The Whale $2/24 hr. pass)*
Airport: Ocean City/Salisbury *(2 mi./32 mi.)*

Medical Services
911 Service **Under 1 mi:** Doctor *(10th St Medical 289-6241)*
1-3 mi: Dentist, Chiropractor, Veterinarian *(OC Animal Hospital 213-1170)*
Hospital: Atlantic General 641-0430 *(6 mi.)*

Setting -- A half mile from the inlet, on the west side of the bay south of the Route 50/Kelley Bridge, OCFC has long been the center of the white marlin capital. Development has changed the surroundings significantly - with more to come. But the heart of this sportfish mecca remains true; over 35 charter boats are based here. In the "L" shaped basin, slips flank two free-standing piers and then edge that entire basin plus the long, slender cut that heads west.

Marina Notes -- DCM. Acquired by Sunset Marina in '03. A 35-ton travelift for haul and launch only; now BY services provided by outside contractors. Basin dredged yearly. Stationary docks have half-length finger piers, high-end pedestals. Two fueling stations; one at the basin entrance, one next to the weigh station. Professional staffed fish cleaning station. In '04 & '05, construction began on 72 townhouses along the north side of the basin. Construction will begin in '06 on 13 single-family homes just east of the basin - on the site of the former Shanty Town shopping village. All new bathhouse in '05 and laundry in '06.

Notable -- In '05, a new pool was perched at the head of the long stretch of narrow basin lined with sport fish boats, with spectacular views down the fairway and beyond. Adjacent is a contemporary, upscale bathhouse - the baby blue clapboard siding with white trim is topped by a teal pyramidal metal roof with cupola. For the '06 season, a matching two story building is planned to replace the old mini-mall that edged the front basin, to house Mickey Finn's waterfront restaurant, an observation deck, the main office, and a new bait and tackle shop. Across the street, a shuttle goes over the bridge to the beach & boardwalk. Under a half mile is the OC Outlet Mall with 30 upscale shops, two eateries & a supermarket - free trolley 10am-9pm daily in season, weekends only off-season.

Harbour Island Marina

419 14th Street, #66; Ocean City, MD 21842

Tel: (410) 289-3511 **VHF: Monitor** 12 **Talk** 72
Fax: (410) 352-9963 **Alternate Tel:** n/a
Email: reelinnbar@aol.com **Web:** n/a
Nearest Town: Ocean City **Tourist Info:** (800) 626-2326

Navigational Information
Lat: 38°20.633' **Long:** 075°05.001' **Tide:** 3 ft. **Current:** 0 kt. **Chart:** 12211
Rep. Depths (*MLW*): Entry 8 ft. **Fuel Dock** 8 ft. **Max Slip/Moor** 6 ft./-
Access: Past R4, private channel to starboard that leads to the basin

Marina Facilities *(In Season/Off Season)*
Fuel: *Ocean City Fuel* - Gasoline, Diesel, High-Speed Pumps
Slips: 30 Total, 10 Transient **Max LOA:** 70 ft. **Max Beam:** 22 ft.
Rate *(per ft.)*: **Day** $2.00 **Week** n/a **Month** n/a
Power: 30 amp Incl., **50 amp** Incl., **100 amp** n/a, **200 amp** n/a
Cable TV: No **Dockside Phone:** No
Dock Type: Fixed, Short Fingers, Wood
Moorings: 0 Total, 0 Transient **Launch:** n/a
Rate: Day n/a **Week** n/a **Month** n/a
Heads: 2 Toilet(s), 2 Shower(s)
Laundry: None **Pay Phones:** No
Pump-Out: OnSite **Fee:** n/a **Closed Heads:** Yes

Marina Operations
Owner/Manager: Scott Lathroum **Dockmaster:** Same
In-Season: May-Sep **Off-Season:** Nov-Apr
After-Hours Arrival: Open until 2am
Reservations: Yes, Preferred **Credit Cards:** Visa/MC, Dscvr, Amex
Discounts: None
Pets: No **Handicap Access:** No

Marina Services and Boat Supplies
Services - Docking Assistance, Security *(24 hrs., guard at gate)*, Trash Pick-Up, Dock Carts **Communication -** FedEx, DHL, UPS, Express Mail **Supplies - OnSite:** Ice *(Block)* **1-3 mi:** Bait/Tackle *(Skip's Bait & Tackle 289-8555)* **3+ mi:** Propane *(Eastern Shore Gas 524-7060, 5 mi.)*

Boatyard Services
Under 1 mi: Travelift, Engine mechanic *(gas, diesel)*, Electrical Repairs, Rigger, Bottom Cleaning, Air Conditioning, Refrigeration.
Nearest Yard: Ocean City Fishing Center (410) 213-1121

Restaurants and Accommodations
OnSite: Restaurant *(Reel Inn 289-3511, L $4-10, D $13-27, 11am-11pm, bar open until 2am; will cook your catch for $8)* **OnCall:** Pizzeria *(Domino's 723-5400)* **Near:** Restaurant *(Phillip's Crab House 289-6821, L $5- 15, D $5- 20)*, *(Buxy's Salty Dog Saloon 289-0973, L & D $4-10)*, *(Adolpho's Italian 289-4001)*, *(Biggie's Seafood & Subs 289-3222)*, Motel *(Sea Breeze 289-6900, $59-109)*, *(Stowaway Grand Hotel 289-7480, $59-329)*, Hotel *(King Charles 289-6141, $45-200)*, Inn/B&B *(Atlantic House 289-2333)* **Under 1 mi:** Seafood Shack *(Mario's 289-9445)*

Recreation and Entertainment
OnSite: Pool, Playground, Tennis Courts **Near:** Beach *(6am-10pm - lifeguards 10-5:30)*, Jogging Paths, Roller Blade/Bike Paths, Volleyball *(at the beach - 9th St.)* **Under 1 mi:** Boat Rentals, Fishing Charter, Video Rental *(Maximum 524-6000)* **1-3 mi:** Dive Shop, Bowling *(Ocean Lanes 524-7550)*, Movie Theater *(Fox Theatres 213-1505)*, Video Arcade, Museum *(Life-Saving Station 289-4991 $3/1, 11am-10pm, AAA 2 for 1 discount)* **3+ mi:** Golf Course *(Ocean City Golf 213-7050, Eagle's Landing 213-7277, 4 mi.)*, Fitness Center *(World Gym 524-1900, 4 mi.)*

Provisioning and General Services
OnSite: Wine/Beer **Near:** Supermarket *(Village Market 289-6461)*, Delicatessen, Liquor Store *(Anthony's Beer Wine & Deli 289-7853)*, Library *(OC 289-7297)*, Beauty Salon *(Hair Works 289-6770)*, Barber Shop **Under 1 mi:** Gourmet Shop, Bank/ATM, Post Office, Catholic Church, Dry Cleaners *(Wilgus 289-0009)*, Copies Etc. *(Beach Copy 524-2300)* **1-3 mi:** Convenience Store, Laundry, Bookstore *(Atlantic Books 289-1776)*, Pharmacy *(CVS 289-6513)*, Hardware Store *(True Value 524-2300)* **3+ mi:** Department Store *(Wal-Mart 221-0292, 6 mi.)*

Transportation
OnSite: Water Taxi *(Buzz Boat 561-512-ASAP, Ch.72, $10)* **OnCall:** Rental Car *(Enterprise 213-0886)*, Taxi *(B&C 326-8200)*, Airport Limo *(Limo Masters 250-7400)* **Near:** Bikes *(14th St. Bikes 289-3310)*, Local Bus *(The Whale $2/24 hr. pass; Boardwalk Tram $2.50/pp each way)*
Airport: Ocean City/Salisbury *(4 mi./30 mi.)*

Medical Services
911 Service **OnCall:** Ambulance **Near:** Doctor *(10th St. Medical 289-6241)* **1-3 mi:** Dentist *(43rd Street 289-8828)*, Chiropractor *(OC Chiropractic Clinic 213-1233)*, Veterinarian *(OC Animal Hosp. 213-1170)*
Hospital: Atlantic General 641-0430 *(8 mi.)*

Setting -- Just two-tenths of a mile off glitzy Ocean City's main drag is a little oasis called Harbour Island. A contemporary take on Cape Cod, this condominium/townhouse complex has gray shingles and white trim. It sits on a small peninsula that juts into the Bay. Townhouses line the perimeter, and in the core are 2 immaculately maintained tennis courts, a small children's playground, and a pool. The docks are bayside, in a very protected basin.

Marina Notes -- A wide range of vessels, including some sportfish and bluewater sailboats make their home here. Scott Lathroum manages about 30 of the dockominium slips, which may be available for transient dockage (the phone number is his cell). Transient slips are in the inner basin. The fuel dock is at the entrance to the basin, and adjacent to some of the permanent bayside slips; it's managed by Ocean City Fuel - 6am-9pm, seven days. They have diesel and gas - (Ch.10 or call 289-4528) - for fuel only. The bathhouse is at the pool: two heads and a shower (twhich seems to be used for umbrella storage).

Notable -- The diminutive Reel Inn Restaurant is neatly tucked in between the pool on the west side and the yacht harbor basin on the east side, with wide doors opening onto both the docks and pool. A boardwalk, which anchors the docks, circles the peninsula and makes a very nice morning or evening stroll. A new housing complex in the northeast corner of the basin is multiple shades of ochre and pale yellow. Buzz Boat Water Taxi is based here (VHF 72) $10/pp. Call or hail them, anywhere from the Route 90 bridge south to the Inlet area. The spectacular ten-mile Ocean City beach is a short walk across the island, with its famous three-mile boardwalk running south to the inlet. Take the boardwalk tram south to the honky-tonk and the excellent Lifesaving Museum.

Navigational Information
Lat: 38°21.077' **Long:** 075°04.733' **Tide:** 3 ft. **Current:** n/a **Chart:** 12211
Rep. Depths (*MLW*): Entry 6 ft. **Fuel Dock** 6 ft. **Max Slip/Moor** 5 ft./-
Access: Channel past Mallard Island then follow private markers into Bahia

Marina Facilities *(In Season/Off Season)*
Fuel: Gasoline, Diesel, On Call Delivery
Slips: 75 Total, 1 Transient **Max LOA:** 100 ft. **Max Beam:** n/a
Rate *(per ft.)*: **Day** $55.00* **Week** $330 **Month** $900
Power: 30 amp Incl., **50 amp** Incl., **100 amp** n/a, **200 amp** n/a
Cable TV: No **Dockside Phone:** No
Dock Type: Fixed, Long Fingers, Short Fingers, Pilings, Wood
Moorings: 0 Total, 0 Transient **Launch:** Yes ($5)
Rate: Day n/a **Week** n/a **Month** n/a
Heads: 6 Toilet(s), 2 Shower(s)
Laundry: None **Pay Phones:** No
Pump-Out: OnSite, Full Service, 1 Central **Fee:** $5 **Closed Heads:** Yes

Marina Operations
Owner/Manager: Shawn Harman **Dockmaster:** Same
In-Season: MemDay-LabDay, 24 hrs. **Off-Season:** Spring/Fall**, 5am-9pm
After-Hours Arrival: Call in advance
Reservations: Yes **Credit Cards:** Visa/MC, Dscvr, Amex
Discounts: None
Pets: Welcome **Handicap Access:** Yes, Heads, Docks

Bahia Marina

2107 Herring Way; Ocean City, MD 21842

Tel: (410) 289-7438; (888) 575-3625 **VHF: Monitor** 68 **Talk** 68
Fax: (410) 289-5720 **Alternate Tel:** (410) 289-7438
Email: fish@bahiamarina.com **Web:** www.bahiamarina.com
Nearest Town: Ocean City **Tourist Info:** (800) 626-2326

Marina Services and Boat Supplies
Services - Docking Assistance, Security, Trash Pick-Up, Dock Carts
Communication - Phone Messages, Fax in/out, Data Ports *(Office)*, FedEx, UPS **Supplies - OnSite:** Ice *(Block, Cube)*, Ships' Store, Bait/Tackle

Boatyard Services
OnSite: Launching Ramp, Engine mechanic *(gas)*, Bottom Cleaning
OnCall: Engine mechanic *(diesel)*, Electrical Repairs, Electronics Repairs, Hull Repairs, Rigger, Sail Loft, Canvas Work, Brightwork, Air Conditioning, Refrigeration, Divers, Compound, Wash & Wax, Interior Cleaning
Under 1 mi: Travelift, Forklift **Nearest Yard:** Sunset Marina (410) 213-9600

Restaurants and Accommodations
OnSite: Restaurant *(Fish Tales 289-0990, L $6-9, D $6-26, kids' $6 - Mon-Sat 11am-2am, Sun Noon-'til)* **OnCall:** Pizzeria *(Pizza Hut 289-5331)* **Near:** Restaurant *(Cafe Milan 289-6341)*, *(Mario's Restaurant 289-9445, D $10-25)*, *(Layton's Family)*, Seafood Shack *(Biggie's Seafood & Subs 289-3222)*, Crab House *(Philip's Crabhouse 289-6821, L $5-15, D $5-20)*, Pizzeria *(Papa Johns 524-1300)*, Motel *(Barefoot Mailman 289-5343, $40-75)*, Hotel *(Ocean Mecca 289-6133, $85-150)*, *(Dunes Manor 289-1100, $100-175)*, *(Days Inn Oceanfront 289-7161, $50-300)* **1-3 mi:** Hotel *(Surf Villa 289-9434, $55-125)*, Inn/B&B *(Atlantic House B&B 289-2333)*

Recreation and Entertainment
OnSite: Playground, Boat Rentals *(16-18 ft. skiffs w/ 8 hp motors $75/4hrs., WaveRunners, pontoon boats $200-300/4 hrs.)*, Fishing Charter *(Hot Pursuit, Capt. Bill 641-8455; Emily 960-4868; Last Call 289-1915; Let-er-Eat 320-420-5083)*, Group Fishing Boat *(75 ft. Judith M, deep sea 1/2 day $29/21, Tortuga Bay 3 hrs. $20/16)*, Video Arcade, Sightseeing *(Assateague Island, Parasailing)* **Near:** Beach **Under 1 mi:** Volleyball **1-3 mi:** Tennis Courts *(OC Tennis 524-8337 $10-14/hr.)*, Fitness Center *(Mussell 289-5656)*, Bowling *(Ocean Lanes 524-7550)*, Movie Theater *(White Marlin 213-1505)*, Video Rental *(Maximum 524-6000)*, Museum *(OC Lifesaving 289-4991 $3/1)* **3+ mi:** Golf Course *(Assateague 213-7526, 4 mi.)*

Provisioning and General Services
OnSite: Wine/Beer *(beer)*, Bank/ATM **Near:** Convenience Store *(7-11)*, Supermarket *(Village 289-6461)*, Liquor Store *(21st St.)*, Pharmacy *(CVS 289-6513)* **Under 1 mi:** Delicatessen *(Anthony's 289-7853)*, Fishmonger, Post Office, Catholic Church, Protestant Church, Library *(OC 289-7297)*, Beauty Salon, Laundry, Bookstore *(Atlantic Books 289-1776)*, Florist, Copies Etc. *(Beach Copy 524-0588)* **1-3 mi:** Health Food *(OC Organics 213-9818)*, Bakery, Dry Cleaners, Hardware Store *(True Value 250-1115)*

Transportation
OnCall: Water Taxi, Rental Car *(Enterprise 213-0886)*, Airport Limo *(Limo Masters 250-7400)* **Near:** Local Bus *(The Whale $2/24 hr. pass; Boardwalk Tram $2.50/pp.)*, InterCity Bus *(O.C. $2/24 hrs.)* **Under 1 mi:** Bikes *(Ann's Rental 289-9189)* **1-3 mi:** Taxi *(Atlantic 289-4011)*
Airport: Ocean City/Salisbury *(3 mi./30 mi.)*

Medical Services
911 Service **OnCall:** Ambulance **Under 1 mi:** Doctor *(10th St. Medical 289-6241)* **1-3 mi:** Dentist *(43rd St. Dental 289-8828)*, Chiropractor *(Family Chiro 213-0900)*, Holistic Services *(A Touch of Energy 723-5533)*, Veterinarian *(OC 213-1170)* **Hospital:** Atlantic General 641-0430 *(8 mi.)*

Setting -- A serious sportfish charter center with a fun and funky Caribbean ambiance: signature red and yellow skiffs and matching adirondack chairs, plus bright purple, yellow and turquoise buildings. The complex sits on a peninsula that juts out into the Isle of Wight Bay, and is centered around the newly enlarged indoor-outdoor, sand-floored Fish Tales eatery. The big-boat docks are strung out along the parking lot directly south of the restaurant.

Marina Notes -- *Flat Rate 30 ft. $55/day, $330/wk., $900/mo.; Up to 52 ft. $85/day, $500/wk., $1500/mo. **Spring/Fall - Apr 1-MemDay, LabDay-Nov 1. DCM. Family-owned & operated. Nicely maintained stationary docks with good pedestals. Fuel dock at the head of the sportfish dock; on call delivery. Fully stocked tackle shop; offshore bait avail. 24 hrs. in season. Prof. fish cleaner, official scales. Plug in your laptop at the office. Deep sea/bay fishing trips and scenic cruises. 14 sportfish charters 28-46 ft. $400-2000 or $225/pp. 12 hr. trip. Fish Tourneys: Mako Mania Shark - first wknd June, Poor Girls open - 3rd wknd in Aug. Tuna Mania Roundup - mid-July. BarTenders Open, 2nd week Sept. Basic heads are shared with the restaurant; but very nice, locked tile showers.

Notable -- The combination of small rental boats, private and charter sportfish vessels and a plethora of water-based activities creates a bustling scene. The counterpoint is relaxing Fish Tales, which tripled in size in '04 - enlarging the dining room and adding two bars. The sand floor gives the outside dining and billards area a beachy feel - shoes not required! Adirondack chairs line the water, the Swinging Lizard Lounge hosts a slew of hammock chairs and part of a ship creates a sandy kids' playground. Five blocks south (27th Street) is the northern terminus of the 3 mile O.C. boardwalk & beach - take the tram south.

PHOTOS ON CD-ROM: 13

Ocean Pines Marina

239 Ocean Parkway; Berlin, MD 21811

Tel: (410) 641-7447 **VHF: Monitor** n/a **Talk** n/a
Fax: (410) 641-8413 **Alternate Tel:** n/a
Email: n/a **Web:** n/a
Nearest Town: Ocean City *(3 mi.)* **Tourist Info:** (800) 626-2326

Navigational Information

Lat: 38°23.233' **Long:** 075°07.800' **Tide:** n/a **Current:** n/a **Chart:** 12211
Rep. Depths (*MLW*): Entry 12 ft. **Fuel Dock** n/a **Max Slip/Moor** -/-
Access: West side of Assawoman Bay, just south of the Rt. 90 bridge

Marina Facilities *(In Season/Off Season)*

Fuel: Yes
Slips: 86 Total, 5 Transient **Max LOA:** 110 ft. **Max Beam:** n/a
Rate *(per ft.)*: **Day** $1.50 **Week** n/a **Month** n/a
Power: 30 amp Incl., **50 amp** Incl., **100 amp** n/a, **200 amp** n/a
Cable TV: No **Dockside Phone:** No
Dock Type: Floating, Long Fingers
Moorings: 0 Total, 0 Transient **Launch:** n/a
Rate: Day n/a **Week** n/a **Month** n/a
Heads: 10 Toilet(s), 4 Shower(s) *(with dressing rooms)*
Laundry: None **Pay Phones:** No
Pump-Out: OnSite, Self Service **Fee:** n/a **Closed Heads:** Yes

Marina Operations

Owner/Manager: Wayne Derewesky **Dockmaster:** Same
In-Season: Apr 15-Sep 30, 8am-6pm* **Off-Season:** Oct 1- Apr 14, Closed
After-Hours Arrival: n/a
Reservations: No **Credit Cards:** Visa/MC
Discounts: None
Pets: No **Handicap Access:** No

Marina Services and Boat Supplies

Communication - FedEx, UPS, Express Mail
Supplies - 3+ mi: Bait/Tackle *(Joe's Bait & Tackle 213-9378, 9 mi.)*

Restaurants and Accommodations

OnSite: Restaurant *(Ocean Pines 641-7447, L $5-13, D $14-24)*, Snack Bar *(Tiki Bar)*, Lite Fare *(Dockside Grill 641-7501, L $5-13, D $5-13, poolside entertainment, buffet breakfast on weekends)* **OnCall:** Pizzeria *(Pizza Hut 208-1916)*, *(Domino's 641-6900)* **1-3 mi:** Restaurant *(Al Casapulla's Subs Steaks 208-2782, L $5-14, D $5-$14, also Pizzas, beer and wine)*, *(Breakfast at Bill's 208-1343)*, *(Hunan Garden 641-4460)*, *(Taylor's 208-4260)*, *(Whiskers Bar and Grill 208-3922)*, *(House of Crabs 524-1118)*, Coffee Shop *(Espresso Wave 208-1596)*, Fast Food *(Subway, McDonalds)*, Pizzeria *(Woobie's 208-6700)*, Hotel *(Paradise Plaza Inn 289-6381, $40-184)*
3+ mi: Motel *(Francis Scott Key Motel 213-0088, $36-200, 5 mi.)*, Hotel *(Atlantic 641-3589, $85-215, 7 mi.)*, *(Days Inn Oceanfront 289-7161, $50-300,5 mi.)*, Inn/B&B *(Merry Sherwood Plantation 641-2112, $125-175, 7 mi.)*, *(Holland House B&B 641-1956, 7 mi.)*

Recreation and Entertainment

Near: Picnic Area, Golf Course *(Ocean Pines Golf Course 641-6057 $66/18 holes before 2pm)*, Jogging Paths, Roller Blade/Bike Paths **1-3 mi:** Playground, Tennis Courts, Fitness Center, Bowling *(Ocean City)*, Fishing Charter *(Ocean City)*, Group Fishing Boat *(Ocean City)*, Park, Sightseeing *(Ocean City)* **3+ mi:** Other *(Ocean Downs Racetrack 641-0600, 6 mi.)*, Video Rental *(Video One 208-1100, 3 mi.)*, Museum *(Calvin Taylor House 641-1019, 7 mi.)*, Cultural Attract *(Globe Theatre 641-0784: music, shows, gallery & gift shop; brunch, dinner & wine bar at the Globe Bistro, 7 mi.)*

Provisioning and General Services

1-3 mi: Convenience Store *(7-Eleven 641-5118)*, Supermarket *(Food Lion 629-1576)*, Delicatessen *(South Side Deli & Seafood Market 208-3343)*, Wine/Beer *(Noble Grape 641-5119)*, Bakery *(Expresso Wave 208-1596)*, Farmers' Market *(Main St, Berlin, MD)*, Fishmonger *(Backfin's Seafood)*, Bank/ATM, Post Office, Protestant Church, Library *(Berlin PL 641-0650)*, Beauty Salon *(Ben's Hair Way 641-5208)*, Dry Cleaners *(Venable's 641-1400)*, Laundry *(Wash N Fold 208-6177)*, Bookstore *(First Editions 641-5211)*, Pharmacy *(Happy Harry's 208-3811, Rite Aid 629-0536)*, Hardware Store *(Home Depot 629-1465)*, Department Store *(Wal-Mart 221-0292)*, Copies Etc. *(Copy Central 208-0641)* **3+ mi:** Gourmet Shop *(Just a Taste 629-1984, 6 mi.)*, Liquor Store *(Whiskers 208-3922, 6 mi.)*, Market *(Shore Stop 641-5015, 6 mi.)*

Transportation

OnCall: Taxi *(Ace Taxi 641-4280)*, Airport Limo *(A Class Act 641-8500)*
1-3 mi: Bikes *(Continental Cycles 524-6942)*, Rental Car *(Xpress Rent-A-Car 213-7336)* **Airport:** Ocean City /Salisbury *(5 mi./25 mi.)*

Medical Services

911 Service **1-3 mi:** Doctor *(Ocean Pines Family Medicine 641-8585)*, Dentist *(Plack 208-0379)*, Chiropractor *(Healing Hands 629-0610)*, Veterinarian *(Watson 208-0910)*, Optician *(Ocean Pines Vision Care)*
Hospital: Atlantic General 641-0430 *(7 mi.)*

Setting -- Tucked away on the quiet, western side of Assawoman Bay, just south of the Route 90 bridge, the docks are away from the hustle and bustle of Ocean City. The yacht club-like marina is part of a 3,500-acre residential complex that sports more than nine miles of waterfront. At the head of the docks, verandas front both stories of a contemporary tan building that houses two restaurants and the bathhouse.

Marina Notes -- *Mon-Fri 8am-6pm, Sat & Sun 7am-6pm. DCM. Mostly smaller boats, but some good-sized sportfish vessels berth here, too. Note: The pool complex directly dockside is not available to transients. Wide floating docks have vinyl-wrapped corners and fairly new pedestals on the outer, bigger-boat, beamy slips. Fuel dock ("C") the third one in. Bathhouses, shared with the restaurant, are quite nice; each sports 5 stalls and a pair of tiled showers.

Notable -- Three eateries with views of the docks and bay serve lunch and dinner daily (MemDay-Oct 1). The casual Dockside Grill serves salads, sandwiches, barbeque, pasta platters and a breakfast buffet on weekends; entertainment several nights a week.The Ocean Pines dining room upstairs serves full-course meals with a varied menu. Poolside Tiki Bar (available even though the pool is not) serves lighter fare. Flat bike paths wind through the community. Tennis courts are available about a mile away (small fee); a bit futher is Ocean Pines Golf Course - an 18-hole Robert Trent design which welcomes overnight marina guests. About three miles is the community's members-only recreation complex (a terrific playground, picnic tables and a gazebo pavilion, basketball hoop, softball field, tennis and paddle tennis courts). Near the recreation complex are three good-size shopping centers - with most services and more eateries.

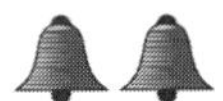

Navigational Information
Lat: 37°56.024' **Long:** 075°22.791' **Tide:** 2.5 ft. **Current:** 5 kt. **Chart:** 12210
Rep. Depths (*MLW*): **Entry** 12 ft. **Fuel Dock** n/a **Max Slip/Moor** 7 ft./-
Access: Chincoteague Channel just before the swing bridge

Marina Facilities *(In Season/Off Season)*
Fuel: No
Slips: 16 Total, 2 Transient **Max LOA:** 40 ft. **Max Beam:** n/a
Rate *(per ft.)*: **Day** $1.00 **Week** n/a **Month** n/a
Power: 30 amp Incl., **50 amp** n/a, **100 amp** n/a, **200 amp** n/a
Cable TV: No **Dockside Phone:** No
Dock Type: Fixed, Wood
Moorings: 0 Total, 0 Transient **Launch:** n/a
Rate: Day n/a **Week** n/a **Month** n/a
Heads: 2 Toilet(s)
Laundry: None **Pay Phones:** Yes, 1
Pump-Out: No **Fee:** n/a **Closed Heads:** Yes

Marina Operations
Owner/Manager: Paul Tatum **Dockmaster:** Same
In-Season: Year Round, 11am-8pm **Off-Season:** n/a
After-Hours Arrival: Call ahead
Reservations: yes **Credit Cards:** Visa/MC, Amex
Discounts: None
Pets: Welcome **Handicap Access:** No

Chincoteague Inn & Marina

6262 Marlin Street; Chincoteague Island, VA 23336

Tel: (757) 336-6110 **VHF: Monitor** n/a **Talk** n/a
Fax: (757) 336-5101 **Alternate Tel:** n/a
Email: n/a **Web:** n/a
Nearest Town: Chincoteague Island **Tourist Info:** (757) 336-6519

Marina Services and Boat Supplies
Communication - Data Ports *(In Library, Free)*, FedEx, UPS, Express Mail
Supplies - Near: Bait/Tackle *(Barnacle Bill's 336-5920)*

Restaurants and Accommodations
OnSite: Restaurant *(Chincoteague Inn 336-6110, D $13-26, most entrees in the teens, kids' $4-6)*, Lite Fare *(P.T. Pelican's Intracoastal Deck Bar L $5-11, D $5-11, steamed crab & pizza, too)* **Near:** Restaurant *(Skipper's Family Restaurant 336-6904, B $3-8, L $8.50-$10, D 13-$19, soups, salad bar, main entrees, breakfast too)*, *(Don's Seafood 336-5715, L $9-$20, D $9-$20, data-ports, library)*, *(Bill's Seafood 336-5831)*, *(Saigon Village)*, Crab House *(Landmark Crab House 336-5552)*, Snack Bar *(Muller's Ice Cream Parlor)*, Hotel *(Hampton Inn 336-1616)*, Inn/B&B *(1848 Island Manor House 336-5436, $100-170, historic, romantic, site of many small elegant events)*, *(Miss Molly's 336-6686, $95-175, a historical B&B where Marguerite Henry wrote her famous book "Misty")*

Recreation and Entertainment
Near: Boat Rentals *(Oyster Bay Outfitters 336-4547, jet skis at Pirates Propulsion 336-6165)*, Fishing Charter *(Reel Time Charters 336-5191)*, Movie Theater *(Island Roxy 336-6301)*, Video Rental *(House of Video)*, Park *(Chincoteague City Park)*, Galleries *(Osprey Nest 336-6042)*
Under 1 mi: Horseback Riding *(Chincoteague Pony Center - half hour - Mon-Sat, 9am-1pm 336-2776)*, Museum *(Oyster & Maritime Museum 336-6117, Chincoteague Pony Centre Museum)*, Cultural Attract *(Island Aquarium 336-2212)* **3+ mi:** Beach *(Chincoteague Nat'l Wildlife Refuge, 5 mi.)*

Provisioning and General Services
Near: Supermarket *(Fresh Pride 336-5829)*, Gourmet Shop *(Sea Star 336-5442)*, Delicatessen *(J&B Subs 336-550, Grubsteak 336-3166)*, Wine/Beer *(Wine, Cheese & More 336-2610)*, Liquor Store *(ABC 336-6162)*, Bakery *(Sugarbaker's)*, Fishmonger *(Sea Best)*, Bank/ATM, Post Office *(336-2934)*, Catholic Church, Protestant Church, Library *(Island Library 336-3460 Mon, Wed, Fri, & Sat 1-5pm, Tue10am-5pm, Thu 4-8pm, Closed Sun, Internet access)*, Beauty Salon *(Headquarters Hair Styling Salon)*, Barber Shop *(Bob's)*, Laundry, Bookstore *(Irene Rouse Book Cellar, Pony Tales)*, Pharmacy *(H&H 336-3115)*, Hardware Store *(Showard Bros. 336-6251)*, Retail Shops *(By the Sea Gift Shop, Twisted Sisters, Decoys)*

Transportation
Near: Bikes *(Mid-Town 336-2700 $8/day, $35/wk.)*, Local Bus *(Trolley)*, Airport Limo *(Island Limo 877-815-LIMO)* **Airport:** Salisbury *(50 mi.)*

Medical Services
911 Service **Near:** Dentist *(Baczek 336-5115)* **Under 1 mi:** Doctor *(Community Health Center, Island Medical 336-2200)*
Hospital: Atlantic General 410-641-0430 *(50 mi.)*

Setting -- Just before the Rt. 175 bridge, the docks of the simple Chincoteague Inn restaurant come into view. Two sets of single piers with alongside dockage plus bulkhead dockage just outboard of the eatery's dining decks. Views are across a large expanse of water and marsh and of the double-span bridge - be on the deck at sunset. Just south, a gaggle of two abreast fishing trawlers provide local color; at night they deliver a surreal light show, an otherworldly specter of ghost ships glowing in the mist. The charming, engaging village of Chincoteague is literally out the back door.

Marina Notes -- Transient dockage is limited. There is power on one of the docks and just water on the other. The bulkhead dockage, if the depths are sufficient, might provide a bit more privacy. An outside dining deck surrounds two sides of the restaurant. The outer section has views across the bay and marsh and of the bridge, and the southern section looks out over the docks. The inside dining room is very attractive, done with natural wood tables and upholstered chairs. Lunch: 11:30am-4pm, Dinner: 4-9pm. P.T. Pelican's is the on-site waterfront deck bar - the Island's first; and offers a more casual menu.

Notable -- The restaurant with docks is right up the street from the shops and services of Chincoteague. Adjacent is a bike rental store and Barnacle Bill's Bait-n-Tackle. The nearby all-volunteer diminutive Island Library has three free Internet access stations (a maximum of one hour per person, per day in the season; when it's crowded, half-hour blocks at a time) and a wonderful young children's section. A couple of blocks north, the elegant, historic 1848 Island Manor House, built in a traditional Maryland "T" style, has a rose-filled courtyard garden and showers that don't rock.

PHOTOS ON CD-ROM: 9

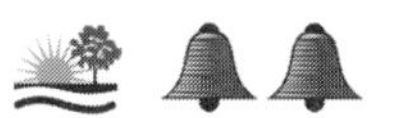

Chincoteague Town Docks

4150 Community Drive; Chincoteague Island, VA 23336

Tel: (757) 336-6519 **VHF: Monitor** n/a **Talk** n/a
Fax: (757) 336-1965 **Alternate Tel:** n/a
Email: n/a **Web:** n/a
Nearest Town: Chincoteague Island **Tourist Info:** (757) 336-6519

Navigational Information

Lat: 37°56.050' **Long:** 075°22.666' **Tide:** 3 ft. **Current:** 5 kt. **Chart:** 12210
Rep. Depths (*MLW*): Entry 12 ft. **Fuel Dock** n/a **Max Slip/Moor** 15 ft./-
Access: Cincoteague Channel just past the swing bridge

Marina Facilities *(In Season/Off Season)*

Fuel: *Mason Oil**** - Diesel, On Call Delivery
Slips: 10 Total, 10 Transient **Max LOA:** 50 ft. **Max Beam:** 18 ft.
Rate *(per ft.)*: **Day** $1.00* **Week** n/a **Month** n/a
Power: 30 amp Incl., **50 amp** n/a, **100 amp** n/a, **200 amp** n/a
Cable TV: No **Dockside Phone:** No
Dock Type: Fixed, Short Fingers, Alongside, Wood
Moorings: 0 Total, 0 Transient **Launch:** n/a
Rate: Day n/a **Week** n/a **Month** n/a
Heads: 4 Toilet(s), 4 Shower(s)
Laundry: None **Pay Phones:** No
Pump-Out: OnSite, 1 Central **Fee:** Free **Closed Heads:** Yes

Marina Operations

Owner/Manager: Town of Chincoteague **Dockmaster:** Wayne Merritt
In-Season: Year Round **Off-Season:** n/a
After-Hours Arrival: Call Chincoteague PD 757-336-3155
Reservations: Preferred** **Credit Cards:** Cash only
Discounts: None
Pets: Welcome **Handicap Access:** Yes, Heads, Docks

Marina Services and Boat Supplies

Communication - Data Ports *(Library, Free)*, FedEx, Express Mail
Supplies - Near: Ice *(Cube)*, Bait/Tackle *(Barnacle Bill's 336-5920)*

Restaurants and Accommodations

OnSite: Restaurant *(Saigon Village 336-7299)* **Near:** Restaurant *(Chincoteague Inn D $13-26, most in the teens, Kids' $4-6)*, *(Wright's Seafood 824-4012, Tue-Sat 4-9pm, Sun 12-9pm, all-you-can-eat crabs, shrimp and ribs)*, *(Sugarbakers Bakery and Café 336-3712, soups, salads, overstuffed sandwiches)*, *(Skipper's 336-6904, L $8.50-10, D 13-19 B, too - soups, salad bar, etc.)*, *(Ray's Shanty 824-3429, 11am-9pm, til 10 pm Fri-Sat, L specials)*, *(Don's Seafood 336-5715, L $9-20, D $9-20, B, too - entertainment on weekends)*, *(Bill's Seafood 336-5831, B, L & D, daily 5am-9pm)*, *(A.J's on the Creek 336-5888, L $4-$10, D $15-$30, oysters, seafood specials)*, Seafood Shack *(Steamers 336-5478, all-you-can-eat crabs, shrimp and chicken)*, Crab House *(Landmark Crab House 336-5552, B & L, waterfront)*, Lite Fare *(P.T Pelican's L $5-11, D $5-11, at Chincoteague Inn)*, Pizzeria *(Ledo 336-6597)*, Motel *(Comfort Suites 336-3700)*, *(Hampton Inn 336-1616)*, *(Lighthouse 336-5091)*, Inn/B&B *(Miss Molly's 336-6686, $95-175, historical B&B where Marguerite Henry wrote "Misty")*, *(Channel Bass Inn)*, *(1848 Island Manor 336-5436, $90-195, traditional MD "T" style building, rose courtyard garden)*

Recreation and Entertainment

OnSite: Picnic Area, Park **Near:** Boat Rentals *(Oyster Bay Outfitters 336-4547, jet skis at Pirates Propulsion 336-6165)*, Fishing Charter *(Reel Time Charters 336-2236, Fishawn 336-1953, Island Charters 336-5191)*, Movie Theater *(Island Roxy 336-6301)*, Video Rental *(House of Video)*, Sightseeing *(National Wildlife Refuge 336-6122, Assateague Explorer Cruises 866-PONY SWIM, Day Sail Charters 336-5271, Back Bay Cruises 336-6508, Spiders Explorer 990-4242)*, Galleries *(Osprey Nest 336-6042)*, Special Events *(Annual pony penning and pony swim - last Wed/Thu of Jul)* **Under 1 mi:** Museum *(Oyster & Maritime Museum 336-6117, Chincoteague Pony Centre 336-2776, Island Aquarium 336-2212)*

Provisioning and General Services

Near: Supermarket *(Fresh Pride 336-9707)*, Gourmet Shop *(Sea Star Carryout 336-5442, year-round)*, Wine/Beer *(Wine, Cheese and More 336-2610)*, Fishmonger *(Sea Best)*, Bank/ATM, Post Office *(336-2934)*, Catholic Church, Protestant Church, Library *(336-3460 - Mon, Wed, Fri & Sat 1-5pm, Tue 10am-5pm, Thu 4-8pm, Closed Sun)*, Beauty Salon *(Ann's Hairport 336-1111, Perfect Wave 336-7366)*, Barber Shop *(Bob's)*, Laundry *(F&G Laundromat 336-3191)*, Bookstore *(Irene Rouse; Pony Tales 336-6688, Kite Coup)*, Hardware Store *(Showard Brothers 336-6251)*, Retail Shops *(By the Sea Gift Shop, Crazy Lady, Twisted Sisters, Decoys)* **Under 1 mi:** Delicatessen *(J&B Subs 336-5500, Grubstake 336-3166)*, Liquor Store *(ABC 336-6162)*, Bakery *(Sugarbaker's)*, Pharmacy *(H&H 336-3115)*

Transportation

OnCall: Airport Limo *(Island Limo 877-815-LIMO)* **Near:** Bikes *($8/day, $35/wk., Mid Town 336-2700)*, Local Bus *(trolley)*
Airport: Salisbury *(50 mi.)*

Medical Services

911 Service **Near:** Dentist *(Baczek 336-5116)* **Under 1 mi:** Doctor *(Island Medical 336-2200)* **Hospital:** Atlantic General 410-641-0430 *(50 mi.)*

Setting -- Chincoteague now sports a wonderful waterfront park with ten new high-end transient docks (docks went in in '03 and pedestals and park in '04). A band pavilion surrounded by a brick patio will sit dockside. Open grassy areas host picnic tables and scattered park benches. Views across the channel are magical at sunset: past a small row of tidewater-themed private houses and a low rise condominium complex, over the marsh to Chincoteague Bay.

Marina Notes -- *Max. 10 days. Stay 10 days, pay for 7. **Reserve via cell phone. After hours: 757-336-6519, ext.119. ***Fuel delivery: Mason Oil Co. 336-3171 or Mears Oil 824-4211. Stationary, short finger piers except for one floating ADA dock. Additional alongside dockage with 6 feet of water is available just south of the bridge, near the launching ramp - no power. New heads & key coded showers are a block away in the white "bathhouse," a little past Bob's Barber Shop. The town also manages the Curtis Merritt Harbor just off The Canal, available only Nov-Apr as soon as the new bathhouses are "permitted;" it's completely filled in the summer except for emergencies. Note: There are no restaurants, services, electric or any way to get anywhere from Curtis Merrit.

Notable -- Everything in this sweet little town is an easy walk; restaurants abound. The tiny, adjacent library has internet access. WCTG, 96.5 FM, broadcasts classic, timeless greats right across the street. For a night off the boat, charming 1848 Island Manor House, just up the block, is particularly inviting. Go clamming, crabbing or fishing - there are several excursions - or take a nature cruise. To get to the beach you'll need a bike (no cabs on the island). It's about 3 miles to the first Chincoteague National Wildlife Refuge Visitors' Center (with lots of civilization along the way) and another two miles to the actual beach.

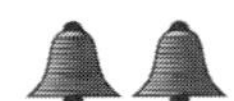

Captain Zed's Marina

PO Box 360; 1 Main Street; Wachapreague, VA 23480

Tel: (757) 789-3222 **VHF: Monitor** 72 **Talk** n/a
Fax: (757) 787-8911 **Alternate Tel:** n/a
Email: info@wachapreague.com **Web:** www.wachapreague.com
Nearest Town: Wachapreague **Tourist Info:** (757) 787-2460

Navigational Information

Lat: 37°36.233' **Long:** 075°41.266' **Tide:** n/a **Current:** n/a **Chart:** 12210
Rep. Depths (*MLW*): Entry 17 ft. **Fuel Dock** 10 ft. **Max Slip/Moor** 10 ft./-
Access: Follow the serpentine Wachapreague Channel

Marina Facilities *(In Season/Off Season)*

Fuel: Gasoline, Diesel
Slips: 18 Total, 6 Transient **Max LOA:** 90 ft. **Max Beam:** 20 ft.
Rate *(per ft.)*: **Day** $1.00 **Week** n/a **Month** n/a
Power: 30 amp Incl., **50 amp** Incl., **100 amp** n/a, **200 amp** n/a
Cable TV: No **Dockside Phone:** No
Dock Type: Fixed
Moorings: 0 Total, 0 Transient **Launch:** Yes
Rate: Day n/a **Week** n/a **Month** n/a
Heads: 2 Toilet(s), 2 Shower(s)
Laundry: 1 Washer(s), 1 Dryer(s) **Pay Phones:** Yes, Yes
Pump-Out: OnSite **Fee:** $10 **Closed Heads:** Yes

Marina Operations

Owner/Manager: Debbie Shrieves **Dockmaster:** Mark Coulbourne
In-Season: May-Oct, 5am-10pm **Off-Season:** Apr-Sep, 5am-8pm
After-Hours Arrival: n/a
Reservations: No **Credit Cards:** Visa/MC
Discounts: Boat/US **Dockage:** n/a **Fuel:** $0.05/gal. **Repair:** n/a
Pets: Welcome **Handicap Access:** Yes

Marina Services and Boat Supplies

Services - Dock Carts **Communication -** Mail & Package Hold, Phone Messages, Fax in/out, FedEx, UPS, Express Mail **Supplies - OnSite:** Ice *(Block, Cube)*, Bait/Tackle *(Captain Zed's)*

Boatyard Services

OnSite: Railway *(50T)*, Launching Ramp, Engine mechanic *(gas, diesel)*, Bottom Cleaning **OnCall:** Divers

Restaurants and Accommodations

OnSite: Restaurant *(Island House 787-4242, D $9-22, raw bar, steamed shellfish, fish, steaks, ribs)*, Motel *(Wachapreague 787-2105, $70-150, 30 rooms, efficiencies & 2 bedroom apartments; special rates off-season)* **Near:** Restaurant *(Henry's Marina Restaurant 787-4110, L $7-$10, lunch only, open Fri-Sun at Seaside Marina)* **3+ mi:** Restaurant *(Lockwood's Tavern 787-7381, L $3-21, D $3-21, 4 mi., in Melfa, VA, formerly called "Paradise Cove")*, Motel *(Captain's Quarters 787-4545, 5 mi.)*, Hotel (Comfort *Inn 787-7787, 7 mi.)*

Recreation and Entertainment

OnSite: Picnic Area, Grills, Playground, Boat Rentals *(16 ft. Carolina Skiffs)*, Fishing Charter *(36 ft. Foxy Lady 787-2105, 42 ft. Canyon Lady 787-2105, American Maid, 40 ft. Scorpio, 31 ft. Marlin Magic)*, Special Events *(Tournaments: Flounder - late Apr; Billfish, late July; Ladies' Tuna - Aug.)* **Near:** Tennis Courts, Jogging Paths, Video Rental, Park, Galleries **3+ mi:** Golf Course *(Back 9 Golf 414-0159, 12 mi.)*,

Provisioning and General Services

Near: Convenience Store, Wine/Beer, Bakery, Market *(Carpenter's Grocery 787-4660, Doughty's Market 787-2497)*, Bank/ATM, Post Office, Protestant Church **3+ mi:** Supermarket *(Food Lion 787-7546, 7 mi.)*, Liquor Store *(Onley Beverage 787-9410, 7 mi.)*, Beauty Salon *(Jolynn's European Hairart 787-8123, 7 mi.)*, Dry Cleaners *(Shore Cleaners 789-3400, 7 mi.)*, Bookstore *(The Book Bin 787-7866, 7 mi.)*, Pharmacy *(CVS 787-5608, Rite Aid 787-7154, 7 mi.)*, Department Store *(Peebles 787-1805, 7 mi.)*

Transportation

OnSite: Courtesy Car/Van **Airport:** Accomack/Norfolk *(9 mi./70 mi.)*

Medical Services

911 Service **OnCall:** Ambulance **Near:** Dentist *(Parker 787-3786)* **3+ mi:** Doctor *(7 mi.)*, Chiropractor *(Accomack Chiropractic 787-4500, 7 mi.)*, Veterinarian *(Accomack Animal Hosp. 787-3112, 7 mi.)*
Hospital: Shore Memorial 789-5000 *(8 mi.)*

Setting -- A long way up the winding Wachapreague Channel, the weathered shingled facade of the sprawling Captain Zed's and Island House restaurant complex welcomes transients. The expansive restaurant's windows and screened porches overlook the protected berths. The full-service marina offers fuel, on-shore lodgings, charter sport fishing and a bait and tackle shop. Ask about climbing up the lookout tower - the views are spectacular.

Marina Notes -- Lovely Island House Restaurant has a large indoor windowed dining room and a deck overlooking the docks, channel and wetlands beyond. It specializes in seafood and has a raw bar and steamer. Also on-site is the well-equipped Zed's Bait and Tackle. Boaters' heads are two simple full baths with quarry tile floors and glass-doored shower stalls. Across the street is the Wachapreague Hotel, a pleasant, simple, single-story brick motel. Additional transient dockage (stern-to, no finger piers) may be available next door at the Wachapreague Seaside Marina, also home to Uncle Henry's luncheonette.

Notable -- Once an internationally recognized fishing destination with elegant lodgings and roots back to 1836, this little seaside village is now a quiet outpost tucked behind pristine barrier islands and surrounded by a U.N. designated Biosphere Reserve - one of the last large wetland habitats in the world. Today amenities are limited - a block up the road is Carpenter's Grocery; next door are a small gift and coffee shop, a gallery, post office and two churches. The fishing is still reportedly excellent; the fleet heads out daily at the crack of dawn - at full plane. Inshore, wreck and offshore fishing features sea bass, tautog, trout, drum, croakers, marlin, bluefin tuna and dolphinfish. Day Rates: Flounder $475+, Seabass & Tautog $575, Tuna & Dolphin $900, Marlin $950.

PHOTOS ON CD-ROM: 10

Boaters' Notes

Add Your Ratings and Reviews at www.AtlanticCruisingClub.com

AtlanticCruisingClub.com provides updated Marina Reports, Destination and Harbor Articles, a Boaters' Forum and much more — including an option within each on-line Marina Report for Boaters to add their ratings and comments regarding that facility. Please log on frequently to share your experiences — and to read other boaters' comments.

On the website, boaters may rate marinas on one or more of the following categories — on a scale of 1 (basic) to 5 (world class) — and also enter additional commentary.

- **Facilities & Services** (Fuel, Reservations, Concierge Services and General Helpfulness):
- **Amenities** (Pool, Beach, Internet Access, including Wi-Fi, Picnic/Grill area, Boaters' Lounge):
- **Setting** (Views, Design, Landscaping, Maintenance, Ship-Shapeness, Overall Ambiance):
- **Convenience** (Access — including delivery services — to Supermarkets, other provisioning sources, Shops, Services. Attractions, Entertainment, Sightseeing, Recreation, including Golf and Sport Fishing & Medical Services):
- **Restaurants/Eateries/Lodgings** (Availability of Fine Dining, Snack Bars, Lite Fare, On Call food service, and Lodgings ashore):
- **Transportation** (Courtesy Car/Vans, Buses, Water Taxis, Bikes, Taxis, Rental Cars, Airports, Amtrak, Commuter Trains):
- **Please Add Any Additional Comments**

2. Top Of The Bay

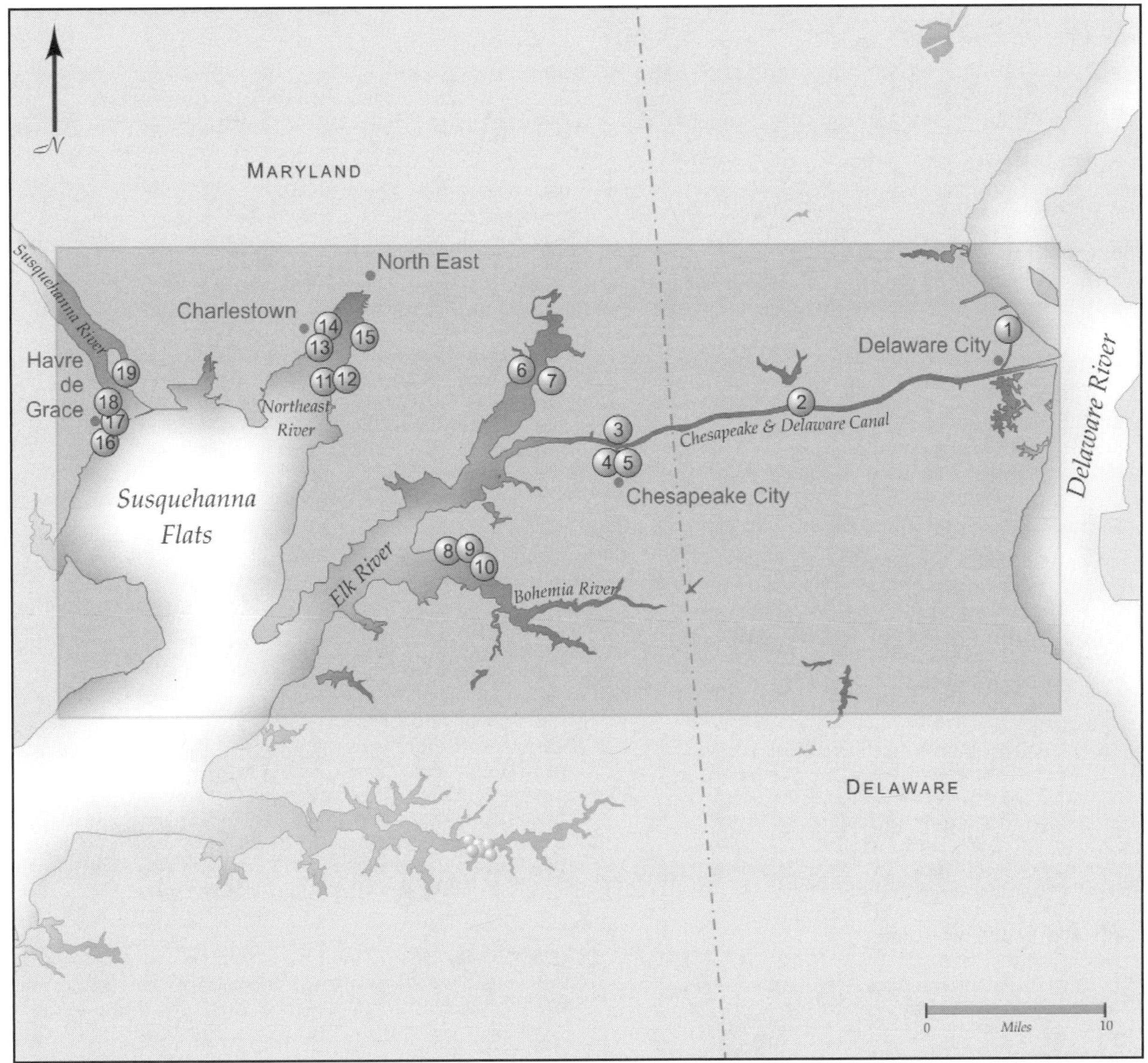

MAP	MARINA	HARBOR	PAGE
1	**Delaware City Marina**	*Delaware City Channel*	38
2	**Summit North Marina**	*C & D Canal*	39
3	**Schaefer's Canal House & Marina**	*C & D Canal*	40
4	**Chesapeake City Floating Docks**	*C & D Canal/Back Creek Basin*	41
5	**Chesapeake Inn & Marina**	*C & D Canal/Back Creek Basin*	42
6	**Triton Marina**	*Elk River*	43
7	**Cove Marina**	*Elk River*	44
8	**Two Rivers Yacht Basin**	*Bohemia River*	45
9	**Bohemia Vista Yacht Basin**	*Bohemia River*	46
10	**Bohemia Bay Yacht Harbour**	*Bohemia River*	47
11	**Jackson Marine**	*Northeast River*	48
12	**Bay Boat Works**	*Northeast River*	49
13	**Charlestown Marina**	*Northeast River*	50
14	**Lee's Marina**	*Northeast River*	51
15	**McDaniel Yacht Basin**	*Northeast River*	52
16	**Havre de Grace City Yacht Basin**	*Susquehanna River*	53
17	**Havre De Grace Marina — Log Pond**	*Susquehanna River*	54
18	**Tidewater Havre de Grace Marina**	*Susquehanna River*	55
19	**Perryville Yacht Club**	*Susquehanna River*	56

- **A "DCM" symbol in Marina Notes means Designated Clean Marina** — This is a coveted state-level award given to marinas that meet stringent, environmentally supportive requirements (see page 307). *For a list of DCM's & pump-out facilities, see page 308.*
- **Ratings & Reviews** — An explanation of the Atlantic Cruising Club's rating system, and a detailed explanation of what is in each section of the Marina Report is on pages 6 – 11. *The Data-Gathering Process is detailed on page 322.*
- **Marina Report Updates** — Updates to Marina Reports (from readers, ACC reviewers, and marinas) are posted regularly on *www.AtlanticCruisingClub.com*.

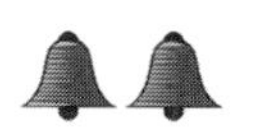

Delaware City Marina

PO Box ; 302 Canal Street; Delaware City, DE 19706

Tel: (302) 834-4172 **VHF: Monitor** 16 **Talk** 9
Fax: (302) 834-5187 **Alternate Tel:** n/a
Email: marinamom302@aol.com **Web:** www.delawarecitymarina.com
Nearest Town: Delaware **Tourist Info:** (302) 652-4088

Navigational Information
Lat: 39°34.200' **Long:** 075°35.383' **Tide:** 7 ft. **Current:** 2 kt. **Chart:** 12273
Rep. Depths (*MLW*): Entry 7 ft. **Fuel Dock** 9 ft. **Max Slip/Moor** 11 ft./-
Access: 2 mi. north of C&D Canal, on the Del side of the Del river

Marina Facilities *(In Season/Off Season)*
Fuel: Gasoline, Diesel
Slips: 100 Total, 10 Transient **Max LOA:** 45 ft. **Max Beam:** n/a
Rate *(per ft.)*: **Day** $1.25 **Week** $6.00 **Month** $15.00
Power: 30 amp $5, **50 amp** $10, **100 amp** n/a, **200 amp** n/a
Cable TV: No **Dockside Phone:** No
Dock Type: Floating, Alongside, Wood
Moorings: 0 Total, 0 Transient **Launch:** n/a
Rate: Day n/a **Week** n/a **Month** n/a
Heads: 2 Toilet(s), 2 Shower(s) *(with dressing rooms)*
Laundry: 2 Washer(s), 2 Dryer(s), Book Exchange **Pay Phones:** Yes
Pump-Out: OnSite, 1 Central **Fee:** $5 **Closed Heads:** Yes

Marina Operations
Owner/Manager: Jo Ann Barnard **Dockmaster:** Patty Hemphill
In-Season: Apr-Sep, 8am-6pm **Off-Season:** Oct-Nov15, 9am-5pm*
After-Hours Arrival: Call ahead
Reservations: Preferred **Credit Cards:** Visa/MC, Dscvr
Discounts: None
Pets: Welcome, Dog Walk Area **Handicap Access:** Yes, Heads, Docks

Marina Services and Boat Supplies
Services - Docking Assistance, Boaters' Lounge, Dock Carts **Communication -** Mail & Package Hold, Phone Messages, Fax in/out *($1/pp)*, FedEx, UPS, Express Mail *(Sat Del)* **Supplies - OnSite:** Ice *(Block, Cube)*, Bait/Tackle, Live Bait *(bloodworms, nightcrawlers)* **Near:** Ships' Store **3+ mi:** West Marine *(836-2766, 6 mi.)*

Boatyard Services
OnSite: Travelift *(20T)*, Crane, Forklift, Engine mechanic *(gas, diesel)*, Hull Repairs, Rigger, Bottom Cleaning, Propeller Repairs *(Mon-Thu turn-around)*, Yacht Broker **OnCall:** Electrical Repairs, Air Conditioning, Refrigeration, Divers, Interior Cleaning **Near:** Launching Ramp. Other Certifications: DMTA, MMRA **Yard Rates:** $60/hr., Haul & Launch $2.50/ft. *(blocking $2.50/ft.)*, Power Wash $2/ft., Bottom Paint $15-20/ft. **Storage:** In-Water $20-25/ft. season, On-Land $15-20/ft./season

Restaurants and Accommodations
Near: Restaurant *(Olde Canal Inn 832-5100, L $6-16, D $17-27, inside and patio - right on the point, great views from the deck)*, *(Wiso's Crab House 834-2279, L $10-16, D $10-16)*, *(La Matesina Italian 836-1855, L $6-13, D $6-13, pizza, too - delivers)*, *(Cofee Roaster Cafe 832-3303)*, Lite Fare *(Ice Cream Parlor)* **Under 1 mi:** Inn/B&B *(Olde Canal Inn 832-5100, $69-99)* **3+ mi:** Motel *(Super 8 322-9480, $55-80, 5 mi.)*, Inn/B&B *(Terry House 322-2505, $90-110, 4 mi.)*

Recreation and Entertainment
OnSite: Picnic Area, Grills, Park *(Battery Park)* **Near:** Museum *(Fort Delaware, a Civil War prison on Pea Patch Island 834-7941 $6/4 Wed-Sun - Fee includes ferry & permits journeying a half-hour further to Fort Mott State Park)*, Special Events *(Del City Days-Jul, Canal Fest- Sep)* **Under 1 mi:** Playground *(Dragon Run Park)*, Jogging Paths **1-3 mi:** Tennis Courts *(Southern Elementary)*, Sightseeing *(Fort Dupont 834-9201- 322 acres along Delaware River and C&D Canal - self-guided hiking trails)* **3+ mi:** Golf Course *(DE Golf Academy 378-3665, 10 mi.)*

Provisioning and General Services
Near: Wine/Beer, Liquor Store *(Delaware City Liquors 834-1941)*, Bank/ATM, Post Office, Catholic Church, Protestant Church, Library *(Delaware City 834-4148)*, Beauty Salon *(Jul's)*, Barber Shop, Retail Shops *(several antique shops)* **Under 1 mi:** Supermarket *(Sunset Market 836-1734)*, Delicatessen *(Sunset Market)* **3+ mi:** Farmers' Market *(Rt. 13 just outside Del City, Thu May-Oct 832-3303, 3 mi.)*, Hardware Store *(Lowes 834-8508, 5 mi.)*, Department Store *(Christiana Mall, 15 mi.)*

Transportation
OnSite: Courtesy Car/Van, Ferry Service *(Three Forts Ferry $6/4 kids, every hour from 10am to Fort Delaware and Fort Mott State Park)* **OnCall:** Rental Car *(Enterprise 323-0850 or Avis, National, 10 mi.)*, Taxi *(Seacoast 834-7575)* **Airport:** Philadelphia *(38 mi.)*

Medical Services
911 Service **OnCall:** Ambulance **Near:** Doctor *(Burdock 834-3600)* **3+ mi:** Veterinarian *(Red Lion Veterinary Hosp 834-2250, 6 mi.)*
Hospital: Christiana 733-1000 *(13 mi.)*

Setting -- Off Delaware Bay's Shore Channel, two miles north of the C&D Canal entrance, the Delaware City Branch Canal (the original C&D) hosts four sets of alongside floating docks that paralell the shore - head to toe - just south of town and Port Park. The feeling is more that of a long protected cove than an active channel. Overlooking the canal and the fuel dock is a gray-stained deck with attractive umbrella-topped picnic tables.

Marina Notes -- *Nov15-Jan 10am-4pm, Feb & Mar by appt. Founded in 1990. Delaware City Towboat lives here. Small Lighthouse pedestals populate four unconnected floating docks - each with its own quality aluminum ramp to the road. "D" Dock is also the fuel dock. "C" is close to the well-supplied ships' store (bait and tackle, too) and the heads. "D" is much newer - with larger lighthouse pedestals and IPE decking. On-the-hard storage surrounds the store - 20-ton travelift & repair services. Inviting bathhouses have faux tile walls, sinks inset into Formica vanities, hanging plants and glass-walled fiberglass shower stalls.

Notable -- At the end of "A" Dock a short brick path leads north to delightful, emerging and gentrifying Delaware City. Unique, local shops, galleries, boutiques, antiques, markets, houses and eateries line Clinton Street on the western shore of the waterway. From downtown Port Park, every hour (10am-4pm) a ferry makes the 10-minute cruise to Fort Delaware State Park - a living history museum on Pea Patch Island. Once there, a jitney provides transportation from the island dock to the massive pentagon-shaped granite and brick fortress. Authentically-clad historic interpreters describe the summer of 1863 when thousands of Confederate soldiers were imprisioned here. Port Park offers courtesy dockage (to 50 ft.) with a 4 hr. maximum - for dining, shopping, visiting Fort Delaware.

PHOTOS ON CD-ROM: 12

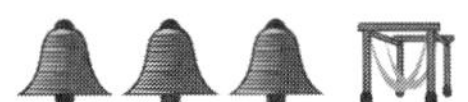

Navigational Information
Lat: 39°32.828' **Long:** 075°42.365' **Tide:** 4ft. **Current:** n/a **Chart:** 12273
Rep. Depths (*MLW*): Entry 10 ft. **Fuel Dock** n/a **Max Slip/Moor** 20 ft./-
Access: Mile #8 on the C & D Canal at Conrail Lift Bridge

Marina Facilities *(In Season/Off Season)*
Fuel: Gasoline, Diesel
Slips: 250 Total, 20 Transient **Max LOA:** 125 ft. **Max Beam:** n/a
Rate *(per ft.)*: **Day** $1.50/Inq.* **Week** Inq. **Month** Inq.
Power: 30 amp $5, **50 amp** $10, **100 amp** n/a, **200 amp** n/a
Cable TV: Yes, Incl. Direct TV **Dockside Phone:** Yes, 2 line(s)
Dock Type: Floating, Long Fingers, Alongside, Wood
Moorings: 1 Total, 0 Transient **Launch:** n/a, Dinghy Dock
Rate: Day n/a **Week** n/a **Month** n/a
Heads: 10 Toilet(s), 10 Shower(s) *(with dressing rooms)*
Laundry: 2 Washer(s), 2 Dryer(s) **Pay Phones:** No
Pump-Out: OnSite, 1 Central **Fee:** $5 **Closed Heads:** Yes

Marina Operations
Owner/Manager: Chris Lloyd **Dockmaster:** Phyllis Drupieski
In-Season: Year-Round, 24 hrs. **Off-Season:** n/a
After-Hours Arrival: Call security Ch. 16
Reservations: Preferred **Credit Cards:** Visa/MC, Dscvr
Discounts: None **Dockage:** n/a **Fuel:** 100 gals **Repair:** n/a
Pets: Welcome, Dog Walk Area **Handicap Access:** Yes, Heads, Docks

Summit North Marina

Summit North Marina

3000 Summit Harbour Place; Bear, DE 19701

Tel: (302) 836-1800 **VHF: Monitor** 16 **Talk** 9
Fax: (302) 836-3647 **Alternate Tel:** n/a
Email: info@summitnorthmarina.com **Web:** www.summitnorthmarina.com
Nearest Town: Kirkwood *(1 mi.)* **Tourist Info:** (302) 737-4059

Marina Services and Boat Supplies
Services - Docking Assistance, Boaters' Lounge, Security *(24 hrs., Guards)*, Trash Pick-Up, Dock Carts **Communication -** Mail & Package Hold, Data Ports *(Office)*, FedEx, DHL, UPS, Express Mail *(Sat Del)* **Supplies - OnSite:** Ice *(Block, Cube)*, Ships' Store **1-3 mi:** Boat/US, Propane *(Kirkwood Gas 834-7694)* **3+ mi:** West Marine *(836-2766, 8 mi.)*, Bait/Tackle *(Tackle Box 322-4307, 6 mi.)*

Boatyard Services
OnSite: Travelift *(50T)*, Engine mechanic *(gas, diesel)* **OnCall:** Electronics Repairs, Hull Repairs, Rigger, Sail Loft, Canvas Work, Bottom Cleaning, Brightwork, Air Conditioning, Refrigeration, Divers, Compound, Wash & Wax, Interior Cleaning, Propeller Repairs, Woodworking, Inflatable Repairs, Life Raft Service, Upholstery, Yacht Interiors, Metal Fabrication, Painting, Total Refits **Under 1 mi:** Launching Ramp. **Dealer for:** Sea Ray.
Yard Rates: Haul & Launch $8/ft. *(blocking $3/ft.)*, Power Wash $3/ft.

Restaurants and Accommodations
OnSite: Restaurant *(Captain's Cove 834-2000, L $5-10, D $15-20, Mon-Thu 11am-9pm, Fri &Sat 'til 11pm, Sun 'til 10pm, kids menu, breakfast-to-go, Sat & Sun 8-11am)* **OnCall:** Pizzeria *(Domino's 376-7000)* **3+ mi:** Restaurant *(Yankee 834-2848, 8 mi.)*, Fast Food *(Subway 834-6632, L $3-7, D $3-7, 4 mi.)*, Lite Fare *(Red Lion Inn 834-7931, 4 mi.)*, Pizzeria *(Amore 834-1434, L $3-9, D $6-10, 4 mi.)*, Motel *(Fairwinds 322-4688, $40, 7 mi., $250/wk.)*, Hotel *(America Inn 326-2500, $79-200, 7 mi.)*

Recreation and Entertainment
OnSite: Pool, Picnic Area, Grills, Jogging Paths, Roller Blade/Bike Paths
Near: Park *(Lum's Pond State Park, boat ramp)* **1-3 mi:** Video Rental *(Big Herb's 834-8457)*, Video Arcade **3+ mi:** Tennis Courts *(Elkton Indoor Tennis 398-8282, 10 mi.)*, Golf Course *(Cedar Run 832-0992, 6 mi.)*, Fitness Center *(YMCA 571-6908, 7 mi.)*, Bowling *(Delaware City Bowling Lanes 834-4480, 9 mi.)*, Movie Theater *(Regal 834-8510, free shuttle, 12 mi.)*

Provisioning and General Services
OnSite: Convenience Store **Under 1 mi:** Bank/ATM, Post Office
1-3 mi: Supermarket *(Acme 453-2335)*, Delicatessen *(Oceanmart Deli 834-1106)*, Market *(Woody's 656-5020, Natalie's Food 836-2796)*, Catholic Church, Protestant Church, Newsstand *(News Basket)*, Florist *(Glasgow Florist)* Florist), Clothing Store **3+ mi:** Liquor Store *(Fox Run 836-9463, 7 mi.)*, Library *(Bear PL 838-3300, 8 mi.)*, Dry Cleaners *(Elim Cleaners 838-9727, 5 mi.)*, Pharmacy *(Rite Aid 836-1004, 7 mi.)*, Hardware Store *(Red Lion 834-1903, 4 mi.)*, Department Store *(Kohl's 834-7300, 9 mi.)*

Transportation
OnSite: Courtesy Car/Van *(8:30am-4:30pm in season)* **OnCall:** Rental Car *(Enterprise 454-2939)*, Taxi *(Bear Transportation (also airport limo) 838-7606)* **3+ mi:** Rail *(Newark, 8 mi.)* **Airport:** Philadelphia *(33 mi.)*

Medical Services
911 Service **OnCall:** Ambulance **3+ mi:** Doctor *(Glasgow Medical Center 836-3539, 6 mi.)*, Dentist *(Bear Glasgow Dental 836-9330, 6 mi.)*, Chiropractor *(Feeney Chiropractic 328-0200, 8 mi.)*, Veterinarian *(Lums Pond Animal Hospital 836-5585, 4 mi.)*
Hospital: Christiana 733-3500/Union 398-5941 *(12 mi.)*

Setting -- The landmark Summit North Bridge marks the entrance to this large, quiet marina protected by high bluffs. Just off the Canal, surrounded by Lum's Pond State Park, the floating, vinyl-edge docks literally fill the basin. There's no development, just trees and marsh. A floating boardwalk runs the full length of the basin; docks radiate from it. A pool, backed by a 2-story cream-colored stucco restaurant and bathhouse, perches on a hill overlooking the basin.

Marina Notes -- *Weekends $2/ft. Well-designed floating docks (with wide, full-length finger piers) are being replaced with grooved mahogany, screwed-down decking. Corner insets create trapezoidal slips, making room for dock boxes, pedestals, and walkways. Docks go from "A," at the basin's head, to "I" at the entrance from the canal. They are varying lengths and include some double-wides for cats. The cut for the ramp that leads to the restaurant and pool is between "C" &" D" dock. On the north side of the eatery, a keycoded bathhouse entrance has six very nice individual, fully-tiled bathrooms and a small laundry room. Another set of heads is near "A" dock, along with a small ships' store, the office, two picnic tables, a parking lot, haul out and dry storage.

Notable -- The basin, part of the C&D Canal before it was straightened, is owned by the state and leased to the marina. Captain's Cove restaurant overlooks the pool; for water views, move to the patio which sports a rope fence and lighthouse sculptures. Lunch all day, dinner, specials on weekends, and 36 varieties of beer. A banquet room seating 80 makes this an interesting club cruise venue. Entertainment Fri & Sat 7-11pm, Sun 4-8pm: easy-listening, dance & beach music. Less than a mile away, a boat ramp provides the nearest access to Lum's Pond State Park and steps lead up to the trails.

PHOTOS ON CD-ROM: 12

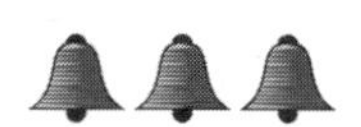

Schaefer's Marina

208 Bank Street; Chesapeake City, MD 21915

Tel: (410) 885-2204 **VHF: Monitor** 16 **Talk** 68
Fax: (410) 885-2206 **Alternate Tel:** (410) 885-2200
Email: n/a **Web:** www.newschaeferscanalhouse.com
Nearest Town: Elkton *(6 mi.)* **Tourist Info:** (410) 398-5076

Navigational Information

Lat: 39°31.768' **Long:** 075°48.776' **Tide:** 3 ft. **Current:** 2 kt. **Chart:** 12273
Rep. Depths (*MLW*): Entry 36 ft. **Fuel Dock** 14 ft. **Max Slip/Moor** 14 ft./-
Access: From Delaware/Chesapeake Bays to the C & D Canal

Marina Facilities *(In Season/Off Season)*

Fuel: *private* - Gasoline, Diesel, High-Speed Pumps
Slips: 35 Total, 35 Transient **Max LOA:** 260 ft. **Max Beam:** n/a
Rate *(per ft.)*: **Day** $1.00* **Week** Inq. **Month** Inq.
Power: 30 amp $5, **50 amp** $10, **100 amp** n/a, **200 amp** n/a
Cable TV: No **Dockside Phone:** No
Dock Type: Fixed
Moorings: 0 Total, 0 Transient **Launch:** n/a
Rate: Day n/a **Week** n/a **Month** n/a
Heads: 8 Toilet(s)
Laundry: None **Pay Phones:** Yes
Pump-Out: No **Fee:** n/a **Closed Heads:** Yes

Marina Operations

Owner/Manager: Rich Ostrander **Dockmaster:** Stacey Byerly
In-Season: Mar-Nov, 8am-8pm **Off-Season:** Dec-Feb, Closed
After-Hours Arrival: Call in advance
Reservations: Yes, Preferred **Credit Cards:** Visa/MC, Dscvr, Amex
Discounts: Boat/US **Dockage:** 10% **Fuel:** n/a **Repair:** n/a
Pets: Welcome, Dog Walk Area **Handicap Access:** No

Marina Services and Boat Supplies

Services - Docking Assistance, Boaters' Lounge **Communication -** Phone Messages, Fax in/out, FedEx, UPS, Express Mail **Supplies - OnSite:** Ice *(Cube)* **3+ mi:** West Marine *(287-6600, 12 mi.)*, Bait/Tackle *(Sarge's Bait Tackle 620-9183, 6 mi.)*, Propane *(Summit Bridge 836-0800, 5 mi.)*

Boatyard Services

OnCall: Engine mechanic *(gas, diesel)*, Electrical Repairs, Electronics Repairs, Hull Repairs, Rigger, Refrigeration, Divers **1-3 mi:** Travelift. **Nearest Yard:** Bohemia Bay Yacht Harbor (410) 885-2601

Restaurants and Accommodations

OnSite: Restaurant *(Schaefer's Canal House, 885-2200, B $5-9, L $6-15, D $16-27, Mon-Fri 11am-10pm, Sat 8am-11pm, Sun 'til 10pm; B Sat & Sun only; L 'til 4pm)*, Lite Fare *(The Terrace L $5-14, D $5-14, outside Thu 4-10pm, Fri 'til 11pm, Sat 11am-11pm, Sun 'til 10pm; entertainment Mon-Thu), (The Canal House Bar L $5-10, D $5-10, inside Sat & Sun 'til 11pm)*, Condo/Cottage *(Schaefer's Canal House 885-2200, $150)* **Near:** Seafood Shack *(Crab Shack 885-2662)* **Under 1 mi:** Restaurant *(Chesapeake Inn 885-2040, L $8-16, D $19-32, deck May-Oct $5-16 - by dinghy/water taxi), (The Yacht Club Restaurant 885-2267, D $13-28, Mon-Thu & Sun 3-9pm, Fri-Sat 3-10pm; early bird daily 3-5pm, $12), (The Bayard House 885-5040, L $10-18, D $21-39, or by dinghy/water taxi; opened in 1780; canal views), (Tap Room 885-2344, or by dinghy/water taxi; classic, old-time crab house)*, Lite Fare *(Bohemia Café & Bakery 885-3066)*, Pizzeria *(Roma 885-2844)*, Inn/B&B *(Ship Watch 885-5300, $115), (Blue Max 885-2781), (Inn at the Canal 885-5995, $85-195, gracious hosts will pick up boaters; antiques, water view, gorgeous garden, center of historic district)*

Recreation and Entertainment

OnSite: Special Events *(Canal Day)* **Under 1 mi:** Jogging Paths, Museum *(C&D Canal 885-5621 Mon-Fri 8am-4pm)*, Sightseeing *(Canal Town Tours 885-5263 $5/Free, $15- 3 people min. Sat & Sun 1pm & 4pm, weekdays by appt. at Franklin Hall; Miss Claire Canal Tours 885-5088)* **1-3 mi:** Golf Course *(Brantwood 398-8818)* **3+ mi:** Tennis Courts *(Elkton Indoor 398-8282, 7 mi.)*, Fitness Center *(Curves 398-9864, 6 mi.)*, Bowling *(Cecil Lanes 398-1664, 7 mi.)*, Movie Theater *(Regal 834-8510, 9 mi.)*

Provisioning and General Services

OnSite: Wine/Beer **Near:** Catholic Church **Under 1 mi:** Convenience Store, Liquor Store *(Chesapeake Wine & Spirits 885-5858)*, Farmers' Market *(Fri 4-7pm at Ches Wine & Spirits)*, Bank/ATM, Post Office, Library *(885-2552)*, Retail Shops *(South Chesapeake City)* **1-3 mi:** Delicatessen *(Brantwood Deli 398-9783)* **3+ mi:** Supermarket *(Acme 398-4925, 5 mi.)*, Pharmacy *(Acme 620-0602, 5 mi.)*, Hardware Store *(Home Depot 838-6818, 9 mi.)*, Department Store *(Wal-Mart 398-1070, 6 mi.)*

Transportation

OnCall: Rental Car *(Enterprise 398-0030)*, Taxi *(Joe's Taxi 392-8070)*, Airport Limo *(Town Car 885-9228)* **Near:** Water Taxi *(From Town Docks just north of Schaefer's to Chesapeake City Floating Docks)* **3+ mi:** Rail *(Wilmington, 30 min.)* **Airport:** Philadelphia/Cecil County *(50 mi./9 mi.)*

Medical Services

911 Service **OnCall:** Ambulance **1-3 mi:** Doctor *(Family Practice 275-8157)*, Dentist *(Cohn 275-2225)*, Veterinarian *(Benner 885-3700)* **3+ mi:** Chiropractor *(Clifford 620-4322, 6 mi.)* **Hospital:** Union 398-4000 *(6 mi.)*

Setting -- Near the western end of the C&D Canal, in the shadow of the massive 135 foot high Rt. 213 Bridge, historic Schaefer's Canal House - with its long fuel dock and red pilings - dominates the northern shore. The white clapboard, mostly windowed, hip-roofed main building houses three eateries. Adjacent is a banquet facility with contemporary dormers and in between a canal-front terrace with a bar in an octagonal pavilion topped by a cuploa. The transient dockage includes the fuel dock and continues under the bridge for 1200 ft. with additional slips tucked into a basin set-back from the canal.

Marina Notes -- NOTE: As of November '05, Schaefer's was again transitioning between owners. The docks had suffered some damage and were closed for extensive repairs. Staff anticipates that the marina will be fully functional by Spring '06, but CALL AHEAD!! *Credit Card Rate $1.35/ft., Boat/US 10%, Cash $1/ft. Inquire about discounts for large fuel quantities. Dockmaster recommends docking into the current - which can be 2 knots. Historic rental houses are available. Schaefer's no longer has a dedicated bath house (formerly in Canvasback). The only heads are those in the restaurant and next to the terrace.

Notable -- The historic main dining room (now The "New" Canal House) has huge windows filled with ships transiting the canal - their names and home port are announced. Thursday to Sunday entertainment keeps The Terrace high energy and crowded. On weekends, the bar serves more casual fare. The Canal House Banquet Room overlooks the terrace and the canal; it can accommodate at least 200 people, with a dance floor, making this a potential cruise event site. Many services, boutiques, galleries, antique shops, more restaurants and B&Bs are in charming South Chesapeake City across the canal.

Navigational Information
Lat: 39°31.605' **Long:** 075°48.665' **Tide:** n/a **Current:** n/a **Chart:** 12273
Rep. Depths (*MLW*): Entry 12 ft. **Fuel Dock** n/a **Max Slip/Moor** 6 ft./-
Access: C&D Canal to Back Creek Basin

Marina Facilities *(In Season/Off Season)*
Fuel: No
Slips: 8 Total, 4 Transient **Max LOA:** 200 ft. **Max Beam:** n/a
Rate *(per ft.)*: **Day** Free* **Week** n/a **Month** n/a
Power: 30 amp n/a, **50 amp** n/a, **100 amp** n/a, **200 amp** n/a
Cable TV: No **Dockside Phone:** No
Dock Type: Floating, Alongside, Wood
Moorings: 10 Total, 10 Transient **Launch:** n/a
Rate: Day n/a **Week** n/a **Month** n/a
Heads: None
Laundry: None **Pay Phones:** No
Pump-Out: No **Fee:** n/a **Closed Heads:** Yes

Marina Operations
Owner/Manager: Chesapeake City **Dockmaster:** None
In-Season: Year-Round **Off-Season:** n/a
After-Hours Arrival: Call ahead
Reservations: No; first-come first-serve **Credit Cards:** n/a
Discounts: None
Pets: Welcome **Handicap Access:** No

Chesapeake City Floating Docks

PO Box 205; 108 Bohemia Avenue; Chesapeake City, MD 21915
Tel: (410) 885-5298 **VHF: Monitor** n/a **Talk** n/a
Fax: (410) 885-2515 **Alternate Tel:** n/a
Email: n/a **Web:** www.chesapeakecity.com
Nearest Town: Elkton *(7 mi.)* **Tourist Info:** (410) 398-5076

Marina Services and Boat Supplies
Supplies - Near: Ice *(Cube)* **3+ mi:** Ships' Store *(Martin Marine Supply 885-2455, 4 mi.)*, Bait/Tackle *(Sarge's Bait Tackle 620-9183, 7 mi.)*

Boatyard Services
OnCall: Engine mechanic *(gas, diesel)* **Near:** Launching Ramp
1-3 mi: Travelift. **Nearest Yard:** Bohemia Bay (410) 885-2601

Restaurants and Accommodations
Near: Restaurant *(The Hole in the Wall L $5-17, D $5-17, 18thC. Pub below Bayards; bar food & Bayard House menu, 11:30am-9:30pm)*, *(Bayard House 885-5040, L $5-18, D $20-40, 11:30am-3pm, 4-9pm)*, *(Chesapeake Inn 885-2040, L $8-16, D $19-32, deck May-Oct $5-16)*, *(The Yacht Club 885-2267, D $13-28, early bird 3-5pm, $12)*, Seafood Shack *(Tap Room 885-9873, steamed crabs)*, Lite Fare *(Bohemia Café & Bakery 885-3066, B, L, D - take-out)*, Pizzeria *(Roma 885-2844)*, Inn/B&B *(Ship Watch Inn 885-5300, $95-245, waterfront, recently renovated)*, *(Blue Max 885-2781, $95-230)*, *(Inn at the Canal 885-5995, $85-195)*, Condo/Cottage *(Old Wharf Cottage 885-5040, $100-120, owned by Bayard House, weekend & week rates)* **Under 1 mi:** Restaurant *(Jack & Helen's 885-5477, B & L)*, *(Schaefer's Canal House 885-2200, B $5-9, L $6-15, D $16-27, water taxi)*, Lite Fare *(Schaefer's Terrace L $5-14, D $5-14, Thu-Sun; inside bar $5-10 weekends, entertainment nightly)*

Recreation and Entertainment
OnSite: Sightseeing *(Ms. Claire Cruises 885-5088; Canal Town Tours Sat & Sun 1 & 4pm 885-5263 $5/Free - 3 person, $15 min.)*, Special Events *(Music in Pell Park; Sun Jul-Aug, Canal Day)* **Near:** Picnic Area *(Ferry Slip Park)* Jogging Paths, Park *(Ferry Slip Park - horseshoe pit; borrow shoes at Town Hall)*, Galleries *(Canal Artworks 885-5083; Neil's 885-5094; Cecil Arts -Town Hall on weekend)* **Under 1 mi:** Museum *(C&D Canal 885-5621 Mon-Fri 8am-4pm)* **1-3 mi:** Horseback Riding *(Irish Tulip 275-8455)* **3+ mi:** Tennis Courts *(Elkton 398-8282, 8 mi.)*, Golf Course *(Brantwood 398-8848, 4 mi.)*, Movie Theater *(Regal 834-8510, 13 mi.)*

Provisioning and General Services
Near: Gourmet Shop *(Back Creek General Store 885-5377)*, Bakery *(Bohemia 885-3066)*, Bank/ATM, Catholic Church, Protestant Church, Clothing Store, Retail Shops *(gifts, antiques, etc.; Almost History 885-2655)* **Under 1 mi:** Convenience Store, Delicatessen *(C&D Market)*, Wine/Beer *(Chesapeake Wine & Spirits 885-5858)*, Farmers' Market *(at Ches Wine Jun-Oct, Fri 4-7pm)*, Fishmonger, Market *(C&D Market & Deli 885-3910)*, Post Office **1-3 mi:** Liquor Store *(Brantwood 392-4295)* **3+ mi:** Pharmacy *(Happy Harry's 620-1325, 8 mi.)*, Department Store *(Wal-Mart 398-1070, 7 mi.)*

Transportation
OnSite: Water Taxi *(Miss Clare - to public dock on Western shore north of Schaefer's)* **OnCall:** Rental Car *(Enterprise 398-0030)*, Taxi *(Joe's 392-8070)*, Airport Limo *(Town Car 885-9228)* **Near:** Bikes
Airport: Philadelphia/Cecil County *(50 mi./9 mi.)*

Medical Services
911 Service **OnCall:** Ambulance **Near:** Doctor *(Chesapeake Family 275-8157)*, Dentist *(Cohn 275-2225)*, Veterinarian *(Benner 885-3700)* **3+ mi:** Chiropractor *(Clifford 620-4322, 7 mi.)* **Hospital:** Union 398-4000 *(7 mi.)*

Setting -- Right in front of Pell Park, in the heart of gentrified and utterly delightful South Chesapeake City, is the new City Floating Dock, with room for about three vessels. In front of Town Hall, adjacent to the the dock, are four private slips. Perpendicular, in the same basin, will be four new slips.

Marina Notes -- *No charge for tie-ups on the Chesapeake City 200 ft. Floating Dock - also no services. Rafting two deep is permitted. Currently dredged to 6.5 feet, it quickly falls off to 2.5 feet; deeper draft vessels need to be on the first bulkhead - the canal end of the float. The four new "Beck's Landing" slips, along 2nd Street, are slated for '06 and will connect to the Chesapeake Inn dockage. Miss Clare, a 42-foot bay dead-rise fishing vessel, docks here and serves as cross-canal water taxi; it also offers tours narrated by local historian Capt. Ralph H. Hazel (885-5088) - Sat & Sun 1 hr. sightseeing, 2 hrs. sunset.

Notable -- In this charming village, which has completely reinvented itself over the last decade, there's entertainment on weekends and quiet during the week. On Sundays, from 6-8pm, Pell Park's professional concerts - bluegrass to cajun to rock 'n' roll - attract an enthusiastic crowd. Up the hill, a gate leads to the Inn at the Canal's beautiful garden (from their Chesapeake Room, you can watch your boat!). Pick up a copy of the Walking & Shopping Guide Map for a 10-block guide to the 19thC. buildings and their shops, galleries, restaurants and B&B's -- now on the National Historic Registry. Acclaimed 1780 Bayard House (one of the brick buildings owned and renovated by Allaire DuPont) has 3 dining rooms featuring Euro-Eastern Shore cuisine - wraparound windows make the ever-changing canal a dining companion. The nearby Canal Museum interprets the history of the 14-mile long, 450 feet wide canal begun in 1804.

PHOTOS ON CD-ROM: 14

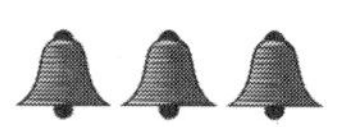

Chesapeake Inn & Marina

605 Second Street; So. Chesapeake City, MD 21915

Tel: (410) 885-2040 **VHF: Monitor** 16 **Talk** 69
Fax: (410) 885-2620 **Alternate Tel:** n/a
Email: peakeinn@aol.com **Web:** www.chesapeakeinn.com
Nearest Town: Elkton *(5 mi.)* **Tourist Info:** (410) 398-5076

Navigational Information
Lat: 39°31.560' **Long:** 075°48.624' **Tide:** n/a **Current:** n/a **Chart:** 12273
Rep. Depths (*MLW*): Entry 12 ft. **Fuel Dock** n/a **Max Slip/Moor** 8 ft./-
Access: C&D Canal to Back Creek Basin & Engineer's Cove

Marina Facilities *(In Season/Off Season)*
Fuel: No
Slips: 60 Total, 50 Transient **Max LOA:** 60 ft. **Max Beam:** n/a
Rate *(per ft.)*: **Day** $1.75/1.50 **Week** $5.95/4.55 **Month** $19.50/16.50
Power: 30 amp Incl., **50 amp** Incl. some slips, **100 amp** n/a, **200 amp** n/a
Cable TV: No **Dockside Phone:** No
Dock Type: Floating, Short Fingers, Wood
Moorings: 0 Total, 0 Transient **Launch:** n/a
Rate: Day n/a **Week** n/a **Month** n/a
Heads: 2 Toilet(s), 3 Shower(s) *(with dressing rooms)*
Laundry: None **Pay Phones:** Yes, 2
Pump-Out: OnSite, Self Service **Fee:** $5 **Closed Heads:** Yes

Marina Operations
Owner/Manager: GianMarco Martuscelli **Dockmaster:** Andy Upp
In-Season: May-Sep, 11am-11pm **Off-Season:** Oct-Apr, 11am-9pm
After-Hours Arrival: n/a
Reservations: No **Credit Cards:** Visa/MC, Dscvr, Din, Amex, yes
Discounts: None
Pets: Welcome **Handicap Access:** Yes, Heads, Docks

Marina Services and Boat Supplies
Services - Docking Assistance **Communication -** FedEx, UPS, Express Mail **Supplies - OnSite:** Ice *(Cube)* **3+ mi:** Ships' Store *(Martin Marine Supply 885-2455, 4 im.)*, Bait/Tackle *(Sarge's Bait Tackle 620-9183, 7 mi.)*, Propane *(Schagrin Gas Co 398-3400, 7 mi.)*

Boatyard Services
OnCall: Engine mechanic *(gas, diesel)* **Near:** Launching Ramp. **1-3 mi:** Travelift **Nearest Yard:** Bohemia Bay (410) 885-2601

Restaurants and Accommodations
OnSite: Restaurant *(Chesapeake Inn Dining Room 885-2040, L $8-16, D $19-32, Mon-Thu 11am-10pm, Fri & Sat to 11pm, Sun 10am-10pm)*, Lite Fare *(Chesapeake Inn Deck L $5-14, D $5-16, Mon-Thu 11am-1am, Fri & Sat 'til 2am, Sun 10am-10pm)* **Near:** Restaurant *(The Yacht Club 885-2267, D $13-28, Mon-Thu & Sat 3-9pm, Fri-Sat 3-10pm, $12 early bird daily 3-5pm)*, *(Hole in the Wall pub atmosphere - below Bayard; bar food plus Bayard menu)*, *(The Bayard House 885-5040, L $10-18, D $21-39, historic, elegant, on the canal; spectacular views; award-winning crab soup)*, *(The Tap Room 885-9873, seafood & classic steamed crabs)*, Snack Bar *(Canal Creamery 885-3314, ice cream)*, Lite Fare *(Bohemia Café & Bakery 885-3066, take-out and baked goods)*, Inn/B&B *(Inn at the Canal 885-5995, $85-195, romantic, 19thC atmosphere, central location, gorgeous garden)*, *(Blue Max 885-2781, $95-230)*, *(Ship Watch Inn 885-5300, $95-245, newly renovated, all rooms direct waterfront)*, Condo/Cottage *(The Old Wharf Cottage 885-5040, $100-120, wkly & wknd rates)* **Under 1 mi:** Restaurant Restaurant *(Jack & Helen's 885-5477, B & L)*, *(Schaefer's Canal House 885-2200, B $5-9, L $6-15, D $6-27, water taxi)*, Pizzeria *(Roma 885-2844)*

Recreation and Entertainment
OnSite: Special Events *(Canal Day, Music in the park Sun Jul-Aug)* **Near:** Picnic Area, Grills, Playground, Park, Sightseeing *(Ms. Claire 885-5088)*,Galleries *(Canal Artworks 885-5083)* **Under 1 mi:** Museum *(C&D Canal 885-5621 Mon-Fri 8am-4pm)* **1-3 mi:** Horseback Riding *(Irish Tulip 275-8455)* **3+ mi:** Tennis Courts *(Elkton Indoor 398-8282, 8 mi.)*, Golf Course *(Brantwood 398-8848, 4 mi.)*

Provisioning and General Services
OnSite: Bank/ATM **Near:** Bakery *(Bohemia 885-3066)*, Post Office, Catholic Church, Retail Shops *(gifts, antiques, gourmet foods: Back Creek General Store 885-5377, Almost History 885-2655)* **Under 1 mi:** Wine/Beer *(Chesapeake Wine & Spirits 885-5858)*, Farmers' Market *(at Ches Wine, Fri 4-7pm Jun-Oct)*, Market *(C&D Market & Deli 885-3910)*, Library *(885-2552)* **1-3 mi:** Liquor Store *(Brantwood 392-4295)*, Laundry **3+ mi:** Pharmacy *(Happy Harry's 620-1325, 8 mi.)*, Department Store *(Wal Mart 398-1070, 7 mi.)*

Transportation
OnCall: Rental Car *(Enterprise 398-0030)*, Taxi *(Joe's Taxi 392-8070)*, Airport Limo *(Town Car Service 885-9228)* **Near:** Bikes, Water Taxi
Airport: Philadelphia/Cecil County *(50 mi./9 mi.)*

Medical Services
911 Service **OnCall:** Ambulance **Near:** Doctor *(Chesapeake Family Practice 275-8157)*, Dentist *(Cohn 275-2225)*, Veterinarian *(Benner 885-3700)* **3+ mi:** Chiropractor *(Clifford Chiropractic 620-4322, 7 mi.)*
Hospital: Union Hospital 398-4000 *(7 mi.)*

Setting -- Snugly situated on the eastern shore of Back Creek Basin - right off the C&D Canal - Chesapeake Inn's 2-story gray contemporary building with hunter green trim hosts two quite different dining options and backs an extensive network of well maintained floating docks. The charming, historic "downtown" of South Chesapeake City is a very short stroll away, with more eateries, boutiques, antique shops, B&B's and lots of small-town Americana.

Marina Notes -- Built in 1996 on the site of Dockside Yacht Club, family owned & operated. Popular destination for day trips as well as for multi-day transients. Five sets of docks run all along the waterfront - the more northerly ones ("E" and "D" docks) host smaller boats, but have the most privacy. "C" dock is just north of the restaurant terrace. On "A" dock (right off the dining deck) and B dock (outboard of the Tiki Bar), your boat is the view. Water taxi to the anchorage - to come in for dinner, just hail them. Two large, tiled, individual bathrooms (a sink, toilet, and 2 showers) are great for a couple or family.

Notable -- The casual dining deck (sandwiches, baskets and great brick-oven pizza) features live bands nightly from May to October. This is clearly where the action is. A magnet for Formula Ones and other high-speed boats, so if "go-fast" intrigues, it can be found here. On the 2nd level, the formal Dining Room serves an upscale menu in elegant surroundings with expansive views, piano music Fri and Sat nights, and a dining terrace. A half-mile north is the "must-see" Canal Museum, housed in the original pump house - the waterwheel and steam pumping engines are the oldest in the U.S. that are still intact. Interactive displays tell the canal's history and live TVs track ships as they transit the Canal. A picnic area overlooks Back Creek.

PHOTOS ON CD-ROM: 12

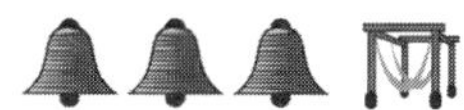

Navigational Information
Lat: 39°33.650' **Long:** 075°51.450' **Tide:** 3 ft. **Current:** 2 kt. **Chart:** 12273
Rep. Depths (*MLW*): Entry 5 ft. **Fuel Dock** 5 ft. **Max Slip/Moor** 5 ft./-
Access: Exit C&D Canal, turn to port up Elk River at Welches Point

Marina Facilities *(In Season/Off Season)*
Fuel: Gasoline, High-Speed Pumps
Slips: 210 Total, 3+ Transient **Max LOA:** 40 ft. **Max Beam:** 14 ft.
Rate *(per ft.)*: **Day** $1.00 **Week** $7.25 **Month** n/a
Power: 30 amp Incl., **50 amp** Incl., **100 amp** n/a, **200 amp** n/a
Cable TV: No **Dockside Phone:** No
Dock Type: Fixed, Floating, Short Fingers, Pilings, Alongside, Wood
Moorings: 0 Total, 0 Transient **Launch:** n/a
Rate: Day n/a **Week** n/a **Month** n/a
Heads: 4 Toilet(s), 4 Shower(s), AC, heat
Laundry: None **Pay Phones:** No
Pump-Out: Full Service, 1 Central, 1 Port **Fee:** $5 **Closed Heads:** Yes

Marina Operations
Owner/Manager: Bill Gravlee **Dockmaster:** Glenn Hines
In-Season: May-Oct, 8am-6pm **Off-Season:** Nov-Apr, 8am-4pm
After-Hours Arrival: Call ahead
Reservations: Required **Credit Cards:** Visa/MC, Dscvr
Discounts: 10% storage **Dockage:** n/a **Fuel:** n/a **Repair:** n/a
Pets: Welcome **Handicap Access:** No

Triton Marina

Triton Marina

PO Box 8216; 285 Plum Point Rd.; Elkton, MD 21921

Tel: (410) 620-3060 **VHF: Monitor** 9 **Talk** 9
Fax: (410) 620-3064 **Alternate Tel:** n/a
Email: bill@tritonmarina.com **Web:** www.tritonmarina.com
Nearest Town: Elkton *(4 mi.)* **Tourist Info:** (410) 398-5076

Marina Services and Boat Supplies
Services - Docking Assistance, Dock Carts **Communication -** FedEx, UPS, Express Mail **Supplies - OnSite:** Ice *(Cube)*, Ships' Store **3+ mi:** West Marine *(287-6600, 8 mi.)*, Bait/Tackle *(Sarge's 620-9183, 5 mi.)*

Boatyard Services
OnSite: Travelift, Forklift *(up to 44 ft. LOA and 15 ft. beam)*, Launching Ramp, Engine mechanic *(gas, diesel)*, Electrical Repairs, Hull Repairs, Bottom Cleaning, Air Conditioning, Refrigeration, Compound, Wash & Wax, Interior Cleaning, Metal Fabrication, Painting, Awlgrip **OnCall:** Propeller Repairs, Inflatable Repairs **Yard Rates:** $40/hr., Haul & Launch $6/ft. *(blocking $8/ft.)*, Power Wash $2.5/ft., Bottom Paint $12.50/ft. *(paint incl.)* **Storage:** On-Land $15.75/ft.

Restaurants and Accommodations
OnSite: Restaurant *(Walsh's Dockside 392-6859, live music weekends)* **OnCall:** Lite Fare *(Brother's Pizza 392-9300)* **3+ mi:** Restaurant *(McCooley's Sports Bar & Grill 392-3122, 5 mi.)*, *(Symphony Steak and Sushi 392-8151, 5 mi.)*, *(Fair Hill Inn 398-4187, D $14-28, 4 mi.)*, *(Ruby Tuesday 398-5134, 5 mi.)*, *(Joker's 398-7551, 4 mi.)*, Fast Food *(McDonalds, Taco Bell 5 mi.)*, Lite Fare *(Northside Market & Deli 398-6633, 6 mi.)*, Pizzeria *(Ninos 287-3737, 5 mi.)*, Motel *(Keystone 398-3300, 5 mi.)*, *(Sutton 398-3830, 5 mi.)*, Hotel *(Elkton Inn 398-0530, $48-56, 5 mi.)*

Recreation and Entertainment
OnSite: Beach *(3 sandy)*, Picnic Area, Grills, Volleyball, Video Arcade, Park *(Horseshoe pit)* **Near:** Jogging Paths, Boat Rentals *(Elk River Outfitters - kayaks, canoes, sunfish - at Locust Point 392-4994 - right across the river)*, Sightseeing *(Elk River Tours - 4 hr. historical tour of the upper Bay 446-3237 $35 - a 32 ft. Tracker pontoon boat leaves from Locust Point across the river.)* **1-3 mi:** Tennis Courts, Cultural Attract *(Historic Elk Landing 620-6400 2.5 mi. by dinghy)* **3+ mi:** Golf Course *(Patriots Glen 392-9552, 6mi./Brantwood 398-8848, 8 mi.)*, Movie Theater *(Regal Cinemas 834-8510, 7 mi.)*, Video Rental *(Blockbuster 620-9550, 6 mi.)*

Provisioning and General Services
OnSite: Convenience Store, Wine/Beer *(or Elk Landing 392-5056, 4 mi.)* **Under 1 mi:** Delicatessen *(Fresh Market & Deli 620-0077)*, Bank/ATM **1-3 mi:** Market *(Elkmore Market 392-4828)* **3+ mi:** Supermarket *(Acme 398-4925, 5 mi./Food Lion 620-3664, 7 mi.)*, Farmers' Market *(Sat 9am-Noon at Fair Hill-Route 273, 996-6292, 5 mi.)*, Post Office, Catholic Church, Protestant Church, Library *(Elkton 620-3808, 6 mi.)*, Beauty Salon, Dry Cleaners, Laundry *(Bridge St. 398-2115, 5 mi.)*, Bookstore *(Main St. 287-2007, 7 mi.)*, Pharmacy *(Medicine Shoppe 398-6100, 5 mi.)*, Hardware Store *(Ace 398-1111, 7 mi.)*, Department Store *(Wal-Mart, 5 mi.)*

Transportation
OnCall: Taxi *(Elkton Cab 398-1551)*, Airport Limo *(About Town 287-6400)* **Airport:** Philadelphia/Cecil County *(45 mi./6 mi.)*

Medical Services
911 Service **OnCall:** Ambulance **1-3 mi:** Optician **3+ mi:** Doctor *(Mulvey Family Practice 996-8912, 5 mi.)*, Dentist *(Greenwald/Riger 398-1221, 5 mi.)*, Chiropractor *(Clifford Chiropratic 620-4322, 5 mi.)*, Veterinarian *(Elkton Veterinary 398-8777, 5 mi.)* **Hospital:** Union Hospital 398-4000 *(5 mi.)*

Setting -- Triton sits on a nicely grassed and treed 8-acre point that's sprinkled with picnic tables and grills, edged by three sandy beaches and anchored by a two-story, hip-roofed stone building that houses a restaurant, bathhouse and offices. From this park-like setting radiate three major sets of docks - stained a light gray that contrasts nicely with the bright blue pedestals. A brand-new dry stack "high & dry" storage shed is further up the creek.

Marina Notes -- New owners in '99. The main floating dock has 2 perpendicular piers with vinyl-edged slips on both sides. The other floating pier runs out to a stationary fuel dock, and a third set of slips hosts smaller boats. There is a good-sized ships' store and repair shop. The new ('05) 200-unit dry-stack operation is situated around the peninsula in a creek that runs alongside the marina and is completely separate from the rest of the operation - it should have little impact on slip tenants or transients. Dealer for Yamaha, Mercury, Volvo-Penta, Angler Boats and Tidewater Trailers. Bathhouse has four very nice, private bathrooms with painted walls, lots of hooks, plugs and good lighting. Each sports a fiberglass stall shower with brightly colored curtain, toilet, & sink with vanity.

Notable -- Walsh's Dockside Restaurant and Raw Bar occupies the first floor of the stone house. Inside is a casual, cozy wood-paneled dining room with bar; ouside, the awninged and curtained dining deck has expansive views of the water and marshland. In addition to being a favorite destination for local boaters, it also welcomes private pilots from nearby Cecil County Airport. A game room is adjacent to the restaurant and outdoor activities include volleyball and horseshoes. This is a good place to get out the dinghy and tour the upper reaches of the recently dredged Elk including Historic Elk Landing.

PHOTOS ON CD-ROM: 13

Cove Marina

11 Mainsail Drive; Elkton, MD 21921

Tel: (410) 620-5505 **VHF: Monitor** 16 **Talk** n/a
Fax: (410) 620-5709 **Alternate Tel:** n/a
Email: petree2121@aol.com **Web:** n/a
Nearest Town: Elkton *(5 mi.)* **Tourist Info:** (410) 398-5076

Navigational Information

Lat: 39°33.500' **Long:** 075°50.767' **Tide:** 3 ft. **Current:** 2 kt. **Chart:** 12273
Rep. Depths (*MLW*): Entry 5 ft. **Fuel Dock** n/a **Max Slip/Moor** 4 ft./-
Access: Exit C&D Canal, turn to port up Elk River at Welches Point

Marina Facilities *(In Season/Off Season)*

Fuel: No
Slips: 80 Total, 5 Transient **Max LOA:** 42 ft. **Max Beam:** 13 ft.
Rate *(per ft.)*: **Day** $1.00 **Week** n/a **Month** n/a
Power: 30 amp Incl., **50 amp** Incl., **100 amp** n/a, **200 amp** n/a
Cable TV: No **Dockside Phone:** No
Dock Type: Fixed, Floating, Short Fingers, Wood
Moorings: 0 Total, 0 Transient **Launch:** n/a
Rate: Day n/a **Week** n/a **Month** n/a
Heads: 4 Toilet(s), 4 Shower(s) *(with dressing rooms)*
Laundry: 1 Washer(s), 1 Dryer(s) **Pay Phones:** No
Pump-Out: OnSite **Fee:** n/a **Closed Heads:** Yes

Marina Operations

Owner/Manager: Ellen & Kurt Gunther **Dockmaster:** Same
In-Season: Apr-Nov, 8am-5pm **Off-Season:** n/a
After-Hours Arrival: Call ahead
Reservations: Yes **Credit Cards:** Visa/MC
Discounts: None
Pets: Welcome **Handicap Access:** Yes, Heads

Marina Services and Boat Supplies

Services - Security *(owners live onsite)*, Dock Carts **Communication -** Mail & Package Hold, FedEx, UPS, Express Mail **Supplies - OnSite:** Ice *(Block)* **Under 1 mi:** Propane *(Mobil)* **3+ mi:** Ships' Store *(Martin Marine Supply 885-2455, 5 mi.)*, Bait/Tackle *(Sarge's Bait Tackle 620-9183, 5 mi.)*

Boatyard Services

OnSite: Travelift, Launching Ramp, Engine mechanic *(gas)*, Electrical Repairs, Hull Repairs, Canvas Work, Bottom Cleaning, Brightwork, Air Conditioning, Refrigeration, Compound, Wash & Wax, Interior Cleaning, Propeller Repairs **Yard Rates:** $65/hr., Haul & Launch $8.50/ft.. *(blocking $14)*, Power Wash $4.50/ft., Bottom Paint $8.50/ft. **Storage:** In-Water $1.00/ft./day

Restaurants and Accommodations

OnCall: Pizzeria *(Domino's 392-3000)* **Under 1 mi:** Restaurant *(Walsh's Dockside 392-6859, by dinghy)* **1-3 mi:** Restaurant *(Fair Hill Inn 398-4187, D $14-28, L, D & Sun Brunch)*, *(Baker's Restaurant 398-2435, L $6-15, D $6-17)*, Motel *(Elkton Inn 398-0530, $42-56)* **3+ mi:** Restaurant *(Bayard House 885-5040, L $10-18, D $20-30, 6 mi.)*, *(Bohemia Cafe 885-3066, 6 mi.)*, *(McCooley's Sports Bar & Grill 392-3122, 5 mi.)*, *(Symphony Steak and Sushi 392-8151, 5 mi.)*, Motel *(Elkton Inn 398-0530, 5 mi.)*, Hotel *(Hampton Inn 398-7777, 8 mi.)*, Inn/B&B *(Chesapeake City B&B 885-3300, 6 mi.)*, *(Elk Forge Inn, Retreat & Spa 392-9007, $90-185, 6 mi.)*

Recreation and Entertainment

OnSite: Picnic Area *(umbrellaed)*, Grills *(propane)*, Playground, Video Rental, Park **Near:** Boat Rentals *(Elk River Outfitters - kayaks, canoes, sunfish - at Locust Point 392-4994)*, Sightseeing *(Elk River Tours 466-3237, 4 hrs, $35, or tour the quiet backwaters in your dinghy)* **1-3 mi:** Golf Course *(Brantwood 398-8848)*, Cultural Attract *(Historic Elk Landing 620-6400, 2.5 mi. by dinghy)* **3+ mi:** Fitness Center *(Curves 398-9864, 5 mi.)*, Bowling *(Cecil Lanes 398-1664, 6 mi.)*, Movie Theater *(Regal Cinemas 834-8510, 8 mi.)*, Museum *(C&D Canal Museum 885-5621 Mon-Fri 8am-4pm, 6 mi.)*

Provisioning and General Services

Under 1 mi: Bank/ATM, Post Office **1-3 mi:** Convenience Store *(Brantwood Convenience)*, Delicatessen *(Brantwood Gas & Deli 398-9783)*, Liquor Store *(Brantwood Discount Liquor 392-4295)*, Green Grocer *(Dettweiler's Produce Stand)*, Barber Shop, Retail Shops **3+ mi:** Supermarket *(Acme 398-4925, Food Lion 620-3664, 5 mi.)*, Bakery *(Williams Bakery 996-8888, 5 mi.)*, Library *(Elkton 996-6269, 7 mi.)*, Dry Cleaners *(Sun Cleaners 398-7214, 5 mi.)*, Laundry *(Bridge St. Laundry 398-2115, 5 mi.)*, Bookstore *(Main St. Books 287-2007, 6 mi.)*, Pharmacy *(Rite Aid 398-9595, 5 mi.)*, Hardware Store *(Ace 398-1111, 6 mi.)*, Department Store *(K-Mart 398-8000, Walmart 398-1070, 5 mi.)*

Transportation

OnCall: Rental Car *(Enterprise 398-0030)*, Taxi *(Elkton Cab 398-1551)*, Airport Limo *(Town Car 885-9228)* **Airport:** Philadelphia/Cecil County *(47 mi./14 mi.)*

Medical Services

911 Service **OnCall:** Ambulance **3+ mi:** Doctor *(North Bay Medical 398-8300, 6 mi.)*, Chiropractor *(Clifford Chiropratic 620-4322, 6 mi.)*, Veterinarian *(Benner 885-3700, 6 mi.)* **Hospital:** Union Hospital 398-4000 *(6 mi.)*

Setting -- Small, shipshape Cove Marina sits at a wide point on the recently dredged Elk's east side; the distant views of the lightly-developed far shore create a sense of away. The primary dock has a generous T-head with wide slips and a few picnic tables that enjoy expansive river views and memorable sunsets. Onshore the ships' store is in a cream-colored, rust-roofed house and other amenities in a tan boat shed.

Marina Notes -- Service-oriented, accommodating owners live on-site and take a personal approach to management. While there are taxis available, they are just as likely to lend you a car. (The furry little assistant dockmaster is named Dudley.) The T-head can take up to a 50-footer, and it's catamaran-friendly - the slips off the T-head are very wide. An additional floating dock without power or water and an additional stationary dock provide overflow space for transients, if the need arises. Half-length finger piers with two steps down. There are plans for considerable improvements in '06: two motel rooms and an apartment above the office, all with decks, plus an eatery. The simple, perfectly fine bathhouses each have 2 toilets, 2 sinks and 2 fibergalss shower stalls.

Notable -- An attractive deck populated by umbrellaed tables serves as the outdoor boaters' lounge. Propane grills, picnic tables and a casual play gym are nearby, and benches along the bulkhead are perfect for watching the river action. Most services are about 5-6 miles in either Chesapeake City or in Elkton. Across the river, Walsh's Dockside, at Triton Marina, makes a good mealtime destination. Elk River Tours leaves from nearby Locust Point Marina; they offer a 4-hour historical cruise to the "Head of the Elk" (disembarking at Elk Landing) and down to the C&D Canal aboard a 32-foot pontoon boat ($35).

Navigational Information
Lat: 39°29.236' **Long:** 075°54.211' **Tide:** 3 ft. **Current:** 2 kt. **Chart:** 12273
Rep. Depths (*MLW*): Entry 5 ft. **Fuel Dock** 5 ft. **Max Slip/Moor** 4 ft./5 ft.
Access: Elk River to Bohemia, north shore at Rich Point

Marina Facilities *(In Season/Off Season)*
Fuel: Gasoline
Slips: 150 Total, 2 Transient **Max LOA:** 45 ft. **Max Beam:** 15'6"' ft.
Rate *(per ft.)*: **Day** $3.00* **Week** Inq. **Month** Inq.
Power: 30 amp Incl., **50 amp** n/a, **100 amp** n/a, **200 amp** n/a
Cable TV: No **Dockside Phone:** No
Dock Type: Fixed, Short Fingers, Wood
Moorings: 12 Total, 1 Transient **Launch:** n/a, Dinghy Dock
Rate: Day $20 **Week** n/a **Month** n/a
Heads: 6 Toilet(s), 6 Shower(s)
Laundry: None **Pay Phones:** No
Pump-Out: OnSite **Fee:** $5 **Closed Heads:** Yes

Marina Operations
Owner/Manager: Tom Pakradooni **Dockmaster:** Kathleen
In-Season: MemDay-LabDay, 8am-5pm **Off-Season:** n/a
After-Hours Arrival: Call in Advance
Reservations: Yes, Preferred **Credit Cards:** Visa/MC, Dscvr, Amex
Discounts: None
Pets: Welcome **Handicap Access:** No

Two Rivers Yacht Basin

64 Two Rivers Lane; Chesapeake City, MD 21915

Tel: (410) 885-2257 **VHF: Monitor** 16 **Talk** n/a
Fax: (410) 885-2255 **Alternate Tel:** n/a
Email: tworiversyachtbasin@yahoo.com **Web:** n/a
Nearest Town: Chesapeake City *(7 mi.)* **Tourist Info:** (410) 398-5076

Marina Services and Boat Supplies
Services - Dock Carts **Communication -** FedEx, DHL, UPS, Express Mail **Supplies - OnSite:** Ice *(Block, Cube)* **Near:** Bait/Tackle **3+ mi:** Ships' Store *(Martin Marine Supply 885-2455, 7 mi.)*, West Marine *(287-6600, 14 mi.)*

Boatyard Services
OnSite: Travelift *(25T)*, Engine mechanic *(gas)*, Bottom Cleaning **OnCall:** Engine mechanic *(diesel)*, Electrical Repairs, Hull Repairs, Brightwork, Air Conditioning **Near:** Launching Ramp. **1-3 mi:** Electronics Repairs, Rigger, Sail Loft, Canvas Work. **Yard Rates:** $40/hr., Haul & Launch $6/ft. *(blocking $2.50/ft.)*, Power Wash $2/ft., Bottom Paint $5/ft. **Storage:** In-Water $17/ft., On-Land $25/ft.

Restaurants and Accommodations
3+ mi: Restaurant *(Coakley's Pub 939-8888, L $6-10, D $10-20, 11 mi.)*, *(Joanie's Restaurant 885-9979, 6 mi.)*, *(Bayard House 885-5040, L $10-18, D $10-18, 6 mi.)*, Seafood Shack *(Yankee Restaurant 885-2844, D $13-28, 6 mi.)*, Fast Food *(Burger King 12.5 mi.)*, Pizzeria *(Roma 885-2844, L $5-9, D $5-9, 7 mi., offers subs, pizza, pastas)*, Inn/B&B *(Blue Max 885-2781, $95-230, 7 mi.)*, *(Ship Watch Inn 885-5300, $95-245, 7 mi.)*, *(Inn at the Canal 885-5995, $75-130, 7 mi.)*

Recreation and Entertainment
OnSite: Pool, Beach, Picnic Area **3+ mi:** Tennis Courts *(Elkton Indoor Tennis 398-8282, 7 mi.)*, Golf Course *(Back Creek Golf Club 378-6499, 8 mi.)*, Bowling *(Cecil Lanes 398-1664, 6 mi.)*, Movie Theater *(Regal Cinemas 834-8510, 13 mi.)*, Video Rental *(Brantwood 398-9783, 10 mi.)*, Museum *(C&D Canal Museum 885-5621 Mon-Fri 8am-4pm, 7 mi.)*

Provisioning and General Services
OnSite: Convenience Store *(snacks and some marine supplies)* **3+ mi:** Liquor Store *(Bennett's Liquors 885-2419, 6 mi.)*, Market *(C&D Market & Deli 885-3910, 7 mi.)*, Library *(Chesapeake City 885-2552, 7 mi.)*, Pharmacy *(Happy Harry's Drug Stores 620-1325, 12 mi.)*, Hardware Store *(Builders Choice 398-1111, 17 mi.)*, Department Store *(Wal Mart 398-1070, 13 mi.)*

Transportation
OnCall: Taxi *(Elkton Cab 398-1551)*, Airport Limo *(Town Car Service 885-9228)* **3+ mi:** Rental Car *(Enterprise 398-0030, 14 mi.)*
Airport: Philadelphia/Cecil County *(55 mi./20 mi.)*

Medical Services
911 Service **OnCall:** Ambulance **1-3 mi:** Doctor *(Heller 885-2324)*
3+ mi: Dentist *(Van Venrooy 275-1462, 7 mi.)*, Chiropractor *(Clifford Chiropractic 620-4322, 12 mi.)*, Veterinarian *(Benner 885-3700, 7 mi.)*
Hospital: Union Hospital 398-4000 *(14 mi.)*

Setting -- A mile east of Town Point, on the Bohemia River's north shore, the bright blue main building, with flags flying, signals your arrival at Two Rivers. Head past the fuel dock into a very protected basin ringed with slips. Down the center of the basin, two main docks host a series of slips in various configurations. The rim of the basin is dense with foliage, which gives the individual slips a delightful sense of being in the woods.

Marina Notes -- *$45 minimum. The on-site mechanic is Skip's Ship Shack. The long fuel dock has two sets of pumps and pumpout. Large dry-storage area. A small crescent-shaped beach is backed by picnic tables and a small stand of trees. The occasional deck hosts additional picnic tables with views of the basin. On a rise just above the eastern edge is the pool. The mooring field is just outboard of the beach. There are bathhouses - small white buildings with blue trim - on both sides of the basin - 2 men's and 2 women's on the west side and one of each on the east - well-maintained single bathrooms with fiberglass walls, tile floors, stall shower with glass door, toilet, and sink.

Notable -- A hike outside the marina will net beautiful rolling land and a pleasant, sparsely-populated residential community with a few ranchettes, antique stone houses and ponds - but no services or supplies. However there are some spectacular vistas across rolling farmland to the Elk River beyond. The dinghy will be the best bet for transportation all the way to the navigable head of the river.

PHOTOS ON CD-ROM: 10

Bohemia Vista Yacht Basin

PO Box 540; 140 Vista Marina Rd.; Chesapeake City, MD 21915

Tel: (410) 885-5402 **VHF: Monitor** 16 **Talk** 68
Fax: (410) 885-3082 **Alternate Tel:** n/a
Email: bovista@dmv.com **Web:** www.bovistamarina.com
Nearest Town: Chesapeake City *(6 mi.)* **Tourist Info:** (410) 398-5076

Navigational Information

Lat: 39°29.241' **Long:** 075°53.706' **Tide:** 3 ft. **Current:** 2 kt. **Chart:** 12273
Rep. Depths (*MLW*): Entry 5 ft. **Fuel Dock** n/a **Max Slip/Moor** 5 ft./6 ft.
Access: Elk River to Bohemia River to north shore

Marina Facilities *(In Season/Off Season)*

Fuel: No
Slips: 124 Total, 5 Transient **Max LOA:** 40 ft. **Max Beam:** 14 ft.
Rate *(per ft.)*: **Day** $1.50 **Week** n/a **Month** n/a
Power: 30 amp Incl., **50 amp** n/a, **100 amp** n/a, **200 amp** n/a
Cable TV: Yes, Free **Dockside Phone:** No
Dock Type: Fixed, Short Fingers, Wood
Moorings: 10 Total, 5 Transient **Launch:** n/a, Dinghy Dock
Rate: Day Inq.* **Week** n/a **Month** n/a
Heads: 6 Toilet(s), 4 Shower(s)
Laundry: 1 Washer(s), 1 Dryer(s) **Pay Phones:** No
Pump-Out: OnSite, Full Service, 1 Port **Fee:** $10 **Closed Heads:** Yes

Marina Operations

Owner/Manager: Kurt & Jody Sarac **Dockmaster:** William Parker
In-Season: May-Oct, 9am-5pm **Off-Season:** Nov-Apr
After-Hours Arrival: Call in advance
Reservations: Yes, Preferred **Credit Cards:** Visa/MC, Dscvr, Amex
Discounts: None
Pets: Welcome **Handicap Access:** No

Marina Services and Boat Supplies

Services - Dock Carts **Communication -** Phone Messages, Fax in/out *($1)*, FedEx, UPS, Express Mail **Supplies - OnSite:** Ice *(Block, Cube)*, Ships' Store, Bait/Tackle **3+ mi:** West Marine *(287-6600, 14 mi.)*

Boatyard Services

OnSite: Travelift *(20T)*, Launching Ramp, Bottom Cleaning, Compound, Wash & Wax **Near:** Woodworking. **Dealer for:** Interlux, Westerbeke. **Yard Rates:** $69/hr., Haul & Launch $4/ft. *(blocking $10/ft.)*, Power Wash $4/ft., Bottom Paint $10.50/ft. **Storage:** On-Land $16.25/ft.

Restaurants and Accommodations

3+ mi: Restaurant *(Canal House 885-2200, B $5-9, L $6-15, D $16-27, 7 mi.)*, *(Bayard House 885-5040, L $10-18, D $21-39, 7 mi.)*, *(The Yacht Club Restaurant 885-2267, L $6-13, D $14-28, 7 mi.)*, *(Jack 'n Helen's 885-5477, 7 mi.)*, Fast Food *(Burger King 7 mi.)*, Pizzeria *(Roma Pizzeria 885-2844, L $5-9, D $5-9, 7 mi., offers subs, sandwiches, pizza, pasta)*, Inn/B&B *(Bohemia House 7 mi.)*, *(Inn at the Canal 885-5995, $75-130, 7 mi.)*

Recreation and Entertainment

3+ mi: Tennis Courts *(Elkton Indoor Tennis 398-8282, 7 mi.)*, Golf Course *(Back Creek Golf Club 378-6499, 8 mi.)*, Fitness Center *(Curves for Women 398-9864, 12 mi.)*, Bowling *(Cecil Lanes 398-1664, 6 mi.)*, Movie Theater *(Regal Cinemas 834-8510, 13 mi.)*, Museum *(C&D Canal Museum 885-5621 Mon-Fri 8am-4pm, 7 mi.)*

Provisioning and General Services

3+ mi: Convenience Store *(Country Grocery, 5 mi.)*, Supermarket *(C&D Market & Deli 885-3910, 7 mi.)*, Gourmet Shop *(Hot Stuff 368-3586, 5 mi.)*, Delicatessen *(Brantwood Gas & Deli 398-9783, 7 mi.)*, Wine/Beer *(Bennett's Liquors 885-2419, 6 mi.)*, Farmers' Market *(Fri 4-7pm Jun-Oct at Chesapeake Wine & Spirits, 6 mi.)*, Library *(Chesapeake City 885-2552, 7 mi.)*, Pharmacy *(Happy Harry's 620-1325, 12 mi.)*, Hardware Store *(Markie's, 5 mi.)*, Department Store *(Wal-mart 398-1070, 12 mi.)*

Transportation

OnCall: Taxi *(Joe's Taxi Service 392-8070)*, Airport Limo *(Town Car Service 885-9228)* **3+ mi:** Rental Car *(Enterprise 398-0030, 14 mi.)*, Rail *(Elkton)*
Airport: Philadelphia/Cecil County *(55 mi./20 mi.)*

Medical Services

911 Service **OnCall:** Ambulance **1-3 mi:** Doctor *(Heller 885-2324)* **3+ mi:** Dentist *(Van Venrooy 275-1462, 7 mi.)*, Chiropractor *(Clifford Chiropractic Center 620-4322, 12 mi.)*, Veterinarian *(Benner 885-3700, 7 mi.)*
Hospital: Union Hospital 398-4000 *(12 mi.)*

Setting -- The second of three closely-set marinas on the northern shore of Bohemia River, Bohemia Vista Yacht Basin is basically a boatyard with docks. Now in the throes of a major makeover, it will soon offer boaters a more upscale experience with a new pool and bathhouse. Because this is a wide stretch of the river, views across the water are fairly distant and bucolic. Houses can be seen tucked among the trees, but the overall feeling is still quite rural.

Marina Notes -- A family-owned and family-oriented marina, founded in 1966 by Augustice Brice Moore and purchased by Kurt and Jody Sarac of Elkton in 2004. Two main piers lie perpendicular to the shore, with slips on either side. *The mooring field, right off the basin, can only manage boats under 30 feet (28-30ft $1120/season). A carved hula maiden guards the gazebo that leads to the dinghy dock. A new bulkhead has just been installed and approvals are in the works for a 490 x 6-ft. pier which will host 27 more slips with 3x15-foot long piers. A petition for a fuel dock is also pending. Current heads are well-mantained cinderblock: 2 showers, 3 stalls, 2 sinks each. A new bathhouse is anticipated as part of the renovation.

Notable -- The original office building has been torn down and is being replaced by a pool and patio complex, which should open in April '06. The tan building sitting at the back of the property - on a short rise overlooking a little pond - was originally designed to be the much-anticipated Barnacle Restaurant, but has been converted into a single-family rental home. It seems that the pond is home to a rare species of endangered turtles. As a result, construction permits for the restaurant were revoked and the marina has created a sanctuary for these endangered Bogie Turtles.

Navigational Information
Lat: 39°29.120' **Long:** 075°53.540' **Tide:** 2 ft. **Current:** 2 kt. **Chart:** 12273
Rep. Depths (*MLW*): Entry 5 ft. **Fuel Dock** 5 ft. **Max Slip/Moor** 5 ft./5 ft.
Access: One mile from markers R-14, G-15 on the Bohemia River

Marina Facilities *(In Season/Off Season)*
Fuel: Gasoline, Diesel
Slips: 300 Total, 20 Transient **Max LOA:** 60 ft. **Max Beam:** n/a
Rate *(per ft.)*: **Day** $1.50 **Week** $5.75 **Month** 11.5% of annual rate
Power: 30 amp $5, **50 amp** $10, **100 amp** n/a, **200 amp** n/a
Cable TV: Yes **Dockside Phone:** No
Dock Type: Fixed, Long Fingers, Short Fingers, Alongside, Wood
Moorings: 60 Total, 0 Transient **Launch:** yes
Rate: Day n/a **Week** n/a **Month** n/a
Heads: 16 Toilet(s), 16 Shower(s)
Laundry: 6 Washer(s), 6 Dryer(s), Book Exchange **Pay Phones:** Yes, 3
Pump-Out: OnSite **Fee:** $5 **Closed Heads:** Yes

Marina Operations
Owner/Manager: Ken Long **Dockmaster:** John Rajchel
In-Season: Mar-Nov, 8am-5pm **Off-Season:** n/a, Dec-Feb closed
After-Hours Arrival: Call ahead
Reservations: Yes **Credit Cards:** Visa/MC, Dscvr, Amex
Discounts: None **Dockage:** n/a **Fuel:** over 200 gal. **Repair:** n/a
Pets: Welcome, Dog Walk Area **Handicap Access:** Yes, Heads, Docks

Bohemia Bay Yacht Harbour

1026 Town Point Road; Chesapeake City, MD 21915

Tel: (410) 885-2706 **VHF: Monitor** 16 **Talk** 9
Fax: (410) 885-5548 **Alternate Tel:** n/a
Email: bohemiabay@dol.net **Web:** www.bbyh.com
Nearest Town: Chesapeake City *(8 mi.)* **Tourist Info:** (410) 398-5076

Marina Services and Boat Supplies
Services - Docking Assistance, Boaters' Lounge, Dock Carts **Communication -** Mail & Package Hold, Phone Messages, Fax in/out, FedEx, DHL, UPS, Express Mail *(Sat Del)* **Supplies - OnSite:** Ice *(Block, Cube)*, Ships' Store, Marine Discount Store **Near:** Bait/Tackle **3+ mi:** West Marine *(287-6600, 14 mi.)*, Propane *(Allied Propane 392-9602, 13 mi.)*

Boatyard Services
OnSite: Travelift *(55T)*, Engine mechanic *(gas, diesel)*, Electrical Repairs, Electronics Repairs, Hull Repairs, Bottom Cleaning, Brightwork, Refrigeration, Compound, Wash & Wax, Propeller Repairs, Painting, Total Refits, Yacht Broker **OnCall:** Rigger, Air Conditioning, Divers, Interior Cleaning, Woodworking, Inflatable Repairs, Life Raft Service, Metal Fabrication, Awlgrip, Yacht Design **Near:** Launching Ramp, Sail Loft. **Member:** ABYC **Yard Rates:** $55-70/hr.*, Haul & Launch $4.50/ft. *(blocking 3.25/ft.)*, Power Wash $1.75/ft., Bottom Paint Up to 36' $13/ft., 37-46' $15/ft., 47-52' $17/ft.

Restaurants and Accommodations
3+ mi: Restaurant *(Bayard House 885-5040, L $10-18, D $20-30, 7 mi.)*, *(Schaefer's Canal House 885-2200, 8 mi.)*, Seafood Shack *(Yankee 834-2848, D $13-28, 7 mi., Mon-Thu 3-9pm, Fri-Sat 3-10pm, Sunday 3-9pm, $12 early bird daily 3-5pm)*, Pizzeria *(Roma 885-2844, 6 mi., L & D $5-9)*, Inn/B&B *(Blue Max 885-2781, $95-230, 7 mi.)*, *(Ship Watch Inn 885-5300, $95-245, 7 mi.)*

Recreation and Entertainment
OnSite: Pool *(Mon-Thu 10am-6pm, Fri-Sat 10am-8pm, Sun 10am-7pm; also kids pool)*, Beach, Picnic Area, Grills *(charcoal)*, Playground **3+ mi:** Tennis Courts *(Elkton Indoor Tennis 398-8282, 14 mi.)*, Golf Course *(Back Creek Golf Club 378-6499, 8 mi.)*, Fitness Center *(Curves for Women 398-9864, 12 mi.)*, Bowling *(Cecil Lanes 398-1664, 12 mi.)*, Video Rental *(Brantwood 398-9783, 9 mi.)*, Museum *(C&D Canal Museum 885-5621 Mon-Fri 8am-4pm, Upper Bay Museum 287-2675, 7 mi.)*

Provisioning and General Services
OnSite: Convenience Store **3+ mi:** Supermarket *(C&D Market & Deli 885-3910, 7 mi.)*, Delicatessen *(Brantwood Deli 398-9783, 9 mi.)*, Liquor Store *(Bennett's Liquors 885-2419, 6 mi.)*, Farmers' Market *(Jun-Oct at Ches Wine & Spirits, Fri 4-7pm, 6 mi.)*, Bank/ATM, Post Office, Catholic Church, Beauty Salon *(Cecilton)*, Barber Shop *(Chesapeake City)*, Dry Cleaners *(Elkton, 11 mi.)*, Pharmacy *(Happy Harry's 620-1325, 12 mi.)*, Hardware Store *(Mackies, 5 mi.)*, Department Store *(Wal Mart 398-1070, 12 mi.)*

Transportation
OnCall: Taxi *(Joe's Taxi 392-8070)*, Airport Limo *(Town Car Service 885-9228)* **3+ mi:** Rental Car *(Enterprise 398-0030, 14 mi.)*
Airport: Philadelphia/Cecil County *(55 mi./20 mi.)*

Medical Services
911 Service **1-3 mi:** Doctor *(Heller 885-2324)* **3+ mi:** Dentist *(Van Venrooy 275-1462, 7 mi.)*, Chiropractor *(Clifford Chiropractic 620-4322, 12 mi.)*, Veterinarian *(Benner 885-3700, 7 mi.)*
Hospital: Union Hospital 398-4000 *(12 mi.)*

Setting -- This upscale, well thought-out resort marina is the most eastern of the Bohemia River's transient facilities; it's also the biggest and offers the most services and amenities. The little lighthouse at the end of the point makes it easy to spot; alongside transient dockage is on the wharf at the entrance. Inside the protected basin, ringed with trees and attractive street lamps, are four sets of covered slips and five open docks. The quiet country setting, impeccably landscaped and maintained, includes a really lovely picnic pavilion above the river and a set of sparkling pools overlooking the docks.

Marina Notes -- Full-service boatyard, large travelift & mechanic on duty six days (*$70/hr. engine mechanic). Some slips are dockominiums. Long fuel dock at the entrance has two sets of pumps. Open slips have 3/4-length, full-width finger piers; covered slips full-length piers. Three comfortable, upscale all-tile bathhouses with large showers & two laundry rooms; two have 4 individual bathrooms, the third, under the office, has a group configuration.

Notable -- Inviting gathering places abound: the picnic pavilion deck is surrounded by some additional tables and grills plus a playground. On the starboard side as you approach the marina, there's a nicely treed grassy peninsula that juts out into the the river; it, too, is scattered with picnic tables and charcoal grills. An attractive second-floor clubroom sports a large deck ("The Party Deck") that overlooks the entrance to the marina; it has a kitchenette, sofas, tables and chairs, and a lending library. The good-sized, nicely furnished pool and adjacent kiddie pool (with an unfortunate, but necessary chain-link fence) are open Mon-Thu 10am-6pm, Fri & Sat 10am-8pm, Sun 10am-7pm. Most services are 6-8 miles away in South Chesapeake City.

PHOTOS ON CD-ROM: 14

Jackson Marine Yacht Basin

PO Box 483; 230 Riverside Drive; North East, MD 21901

Tel: (410) 287-9400 **VHF: Monitor** n/a **Talk** n/a
Fax: (410) 287-9034 **Alternate Tel:** n/a
Email: info@jacksonmarinesales.com **Web:** www.jacksonmarinesales.com
Nearest Town: North East *(4 mi.)* **Tourist Info:** (410) 287-2658

Navigational Information

Lat: 39°33.550' **Long:** 075°58.100' **Tide:** 2 ft. **Current:** .5 kt **Chart:** 12274
Rep. Depths (*MLW*): Entry 6 ft. **Fuel Dock** 6 ft. **Max Slip/Moor** 6 ft./6 ft.
Access: Directly on the Northeast River at Hance Point

Marina Facilities *(In Season/Off Season)*

Fuel: Gasoline, Diesel
Slips: 175 Total, 5 Transient **Max LOA:** 50 ft. **Max Beam:** 17 ft.
Rate *(per ft.)*: **Day** $40.00 **Week** $150 **Month** $350
Power: 30 amp Inq., **50 amp** Inq., **100 amp** n/a, **200 amp** n/a
Cable TV: Yes **Dockside Phone:** No
Dock Type: Fixed, Floating, Short Fingers, Wood
Moorings: 0 Total, 0 Transient **Launch:** n/a
Rate: Day n/a **Week** n/a **Month** n/a
Heads: Toilet(s), Shower(s)
Laundry: 1 Washer(s), 1 Dryer(s) **Pay Phones:** No
Pump-Out: OnSite, OnCall, 1 Central, 1 Port **Fee:** $5 **Closed Heads:** Yes

Marina Operations

Owner/Manager: Gary Parker **Dockmaster:** same
In-Season: Mar-Dec, 8am-5pm **Off-Season:** Jan-Feb, 8am-4pm
After-Hours Arrival: Call ahead
Reservations: Preferred **Credit Cards:** Visa/MC, Dscvr, Amex
Discounts: Boat/US **Dockage:** Inq. **Fuel:** $0.10/gal **Repair:** n/a
Pets: Welcome, Dog Walk Area **Handicap Access:** Yes, Heads, Docks

Marina Services and Boat Supplies

Services - Docking Assistance, Security *(owner lives onsite)* **Communication -** FedEx, UPS, Express Mail **Supplies - OnSite:** Ice *(Cube)*, Ships' Store **1-3 mi:** West Marine *(287-6600)*, Bait/Tackle *(Herb's 287-5490)* **3+ mi:** Propane *(Kirkwood, 4 mi.)*

Boatyard Services

OnSite: Travelift *(25T)*, Forklift, Engine mechanic *(gas, diesel)*, Electrical Repairs, Electronics Repairs, Hull Repairs, Canvas Work *(The Canvas Shop 967-0009)*, Bottom Cleaning *($39/hr.)*, Brightwork, Air Conditioning, Refrigeration, Compound, Wash & Wax, Interior Cleaning *($39/hr.)*, Woodworking, Painting, Yacht Broker *(Jackson Marine)* **OnCall:** Pro-Propeller Repairs **Dealer for:** Donzi, Regal, Mercury. Other Certifications: Mercury, Volvo, Regal, Donzi **Yard Rates:** $87/hr., Haul & Launch $3/ft. + labor *(blocking incl.)*, Power Wash $2/ft., Bottom Paint $8.50/ft. + materials

Restaurants and Accommodations

OnSite: Snack Bar *(The Galley B & L Fri-Mon; sandwiches, burgers, hotdogs, ice cream)* **OnCall:** Pizzeria *(Pat's 30-283-2660)* **Under 1 mi:** Inn/B&B *(North Bay 287-5948, $65-125)* **1-3 mi:** Restaurant *(Nauti-Goose Saloon 287-7880, L $4-14, D $4-26, by water; indoor & waterside deck; free docking with Dinner; Buffet $24)*, Inn/B&B *(Mill House 287-3532)* **3+ mi:** Restaurant *(Woody's Crabhouse 287-3541, L $5-10, D $13-30, 5 mi., voted best crabhouse for last 6 years)*, *(Steak & Main 287-3512, L $10-15, D $16-40, 5 mi., oyster bar too)*, Lite Fare *(Pier One 287-6599, 4 mi., local hangout)*, *(Highborn Café 287-3300, 4 mi., 6:30am-3pm, carryout, D Thu-Sat 6:30-8pm $4-12/lb.- delivers; Internet access)*, Pizzeria *(Bella 287-6300, 4 mi.)*, Hotel *(Crystal Inn 287-7100, $80-100, 5 mi.)*

Recreation and Entertainment

OnSite: Beach, Picnic Area, Grills *(charcoal)*, Playground **Under 1 mi:** Park *(Elk Neck State Park 287-5333, Turkey Point Lighthouse 287-8170)* **1-3 mi:** Golf Course *(Chesapeake Bay 287-0200)*, Video Rental *(Movie King 287-3409)*, Museum *(Upper Bay 287-2675)* **3+ mi:** Fitness Center *(Pro-Fitness 287-4600, 5 mi.)*, Horseback Riding *(Fairwinds 620-3883, Double S Arabians 287-2539, 8 mi.)*, Cultural Attract *(Milbourne Theatre 287-1037, 7 mi.)*

Provisioning and General Services

Near: Liquor Store, Market *(Weaver's Plum Creek Market and Liquor 287-8474)* **1-3 mi:** Bank/ATM, Post Office, Catholic Church, Protestant Church *(St. Mary Anne's Episcopal)*, Laundry **3+ mi:** Supermarket *(Acme 287-9008/Food Lion 287-5177, 5 mi.)*, Gourmet Shop *(Bay Gourmet Seafood Mkt. & Café 287-4300, 5 mi.)*, Delicatessen *(Schroeder's 287-6465, 5 mi.)*, Library *(287-1005, 7 mi.)*, Bookstore *(Main St. 287-2007, 5 mi.)*, Pharmacy *(Happy Harry's 287-8887, 5 mi.)*, Hardware Store *(Ace 398-1111, 7 mi.)*

Transportation

OnCall: Taxi *(Grab-a-Cab 287-2200)*, Airport Limo *(About Town 838-6449)* **3+ mi:** Rental Car *(North East Auto 287-2040, 5 mi.)*
Airport: Philadelphia/Cecil County *(52 mi./8 mi.)*

Medical Services

911 Service **OnCall:** Ambulance **3+ mi:** Doctor *(North Bay 287-5570, 5 mi.)*, Dentist *(Gwiazdowski 287-6988, 5 mi.)*, Chiropractor *(North East 287-9110, 5 mi.)*, Holistic Services *(Blue Iris Wellness & Yoga 287-1331, 4 mi.)*, Veterinarian *(North East 398-8100, 6 mi.)*
Hospital: Union Hospital 398-4000 *(11 mi.)*

Setting -- At the mouth of Northeast River at Hance Point, Jackson's extensive and professionally-managed dockage rings two basins. An almost closed "C" shaped peninsula, part of which is a paved parking area, creates a keyhole interior basin; an outside basin adds another set of riverside docks. Two sets of slips are covered. The top of the "keyhole" is a broad, grassy area and a wedge-shaped sandy beach right on the river.

Marina Notes -- Very service-oriented; in business since 1954. The owner, Woody Jackson, lives on-site. A Mercury repair facility open six days a week, with 6 Mercury-certified technicians. Large dry-stack storage operation that manages up to 31 ft. LOA. Remarkably large and well-stocked ships' store. The Canvas Shop is also on-site (967-0009) along with a new boat showroom. The white cinderblock building, in the parking area between the two basins, houses the Galley snack bar and the basic bathhouse. Bay Boat Work's pump-out boat (287-8113).

Notable -- The Galley has picnic tables inside and out and is open for breakfast and lunch, usually Thursday through Monday starting at 7:30am. There's a great picnic pavilion (and charcoal grills) between the two basins, just past the first set of covered slips. It's named for the service manager who has been there for 30 years and is responsible for the extraordinary parts department. Adjacent is a nice wooden play gym enclosed by a white picket fence. The nearest market is Weaver's Plum Creek Market and Liquor Store. The shops of North East are a bit of a hike up river and require a cab - but the village is worth it. At Day Basket Factory (287-6100) artisans weave split oak baskets. The Nauti-Goose restaurant has dockage for patrons - walk to the museum from there.

PHOTOS ON CD-ROM: 10

Navigational Information

Lat: 39°33.533' **Long:** 075°57.850' **Tide:** 3 ft. **Current:** n/a **Chart:** 12274
Rep. Depths (*MLW*): Entry 6 ft. **Fuel Dock** 6 ft. **Max Slip/Moor** 6 ft./8 ft.
Access: Around Hance Point in to Hance Creek on the south shore

Marina Facilities *(In Season/Off Season)*

Fuel: *Shell* - Gasoline, Diesel
Slips: 137 Total, 6 Transient **Max LOA:** 55 ft. **Max Beam:** 16 ft.
Rate *(per ft.)*: **Day** $1.00/Inq. **Week** $50* **Month** $200
Power: 30 amp Incl., **50 amp** Incl., **100 amp** n/a, **200 amp** n/a
Cable TV: No **Dockside Phone:** No
Dock Type: Fixed, Floating, Long Fingers, Wood
Moorings: 30 Total, 1 Transient **Launch:** n/a, Dinghy Dock
Rate: Day $0.75/ft. **Week** n/a **Month** n/a
Heads: 6 Toilet(s), 4 Shower(s) *(with dressing rooms)*
Laundry: None **Pay Phones:** No
Pump-Out: OnSite, Full Service, 1 Port **Fee:** $5 **Closed Heads:** Yes

Marina Operations

Owner/Manager: Donald J. Green **Dockmaster:** Same
In-Season: Apr-Oct, 8am-4:30pm **Off-Season:** Nov-Mar, 8am-4:30pm
After-Hours Arrival: Tie up to fuel dock
Reservations: Yes **Credit Cards:** Visa/MC, Cash or checks
Discounts: None
Pets: Welcome **Handicap Access:** No

Bay Boat Works

PO Box 340; 145 Hance Point Road; North East, MD 21901

Tel: (410) 287-8113 **VHF: Monitor** n/a **Talk** n/a
Fax: (410) 287-5666 **Alternate Tel:** n/a
Email: mary@bayboatworks.com **Web:** bayboatworks.com
Nearest Town: North East *(4 mi.)* **Tourist Info:** (410) 939-9009

Marina Services and Boat Supplies

Services - Dock Carts **Communication -** Data Ports, FedEx, DHL, UPS, Express Mail **Supplies - OnSite:** Ice *(Block, Cube)*, Ships' Store
1-3 mi: Bait/Tackle *(Herb's Tackle Shop 287-5490)* **3+ mi:** West Marine *(287-6600, 4 mi.)*, Propane *(Kirkwood Gas 378-2900, 4 mi.)*

Boatyard Services

OnSite: Travelift *(50T)*, Railway, Launching Ramp, Engine mechanic *(gas)*, Electrical Repairs, Bottom Cleaning, Brightwork, Compound, Wash & Wax, Interior Cleaning, Woodworking, Metal Fabrication, Yacht Broker *(Giordano & Dour)* **Yard Rates:** $65/hr., Haul & Launch $6/ft. *(blocking $88)*, Power Wash $2/ft., Bottom Paint $20/ft.

Restaurants and Accommodations

OnSite: Inn/B&B *(Boat & Breakfast on Journey $120)*, *(North Bay B&B 287-5948, $65-125, ask about sailing packages)* **Under 1 mi:** Hotel *(Holiday Inn 287-0008)* **1-3 mi:** Restaurant *(Nauti-Goose Saloon 287-7880, L $4-14, D $4-26, dinner buffet $24. By water - indoor and waterside deck; free docking with dinner)* **3+ mi:** Restaurant *(Woody's Crabhouse 287-3541, L $5-10, D $13-30, 3+ mi., voted best crabhouse in Maryland and Delaware for the last six years)*, *(Highborne Café 287-3300, 5 mi.)*, *(Pier One 287-6599, 5 mi.)*, *(Bay Gourmet 287-4300, 5 mi.)*, Fast Food *(Wendy's 6 mi.)*, Pizzeria *(Jengerbee's 287-6111, 5 mi.)*, Motel *(Crystal Inn 287-7100, 6 mi.)*, Inn/B&B *(Mill House 287-3532, 4 mi.)*

Recreation and Entertainment

OnSite: Boat Rentals *(J-24 sailboat $130/day, $90/half-day, 287-5948)*, Sightseeing *(Upper Bay sail on "Journey" - $150 half-day/235 day per couple)* **Under 1 mi:** Park *(Elk Neck State Park 287-5333, Turkey Point Lighthouse 287-8170)* **1-3 mi:** Golf Course *(Chesapeake Bay 287-0200)*, Museum *(Upper Bay Museum 287-2675)* **3+ mi:** Fitness Center *(Curves 287-8380, 4 mi.)*, Video Rental *(Jo's 287-6994, 4 mi.)*, Cultural Attract *(Milbourne Stone Theatre 287-1037, 7 mi.)*

Provisioning and General Services

Near: Liquor Store, Market *(Weaver's Plum Creek Market and Liquor Store 287-8474)* **1-3 mi:** Bank/ATM, Post Office, Protestant Church *(United Methodist, 18th C. St. Mary Anne's Episcopal)* **3+ mi:** Supermarket *(Anchorage Enterprise 287-8120, 5 mi.)*, Gourmet Shop *(Bay Gourmet Seafood Market & Cafe 287-4300, 5 mi.)*, Delicatessen *(Schroeder's Deli 287-6465, 5 mi.)*, Bakery *(5 mi.)*, Fishmonger *(5 mi.)*, Library *(North East 287-1005, 7 mi.)*, Bookstore *(Main St. Books 287-2007, 5 mi.)*, Pharmacy *(Happy Harry's 287-8887, 5 mi.)*, Hardware Store *(Builders Choice 398-1111, 8 mi.)*, Copies Etc. *(Bayside Office 287-0999, 5 mi.)*

Transportation

OnCall: Taxi *(Grab-a-Cab 287-2200)*, Airport Limo *(Nationwide 287-0722)*
3+ mi: Rental Car *(North East Auto Rental 287-2040, 5 mi.)*
Airport: Philadelphia/Cecil County *(52 mi./8 mi.)*

Medical Services

911 Service **OnCall:** Ambulance **3+ mi:** Doctor *(North Bay 287-5570, 5 mi.)*, Dentist *(Indian Falls 287-2323, 5 mi.)*, Chiropractor *(North East 287-9110, 5 mi.)*, Holistic Services *(Blue Iris Wellness & Yoga 287-1331, 4 mi.)*, Veterinarian *(North East 398-8100, 6 mi.)*
Hospital: Union Hospital 398-4000 *(11 mi.)*

Setting -- Just around Northeast River's Hances Point, Bay Boat Works is tucked in a cove at the mouth of Hance Pt. Creek. A small blue dockhouse sits at the head of the two main piers. In the creek itself, there's a set of covered slips, some additioinal open dockage, and, farther up the creek, another set of covered slips. Just starboard of the main docks is the North Bay Bed and Breakfast, an updated classic bay cottage, dripping with wisteria.

Marina Notes -- *Weekly and Monthly rates are flat fees, not per foot. DCM. A Clean Marina designated "model facility." Stationary docks sport good pedestals and full-length finger piers, all in very nice condition. Long, easy access fuel dock. In '03, the marina received the 3rd grant for a Bay pumpout vessel - it covers all of Northeast River, 7 days 8am-4:30pm (287-8113). Eventually, it will be equipped with a radio or cell phone. ($5 for the first 50 gal., $0.10/gal. thereafter). Onsite Giordano and Dour Yacht Sales specializes in brokerage power vessels and new Silverton yachts. Bathhouse completely remodeled in '05.

Notable -- On-site North Bay B&B has veiws of the docks and out to the river. In addition to rooms and breakfast, Bob & Pam Appletom offer sails on their 50 foot Gulfstar ketch "Journey," or on 42 foot schooner, Island Time, as well as "boat & breakfast" - a fun option if you have a crew overflow. If you're on your own boat (and it's breakfast time) consider giving them a call to ask if there's room at the table. They also bareboat charter smaller vessels & give sailing lessons. The bustling village of North East is 4 miles and well worth a cab ride - eateries, including famed Woody's Crabhouse, shops, and an interesting basket weaving atelier. Or dinghy or big-boat to the Natui-Goose Saloon - which offers dock 'n' dine and is a short walk to the Upper Bay Museum and town park.

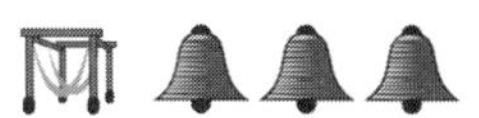

Charlestown Marina

PO Box 26; 4 Water Street; Charlestown, MD 21914

Tel: (410) 287-8125 **VHF: Monitor** 16 **Talk** 72
Fax: (410) 287-0292 **Alternate Tel:** n/a
Email: charlestownmarina@hotmail.com **Web:** charlestownmarina.com
Nearest Town: Charlestown **Tourist Info:** (410) 939-9009

Navigational Information

Lat: 39°34.339' **Long:** 075°58.253' **Tide:** 3 ft. **Current:** 1 kt. **Chart:** 12274
Rep. Depths (*MLW*): Entry 8 ft. **Fuel Dock** 8 ft. **Max Slip/Moor** 8 ft./-
Access: Daymarker 12 on the western shore of the Northeast River

Marina Facilities *(In Season/Off Season)*

Fuel: Gasoline
Slips: 265 Total, 40 Transient **Max LOA:** 65 ft. **Max Beam:** 22 ft.
Rate *(per ft.)*: **Day** $1.75/1.25 **Week** Inq. **Month** Inq.
Power: 30 amp Incl., **50 amp** Incl., **100 amp** n/a, **200 amp** n/a
Cable TV: Yes Trans-Free, 6 mo./$125 **Dockside Phone:** No
Dock Type: Fixed, Long Fingers, Short Fingers, Pilings, Alongside, Wood
Moorings: 0 Total, 0 Transient **Launch:** n/a
Rate: Day n/a **Week** n/a **Month** n/a
Heads: 3 Toilet(s), 3 Shower(s) *(with dressing rooms)*
Laundry: 2 Washer(s), 2 Dryer(s), Book Exchange **Pay Phones:** Yes, 1
Pump-Out: Full Service, 1 Central, 1 Port **Fee:** $5 **Closed Heads:** Yes

Marina Operations

Owner/Manager: Phil Price **Dockmaster:** Ty Price
In-Season: Year-Round, 8am-4:30pm **Off-Season:** n/a
After-Hours Arrival: Call ahead
Reservations: Yes **Credit Cards:** Visa/MC, Amex
Discounts: None
Pets: Welcome, Dog Walk Area **Handicap Access:** No

Marina Services and Boat Supplies

Services - Docking Assistance, Dock Carts **Communication -** Mail & Package Hold, Phone Messages, Fax in/out, FedEx, DHL, UPS, Express Mail *(Sat Del)* **Supplies - OnSite:** Ice *(Block, Cube)*, Ships' Store **Near:** Bait/Tackle, Live Bait, Propane **Under 1 mi:** West Marine *(287-6600)*

Boatyard Services

OnSite: Travelift *(25 & 50T)*, Forklift, Engine mechanic *(gas, diesel)*, Electrical Repairs, Hull Repairs, Canvas Work, Bottom Cleaning, Brightwork, Air Conditioning, Refrigeration, Compound, Wash & Wax, Interior Cleaning, Woodworking, Upholstery, Painting, Awlgrip, Yacht Broker **OnCall:** Crane, Electronics Repairs, Rigger, Propeller Repairs, Inflatable Repairs **Near:**Launching Ramp. **Under 1 mi:** Railway. **Dealer for:** Interlux. **Yard Rates:** $75/hr., Haul & Launch $8/ft. *(blocking $70)*, Power Wash $2/ft., Bottom Paint $14/ft., Incl haul & wash **Storage:** In-Water $22/ft. open, $40/ft. covered, On-Land $27/ft. Incl. haul, launch, block, wash.

Restaurants and Accommodations

OnSite: Restaurant *(The Wellwood 287-6666, L $6-12, D $9-22, motown inside, acoustic guitar on patio)* **OnCall:** Pizzeria *(Bella's 287-6300)*, *(Pat's 939-6060)* **Near:** Restaurant *(Market St. Café 287-6374, L $4-8, D $4-25, Tue-Thu 11am-8pm, Fri-Sat 11am-10pm, Mon specials 3-8pm)*, Seafood Shack *(The River Shack $22 crab feast incl. crab, chicken & corn - takeout too; B Sat & Sun)*, Condo/Cottage *(The Wellwood 287-6666, $125, 3 rental houses, one right over the river, avail. by the night)* **Under 1 mi:** Restaurant *(Beach Comber 287-0580)* **1-3 mi:** Restaurant *(Nauti-Goose 287-7880, L $4-14, D $4-26, dock 'n' dine)*, Fast Food, Hotel *(Holiday Inn 531-5084, $100)* **3+ mi:** Restaurant *(Woody's 287-3541, L $6-9, D $13-30, 4 mi.)*

Recreation and Entertainment

Near: Beach *(town park)*, Picnic Area, Grills, Tennis Courts, Jogging Paths, Volleyball, Video Rental *(Movie King 287-3409)*, Park, Sightseeing *(the village, incorporated 1742)*, Special Events *(Riverfest - 2nd week Sep - vendors, fireworks, historic house tours, kids activities, classic cars, antique boats)* **Under 1 mi:** Playground **1-3 mi:** Golf Course *(Chesapeake Bay 287-0200)*, Fitness Center *(Curves 287-8380)*, Museum *(Upper Bay Museum 287-2675 $4)*, Cultural Attract *(Summer stock at the Community College)*

Provisioning and General Services

Near: Convenience Store, Delicatessen *(Market Street Café 287-6374)*, Wine/Beer *(Beaverbrook 287-0339)*, Bank/ATM, Post Office, Catholic Church, Beauty Salon, Dry Cleaners **Under 1 mi:** Liquor Store *(Weaver's 287-5710)*, Hardware Store *(Ace 398-1111)*, Florist **1-3 mi:** Supermarket *(Food Lion 287-5177)*, Gourmet Shop *(Bay Gourmet 287-4300)*, Bakery, Fishmonger, Meat Market, Library *(North East 287-1005)*, Bookstore *(Main St. 287-2007)*, Pharmacy *(Happy Harry's 287-8887)*

Transportation

OnCall: Taxi *(Grab-a-Cab 287-2200)*, Airport Limo **Near:** Local Bus *(trolley in-season; Charlestown - North East)* **1-3 mi:** Rental Car *(North East Auto Rental 287-2040)* **3+ mi:** Rail *(Perryville, 4 mi.)*
Airport: BWI/Philadelphia *(55 mi./55 mi.)*

Medical Services

911 Service **OnCall:** Ambulance **1-3 mi:** Doctor *(North Bay 287-5570)*, Dentist, Chiropractor *(North East 287-9110)*, Holistic Services *(Blue Iris 287-1331)* **Hospital:** Union 398-4000 *(6 mi.)*

Setting -- The sleepy little burg of Charlestown has deep historical roots, some fascinating residents and 3 marinas. The first is Charlestown, a fairly large, well-maintained facility with 4 long main piers poking into the river, protected from the chop by a wave attenuator. Each berths about 35 vessels in a mix of open and covered docks. About midway along "C" dock, which is managed by The Wellwood Club across the street, a furnished deck serves as a gathering place.

Marina Notes -- Caters to powerboaters. Four sets of docks, many rebuilt since Isabel (including the fuel dock): "A" dock is the 1st covered dock, "B" is open, "C" dock, managed by The Wellwood (287-6666), is half open (to 45-ft.) and "D" is the last covered dock. Small sitting decks are interspersed. Mix of craft includes many classic vessels, some lovingly restored. About 50 live aboard year-round. Nice cinderblock bathhouses adjacent to the ships' store - tile floors, 4 sinks in a Formica vanity, tile shower stalls with glass doors & dressing rooms. Another set, beyond the mechanical building, has a washer & dryer.

Notable -- Adjacent is a town park with a big, grassy picnic area, a small, crescent-shaped sand beach, a pavilion and grills. The Wellwood, which has been in owner Larry Metz's family since the early 60's, is a culinary magnet. Originally a hunting and fishing retreat founded by the Union League & Gridiron Clubs, it once hosted famous politicians, including Teddy Roosevelt. Today, it's better known for its seafood (as well as steaks & ribs), delightful garden patio overlooking the docks, and antique-studded dining rooms (Wed-Sun). The Wellwood also manages a banquet room for up to 150, the nearby River Shack, (crab feasts & take out), and three rental cottages. Northeast, across the river, offers many services & eateries - dinghy to the Nauti-Goose to dock 'n' dine.

PHOTOS ON CD-ROM: 13

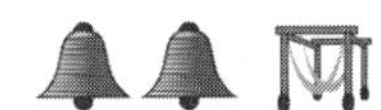

Navigational Information
Lat: 38°34.442' **Long:** 075°58.167' **Tide:** 3 ft. **Current:** 1 kt. **Chart:** 12274
Rep. Depths (*MLW*): Entry 4 ft. **Fuel Dock** n/a **Max Slip/Moor** 8 ft./-
Access: Past Daymarker 12, 3rd marina on Northeast River's western shore

Marina Facilities *(In Season/Off Season)*
Fuel: No
Slips: 70 Total, 4 Transient **Max LOA:** 45 ft. **Max Beam:** 12 ft.
Rate *(per ft.)*: **Day** $1.50 **Week** n/a **Month** n/a
Power: 30 amp Incl., **50 amp** n/a, **100 amp** n/a, **200 amp** n/a
Cable TV: No **Dockside Phone:** No
Dock Type: Fixed, Floating, Short Fingers, Pilings, Alongside, Wood
Moorings: 0 Total, 0 Transient **Launch:** n/a
Rate: Day n/a **Week** n/a **Month** n/a
Heads: 4 Toilet(s), 4 Shower(s) *(with dressing rooms)*
Laundry: None **Pay Phones:** No
Pump-Out: OnSite, Self Service, 1 Central **Fee:** $5 **Closed Heads:** Yes

Marina Operations
Owner/Manager: Thomas Brittingham **Dockmaster:** same
In-Season: May-Sep, 8am-4pm **Off-Season:** Oct-Apr, 9am-3pm
After-Hours Arrival: n/a
Reservations: No **Credit Cards:** Visa/MC, Dscvr, Amex
Discounts: None
Pets: Welcome, Dog Walk Area **Handicap Access:** No

Lee's Marina

PO Box 380; 726 Water Street; Charlestown, MD 21914

Tel: (410) 287-5100 **VHF: Monitor** n/a **Talk** n/a
Fax: (410) 287-5101 **Alternate Tel:** n/a
Email: lmarina726@cs.com **Web:** n/a
Nearest Town: Charlestown **Tourist Info:** (410) 939-9009

Marina Services and Boat Supplies
Services - Docking Assistance, Boaters' Lounge, Trash Pick-Up, Dock Carts **Communication -** Mail & Package Hold, Phone Messages, Fax in/out *($3)*, FedEx, DHL, UPS, Express Mail *(Sat Del)* **Supplies - OnSite:** Ice *(Block, Cube)*, Ships' Store **Under 1 mi:** West Marine (287-6600), Bait/Tackle *(Warrior Rods 287-3282)* **1-3 mi:** CNG

Boatyard Services
OnSite: Travelift, Engine mechanic *(gas, diesel)*, Electrical Repairs, Hull Repairs, Bottom Cleaning, Brightwork, Air Conditioning, Refrigeration, Woodworking, Upholstery, Yacht Interiors **OnCall:** Canvas Work *(Caudill's)*, Compound, Wash & Wax, Interior Cleaning, Propeller Repairs
Near: Launching Ramp. **Yard Rates:** $60/hr., Haul & Launch $10/ft. *(blocking inq.)*, Power Wash $3/ft., Bottom Paint $9/ft. *(paint incl.)*
Storage: On-Land $100/mo.

Restaurants and Accommodations
OnCall: Pizzeria *(Pat's 832-6606, delivers)* **Near:** Restaurant *(The Wellwood 287-6666, L $6-12, D $9-22)*, Seafood Shack *(River Shack all-you-can-eat crabs, chicken & corn $22, take out also; B Sat & Sun)*, Condo/Cottage *(The Wellwood 287-6666, three houses avail. nightly)*
Under 1 mi: Restaurant *(Nauti-Goose 287-7880, L $4-14, D $4-26, by water - dock 'n' dine)*, *(Market Street Café 287-6374, L $4-8, D $4-25, Entrees mostly mid-teens, Fri-Sat 11am-8pm, Fri-Sat 11am-10pm, Mon Seafood Specials 3-8pm)*, *(Beachcomber 287-5629)* **1-3 mi:** Hotel *(Crystal Inn 287-7100, $100)*, Inn/B&B *(Holiday Inn Express 287-7851, $100)* **3+ mi:** Restaurant *(Pier One 287-6599, 4 mi.)*, *(Woody's Crabhouse 287-3541, L $6-9, D $13-30, 4 mi., kids' menu, peanut shells & brown paper tablecloths)*

Recreation and Entertainment
OnSite: Picnic Area, Grills **Near:** Beach, Tennis Courts *(Charlestown athletic complex)*, Jogging Paths, Park *(town park)*, Sightseeing *(historic district)*, Special Events *(Riverfest - 2nd week Sep)* **Under 1 mi:** Video Rental *(Movie King 287-3409)* **1-3 mi:** Golf Course *(Chesapeake Bay 287-0200)*, Fitness Center *(Curves 287-8380)*, Boat Rentals, Fishing Charter, Museum *(Upper Bay 287-2675 $4)*, Cultural Attract *(Summer stock at Cecil County Community College - the covered Bridge 287-1037)*

Provisioning and General Services
Near: Wine/Beer *(Beaverbrook 287-0339)*, Liquor Store *(Weaver's 287-5710)*, Bank/ATM, Post Office, Catholic Church, Protestant Church, Newsstand, Retail Shops **Under 1 mi:** Delicatessen *(Market Street Café 287-6374)*, Market *(Lewis Market 287-6130)* **1-3 mi:** Supermarket *(Food Lion 287-5177)*, Library *(North East 287-1005)*, Beauty Salon, Barber Shop, Dry Cleaners, Laundry *(Laundry Care 287-6775)*, Bookstore *(Main St. Books 287-2007)*, Pharmacy *(Happy Harry's 287-8887)*, Hardware Store *(Ace 398-1111)*, Florist, Clothing Store, Copies Etc. *(Bayside Office 287-0999)*

Transportation
OnCall: Taxi *(Grab-a-Cab 287-2200)*, Airport Limo **Near:** Local Bus *(Trolley in-season from Charlestown to North East)* **1-3 mi:** Rental Car *(North East Auto Rental 287-2040)* **Airport:** BWI/Philadelphia *(55 mi.)*

Medical Services
911 Service **OnCall:** Ambulance **1-3 mi:** Doctor *(North Bay 287-5570)*, Dentist, Chiropractor *(North East 287-9110)*
Hospital: Union Hospital398-4000 *(8 mi.)*

Setting -- Lee's is the third marina on the southern shore of Northeast River. A boardwalk runs parallel to the shore and 3 piers flow out into the river. Two have floating slips on both sides; the third has slips inside and alongside dockage on the outside. A large, gray, vertical-sided building with blue trim sits at the head of the dock and houses the offices and ships' store. Nicely varnished picnic tables sit on a patch of grass overlooking the docks.

Marina Notes -- A very nicely furnished little boaters' lounge is in a corner in the ships' store; a phone's available for local calls. Two basic, but quite serviceable, complete bathrooms have fiberglass shower stalls with fresh curtains, asphalt tile flooring, and Formica walls. Pat's Marina, between Charlestown and Lee's, accepts transients under 32 ft. only when space is available; Charlestown Dock has 2 free slips. Stay tuned for a 36-slip municipal marina.

Notable -- Directly adjacent to Lee's is a town park with the Fire and Rescue Boat Pier. Next to that, past the trailer parking lot, a new condo and marina is being developed on the Avalon Yacht Basin site. Charlestown merits a stroll along its leafy waterfront lanes - it has the feeling of being on the verge of discovery (although a few lovely waterfornt homes suggest that some have.) About three blocks from the docks is the Market Street Café and grocery store - a smoky, local hangout featuring a kind of "shuffleboard on legs" that's played on two long tables - with great enthusiasm. On the lower level, under the café, is a fairly well-stocked convenience store and deli. At the edge of town is Beachcomber, an eatery housed in a modular building. The Wellwood restaurant is an experience and makes Charlestown a real destination. Alternatively, dinghy across the river to North East and tie up at the dock 'n' dine Nauti-Goose Saloon.

McDaniel Yacht Basin

15 Grandview Avenue; North East, MD 21901

Tel: (410) 287-8121 **VHF: Monitor** 16 **Talk** 13
Fax: (410) 287-8127 **Alternate Tel:** n/a
Email: office@mcdanyacht.com **Web:** www.mcdanielyacht.com
Nearest Town: North East *(1.5 mi.)* **Tourist Info:** (410) 287-2658

Navigational Information

Lat: 39°34.629' **Long:** 075°56.966' **Tide:** 2 ft. **Current:** n/a **Chart:** 12274
Rep. Depths (*MLW*): Entry 6 ft. **Fuel Dock** 6 ft. **Max Slip/Moor** 6 ft./-
Access: Eastern shore of Northeast River

Marina Facilities *(In Season/Off Season)*

Fuel: *Unbranded* - Gasoline, Diesel, High-Speed Pumps
Slips: 175 Total, 6 Transient **Max LOA:** 65 ft. **Max Beam:** 18 ft.
Rate *(per ft.)*: **Day** $1.25 **Week** Inq. **Month** Inq.
Power: 30 amp Incl., **50 amp** Incl., **100 amp** n/a, **200 amp** n/a
Cable TV: Yes Incl. **Dockside Phone:** Yes On request
Dock Type: Fixed, Long Fingers, Short Fingers, Pilings, Alongside, Wood
Moorings: 0 Total, 0 Transient **Launch:** None
Rate: Day n/a **Week** n/a **Month** n/a
Heads: 12 Toilet(s), 6 Shower(s)
Laundry: 2 Washer(s), 2 Dryer(s), Iron Board **Pay Phones:** Yes, 1
Pump-Out: Full Service, 2 Central, 1 Port **Fee:** $5 **Closed Heads:** Yes

Marina Operations

Owner/Manager: Thomas W. Trainer **Dockmaster:** Bill Faul
In-Season: Summer, 8am-4:30pm **Off-Season:** Fall-Win-Sprg, 8am-4:30pm
After-Hours Arrival: Security Guards
Reservations: Yes, Required **Credit Cards:** Visa/MC, Dscvr, Amex
Discounts: None
Pets: Welcome, Dog Walk Area **Handicap Access:** Yes, Heads

Marina Services and Boat Supplies

Services - Docking Assistance, Boaters' Lounge, Trash Pick-Up, Dock Carts **Communication -** Mail & Package Hold, Phone Messages, Fax in/out, Data Ports *(lounge)*, FedEx, DHL, UPS, Express Mail *(Sat Del)* **Supplies - OnSite:** Ice *(Cube)*, Ships' Store **Near:** Bait/Tackle *(Herb's 287-5490)* **Under 1 mi:** West Marine *(287-6600)*, Live Bait, Propane

Boatyard Services

OnSite: Travelift *(50 & 35T)*, Railway *(70T)*, Crane *(20T)*, Forklift *(4T)*, Hydraulic Trailer, Engine mechanic *(gas, diesel)*, Electrical Repairs, Electronics Repairs, Hull Repairs, Rigger, Canvas Work, Bottom Cleaning, Brightwork, Air Conditioning, Refrigeration, Compound, Wash & Wax, Interior Cleaning, Propeller Repairs, Woodworking, Inflatable Repairs, Life Raft Service, Upholstery, Painting, Awlgrip, Yacht Broker **OnCall:** Metal Fabrication **Near:** Launching Ramp **Member:** ABBRA, ABYC **Yard Rates:** $70/hr., Haul & Launch $7/ft. *(blocking incl.)*, Power Wash $1.25/ft., Bottom Paint $15/ft. *(paint incl.)* **Storage:** In-Water $16/ft., On-Land $25/ft.

Restaurants and Accommodations

Near: Restaurant *(Aft Deck 287-6200)* **1-3 mi:** Restaurant *(Steak and Main 287-3512, oyster bar)*, *(Highbourne Café 287-3300, delivers)*, *(Woody's Crab House 287-3541, L $6-9, D $7-28, kids' menu)*, *(Nauti-Goose 287-7880, L $4-14, D $4-26, dockage)*, Seafood Shack *(Pier One 287-6599)*, Fast Food, Lite Fare *(Victorian Tea Cup 287-9500)*, *(Bay Gourmet 287-4300, L $10-26, D $10-26, menu changes daily)*, Pizzeria *(Bella's 287-6300)*, Hotel *(Crystal Inn 287-7100, $100)*, *(Holiday Express 287-0008, $100)*

Recreation and Entertainment

OnSite: Pool, Beach, Picnic Area **Near:** Boat Rentals *(Sail only)* **Under 1 mi:** Golf Course *(Chesapeake Bay 287-0200)*, Video Rental *(Jo's 287-6994)*, Park, Museum *(Upper Bay 287-2675 $4)*, Sightseeing *(Elk Neck State Park 287-5333, Turkey Point Lighthouse 287-5333)* **1-3 mi:** Galleries *(East of the Bay 287-4373)* **3+ mi:** Fitness Center *(Pro Fitness 287-4600, 4 mi.)*

Provisioning and General Services

Near: Delicatessen *(Schroeder's 287-6465)*, Wine/Beer *(Weaver's 287-5710)*, Market *(Howards 287-5544)*, Barber Shop, Laundry **Under 1 mi:** Bank/ATM, Post Office, Catholic Church, Protestant Church *(Methodist, Episcopal)* **1-3 mi:** Supermarket *(Food Lion 287-5177, Acme 287-9008)*, Gourmet Shop *(Bay Gourmet 287-4300)*, Bakery, Fishmonger, Beauty Salon, Dry Cleaners, Bookstore *(Main St. 287-2007)*, Pharmacy *(Happy Harry's 287-8887)* **3+ mi:** Library *(287-1005, 5 mi.)*, Hardware Store *(Ace 398-1111, 4 mi.)*

Transportation

OnSite: Courtesy Car/Van *(9am-5pm)* **OnCall:** Taxi *(Grab-a-Cab 287-2200)*, Airport Limo *(Nationwide 287-0722)* **1-3 mi:** Rental Car *(North East Auto Rental 287-2040)* **Airport:** Philadelphia/Cecil County *(50 mi./8 mi.)*

Medical Services

911 Service **OnCall:** Ambulance **1-3 mi:** Doctor *(North Bay 287-5570)*, Dentist *(Jackson 287-8644)*, Chiropractor *(North East 287-9110)*, Holistic Services *(Blue Iris Wellness & Yoga 287-1331)*, Veterinarian *(North East 398-8100)* **Hospital:** Union 398-4000 *(9 mi.)*

Setting -- A beige, three-story glass-front contemporary topped with a French-blue roof and cupola rises steeply above the docks, announcing McDaniel's very protected 31-acre facility. That theme is replicated throughout this beautifully renovated, immaculate facility. Past the wave fence, the marina divides into two basins - imagine a reverse "check mark." To starboard is the shorter basin, ringed with slips; to port is a long meandering waterway, hosting covered and uncovered slip, that ends at the boatyard operation and the pool. The central peninsula houses the sparkling new amenities building.

Marina Notes -- A large, well-equipped ships' store and beautiful new boaters' lounge sit on the central pier. Easy chairs surround several sets of tables & chairs; there's a big-screen TV plus broadband access (cables available in the main office). A picnic area on the deck provides views of the passing boat traffic. The serious boatyard operation, on-the-hard storage, and inauspiciously-sited pool are set farther up the waterway, away from the main slips. Certified Clean Marina. Dealer for Carver, Navagator, Kohler, Criuse Air, Mercruiser. Adjacent to the boaters' lounge is the inviting main bathhouse; the vanity has skirted molded sinks with assorted toiletries. Across the waterway is a second, brightly painted cinderblock bathhouse.

Notable -- McDaniel's provides daytime transport into the nearby, bustling village of North East (for dinner, take a cab back). About a half-dozen interesting restaurants, a plethora of antique, collectible and clothing shops, galleries, plus the Upper Bay Museum have made North East a destination. The renaissance was kicked off by now nationally-famous Woody's Crab House, which spun off a mini Woody's industry and ultimately, a whole new town.

Havre de Grace Yacht Basin

352 Commerce Street; Havre De Grace, MD 21078

Tel: (410) 939-0015 **VHF: Monitor** 68 **Talk** 9
Fax: (410) 939-3692 **Alternate Tel:** n/a
Email: geref@havredegracemd.com **Web:** www.havredegracemd.com
Nearest Town: Havre de Grace *(0.5 mi.)* **Tourist Info:** (800) 851-7756

Navigational Information
Lat: 39°32.272' **Long:** 076°05.317' **Tide:** 2 ft. **Current:** n/a **Chart:** 12274
Rep. Depths (*MLW*): Entry 6 ft. **Fuel Dock** 6 ft. **Max Slip/Moor** 6 ft./-
Access: North to Susquehanna River west at #17 FL

Marina Facilities *(In Season/Off Season)*
Fuel: Gasoline, Diesel
Slips: 275 Total, 25 Transient **Max LOA:** 55 ft. **Max Beam:** 25 ft.
Rate *(per ft.)*: **Day** $1.00/Inq. **Week** $3.50 **Month** $9.00
Power: 30 amp $5, **50 amp** $10, **100 amp** n/a, **200 amp** n/a
Cable TV: No **Dockside Phone:** No
Dock Type: Fixed, Short Fingers, Pilings, Wood
Moorings: 0 Total, 0 Transient **Launch:** n/a
Rate: Day n/a **Week** n/a **Month** n/a
Heads: 5 Toilet(s), 8 Shower(s)
Laundry: None **Pay Phones:** Yes
Pump-Out: OnSite, Full Service **Fee:** $5 **Closed Heads:** Yes

Marina Operations
Owner/Manager: Gerard Frailey **Dockmaster:** Same
In-Season: Apr-Nov, 8am-6pm **Off-Season:** Dec-Mar, 8am-4pm
After-Hours Arrival: Call in advance
Reservations: Preferred **Credit Cards:** Visa/MC
Discounts: None
Pets: Welcome, Dog Walk Area **Handicap Access:** No

Marina Services and Boat Supplies
Services - Docking Assistance **Communication -** Mail & Package Hold, FedEx, UPS, Express Mail *(Sat Del)* **Supplies - OnSite:** Ice *(Block, Cube)*, Live Bait **Near:** Ships' Store **Under 1 mi:** West Marine *(939-6282)*, Bait/Tackle *(Extreme Bait 942-0700)* **1-3 mi:** Propane *(U-Haul 939-7971)*

Boatyard Services
OnSite: Launching Ramp **OnCall:** Engine mechanic *(gas, diesel)*, Divers, Propeller Repairs, Inflatable Repairs **Near:** Electrical Repairs, Hull Repairs, Rigger. **Under 1 mi:** Railway *(50T)*, Crane, Forklift, Sail Loft, Canvas Work, Bottom Cleaning, Brightwork, Air Conditioning, Refrigeration, Compound, Wash & Wax, Woodworking, Upholstery, Painting, Awlgrip.

Restaurants and Accommodations
OnSite: Snack Bar *(Top of the Bay Grill 939-0304, burgers, hot dogs, ice-cream)* **Near:** Restaurant *(Promenade Grille 939-1416)*, Inn/B&B *(Currier House 939-7886, $110-140)* **Under 1 mi:** Restaurant *(Laurrapin Grille 939-3663)*, *(Havre de Grace Ritz Cafe 939-5858, L $7-10, D $7-10)*, *(MacGregor's 939-3003, L $8-13, D $17-23)*, *(Tidewater Grille 939-3313, D $15-25)*, Coffee Shop *(Java by the Bay 939-0227)*, Pizzeria *(Deli Mart Carryout 939-0090, packaged beer to go)*, Inn/B&B *(Spencer Silver Mansion 939-1485, $80-150)*, *(Vandiver Inn 939-5200, $75-105)*, *(La Cle D'Or Guesthouse 939-6502)* **1-3 mi:** Restaurant *(Aquatica 939-7686, L $8-30, D $8-30)*, *(Coakley's Pub 939-8888, L $6-10, D $10-20)*

Recreation and Entertainment
OnSite: Picnic Area, Grills, Playground, Tennis Courts, Jogging Paths *(0.4 mi. Promenade - sunrise to 11pm, biking 'til 10am)*, Park *(Tydings)*, Special Events *(Seafood Fest - Aug)* **Near:** Museum *(Maritime 939-4800, Decoy 939-3739, Susquehanna 939-5780)*, Sightseeing *(Concord Point Lighthouse 939-9040)* **Under 1 mi:** Golf Course *(Bulle Rock 939-8887)*, Video Rental *(Blockbuster 939-6293)* **1-3 mi:** Fitness Center *(Curves 939-3555)*, Boat Rentals *(Starrk Moon Kayaks 939-9500)*

Provisioning and General Services
OnCall: Delicatessen *(St. John Gourmet Deli, under 1 mi. 939-3663, delivers)* **Near:** Convenience Store, Farmers' Market *(Sat 9am-noon)*, Bank/ATM, Post Office, Catholic Church, Protestant Church, Beauty Salon, Pharmacy *(Citizen's 939-4404)*, Florist **Under 1 mi:** Supermarket *(Save-A-Lot 939-3116)*, Health Food *(Washington Sq.)*, Liquor Store *(Cork & Barrel 939-8002)*, Bakery *(Goll's 939-4321)*, Fishmonger, Library *(939-6700)*, Dry Cleaners *(Post Road 939-3070)*, Laundry, Bookstore *(Washington St. 939-6215)*, Hardware Store *(Walton's 939-1117)*, Department Store *(Joseph's 939-4114)*, Copies Etc. *(Hickory 939-1790)* **1-3 mi:** Synagogue

Transportation
OnCall: Rental Car *(Enterprise 273-7711 or Budget 939-3333, 2 mi.)*, Taxi *(Yellow Cab 939-6000)*, Airport Limo *(Akini 939-9756)* **Near:** Local Bus, InterCity Bus **3+ mi:** Rail *(Amtrak Perryville 642-2620, 4 mi.)*
Airport: BWI/Philadelphia *(52 mi./60 mi.)*

Medical Services
911 Service **OnCall:** Ambulance **Near:** Doctor *(Landmark 939-5358)* **Under 1 mi:** Dentist *(Union 939-3950)*, Chiropractor *(McDermott 939-1111)* **1-3 mi:** Veterinarian *(Animal Hospital 272-8656)* **3+ mi:** Holistic Services *(Acupuncture 272-0665, 5 mi.)* **Hospital:** Harford 575-7550 *(0.5 mi.)*

Setting -- At the mouth of the river, snuggled between Tydings Park and Tydings Island (made from dredging spoil) are six mainland piers, with slips on both sides, and a seventh on the island accessible only by dinghy. A wave attenuator protects the docks from the river's wakes and a clearly marked channel leads to the marina. Shoreside is a lovely park, a fun dockhouse that looks like a cab ripped from a tugboat - built by the dockmaster - and a spectacular boardwalk.

Marina Notes -- An island, formed by the dredging spoil, provides some protection for the six piers. Perfectly maintained stationary wood docks with creosoted pilings have full power pedestals and half-length finger piers with boarding ladders at the end - deeper slips have three-quarter fingers. Big T-heads at the end of each pier handle larger boats. The on-site snack bar sells burgers, hot dogs, & ice cream. Refurbished, very lovely cinderblock bathhouses courtesy of Isabel - Formica vanities with inset sinks plus 3 heads, 3 fiberglass shower stalls & dressing areas with benches (divided with shower curtains).

Notable -- Eight-acre Tydings Park, on a hill directly above the marina's parking lot, has picnic tables, a gazebo, an inventive playground, and a winding brick path - all with views of the docks; it's also home to the Center for Environmental and Estuarine Studies run by the University of MD. The surrounding community's lovely homes invite a stroll, but the best walk is along the beautiful, newly rebuilt 4/10 mi. promenade that begins at the gazebo by the docks and ends at Concord Point Lighthouse, one of the oldest on the Bay. The stone mansion, once the Bayou Hotel, is now the Bayou Condos. Within a block is the famous Decoy Museum - carving demonstrations on Sat and Sun. Just beyond is the Havre de Grace Maritime Museum - Mon, Wed & Fri, 11am-5pm.

PHOTOS ON CD-ROM: 13

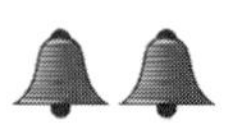

Havre de Grace Marina

401 Concord Street; Havre de Grace, MD 21078

Tel: (410) 939-2221 **VHF: Monitor** 16 **Talk** n/a
Fax: (410) 939-0220 **Alternate Tel:** (410) 939-2161
Email: hdgys@msn.com **Web:** www.yachtworld.com/hdgys
Nearest Town: Havre de Grace *(0.5 mi.)* **Tourist Info:** (800) 851-7756

Navigational Information

Lat: 39°32.697' **Long:** 076°05.082' **Tide:** 2 ft. **Current:** n/a **Chart:** 12274
Rep. Depths (*MLW*): Entry 9 ft. **Fuel Dock** 9 ft. **Max Slip/Moor** 9 ft./-
Access: Chesapeake Bay to Susquehanna River past R18 on western shore

Marina Facilities *(In Season/Off Season)*

Fuel: Gasoline, Diesel
Slips: 65 Total, 5 Transient **Max LOA:** 44 ft. **Max Beam:** 14 ft.
Rate *(per ft.)*: **Day** $1.50 **Week** n/a **Month** $450-350
Power: 30 amp $5, **50 amp** $10, **100 amp** n/a, **200 amp** n/a
Cable TV: No **Dockside Phone:** No
Dock Type: Floating, Long Fingers, Short Fingers, Alongside, Wood
Moorings: 0 Total, 0 Transient **Launch:** n/a
Rate: Day n/a **Week** n/a **Month** n/a
Heads: 3 Toilet(s), 3 Shower(s)
Laundry: 1 Washer(s), 1 Dryer(s) **Pay Phones:** Yes
Pump-Out: OnSite **Fee:** $10 **Closed Heads:** Yes

Marina Operations

Owner/Manager: Donna Scherpf **Dockmaster:** Arvid Scherpf
In-Season: Apr-Nov, 9am-6pm **Off-Season:** Dec-Mar, closed
After-Hours Arrival: Call ahead
Reservations: Preferred **Credit Cards:** Visa/MC
Discounts: Boat/US **Dockage:** $0.25/ft **Fuel:** $0.10 **Repair:** n/a
Pets: Welcome, Dog Walk Area **Handicap Access:** Yes, Heads

Marina Services and Boat Supplies

Services - Docking Assistance, Security, Trash Pick-Up, Dock Carts **Communication -** Phone Messages, Fax in/out, FedEx, DHL, UPS, Express Mail **Supplies - OnSite:** Ice *(Block, Cube)* **Near:** CNG **Under 1 mi:** West Marine *(939-6282)* **1-3 mi:** Bait/Tackle *(Extreme Bait & Tackle 942-0700)*, Propane *(U-Haul 939-7971)*

Boatyard Services

OnSite: Yacht Broker **OnCall:** Engine mechanic *(gas, diesel)*, Electrical Repairs, Electronics Repairs, Hull Repairs, Rigger, Canvas Work, Brightwork **Near:** Awlgrip *(Roundebush 939-6195).* **Under 1 mi:** Travelift *(15T HDGM 939-2161)*, Crane, Bottom Cleaning, Compound, Wash & Wax, Interior Cleaning. **1-3 mi:** Launching Ramp. **Member:** ABBRA, ABYC

Restaurants and Accommodations

Near: Restaurant *(Havre de Grace Ritz 939-5858, L $7-10, D $7-10)*, *(La Cucina 939-1401)*, *(MacGregor's 939-3003, L $8-13, D $17-23)*, Snack Bar *(Bomboy's Homemade Ice Cream)*, Coffee Shop *(Java by the Bay 939-0227)*, Inn/B&B *(Union Ave. 939-7023)*, *(Currier House 939-7886)*, *(Spencer Silver Mansion 939-1485)* **Under 1 mi:** Restaurant *(The Crazy Swede 939-5440, L $3-12, D $8-25)*, Seafood Shack *(Price's 939-2782)*, Pizzeria *(Deli Mart Carryout 939-0090)*, Inn/B&B *(Vandiver Inn 939-5200, $75-105)* **1-3 mi:** Fast Food *(McDonalds, Burger King)*

Recreation and Entertainment

OnSite: Picnic Area **Near:** Playground, Tennis Courts, Jogging Paths, Boat Rentals, Park *(Tydings)*, Museum *(Maritime 939-4800, Decoy 939-3739, Susquehanna 939-5780, 1 mi.)*, Cultural Attract, Sightseeing *(Concord Point Lighthouse 939-9040)* **Under 1 mi:** Grills, Dive Shop, Fitness Center *(Curves 939-3555)*, Video Rental *(Blockbuster 939-6293)* **1-3 mi:** Golf Course *(Bulle Rock 939-8887)* **3+ mi:** Bowling *(Harford 272-3555, 5 mi.)*

Provisioning and General Services

OnCall: Delicatessen *(St. John Gourmet Deli, under 1 mi, 939-3663, delivers)* **Near:** Convenience Store *(WAWA)*, Bakery *(Goll's 939-4321)*, Farmers' Market *(Sat 9am-noon)*, Market *(Save-A-Lot 939-3116)*, Bank/ATM, Library *(939-6700)*, Beauty Salon, Pharmacy *(Citizen's 939-4404)*, Hardware Store *(Walton's 939-1117)*, Department Store *(Joseph's 939-4114)* **Under 1 mi:** Wine/Beer *(Deli Mart 939-0090, Chevron 939-5584)*, Liquor Store *(Cork & Barrel 939-8002)*, Fishmonger, Post Office, Dry Cleaners *(Post Road 939-3070)*, Laundry, Bookstore *(Washington St. Books 939-6215)*, Copies Etc. *(Hickory 939-1790)* **1-3 mi:** Supermarket *(Acme 939-9015)*

Transportation

OnCall: Rental Car *(Enterprise 273-7711 or Budget 939-3333 2 mi.)*, Taxi *(Montville Taxi 939-0900)*, Airport Limo *(Akini 939-9756)* **Near:** Local Bus **Under 1 mi:** Bikes **3+ mi:** Rail *(Amtrak Perryville 642-2620, 4 mi.)*
Airport: BWI/Philadelphia *(52 mi./60 mi.)*

Medical Services

911 Service **OnCall:** Ambulance **Near:** Doctor *(Landmark Medical 939-5358)*, Holistic Services *(Par Excellence Day Spa 939-0029)* **Under 1 mi:** Dentist *(Union Dental 939-3950)*, Chiropractor *(McDermott 939-1111)* **1-3 mi:** Veterinarian *(Animal Hospital of Havre de Grace 272-8656)*
Hospital: Harford Memorial 575-7550 *(0.5 mi.)*

Setting -- Nestled in a basin backed on two sides by a gray & white three-story contemporary condominium complex, this network of high-end floating docks features wide alleys for easy manueuverability. The main pier, perpendicular to the shoreline, anchors two well-spaced floating docks that paralell the mainland. Alongside dockage for cats and larger boats lines one side of the primary pier. A fuel dock on the T-head of outer dock is easily accessible from the river.

Marina Notes -- Alongside can accommodates up to 125 ft. This shipshape faciity, managed by Havre de Grace Marina, is protected from the roll of the river by a wave fence. Even mix of power and sail. Good pedestals. Boat US discounts. A part-time dockmaster is on the second floor above the bathhouse. The docks are now being repaired and refurbished. Sailboat multihull dealers: Seawind Catamarans, Corsair & Wind Rider Trimarans. Boatyard services are available from HDG Marina or nearby Tidewater. Brand new, gorgeous key-coded bathhouse has glass-block wall sections for natural light, tile floors & walls inset with decorative strips; full bathrooms have glass shower doors. Plus a larger handicapped bathroom and a washer and dryer.

Notable -- Bomboy's Homemade Ice Cream & Candy is right outside the complex. It's a short, three-block walk north to the bustling, thriving 18thC river town of Havre de Grace with antique stores, restaurants, shops and a weekend flea market. Pick up the 28-stop self-guided tour of the Nationally Registered Historic District (939-1800). Or walk 0.2 mile south to the Concord Point Lighthouse (Sat & Sun 1-5pm) and the beginning of the spectacular new waterfront promenade that overlooks the Susquehanna Flats. Adjacent to the boardwalk are the Harvre de Grace Maritime Museum and the Decoy Museum (11am-4pm, 7 days).

Navigational Information
Lat: 39°32.752' **Long:** 076°05.054' **Tide:** 2 ft. **Current:** n/a **Chart:** 12274
Rep. Depths (*MLW*): Entry 8 ft. **Fuel Dock** 6 ft. **Max Slip/Moor** 6 ft./-
Access: Susquehanna River past R18 on western shore

Marina Facilities *(In Season/Off Season)*
Fuel: Gasoline, Diesel
Slips: 160 Total, 15 Transient **Max LOA:** 60 ft. **Max Beam:** 18 ft.
Rate *(per ft.)*: **Day** $1.50 **Week** Inq. **Month** Inq.
Power: 30 amp $6, **50 amp** $6, **100 amp** n/a, **200 amp** n/a
Cable TV: No **Dockside Phone:** No
Dock Type: Fixed, Short Fingers, Wood
Moorings: 12 Total, 0 Transient **Launch:** n/a
Rate: Day n/a **Week** n/a **Month** n/a
Heads: 10 Toilet(s), 10 Shower(s)
Laundry: None **Pay Phones:** No
Pump-Out: OnSite **Fee:** $5 **Closed Heads:** Yes

Marina Operations
Owner/Manager: Susan Burchette **Dockmaster:** Jeff Andrews
In-Season: Apr-Nov, 8am-5pm **Off-Season:** Dec-Mar, 8am-5pm
After-Hours Arrival: Call in Advance
Reservations: Yes, Preferred **Credit Cards:** Visa/MC, Dscvr
Discounts: None
Pets: Welcome **Handicap Access:** No

Tidewater Havre de Grace

100 Bourbon Street; Havre de Grace, MD 21078

Tel: (410) 939-0950; (800) 960-8433 **VHF: Monitor** 16 **Talk** 9
Fax: (410) 939-0960 **Alternate Tel:** n/a
Email: dockmaster@tidewatermarina.com **Web:** www.tidewatermarina.com
Nearest Town: Havre de Grace **Tourist Info:** (800) 851-7756

Marina Services and Boat Supplies
Services - Docking Assistance, Concierge **Communication -** Mail & Package Hold, Phone Messages, Fax in/out, Data Ports *(Cable)*, FedEx, DHL, UPS **Supplies - OnSite:** Ice *(Block, Cube)*, Ships' Store *(Tidewater Marine)*, CNG **1-3 mi:** West Marine *(939-6282)*, Bait/Tackle, Propane

Boatyard Services
OnSite: Travelift *(35T/30T/20T)*, Crane, Forklift, Hydraulic Trailer, Launching Ramp, Engine mechanic *(gas, diesel)*, Electrical Repairs, Electronics Repairs, Hull Repairs, Rigger, Brightwork, Air Conditioning, Refrigeration, Compound, Wash & Wax, Interior Cleaning, Propeller Repairs, Woodworking, Painting, Awlgrip *(Caribbean 939-6578)*, Total Refits, Yacht Broker **OnCall:** Canvas Work, Inflatable Repairs, Life Raft Service, Metal Fabrication **Yard Rates:** $65/hr., Haul & Launch $6/ft. *(blocking $8.50/ft.)*, Power Wash Incl., Bottom Paint $6.25/ft. **Storage:** On-Land $30/ft.

Restaurants and Accommodations
Near: Restaurant *(McGregor's 939-3003, L $8-13, D $17-23)*, *(Vancheri's 942-0199)*, *(White House B $4-10, L $4-8, D $9-17, kids' menu $5)*, *(The Bayou 939-3565, L $5-7, D $10-18, luncheon buffet)*, *(The Tidewater Grill 575-7045, D $15-25)*, *(Coakley's Pub 939-8888, L $6-9, D $7-22)*, Pizzeria *(Fortunato Brothers 939-1401)* **Under 1 mi:** Pizzeria *(Deli Mart Carryout & Restaurant 939-0090)*, Motel *(Super 8 939-1880)*, Inn/B&B *(Crazy Swede 939-5440)*, *(Currier House 939-7886, $110-140)*, *(Spencer Silver Mansion 939-1485, $80-150)*, *(Vandiver Inn 939-5200, $75-105)*

Recreation and Entertainment
OnSite: Picnic Area, Grills, Boat Rentals *(Bay Sail School & Charters 939-2869)* **Near:** Park *(Hutchins Mem.)*, Cultural Attract, Sightseeing *(Walking tours; Concord Pt. Lighthouse 939-9040)*, Galleries **Under 1 mi:** Tennis Courts, Fitness Center *(Curves 939-3555)*, Jogging Paths, Museum *(Decoy 939-3739, Maritime 939-4800, Susquehanna 939-5780)* **1-3 mi:** Golf Course *(Bulle Rock 939-8887)*, Video Rental *(Blockbuster 939-6293)*

Provisioning and General Services
OnSite: Clothing Store **Near:** Delicatessen *(St. John Gourmet Deli 939-3663, Sam's 939-9594, delivers)*, Wine/Beer *(Deli Mart 939-0090)*, Liquor Store *(Cork and Barrel 939-8002)*, Bakery *(Gull's)*, Farmers' Market *(Sat 9am-Noon)*, Market *(Save-A-Lot 939-3116)*, Bank/ATM, Post Office, Catholic Church, Protestant Church, Library *(Havre de Grace 939-6700)*, Beauty Salon, Pharmacy *(Citizen's 939-4404)*, Hardware Store *(Walton's 939-1117)*, Florist, Department Store *(Joseph's 939-4114)* **Under 1 mi:** Convenience Store, Dry Cleaners *(TC Cleaners 939-9177)*, Laundry, Bookstore *(Washington St. Books 939-6215)*, Copies Etc. *(Hickory 939-1790)* **1-3 mi:** Supermarket *(Acme 939-9015)*

Transportation
OnSite: Courtesy Car/Van, Bikes, Local Bus **OnCall:** Rental Car *(Enterprise 273-7711 or Budget 939-3333, 2 mi.)*, Taxi *(Yellow Cab 939-6000)* **Under 1 mi:** Airport Limo **3+ mi:** Rail *(Amtrak Perryville 642-2620, 4 mi.)* **Airport:** BWI/Philadelphia *(52 mi./60 mi.)*

Medical Services
911 Service **OnCall:** Ambulance **Near:** Doctor, Dentist *(Union Dental 939-3950)*, Chiropractor *(McDermott 939-1111)* **1-3 mi:** Veterinarian *(Havre de Grace 272-8656)* **Hospital:** Harford Memorial 575-7550 *(0.5 mi.)*

Setting -- It's easy to spot Tidewater. Directly riverside is a two-story white building with blue-gray trim and a single-story annex - flags flying from a three post flagpole. On the north side is a fuel dock; on the south side a large grassy picnic area with tables, a grill, and benches for watching the river traffic. Behind this riverfront complex are three basins lined with slips, created by two paved peninsulas, which house the service facilities. Each basin has a separate entrance.

Marina Notes -- DCM. Founded in 1956, still owned by the same family. A serious, service-focused boat yard with 3 travelifts serving lots of big boats, frequently cited as "a best service marina." Brand-new attractive 4-story brick & granite Tidewater Marine Outfitters opened late '05. Paved peninsulas, edged with swaths of grass, house service yards, storage buildings, and work sheds. The first narrow basin, south of the picinic area, has slips along the northern shore. The next long basin, past the fuel dock, has slips on both sides.The third basin, at the end of the grass jetty, has slips on three sides and a pier down the middle. Dealer for Hunter & Catalina. Bay Sail Sailing School is onsite. The bathhouse has eight locked, private bathrooms with tile floors and walls.

Notable -- Right outside the entrance is a Sav-A-Lot market. Just north is Hutchins Memorial Park, home to the sternwheeler Lantern Queen and the skipjack Martha Lewis (which may be at the Concord Lighthouse Pier). Two blocks away is Washington Street, lined with shops. Havre de Grace is one of those great destination towns where you can actually walk from the docks to virtually everything that might be needed or desired, all wrapped in a preserved and thriving 18th C. city. Two useful maps: Visitor Center's Events & Attractions, and the Self-guided Walking Tour of the Nationally Registered Historic District.

PHOTOS ON CD-ROM: 13

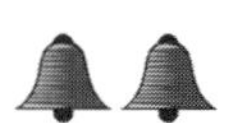

Perryville Yacht Club

31 River Road; Perryville, MD 21903

Tel: (410) 642-6364 **VHF: Monitor** n/a **Talk** n/a
Fax: n/a **Alternate Tel:** n/a
Email: n/a **Web:** n/a
Nearest Town: Perryville *(0.2 mi.)* **Tourist Info:** (410) 939-0990

Navigational Information

Lat: 39°33.680' **Long:** 076°04.866' **Tide:** 5 ft. **Current:** n/a **Chart:** 12274
Rep. Depths (*MLW*): Entry n/a **Fuel Dock** 10 ft. **Max Slip/Moor** 50 ft./-
Access: Stabroard side of Susquehanna, past the RR bridge

Marina Facilities *(In Season/Off Season)*

Fuel: Gasoline
Slips: 100 Total, 6 Transient **Max LOA:** 40 ft. **Max Beam:** 14 ft.
Rate *(per ft.)*: **Day** $1.00 **Week** $75 **Month** $300
Power: 30 amp $2, **50 amp** n/a, **100 amp** n/a, **200 amp** n/a
Cable TV: No **Dockside Phone:** No
Dock Type: Fixed, Floating, Long Fingers, Short Fingers, Concrete, Wood
Moorings: 0 Total, 0 Transient **Launch:** n/a
Rate: Day n/a **Week** n/a **Month** n/a
Heads: 3 Toilet(s), 2 Shower(s) *(with dressing rooms)*
Laundry: None **Pay Phones:** No
Pump-Out: OnSite, 1 Central, 1 Port **Fee:** $10 **Closed Heads:** Yes

Marina Operations

Owner/Manager: Tony Trapani **Dockmaster:** Ken Chilcoat
In-Season: Apr 15-Nov 1, 9am-6pm **Off-Season:** Nov 2-Apr 14, closed
After-Hours Arrival: Call ahead
Reservations: Preferred **Credit Cards:** Visa/MC, Dscvr
Discounts: None
Pets: Welcome, Dog Walk Area **Handicap Access:** No

Marina Services and Boat Supplies

Services - Docking Assistance, Security *(Management lives OnSite)*, Trash Pick-Up, Dock Carts **Communication -** FedEx, DHL, UPS, Express Mail **Supplies - Under 1 mi:** Bait/Tackle *(The Bait Shack 642-9166)* **1-3 mi:** Propane *(Collette's 642-2506)* **3+ mi:** Ships' Store *(River City Marine Supply 939-3229, 4 mi.)*, West Marine *(939-6282, 4 mi.)*

Boatyard Services

OnSite: Travelift, Launching Ramp

Restaurants and Accommodations

Near: Restaurant *(Rendezvous Inn 642-0045, L $7-15, D $15-25)*, Lite Fare *(Box Car Avenue 642-3445, L $2-4, D $2-4, take out, sandwiches and ice cream)* **Under 1 mi:** Restaurant *(Ercole Pizza & Pasta 642-3200)*, Motel *(Perryville Motel 642-2044, $42-54)* **1-3 mi:** Restaurant *(China Star 642-9978)*, *(Sub Works Pizzeria & Restaurant 642-6722, L $5-16, D $9-17)*, Lite Fare *(Chesapeake Food Works 642-3844, B $1-4, L $3-8, at outlets 3 mi., Mon-Sat 7am-7pm, Sun 11am-6pm)*, Motel *(Ramada 642-2866)* **3+ mi:** Motel *(Super 8 939-1880, $39-80, 4 mi.)*

Recreation and Entertainment

Near: Boat Rentals *(Watersport Rentals 642-9898)* **1-3 mi:** Golf Course *(Furnace Bay Golf Course 642-6816)*, Fitness Center *(Curves 642-9150)*, Video Rental *(Video Visions 642-3332)* **3+ mi:** Museum *(Havre de Grace Maritime 939-4800, Susquehanna Museum 939-5780, 4 mi.)*

Provisioning and General Services

Under 1 mi: Delicatessen *(Texaco Deli or Lindy's Market, 2 mi.)*, Liquor Store *(Martino's Liquors 642-0058)*, Market *(Riverside Market 642-6536 or Lindy's Market 642-2323, 2 mi.)*, Post Office *(642-6012)*, Protestant Church *(United Methodist)*, Laundry *(Laundry Center 642-2799)* **1-3 mi:** Convenience Store *(7-Eleven 642-6770, Royal Farms 642-2478)*, Gourmet Shop *(Chesapeake Food Works 642-3844)*, Green Grocer *(KT Farm Market 642-6450)*, Dry Cleaners *(Sun Cleaners 642-6449)*, Bookstore *(Book Cellar 378-2054)*, Retail Shops *(Perryville Outlets 378-9399, Mon-Thu 10am-6pm, Fri & Sat 10am-9pm, Sun 11am-6pm, 33 shops)* **3+ mi:** Library *(Havre De Grace 939-6700, 4 mi.)*, Pharmacy *(Lyon's 939-4545, 4 mi.)*, Hardware Store *(Walton's 939-1117, 4 mi.)*

Transportation

OnCall: Rental Car *(Enterprise 273-7711 or Budget 939-3333 4 mi.)*, Taxi *(Route 40 Taxi 642-9995)*, Airport Limo *(Business Car 272-2710)*
Under 1 mi: Rail *(MARC commuter line 800-325-RAIL)*
Airport: BWI/Philadelphia *(48 mi./56 mi.)*

Medical Services

911 Service **OnCall:** Ambulance **1-3 mi:** Dentist *(Smith 642-3370)*, Veterinarian *(Post Road Vet 642-9255)* **3+ mi:** Doctor *(Havre de Grace Family Care 939-5358, 4 mi.)*, Chiropractor *(Havre de Grace Chiropractic 307-0585, 4 mi.)* **Hospital:** Harford Memorial 575-7550 *(5 mi.)*

Setting -- On the starboard side of the Susquehanna, past the railroad swing bridge and The Marina at Owens Landing, almost to the Route 40 Bridge, is this smaller boat facility that can accommodate an occasional large boat. The pale blue clapboard three-story building with white trim houses the marina office.

Marina Notes -- Perryville Yacht Club is very much a facility in transition. There is a combination of docks: outer ones are floating cement with full-length finger piers, and the inner docks are stationary wood with short finger piers. The end slips have newer lighthouse pedestals. A combination of Isabel, a tornado, and a flood left this facility a little bit at its wits' end. Plans are to build a new bathhouse by the beginning of the '06 season. (Currently using a Porta-Trailer w/showers). As management is also in flux, it would be advisable to check before arriving to confirm what has been done and where the renovation stands. Directly adjacent, The Marina at Owens Landing is part of a very nicely executed and maintained condominium complex with recently renovated floating cement docks and excellent amenities; they will, on occasion, have a transient slip - but that is not their focus.

Notable -- Nearby is Box Car Avenue, which is a little takeout stand, and the Rendezvous restaurant. Within three tenths of a mile is the train station, circa 1905, which is also home of the Perryville Chapter of the National Railway Historical Society. Four tenths of a mile is Perryville Town Hall and within two miles are a number of other historic sites: 1740 Rodgers Tavern, which hosted George Washington, Lafayette and Rochambeau; Perryville Methodist and Presbyterian Churches, the Principio Iron Company, and 1812 Woodlands. The Perryville Outlets are just three miles away with 33 shops on-site.

PHOTOS ON CD-ROM: 9

3. Western Shore: Baltimore Region

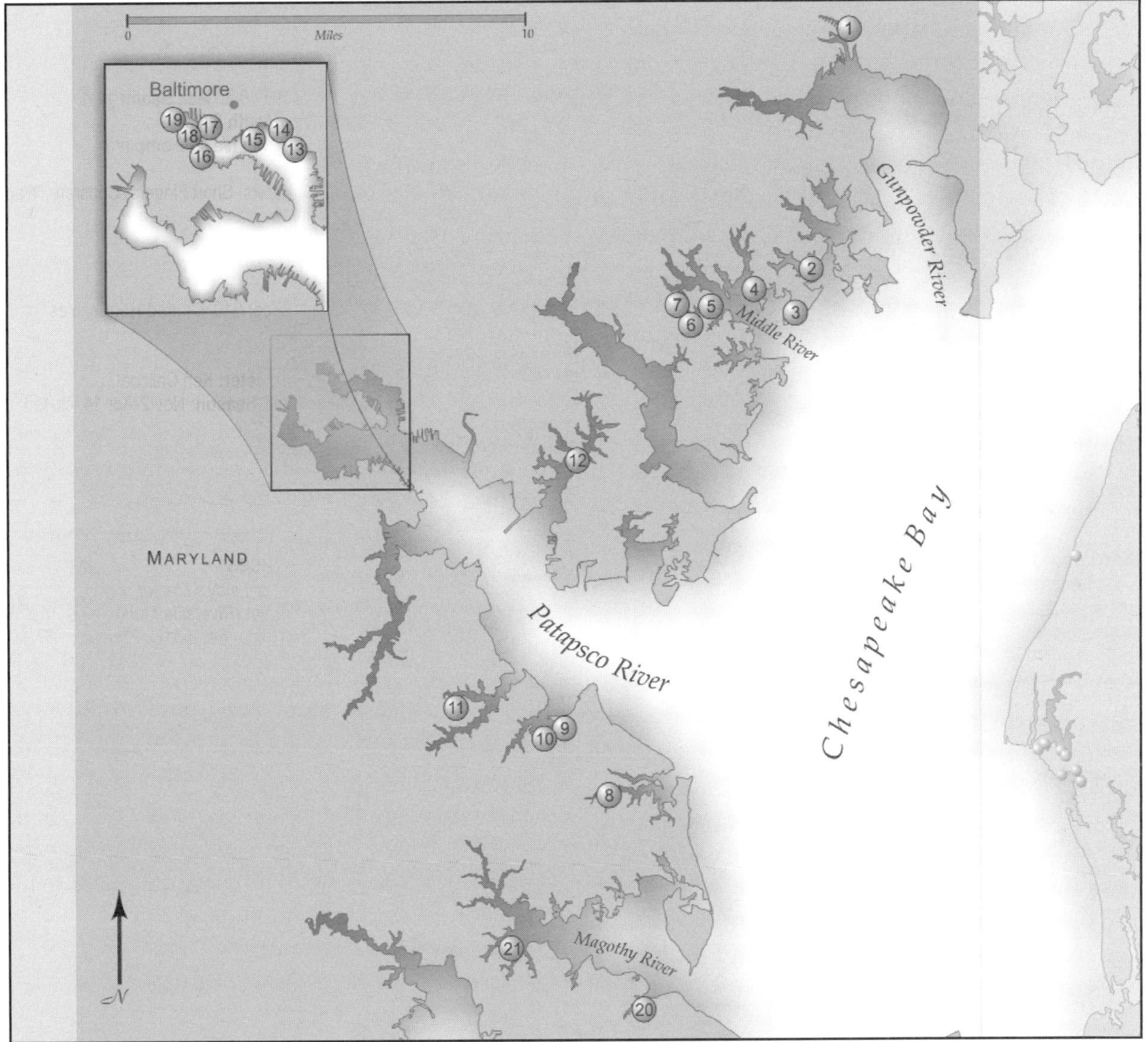

- **A "DCM" symbol in Marina Notes means Designated Clean Marina** — This is a coveted state-level award given to marinas that meet stringent, environmentally supportive requirements (see page 307). *For a list of DCM's & pump-out facilities, see page 308.*
- **Ratings & Reviews** — An explanation of the Atlantic Cruising Club's rating system, and a detailed explanation of what is in each section of the Marina Report is on pages 6 – 11. *The Data-Gathering Process is detailed on page 322.*
- **Marina Report Updates** — Updates to Marina Reports (from readers, ACC reviewers, and marinas) are posted regularly on *www.AtlanticCruisingClub.com.*

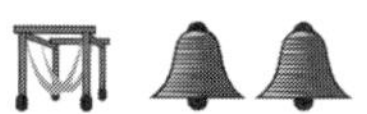

Marine Max Gunpowder Cove

PO Box 229; 510 Riviera Drive; Joppa, MD 21085

Tel: (410) 679-5454 **VHF: Monitor** n/a **Talk** n/a
Fax: (410) 679-5843 **Alternate Tel:** (410) 679-5454
Email: n/a **Web:** www.marinemax.com
Nearest Town: Joppa *(3 mi.)* **Tourist Info:** (410) 877-0000

Navigational Information

Lat: 39°24.430' **Long:** 076°20.990' **Tide:** 2 ft. **Current:** n/a **Chart:** 12273
Rep. Depths (*MLW*): Entry 5 ft. **Fuel Dock** 5 ft. **Max Slip/Moor** 5 ft./-
Access: Follow marked channel to the head of the Gunpowder River

Marina Facilities *(In Season/Off Season)*

Fuel: *Citgo* - Gasoline
Slips: 290 Total, 10 Transient **Max LOA:** 45 ft. **Max Beam:** n/a
Rate *(per ft.)*: **Day** $1.00 **Week** Inq. **Month** Inq.
Power: 30 amp Incl., **50 amp** n/a, **100 amp** n/a, **200 amp** n/a
Cable TV: No **Dockside Phone:** No
Dock Type: Fixed, Floating, Long Fingers, Short Fingers, Concrete, Wood
Moorings: 0 Total, 0 Transient **Launch:** n/a
Rate: Day n/a **Week** n/a **Month** n/a
Heads: 12 Toilet(s), 8 Shower(s)
Laundry: None **Pay Phones:** Yes, 2
Pump-Out: OnSite **Fee:** $5 **Closed Heads:** Yes

Marina Operations

Owner/Manager: Marine Max **Dockmaster:** Don Rogers
In-Season: Sum, 8am-6pm **Off-Season:** Fall-Win-Sprg, 8am-4:30pm
After-Hours Arrival: Check in with attendant on duty
Reservations: No **Credit Cards:** Visa/MC, Dscvr, Citgo
Discounts: None
Pets: Welcome **Handicap Access:** No

Marina Services and Boat Supplies

Services - Docking Assistance, Dock Carts **Communication -** Phone Messages, Fax in/out, FedEx, DHL, UPS, Express Mail *(Sat Del)* **Supplies - OnSite:** Ice *(Cube)*, Ships' Store **1-3 mi:** Bait/Tackle, Propane *(Holters 676-0600)* **3+ mi:** West Marine *(335-7896, 11 mi.)*, Marine Discount Store *(Imperial Marine 335-6501, 6 mi.)*

Boatyard Services

OnSite: Travelift *(15T)*, Forklift, Launching Ramp, Engine mechanic *(gas)*, Electrical Repairs, Hull Repairs, Bottom Cleaning, Propeller Repairs **OnCall:** Compound, Wash & Wax, Interior Cleaning **Dealer for:** Sea Ray, Key West. **Yard Rates:** $75/hr., Haul & Launch $4-6/ft., Power Wash $3/ft. **Storage:** On-Land Inq.

Restaurants and Accommodations

OnSite: Restaurant *(Sapore di Mare 538-8066, L $6-15, D $6-15)*, *(Beefeaters The Pit 538-7810, take-out)* **Under 1 mi:** Restaurant *(Chinese Boys 679-8878, L $4-6, D $7-10, serves all kinds of Chinese food at low prices)*, *(Handlebar & Grille, 538-1000)*, Pizzeria *(Moore's Pizza & Subs 538-8955, L $4-12, D $4-15, open from 11am-11pm daily)* **1-3 mi:** Seafood Shack *(Mariner Seafood & Subs 538-4590, take-out and fresh seafood also)*, *(Baldwin's Crab House 679-0957)*, Fast Food *(Burger King, Wendys)* **3+ mi:** Motel *(Edgewood Motel 676-4466, $48-55, 5 mi., friendly staff)*, *(Super 8 676-2700, $65-83, 4 mi.)*

Recreation and Entertainment

OnSite: Picnic Area *(umbrellaed tables)* **Near:** Heated Pool *(Joppa Municipal)*, Grills, Tennis Courts **Under 1 mi:** Playground, Volleyball, Park *(Mariner Park, Gunpowder Falls State 592-2897)* **3+ mi:** Golf Course *(Mount Vista Golf Course 592-5467, 4 mi.)*, Fitness Center *(Nick's Fitness 676-3832, 5 mi.)*, Bowling *(AMF Edgewood 679-8444, 6 mi.)*, Movie Theater *(Regal Cinemas 569-8276, 8 mi.)*, Video Rental *(Blockbuster 671-6354, 6 mi.)*, Museum *(Glenn Martin Aviation Museum 682-6122, 11 mi.)*

Provisioning and General Services

Near: Convenience Store, Market *(Royal Farms 679-2698 subs, cheesesteaks)*, Bank/ATM, Post Office, Catholic Church, Protestant Church **Under 1 mi:** Delicatessen *(Appetite's Deli Mart 679-9500)*, Bakery, Library *(Joppa 612-1660)* **1-3 mi:** Wine/Beer *(Island Liquors 679-9463)*, Liquor Store *(Midway Liquors 679-5511)*, Farmers' Market, Beauty Salon, Barber Shop, Pharmacy *(Rite Aid 549-6250)* **3+ mi:** Dry Cleaners *(Best Dry Cleaners 679-4432, 5 mi.)*, Laundry *(Laundry Room 679-2444, 5 mi.)*, Hardware Store *(Home Depot 612-8114, 6 mi.)*, Copies Etc. *(Edgewood Copy & Print 676-8080, 5 mi.)*

Transportation

OnCall: Rental Car *(Enterprise 538-4583)*, Taxi *(United Taxi 679-6100)*, Airport Limo *(Augusta Limousines 676-6771)*
Airport: Baltimore-Washington Int'l. *(30 mi.)*

Medical Services

911 Service **OnCall:** Ambulance **1-3 mi:** Dentist *(Forno Family Dentistry 679-8813)* **3+ mi:** Doctor *(Edgewood Walk-In 676-2600, 5 mi.)*, Chiropractor *(Sigafoose Chiropractic 679-0022, 5 mi.)*, Holistic Services *(Center of Well Being 676-3375, 4 mi.)*, Veterinarian *(White Marsh Animal Hospital 335-8400, 4 mi.)* **Hospital:** Union Memorial 838-9200 *(8 mi.)*

Setting -- Located in a residential community at the head of Gunpowder River. The docks, which fill most of this narrow stretch of water, are in two basins divided by the central service complex. Condos ring one side of one basin and the opposite shore is lined with single-family homes and townhouses.

Marina Notes -- Gunpowder Cove is now a part of Marine Max - it's strictly powerboats, as navigation is restricted by an 11 ft. clearance under the railroad bridge. As you approach, there are two paralell sets of docks, one of them on the bulkhead. This is followed by the facilities: a fuel dock, a small white dockhouse, a brown house with screen porch, and the large main building that houses a good-size service facility and dry stack operation. Then a second set of piers with slips continues along the shore. Three quite nice, standard-issue tiled bathhouses - one right in the office complex and one in each basin.

Notable -- Note that to get to the marina, it is necessary to pass through the Aberdeen Proving Ground Military Reservation's restricted area. Guidelines prohibit being outside any vessel within the area - no beaching boats or swimming - at any time. When testing is in progress, the APG postions hard-to-miss patrol boats at the perimeter with loudspeakers and flashing lights. The area surrounding Maxwell Point is always closed. The upside is that the area is undeveloped and the views are verdant and pristine. From the marina, 38-acre Mariner Point Park (612-1608) is an easy walk down Kearny Drive. It's open Memorial Day through October, with a fishing pier, boat launch, picnic tables, playgrounds, volleyball courts, hiking trails, horseshoe pits and lots of room to spread out a picnic blanket.

Navigational Information
Lat: 39°19.201' **Long:** 076°22.321' **Tide:** 3ft. **Current:** n/a **Chart:** 12273
Rep. Depths (*MLW*): **Entry** 8 ft. **Fuel Dock** 6 ft. **Max Slip/Moor** 8 ft./-
Access: Just off the Bay by the Crane Power Plant

Marina Facilities *(In Season/Off Season)*
Fuel: Gasoline
Slips: 100 Total, 10 Transient **Max LOA:** 50 ft. **Max Beam:** 16 ft.
Rate *(per ft.)*: **Day** $1.00 **Week** n/a **Month** n/a
Power: 30 amp $2, **50 amp** $4, **100 amp** n/a, **200 amp** n/a
Cable TV: No **Dockside Phone:** No
Dock Type: Fixed, Short Fingers, Pilings
Moorings: 0 Total, 0 Transient **Launch:** none
Rate: Day n/a **Week** n/a **Month** n/a
Heads: 2 Toilet(s), 2 Shower(s), Hair Dryers, heated/air-conditioned
Laundry: None **Pay Phones:** No
Pump-Out: OnSite, Full Service, 1 Central **Fee:** n/a **Closed Heads:** Yes

Marina Operations
Owner/Manager: Raymond Porter **Dockmaster:** Same
In-Season: Apr-Oct, 9am-6pm **Off-Season:** Nov-Mar, 9am-5pm
After-Hours Arrival: Check in in the morning
Reservations: Call in advance **Credit Cards:** Visa/MC
Discounts: None
Pets: Welcome **Handicap Access:** Yes, Heads, Docks

Porter's Seneca Marina

918 Seneca Park Road; Middle River, MD 21220

Tel: (410) 335-6563 **VHF: Monitor** n/a **Talk** n/a
Fax: (410) 335-7447 **Alternate Tel:** n/a
Email: n/a **Web:** www.porterssenecamarina.com
Nearest Town: Baltimore *(9 mi.)* **Tourist Info:** (410) 686-2233

Marina Services and Boat Supplies
Services - Docking Assistance, Dock Carts **Communication -** Mail & Package Hold, Fax in/out, FedEx, UPS **Supplies - OnSite:** Ice *(Cube)*, Ships' Store **1-3 mi:** West Marine *(335-7896)*, Marine Discount Store, Bait/Tackle *(Bowleys Bait & Tackle 687-2107)* **3+ mi:** Boat/US *(918-9344, 8 mi.)*, Propane *(Hodges, True Value 686-1389, 7 mi.)*

Boatyard Services
OnSite: Travelift *(30T)*, Forklift, Launching Ramp, Engine mechanic *(gas, diesel)*, Electrical Repairs, Hull Repairs, Rigger, Canvas Work, Bottom Cleaning, Brightwork, Air Conditioning, Refrigeration, Compound, Wash & Wax, Interior Cleaning, Propeller Repairs, Woodworking, Painting **1-3 mi:** Inflatable Repairs **Dealer for:** Mercruiser **Yard Rates:** $75/hr., Haul & Launch $5.50-8/ft. *(blocking incl.)*, Bottom Paint $9/ft. *(paint incl.)*

Restaurants and Accommodations
OnCall: Pizzeria *(Domino's 682-4200)* **1-3 mi:** Restaurant *(Carroll Island Diner 335-2004, L $6-13, D $6-13)*, *(Crab Quarters 686-2222)*, *(Bruno's Italian Quarters 344-1506, L $5-12, D $5-12)*, *(Wild Duck Café 335-2121, L $5-10, D $14-28, music & tables down on the beach on the weekends)*, *(Chinatown Express 335-7800)*, Fast Food *(KFC, Taco Bell)*, Lite Fare *(Mama Maria's Carry-out 335-7430)*, *(Super Subs 391-1585)*, Motel *(Star 687-3169, $50-55)* **3+ mi:** Motel *(Super 8 676-2700, $65-83, 9 mi.)*, *(Colony 335-6577, $36-75, 4 mi.)*

Recreation and Entertainment
OnSite: Pool, Picnic Area, Grills **1-3 mi:** Fishing Charter, Video Rental *(Blockbuster 335-2807)*, Park **3+ mi:** Golf Course *(Rocky Point 887-4653, 11 mi.)*, Fitness Center *(Middle River Gym 682-4044, 5 mi.)*, Museum *(Glenn L Martin Aviation Museum 682-6122, 11am-3pm Wed-Sat, Free, 4 mi.)*

Provisioning and General Services
1-3 mi: Convenience Store *(7-Eleven 335-7932; Royal Farm 335-7567)*, Supermarket *(Safeway 335-3668)*, Wine/Beer, Liquor Store *(Island Spirits 335-7200)*, Farmers' Market, Fishmonger *(Carolina Gardens 335-7775)*, Crabs/Waterman, Bank/ATM, Post Office, Catholic Church, Beauty Salon, Barber Shop, Dry Cleaners *(Magic Professional 1 hr. 335-3232)*, Pharmacy *(Rite Aid 335-2323)*, Newsstand, Hardware Store *(Carroll Island True Value 335-5434)*, Florist, Department Store *(Wal-Mart 335-5669)* **3+ mi:** Laundry *(Sudsville 433-9620, 4 mi.)*, Retail Shops *(7 mi.)*

Transportation
OnCall: Water Taxi *(Middle River 375-1131)*, Rental Car *(Enterprise 931-7455 or Alamo 661-6900, 3 mi.)*, Taxi *(Atwater Cab 391-4040)*, Airport Limo *(Baltimore Limousine 335-1160)*
Airport: Baltimore-Washington Int'l. *(20 mi.)*

Medical Services
911 Service **OnCall:** Ambulance **1-3 mi:** Doctor, Dentist *(Hepner 335-9661)* **3+ mi:** Chiropractor *(Eastern Chiropractic 686-1117, 5 mi.)*, Veterinarian *(Pulaski Vet Clinic 686-6310, 7 mi.)*
Hospital: Franklin Square 443-777-7000 *(8 mi.)*

Setting -- Easily accessed right off the Bay at the mouth of Seneca Creek, Porter's has four main piers, most with two slips on both sides; a fuel dock is at the end of the second pier and a pool. Views from the slips include the Crane Power Plant at the Tipple Industrial Complex.

Marina Notes -- DCM. Family-owned since 1979. The new bulkhead constructed at the end of '04 was the final restoration from Isabel. In fall '05, new 40 ft.x70 ft. service building with 32 foot doors was completed increasing the capacity for fiberglass, blister, gelcoat and mechanical work. Fuel, ice, and pump-out open 7 days during the season. There is a mix of power options, depending on the dock - full-race lighthouse pedestals or power outlets on posts. "A" pier has new pedestals. "B" pier has the fuel dock. "C" pier is called "the official party pier," and "D" pier is just past the travelift. Good size travelift and basic BY services. Large, well-stocked ships' store and parts department, including a large inventory of Mercury Marine parts. Perfectly fine cinderblock, climate controlled bathhouses have bathrooms with quarry tile floors, vanities and fresh shower curtains.

Notable -- A nice-size (20 ft. x 40 ft.) pool surrounding a cement patio populated by white chaises, tables and chairs, overlooks the creek and the marina. Nearby is a picnic area beneath a blue vinyl hooped cover. Several restaurants are a short boat ride away. The Carroll Island Shopping Center is about three miles - Wal-Mart, a Dollar Tree, True Value Hardware, First Mariner Bank, Blockbuster, Nails, Middle River Gym, Advanced Auto Parts, Magic Professional One-hour Cleaners, and the Carroll Island Diner.

Bowleys Marina

1700 Bowleys Quarters Road; Middle River, MD 21220

Tel: (410) 335-3553 **VHF: Monitor** 9 **Talk** 9
Fax: (410) 335-5478 **Alternate Tel:** n/a
Email: mary@bowleysmarina.com **Web:** www.bowleysmarina.com
Nearest Town: Baltimore *(9 mi.)* **Tourist Info:** (410) 686-2233

Navigational Information

Lat: 39°18.150' **Long:** 076°26.200' **Tide:** 2 ft. **Current:** 1 kt. **Chart:** 12273
Rep. Depths (*MLW*): Entry 8 ft. **Fuel Dock** 8 ft. **Max Slip/Moor** 8 ft./-
Access: Chesapeake Bay to the mouth of Middle River

Marina Facilities *(In Season/Off Season)*

Fuel: Gasoline, Diesel
Slips: 505 Total, 20 Transient **Max LOA:** 60 ft. **Max Beam:** n/a
Rate *(per ft.)*: **Day** $1.75/Inq. **Week** $8 **Month** $10
Power: 30 amp $5, **50 amp** $10, **100 amp** n/a, **200 amp** n/a
Cable TV: No **Dockside Phone:** No
Dock Type: Fixed, Wood
Moorings: 0 Total, 0 Transient **Launch:** n/a, Dinghy Dock
Rate: Day n/a **Week** n/a **Month** n/a
Heads: 14 Toilet(s), 8 Shower(s) *(with dressing rooms)*
Laundry: 2 Washer(s), 2 Dryer(s), Book Exchange **Pay Phones:** Yes, 1
Pump-Out: OnSite, Full Service **Fee:** $10 **Closed Heads:** Yes

Marina Operations

Owner/Manager: Rich Yarborough **Dockmaster:** Same
In-Season: Year-Round, 8am-5pm* **Off-Season:** n/a
After-Hours Arrival: Call ahead
Reservations: Yes **Credit Cards:** Visa/MC, Amex
Discounts: None
Pets: Welcome **Handicap Access:** No

Marina Services and Boat Supplies

Services - Docking Assistance, Boaters' Lounge, Security *(24 hrs., gate)*, Trash Pick-Up, Dock Carts **Communication -** FedEx, DHL, UPS, Express Mail **Supplies - OnSite:** Ice *(Block, Cube, Shaved)*, Ships' Store *(ice-cream and gifts)* **1-3 mi:** West Marine *(335-7896)*, Marine Discount Store **3+ mi:** Boat/US *(918-9344, 8 mi.)*, Bait/Tackle *(Bowleys Bait & Tackle 687-2107, 4 mi.)*, Propane *(Hodges True Value 686-1389, 7 mi.)*

Boatyard Services

OnSite: Travelift *(35T)*, Forklift, Launching Ramp, Engine mechanic *(gas, diesel)*, Bottom Cleaning, Compound, Wash & Wax **Yard Rates:** $35/hr., Haul & Launch $8-12/ft. *(blocking $150)*, Bottom Paint $9.50/ft.

Restaurants and Accommodations

OnSite: Lite Fare *(Bowley's Snack Bar L $2-6, D $2-6, hamburgers, hot dogs, pizza at the rec room - Fri 6pm-1am, Sat 9am-1am, Sun 9am-3pm)* **OnCall:** Pizzeria *(Domino's 682-5315)* **1-3 mi:** Restaurant *(Caroll Island Diner 335-2004, L $6-13, D $6-13)*, *(Bruno's Italian Quarter 344-1506)*, *(Wild Duck Café 335-2121, L $5-10, D $14-28)*, *(China Town Express 335-7800)*, *(Legendary's Classic 344-9183)*, Lite Fare *(Mama Maria's Carryout 335-7430)* **3+ mi:** Restaurant *(The Mariner's Landing 477-1261, L $5-15, D $15-30, 6 mi.)*, Seafood Shack *(Al's Seafood Restaurant 687-3264, 8 mi.)*, Motel *(Super 8 780-0030, $65-83, 7 mi.)*, *(Star Motel 687-3169, 7 mi.)*, *(Blue Star 335-6653, 9 mi.)*, *(Colony Motel 335-6577, $36-75, 6 mi.)*

Recreation and Entertainment

OnSite: Pool, Picnic Area, Grills, Playground *(and horseshoes)*, Volleyball **Near:** Park **1-3 mi:** Fitness Center *(Middle River Gym 682-4044)*, Video Rental *(Blockbuster 335-2807)* **3+ mi:** Golf Course *(Rocky Point 887-4653, 11 mi.)*, Bowling *(AMF Bowling Centers 686-2556, 8 mi.)*, Museum *(Glenn L Martin Aviation Museum 682-6122, 11am-3pm Wed-Sat, Free, 6 mi.)*

Provisioning and General Services

Under 1 mi: Green Grocer *(Howell's Blue Farm)* **1-3 mi:** Convenience Store *(7-Eleven 335-7932; Royal Farm 335-7567)*, Supermarket *(Safeway 335-3668)*, Wine/Beer, Liquor Store *(Island Spirits 335-7200)*, Fishmonger *(Carolina Gardens 335-7775)*, Bank/ATM, Post Office, Catholic Church, Protestant Church, Beauty Salon, Dry Cleaners *(Magic Professional 1 hr. 335-3232)*, Laundry *(Sudsville 433-9620)*, Pharmacy *(Rite Aid 335-2323)*, Florist, Department Store *(Wal-Mart 335-5669)* **3+ mi:** Hardware Store *(Carroll Island 335-5434, 6 mi.)*, Copies Etc. *(Cogar Printing 391-8888, 6 mi.)*

Transportation

OnCall: Rental Car *(Enterprise 931-7455; Alamo 661-6900, 3 mi.)*, Taxi *(Reliable Sedan 686-2180)*, Airport Limo *(Baltimore Limo 335-1160)*
Airport: Baltimore-Washington Int'l. *(20 mi.)*

Medical Services

911 Service **OnCall:** Ambulance **1-3 mi:** Doctor **3+ mi:** Dentist *(Hepner 335-9661, 6 mi.)*, Chiropractor *(Eastern Chiropractic 686-1117, 6 mi.)*, Veterinarian *(Essex Dog & Cat Hospital 687-1111, 6.5 mi.)*
Hospital: Franklin Square 443-777-7000 *(9 mi.)*

Setting -- Just inside the mouth of Middle River, Bowley's is a destination family resort marina and a self-contained kids' paradise. The recreational facilities surround a renovated 1887 two-story manor house once home to Baltimore sea-captain Daniel Bowley. Trees punctuate the grassy expanses and willows weep over the bulkhead. Gazebos and benches are scattered about; picnic areas poke out over the bulkhead. An extensive network of docks hosts over 500 vessels, protected from wakes and the Bay by a wave fence. Signature blue & white striped awnings annotate the buildings and step up the atmosphere.

Marina Notes -- *Nov-Mar, Sat & Sun 10am-3pm. DCM. Service oriented staff: just ask - if it can be done, it will be. Member-owned slips are managed by Coastal Properties (transient fees are shared with owners). Private club atmosphere. Five main piers flanked by slips; the two end piers with slips on one side, all renovated with new power pedestals courtesy of Isabel. The fuel dock is at the end of "D" dock. The small ships' store also has T-shirts and ice cream. Lovely climate controlled bathhouses have tiled floors, fiberglass shower stalls with glass doors & dressing rooms; sinks set in well-lighted Corian vanities.

Notable -- Close as it is to the Bay, but far from everything on land. Come fully provisioned to kick back and enjoy the resort - that is how it was designed. There's lots to do right here and there's really no place to walk or ride your bike. There's a big pool with a cement surround and lots of chaises on the grass patio, plus volleyball, horseshoes, playground, picnic tables, grills, a clubhouse and covered pavilions. The big rec hall has a bar that serves hot dogs, hamburgers and pizza - kids welcome - karaoke twice a month. Club or group cruises are graciously accommodated.

Navigational Information
Lat: 39°18.975' **Long:** 076°24.004' **Tide:** 2 ft. **Current:** n/a **Chart:** 12273
Rep. Depths (*MLW*): Entry 12 ft. **Fuel Dock** 8 ft. **Max Slip/Moor** 8 ft./-
Access: Middle River to Frog Mortar Creek past Galloway Point

Marina Facilities *(In Season/Off Season)*
Fuel: Gasoline, Diesel
Slips: 327 Total, 6 Transient **Max LOA:** 70 ft. **Max Beam:** 18 ft.
Rate *(per ft.)*: **Day** $1.25 **Week** n/a **Month** n/a
Power: 30 amp $5, **50 amp** $10*, **100 amp** n/a, **200 amp** n/a
Cable TV: No **Dockside Phone:** No
Dock Type: Fixed
Moorings: 0 Total, 0 Transient **Launch:** n/a
Rate: Day n/a **Week** n/a **Month** n/a
Heads: 3 Toilet(s), 3 Shower(s)
Laundry: 1 Washer(s), 1 Dryer(s) **Pay Phones:** No
Pump-Out: OnSite, Full Service, 1 Central **Fee:** $5 **Closed Heads:** Yes

Marina Operations
Owner/Manager: Vern Davis **Dockmaster:** Same
In-Season: Apr-Nov, 8am-5pm** **Off-Season:** Dec-Mar, 9am-1pm
After-Hours Arrival: Call ahead
Reservations: Required **Credit Cards:** Visa/MC, Dscvr, Amex
Discounts: None
Pets: Welcome **Handicap Access:** No

Long Beach Marina

800 Chester Road; Middle River, MD 21220

Tel: (410) 335-8602 **VHF: Monitor** 16 **Talk** 9
Fax: (410) 335-8614 **Alternate Tel:** n/a
Email: longbeachmarina@aol.com **Web:** www.longbeachmarinaonline.com
Nearest Town: Middle River *(3 mi.)* **Tourist Info:** (410) 686-2233

Marina Services and Boat Supplies
Services - Docking Assistance, Boaters' Lounge, Security *(24 hrs.)*, Dock Carts **Communication -** Data Ports *(Wi-Fi, $5)*, FedEx, DHL, UPS, Express Mail *(Sat Del)* **Supplies - OnSite:** Ice *(Block, Cube)* **Under 1 mi:** West Marine *(335-7896)* **1-3 mi:** Marine Discount Store, Bait/Tackle *(Bowleys Bait & Tackle 687-2107)* **3+ mi:** Propane *(Hodges True Value 686-1389, 5 mi.)*

Boatyard Services
OnSite: Travelift *(2-35T)*, Launching Ramp, Engine mechanic *(gas)*, Electrical Repairs, Hull Repairs, Bottom Cleaning, Compound, Wash & Wax, Interior Cleaning, Propeller Repairs, Painting **Yard Rates:** Haul & Launch $7.50/ft., Power Wash $1.50/ft., Bottom Paint $10/ft.

Restaurants and Accommodations
OnCall: Restaurant *(China Town Express 335-7800)*, Pizzeria *(Domino's 682-4200)* **Near:** Restaurant *(Wild Duck 335-2121)*, *(Bruno's Italian Quarter 344-1506, L $5-12, D $5-12)*, *(Legendary Classics 334-9138)* **Under 1 mi:** Restaurant *(Carroll Island Diner 335-2004, L $6-13, D $6-13)*, Crab House *(Angie's Crabs)* **1-3 mi:** Lite Fare *(Mama Maria's Carry-out 335-7430)* **3+ mi:** Restaurant *(The Mariner's Landing 477-1261, L $5-15, D $15-30, 6 mi.)*, Motel *(Colony 335-6577, 7 mi.)*, *(Williamsburg Inn 335-3172, 7 mi.)*, *(Blue Star 335-6653, 6 mi.)*

Recreation and Entertainment
OnSite: Pool, Beach *(sand)*, Picnic Area, Grills **1-3 mi:** Fitness Center *(Bowleys Quarters Fitness Club 344-1181)*, Movie Theater *(Bengies Drive in Theatre 687-5627)*, Video Rental *(Blockbuster 335-2807)*, Park **3+ mi:** Golf Course *(Rocky Point 887-4653, 10 mi.)*, Bowling *(AMF 686-2556, 6 mi.)*, Museum *(Glenn L. Martin Aviation Museum 682-6122, 11am-3pm Wed-Sat, Free, 5 mi.)*

Provisioning and General Services
Under 1 mi: Convenience Store *(Royal Farm 335-7567)*, Bank/ATM, Post Office, Beauty Salon *(Noelle's 335-0282)*, Barber Shop, Dry Cleaners *(Magic Professional 1 hr. 335-3232)*, Laundry *(Sudsville 433-9620)*, Pharmacy *(Rite Aid 335-2323)*, Newsstand **1-3 mi:** Supermarket *(Safeway 335-3668)*, Gourmet Shop, Delicatessen *(Your Deli 335-9290)*, Liquor Store *(Island Spirits 335-7200)*, Bakery, Farmers' Market, Green Grocer, Catholic Church, Hardware Store *(Carrol Island 335-5434)*, Department Store *(Wal-Mart 335-5669)* **3+ mi:** Buying Club *(Costco 648-4000, 5 mi.)*

Transportation
OnSite: Courtesy Car/Van **OnCall:** Water Taxi *(Middle River, Ch.68, 375-1131 Thu 6-11pm, Fri 6pm-Mid, Sat Noon-Mid, Sun 11am-9pm, $4/1way)*, Rental Car *(Enterprise 931-7455 or Alamo 661-6900, 3 mi.)*, Taxi *(Atwater Cab 391-4040)*, Airport Limo *(Baltimore Limo 335-1160)* **1-3 mi:** Rail *(Eastern Blvd.)* **Airport:** Baltimore/Washington Int'l. *(22 mi.)*

Medical Services
911 Service **OnCall:** Ambulance **1-3 mi:** Doctor, Dentist *(Berman & Platt 687-0900)* **3+ mi:** Chiropractor *(Eastern Chiropractic 686-1117, 4 mi.)*
Hospital: Franklyn Square 443-777-2000 *(6 mi.)*

Setting -- On a small peninsula near the mouth of Frog Mortar Creek sits sparkling Long Beach Marina - the beneficiary of a 3-year stem-to-stem renovation. Four main piers flanked by slips are separated by wide fairways for comfortable maneuvering. Almost at the end of "B" dock, a dockhouse sits near the fuel pumps. A small sand beach fronts the office building and nearby are the brand new bathhouse, a new pool, and an event room with sundeck above.

Marina Notes -- *Twin-30A cords. **Fuel dock 7 days, 7am-7pm., Summer Fri-Sun 'til Dusk. New management and a major renovation started in October '02 -- everything is new. Stationary slips tend to house medium-sized boats, but occasional larger vessels are welcome. Two travelifts are next to "D" dock. At the time of the site visit, Long Beach was not quite complete - so look beyond the photos. When work is finished this will likely be one of the nicest marinas on Middle River. Wi-Fi available for $5/night. Courtesy van for provisioning runs or restaurant visits. In the planning stages for '07-'08 is a small restaurant in the pool house - the first step will likely be a bar. A laundry will be installed by Summer '06. Each of the new, well-done bathhouses have three fiberglass shower stalls with shower curtains, tiled floors, two sinks set in a vanity, hair-dryer plugs and three generous-size toilet compartments.

Notable -- Next to the pool, a large event room that can accommodate up to 50, is topped by a sun deck with expansive views of the nicely landscaped 4.5-acre site, the docks, and across the creek, the Glen L. Martin State Airport. The surrounding area is residential with modest houses. About 0.3-mile out to the main road are Bruno's Italian American Seafood and Legendary's Classic restaurant. About 0.5-mile is Angie's Crabs.

PHOTOS ON CD-ROM: 9

Norman Creek Marina

2229 Corsica Road; Essex, MD 21221

Tel: (410) 686-9343 **VHF: Monitor** n/a **Talk** n/a
Fax: (410) 686-9343 **Alternate Tel:** (410) 391-5816
Email: n/a **Web:** n/a
Nearest Town: Essex *(1 mi.)* **Tourist Info:** (410) 686-2233

Navigational Information

Lat: 39°18.383' **Long:** 076°25.216' **Tide:** n/a **Current:** n/a **Chart:** 12273
Rep. Depths (*MLW*): Entry 5 ft. **Fuel Dock** 5 ft. **Max Slip/Moor** 5 ft./-
Access: Norman Creek, first commercial facility on starboard side

Marina Facilities *(In Season/Off Season)*

Fuel: Gasoline, Diesel
Slips: 30 Total, 2 Transient **Max LOA:** 45 ft. **Max Beam:** n/a
Rate *(per ft.)*: **Day** $1.25* **Week** n/a **Month** n/a
Power: 30 amp Incl., **50 amp** Incl., **100 amp** n/a, **200 amp** n/a
Cable TV: No **Dockside Phone:** No
Dock Type: Fixed, Short Fingers, Wood
Moorings: 0 Total, 0 Transient **Launch:** n/a
Rate: Day n/a **Week** n/a **Month** n/a
Heads: 2 Toilet(s), 2 Shower(s), heat/air
Laundry: None **Pay Phones:** No
Pump-Out: OnSite, Full Service, 1 Central **Fee:** $5 **Closed Heads:** Yes

Marina Operations

Owner/Manager: Mark & Lisa Hoos **Dockmaster:** Same
In-Season: May-Oct, 8am-8pm **Off-Season:** n/a
After-Hours Arrival: Call 24 hrs. ahead
Reservations: Yes **Credit Cards:** Visa/MC, Dscvr, Amex
Discounts: Fuel **Dockage:** n/a **Fuel:** $0.10/100 gal **Repair:** n/a
Pets: Welcome, Dog Walk Area **Handicap Access:** Yes, Docks

Marina Services and Boat Supplies

Services - Security *(24 hrs., owners live onsite)*, Dock Carts **Communication -** FedEx, DHL, UPS, Express Mail **Supplies - OnSite:** Ice *(Block)*, Bait/Tackle **Under 1 mi:** Ships' Store *(Anchor Bay 574-0777)*, Marine Discount Store *(Bay Boat Supplies)* **3+ mi:** Boat/US *(918-9344, 5 mi.)*

Boatyard Services

Under 1 mi: Travelift, Launching Ramp, Engine mechanic *(gas, diesel)*, Electrical Repairs, Electronics Repairs, Hull Repairs, Rigger, Sail Loft, Canvas Work, Bottom Cleaning, Brightwork, Air Conditioning, Refrigeration, Compound, Wash & Wax, Interior Cleaning, Woodworking, Inflatable Repairs, Life Raft Service, Painting, Awlgrip. **1-3 mi:** Propeller Repairs.

Restaurants and Accommodations

OnCall: Pizzeria *(Domino's 682-5315)* **Under 1 mi:** Restaurant *(River Watch Restaurant 687-1422)*, *(Doughboy's Family Carry-out 686-9161, across the way)*, *(Decoy's Bar & Grill 391-5798, L $6-15, D $16-30, across the way)*, *(Driftwood Inn 391-3493, B $6, L $10, D $20)* **1-3 mi:** Restaurant *(Bobby B's 687-4522, L $3-10, D $3-23, karaoke and variety shows/music guests)*, *(Runabouts Restaurant & Lounge 682-5930, L $2-13, D $2-13, different specials throughout the week)*, *(China House 238-3188)*, Pizzeria *(Philadelphia Style Pizza & Subs 682-6900)*, Motel *(Super 8 780-0030, $35-80)* **3+ mi:** Motel *(Colonial 687-4900, 8 mi.)*, *(Star Motel 687-3169, $50-55, 8 mi.)*

Recreation and Entertainment

OnSite: Picnic Area, Playground **Under 1 mi:** Fishing Charter *(Green's Charter 574-7067)* **1-3 mi:** Fitness Center *(Curves 391-0700)*, Video Rental *(Blockbuster 391-8800)*, Park *(Sue Creek Park)* **3+ mi:** Golf Course *(Rocky Point 887-4653, 6 mi.)*, Bowling *(AMF 686-2556, 6 mi.)*, Museum *(Glenn L Martin Aviation Museum 682-6122, 11am-3pm Wed-Sat, Free, 5 mi.)*

Provisioning and General Services

OnSite: Convenience Store *(snacks, sodas, crabs)* **Near:** Delicatessen *(Middleborough Grocery & Deli)*, Liquor Store *(Ventures Four 391-4092, crabs also)*, Market *(Middleborough Grocery & Deli 686-5059)*, Catholic Church, Protestant Church, Hardware Store *(Dundalk Lumber 285-0080)* **1-3 mi:** Supermarket *(Food Lion 918-0171, Giant 995-4322)*, Wine/Beer *(Compass Liquors 238-7904)*, Bank/ATM, Post Office *(687-5568)*, Beauty Salon *(Donna's 238-2400)*, Dry Cleaners *(Martin 1 Hr. Cleaners & Laundry 686-0192)*, Laundry *(Martin)*, Bookstore *(That's My Story 686-8316)*, Pharmacy *(CVS 687-6313)*, Department Store *(Wal-Mart 687-4858)*, Copies Etc. *(Minuteman 574-2668)*

Transportation

OnCall: Water Taxi *(Middle River, Ch.68, 375-1131 Thu 6-11pm, Fri 6-Mid, Sat Noon-Mid, Sun 11am-9pm, $4/1way)*, Rental Car *(Enterprise 682-6474, Thrifty 391-3103)*, Taxi *(Atwater Cab 682-2100)*, Airport Limo *(Bayview 574-2491)* **Airport:** Baltimore-Washington Int'l. *(17 mi.)*

Medical Services

911 Service **OnCall:** Ambulance **1-3 mi:** Doctor, Dentist *(Kurek 574-5330)*, Chiropractor *(Eastern Chiropractic 686-1117)*, Holistic Services *(About Your Body 687-3200)*, Veterinarian *(White Marsh 335-8400)*
Hospital: Franklin Square 443-777-7950 *(7 mi.)*

Setting -- Located in a small residential community, this single pier marina is tucked up Norman Creek; it's the first commercial facility on the starboard side, just past red Marker Number Two. There's a low-slung gray clapboard building that serves as the dock house, and a long T-head fuel dock. A picnic table and a gazebo sit on the lawn at the head of the docks - an eye for detail and a caring hand is evident throughout.

Marina Notes -- *Call first - ACC was informed at press time that they may now not take transients. Family-operated -- a member of the Hoos family is almost always on the premises; the owners' house sits at the head of the dock. Their parents live in an adjacent house, and a rental cottage is also on the property. Stationary docks are in good condition, with short finger piers and power on pedestals. Most boats in the 30-35 foot range with a few larger ones; they can accommodate a larger vessel on the fuel dock T-head. Two really well done key-coded individual bathrooms each have gray quarry tile floors with carpets, an immaculate fiberglass shower stall with lovely curtains plus plugs for hair dryers - you'll want to take a shower here. Leashed pets are welcomed.

Notable -- There's a very inviting sitting area on the lawn directly in front of the house which is available to boaters. A decidedly green thumb is at work here, and the facility is immaculate and shipshape. The dockhouse is also a small concession stand that sells snacks and sodas, bait, and CRABS! Soft-shell and hard-shell - which makes this, obviously, a destination. This is a residential area, so getting anywhere is a bit of a hike. 0.4 mile to Venture's Four, a liquor store and crab place. About 0.85 mile is the River Watch Restaurant, Anchor Bay Marina and Bay Boat Supplies.

Navigational Information

Lat: 39°18.706' **Long:** 076°25.957' **Tide:** 4 ft. **Current:** 3 kt. **Chart:** 12273
Rep. Depths (*MLW*): Entry 15 ft. **Fuel Dock** 20 ft. **Max Slip/Moor** 25 ft./-
Access: Middle River to mouth of Hopkins Creek off western shore

Marina Facilities *(In Season/Off Season)*

Fuel: *Carrollind* - Gasoline, Diesel
Slips: 110 Total, 15 Transient **Max LOA:** 60 ft. **Max Beam:** n/a
Rate *(per ft.)*: **Day** $1.00* **Week** n/a **Month** n/a
Power: 30 amp $10, **50 amp** n/a, **100 amp** n/a, **200 amp** n/a
Cable TV: No **Dockside Phone:** No
Dock Type: Fixed, Short Fingers, Pilings, Wood
Moorings: 0 Total, 0 Transient **Launch:** n/a
Rate: Day n/a **Week** n/a **Month** n/a
Heads: 4 Toilet(s), 4 Shower(s) *(with dressing rooms)*
Laundry: None **Pay Phones:** No
Pump-Out: OnSite **Fee:** $5 **Closed Heads:** Yes

Marina Operations

Owner/Manager: Traci and Mark Sullivan **Dockmaster:** Same
In-Season: Apr-Oct, 10am-8pm **Off-Season:** Nov-Mar
After-Hours Arrival: Must call ahead
Reservations: Preferred **Credit Cards:** Visa/MC, Dscvr
Discounts: None
Pets: No **Handicap Access:** No

River Watch Marina

207 Nanticoke Road; Baltimore, MD 21221

Tel: (410) 687-1422 **VHF: Monitor** n/a **Talk** n/a
Fax: (410) 687-2202 **Alternate Tel:** n/a
Email: n/a **Web:** www.riverwatchrestaurant.com
Nearest Town: Essex *(1mi.)* **Tourist Info:** (401) 686-2033

Marina Services and Boat Supplies

Services - Docking Assistance, Dock Carts **Communication -** FedEx, DHL, UPS, Express Mail **Supplies - OnSite:** Ice *(Cube)* **Near:** Ships' Store *(Anchor Bay 574-0777)* **Under 1 mi:** Bait/Tackle *(Outdoor Sportsman 391-0222)* **1-3 mi:** Propane *(U-Haul 687-5400)* **3+ mi:** Boat/US *(918-9344, 5 mi.)*

Boatyard Services

Near: Travelift, Crane, Engine mechanic *(gas, diesel)*, Electrical Repairs, Hull Repairs, Bottom Cleaning, Brightwork, Air Conditioning, Refrigeration, Compound, Wash & Wax, Propeller Repairs. **Nearest Yard:** Essex Marina & Boat Sales (410) 686-3435

Restaurants and Accommodations

OnSite: Restaurant *(River Watch 687-1422, B $13, L $6-15, D $16-30, inside & deck, entertainment in-season, same menu all day)* **OnCall:** Pizzeria *(Domino's 682-5315)* **Under 1 mi:** Restaurant *(Wolfe's 686-7900)*, Lite Fare *(Shea's Pancake & Waffle House 238-4877)*, Pizzeria *(Pronto Pizza & Subs 780-3330)* **1-3 mi:** Restaurant *(Carroll Island Diner 335-2004, L $6-13, D $6-13)*, Seafood Shack *(Schultz's Crab House 687-1020)*, Lite Fare *(Maria's Delight Carry-Out 391-6398)*, Motel *(Super 8 780-0030, $35-85)* **3+ mi:** Motel *(Fairfield Inn 7 mi., 800-228-2800)*, *(Colonial 687-4900, 7 mi.)*, *(Star Motel 687-3169, $50-55, 7 mi.)*

Recreation and Entertainment

OnSite: Special Events *(entertainment)* **Under 1 mi:** Fishing Charter *(Green's Charter 574-7067)* **1-3 mi:** Fitness Center *(Curves 391-0700)*, Video Rental *(Blockbuster 391-8800)*, Park *(Sue Creek Park)* **3+ mi:** Golf Course *(Rocky Point 887-4653, 5 mi.)*, Bowling *(AMF 686-2556, 4 mi.)*, Museum *(Glenn L. Martin Aviation Museum 682-6122, Free, Wed-Sat 11am-3pm, 5 mi.)*

Provisioning and General Services

OnSite: Bank/ATM **Near:** Convenience Store, Delicatessen *(Middleborough)*, Wine/Beer *(Ventures Four 391-4092, crabs too)*, Bakery, Market *(Middleborough Grocery & Deli 686-5059)*, Catholic Church, Protestant Church **Under 1 mi:** Fishmonger *(Skipjack Seafood 391-9284)*, Newsstand, Hardware Store *(Essex Home Improvement 391-6227)* **1-3 mi:** Supermarket *(Food Lion 918-0171, Giant 995-4322)*, Liquor Store *(Compass 238-7904)*, Farmers' Market, Post Office *(687-5568)*, Library *(Essex 887-0295)*, Beauty Salon *(Donna's 238-2400)*, Barber Shop, Dry Cleaners *(Martin 1 Hr. 686-0192)*, Laundry *(Martin)*, Bookstore *(That's My Story 686-8316)*, Pharmacy *(CVS 687-6313)*, Department Store *(Wal-Mart 687-4858)*, Copies Etc. *(Minuteman 574-2668)*

Transportation

OnCall: Water Taxi *(Middle River, Ch.68, 375-1131 Thu 6-11pm, Fri 6-Mid, Sat Noon-Mid, Sun 11am-9pm, $4/1way)*, Rental Car *(Enterprise 682-6474, Thrifty 391-3103)*, Taxi *(Atwater Cab 682-2100)*, Airport Limo *(Bayview 574-2491)* **Airport:** Baltimore-Washington Int'l.*(17 mi.)*

Medical Services

911 Service **OnCall:** Ambulance **Under 1 mi:** Dentist *(Amsterdam 574-1555)* **1-3 mi:** Doctor, Chiropractor *(Eastern Chiropractic 686-1117)*, Holistic Services *(About Your Body 687-3200)*, Veterinarian *(Schoeberlein 686-3862)* **Hospital:** Franklin Square 443-777-7950 *(5 mi.)*

Setting -- Toward the head of Middle River at the mouth of Hopkins Creek, River Watch Restaurant's expansive windows overlook a 110 slip marina -- four main piers whose slips house a wide variety of boats. Ceiling fans whir lazily on the covered deck and a fireplace creates a cozy atmosphere inside on rainy days. Surrounding are single-family homes with private docks.

Marina Notes -- *Under 29 ft, power is $5/night. Owned by current management since 1991. Good stationary docks with half-length finger piers. The fuel dock is at the end of "B" dock; fuel supplied by Carroll Fuel. The larger boats seem to be at the end of "A" dock. The heads and showers are quite acceptable: two full bathrooms with tile floors and glass-doored shower stalls. Launch service is available for anchored boats. Dock 'n' dine also available.

Notable -- One of the most highly regarded restaurants in the area, River Watch has had its share of media attention. Three public eating areas: a main inside dining room, a covered deck, and a sunset bar area. Inside there's entertainment year round on Friday & Saturday - usually a Top 40 group; outside on the deck near the tiki bar, entertainment in season Thursdays at 7pm and Sundays at 5pm - anything from jazz to Zydeco to Raggae to swing to Jimmy Buffett. Opens 11:30am daily except holidays (then it's Noon) - until 11pm; Midnight on Friday and Saturday in the summer. Sunday Deck Parties from May to September. Function rooms overlooking the deck and the docks accommodate up to 110 people, so this is an interesting group cruise stop. Anchor Bay Marine store is within walking distance.

Essex Marina and Boat Sales

1755 Hilltop Avenue; Essex, MD 21221

Tel: (410) 686-3435 **VHF: Monitor** n/a **Talk** n/a
Fax: (410) 686-1017 **Alternate Tel:** (443) 928-2851
Email: essexboats@aol.com **Web:** www2.yachtworld.com/essexboats
Nearest Town: Essex *(0.5 mi.)* **Tourist Info:** (410) 686-2233

Navigational Information

Lat: 39°18.600' **Long:** 076°26.179' **Tide:** 3 ft. **Current:** n/a **Chart:** 12273
Rep. Depths (*MLW*): Entry 9 ft. **Fuel Dock** n/a **Max Slip/Moor** 9 ft./-
Access: n/a

Marina Facilities *(In Season/Off Season)*

Fuel: No
Slips: 70 Total, 20 Transient **Max LOA:** 45 ft. **Max Beam:** 16 ft.
Rate *(per ft.)*: **Day** $1.00 **Week** n/a **Month** n/a
Power: 30 amp $5, **50 amp** $10, **100 amp** n/a, **200 amp** n/a
Cable TV: No **Dockside Phone:** No
Dock Type: Fixed, Short Fingers, Alongside, Wood
Moorings: 0 Total, 0 Transient **Launch:** n/a, Dinghy Dock (0)
Rate: Day n/a **Week** n/a **Month** n/a
Heads: 2 Toilet(s), 2 Shower(s) *(with dressing rooms)*
Laundry: None **Pay Phones:** No
Pump-Out: OnSite, 1 Central, 1 Port **Fee:** n/a **Closed Heads:** Yes

Marina Operations

Owner/Manager: Michael Dardenberg **Dockmaster:** Doug Crowe
In-Season: Apr-Nov, 9am-5pm **Off-Season:** Nov-Apr, 10am-5pm
After-Hours Arrival: n/a
Reservations: No **Credit Cards:** Visa/MC, Dscvr
Discounts: None
Pets: Welcome, Dog Walk Area **Handicap Access:** Yes, Heads, Docks

Marina Services and Boat Supplies

Services - Docking Assistance, Security *(24 hrs., manager/gated)*, Trash Pick-Up, Dock Carts **Communication -** Mail & Package Hold, Phone Messages, Fax in/out *(Free)*, Data Ports *(Office)*, FedEx, UPS *(Sat Del)* **Supplies - OnSite:** Ice *(Cube)*, Ships' Store **Near:** Boat/US *(918-9344)* **Under 1 mi:** Bait/Tackle *(Outdoor Sportsman 391-0222)*, Propane *(B&T Hardware)*

Boatyard Services

OnSite: Travelift *(27T)*, Crane, Forklift, Engine mechanic *(gas, diesel)*, Electrical Repairs, Electronic Sales, Electronics Repairs, Hull Repairs, Bottom Cleaning, Brightwork, Air Conditioning, Compound, Wash & Wax, Interior Cleaning, Propeller Repairs, Painting, Yacht Broker *(Essex Boat Sales)* **OnCall:** Rigger, Canvas Work **Dealer for:** Mercury, Yanmar, Crusaders, Marine Power, Jasper, Sealand, Mermaid, Polar Bay, Waeco Refrig, SeaVac. **Yard Rates:** $75/hr., Haul & Launch $8/ft., Power Wash $1/ft., Bottom Paint $8/ft. **Storage:** On-Land $3/ft./mo.

Restaurants and Accommodations

Near: Restaurant *(River Watch 687-1422, B $13, L $6-15, D $16-30)*, *(Driftwood 391-3493)*, *(Jaz Nick's 391-5700)*, *(Wolfe's 686-7900)*, *(Neptune's Bar & Grill 238-7800)*, Seafood Shack *(Lady Frances Crabhouse 682-6100)*, Fast Food *(McDonald's)*, Lite Fare *(Maria's Delight Carryout 391-6398)*, Pizzeria *(Vizzini's 686-6600)*, *(Prima / John's 574-1100)* **1-3 mi:** Motel *(Fairfield Inn 574-8100, $90-100)*, *(Super 8 780-0030)*

Recreation and Entertainment

OnSite: Picnic Area, Playground **Under 1 mi:** Fishing Charter *(Green's Charter 574-7067)*, Park *(Sue Creek Park & Rocky Point)*, Galleries **1-3 mi:** Beach *(Miami Beach)*, Jogging Paths *(Tall Trees)*, Video Rental *(Block-3buster 91-5500)* **3+ mi:** Golf Course *(Rocky Point 887-0215, 5 mi.)*, Bowling *(AMF 686-2556, 6 mi.)*, Movie Theater *(Lowes, 7 mi.)*, Museum *(G.L. Martin Maryland Aviation 682-6122, 11am-3pm Wed-Sat, Free, 5 mi.)*

Provisioning and General Services

Near: Convenience Store *(7-Eleven)*, Supermarket *(Food Lion 918-0171)*, Delicatessen *(Middleborough 686-5059)*, Wine/Beer, Liquor Store *(Bi-Rite 686-7001)*, Bakery *(Schimidt 687-8052)*, Fishmonger *(Skipjack 391-9284)*, Crabs/Waterman, Bank/ATM *(Bank of America)*, Pharmacy *(Rite Aid 238-0511)*, Newsstand **Under 1 mi:** Health Food, Catholic Church, Library *(Essex 887-0295)*, Beauty Salon *(Donna's 238-2400)*, Barber Shop, Dry Cleaners *(Admiral 682-5579)*, Hardware Store *(Essex 391-6227)*, Copies Etc. **1-3 mi:** Green Grocer, Post Office *(687-0326)*, Laundry *(Laundry Works 574-6257)*, Bookstore *(Book Warehouse 391-1045)*, Florist, Buying Club **3+ mi:** Department Store *(White Marsh Mall, 7.5 mi.)*

Transportation

OnCall: Water Taxi *(Middle River, Ch.68, 375-1131 Thu 6-11pm, Fri 6pm-Mid, Sat Noon-Mid, Sun 11am-9pm, $4/1way)*, Rental Car *(Enterprise 682-6474 or Thrifty 391-3103 1 mi.)*, Taxi *(New Eastern 687-3232)*, Airport Limo *(Bayview 574-2491)* **Airport:** Baltimore-Washington Int'l. *(15 mi.)*

Medical Services

911 Service **Near:** Dentist *(Amsterdam 574-1555)* **Under 1 mi:** Doctor, Chiropractor *(Murveit 686-0500)* **1-3 mi:** Holistic Services *(About Your Body 687-3200)*, Veterinarian **Hospital:** Franklyn Square 443-777-2000 (5 mi.)

Setting -- This small, charming, full-service marina is tucked into a quiet cove off crowded but scenic Hopkins Creek. Rising above Essex's two main docks is a three-story brick building with twin railed porches fronting each floor. A flower bedecked gazebo and long stretches of off-white railings backed by gardens line the shore. Overlooking the impeccable, brown-stained docks is a large delightful sun deck populated with tables and chairs topped by cream market umbrellas - more crisp off-white railings rim the perimeter.

Marina Notes -- Each of the main piers is L-shaped with slips on either side and short finger piers - all carefully stained. Power is on posts on the docks. Full-service boatyard with travelift and crane plus extensive on-the-hard storage. Welcoming tubs of flowers at the end of each pier. The talented and committed residential green thumb is reportedly Service Manager Doug Crow. Sundeck available for private parties. Very nice, all tiled heads, showers with glass doors.

Notable -- An eye for detail along with a serious effort to soften the boatyard atmosphere lifts this marina out of the ordinary. Every place the eye falls is a little corner of green, a special sitting area, an overflowing planter. Cream-colored railings, backed by beds of annuals and perennials, line the shore - greenery trails down to the docks below. The gazebo is the centerpiece of a beautiful garden that invites boaters to stop and listen - to the wind chimes or to the gurgling fountain flowing into the diminutive pond. Supermarkets, restaurants, and services are within walking distance and cabs are readily available. An interesting rainy day ride is the Glenn L. Martin Maryland Aviation Museum at Martin Airport. It focuses on space and aviation history with 13 historic aircraft.

Navigational Information
Lat: 39°07.650' **Long:** 076°28.367' **Tide:** n/a **Current:** 0 **Chart:** 12272
Rep. Depths (*MLW*): Entry 8 ft. **Fuel Dock** 8 ft. **Max Slip/Moor** 8 ft./-
Access: Patapsco River to Bodkin Creek almost to the head of Main Creek

Marina Facilities *(In Season/Off Season)*
Fuel: Gasoline, Diesel, High-Speed Pumps
Slips: 58 Total, 5 Transient **Max LOA:** 85 ft. **Max Beam:** n/a
Rate *(per ft.)*: **Day** $2.00* **Week** n/a **Month** n/a
Power: 30 amp $5, **50 amp** $10, **100 amp** $20**, **200 amp** n/a
Cable TV: Yes **Dockside Phone:** Yes
Dock Type: Fixed, Long Fingers, Wood
Moorings: 0 Total, 0 Transient **Launch:** n/a
Rate: Day n/a **Week** n/a **Month** n/a
Heads: 6 Toilet(s), 4 Shower(s) *(with dressing rooms)*
Laundry: 2 Washer(s), 2 Dryer(s) **Pay Phones:** No
Pump-Out: OnSite, Full Service **Fee:** $10 **Closed Heads:** Yes

Marina Operations
Owner/Manager: Jeff Barger **Dockmaster:** Don Walker
In-Season: Mem-LabDay, 8am-6pm **Off-Season:** Lab-MemDay, 8am-5pm**
After-Hours Arrival: Tie up, check-in in morning
Reservations: Yes **Credit Cards:** Visa/MC, Amex
Discounts: Boat/US **Dockage:** 25% **Fuel:** $0.10 **Repair:** 10%
Pets: Welcome **Handicap Access:** No

Pleasure Cove Marina

1701 Poplar Ridge Road; Pasadena, MD 21122

Tel: (410) 437-6600 **VHF: Monitor** 69 **Talk** 69
Fax: (410) 437-6127 **Alternate Tel:** (410) 360-2220
Email: info@pleasurecovemarine.com **Web:** www.pleasurecovemarina.com
Nearest Town: Pasadena **Tourist Info:** (410) 647-3900

Marina Services and Boat Supplies
Services - Docking Assistance, Dock Carts **Communication -** FedEx, DHL, UPS, Express Mail **Supplies - OnSite:** Ships' Store *(well-stocked ship store also includes sundries)* **1-3 mi:** Bait/Tackle *(Cobe Marine 255-9488)* **3+ mi:** West Marine *(431-5100, 11 mi.)*, Propane *(Suburban 647-4690, 8 mi.)*

Boatyard Services
OnSite: Travelift *(80T, 25 ft. wide)*, Engine mechanic *(gas, diesel)*, Hull Repairs, Bottom Cleaning, Air Conditioning, Refrigeration, Compound, Wash & Wax, Propeller Repairs, Painting **Dealer for:** CAT, Cummins, Detroit, MerCruiser, Volvo, Galley Maid, Twin Disc, Arnison (Repower Specialists).

Restaurants and Accommodations
OnSite: Restaurant *(Cheshire Crab 360-2220, L $7-12, D $11-28, steamed hard shells & seafood dinners - market price; Sun brunch $7-12, kids' $4.50)* **1-3 mi:** Restaurant *(Windows On the Bay 255-1413, L $8-15, D $15-30)*, *(Blazing Steaks 439-4400)*, *(Sterling Seafood 467-7710)*, Lite Fare *(Pampered Palate 255-7626, B $6-10, D $25-45, breakfast served Sat & Sun)*, Pizzeria *(Carini's Pizza 255-7100)* **3+ mi:** Fast Food *(Hardee's, Subway 4 mi.)*, Motel *(Candlewood Suites 850-9214, 3 mi.)*, Inn/B&B *(Quality Inn 974-4440, $70-130, 8 mi.)*, *(Magothy Manor 647-2995, 6 mi.)*

Recreation and Entertainment
OnSite: Pool *(next to Cheshire Crab, Mon-Thu 8am-6pm, Fri-Sun 8am-8pm)*, Spa *(Jacuzzi)*, Picnic Area, Fitness Center *(Jerry's Gymers: ellipticals, treadmills, recumbent bicycles, weight training equipment)* **Near:** Golf Course *(Anne Arundel County's 36-hole Compass Pointe Golf Courses 255-7764 - designed by Lindsay Ervin, 4 "9"s cover 800 acres - $35-55 cart incl.)*, Jogging Paths, Roller Blade/Bike Paths **Under 1 mi:** Park *(Poplar Ridge Park)* **3+ mi:** Bowling *(Sandusky's Riviera Bowl 255-3550, 6 mi.)*, Movie Theater *(Jumpers Cinemas 768-9999, 8 mi.)*, Video Rental *(Blockbuster 439-5370, 4 mi.)*

Provisioning and General Services
1-3 mi: Convenience Store *(Seven-11 255-2094)* **3+ mi:** Supermarket *(Safeway 439-4560, 4 mi.)*, Delicatessen *(Subway 360-1926, 4 mi.)*, Health Food *(Nature's Good Earth 437-5028, 8 mi.)*, Liquor Store *(Plaza 255-3593; Phelps 255-0151, 4 mi.)*, Bank/ATM *(Susquehanna 360-8112, 4 mi.)*, Post Office *(4 mi.)*, Library *(Anne Arrundel Riviera Beach 222-6285, 4 mi.)*, Pharmacy *(CVS 437-6450, 4 mi.)*, Hardware Store *(Ace Hardware 437-4300, 4 mi.)*, Department Store *(Kmart 760-2222, 8 mi.)*, Copies Etc. *(Mail Boxes Etc 437-9286, 4 mi.)*

Transportation
OnCall: Rental Car *(Enterprise 315-7980, or Reliable Rent-A-Car 255-9970, 4 mi.)*, Taxi *(Gentle Touch 437-1444)*, Airport Limo *(Gentle Touch Limousine)* **Airport:** Baltimore-Washington Int'l. *(17 mi.)*

Medical Services
911 Service **3+ mi:** Doctor *(Marion Outpatient Clinic 304-363-0222, 4 mi.)*, Dentist *(Pasadena Dental Cares 437-5900, 4 mi.)*, Chiropractor *(Horne Chiropractic Center 437-2600, 4 mi.)*, Holistic Services *(Graceful Touch Therapeutic Massage 439-5843, 8 mi.)*, Veterinarian *(Pasadena Animal Hospital 255-2300, 4 mi.)* **Hospital:** North Arundel 787-4000 *(11 mi.)*

Setting -- Tucked far up bucolic Bodkin's Main Creek at the mouth of the Patapsco, this full-service marina has a resort-like ambiance. Three sets of slips are backed by the popular Chesire Crab Restaurant and a particularly inviting, nicely foliaged pool - both with views of the pretty creek lined with private homes. Jerry's Gymers' fitness center is adjacent to the bathhouse and up the hill is a ships' store and boatyard operation with extensive on-the-hard storage.

Marina Notes -- *$2.25/ft. holidays. **Mon-Thu 8am-6pm, Fri-Sun 8am-8pm; Main office closed Sat & Sun. Two sets of fixed docks in front of the travelift have wide, full-length finger piers and large lighthouse pedestals. Main dock slips are inboard, with 1500 ft. side-to outboard to handle larger vessels. Shorefront slips have smaller pedestals for smaller boats. Up the side creek, seasonal docks have built in lifts. 25-ft. wide travelift manages most cats, and a dry storage operation takes up to 45-footers. Well-stocked ships' store includes most necessary sundries. Pleasant bathhouse - shower rooms sport full doors & fiberglass stalls with dressing rooms. An adjacent laundry room has a deck with picnic tables overlooking the docks, and nearby is the well-equipped fitness center.

Notable -- The Cheshire Crab has a large open deck overlooking the docks, plus an expansive glass room with sliding doors that can open to the outside - both populated with picnic tables. A more formal dining room is inside (11:30am-10pm, Fri & Sat 'til 11pm , Sun 10am-10pm). The large, pristine pool is nicely sited amid greenery and has dock views. Surrounding it is a wide concrete deck furnished with comfortable matching chaises and an attractive black wrought iron fence. Directly across the creek is Bodkin Y.C. Further up the small, undeveloped tributary is Bodkin Marina - no services, just the peaceful sound of ducks.

PHOTOS ON CD-ROM: 12

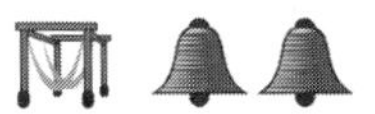

Fairview Marina

1575 Fairview Beach Road; Pasadena, MD 21122

Tel: (410) 437-3400 **VHF: Monitor** n/a **Talk** n/a
Fax: (410) 360-9526 **Alternate Tel:** (410) 299-3406
Email: info@fairviewmarina.com **Web:** www.fairviewmarina.com
Nearest Town: Pasadena *(3 mi.)* **Tourist Info:** (410) 647-3900

Navigational Information

Lat: 39°09.083' **Long:** 076°29.717' **Tide:** 2 ft. **Current:** n/a **Chart:** 12272
Rep. Depths (*MLW*): Entry 12 ft. **Fuel Dock** n/a **Max Slip/Moor** 12 ft./-
Access: Patapsco Brewerton Channel to G5B; Rock Creek to R4

Marina Facilities *(In Season/Off Season)*

Fuel: No
Slips: 115 Total, 7 Transient **Max LOA:** 80 ft. **Max Beam:** 24 ft.
Rate *(per ft.)*: **Day** $1.40/Inq. **Week** $6 **Month** Inq.
Power: 30 amp $5, **50 amp** $10, **100 amp** n/a, **200 amp** n/a
Cable TV: No **Dockside Phone:** No
Dock Type: Fixed, Short Fingers, Pilings, Wood
Moorings: 0 Total, 0 Transient **Launch:** n/a, Dinghy Dock
Rate: Day n/a **Week** n/a **Month** n/a
Heads: 2 Toilet(s), 1 Shower(s) *(with dressing rooms)*
Laundry: 1 Washer(s), 1 Dryer(s) **Pay Phones:** No
Pump-Out: OnSite, Self Service **Fee:** $5 **Closed Heads:** Yes

Marina Operations

Owner/Manager: Marc Kahan **Dockmaster:** Same
In-Season: Year-Round, 8:30am-4:30pm* **Off-Season:** n/a
After-Hours Arrival: Call 299-3406
Reservations: No **Credit Cards:** Visa/MC
Discounts: Boat/US **Dockage:** Yes **Fuel:** Yes **Repair:** Yes
Pets: Welcome, Dog Walk Area **Handicap Access:** No

Marina Services and Boat Supplies

Services - Docking Assistance, Security *(24 hrs.)*, Trash Pick-Up, Dock Carts **Communication -** Mail & Package Hold, Data Ports *(Office)*, FedEx, DHL, UPS, Express Mail *(Sat Del)* **Supplies - OnSite:** Ice *(Block, Cube)*, Ships' Store, Marine Discount Store **1-3 mi:** Bait/Tackle *(COBE Marine 255-9488)*, Propane **3+ mi:** West Marine *(431-5100, 10 mi.)*

Boatyard Services

OnSite: Travelift *(27T)*, Launching Ramp, Engine mechanic *(gas, diesel)*, Electrical Repairs, Electronics Repairs, Hull Repairs *(Fiberglass core & Osmotic blister repairs)*, Rigger, Canvas Work, Bottom Cleaning, Brightwork, Air Conditioning, Refrigeration, Divers, Compound, Wash & Wax, Interior Cleaning, Propeller Repairs, Woodworking, Upholstery, Yacht Interiors, Metal Fabrication, Painting, Awlgrip, Total Refits **Member:** ABBRA
Yard Rates: $80/hr., Haul & Launch $10/ft. *(blocking incl.)*, Power Wash Incl., Bottom Paint $15/ft. *(paint incl.)* **Storage:** In-Water Inq. , On-Land Outside $4.50/ft./mo. Inside, Inq. for rates

Restaurants and Accommodations

Near: Restaurant *(Tall Oaks 255-1438, L $5-10, D $5-35)* **Under 1 mi:** Restaurant *(Anchor Inn 437-0696, L $8-22, D $8-22)*, *(Windows On the Bay 255-1413, L $8-17, D $5-27, or by dinghy)* **1-3 mi:** Restaurant *(Rock Creek Diner 439-1214)*, Pizzeria *(Carini's 255-7100)* **3+ mi:** Motel *(Holiday Inn 636-4300, $130, 8 mi.)*, *(Candlewood Suites 850-9214, $100-160, 4 mi.)*

Recreation and Entertainment

OnSite: Pool *(hurricane-fenced, overlooking the cove)*, Beach, Picnic Area *(above the cove nestled under trees)*, Grills **1-3 mi:** Playground, Tennis Courts, Golf Course *(Anne Arundel County's 36-hole Compass Pointe Golf Courses 255-7764 - designed by Lindsay Ervin, 4 "9"s cover 800 acres - $35-55 cart incl.)*, Fitness Center *(Curtis Bay Athletic 437-8064)*, Jogging Paths, Park *(Fort Smallwood)*, Cultural Attract **3+ mi:** Bowling *(Sandusky's 255-3550, 5 mi.)*, Movie Theater *(Jumpers 768-9999, 9 mi.)*, Video Rental *(Blockbuster 439-5370, 4 mi.)*

Provisioning and General Services

1-3 mi: Convenience Store *(7-Eleven 255-2094)*, Delicatessen *(Sandy's Subs 360-7827)*, Wine/Beer, Bakery, Green Grocer, Lobster Pound, Bank/ATM, Post Office, Catholic Church, Protestant Church, Beauty Salon, Barber Shop, Dry Cleaners, Laundry *(Spin & Trim 360-0112)*, Newsstand, Florist **3+ mi:** Supermarket *(Safeway 439-4560, 5 mi.)*, Health Food *(Nature's Good Earth 437-5028, 8 mi.)*, Liquor Store *(Key Bridge 360-0055, 4 mi.)*, Library *(Riviera Beach 222-6270, 5 mi.)*, Pharmacy *(CVS 437-6855, 4 mi.)*, Hardware Store *(Hometown 360-8200, 5 mi.)*, Department Store *(Kmart 760-2222, 8 mi.)*, Copies Etc. *(Mail Boxes 437-9286, 4 mi.)*

Transportation

OnCall: Rental Car *(Enterprise 315-7980, or Reliable Rent-A-Car 255-9970, 4 mi.)*, Taxi *(Gentle Touch 437-1444)*, Airport Limo *(Gentle Touch Limousine 437-1444)* **Airport:** Baltimore-Washington Int'l. *(15 mi.)*

Medical Services

911 Service **OnCall:** Ambulance **Under 1 mi:** Dentist *(Leary 360-9061)*
3+ mi: Doctor *(Primary Care 255-2700, 4 mi.)*, Chiropractor *(Fish Family Chiro 360-5022, 4 mi.)*, Veterinarian *(Pasadena Animal 255-2300, 4 mi.)*
Hospital: North Arrundel 787-4000 *(10 mi.)*

Setting -- Beyond Fairview Point, Wall Cove, off Rock Creek, shelters low-key Fairview Marina - a serious boatyard with an extensive network of docks. Approaching boaters see a small gray dockhouse out on L-shaped "F" dock, followed by five more docks and a long metal quonset hut covering a work slip. A pool, a porch swing and picnic tables with grills are perched up on the bank with views across the creek. Upland are a two-story natural clapboard work building; adjacent is a gray modular marina office with a green awning and the white bathhouse cottage. Rising above them is a tall white vinyl work shed.

Marina Notes -- *Sun 8:30am-1pm. DCM. Founded in 1934. The Kahns, a husband & wife team, have been at the helm since 1994 and live on the property; they are accommodating and service focused - just ask. (Actually an adorable trio really rule the roost - Nelson, the little ringleader, manages a couple of bull-terriers.) F dock hosts the larger boats with full-length finger piers and good pedestals. "D" dock has covered slips and full-length finger piers. Remaining four stationary docks have short finger piers with power and water tucked beneath the docks. The rare long covered work slip plus the vinyl work shed support a fulll-service boatyard. The quite nice bathhouse has faux beige tile walls, Formica-walled showers with glass doors, changing rooms plus full-length mirrors.

Notable -- An effort has been made to soften the boatyard ambiance with plantings and thoughtful touches. The combination of convenient airport access, owner oversight and the quiet, protected cove make this a logical place to leave the boat. Enterprise will deliver, and there are cabs. The Maryland Yacht Club is next door backed by red and white-striped smoke stacks and welcomes reciprocal boaters. (NOTE: Nearby White Rocks no longer takes transients.)

Navigational Information
Lat: 39°08.766' **Long:** 076°30.859' **Tide:** 2 ft. **Current:** n/a **Chart:** 12272
Rep. Depths (*MLW*): Entry 10 ft. **Fuel Dock** n/a **Max Slip/Moor** 10 ft./-
Access: Brewerton Channel to G5B to Rock Creek halfway on port side

Marina Facilities *(In Season/Off Season)*
Fuel: No
Slips: 98 Total, 2 Transient **Max LOA:** 60 ft. **Max Beam:** 17 ft.
Rate *(per ft.)*: **Day** $1.00 **Week** $4.00 **Month** $8.00
Power: 30 amp $5, **50 amp** n/a, **100 amp** n/a, **200 amp** n/a
Cable TV: No **Dockside Phone:** No
Dock Type: Fixed, Long Fingers, Short Fingers, Pilings, Wood
Moorings: 0 Total, 0 Transient **Launch:** n/a, Dinghy Dock
Rate: Day n/a **Week** n/a **Month** n/a
Heads: 4 Toilet(s), 4 Shower(s)
Laundry: 1 Washer(s), 1 Dryer(s), Iron, Iron Board **Pay Phones:** Yes
Pump-Out: OnSite, Self Service, 1 Central **Fee:** $5 **Closed Heads:** Yes

Marina Operations
Owner/Manager: Kendall E. Broman **Dockmaster:** Chris Broman
In-Season: Year-Round, 7:30am-4pm **Off-Season:** n/a
After-Hours Arrival: Call in advance
Reservations: Yes **Credit Cards:** Visa/MC, Amex
Discounts: None
Pets: Welcome **Handicap Access:** No

Oak Harbor Marina

1343 Old Water Oak Point Road; Pasadena, MD 21122

Tel: (410) 255-4070 **VHF: Monitor** 16 **Talk** 12
Fax: (410) 360-9737 **Alternate Tel:** n/a
Email: Seakris3@home.com **Web:** www.oakharbor.8m.com
Nearest Town: Pasadena **Tourist Info:** (410) 647-3900

Marina Services and Boat Supplies
Services - Docking Assistance, Boaters' Lounge, Dock Carts
Communication - Mail & Package Hold, Phone Messages, Fax in/out, Data Ports *(boater's lounge, Free)*, FedEx, UPS **Supplies - OnSite:** Ice *(Block, Cube)*, Ships' Store **1-3 mi:** Bait/Tackle *(COBE Marine 255-9488)* **3+ mi:** West Marine *(431-5100, 8 mi.)*, Propane *(Suburban 647-4690, 8 mi.)*

Boatyard Services
OnSite: Travelift *(30T)*, Crane, Forklift, Engine mechanic *(gas, diesel)*, Electrical Repairs, Electronics Repairs, Hull Repairs, Rigger, Sail Loft, Canvas Work *(Canvas by Nancy 439-9100)*, Bottom Cleaning, Brightwork, Air Conditioning, Compound, Wash & Wax, Interior Cleaning, Propeller Repairs, Woodworking, Painting, Awlgrip, Yacht Broker **OnCall:** Refrigeration, Upholstery **Near:** Metal Fabrication. **Yard Rates:** $85/hr., Haul & Launch $5/ft. *(blocking $2.50/ft.)*, Power Wash $2.50/ft., Bottom Paint $10/ft. **Storage:** On-Land $4/ft./mo.

Restaurants and Accommodations
OnCall: Pizzeria *(Domino's 437-6200)* **Under 1 mi:** Restaurant *(Anchor Inn 437-0696, L $8-22, D $8-22)*, *(Windows on the Bay 255-1413, L $8-17, D $5-27, or by dinghy)*, *(Tall Oaks 255-1438, L $5-10, D $5-35)* **1-3 mi:** Restaurant *(Rock Creek Diner 439-1214)*, *(Sterling Seafood 467-7710)*, Fast Food *(Burger King, McDonalds)*, Pizzeria *(Carini's 255-7100)* **3+ mi:** Motel *(Candlewood Suites 850-9014, $100-160, 4 mi.)*, Inn/B&B *(Magothy Manor 647-2995, 5 mi.)*, *(Rigby Valliant House 745-3977, 7 mi.)*

Recreation and Entertainment
OnSite: Beach, Picnic Area, Grills **1-3 mi:** Golf Course *(36-hole Compass Pointe County G.C. 255-7764 $35-55 incl. cart)*, Fitness Center *(Curtis Bay A.C. 437-8064)*, Video Rental *(Blockbuster 439-5370)*, Video Arcade, Park *(Fort Smallwood)* **3+ mi:** Bowling *(Sandusky's Riviera 255-3550, 5 mi.)*, Movie Theater *(Jumpers 768-9999, 8 mi.)*

Provisioning and General Services
Under 1 mi: Newsstand, Florist **1-3 mi:** Provisioning Service, Convenience Store *(7-Eleven 255-2094)*, Gourmet Shop, Delicatessen *(Sandy's Subs & Stuff 360-7827)*, Wine/Beer, Liquor Store *(Plaza Liquors 255-3593)*, Bakery, Bank/ATM, Post Office, Catholic Church, Protestant Church, Beauty Salon, Barber Shop, Dry Cleaners, Laundry *(Spin & Trim 360-0112)*, Bookstore, Pharmacy *(CVS 437-6855)*, Hardware Store *(Hometown 360-8200)*, Clothing Store, Retail Shops, Buying Club **3+ mi:** Supermarket *(Safeway 439-4560, 4 mi.)*, Health Food *(Nature's Good Earth 437-5028, 8 mi.)*, Library *(Riviera Beach 222-6270, 5 mi.)*, Department Store *(Kmart 760-2222, 8 mi.)*, Copies Etc. *(Mail Boxes 437-9286, 4 mi.)*

Transportation
OnCall: Rental Car *(Enterprise 315-7980, or Reliable Rent-A-Car 255-9970, 4 mi.)*, Taxi *(Gentle Touch Limousine 437-1444)*, Airport Limo *(Gentle Touch Limo)* **Airport:** Baltimore-Washington Int'l. *(15 mi.)*

Medical Services
911 Service **OnCall:** Ambulance **Near:** Dentist *(Leary 360-9061)* **1-3 mi:** Doctor *(Primary Care Physicians 255-2700)*, Chiropractor *(Fish Family Chiropractic 360-5022)*, Veterinarian *(Pasadena Animal Hospital 255-2300)* **3+ mi:** Holistic Services *(Graceful Touch Therapeutic Massage Center 439-5843, 6 mi.)* **Hospital:** North Arundel 787-4000 *(9 mi.)*

Setting -- Further up Rock Creek, Oak Harbor is in a quiet, protected harbor. The rustic, casual boatyard atmosphere belies the community spirit and useful boater amenities beneath the surface. A picnic deck overlooking the docks, with tables and grills, serves as a gathering place - particularly for the liveaboards.

Marina Notes -- DCM. Run by the Broman family - two generations at the helm. Very service-oriented staff. Only some of the stationary wood docks with half-length finger piers have power - "A" dock has power; it's on short pilings. Behind the "Canvas by Nancy" building is a boaters' lounge (open from 8am-8pm). It has a sofa, lending library, latest boaters' newspapers, a book exchange, a television, a coin operated washer and dryer, and two phone lines, one for internet access and one for complimentary local calls. Sailboats greatly outnumber powerboats. Most boatyard services are available onsite and do-it-yourselfers are welcome. Small dry storage operation also on-site. Located in the gray cinderblock bathhouse with barn roof are the quite acceptable heads - tile floors, composite dividers and fiberglass shower stalls with glass doors and a group dressing room.

Notable -- Situated in a residential area, Oak Harbor encourages a community atmosphere among the liveaboards, seasonal tenants and transient boaters. If you need to get somewhere, there'll likely be someone to help. This also makes it an interesting choice for leaving the boat. A short dinghy ride down the creek, at White Rocks Marina (which no longer accepts transients), is Windows on the Bay Restaurant. A large, bright, airy main dining room looks out over the open, covered deck, and the covered deck looks out over the docks and creek. The bar area is calls Doc's.

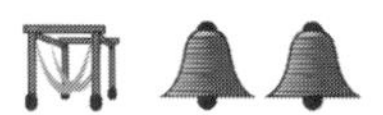

Maurgale Marina

864 Nabbs Creek Road; Glen Burnie, MD 21060

Tel: (410) 437-0402 **VHF: Monitor** n/a **Talk** n/a
Fax: (410) 437-0484 **Alternate Tel:** (443) 623-3673
Email: n/a **Web:** n/a
Nearest Town: Glen Burnie *(6 mi.)* **Tourist Info:** (410) 647-3900

Navigational Information

Lat: 39°09.716' **Long:** 076°32.733' **Tide:** 2 ft. **Current:** n/a **Chart:** 12272
Rep. Depths (*MLW*): Entry 9 ft. **Fuel Dock** 9 ft. **Max Slip/Moor** 9 ft./-
Access: Patapsco to Stony Creek to Nabb's Creek

Marina Facilities *(In Season/Off Season)*

Fuel: Gasoline, Diesel
Slips: 141 Total, 6 Transient **Max LOA:** 60 ft. **Max Beam:** 18 ft.
Rate *(per ft.)*: **Day** $2.00 **Week** n/a **Month** n/a
Power: 30 amp $5, **50 amp** n/a, **100 amp** n/a, **200 amp** n/a
Cable TV: No **Dockside Phone:** No
Dock Type: Fixed, Short Fingers, Pilings, Wood
Moorings: 0 Total, 0 Transient **Launch:** yes
Rate: Day n/a **Week** n/a **Month** n/a
Heads: 3 Toilet(s), 2 Shower(s)
Laundry: None **Pay Phones:** No
Pump-Out: OnCall, Full Service **Fee:** $5 **Closed Heads:** Yes

Marina Operations

Owner/Manager: Harry L. Erbe **Dockmaster:** Same
In-Season: Year-Round, 8am-6pm **Off-Season:** n/a
After-Hours Arrival: Call 443-623-3673
Reservations: Yes, Required **Credit Cards:** Cash or Check
Discounts: None
Pets: Welcome, Dog Walk Area **Handicap Access:** No

Marina Services and Boat Supplies

Services - Security *(Owner on premises)*, Dock Carts **Communication -** FedEx, DHL, UPS **Supplies - 3+ mi:** West Marine *(431-5100, 6 mi.)*, Boat/US *(761-5901, 6 mi.)*, Bait/Tackle *(Cobe Marine 255-9488, 4 mi.)*, Propane *(Texaco 761-5970, 7 mi.)*

Boatyard Services

OnSite: Travelift *(20T)* **Yard Rates:** Haul & Launch $4/ft each way *(blocking incl.)*, Power Wash $3/ft. **Storage:** In-Water $95/mo., On-Land $3/ft./mo.

Restaurants and Accommodations

OnSite: Restaurant *(The Original Nabbs Creek Cafe 437-0400)* **3+ mi:** Restaurant *(Stoney Creek Inn 439-3123, L $6-22, D $12-30, 4 mi.)*, *(Captain K's 360-7010, 4 mi.)*, *(Garvins Grill 437-8500, 4 mi.)*, *(Pete's 437-1779, L $6-8, D $10-17, 4 mi., "good food")*, *(Ocean Chinese 439-8622, 4 mi.)*, Lite Fare *(Sub Shack 439-8500, 4 mi.)*, Pizzeria *(Italiano Supreme 255-8888, L $6-13, D $6-13, 4 mi.)*, *(Gourmet Pizza 360-8777, 4 mi.)*, Motel *(Holiday Inn 470-3431, $80-150, 5 mi.)*, *(Days Inn 761-8300, $90-160, 4 mi.)*

Recreation and Entertainment

OnSite: Picnic Area **3+ mi:** Golf Course *(Compass Pointe Golf Course 255-7764, 7 mi.)*, Fitness Center *(Curves 439-4202, Club One Fitness 760-8746, 4 mi.)*, Bowling *(Sandusky's Riviera Bowl 255-3550, 4 mi.)*, Movie Theater *(Jumpers Cinemas 768-9999, 5 mi.)*, Video Rental *(Blockbuster 360-7229, 4 mi.)*

Provisioning and General Services

Under 1 mi: Bank/ATM **1-3 mi:** Convenience Store, Health Food, Bakery, Post Office, Catholic Church, Protestant Church, Barber Shop, Florist
3+ mi: Supermarket *(Mars 360-0200, Food Lion 255-4626, 5 mi.)*, Delicatessen *(Sandy's Subs & Stuff 360-7827, 4 mi.)*, Wine/Beer *(Arundel Liquors 255-9122, 4 mi.)*, Liquor Store *(Harbour Liquor 255-4395, 4 mi.)*, Library *(Riviera Beach 222-6285, 5 mi.)*, Beauty Salon *(Della's Day Spa 360-0900,* 4 mi.), Laundry *(Danny's Laundry & Dry Cleaning 437-8090, 4 mi.)*, Pharmacy *(CVS 437-1149, 4 mi.)*, Hardware Store *(Home Depot 443-572-0077, 6 mi.)*, Department Store *(Marley Station Mall, 6 mi.)*

Transportation

OnCall: Rental Car *(Enterprise 315-7980, or Hertz 850-7400)*, Taxi *(Glen Burnie Taxi 766-1000)*, Airport Limo *(Blue Star Limo 766-9219)*
Airport: Baltimore-Washington Int'l. *(14 mi.)*

Medical Services

911 Service **OnCall:** Ambulance **1-3 mi:** Doctor **3+ mi:** Dentist *(Hittle 255-6611, 4 mi.)*, Chiropractor *(Mandell Chiropractic Center 439-4466, 5 mi.)*, Veterinarian *(Pasadena Animal Hospital 255-2300, 5 mi.)*
Hospital: North Arundel 787-4000 *(7 mi.)*

Setting -- Follow deep Stony Creek through the Rt. 173 drawbridge into equally deep Nabbs Creek. A large, bark brown, mostly glass modified A-frame, housing the Original Nabbs Creek Café, rises behind Maurgale's four main piers. Each pier hosts slips on either side, and two small picnic decks with tables and grills are at the head of "C" and "B" docks. Eighteen dock 'n dine slips directly in front of the restaurant are easily identified by their pink and blue stripes.

Marina Notes -- Owner lives on premises. A hurricane haven - no damage from Isabel. Larger boats are on " A" & " B" docks. Stationary docks, narrow half-length fingers and 30A power on pilings. Boatyard services are limited to haulout, storage & power wash. Interesting mix of boats run the gamut from large, old wooden vessels that have suffered at the hands of time to spiffy new power boats in pristine condition. The bathhouse's two full bathrooms are rustic at best.

Notable -- Situated on 5 acres, the Original Nabbs Creek Café is a bit of a magnet in this neighborhood - for locals, especially watermen, during the week, and for boaters on weekends. In summer, there's full service outside on the decks overlooking the docks and waterway, a tiki bar, and a DJ Friday and Saturday nights. Open 7 days, 11am to Midnight and beyond - same menu all day plus lunch specials from 11am-4pm. The varied menu includes a steamer bar, salads, seafood, steaks, ribs, or combination platters, sandwiches, gourmet pizza, and burgers. Multiple TVs reinforce a sports theme as do specials on game days and bus trips to see the Orioles play. Upstairs is a long bar, a big screen TV, a pool table for tournaments and a dance floor. Formerly called Marguale Restaurant and Nabbs Creek before that. Nearest fuel is at Stony Creek Marina. (Note: Adjacent Hand Bros. Marina does not accept transients.)

Navigational Information

Lat: 39°15.025' **Long:** 076°29.152' **Tide:** 2 ft. **Current:** n/a **Chart:** 12272
Rep. Depths (*MLW*): Entry 12 ft. **Fuel Dock** 12 ft. **Max Slip/Moor** 12 ft./-
Access: Thru 53 ft. fixed bridge, Peninsula Bridge & RR swing bridge

Marina Facilities *(In Season/Off Season)*

Fuel: *Carroll* - Gasoline, Diesel
Slips: 65 Total, 10 Transient **Max LOA:** 150 ft. **Max Beam:** 30 ft.
Rate *(per ft.)*: **Day** $1.00 **Week** $7.00 **Month** $30
Power: 30 amp Incl., **50 amp** Incl., **100 amp** Incl., **200 amp** n/a
Cable TV: No **Dockside Phone:** No
Dock Type: Fixed, Long Fingers, Short Fingers, Pilings
Moorings: 0 Total, 0 Transient **Launch:** n/a
Rate: Day n/a **Week** n/a **Month** n/a
Heads: 6 Toilet(s), 3 Shower(s) *(with dressing rooms)*
Laundry: 1 Washer(s), 1 Dryer(s) **Pay Phones:** No
Pump-Out: Full Service, 1 Central **Fee:** Free w/fuel **Closed Heads:** Yes

Marina Operations

Owner/Manager: Art and Tina Cox **Dockmaster:** Same
In-Season: May-Oct, 7am-7pm **Off-Season:** Nov-Apr, 7am-6pm
After-Hours Arrival: Tie up to piers or any open slip
Reservations: Yes, Preferred **Credit Cards:** Visa/MC, Dscvr, Amex
Discounts: Boat/US; Marina Life **Dockage:** n/a **Fuel:** $0.05 **Repair:** n/a
Pets: Welcome, Dog Walk Area **Handicap Access:** No

Anchor Bay East Marine

8500 Cove Road; Dundalk, MD 21222

Tel: (410) 284-1044 **VHF: Monitor** 16 **Talk** 69
Fax: (410) 284-2534 **Alternate Tel:** (443) 562-7879
Email: n/a **Web:** www.anchorbayeastmarina.com
Nearest Town: Dundalk *(1 mi.)* **Tourist Info:** (410) 647-3900

Marina Services and Boat Supplies

Services - Docking Assistance, Boaters' Lounge, Security, Trash Pick-Up, Dock Carts, Megayacht Facilities **Communication -** Mail & Package Hold, Phone Messages, Fax in/out, Data Ports *(Lobby)*, FedEx, DHL, UPS, Express Mail *(Sat Del)* **Supplies - OnSite:** Ice *(Cube)*, Ships' Store *(ship supplies, sundries, drinks)* **3+ mi:** Boat/US *(918-9344, 8 mi.)*, Bait/Tackle *(Bluefin's Bait & Tackle 477-9244, 4 mi.)*, Propane *(ABC 282-2550, 4 mi.)*

Boatyard Services

OnSite: Travelift *(60 & 80T)*, Crane *(8.5T)*, Launching Ramp, Engine mechanic *(gas, diesel)*, Electrical Repairs, Electronic Sales, Electronics Repairs, Hull Repairs, Rigger, Bottom Cleaning, Air Conditioning, Refrigeration, Compound, Wash & Wax, Propeller Repairs, Woodworking, Metal Fabrication, Painting, Awlgrip **Dealer for:** Cummins, Volvo, Cat, Kohler, Onan, Merc. **Member:** ABBRA, ABYC - 4 Certified Tech(s) **Yard Rates:** $65/hr., Haul & Launch $3/ft. *(blocking $5/ft.)*, Power Wash Incl., Bottom Paint $8/ft. **Storage:** On-Land Inq.

Restaurants and Accommodations

OnCall: Restaurant *(Domino's 282-1919)* **Under 1 mi:** Restaurant *(The Mariner's Landing 477-1261, L $5-15, D $15-30)* **1-3 mi:** Restaurant *(Philly Steak & Burgers 288-2539, carry-out in a mall)*, *(Filippo's Pizza 284-7997)*, Crab House *(Ross' Crab House 282-1235)*, *(Blue Claw Crabhouse 284-9800, carry-out)*, Lite Fare *(B&K Carryout 285-8113)* **3+ mi:** Restaurant *(Five Seasons 625-9787, L $7, D $15-25, 7 mi., Ethiopian and international cuisine)*, *(Seahorse Inn 388-1150, L $8-20, D $8-20, 4 mi., daily specials)*, Motel *(Best Western Baltimore 633-9500, $100-130, 4 mi.)*, Hotel *(Fairfield Inn Baltimore North 574-8100, $80-100, 6 mi.)*

Recreation and Entertainment

OnSite: Pool **Under 1 mi:** Park *(Stansbury Park)* **1-3 mi:** Fitness Center *(Middle River Gym 682-4044)*, Video Rental *(Blockbuster 391-8800)* **3+ mi:** Golf Course *(Rocky Point 887-0215, 5 mi.)*, Bowling *(6 mi.)*

Provisioning and General Services

OnSite: Crabs/Waterman **OnCall:** Market *(Sysco)* **1-3 mi:** Delicatessen *(Merritt Filleti Sub Shop 288-5628)*, Wine/Beer, Liquor Store *(Hoover's Liquors 282-0700)*, Bakery *(Herman's Bakery & Deli 284-5590)*, Farmers' Market *(Sat 8am-Noon, Veterans Park behind post office 285-3476)*, Post Office *(284-4326)*, Protestant Church, Beauty Salon *(Heavenly Hair 2855700)*, Dry Cleaners *(Roh's Cleaners 285-1788)*, Laundry *(Sudsy's Laundromat 282-2427)*, Pharmacy *(Drug City 284-2424)*, Newsstand, Hardware Store *(Poplar Place Hardware 284-9850)*, Florist, Retail Shops, Department Store *(Eastpoint Mall, Wal-Mart 284-5412)*, Buying Club *(Sam's 284-2501)*, Copies Etc. *(Minuteman 282-6660)* **3+ mi:** Fishmonger *(M & I Seafood 477-0050, 5 mi.)*, Library *(Fells Point 396-0992, 6 mi.)*

Transportation

OnSite: Airport Limo **OnCall:** Rental Car *(Enterprise 282-9575, Alamo 288-5657, Thrifty 282-0482)*, Taxi *(Statewide Sedan 285-3330)* **3+ mi:** Rail
Airport: Baltimore-Washington Int'l. *(15 mi.)*

Medical Services

911 Service **OnCall:** Ambulance **1-3 mi:** Doctor, Dentist *(Beautiful Smile 288-1162)*, Chiropractor *(Adio Chiropractor 288-1800)*, Veterinarian *(Dundalk Animal Hospital 282-2250)* **Hospital:** Johns Hopkins 955-5000 *(7 mi.)*

Setting -- On the northeast side of the Patapsco, on a point formed by Bear Creek and Lynch Cove, Anchor Bay East is immediately beyond the railroad bridge (usually open). Extensive land-side boatyard and storage facilities support the "F" shaped stationary docks. Stretching out into the creek, a long, three-pump, easy-access fuel dock hosts a two-story gray clapboard dockhouse with blue and white striped awnings (look for Isabel's high-water mark). An above-ground pool sits at the entrance to that same pier.

Marina Notes -- DCM. Founded in 1988, family owned and operated with an obvious affinity for customer care (i.e. rides can usually be found). Full-service boatyard with large lifts. Outer docks are designed for larger boats, with appropriate power options. The yard next door has just been acquired, doubling the on-the-hard storage space. An indoor boaters' lounge has a kitchen and two friendly dogs help out - the white one is Trevor and the black one is Little Dog. Well-stocked parts department plus ships' store has a wide variety of maintenance supplies, sundries, ice cream and drinks. A cement floor, cinderblock bathhouse has three full-baths with cement shower stalls (men's, women's & unisex) plus a washer and dryer, a folding table and a snack vending machine.

Notable -- Pots of flowers here and there and planters filled with brightly colored flowers soften the boatyard atmosphere. The surrounding area is rural, quiet and green - particularly pretty in the fall. The combination of big haul out capability, reportedly great customer service and convenience to the airport makes this a frequent stop for part-time cruisers, and a nice cozy little area to leave the boat - especially if there is work to be done.

3. WS: BALTIMORE REGION

PHOTOS ON CD-ROM: 12

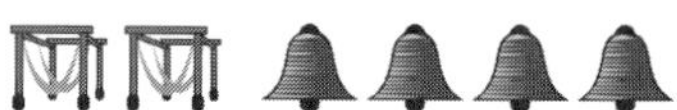

Baltimore Marine Center

2738 Lighthouse Point East; Baltimore, MD 21224

Tel: (410) 675-8888 **VHF: Monitor** 16 **Talk** 68
Fax: (410) 675-3568 **Alternate Tel:** (410) 675-1288
Email: n/a **Web:** www.baltimoremarinecenter.com
Nearest Town: Baltimore/Canton *(2.5 mi.)* **Tourist Info:** (410) 558-3515

Navigational Information

Lat: 39°16.658' **Long:** 076°34.683' **Tide:** 2 ft. **Current:** n/a **Chart:** 12272
Rep. Depths (*MLW*): Entry 15 ft. **Fuel Dock** 20 ft. **Max Slip/Moor** 25 ft./-
Access: Patapsco River use Northwest channel

Marina Facilities *(In Season/Off Season)*

Fuel: Gasoline, Diesel, High-Speed Pumps
Slips: 500 Total, 100 Transient **Max LOA:** 200 ft. **Max Beam:** n/a
Rate *(per ft.)*: **Day** $2.50/Inq.* **Week** Inq. **Month** $25
Power: 30 amp $13, **50 amp** $15, **100 amp** $40, **200 amp** n/a
Cable TV: Yes Incl. **Dockside Phone:** Yes Verizon
Dock Type: Fixed, Floating, Long Fingers, Alongside, Concrete
Moorings: 0 Total, 0 Transient **Launch:** n/a
Rate: Day n/a **Week** n/a **Month** n/a
Heads: 20 Toilet(s), 10 Shower(s) *(with dressing rooms)*
Laundry: 3 Washer(s), 3 Dryer(s) **Pay Phones:** Yes, 2
Pump-Out: OnSite, Full Service, 5 Central **Fee:** $5 **Closed Heads:** Yes

Marina Operations

Owner/Manager: Jack Gardner **Dockmaster:** Dave Bezos
In-Season: Apr-Oct, 9am-8pm **Off-Season:** Nov-Mar, 9am-4pm
After-Hours Arrival: Call 675-1288
Reservations: Preferred **Credit Cards:** Visa/MC, Dscvr, Din, Amex, ATM
Discounts: Boat/US; MarinaLife **Dockage:** n/a **Fuel:** $.10/gal **Repair:** n/a
Pets: Welcome, Dog Walk Area **Handicap Access:** Yes, Heads, Docks

Marina Services and Boat Supplies

Services - Docking Assistance, Concierge, Room Service to the Boat, Security *(24 hrs., live & camera)*, Trash Pick-Up, Dock Carts, Megayacht Facilities, 3 Phase **Communication -** Mail & Package Hold, Phone Messages, Fax in/out, Data Ports *(Wi-Fi)*, FedEx, DHL, UPS *(Sat Del)* **Supplies - OnSite:** Ice *(Block)*, West Marine *(563-8905)*, Bait/Tackle

Boatyard Services

OnSite: Travelift *(88T, 55T)*, Crane *(18T hydraulic)*, Forklift *(27000 lb.)*, Hydraulic Trailer *(30T)*, Engine mechanic *(gas, diesel)*, Electrical Repairs, Electronics Repairs, Hull Repairs, Rigger, Bottom Cleaning, Brightwork, Air Conditioning, Refrigeration, Compound, Wash & Wax, Interior Cleaning, Woodworking, Yacht Broker **OnCall:** Sail Loft, Canvas Work, Divers, Inflatable Repairs, Life Raft Service, Upholstery, Yacht Interiors, Metal Fabrication **Under 1 mi:** Launching Ramp. **Member:** ABYC - 3 Certified Tech(s) **Yard Rates:** $60-100, Haul & Launch $8-10 *(blocking incl.)*, Power Wash Incl. **Storage:** On-Land $25-35/day

Restaurants and Accommodations

OnSite: Restaurant *(Bo Brooks 558-0202, L $6-14, D $12-30, kids' $8)*, *(Sushi San & Thai Jaidee 534-8888, L $7-15, D $9-15)*, Lite Fare *(Bagel Works Canton 563-0550)*, *(Park Avenue B, L Mon-Fri 6am-4pm, Sat-Sun 7am-4pm)* **OnCall:** Pizzeria *(Papa Johns 732-7722)* **Near:** Restaurant *(Buddy's Elliott Street Bar & Grill 522-0222)*, Lite Fare *(Bay Cafe L $7-21, D $7-21)*, Inn/B&B *(Inn at 2920 342-4450, $155-225)* **Under 1 mi:** Restaurant *(Outback 522-7757, 1 mi.)*, Seafood Shack *(Captain James Landing 327-8600)*, Fast Food, Pizzeria *(Pizza Magoo 534-9555)*, Motel *(Best Western 633-9500, $100-130)*, Hotel *(Hendersons Wharf 522-7777, $120-300)*

Recreation and Entertainment

OnSite: Heated Pool, Spa, Picnic Area, Fitness Center *(Canton)*, Jogging Paths, Boat Rentals, Video Rental *(Blockbuster)*, Video Arcade **OnCall:** Fishing Charter *(Capt. Chuck 327-7923)*, Sightseeing *(Ft. McHenry 962-4290 $5)* **1-3 mi:** Movie Theater *(Fells Pt 276-7837)*, Museum *(Flag House 837-1793, American Visionary Art 244-1900, Port Discovery 727-8120)*, Cultural Attract *(Performing Arts 625-4230)*, Galleries *(Walter's)*, Special Events *(Ches. Challenge, Street Fest)*

Provisioning and General Services

OnSite: Delicatessen *(Taste of Home 342-4943)*, Wine/Beer, Bank/ATM, Dry Cleaners *(Anna Plaza)* **Near:** Supermarket *(Safeway 675-3704)*, Gourmet Shop *(Rosina 675-9300)*, Health Food *(Touch the Earth 522-1500)*, Catholic Church, Library *(396-8548)*, Laundry *(O'Donnell Square 327-0544)*, Pharmacy *(Safeway)*, Hardware Store *(Kurek's 732-3397)* **Under 1 mi:** Liquor Store *(DAP 675-2100)*, Fishmonger *(Chris's Seafood 675-0117)*, Lobster Pound, Beauty Salon, Bookstore *(Book Market 327-6717)*

Transportation

OnCall: Water Taxi *(382-1014 or 563-3901 whistle stop $8/day)*, Rental Car *(Enterprise 276-4850)*, Taxi *(Baltimore 685-1212)*, Airport Limo
Under 1 mi: Local Bus, InterCity Bus **3+ mi:** Rail *(Amtrak 727-3210, 4 mi.)*
Airport: Baltimore-Washington Int'l. *(8 mi.)*

Medical Services

911 Service **OnSite:** Dentist *(Canton Dental 675-3300)*, Chiropractor *(Lighthouse Point)* **OnCall:** Ambulance **Near:** Doctor *(Friends Medical 534-1203)* **Hospital:** Johns Hopkins 955-5600 *(3 mi.)*

Setting -- The first marina after entering the northwest Ft. McHenry channel, BMC's network of 500 high-end docks - with aqua and black pilings - sits at the center of historic Canton. A cream-colored "dockhouse" barge is flanked by 4 of the 7 fuel pumps. Along the outer dock are umbrellaed picnic tables with views of the Port of Baltimore shipping traffic. Inland Lighthouse Point, a 16-acre waterfront development, now encloses the marina with an array of services and amenities: a large pool, fitness center, and a plethora of eateries & shops. Nearby Fort McHenry and more distant inner harbor are accessible via water taxis.

Marina Notes -- *$2 wkdys, $2.50 Fri-Sun, Hols - includes pool privileges for one person per 10 feet of LOA (Mon-Wed 11am-8pm, Fri-Sat 10am-8pm) and the very nicely appointed Health Club. Built in 1996. Full service boatyard. 3-phase $60. Big, green mesh dock carts. 5-story covered "boatel." Inviting, comfortable bathhouse has multicolored tile floors & walls, sinks set in tiled vanities, plugs for hair dryers, showers with private dressing rooms & benches.

Notable -- A gorgeous 40 x 80 ft. ideally angled pool, plus kids' pool and heated spa, are surrounded by a large patio populated with cushioned chaises and tables & chairs - overlooking the docks and river beyond. The adjacent pale yellow Cabana Club with deep blue roof houses the bathhouse, laundry, game room and sno-cone kiosk. Right in the center - between the two main piers is Bo Brook's Crab House with views right down the fairway (Sun-Thu 11:30am-11:30pm, Sat & Sun 'til 1am). Behind Bo Brooks is the on-site mini-mall. The Black-eyed Susan Paddle Wheeler makes her home here. BMC is considerably east of the tourist area, but Fells Point is 0.75 miles away and is the closest marina to Ft. McHenry. A large new supermarket is across the street.

Navigational Information
Lat: 39°16.847' **Long:** 076°34.929' **Tide:** 2 ft. **Current:** n/a **Chart:** 12272
Rep. Depths (*MLW*): Entry 18 ft. **Fuel Dock** 18 ft. **Max Slip/Moor** 18 ft./-
Access: Brewerton Cannel to Ft. McHenry Channel to Northwest Channel

Marina Facilities *(In Season/Off Season)*
Fuel: No
Slips: 547 Total, 50 Transient **Max LOA:** 110 ft. **Max Beam:** n/a
Rate *(per ft.)*: **Day** $1.75 **Week** $6.50 **Month** Inq.
Power: 30 amp $5, **50 amp** $8, **100 amp** n/a, **200 amp** n/a
Cable TV: Yes, $5/night **Dockside Phone:** Yes Verizon
Dock Type: Floating, Long Fingers, Alongside, Wood
Moorings: 0 Total, 0 Transient **Launch:** n/a, Dinghy Dock
Rate: Day n/a **Week** n/a **Month** n/a
Heads: 17 Toilet(s), 12 Shower(s)
Laundry: 4 Washer(s), 4 Dryer(s), Book Exchange **Pay Phones:** Yes
Pump-Out: Full Service, 1 Central, 1 Port **Fee:** $5 **Closed Heads:** Yes

Marina Operations
Owner/Manager: Jacob Pinkham **Dockmaster:** Same
In-Season: Year-Round, 8am-6pm **Off-Season:** n/a
After-Hours Arrival: Call security on Ch. 16
Reservations: Preferred **Credit Cards:** Visa/MC, Amex
Discounts: Boat/US; Marina Life **Dockage:** $1.25 **Fuel:** n/a **Repair:** n/a
Pets: Welcome, Dog Walk Area **Handicap Access:** Yes, Heads, Docks

Anchorage Marina

2501 Boston Street; Baltimore, MD 21224

Tel: (410) 522-7200 **VHF: Monitor** 16, 9 **Talk** 68
Fax: (410) 675-1352 **Alternate Tel:** n/a
Email: office@anchoragemarina.com **Web:** www.anchoragemarina.com
Nearest Town: Baltimore/Canton **Tourist Info:** (410) 276-3212

Marina Services and Boat Supplies
Services - Docking Assistance, Concierge, Boaters' Lounge, Security *(Security Guards)*, Dock Carts **Communication -** Mail & Package Hold, Phone Messages, Fax in/out *($1)*, Data Ports *(Wi-Fi)*, FedEx, DHL, UPS, Express Mail *(Sat Del)* **Supplies - OnSite:** Ice *(Block, Cube)* **Near:** Bait/Tackle **Under 1 mi:** West Marine *(563-8905)* **1-3 mi:** Propane *(U-Haul 327-7100)*, CNG

Boatyard Services
OnSite: Canvas Work, Upholstery, Yacht Broker **OnCall:** Electrical Repairs, Electronics Repairs, Hull Repairs, Rigger, Bottom Cleaning, Brightwork, Air Conditioning, Refrigeration, Divers, Compound, Wash & Wax, Interior Cleaning, Propeller Repairs, Woodworking **Near:** Travelift, Forklift, Launching Ramp, Engine mechanic *(gas, diesel)*. **Nearest Yard:** Tidewater (410) 625-4992

Restaurants and Accommodations
Near: Restaurant *(Kiss Café 327-9889, L $5-12, currently L only)*, *(Ray Lewis Full Moon BBQ 327-5200, L $12-20, D $12-20)*, *(Outback 522-7757)*, *(Austin Grill 534-0606, L $10-20, D $10-20)*, *(Atlantic 675-4565)*, Seafood Shack *(Captain James Landing 327-8600, L $4-39, D $8-45)*, *(Chris's Seafood 675-0117)*, Fast Food *(Subway at Safeway)* **Under 1 mi:** Inn/B&B *(Hendersons Wharf Inn 522-7777, $120-300)*, *(Ann Street 342-5883)*, *(Inn at 2920 342-4450, $155-225)*

Recreation and Entertainment
OnSite: Pool, Picnic Area, Grills, Boat Rentals, Video Arcade *(and a pool table)* **Near:** Fitness Center *(Curves 534-8500)*, Jogging Paths, Video Rental *(Blockbuster 534-0415)*, Special Events **Under 1 mi:** Fishing Charter, Park, Sightseeing *(Tourmobile Sightseeing 732-7328)* **1-3 mi:** Golf Course *(Clifton Park 243-5326)*, Bowling, Movie Theater *(Fells Point Theater 276-7837)*, Museum *(Civil War 385-5188, Flag House 837-1793, National Aquarium 576-3800)*, Cultural Attract *(Performing Arts Center 625-4230)*, Galleries **3+ mi:** Tennis Courts *(Bolton 728-1634, 4 mi.)*

Provisioning and General Services
Near: Supermarket *(Safeway 675-3704)*, Delicatessen *(Taste of Home 342-4943)*, Health Food *(Touch the Earth 522-1500)*, Wine/Beer *(Ches. Wine 522-4556)*, Liquor Store *(DAP 675-2100)*, Fishmonger *(Chris's Seafood 675-0117)*, Bank/ATM, Catholic Church, Beauty Salon *(Calabrese 342-5577)*, Barber Shop, Dry Cleaners *(Express 675-0919)*, Bookstore *(Book Market 327-6717)*, Pharmacy *(Safeway 675-3802)* **Under 1 mi:** Protestant Church, Library *(396-8548)*, Laundry *(O'Donnell 327-0544)*, Hardware Store *(Kurek's 732-3397)* **1-3 mi:** Farmers' Market *(Sun 8am-noon, 752-8632)*, Department Store *(Wal-Mart 625-1971)*, Buying Club *(Sam's 837-1142)*

Transportation
OnCall: Water Taxi *(563-3901 $8/4)*, Rental Car *(Enterprise 276-4850, Hertz 837-8336)*, Taxi *(732-1600)*, Airport Limo *(1st Class 276-6511)* **Near:** Local Bus **3+ mi:** Rail *(Amtrak 727-3210, 3 mi.)* **Airport:** BWI *(8 mi.)*

Medical Services
911 Service **OnCall:** Ambulance **Near:** Dentist *(Collier 522-9680)*, Chiropractor *(Lighthouse Point 534-5900)* **Under 1 mi:** Doctor *(Friends 534-1203)*, Veterinarian *(Doc Side Vet 522-0055)* **1-3 mi:** Holistic Services *(Albertos Spa 342-0710)* **Hospital:** Johns Hopkins 955-5000 *(3 mi.)*

Setting -- Anchorage's gray clapboard dockhouse and three-story facilities' building are adorned by trademark bright blue canvas pyramids, awnings and terrace windbreaks. On the breakwater are the inviting floating pool, a small sundeck and a very nice picnic area with grill - all with great views of the passing traffic. A canvas awning protects the entrance to the locked main pier and the brick Harborwalk Promenade, which continues around to the Inner Harbor.

Marina Notes -- *Boat US rate $1.25/ft. DCM. On the 3rd floor is a sun deck with spectacular views of the docks and the outer harbor; it's a great place to watch the shipping lanes. On the 1st floor, a large boaters' lounge overlooks the docks. It has a comfortable seating area with large-screen television and VCR, vending machines, video games, a pool table, menu book, active bulletin board and, just outside, picnic tables. The marina is wired for Wi-Fi. Each quite nice all-tile bathhouse has 4 fiberglass shower stalls with glass doors and little dressing rooms; a vanity with three drop-in sinks, a thoughtful shelf, plugs for hair dryers and big mirrors, including makeup mirrors. A second less inviting set of heads is by the pool. Excellent place to leave the boat.

Notable -- This is a very functional marina; designed as much for the fifty live-aboard boats that are here permanently as it is for the seasonal slip owners and the transients - which makes for a very interesting mix and great laundry room conversations. Across the way is The Can Company, a factory converted to a mall, that hosts an array of shops & eateries. Historic Canton is just outside the door and Fells Point is 0.5/mi. away - both offer more shops and eating establishments. Water taxi to downtown Baltimore, Harbor Place and out to Fort McHenry from here.

PHOTOS ON CD-ROM: 10

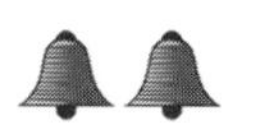

Henderson's Wharf Marina & Inn

1001 Fell Street; Baltimore, MD 21231

Tel: (410) 732-1049 **VHF: Monitor** 9 **Talk** 72
Fax: (410) 276-1075 **Alternate Tel:** (410) 522-7777
Email: john@hendersonswharf.com **Web:** www.hendersonswharf.com
Nearest Town: Baltimore/Fells Point **Tourist Info:** (410) 276-3212

Navigational Information

Lat: 39°16.778' **Long:** 076°35.351' **Tide:** 3 ft. **Current:** 3 kt. **Chart:** 12272
Rep. Depths (*MLW*): Entry 40 ft. **Fuel Dock** n/a **Max Slip/Moor** 20 ft./-
Access: Brewerton Cannel to Ft. McHenry Channel to Northwest Channel

Marina Facilities *(In Season/Off Season)*

Fuel: No
Slips: 255 Total, 30 Transient **Max LOA:** 55 ft. **Max Beam:** 16 ft.
Rate *(per ft.)*: **Day** $1.50/$1.25 **Week** $6 **Month** $12
Power: 30 amp $5, **50 amp** $8, **100 amp** n/a, **200 amp** n/a
Cable TV: Yes **Dockside Phone:** Yes
Dock Type: Floating, Short Fingers, Pilings, Alongside, Wood
Moorings: 0 Total, 0 Transient **Launch:** n/a
Rate: Day n/a **Week** n/a **Month** n/a
Heads: 4 Toilet(s), 4 Shower(s) *(with dressing rooms)*
Laundry: 1 Washer(s), 1 Dryer(s), Book Exchange **Pay Phones:** Yes, 1
Pump-Out: OnCall, 1 Central **Fee:** $5 **Closed Heads:** Yes

Marina Operations

Owner/Manager: John Guildener **Dockmaster:** Paul DeLuca
In-Season: Apr-Oct, 8am-6pm **Off-Season:** Nov-Mar, 8am-4pm
After-Hours Arrival: Check in at Henderson's Wharf Inn
Reservations: Yes, Required **Credit Cards:** Visa/MC, Dscvr, Amex
Discounts: Groups of 10 **Dockage:** n/a **Fuel:** n/a **Repair:** n/a
Pets: No **Handicap Access:** Yes, Docks

Marina Services and Boat Supplies

Services - Docking Assistance, Security *(24 hrs., Staff lives OnSite)*, Dock Carts **Communication -** Fax in/out *($1)*, Data Ports *(Office)* **Supplies - OnSite:** Ice *(Block, Cube)* **Under 1 mi:** Ships' Store, West Marine *(563-8905)*, Bait/Tackle *(S&S 563-3243)* **1-3 mi:** Propane *(U-Haul 327-7100)*

Boatyard Services

OnCall: Divers *(Gary Sadowski 340-2466)*, Propeller Repairs
Near: Launching Ramp *(City Park - Boston St.)* **Under 1 mi:** Travelift, Engine Mechanic *(gas, diesel)*, Electrical Repairs, Electronics Repairs, Hull Repairs, Rigger, Sail Loft, Canvas Work, Bottom Cleaning, Air Conditioning,Refrigeration, Compound, Wash & Wax, Woodworking, Inflatable Repairs, Painting, Awlgrip **Nearest Yard:** Tidewater Marine (410) 625-4992

Restaurants and Accommodations

OnSite: Inn/B&B *(Hendersons Wharf Inn 522-7777, $120-160)*, Condo/Cottage *(Residence at Henderson's Wharf 522-7900, $1000/month and up)* **OnCall:** Pizzeria *(Bop's 563-1600)* **Near:** Restaurant *(Capt. James 327-8600, B $4-12, L $6-17, D $6-26)*, *(Kawasaki Café 327-9400)*, *(Jimmy's 327-3273, B $4, L $5, D $10)*, *(The Waters Edge 327-4416)*, *(Deadend 732-3602, L $8-10, D $15-20)*, Seafood Shack *(Broadway Market)*, *(Bertha's Dining Room 327-5795, D $6-28)*, Lite Fare *(Bonaparte Bread & Café 342-4000)*, *(Daily Grind 558-0399, B $2-5, L $10-15)* **Under 1 mi:** Fast Food *(Burger King)*, Motel *(Rodeway 633-4611)*

Recreation and Entertainment

OnSite: Picnic Area, Fishing Charter *(Capt. Don's)* **Near:** Jogging Paths, Park, Special Events *(Fells Pt Festival first weekend Oct)* **Under 1 mi:** Video Rental *(Blockbuster 534-0415)*, Museum *(Civil War 385-5188, Flag House 837-1793, Fells Point Maritime)*, Sightseeing *(Harbor Palace, Fells Point walking tour)* **1-3 mi:** Tennis Courts *(Bolton Club 728-1634)*, Golf Course *(Clifton Park 243-5326)*, Movie Theater *(Fells Point Theater 276-7837)*, Cultural Attract *(Performing Arts Center 625-4230)*

Provisioning and General Services

OnSite: Dry Cleaners **Near:** Gourmet Shop, Delicatessen *(Broadway Deli 522-2262)*, Liquor Store *(House of Spirits 342-7494)*, Bakery, Green Grocer, Fishmonger, Bank/ATM, Catholic Church, Laundry *(Fleet St 276-9050)*, Retail Shops **Under 1 mi:** Convenience Store, Supermarket *(Safeway 675-3704, Mars 687-9400)*, Health Food *(Whole Foods 539-7487)*, Post Office, Protestant Church, Library *(Fells Point 396-0992)*, Bookstore *(Book Market 327-6717)*, Pharmacy *(Rite Aid 780-7020)*, Newsstand, Hardware Store *(Lombard 276-1294)*, Florist, Copies Etc. **1-3 mi:** Farmers' Market *(Sun 8am-nNon, 752-8632)*, Beauty Salon, Barber Shop, Clothing Store, Department Store *(Wal-Mart 625-1971)*, Buying Club *(Sam's 837-1142)*

Transportation

OnCall: Water Taxi *($8/4 day)*, Rental Car *(Enterprise 276-4850/ Hertz)*, Taxi *(Baltimore 685-1212)* **Near:** Local Bus, Airport Limo *(Airporter 336-2828)* **3+ mi:** Rail *(Amtrak 727-3210, 3 mi.)* **Airport:** BWI *(7 mi.)*

Medical Services

911 Service **OnCall:** Ambulance **Near:** Doctor *(MD Physicians 342-0333)*, Chiropractor *(Back Pain 675-3332)* **Under 1 mi:** Dentist *(Boston St. 276-4455)*, Veterinarian *(Doc Side 522-0055)* **1-3 mi:** Holistic Services *(Albertos Spa 342-0710)* **Hospital:** Johns Hopkins 955-5000 *(3 mi.)*

Setting -- A red & white shed with lighthouse atop marks the most eastern of the docks. Rising above the slips is an historic 7-story tobacco warehouse - now the elegant, exquisitely restored Henderson's Wharf - Inn, Residences and Marina. The ground-floor Inn features the original arched bays, annotated with turquoise shutters. Picnic tables populate an adjacent dock; a gravel parking lot juts into the harbor - piers hosting 250 full-service slips radiate from this hub.

Marina Notes -- Closed Sat & Sun Nov-Mar. No Pets. 10% disc. for 10 or more boats. A long, angled face dock serves as a wave fence that shelters the boats. Floating vinyl-edged docks with half-length finger piers, good pedestals with cable TV. Transients tend to be on the outer docks (guests of the Inn may request slips adjacent to their room). Dockmaster permits boaters to plug in their laptops for very short time periods. Pleasant, linoleum-floored bathouse is in a large trailer in the parking lot (fiberglass shower stalls with dressing rooms divided by curtains, 2 toilets & 2 sinks). A small laundry room and the dockmaster's office are here too. NOTE: Owner Robert Gunn plans to build 30 luxury townhouses on the parking lot which will impact the marina considerably - so call!

Notable -- The 1st floor of the Inn features 38 impeccably appointed rooms with old-world ambiance, an inviting lobby, and gorgeous interior garden with teak furnishings. Above, The Residences' 15 stylish longer-stay apartments & 115 rental units have spectacular views. The wide boardwalk that skirts the Inn's two waterside faces connects with a brick promenade that will soon edge the entire Inner Harbor. A short block away, trendy, historic Fells Point promises restaurants, nightlife and shops - the Maritime Museum explores much of Baltimore's nautical history. Across the river, an old P&G plant is now upscale offices.

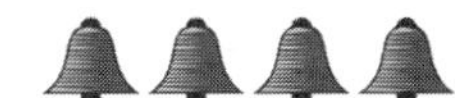

Navigational Information
Lat: 39°16.581' **Long:** 076°36.263' **Tide:** 3 ft. **Current:** 3 kt. **Chart:** 12272
Rep. Depths (*MLW*): Entry 40 ft. **Fuel Dock** n/a **Max Slip/Moor** 40 ft./-
Access: Brewerton Cannel to Ft. McHenry Channel to Northwest Channel

Marina Facilities *(In Season/Off Season)*
Fuel: No
Slips: 278 Total, 10 Transient **Max LOA:** 250 ft. **Max Beam:** n/a
Rate *(per ft.)*: **Day** $1.75* **Week** $9.00 **Month** $20
Power: 30 amp $6, **50 amp** $9, **100 amp** $17, **200 amp** $34
Cable TV: No **Dockside Phone:** No
Dock Type: Floating, Long Fingers
Moorings: 0 Total, 0 Transient **Launch:** n/a
Rate: Day n/a **Week** n/a **Month** n/a
Heads: 14 Toilet(s), 14 Shower(s)
Laundry: 2 Washer(s), 2 Dryer(s), Book Exchange **Pay Phones:** Yes, 1
Pump-Out: OnSite **Fee:** $5 **Closed Heads:** Yes

Marina Operations
Owner/Manager: Jason Rangas **Dockmaster:** Charles Dibley
In-Season: Year-Round, 24 hrs. **Off-Season:** n/a
After-Hours Arrival: Call in Advance
Reservations: Yes **Credit Cards:** Visa/MC, Amex
Discounts: None
Pets: Welcome, Dog Walk Area **Handicap Access:** No

Harborview Marina & Yacht Club

500 Harbor View Drive; Baltimore, MD 21230

Tel: (410) 752-1122 **VHF: Monitor** 16 **Talk** 8
Fax: (410) 576-8509 **Alternate Tel:** n/a
Email: dockmasterharborview@fscv.net **Web:** www.coastal-properties.com
Nearest Town: Baltimore **Tourist Info:** (410) 837-7100

Marina Services and Boat Supplies
Services - Docking Assistance, Concierge, Boaters' Lounge, Security, Dock Carts, Megayacht Facilities, 3 Phase **Communication -** Mail & Package Hold, Phone Messages, Fax in/out, Data Ports *(Office)*, FedEx, DHL, UPS, Express Mail *(Sat Del)* **Supplies - OnSite:** Ice *(Block, Cube)* **Near:** Marine Discount Store *(Tidewater)* **1-3 mi:** West Marine *(563-8905)*, Bait/Tackle *(S&S 563-3243)*, Propane *(728-6624)*, CNG

Boatyard Services
OnCall: Electrical Repairs, Electronics Repairs, Hull Repairs, Rigger, Canvas Work, Bottom Cleaning, Brightwork, Refrigeration, Divers
Near: Travelift, Air Conditioning, Compound, Wash & Wax, Interior Cleaning, Propeller Repairs, Woodworking, Inflatable Repairs, Life Raft Service, Yacht Broker. **Nearest Yard:** Tidewater Marina (410) 625-4992

Restaurants and Accommodations
OnSite: Restaurant *(Catalina D $18-24, indoor & out, 4-10pm, 7 days, Sun brunch 11am-3pm $16)*, Lite Fare *(Barista Espresso Cafe B $3-6, L $6-9, D $6-9, Mon-Fri 6:30am-8pm, Sat-Sun 8am-8pm)*, Condo/Cottage *(Call 528-1122 for res.)* **Near:** Restaurant *(Little Havana 837-9903, outdoor deck)*, Pizzeria *(Brunos 727-3663)* **Under 1 mi:** Seafood Shack *(Crazy Lil's 347-9793)*, Hotel *(Harbor Court 234-0550, $270-340)*, Inn/B&B *(Scarborough Fair 837-0010)* **1-3 mi:** Restaurant *(Kobe Teppan & Sushi 468-4468, L $6-10, D $10-29)*, Hotel *(Hyatt Regency 528-1234, $245-275)*

Recreation and Entertainment
OnSite: Pool *(2 - outside on the floating barge; inside at health club)*, Fitness Center *(Harborview Health 752-3488)* **Near:** Video Rental *(Blockbuster 244-0376)*, Park *(Federal Hill Park & promenade)*, Museum *(Museum of Industry 727-4808)*, Sightseeing *(Ride The Ducks 962-8236)* **Under 1 mi:** Movie Theater *(IMAX 685-5225)* **1-3 mi:** Tennis Courts *(Bolton Tennis728-1634)*, Cultural Attract *(Performing Arts 625-4230)* **3+ mi:** Golf Course *(Carroll Park 685-8344, 4 mi.)*, Bowling *(Charm City 355-2196, 4 mi.)*

Provisioning and General Services
OnSite: Convenience Store **OnCall:** Wine/Beer *(Charles St. 685-6929)*, Liquor Store *(Geldmans 539-7000)*, Bakery **Near:** Supermarket *(Metro Food 727-1246)*, Health Food *(Healthware Solutions 752-6779)*, Fishmonger, Bank/ATM, Post Office, Catholic Church, Protestant Church, Library *(396-1096)*, Beauty Salon, Dry Cleaners *(American 727-7389)*, Laundry *(Opes 332-4002)*, Bookstore *(Book Escape 576-8885)*, Florist, Copies Etc. *(Work Printing 244-0968)* **Under 1 mi:** Delicatessen *(NY Deli 234-0950)*, Pharmacy *(James Pharmacy 752-5810)*, Hardware Store *(Singer's 685-3720)* **1-3 mi:** Farmers' Market *(W Preston St. Wed 10am-2pm, 767-6778)*, Department Store *(Wal-Mart 625-1971)*, Buying Club *(Sam's 837-1142)*

Transportation
OnCall: Water Taxi *($8/4)*, Rental Car *(Enterprise 547-1855/ Budget 3 mi.)*, Taxi *(685-1212)*, Airport Limo *(Airporter 336-2828)* **Under 1 mi:** Bikes *(Light St. 685-2234)* **3+ mi:** Rail *(Amtrak 727-3210, 4 mi.)* **Airport:** BWI *(7 mi.)*

Medical Services
911 Service **OnSite:** Holistic Services *(Harborview Health 752-3488 massage, acupuncture)* **Near:** Dentist *(Fort Ave. 244-8994)* **Under 1 mi:** Doctor *(Inner Harbor 234-0444)*, Chiropractor *(Southside 332-0044)*, Veterinarian *(Light St. 547-8385)* **Hospital:** Johns Hopkins 955-5000 *(3 mi.)*

Setting -- In the shadow of the Domino Sugar sign, on the outskirts of the Inner Harbor, upscale Harborview Marina is in a high-end multimillion dollar waterfront complex that includes condos, townhouses, 2 restaurants and a health club. It's a retreat from the city, but a water-taxi ride to the attractions. Approaching, multicolored flags flutter along the outermost docks next to a floating barge that hosts a swimming pool and second floor sundeck. A wide concrete wharf divides the basin and ends at the three-story, stucco main facilities building. New set of docks in '06 on the west side of the condo building.

Marina Notes -- *$2.25/ft. weekends & holidays. Staffed 24/7. DCM. Vintage floating docks & pedestals in good condition; T-heads accommodate larger vessels. 11 docks ("A"-"L") radiate from the central pier with generous fairways for big yachts. Cable not available. Nautically-inspired turquoise canvas awnings, wind screens & trash containers. Golf cart servce to slips. Boaters gather next to marina office - tables & chairs, coffee, TV & book exchange.A djacent bathhouse has brightly-colored tile, wallpaper, fresh flowers; a more modest bathhouse is on the floating barge; the best is at the Health Club.

Notable -- The main building hosts two restaurants: light fare Barista Espresso Café and serious dining Catalina; on the 2nd floor, the Princess Ballroom accommodates 250 with spectacular views of the docks. Landside it faces Harbor Island's brick streeets and "neo old-world village" atmosphere. Included is use of the fabulous Health Club in the sky-scraper condominium - lap & wading pools, Jacuzzi, sauna, steam room, fitness center, Pilates, yoga, aqua aerobics plus towels, hair dryers, etc. Massage, trainers & acupuncture by appointment. Mon-Thu 5:45am-8:45pm, Fri to 7:45pm, Sat 7:15am-5:45pm, Sun 8:15am-5:45pm.

PHOTOS ON CD-ROM: 16

Inner Harbor East Marina

801 Lancaster Street; Baltimore, MD 21202

Tel: (410) 625-1700 **VHF: Monitor** 16 **Talk** 68
Fax: (410) 625-1724 **Alternate Tel:** (410) 625-1700
Email: dkmastr@aol.com **Web:** www.innerharboreastmarina.com
Nearest Town: Baltimore **Tourist Info:** (410) 837-7100

Navigational Information

Lat: 39°16.910' **Long:** 076°36.159' **Tide:** 2 ft. **Current:** 1.5 kt. **Chart:** 12272
Rep. Depths (*MLW*): Entry 16 ft. **Fuel Dock** 8 ft. **Max Slip/Moor** 16 ft./-
Access: Brewerton Channel to Ft. McHenry Channel to Northwest Channel

Marina Facilities *(In Season/Off Season)*

Fuel: No
Slips: 185 Total, 80 Transient **Max LOA:** 180 ft. **Max Beam:** n/a
Rate *(per ft.)*: **Day** $1.85* **Week** n/a **Month** n/a
Power: 30 amp $5, **50 amp** $10, **100 amp** n/a, **200 amp** n/a
Cable TV: Yes, $5 /night **Dockside Phone:** No
Dock Type: Floating, Long Fingers, Wood
Moorings: 0 Total, 0 Transient **Launch:** n/a
Rate: Day n/a **Week** n/a **Month** n/a
Heads: 3 Toilet(s), 6 Shower(s) *(with dressing rooms)*
Laundry: 2 Washer(s), 2 Dryer(s), Book Exchange **Pay Phones:** Yes, 1
Pump-Out: OnSite, Full Service, 1 Central **Fee:** $5 **Closed Heads:** Yes

Marina Operations

Owner/Manager: Capt. William Flohr **Dockmaster:** Same
In-Season: Year-Round, 24 hrs. **Off-Season:** n/a
After-Hours Arrival: Call Ch. 68
Reservations: Yes, Preferred **Credit Cards:** Visa/MC, Dscvr, Amex
Discounts: *Nauticard **Dockage:** 10% **Fuel:** n/a **Repair:** n/a
Pets: Welcome, Dog Walk Area **Handicap Access:** Yes, Heads, Docks

Marina Services and Boat Supplies

Services - Docking Assistance, Concierge, Security *(24 hrs., night guard 4pm-8am)*, Dock Carts, Megayacht Facilities **Communication -** Mail & Package Hold, Phone Messages, Fax in/out *(Free)*, Data Ports *(Lobby)*, FedEx, DHL, UPS, Express Mail *(Sat Del)* **Supplies - OnSite:** Ice *(Cube)* **Under 1 mi:** Bait/Tackle *(S&S 563-3243)*, CNG **1-3 mi:** West Marine *(563-8905)*, Propane *(U-Haul 327-7100)*

Boatyard Services

OnCall: Compound, Wash & Wax, Interior Cleaning, Propeller Repairs **Under 1 mi:** Travelift, Launching Ramp, Engine mechanic *(gas)*, Electrical Repairs, Electronics Repairs, Hull Repairs, Rigger, Sail Loft, Inflatable Repairs, Painting. **Nearest Yard:** Tidewater (410) 625-4992

Restaurants and Accommodations

OnSite: Restaurant *(Victors Café 244-1722, B $6-12, L $8-15, D $12-25, brunch Sat-Sun 11am-2pm, kids' menu $6)* **Near:** Restaurant *(Chef Cindy Wolf's Charleston 332-7373, L $8-35, D $8-35, 7-course w/wine $115)*, *(Fleming's Steakhouse 332-0432, D $26-36)*, *(Della Notte Ristorante 837-5500, L $10-17, D $16-36)*, *(McCormick & Schmick's 234-1300, L $6-21, D $7-30)*, *(Roy's - Hawaiian Fusion 659-0099, Prix Fixe $33)*, *(Marriott's Grille 700 385-3000)*, Lite Fare *(Rigano's Bakery & Deli 385-3000, B, L, D)*, Pizzeria *(Marinellis 558-3737)*, Hotel *(Marriott Waterfront 385-3000, $250-280)*, *(Mariott Courtyard 321-2211)*, *(Hyatt Regency 528-1234, $245-275)*

Recreation and Entertainment

Near: Picnic Area, Park, Museum *(Baltimore Civil War 385-5188 $4/3 & Baltimore Maritime 732-0278 $7/4 - 3 ships & a lighthouse at piers 3 & 5)*, Cultural Attract *(National Aquarium 576-3869 $19.50/13.50)*, Sightseeing *(Baltimore!)*, Special Events **Under 1 mi:** Fitness Center *(Golds Gym 576-7771)*, Video Rental *(Blockbuster 534-0415)* **1-3 mi:** Tennis Courts *(Bolton Tennis 728-1634)*, Golf Course *(Clifton Park 243-5326)*, Bowling *(Parkville 444-6100)*, Movie Theater *(Fells Point 276-7837)*

Provisioning and General Services

OnSite: Newsstand **Near:** Convenience Store, Delicatessen *(Waterfront Deli 332-9969)*, Health Food *(Whole Foods 539-7487)*, Wine/Beer *(Bin 604 576-0444)*, Liquor Store *(Bristol 732-8394)*, Bakery, Fishmonger, Bank/ATM, Post Office, Catholic Church, Pharmacy *(Drug Counter 752-7206)*, Hardware Store *(Value Express 327-7041)* **Under 1 mi:** Supermarket *(Safeway 675-3704, Mars 687-9400)*, Protestant Church, Library *(Fells Point 396-0992)*, Beauty Salon *(Heads Up 284-0711)*, Barber Shop, Dry Cleaners *(Dry Clean Express 675-0919)*, Laundry *(O'Donnell 327-0544)*, Bookstore *(Barnes & Noble 385-1709)*, Florist, Clothing Store, Copies Etc. *(ABC 779-4550)* **1-3 mi:** Farmers' Market *(Saratoga & Gay St, Sun 8am-noon, 752-8632)*, Department Store *(Wal-Mart 625-1971)*, Buying Club *(Sam's 837-1142)*

Transportation

OnSite: Water Taxi *($8/day)* **OnCall:** Rental Car *(Enterprise 276-4850, Hertz 837-8336)*, Taxi *(Baltimore 685-1212)*, Airport Limo *(1st Class 276-6511)* **3+ mi:** Rail *(Amtrak 727-3210, 3 mi.)* **Airport:** BWI *(7 mi.)*

Medical Services

911 Service **Under 1 mi:** Doctor *(MD Physicians 342-0333)*, Dentist *(Boston St. 276-4455)*, Chiropractor *(Back Pain 675-3332)*, Veterinarian *(Doc Side 522-0055)* **Hospital:** Johns Hopkins 955-5000 *(3 mi.)*

Setting -- Conveniently situated in the northeast corner of Inner Harbor, most of the 200 high-end docks are sheltered within a long, curved breakwater that serves as alongside dockage for larger yachts. Picnic tables line the main pier that leads from the docks to the striking two-story, three-quarter round Victor's Café; a huge waterside deck is crowded with dozens of umbrella-topped tables. Portholes punctuate the attached single-story gray amenties building.

Marina Notes -- *10% disc. to Power Squadrom & USCG Aux Members. No longer has fuel. Floating docks with beige vinyl edging, full finger piers and full pedestals. Quite nice, all tile bathhouse. The showers have private dressing rooms, brightly colored composite doors, vanity with mirror, and hair dryer plugs. Adjacent empty lot on the east side was named a Super Fund site; $100 million invested in cleaning it up and readying it for, possibly, a new hotel.

Notable -- Popular Victor's Café (Sun-Thu 11am-10pm, Fri & Sat 11am-11pm) serves sandwiches, pizza, entrees all day. The round, all-glass ground floor dining room spills out onto the deck; the second floor glass room sports a narrow dining terrace that curves around the building. There isn't a bad seat - the view of the entire Inner Harbor is simply spectacular. The marina is located in Little Italy with easy access to Fells Point and Harbor Place. The nicely planted, well-lit, engraved-brick Baltimore Waterfront Promenade runs right in front of the marina. It's dotted with benches and skirts the shoreline east to Canton Park and west around the edge of the Inner Harbor. The surrounding area has seen a tremendous amount of recent development. The new Marriott is finally complete as is the adjacent condo complex with another on the way. The on-site water taxi makes the whole basin immediately accessible.

Navigational Information
Lat: 39°16.901' **Long:** 076°36.504' **Tide:** 2 ft. **Current:** n/a **Chart:** 12272
Rep. Depths (*MLW*): Entry 16 ft. **Fuel Dock** 19 ft. **Max Slip/Moor** 30 ft./-
Access: Brewerton Channel to Ft. McHenry Channel to Northwest Channel

Marina Facilities *(In Season/Off Season)*
Fuel: *Crown* - Gasoline, Diesel, High-Speed Pumps
Slips: 158 Total, 90+ Transient **Max LOA:** 200 ft. **Max Beam:** n/a
Rate *(per ft.)*: **Day** $2.00* **Week** n/a **Month** $25
Power: 30 amp $13, **50 amp** $15, **100 amp** $40, **200 amp** n/a
Cable TV: Yes, Incl. **Dockside Phone:** No
Dock Type: Floating, Long Fingers, Concrete
Moorings: 0 Total, 0 Transient **Launch:** n/a
Rate: Day n/a **Week** n/a **Month** n/a
Heads: 4 Toilet(s), 6 Shower(s) *(with dressing rooms)*
Laundry: 2 Washer(s), 2 Dryer(s) **Pay Phones:** Yes, 1
Pump-Out: OnSite, Full Service **Fee:** $5 **Closed Heads:** Yes

Marina Operations
Owner/Manager: Ben Ayres **Dockmaster:** Same
In-Season: Jun-Oct, 9am-8pm** **Off-Season:** Nov-May, 10am-4pm
After-Hours Arrival: Call in advance
Reservations: Yes **Credit Cards:** Visa/MC, Dscvr, Amex
Discounts: Fuel **Dockage:** n/a **Fuel:** $.10 **Repair:** n/a
Pets: Welcome, Dog Walk Area **Handicap Access:** Yes, Heads, Docks

Inner Harbor Marine Center

400 Key Highway; Baltimore, MD 21230

Tel: (410) 837-5339 **VHF: Monitor** 16 **Talk** 69
Fax: (410) 539-0722 **Alternate Tel:** n/a
Email: (see marina notes) **Web:** baltimoreinnerharbormarinecenter.com
Nearest Town: Baltimore **Tourist Info:** (410) 837-7100

Marina Services and Boat Supplies
Services - Docking Assistance, Concierge, Boaters' Lounge, Security, Trash Pick-Up, Dock Carts, Megayacht Facilities **Communication -** Mail & Package Hold, Phone Messages, Fax in/out *(Free)*, Data Ports *(Wi-Fi)*, FedEx, DHL, UPS, Express Mail *(Sat Del)* **Supplies - OnSite:** Ice *(Block, Cube)*, Ships' Store **Near:** Propane **Under 1 mi:** CNG **1-3 mi:** West Marine *(563-8905)*, Bait/Tackle *(S&S 563-3243)*

Boatyard Services
OnCall: Bottom Cleaning, Brightwork, Refrigeration, Divers, Compound, Wash & Wax, Interior Cleaning, Propeller Repairs, Woodworking
Near: Travelift, Forklift, Engine mechanic *(gas, diesel)*, Electrical Repairs, Electronics Repairs, Hull Repairs, Rigger, Sail Loft, Canvas Work, Air Conditioning, Inflatable Repairs, Life Raft Service, Yacht Interiors, Metal Fabrication, Painting, Awlgrip. **Nearest Yard:** Tidewater (410) 625-4992

Restaurants and Accommodations
OnSite: Restaurant *(Rusty Scupper 234-1084, L $8-15, D $20-30, Sun brunch buffet)* **Near:** Restaurant *(Hamptons at Harbor Court 234-0550, D $30-40)*, *(Joy America Café 244-6500, D $19-29)*, *(Kiku Shushi 468-4468, L&D)*, *(Blue Agave 576-3938, D $11-22)*, Fast Food *(Subway)*, Pizzeria *(Ultimate Pizza 385-2131)*, Hotel *(Harbor Court 234-0550, $270-340)*, Inn/B&B *(Scarborough Fair 837-0010)* **Under 1 mi:** Hotel *(Hyatt 528-1234, $245-275)*, *(Reinassance 547-1200)*

Recreation and Entertainment
OnSite: Picnic Area, Grills, Jogging Paths, Roller Blade/Bike Paths
Near: Heated Pool *(Harbor Court 234-0550, Incl.)*, Spa, Playground, Fitness Center *(Harbor Court)*, Fishing Charter, Movie Theater *(IMAX 685-5225)*, Video Rental *(Movie Time 528-8888)*, Park *(Rash Field)*, Museum *(Maryland Science Ctr 539-7827 $16/12 & Davis Planetarium 685-5225 American Visionary Art 244-1900 $11/7; Museum of Industry 727-4808 $10/6)*, Cultural Attract *(Oriole Park at Camden Yards 685-9800 Tour $7/5)* **Under 1 mi:** Bowling *(Parkville 444-6100)*, Sightseeing *(Ride The Ducks 962-8236, Clipper City Schooner 539-6277 $20)* **1-3 mi:** Tennis Courts *(Bolton 728-1634)* **3+ mi:** Golf Course *(Carroll Park 685-8344, 4 mi.)*

Provisioning and General Services
Near: Convenience Store *(7-Eleven)*, Delicatessen *(NY Deli 234-0950)*, Health Food *(Natures Way 528-1837)*, Wine/Beer, Liquor Store *(Federal Hill 539-7757)*, Bakery, Bank/ATM, Post Office, Catholic Church, Library *(396-1096)*, Dry Cleaners *(American 727-7389)*, Laundry *(Opes 332-4002)*, Bookstore *(Book Escape 576-8885)*, Pharmacy *(James 752-5810)* **Under 1 mi:** Supermarket *(Safeway 675-3704)*, Gourmet Shop *(Cross St. Market)*, Fishmonger, Hardware Store *(Singer's 685-3720)* **1-3 mi:** Farmers' Market *(Wed 10am-2pm, 767-6778)*, Department Store *(Wal-Mart)*, Buying Club

Transportation
OnCall: Water Taxi *(563-3901, $8/day)*, Rental Car *(Enterprise 547-1855)*, Taxi *(685-1212)*, Airport Limo *(Airporter 336-2828)* **Near:** Bikes *(Light St. 685-2234)*, Local Bus **Under 1 mi:** Rail *(Amtrak)* **Airport:** BWI *(7 mi.)*

Medical Services
911 Service **Near:** Dentist *(Balciunas 659-0900)*, Chiropractor *(Southside 332-0044)* **Under 1 mi:** Doctor *(Inner Harbor 234-0444)*, Veterinarian *(Light St. 547-9394)* **Hospital:** Johns Hopkins 955-5000 *(3 mi.)*

Setting -- Head for the Rusty Scupper - three-stories of contemporary steel and concrete touched with red - on the port side as you approach the head of the Inner Harbor. The marina office and amenities occupy the first floor, with the 24/7 fuel dock right in front. Five sets of high-end floating docks, annotated with bright blue awnings, flow toward the harbor's head - the main piers connect to the treed, well-lit, brick South Shore Promenade. Adjacent to the Promenade is Rash Field, affording the slips lovely, verdant views in one direction and a striking cityscape in the other. Perfect.

Marina Notes -- *$2/ft. Mon-Thu, $2.50/ft. Fri-Sun **In-Season Hours: Wed-Sat 9am-8pm, Sun-Tue, 9am-6pm, closed Sun off-season). Founded in 1976 as a privately run, city-owned facility, in Feb '05 Marine Associates took the helm. Floating vinyl-edged cement docks. Complimentary access to Harbor Court Hotel's Fitness Center & Pool (1 person per 10 ft. of LOA). On-site parking discounted at $6/day for marina guests/visitors. Very nice, simple tile heads have showers with dressing rooms and sinks with vanities. Laundry room with large folding table. (email: lwolinski@innerharbormarinecenter.com)

Notable -- Rusty Scupper has three dining levels on the 2nd floor; on weekends the 3rd floor and outdoor deck are open - all with great views. Just east is the American Visionary Art Museum. A short stroll west along the promenade is the Maryland Science Museum, Harbor Place and many Inner Harbor attractions: museums, aquarium, tall ships, USS Constellation. Just a little further is Oriole Park. Alternatively, tie up at the city dinghy dock near the anchorage or take the water taxi (it stops at 35 attractions). Get a Harbor Pass at the Visitors' Center $46/30 - 3-day access to 4 attractions, water taxi, plus discounts.

City of Baltimore Docks

561 Light Street; Baltimore, MD 21202

Tel: (410) 396-3174 **VHF: Monitor** 68 **Talk** n/a
Fax: (410) 545-7973 **Alternate Tel:** n/a
Email: n/a **Web:** n/a
Nearest Town: Baltimore **Tourist Info:** (410) 837-7100

Navigational Information

Lat: 39°16.993' **Long:** 076°36.685' **Tide:** 2 **Current:** n/a **Chart:** 12272
Rep. Depths (*MLW*): Entry 12 ft. **Fuel Dock** n/a **Max Slip/Moor** 8 ft./-
Access: Brewerton Channel to Ft. McHenry Ch. to head of Northwest Ch.

Marina Facilities *(In Season/Off Season)*

Fuel: No
Slips: 125 Total, 25 Transient **Max LOA:** 300 ft. **Max Beam:** n/a
Rate *(per ft.)*: **Day** $1.00/$0.50* **Week** n/a **Month** n/a
Power: 30 amp $4, **50 amp** $4, **100 amp** n/a, **200 amp** n/a
Cable TV: Incl. **Dockside Phone:** No
Dock Type: Fixed, Pilings, Alongside, Concrete
Moorings: 0 Total, 0 Transient **Launch:** n/a, Dinghy Dock
Rate: Day n/a **Week** n/a **Month** n/a
Heads: 5 Toilet(s), 1 Shower(s)
Laundry: None **Pay Phones:** Yes
Pump-Out: No **Fee:** n/a **Closed Heads:** Yes

Marina Operations

Owner/Manager: Frances Knauff **Dockmaster:** Same
In-Season: May-Oct, 8:30am-7pm **Off-Season:** Nov-April, 8:30am-5pm
After-Hours Arrival: Call ahead
Reservations: No **Credit Cards:** Cash or Check
Discounts: None
Pets: Welcome, Dog Walk Area **Handicap Access:** Yes, Heads

Marina Services and Boat Supplies

Services - Docking Assistance, Security *(City Police patrol area)* **Communication -** FedEx, DHL, UPS, Express Mail **Supplies - Near:** Ice *(Cube)* **1-3 mi:** West Marine *(563-8905)*, Bait/Tackle *(S&S Bait & Tackle 563-3243)*, Propane *(Fountain Albert 728-6624)*

Boatyard Services

Nearest Yard: Baltimore Marine Center (410) 675-8888

Restaurants and Accommodations

Near: Restaurant *(Sealight Seafood)*, *(Phillips Harborplace 685-6600, L $10-20, D $10-50)*, *(Hamptons Restaurant 234-0550, D $31-41)*, *(Peacock Café 539-8400, Pier 5)*, *(Eurasian Harbor Bistro 230-9992, Pier 5)*, *(McCormick & Schmick's 234-1300, Pier 5)*, *(Rusty Scupper 234-1084, L $8-15, D $8-30)*, *(City Lights 244-8811, D $10-26, kids $5)*, *(Paolo's 539-7060, D $9-22)*, *(Port Welcome 727-3113)*, *(Capital City Brewing L $7-13, D $8-23, kids $4)*, Pizzeria *(Mangia Italian Grill 685-5080)*, Hotel *(Harbor Court 234-0550, $270-340)*, *(Renaissance 547-1200, $200-300)*, *(Pier 5 539-2000)*

Recreation and Entertainment

OnSite: Museum *(Maryland Science Ctr 545-5927 $16/12, combo w/ IMAX & Titanic add $4/3; Maritime Museum 396-3453 $7/4; Port Discovery 727-8120 - top kids' musuem $11/8.50)*, Sightseeing *(Boat tours: Miss Caroline, Prince Charming, Ride The Ducks 962-8236, the schooners Pride of Baltimore 539-1151 & Clipper City 837-6277)* **OnCall:** Fishing Charter *(Capt. Don's 342-2004)* **Near:** Picnic Area, Fitness Center *(Federal Hill 752-3004, Golds)*, Jogging Paths, Boat Rentals, Roller Blade/Bike Paths, Movie Theater *(IMAX 685-5225)*, Video Arcade, Park *(Federal Hill, promenade)*, Cultural Attract *(Nat'l Aquarium 576-3800 $18/11; 1 mi: Performing Arts Center 625-4230, Oriole Park at Camden Yards)*, Special Events **Under 1 mi:** Video Rental *(Blockbuster 244-0376)* **1-3 mi:** Tennis Courts *(Bolton Tennis & Swim 728-1634)* **3+ mi:** Golf Course *(Carroll Park 685-8344, 4 mi.)*, Bowling *(Charm City Duckpin 355-2196, 4 mi.)*

Provisioning and General Services

Near: Convenience Store, Delicatessen *(New York 234-0950)*, Health Food *(D' Natures Way 528-1837)*, Bakery, Fishmonger, Lobster Pound, Bank/ATM, Post Office, Catholic Church, Library *(396-1096)*, Beauty Salon, Laundry *(Opes 332-4002)*, Bookstore *(Book Escape 576-8885)*, Florist, Copies Etc. *(Work Printing 244-0968)* **Under 1 mi:** Supermarket *(Safeway 675-3704)*, Wine/Beer *(Charles St. Liquors 685-6929)*, Liquor Store *(Federal Hill 539-7757)*, Farmers' Market *(W Preston Street, Wed 10am-2pm, 767-6778)*, Dry Cleaners *(American Cleaners 727-7389)*, Pharmacy *(James 752-5810)*, Hardware Store *(Singer's 685-3720)* **1-3 mi:** Department Store *(Wal-Mart 625-1971)*, Buying Club *(Sam's 837-1142)*

Transportation

OnCall: Water Taxi *(675-2900)*, Rental Car *(Enterprise 547-1855)*, Taxi *(Baltimore 685-1212)*, Airport Limo *(Airporter 336-2828)* **Near:** Bikes *(Light St. Cycles 685-2234)*, Local Bus **3+ mi:** Rail *(Amtrak 727-3210, 4 mi.)*
Airport: Baltimore-Washington Int'l. *(7 mi.)*

Medical Services

911 Service **OnCall:** Ambulance **Near:** Dentist *(Balciunas 659-0900)*, Chiropractor *(Southside 332-0044)* **Under 1 mi:** Doctor *(Inner Harbor 234-0444)*, Veterinarian *(Light St.)* **Hospital:** Johns Hopkins 955-5000 *(3 mi.)*

Setting -- In the heart of the action at Baltimore's Inner Harbor is one of the city's three pleasure craft docking areas - right in front of the Visitors' Center. Three main parallel piers, two connecting piers plus the wharf itself offer unreserved alongside dockage to transient vessels. The other two city docks are on the face of Pier 4 (in front of the Aquarium) and in the canal on its east side and on the face of Pier 5 (in front of Pier 5 Hotel) and on the hotel's west side.

Marina Notes -- *Hourly rate $5/4 hrs. Check-out at noon. Look for the black cleats - dock anywhere unless there is a "no docking" sign or the cleats are red. Assistance is available 7 days. Most of the Harbor Place piers have new pedestals (cable incl.); the farthest south has older wooden pedestals - all with water. Power for the boats docked along the face wharf are in the bases of the streetlights - but no water. Stay clear of the water taxis and tour boats. The Visitors Center's very nice stainless steel heads are open 7 days 9am-7pm; modest showers are in the dockhouse. No amenities at the Pier 4 & 5 locations.

Notable -- The best of Baltimore's Inner Harbor attractions are practically dockside. Start with the free movie in the Visitors' Center; a 3-day Harbor Pass $46/30 accesses 4 attractions & water taxis. Kids love innovative Maryland Science Center's interactive Newton's Alley, Your Body, Blue Crab & Terra Link, along with IMAX films. Adjacent Harborplace (The Gallery and Light & Pratt Street Pavilions) has over 100 shops, 14 restaurants and 40 "snackeries." Just beyond, the National Aquarium features more than 11,000 animals including bottlenose dolphins and new Planet Australia. Next is Port Discovery, a superb childen's museum, and the Maritime Museum on Piers 3 & 5 with 3 boardable vessels. Don't miss the 1854 USS Constellation, the last all-sail warship.

Navigational Information

Lat: 39°04.306' **Long:** 076°31.058' **Tide:** 2 ft. **Current:** n/a **Chart:** 12272
Rep. Depths (*MLW*): Entry 15 ft. **Fuel Dock** 15 ft. **Max Slip/Moor** 15 ft./-
Access: Follow markers from the Bay 4.4 NM to Crystal Beach

Marina Facilities *(In Season/Off Season)*

Fuel: Gasoline, Diesel
Slips: 182 Total, Inq Transient **Max LOA:** 55 ft. **Max Beam:** n/a
Rate *(per ft.)*: **Day** $1.25 **Week** $6 **Month** $12
Power: 30 amp $5, **50 amp** $10, **100 amp** n/a, **200 amp** n/a
Cable TV: Yes **Dockside Phone:** Yes overnight possible
Dock Type: Fixed, Wood
Moorings: 0 Total, 0 Transient **Launch:** n/a
Rate: Day n/a **Week** n/a **Month** n/a
Heads: 6 Toilet(s), 6 Shower(s)
Laundry: 2 Washer(s), 2 Dryer(s), Iron, Iron Board **Pay Phones:** No
Pump-Out: Full Service, 2 Central **Fee:** $5/3 guests **Closed Heads:** Yes

Marina Operations

Owner/Manager: Victoria Shiroky **Dockmaster:** Mary Heinritz
In-Season: May-Sept, 8am-8pm **Off-Season:** Oct-Apr, 9am-5:30pm
After-Hours Arrival: Pull up alongside fuel pier
Reservations: Yes, Preferred **Credit Cards:** Visa/MC
Discounts: Boat/US **Dockage:** 25% **Fuel:** n/a **Repair:** n/a
Pets: Welcome, Dog Walk Area **Handicap Access:** Yes, Heads, Docks

Magothy Marina

360 Magothy Road; Severna Park, MD 21146

Tel: (410) 647-2356 **VHF: Monitor** 16 **Talk** 69
Fax: (410) 647-2239 **Alternate Tel:** (410) 647-2356
Email: magothymar@aol.com **Web:** www.magothymarina.com
Nearest Town: Severna Park *(3 mi.)* **Tourist Info:** (410) 268-7677

Marina Services and Boat Supplies

Services - Docking Assistance, Boaters' Lounge, Security *(key card entry)*, Trash Pick-Up, Dock Carts **Communication -** Mail & Package Hold, Phone Messages, Fax in/out *($1)*, Data Ports *(Wi-Fi, Free)*, FedEx, DHL, UPS, Express Mail *(Sat Del)* **Supplies - OnSite:** Ice *(Block, Cube)* **OnCall:** CNG *(Ray Dunentat 321-3721)* **1-3 mi:** West Marine *(431-5100)*, Marine Discount Store *(Fawcett's)*, Bait/Tackle *(Angler's 757-3442)*, Live Bait, Propane *(Fishpaw's 642-7363)*

Boatyard Services

OnSite: Launching Ramp **OnCall:** Engine mechanic *(gas, diesel)*, Hull Repairs *(A1A 267-6663)*, Rigger, Sail Loft *(Hoosley 263-4913)*, Canvas Work, Bottom Cleaning, Brightwork, Air Conditioning, Refrigeration, Divers *(Chuck's 885-2479)*, Compound, Wash & Wax, Interior Cleaning, Propeller Repairs, Woodworking, Inflatable Repairs *(Air Works 268-7332)*, Life Raft Service, Upholstery **Nearest Yard:** Cypress Marine (410) 647-7940

Restaurants and Accommodations

OnCall: Pizzeria *(Domino's 421-9400)*, *(Papa John's 544-6262)*
Near: Seafood Shack *(Magothy Seafood 647-5793, dinghy)*
1-3 mi: Restaurant *(Cafe Mezzanotte 647-1100, L $8-15, D $20-25)*, *Woodfire 315-8100, L $7-17, D $18-30)*, *(Café Bretton 647-8222,* D $19-29), Coffee Shop (Big Bean), Fast Food *(McDonalds, Taco Bell,* Wendys), *Pizzeria (Scilipote's Pizzeria 421-5414)*, Inn/B&B *(Magothy Manor B&B 647-2995)*, *(Comfort Inn Annapolis 757-8500, $100-150, 4 mi.)*

Recreation and Entertainment

OnSite: Pool, Picnic Area, Grills **OnCall:** Fishing Charter *(Admirals of the Bay 263-5196)* **Near:** Roller Blade/Bike Paths **1-3 mi:** Dive Shop *(Sea Colony 544-3607)*, Fitness Center *(Big Vanilla 544-2005 tennis courts too)*, Jogging Paths *(B&A Trail Park 222-6244)*, Bowling *(Severna Park 647-0811)* **3+ mi:** Golf Course *(Bay Hills 757-8104, 5 mi.)*, Video Rental *(Blockbuster 544-1313, 5 mi.)*, Park *(Sandy Point State Park, 8 mi.)*

Provisioning and General Services

1-3 mi: Convenience Store *(7-Eleven)*, Supermarket *(Giant 760-8443)*, Delicatessen *(Fishpaws 647-7363)*, Wine/Beer *(Fishpaws)*, Liquor Store *(Severna Park 518-6750)*, Green Grocer *(Diane's Produce)*, Fishmonger *(Annapolis Seafood 544-4901)*, Post Office *(647-5031)*, Library *(Severna Park 222-6290)*, Beauty Salon *(Morgan Gerard 263-1812)*, Barber Shop *(647-9843)*, Dry Cleaners *(College Village 544-8984)*, Laundry, Pharmacy *(Rite Aid 647-0451)*, Department Store *(Kohl's)* **3+ mi:** Bakery *(Panera 544-6400, 4 mi.)*, Bank/ATM *(4 mi.)*, Catholic Church, Protestant Church, Hardware Store *(Clement 647-4611, 5 mi.)*, Buying Club *(BJ's, 8 mi.)*

Transportation

OnCall: Rental Car *(Enterprise 315-7980, Budget 766-9371)*, Taxi *(766-1234)*, Airport Limo *(Agentie Touch 437-1444)* **Under 1 mi:** Local Bus *(866-RIDE-MTA)* **3+ mi:** Bikes *(Pedal Pusher's 544-2323, 4 mi.)*, Rail *(Penn Sta., 20 mi.)* **Airport:** Baltimore-Washington Int'l. *(15 mi.)*

Medical Services

911 Service **OnSite:** Holistic Services *(Massages by Kathleen 533-8261)*
1-3 mi: Doctor *(Primary Care 647-8600)*, Dentist (Woods 647-1800), Veterinarian *(Severna Park 647-8366)* **3+ mi:** Chiropractor *(Thorne 544-1957)* **Hospital:** Anne Arundel 432-1000 *(8 mi.)*

Setting -- On the southwestern shore of the Magothy, about 4.4 NM from the Bay, beautifully managed and maintained Magothy Marina sits on a peninsula formed by Dividing and Cypress Creeks. Nine sets of slips radiate on either side of the main pier. A second pier ends at the fuel dock, with slips on one side plus alongside dockage for larger vessels and catamarans. Dinghy slips front the nicely grassed bulkhead.

Marina Notes -- DCM. A 182 slip dockominium run like a yacht club - service-oriented staff, twice daily dock-walks. Women are at the helm - and it shows. Cable TV is in progress; overnight phone service available. Attended pumpout $3 for guests, $5 for others. Majority of boats are sail, but some good-size power vessels home here as well. Previously this site was Crystal Beach - a popular summer attraction with dancing, bingo and a crab shack. Several very, very nice full bathrooms: the floors are high gloss, painted cement; all tile walls and fiberglass shower stalls - plus full-length mirrors and an electrical outlet.

Notable -- A nice-sized pool - well-shrubbed for privacy, but with views across the docks - sits on a raised platform with a nicely furnished surrounding patio. Just seaward of the pool are picnic tables with brightly-striped umbrellas and grills. On the second floor of the marina facilities building is a small boaters' lounge that's really part of the office; it has a remarkably extensive lending library. The second-floor deck provides a protective overhang for the first floor patio - picnic tables and chairs create a much-used gathering place for boaters. The nearest grocery store is 3.2 miles, and the only way to get there is by taxi. A 7-Eleven is a little closer. Magothy Seafood eatery is nearby by dinghy.

PHOTOS ON CD-ROM: 13

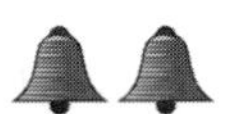

Deep Creek Restaurant & Marina

1050 Deep Creek Avenue; Arnold, MD 21012

Tel: (410) 757-4045 **VHF: Monitor** n/a **Talk** n/a
Fax: (410) 757-4186 **Alternate Tel:** (410) 974-1408
Email: (see below) **Web:** www.deepcreekrestaurantandmarina.com
Nearest Town: Arnold *(5 mi.)* **Tourist Info:** (410) 268-7676

Navigational Information

Lat: 39°02.950' **Long:** 076°27.633' **Tide:** 2 ft. **Current:** 0 kt. **Chart:** 12282
Rep. Depths (*MLW*): Entry 8 ft. **Fuel Dock** 6 ft. **Max Slip/Moor** 6 ft./-
Access: Magothy River to Deep Creek

Marina Facilities *(In Season/Off Season)*

Fuel: Gasoline, Diesel
Slips: 12 Total, 3 Transient **Max LOA:** 45 ft. **Max Beam:** n/a
Rate *(per ft.)*: **Day** $1.50* **Week** n/a **Month** n/a
Power: 30 amp $5, **50 amp** n/a, **100 amp** n/a, **200 amp** n/a
Cable TV: No **Dockside Phone:** No
Dock Type: Fixed
Moorings: 0 Total, 0 Transient **Launch:** n/a
Rate: Day n/a **Week** n/a **Month** n/a
Heads: 4 Toilet(s)
Laundry: None **Pay Phones:** No
Pump-Out: No **Fee:** n/a **Closed Heads:** Yes

Marina Operations

Owner/Manager: Phil & Rene Hundemann **Dockmaster:** Same
In-Season: Year-Round, 11am-11pm **Off-Season:** n/a
After-Hours Arrival: Restaurant open until 11pm
Reservations: Dinner reservation **Credit Cards:** Visa/MC, Dscvr, Amex
Discounts: None
Pets: Welcome **Handicap Access:** No

Marina Services and Boat Supplies

Communication - FedEx, UPS, Express Mail **Supplies - OnSite:** Ice *(Cube)* **3+ mi:** Ships' Store *(Fairwinds 974-0758, 5 mi.)*, West Marine *(266-7766, 9 mi.)*, Boat/US *(573-5744, 10 mi.)*, Bait/Tackle *(4 mi.)*, Propane *(Bay Mart 757-5926, 4 mi.)*

Boatyard Services

Near: Travelift, Engine mechanic *(gas, diesel)*, Electrical Repairs, Electronic Sales, Electronics Repairs, Hull Repairs, Rigger, Sail Loft, Bottom Cleaning, Brightwork, Air Conditioning, Refrigeration, Divers, Compound, Wash & Wax, Interior Cleaning, Propeller Repairs, Woodworking, Inflatable Repairs, Life Raft Service, Upholstery, Yacht Interiors, Metal Fabrication, Painting, Awlgrip, Yacht Broker.

Restaurants and Accommodations

OnSite: Restaurant *(Deep Creek Restaurant 757-4045, L $7-15, D $15-35, seafood, steaks, crabs, American)* **1-3 mi:** Restaurant *(City Dock Café 757-2405)*, *(O'Loughlin's 349-0200)*, *(George's Restaurant & Carry-Out 974-0405)*, *(China Garden 757-3388)*, Motel *(Super 8 Annapolis 757-2222, $50-80)* **3+ mi:** Restaurant *(Red Parrot Asian Café 280-8817, L $6-15, D $10-15, 6 mi., Japanese, Chinese, & Thai food)*, *(O'Learys Seafood Restaurant 263-0884, L $10-15, D $15-30, 5 mi.)*, Motel *(Village Inn 349-1600, 4 mi.)*, Hotel *(Comfort Inn Annapolis 757-8500, $100-140, 4 mi.)*, Inn/B&B *(Barn On Howards Cove 571-9511, 8 mi.)*

Recreation and Entertainment

Under 1 mi: Golf Course *(Bay Hills 757-8104)* **1-3 mi:** Fitness Center *(Curves 349-9305)* **3+ mi:** Tennis Courts *(Big Vanilla Athletic Club 544-2525, 5 mi.)*, Bowling *(Annapolis Bowl 266-0700, 10 mi.)*, Movie Theater *(Crown Annapolis 224-1145, 10 mi.)*, Video Rental *(Blockbuster 626-7770, 5 mi.)*, Park *(Sandy Point State Park 974-5975, 7 mi.)*, Museum *(Annapolis, 10 mi.)*, Sightseeing, Galleries

Provisioning and General Services

OnSite: Wine/Beer **Near:** Bank/ATM, Post Office **1-3 mi:** Convenience Store, Delicatessen *(Bay Hill Deli 974-1310)*, Liquor Store *(Port Tack 974-0800)*, Fishmonger *(Wild Goose Seafood Market 757-7500)*, Beauty Salon *(Great Clips 757-7447)*, Pharmacy *(Rite Aid 757-0027)* **3+ mi:** Supermarket *(Safeway 757-2449, 5 mi.)*, Market *(Fishpaws Market Place 647-7363, 5 mi.)*, Catholic Church, Protestant Church, Library *(Broadneck 222-1905, 6 mi.)*, Dry Cleaners *(College Village 544-8984, 5 mi.)*, Bookstore *(Borders 990-0955, 9 mi.)*, Hardware Store *(84 Lumber 757-4684, 5 mi.)*, Department Store *(Annapolis Mall, 10 mi.)*

Transportation

OnCall: Rental Car *(Enterprise 268-7751/Budget 263-7622, 9 mi.)*, Taxi *(Yellow Cab 268-2626)*, Airport Limo *(A & W 263-8715)* **3+ mi:** Rail *(Amtrak BWI 672-6167, 20 mi.)* **Airport:** Baltimore-Washington Int'l. *(20 mi.)*

Medical Services

911 Service **OnCall:** Ambulance **1-3 mi:** Dentist *(Bay Hills Family Dentistry 757-9222)*, Holistic Services *(Chesapeake Holistic Health 349-9043)* **3+ mi:** Doctor, Chiropractor *(Kelly 757-8989, 5 mi.)*, Veterinarian *(Arnold Veterinary Hospital 757-7645, 5 mi.)* **Hospital:** Anne Arundel 267-1000 *(8 mi.)*

Setting -- At the confluence of the Magothy River and Deep Creek, this casual, very popular waterfront eatery hosts slips for diners and overnight transients. The small, gray, two-story main building with hip roof backs 2 sets of docks -- one directly in front of the restaurant. Another set, the main pier, anchors two docks that paralell the bulkhead and ends out at the fuel dock. Brightly colored umbrella-topped picnic tables dot the shoreline - perfect for steamed crabs.

Marina Notes -- *$1.50/ft. overnight; if boaters have dinner, then dockage is free. Power $5/cord. Dock 'n' Dine, too. There's been a docking facility on this site for forty years. The current owners have been at the helm since 1997. Fuel dock has both gas and diesel. On the restaurants' ground level, an event room doubles as overflow room for dinner in the height of the season. It holds about 50 people and is available for special events, including small club cruises.

Notable -- Deep Creek (open 7 days, year-round) specializes in seafood, particularly Chesapeake oysters, bought right off the three skipjacks that make their home here during the oyster season. Seafood doesn't get any fresher than that. The upper level main dining room is all windows; attractive natural wood Windsor chairs and tables - with sweet candle lamps - look right over the docks to the Creek. Specials most nights, early bird Mon-Thu 4-6pm, and Sunday buffet brunch. Lunch Mon-Sat, 11:30am-4pm, Dinner daily 4-11pm, Sun brunch 10am-2:30pm. Deep Creek also has an "off-premise license" - they can sell beer and wine to go. The surrounding area is residential. You can take a cab two miles to College Parkway, just before Ritchie Highway, and there's a small shopping center that should meet most boaters' needs. (email: deepcreekrestaurant@comcast.net)

PHOTOS ON CD-ROM: 9

4. Eastern Shore: Sassafras River To Rock Hall

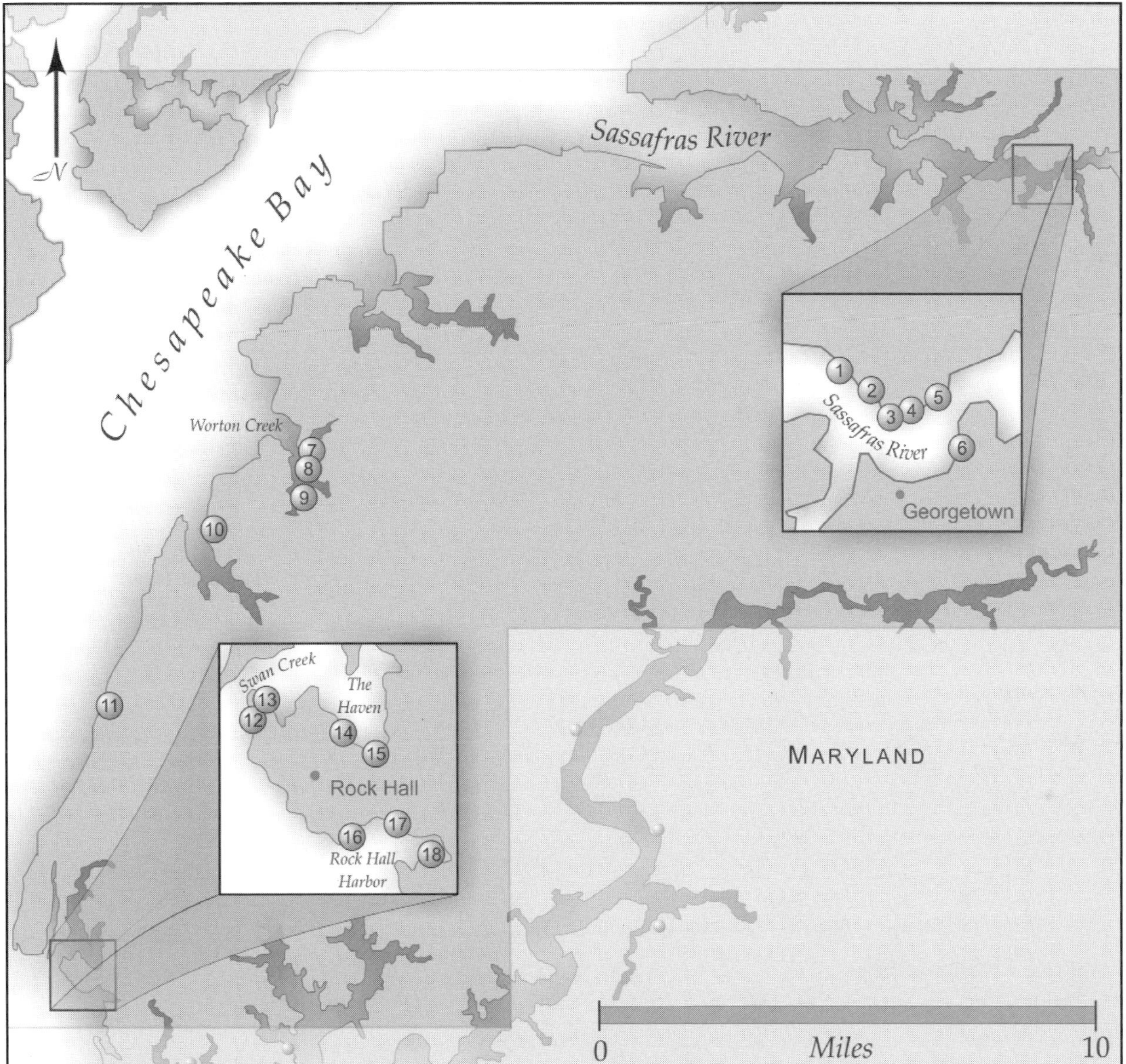

MAP	MARINA	HARBOR	PAGE
1	**Skipjack Cove Yachting Resort**	*Sassafras River*	80
2	**Duffy Creek Marina**	*Sassafras River*	81
3	**Granary Marina**	*Sassafras River*	82
4	**Sailing Associates**	*Sassafras River*	83
5	**Sassafras Harbor Marina**	*Sassafras River*	84
6	**Georgetown Yacht Basin**	*Sassafras River*	85
7	**Green Point Landing**	*Worton Creek*	86
8	**The Wharf at Handy's Point**	*Worton Creek*	87
9	**Worton Creek Marina**	*Worton Creek*	88
10	**Mear's Great Oak Landing**	*Fairlee Creek*	89
11	**Tolchester Marina**	*Chesapeake Bay*	90
12	**Moonlight Bay Marina & Inn**	*Swan Creek*	91
13	**Swan Creek Marina**	*Swan Creek*	92
14	**Osprey Point Marina**	*Swan Creek*	93
15	**Haven Harbour at Port of Rock Hall**	*Swan Creek*	94
16	**North Point Marina**	*Rock Hall Harbor*	95
17	**Rock Hall Landing Marina**	*Rock Hall Harbor*	96
18	**The Sailing Emporium**	*Rock Hall Harbor*	97

- **A "DCM" symbol in Marina Notes means Designated Clean Marina** — This is a coveted state-level award given to marinas that meet stringent, environmentally supportive requirements (see page 307). *For a list of DCM's & pump-out facilities, see page 308.*
- **Ratings & Reviews** — An explanation of the Atlantic Cruising Club's rating system, and a detailed explanation of what is in each section of the Marina Report is on pages 6 – 11. *The Data-Gathering Process is detailed on page 322.*
- **Marina Report Updates** — Updates to Marina Reports (from readers, ACC reviewers, and marinas) are posted regularly on *www.AtlanticCruisingClub.com.*

Skipjack Cove Yachting Resort

PO Box 208; 150 Skipjack Lane; Georgetown, MD 21930

Tel: (410) 275-2122; (800) 262-8754 **VHF: Monitor** 16 **Talk** 69
Fax: (410) 275-1133 **Alternate Tel:** n/a
Email: scyr@intercom.net **Web:** www.skipjackcove.com
Nearest Town: Galena *(3 mi.)* **Tourist Info:** (302) 378-6260

Navigational Information

Lat: 39°21.942' **Long:** 075°53.544' **Tide:** 2 ft. **Current:** n/a **Chart:** 12273
Rep. Depths (*MLW*): Entry 22 ft. **Fuel Dock** 17 ft. **Max Slip/Moor** 17 ft./-
Access: Chesapeake Bay to Sassafras 4.5mi. past Ordinary Point

Marina Facilities *(In Season/Off Season)*

Fuel: Gasoline, Diesel, High-Speed Pumps
Slips: 360 Total, 50 Transient **Max LOA:** 150 ft. **Max Beam:** n/a
Rate *(per ft.)*: **Day** $2.00/$1.25* **Week** Inq. **Month** Inq.
Power: 30 amp $5, **50 amp** $10, **100 amp** $20, **200 amp** n/a
Cable TV: Yes Incl. **Dockside Phone:** No
Dock Type: Fixed, Long Fingers, Pilings
Moorings: 0 Total, 0 Transient **Launch:** Yes (Free)
Rate: Day n/a **Week** n/a **Month** n/a
Heads: 28 Toilet(s), 28 Shower(s)
Laundry: 4 Washer(s), 4 Dryer(s), Book Exchange **Pay Phones:** Yes, 3
Pump-Out: OnSite, Full Service, 3 Central **Fee:** $5 **Closed Heads:** Yes

Marina Operations

Owner/Manager: Rich Lauser **Dockmaster:** Lance Bernardo
In-Season: May-Sep, 8am-6pm** **Off-Season:** Oct-Apr, 8am-4:30pm
After-Hours Arrival: See security
Reservations: Yes, Required **Credit Cards:** Visa/MC, Dscvr, Amex
Discounts: None
Pets: Welcome, Dog Walk Area **Handicap Access:** Yes, Heads, Docks

Marina Services and Boat Supplies

Services - Docking Assistance, Concierge, Boaters' Lounge, Trash Pick-Up, Dock Carts, Megayacht Facilities **Communication -** Mail & Package Hold, Phone Messages, Fax in/out, Data Ports *(Boater's Lounge)*, FedEx, DHL, UPS, Express Mail **Supplies - OnSite:** Ice *(Block, Cube)*, Ships' Store **Near:** Bait/Tackle, CNG *(Georgetown Yacht Basin 648-5112)*
1-3 mi: Propane *(Turner's 648-5443)*

Boatyard Services

OnSite: Travelift *(70T)*, Forklift, Engine mechanic *(gas, diesel)*, Electrical Repairs, Electronics Repairs, Hull Repairs, Rigger, Bottom Cleaning, Brightwork, Compound, Wash & Wax, Propeller Repairs, Woodworking, Painting, Awlgrip, Yacht Broker **OnCall:** Divers **Near:** Launching Ramp, Sail Loft, Canvas Work, Air Conditioning, Refrigeration, Interior Cleaning, Inflatable Repairs, Life Raft Service, Metal Fabrication. **Yard Rates:** $39-58/hr., Haul & Launch $5.50/ft. *(blocking $3.25/ft.)*, Power Wash $1.75/ft., Bottom Paint $7/ft. *(paint incl.)* **Storage:** In-Water $20/ft., On-Land $27/ft.

Restaurants and Accommodations

OnSite: Restaurant *(Signals Pub 275-2122, L $3-11, D $5-25, open Thu-Sun, kids' menu $4)* **Near:** Restaurant *(The Granary 275-1603, L $6-12, D $16-25)*, Lite Fare *(Sassafras Harbor Café & Pizzeria 275-2963, B $2-5, L $3-13, D $3-13)* **Under 1 mi:** Restaurant *(Kitty Knight House 648-5200, B $5-9, L $7-13, D $13-33, , by launch)*, Inn/B&B *(Kitty Knight House 648-5777, $95-160)* **1-3 mi:** Restaurant *(Twinny's 648-5784, B $5, L $7, D $10)*, Snack Bar *(Dixie-Jo's 648-5521)*, Pizzeria *(Galena 648-5945)*, Inn/B&B *(Carousel Horse 648-5476, $80-90, cont. Break Incl.)*, *(Rosehill Farm 648-5334)*

Recreation and Entertainment

OnSite: Pool, Picnic Area, Grills, Playground, Tennis Courts, Jogging Paths, Volleyball **Near:** Beach, Sightseeing *(East through or under the drawbridge to the Upper Sassafras)* **Under 1 mi:** Cultural Attract *(Mt. Harmon - by dinghy to the point between McGill & Back Creeks - Tue & Thu 10am-3pm, Sun 1-4pm, 275-8819/8502, $5)*

Provisioning and General Services

OnSite: Convenience Store *(beverages, beer snacks)*, Wine/Beer, Liquor Store, Retail Shops *(ships' store has gifts & clothing)* **1-3 mi:** Supermarket *(Otwell's Market 648-5111)*, Gourmet Shop, Delicatessen *(Galena Mini Mart 648-5000)*, Bakery *(Village Bakery & Cafe 648-6400)*, Farmers' Market, Fishmonger, Market *(Ripples 648-6180)*, Bank/ATM, Post Office *(648-5783)*, Catholic Church, Protestant Church, Beauty Salon *(Hidden Beauty 648-5502)*, Laundry, Bookstore *(Last Page Bookshop 648-6560)*, Pharmacy, Newsstand, Florist **3+ mi:** Library *(Cecilton 275-1091, 3 mi.)*

Transportation

OnSite: Water Taxi *(to town and restaurants)* **OnCall:** Rental Car *(Enterprise 302-398-0030)*, Taxi *(Joe's Taxi 392-8070)*, Airport Limo *(Town Car 885-9228)* **Airport:** Baltimore-Washington Int'l./Philadelphia *(70 mi./60 mi.)*

Medical Services

911 Service **OnCall:** Ambulance **1-3 mi:** Doctor *(Donaher 648-6011)*
3+ mi: Veterinarian *(Middletown Vet 302-378-2342, 7 mi.)*
Hospital: Union in Elkton 410-398-4000 *(17 mi.)*

Setting -- This 18-acre, upscale destination marina is tucked into a quiet cove on the north shore of the Sassafras about 4.5 miles from Ordinary Point. The octagonal two-story pub and office building, the pools, gazebo, picnic area and bathhouse sit on a bluff overlooking the vast network of slips and river beyond.

Marina Notes -- *In season rates: $2.00/ft. weekends, $1.75/ft. Mon-Thu, $2.50/ft. holidays (2 night min). **Hours: MemDay-LabDay: DCM. Fuel: Sun-Thu 8am-6pm, Fri & Sat 8am-8pm; Launch: Sun-Thu 10am-10pm, Fri & Sat 10am-Mid; Pool: (MemDay-Sep 30) 10am-Sunset; Office & Service: week 8am-4:30pm, weekends 8:30am-5pm. DCM. 21 slips are covered. The focus is service - ever-present dockhands and marine services six days a week (note that for yard services, Saturdays are charged a time & a half rate, $85 min); emergency mechanic on Sundays. Bathhouse: 28 superb individual, pale-blue & cream tiled, climate-controlled units. Facilities available to anchored boats for $30/day. Shuttle launch is available to nearby restaurants.

Notable -- On-site Signals Pub is open Thu 4-10pm, Fri Noon-10pm, Sat 9am-10pm, Sun 9am-9pm, closed Mon-Wed. It offers inside or deck dining and live entertainment Saturday nights. The Olympic-size swimming pool, perched at the edge of the bluff, is surrounded by an attractively furnished deck with spectacular views, especially at sunset. A small, round children's pool is adjacent. The "Family Lounge" above the bathhouse sports a wide-screen TV, comfortable sofas and easy chairs, 2 internet access cubbies, game tables and a little play area - parents required at all times. Beyond the parking lot are a tennis court, basketball court, and playground. Event catering available - can manage up 10 boats at dock, many more anchored out and 200 for an event.

PHOTOS ON CD-ROM: 15

Navigational Information
Lat: 39°21.878' **Long:** 075°53.346' **Tide:** 1.5 ft. **Current:** n/a **Chart:** 12273
Rep. Depths (*MLW*): Entry 6 ft. **Fuel Dock** 5 ft. **Max Slip/Moor** 8 ft./-
Access: Chesapeake Bay to Sassafras to port entrance to marina

Marina Facilities *(In Season/Off Season)*
Fuel: Gasoline, Diesel
Slips: 117 Total, 10 Transient **Max LOA:** 70 ft. **Max Beam:** 15.5 ft.
Rate *(per ft.)*: **Day** $1.25/1.00 **Week** n/a **Month** n/a
Power: 30 amp $5, **50 amp** $8, **100 amp** n/a, **200 amp** n/a
Cable TV: Yes, $20 /month **Dockside Phone:** No
Dock Type: Fixed, Wood
Moorings: 0 Total, 0 Transient **Launch:** n/a, Dinghy Dock
Rate: Day n/a **Week** n/a **Month** n/a
Heads: 6 Toilet(s), 5 Shower(s)
Laundry: 1 Washer(s), 1 Dryer(s), Book Exchange **Pay Phones:** No
Pump-Out: OnSite, OnCall, Self Service **Fee:** $5 **Closed Heads:** Yes

Marina Operations
Owner/Manager: Richard Wicks **Dockmaster:** Marcia Mabry
In-Season: May-Oct 15, 8:30am-5pm **Off-Season:** Oct 16-Apr, 8am-4pm
After-Hours Arrival: Call ahead
Reservations: Preferred **Credit Cards:** Visa/MC, Dscvr
Discounts: Boat/US **Dockage:** 25% **Fuel:** n/a **Repair:** n/a
Pets: Welcome, Dog Walk Area **Handicap Access:** No

Duffy Creek Marina

PO Box 116; 20 Duffy Creek Road; Georgetown, MD 21930

Tel: (410) 275-2141; (800) 451-4416 **VHF: Monitor** n/a **Talk** n/a
Fax: (410) 275-0096 **Alternate Tel:** n/a
Email: duffy@crosslink.net **Web:** www.duffycreekmarina.com
Nearest Town: Galena *(2.5 mi.)* **Tourist Info:** (302) 378-6260

Marina Services and Boat Supplies
Services - Dock Carts **Communication -** Mail & Package Hold, Phone Messages, FedEx, UPS, Express Mail *(Sat Del)* **Supplies - OnSite:** Ice *(Block, Cube)*, Ships' Store **Near:** Bait/Tackle, Live Bait, CNG *(Georgetown Yacht Basin 648-5112)* **1-3 mi:** Propane *(Turner's 648-5443)*

Boatyard Services
OnSite: Travelift *(35T)*, Forklift, Hydraulic Trailer, Launching Ramp, Engine mechanic *(gas)*, Hull Repairs, Bottom Cleaning, Brightwork, Compound, Wash & Wax, Interior Cleaning, Painting, Total Refits, Yacht Broker
OnCall: Engine mechanic *(diesel)*, Electrical Repairs, Electronics Repairs, Canvas Work, Air Conditioning, Refrigeration, Propeller Repairs, Upholstery, Yacht Interiors **Near:** Rigger, Sail Loft. **Member:** ABBRA, ABYC
Yard Rates: Haul & Launch $5/ft. *(blocking $2/ft.)*, Power Wash $2/ft., Bottom Paint $9/ft. **Storage:** On-Land $150/mo.

Restaurants and Accommodations
Near: Restaurant *(The Granary 275-1603, L $6-12, D $25, Fri & Sat 4-11pm, Sun brunch 10am-1pm, dinner 1-10pm)*, *(Kitty Knight House 648-5200, B $5-9, L $3-13, D $16-25)*, Lite Fare *(Sassafras Harbor Cafe & Pizzeria 275-2963, B $2-5, L $3-13, D $3-13)*, *(Sassafras Grill 275-1603, L $6-12, D $6-12, only open weekends MemDay-LabDay; Fri 4pm-mid, Sat 11am-1am,Sun 11am-10pm)*, Inn/B&B *(Kitty Knight House 275-8600, $95-160)*
1-3 mi: Restaurant *(Twinny's 648-5784, B $5, L $7, D $10)*, Snack Bar *(Dixie-Jo's 648-5521)*, Pizzeria *(Galena Pizza 648-5945)*, Inn/B&B *(Carousel Horse 648-5476, $80-90)*, *(Rosehill Farm 648-5334)*
3+ mi: Inn/B&B *(Achorage B&B 275-1972, 5 mi.)*

Recreation and Entertainment
OnSite: Pool *(10am-8pm)*, Picnic Area, Grills **Under 1 mi:** Cultural Attract *(Mt. Harmon - 275-8819/8502 Tue & Thu 10am-3pm, Sun 1-4pm, $5)*, Sightseeing *(Upper Sassafrass)* **1-3 mi:** Park *(Toad Park)* **3+ mi:** Golf Course *(Frog Hollow Golf Course 376-6500, 16 mi.)*, Movie Theater *(Chester 5 778-2227, 16 mi.)*, Video Rental *(Video Scene 376-6111, 15 mi.)*, Museum *(Historic Houses of Odessa 378-4069, 15 mi.)*

Provisioning and General Services
1-3 mi: Convenience Store *(Glena Mini Mart 648-5000)*, Supermarket *(Otwell's Market 648-5111)*, Delicatessen, Wine/Beer, Liquor Store *(Galena Liquors 648-5484)*, Bakery *(Village Bakery & Cafe 648-6400)*, Fishmonger, Meat Market, Market *(Ripples 648-6180)*, Bank/ATM, Post Office *(648-5783)*, Catholic Church, Beauty Salon *(Hidden Beauty 648-5502)*, Bookstore *(Last Page Bookshop 648-6560)*, Pharmacy *(Galena 648-5662)* **3+ mi:** Library *(Cecilton 275-1091, 3 mi.)*, Hardware Store *(Home Center 648-5822 / Millington Service 928-5060, 10 mi.)*, Department Store *(Wal-Mart 398-1070, 19 mi.)*

Transportation
OnCall: Rental Car *(Enterprise 302-398-0030)*, Taxi *(Joe's Taxi 392-8070)*, Airport Limo *(Town Car 885-9228)*
Airport: BWI 636-9070/Philadelphia 215-937-6800 *(70 mi./60 mi.)*

Medical Services
911 Service **OnCall:** Ambulance **1-3 mi:** Doctor *(Donaher 648-6011)*
3+ mi: Veterinarian *(Middletown Vet 302-378-2342, 7 mi.)*
Hospital: Union, Elkton 302-378-9672 *(17 mi.)*

Setting -- Duffy Creek's docks are in an almost-enclosed, wind and wake-free basin rimmed with slips -- with additional dockage down the center of the basin. A white, two-story building with bright blue trim and roof announces the marina with a large sign. The eastern shore of the basin is terraced and handsomely landscaped. The pool sits high above the docks with views that stretch over the basin to the river beyond. The ambiance is "down-home" and casual.

Marina Notes -- DCM. Family owned and operated since 1960, Duffy Creek takes a personal approach to service. The fuel dock, with its matching bright blue roof, is in front of the main office building. The travelift, on-the-hard storage and other boatyard services are at the back of the basin. On the first level above the docks a natural woven fence and some very healthy bushes create a privacy screen for the quite nice and well-maintained, tile-floored bathhouse with individual bathrooms. The next level up is the pool, which is surrounded by a modest concrete terrace and some chairs and chaises.

Notable -- Explore the Sassafras, by big boat or dink. Consider a cruise upriver - clearance under the bridge is 5-feet, so hail the bridge tender (Ch.13 or 648-5752). Pass through and step back in time - very little boat traffic, quiet, verdant riverbanks, and 11-feet of water for at least a mile. Gregg Neck BY is about 0.75 mile upstream. Or head downriver to Mount Harmon Plantation, a 1730 brick Georgian manor house. Round Knight Island and cruise up Back Creek. The plantation is on the point between Back and McGill Creeks. Reportedly the channel has 6 ft. of water but check. Tie up at the pier by Tobacco Prize House. It's a one mile hike to the Manor House, but you'll slip back 200 years in the process.

PHOTOS ON CD-ROM: 12

Granary Marina

Granary Marina

PO Box 8; 97 George Street; Georgetown, MD 21930

Tel: (410) 648-5112 **VHF: Monitor** 9, 16 **Talk** 71
Fax: (410) 648-5321 **Alternate Tel:** n/a
Email: n/a **Web:** www.georgetownyachtbasin.com
Nearest Town: Galena *(2 mi.)* **Tourist Info:** (302) 378-6260

Navigational Information

Lat: 39°21.800' **Long:** 075°53.266' **Tide:** 3 ft. **Current:** 3 kt. **Chart:** 12274
Rep. Depths (*MLW*): Entry 13 ft. **Fuel Dock** n/a **Max Slip/Moor** 10 ft./-
Access: Chesapeake Bay to Sassafras River

Marina Facilities *(In Season/Off Season)*

Fuel: Gasoline, Diesel
Slips: 150 Total, 20 Transient **Max LOA:** 200 ft. **Max Beam:** n/a
Rate *(per ft.)*: **Day** $1.75/1.50 **Week** $6.30 **Month** $21
Power: 30 amp Incl., **50 amp** Incl., **100 amp** Incl., **200 amp** n/a
Cable TV: No **Dockside Phone:** Yes
Dock Type: Fixed
Moorings: 0 Total, 0 Transient **Launch:** n/a
Rate: Day n/a **Week** n/a **Month** n/a
Heads: 6 Toilet(s), 6 Shower(s)
Laundry: 4 Washer(s), 4 Dryer(s) **Pay Phones:** Yes
Pump-Out: No **Fee:** n/a **Closed Heads:** Yes

Marina Operations

Owner/Manager: Ford Hall Sr. **Dockmaster:** Ivan Wade
In-Season: MemDay-LabDay, 8am-8pm **Off-Season:** Spring & Fall, 8am-5pm
After-Hours Arrival: n/a
Reservations: No **Credit Cards:** Visa/MC, Dscvr
Discounts: None
Pets: Welcome, Dog Walk Area **Handicap Access:** No

Marina Services and Boat Supplies

Services - Docking Assistance, Concierge, Boaters' Lounge, Dock Carts, Megayacht Facilities **Communication -** Mail & Package Hold, Phone Messages, Fax in/out, Data Ports *(Georgetown Yacht Basin)*, FedEx, UPS, Express Mail **Supplies - OnSite:** Ice *(Block, Cube)*, Ships' Store, Marine Discount Store **Near:** CNG *(Georgetown Yacht Basin 648-5112)* **1-3 mi:** Propane *(Turner's 648-5443)*

Boatyard Services

Near: Travelift *(110T)*, Launching Ramp, Engine mechanic *(gas, diesel)*, Electrical Repairs, Electronics Repairs, Hull Repairs, Rigger, Sail Loft, Canvas Work, Bottom Cleaning, Brightwork, Air Conditioning, Refrigeration, Compound, Wash & Wax, Interior Cleaning, Propeller Repairs, Woodworking, Inflatable Repairs, Life Raft Service, Upholstery, Yacht Interiors, Painting, Awlgrip, Yacht Broker. **Nearest Yard:** Georgetown Yacht Basin (401) 648-5112

Restaurants and Accommodations

OnSite: Restaurant *(The Granary 275-1603, L $6-12, D $10-25, Kobe beef $37, Mon-Thu 4-10pm, Fri & Sat 4-11pm, Sun brunch 10am-1pm $5-11, Sun dinner 1-10pm)*, Lite Fare *(Sassafras Grill 275-1603, L $6-12, D $6-12, only open weekends, MemDay-LabDay; Fri 4pm-Mid, Sat 11am-11pm, Sun 11am-10pm)* **Near:** Restaurant *(Kitty Knight House 648-5200, B $5-9, L $3-13, D $16-25)*, *(Village Cafe 648-6400)*, Lite Fare *(Sassafras Harbor Cafe & Pizzeria 275-2963, B $2-5, L $3-13, D $3-13)*, Pizzeria *(Galena Pizzeria 648-5945)*, Inn/B&B *(Kitty Knight House 275-8600, $95-160)* **1-3 mi:** Restaurant *(Cross Street 648-5776)*, Snack Bar *(Dixie-Jo's 648-5521)*, Inn/B&B *(Rosehill Farm 648-5334)*, *(Carousel Horse 648-5476, $80-90)*

Recreation and Entertainment

OnSite: Picnic Area, Grills **Near:** Pool, Beach **Under 1 mi:** Cultural Attract *(1730 Mt. Harmon Plantation - by water - 275-8819 $5)*, Sightseeing *(The Mighty Tug Cornell - cruise the Sassafras on a real 106-ft. tug - leaves from Gregg Neck BY 275-2464 - $25)* **1-3 mi:** Video Rental *(Video Scene 376-6111 R 13.5 mi.)*, Park **3+ mi:** Movie Theater *(Chester 5 Theatres 778-2227, 18 mi.)*

Provisioning and General Services

Near: Florist **1-3 mi:** Convenience Store *(Glena Mini Mart 648-5000)*, Supermarket *(Otwell's Market 648-5111)*, Liquor Store *(Galena Liquors 648-5484)*, Bakery *(Village Bakery & Cafe 648-6400)*, Farmers' Market, Meat Market, Market *(Ripples 648-6180)*, Bank/ATM, Post Office *(648-5783)*, Catholic Church, Protestant Church, Beauty Salon *(Hidden Beauty 648-5502)*, Bookstore *(Last Page Bookshop 648-6560)*, Pharmacy *(Galena 648-5662)*, Hardware Store *(Mackie's Home Ctr in Cecilton 648-5822)* **3+ mi:** Library *(Cecilton 275-1091, 3 mi.)*

Transportation

OnSite: Bikes *(comp. at Georgetown Y.B.)*, Rental Car **OnCall:** Water Taxi *(from Georgetown Y.B.)*, Taxi *(Joe's Taxi 392-8070)*, Airport Limo *(Town Car 885-9228)* **Near:** InterCity Bus *(Rock Hall Trolley -639-2775 - A Day in Galena $5)* **Airport:** BWI/Philadelphia *(70 mi./60 mi.)*

Medical Services

911 Service **OnCall:** Ambulance **1-3 mi:** Doctor *(Donaher 648-6011)* **3+ mi:** Veterinarian *(Buckle 778-2455, 7 mi.)* **Hospital:** Chester River 778-3300 *(17 mi.)*

Setting -- The distinctive cedar roof of the large, 2-story natural-sided Granary Restaurant beckons boaters with an inviting wrap-around deck and contemporary flair. The sleek all-glass design, equally at home on a Colorado ski slope as it is on this busy river bank, takes full advantage of the spectacular views. Four networks of slips from 25 to 50 ft flank the main building; across the parking lot a second matching structure houses the bathhouse and boaters' lounge.

Marina Notes -- Owned & operated by the Hall family which has also owned Georgetown Yacht Basin since the early 1950's. The Granary Marina office, next to the Sassafras Grill, is only open Fri 4pm-Mid, Sat 11am-11pm & Sun 11am-10pm. The dockmaster monitors both VHF and cell phone seven days a week from Georgetown Marina just up the river (Ch.9 or 275-2911). 300 ft. T-head and ample power for megayachts. All of the facilities and services at Georgetown Y.B. are available to Granary transient dockers -- Internet access, complimentary bikes (open Mon-Thu 8am-5pm, Fri & Sat 'til 6pm, Sun 9am-5pm), and use of the pool. Just call, they'll send a launch.The small boaters' lounge features a television and truly excellent adjacent heads and showers.

Notable -- Onsite are two very popular eateries. On the second floor, three sides of the year-round Granary Restaurant are windowed with truly magical views; especially at sunset looking west across the docks and down six of the river's twelve miles. Add to that a menu specializing in classic Eastern Shore cuisine with a well-priced wine list and mid-week specials. Tue specials $8/3, Wed shrimp $13, Thu lobster $15. A popular pub is in the back. Downstairs the Sassafras Grill has a tropically-inspired menu with weekend entertainment. MemDay-LabDay only. Dock 'n' Dine. Four event spaces accommodate up to 125.

Navigational Information
Lat: 39°21.830' **Long:** 075°53.200' **Tide:** 3 ft. **Current:** 1 kt. **Chart:** 12273
Rep. Depths (*MLW*): Entry 12 ft. **Fuel Dock** n/a **Max Slip/Moor** 15 ft./15 ft.
Access: Chesapeake Bay to Sassafras River

Marina Facilities *(In Season/Off Season)*
Fuel: No
Slips: 80 Total, 12 Transient **Max LOA:** 60 ft. **Max Beam:** 19 ft.
Rate *(per ft.)*: **Day** $1.60 **Week** $8.40 **Month** $18
Power: 30 amp Incl.**, **50 amp** $8, **100 amp** n/a, **200 amp** n/a
Cable TV: No **Dockside Phone:** Yes
Dock Type: Fixed, Long Fingers, Pilings, Wood
Moorings: 45 Total, 10 Transient **Launch:** Yes (Incl.), Dinghy Dock
Rate: Day $0.60/ft. **Week** $3.15/ft. **Month** $10.50/ft..
Heads: 6 Toilet(s), 4 Shower(s), Hair Dryers
Laundry: None, Book Exchange **Pay Phones:** No
Pump-Out: OnSite **Fee:** $5 **Closed Heads:** Yes

Marina Operations
Owner/Manager: Patrick Grieb **Dockmaster:** Same
In-Season: May-Sep, 9am-7pm* **Off-Season:** Nov-Apr, 9am-5pm
After-Hours Arrival: Call ahead
Reservations: Preferred **Credit Cards:** Visa/MC, Dscvr
Discounts: None
Pets: Welcome, Dog Walk Area **Handicap Access:** No

Sailing Associates

PO Box 6; 78 George Street; Georgetown, MD 21930

Tel: (410) 275-8171 **VHF: Monitor** 16 **Talk** 68
Fax: (410) 275-8835 **Alternate Tel:** n/a
Email: sailassoc@dmv.com **Web:** www.sailingassociates.com
Nearest Town: Galena *(2 mi.)* **Tourist Info:** (302) 378-6260

Marina Services and Boat Supplies
Services - Docking Assistance, Concierge, Boaters' Lounge, Security, Trash Pick-Up, Dock Carts **Communication -** Mail & Package Hold, Phone Messages, Fax in/out, FedEx, DHL, UPS, Express Mail **Supplies - OnSite:** Ice *(Block, Cube)*, Ships' Store *(coffee, snacks)* **Near:** Bait/Tackle, Live Bait **Under 1 mi:** CNG *(Georgetown Yacht Basin 648-5112)* **1-3 mi:** Propane *(Turner's 648-5443)*

Boatyard Services
OnSite: Engine mechanic *(gas, diesel)*, Electrical Repairs, Electronics Repairs, Hull Repairs, Rigger, Canvas Work, Bottom Cleaning, Brightwork, Refrigeration, Compound, Wash & Wax, Propeller Repairs, Woodworking, Yacht Broker **OnCall:** Sail Loft, Air Conditioning, Divers, Interior Cleaning, Inflatable Repairs, Life Raft Service, Metal Fabrication **Near:** Travelift *(45T)*, Launching Ramp. **Dealer for:** Westerbeke, Yanmar, Volvo. **Member:** ABBRA, ABYC **Yard Rates:** $71/hr.

Restaurants and Accommodations
Near: Restaurant *(Granary Restaurant 275-1603, L $6-12, D $14-25, $37 for Kobe beef + mid-week specials)*, Lite Fare *(Sassafras Harbor Cafe 275-2963, B $2-5, L $3-13, D $3-13)*, *(Sassafras Grill 275-1603, L $6-12, D $6-12, only open weekends MemDay-LabDay; Fri 4pm-Mid, Sat 11am-1am, Sun 11am-10pm)* **Under 1 mi:** Restaurant *(Kitty Knight House 275-8600, B $5-9, L $3-13, D $16-25)*, Inn/B&B *(Kitty Knight House Restaurant 275-8600, $95-160)* **1-3 mi:** Restaurant *(Dixie Jo's 648-5521)*, Snack Bar *(Twinny's 648-5784, B $5, L $7, D $10)*, Pizzeria *(Galena Pizzeria 648-5945)*, Inn/B&B *(Carousel Horse 648-5476, $80-90)*, *(Rosehill Farm 648-5334)*

Recreation and Entertainment
OnSite: Pool *(11am-5pm Mon-Thu, 11am-7pm Fri-Sun)*, Beach *(2 including The Cove)*, Picnic Area, Grills, Playground, Special Events *(July 4th, etc.)* **Near:** Jogging Paths, Fishing Charter, Park **Under 1 mi:** Sightseeing *(Upper Sassafras by dinghy or take the Mighty Tug Cornell Sassafras Cruise 275-2464 $25)* **1-3 mi:** Cultural Attract *(1730 Harmon Plantation 275-8819, Tue & thu 10am-3pm, Sun 1-4pm, $5 - or dinghy)*

Provisioning and General Services
OnSite: Copies Etc. **Near:** Newsstand, Retail Shops, Department Store **1-3 mi:** Convenience Store *(Glena Mini Mart 648-5000)*, Supermarket *(Otwell's Market 648-5111)*, Wine/Beer, Liquor Store *(Galena Liquors 648-, 5484)*,Bakery *(Village Bakery & Cafe 648-6400)*, Farmers' Market, Fishmonger, Meat Market, Market *(Ripples 648-6180)*, Bank/ATM, Post Office *(648-5783)*, Catholic Church, Protestant Church, Library *(Cecilton 275-1091)*, Beauty Salon *(Hidden Beauty 648-5502)*, Dry Cleaners, Laundry, Bookstore *(Last Page 648-6560)*, Pharmacy *(Galena 648-5662)*, Hardware Store *(Mackie's Home Ctr 648-5822)*, Florist *(Turners 648-5443)*

Transportation
OnSite: Bikes **OnCall:** Rental Car *(Enterprise 302-398-0030)*, Taxi *(Joe's 392-8070)*, Airport Limo *(Town Car 885-9228)* **Near:** InterCity Bus *(Rock Hall Trolley -639-2775 - to Galena $5)* **Airport:** BWI/Phil *(70 mi./60 mi.)*

Medical Services
911 Service **OnCall:** Ambulance **1-3 mi:** Doctor *(Donaher 648-6011)*
3+ mi: Veterinarian *(Middletown Vet 302-378-2342, 7 mi.)*
Hospital: Union, Elkton 302-378-9672 *(17 mi.)*

Setting -- Nestled in the trees is a charming eighteenth-century Eastern shore house surrounded by impeccably maintained facilities; Sailing Associates has a very special ambiance: small, charming, comfortable, with rocking chairs on the porch, hammocks in the trees, Adirondack chairs along the waterfront. Plus a delightful kidney-shaped pool overlooking the docks, a little kids' playground, a large screened gazebo, picnic tables on the lawn, charcoal grills, and two nice little beaches.

Marina Notes -- *In-season weekdays 9am-5pm, weekends 9am-7pm. **2nd 30amp elec $5. Founded in 1964. Two main piers head straight out into the river with slips on both sides with wide, full-length finger piers. The large mooring field is outboard of the docks and a new floating dinghy dock is adjacent to the gazebo. Launch in season only. No longer a sail only marina, there are many power boats at the docks. An attractively furnished pool is open Mon-Thu from 11am-5pm, Fri-Sun until 7pm. The nicely restored house serves as marina office and also houses a lending library with a constantly rotating stock of books, magazines, books-on-tape & videos. The coffeepot is always on and boaters are welcome to plug their laptops into the fax line for a quick download.

Notable -- The landscaping is natural and lovely. One small sandy beach, populated by Adirondack-style chairs, is right at the foot of the gazebo. Around the bend, on the eastern edge of the property, is a new beach called "The Cove" with a picnic table, a gaggle of chairs and a dinghy rack - kids seem to love it. The highly regarded Granary Restaurant and Sassafras Grill are just a short walk up the road.

PHOTOS ON CD-ROM: 12

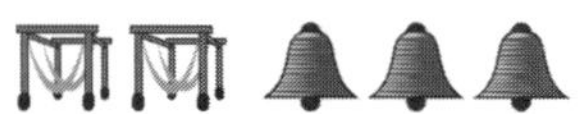

Sassafras Harbor Marina

Sassafras Harbor Marina

PO Box 68; 2 George Street; Georgetown, MD 21930

Tel: (410) 275-1144 **VHF: Monitor** 16 **Talk** 71
Fax: (410) 275-9966 **Alternate Tel:** n/a
Email: shmyacht@dmv.com **Web:** www.sassafrasharbormarina.com
Nearest Town: Galena *(2 mi.)* **Tourist Info:** (302) 378-6260

Navigational Information
Lat: 39°21.857' **Long:** 075°53.013' **Tide:** 2 ft. **Current:** n/a **Chart:** 12273
Rep. Depths (*MLW*): Entry 20 ft. **Fuel Dock** n/a **Max Slip/Moor** 20 ft./-
Access: Buoy markers 54/55 off Howell Point follow markers in to buoy 14

Marina Facilities *(In Season/Off Season)*
Fuel: No
Slips: 200 Total, 15 Transient **Max LOA:** 125 ft. **Max Beam:** n/a
Rate *(per ft.)*: **Day** $1.25 **Week** Inq. **Month** Inq.
Power: 30 amp $4, **50 amp** $8, **100 amp** n/a, **200 amp** n/a
Cable TV: Yes **Dockside Phone:** Yes
Dock Type: Fixed, Floating, Long Fingers, Pilings, Wood
Moorings: 0 Total, 0 Transient **Launch:** n/a, Dinghy Dock
Rate: Day n/a **Week** n/a **Month** n/a
Heads: 14 Toilet(s), 14 Shower(s) *(with dressing rooms)*
Laundry: 1 Washer(s), 1 Dryer(s), Book Exchange **Pay Phones:** No
Pump-Out: Full Service, 3 Central, 5 InSlip **Fee:** $5 **Closed Heads:** Yes

Marina Operations
Owner/Manager: Joseph Smith **Dockmaster:** Tracy Henry
In-Season: Apr-Oct, 8am-5pm **Off-Season:** Nov-Mar, 8:30am-4:30pm
After-Hours Arrival: Tie onto T head, check in next morning
Reservations: Yes, Preferred **Credit Cards:** Visa/MC, Dscvr
Discounts: None
Pets: Welcome, Dog Walk Area **Handicap Access:** No

Marina Services and Boat Supplies
Services - Docking Assistance, Boaters' Lounge, Crew Lounge, Dock Carts, Megayacht Facilities **Communication -** Mail & Package Hold, Phone Messages, Fax in/out, FedEx, UPS, Express Mail **Supplies - OnSite:** Ice *(Block, Cube)*, Ships' Store *(Harbor Marine daily until 4:30pm, Sun 'til 4pm* Bait/Tackle **Near:** Live Bait, CNG *(Georgetown Y.B. 648-5112)*
1-3 mi: Propane *(Turner's 648-5443)*

Boatyard Services
OnSite: Travelift *(70T)*, Hydraulic Trailer, Engine mechanic *(gas, diesel)*, Electrical Repairs, Hull Repairs, Bottom Cleaning, Compound, Wash & Wax, Interior Cleaning, Propeller Repairs, Woodworking, Painting, Yacht Broker *(Sassafras Harbor Marina Yacht Sales)* **OnCall:** Electronics Repairs, Canvas Work, Brightwork, Air Conditioning, Refrigeration, Divers, Inflatable Repairs, Life Raft Service, Upholstery, Yacht Interiors, Metal Fabrication
Near: Launching Ramp, Rigger, Sail Loft **Under 1 mi:** Awlgrip
Dealer for: Egg Harbor Yachts. **Yard Rates:** $55/hr., Haul & Launch $5/ft., Power Wash $2/ft., Bottom Paint $9.50/ft.

Restaurants and Accommodations
OnSite: Lite Fare *(Sassafras Harbor Cafe & Pizzeria 275-2963, B $2-5, L $3-13, D $3-13, kids' $2-4, Pizza $6-12; Mon & Tue 9am-8:30pm, Wed, Thu & Sun 7am-8:30pm, Fri & Sat 7am-9pm)* **Near:** Restaurant *(The Granary 275-1603, L $6-12, D $14-25)*, *(Kitty Knight House 275-8600, B $5-9, L $5-12, D $16-25)*, Lite Fare *(Sassafras Grill L $6-12, D $6-12)*, Inn/B&B *(Kitty Knight House 275-8600, $95-160)* **1-3 mi:** Restaurant *(Village Café 648-6400, B $7, L $12)*, Lite Fare *(Twinny's 648-5784, B $5, L $7, D $10)*

Recreation and Entertainment
OnSite: Pool, Picnic Area, Grills, Playground, Fitness Center *(some equipment onsite, or Curves)*, Video Arcade *(video games, ping pong, pool tables, TV)*, Special Events *(Fireworks Jul 4th)* **Near:** Beach
Under 1 mi: Sightseeing *(The Mighty Tug Cornell - Sassafras cruise 275-2464, $25)* **1-3 mi:** Tennis Courts, Park, Museum *(1730 Mt. Harmon Plantation 275-8819 Tue & Thu 10am-3pm, Sun 1-4pm, $5 - area was* known as "World's End Galleries *(Cross St. Station Antiques 648-5776 & Galena Antique Ctr. 1.5 miles from bridge)*

Provisioning and General Services
OnSite: Clothing Store *(Heron's Nest)*, Copies Etc. **Under 1 mi:** Bank/ATM, Laundry, Florist **1-3 mi:** Convenience Store *(Glena Mini Mart 648-5000)*, Supermarket *(Otwells Market 648-5111)*, Liquor Store *(Galena Liquors 648-5484)*, Bakery *(Village Bakery & Cafe 648-6400)*, Market *(Ripples 648-6180)*, Post Office *(648-5783)*, Catholic Church, Protestant Church, Beauty Salon *(Hidden Beauty 648-5502)*, Bookstore *(Last Page 648-6560)*, Pharmacy *(Galena 648-5662)*, Hardware Store *(Mackie's Home Ctr 648-5822)*
3+ mi: Library *(Cecilton 275-1091, 3 mi.)*

Transportation
OnCall: Rental Car *(Enterprise 302-398-0030)*, Taxi *(Joe's Taxi 392-8070)*, Airport Limo *(About Town 287-6400)* **Near:** InterCity Bus *(Rock Hall Trolley 639-2775, Day in Galena $5)* **Airport:** BWI/Philadelphia *(70 mi./60 mi.)*

Medical Services
911 Service **OnCall:** Ambulance **Under 1 mi:** Doctor *(Donaher 648-6011)*
Hospital: Union 302-378-9672 *(17 miles)*

Setting -- Look for the two large hunter green dock sheds emblazoned with "Sassafras Harbor Marina;" open slips line the south shore all the way to the Route 213 Bridge. Ashore, great stands of sea grasses and azaleas punctuate the entrances to each of the seven main docks, protecting them from the road. Gazebos are tucked among the greenery. Across the road are the faciities building and the attractive, well-furnished pool surrounded by a white picket fence.

Marina Notes -- Family owned & operated since 1993. In the activities center, on the first floor by the pool is the game room - a ping pong table, two pool tables, some pinball machines, a jukebox, a television and five video games. Upstairs are two function rooms - a smaller one with kitchen and a deck overlooking the pool, and a larger one with a dance floor that might handle 100 or more. Sassafras Harbor Marina Yacht Sales is above the shops. There are two excellent, comfortable bathhouses - one in the office building across from the covered slips (5 men's & 5 women's) and another adjacent to the pool (4 full baths) -- with composite floors, cinderblock walls, glass-doored shower, sink and toilet.

Notable -- Next to the pool is a small strip mall. Harbor Marine, large and well-supplied with just about anything a boater might need, including fishing tackle, marine supplies and parts, promises serious discounts. Summer hours: Mon-Sat 8am-5pm, Sun 9am-4:30pm (in winter it's a half hour earlier). Next door are Heron's Nest nautical gift and clothing shop and Sassafras Harbor Restaurant (also called The Harbor Café and Pizzeria); its hours are Monday & Tuesday 9am-8:30pm, Wed 7am-8:30pm, Thur 7am-8:30pm, Fri 7am-9pm, Sat 7am-9pm, Sun 7am-8:30pm. The Kitty Hawk House is a quick walk over the bridge.

PHOTOS ON CD-ROM: 15

Navigational Information
Lat: 39°21.660' **Long:** 075°52.922' **Tide:** 3 ft. **Current:** 3 kt. **Chart:** 12274
Rep. Depths (*MLW*): Entry 13 ft. **Fuel Dock** 15 ft. **Max Slip/Moor** 15 ft./15 ft.
Access: Chesapeake Bay to the northern shore of the Sassafras at the bridge

Marina Facilities *(In Season/Off Season)*
Fuel: Gasoline, Diesel
Slips: 300 Total, 30 Transient **Max LOA:** 120 ft. **Max Beam:** n/a
Rate *(per ft.)*: **Day** $1.75/0.70 **Week** $6.30 **Month** $21
Power: 30 amp Incl., **50 amp** Incl., **100 amp** Incl., **200 amp** n/a
Cable TV: No **Dockside Phone:** No
Dock Type: Fixed, Floating, Pilings, Wood
Moorings: 90 Total, 6 Transient **Launch:** Yes (Included), Dinghy Dock
Rate: Day $0.75 **Week** $3.15 **Month** $12
Heads: 12 Toilet(s), 12 Shower(s)
Laundry: 1 Washer(s), 1 Dryer(s), Book Exchange **Pay Phones:** Yes
Pump-Out: OnSite, Self Service **Fee:** $5 **Closed Heads:** Yes

Marina Operations
Owner/Manager: Ford Hall Sr. **Dockmaster:** Ivan Wade
In-Season: MemDay-LabDay, 8am-8pm **Off-Season:** Sep-May, 9am-5pm
After-Hours Arrival: n/a
Reservations: No **Credit Cards:** Visa/MC, Dscvr
Discounts: None
Pets: Welcome, Dog Walk Area **Handicap Access:** No

Georgetown Yacht Basin

14020 Augustine Herman Hwy; Georgetown, MD 21930

Tel: (410) 648-5112 **VHF: Monitor** 16 **Talk** 71
Fax: (410) 648-5321 **Alternate Tel:** (410) 648-5113
Email: pwallace@georgetownyachtbasin.com **Web:** georgetownyachtbasin.
Nearest Town: Galena *(1.5 mi.)* **Tourist Info:** (302) 378-6260

Marina Services and Boat Supplies
Services - Docking Assistance, Concierge, Dock Carts, Megayacht Facilities **Communication -** Mail & Package Hold, Phone Messages, Fax in/out, Data Ports *(Club Room)*, FedEx, UPS, Express Mail **Supplies - OnSite:** Ice *(Block, Cube)*, Ships' Store *(Mon-Thu 8am-5pm, Fri & Sat 'til 6pm, Sun 9am-5pm; also sundries, ice cream, bikes)*, CNG
1-3 mi: Propane *(Turner's 648-5443)*

Boatyard Services
OnSite: Travelift *(110T)*, Engine mechanic *(gas, diesel)*, Electrical Repairs, Electronics Repairs, Hull Repairs, Rigger, Sail Loft, Canvas Work, Bottom Cleaning, Brightwork, Air Conditioning, Refrigeration, Compound, Wash & Wax, Woodworking, Inflatable Repairs, Upholstery, Yacht Interiors, Painting, Awlgrip, Yacht Broker **OnCall:** Interior Cleaning, Propeller Repairs
Yard Rates: Up to $85/hr., Haul & Launch $16.50/ft., Power Wash $0.50/ft.
Storage: In-Water $15/ft. open, $52/ft. covered, On-Land $15 /ft. open, $50/ft. covered

Restaurants and Accommodations
Near: Restaurant *(The Granary 275-1603, L $6-12, D $25, by launch)*, *(Kitty Knight House Restaurant 648-5200, B $5-9, L $5-12, D $16-25)*, Lite Fare *(Harbor Cafe & Pizzeria 275-2963, B $5, L $8, D $10)*, *(Sassafras Grill 275-1603, B $6-12, L $6-12, by launch, only open weekends MemDay-LabDay; Fri 4pm-mid, Sat 11am-11pm, Sun 11am-10pm)*, Inn/B&B *(Kitty Knight House Restaurant 648-5200, $95-160)* **1-3 mi:** Restaurant *(Dixie-Jo's 648-5521)*, *(Village Cafe' 648-6400, B $7, L $9)*, Pizzeria *(Galena Pizzeria 648-5945)*, Inn/B&B *(Carousel Horse 648-5476, $80-90)* **3+ mi:** Inn/B&B *(Anchorage B&B 275-1972, 5 mi.)*

Recreation and Entertainment
OnSite: Pool, Beach, Picnic Area, Grills *(propane)* **Under 1 mi:** Sightseeing *(The Mighty Tug Cornell Sasafras cruises 275-2464 $25)* **1-3 mi:** Playground, Tennis Courts, Park, Museum *(Mt. Harmon Plantation at World's End's 275-8819 Tue & Thu 10am-3pm, Sun 1-4pm $25)*, Galleries *(Galena Antique Center, 1.5 miles from the drawbridge)*

Provisioning and General Services
OnSite: Convenience Store, Wine/Beer, Liquor Store, Laundry **1-3 mi:** Supermarket *(Otwell's Market 648-5111)*, Bakery *(Village Bakery & Cafe 648-6400)*, Farmers' Market, Meat Market, Market *(Ripples 648-6180)*, Bank/ATM, Post Office *(648-5783)*, Catholic Church, Protestant Church, Beauty Salon *(Hidden Beauty 648-5502)*, Bookstore *(Last Page Bookshop 648-6560)*, Pharmacy *(Galena Pharmacy 648-5662)*, Florist *(Turner's Unlimited 648-5443)*, Retail Shops **3+ mi:** Library *(Cecilton 275-1091, 3 mi.)*, Department Store *(15 mi.)*

Transportation
OnSite: Bikes *(comp. at the store - check hours)*, Water Taxi *(Two Toots, complimentary)*, Rental Car **OnCall:** Taxi *(Joe's Taxi 392-8070)*, InterCity Bus *(Rock Hall Trolley -639-2775 - A Day in Galena $5)*, Airport Limo *(Town Car 885-9228)* **Airport:** BWI/Philadelphia *(70 mi./60 mi.)*

Medical Services
911 Service **OnCall:** Ambulance **1-3 mi:** Doctor *(Donaher 648-6011)*
3+ mi: Veterinarian *(Buckle 778-2455, 15 mi.)*
Hospital: Chester River, Chestertown 778-3300 *(17 mi.)*

Setting -- At the head of the Sassafras River, just before the bridge, the entire northern shore is occupied by Georgetown Yacht Basin's two sets of docks - each with a combination of open and covered slips. On a grassy knoll above the docks are the pool and picnic area and above that the famous Kitty Knight House. It's a beautiful spot with great views of the Sassafras and lots of traffic on weekends.

Marina Notes -- Founded in 1949, by the Hall family who own and operate it today - second & third generations are among the workforce. 110 ton lift serves both a full-service and do-it-yourself yard. Dry inside or outside storage. The ships' store has marine supplies, sundries, basic convenience items, ice cream, and complimentary bicycles (Note: bikes available when the store is open). Internet access is in the little club room, which is part of the amenities building for the northern "I"-"J"-"K" docks. Halfway up the hill is an attractive dog walk area. Heads and showers are cute, well-maintained fully-tiled individual rooms with portholes that sit out on the main pier flanking two sides of the dockhouse. A covered waiting area near the fuel dock has soda machines.

Notable -- The pool is midway up the hill overlooking Georgetown and the Sassafras. Nearby are 5 attractive picnic tables, with the same spectacular view, and 3 propane grills with utensils thoughtfully hanging by their sides. A path leads up to the Kitty Knight House. (Kitty Knight is credited with saving 4 Georgetown houses from being burned in the War of 1812.) Today, the impeccable, flower-bedecked complex features 11 recently renovated rooms, a restaurant that serves "traditional Eastern Shore cuisine with Philadelphia flair," a casual Tavern offering pub food plus an expansive dining deck with long river views.

PHOTOS ON CD-ROM: 16

Green Point Landing

23150 Green Point Road; Worton, MD 21678

Tel: (410) 778-1615 **VHF: Monitor** 16 **Talk** 79
Fax: (410) 778-1402 **Alternate Tel:** n/a
Email: greenpt@dmv.com **Web:** n/a
Nearest Town: Worton *(8 mi.)* **Tourist Info:** (410) 810-2968

Navigational Information

Lat: 39°16.950' **Long:** 076°10.097' **Tide:** 2 ft. **Current:** n/a **Chart:** 12278
Rep. Depths (*MLW*): Entry n/a **Fuel Dock** n/a **Max Slip/Moor** -/-
Access: Tim's Creek past Worton Creek - portside

Marina Facilities *(In Season/Off Season)*

Fuel: Gasoline, Diesel
Slips: 57 Total, 1 Transient **Max LOA:** 60 ft. **Max Beam:** 16 ft.
Rate *(per ft.)*: **Day** $1.00/Inq. **Week** Inq. **Month** Inq.
Power: 30 amp Incl., **50 amp** n/a, **100 amp** n/a, **200 amp** n/a
Cable TV: No **Dockside Phone:** No
Dock Type: Fixed
Moorings: 33 Total, 2 Transient **Launch:** n/a, Dinghy Dock
Rate: Day $15 **Week** n/a **Month** n/a
Heads: 6 Toilet(s), 6 Shower(s)
Laundry: None, Book Exchange **Pay Phones:** Yes, 1
Pump-Out: OnSite, 1 Central **Fee:** $5 **Closed Heads:** Yes

Marina Operations

Owner/Manager: Ray Clark **Dockmaster:** Same
In-Season: Apr-Nov, 9am-4pm **Off-Season:** closed, Closed
After-Hours Arrival: Call ahead
Reservations: Preferred **Credit Cards:** Visa/MC, Dscvr
Discounts: None
Pets: Welcome, Dog Walk Area **Handicap Access:** No

Marina Services and Boat Supplies

Services - Boaters' Lounge, Security *(24 hrs, owners live onsite)*, Dock Carts **Communication -** FedEx, UPS, Express Mail **Supplies - OnSite:** Ice *(Block, Cube)*, Ships' Store *(minimal)* **Under 1 mi:** Marine Discount Store *(Worton Creek Marina 778-3282)*, Propane *(Worton Creek Marina)* **3+ mi:** West Marine *(639-9959 in Rock Hall, 15 mi.)*

Boatyard Services

OnSite: Travelift *(15T)*, Launching Ramp, Engine mechanic *(gas, diesel)*, Electrical Repairs, Hull Repairs, Bottom Cleaning, Brightwork, Compound, Wash & Wax, Interior Cleaning, Woodworking, Painting **Dealer for:** Mercury/Mercruiser - onsite. **Yard Rates:** $50-65/hr., Haul & Launch $6/ft. *(blocking $7/ft.)*, Power Wash $7, Bottom Paint $15/ft. *(paint incl.)*
Storage: In-Water $25/ft., On-Land $4/ft./mo.

Restaurants and Accommodations

1-3 mi: Restaurant *(Harbor House 778-0669, D $16-22)*, *(China House 778-3939, L $3-11, D $3-12)*, Pizzeria *(Procolino Pizza 778-5900, L $7-14, D $7-14)* **3+ mi:** Restaurant *(Great Oak Landing 778-2100, L $6-10, D $15-30, 6 mi.)*, *(Old Wharf Inn 778-3055, 7 mi.)*, Pizzeria *(Pizza Hut 778-1070, 4 mi.)*, Motel *(Comfort Suites 810-0555, $100-200, 6 mi.)*, Hotel *(Great Oak Landing 778-2100, 4 mi.)*, Inn/B&B *(Great Oaks Manor B&B 778-5943, $140-275, 6 mi.)*

Recreation and Entertainment

OnSite: Picnic Area, Grills, Boat Rentals *(Upper Bay Sailing School 888-302-7245 - Beneteau First 35 & Beneteau 411- $625 2-day weekend, $1950 week)* **Near:** Beach **3+ mi:** Golf Course *(Great Oak Landing, 7 mi.)*, Fitness Center *(Kent Athletic Club 778-3148, 8 mi.)*, Horseback Riding *(Crimson Stables 778-7304, 9 mi.)*, Bowling *(Queen Anne's 778-5800, 10 mi.)*, Movie Theater *(Chester 5 Theatres 778-2227, 8 mi.)*, Video Rental *(Video Scene 778-7900, 8 mi.)*

Provisioning and General Services

1-3 mi: Liquor Store *(Pip's Liquors 778-0123)*, Fishmonger *(E & E Seafood 778-6333)* **3+ mi:** Supermarket *(Super Fresh 778-9535, 8 mi.)*, Delicatessen *(C-Town Deli 778-3119, 8 mi.)*, Health Food *(Chestertown Natural Foods 778-1677, 8 mi.)*, Post Office *(Chestertown 778-0690, 8 mi.)*, Library *(810-0531, 8 mi.)*, Dry Cleaners *(Mcbride's 778-4790, 8 mi.)*, Bookstore *(Mustard Seed 778-6707, 8 mi.)*, Pharmacy *(Eckerd 778-6214, 8 mi.)*, Hardware Store *(True Value 778-9600, 8 mi.)*, Department Store *(Peebles 778-6011, 8 mi.)*, Copies Etc. *(The UPS Store 778-9446, 8 mi.)*

Transportation

OnCall: Rental Car *(Enterprise 810-0971)* **3+ mi:** Taxi *(Country Sedan 810-0139, 8 mi.)*, Rail *(Amtrak Caudon Bridge 642-2620, 50 mi.)*, Airport Limo *(Prince 778-4860, 8 mi.)* **Airport:** Philadelphia/Cecil County *(90 mi./40 mi.)*

Medical Services

911 Service **3+ mi:** Doctor *(Shanahan & Ferguson 778-9300, 7 mi.)*, Dentist *(Brayton 778-1104, 7 mi.)*, Chiropractor *(Chestertown Chiropractic Center 810-0530, 8 mi.)*, Veterinarian *(Hash 778-9627, 8 mi.)*
Hospital: Chester River Hospital Center 778-3300 *(8.3 mi.)*

Setting -- Just past Tim's Creek on Worton Creek, Green Point is the first public facility on the port side and directly adjacent to the Wharf at Handy's Point. Three docks radiate from the shoreside bulkhead, backed by a gray two-story office building with hunter green trim. Two additional docks stretch out from a pier that runs paralell to the land. A fairly extensive network of docks, with nearly 60 protected slips. A green thumb seems to be at work here - a vegetable patch is right outside the office. The area around the marina is quite rural.

Marina Notes -- A family-run business founded in 1984; the second-generation owners live on-site, in the house on the ridge overlooking the docks. A separate marine service facility is onsite as well. There's a nice little first-floor lounge with a couple of "ice cream parlor" tables and chairs and a coffee machine, ice cream, freezer, microwave, and a few boating supplies. A couple of picnic tables overlook the docks. The 2 full baths are located in two small tandem green-rimmed gray buldings edged with flowers.

Notable -- The Upper Bay Sailing School, an American Sailing Association-certified training facility, is onsite (www.upperbaysailing.com). It received the American Sailing Association's Gold Standard Rating, and offers affordable lessons on the boats here, plus in the BVIs. Courses range from weekend basic coastal cruising classes ($475) to 4-day advanced coastal cruising ($725) to blue water passages to Bermuda or the BVIs ($1195-1495).

PHOTOS ON CD-ROM: 11

Navigational Information
Lat: 39°16.905' **Long:** 076°10.130' **Tide:** n/a **Current:** n/a **Chart:** 12278
Rep. Depths (*MLW*): Entry n/a **Fuel Dock** n/a **Max Slip/Moor** -/-
Access: Tim's Creek to Worton Creek portside

Marina Facilities *(In Season/Off Season)*
Fuel: No
Slips: 59 Total, varies Transient **Max LOA:** 50 ft. **Max Beam:** 18 ft.
Rate *(per ft.)*: **Day** $1.50/1.00 **Week** Inq **Month** n/a
Power: 30 amp Incl., **50 amp** Incl., **100 amp** n/a, **200 amp** n/a
Cable TV: No **Dockside Phone:** No
Dock Type: Fixed, Wood
Moorings: 0 Total, 0 Transient **Launch:** n/a
Rate: Day n/a **Week** n/a **Month** n/a
Heads: 4 Toilet(s), 4 Shower(s)
Laundry: 2 Washer(s) **Pay Phones:** No
Pump-Out: OnSite, Self Service, 1 Central **Fee:** n/a **Closed Heads:** Yes

Marina Operations
Owner/Manager: Alice Smith **Dockmaster:** n/a
In-Season: Apr-Nov, 8am-5pm **Off-Season:** n/a
After-Hours Arrival: Tie up - discuss next day
Reservations: Yes, Preferred **Credit Cards:** n/a
Discounts: None
Pets: Welcome, Dog Walk Area **Handicap Access:** No

The Wharf at Handy's Point

23153 Green Point Road; Worton, MD 21678

Tel: (410) 778-4363 **VHF: Monitor** 16 **Talk** n/a
Fax: (410) 778-0446 **Alternate Tel:** n/a
Email: n/a **Web:** n/a
Nearest Town: Chestertown *(10 mi.)* **Tourist Info:** (410) 810-2968

Marina Services and Boat Supplies
Services - Docking Assistance, Security *(owners live on-site)*, Dock Carts
Communication - Fed Ex, UPS **Supplies - OnSite:** Ice *(Block, Cube)*
Under 1 mi: Marine Discount Store *(Worton Creek 778-3282)*, Propane *(Worton Creek 778-3282)* **3+ mi:** West Marine *(639-9959 - Rock Hall, 15 mi.)*

Boatyard Services
OnSite: Travelift *(35T)*, Launching Ramp, Painting **Near:** Engine mechanic *(gas, diesel)*, Electrical Repairs, Hull Repairs, Bottom Cleaning, Brightwork, Compound, Wash & Wax, Woodworking. **Yard Rates:** $52/hr., Haul & Launch $8/ft., Bottom Paint $10

Restaurants and Accommodations
1-3 mi: Restaurant *(China House 778-3939, L $3-11, D $3-11)*, *(Harbor House 778-0669, D $16-22)*, Pizzeria *(Procolino Pizza 778-5900, L $7-14, D $7-14)* **3+ mi:** Restaurant *(Great Oak Landing 778-2100, L $6-10, D $15-30, 4 mi.)*, Pizzeria *(Pizza Hut 778-1070, 4 mi.)*, Motel *(Comfort Suites 810-0555, $100-200, 6 mi.)*, Hotel *(Great Oak Landing 778-2100, 4 mi.)*, Inn/B&B *(Inn at Mitchell House 778-6500, 11 mi.)*, *(Great Oaks Manor B&B 778-5943, $140-275, 6 mi.)*

Recreation and Entertainment
3+ mi: Golf Course *(Great Oak Landing, 7 mi.)*, Fitness Center *(Kent Athletic Club 778-3148, 8 mi.)*, Horseback Riding *(Crimson Stables 778-7304, 9 mi.)*, Bowling *(Queen Anne's 778-5800, 10 mi.)*, Movie Theater *(Chester 5 Theatres 778-2227, 8 mi.)*, Video Rental *(Video Scene 778-7900, 8 mi.)*

Provisioning and General Services
1-3 mi: Liquor Store *(Pip's Liquors 778-0123)*, Fishmonger *(E & E Seafood 778-6333)* **3+ mi:** Supermarket *(Super Fresh 778-9535, 8 mi.)*, Delicatessen *(C-Town Deli 778-3119, 8 mi.)*, Health Food *(Chestertown Natural Foods 778-1677, 8 mi.)*, Post Office *(Chestertown 778-0690, 8 mi.)*, Library *(810-0531, 8 mi.)*, Dry Cleaners *(McBride's 778-4790, 8 mi.)*, Bookstore *(Mustard Seed 778-6707, 8 mi.)*, Pharmacy *(Eckerd 778-6214, 8 mi.)*, Hardware Store *(True Value 778-9600, 8 mi.)*, Department Store *(Peebles 778-6011, 8 mi.)*, Copies Etc. *(The UPS Store 778-9446, 8 mi.)*

Transportation
OnCall: Rental Car *(Enterprise 810-0971)* **3+ mi:** Taxi *(Country Sedan 810-0139, 8 mi.)*, Rail *(Amtrak Caudon Bridge 642-2620, 50 mi.)*, Airport Limo *(Prince 778-4860, 8 mi.)*
Airport: Philadelphia/Cecil County *(90 mi./40 mi.)*

Medical Services
911 Service **3+ mi:** Doctor *(Shanahan & Ferguson 778-9300, 7 mi.)*, Dentist *(Brayton 778-1104, 7 mi.)*, Chiropractor *(Chestertown Chiropractic Center 810-0530, 8 mi.)*, Veterinarian *(Hash 778-9627, 8 mi.)*
Hospital: Chester River Hospital Center 778-3300 *(8.3 mi.)*

Setting -- A 3-arm flagpole sits in front of the contemporary greige clapboard two-story main building with a second-story balcony punctuated by dark brown trim . The network of recent, well-maintained, stationary docks winds its way among the reeds and grasses that line the bank. A swath of green hosts comfortable Adirondack-style chairs adjacent to the large travelift. Right off Worton Creek, on protected little Tim's Creek, this lovely, quiet spot makes the most of its natural setting.

Marina Notes -- DCM. A family operation - Alice Smith and Pepper Gilbert live onsite with their two little boys - and the office doubles as a playroom. While there are no dedicated transient slips, when the slipholders are gone, dockage is usually available with considerable on-the-hard storage. Generous partial finger piers. If you have serious draft, you probably want to be on their closest docks. Some haulout for winter. A large single-story bathhouse surrounded by decks sits back from the docks. Across the front are four individual, private shower rooms; on each side of the bathhouse are the ladies' room and men's heads - each with two toilets, three sinks, a snack machine, and thoughtful basket of shampoos and soaps (and baby wipes too). Although the heads are cinderblock, they're quite inviting and nicely maintained.

Notable -- One set of slips is a bit remote and reached via a wide and comfortable boardwalk that runs though a sea of salt grass.- which adds a delightful element to an already peaceful, rural environment. An occasional flower garden and festive planter supplement the natural ambiance.

PHOTOS ON CD-ROM: 11

Worton Creek Marina

23145 Buck Neck Road; Chestertown, MD 21620

Tel: (410) 778-3282 **VHF: Monitor** 16 **Talk** 68
Fax: (410) 778-3395 **Alternate Tel:** n/a
Email: wortoncrek@friend.ly.net **Web:** www.wortoncreek.com
Nearest Town: Chestertown *(8 mi.)* **Tourist Info:** (410) 810-2968

Navigational Information
Lat: 39°16.457' **Long:** 076°10.142' **Tide:** 2 ft. **Current:** n/a **Chart:** 12278
Rep. Depths (*MLW*): Entry 6 ft. **Fuel Dock** 6 ft. **Max Slip/Moor** 6 ft./6 ft.
Access: 1.5 miles from Chesapeake Bay on Worton Creek,

Marina Facilities *(In Season/Off Season)*
Fuel: Gasoline, Diesel
Slips: 110 Total, 20 Transient **Max LOA:** 90 ft. **Max Beam:** 30 ft.
Rate *(per ft.)*: **Day** $1.35 **Week** $175-285* **Month** $540-865
Power: 30 amp Incl., **50 amp** $3, **100 amp** n/a, **200 amp** n/a
Cable TV: No **Dockside Phone:** No
Dock Type: Fixed, Long Fingers, Pilings
Moorings: 77 Total, 30 Transient **Launch:** None, Dinghy Dock
Rate: Day $15 **Week** $95 **Month** $290
Heads: 8 Toilet(s), 6 Shower(s)
Laundry: 1 Washer(s), 1 Dryer(s), Book Exchange **Pay Phones:** Yes, 1
Pump-Out: OnSite, Full Service, 1 Central **Fee:** $5 **Closed Heads:** Yes

Marina Operations
Owner/Manager: John & Libby Patnovic **Dockmaster:** Libby Patnovic
In-Season: Apr-Oct, 8am-6pm **Off-Season:** Nov-Mar, 8am-5pm
After-Hours Arrival: Call in advance
Reservations: Yes, Preferred **Credit Cards:** Visa/MC, Dscvr, Amex
Discounts: None
Pets: Welcome, Dog Walk Area **Handicap Access:** No

Marina Services and Boat Supplies
Services - Docking Assistance, Trash Pick-Up, Dock Carts **Communication -** Mail & Package Hold, Fax in/out *($1)*, FedEx, DHL, UPS, Express Mail **Supplies - OnSite:** Ice *(Block, Cube)*, Ships' Store, Bait/Tackle, Propane, CNG **3+ mi:** West Marine *(639-9959, 15 mi.)*

Boatyard Services
OnSite: Travelift *(25T & 70T**)*, Crane, Engine mechanic *(gas, diesel)*, Electrical Repairs, Hull Repairs, Bottom Cleaning, Brightwork, Compound, Wash & Wax, Interior Cleaning, Woodworking, Metal Fabrication, Painting, Awlgrip, Total Refits **OnCall:** Electronics Repairs, Sail Loft, Canvas Work, Air Conditioning, Refrigeration, Divers, Propeller Repairs, Inflatable Repairs, Life Raft Service, Upholstery, Yacht Interiors, Yacht Design, Yacht Building, Yacht Broker **1-3 mi:** Rigger. **3+ mi:** Launching Ramp *(4 mi.)*.
Member: ABBRA, ABYC - 3 Certified Tech(s), Other Certifications: Sealand, Onan **Yard Rates:** $70/hr., Haul & Launch $4.75-7.50/ft. + Labor *(blocking incl.)*, Power Wash Yes, Bottom Paint $70/hr.
Storage: In-Water $580-850 per winter, On-Land $25.50/ft.

Restaurants and Accommodations
OnSite: Restaurant *(Harbor House 778-0669, D $16-22, Tue-Sun 5-8pm)* **3+ mi:** Restaurant *(China House 778-3939, 4 mi.)*, *(Great Oak Landing 778-2100, L $6-10, D $15-30, 4 mi.)*, Pizzeria *(Procolino Pizza 778-5900, L $7-14, D $7-14, 4 mi.)*, Motel *(Comfort Suites 810-0555, $100-200, 8 mi.)*, Hotel *(Great Oak Landing 778-2100, 4 mi.)*, Inn/B&B *(Inn at Mitchell House 778-6500, 11 mi.)*, *(Great Oaks Manor 778-5943, $140-275, 4 mi.)*

Recreation and Entertainment
OnSite: Pool *(10am-8pm)*, Picnic Area, Grills *(propane)*, Playground **Near:** Beach **3+ mi:** Fitness Center *(Kent Athletic Club 778-3148, 8 mi.)*, Horseback Riding *(Crimson Stables 778-7304, 9 mi.)*, Bowling *(Queen Anne's 778-5800, 10 mi.)*, Movie Theater *(Chester 5 Theatres 778-2227, 8 mi.)*, Video Rental *(Video Scene 778-7900, 8 mi.)*

Provisioning and General Services
OnSite: Convenience Store *(gift, clothing, sandwiches, and drinks)*, Wine/Beer **1-3 mi:** Fishmonger *(E & E Seafood 778-6333)* **3+ mi:** Super market *(Super Fresh 778-9535, 8 mi.)*, Delicatessen *(C-Town Deli 778-3119, 8 mi.)*, Health Food *(Natural Foods 778-1677, 8 mi.)*, Liquor Store *(Pip's Liquors 778-0123, 8 mi.)*, Post Office *(Chestertown 778-0690, 8 mi.)*, Library *(810-0531, 8 mi.)*, Dry Cleaners *(McBride's 778-4790, 8 mi.)*, Bookstore *(Mustard Seed 778-6707, 8 mi.)*, Pharmacy *(Eckerd 778-6214, 8 mi.)*, Hardware Store *(True Value 778-9600, 8 mi.)*, Department Store *(Peebles 778-6011, 8 mi.)*, Copies Etc. *(UPS Store 778-9446, 8 mi.)*

Transportation
OnCall: Rental Car *(Enterprise 810-0971)*, InterCity Bus *(Rock Hall Trolley - 639-2775 $5)* **3+ mi:** Taxi *(Country Sedan 810-0139, 8 mi.)*, Airport Limo *(Prince 778-4860, 8 mi.)* **Airport:** Philadelphia/Cecil County *(90 mi./40 mi.)*

Medical Services
911 Service **3+ mi:** Doctor *(Ferguson 778-9300, 7 mi.)*, Dentist *(Brayton 778-1104, 7 mi.)*, Chiropractor *(Chestertown 810-0530, 8 mi.)*, Veterinarian *(Hash 778-9627, 8 mi.)* **Hospital:** Chester River 778-3300 *(9 mi.)*

Setting -- A country marina far from "town," Worton Creek seems to embody a relaxed Eastern Shore, rural tradition - it has an old-time feeling in the very best sense of the word. Barn-red buildings house the workshops, offices, and enticing country store. Up the hill from the docks are a pool, a casual picnic area, and a seasonal restaurant - all overlooking the snug harbor below.

Marina Notes -- *Weekly & monthly fees are flat rates. Founded in 1949. Family-owned by John & Libby Patnovic since 1997. Closed Mondays. Extensive staff of craftsmen for yacht repairs, two large travelifts, and mechanic available on weekends (**25 ton lift $4.75/ft., 70 ton lift $7.50/ft). DCM. Three uncovered docks and two covered sheds. Large yachts can be accommodated here - there were several on each visit. Adjacent to the store is a well-stocked chandlery. On a bluff above the docks is a small pool (10am-8pm). Nearby is the picnic area with propane grills. Considerable on-the-hard storage is also on that upper level. One set of heads and showers is immediately adjacent. The second set is down in the red building next to the big set of covered shed docks.

Notable -- The charming, well-merchandised store is housed in one of the original boat sheds; the cathedral ceiling has been left raw with open beams, and the original floors are intact and refurbished. It's stocked with a wide array of delightful gifts and clothing, as well as sundries, some sandwiches and drinks. There's always hot coffee, ice cream, and cold sodas. Harbor House Restaurant, up on the ridge, is open for dinner 5-8pm, Tue-Sun. Furnished with blonde bentwood chairs and attractive green tablecloths, it sports a view of the marina and beyond.

Navigational Information

Lat: 39°15.857' **Long:** 076°12.163' **Tide:** 2 ft. **Current:** 4 kt. **Chart:** 12278
Rep. Depths (*MLW*): Entry 8 ft. **Fuel Dock** 6 ft. **Max Slip/Moor** 6 ft./-
Access: Chesapeake Bay to Fairlee Creek to Red buoy #34

Marina Facilities *(In Season/Off Season)*

Fuel: Gasoline, Diesel
Slips: 350 Total, 60 Transient **Max LOA:** 70 ft. **Max Beam:** n/a
Rate *(per ft.)*: **Day** $1.75/0.75* **Week** $7.00 **Month** Inq.
Power: 30 amp $6, **50 amp** $12, **100 amp** $20, **200 amp** n/a
Cable TV: Yes Incl. **Dockside Phone:** No
Dock Type: Fixed, Long Fingers, Short Fingers, Pilings
Moorings: 0 Total, 0 Transient **Launch:** n/a, Dinghy Dock
Rate: Day n/a **Week** n/a **Month** n/a
Heads: 18 Toilet(s), 18 Shower(s)
Laundry: 2 Washer(s), 2 Dryer(s) **Pay Phones:** Yes
Pump-Out: OnSite, OnCall **Fee:** $5 **Closed Heads:** Yes

Marina Operations

Owner/Manager: Mark Grahamer **Dockmaster:** Brad Willson
In-Season: May-Oct, 8:30am-8pm **Off-Season:** Nov-Apr, 9am-4:30pm
After-Hours Arrival: Look for open slip on bulletin board at dock office
Reservations: Recommended **Credit Cards:** Visa/MC, Dscvr, Amex
Discounts: None
Pets: Welcome, Dog Walk Area **Handicap Access:** Yes, Heads, Docks

Mear's Great Oak Landing

22170 Great Oak Landing Rd.; Chestertown, MD 21620

Tel: (410) 778-5007 **VHF: Monitor** 9 **Talk** 9
Fax: (410) 778-4980 **Alternate Tel:** n/a
Email: info@mearsgreatoaklanding.com **Web:** mearsgreatoaklanding.com
Nearest Town: Chestertown *(7 mi.)* **Tourist Info:** (410) 810-2968

Marina Services and Boat Supplies

Services - Docking Assistance, Security, Dock Carts **Communication -** Phone Messages, Fax in/out, FedEx, DHL, UPS **Supplies - OnSite:** Ice *(Block, Cube)*, Ships' Store **3+ mi:** West Marine *(639-9959 in Rock Hall, 15 mi.)*, Marine Discount Store *(Worton Creek Marina 778-3282, 4 mi.)*, Propane *(Worton Creek, 4 mi.)*, CNG *(Worton Creek, 4 mi.)*

Boatyard Services

OnSite: Travelift *(50T)*, Forklift, Hydraulic Trailer, Launching Ramp, Engine mechanic *(gas, diesel)*, Electrical Repairs, Electronics Repairs, Hull Repairs, Rigger, Canvas Work, Bottom Cleaning, Brightwork **OnCall:** Air Conditioning, Refrigeration, Divers, Compound, Wash & Wax, Interior Cleaning, Propeller Repairs

Restaurants and Accommodations

OnSite: Restaurant *(Mears Great Oak Landing 778-2100, L $6-14, D $9-28, kids' $4.50; specials Mon-Wed, pool menu - sandwiches & salads)*, Lite Fare *(Erica's Food Stand at Jellyfish Joel's Tiki Bar - walk, jitney or dinghy)*, Hotel *(Great Oak Landing Lodge 778-2100, $79-129, 28 units)* **Near:** Inn/B&B *(Great Oaks Manor B&B 778-5943)* **1-3 mi:** Restaurant *(China House 778-3939, L $3-11, D $3-11)*, Pizzeria *(Procolino 778-5900, L $7-14, D $7-14)* **3+ mi:** Motel *(Comfort Suites 810-0555, 9 mi.)*

Recreation and Entertainment

OnSite: Pool, Spa, Beach *(600 ft. of sand)*, Picnic Area, Grills, Playground, Tennis Courts, Golf Course *(9 hole)* **3+ mi:** Fitness Center *(Kent Athletic Club 778-3148, 9 mi.)*, Horseback Riding *(Crimson Stables 778-7304, 10 mi.)*, Bowling *(Queen Anne's 778-5800, 11 mi.)*, Movie Theater *(Chester 5 Theatres 778-2227, 9 mi.)*, Video Rental *(Video Scene 778-7900, 9 mi.)*

Provisioning and General Services

OnSite: Convenience Store *(limited groceries)*, Wine/Beer **1-3 mi:** Liquor Store *(Pip's Liquors 778-0123)*, Fishmonger *(E & E Seafood 778-6333)* **3+ mi:** Supermarket *(Super Fresh 778-9535, 9 mi.)*, Delicatessen *(C-Town Deli 778-3119, 9 mi.)*, Health Food *(Chestertown Natural Foods 778-1677), 9 mi.)*,Post Office *(Chestertown 778-0690, 9 mi.)*, Library *(810-0531, 9 mi.)*, Dry Cleaners *(Mcbride's 778-4790, 9 mi.)*, Bookstore *(Mustard Seed 778-6707, 9 mi.)*, Pharmacy *(Eckerd 778-6214, 9 mi.)*, Hardware Store *(True Value 778-9600, 9 mi.)*, Department Store *(Peebles 778-6011, 9 mi.)*, Copies Etc. *(The UPS Store 778-9446, 9 mi.)*

Transportation

OnCall: Rental Car *(Enterprise 810-0971)*, Taxi *(Country Sedan 810-0139, 9 mi.)*, Local Bus *(Rock Hall Trolley 866-748-7659 $5)*, Airport Limo *(Prince 778-4860 9 mi.)* **3+ mi:** Rail *(Amtrak Caudon Bridge 642-2620, 50 mi.)*
Airport: Philadelphia/Cecil County *(90 mi./40 mi.)*

Medical Services

911 Service **3+ mi:** Doctor *(Shanahan & Ferguson 778-9300, 8 mi.)*, Dentist *(Brayton 778-1104, 8 mi.)*, Chiropractor *(Chestertown 810-0530,* 9 mi.), Veterinarian *(Hash 778-9627, 9 mi.)*
Hospital: Chester River 778-3300 *(9 mi.)*

Setting -- A secluded 70-acre resort set in the midst of farmlands, 350 well-maintained slips, eateries, a golf course and a host of amenities make Fairlee Creek's Great Oak Landing a true desination marina. A long one and two-story brick and yellow clapboard building sits at the top of a manicured rise and houses many of the services. A restaurant, hotel and a large, nicely furnished and landscaped pool all overlook the expansive harbor filled with docks.

Marina Notes -- *In-season $55/night minimum, weekends $2.50/ft., holidays $2.75/ft. - 2 night min. DCM. Established in 1955 as a yacht club & hunting lodge. Dockmaster, most transients, and fuel are on "D" dock. Fuel Mon-Thu 8:30am-7pm, Fri-Sun 8am-8pm. Onsite Chesapeake Marine Services handles most of the boat work. Grab your foursome for the midweek golf special - $1.25/ft. includes nine holes of golf for up to four people and dockage. Club cruises & rendezvous are welcome. Several bathhouses plus a beach shower. Adequate key coded individual tile full bathrooms with fiberglass showers stalls.

Notable -- On the site of 1,100 acre Great Oak Manor, established in 1658. Well-reviewed Great Oak Restaurant (Mon-Thu noon-9pm, Fri-Sat, noon-10pm, Sun noon-8pm; continental breakfast Sat-Sun 8-10am) features seafood and country buffets - live bands Fri, Sat & Sun. Jellyfish Joel's peninsula (open Fri night, Sat & Sun) is around the cove - walk, take the jitney golf cart or dinghy (8 dinghy slips). It has a 200-ft. sandy beach with chaises, a bar, the Caribbean Grill (which is Erica's Food Stand), a picnic area, and a gift shop with T-shirts, snacks, frozen drinks and live music every weekend 1-9pm. Palm trees strung with twinkling lights add to the tropical ambience. Tennis courts, a beach, and 3 playgrounds are also onsite. Seven to nine mile trek to all services.

PHOTOS ON CD-ROM: 16

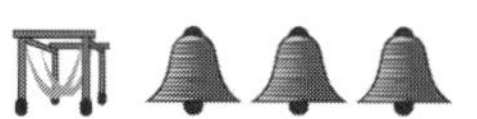

Tolchester Marina

21085 Tolchester Beach Road; Chestertown, MD 21620

Tel: (410) 778-1400 **VHF: Monitor** 16 **Talk** n/a
Fax: (410) 778-6570 **Alternate Tel:** n/a
Email: office@tolchestermarina.com **Web:** www.tolchestermarina.com
Nearest Town: Chestertown *(7 mi.)* **Tourist Info:** (410) 810-2968

Navigational Information

Lat: 39°12.848' **Long:** 076°14.563' **Tide:** 2 ft. **Current:** n/a **Chart:** 12278
Rep. Depths (*MLW*): Entry 6 ft. **Fuel Dock** 6 ft. **Max Slip/Moor** 6 ft./-
Access: Right off the Chesapeake Bay at Buoy #24

Marina Facilities *(In Season/Off Season)*

Fuel: Gasoline, Diesel
Slips: 264 Total, 15 Transient **Max LOA:** 60 ft. **Max Beam:** n/a
Rate *(per ft.)*: **Day** $1.75 **Week** Inq. **Month** Inq.
Power: 30 amp $6, **50 amp** $12, **100 amp** n/a, **200 amp** n/a
Cable TV: No **Dockside Phone:** No
Dock Type: Fixed, Long Fingers, Pilings, Wood
Moorings: 0 Total, 0 Transient **Launch:** n/a
Rate: Day n/a **Week** n/a **Month** n/a
Heads: 10 Toilet(s), 10 Shower(s)
Laundry: 2 Washer(s), 2 Dryer(s) **Pay Phones:** Yes, 1
Pump-Out: OnSite, Full Service, 2 Central **Fee:** $5 **Closed Heads:** Yes

Marina Operations

Owner/Manager: Alam Bramble **Dockmaster:** Cathy Bramble
In-Season: Year-Round, 9am-5pm **Off-Season:** n/a
After-Hours Arrival: Check in at fuel dock
Reservations: Yes **Credit Cards:** Visa/MC, Dscvr, Amex
Discounts: None
Pets: Welcome, Dog Walk Area **Handicap Access:** Yes, Heads

Marina Services and Boat Supplies

Services - Docking Assistance, Security *(8 hrs., Night Time)*, Dock Carts **Communication -** Mail & Package Hold, Phone Messages, Fax in/out *(0.25)*, FedEx, DHL, UPS, Express Mail **Supplies - OnSite:** Ice *(Block, Cube)*, Ships' Store, Bait/Tackle, Propane *(or Bayside Gas 778-2787, 7 mi.)* **3+ mi:** West Marine *(639-9959, 8 mi.)*

Boatyard Services

OnSite: Travelift *(50T)*, Crane, Forklift, Hydraulic Trailer, Engine mechanic *(gas, diesel)*, Electrical Repairs, Hull Repairs, Rigger, Bottom Cleaning, Brightwork, Air Conditioning, Compound, Wash & Wax, Woodworking, Painting, Awlgrip **OnCall:** Electronics Repairs, Canvas Work, Refrigeration, Propeller Repairs, Upholstery, Yacht Interiors **3+ mi:** Sail Loft *(7 mi.)*, Yacht Broker *(7 mi.)*. **Dealer for:** John Deere, CAT, MAN, ZF, Twin Disc. **Member:** ABYC - 1 Certified Tech(s) **Yard Rates:** $60/hr., Haul & Launch $6/ft., Bottom Paint Inq.

Restaurants and Accommodations

OnSite: Restaurant *(The Channel 778-0751, B $3-8, L $3-10, D $11-25,* Lite Fare *(Shanty Beach Bar poolside)* **Under 1 mi:** Inn/B&B *(Inn at Mitchell House 778-6500, built in 1743)* **3+ mi:** Restaurant *(Waterman's Crab House 639-2261, L $5-16, D $5-16, 8 mi.)*, *(Inn at Osprey 639-2762, 8 mi.)*, Snack Bar *(Rockhall Snack Bar 639-7427, 7 mi.)*, Lite Fare *(Pasta Plus 639-7916, 8 mi.)*, Pizzeria *(Procolino 778-5900, L & D $7-14, D, 8 mi.)*, Hotel *(Great Oak Landing 778-2100, 11 mi.)*, *(Comfort Suites 810-0555, $100-200, 10 mi.)*, *(North Point Marina 639-2907, 8 mi.)*, Inn/B&B *(Swan Point Inn 639-2500, 8 mi.)*, *(Inn at Osprey 639-2194, $150-200, 8 mi.)*

Recreation and Entertainment

OnSite: Pool, Beach, Picnic Area *(floating picnic dock)*, Grills *(propane)*, Playground, Tennis Courts, Volleyball **3+ mi:** Fitness Center *(Kent Athletic Club 778-3148, 10 mi.)*, Horseback Riding *(Crimson Stables 778-7304, 13 mi.)*, Bowling *(Queen Anne's 778-5800, 15 mi.)*, Movie Theater *(Chester 5 Theatres 778-2227, 12 mi.)*, Video Rental *(Video Scene 778-7900, 12 mi.)*

Provisioning and General Services

1-3 mi: Florist *(Eagle Hill Florist 778-2230)* **3+ mi:** Convenience Store *(Caulk's Field One Stop 778-4373, 8 mi.)*, Liquor Store (Rock Hall *Liquors 639-2177, 7 mi.)*, Fishmonger *(J & J Wholesale 639-2325,7 mi.)*, Market *(Bayside Foods 639-2552, 8 mi.)*, Post Office *(Rock Hall 639-7054, 7 mi.)*, Library *(639-7162, 7 mi.)*, Pharmacy *(Happy Harry's 639-9140, 7 mi.)*, Hardware Store *(Village 639-7014, 7 mi.)*, Copies Etc. *(The UPS Store 778-9446, 12 mi.)*

Transportation

OnCall: Rental Car *(Enterprise 810-0971)*, InterCity Bus *(Rock Hall Trolley - 639-2775 $5)* **3+ mi:** Taxi *(Country Sedan 810-0139, leave message, 11 mi.)*, Rail *(Amtrak Caudon Bridge 642-2620, 55 mi.)*, Airport Limo *(Prince 778-4860, 11 mi.)* **Airport:** Philadelphia/Cecil County *(95 mi./45 mi.)*

Medical Services

911 Service **OnCall:** Ambulance **3+ mi:** Doctor *(Seymour 778-6335, 5 mi.)*, Dentist *(Roth 778-1234, 7 mi.)*, Veterinarian *(Hall 639-7084, 7 mi.)*
Hospital: Chester River 778-3300 *(11 mi.)*

PHOTOS ON CD-ROM: 11

Setting -- Directly off the Bay, Tolchester Marina sports a long sand beach, picnic area, small inviting pool, play gym, two eateries and, up a narrow channel - a very protected "U" shaped basin filled with dockage. It's an out-ofthe-way location with a relaxed atmosphere. A three-story gray dormered building, surrounded by a plethora of Black-eyed Susans, hosts the office and the Channel Restaurant.

Marina Notes -- Established 1971 - family owned and operated. The only harbor of refuge in the area. Three sets of large covered slips radiate out from the shore, plus additional open slips. A floating picnic dock is at the head of the center dock. Extensive boatyard services and on-the-hard storage (most of it is occupied), plus a travelift. A fairly nice cement-floored bathhouse, with two sets of showers and two toilets each, is adjacent to the pool.

Notable -- The amenities area is right on the Bay. Stretched along the wide sandy beach is a low deck populated with chaises and chairs - on the beach itself is a play gym and scattered picnic tables with propane grills. One level up is the pool and pool deck - all nicely furnished and quite inviting, with views of the Bay and marina. Poolside is the Shanty Beach Bar - with umbrellaed tables overlooking the Bay - that serves lite fare (including some of the best crab cakes on the Bay), drinks and spectacular sunsets. A rustic tennis court sits above the beach. Inland, on the far side of the basin, the Channel Restaurant is a lovely little bistro with tables that hug the windows; it serves breakfast 7-11:30am and serves sandwiches, baskets, burgers, salads for lunch and features fresh local crabcakes & rockfish plus ribs for dinner. Other area restaurants will also transport customers; also consider the Rock Hall Trolley.

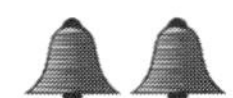

Navigational Information
Lat: 39°08.598' **Long:** 076°15.649' **Tide:** 2 ft. **Current:** n/a **Chart:** 12278
Rep. Depths (*MLW*): Entry 7 ft. **Fuel Dock** n/a **Max Slip/Moor** 6 ft./-
Access: Chesapeake Bay to Swan Creek

Marina Facilities *(In Season/Off Season)*
Fuel: No
Slips: 52 Total, 52 Transient **Max LOA:** 42 ft. **Max Beam:** n/a
Rate *(per ft.)*: **Day** $1.00 **Week** $4.55 **Month** $16.50
Power: 30 amp $3, **50 amp** $5, **100 amp** n/a, **200 amp** n/a
Cable TV: No **Dockside Phone:** No
Dock Type: Fixed, Long Fingers, Short Fingers, Pilings
Moorings: 0 Total, 0 Transient **Launch:** Yes
Rate: Day n/a **Week** n/a **Month** n/a
Heads: 4 Toilet(s), 4 Shower(s), Hair Dryers
Laundry: None **Pay Phones:** Yes
Pump-Out: No **Fee:** n/a **Closed Heads:** Yes

Marina Operations
Owner/Manager: Bob & Dorothy Santangelo **Dockmaster:** Bob Santangelo
In-Season: Apr-Nov, 9am-5pm **Off-Season:** Dec-Mar, Closed
After-Hours Arrival: Call innkeeper
Reservations: Preferred **Credit Cards:** Visa/MC, Dscvr
Discounts: Boat/US* **Dockage:** 15% **Fuel:** n/a **Repair:** n/a
Pets: No **Handicap Access:** No

Moonlight Bay Marina & Inn

6002 Lawton Avenue; Rock Hall, MD 21661

Tel: (410) 639-2660 **VHF: Monitor** n/a **Talk** n/a
Fax: (410) 639-7739 **Alternate Tel:** (410) 639-2660
Email: moonbay@friendly.net **Web:** www.moonlightbayinn.com
Nearest Town: Rock Hall *(1.5 mi.)* **Tourist Info:** (410) 778-0416

Marina Services and Boat Supplies
Services - Docking Assistance, Security, Trash Pick-Up, Dock Carts
Communication - Data Ports, FedEx, DHL, UPS, Express Mail *(Sat Del)*
Supplies - Near: Ice *(Cube)*, West Marine *(639-9959)* **Under 1 mi:** Ships' Store *(Ditty Bag 778-6697)*, Live Bait *(J & J Seafood 639-2325)*
1-3 mi: Bait/Tackle *(Toy's 778-2561)*, Propane *(Bayside 778-2787)*

Boatyard Services
OnCall: Electrical Repairs, Divers, Interior Cleaning, Propeller Repairs, Woodworking, Inflatable Repairs, Upholstery, Yacht Interiors, Metal Fabrication **Near:** Painting, Awlgrip. **Under 1 mi:** Launching Ramp.
Nearest Yard: Swan Creek Marina (410) 639-7813

Restaurants and Accommodations
OnSite: Inn/B&B *(Moonlight Bay 639-2660, $135-180)* **Near:** Restaurant *(Osprey Point 639-2194, L $5-16, D $20-26), (Swan Point Inn 639-2500, D $13-23), (Pruitt's 639-7454, L $7-11, D $12-26, delivers Thu-Sun)*, Inn/B&B *(Swan Point Inn 639-2500), (Inn at Osprey 639-2194, $150-200), (Swan Haven 639-2527)* **Under 1 mi:** Restaurant *(Waterman's Crab House 639-2261, L $5-16, D $5-16, kids' $4, crab feast Tue & Thu)*
1-3 mi: Restaurant *(Martel's Old Oars 639-2541), (Bay Wolf 639-2000, L $4-11, D $17-25)*, Seafood Shack *(J & J Seafood 639-2325)*, Lite Fare (Pasta Plus 639-7916, *B $2-6, L $3-7, D $3-8, kids' $3)*, Pizzeria *(Chessie's 639-7727, L $3-13, D $3-13, carry-out; kids' $2-4)*, Inn/B&B *(Black Duck 639-2478, Sun brunch 7:30am-1pm)*

Recreation and Entertainment
OnSite: Beach, Picnic Area, Grills, Roller Blade/Bike Paths
Near: Jogging Paths, Video Rental, Museum *(Waterman's 778-6697, Rock Hall)* **Under 1 mi:** Pool, Playground, Dive Shop, Tennis Courts, Boat Rentals *(Swan Haven 639-2527)*, Volleyball, Cultural Attract *(The Mainstay 639-9133 - regional & natl. - blues, jazz, blue grass)* **1-3 mi:** Fitness Center, Fishing Charter *(Daddy's Girl Charters 778-9424)*, Park *(Bayside Landing Park 778-7439)* **3+ mi:** Movie Theater *(Chester 5 778-2227, 10 mi.)*

Provisioning and General Services
Near: Delicatessen *(The Haven Deli)*, Laundry *(Jesse's)*, Bookstore, Newsstand **Under 1 mi:** Wine/Beer, Bakery, Crabs/Waterman *(Waterman's)*, Bank/ATM, Post Office *(639-7054)*, Catholic Church, Library *(639-7162)*, Beauty Salon *(Mirror Image 639-2377)*, Dry Cleaners
1-3 mi: Convenience Store *(Shore Stop 639-7441)*, Supermarket *(Bayside Foods 639-2552 7am-10pm 7 days)*, Gourmet Shop *(Bayleaf Gourmet 639-2700)*, Liquor Store *(Rock Hall 639-2177)*, Fishmonger *(J & J Seafood 639-2325)*, Pharmacy *(Happy Harry's 639-9140)*, Hardware Store *(Village 639-7014)*, Florist *(Eagle Hill Florist 639-2230)*

Transportation
OnSite: Courtesy Car/Van, Bikes *(complimentary)* **OnCall:** Rental Car *(Enterprise 810-0971)*, Airport Limo *(Prince 778-4860)* **Near:** Local Bus *(Rock Hall Trolley 639-2775,, Ch.71 $3/1)* **3+ mi:** Rail *(Amtrak Caudon Bridge 642-2620, 60 mi.)* **Airport:** BWI/Cecil County *(80 mi./50 mi.)*

Medical Services
911 Service **OnCall:** Ambulance **1-3 mi:** Doctor *(Seymour 778-6335)*, Dentist *(Roth 778-1234)*, Chiropractor, Holistic Services, Veterinarian *(Hall 639-7084)* **Hospital:** Chester River 778-3300 *(15 mi.)*

Setting -- Right on the Bay, just south of Swan Creek, two main piers hosting stationary slips end at the bulk-headed grounds of this recently renovated and expanded Bed & Breakfast complex. The Main Inn, a charming 19th C. white Victorian with hunter green trim and black shutters dominates the shore. A large wrap-around porch with rocking chairs leads to the adjacent West Wing, a two-story water-front lodge.

Marina Notes -- *15% dicount dockage only. 50 docks radiate from the 2 well-lit piers - 30 amp service and water. Built in the late 1800s, the Inn was originally a Post Office, then a commercial ferry dock, then a restaurant, then a rooming house and now a full-service bed and breakfast. Complimentary bicycles make all of Rock Hall immediately accessible. Full breakfast is available. A screened gazebo and glider sit dockside. Nearby is a picnic and grill area, an English garden and a sliver of sandy beach. Largely open to the west - a night's stay onboard could be rolly, so consider checking in at this lovely establishment. Dedicated boaters' bathhouse.

Notable -- Moonlight Bay offers five rooms in the main Inn and five waterfront rooms in the West Wing. Several public rooms are available to all - the dining room, comfortable Parlor and West Wing parlor - all with period furnishings. Excellent rock fish angling has been reported off the end of the docks at night. The burgeoning town of Rock Hall and its many restaurants are nearby: Swan Point Inn (picks up), Osprey Point, P.E. Pruitt, Waterman's Crab House - and in town Pasta Plus, Tony's Pizza, Chessie's, Bay Wolfe and more. 34-stop R.H. Trolley loops the town every hour ($3/1 all day) and round-trips to Chestertown ($5).

PHOTOS ON CD-ROM: 12

Swan Creek Marina

6043 Lawton Avenue; Rock Hall, MD 21661

Tel: (410) 639-7813 **VHF: Monitor** 16 **Talk** n/a
Fax: (410) 639-7893 **Alternate Tel:** n/a
Email: swancrk@intercom.net **Web:** www.rockhallmd.com/swancreek
Nearest Town: Rock Hall *(1 mi.)* **Tourist Info:** (410) 778-0416

Navigational Information

Lat: 39°08.695' **Long:** 076°15.561' **Tide:** 2 ft. **Current:** n/a **Chart:** 12278
Rep. Depths (*MLW*): Entry 7 ft. **Fuel Dock** n/a **Max Slip/Moor** 8 ft./-
Access: Chesapeake Bay to Swan Creek

Marina Facilities *(In Season/Off Season)*

Fuel: No
Slips: 110 Total, 10 Transient **Max LOA:** 60 ft. **Max Beam:** 18 ft.
Rate *(per ft.)*: **Day** $1.50* **Week** Inq. **Month** Inq.
Power: 30 amp Incl., **50 amp** $6, **100 amp** n/a, **200 amp** n/a
Cable TV: No **Dockside Phone:** No
Dock Type: Fixed, Short Fingers, Pilings, Wood
Moorings: 31 Total, 5 Transient **Launch:** None, Dinghy Dock
Rate: Day $20 **Week** Inq. **Month** Inq.
Heads: 4 Toilet(s), 4 Shower(s) *(with dressing rooms)*
Laundry: None, Book Exchange **Pay Phones:** No
Pump-Out: OnSite, Self Service, 1 Central **Fee:** n/a **Closed Heads:** Yes

Marina Operations

Owner/Manager: Cindy Bair **Dockmaster:** Same
In-Season: Apr-Nov, 8am-5pm **Off-Season:** n/a
After-Hours Arrival: Call ahead
Reservations: yes **Credit Cards:** n/a
Discounts: None
Pets: Welcome **Handicap Access:** No

Marina Services and Boat Supplies

Services - Docking Assistance, Security *(owner lives onsite)*, Dock Carts **Communication -** Mail & Package Hold, Phone Messages, Fax in/out, FedEx, DHL, UPS, Express Mail **Supplies - OnSite:** Ice *(Block, Cube)* **Near:** West Marine *(639-9959)* **Under 1 mi:** Ships' Store *(Ditty Bag 778-6697)*, Live Bait *(J & J 639-2325)*, CNG *(Haven Harbour 778-5884)* **1-3 mi:** Bait/Tackle *(Toy's Outdoor 778-2561)*, Propane *(Bayside Gas 778-2787)*

Boatyard Services

OnSite: Travelift *(40T)*, Crane *(15T)*, Engine mechanic *(gas, diesel)*, Electrical Repairs, Electronics Repairs, Hull Repairs, Rigger, Bottom Cleaning, Brightwork, Refrigeration, Compound, Wash & Wax, Painting, Awlgrip, Total Refits **OnCall:** Air Conditioning, Divers, Interior Cleaning, Propeller Repairs, Woodworking, Upholstery, Yacht Interiors, Metal Fabrication **Near:** Canvas Work, Yacht Broker. **Under 1 mi:** Sail Loft. **Dealer for:** Interlux, Sea Hawk. **Member:** ABBRA, ABYC - 2 Certified Tech (s) **Yard Rates:** $55, Haul & Launch $3/ft. *(blocking $55)*, Power Wash $3/ft., Bottom Paint $9/ft. **Storage:** In-Water $15/ft., On-Land $13/ft.

Restaurants and Accommodations

Near: Restaurant *(Swan Point Inn 639-2500, D $13-23)*, *(Osprey Point 639-2762, L $5-16, D $21-23)*, Inn/B&B *(Carriage House)*, *(Moonlight Bay Marina 639-2660, $135-180)*, *(Inn at Osprey 639-2194, $150-200)*, *(Swan Haven 639-2527)*, *(Swan Point 639-2500)* **Under 1 mi:** Restaurant *(P.E. Pruitt's 639-7454, L $7-11, D $12-26, kids' $4; delivers)* **1-3 mi:** Restaurant *(Waterman's 639-2261, L $5-16, D $5-16, kids' $4)*, Seafood Shack *(Ford's 639-2032, L $5-9, D $5-9)*, Lite Fare *(Pasta Plus 639-7916, B $2-6, L $3-7, D $3-8, kids' $4)*, Pizzeria *(Chessies 639-7727, carry-out)*

Recreation and Entertainment

OnSite: Picnic Area, Grills **Near:** Beach, Boat Rentals *(Swan Haven 639-2527)*, Museum *(Waterman's Museum 778-6697)*, Sightseeing *(Blue Heron Park - new sightseeing pier)* **Under 1 mi:** Pool **1-3 mi:** Playground, Tennis Courts, Fishing Charter *(Daddy's Girl 778-9424)*, Video Rental, Park *(Bayside Landing Park 778-7439)*, Cultural Attract *(The Mainstay 639-9133 - regional & natl. - blues, jazz, blue grass)*, Special Events *(Fabulous 4th)*

Provisioning and General Services

Under 1 mi: Delicatessen *(The Haven Deli)*, Post Office *(639-7054)*, Library *(639-7162)*, Beauty Salon *(Mirror Image 639-2377)*, Laundry *(Jesse's)* **1-3 mi:** Convenience Store *(Shore Stop 639-7441)*, Supermarket *(Bayside Foods 639-2552 7am-10pm 7 days)*, Gourmet Shop *(Bayleaf 639-2700)*, Liquor Store *(Rock Hall 639-2177)*, Bakery, Farmers' Market, Fishmonger *(J & J Seafood 639-2325)*, Bank/ATM, Catholic Church, Protestant Church, Barber Shop, Pharmacy *(Happy Harry's 639-9140)*, Hardware Store *(Village 639-7014)*, Florist *(Eagle Hill 639-2230)*

Transportation

OnSite: Bikes *(free)* **OnCall:** Rental Car *(Enterprise 810-0971)*, Airport Limo *(Prince 778-4860 14 mi.)* **Near:** Local Bus *(Trolley 639-2775 $3/1 day)* **1-3 mi:** Ferry Service *(Ches. Flyer to Balt., Annapolis, St. Michaels)* **Airport:** BWI/Cecil County *(80 mi./50 mi.)*

Medical Services

911 Service **OnCall:** Ambulance **1-3 mi:** Doctor *(Seymour 778-6335)*, Dentist *(Roth 778-1234)*, Veterinarian *(Hall 639-7084)* **Hospital:** Chester River 778-3300 *(15 mi.)*

PHOTOS ON CD-ROM: 11

Setting -- Located in a beautiful, tranquil setting just inside Swan Creek, this sweet place at the end of the road delivers full marina services while still retaining its charming, rural flavor. Brick paths edged with very lovely perennial borders lead to the nicely protected docks. Additional flower borders punctuate the grounds.

Marina Notes -- *$20 min. In the same family since 1951, this is a multigenerational operation, and the very accommodating owners live onsite. Sheltered by an oak tree and an old swamp maple, 2 sets of picnic tables surround the bathhouse and overlook the docks. Two propane grills are nearby. The area's oldest working yard, it offers full boatyard services and an extensive network of docks. Member ABBRA. Lenox company fiberglass. Docks are in excellent condition with full-width half finger piers. Accommodates cats, even in slips. If you draw over 6 ft., it will be difficult to get into a slip -- take a mooring. The very simple but impeccably maintained bathhouses have two showers, a separate dressing room with a vanity and mirror, two toilets, and two sinks each.

Notable -- This is perfect biking territory and the bicycles are complimentary. Nearby Blue Heron Park is a wetlands with raised walkways for sightseeing. Most basic services and a number of interesting restaurants and shops can be found in slowly emerging Rock Hall. Once a sleepy fishing village, it is now a curiously delightful mix of pleasure boaters and traditional watermen still plying their trade - each holding his/her own. The Rock Hall Trolley's twice an hour circuit makes everything accessible. Major shopping is 12 miles away in Chestertown - trolley makes a round trip ($5). Pruitt's will deliver Thu-Sun Noon-7pm.

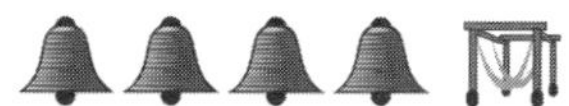

Osprey Point Marina

20786 Rock Hall Avenue; Rock Hall, MD 21661

Tel: (410) 639-2663 **VHF: Monitor** 16 **Talk** 69
Fax: (410) 639-7716 **Alternate Tel:** (410) 639-2663
Email: innkeeper@ospreypoint.com **Web:** www.ospreypoint.com
Nearest Town: Rock Hall *(0.8 mi.)* **Tourist Info:** (410) 778-0416

Navigational Information

Lat: 39°08.532' **Long:** 076°15.049' **Tide:** 1.5 ft. **Current:** n/a **Chart:** 12278
Rep. Depths (*MLW*): Entry 8 ft. **Fuel Dock** n/a **Max Slip/Moor** 6 ft./-
Access: Chesapeake Bay, 10 miles north of the Bay Bridge

Marina Facilities *(In Season/Off Season)*

Fuel: No
Slips: 160 Total, 5-10 Transient **Max LOA:** 50 ft. **Max Beam:** 16 ft.
Rate *(per ft.)*: **Day** $2.00 **Week** Inq. **Month** $700 + elec
Power: 30 amp $6, **50 amp** $12, **100 amp** n/a, **200 amp** n/a
Cable TV: No **Dockside Phone:** No
Dock Type: Floating, Long Fingers, Wood
Moorings: 0 Total, 0 Transient **Launch:** n/a
Rate: Day n/a **Week** n/a **Month** n/a
Heads: 10 Toilet(s), 8 Shower(s) *(with dressing rooms)*, Hair Dryers, A/C
Laundry: 1 Washer(s), 1 Dryer(s), Iron, Iron Board **Pay Phones:** Yes, 1
Pump-Out: OnSite **Fee:** $5 **Closed Heads:** Yes

Marina Operations

Owner/Manager: Jonathan Wright **Dockmaster:** Becky Sullivian
In-Season: Apr1-Nov15, 8am-5pm **Off-Season:** Nov15-Apr30, 9am-4pm
After-Hours Arrival: Call ahead
Reservations: Yes, Preferred **Credit Cards:** Visa/MC, Dscvr
Discounts: None
Pets: Welcome, Dog Walk Area **Handicap Access:** Yes

Marina Services and Boat Supplies

Services - Docking Assistance, Concierge, Boaters' Lounge, Dock Carts **Communication -** Phone Messages, FedEx, UPS **Supplies - OnSite:** Ice *(Block, Cube)* **Near:** Ships' Store *(Ditty Bag 778-6697)* **Under 1 mi:** West Marine *(639-9959)* **1-3 mi:** Bait/Tackle *(Toy's Outdoor Store 778-2561)*, Live Bait *(J & J Wholesale 639-2325)*, Propane *(Bayside Gas 778-2787)*

Boatyard Services

OnSite: Travelift *(35T)*, Engine mechanic *(gas, diesel)*, Electrical Repairs, Electronics Repairs, Hull Repairs, Rigger, Bottom Cleaning, Brightwork, Air Conditioning, Compound, Wash & Wax, Interior Cleaning, Woodworking, Painting, Total Refits **OnCall:** Refrigeration **Near:** Launching Ramp, Sail Loft, Propeller Repairs. **Member:** ABBRA, ABYC - 3 Certified Tech(s) **Yard Rates:** $45/hr., Haul & Launch $4.50/ft. *(blocking $22)*, Bottom Paint $7.50/ft. **Storage:** In-Water $10/ft./mo., On-Land $14.50/ft./mo.

Restaurants and Accommodations

OnSite: Restaurant *(Osprey Point 639-2762, D $19-26)*, Inn/B&B *(Inn at Osprey 639-2194, $150-200)* **Near:** Restaurant *(Swan Point Inn 639-2500, D $13-23)*, *(Passages Bar & Grill 639-7427, L $5-10, Fri-Sun)*, Inn/B&B *(Moonlight Bay Marina 639-2660)*, *(Swan Haven B&B 639-2527, $105-160, B incl., all rooms A/C)*, *(Swan Point 639-2500, $80-90, min. 2-days wknds)* **Under 1 mi:** Restaurant *(Waterman's Crab House 639-2261, L $5-16, D $5-16, kids' plate $4, crab feazt Tue & Thu)*, *(Old Oars Inn 639-2541)*, *(Pruitt's 639-7454, L $7-11, D $12-26)*, *(Bay Wolf 639-2000, L $4-11, D $17-25)*, Lite Fare *(Pasta Plus 639-7916, B $2-6, L $3-7, D $3-8, kids' $3)*, *(Sweet Rick's 639-7700)*, Pizzeria *(Chessies 639-7727, L $3-13, D $3-13)*, Inn/B&B *(Black Duck 639-2478, Sun brunch)*, *(Old Oars 639-2541)*

Recreation and Entertainment

OnSite: Pool, Picnic Area, Grills, Playground, Volleyball **Near:** Beach, Boat Rentals *(Swan Haven 639-2527)*, Roller Blade/Bike Paths, Park *(Blue Heron)*, Museum *(Waterman's Museum 778-6697)* **Under 1 mi:** Cultural Attract *(The Mainstay 639-9133 - blues, jazz, blue grass; Rock Hall Museum)* **1-3 mi:** Fishing Charter, Video Rental

Provisioning and General Services

Near: Delicatessen *(The Haven Deli)*, Beauty Salon *(Mirror Image 639-2377)* **Under 1 mi:** Convenience Store *(Shore Stop 639-7441)*, Supermarket *(Bayside Foods 639-2552 7am-10pm 7 days)*, Gourmet Shop *(Bayleaf 639-2700)*, Liquor Store *(Rock Hall Liquors 639-2177)*, Crabs/Waterman, Bank/ATM *(People's 693-2233)*, Post Office *(639-7054)*, Library *(639-7162)*, Newsstand **1-3 mi:** Fishmonger *(J & J Seafood 639-2325)*, Catholic Church, Protestant Church, Barber Shop, Laundry *(Jesse's)*, Pharmacy *(Happy Harry's 639-9140)*, Hardware Store *(Village 639-7014)*, Florist *(Eagle Hill 639-2230)*

Transportation

OnSite: Bikes *(complimentary)* **OnCall:** Rental Car *(Enterprise 810-0971)*, Airport Limo *(Prince 778-4860 14 mi.)* **Near:** Local Bus *(Trolley 639-2775 or Ch.71 $3/1-day)* **Under 1 mi:** Ferry Service *(Annapolis, Baltimore)*
Airport: BWI/Cecil County *(80 mi./50 mi.)*

Medical Services

911 Service **OnCall:** Ambulance **1-3 mi:** Doctor *(Seymour 778-6335)*, Dentist *(Roth 778-1234)*, Veterinarian *(Hall 639-7084)*
Hospital: Chester River 778-3300 *(15 mi.)*

Setting -- Tucked into Swan Creek's The Haven are 160 top-drawer slips surrounded by pristine Eastern Shore greenery, marsh and trees. Upland views are of a classic three-story white clapboard 17th century-style country inn with black shutters - the centerpiece of a 30-acre, lushly landscaped waterfront estate.

Marina Notes -- DCM. The floating, screwed-down grooved mahogany docks sport full-length, wide, comfortable finger piers, all edged in vinyl - additional corner fill-ins hold dock boxes. The docks are divided into two groups; "A" and "B" docks radiate from the main boardwalk (right in front of the inn) and "C" and "D" docks from a more secluded boardwalk just across from the bicycle barn. Each elegantly executed air conditioned bathhouse has a single Corian vanity with five molded sinks, flanked by two hair dryers, five heads and four very commodious, comfortable showers with separate dressing rooms that feature double sets of French-blue curtains. In the anteroom are a washer, dryer and a book exchange.

Notable -- Built in 1993, the country inn and outbuildings are in the style of Williamsburg's Cole-Garret House, reflective of area farms settled in the 1600s. The lovely hostelry has 7 well-appointed rooms-- all furnished in good-quality antique reproductions and four-posters. The well-reviewed restaurant serves Eastern Shore cusine for lunch and dinner. A gracefully designed pool is immediately adjacent surrounded by a patio comfortably furnished with umbrella-topped tables, chairs and chaise lounges. A small, shaded pavilion provides a respite from the summer sun. Adjacent to the pool, the Inn's screened back porch - used as a breakfast room - overlooks a little pond (inquire about joining the Inn guests for breakfast). Nearby are picnic tables, grills and a small play gym.

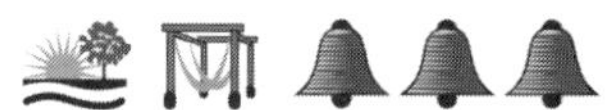

Haven Harbour

20880 Rock Hall Avenue; Rock Hall, MD 21620

Tel: (410) 778-6697; (800) 506-6697 **VHF: Monitor** 16 **Talk** 68
Fax: (410) 639-2971 **Alternate Tel:** (800) 506-6697
Email: email@havenharbour.com **Web:** www.havenharbour.com
Nearest Town: Rock Hall *(0.5 mi.)* **Tourist Info:** (410) 778-0416

Navigational Information

Lat: 39°08.412' **Long:** 076°14.852' **Tide:** 2 ft. **Current:** n/a **Chart:** 12278
Rep. Depths (*MLW*): Entry 6 ft. **Fuel Dock** 6 ft. **Max Slip/Moor** 6 ft./-
Access: Swan Creek to The Haven

Marina Facilities *(In Season/Off Season)*

Fuel: *Mobil* - Gasoline, Diesel
Slips: 217 Total, 35 Transient **Max LOA:** 60 ft. **Max Beam:** 22 ft.
Rate *(per ft.)*: **Day** $1.75* **Week** Inq. **Month** Inq.
Power: 30 amp $6.50, **50 amp** $13, **100 amp** n/a, **200 amp** n/a
Cable TV: No **Dockside Phone:** No
Dock Type: Fixed, Long Fingers, Short Fingers, Pilings, Wood
Moorings: 4 Total, 0 Transient **Launch:** None, Dinghy Dock
Rate: Day n/a **Week** n/a **Month** n/a
Heads: 15 Toilet(s), 15 Shower(s) *(with dressing rooms)*
Laundry: 1 Washer(s), 1 Dryer(s), Book Exchange **Pay Phones:** Yes, 2
Pump-Out: OnSite, Full Service, 1 Central **Fee:** $5 **Closed Heads:** Yes

Marina Operations

Owner/Manager: Jonathan L. A. Jones **Dockmaster:** Dennis Herrmann
In-Season: May-Sep, 8am-6pm **Off-Season:** Oct-Apr, 8am-5pm
After-Hours Arrival: Call in advance
Reservations: Yes **Credit Cards:** Visa/MC, Dscvr, Amex
Discounts: Boat/US **Dockage:** n/a **Fuel:** $0.10/gal** **Repair:** n/a
Pets: Welcome, Dog Walk Area **Handicap Access:** No

Marina Services and Boat Supplies

Services - Docking Assistance, Concierge, Boaters' Lounge, Security, Trash Pick-Up, Dock Carts **Communication -** Mail & Package Hold, Phone Messages, Fax in/out *(Free)*, Data Ports *(Wi-Fi & Office)*, FedEx, DHL, UPS, Express Mail **Supplies - OnSite:** Ice *(Block, Cube)*, Ships' Store *(Ditty Bag 778-6697)*, CNG **Under 1 mi:** West Marine *(639-9959)*, Bait/Tackle *(Toy's 778-2561)*, Live Bait *(J & J 639-2325)*, Propane *(Bayside 778-2787)*

Boatyard Services

OnSite: Travelift *(35T)*, Crane, Engine mechanic *(gas, diesel)*, Electrical Repairs, Electronics Repairs, Hull Repairs, Rigger, Canvas Work, Bottom Cleaning, Brightwork, Air Conditioning, Refrigeration, Compound, Wash & Wax, Interior Cleaning, Propeller Repairs, Woodworking, Metal Fabrication, Painting, Awlgrip, Total Refits, Yacht Broker **OnCall:** Inflatable Repairs **Near:** Launching Ramp. **Member:** ABBRA - 12 Certified Tech(s), ABYC - 12 Certified Tech(s), Other Certifications: welding, refrigeration, EPA
Yard Rates: $74/hr., Haul & Launch $8.00/ft., Power Wash $3.50/ft., Bottom Paint $10.75/ft. **Storage:** In-Water $750/mo., On-Land $200/mo.

Restaurants and Accommodations

OnSite: Snack Bar *(The Haven Deli)*, Lite Fare *(Passages Bar & Grill 639-7427, L $5-10, D $5-10, Fri-Sun: sandwiches, burgers, pork BBQ, crab cakes)* **Near:** Restaurant *(Inn at Osprey 639-2762, L $5-16, D $20-26)*, Inn/B&B *(Swan Point Inn 639-2500, $80-90)*, *(Inn at Osprey 639-2194, $150-200)*, *(Swan Haven B&B 639-2527, $105-160)*, Condo/Cottage *(The Hamlet 778-6697, across the street - bungalows)* **Under 1 mi:** Restaurant *(Pruitt's 639-7454, L $7-11, D $12-26)*, *(Waterman's 639-2261, L $5-16, D $5-16)*, Lite Fare *(Pasta Plus 639-7916)*, Pizzeria *(Chessie's 639-7727)*

Recreation and Entertainment

OnSite: Pool *(2 - extended hours)*, Spa *(Jacuzzi)*, Picnic Area, Grills, Playground, Jogging Paths *(nature walk)*, Boat Rentals *(kayaks or Swan Haven 639-2527)*, Volleyball, Museum *(Waterman's, 10am-5pm - get key from The Ditty Bag)* **Near:** Beach, Fishing Charter, Park *(Blue Heron)*, Sightseeing, Special Events *(4th of July, Party on bay)* **Under 1 mi:** Tennis Courts, Video Rental, Cultural Attract *(The Mainstay 639-9133)*

Provisioning and General Services

OnSite: Delicatessen, Wine/Beer, Clothing Store *(Ditty Bag, gifts)* **Near:** **Near:** Beauty Salon *(Mirror Image 639-2377)* **Under 1 mi:** Convenience Store *(Shore Stop 639-7441)*, Supermarket *(Bayside Foods 639-2552)*, Gourmet Shop *(Bayleaf 639-2700)*, Liquor Store *(Rock Hall 639-2177)*, Bank ATM, Post Office *(639-7054)*, Catholic Church, Protestant Church, Library *(639-7162)*, Barber Shop, Laundry *(Jesse's)*, Bookstore **1-3 mi:** Fishmonger *(J & J Seafood 639-2325)*, Pharmacy *(Happy Harry's 639-9140)*, Hardware Store *(Village 639-7014)*, Florist

Transportation

OnSite: Bikes **OnCall:** Rental Car *(Enterprise 810-0971)*, Airport Limo *(Prince 778-4860 14 mi.)* **Near:** Local Bus *(Trolley 639-2775 $3/1-day)*
3+ mi: Rail *(Amtrak Caudon Bridge 642-2620, 60 mi.)*
Airport: BWI/Cecil County *(80 mi./50 mi.)*

Medical Services

911 Service **OnCall:** Ambulance **1-3 mi:** Doctor *(Seymour 778-6335)*, Dentist *(Roth 778-1234)*, Veterinarian *(Hall 639-7084)*
Hospital: Chester River 778-3300 *(14 mi.)*

Setting -- Snugged into the protected upper reaches of The Haven, this superbly conceived and executed marina provides top quality dockage in a resort environment. It's neatly divided into distinct areas: Dockage and waterfront Reception (a handsome three-story clapboard lighthouse contemporary with a cupola and decks); an engaging, deftly landscaped street-side Resort zone, and, sufficiently isolated from the marina so as not to intrude, the Boatyard.

Marina Notes -- *$2.50/ft. holidays. **Disc. over 50 gal. DCM. Originally Y&W Yacht Basin, then Port of Rock. Current owners at the helm since 1990. Environmentally sensitive. Fuel dock Sun-Thu 8am-5pm, Fri & Sat 8am-6pm. Full service yard. Dealer for Sealand, Seafrost, RayMarine, Yanmar, etc. Main piers are edged with wide, painted stripes - blue dock, red dock, etc. At the main entrance, the Ditty Bag sells gifts, clothing and extensive marine supplies. Reception building hosts a pine-paneled boaters' lounge with area reading material, very comfortable sofas and chairs, TV, VCR, computer, plus the dockmaster's office and The Haven Deli - a mini convenience store, with sandwiches, drinks and basics. Below are a plethora of nicely done full bathrooms.

Notable -- On Reception's 2nd floor, Passages Bar & Grill opens Fri at 5pm, Sat & Sun at noon - additional seating on the 3rd floor tower deck with distant vistas. The surrounding water-view picnic area is a mosaic of grass and brick under retractable canvas canopies or stands of old maples - hammock chairs, gliders and a gazebo. Across the parking lot, the Resort zone is a world apart. Two pools (one adults only, Jacuzzi & lights for extended hours), more picnic areas with grills, playground, shuffleboard, croquet court (flanked by two gazebos), snack bar, and lushly planted gardens populated by Adirondack chairs.

PHOTOS ON CD-ROM: 9

Navigational Information
Lat: 39°08.000' **Long:** 076°15.000' **Tide:** n/a **Current:** n/a **Chart:** 12278
Rep. Depths (*MLW*): Entry 7 ft. **Fuel Dock** 8 ft. **Max Slip/Moor** 8 ft./-
Access: Just inside the breakwater, on port side

Marina Facilities *(In Season/Off Season)*
Fuel: Gasoline, Diesel, High-Speed Pumps
Slips: 127 Total, varies Transient **Max LOA:** 100 ft. **Max Beam:** 22 ft.
Rate *(per ft.)*: **Day** $1.75/1.50 **Week** 5.25 **Month** 15
Power: 30 amp $5, **50 amp** $10, **100 amp** n/a, **200 amp** n/a
Cable TV: No **Dockside Phone:** No
Dock Type: Fixed, Short Fingers, Wood
Moorings: 0 Total, 0 Transient **Launch:** n/a, Dinghy Dock
Rate: Day n/a **Week** n/a **Month** n/a
Heads: 8 Toilet(s), 8 Shower(s) *(with dressing rooms)*
Laundry: 2 Washer(s), 2 Dryer(s), Book Exchange **Pay Phones:** Yes, 1
Pump-Out: OnSite, 1 Central **Fee:** $5 **Closed Heads:** Yes

Marina Operations
Owner/Manager: Joe & Lori Campbell **Dockmaster:** Same
In-Season: Year-Round, 8am-6pm **Off-Season:** 9am-5pm
After-Hours Arrival: Call ahead and get slip assignment
Reservations: Preferred **Credit Cards:** Visa/MC
Discounts: None
Pets: No **Handicap Access:** No

North Point Marina

PO Box 298; 5639 Walnut Street; Rock Hall, MD 21681

Tel: (410) 639-2907 **VHF: Monitor** 16 **Talk** 72
Fax: (410) 639-7859 **Alternate Tel:** n/a
Email: npm@dmv.com **Web:** www.rockhallmd.com/npoint
Nearest Town: Rock Hall *(1 mi.)* **Tourist Info:** (410) 778-0416

Marina Services and Boat Supplies
Services - Docking Assistance, Security *(24 hrs., Owners live onsite)*, Trash, Pick-Up, Dock Carts **Communication -** Mail & Package Hold, Fax in/out *($1.00)*, Fed-Ex, UPS, DHL **Supplies - OnSite:** Ice *(Block)* **Near:** Ships' Store *(Waterman's 639-2615)* **Under 1 mi:** Live Bait *(J & J 639-2325)*, Propane *(Bayside Gas 778-2787)* Bait & Tackle *(Toy's Outdoor* **1-3 mi:** West Marine *(639-9959)778-2561)*

Boatyard Services
OnCall: Electrical Repairs, Electronics Repairs, Canvas Work, Brightwork, Air Conditioning, Divers, Interior Cleaning, Propeller Repairs, Woodworking, Inflatable Repairs, Upholstery **Near:** Travelift. **Under 1 mi:** Launching Ramp. **Nearest Yard:** Rock Hall Marine Railway (410) 639-2263

Restaurants and Accommodations
OnSite: Motel *(North Point - bay views)* **Near:** Restaurant *(Pruitt's 639-7454, L $7-11, D $12-26, kids' $3.50; delivers Thu-Sun)*, Inn/B&B *(Black Duck Inn 639-2478, Dockside Cafe - Sun brunch 7:30am-1pm - dock 'n' dine)* **Under 1 mi:** Restaurant *(Old Oars Inn 639-2541), (Swan Point Inn 639-2500, D $13-23), (Waterman's Crab House 639-2261, L $5-16, D $5-16, kids' plate $4, crab feast Tue & Thu), (Bay Wolf 639-2000, L $4-11, D $17-25), (Osprey Point 639-2762, L $5-16, D $20-16)*, Snack Bar *(Durding's Store 778-7957, old fashion ice cream parlor)*, Lite Fare *(Sweet Rick's 639-7700), (Bay Leaf Gourmet 639-2700)*, Motel *(Mariner's 639-2291)*, Inn/B&B *(Inn at Osprey 639-2194, $150-200), (Swan Haven B&B 639-2527, $105-160)* **1-3 mi:** Lite Fare *(Pasta Plus 639-7916, B $2-6, L $3-7, D $3-8), (Chessies 639-7727, L $3-13, D $3-13, pizza & carryout)*

Recreation and Entertainment
OnSite: Pool, Picnic Area, Grills, Fishing Charter *(Captain Richard Manley 639-7420)* **Near:** Beach, Museum *(Waterman's Museum 778-6697 - get key from Ditty Bag)*, Sightseeing **Under 1 mi:** Cultural Attract *(The Mainstay 639-9133 - regional & nat'l - blues, jazz, blue grass)* **1-3 mi:** Boat Rentals *(Swan Haven 639-2527)*, Park *(Bayside Landing Park 778-7439)*

Provisioning and General Services
OnSite: Wine/Beer **Near:** Bank/ATM, Post Office *(639-7054)* **Under 1 mi:** Convenience Store *(Shore Stop 639-7441)*, Supermarket *(Bayside Foods 639-2552 7am-10pm 7 days)*, Gourmet Shop *(Bayleaf Gourmet 639-2700)*, Liquor Store *(Rock Hall Liquors 639-2177)*, Green Grocer, Catholic Church, Library *(639-7162)*, Beauty Salon *(Mirror Image 639-2377)*, Laundry *(Jesse's Laundromat)*, Retail Shops **1-3 mi:** Fishmonger *(J & J Seafood 639-2325)*, Pharmacy *(Happy Harry's 639-9140)*, Hardware Store *(Village 639-7014)*, Florist *(Eagle Hill Florist 639-2230)*

Transportation
OnSite: Bikes *(Complimentary)* **OnCall:** Rental Car *(Enterprise 810-0971)*, Airport Limo *(Prince 778-4860)* **Near:** Local Bus *(Trolley 639-7996 $3/1-day; Chestertown $5 RT)* **3+ mi:** Rail *(Amtrak Caudon Bridge 642-2620, 60mi.)* **Airport:** BWI/Cecil County *(80 mi./50 mi.)*

Medical Services
911 Service **OnCall:** Ambulance **1-3 mi:** Doctor *(Seymour 778-6335)*, Dentist *(Roth 778-1234)*, Veterinarian *(Hall 639-7084)*
Hospital: Chester River 778-3300 *(14 mi.)*

Setting -- Right on the Rock Hall Harbor jetty, North Point is the first marina immediately off your port bow. Directly inside the deep, rip-rapped breakwater, one of the two fuel docks is adjacent to day marker number six. An inviting pool sits right on the bank overlooking the Bay - carefully furnished with fresh tables, cushioned chairs and chaises. At the other end of the bank is a large pavilion with five long picnic tables and two propane grills - all in perfect condition and all with spectacular views of the Bay and the sunsets. Overlooking the docks is a two-story blue-gray shingle and beige stucco motel.

Marina Notes -- Owners Joe & Lori Campbell live onsite and it shows. Immaculate covered slips are available to transients. The docks are very protected by the jetty that runs the full length of the marina. Attractive second-floor motel units have completely equipped little kitchenettes with refrigerators and sinks, coffeemakers, tables and chairs and a television, two double beds, and sliding glass doors out to a porch - with expansive beachfront views. Room no. 1 affords the most privacy but the pool interrupts the view of the Bay. On the first floor of the motel building, the carefully painted and maintained cinderblock and cement heads -- with varnished redwood floor slats and seats in the shower stall dressing rooms - set a new standard for quality.

Notable -- Up the street, P.E. Pruitt's Waterside Restaurant (pictured) serves New Orleans style seafood and fresh off-the-boat steamed crabs. They'll also deliver to the marina Thu-Sun Noon-7pm. Directly across the harbor is Waterman's Crab House - walk, dinghy or take the Rock Hall Trolley (stops at the marina every 20 minutes & makes a complete loop of Rock Hall). Bay Leaf Gourmet, in town, is a good provisioning resource (Tue-Sat 7:30am-7pm; Sun 7:30am-5pm.

PHOTOS ON CD-ROM: 13

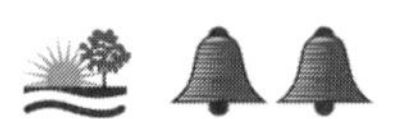

Rock Hall Landing Marina

PO Box 448; 5657 S Hawthorne Avenue; Rock Hall, MD 21661

Tel: (410) 639-2224 **VHF: Monitor** 16 **Talk** 18
Fax: (410) 639-2081 **Alternate Tel:** n/a
Email: rockhall@dmv.com **Web:** www.rockhallmd.com/rhlanding
Nearest Town: Rock Hall *(0.5 mi.)* **Tourist Info:** (410) 778-0416

Navigational Information

Lat: 39°08.058' **Long:** 076°14.696' **Tide:** 1.5 ft. **Current:** n/a **Chart:** 12278
Rep. Depths (*MLW*): Entry 8 ft. **Fuel Dock** n/a **Max Slip/Moor** 10 ft./-
Access: Chesapeake Bay, 0.5 mi. to head of Rock Hall Harbor

Marina Facilities *(In Season/Off Season)*

Fuel: No
Slips: 75 Total, 10 Transient **Max LOA:** 90 ft. **Max Beam:** n/a
Rate *(per ft.)*: **Day** $1.75 **Week** $10.50 **Month** Inq.
Power: 30 amp $5, **50 amp** $10, **100 amp** n/a, **200 amp** n/a
Cable TV: Yes, $5 **Dockside Phone:** No
Dock Type: Floating, Long Fingers, Wood
Moorings: 0 Total, 0 Transient **Launch:** n/a
Rate: Day n/a **Week** n/a **Month** n/a
Heads: 8 Toilet(s), 8 Shower(s)
Laundry: 1 Washer(s), 1 Dryer(s), Book Exchange **Pay Phones:** No
Pump-Out: OnSite, Full Service, 1 Central **Fee:** $5 **Closed Heads:** Yes

Marina Operations

Owner/Manager: James & Mary Anne Lancaster **Dockmaster:** J. Lancaster
In-Season: Apr-Nov 15, 8am-6pm **Off-Season:** Nov 16-Mar, Closed
After-Hours Arrival: Call in advance
Reservations: Recommended **Credit Cards:** Visa/MC, Dscvr, Amex
Discounts: None
Pets: Welcome, Dog Walk Area **Handicap Access:** Yes, Heads, Docks

Marina Services and Boat Supplies

Services - Docking Assistance, Dock Carts **Communication -** Mail & Package Hold, Phone Messages, Fax in/out, Data Ports *(Office)*, FedEx, UPS, Express Mail **Supplies - OnSite:** Ice *(Cube, Shaved)* **Near:** Ice *(Block)*, Ships' Store *(Waterman's 639-2615)*, Live Bait *(J & J Seafood 639-2325)* **Under 1 mi:** West Marine *(639-9959)*, Bait/Tackle *(Toy's Outdoor 778-2561)*, Propane *(Bayside 778-2787)*, CNG *(Haven Harbour 778-5884)*

Boatyard Services

OnSite: Forklift **OnCall:** Engine mechanic *(gas, diesel)*, Electrical Repairs, Electronics Repairs, Hull Repairs, Canvas Work, Bottom Cleaning, Brightwork, Air Conditioning, Refrigeration, Divers, Upholstery, Metal Fabrication, Painting, Awlgrip **Near:** Travelift *(30T)*, Railway, Rigger, Sail Loft. **1-3 mi:** Launching Ramp, Woodworking. **3+ mi:** Propeller Repairs *(5 mi.)*. **Nearest Yard:** Rock Hall Marine Railway (410) 639-2263

Restaurants and Accommodations

OnSite: Motel *(Mariner's 639-2291, $75-85)*, Condo/Cottage *(Rock Hall Landing)* **Near:** Restaurant *(P.E. Pruitt's 639-7454, L $7-11, D $12-26)*, *(Dockside Café 639-2478, Sun brunch only)*, Seafood Shack *(Waterman's Crab House 639-2261, L $5-16, D $5-16, crab feasts Tue & Thu)* **Under 1 mi:** Restaurant *(Upstairs 639-2541)*, *(Bay Wolf 639-2000, L $4-11, D $17-25)*, Seafood Shack *(Ford's Seafood 639-2032)*, Snack Bar *(Rock Hall Snack Bar 639-7427)*, *(Durding Store 778-7957)*, Lite Fare *(Pasta Plus 639-7916, B $2-6, L $3-7, D $3-8)*, Pizzeria *(Chessie's 639-7727, L $3-13, D $3-13, carryout)*, Motel *(Bay Breeze Inn 639-2061)*, Hotel *(Inn at Osprey 639-2194, $150-200)*, Inn/B&B *(Swan Haven B&B 639-2527, $105-160)*
1-3 mi: Inn/B&B *(Black Duck Inn 639-2478, Sun brunch 7:30am-1pm)*

Recreation and Entertainment

OnSite: Pool, Picnic Area, Grills, Playground, Boat Rentals *(or Swan Haven 639-2527)* **Near:** Tennis Courts, Park *(Bayside Landing Park 778-7439)*, Museum *(Waterman's Museum 778-6697)*, Cultural Attract *(The Mainstay 639-9133 - regional & nat'l - blues, jazz, blue grass)*, Special Events
Under 1 mi: Beach *(Rock Hall)*

Provisioning and General Services

Near: Delicatessen, Crabs/Waterman *(Waterman's)*, Meat Market **Under 1 mi:** Convenience Store *(Shore Stop 639-7441)*, Supermarket *(Bayside Foods 639-2552 7am-10pm 7 days)*, Gourmet Shop *(Bayleaf Gourmet 639-2700)*, Liquor Store *(Rock Hall Liquors 639-2177)*, Fishmonger *(J & J Seafood 639-2325)*, Bank/ATM, Post Office *(639-7054)*, Catholic Church, Protestant Church, Library *(639-7162)*, Beauty Salon *(Mirror Image 639-2377)*, Barber Shop, Laundry *(Jesse's)*, Bookstore, Clothing Store, Retail Shops **1-3 mi:** Pharmacy *(Happy Harry's 639-9140)*, Hardware Store *(Village 639-7014)*, Florist *(Eagle Hill 639-2230)*

Transportation

OnSite: Bikes *($3/hr.)* **OnCall:** Rental Car *(Enterprise 810-0971)*
Near: Local Bus *(Trolley 639-7996 $3/1-day - Chester $5/RT)* **3+ mi:** Rail *(Amtrak Caudon Bridge 642-2620, 60 mi.)*, Airport Limo *(Prince 778-4860, 14 mi.)* **Airport:** BWI/Cecil County *(80 mi./50 mi.)*

Medical Services

911 Service **OnCall:** Ambulance **1-3 mi:** Doctor *(Seymour 778-6335)*, Dentist *(Roth 778-1234)*, Veterinarian *(Hall 639-7084)*
Hospital: ChesterRiver 778-3300 *(14 mi.)*

Setting -- Directly ahead as you pass through the breakwater are three piers of high quality floating docks. All the amenities are directly across the road. An attractive, carefully shrubbed and walled pool with chaises and chairs has a view of the masts. Beyond it is a large, grassy area with picnic tables and charcoal grills; at the far end of it is a smal strip motel. A three-story gray clapboard condo building punctuated with natural wood balconies is directly next to the pool.

Marina Notes -- Midweek, 3rd night of dockage free. The marina was built in 1990 and purchased by onsite owner-managers Jim and Mary Lancaster in 1996. If drawing more than 5 feet, stick to south side of the channel entrance. There are three main piers: single-sided "A" pier runs along the side of Waterman's. "B" pier is the double-sided one in the middle, and "C" is single-sided. The nicely done floating docks have a cut-in to provide space for dock boxes plus wide, long fingers all with vinyl edging. Full service pedestals have cable TV. A dry stack storage operation is at the back of the property. Very nice all-tile individual bathrooms are in a bathhouse near the pool. The washer and a dryer are outside, underneath the overhang of the motel.

Notable -- The onsite Mariners Motel, a basic 1950s-style cinderblock motel, has twelve rooms -- each with two double beds, knotty pine wainscoting and semi-nautical decor. The adjacent contemporary condo complex has one villa unit available for rental. Eastern Shore seafood, including steamed crabs, is served next-door at the well-known, casual Waterman's Crab House, with live outdoor entertainment on weekends. Waterman's also has dockage available for Dock 'n' Dine and some full-service dockage for overnight transients. These are the closest docks to town, with 7 restaurants within a 0.6 mile walk.

PHOTOS ON CD-ROM: 11

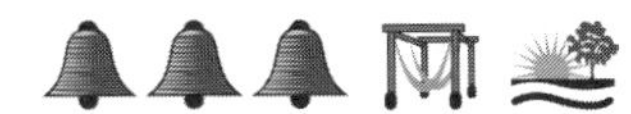

Navigational Information
Lat: 39°07.910' **Long:** 076°14.470' **Tide:** 1.5 ft. **Current:** n/a **Chart:** 12278
Rep. Depths (*MLW*): Entry 8 ft. **Fuel Dock** 8 ft. **Max Slip/Moor** 10 ft./-
Access: 1/2 mile to Chesapeake Bay

Marina Facilities *(In Season/Off Season)*
Fuel: Gasoline, Diesel, On Call Delivery
Slips: 160 Total, 60 Transient **Max LOA:** 120 ft. **Max Beam:** 22 ft.
Rate *(per ft.)*: **Day** $1.75/Inq.* **Week** Inq. **Month** Inq.
Power: 30 amp $5, **50 amp** $10, **100 amp** $20, **200 amp** n/a
Cable TV: No **Dockside Phone:** No
Dock Type: Fixed, Long Fingers, Pilings, Wood
Moorings: 0 Total, 0 Transient **Launch:** n/a, Dinghy Dock
Rate: Day n/a **Week** n/a **Month** n/a
Heads: 12 Toilet(s), 12 Shower(s) *(with dressing rooms)*
Laundry: 2 Washer(s), 2 Dryer(s), Book Exchange **Pay Phones:** Yes
Pump-Out: OnSite, Full Service, 1 Central **Fee:** Free **Closed Heads:** Yes

Marina Operations
Owner/Manager: Art Willis **Dockmaster:** Bob Willis
In-Season: May-Oct, 8am-8pm **Off-Season:** Nov-Apr, 8am-6pm
After-Hours Arrival: Call ahead
Reservations: No **Credit Cards:** Visa/MC, Dscvr
Discounts: None
Pets: Welcome, Dog Walk Area **Handicap Access:** No

The Sailing Emporium

PO Box 597; Green Lane; Rock Hall, MD 21661

Tel: (410) 778-1342 **VHF: Monitor** 16 **Talk** 68
Fax: (410) 778-3264 **Alternate Tel:** n/a
Email: sailemp@dmv.com **Web:** www.sailingemporium.com
Nearest Town: Rock Hall *(1.5 mi.)* **Tourist Info:** (410) 778-0416

Marina Services and Boat Supplies
Services - Docking Assistance, Concierge, Boaters' Lounge, Security *(24 hrs., on premises)*, Trash Pick-Up, Dock Carts **Communication -** Mail & Package Hold, Phone Messages, Fax in/out, Data Ports *(Broadband)*, FedEx, DHL, UPS, Express Mail *(Sat Del)* **Supplies - OnSite:** Ice *(Block, Cube)*, Ships' Store *(The Chandlery)*, Propane, CNG **1-3 mi:** West Marine *(639-9959)*, Bait/Tackle *(Toy's 778-2561)*

Boatyard Services
OnSite: Travelift *(35T)*, Crane *(15T)*, Launching Ramp, Engine mechanic *(gas, diesel)*, Electrical Repairs, Electronics Repairs, Hull Repairs, Rigger, Canvas Work, Bottom Cleaning, Brightwork, Air Conditioning, Refrigeration, Compound, Wash & Wax, Interior Cleaning, Woodworking, Painting, Awlgrip, Total Refits, Yacht Broker **OnCall:** Divers **Dealer for:** Gozzard Yachts, CS Yachts, Brokerage Boats. **Member:** ABYC - 2 Certified Tech(s)
Yard Rates: $65/hr., Wknds $97.50/hr., Haul & Launch $6-10/ft., Bottom Paint $9.50/ft. **Storage:** In-Water $16/ft., On-Land $18/ft.

Restaurants and Accommodations
OnSite: Snack Bar *(Galley)* **Near:** Restaurant *(Waterman's Crab House 639-2261, L $5-16, D $5-16, by dinghy - crab feasts Tue & Thu)* **Under 1 mi:** Lite Fare *(Dockside Café 639-2478)* **1-3 mi:** Restaurant *(Old Oars Inn 639-2541)*, *(Bay Wolf 639-2000, L $4-11, D $17-25)*, Seafood Shack *(Ford's Seafood 639-2032)*, Snack Bar *(Durding Store 778-7957, old fashion ice cream store circa 1800s - same ownership)*, Lite Fare *(Pasta Plus 639-7916, B $2-6, L $3-7, D $3-8)*, *(Bayleaf Gourmet)*, Pizzeria *(Chessie's 639-7727, L $3-13, D $3-13, carry-out)*, Motel *(Mariner's 639-2291, $70-85)*, Inn/B&B *(Bay Breeze Inn 639-2061, $90-150)*, *(Inn at Osprey 639-2194, $150-200)*

Recreation and Entertainment
OnSite: Pool, Picnic Area *(umbrella-topped tables poolside or a tree-shaded picnic grove)*, Grills *(10 grills)*, Playground, Boat Rentals *(31-42 ft. sailboats $1300-2150/wk.)* **Near:** Jogging Paths, Fishing Charter *(dinghy)* **Under 1 mi:** Park *(Rock Hall Civic Center)* **1-3 mi:** Beach *(Rock Hall/Ferry Park)*, Tennis Courts *(Rock Hall M.S.)*, Fitness Center, Volleyball, Video Rental, Museum *(Waterman's 778-6697)*, Cultural Attract *(The Mainstay 639-9133)*

Provisioning and General Services
OnSite: Crabs/Waterman *("Carol Ann")*, Clothing Store *(The Cat's Paw Gift Shop)* **Under 1 mi:** Library *(639-7162)* **1-3 mi:** Convenience Store *(Shore Stop 639-7441)*, Supermarket *(Bayside Foods 639-2552)*, Gourmet Shop *(Bayleaf 639-2700)*, Delicatessen, Liquor Store *(Rock Hall 639-2177)*, Bakery, Fishmonger *(J & J Seafood 639-2325)*, Bank/ATM, Post Office *(639-7054)*, Catholic Church, Protestant Church, Beauty Salon, Barber Shop, Laundry *(Jesse's)*, Pharmacy *(Happy Harry's 639-9140)*, Hardware Store *(Village 639-7014)*, Florist

Transportation
OnSite: Courtesy Car/Van, Bikes *(Free)*, Water Taxi **OnCall:** Rental Car *(Enterprise 810-0971)* **Near:** Local Bus *(Trolley 639-2775 $3/1-day)*
3+ mi: Airport Limo *(Prince 778-4860, 14 mi.)*
Airport: BWI/Cecil County *(80 mi./50 mi.)*

Medical Services
911 Service **OnCall:** Ambulance **1-3 mi:** Doctor *(Seymour 778-6335)*, Dentist *(Roth 778-1234)*, Veterinarian *(Hall 639-7084)*
Hospital: Chester River 778-3300 *(14 mi.)*

Setting -- In the southeast corner of Rock Hall Harbor, a colonial-style fuel pavilion welcomes boaters to The Sailing Emporium - likely the most impeccably manicured marina on the Bay. Six sets of docks are backed by an array of charming two-story barn red buildings trimmed with buttercream-colored porches, festooned with flowers and topped with an easy-to-spot observation cupola. Gorgeous gardens, brick pathways, a pool, picnic areas, gazebos, sitting areas and exquisite boater amenities seem to be ageless. Boardwalks edge the bulkheads - two are connected by a bridge with Chinese chippendale railings.

Marina Notes -- *$5 per electric cord. DCM. Family-owned & managed since 1978, there is obvioulsy a fastidious, "eagle-eye" at the helm. A full-service & do-it-yourself boatyard, dry-storage area and 5300 sq. ft. repair shed, discretely out of sight, can manage up to a 60 ft. yacht on a travelift under cover. A large pavilion with roll-down sides, new in '05/6, will accommodate up to 300 people. The inspired Cat's Paw has a large selection of resort wear, gifts, gourmet foods, even nautically-styled furniture. Guests can help themselves from the "secret" vegetable garden and buy direct from the Carol Ann crab boat (about noon every day). The bathhouse features designer tilework on the floors & walls, dressing rooms, vanities atop wood cabinets and flowers - all in perfect condition.

Notable -- The Carriage House's 2nd floor boaters' lounge is decorated with comfortable upholstered pieces, game tables, bookcases, and a baker's rack filled with games; the rockers on its front porch have the best views. Another lovely sitting porch is on the 2nd floor of the bathhouse. On the waterfront, Adirondack chairs line the 200 ft. deck. The sparkling pool is surrounded by greenery and flanked by brick barbecue areas, picnic spots and a putting green.

PHOTOS ON CD-ROM: 17

Boaters' Notes

Add Your Ratings and Reviews at www.AtlanticCruisingClub.com

AtlanticCruisingClub.com provides updated Marina Reports, Destination and Harbor Articles, a Boaters' Forum and much more — including an option within each on-line Marina Report for Boaters to add their ratings and comments regarding that facility. Please log on frequently to share your experiences — and to read other boaters' comments.

On the website, boaters may rate marinas on one or more of the following categories — on a scale of 1 (basic) to 5 (world class) — and also enter additional commentary.

- **Facilities & Services** (Fuel, Reservations, Concierge Services and General Helpfulness):
- **Amenities** (Pool, Beach, Internet Access, including Wi-Fi, Picnic/Grill area, Boaters' Lounge):
- **Setting** (Views, Design, Landscaping, Maintenance, Ship-Shapeness, Overall Ambiance):
- **Convenience** (Access — including delivery services — to Supermarkets, other provisioning sources, Shops, Services. Attractions, Entertainment, Sightseeing, Recreation, including Golf and Sport Fishing & Medical Services):
- **Restaurants/Eateries/Lodgings** (Availability of Fine Dining, Snack Bars, Lite Fare, On Call food service, and Lodgings ashore):
- **Transportation** (Courtesy Car/Vans, Buses, Water Taxis, Bikes, Taxis, Rental Cars, Airports, Amtrak, Commuter Trains):
- **Please Add Any Additional Comments**

5. Western Shore: Severn River To South River

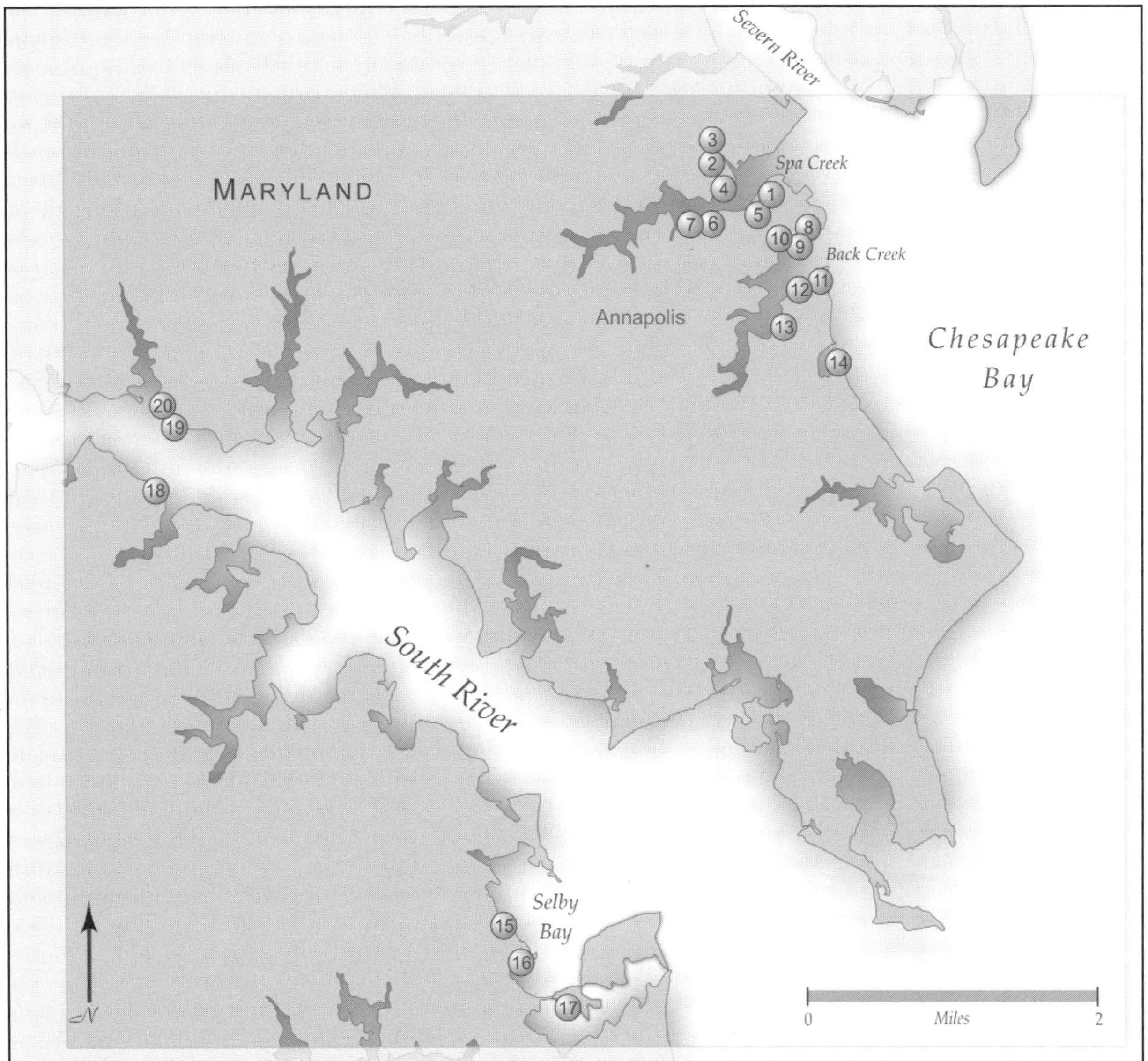

MAP	MARINA	HARBOR	PAGE	MAP	MARINA	HARBOR	PAGE
1	**W & P Nautical**	*Severn River/Spa Creek*	100	11	**Annapolis Landing Marina**	*Severn River/Back Creek*	110
2	**The Waterfront at Annapolis Marina**	*Severn River/Spa Creek*	101	12	**Port Annapolis Marina**	*Severn River/Back Creek*	111
3	**Annapolis City Dock**	*Severn River/Spa Creek*	102	13	**Bert Jabin's Yacht Yard**	*Severn River/Back Creek*	112
4	**The Yacht Basin**	*Severn River/Spa Creek*	103	14	**Chesapeake Harbour Marina**	*Chesapeake Bay*	113
5	**Annapolis City Marina**	*Severn River/Spa Creek*	104	15	**Selby Bay Yacht Basin**	*South River/Selby Bay*	114
6	**Petrini Shipyard & Marina**	*Severn River/Spa Creek*	105	16	**Holiday Point Marina**	*South River/Selby Bay*	115
7	**Sarles Boat and Engine Shop**	*Severn River/Spa Creek*	106	17	**Turkey Point Marina**	*South River/Selby Bay*	116
8	**Horn Point Harbor Marina**	*Severn River/Back Creek*	107	18	**Pier 7 Marina**	*South River*	117
9	**Eastport Yacht Center**	*Severn River/Back Creek*	108	19	**Liberty Yacht Club & Marina**	*South River*	118
10	**Mears Marina Annapolis**	*Severn River/Back Creek*	109	20	**Oak Grove Marine Center**	*South River*	119

- **A "DCM" symbol in Marina Notes means Designated Clean Marina** — This is a coveted state-level award given to marinas that meet stringent, environmentally supportive requirements (see page 307). *For a list of DCM's & pump-out facilities, see page 308.*
- **Ratings & Reviews** — An explanation of the Atlantic Cruising Club's rating system, and a detailed explanation of what is in each section of the Marina Report is on pages 6 – 11. *The Data-Gathering Process is detailed on page 322.*
- **Marina Report Updates** — Updates to Marina Reports (from readers, ACC reviewers, and marinas) are posted regularly on *www.AtlanticCruisingClub.com.*

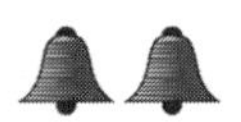

W & P Nautical

222 Severn Avenue; Annapolis, MD 21403

Tel: (410) 268-7700 **VHF: Monitor** n/a **Talk** n/a
Fax: (410) 268-7750 **Alternate Tel:** (410) 268-7700
Email: judy@wpnautical.com **Web:** www.wpnautical.com
Nearest Town: Annapolis **Tourist Info:** (410) 268-7676

Navigational Information

Lat: 38°58.432' **Long:** 076°28.863' **Tide:** 3 ft. **Current:** 5 kt. **Chart:** 12282
Rep. Depths (*MLW*): Entry 11 ft. **Fuel Dock** 11 ft. **Max Slip/Moor** 11 ft./-
Access: SE Side of Spa Creek off Severn River off Chesapeake Bay

Marina Facilities *(In Season/Off Season)*

Fuel: No
Slips: 48 Total, 2 Transient **Max LOA:** 100 ft. **Max Beam:** 25 ft.
Rate *(per ft.)*: **Day** $2.50/1.50 **Week** n/a **Month** 16/11.50
Power: 30 amp $5, **50 amp** $10, **100 amp** n/a, **200 amp** n/a
Cable TV: Yes Tenant arranges **Dockside Phone:** Yes Tenant arranges
Dock Type: Fixed, Short Fingers, Alongside, Wood
Moorings: 0 Total, 0 Transient **Launch:** n/a
Rate: Day n/a **Week** n/a **Month** n/a
Heads: 2 Toilet(s), 2 Shower(s)
Laundry: None **Pay Phones:** Yes
Pump-Out: No **Fee:** n/a **Closed Heads:** Yes

Marina Operations

Owner/Manager: Judy Templeton **Dockmaster:** Same
In-Season: Year-Round, 9am-5pm **Off-Season:** n/a
After-Hours Arrival: Call ahead
Reservations: Yes, Required **Credit Cards:** Checks or Cash only
Discounts: None
Pets: Welcome, Dog Walk Area **Handicap Access:** No

Marina Services and Boat Supplies

Communication - Mail & Package Hold, FedEx, DHL, UPS, Express Mail *(Sat Del)* **Supplies - OnSite:** Ice *(Block)* **Near:** Ice *(Cube)* **Under 1 mi:** Propane *(Trans-Tech Energy 990-0696)* **1-3 mi:** Ships' Store (268-0129), Bait/Tackle *(Angler's 974-4013)* **3+ mi:** West Marine *(266-7766,* 4 mi.),Boater's World *(573-5744, 4 mi.)*

Boatyard Services

OnSite: Rigger, Sail Loft, Inflatable Repairs, Yacht Design **OnCall:** Engine mechanic *(gas, diesel)*, Electrical Repairs, Electronics Repairs, Hull Repairs, Bottom Cleaning, Brightwork, Divers, Compound, Wash & Wax, Interior Cleaning, Propeller Repairs, Woodworking, Upholstery, Metal Fabrication
Nearest Yard: Steve's Yacht Repair (410) 625-4992

Restaurants and Accommodations

OnSite: Restaurant *(Chart House 268-7166, D $15-41, lounge menu $8-13, Sun brunch 11am-2pm $24; Mon-Thu 5-10pm, Sat & Sun 5-11pm)*
Near: Restaurant *(O'Learys Seafood 263-0884, L $10-15, D $15-30)*, *(Boatyard Bar & Grill 216-6206)*, *(Rockfish Raw Bar & Grill 267-1800, L & D $9-30)*, *(Eastport Clipper 280-6400)*, *(Carrol's Creek Café 263-8102, L $6-11, D $10-20)*, *(Adam's the Place for Ribs 267-7001, L $7-20, D $10-20,* carryout), *(Feed Your Crew 280-0973)*, *(Lewnes Steakhouse 263-1617)*, *(Cafe Gurus 295-0601)*, Lite Fare *(Davis Pub 268-7432)*, Inn/B&B *(Peninsula House 267-8796, $165-225, 3 charming rooms, picks up boaters, 2 nt. min* wknds) **Under 1 mi:** Hotel *(Marriott Waterfront 268-7755, $160-270)*

Recreation and Entertainment

OnSite: Picnic Area, Boat Rentals *(Spring River Kayaks 263-2303; Let's Go Cruising 263-1818 bareboat charters)*, Sightseeing *(Sea Gypsy 263-0002, $17/8.50)* **Near:** Playground, Fitness Center *(Annapolis Athletic Club 990-1095)*, Museum *(Barge House, Maritime 295-0104)* **Under 1 mi:** Movie Theater *(Crown 263-3747)* **1-3 mi:** Beach *(Sandy Point)*, Golf Course *(Annapolis GC 263-6771)*, Video Rental *(Blockbuster 626-0090)*

Provisioning and General Services

Near: Convenience Store *(Royal Farm 269-1052)*, Delicatessen *(Harbour Deli 263-5276)*, Bank/ATM, Protestant Church *(St. Philips)*, Beauty Salon *(House of Ebbitt 268-4033)*, Barber Shop *(Eastport 268-8040)*, Dry Cleaners *(Rainbow 626-1112)*, Copies Etc. *(Eastport Copy 269-6399)* **Under 1 mi:** Gourmet Shop *(Palate Pleasers 263-6941)*, Liquor Store *(Eastport 263-4747)*, Bakery, Fishmonger, Post Office *(269-0442)*, Catholic Church, Laundry, Bookstore *(Insight Concepts 263-1540)*, Pharmacy *(Rite Aid 267-8600)*, Hardware Store *(Stevens 269-0629)* **1-3 mi:** Supermarket *(Safeway 262-3436, Giant 261-8095)*, Health Food *(Sun & Earth 266-6862)*, Farmers' Market *(Calvert St. Thu 11am-2pm, 987-6034)*, Library *(Eastport 222-1770)*

Transportation

OnSite: Water Taxi *(Ch.68; 263-0033 $2-4.50)* **OnCall:** Rental Car *(Enterprise 268-7751)*, Taxi *(Yellow Cab 268-2626)*, Airport Limo *(Airport Sedan 269-6226)* **Near:** Local Bus **3+ mi:** Rail *(Amtrak BWI 672-6167, 20 mi.)* **Airport:** Baltimore-Washington Int'l. *(20 mi.)*

Medical Services

911 Service **OnCall:** Ambulance **Near:** Dentist *(Stewart 268-2072)*
1-3 mi: Doctor, Chiropractor, Holistic Services *(Natural Healing 626-0045)*, Veterinarian **Hospital:** Anne Arundel 267-1000 *(4 mi.)*

Setting -- W & P Nautical sits on the site of the three-acre Trumpy boatyard. The centerpiece of the W & P docks, Chart House Restaurant, with its walls of glass and soaring ceilings, was the original Trumpy service facility. Two of the four docks sandwich the Chart House. A third dock is anchored by Let's Go Cruising's bright little turquoise, yellow, and peach charter headquarters - a touch of the Bahamas so that you can't miss it. A fourth dock lies directly west.

Marina Notes -- The management office is a short distance from the docks in a converted warehouse on the main road. This is primarily a seasonal marina, but empty slips from seasonal holders are generally available and they happily offer those to transients. Note: Alongside dockage flanking the Chart House makes your boat the primary table-side view. Two sets of heads and showers plus two separate shower rooms provide adequate facilities.

Notable -- In 1947, the luxury wooden yacht builder John Trumpy & Sons relocated to Eastport and built boats until fiberglass, unions and real estate development zoning laws forced the yard to close in 1974. As a result, this Chart House has, without a doubt, the most spectacular location, stylish interior and maritime historic significance of the entire restaurant chain. Plush deep blue and tan leather seating surrounds a copper hooded round fireplace backed by a window wall that looks right across the mooring field and up Ego Alley (The result of a million-dollar post-Isabel renovation). Snag one of the 13 waterside tables that rim the lounge windows - first-come basis. Sunday to Thursday ask to have the dinner menu served there. "Pirate Adventures on the Chesapeake" makes its home on the western-most dock. Its "Sea Gypsy" sails 6 times daily - make-up and costumes transform kids into pirates.

PHOTOS ON CD-ROM: 15

Navigational Information

Lat: 38°58.524' **Long:** 076°26.095' **Tide:** 2 ft. **Current:** n/a **Chart:** 12282
Rep. Depths (*MLW*): Entry 15 ft. **Fuel Dock** n/a **Max Slip/Moor** 10 ft./-
Access: Severn River to Spa Creek to port side of Ego Alley

Marina Facilities *(In Season/Off Season)*

Fuel: No
Slips: 5 Total, 5 Transient **Max LOA:** 50 ft. **Max Beam:** n/a
Rate *(per ft.)*: **Day** $2.25* **Week** Inq. **Month** n/a
Power: 30 amp $6, **50 amp** n/a, **100 amp** n/a, **200 amp** n/a
Cable TV: No **Dockside Phone:** No
Dock Type: Fixed, Alongside
Moorings: 0 Total, 0 Transient **Launch:** n/a
Rate: Day n/a **Week** n/a **Month** n/a
Heads: 10 Toilet(s)
Laundry: None **Pay Phones:** Yes, 2
Pump-Out: OnCall **Fee:** $5 **Closed Heads:** Yes

Marina Operations

Owner/Manager: Dan Brest **Dockmaster:** Same
In-Season: Apr-Oct, 9am-5pm **Off-Season:** Nov-Mar
After-Hours Arrival: Call ahead
Reservations: Yes **Credit Cards:** Visa/MC, Dscvr, Amex
Discounts: None
Pets: Welcome **Handicap Access:** No

The Waterfront at Annapolis

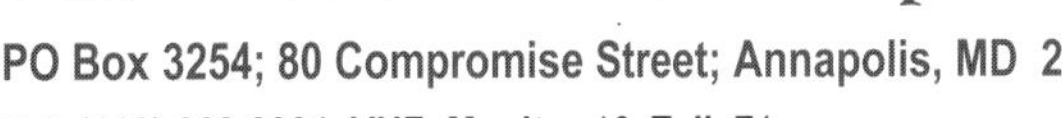

PO Box 3254; 80 Compromise Street; Annapolis, MD 21403

Tel: (410) 263-8994 **VHF: Monitor** 16 **Talk** 71
Fax: (410) 280-6952 **Alternate Tel:** (410) 263-8619
Email: woodwin@pipeline.com **Web:** www.annapolismarriott.com
Nearest Town: Annapolis **Tourist Info:** (410) 268-7676

Marina Services and Boat Supplies

Services - Docking Assistance, Concierge, Security, Trash Pick-Up **Communication -** Fax in/out *(Inq.)*, FedEx, UPS, Express Mail **Supplies - OnSite:** Ice *(Cube)* **Near:** Ice *(Block)*, Ships' Store *(Fawcett 267-8681)* **Under 1 mi:** Propane *(Trans-Tech 990-0696)* **1-3 mi:** West Marine *(268-0129)*, Boater's World *(266-7766)*, Bait/Tackle *(Angler's 974-4013)* **3+ mi:** Boat/US *(573-5744, 4 mi.)*, CNG *(Bert Jabins, 4 mi.)*

Boatyard Services

Near: Travelift, Engine mechanic *(gas, diesel)*, Electrical Repairs, Electronics Repairs, Hull Repairs, Rigger, Sail Loft, Canvas Work, Bottom Cleaning, Brightwork. **Nearest Yard:** Harbor Boatyard (410) 267-9050

Restaurants and Accommodations

OnSite: Restaurant *(Pusser's Landing 626-0004, B $8-14, L $7-20, D $9-22)*, Hotel *(Marriott 268-7755, $160-270)*, Inn/B&B *(Schooner Woodwind 263-7837, $185-245, Boat & Breakfast + 2 hr. sail)* **Near:** Restaurant *(Maria's Sicilian 268-2112)*, *(Buddy's Crabs & Ribs 626-1100)*, *(O'Brien Oyster Bar 268-6288, L $15-33, D $15-33)*, *(Griffins City Deck 268-2576, L $8-20, D $16-20)*, *(Acme Bar & Grill 280-6486, L $10-15, D $8-17)*, *(Nikko Japanese 267-6688)*, *(Phillips Annapolis Harbor 990-9888)*, *(King of France 261-2206)*, Inn/B&B *(Georgian House 557-2068, $160-220)*, *(Harbor View 626-9802, $160-225)*

Recreation and Entertainment

OnSite: Picnic Area, Fitness Center, Fishing Charter, Sightseeing *(74-ft. schooners Woodwind I & II 263-7837 $29-32/18; near - Three-Centuries Walking Tour of State Capital 268-7601)* **Near:** Playground, Park *(near)*, Museum *(Charles Carroll House 263-1737 $5/2; US Naval Academy Museum 263-6933 $6/4)*, Cultural Attract *(Wm. Paca House & Garden $7/3.50)*, Galleries *(Marine Art Gallery 263-4100)*, Special Events *(Naval Academy)* **1-3 mi:** Pool, Movie Theater *(Crown 263-3747)*, Video Rental *(Blockbuster 626-0090)* **3+ mi:** Golf Course *(Annapolis 263-6771, 4 mi.)*

Provisioning and General Services

OnSite: Bank/ATM, Laundry *(Hotel's valet service)*, Clothing Store **Near:** Liquor Store *(Mills 263-2888)*, Fishmonger, Catholic Church, Bookstore *(Hard Bean)*, Hardware Store *(Stevens 263-3390)*, Retail Shops *(Peppers 267-8722 navy clothing, Sign O' the Whale 268-2161 nautical crafts)* **Under 1 mi:** Supermarket *(Graul's, Safeway 262-3436, 3 mi.)*, Gourmet Shop *(Palate Pleasers 263-6941)*, Delicatessen *(Chick & Ruth's 269-6737)*, Farmers' Market *(Thu 11am-2pm, 987-6034)*, Post Office *(269-0442)*, Protestant Church, Beauty Salon, Dry Cleaners *(West Cleaners 268-4274)*, Pharmacy *(Rite Aid 268-5007)*, Copies Etc. *(Post Box 268-6245)* **1-3 mi:** Health Food *(Sun & Earth 266-6862)*, Synagogue, Library *(222-1750)*

Transportation

OnCall: Water Taxi *(Ch.68; 263-0033 $2-4.50)*, Rental Car *(Enterprise 268-7751)*, Taxi *(Arundel 263-2555)*, Airport Limo *(Better Limo 261-8860)* **Near:** Local Bus **3+ mi:** Rail *(Baltimore 672-6167, 20 mi.)* **Airport:** Baltimore/Washington Int'l *(20 mi.)*

Medical Services

911 Service **OnCall:** Ambulance **Under 1 mi:** Doctor *(Clifford 268-0959)*, Dentist *(Whittaker 268-9336)*, Chiropractor *(Chiropractic Life 267-0033)* **Hospital:** Anne Arundel 267-1000 *(4 mi.)*

Setting -- Docking side-to along the 220 feet of bulkhead that flanks two sides of Pusser's Landing Restaurant - at the brick 6-story mansard roofed Annapolis Marriott -- puts boaters right in the midst of bustling Ego Alley - a narrow spur off Spa Creek. Copper green multi-level roofs hover above lattice archways; tables and chairs, topped with marine blue umbrellas, spill out onto the deck. Across the waterway are distant views of the Naval Academy 's green domed chapel and the enormous field house; closer is the harbor and municipal mooring field filled with all manner of craft.

Marina Notes -- *$3/ft. over 50/ft. Family managed. On weekends, overnight dockage is available to hotel-room guests only (160 rooms - many waterview). 2-hr. temporary tie-ups. Short-term drop-off/pick-up only. More private dockage for overnight transients lies around the corner, along the southern bulkhead - good pedestals and teak benches line the boardwalk. No discounts during the boat shows. Heads are in the hotel - no showers.

Notable -- Twin 74 ft. replica schooners, Woodwind I & II, base along the same bulkhead carrying up to 48 passengers, all invited to help. Four 2-hour sailings daily chart a variety of routes; some include special events, like beer tastings or race watching. The Waterfront Annapolis Marriott has a unique tented roof-top terrace accommodating up to 400 for cruises and rendezvous. Pusser's Landing features seafood with a Virgin Islands lilt in an array of 19th C. English-style venues - cozy wood-paneled bar, airy, windowed waterview dining room, and the alfresco waterfront deck. Breakfast Mon-Fri 7-11am, Sat & Sun 'til noon, Lunch 11am-4:45pm, Dinner 5pm 'til ? Historic Annapolis, including the State Capital, is a very short walk past famous Fawcett's Marine Supply.

PHOTOS ON CD-ROM: 12

Annapolis City Dock

1 Dock Street; Annapolis, MD 21401

Tel: (410) 263-7973 **VHF: Monitor** 9, 17 **Talk** 17
Fax: (410) 295-9018 **Alternate Tel:** n/a
Email: harbormaster@annapolis.gov **Web:** n/a
Nearest Town: Annapolis **Tourist Info:** (410) 268-7676

Navigational Information

Lat: 38°58.641' **Long:** 076°29.121' **Tide:** 2 ft. **Current:** n/a **Chart:** 12282
Rep. Depths (*MLW*): Entry 12 ft. **Fuel Dock** 12 ft. **Max Slip/Moor** 12 ft./-
Access: Severn River to Spa Creek for moorings - up Ego Alley for dockage

Marina Facilities *(In Season/Off Season)*

Fuel: No
Slips: 19 Total, 19 Transient **Max LOA:** 45 ft. **Max Beam:** n/a
Rate *(per ft.)*: **Day** $2.00* **Week** Inq. **Month** Inq.
Power: 30 amp Yes, **50 amp** n/a, **100 amp** n/a, **200 amp** n/a
Cable TV: No **Dockside Phone:** No
Dock Type: Fixed, Wood
Moorings: 76 Total, 76 Transient **Launch:** Water Taxi**, Dinghy Dock
Rate: Day $25 **Week** $150 **Month** $375
Heads: 6 Toilet(s), 6 Shower(s)
Laundry: 2 Washer(s), 2 Dryer(s), Book Exchange **Pay Phones:** Yes, 3
Pump-Out: OnSite, 1 Port **Fee:** $5 **Closed Heads:** Yes

Marina Operations

Owner/Manager: City of Annapolis **Dockmaster:** Rick Dahlgren
In-Season: May-Sep, 8am-9pm **Off-Season:** Oct-Apr, 8:30am-4:30pm
After-Hours Arrival: Take empty slip, check in next morning*
Reservations: No **Credit Cards:** Visa/MC
Discounts: None
Pets: Welcome, Dog Walk Area **Handicap Access:** Yes, Heads

Marina Services and Boat Supplies

Services - Docking Assistance **Communication -** Mail & Package Hold, Phone Messages, Fax in/out, Data Ports *(Office, $1)* **Supplies - Near:** Ice *(Cube)*, Ships' Store *(Fawcett 267-8681- practically onsite, has own dockage)* **Under 1 mi:** Propane *(Trans-Tech 990-0696)* **1-3 mi:** West Marine *(268-0129)*, Boater's World *(266-7766)*, Bait/Tackle *(Angler's 974-4013)* **3+ mi:** Boat/US *(573-5744, 4 mi.)*

Boatyard Services

Under 1 mi: Travelift, Railway, Engine mechanic *(gas, diesel)*, Electrical Repairs, Electronics Repairs, Hull Repairs, Rigger, Sail Loft, Canvas Work, Bottom Cleaning. **Nearest Yard:** Harbor Boatyard (410) 267-9050

Restaurants and Accommodations

Near: Restaurant *(Buddy's Crabs & Rib 269-1800, L $8-12, D 9-17)*, *(Griffins City Docks 268-2576, L $8-20, D $16-20)*, *(Middleton Tavern 263-3323, L $6-11, D $14-26)*, *(Bay Brewing Co. 267-9200)*, *(Ego Alley Tropical Grill 269-6656)*, *(Phillips 990-9888)*, *(Governor's Grille D $20-32)*, *(O'Brien's Oyster Bar 269-0099, L $15-33, D $15-33)*, *(Joy Luck III 267-7700)*, *(Café Normandie 263-3382, L $6-12, D $9-24)*, *(Nikko Japanese 267-6688)*, Hotel *(Marriott 888-773-0786, $160-270)*, Inn/B&B *(William Page Inn 626-1506, $140-250)*, *(Annapolis Inn 295-5200, $200-475)*, *(Blue Heron B & B 263-9171)*

Recreation and Entertainment

OnSite: Sightseeing *(Watermark Cruises 268-7601, 40 min Harbor $8/4, 90 min River-St. Thomas Pt. $16/8, St. Michaels $55/27)* **Near:** Grills, Park, Museum *(Maryland State House 974-3400 Free; Wm. Paca House & Garden 263-5553 $5/2.50; St. John's College)*, Cultural Attract *(US Naval Academy 263-6933, $7.50/5.50 - start at Armel-Leftwich Visitors Center, foot King George St)*, Galleries, Special Events **Under 1 mi:** Fitness Center *(Southriver 263-2440)*, Movie Theater *(Crown 263-3747)* **1-3 mi:** Pool, Tennis Courts, Golf Course *(Annapolis GC 263-6771)*

Provisioning and General Services

Near: Convenience Store *(The Market Place)*, Delicatessen *(Chick & Ruths 269-6737)*, Liquor Store *(Mills 263-2888)*, Bakery, Fishmonger, Bank/ATM, Catholic Church, Beauty Salon, Dry Cleaners *(West Cleaners 268-4274)*, Laundry *(Self Service 267-9092)*, Bookstore *(Borders 990-0955)*, Hardware Store *(Stevens 263-3390)*, Retail Shops *(Peppers 267-8722 navy clothing, Sign O' the Whale 268-2161nautical crafts)* **Under 1 mi:** Farmers' Market *(Thu 11am-2pm, 987-6034)*, Post Office, Protestant Church, Pharmacy *(Rite Aid 268-5007)* **1-3 mi:** Supermarket *(Giant 261-8095)*, Gourmet Shop *(Trader Joe's 573-0505)*, Synagogue, Library *(222-1750)*

Transportation

OnSite: Water Taxi *(Ch.68; 263-0033 $2-4.50)* **OnCall:** Rental Car *(Enterprise 268-7751)*, Taxi *(Reliable268-4714)*, Airport Limo *(Airport Sedan 269-6226)* **Near:** Bikes *(Net Ped@llers 263-2344)*, Local Bus *(ACT)*, InterCity Bus **3+ mi:** Rail *(Amtrak BWI 672-6167, 20 mi.)*
Airport: Baltimore-Washington Int'l *(20 mi.)*

Medical Services

911 Service **OnCall:** Ambulance **Under 1 mi:** Doctor *(Clifford 268-0959)*, Dentist *(Handelsman 268-3347)* **1-3 mi:** Chiropractor, Holistic Services *(Natural Healing 626-0045)* **Hospital:** Anne Arundel 267-1000 *(4 mi.)*

Setting -- The city of Annapolis' municipal dockage lines Ego Alley's north bulkhead - right in the middle of the historic district and the tourist action. Views are of an 18th C. skyline topped by the 1772 State House wedding-cake cypress dome and the Naval Academy's chapel and field house. Colonial-era buildings host shops and restaurants that spill onto the brick-paved streets and sidewalks. Benches dot Market Space - site of a downtown market since 1750 - that backs the dinghy dock and morphs into charming Main Street. Water taxis and sightseeing cruises crisscross the inner harbor and municipal mooring field.

Marina Notes -- City-owned dockage - first come, first served slips and moorings. *If arriving after hours, there's a courtesy payment-envelope drop at the door. All-tile heads and showers are on the second floor of the elevated brick "Visitor Information" building on the north side of the harbor - which also houses the dockmaster's office. Dinghy dockage (max 17 ft.) and bike rentals at the head of Ego Alley. Showers are $1 per person (tokens at the dockmaster's office). **The water taxi plies the harbor and functions as a launch. Dataports in dockmaster's office and at Net Ped@llers 263-2344.

Notable -- Once the nation's capital, America's Sailing Capital is rich with history and treasured artifacts; it boasts the largest number of 18thC. houses (over 1500) of any city in the country. Overlooking the dinghy dock is the Kunta Kinte-Alex Haley Memorial and the Market House (open stall and a variety of foods). The 338-acre U.S. Naval Academy campus ("the Yard") is nearby - don't miss the noon formation - as is St. John's College (circa 1696) - both on the Natl. Historic Register. Waterfront events start in April, with the Annapolis Spring Boat Show, and run right through the fall with two large October in-water boat

Navigational Information
Lat: 38°58.469' **Long:** 076°29.086' **Tide:** 2 ft. **Current:** n/a **Chart:** 12282
Rep. Depths (*MLW*): Entry 11 ft. **Fuel Dock** 11 ft. **Max Slip/Moor** 13 ft./-
Access: Severn River to Spa Creek at the entrance to Ego Alley

Marina Facilities *(In Season/Off Season)*
Fuel: *Amoco / BP* - Gasoline, Diesel, High-Speed Pumps
Slips: 107 Total, 45 Transient **Max LOA:** 234 ft. **Max Beam:** n/a
Rate *(per ft.)*: **Day** $2.00/$1.50 **Week** $10.50 **Month** $21*
Power: 30 amp $5, **50 amp** $10, **100 amp** $20, **200 amp** $40
Cable TV: Yes, $3 **Dockside Phone:** Yes, $5
Dock Type: Fixed, Long Fingers, Pilings, Alongside, Wood
Moorings: 0 Total, 0 Transient **Launch:** n/a
Rate: Day n/a **Week** n/a **Month** n/a
Heads: 5 Toilet(s), 6 Shower(s) *(with dressing rooms)*
Laundry: 3 Washer(s), 3 Dryer(s), Book Exchange **Pay Phones:** No
Pump-Out: OnSite **Fee:** $10 **Closed Heads:** Yes

Marina Operations
Owner/Manager: Steve Grace **Dockmaster:** Dick Hall
In-Season: MemDay-LabDay, 7am-7pm **Off-Season:** Oct-May, 9am-5pm
After-Hours Arrival: Call in advance
Reservations: Recommended **Credit Cards:** Visa/MC, Dscvr, Din, BP
Discounts: Fuel **Dockage:** n/a **Fuel:** 500+ gals. **Repair:** n/a
Pets: Welcome, Dog Walk Area **Handicap Access:** Yes

The Yacht Basin

#2 Compromise Street; Annapolis, MD 21401

Tel: (410) 263-3544 **VHF: Monitor** 9 **Talk** 74
Fax: (410) 269-1319 **Alternate Tel:** n/a
Email: n/a **Web:** www.yachtbasin.com
Nearest Town: Annapolis **Tourist Info:** (410) 268-7676

Marina Services and Boat Supplies
Services - Docking Assistance, Dock Carts, Megayacht Facilities **Communication -** Mail & Package Hold, Phone Messages, Fax in/out, Data Ports *(Laundry)*, FedEx, DHL, UPS, Express Mail *(Sat Del)* **Supplies - OnSite:** Ice *(Block, Cube)* **Near:** Ships' Store *(Fawcett 267-8681)* **Under 1 mi:** Propane *(Trans-Tech 990-0696)* **1-3 mi:** West Marine *(268-0129)*, Boater's World *(266-7766)*, Bait/Tackle *(Angler's 974-4013)* **3+ mi:** CNG

Boatyard Services
OnSite: Bottom Cleaning, Yacht Broker *(Blue Water Yacht Sales)* **OnCall:** Divers, Compound, Wash & Wax **Near:** Electrical Repairs, Hull Repairs, Rigger, Woodworking, Inflatable Repairs, Life Raft Service, Painting, Awlgrip. **Nearest Yard:** Harbor Boat Yard (410) 267-9050

Restaurants and Accommodations
Near: Restaurant *(Phillips Annapolis Harbor 990-9888)*, *(Buddy's Crabs & Ribs 626-1100, L $8-12, D $9-17)*, *(Pusser's Landing 626-0004, B $8-14, L $7-20, D $9-22)*, *(Aromi D'Italia 263-1300)*, Coffee Shop *(City Dock 269-0961)*, Hotel *(Marriott Waterfront 268-7555, $160-270)*, Inn/B&B *(William Page Inn 626-1506, $140-250)* **Under 1 mi:** Restaurant *(Carrol's Creek Waterfront 263-8102, L $6-10, D $10-20)*, *(Adam's 267-7001, L $7-20, D $10-20)*, Inn/B&B *(Peninsula House 267-8796, $154-225, picks up)*

Recreation and Entertainment
OnSite: Picnic Area **Near:** Museum *(Maritime Museum 295-0104, Sailing Hall of Fame 295-3022)*, Sightseeing *(Watermark Cruises 268-7601; Mini-Bus tours 626-6000 $10/3)* **Under 1 mi:** Playground, Dive Shop, Tennis Courts, Fitness Center *(Southriver 263-2440)*, Boat Rentals *(Spring River Kayaks 263-2303)*, Fishing Charter, Park, Cultural Attract *(US Naval Academy 263-6933 $7.50/5.50 - Armel-Leftwich Visitors Ctr.)* **1-3 mi:** Pool, Beach, Movie Theater *(Crown Eastport 263-3747)*, Video Rental *(Hollywood Video 626-9993)* **3+ mi:** Golf Course *(Annapolis GC 263-6771, 4 mi.)*

Provisioning and General Services
Near: Convenience Store *(Market Place)*, Liquor Store *(Mills 263-2888)*, Fishmonger, Bank/ATM, Bookstore *(Insight Concepts 263-1540)*, Hardware Store *(Stevens 263-3390)* **Under 1 mi:** Gourmet Shop *(Palate Pleasers 263-6941)*, Delicatessen *(Chick & Ruth's 269-6737)*, Farmers' Market *(Calvert & Clay St. Thu 11am-2pm)*, Post Office *(269-0442)*, Catholic Church, Protestant Church, Beauty Salon *(Pasqualucci 263-4842)*, Barber Shop *(Eastport 268-8040)*, Dry Cleaners *(West 268-4274)*, Laundry *(267-9092)*, Pharmacy *(Rite Aid 267-8600)*, Retail Shops *(Peppers 267-8722 navy clothing; Sign O' the Whale - maritime crafts)*, Copies Etc. *(Sir Speedy 280-2884)* **1-3 mi:** Supermarket *(Giant 261-8095)*, Library *(222-1750)*

Transportation
OnSite: Water Taxi **OnCall:** Rental Car *(Budget 266-5030, Enterprise 268-5955)*, Taxi *(Yellow 268-3737, Reliable 268-4714)*, Airport Limo *(Airport Sedan 269-6226)* **Near:** Local Bus, InterCity Bus **3+ mi:** Rail *(Amtrak BWI 672-6167, 20 mi.)* **Airport:** Baltimore-Washington Int'l *(20 mi.)*

Medical Services
911 Service **OnCall:** Ambulance **Under 1 mi:** Doctor, Dentist **1-3 mi:** Chiropractor *(Atlas 263-3970)*, Holistic Services *(Natural Healing 626-0045)*, Veterinarian *(Annapolis 263-4112)* **Hospital:** Anne Arundel 267-1000 *(4mi.)*

Setting -- Just past the Annapolis Yacht Club, at the entrance to "Ego Alley" (the Spa Creek spur that plows into the center of historic Annapolis), The Yacht Basin is the closest full-service marina to the city sights. A contemporary two-story gray clapboard building with green metal roof and striking deep red roof braces, sits on the fuel dock; it anchors a network of quite new, high-end docks that serve megayachts along with smaller power boats. In season, there's usually a waiting list for slips. Views are across the main harbor and mooring field to the roofs of the Naval Academy. Club cruises and rendezvous welcomed.

Marina Notes -- *Monthly $21/ft. to 60', $23/ft. 61-75 ft., $25/ft. 76-200 ft.. Power $125-450/mo. Founded in 1937, it is still operated by the original owners. A horse-shoe of 107 docks can handle up to fifteen 100' vessels at one time - with 200A electrical service for each. The first floor of the main building houses the dockmaster's office, ice, a laundry room with folding table, and an internet access counter - just plug in. Upstairs is Bluewater Yacht Sales. Right outside is the long, easy-access fuel dock with five stations and volume discounts. Full-length finger piers throughout. Simple, but sparkling all-tile heads are located at the far corner of the facility, near the parking lot, in a white building with blue awnings - three showers in each bathhouse with a communal dressing room.

Notable -- Arguably the most desirable public dockage in historic Annapolis, the Yacht Basin offers an unbeatable combination of high-end, first class dock service and a great location - an easy walk from the historic district. It is flanked by the Japanese-modern Annapolis Yacht Club on one side and the 6-story brick Annapolis Waterfront Marriott (with brown mansard roof) on the other. Fawcett's enormous Chandlery is close by - on the way to the district's hub.

PHOTOS ON CD-ROM: 10

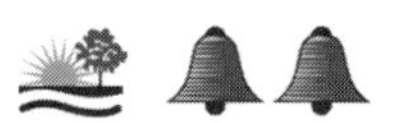

Annapolis City Marina

410 Severn Avenue; Annapolis, MD 21403

Tel: (410) 268-0660 **VHF: Monitor** 16 **Talk** 72
Fax: (410) 268-1761 **Alternate Tel:** n/a
Email: dockmaster@annapoliscitymarina.com **Web:** see marina notes***
Nearest Town: Annapolis *(0.5 mi.)* **Tourist Info:** (410) 268-7676

Navigational Information

Lat: 38°58.321' **Long:** 076°28.975' **Tide:** 2 ft. **Current:** n/a **Chart:** 12282
Rep. Depths (*MLW*): Entry 22 ft. **Fuel Dock** 12 ft. **Max Slip/Moor** 12 ft./-
Access: Severn River to Spa Creek to port side before bridge

Marina Facilities *(In Season/Off Season)*

Fuel: Gasoline, Diesel
Slips: 87 Total, 10 / 30 Transient **Max LOA:** 100 ft. **Max Beam:** 20 ft.
Rate *(per ft.)*: **Day** $2.00* **Week** Inq. **Month** Inq.
Power: 30 amp $5, **50 amp** $10, **100 amp** n/a, **200 amp** n/a
Cable TV: Yes **Dockside Phone:** Yes
Dock Type: Fixed, Long Fingers
Moorings: 0 Total, 0 Transient **Launch:** n/a
Rate: Day n/a **Week** n/a **Month** n/a
Heads: 4 Toilet(s), 4 Shower(s)
Laundry: 2 Washer(s), 2 Dryer(s), Book Exchange **Pay Phones:** No
Pump-Out: OnSite **Fee:** $5 **Closed Heads:** Yes

Marina Operations

Owner/Manager: Jeff Turken **Dockmaster:** Same
In-Season: May-Sep, 8am-8pm **Off-Season:** Oct-Apr, 9am-5pm
After-Hours Arrival: Call ahead
Reservations: Yes **Credit Cards:** Visa/MC, Dscvr, Amex, Debit
Discounts: Fuel **Dockage:** n/a **Fuel:** vol. disc. **Repair:** n/a
Pets: Welcome, Dog Walk Area **Handicap Access:** No

Marina Services and Boat Supplies

Services - Docking Assistance, Security, Dock Carts **Communication -** Mail & Package Hold, Phone Messages, Fax in/out, FedEx, UPS, Express Mail **Supplies - OnSite:** Ice *(Block, Cube)*, Ships' Store **Under 1 mi:** Propane *(Trans-Tech 990-0696)*, CNG *(Bert Jabin's 280-0339)* **1-3 mi:** West Marine *(268-0129)*, Bait/Tackle *(Angler's 974-4013)*

Boatyard Services

OnCall: Air Conditioning, Refrigeration **Near:** Travelift, Launching Ramp, Engine mechanic *(gas, diesel)*, Electrical Repairs, Electronics Repairs, Hull Repairs, Rigger, Sail Loft, Canvas Work, Bottom Cleaning, Divers. **Nearest Yard:** Harbor Boatyard (410) 267-9050

Restaurants and Accommodations

OnSite: Restaurant *(Carroll's Creek Waterfront 263-8102, L $7-15, D $19-30, Sun brunch $22/11- nuevo Mediterranean takes on Chesapeake traditional)* **Near:** Restaurant *(Lewnes Steakhouse 263-1617, D $15-27)*, *(Boatyard Bar & Grill 216-6206, L $7-22, D $7-22, voted one of the best sailing bars in the world, Carribean specialties, kids' menu)*, *(O'Leary's Seafood 263-0884, L $9-25, D $25-35)*, Hotel *(Inn at Spa Creek 263-8866, $160-250)*, *(Marriott 268-7755, $160-270)* **Under 1 mi:** Restaurant *(Café Normandie 263-3382, L $5-12, D $9-25, 1 mi.)*, Pizzeria *(Squisito NY 990-9800)*, Inn/B&B *(Peninsula House 267-8796, $154-225)*

Recreation and Entertainment

OnSite: Picnic Area, Grills, Fishing Charter, Sightseeing *("Independent" Alura 30 Express Cruises 994-2424 $30-125; Three Centuries Walking Tour of State Capital 268-7601)* **Near:** Playground, Tennis Courts, Fitness Center *(South River 263-2440)*, Boat Rentals, Cultural Attract *(U.S. Naval Academy 263--6933 $7.50/5.50)* **Under 1 mi:** Movie Theater *(Crown 263-3747)*, Museum *(Maritime 295-0104, Sailing Hall of Fame 295-3022)* **1-3 mi:** Golf Course *(Annapolis GC 263-6771)*, Video Rental

Provisioning and General Services

OnSite: Convenience Store **Near:** Gourmet Shop *(Palate Pleasers 263-6941)*, Delicatessen *(Liquor Mart & Deli 224-2166)*, Bank/ATM, Post Office *(269-0442)*, Catholic Church, Protestant Church, Beauty Salon *(House of Ebbitt 268-4033)*, Barber Shop, Dry Cleaners *(Rainbow 626-1112)*, Laundry *(Economy)*, Copies Etc. *(Eastport Copy 269-6399)* **Under 1 mi:** Liquor Store *(Eastport Liquors 263-4747)*, Bookstore *(Insight Concepts 263-1540)*, Pharmacy *(Rite Aid 267-8600)*, Hardware Store *(Stevens 263-3390)*, Florist **1-3 mi:** Supermarket *(Giant 261-8095)*, Health Food *(Sun & Earth 266-6862)*, Bakery, Farmers' Market *(Calvert & Clay St. Thu 11am-2pm, 987-6034)*, Fishmonger, Library *(Eastport 222-1770)*

Transportation

OnSite: Water Taxi *(Ch.68; 263-0033 $2-4.50)* **OnCall:** Rental Car *(Enterprise 268-7751)*, Taxi *(Reliable Cab 268-4714)*, Airport Limo *(Airport Sedan 269-6226)* **Near:** Local Bus **3+ mi:** Rail *(Amtrak BWI 672-6167, 20 mi.)* **Airport:** Baltimore-Washington Int'l. *(20 mi.)*

Medical Services

911 Service **OnCall:** Ambulance **Near:** Dentist *(Stewart 268-2072)* **Under 1 mi:** Doctor **1-3 mi:** Chiropractor, Holistic Services *(Natural Healing 626-0045)*, Veterinarian **Hospital:** Anne Arundel 267-1000 *(4 mi.)*

Setting -- In the Eastport area of Annapolis, on the port side of Spa Creek just before Bascule Bridge, are Annapolis City Marina's four sets of docks; they're backed by an "L" shaped, 4-story gray contemporary office complex with bright red awnings and tubular railings. The long fuel dock and dockhouse sit right on the waterway. The slips and on site restaurant share wide open views across the harbor - the city skyline and the Naval Academy in the distance.

Marina Notes -- *$2.50/ft. holidays & special events. Accommodates yachts to 85-ft. in slips and to 100-ft. on face docks. Aging docks are being quickly replaced with high-end new ones. Repairs not available at marina are available next door. Winter deicing system. Complimentary coffee, bagels, and newspapers on Sundays. Incoming faxes only. Octagonal picnic tables with red umbrellas overlook the docks from the promenade; a second set sits dockside with propane grills. Small laundry room area. Cinderblock and tile bathhouse; showers share communal dressing area. **www.annapoliscitymarina.com

Notable -- This quieter alternative to the bustle of downtown is an easy walk right across the bridge to shopping and the historic district - or dinghy to the city landing at the head of Ego Alley. On site Carroll's Creek waterfront (honoring Spa Creek's original name) is on the leading edge of the complex, one flight up, overlooking the docks and harbor. Its three recently and elegantly redesigned dining areas feature subtle nautical decor, stainless steel, blue leather, burnished wood, and a gorgeous curved marble bar. Well-priced, highly rated cusine is matched by an underpriced wine list. Deli fare to go as well. Lunch 11:30am-4pm, dinner 5-10pm; Sun brunch 10am-1:30pm, dinner 3-10pm. (Private parties up to 60.) The office complex houses many of Annapolis' major marine facilities.

Navigational Information
Lat: 38°58.296' **Long:** 076°29.247' **Tide:** 18 ft. **Current:** n/a **Chart:** 12282
Rep. Depths (*MLW*): Entry 11 ft. **Fuel Dock** n/a **Max Slip/Moor** 17 ft./-
Access: Chesapeake Bay to Severn River to Spa Creek

Marina Facilities *(In Season/Off Season)*
Fuel: Yes
Slips: 50 Total, 6 Transient **Max LOA:** 140 ft. **Max Beam:** n/a
Rate *(per ft.)*: **Day** $2.00 **Week** n/a **Month** $15
Power: 30 amp $5, **50 amp** $10, **100 amp** smart-box, **200 amp** n/a
Cable TV: No **Dockside Phone:** Yes
Dock Type: Fixed, Long Fingers, Pilings
Moorings: 0 Total, 0 Transient **Launch:** n/a
Rate: Day n/a **Week** n/a **Month** n/a
Heads: 1 Toilet(s), 1 Shower(s)
Laundry: None **Pay Phones:** No
Pump-Out: OnCall **Fee:** n/a **Closed Heads:** Yes

Marina Operations
Owner/Manager: John Petrini **Dockmaster:** Same
In-Season: Apr-Oct, 8am-4:30pm **Off-Season:** Nov-Mar, 8am-4:30pm
After-Hours Arrival: Call dockmaster
Reservations: No **Credit Cards:** n/a
Discounts: None
Pets: Welcome, Dog Walk Area **Handicap Access:** No

Petrini Shipyard & Marina

1 Walton Lane; Annapolis, MD 21403

Tel: (410) 263-4278 **VHF: Monitor** 16 **Talk** 9
Fax: (410) 263-4917 **Alternate Tel:** (410) 263-4278
Email: Petrinishipyard@aol.com **Web:** n/a
Nearest Town: Annapolis *(0.5 mi.)* **Tourist Info:** (410) 268-7676

Marina Services and Boat Supplies
Services - Docking Assistance, Security *(owners on site)*, Megayacht Facilities **Communication -** Mail & Package Hold, Phone Messages, Fax in/out, FedEx, DHL, UPS, Express Mail *(Sat Del)* **Supplies - Near:** Ice *(Cube)*, Ships' Store, CNG **Under 1 mi:** Propane *(Trans-Tech 990-0696)* **1-3 mi:** West Marine *(268-0129)*, Bait/Tackle **3+ mi:** Boater's World *(266-7766, 4 mi.)*, Boat/US *(573-5744, 4 mi.)*

Boatyard Services
OnSite: Travelift *(50T Ultrawide/20T Algonac)*, Electrical Repairs, Electronics Repairs, Hull Repairs, Rigger, Sail Loft, Canvas Work, Bottom Cleaning, Brightwork, Air Conditioning, Refrigeration, Divers, Compound, Wash & Wax, Interior Cleaning, Propeller Repairs, Woodworking, Inflatable Repairs, Metal Fabrication, Painting, Awlgrip **Yard Rates:** $35-75/ft., Haul & Launch $8/ft., Power Wash $6, Bottom Paint $24/ft. *(paint incl.)*

Restaurants and Accommodations
Near: Restaurant *(Adam's the Place for Ribs 267-7001, L $7-20, D $10-20)*, *(Lewnes Steakhouse 263-1617, D $15-27)*, *(Carroll's Creek Waterfront 263-8102, L $6-11, D $10-30)*, *(Rockfish Raw Bar & Grill 267-1800, L $9-30, D $9-30)*, Seafood Shack *(O'Leary's Seafood 263-0884, L $9-25, D $25-35)*, Inn/B&B *(Inn at Spa Creek 263-8866, $160-250)* **Under 1 mi:** Motel *(Gibson's Lodgings 268-5555)*, Hotel *(Marriott 888-773-0786, $160-270)*, Inn/B&B *(Harbor View 626-9802, $160-225)*

Recreation and Entertainment
Near: Fitness Center *(Southriver 263-2440)*, Movie Theater *(Crown 263-3747)* **Under 1 mi:** Playground, Dive Shop, Boat Rentals, Roller Blade/Bike Paths, Park *(Truxtun Park)*, Museum *(Maritime Museum 295-0104, Sailing Hall of Fame 295-3022)*, Cultural Attract *(Wm. Paca House)*, Sightseeing *(Discover Annapolis Mini-Bus Tours 626-6000 $10/3, U.S. Naval Academy $7/3.50)*, Galleries, Special Events **1-3 mi:** Pool, Beach, Tennis Courts, Golf Course *(Annapolis GG 263-6771)*, Jogging Paths, Video Rental *(Blockbuster 626-0090)*

Provisioning and General Services
Near: Convenience Store, Gourmet Shop *(Palate Pleasers 263-6941)*, Delicatessen *(Harbour Deli 263-5276)*, Liquor Store *(Eastport 263-4747)*, Post Office *(269-0442)*, Beauty Salon *(House of Ebbitt 268-4033)*, Barber Shop *(Eastport 268-8040)*, Dry Cleaners *(Snow White 295-6755)*, Laundry *(Economy)* **Under 1 mi:** Bank/ATM, Catholic Church, Protestant Church, Bookstore *(Insight Concepts 263-1540)*, Pharmacy *(Rite Aid 267-8600)*, Hardware Store *(Stevens 263-3390)*, Florist, Copies Etc. *(Eastport Copy 269-6399)* **1-3 mi:** Supermarket *(Giant 261-8095)*, Health Food *(Sun & Earth 266-6862)*, Farmers' Market *(Calvert & Clay St. Thu 11am-2pm, 987-6034)*, Fishmonger, Synagogue, Library *(Eastoprt 222-1770)*, Buying Club

Transportation
OnCall: Water Taxi, Rental Car *(Enterprise 268-7751)*, Taxi *(Reliable 268-4714)*, Airport Limo *(Bay Area 268-0509)* **Near:** Local Bus **3+ mi:** Rail *(Amtrak BWI 672-6167, 20 mi.)* **Airport:** BWI *(20 mi.)*

Medical Services
911 Service **OnCall:** Ambulance **Near:** Doctor, Dentist *(Block 269-6713)* **1-3 mi:** Chiropractor *(267-0033)*, Holistic Services, Veterinarian *(Bay Ridge 268-6994)* **Hospital:** Anne Arundel 267-1000 *(4 mi.)*

Setting -- Tucked above the 6th Street/Spa Creek Bridge, this rustic boatyard sprawls along the southern shore of Spa Creek in an otherwise quiet residential area of Eastport. The maze like docks are well sheltered from wind and weather and host some very nice looking sailing yachts. A run of low white buildings, punctuated by a cape cod with dormers, a white Quonset hut, a large blue travelift and a big sign announce your arrival.

Marina Notes -- Family owned and operated since 1947; the Petrini's live on site. Covered and open slips - some are right on the bulkheads, others on piers parallel to the shore - with quite long finger piers. Emphasis is on the very complete boatyard services although they no longer provide dry storage except for repair. The man in the office is often the man who is working on your boat - which makes for a very personal level of service and interaction. There's a "big boat room" - temperature-controlled environment for paint and varnish work. Telephone hookups for long-term guests only. Significant damage from Isabel is mostly fully repaired. The single basic head is located in the covered passageway that runs under the house between the docks and the parking lot.

Notable -- The Eastport Shopping Center is within walking distance with restaurants, services, and a movie theater. Historic Annapolis is the other direction - a reasonable dinghy ride down the creek and up Ego Alley to the city landing, or a healthy walk across the bridge. If you're looking to get out of the hustle and bustle of Annapolis, and don't mind a boatyard atmosphere, this is an interesting choice - also a good possibility for leaving the boat, especially if you want work done.

PHOTOS ON CD-ROM: 7

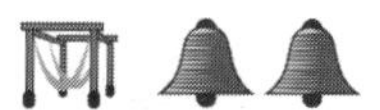

Sarles Boat and Engine Shop

808 Boucher Avenue; Annapolis, MD 21403

Tel: (410) 263-3661; (888) 837-6526 **VHF: Monitor** n/a **Talk** n/a
Fax: (410) 263-3771 **Alternate Tel:** n/a
Email: sarles@annapolis.net **Web:** www.sarlesboat.com
Nearest Town: Annapolis *(1 mi.)* **Tourist Info:** (410) 268-7676

Navigational Information

Lat: 38°58.287' **Long:** 076°29.329' **Tide:** 18 ft. **Current:** n/a **Chart:** 12282
Rep. Depths (*MLW*): Entry 11 ft. **Fuel Dock** n/a **Max Slip/Moor** 11 ft./-
Access: Chesapeake Bay to Severn River to Spa Creek

Marina Facilities *(In Season/Off Season)*

Fuel: No
Slips: 48 Total, 5 Transient **Max LOA:** n/a **Max Beam:** n/a
Rate *(per ft.)*: **Day** $1.75 **Week** n/a **Month** n/a
Power: 30 amp $10, **50 amp** $10, **100 amp** n/a, **200 amp** n/a
Cable TV: No **Dockside Phone:** No
Dock Type: Fixed, Long Fingers, Pilings
Moorings: 0 Total, 0 Transient **Launch:** n/a
Rate: Day n/a **Week** n/a **Month** n/a
Heads: 2 Toilet(s), 2 Shower(s)
Laundry: None **Pay Phones:** Yes
Pump-Out: No **Fee:** n/a **Closed Heads:** Yes

Marina Operations

Owner/Manager: Ben Sarles **Dockmaster:** Same
In-Season: Year-Round, 8am-4:30pm **Off-Season:** n/a
After-Hours Arrival: Call and will meet
Reservations: Yes **Credit Cards:** Visa/MC
Discounts: None
Pets: Welcome, Dog Walk Area **Handicap Access:** No

Marina Services and Boat Supplies

Services - Docking Assistance, Security *(night watchman)*, Trash Pick-Up, Dock Carts **Communication -** Fax in/out, FedEx, DHL, UPS, Express Mail *(Sat Del)* **Supplies - Near:** Ships' Store **Under 1 mi:** Propane *(Trans-Tech Energy 990-0696)* **1-3 mi:** West Marine *(268-0129)*, Bait/Tackle *(Angler's 974-4013)* **3+ mi:** Boater's World *(266-7766, 4 mi.)*, Boat/US *(573-5744, 4 mi.)*

Boatyard Services

OnSite: Travelift, Railway, Launching Ramp, Electrical Repairs, Electronics Repairs, Hull Repairs, Bottom Cleaning, Brightwork **Near:** Rigger, Canvas Work. **1-3 mi:** Refrigeration.

Restaurants and Accommodations

Near: Restaurant *(China Wok 268-1250)*, *(Rockfish Raw Bar & Grill 267-1800, L $9-30, D $9-30)*, *(Squisito Pizzeria & Ristorante 990-9800)*, *(Eastport Clipper 280-6400)*, *(Boatyard Bar & Grill 216-6206)*, *(Lewnes Steakhouse 263-1617, D $15-27)*, *(Ruth's Chris Steakhouse 990-0033)*, *(Carroll's Creek Café 263-8102, L $6-11, D $10-30)*, Seafood Shack *(O'Leary's 263-0884, L $9-25, D $25-35)*, Motel *(Inn at Spa Creek 263-8866, $160-250)* **Under 1 mi:** Motel *(Harbor View 626-9802, $160-225)*, Hotel *(Marriott 268-7555, $160-270)*, Inn/B&B *(Charles Inn 268-1451)*

Recreation and Entertainment

OnSite: Picnic Area, Grills **Near:** Fitness Center *(Southriver Fitness 263-2440)*, Movie Theater *(Crown Eastport 263-3747)* **Under 1 mi:** Playground, Dive Shop, Boat Rentals, Park *(Truxtun Park)*, Museum *(Annapolis Maritime Museum 295-0104, Sailing Hall of Fame 295-3022)*, Cultural Attract *(U.S. Naval Academy)*, Sightseeing *(Annapolis Historic District)*, Galleries, Special Events *(Blue Angels Navy graduates, boat shows and fireworks.)* **1-3 mi:** Pool, Beach, Tennis Courts, Golf Course *(Annapolis Golf Club 263-6771)*, Volleyball, Video Rental *(Blockbuster 626-0090)*

Provisioning and General Services

Near: Convenience Store, Gourmet Shop *(Palate Pleasers 263-6941)*, Liquor Store *(Eastport Liquors 263-4747)*, Post Office *(269-0442)*, Barber Shop *(Eastport Barber 268-8040)*, Dry Cleaners *(Rainbow Cleaners 626-1112)*, Laundry *(Economy)*, Copies Etc. *(Eastport Copy 269-6399)* **Under 1 mi:** Delicatessen *(Liquor Mart & Deli 224-2166)*, Bakery, Bank/ATM, Catholic Church, Beauty Salon *(House of Ebbitt Touch 268-4033)*, Bookstore *(Insight Concepts 263-1540)*, Pharmacy *(Rite Aid 267-8600)*, Newsstand, Hardware Store *(Stevens 263-3390)*, Florist, Clothing Store **1-3 mi:** Supermarket *(Safeway 262-3436, Giant 261-8095)*, Health Food *(Sun & Earth Natural Foods 266-6862)*, Farmers' Market *(Calvert & Clay St. Thu 11am-2pm, 987-6034)*, Fishmonger, Library *(Eastoprt 222-1770)*, Buying Club

Transportation

OnCall: Rental Car *(Enterprise 268-7751)*, Taxi *(Yellow Cab 268-2626)*, Airport Limo *(Bay Area 268-0509)* **Near:** Local Bus **3+ mi:** Rail *(Amtrak BWI 672-6167, 20 mi.)* **Airport:** Baltimore-Washington Int'l. *(20 mi.)*

Medical Services

911 Service **OnCall:** Ambulance **Near:** Dentist *(Block 269-6713)* **Under 1 mi:** Doctor **1-3 mi:** Chiropractor *(Chiropractic Life 267-0033)*, Holistic Services *(Natural Healing 626-0045)*, Veterinarian *(Bay Ridge 268-6994)*
Hospital: Anne Arundel 267-1000 *(4 mi.)*

Setting -- Just past Petrini, from the water Sarles appears to be just a series of covered slips housing high-end, beautifully maintained classic power boats, and some open slips occupied by a few sailboats and more powerboats. Behind the boat sheds is a quiet, old-fashioned, family-run boatyard - the oldest in Annapolis. A rustic free standing roof shelters picnic tables, grills and a handful of Adirondack-chairs for watching the boat traffic on the Creek.

Marina Notes -- Sarles is a family operation and has been since 1907. Today, manager Ben Sarles is at the helm. Reasonably-priced dockage and a long history in the area makes this a good place to leave the boat. Open and covered slips. The full-service boatyard focuses on powerboats and specializes in restorations and woodworking; it includes a travelift and a rare covered railway. Two quite adequate all-tile full bathrooms have their own little house and sport freshly varnished dividers and doors.

Notable -- The gorgeous custom, made-to-order, mahogany Sarles Skiffs are available in lengths from 14 to 19 feet. Above the 6th Street/Spa Creek Bridge, Sarles is quietly insinuated into a residential neighborhood. It's less than half a mile to the Eastport Shopping Center which has a couple of restaurants and a movie theater. It's also a doable dinghy ride or a good hike to downtown Annapolis' historic district.

PHOTOS ON CD-ROM: 9

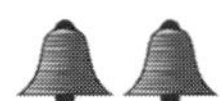

Navigational Information
Lat: 38°58.212' **Long:** 076°28.517' **Tide:** 2 ft. **Current:** 0 kt. **Chart:** 12282
Rep. Depths (*MLW*): Entry 12 ft. **Fuel Dock** n/a **Max Slip/Moor** 12 ft./-
Access: Mouth of Back Creek on starboard side

Marina Facilities *(In Season/Off Season)*
Fuel: No
Slips: 54 Total, 4 Transient **Max LOA:** 120 ft. **Max Beam:** n/a
Rate *(per ft.)*: **Day** $2.00 **Week** n/a **Month** n/a
Power: 30 amp $5, **50 amp** $10, **100 amp** $20, **200 amp** n/a
Cable TV: Yes, Free **Dockside Phone:** Yes - longer term
Dock Type: Fixed, Short Fingers, Alongside, Vinyl
Moorings: 0 Total, 0 Transient **Launch:** n/a
Rate: Day n/a **Week** n/a **Month** n/a
Heads: 3 Toilet(s), 3 Shower(s) *(with dressing rooms)*
Laundry: 1 Washer(s), 1 Dryer(s) **Pay Phones:** No
Pump-Out: OnSite **Fee:** $5 **Closed Heads:** Yes

Marina Operations
Owner/Manager: Greg Holochwost **Dockmaster:** Rob Fettis
In-Season: Year-Round, Mon-Fri 8:30am-5pm **Off-Season:** n/a
After-Hours Arrival: Pull into assigned slip
Reservations: Yes, Required **Credit Cards:** Visa/MC
Discounts: None
Pets: Welcome **Handicap Access:** No

Horn Point Harbor Marina

PO Box 4358; 105 Eastern Avenue; Annapolis, MD 21403

Tel: (410) 263-0550 **VHF: Monitor** n/a **Talk** n/a
Fax: (410) 269-1755 **Alternate Tel:** n/a
Email: cpm@erols.com **Web:** www.hornpointharbor.com
Nearest Town: Annapolis *(0.5 mi.)* **Tourist Info:** (410) 268-7676

Marina Services and Boat Supplies
Services - Dock Carts, Megayacht Facilities **Communication -** FedEx, UPS, Express Mail **Supplies - Near:** Ice *(Block, Cube)* **Under 1 mi:** Ships' Store, Propane *(Trans-Tech 990-0696)* **1-3 mi:** West Marine *(268-0129)*, Bait/Tackle *(Angler's 974-4013)* **3+ mi:** Boater's World *(266-7766, 4 mi.)*, Boat/US *(573-5744, 4 mi.)*

Boatyard Services
OnCall: Engine mechanic *(gas, diesel)*, Electrical Repairs, Compound, Wash & Wax, Propeller Repairs **Near:** Travelift, Railway, Crane, Forklift, Electronics Repairs, Hull Repairs, Rigger, Sail Loft, Canvas Work, Brightwork, Interior Cleaning. **Under 1 mi:** Launching Ramp.
Nearest Yard: Eastport Marina (410) 280-9988

Restaurants and Accommodations
OnSite: Condo/Cottage *(Horn Harbor 994-9990, $150-325, 2 nite-min. weekends, $500/nt. boatshow)* **Near:** Restaurant *(Café Guru's 295-0601)*, *(Rockfish Raw Bar & Grill 267-1800, L $9-30, D $9-30)*, *(O'Leary's Seafood 263-0884, L $9-25, D $25-35)*, *(Ruth's Chris Steak House 990-0033)*, *(Feed Your Crew 280-0973)*, *(Lewnes Steakhouse 263-1617, D $15-27)*, *(Carroll's Creek Café 263-8102, L $6-11, D $10-30)*, Inn/B&B *(Penninsula House 267-8796, $154-225, picks up)*, *(Inn at Spa Creek 263-8866, $160-250)*, *(Sanctuary)* **Under 1 mi:** Hotel *(Marriott 268-7755, $160-270)*, Inn/B&B *(Chez Amis B&B 623-6631, $150-180)*, *(State House 990-0024)*

Recreation and Entertainment
Near: Playground, Fitness Center *(Southriver Fitness 263-2440)*, Boat Rentals, Fishing Charter, Museum *(Barge House Museum, Maritime Museum 295-0104)* **Under 1 mi:** Movie Theater *(Crown Eastport 263-3747)* **1-3 mi:** Golf Course *(Annapolis Country Club 263-6771)*, Video Rental *(Blockbuster 626-0090)*, Park, Cultural Attract, Sightseeing

Provisioning and General Services
Near: Convenience Store *(Royal Farm 269-1052)*, Wine/Beer *(Eastport Liquors 263-4747)*, Liquor Store *(Liquor Mart & Deli 224-2166)*, Bank/ATM, Protestant Church *(St Philips)*, Barber Shop *(Eastport Barber Shop 268-8040)*, Dry Cleaners *(Rainbow Cleaners 626-1112)*, Laundry, Copies Etc. *(East Port Copy 263-3157)* **Under 1 mi:** Gourmet Shop *(Palate Pleasers 263-6941)*, Bakery, Fishmonger, Post Office *(269-0442)*, Catholic Church, Beauty Salon *(House of Ebbitt 268-4033)*, Bookstore *(Borders 990-0955)*, Pharmacy *(Rite Aid 267-8600)*, Hardware Store *(Stevens Hardware 263-3390)* **1-3 mi:** Supermarket *(Safeway 262-3436, Giant 261-8095)*, Delicatessen *(Harbour Deli 263-5276)*, Health Food *(Sun & Earth Natural Foods 266-6862)*, Farmers' Market *(Calvert & Clay St. Thu 11am-2pm, 987-6034)*, Library *(Eastport 222-1770)* **3+ mi:** Department Store *(4 mi.)*

Transportation
OnCall: Water Taxi, Rental Car *(Enterprise 268-7751)*, Taxi *(Arundel 263-2555)*, Airport Limo *(Airport Sedan 269-6226)* **Near:** Local Bus **3+ mi:** Rail *(Amtrak BWI 672-6167, 20 mi.)* **Airport:** Baltimore-Washington Int'l. *(20 mi.)*

Medical Services
911 Service **OnCall:** Ambulance **Near:** Dentist *(Stewart 268-2072)*
1-3 mi: Doctor, Chiropractor, Holistic Services, Veterinarian *(Bay Ridge 268-6994)* **Hospital:** Anne Arundel 267-1000 *(4 mi.)*

Setting -- With Annapolis' most spectacular bay vistas, Horn Harbor is at the mouth of the Severn River with views up Back Creek and out to the Bay. Two recently renovated docks are protected by a six-foot asphalt pier and breakwater which also provides additional dockage. At the head of the docks, the land base is occupied by a large, two-story, contemporary "L"-shaped office building - tan with a brick red roof and awnings highlighted by aqua trim and railings. A courtyard nestles into the "L" and serves as a picnic and special event site.

Marina Notes -- Dockmaster lives onsite. Make reservations directly with Coastal Properties; they don't monitor the radio. The docks were replaced in '02 when the basin was dredged to 6-1/2 feet (and very recently rebuilt again as a result of hurricane damage). There's also 240 feet of alongside bulkhead for larger yachts and cats. Mostly sailboats but there a few powerboats mixed in. New pedestals offer 30-100amp service. All landscaping has been redone as well. Three very lovely, immaculately maintained all-tile full bathrooms have glass-doored showers and varnished natural wood benches and hooks.

Notable -- Located in the Eastport section of Annapolis, Horn Point Harbor Marina is an easy walk to some Eastport services, and approx. six blocks from City Dock. A couple of blocks away is one of Annapolis' 25 B&Bs, the delightful, boater-friendly Peninsula House- with 3 elegantly appointed rooms and an accommodating "we pick-up and deliver, how can we help" attitude. Café Guru is a local hangout with Internet access and eat-in/take out available.

PHOTOS ON CD-ROM: 7

Eastport Yacht Center

726 2nd Street; Annapolis, MD

Tel: (410) 280-9988 **VHF: Monitor** n/a **Talk** n/a
Fax: (410) 280-3428 **Alternate Tel:** n/a
Email: n/a **Web:** www.eastportyachtcenter.com
Nearest Town: Annapolis *(0.5 mi.)* **Tourist Info:** (410) 268-7676

Navigational Information

Lat: 38°58.109' **Long:** 076°28.614' **Tide:** 2 ft. **Current:** 0 kt. **Chart:** 12282
Rep. Depths (*MLW*): Entry 9 ft. **Fuel Dock** n/a **Max Slip/Moor** 7 ft./-
Access: Starboard side Back Creek between Markers 5 & 7

Marina Facilities *(In Season/Off Season)*

Fuel: No
Slips: 106 Total, 10 Transient **Max LOA:** 60 ft. **Max Beam:** n/a
Rate *(per ft.)*: **Day** $1.75* **Week** n/a **Month** $13-15.50
Power: 30 amp Incl., **50 amp** n/a, **100 amp** n/a, **200 amp** n/a
Cable TV: No **Dockside Phone:** No
Dock Type: Fixed, Short Fingers, Wood
Moorings: 0 Total, 0 Transient **Launch:** n/a
Rate: Day n/a **Week** n/a **Month** n/a
Heads: 4 Toilet(s), 4 Shower(s)
Laundry: 1 Washer(s), 1 Dryer(s) **Pay Phones:** No
Pump-Out: No **Fee:** n/a **Closed Heads:** Yes

Marina Operations

Owner/Manager: Kimberly Brown **Dockmaster:** Same
In-Season: Year-Round, 9am-5pm **Off-Season:** n/a
After-Hours Arrival: Call ahead
Reservations: Yes **Credit Cards:** Visa/MC, Amex
Discounts: None
Pets: Welcome **Handicap Access:** No

Marina Services and Boat Supplies

Services - Docking Assistance, Trash Pick-Up, Dock Carts **Communication -** Phone Messages, Fax in/out, FedEx, DHL, UPS, Express Mail *(Sat Del)* **Supplies - OnSite:** Ice *(Block, Cube)* **Near:** CNG *(Bert Jabin's)* **Under 1 mi:** Ships' Store *(Fawcett's 267-8681)* **1-3 mi:** West Marine *(268-0129)*, Bait/Tackle, Propane *(Hardware House 268-3939)* **3+ mi:** Boater's World *(266-7766, 4 mi.)*, Boat/US *(573-5744, 4 mi.)*

Boatyard Services

OnSite: Travelift *(35T - J. Gordon & Co. 263-0054)*, Crane, Engine mechanic *(gas, diesel)*, Electrical Repairs, Hull Repairs, Propeller Repairs, Yacht Broker *(Several)* **OnCall:** Rigger, Sail Loft, Canvas Work, Bottom Cleaning, Brightwork, Divers, Compound, Wash & Wax, Inflatable Repairs, Upholstery **Near:** Air Conditioning, Refrigeration. **Dealer for:** Nautor Swan. **Yard Rates:** Haul & Launch $7-9/ft, For Survey $5-7 *(blocking $2.25-2.50/ft.)*, Power Wash $2-3.50/ft. **Storage:** On-Land $360/mo.

Restaurants and Accommodations

Near: Restaurant *(Carroll's Creek Café 263-8102, L $6-11, D $10-30)*, *(Lewnes Steakhouse 263-1617, D $15-27)*, *(Rockfish Raw Bar & Grill 267-1800, L $9-30, D $9-30)*, *(Ruth's Chris Steak House 990-0033)*, *(Chart House 268-7166, D $21-41, lounge $)*, *(Boatyard Bar & Grill 216-6206)*, *(La Rose de Saigon 268-8484)*, Seafood Shack *(O'Leary's Seafood 263-0884, L $9-25, D $25-35)*, Lite Fare *(Café Guru 295-0601, Internet)*, Inn/B&B *(Inn at Spa Creek 263-8866, $160-250)*, *(Peninsula House 267-8796, $154-225, picks up)* **Under 1 mi:** Restaurant *(Rocco's 263-9444)*, Seafood Shack *(Ego Alley Tropical Grill 263-3353)*, Motel *(Academy Motel 757-2222)*, Hotel *(Loew's 263-7777)*, *(Marriott 268-7555, $160-270)*

Recreation and Entertainment

Near: Playground, Fitness Center *(Southriver Fitness 263-2440)*, Boat Rentals, Fishing Charter, Museum *(Barge House at Annapolis Maritime Museum 295-0104 - soon)* **Under 1 mi:** Movie Theater *(Crown Eastport 263-3747)* **1-3 mi:** Golf Course *(Annapolis Country Club 263-6771)*, Video Rental *(Blockbuster 626-0090)*

Provisioning and General Services

Near: Convenience Store *(Royal Farm 269-1052)*, Delicatessen *(Liquor Mart & Deli 224-2166)*, Liquor Store *(Eastport Liquor 263-4747)*, Bank/ATM, Protestant Church, Beauty Salon *(House of Ebbitt 268-4033)*, Barber Shop *(Eastport 268-8040)*, Dry Cleaners *(Rainbow 626-1112)*, Laundry, Copies Etc. *(East Port Copy 263-3157)* **Under 1 mi:** Gourmet Shop *(Palate Pleasers 263-6941)*, Fishmonger, Post Office *(269-0442)*, Catholic Church, Bookstore *(Borders 990-0955)*, Pharmacy *(Rite Aid 267-8600)*, Hardware Store *(Stevens 263-3390)* **1-3 mi:** Supermarket *(Safeway 262-3436, Giant 261-8095)*, Health Food *(Sun & Earth 266-6862)*, Farmers' Market *(Calvert & Clay St. Thu 11am-2pm, 987-6034)*, Library *(222-1770)*

Transportation

OnSite: Water Taxi **OnCall:** Rental Car *(Enterprise 268-7751)*, Taxi *(A&W Taxi 263-8715)*, Airport Limo *(Airport Sedan 269-6226)* **Near:** Local Bus **3+ mi:** Rail *(Amtrak BWI 672-6167, 20 mi.)* **Airport:** BWI *(20 mi.)*

Medical Services

911 Service **Near:** Dentist *(Stewart 268-2072)* **1-3 mi:** Doctor, Chiropractor *(Chiropractic Life 267-0033)*, Holistic Services *(626-0045)* **Hospital:** Anne Arundel 267-1000 *(4 mi.)*

Setting -- Eastport Yacht Center is on the northern shore of Back Creek on the Eastport Peninsula. Its extensive network of 106 docks is divided among four main piers and backed by a 3-story gray contemporary complex, with white tubular staircase and deck railings, which houses many maritime services.

Marina Notes -- *Rates, from $1.75-2.50/ft., are based on length of vessel - from bowsprit to swim platform. Monthly liveaboard extra $200/mo. Formerly Bert Jabin's Eastport Yard, under new ownership as of 2003. Sustained significant hurricane damage but was completely rebuilt. EYC's boatyard services limited to haul/launch/storage and attendant services - 35T travelift and crane. But many independent services base here - a Nautor Swan official dealership, J. Gordon & Co. (263-0054) - a full-service yacht repair center, plus Annapolis Yacht Management and Walczak Yacht brokerage. Also virtually onsite is OzmoTech and Nautech which commissions, repairs, and restores Swans and J Boats (280-9704). Sea-Tow bases here as well. Internet access is at Café Guru. The heads sport rosy tile floors, attractive gray dividers, and counters with rosewood cabinets. Two glass-doored shower stalls share a dressing room.

Notable -- Across the street are the Maritime Café at McNasby's and the Annapolis Maritime Museum, which was destroyed by Isabel and is temporarily closed; The Barge House, the main edifice, is being reconstructed, but the docks are now operational and will soon host the "Peg Wallace", their draketail deadrise workboat. Weems & Plath is a block away and their joint exhibit "Before GPS: the Genius of Captain Philip Van Horn Weems" is temporarily at the Maritime Institute of Technology. The surrounding neighborhood is largely residential; the yellow bus line stops two blocks away at Fourth and Chesapeake.

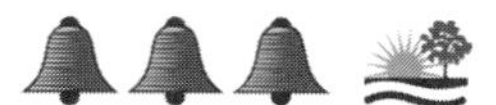

Navigational Information
Lat: 38°58.109' **Long:** 076°28.799' **Tide:** 2 ft. **Current:** 0 kt. **Chart:** 12282
Rep. Depths (*MLW*): Entry 8 ft. **Fuel Dock** n/a **Max Slip/Moor** 7 ft./-
Access: N side of Back Creek on East Port Peninsula past G7

Marina Facilities *(In Season/Off Season)*
Fuel: No
Slips: 232 Total, 15 Transient **Max LOA:** 70 ft. **Max Beam:** n/a
Rate *(per ft.)*: **Day** $3.00/Inq. **Week** 5 **Month** Inq.
Power: 30 amp Incl., **50 amp** Incl., **100 amp** n/a, **200 amp** n/a
Cable TV: Yes, $5.00 **Dockside Phone:** Yes
Dock Type: Fixed, Long Fingers, Short Fingers, Wood
Moorings: 0 Total, 0 Transient **Launch:** n/a, Dinghy Dock
Rate: Day n/a **Week** n/a **Month** n/a
Heads: 7 Toilet(s), 7 Shower(s) *(with dressing rooms)*, Hair Dryers
Laundry: 3 Washer(s), 3 Dryer(s), Iron, Iron Board **Pay Phones:** No
Pump-Out: OnSite **Fee:** n/a **Closed Heads:** Yes

Marina Operations
Owner/Manager: Desiree Bell **Dockmaster:** John Kamrath
In-Season: Year-Round, 8:30am-5pm **Off-Season:** n/a, Winter 8:30am-4pm
After-Hours Arrival: Call in advance
Reservations: Yes **Credit Cards:** Visa/MC, Dscvr
Discounts: None
Pets: Welcome, Dog Walk Area **Handicap Access:** No

Mears Marina Annapolis

519 Chester Avenue; Annapolis, MD 21403

Tel: (410) 268-8282 **VHF: Monitor** 09 **Talk** 72
Fax: (410) 268-7161 **Alternate Tel:** n/a
Email: mears@mearsannapolis.com **Web:** www.mearsannapolis.com
Nearest Town: Annapolis *(1 mi.)* **Tourist Info:** (410) 268-3034

Marina Services and Boat Supplies
Services - Docking Assistance, Security *(Keycard entry)*, Dock Carts **Communication -** Phone Messages, Fax in/out, Data Ports *(Wi-Fi)*, FedEx, UPS, Express Mail **Supplies - OnSite:** Ice *(Block, Cube)* **Under 1 mi:** Ships' Store, Propane *(Arundel 956-2400)* **1-3 mi:** West Marine *(268-0129)*, Bait/Tackle *(Angler's)*, CNG *(Bert Jabin's)* **3+ mi:** Boater's World *(266-7766, 4 mi.)*, Boat/US *(573-5744, 4 mi.)*

Boatyard Services
OnSite: Crane, Electrical Repairs, Electronics Repairs, Hull Repairs, Rigger, Bottom Cleaning, Brightwork, Refrigeration, Compound, Wash & Wax, Woodworking, Awlgrip, Yacht Broker *(Bristol Yacht Sales)* **OnCall:** Canvas Work, Divers **Member:** ABYC - 1 Certified Tech(s)

Restaurants and Accommodations
OnSite: Lite Fare *(Zephyr's Poolside Café & Bar L plus omlettes cooked to order)*, *(Mear's B Sat & Sun - last week Apr to mid-Oct - coffee, bagels & donuts)* **Near:** Restaurant *(Boatyard Bar & Grill 216-6206)*, *(Rockfish Raw Bar & Grill 267-1800, L $9-30, D $9-30)*, *(Lewnes Steakhouse 263-1617, D $15-27)*, *(Chart House 268-7166, D $21-41)*, *(Carroll's Creek Café 263-8102, L $6-11, D $10-30)*, *(Wild Orchid 268-8009, mid-Oct)*, Seafood Shack *(O'Leary's Seafood 263-0884, L $9-25, D $25-35)*, Inn/B&B *(Inn at Spa Creek 263-8866, $160-250)*, *(Peninsula House picks up boaters)* **Under 1 mi:** Pizzeria *(Papa John's 280-1500)*, *(Squisito NY 990-9800)*, Hotel *(Marriott 268-7555, $160-270)*, Inn/B&B *(Chez Amis 263-6631, $150-180)*

Recreation and Entertainment
OnSite: Pool *(until 8:30pm MemDay-LabDay; poolside bar & kids' pool)*, Picnic Area, Grills *(charcoal)*, Tennis Courts, Boat Rentals *(Annapolis Sailing School)*, Volleyball **Near:** Fitness Center *(Southriver Fitness 263-2440)*, Park **Under 1 mi:** Movie Theater *(Crown Eastport 263-3747)*, Museum *(Annapolis Maritime 295-0104, Sailing Hall of Fame 295-3022)*, Sightseeing, Galleries **1-3 mi:** Golf Course *(Annapolis GC 263-6771)*, Video Rental

Provisioning and General Services
Near: Convenience Store *(Royal Farm 269-1052)*, Gourmet Shop *(Palate Pleasers 263-6941)*, Delicatessen *(Harbour 263-5276)*, Wine/Beer *(Mills Wine 263-2888)*, Liquor Store *(Liquor Mart & Deli 224-2166)*, Bank/ATM, Post Office *(269-0442)*, Catholic Church, Protestant Church *(St. Philips Episcopal)*, Beauty Salon, Barber Shop *(Eastport 268-8040)*, Dry Cleaners *(Rainbow 626-1112)*, Laundry, Copies Etc. *(269-6399)* **Under 1 mi:** Health Food, Bookstore *(Borders 990-0955)*, Pharmacy *(Rite Aid 267-8600)*, Hardware Store *(Stevens 263-3390)* **1-3 mi:** Supermarket *(Giant 261-8095)*, Farmers' Market, Library *(Eastport 222-1770)*

Transportation
OnSite: Bikes **OnCall:** Water Taxi *(Ch.68, 263-0033 -15 min. after hour - must call)*, Rental Car *(Enterprise 268-7751)*, Taxi *(Yellow Cab 268-2626)*, Airport Limo *(Better Limousine 261-8860)* **Near:** Local Bus **3+ mi:** Rail *(Baltimore 672-6167, 20 mi.)* **Airport:** Baltimore-Washington Int'l. *(20 mi.)*

Medical Services
911 Service **Near:** Dentist *(Stewart 268-2072)* **Under 1 mi:** Doctor **1-3 mi:** Chiropractor *(267-0033)*, Holistic Services *(626-0045)*, Veterinarian *(Bay Ridge 268-6994)* **Hospital:** Anne Arundel 267-1000 *(1-3 mi)*

Setting -- An unassuming two-story white bulding, with a signature "M", anchors this resort-style marina on the south shore of the Eastport Peninsula. The spacious, well-tended grounds are highlighted by perennial borders and a profusion of flowers. Four piers jut into Back Creek from the bulkheaded lawn, hosting 232 nicely maintained slips. The facilities of the well-appointed, on site Marina Swim and Tennis Club are available to transient boaters - including lessons.

Marina Notes -- DCM. Advance reservations are critical. A combination of older bulkhead pedestals attached to the bulkhead and new, white contemporary power pedestals on some T-heads and larger docks. The heads are superb - custom tile floors and walls, blue striped wallpaper, Corian vanities with upholstered benches, flowers and hairdryers. An airy laundry has a folding counter, iron & ironing board. An adjacent "bath house" features a large bench and another vanity plus 7 private shower rooms. Additional heads are at the pool and the Severn River YC (facilities also available).

Notable -- The Olympic-size pool is surrounded by layers of comfortable chaises; "adults-only" swim 15 min. each hour. Zephyr's Poolside Café has a tiki bar theme featuring healthy sandwiches, "to-order" omlettes, fun kid-food and beverages including beer & wine. Adjacent are 7 championship tennis courts with a well-attended kids' program. A large picnic pavillion is perfect for groups & club cruises (200 for cocktails, 80 for sit-down, plus the lawn can be tented); plus it overlooks the docks. Adjacent are picnic tables pleasantly shaded by umbrellas plus two propane grills with a benches for the griller and a second picnic area east of the bath house. It's about a half mile walk to historic Annapolis.

PHOTOS ON CD-ROM: 14

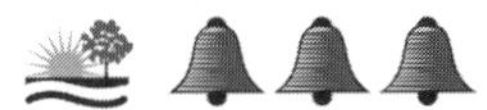

Annapolis Landing Marina

980 Awald Road, Suite 500; Annapolis, MD 21403

Tel: (410) 263-0090 **VHF: Monitor** 9 **Talk** 72
Fax: (410) 263-9109 **Alternate Tel:** (443) 994-9529
Email: annapolislandingmarina@comcast.net **Web:** www.annapolismarina.c
Nearest Town: Annapolis *(3.5 mi.)* **Tourist Info:** (410) 268-7676

Navigational Information

Lat: 38°57.920' **Long:** 076°28.655' **Tide:** 2 ft. **Current:** 0 kt. **Chart:** 12282
Rep. Depths (*MLW*): Entry 10 ft. **Fuel Dock** 10 ft. **Max Slip/Moor** 10 ft./-
Access: Severn River to Back Creek keep DM 7 to port to ALM fuel dock

Marina Facilities *(In Season/Off Season)*

Fuel: Gasoline, Diesel
Slips: 122 Total, 20 / 50 Transient **Max LOA:** 165 ft. **Max Beam:** n/a
Rate *(per ft.)*: **Day** $1.75* **Week** Inq. **Month** Inq.
Power: 30 amp $5, **50 amp** $10, **100 amp** $20, **200 amp** n/a
Cable TV: Yes, $3/day $5/week-end **Dockside Phone:** Yes
Dock Type: Fixed, Long Fingers, Pilings, Wood
Moorings: 0 Total, 0 Transient **Launch:** n/a, Dinghy Dock
Rate: Day n/a **Week** n/a **Month** n/a
Heads: 8 Toilet(s), 8 Shower(s)
Laundry: 4 Washer(s), 4 Dryer(s), Book Exchange **Pay Phones:** Yes
Pump-Out: OnSite, Self Service, 2 Central **Fee:** $8 **Closed Heads:** Yes

Marina Operations

Owner/Manager: C. Edward Hartman **Dockmaster:** Eric Bradley
In-Season: May-Oct, 8am-7pm **Off-Season:** Nov-Apr, 9am-5pm
After-Hours Arrival: Call in advance
Reservations: Preferred **Credit Cards:** Visa/MC, Dscvr, Amex
Discounts: None
Pets: Welcome, Dog Walk Area **Handicap Access:** Yes, Heads

Marina Services and Boat Supplies

Services - Docking Assistance, Trash Pick-Up, Dock Carts, Megayacht Facilities **Communication -** Mail & Package Hold, Phone Messages, Fax in/out *($0.50)*, Data Ports *(Beacon Wi-Fi)*, FedEx, DHL, UPS, Express Mail *(Sat Del)* **Supplies - OnSite:** Ice *(Block, Cube)*, Ships' Store **Near:** Bait/Tackle, CNG *(Bert Jabin's)* **1-3 mi:** West Marine *(268-0129)*, Propane *(Hardware House 268-3939)* **3+ mi:** Boater's World *(266-7766)*, Boat/US *(573-5744)*

Boatyard Services

OnSite: Canvas Work *(Annapolis Custom Yacht Canvas 263-6006)*, Bottom Cleaning, Brightwork, Divers *(Harbor Diving 991-7767)*, Compound, Wash & Wax *(Williams Yacht 268-1634 - much more)*, Yacht Interiors *(Chesapeake Yacht Interiors)* **OnCall:** Propeller Repairs

Restaurants and Accommodations

OnSite: Lite Fare *(The Back Porch at Ken's Creative Kitchen 280-0380, B $4-8, L $7-15, Wed-Sun 8am-2pm)* **Near:** Lite Fare *(Wet Dog Café 263-7914)*, Motel *(Super 8 Motel 757-2222, $50-80)*, Inn/B&B *(Inn at Spa Creek 263-8866, $160-250), (Peninsula House)* **Under 1 mi:** Restaurant *(Chesapeake Harbour 263-3600)* **1-3 mi:** Restaurant *(Adam's Ribs 267-7001, L $7-20, D $10-20, carry-out), (Benvenuti Squisito Pizza Pasta & More 990-9800), (La Braza 990-4747), (Sam's Waterfront Café 263-3200), (La Rose de Saigon 268-8484)*, Seafood Shack *(O'Leary's Seafood 263-0884, L $9-25, D $25-35)*, Pizzeria *(Rocco's 263-9444)*

Recreation and Entertainment

OnSite: Pool, Picnic Area, Grills, Boat Rentals *(Sunsail 280-2553 sail & power catamaran charters)*, Sightseeing *(Watermark Cruises 268-7601 40 min. Harbor, $8/4, 90 min. River-St.Thomas Pt. $16/8, St. Michaels $55/27)* **Near:** Beach, Playground, Dive Shop, Tennis Courts, Jogging Paths, Park, Cultural Attract, Special Events **Under 1 mi:** Roller Blade/Bike Paths **1-3 mi:** Golf Course *(Annapolis GC 263-6771)*, Fitness Center, Movie Theater *(Crown 263-3747)*, Video Rental *(Blockbuster 626-0090)*

Provisioning and General Services

Near: Delicatessen *(Wet Dog 263-7914)*, Fishmonger *(Ruggiero & Son 263-6627)* **Under 1 mi:** Convenience Store, Bakery, Bank/ATM, Catholic Church **1-3 mi:** Supermarket *(Giant 261-8095)*, Gourmet Shop, Wine/Beer *(Bay Ridge 268-1961)*, Liquor Store *(Ebb Tide 269-1500)*, Post Office, Protestant Church, Library *(Eastport 222-1770)*, Beauty Salon *(Saphire 990-4890)*, Dry Cleaners *(Admiral 268-8894)*, Pharmacy *(CVS 268-5253)*, Hardware Store *(Hardware House 268-3939)*, Copies Etc. *(Kinko's 573-5600)*

Transportation

OnSite: Courtesy Car/Van **OnCall:** Water Taxi *(Ch.68, 263-0033 - must call)*, Rental Car *(Enterprise 268-7751)*, Taxi *(Reliable 268-4714)*, Airport Limo *(Carey Limo 269-5500)* **Near:** Local Bus **3+ mi:** Rail *(Amtrak BWI 672-6167, 20 mi.)* **Airport:** Baltimore-Washington Int'l *(20 mi.)*

Medical Services

911 Service **OnSite:** Holistic Services *(Innersource 269-6298; California Therapeutic Massage 280-2726)* **OnCall:** Ambulance **1-3 mi:** Doctor, Dentist *(Boyd 626-1797)*, Chiropractor *(Chiropractic Life 267-0033)*, Veterinarian *(Bay 268-6994)* **Hospital:** Anne Arundel 267-1000 *(6 mi.)*

Setting -- This small, lushly planted peninsula sits on the southern shore of Back Creek and is blanketed on two sides by seven sets of docks. On a rise above the docks is the signature two-story gray contemporary Cape Cod with white trim and red roof punctuated by dormers. The wrap-around porches offer spectacular views of the Bay and across to the Annapolis skyline. A pool is sequestered to the west by the small brick marina office and large picnic pavilion.

Marina Notes -- *Fri-Sat 8am-8pm. Dockage fee $35 ft.minimum. 95 ft. fuel dock; all piers were recently renovated or replaced along with high-quality pedestals. Graciously-spaced stone-floor picnic nooks, with tables and grills, are cut into the hill. The picnic pavilion has 8 long picnic tables (ideal for groups) topped with a curved canvas awning. Adjacent is the pool, well furnished with chaises. There are two bathhouses - one adjacent to the pool and one in the main building that also houses the Watermark Tours and a few other services. Each is all-tile with pretty awning-stripe curtains.

Notable -- The Back Porch Café at Ken's Creative Kitchen, open Wednesday to Sunday from 8am-2pm, serves breakfast and lunch on "the deck" - the front porch of the main building, furnished with lovely wrought-iron tables and chairs. It will also create picnic lunches to take on the boat. On site Watermark Cruises offers 40 and 90 minute cruises of Spa Creek, the river, and Thomas Pt. Light, plus all-day trips to St. Michaels & Rock Hall. They also run the water taxi (discount to Annapolis Landing guests), which gives this quiet, serene area quick access to downtown Annapolis. Sail Magazine's office is here as well. Courtesy car for provisioning and boat supplies $5 for 2 hours.

PHOTOS ON CD-ROM: 17

Navigational Information

Lat: 38°57.998' **Long:** 076°28.521' **Tide:** 2 ft. **Current:** 0 kt. **Chart:** 12282
Rep. Depths (*MLW*): Entry 10 ft. **Fuel Dock** n/a **Max Slip/Moor** 12 ft./-
Access: Severn River to Back Creek, past G4 on port bow

Marina Facilities *(In Season/Off Season)*

Fuel: No
Slips: 265 Total, 40 Transient **Max LOA:** 65 ft. **Max Beam:** n/a
Rate *(per ft.)*: **Day** $2.00 **Week** $9.00 **Month** $19
Power: 30 amp Incl., **50 amp** Incl., **100 amp** n/a, **200 amp** n/a
Cable TV: Yes **Dockside Phone:** No
Dock Type: Fixed, Long Fingers, Pilings, Wood
Moorings: 0 Total, 0 Transient **Launch:** n/a
Rate: Day n/a **Week** n/a **Month** n/a
Heads: 14 Toilet(s), 11 Shower(s)
Laundry: 2 Washer(s), 3 Dryer(s), Book Exchange **Pay Phones:** Yes, 2
Pump-Out: OnSite, Full Service **Fee:** Free* **Closed Heads:** Yes

Marina Operations

Owner/Manager: Scott Tinkler **Dockmaster:** Jan Kanner
In-Season: Mem-LabDay, 8am-6pm **Off-Season:** Sep-May, 8am-4:30pm
After-Hours Arrival: Call ahead
Reservations: Yes **Credit Cards:** Visa/MC, Dscvr, Amex
Discounts: None
Pets: Welcome, Dog Walk Area **Handicap Access:** Yes

Port Annapolis Marina

PO Box; 7074 Bembe Beach Road; Annapolis, MD 21403

Tel: (410) 269-1990 **VHF: Monitor** 16 **Talk** n/a
Fax: (410) 269-5856 **Alternate Tel:** (410) 269-1944
Email: office@portannapolis.com **Web:** www.portannapolis.com
Nearest Town: Annapolis *(3.5 mi.)* **Tourist Info:** (410) 268-7676

Marina Services and Boat Supplies

Services - Docking Assistance, Boaters' Lounge, Security *(40 hrs./wk.)*, Dock Carts **Communication -** Mail & Package Hold, Phone Messages, Fax in/out *($1)*, Data Ports *(Lounge, Free)*, FedEx, DHL, UPS, Express Mail *(Sat Del)* **Supplies - OnSite:** Ice *(Block, Cube)*, Ships' Store **Near:** CNG *(Bert Jabin's)* **1-3 mi:** West Marine, Bait/Tackle, Propane *(Hardware House)*

Boatyard Services

OnSite: Travelift *(25T)*, Crane, Engine mechanic *(gas, diesel)*, Electrical Repairs, Hull Repairs, Rigger, Bottom Cleaning, Brightwork, Air Conditioning, Refrigeration, Compound, Wash & Wax, Interior Cleaning, Woodworking, Painting, Awlgrip, Yacht Broker **OnCall:** Electronics Repairs, Canvas Work, Divers, Propeller Repairs **Under 1 mi:** Metal Fabrication. **Member:** ABYC, ABBRA **Yard Rates:** $60-70/hr., Haul & Launch $10-12/ft. based on size *(blocking $2/ft.)*, Power Wash Incl., Bottom Paint $16-25/ft. *(paint incl.)*
Storage: In-Water $2/ft./day, On-Land $10-15/day

Restaurants and Accommodations

OnSite: Lite Fare *(The Wet Dog 263-7914, B, L in season; carry-out)*
Near: Lite Fare *(The Back Porch 280-0380, B $4-8, L $7-15)*
Under 1 mi: Restaurant *(Sam's Waterfront Café 263-3200)*, Inn/B&B *(Inn at Spa Creek 263-8866, $160-250)* **1-3 mi:** Restaurant *(O'Leary's Seafood 263-0884, L $9-$25, D $25-35)*, *(Wild Orchid 268-8009)*, *(Adam's Ribs 267-7001, L $7-20, D $10-20)*, Fast Food *(McDonald's, Subway 268-3889)* Pizzeria *(Rocco's 263-9444)*, Hotel *(Chesapeake Hotel 280-9800)*
3+ mi: Hotel *(Marriott 268-7555, $160-270, 4 mi.)*, Inn/B&B *(Prince George Inn B&B 263-6418, 4 mi.)*

Recreation and Entertainment

OnSite: Pool, Picnic Area, Grills, Playground, Boat Rentals, Volleyball
Under 1 mi: Golf Course *(Annapolis Golf Club 263-6771)* **1-3 mi:** Tennis Courts, Fitness Center *(Curves 990-1002)*, Movie Theater *(Crown Eastport 263-3747)*, Video Rental *(Blockbuster 626-0090)*, Cultural Attract, Sightseeing **3+ mi:** Museum *(Annapolis Maritime Museum 295-0104, Sailing Hall of Fame 295-3022, 4 mi.)*

Provisioning and General Services

OnSite: Bank/ATM **Near:** Convenience Store, Delicatessen *(The Wet Dog 263-7914)*, Fishmonger *(Ruggiero & Son Seafood 263-6627)*
1-3 mi: Supermarket *(Giant 261-8095)*, Gourmet Shop *(Butcher Gourmet 263-0793)*, Liquor Store *(Bay Ridge Wine 268-1961)*, Bakery, Post Office, Catholic Church, Library *(Eastport 222-1770)*, Beauty Salon *(Saphire 990-4890)*, Dry Cleaners *(Admiral Laundry & Cleaners 268-8894)*, Pharmacy *(CVS 268-5253)*, Hardware Store *(Hardware House 268-3939)*

Transportation

OnCall: Water Taxi, Rental Car *(Enterprise 268-7751)*, Taxi *(Reliable 268-4714)*, Airport Limo *(Better Limo 261-8860)* **Under 1 mi:** Local Bus
3+ mi: Rail *(Amtrak at BWI 672-6167, 20 mi.)*
Airport: Baltimore-Washington Int'l. *(20 mi.)*

Medical Services

911 Service **OnCall:** Ambulance **Near:** Holistic Services *(Innersource 269-6298)* **1-3 mi:** Doctor, Dentist *(Boyd 626-1797)*, Chiropractor *(Chiropractic Life 267-0033)*, Veterinarian *(Bay Ridge Animal Hospital 268-6994)*
Hospital: Anne Arundel 267-1000 *(6 mi.)*

Setting -- Port Annapolis' 18 park like acres hug the southern shore of Back Creek; more than a dozen sets of docks follow the waters' edge. The pool has water views through the plantings and the poolhouse has a delightful "Summer on the Bay" mural by a local artist on the pool-side wall. Pockets of picnic tables with charcoal grills are scattered about the grounds. Winding brick paths and boardwalks link the amenities and a veritable mall of boaters' services.

Marina Notes -- *Pump-out is $2 for non-slip tenants. DCM. Founded in 1977, Dock Age Magazine's Marina of the Year in 2003. A full-service boatyard with acres of dry storage hosts mostly sailboats. Do-it-yourself option available. Services include fiberglassing and custom carpentry. Thoughtfully appointed lounge with comfortable seating, ATM, broadband Internet (up to a generous one hour), pay phone, soda machine, and one set of heads. The other is by the pool; heads have sparkling white tile with nautical accents and a separate shower area with dressing room - all very nice and very new. Just outside, a large table and chairs sit under an awning overlooking the docks. The laundry is in the poolhouse - a thoughtful location. Southern Cross Marine, Eastport Technologies, Contemporary Yachts, Atlantic Coast Yacht Service, Interyacht Yacht Brokerage, Capital Yacht Sales, Hill's Yacht Sales, and a host of other services.

Notable -- The new 3,000 sq. ft. Overlook Pavilion with 12 ft. vaulted ceiling seats over 200 - perfect for club cruises and parties. A gazebo is adjacent - both have great views. The Wet Dog Café is an eat-in/takeout, light-fare eatery and bakery with a lovely picnic area populated with octagonal, umbreallaed tables. They cater the Pavilion, too. It's a short, lovely walk out the driveway to main Edgewood Road. The Back to Nature Annapolis City Park is close by.

PHOTOS ON CD-ROM: 17

Bert Jabin's Yacht Yard

7310 Edgewood Road; Annapolis, MD 21403

Tel: (410) 268-9667 **VHF: Monitor** n/a **Talk** n/a
Fax: (410) 280-3163 **Alternate Tel:** n/a
Email: n/a **Web:** www.bjyy.com
Nearest Town: Annapolis *(5 mi.)* **Tourist Info:** (410) 268-7676

Navigational Information

Lat: 38°57.738' **Long:** 076°28.784' **Tide:** 1 ft. **Current:** 0 kt. **Chart:** 12282
Rep. Depths (*MLW*): Entry 10 ft. **Fuel Dock** n/a **Max Slip/Moor** 10 ft./-
Access: Severn River to Back Creek to a jog in the waterway

Marina Facilities *(In Season/Off Season)*

Fuel: No
Slips: 200 Total, 50 Transient **Max LOA:** 60 ft. **Max Beam:** 20 ft.
Rate *(per ft.)*: **Day** $2.00* **Week** n/a **Month** n/a
Power: 30 amp by meter, **50 amp** by meter, **100 amp** n/a, **200 amp** n/a
Cable TV: No **Dockside Phone:** No
Dock Type: Fixed, Floating, Short Fingers, Pilings, Alongside
Moorings: 0 Total, 0 Transient **Launch:** n/a, Dinghy Dock
Rate: Day n/a **Week** n/a **Month** n/a
Heads: 12 Toilet(s), Shower(s)
Laundry: 1 Washer(s), 1 Dryer(s), Book Exchange **Pay Phones:** Yes
Pump-Out: OnSite, Full Service **Fee:** $5 **Closed Heads:** Yes

Marina Operations

Owner/Manager: Rod Jabin **Dockmaster:** Same
In-Season: Year-Round, 8am-5pm **Off-Season:** n/a
After-Hours Arrival: Floating dock or travelift well
Reservations: Yes, Preferred **Credit Cards:** Visa/MC, Dscvr, Amex
Discounts: None
Pets: Welcome, Dog Walk Area **Handicap Access:** Yes, Heads

Marina Services and Boat Supplies

Services - Docking Assistance, Boaters' Lounge, Crew Lounge, Security, Trash Pick-Up, Dock Carts **Communication -** Mail & Package Hold, Phone Messages, Fax in/out *($1-2)*, Data Ports, FedEx, DHL, UPS, Express Mail **Supplies - OnSite:** Ice *(Block)*, Ships' Store, CNG **Under 1 mi:** Bait/ Tackle, Live Bait **1-3 mi:** West Marine *(268-0129)*, Propane *(Hardware House 268-3939)*

Boatyard Services

OnSite: Travelift *(3-35T)*, Railway, Crane *(15T)*, Forklift *(4)*, Engine mechanic *(gas, diesel)*, Electrical Repairs, Electronics Repairs, Hull Repairs, Rigger, Sail Loft, Canvas Work, Bottom Cleaning, Brightwork, Air Conditioning, Refrigeration, Divers, Compound, Wash & Wax *(Above the Waterline)*, Interior Cleaning, Propeller Repairs, Woodworking, Inflatable Repairs, Upholstery, Metal Fabrication, Painting, Awlgrip, Total Refits, Yacht Broker *(Tidewater; Annapolis Yacht Sales; Bay Yacht Traders)* **Yard Rates:** $85, Haul & Launch $4.75-6.75/ft. *(blocking $2.50-3.35/ft.)*, Power Wash $1.50-2/ft. **Storage:** In-Water $11.50-15.50/ft., On-Land $11.50-15.50/ft.

Restaurants and Accommodations

OnCall: Pizzeria *(Domino's)* **Near:** Restaurant *(Back Porch Café 280-0380)*, Seafood Shack *(O'Leary's Seafood 263-0884, L $9-25, D $25-35)*, Lite Fare *(Wet Dog Café 263-7914)* **Under 1 mi:** Restaurant *(Sam's Waterfront 263-3200, L $9-13, D $24-30)*, Pizzeria *(Rocco's 263-9444)* **1-3 mi:** Restaurant *(La Rose de Saigon 268-8484)*, *(Adam's Ribs 267-7100, L $7-20, D $10-20)*, *(Mexican Café 626-1520)*, Fast Food *(McDonald's, Subway)*, Inn/B&B *(Inn at Spa Creek 263-8866, $160-250)*, *(Peninsula House 2-678-796,, $154-225, picks up)*

Recreation and Entertainment

OnSite: Fishing Charter **Near:** Beach, Playground, Dive Shop, Tennis Courts, Park **Under 1 mi:** Boat Rentals, Video Arcade **1-3 mi:** Golf Course *(Annapolis GC 263-6771)*, Fitness Center *(Curves 990-1002)*, Movie Theater *(Crown Eastport 263-3747)*, Video Rental *(Blockbuster 626-0090)*, Cultural Attract, Sightseeing

Provisioning and General Services

OnSite: Convenience Store *(Back Creek Cafe & Boat Supply)*, Wine/Beer *(C & C Liquors 268-1391)* **Near:** Fishmonger *(Ruggiero & Son Seafood 263-6627)* **Under 1 mi:** Gourmet Shop, Delicatessen, Liquor Store *(Ebb Tide 269-1500)*, Bakery, Green Grocer, Bank/ATM, Catholic Church, Barber Shop, Florist **1-3 mi:** Supermarket *(Giant 261-8095)*, Farmers' Market, Post Office, Library *(Eastport 222-1770)*, Beauty Salon *(Saphire Salon 990-4890)*, Dry Cleaners *(Admiral Laundry & Cleaners 268-8894)*, Pharmacy *(CVS 268-5253)*, Hardware Store *(Hardware House 268-3939)*, Copies Etc. *(Eastport Copy 263-3157)* **3+ mi:** Bookstore *(Insight Concepts 263-1540, 4 mi.)*

Transportation

OnCall: Water Taxi *(Ch.68, to Annapolis historic district)*, Rental Car *(Enterprise 268-7751)*, Taxi *(Annapolis Cab 268-0022)*, Airport Limo **1-3 mi:** Bikes, Local Bus **3+ mi:** Rail *(Amtrak BWI 672-6167, 20 mi.)* **Airport:** Baltimore-Washington Int'l. *(20 mi.)*

Medical Services

911 Service **OnCall:** Ambulance **Near:** Holistic Services *(Innersource 269-6298)* **1-3 mi:** Doctor, Dentist *(Boyd 626-1797)*, Chiropractor, Veterinarian *(Bay Ridge 268-6994)* **Hospital:** Anne Arundel 267-1000 *(6 mi.)*

PHOTOS ON CD-ROM: 12

Setting -- This enormous boatyard with slips sits at a jog in Back Creek, affording many of the 200 docks long water views. The upland is dominated by rows of 3-story storage racks backed by acres of dry storage for larger vessels and 18 independent contractors. The boatyard atmosphere is interrupted by a nicely designed 2-story gray contemporary highlighted by burgundy awnings. At the water's edge, a pavilion provides respite from the summer sun.

Marina Notes -- *Up to 49' $2/ft., 50-59' $2.25/ft., over 60' $2.75/ft. DCM. One of the middle bay's largest operations, BJYY has an affinity for racing sailors. Plus: a high & dry "boatel" to 27 ft., dry sail area for smaller sailboats, haul & launch, and dry and wet storage. The customers can choose to do-it-themselves or hire one of the onsite contractors: A & B Yachtsmen (263-5836), Annapolis Boat Svc. (280 935), Annapolis Marine Metals (295-7586), Annapolis Rigging (269-8035), Bay Shore Marine Engine (263-8370), Chesapeake Rigging/Annapolis Spars (268-0956), Diversifed Marine Svc (263-8717), E 2 Marine Electronic Systems (626-1022), Engineered Marine Systems (267-8288), First Mate Yacht (267-7782), Glenn Housley Sailmakers (263-4913), Kato Marine (269-1218), Ocean Options (268-9365), Portside Marine (269-7880), Seaside Boat Works (267-9179), Southern Cross Marine (267-9337). Modest heads are all tile.

Notable -- Back Creek Café and Boat Supply is located adjacent to the dry stack storage area - despite the name, it's a modest convenience store with sandwiches, breakfast, beverages - including beer & wine, plus assorted boat maintenance products. The large, sparsely furnished boaters' lounge has a washer & dryer, Internet access, a lending library, and a sofa and chairs. It's 0.3 miles to the Wet Dog Café and another 0.1 mile to the Back Porch Café.

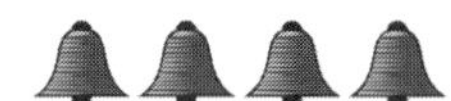

Chesapeake Harbour Marina

2030 Chesapeake Harbor Drive E; Annapolis, MD 21403

Tel: (410) 268-1969 **VHF: Monitor** 16 **Talk** 71
Fax: (410) 268-9654 **Alternate Tel:** n/a
Email: office@chesapeakeharbour.com **Web:** chesapeakeharbour.com
Nearest Town: Annapolis *(3 mi.)* **Tourist Info:** (410) 268-3034

Navigational Information

Lat: 38°57.585' **Long:** 762°8.8.36' **Tide:** 2 ft. **Current:** 0 kt. **Chart:** 12282
Rep. Depths (*MLW*): Entry 8 ft. **Fuel Dock** n/a **Max Slip/Moor** 8 ft./-
Access: At the mouth of the Severn River on the Southern shore

Marina Facilities *(In Season/Off Season)*

Fuel: No
Slips: 200 Total, 20 Transient **Max LOA:** 120 ft. **Max Beam:** 25 ft.
Rate *(per ft.)*: **Day** $2.00* **Week** $1.60 **Month** Inq.
Power: 30 amp $5, **50 amp** $10, **100 amp** $20, **200 amp** n/a
Cable TV: Yes, $0 **Dockside Phone:** Yes
Dock Type: Fixed, Long Fingers, Short Fingers, Pilings, Alongside, Wood
Moorings: 0 Total, 0 Transient **Launch:** n/a
Rate: Day n/a **Week** n/a **Month** n/a
Heads: 8 Toilet(s), 8 Shower(s), Hair Dryers
Laundry: None, Book Exchange **Pay Phones:** Yes, 1
Pump-Out: OnSite, 1 InSlip **Fee:** $15 **Closed Heads:** Yes

Marina Operations

Owner/Manager: n/a **Dockmaster:** Andy Anderson
In-Season: Apr-Oct, 8:30am-5pm **Off-Season:** Nov-Mar, 8:30am-5pm
After-Hours Arrival: Call ahead
Reservations: Preferred **Credit Cards:** Visa/MC
Discounts: None
Pets: Welcome, Dog Walk Area **Handicap Access:** Yes

Marina Services and Boat Supplies

Services - Docking Assistance, Security *(24 hrs.)*, Trash Pick-Up, Dock Carts, Megayacht Facilities **Communication -** Mail & Package Hold, Phone Messages, Fax in/out, Data Ports *(Office)*, FedEx, DHL, UPS, Express Mail *(Sat Del)* **Supplies - OnSite:** Ice *(Block, Cube)* **Under 1 mi:** West Marine *(268-0129)*, CNG *(Bert Jabin's)* **1-3 mi:** Bait/Tackle, Propane *(Hardware House 268-3939)* **3+ mi:** Boater's World *(266-7766)*, Boat/US *(573-5744)*

Boatyard Services

OnCall: Engine mechanic *(gas, diesel)*, Electrical Repairs, Electronics Repairs, Rigger, Sail Loft, Canvas Work, Bottom Cleaning, Brightwork, Air Conditioning, Refrigeration, Divers, Compound, Wash & Wax, Interior Cleaning, Propeller Repairs, Inflatable Repairs, Life Raft Service, Upholstery, Yacht Interiors, Metal Fabrication, Painting, Awlgrip **Near:** Travelift, Crane *(50T)*, Hull Repairs, Woodworking, Yacht Broker. **1-3 mi:** Launching Ramp. **Nearest Yard:** Bert Jabin's (410) 268-9667

Restaurants and Accommodations

OnSite: Restaurant *(Sam's Waterfront Café 263-3200, L $9-13, D $24-30)* **Under 1 mi:** Restaurant *(Mexican Café 626-1520)*, *(Main Ingredient Café 626-0388, L $5-20, D $10-28, premier catering and dining)*, *(Back Porch Café 280-0380, L $6-13, D $11-15, Wed-Sun 8am-2pm)*, *(Asian Café 268-8780)*, Fast Food *(Subway, McDonalds)*, Lite Fare *(The Wet Dog 263-7914)*, Pizzeria *(Rocco's 263-9444)* **1-3 mi:** Pizzeria *(Papa John's 280-1500)*, Inn/B&B *(Inn at Spa Creek 263-8866, $160-250)* **3+ mi:** Hotel *(Marriott 888-773-0786, $160-270, 4 mi.)*, Inn/B&B *(Harbor View 626-9802, $160-225, 4 mi.)*, *(Blue Heron 263-9171, 4 mi.)*

Recreation and Entertainment

OnSite: Pool *(2, 1 w/ beach access)*, Beach, Picnic Area, Grills *(2)*, Tennis Courts *(4)*, Fitness Center **Near:** Park *(Back to Nature)* **Under 1 mi:** Video Rental *(Blockbuster 626-0090)* **1-3 mi:** Playground, Golf Course *(Annapolis GC 263-6771)*, Boat Rentals *(Spring River Kayaks 263-2303)*, Volleyball, Movie Theater *(Crown 263-3747)*, Sightseeing *(Water taxit to Historic downtown)*, Special Events *(Boat Show - Oct)*

Provisioning and General Services

Near: Lobster Pound **Under 1 mi:** Convenience Store *(Shop-N Go)*, Delicatessen *(Wet Dog 263-7914)*, Wine/Beer *(Ebb Tide 269-1500)*, Liquor Store *(Bay Ridge 268-1961)*, Fishmonger *(Ruggiero & Son 263-6627)*, Bank/ATM, Pharmacy *(CVS 268-5253)* **1-3 mi:** Supermarket *(Giant 261-8095)*, Bakery, Market *(Sanky's 263-9032)*, Post Office *(269-0442)*, Catholic Church, Library *(Eastport 222-1770)*, Beauty Salon *(Saphire Salon 990-4890)*, Dry Cleaners *(Admiral Laundry & Cleaners 268-8894)*, Laundry, Hardware Store *(Hardware House 268-3939)*, Florist

Transportation

OnSite: Water Taxi *(Chessie $5)* **OnCall:** Rental Car *(Enterprise 268-7751)*, Taxi *(A&W 263-8715)*, Airport Limo *(269-6226)* **Near:** Bikes, Local Bus **3+ mi:** Rail *(Amtrak 672-6167, 20 mi.)* **Airport:** BWI *(20 mi.)*

Medical Services

911 Service **OnCall:** Ambulance **Near:** Holistic Services *(Innersource 269-6298)* **Under 1 mi:** Dentist *(Boyd 626-1797)*, Chiropractor *(267-0033)* **1-3 mi:** Doctor, Veterinarian *(Bay Ridge 268-6994)* **Hospital:** Anne Arundel 267-1000 *(6 mi.)*

Setting -- Right off the Chesapeake Bay, at the mouth of the Severn River, a protected network of 200 docks lines both sides of a ten-acre man-made basin. A pool, basketball court and four tennis courts are dispersed within an upscale community of contemporary, tan clapboard townhouses. A short walk from the docks, and adjacent to the basin's entrance, is a long stretch of sandy beach, a fishing pier, and a second bayfront pool with its own bathhouse. At the head of the basin, a two-story octagonal building (a copy of the Thomas Point Lighthouse) with copper-green roof houses Sam's Waterfront Café.

Marina Notes -- *$2.25/ft. for holidays & Boat Shows. DCM. Established in 1985. 24-hour security. Chessie, the marina's private water taxi service, runs to the Annapolis City Dock on the hour, 10am-6pm Sat, Sun & holidays, MemDay-LabDay plus Boat Show weeks (return trips are on the half hour). Underwater maintenance services available. Home of the Chesapeake Harbour Yacht Club. Attractive bathhouses, nicely done in all-tile with thoughtful vanities and chairs, are placed at strategic locations on either side of the basin. Both pools also have changing rooms.

Notable -- The marina is extraordinarily well-protected and current-free. White-tablecloth Sam's Waterfront Café, specializes in contemporary riffs on seafood. Mostly glass, it's built out over the water for spectacular views in many directions. Deck dining, too. Tue-Thu 11:30am-9pm, Fri & Sat 'til 10pm, Sun 10:30am-9pm. Dock 'n' Dine also available. It's a very lovely half-mile walk out to the main road, and downtown Annapolis is three miles away.

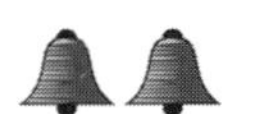

Selby-on-the-Bay Yacht Basin

PO Box 355; 931 Selby Boulevard; Edgewater, MD 21037

Tel: (410) 798-0232 **VHF: Monitor** n/a **Talk** n/a
Fax: (410) 263-3110 **Alternate Tel:** (410) 268-5659
Email: n/a **Web:** n/a
Nearest Town: Mayo *(1 mi.)* **Tourist Info:** (410) 263-7648

Navigational Information

Lat: 38°54.500' **Long:** 076°30.759' **Tide:** 2 ft. **Current:** n/a **Chart:** 12270
Rep. Depths (*MLW*): Entry 10 ft. **Fuel Dock** 7 ft. **Max Slip/Moor** 7 ft./-
Access: South River leave Marks 2 & 4 to starbord

Marina Facilities *(In Season/Off Season)*

Fuel: *Coastal* - Gasoline, Diesel, High-Speed Pumps
Slips: 100 Total, 5 Transient **Max LOA:** 80 ft. **Max Beam:** n/a
Rate *(per ft.)*: **Day** $0.75/Inq. **Week** $4.20 **Month** $15
Power: 30 amp Incl., **50 amp** Incl., **100 amp** n/a, **200 amp** n/a
Cable TV: No **Dockside Phone:** Yes
Dock Type: Fixed, Wood, Aluminum
Moorings: 0 Total, 0 Transient **Launch:** n/a, Dinghy Dock
Rate: Day n/a **Week** n/a **Month** n/a
Heads: 2 Toilet(s), 2 Shower(s) *(with dressing rooms)*
Laundry: None **Pay Phones:** No
Pump-Out: OnSite, Full Service **Fee:** $5 **Closed Heads:** Yes

Marina Operations

Owner/Manager: Theodor Petersen **Dockmaster:** Same
In-Season: Apr-Dec, 9am-5pm **Off-Season:** Dec-Mar, Mon-Fri, 9am-5pm*
After-Hours Arrival: Call ahead
Reservations: Preferred **Credit Cards:** Visa/MC, Coastel
Discounts: Boat/US **Dockage:** 10% **Fuel:** 0.03/gal **Repair:** 10%
Pets: Welcome, Dog Walk Area **Handicap Access:** No

Marina Services and Boat Supplies

Services - Docking Assistance, Security *(24 hrs., employee lives on premises)*, Trash Pick-Up, Dock Carts **Communication -** Mail & Package Hold, Phone Messages, FedEx, UPS, Express Mail *(Sat Del)* **Supplies - OnSite:** Ice *(Block, Cube, Shaved)* **Under 1 mi:** Bait/Tackle *(Peninsula Farms 798-5767)* **1-3 mi:** Ships' Store, Propane *(Loch Haven Amoco 798-4668)* **3+ mi:** West Marine *(956-8920, 4 mi.)*, Live Bait *(PJS Bait & Tackle Shop 956-8660, 4 mi.)*

Boatyard Services

OnSite: Divers, Compound, Wash & Wax, Interior Cleaning, Woodworking, Painting **OnCall:** Launching Ramp, Engine mechanic *(gas, diesel)* **Under 1 mi:** Propeller Repairs. **Nearest Yard:** Anchor Yachts

Restaurants and Accommodations

OnCall: Pizzeria *(Domino's 956-1800)* **Under 1 mi:** Restaurant *(Old Stein Inn 798-1544, D $10-20, German)*, *(Mayo Yacht Club & Grill 956-2722)*, Lite Fare *(Selby Sub Shoppe 798-0700)*, Pizzeria *(Mayo Subs & Pizza 798-9005, L $10-20, D $15-25)* **1-3 mi:** Restaurant *(Original Steak House 956-4494, L $10-20, D $25-35)*, Fast Food *(Popeye's, McDonalds)* **3+ mi:** Pizzeria *(Happy House Pizza & Subs 956-4000, 4 mi.)*, Motel *(Days Inn 224-4317, 9 mi.)*, *(Hampton Inn 571-0200, $140-195, 8 mi., hot "on the house" breakfast)*, *(Best Western 224-4369, 9 mi.)*, Inn/B&B *(Charles Inn 268-1451, $125-225, 8 mi.)*

Recreation and Entertainment

OnSite: Beach, Picnic Area, Grills, Playground **3+ mi:** Golf Course *(South River Golf 798-5865, 5 mi.)*, Fitness Center *(Curves for Women 956-2500, 4 mi.)*, Horseback Riding *(Harmony Ridge Riding Stable 798-5200, 5 mi.)*, Movie Theater *(Crown Eastport Theatres 263-3747, 10 mi.)*, Video Rental *(Potomac Video 261-7596, 4 mi.)*, Museum *(Smithsonian Environmental RC 443-482-2200, 5 mi.)*

Provisioning and General Services

Near: Wine/Beer *(Lou's Corner Stop 798-5055)*, Market *(Sam's Supermarket 798-8001)* **Under 1 mi:** Liquor Store *(Cox Wine & Spirits 798-4111)*, Beauty Salon *(J & B Unisex Hair Salon 798-9560)*, Barber Shop *(Nikki's Barber Shop 798-6650)* **1-3 mi:** Delicatessen *(Sue's Deli 798-6300)*, Bank/ATM, Post Office *(573-0953)*, Catholic Church, Protestant Church, Dry Cleaners *(Admiral 956-4947)*, Laundry *(Mayo 798-1345)* **3+ mi:** Supermarket *(Food Lion 956-6498, Safeway 261-4661, 5 mi.)*, Health Food *(Whole Foods 573-1800, 8 mi.)*, Fishmonger *(Chesapeake Seafood 956-8956, 4 mi.)*, Library *(Edgewater 222-1538, 4 mi.)*, Pharmacy *(Giant Pharmacy 956-4150, 5 mi.)*, Hardware Store *(Ace 956-5123, 4 mi.)*, Department Store *(Kmart 956-0056, 4 mi.)*

Transportation

OnCall: Rental Car *(Enterprise 268-7751)*, Taxi *(Annapolis 268-0022)*, Airport Limo *(Care-L Limo261-7796)* **3+ mi:** Rail *(Amtrak 672-6167, 25 mi.)* **Airport:** Baltimore-Washington Int'l. *(25 mi.)*

Medical Services

911 Service **OnCall:** Ambulance **3+ mi:** Doctor *(4 mi.)*, Dentist *(Muller 798-6341, 4 mi.)*, Chiropractor *(Living Health 56-9180, 5 mi.)*, Holistic Services *(American Healing Arts 956-0055, 4 mi.)*, Veterinarian *(Reichardt Animal Hospital 956-4500, 4 mi.)* **Hospital:** Anne Arundel 267-1000 *(10 mi.)*

Setting -- In the quiet community of Selby Beach, just off South River, Selby-on-the-Bay Yacht Basin is an old-time, rural marina with extensive, particularly nice, quite high, covered slips. The sheds make a horseshoe, and open slips are mixed in. There's nothing spiffy about it, but that's a big part of its down-home charm.

Marina Notes -- *Off season, closed on weekends. DCM. Boat US discounts. The marina was established in 1947 and the current owners have been offering continuous, personal service since 1975. Most of the dock decking is a result of Isabel. Power is generally on the posts. The heads are tiled - full bath, one men's and one women's, each with a shower.

Notable -- Tucked safely into the sheds, mostly on new docks, are some wonderful old classic yachts. A little picnic area sits on a deck and overlooks a wide expanse of bay, offering beautiful water views. There are no other amenities. Walking outside the marina, one will find the Selby Beach area of Selby on the Bay, a residential neighborhood of smaller homes on the Mayo Peninsula; right next door is the Club House. A half mile away is a little shopping area with Sam's Supermarket and Mayo Subs & Pizza - the closest commercial area.

PHOTOS ON CD-ROM: 8

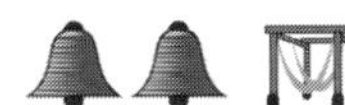

Navigational Information

Lat: 38°54.250' **Long:** 076°30.650' **Tide:** 2 ft. **Current:** 5 kt. **Chart:** 12270
Rep. Depths (*MLW*): Entry 8 ft. **Fuel Dock** n/a **Max Slip/Moor** 8 ft./-
Access: South R. to Selby Bay round Holiday Point

Marina Facilities *(In Season/Off Season)*

Fuel: No
Slips: 160 Total, 1 Transient **Max LOA:** 56 ft. **Max Beam:** 16 ft.
Rate *(per ft.)*: **Day** $50.00* **Week** $125 **Month** $500
Power: 30 amp $10, **50 amp** n/a, **100 amp** n/a, **200 amp** n/a
Cable TV: No **Dockside Phone:** No
Dock Type: Fixed, Long Fingers, Short Fingers, Wood
Moorings: 0 Total, 0 Transient **Launch:** None
Rate: Day n/a **Week** n/a **Month** n/a
Heads: 6 Toilet(s), 2 Shower(s) *(with dressing rooms)*
Laundry: None **Pay Phones:** No
Pump-Out: OnSite, Full Service **Fee:** Free **Closed Heads:** Yes

Marina Operations

Owner/Manager: Ron Sinclair **Dockmaster:** Same
In-Season: Year-Round **Off-Season:** n/a
After-Hours Arrival: Call ahead
Reservations: Yes **Credit Cards:** Visa/MC
Discounts: None
Pets: Welcome, Dog Walk Area **Handicap Access:** No

Holiday Point Marina

PO Box 595; 3774 Beach Drive Boulevard; Edgewater, MD 21037

Tel: (410) 956-2208 **VHF: Monitor** 16 **Talk** 68
Fax: (410) 798-7647 **Alternate Tel:** n/a
Email: n/a **Web:** n/a
Nearest Town: Annapolis *(10 mi.)* **Tourist Info:** (410) 263-7648

Marina Services and Boat Supplies

Services - Trash Pick-Up, Dock Carts **Communication -** Mail & Package Hold, Phone Messages, FedEx, DHL, UPS, Express Mail **Supplies - Under 1 mi:** Ice *(Block, Cube)*, Bait/Tackle *(Peninsula Farms 798-5767)* **1-3 mi:** Ships' Store, Propane *(Amoco 798-4668)* **3+ mi:** West Marine, Boat/US

Boatyard Services

OnSite: Travelift *(35T + 25T)*, Crane, Engine mechanic *(gas, diesel)*, Electrical Repairs, Hull Repairs, Bottom Cleaning, Brightwork, Compound, Wash & Wax, Interior Cleaning, Propeller Repairs, Woodworking, Metal Fabrication, Yacht Design, Yacht Building, Total Refits **OnCall:** Rigger **Yard Rates:** $75/hr., Haul & Launch $5/ft. *(blocking $3/ft.)*, Power Wash $2/ft., Bottom Paint $18/ft. / $21/ft. **Storage:** In-Water $200 +/mo., On-Land $150+/mo.

Restaurants and Accommodations

OnCall: Pizzeria *(Domino's 956-1800)* **Near:** Restaurant *(Old Stein Inn 798-1544, D $10-20)* **1-3 mi:** Restaurant *(Original Steak House 956-4494, L $10-20, D $25-35)*, *(Mayo Beach Yacht Club 956-2722, L $10-20, D $15-25)*, Snack Bar *(Sam's Plaza Deli L $3-8, D $5-15)*, Coffee Shop *(Coffe'no Delay 571-0877)*, Fast Food *(Burger King, McDonalds, Popeye's)*, Lite Fare *(Selby Sub Shoppe 798-0700)* **3+ mi:** Motel *(Best Western 224-4369, 9 mi.)*, *(Econo Lodge 841-2545, 9 mi.)*, *(Hampton Inn 571-0200, $140-195, 8 mi.)*, Inn/B&B *(Charles Inn 268-1451, $125-225, 8 mi.)*

Recreation and Entertainment

OnSite: Fishing Charter **1-3 mi:** Sightseeing *(Londontown Public House)* **3+ mi:** Golf Course *(Atlantic Golf 956-3310, 4 mi.)*, Fitness Center *(South River 956-2665, 4 mi.)*, Horseback Riding *(Harmony Ridge 798-5200, 5 mi.)*, Video Rental *(Potomac Video 261-7596, 4 mi.)*, Museum *(Smithsonian Environmental RC 443-482-2200, 4 mi.)*

Provisioning and General Services

Near: Convenience Store, Wine/Beer *(Lou's Corner Stop 798-5055)*, Market *(Sam's Supermarket 798-8001)* **Under 1 mi:** Liquor Store *(Cox Wine & Spirits 798-4111)*, Bakery *(El Amigo Bakery 798-7600)*, Laundry *(Mayo 798-1345)* **1-3 mi:** Delicatessen *(Sue's Deli 798-6300)*, Farmers' Market, Bank/ATM, Post Office *(573-0953)*, Catholic Church, Protestant Church, Beauty Salon *(J & B Unisex Hair Salon 798-9560)*, Barber Shop *(Nikki's Barber Shop 798-6650)*, Dry Cleaners *(Admiral 956-4947)*, Hardware Store *(Ace 956-5123)*, Florist *(Silver Stems 798-7700)*, Retail Shops, Copies Etc. *(Superior Copier 956-1227)* **3+ mi:** Supermarket *(Food Lion 956-6498, Giant 798-1466, 5 mi.)*, Fishmonger *(Chesapeake Seafood 956-8956, 4 mi.)*, Library *(Edgewater 222-1538, 4 mi.)*, Bookstore *(7 mi.)*, Pharmacy *(Safeway 956-4660, 5 mi.)*, Department Store *(Kmart 956-0056, 4 mi.)*

Transportation

OnCall: Rental Car *(Enterprise 268-7751)*, Taxi *(Annapolis Cab 268-0022)*, Airport Limo *(Care-L Limousine 261-7796)* **3+ mi:** Rail *(Amtrak 672-6167, 25 mi.)* **Airport:** Baltimore-Washington Int'l. *(25 mi.)*

Medical Services

911 Service **OnCall:** Ambulance **3+ mi:** Doctor *(4 mi.)*, Dentist *(Muller 798-6341, 4 mi.)*, Chiropractor *(Living Health 956-9180, 5 mi.)*, Holistic Services *(American Healing Arts 956-0055, 4 mi.)*, Veterinarian *(Reichardt Animal Hospital 956-4500, 4 mi.)* **Hospital:** Anne Arundel 267-1000 *(10 mi.)*

Setting -- At the mouth of the South River and around the point from Selby Bay Yacht Basin, Holiday Point offers extensive, good quality dockage in a natural environment convenient to the Bay. A large, light blue boat shed anchors the 5 main piers that fan out around the point. The most protected piers, "A" and "B", are tucked up into the cove, and then short "C" dock and longer "D" are followed by "E" -- the longest and newest.

Marina Notes -- *Dockage flat rate - not per foot. Family owned since 1974. Short haul July and Aug $6.50/ft.; winter discount on labor 15%. Full service repairs, including machine shop for propeller repairs. Major refit and repairs also available. "E" dock has all brand-new slips, new wiring, new boxes. The slips farthest out have full finger piers, and all the closer in slips have partial finger piers. The cinderblock heads are nicely painted, with four toilets, tiled showers with a dressing room, and fresh louvered doors on the stalls. Pump-out is free but tipping is welcomed.

Notable -- The marina is surrounded by the quiet residential beach community of Selby on the Bay. Initially an area of tobacco farms and fruit orchards, it was broken up into residential plots by the Selby on the Bay Properties Company in 1930 and has grown up over the last seven or eight decades. It's about two-thirds of a mile walk through this neighborhood to a small collection of shops (including Mayo Subs & Pizza and Sam's Supermarket) at Mayo Road and Selby Boulevard.

PHOTOS ON CD-ROM: 9

Turkey Point Marina

1107 Turkey Point Rd; Edgewater, MD 21037

Tel: (410) 798-1369 **VHF: Monitor** 16 **Talk** n/a
Fax: (410) 798-6602 **Alternate Tel:** (410) 798-1369
Email: n/a **Web:** turkeypointmarina.com
Nearest Town: Edgewater *(2 mi.)* **Tourist Info:** (410) 263-7648

Navigational Information

Lat: 38°54.074' **Long:** 076°30.371' **Tide:** n/a **Current:** n/a **Chart:** 12270
Rep. Depths (*MLW*): Entry 10 ft. **Fuel Dock** n/a **Max Slip/Moor** 12 ft./-
Access: Selby Bay, under Turkey Point Rd. Bridge, port side

Marina Facilities *(In Season/Off Season)*

Fuel: *BP* - Gasoline
Slips: 110 Total, 6 Transient **Max LOA:** 45 ft. **Max Beam:** 14 ft.
Rate *(per ft.)*: **Day** $2.50 **Week** n/a **Month** $900/500*
Power: 30 amp Incl., **50 amp** n/a, **100 amp** n/a, **200 amp** n/a
Cable TV: No **Dockside Phone:** No
Dock Type: Short Fingers
Moorings: 0 Total, 0 Transient **Launch:** n/a
Rate: Day n/a **Week** n/a **Month** n/a
Heads: 8 Toilet(s), 6 Shower(s) *(with dressing rooms)*
Laundry: None **Pay Phones:** No
Pump-Out: OnSite, Full Service **Fee:** $15 **Closed Heads:** Yes

Marina Operations

Owner/Manager: Todd Harper **Dockmaster:** Sandy Zimmerman
In-Season: Year-Round, 9am-5pm **Off-Season:** n/a
After-Hours Arrival: Call ahead
Reservations: No **Credit Cards:** Visa/MC, Amex
Discounts: None
Pets: Welcome **Handicap Access:** Yes, Heads, Docks

Marina Services and Boat Supplies

Services - Docking Assistance, Security *(24 hrs, camera and guard)*, Trash Pick-Up, Dock Carts **Communication -** Phone Messages, FedEx, UPS, Express Mail *(Sat Del)* **Supplies - OnSite:** Ice *(Block, Cube)* **Under 1 mi:** Bait/Tackle *(Peninsula Farms 798-5767)* **1-3 mi:** Propane *(Amoco 798-4668)* **3+ mi:** West Marine *(956-8920, order onsite)*, Boat/US *(573-5744)*

Boatyard Services

OnSite: Travelift, Launching Ramp, Bottom Cleaning, Brightwork, Compound, Wash & Wax, Interior Cleaning, Painting, Awlgrip **Near:** Engine mechanic *(gas, diesel)*, Electrical Repairs. **Under 1 mi:** Electronics Repairs, Hull Repairs, Air Conditioning, Refrigeration, Propeller Repairs, Woodworking, Inflatable Repairs. **1-3 mi:** Life Raft Service, Upholstery, Yacht Interiors, Metal Fabrication.

Restaurants and Accommodations

OnCall: Pizzeria *(Domino's 956-1800)* **Near:** Restaurant *(Old Stein Inn 798-1544, D $10-20, German)*, *(Mayo Yacht Club & Grill 957-2722, L $10-20, D $15-25)* **Under 1 mi:** Lite Fare *(Selby Sub Shoppe 798-0700)*, *(Mayo Subs & Pizza 798-9005)* **1-3 mi:** Restaurant *(Original Steak House 956-4494, L $10-20, D $15-35)*, *(Hong Kong Buffet 956-3382)*, Fast Food *(Burger King, Popeye's)* **3+ mi:** Motel *(Residence Inn 800-331-3131, 8 mi.)*, *(Econo Lodge 841-2545, 9 mi.)*, *(Courtyard 800-321-2211, 9 mi.)*, *(Days Inn 224-4317, 9 mi.)*, *(Hampton Inn 571-0200, $140-195, 8 mi.)*, Inn/B&B *(Charles Inn 268-1451, $125-225, 8 mi.)*

Recreation and Entertainment

3+ mi: Golf Course *(Atlantic Golf 956-3310, 4 mi.)*, Fitness Center *(South River Fitness 956-2665, 4 mi.)*, Horseback Riding *(Harmony Ridge Riding Stable 798-5200, 5 mi.)*, Movie Theater *(Crown Eastport 263-3747, 10 mi.)*, Video Rental *(Potomac Video 261-7596, 4 mi.)*, Museum *(Smithsonian Environmental RC 443-482-2200, 5 mi.)*

Provisioning and General Services

Under 1 mi: Convenience Store *(Citgo 798-0968)*, Wine/Beer *(Lou's Corner Stop 798-5055)*, Liquor Store *(Cox Wine & Spirits 798-4111)*, Bakery *(El Amigo Bakery 798-7600)*, Market *(Sam's Supermarket 798-8001)*, Bank/ATM, Post Office *(573-0953)*, Catholic Church, Beauty Salon *(J&B Unisex Hair Salon 798-9560)*, Barber Shop, Laundry *(Mayo 798-1345)* **1-3 mi:** Delicatessen *(Sue's Deli 798-6300)* **3+ mi:** Supermarket *(Food Lion 956-6498, Giant 798-1466, 5 mi.)*, Farmers' Market *(Pennsylvania Dutch Farmers Market 573-0770, 7 mi.)*, Fishmonger *(Chesapeake Seafood 956-8956, 4 mi.)*, Library *(Edgewater 222-1538, 4 mi.)*, Dry Cleaners *(Woodland Cleaners 956-1244, 4 mi.)*, Pharmacy *(Safeway 956-4660, 5 mi.)*, Hardware Store *(Ace 956-5123, 4 mi.)*, Department Store *(Kmart 956-0056, 4 mi.)*

Transportation

OnCall: Rental Car *(Enterprise 268-7751)*, Taxi *(Annapolis 268-0022)*, Airport Limo *(Care-L Limo 261-7796)* **3+ mi:** Rail *(Amtrak 672-6167, 25 mi.)* **Airport:** Baltimore-Washington Int'l. *(25 mil)*

Medical Services

911 Service **OnCall:** Ambulance **3+ mi:** Doctor *(4 mi.)*, Dentist *(Edgewater Dental Arts 956-3525, 5 mi.)*, Chiropractor *(Community Chiro 956-9056, 5 mi.)*, Holistic Services *(American Healing Arts 956-0055, 4 mi.)*, Veterinarian *(Reichardt 956-4500, 4 mi.)* **Hospital:** Anne Arundel 267-1000 *(10 mi.)*

Setting -- Turkey Point's very protected docks are most easily reached through Selby Bay, on the far side of the 14-ft. fixed Turkey Point Road bridge - in Ramsay Lake. On the port side, several piers fan out from a large paved peninsula. Land side is a two-story light blue building with bright blue awning. A small ships' store and the bathhouse are on the ground floor.

Marina Notes -- *Monthly rates are flat, not per foot. Office is closed Mondays. Turkey Point is a powerboat marina; the boats that make their home here tend to be smaller, with a lot of go-fast among them - most of them are up on elevator racks. A variety of services are available, including bottom painting, washing & waxing, winterizing, haul out, docking and storage, boat transport, pressure washing and engine repair.

Notable -- The controlling height to get into Turkey Point from through Selby Bay is 14-ft. To avoid the low bridge, it is possible for shallow draft boats to either circumnavigate Turkey Point Island - if approaching from Selby Bay - or simply cut in below Turkey Point when approaching from South River. However, the whole area is very shallow so call ahead for local knowledge. Just down the road, the Selby Bay Sailing Center is home to the Flying Scot Fleet 42 - about 50 of these venerable one-designs - and offers service, parts and repairs. It's about a half mile to the Mayo convenience store and Old Stein Inn.

PHOTOS ON CD-ROM: 8

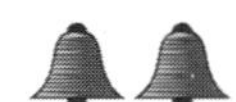

Navigational Information
Lat: 38°56.867' **Long:** 076°33.283' **Tide:** n/a **Current:** n/a **Chart:** 12270
Rep. Depths (*MLW*): Entry n/a **Fuel Dock** n/a **Max Slip/Moor** -/-
Access: southern shore of the South River, just east of bridge

Marina Facilities *(In Season/Off Season)*
Fuel: No
Slips: 195 Total, 4 Transient **Max LOA:** 65 ft. **Max Beam:** 20 ft.
Rate *(per ft.)*: **Day** $1.50 **Week** Inq. **Month** Inq.
Power: 30 amp Incl., **50 amp** n/a, **100 amp** n/a, **200 amp** n/a
Cable TV: No **Dockside Phone:** No
Dock Type: Fixed
Moorings: 0 Total, 0 Transient **Launch:** n/a
Rate: Day n/a **Week** n/a **Month** n/a
Heads: 2 Toilet(s), 2 Shower(s)
Laundry: None **Pay Phones:** No
Pump-Out: OnSite **Fee:** $5.00 **Closed Heads:** Yes

Marina Operations
Owner/Manager: Peter Arndt **Dockmaster:** Same
In-Season: Year-Round, 9am-5pm **Off-Season:** n/a
After-Hours Arrival: Call in advance
Reservations: Required **Credit Cards:** Visa/MC
Discounts: None
Pets: Welcome **Handicap Access:** Yes

Pier 7 Marina

48 South River Road; Edgewater, MD 21037

Tel: (410) 956-2288 **VHF: Monitor** n/a **Talk** n/a
Fax: (410) 956-5507 **Alternate Tel:** n/a
Email: n/a **Web:** n/a
Nearest Town: Edgewater *(1 mi.)* **Tourist Info:** (410) 263-7648

Marina Services and Boat Supplies
Services - Security *(Dockmaster lives on premises)* **Communication -** FedEx, UPS, Express Mail **Supplies - 1-3 mi:** West Marine *(956-8920)*, Bait/Tackle *(PJS Bait & Tackle Shop 956-8660)*, Propane *(Arundel Gas 956-2400)* **3+ mi:** Boat/US *(573-5744, 4 mi.)*

Boatyard Services
Nearest Yard: Liberty Marina (410) 266-5633

Restaurants and Accommodations
OnSite: Restaurant *(Becky's on the Water Comedy Dock 956-3931, Mon-Sat 11am-1:30am, L & D same menu $5-23, Stand-up comedy Wed, Fri, Sat 8:30pm)* **OnCall:** Restaurant *(Dragon House 956-2121)*, Pizzeria *(Domino's 956-1800)* **Near:** Restaurant *(Yellow Fin Steak and Fish House 573-0863, D $14-36, across river by dinghy)* **Under 1 mi:** Restaurant *(Little Panda 956-0504)*, *(Steele Grille 956-5070)*, *(Tapenade 956-1335)*, Fast Food *(KFC, Taco Bell)*, Lite Fare *(Happy House Pizza & Subs 956-4000)*, Pizzeria *(Ledo 956-6700)* **1-3 mi:** Restaurant *(Original Steak House 956-4494, L $10-20, D $15-35)*, *(Adam's the Place for Ribs 956-2995)*, Coffee Shop *(Coffee Beanery 956-7544)*, Hotel *(Hampton In 571-0200, $140-195)* **3+ mi:** Restaurant *(Mayo Yacht Club & Grill 957-2722, L $10-20, D $15-25, 5 mi.)*, Motel *(Annapolis Inn 573-0300, 4 mi.)*, *(Courtyard 800-321-2211, 4 mi.)*, Inn/B&B *(Charles Inn 268-1451, $125-225, 4 mi.)*

Recreation and Entertainment
OnSite: Picnic Area, Volleyball **Under 1 mi:** Boat Rentals *(South River Rentals 956-9729)* **1-3 mi:** Golf Course *(South River 798-5961)*, Fitness Center *(South River Fitness 261-4222)*, Video Rental *(Blockbuster 266-8144)*, Cultural Attract *(Historic London Town & Gardens - 23-acre park & excavation of late 17th C. town, Wm. Brown House Museum & 8-acre garden 222-1919 $4/3)* **3+ mi:** Bowling *(Annapolis Bowl 266-0700, 4 mi.)*, Movie Theater *(Crown Eastport 263-3747, 6 mi.)*

Provisioning and General Services
Under 1 mi: Convenience Store, Delicatessen *(Uptown Deli 798-6300)*, Liquor Store *(Olde Solomon's Wine and Spirits 956-4055)*, Bakery *(Carlson's Doughnut & Pastry 956-0952)*, Fishmonger *(Chesapeake Seafood 956-8956)*, Bank/ATM, Post Office, Beauty Salon *(Shears 798-4600)*, Barber Shop, Dry Cleaners *(South-Edge Cleaners 956-0909)*, Pharmacy *(CVS 798-8715)* **1-3 mi:** Supermarket *(Giant 798-1466)*, Farmers' Market *(Pennsylvania Dutch 573-0770)*, Catholic Church, Protestant Church, Hardware Store *(Ace 956-5123)*, Florist, Department Store *(Kmart 956-0056)*, Copies Etc. **3+ mi:** Health Food *(Whole Foods 573-1800, 4 mi.)*, Bookstore *(Barnes & Noble 573-1115, 4 mi.)*

Transportation
OnCall: Taxi *(Holiday Taxi 266-3448)*, Airport Limo *(Imperial 269-0000)*
Near: Rental Car *(Total Car Rental 956-5915, or Hertz 224-1414, 4 mi.)*
3+ mi: Rail *(Amtrak 672-6167, 20 mi.)* **Airport:** BWI *(20 mi.)*

Medical Services
911 Service **OnCall:** Ambulance **Near:** Dentist *(Doring 956-2505)*, Chiropractor *(Chaney 956-9180)* **Under 1 mi:** Doctor *(1st Medical 956-6800)* **1-3 mi:** Holistic Services *(Traditional Acupuncture 269-6032)*, Veterinarian *(Reichardt Animal Hospital 956-4500)* **Hospital:** Anne Arundel 267-1000 *(5 mi.)*

Setting -- The Pier 7 docks stretch all the way along the southern shore of the South River, just east of the 65-ft. Solomons Island Road bridge. The main marina building is a half-timbered, English-style gray Tudor with French-blue trim; the primary docks are clustered around a small, nicely grassed and treed peninsula. A boardwalk leads along the river to an additional set of docks that sprawl in front of the sloping lawn banks of the restaurant.

Marina Notes -- Pier 7 manages all of the docks in front of its building, the docks in front of the restaurant and all of the docks in between along the boardwalk. Picnic tables with charcoal grills, sheltered by ancient oaks overlook the water. There are two sets of heads. One set is in the main gray half-timbered building - the ladies' room is on the second floor. Each head features two stalls with beadboard trim, a sink and a shower, and asphalt-tiled floor.

Notable -- Becky's on the Water Comedy Dock (formerly South River Cafe, before that Pier Seven Restaurant), opened in November '05. It specializes in seafood and has a sports bar flavor. The club is open 7 days and reservations are required. Sand-volleyball right outside provides a fun distraction during the wait for dinner. There's lots of different kinds of seating inside. Outside on the deck, are brightly-colored umbrella topped tables and on the lower, dock-level deck are bright blue picnic tables. Hours: Mon-Fri, 4-10pm, Sat & Sun 11am-10pm. It's the same menu all day long, lunch and dinner. Directly across the river is the Liberty Yacht Club and Yellow Fin Steak and Fish House (dock 'n' dine).

PHOTOS ON CD-ROM: 11

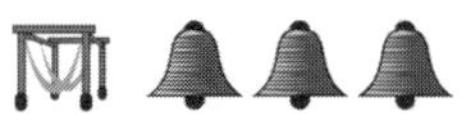

Liberty Yacht Club & Marina

64 Old South River Road; Edgewater, MD 21037

Tel: (410) 266-5633; (800) 971-1300 **VHF: Monitor** n/a **Talk** n/a
Fax: (410) 266-9026 **Alternate Tel:** n/a
Email: n/a **Web:** n/a
Nearest Town: Annapolis *(5 mi.)* **Tourist Info:** (410) 263-7648

Navigational Information

Lat: 38°57.210' **Long:** 076°33.169' **Tide:** 2 ft. **Current:** n/a **Chart:** 12270
Rep. Depths (*MLW*): Entry 10 ft. **Fuel Dock** 10 ft. **Max Slip/Moor** 19 ft./-
Access: South River, under the Solomons Island Road Bridge, north shore

Marina Facilities *(In Season/Off Season)*

Fuel: *Hi-Test* - Gasoline, Diesel
Slips: 300 Total, 30 Transient **Max LOA:** 150 ft. **Max Beam:** n/a
Rate *(per ft.)*: **Day** $1.50 **Week** n/a **Month** Inq.
Power: 30 amp $5, **50 amp** $5, **100 amp** n/a, **200 amp** n/a
Cable TV: No **Dockside Phone:** No
Dock Type: Fixed, Floating, Long Fingers, Short Fingers
Moorings: 0 Total, 0 Transient **Launch:** n/a
Rate: Day n/a **Week** n/a **Month** n/a
Heads: 9 Toilet(s), 8 Shower(s)
Laundry: None, Book Exchange **Pay Phones:** Yes, 1
Pump-Out: OnSite **Fee:** $5 **Closed Heads:** Yes

Marina Operations

Owner/Manager: Capt. Jim Hasty **Dockmaster:** Tim Ryan
In-Season: Mem-LabDay, 8am-7pm **Off-Season:** Lab-MemDay, 9am-4pm
After-Hours Arrival: Call ahead
Reservations: Preferred **Credit Cards:** Visa/MC, Dscvr, Din, Amex
Discounts: None
Pets: Welcome **Handicap Access:** Yes, Docks

Marina Services and Boat Supplies

Services - Docking Assistance, Concierge, Trash Pick-Up, Dock Carts **Communication -** Mail & Package Hold, Phone Messages, FedEx, DHL, UPS, Express Mail *(Sat Del)* **Supplies - OnSite:** Ice *(Cube)*, Ships' Store **1-3 mi:** West Marine *(956-8920)*, Boat/US *(573-5744)*, Bait/Tackle *(PJS Bait & Tackle 956-8660)*, Propane *(Arundel Gas 956-2400)*

Boatyard Services

OnSite: Travelift *(25T)*, Engine mechanic *(gas, diesel)*, Electrical Repairs, Electronics Repairs, Hull Repairs, Rigger, Canvas Work, Bottom Cleaning, Refrigeration **Near:** Launching Ramp, Brightwork. **Yard Rates:** $65/hr, Haul & Launch $7.50/ft., Power Wash $2.50/ft. **Storage:** On-Land $8/ft.

Restaurants and Accommodations

OnCall: Pizzeria *(Domino's 956-1800)* **Near:** Restaurant *(Becky's On-the-Water Comedy Club 956-0739, dinghy across river)*, *(Yellow Fin Steak and Fish House 573-0863, D $14-36, brunch $12-22 11am-2pm, lounge $5-12; D 4-9pm; happy hour Fri 4-7pm, Sun 2-6pm)*, *(Fergie's Waterfront 573-1371)*, Pizzeria *(Ledo 956-6700, L $7-10, D $7-10)* **Under 1 mi:** Fast Food *(Wendy's, KFC, Taco Bell)* **1-3 mi:** Restaurant *(Dragon House 956-2121, delivers)*, *(Original Steak House 956-4494, L $10-20, D $15-35)*, *(Mayo Yacht Club & Grill 957-2722, L $10-20, D $15-25)*, Motel *(Best Western 224-2800, $60-120)*, *(Hampton Inn 571-0200, $140-195)*

Recreation and Entertainment

OnSite: Pool *(and sundeck)*, Picnic Area, Grills, Fitness Center **Near:** Boat Rentals *(South River Rentals 956-9729)* **1-3 mi:** Golf Course *(South River Golf 798-5865)*, Bowling *(Annapolis Bowl 266-0700)*, Video Rental *(Blockbuster 266-8144)*, Museum *(Chesapeake Children's Museum 990-1993)*, Cultural Attract *(Historic London Town & Gardens - 23-acre park & excavation of late 17thC. town, Wm. Brown House Museum & 8-acre garden 222-1919 $4/3)* **3+ mi:** Movie Theater *(Crown 263-3747, 5 mi.)*

Provisioning and General Services

Under 1 mi: Convenience Store, Delicatessen *(Uptown 798-6300)*, Wine/Beer *(Olde Solomon's 956-4054)*, Post Office *(573-0953)* **1-3 mi:** Supermarket *(Safeway 626-2710, Giant 798-1466)*, Gourmet Shop *(Peppercorn 266-9401)*, Health Food *(Whole Foods 573-1800)*, Bakery *(Carlson's Doughnut & Pastry 956-0952)*, Farmers' Market *(Pennsylvania Dutch 573-0770)*, Fishmonger *(Chesapeake Seafood 956-8956)*, Bank/ATM, Beauty Salon *(Sun Deck 266-8450)*, Barber Shop *(Hair Cuttery 573-5128)*, Dry Cleaners *(South-Edge Cleaners 956-0909)*, Bookstore *(Barnes & Noble 573-1115)*, Pharmacy *(CVS 798-8715)*, Hardware Store *(Ace 956-5123)*, Department Store *(Kmart 956-0056)*, Copies Etc. *(Office Depot 573-0020)*

Transportation

OnCall: Taxi *(Holiday Taxi 266-3448)*, Airport Limo *(A Trans 224-4966)*
1-3 mi: Rental Car *(Total Car Rental 956-5915, Hertz 224-1414)*
3+ mi: Rail *(Amtrak 672-6167, 20 mi.)*
Airport: Baltimore-Washington Int'l. *(20 mi.)*

Medical Services

911 Service **OnCall:** Ambulance **Under 1 mi:** Chiropractor *(Cohen 224-3387)* **1-3 mi:** Doctor, Dentist *(Edgewater 956-3525)*, Holistic Services *(Traditional Acupuncture 269-6032)*, Veterinarian *(Reichardt 956-4500)*
Hospital: Anne Arundel 267-1000 *(3 mi.)*

PHOTOS ON CD-ROM: 12

Setting -- Liberty Yacht Club's network of recently replaced docks sits in the shadow of the 65-ft. Solomons Island Road Bridge, filling this whole "corner" of the river. A wide, extremely long floating fuel dock has four pumps and fronts right on the channel. A large "step-down" yellow-trimmed metal boatyard shed sports "Liberty Yacht Club" sprawled across on the roof. As boats arrive, they are greeted by a clock embedded in a big blue liberty bell nailed to a piling.

Marina Notes -- There's a wide range of boats, from smaller dry stack storage, to medium-size boats up on lifts, to good-size sailboats, power, and trawlers - with most of the larger boats occupying the T-heads. If there's one free, the easternmost slips - on the outside of "H" dock - have spectacular views straight down South River. In addition to the boatyard, there's also extensive on-the-hard storage back behind the pool. Clubhouse has a big-screen TV. Two sets of heads and showers are being renovated because of storm damage. Some heads are full designer-tiled bathrooms with a separate shower. Others have a shower and two toilets, plus two sinks with attractive, pebbled, fiberglass dividers.

Notable -- An inviting pool sits well away from the boatyard activity and docks. Clear Lucite panels at either end provide shelter from the wind but allow views out to the river. A separate sundeck is furnished with chaises. Dockage for customers of The Yellow Fin Steak and Fish House is here, but the restaurant is actually at the end of a path that leads underneath the overpass to the other side of the bridge. It features a wild exterior, stylish, contemporary interior, sushi bar and wide open lounge area. (Half price on appetizers during happy hour.) Directly across the river, Becky's On-the-Water Comedy Club has dock 'n' dine.

Navigational Information

Lat: 38°57.300' **Long:** 076°33.233' **Tide:** 3 ft. **Current:** 4 kt. **Chart:** 12270
Rep. Depths (*MLW*): Entry 14 ft. **Fuel Dock** 13 ft. **Max Slip/Moor** 13 ft./-
Access: South River 4 mi. N from Thomas Point next to Solomons Bridge

Marina Facilities *(In Season/Off Season)*

Fuel: *BP* - Gasoline, Diesel, High-Speed Pumps
Slips: 135 Total, 10 Transient **Max LOA:** 50 ft. **Max Beam:** 21 ft.
Rate *(per ft.)*: **Day** $1.50/$1.00 **Week** n/a **Month** n/a
Power: 30 amp $5, **50 amp** $10, **100 amp** n/a, **200 amp** n/a
Cable TV: No **Dockside Phone:** Yes, $0 Tenant Billed
Dock Type: Fixed, Long Fingers, Short Fingers, Pilings
Moorings: 0 Total, 0 Transient **Launch:** n/a
Rate: Day n/a **Week** n/a **Month** n/a
Heads: 6 Toilet(s), 2 Shower(s) *(with dressing rooms)*
Laundry: None **Pay Phones:** Yes, 1
Pump-Out: OnSite, Full Service, 1 Central **Fee:** $5** **Closed Heads:** Yes

Marina Operations

Owner/Manager: David French **Dockmaster:** Gregg Rodgers
In-Season: Jun-Sep, 8am-7pm **Off-Season:** Mar-May,Oct-Nov, 10am-6pm*
After-Hours Arrival: Call ahead
Reservations: No **Credit Cards:** Visa/MC, Dscvr, Amex, Amoco
Discounts: None
Pets: Welcome, Dog Walk Area **Handicap Access:** Yes, Heads, Docks

Oak Grove Marine Center

2820 Solomon Island Road; Edgewater, MD 21037

Tel: (410) 266-6696 **VHF: Monitor** n/a **Talk** n/a
Fax: (410) 349-2245 **Alternate Tel:** (410) 353-7310
Email: n/a **Web:** n/a
Nearest Town: Annapolis *(5 mi.)* **Tourist Info:** (410) 263-7648

Marina Services and Boat Supplies

Services - Docking Assistance, Security *(Night watchman & gated parking lot)*, Trash Pick-Up, Dock Carts **Communication -** Mail & Package Hold, Phone Messages, FedEx, DHL, UPS *(Sat Del)* **Supplies - OnSite:** Ice *(Cube)*, Ships' Store **Under 1 mi:** Live Bait **1-3 mi:** West Marine *(956-8920)*, Boat/US *(573-5744)*, Bait/Tackle *(PJS 956-8660)*, Propane

Boatyard Services

OnSite: Forklift, Launching Ramp *($15)*, Engine mechanic *(gas)*, Bottom Cleaning, Air Conditioning, Refrigeration, Compound, Wash & Wax **OnCall:** Brightwork, Divers, Interior Cleaning, Propeller Repairs **Near:** Hull Repairs. **Dealer for:** Used Powerboats. **Yard Rates:** $70/hr., Haul & Launch $60 to 28 ft. *(blocking $10/ft.)*, Power Wash $1.50/ft., Bottom Paint $10/ft. **Storage:** In-Water $2/ft./mo., On-Land $5/ft/mo., min. $60/mo.

Restaurants and Accommodations

OnSite: Restaurant *(Yellow Fin Steak & Fish House 573-0863, D $14-36, brunch 11am-2pm, D 4-9pm; happy hour Fri 4-7pm, Sun 2-6pm)* **OnCall:** Pizzeria *(Domino's 956-1800, delivers)* **Near:** Restaurant *(Becky's On-the-Water Comedy Club 956-0739, dinghy across the river)*, Pizzeria *(Ledo 956-6700, L $7-10, D $7-10)* **Under 1 mi:** Fast Food **1-3 mi:** Restaurant *(Mona Lisa 266-7595)*, *(Original Steak House 956-4494, L $10-20, D $15-35)*, *(Dragon House 956-2121)*, *(Baja Fresh Mexican Grill 897-0090)*, *(Steele Grille 956-5070)*, Motel *(Hampton Inn 571-0200, $140-195)*, *(Econo Lodge 224-4317)*, Inn/B&B *(State House Inn 990-0024)*

Recreation and Entertainment

Near: Boat Rentals *(South River Rentals 956-9729)* **1-3 mi:** Golf Course *(Atlantic Golf 956-3310)*, Fitness Center *(South River 261-4222)*, Bowling *(Annapolis 266-0700)*, Group Fishing Boat, Video Rental *(Blockbuster 266-8144)*, Video Arcade **3+ mi:** Horseback Riding *(Harmony Ridge 798-5200, 6 mi.)*, Movie Theater *(Crown Eastport 263-3747, 5 mi.)*, Museum *(Chesapeake Children's Museum 990-1993, 4 mi.)*, Cultural Attract *(Historic London Town & Gardens - 23-acre park & excavation of late 17thC. town, Wm. Brown House Museum & 8-acre garden 222-1919 $4/3, 4 mi.)*

Provisioning and General Services

Under 1 mi: Post Office *(573-0953)* **1-3 mi:** Convenience Store, Supermarket *(Safeway 626-2710)*, Gourmet Shop *(Peppercorn 266-9401)*, Health Food *(Whole Foods 573-1800)*, Liquor Store *(Colony 205-0568)*, Bakery *(Carlson's 956-0952)*, Farmers' Market *(PA Dutch 573-0770)*, Bank/ATM, Catholic Church, Beauty Salon *(Sun Deck 266-8450)*, Barber Shop *(Hair Cuttery 573-5128)*, Dry Cleaners *(South-Edge 956-0909)*, Laundry, Bookstore *(Barnes & Noble 573-1115)*, Pharmacy *(CVS 798-8715)*, Hardware Store *(Ace 956-5123)*, Florist, Department Store *(Kmart 956-0056)*

Transportation

OnCall: Taxi *(Holiday 266-3448)*, Airport Limo *(A Trans 224-4966)*
1-3 mi: Rental Car *(Total Car 956-5915, Hertz 224-1414)* **3+ mi:** Rail *(Amtrak 672-6167, 20 mi.)* **Airport:** Baltimore-Washington Int'l. *(20 mi.)*

Medical Services

911 Service **1-3 mi:** Doctor, Dentist *(Doring 956-2505)*, Chiropractor *(Cohen 224-3387)*, Holistic Services *(Healing Arts 956-0055)*, Veterinarian *(Reichardt 956-4500)* **Hospital:** Anne Arundel 267-1000 *(3 mi.)*

Setting -- The six main Oak Grove piers lie along very protected Gingerville Creek. On the northwest side of the 65-ft. bridge, at the corner of South River, make a very sharp right and go past Pier 4. The entire stretch of docks is now all part of Oak Grove. Waterside, a two-story, gray-sided dockhouse is backed by a big, four-story dry stack storage building. A sculptural concrete box-like 2-story building is topped with a deep-brown cornice and Oak Grove Marina sign. Next to it is the two story golden-yellow all-window Yellow Fin Steak and Fish House.

Marina Notes -- *Mar-May & Oct-Nov 10am-6pm, Closed Dec-Feb.**Pumpout $5 up to 50 gal. DCM. Fifty years under same management, same location. An L-shaped gas dock has four pumps. Boatyard services are provided by onsite Persimmon Point Marine Services. The really nice cinderblock heads have tiled floors, three toilets, and one shower with a small dressing room.

Notable -- Yellow Fin Steak and Fish House has a dramatic exterior and elegant, contemporary interior décor - black and cherry furnture, bright blue and mustard yellow floors and walls. On the road level, the large main dining room is surrounded by windows on three sides, netting spectacular views of the marina and up the river. On the ground, at dock level is a banquet room with a wall of glass; it can accommodate up to 200 diners - perfect for club cruises or rendezvous. Brunch is served from 11am-2pm, dinner Mon-Thu 4-10pm, Fri & Sat to 11pm. Sushi and seafood bar. Half price on appetizers in the bar during happy hour: Fri 4-7pm and Sun 2-6pm.

PHOTOS ON CD-ROM: 9

Boaters' Notes

Add Your Ratings and Reviews at www.AtlanticCruisingClub.com

AtlanticCruisingClub.com provides updated Marina Reports, Destination and Harbor Articles, a Boaters' Forum and much more — including an option within each on-line Marina Report for Boaters to add their ratings and comments regarding that facility. Please log on frequently to share your experiences — and to read other boaters' comments.

On the website, boaters may rate marinas on one or more of the following categories — on a scale of 1 (basic) to 5 (world class) — and also enter additional commentary.

- **Facilities & Services** (Fuel, Reservations, Concierge Services and General Helpfulness):
- **Amenities** (Pool, Beach, Internet Access, including Wi-Fi, Picnic/Grill area, Boaters' Lounge):
- **Setting** (Views, Design, Landscaping, Maintenance, Ship-Shapeness, Overall Ambiance):
- **Convenience** (Access — including delivery services — to Supermarkets, other provisioning sources, Shops, Services. Attractions, Entertainment, Sightseeing, Recreation, including Golf and Sport Fishing & Medical Services):
- **Restaurants/Eateries/Lodgings** (Availability of Fine Dining, Snack Bars, Lite Fare, On Call food service, and Lodgings ashore):
- **Transportation** (Courtesy Car/Vans, Buses, Water Taxis, Bikes, Taxis, Rental Cars, Airports, Amtrak, Commuter Trains):
- **Please Add Any Additional Comments**

6. Eastern Shore: Chester River & Kent Island

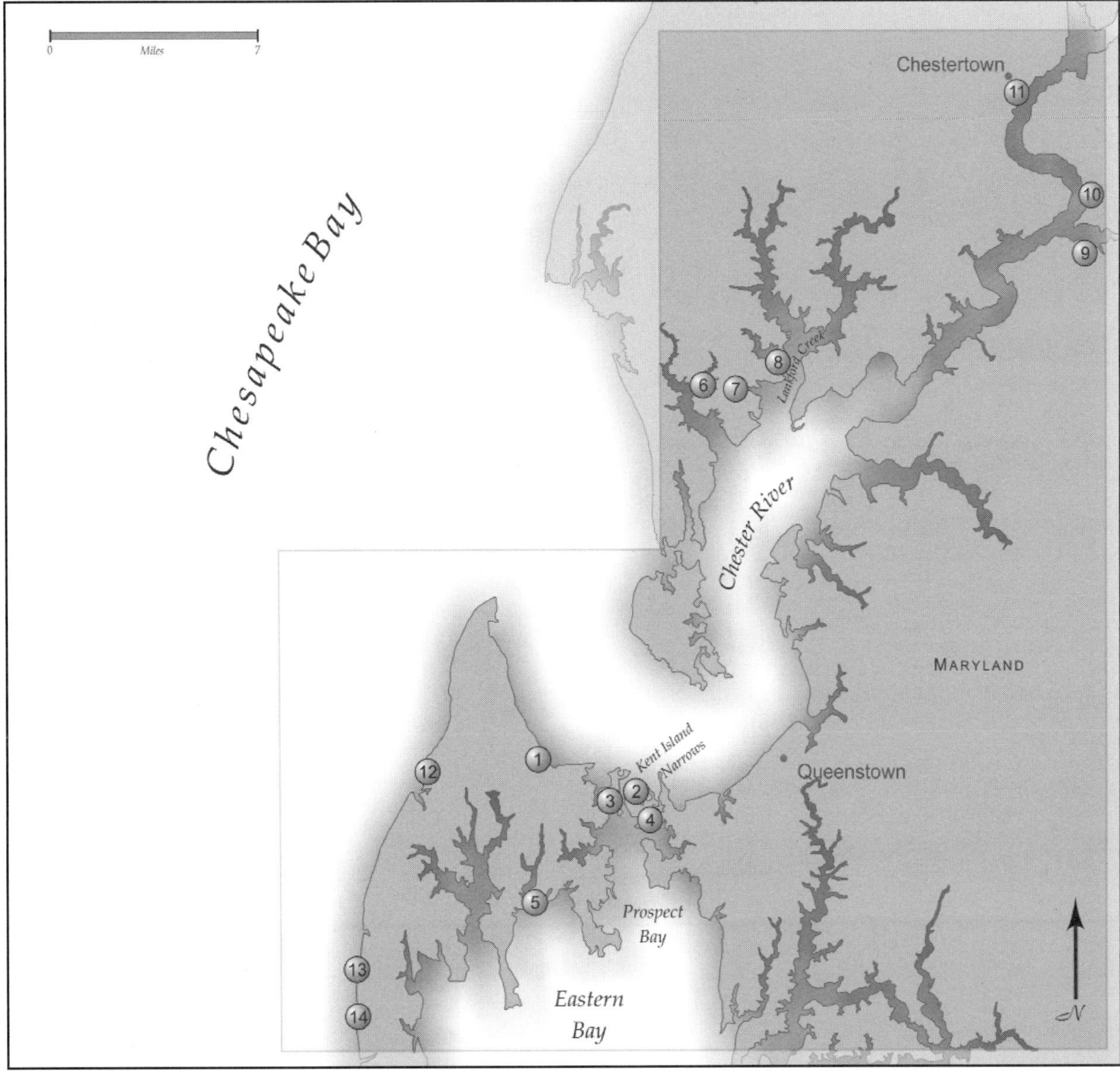

MAP	MARINA	HARBOR	PAGE
1	**Castle Harbor Marina**	*Chester River*	122
2	**Mears Point Marina**	*Chester River/Kent Narrows*	123
3	**Piney Narrows Yacht Haven**	*Chester River/Kent Narrows*	124
4	**Lippincott Marine**	*Kent Narrows*	125
5	**Island View Marina**	*Eastern Bay/Crab Alley*	126
6	**Hill's Marine Railway**	*Chester River/Grays Inn Cr.*	127
7	**Long Cove Marina**	*Chester River*	128
8	**Lankford Bay Marina**	*Chester River/Lankford Bay*	129
9	**Kennersley Point Marina**	*Chester River/Island Creek*	130
10	**Rolph's Wharf Marina & Country Inn**	*Chester River*	131
11	**Chestertown Marina**	*Chester River*	132
12	**Bay Bridge Marina**	*Kent Island*	133
13	**Kentmorr Harbour Marina**	*Chesapeake Bay*	134
14	**Queen Anne Marina**	*Prices Creek*	135

- **A "DCM" symbol in Marina Notes means Designated Clean Marina** — This is a coveted state-level award given to marinas that meet stringent, environmentally supportive requirements (see page 307). *For a list of DCM's & pump-out facilities, see page 308.*
- **Ratings & Reviews** — An explanation of the Atlantic Cruising Club's rating system, and a detailed explanation of what is in each section of the Marina Report is on pages 6 – 11. *The Data-Gathering Process is detailed on page 322.*
- **Marina Report Updates** — Updates to Marina Reports (from readers, ACC reviewers, and marinas) are posted regularly on *www.AtlanticCruisingClub.com.*

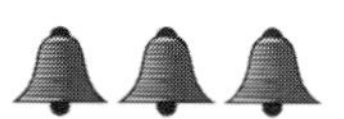

Castle Harbor Marina

PO Box 248; 301 Tackle Circle; Chester, MD 21619

Tel: (410) 643-5599 **VHF: Monitor** 16 **Talk** 68, 69
Fax: (410) 643-3863 **Alternate Tel:** n/a
Email: chm@castlemarina.com **Web:** www.castlemarina.com
Nearest Town: Stevensville *(0.5 mi.)* **Tourist Info:** (410) 643-8530

Navigational Information

Lat: 38°59.105' **Long:** 076°17.106' **Tide:** 2 ft. **Current:** n/a **Chart:** 12270
Rep. Depths (*MLW*): Entry 6 ft. **Fuel Dock** 6 ft. **Max Slip/Moor** 6 ft./-
Access: Chester River to Red Buoy #6, or Kent Narrows

Marina Facilities *(In Season/Off Season)*

Fuel: Gasoline, Diesel
Slips: 347 Total, 15 Transient **Max LOA:** 60 ft. **Max Beam:** n/a
Rate *(per ft.)*: **Day** $2.00/Inq.* **Week** Inq. **Month** Inq.
Power: 30 amp $6, **50 amp** $12, **100 amp** n/a, **200 amp** n/a
Cable TV: Yes, $6/night; satellite TV w/HBO **Dockside Phone:** No
Dock Type: Fixed, Short Fingers, Pilings, Wood
Moorings: 0 Total, 0 Transient **Launch:** n/a
Rate: Day n/a **Week** n/a **Month** n/a
Heads: 4 Toilet(s), 4 Shower(s), Hair Dryers
Laundry: 3 Washer(s), 4 Dryer(s), Book Exchange **Pay Phones:** Yes, 2
Pump-Out: OnSite, Full Service **Fee:** n/a **Closed Heads:** Yes

Marina Operations

Owner/Manager: Richard C.S. Feiner **Dockmaster:** Fred Grady
In-Season: May-Sep, 8am-6pm** **Off-Season:** Oct-Apr, 8am-4:30pm
After-Hours Arrival: Call ahead for slip assignment
Reservations: Yes **Credit Cards:** Visa/MC, Dscvr, Amex
Discounts: None
Pets: Welcome, Dog Walk Area **Handicap Access:** No

Marina Services and Boat Supplies

Services - Docking Assistance, Trash Pick-Up, Dock Carts **Communication -** Mail & Package Hold, Phone Messages, Fax in/out, FedEx, UPS, Express Mail **Supplies - OnSite:** Ice *(Block, Cube)*, Ships' Store **Under 1 mi:** Propane *(Kent Island 643-5277)* **1-3 mi:** West Marine *(604-1752)*, Boater's World *(604-2613)*, Bait/Tackle *(Island Fishing & Hunting 643-4224)*, CNG *(Mears Point 827-7888)*

Boatyard Services

Near: Launching Ramp, Electrical Repairs, Electronics Repairs, Hull Repairs, Rigger, Canvas Work, Bottom Cleaning, Brightwork, Refrigeration. **Nearest Yard:** Piney Narrows (410) 643-6600

Restaurants and Accommodations

OnSite: Restaurant *(Meighan's Pub 643-6554, L $7-26, D $7-26, Wed-Thu 4-11pm, Fri 4pm-2am, Sat 3pm-2am, Sun 3-11pm, Open at Noon for NFL season only)* **Under 1 mi:** Restaurant *(B&B Family Restaurant 604-0035)*, *(Star of China 643-6006)*, *(Lighthouse 604-3344)*, Fast Food *(Subway)*, Pizzeria *(Papa John's 604-0660)* **1-3 mi:** Restaurant *(Narrows Restaurant 827-8113, D $13-25)*, Hotel *(Comfort Inn Kent Narrows 827-6767)*, Inn/B&B *(Kent Manor Inn 643-5757, $135-215)* **3+ mi:** Motel *(Sleep Inn 827-5555, $75-140, 5 mi.)*

Recreation and Entertainment

OnSite: Pool *(kids pool too)*, Spa, Picnic Area, Grills *(charcoal)* **Near:** Playground, Dive Shop, Tennis Courts, Jogging Paths, Boat Rentals, Roller Blade/Bike Paths, Volleyball, Park **1-3 mi:** Fitness Center *(Club One 643-3488)*, Video Rental *(Blockbuster 643-8400)*, Museum *(Cray House, Stevensville Train Depot)* **3+ mi:** Golf Course *(Blue Heron Golf Course 643-5721, 8 mi.)*, Cultural Attract *(Class Act 827-0098, movies & shows, 7 mi.)*

Provisioning and General Services

OnSite: Wine/Beer **Near:** Bank/ATM **Under 1 mi:** Convenience Store *(Exxon)*, Liquor Store *(Baker's Liquor 643-5851)*, Bakery, Post Office, Barber Shop, Pharmacy *(Kent Drug 643-2339)*, Newsstand, Hardware Store *(Rommel's Ace 643-7702)* **1-3 mi:** Supermarket *(Food Lion 643-9687, Safeway 643-4929)*, Delicatessen *(Lovepoint Deli 604-2447)*, Fishmonger *(L&L Seafood 604-0338)*, Catholic Church, Library *(Stevensville 643-8161)*, Beauty Salon, Dry Cleaners *(Thompson Creek 643-4864)*, Department Store *(Kmart 643-9600)*, Copies Etc. *(Copies Plus 643-6383)* **3+ mi:** Gourmet Shop *(Chesapeake Gourmet 827-8686, 8 mi.)*

Transportation

OnSite: Water Taxi *(Kent Narrows Ch.68/212-4070 $4 to Narrows)* **OnCall:** Rental Car *(Enterprise 810-0971)*, Taxi *(Kent Island 604-0486)*, Airport Limo *(Above & Beyond 827-8835)* **1-3 mi:** InterCity Bus *(Greyhound 643-6584)* **Airport:** Baltimore-Washington Int'l./Bay Bridge *(50 mi./4 mi.)*

Medical Services

911 Service **OnCall:** Ambulance **Near:** Doctor *(Queen Anne's Medical 643-6205)* **Under 1 mi:** Dentist *(Billings 643-5500)* **1-3 mi:** Chiropractor *(Mandell 604-0900)*, Holistic Services *(Mid-Shore Massage 643-9910)*, Veterinarian *(Chesapeake Vet Hospital 643-3101)*
Hospital: Anne Arundel 267-1000 *(16 mi.)*

Setting -- Located on peaceful Kent Island, at the mouth of the Chester River, Castle Harbor's slips are in a protected basin accessed through a well-marked private channel. An inverted "V" shaped spit of land divides the two sets of docks and hosts the pool and other amenities. At the end of the main dock, a large hip-roofed dockhouse backs the long fuel dock and greets boats as they arrive. Pine trees and other evergreens shade well-clipped stretches of lawn - creating a woodsy feeling. Two large townhouse complexes flank the basin. The office and a modest ships' store are in the dockhouse.

Marina Notes -- *$1.75/ft. Mon-Thu, $2.00 Weekends & Holidays. 35/ft. min. **8am-6pm Fri & Sat in season. 8am-4pm off-season. DCM. Founded in the 1960s, operated by the same family since 1985. A 1200 foot stone jetty was installed in the channel. Nicely done air-conditioned cinderblock bathhouses feature vinyl grating floors which dramatically steps up the appearance and usability. Showers have separate dressing rooms, sinks are set in a Corian vanity, everything freshly painted and inviting.

Notable -- Rope-and-piling fencing define various areas. A good-size pool is surrounded by tables and rows of turquoise strap chaises, with a poolhouse at one end and views of the docks at the other. A children's wading pool and an adults-only spa are nearby. Picnic tables with charcoal grills are scattered about and a pavilion shelters a dozen tables. On the 1st floor of the Castle Marina Inn, Meighan's, a nicely appointed pub, overlooks the docks. They serve hearty Irish food with entertainment most nights. A pool table is a central feature. The 2nd floor is used for private functions - an interesting option for club cruises.

Mears Point Marina

428 Kent Narrows Way North; Grasonville, MD 21638

Tel: (410) 827-8888 **VHF: Monitor** 9 **Talk** n/a
Fax: (410) 827-8758 **Alternate Tel:** n/a
Email: mearspt@aol.com **Web:** www.mearspoint.com
Nearest Town: Chester *(3 mi.)* **Tourist Info:** (410) 643-8530

Navigational Information

Lat: 38°58.382' **Long:** 076°14.597' **Tide:** 2 ft. **Current:** n/a **Chart:** 12270
Rep. Depths (*MLW*): Entry 8 ft. **Fuel Dock** 6 ft. **Max Slip/Moor** 6 ft./-
Access: Chester River to entrance channel to Kent Narrows

Marina Facilities *(In Season/Off Season)*

Fuel: *Carrol Independ* - Gasoline, Diesel
Slips: 550 Total, 60 Transient **Max LOA:** 80 ft. **Max Beam:** n/a
Rate *(per ft.)*: **Day** $2.00* **Week** Inq. **Month** Inq.
Power: 30 amp $5, **50 amp** $10, **100 amp** n/a, **200 amp** n/a
Cable TV: Yes **Dockside Phone:** Yes
Dock Type: Fixed, Long Fingers, Pilings
Moorings: 0 Total, 0 Transient **Launch:** n/a
Rate: Day n/a **Week** n/a **Month** n/a
Heads: 22 Toilet(s), 24 Shower(s) *(with dressing rooms)*
Laundry: 4 Washer(s), 4 Dryer(s), Book Exchange **Pay Phones:** Yes
Pump-Out: OnSite, Full Service **Fee:** $5 **Closed Heads:** Yes

Marina Operations

Owner/Manager: Bob Wilson **Dockmaster:** Same
In-Season: Apr-Dec, 8:30am-8pm **Off-Season:** Jan-Mar, 9am-4:30pm
After-Hours Arrival: Call in advance
Reservations: Yes **Credit Cards:** Visa/MC, Dscvr, Amex
Discounts: None
Pets: Welcome, Dog Walk Area **Handicap Access:** Yes, Heads

Marina Services and Boat Supplies

Services - Docking Assistance, Concierge, Security *(gated)*, Dock Carts **Communication -** Mail & Package Hold, Phone Messages, Fax in/out, Data Ports *(Laundry)*, FedEx, DHL, UPS, Express Mail *(Sat Del)* **Supplies - OnSite:** Ice *(Block, Cube)*, Ships' Store, CNG **1-3 mi:** West Marine *(604-1752)*, Bait/Tackle *(Island Fishing 643-4224)*, Propane *(United 643-7400)*

Boatyard Services

OnSite: Travelift *(35T)*, Forklift, Engine mechanic *(gas, diesel)*, Electrical Repairs, Electronics Repairs, Hull Repairs, Bottom Cleaning, Brightwork, Air Conditioning, Refrigeration, Compound, Wash & Wax, Interior Cleaning, Propeller Repairs, Woodworking, Metal Fabrication, Painting, Awlgrip, Yacht Broker **OnCall:** Divers **Member:** ABYC - 2 Certified Tech(s)
Yard Rates: Haul & Launch $9/ft. *(blocking $9/ft.)*, Power Wash $1.50/ft., Bottom Paint $8-13/ft. *(paint incl.)*

Restaurants and Accommodations

OnSite: Restaurant *(Annie's Paramount 827-7103, L $7-23, D $9-29, 11am-10pm, Sun 9am-10pm; Sun brunch buffet 9am-2pm, $19)*, Seafood Shack *(Harris' Crab House 827-9500, all-you-can-eat crab feasts Mon-Fri 11am-9pm)*, Lite Fare *(Pool Bar L&D $4-7: sandwiches, burgers, hot dogs, ice cream)*, *(Red Eyes Dock Bar L $4-12, D $4-12, 11am-11pm, wknds 'til 12:30, entertainment)* **Near:** Restaurant *(Angler's 827-6717, L $5-13, D $9-23)*, *(Fisherman's Inn 827-8807)*, *(The Jetty 827-4959)*, *(Narrows 827-8113, D $13-26, water taxi)*, Seafood Shack *(The Crab Deck 827-6666)*, Snack Bar *(Double Dip Ice-Cream)*, Hotel *(Best Western 827-6767, $75-140)*, *(Holiday Inn Express 827-4454, $89-210, overlooks marina, AAA & military discount)* **1-3 mi:** Pizzeria *(Papa John's 604-0660)*, Motel *(Sleep Inn 827-5555)*

Recreation and Entertainment

OnSite: Pool *(Mon-Thu 11am-8pm, Fri-Sun & Hol 10am-10pm)*, Picnic Area, Grills, Playground, Fitness Center *(Island Athletic 827-5527, $5 boaters - Mon-Fri 5am-9pm Sat-Sun 7am-4pm)*, Jogging Paths, Volleyball
Near: Museum *(Chespeake Exploration Ctr 604-2100 - dinghy across)*
Under 1 mi: Boat Rentals, Fishing Charter *(Captain George 643-8964)*, Park *(Cross Island Trail)*, Special Events **1-3 mi:** Video Rental (Blockbuster 643-*8400)* **3+ mi:** Golf Course *(Queenstown Harbor 827-6611, 5 mi.)*

Provisioning and General Services

OnSite: Bank/ATM **Near:** Liquor Store *(Marshy Creek 827-7377)*, Fishmonger *(United Shellfish, Harris' Seafood)* **1-3 mi:** Convenience Store, Supermarket *(Safeway 643-4919)*, Delicatessen *(Baker's 643-5851)*, Post Office, Catholic Church, Protestant Church, Beauty Salon, Dry Cleaners, Pharmacy *(Kent Drug 643-2339)*, Hardware Store *(Kent Island 643-3500)*, Florist **3+ mi:** Gourmet Shop *(Chesapeake Gourmet 827-8686, 5 mi.)*, Library *(Stevensville 643-8161, 4 mi.)*, Bookstore *(Book Warehouse, 5 mi.)*

Transportation

OnCall: Water Taxi *(Kent Narrows, 212-4070, Ch.68)*, Rental Car *(Enterprise 604-6154, Total Car 604-2529)*, Taxi *(Kent Island 827-9522)*, Airport Limo *(Above & Beyond 827-8835)* **Under 1 mi:** Bikes
Airport: Baltimore-Washington Int'l/Bay Bridge *(50 mi./6 mi.)*

Medical Services

911 Service **OnCall:** Ambulance **1-3 mi:** Doctor *(Chester Regional 643-4900)*, Dentist *(Billings 643-5500)*, Chiropractor *(Mandell 604-0900)*, Holistic Services, Veterinarian **Hospital:** Anne Arundel 267-1000 *(18 mi.)*

Setting -- The first marina on the eastern shore of Kent Narrows, Mears' 550 slips surround most of a large key-hole-shaped core that hosts a 2-story postmodern, gray clapboard office building, an enormous pool complex, boatyard services, on-the-hard storage and restaurants. Views are of the Narrows, Narrows Pointe, a large townhouse complex (prices starting at $900,000, not shown in photo), and, from the outer docks, views of undisturbed marsh.

Marina Notes -- *$2 Mon-Thu, $2.75 Fri-Sun and holidays. DCM. Founded in 1981, formerly Seward's Point Marina. Charter boats and towing available. Good quality docks have comfortable, full-width, near or full-length finger piers with new pedestals. Small pavilions with picnic tables and grills anchor each main dock. Security is very tight - take your card if leaving the complex (even to the restaurants). Particularly nice bathhouses have composite floor, Formica or fiberglass walls & dividers, Corian topped vanities, showers with private dressing rooms, and lockers.

Notable -- The marina's centerpiece is a huge pool surrounded by rows of immaculate white chaises, a large kiddie pool, and a snack bar pavilion. The two-story building that backs the pool houses the office, bathhouse, a very convenient laundry (folding table, dataports & book exchange), the Island Athletic Club, and maritime businesses. Immediately adjacent to the marina are 3 eateries: Annie's, two pink-tableclothed dining rooms with dock views; Red Eyes Dock Bar with weekend entertainment, late hours, scads of go-fast boats, and a generally wild ambiance; and "Famous" Harris' Crab House with 2 floors of inside/outside dining and views down the Narrows. Waterfront Shops are between Red's and Harris' - ice-cream, gifts, & a demonstration of the Oyster Recovery Partnership.

PHOTOS ON CD-ROM: 17

Piney Narrows Yacht Haven

500 Piney Narrows Road; Chester, MD 21619

Tel: (410) 643-6600 **VHF: Monitor** 16/9 **Talk** n/a
Fax: (410) 643-6041 **Alternate Tel:** n/a
Email: n/a **Web:** www.pineynarrowsyachthaven.com
Nearest Town: Chester *(2 mi.)* **Tourist Info:** (410) 643-8530

Navigational Information

Lat: 38°58.356' **Long:** 076°15.019' **Tide:** 2 ft. **Current:** n/a **Chart:** 12270
Rep. Depths (*MLW*): Entry 7 ft. **Fuel Dock** 7 ft. **Max Slip/Moor** -/-
Access: Chester River to channel into Kent Narrows

Marina Facilities *(In Season/Off Season)*

Fuel: *89* - Gasoline, Diesel
Slips: 278 Total, varies Transient **Max LOA:** 60 ft. **Max Beam:** n/a
Rate *(per ft.)*: **Day** $1.50/0.75 **Week** $5.50 **Month** based on slip size
Power: 30 amp $5, **50 amp** $8, **100 amp** n/a, **200 amp** n/a
Cable TV: Yes **Dockside Phone:** Yes
Dock Type: Fixed, Long Fingers, Pilings, Wood
Moorings: 0 Total, 0 Transient **Launch:** n/a
Rate: Day n/a **Week** n/a **Month** n/a
Heads: 22 Toilet(s), 20 Shower(s)
Laundry: 2 Washer(s), 2 Dryer(s), Book Exchange **Pay Phones:** Yes, 3
Pump-Out: OnSite, 278 InSlip **Fee:** $5 **Closed Heads:** Yes

Marina Operations

Owner/Manager: Joe Pomerantz **Dockmaster:** Gail Coster
In-Season: MemDay-Sep, 8am-8pm **Off-Season:** Oct-MemDay, 8:30am-5pm
After-Hours Arrival: Call ahead
Reservations: Recommended **Credit Cards:** Visa/MC, Dscvr
Discounts: None
Pets: Welcome, Dog Walk Area **Handicap Access:** No

Marina Services and Boat Supplies

Services - Docking Assistance, Boaters' Lounge, Security, Trash Pick-Up, Dock Carts **Communication -** Mail & Package Hold, Phone Messages, Fax in/out, FedEx, DHL, UPS, Express Mail *(Sat Del)* **Supplies - OnSite:** Ice *(Block, Cube)*, Ships' Store **Near:** Bait/Tackle, CNG *(Mears Point)* **1-3 mi:** West Marine *(604-1752)*, Marine Discount Store *(Kent Narrows)*, Propane *(Kent Island 643-5277)*

Boatyard Services

OnSite: Launching Ramp, Electrical Repairs, Electronics Repairs, Canvas Work, Bottom Cleaning, Brightwork, Air Conditioning, Refrigeration, Woodworking **OnCall:** Painting **Near:** Travelift *(60T)*, Forklift, Engine mechanic *(gas, diesel)*, Hull Repairs, Rigger, Divers, Compound, Wash & Wax, Interior Cleaning, Propeller Repairs, Metal Fabrication, Awlgrip, Yacht Design, Yacht Building, Yacht Broker. **1-3 mi:** Upholstery, Yacht Interiors. **Nearest Yard:** Kent Narrows Yacht Yard (410) 643-4400

Restaurants and Accommodations

Near: Restaurant *(Harris' Crab House 827-9500, dinghy - all-you-can-eat crab feasts Mon-Fri 11am-9pm)*, *(Annie's 827-7103, L $7-23, D $9-29, 11am-10pm, Sun 9am-10pm, enormous Sun brunch buffet 9am-2pm, $19)*, *(The Narrows 827-8113, D $13-25, water taxi)*, *(Lighthouse 604-3344)*, Lite Fare *(Red Eyes L $4-12, D $4-12, dinghy - 11am-11pm, weekends til 12:30, entertainment)* **Under 1 mi:** Restaurant *(Anglers 827-6717, water taxi)*, Crab House *(Crab Deck 827-6666)*, Motel *(Comfort Inn 827-6767, $76-140)*, *(Hilton Garden Inn 827-3877)*, Hotel *(Holiday Inn 866-270-5110)* **1-3 mi:** Seafood Shack *(Meredith Seafood & Carry Out 827-7737)*, Fast Food *(Subway)*, *(The Jetty 827-4959)*, Pizzeria *(Papa John's 604-0660)*

Recreation and Entertainment

OnSite: Pool, Picnic Area, Grills *(propane)*, Volleyball **Near:** Playground, Dive Shop, Fitness Center *(Club One 643-3488)*, Jogging Paths, Boat Rentals, Roller Blade/Bike Paths, Group Fishing Boat, Park *(Cross Island Trail)*, Museum *(Chespeake Exploration Ctr 604-2100 - right outside the marina gates)*, Special Events **Under 1 mi:** Fishing Charter *(Captain George & Sons 643-8964)* **1-3 mi:** Video Rental *(Blockbuster 643-8400)*, Video Arcade **3+ mi:** Golf Course *(Queenstown Harbor 827-6611, 6 mi.)*

Provisioning and General Services

1-3 mi: Supermarket *(Food Lion 643-9687, Safeway 643-4929)*, Gourmet Shop, Liquor Store *(Baker's Liquor 643-5851)*, Bakery, Farmers' Market, Fishmonger *(Fisherman's Seafood 827-7323, 7 days)*, Bank/ATM, Post Office, Catholic Church, Beauty Salon, Dry Cleaners, Laundry, Bookstore, Pharmacy *(Kent Drug 643-2339)*, Hardware Store *(True Value 643-3500)*, Florist **3+ mi:** Delicatessen *(Lovepoint Deli 604-2447, 4 mi.)*, Library *(Stevensville 643-8161, 4 mi.)*, Department Store *(Kmart 643-9600, 5 mi.)*

Transportation

OnCall: Water Taxi *(Kent Narrows, 212-4070, Ch.68 $3)*, Rental Car *(Enterprise 604-6154)*, Taxi *(Kent Island 604-0486)*, Airport Limo *(Associated Sedan 643-1500)* **Near:** Bikes *(Cross-Island Trail Route runs by the marina)* **Airport:** Baltimore-Washington Int'l/Bay Bridge *(50 mi./6 mi.)*

Medical Services

911 Service **OnCall:** Ambulance **1-3 mi:** Dentist *(Wolfe 643-3888)*, Veterinarian *(Chesapeake 643-3101)* **3+ mi:** Doctor *(Chester Regional 643-4900, 4 mi.)* **Hospital:** Anne Arundel 267-1000 *(18 mi.)*

Setting -- Arriving at the marina, one is greeted by a nicely landscaped welcome area that fronts on the west side of Kent Narrows. A gazebo and lots of flowers add a touch of grace. The long fuel dock wraps the corner and hosts five pumps; it's backed by a low, hip-roofed taupe-sided clubhouse and just beyond is the entrance to the marina. The protected basin is filled mostly with covered slips. Behind the dockhouse, on a small rise, is the pool.

Marina Notes -- DCM. Recent dredging of a new strait will improve access to MLW of 8 feet. Managed by Coastal Properties, the marina is private and family-oriented. Condominium slips for sale as well as lease. About half the 300 slips are covered; the open slips have a mix of full and half-length finger pier. Grills, mostly propane, are scattered about. Very secure, gated facility; always know your key-code. No Internet access. A small corner of the marina grounds has been set aside for on-the-hard storage. Heads and showers were all brand new in late '04, with tiled floors and fiberglass showers.

Notable -- A particularly nice boaters' lounge is in the clubhouse - plush sofas, a large-screen TV, maple captains' tables and chairs - all overlooking the water. The adjacent pool, next to the docks, is surrounded by chaises and tables with umbrellas, and has a view of the Narrows and the passing boats. Six restaurants are nearby, three of them a dinghy ride across the Narrows, and 26 factory outlet shops are next door. Just outside the marina, the delightful Chesapeake Exploration Center's "Our Chesapeake Legacy" uses 7 exhibits, with hands-on displays, to explain the Bay's natural and cultural history - accessible by boat, too! Skipjack Anna McGarvey guards the entrance. Mon-Sat 8:30am-4:30pm, Sun 10-4pm. The Visitors' Center is in the same building.

PHOTOS ON CD-ROM: 15

Navigational Information
Lat: 38°57.767' **Long:** 076°14.117' **Tide:** 2 ft. **Current:** n/a **Chart:** 12270
Rep. Depths (*MLW*): Entry 7 ft. **Fuel Dock** 7 ft. **Max Slip/Moor** 7 ft./-
Access: Chester River or Eastern Bay to Kent Narrows

Marina Facilities *(In Season/Off Season)*
Fuel: No
Slips: 200 Total, 3 Transient **Max LOA:** 60 ft. **Max Beam:** 18 ft.
Rate *(per ft.)*: **Day** $1.75 **Week** Inq. **Month** Inq.
Power: 30 amp $5, **50 amp** $10, **100 amp** n/a, **200 amp** n/a
Cable TV: No **Dockside Phone:** Yes
Dock Type: Fixed, Short Fingers, Pilings, Wood, Aluminum
Moorings: 0 Total, 0 Transient **Launch:** n/a
Rate: Day n/a **Week** n/a **Month** n/a
Heads: 7 Toilet(s), 5 Shower(s) *(with dressing rooms)*
Laundry: 1 Washer(s), 1 Dryer(s), Book Exchange **Pay Phones:** Yes, 1
Pump-Out: OnSite, Self Service **Fee:** $5 **Closed Heads:** Yes

Marina Operations
Owner/Manager: Richard Lippincott **Dockmaster:** Art Jeffra
In-Season: Apr-Oct, 8am-5pm **Off-Season:** Nov-Mar, 8am-4:30pm
After-Hours Arrival: Call marina office prior to 4pm
Reservations: Preferred **Credit Cards:** Visa/MC
Discounts: Boat/US **Dockage:** 10% **Fuel:** n/a **Repair:** n/a
Pets: Welcome, Dog Walk Area **Handicap Access:** No

Lippincott Marine

3420 Main Street; Grasonville, MD 21638

Tel: (410) 827-9300 **VHF: Monitor** 16 **Talk** n/a
Fax: (410) 827-9303 **Alternate Tel:** n/a
Email: lippincott@toad.net **Web:** n/a
Nearest Town: Chester *(4 mi.)* **Tourist Info:** (410) 643-8530

Marina Services and Boat Supplies
Services - Docking Assistance, Security *(24 hrs., employee on premises/gate card)*, Dock Carts **Communication -** Mail & Package Hold, Phone Messages, Fax in/out, FedEx **Supplies - OnSite:** Ice *(Block, Cube)*, Ships' Store **Near:** CNG *(Mears Point 827-7888)* **1-3 mi:** West Marine *(604-1752)*, Bait/Tackle *(Island Fishing & Hunting 643-4224)*, Propane *(United Shoregas 643-7400)* **3+ mi:** Boater's World *(604-2613, 7 mi.)*

Boatyard Services
OnSite: Travelift *(35T)*, Crane *(1500 lbs.)*, Launching Ramp, Engine mechanic *(gas, diesel)*, Electrical Repairs, Hull Repairs, Rigger, Bottom Cleaning, Brightwork, Compound, Wash & Wax, Interior Cleaning, Propeller Repairs, Woodworking, Painting, Awlgrip, Total Refits, Yacht Broker *(Lippincott Marine)* **OnCall:** Refrigeration, Upholstery **Near:** Air Conditioning, Metal Fabrication. **Under 1 mi:** Canvas Work, Divers. **1-3 mi:** Electronics Repairs, Sail Loft. **Dealer for:** Mainship Trawlers, Luhrs Sport. **Yard Rates:** $76.50/hr., Haul & Launch $7.50/ft., Bottom Paint $17.95/ft. **Storage:** On-Land $2.60/ft./mo.

Restaurants and Accommodations
OnCall: Pizzeria *(Domino's 643-3002)* **Near:** Restaurant *(The Jetty 827-4959)*, *(Narrows 827-8113, D $13-25)*, Seafood Shack *(Meredith Seafood & Carryout 827-7737)*, Motel *(Hilton Garden Inn 827-3877)*, *(Comfort Inn 827-6767, $76-140)*, Hotel *(Holiday Inn Express 827-4454)* **Under 1 mi:** Restaurant *(Fisherman's 827-8807, L $9-28, D $11-30)*, *(Annie's 827-7103)*, Seafood Shack *(Harris' Crab House 827-9500)* **1-3 mi:** Restaurant *(Anglers 827-7617, L $5-13, D $9-23)*, Fast Food, Pizzeria *(La Piazza 827-9300)*, Motel *(Chesapeake Motel 827-7272)*

Recreation and Entertainment
OnSite: Pool *(8am-7pm)*, Picnic Area, Grills *(charcoal)* **Near:** Group Fishing Boat *(Captain Lloyd Price 827-6700; The Island Queen - at Scott Marine)*, Museum *(Exploratorium)* **Under 1 mi:** Dive Shop, Fitness Center *(Island Athletic 827-5527)*, Jogging Paths, Fishing Charter *(Captain George & Sons 643-8964, Captain Lloyd Price 827-6700)*, Park *(Cross Island Trail)* **3+ mi:** Golf Course *(Queenstown 827-6611, 6 mi.)*,

Provisioning and General Services
Near: Liquor Store *(Marshy Creek 827-7377)*, Fishmonger *(Fisherman's Seafood 827-7323)* **Under 1 mi:** Bank/ATM **1-3 mi:** Delicatessen *(Baker's 643-5851)*, Bakery, Market *(Grasonville Food Mart 827-9330)*, Post Office, Catholic Church, Protestant Church, Beauty Salon, Dry Cleaners, Pharmacy *(Kent Drug 643-2339)*, Hardware Store *(True Value 643-3500)*, Florist **3+ mi:** Supermarket *(Food Lion 643-9687, Safeway 643-4929, 4 mi.)*, Library *(643-8161, 4 mi.)*, Bookstore *(Book Warehouse 827-8474, 5 mi.)*, Department Store *(Kmart 643-9600, 5 mi.)*

Transportation
OnCall: Water Taxi *(Kent Narrows 212-4070, Ch.68 - Oyster Cove $3)*, Rental Car *(Enterprise 604-6154)*, Taxi *(Kent Island 827-9522)*, Airport Limo *(Above & Beyond 827-8835)* **Near:** Bikes
Airport: Baltimore-Washington Int'l./Bay Bridge *(50 mi./6 mi.)*

Medical Services
911 Service **OnCall:** Ambulance **1-3 mi:** Doctor *(Chester Regional 643-4900)*, Dentist *(Chesapeake Dental 827-7119)*, Chiropractor, Veterinarian *(Chesapeake 643-3101)* **Hospital:** Anne Arundel 267-1000 *(20 mi.)*

Setting -- Lippincott is in a quiet and unspoiled part of the Narrows - south of the bridge, on the east side. The views are completely untouched; the only sign of civilization is the immediately adjacent Oyster Cove townhouse complex. It's a lovely, peaceful spot that berths an attractive fleet of boats. A wave attenuator, outboard of the last set of docks, minimizes the wash.

Marina Notes -- DCM. Founded in 1971, Lippincott's is family owned and operated. Boat/U.S. discounts. Quiet, family-oriented marina with a 50-50 sailboat/powerboat mix and a large sportfish contingent. Two sets of docks - the outer set consists of three main piers radiating from the western shore and one from the western side; then a large rectangular man-made basin is completely lined with slips. Considerable amount of dry storage space for boats on the hard - generally pretty full. Two sets of heads: the main bathhouse near the office, and a second set near the pool.

Notable -- A small pool and the adjacent cabana and bathhouse, surrounded by a chain link fence (hours are 8am-7pm), have arresting views of the harbor and the marsh beyond. There are four picnic tables and two charcoal grills that share those same views. A couple of head boats are at nearby Scott Marine. "The Jetty" beach bar (the yellow and chartreuse building) is an easy dinghy ride, and less than a mile is The Fisherman's Village complex. The Cross Island Trail Park begins near the marina entrance and ends at Kent Island's Terrapin Park & Nature Center. It's a six-mile long, ten-foot wide paved surface that runs through forests, near entertainment centers, over bridges and alongside several parks.

PHOTOS ON CD-ROM: 9

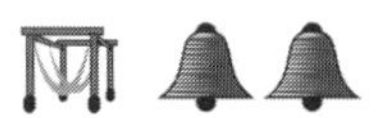

Island View Marina

1814 Crab Alley Drive; Chester, MD 21619

Tel: (410) 643-2842 **VHF: Monitor** n/a **Talk** n/a
Fax: (410) 643-8223 **Alternate Tel:** (410) 643-2842
Email: bruzzmax@dmv.com **Web:** n/a
Nearest Town: Chester *(3 mi.)* **Tourist Info:** (410) 643-8530

Navigational Information

Lat: 38°56.146' **Long:** 076°17.126' **Tide:** 2 ft. **Current:** 0 kt. **Chart:** 12273
Rep. Depths (*MLW*): Entry 10 ft. **Fuel Dock** n/a **Max Slip/Moor** 8 ft./-
Access: Narrows, around Norman Pt. up Crab Alley Bay past Johnson Is.

Marina Facilities *(In Season/Off Season)*

Fuel: *Citgo* - Gasoline
Slips: 40 Total, 2 Transient **Max LOA:** 48 ft. **Max Beam:** 15 ft.
Rate *(per ft.)*: **Day** $2.00/1 **Week** $5 **Month** $10
Power: 30 amp $5, **50 amp** $10, **100 amp** n/a, **200 amp** n/a
Cable TV: No **Dockside Phone:** No
Dock Type: Fixed, Long Fingers, Wood
Moorings: 0 Total, 0 Transient **Launch:** n/a, Dinghy Dock
Rate: Day n/a **Week** n/a **Month** n/a
Heads: 6 Toilet(s), 6 Shower(s) *(with dressing rooms)*
Laundry: None **Pay Phones:** No
Pump-Out: OnSite, Full Service, 1 Central **Fee:** $5 **Closed Heads:** Yes

Marina Operations

Owner/Manager: Bruzz & Maxine Ritter **Dockmaster:** Same
In-Season: Year-Round, 7am-7pm **Off-Season:** n/a
After-Hours Arrival: Call ahead
Reservations: Preferred **Credit Cards:** Visa/MC
Discounts: None
Pets: Welcome, Dog Walk Area **Handicap Access:** No

Marina Services and Boat Supplies

Services - Docking Assistance, Security *(24 hrs., owners live on premises)*, Trash Pick-Up, Dock Carts **Communication -** Fax in/out *($2)*, FedEx, UPS, Express Mail **Supplies - OnSite:** Ice *(Block, Cube)*, Ships' Store **1-3 mi:** Propane *(Kent Island Mobil 643-5277)* **3+ mi:** West Marine *(604-1752, 3 mi.)*, Boater's World *(604-2613, 6 mi.)*, Bait/Tackle *(Island Fishing & Hunting 643-4224, 4 mi.)*

Boatyard Services

OnSite: Travelift *(25T)*, Forklift, Launching Ramp, Engine mechanic *(gas, diesel)*, Electrical Repairs, Hull Repairs, Bottom Cleaning, Compound, Wash & Wax, Propeller Repairs, Woodworking, Metal Fabrication **OnCall:** Rigger, Sail Loft, Canvas Work, Air Conditioning, Refrigeration, Divers, Interior Cleaning, Upholstery **Yard Rates:** $65/hr., Haul & Launch $6/ft. *(blocking $3/ft.)*, Power Wash $3, Bottom Paint $16/ft. *(paint incl.)* **Storage:** On-Land $3/ft./mo.

Restaurants and Accommodations

OnCall: Pizzeria *(Domino's 643-3002)* **1-3 mi:** Restaurant *(Lighthouse 604-3344)* **3+ mi:** Restaurant *(Narrows 827-8113, D $13-26, 5 mi.)*, *(Black-Eyed Susan 778-1214, 3 mi.)*, *(Fishermans Inn 827-8807, L $9-28, D $11-30, 5 mi.)*, *(B&B Family Restaurant 604-0035, L $3-11, D $3-12, 3 mi.)*, *(Island Beef & BBQ 604-2333, L $6-8, 3 mi.)*, Fast Food *(Subway, Hardee's 4 mi.)*, Pizzeria *(Ledos 643-7979, 3 mi.)*, *(Benvenuti 604-2123, 3 mi.)*, Motel *(Comfort Inn Kent Narrows 827-6767, $76-140, 5 mi.)*, Hotel *(Hilton Garden Inn 827-3877, 5 mi.)*, Inn/B&B *(Kent Manor Inn 643-5757, $135-215, 6 mi.)*

Recreation and Entertainment

Near: Boat Rentals **3+ mi:** Golf Course *(Queenstown Harbor Golf 827-6611, 10 mi.)*, Fitness Center *(Club One 643-3488, 4 mi.)*, Video Rental *(Blockbuster 643-8400, 3 mi.)*

Provisioning and General Services

Under 1 mi: Convenience Store *(7-Eleven 643-3369)* **1-3 mi:** Supermarket *(Safeway 643-4919, or Food Lion 643-9687, 5 mi.)*, Bank/ATM, Catholic Church, Protestant Church, Barber Shop, Dry Cleaners, Laundry, Florist, Retail Shops **3+ mi:** Wine/Beer *(L&L 643-2455, 4 mi.)*, Liquor Store *(Baker's 643-5851, 3 mi.)*, Bakery *(4 mi.)*, Farmers' Market *(4 mi.)*, Post Office *(643-6488, 3 mi.)*, Library *(Stevensville 643-8161, 5 mi.)*, Beauty Salon *(Allure Salon & Day Spa 643-8890, 3 mi.)*, Pharmacy *(Rite Aid 604-2337, 3 mi.)*, Hardware Store *(Kent Island True Value 643-3500, 3 mi.)*

Transportation

OnCall: Rental Car *(Enterprise 604-6154, Total Car 604-2529)*, Taxi *(Kent Island 604-0486)*, Airport Limo *(Associated Sedan 643-1500)*
Airport: Baltimore-Washington Int'l./Bay Bridge *(50 mi./7 mi.)*

Medical Services

911 Service **OnCall:** Ambulance **1-3 mi:** Dentist *(Olmstead 643-7367)*, Holistic Services *(Mid-Shore Massage 643-9910)*, Veterinarian *(Kent Island Veterinary 643-4204)* **3+ mi:** Doctor *(Queen Anne's Medical 643-6205, 3 mi.)*, Chiropractor *(Jennings Chiropractic 643-7100, 3 mi.)*
Hospital: Anne Arundel 267-1000 *(19 mi.)*

Setting -- This small marina, with one main pier and a T-head, sits off the southern end of the Narrows, up Crab Alley Bay. Its name stems from the bucolic views of four near and distant islands: Johnson Island (which it is just beyond), Bodkin Island, Little Island, and Parsons Island. Landside is a small boatyard operation, the main office, in a white two-story colonial with gray-blue trim, the bathhouse, and a dry storage area.

Marina Notes -- A family operation founded in 1985. The owners live on site, providing excellent security, and obviously take enormous pride of place. Small boatyard operation with good size lift. ACC's policy dictates no pictures of heads, but we are making an exception. At Island View, what looks like a boaters' lounge is the bathhouse - three sinks sit in a vanity with beautifully varnished trim. Every toiletry imaginable sits on a rack. It's nicely decorated and furnished, with a comfortable sofa, lamps, interesting (and current!) reading matter, wall-to-wall carpeting, and all kinds of fun and funny little tchotchkes - all absolutely immaculate. The men's is as nice as the women's. Every effort has been made to make boaters comfortable.

Notable -- The surrounding area - both on the water and on land - is very rural, and most of the other docks belong to watermen. Right next door is Skipjack Landing Marine, which does not take transients, but can offer boatyard services in addition to those of Island View. Little is nearby, but there are taxis and rental cars that deliver. Island View invites a day of relaxation or dinghy tour of the river islands.

PHOTOS ON CD-ROM: 9

Navigational Information
Lat: 39°06.617' **Long:** 076°12.717' **Tide:** 2 ft. **Current:** 2 kts. **Chart:** 12273
Rep. Depths (*MLW*): Entry 9.5 ft. **Fuel Dock** 9 ft. **Max Slip/Moor** 9 ft./-
Access: Chester River to Nerrington Creek

Marina Facilities *(In Season/Off Season)*
Fuel: Gasoline
Slips: 31 Total, 1 Transient **Max LOA:** 50 ft. **Max Beam:** n/a
Rate *(per ft.)*: **Day** $2.00 **Week** *$100 **Month** n/a
Power: 30 amp Incl., **50 amp** n/a, **100 amp** n/a, **200 amp** n/a
Cable TV: No **Dockside Phone:** No
Dock Type: Fixed, Long Fingers, Wood
Moorings: 0 Total, 0 Transient **Launch:** n/a
Rate: Day n/a **Week** n/a **Month** n/a
Heads: 2 Toilet(s), 2 Shower(s)
Laundry: None **Pay Phones:** No
Pump-Out: No **Fee:** n/a **Closed Heads:** Yes

Marina Operations
Owner/Manager: Doug Hill **Dockmaster:** Same
In-Season: May-Oct, 8am-5pm **Off-Season:** Nov-Apr, 8am-12pm
After-Hours Arrival: Call ahead
Reservations: No **Credit Cards:** n/a
Discounts: None
Pets: Welcome **Handicap Access:** Yes

Hill's Marine Railway

4866 Skinner's Neck Road; Rock Hall, MD 21661

Tel: (410) 639-7267 **VHF: Monitor** n/a **Talk** n/a
Fax: n/a **Alternate Tel:** n/a
Email: n/a **Web:** n/a
Nearest Town: Rock Hall *(3 mi.)* **Tourist Info:** (410) 639-7611

Marina Services and Boat Supplies
Services - Security *(Owner lives on premises)*, Trash Pick-Up, Dock Carts **Communication -** Phone Messages, FedEx, UPS, Express Mail **Supplies - OnSite:** Ice *(Cube)*, Ships' Store **1-3 mi:** West Marine *(639-9959)*, Boater's World, Bait/Tackle *(Toy's Outdoor Store 778-2561)*, Live Bait *(J & J Seafood 639-2325)*, Propane *(Bayside Gas 778-2787)*

Boatyard Services
OnSite: Railway, Engine mechanic *(gas)*, Electrical Repairs, Hull Repairs, Bottom Cleaning, Brightwork, Compound, Wash & Wax, Woodworking **Near:** Canvas Work, Upholstery. **Under 1 mi:** Divers, Propeller Repairs, Painting.

Restaurants and Accommodations
1-3 mi: Restaurant *(Bay Wolf 639-2000, L $7-9, D $17-21)*, *(Bay Way 639-2000)*, *(P.S. Pruitt's 639-7454, L $7-11, D $12-26, delivers to the marinas Thu-Sun 11am-7pm)*, *(Waterman's Crab House 639-2261, L $5-16, D $5-16, crab feasts Tue & Thu)*, Lite Fare *(Pasta Plus 639-7916, B $2-6, L $3-7, D $3-8)*, *(Dockside Café 639-2478)*, Pizzeria *(Chessie's 639-7727, Carryout)*, Motel *(Mariner's 639-2291, $75-85)*, Inn/B&B *(Swan Haven B&B 639-2527, $105-158)*, *(Black Duck Inn 639-2478, Sunday brunch from 7:30am-1pm)*, *(Inn at Osprey 639-2194, $150-200)*

Recreation and Entertainment
OnSite: Picnic Area, Grills **1-3 mi:** Park *(Bayside Landing Park 778-7439)*, Museum *(Waterman's Museum 778-6697; Rock Hall Museum 639-7611 Sat, Sun, Hols 11am-3pm)*, Cultural Attract *(The Mainstay 639-9133 - regional & nat'l - blues, jazz, bluegrass)*

Provisioning and General Services
1-3 mi: Convenience Store *(Caulk's Field One Stop 778-4373)*, Supermarket *(Bayside Foods 639-2552 7am-10pm 7 days)*, Gourmet Shop *(Bayleaf Gourmet 639-2700)*, Wine/Beer, Liquor Store *(Rock Hall Liquors 639-2177)*, Bakery, Fishmonger *(J & J Seafood 639-2325)*, Market *(Bayside Foods 639-2552)*, Bank/ATM, Post Office *(639-7054)*, Catholic Church, Protestant Church, Library *(639-7162)*, Beauty Salon *(Mirror Image 639-2377)*, Laundry *(Jesse's Laundromat)*, Pharmacy *(Happy Harry's 639-9140)*, Newsstand, Hardware Store *(Village 639-7014)*, Florist *(Eagle Hill Florist 639-2230)*

Transportation
OnCall: Rental Car *(Enterprise 810-0971)*, Airport Limo *(Prince 778-4860)*
Near: Local Bus *(639-7996 $3/1 to Chestertown $5 round-trip)*
3+ mi: Rail *(Amtrak Caudon Bridge 642-2620, 60 mi.)*
Airport: Baltimore-Washington Int'l/Bay Bridge *(70 mi./45 mi.)*

Medical Services
911 Service **OnCall:** Ambulance **1-3 mi:** Doctor *(Seymour 778-6335)*, Dentist *(Roth 778-1234)*, Veterinarian *(Hall 639-7084)*
Hospital: Kent & Queen Anne's 778-3300

Setting -- Hill's is a real step back in time, surrounded by the pristine waters of Nerrington Creek. A perfect place to "pull off the road" and spend the evening tied to a tranquil dock. Pleasure craft share the docks with commercial fishing boats. The other wharfs along this side of the creek are all occupied by waterman's boats. The far side of the creek is untouched - the verdant views are of marsh backed by dense forest.

Marina Notes -- *Flat rate for week. Family owned and operated since 1952. The owner lives on site, in the next house up from the marina. One of the oldest marinas in the Rock Hall area, it has a railway for haulout. Two docks with slips have power on the posts at the end of the two-third length finger pier. Gas only at the fuel dock. A waterside screened gazebo has tables and chairs and a new propane grill inside, plus a picnic table outside. Note: According to the owners, Hill's may be for sale - so call first to ensure it is still operating.

Notable -- A pleasant respite from the hubbub of many other Bay tie-ups, this rustic, out-of-the-way spot promises peace and quiet with few amenities. Inquire of the local watermen if they will sell direct form their boats (they tend to return midday to 2 pm) - a crab feast in the cockpit surrounded by this glorious piece of quiet is an increasingly rare opportunity. Especially when more developed civilization is a mere three miles away. Thanks to the trolley, which will stop here on request, Rock Hall's useful services, supplies and interesting restaurants are a short ride.

PHOTOS ON CD-ROM: 7

Long Cove Marina

22589 Hudson Road; Rock Hall, MD 21661

Tel: (410) 778-6777 **VHF: Monitor** 16 **Talk** n/a
Fax: (410) 778-9400 **Alternate Tel:** n/a
Email: n/a **Web:** n/a
Nearest Town: Rock Hall *(5 mi.)* **Tourist Info:** (410) 639-7611

Navigational Information
Lat: 39°06.533' **Long:** 076°11.383' **Tide:** n/a **Current:** n/a **Chart:** 12272
Rep. Depths (*MLW*): Entry 6 ft. **Fuel Dock** 7 ft. **Max Slip/Moor** 6 ft./-
Access: Chester River to Langford Creek to Long Cove

Marina Facilities *(In Season/Off Season)*
Fuel: Slip-Side Fueling, Gasoline, Diesel
Slips: 106 Total, 10 Transient **Max LOA:** 50 ft. **Max Beam:** 16 ft.
Rate *(per ft.)*: **Day** $1.50 **Week** n/a **Month** n/a
Power: 30 amp $3, **50 amp** Inq., **100 amp** n/a, **200 amp** n/a
Cable TV: No **Dockside Phone:** No
Dock Type: Fixed, Short Fingers, Wood
Moorings: 12 Total, 6 Transient **Launch:** n/a
Rate: Day Inq. **Week** Inq. **Month** $1.50/ft.
Heads: 6 Toilet(s), 6 Shower(s) *(with dressing rooms)*
Laundry: None **Pay Phones:** No
Pump-Out: OnSite, Full Service **Fee:** $5 **Closed Heads:** Yes

Marina Operations
Owner/Manager: Mort and Maria Deckelman **Dockmaster:** Same
In-Season: May-Oct, Mon-Sun,9am-5pm **Off-Season:** Nov-Apr, 9am-4pm
After-Hours Arrival: Call ahead
Reservations: Preferred **Credit Cards:** Visa/MC
Discounts: None
Pets: Welcome, Dog Walk Area **Handicap Access:** No

Marina Services and Boat Supplies
Services - Docking Assistance, Trash Pick-Up, Dock Carts **Communication -** FedEx, UPS, Express Mail **Supplies - OnSite:** Ice *(Block, Cube)*, Ships' Store **3+ mi:** West Marine *(639-9959, 5 mi.)*, Bait/Tackle *(Toy's Outdoor Store 778-2561, 5 mi.)*, Propane *(Bayside Gas 778-2787, 4 mi.)*, CNG *(Sailing Emporium 778-1342, 5 mi.)*

Boatyard Services
OnSite: Travelift *(25T/70T)*, Engine mechanic *(gas, diesel)*, Electrical Repairs, Hull Repairs, Bottom Cleaning, Compound, Wash & Wax, Propeller Repairs, Woodworking, Metal Fabrication **OnCall:** Canvas Work, Air Conditioning, Divers, Inflatable Repairs, Upholstery, Yacht Interiors **Near:** Launching Ramp. **Yard Rates:** $60/hr., Bottom Paint $8/ft.

Restaurants and Accommodations
1-3 mi: Restaurant *(Bay Wolf 639-2000, L $7-9, D $17-20)*, *(Main Street Bar & Grill 639-7500, L $7-9, D $7-25)*, *(Chessie's Restaurant 639-7727, L $7-10 D $8-18, pizza is the specialty)*, Seafood Shack *(Ford's Seafood 639-2032)*, *(J & J Seafood 639-2325, L $4-18, Recommended as the best in town - closes at 6pm, Fri & Sat 'til 7pm)* **3+ mi:** Restaurant *(Old Oars Inn 639-2541, 639-2541, 5 mi.)*, Inn/B&B *(Bay Breeze Inn 639-2061, $90-150, 5 mi.)*, *(Black Duck Inn 639-2478, $98-120, 5 mi.)*, *(Carriage House B&B 639-2855, $125, 5 mi.)*, Condo/Cottage *(Inn at Osprey Point 639-2194, $90-200, 5 mi.)*

Recreation and Entertainment
OnSite: Picnic Area, Grills *(charcoal)* **3+ mi:** Boat Rentals *(5 mi.)*, Fishing Charter *(5 mi.)*, Park *(5 mi.)*, Museum *(Rock Hall Museum, weekends 11am-3pm, 5 mi.)*, Cultural Attract *(The Mainstay 639-9133 - regional & nat'l - blues, jazz, bluegrass, 5 mi.)*, Galleries *(Reuben Rodney 639-2494, 5 mi.)*, Special Events *(Rock Hall's Party on the Bay; mid Aug & Fall Fest in late Sep., 5 mi.)*

Provisioning and General Services
3+ mi: Convenience Store *(Shore Stop 639-7441, 5 mi.)*, Supermarket *(Bayside Foods 639-2552 7am-10pm 7 days, 5 mi.)*, Liquor Store *(Rock Hall 639-2177, 4 mi.)*, Market *(Bayside Foods 639-2552, 5 mi.)*, Bank/ATM *(5 mi.)*, Post Office *(5 mi.)*, Catholic Church *(5 mi.)*, Library *(Rock Hall 639-7162, 5 mi.)*, Dry Cleaners *(5 mi.)*, Pharmacy *(Harry's Discount Drug Store 639-9140, 4 mi.)*, Hardware Store *(Village Hardware & Garden 639-7014, 4 mi.)*

Transportation
OnCall: Rental Car *(Enterprise 810-0971)*, Local Bus *(Rock Hall Trolley 639-7996 $3/1-day or $5 round-trip)*
Airport: Baltimore-Washington Int'l./Bay Bridge *(70 mi./45 mi.)*

Medical Services
911 Service **1-3 mi:** Dentist *(Fallowfield 639-7987)* **3+ mi:** Doctor *(Rock Hall Medical Center 639-2221, 4 mi.)*, Veterinarian *(Kent County Vet 639-7084, 4 mi.)* **Hospital:** Kent & Queen Anne's 778-3300 *(16 mi.)*

Setting -- Just past green "3" on Langford Creek, the docks are tucked half way up Long Cove on the western side. Four sets of pleasure craft docks and several sets of commercial waterman's docks are separated by a large travelift haul out bay. Across the cove, the land is untouched and bucolic. Upland from the docks, it's all boatyard. On a small rise are a lovely tree-shaded picnic area, a huge, pale-blue work and storage shed, extensive on-the-hard storage, and a separate single story pale-blue clapboard bathhouse.

Marina Notes -- *Off-season, closed on Sundays. Long Cove hauls and stores some very good-sized boats - there are two haul out bays and two travelifts - 25 & 70 tons. A fairly well-equipped ships' store is in the office. The stationary docks are new, and the gangplank down to them has very attractive rope railings, nicely done. There are wide half finger piers, and power connections are on the finger pier posts. New covered docks were just built for the '05 season. Long Cove also operates the 35-ft. tow-boat called "Popeye." The bathhouse has three complete bathrooms for men and three for women.

Notable -- There are three sets of picnic areas; the best one is on a little rise above the middle docks. Two charcoal grills, two picnic tables, and a bench sit under a huge spreading maple tree. More picnic tables and a charcoal grill are on a cement terrace overlooking the second set of docks, next to the office. The Rock Hall Trolley will stop "on call" and also makes scheduled trips up to Chestertown.

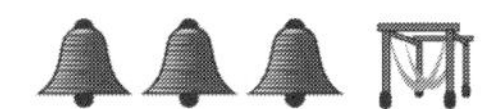

Navigational Information
Lat: 39°07.127' **Long:** 076°10.470' **Tide:** 3 ft. **Current:** n/a **Chart:** 12272
Rep. Depths (*MLW*): Entry 7 ft. **Fuel Dock** 6 ft. **Max Slip/Moor** 8 ft./7 ft.
Access: Chester River to Green #7 Lankford Creek to day marker #2 to Davis

Marina Facilities *(In Season/Off Season)*
Fuel: *Chevron* - Gasoline, Diesel, High-Speed Pumps
Slips: 105 Total, 10 Transient **Max LOA:** 50 ft. **Max Beam:** 15 ft.
Rate *(per ft.)*: **Day** $1.75/1.50 **Week** Inq. **Month** Inq.
Power: 30 amp $5, **50 amp** $10, **100 amp** n/a, **200 amp** n/a
Cable TV: No **Dockside Phone:** No
Dock Type: Fixed, Long Fingers, Alongside, Wood
Moorings: 23 Total, 5 Transient **Launch:** Yes, Dinghy Dock
Rate: Day $25 **Week** $100 **Month** $300
Heads: 6 Toilet(s), 6 Shower(s)
Laundry: 1 Washer(s), 1 Dryer(s) **Pay Phones:** Yes, 1
Pump-Out: OnSite, Self Service **Fee:** $5 **Closed Heads:** Yes

Marina Operations
Owner/Manager: Douglas Edwards **Dockmaster:** John A. Groves
In-Season: Mar-Nov, 8am-4:30pm **Off-Season:** Dec-Feb, 8am-4pm*
After-Hours Arrival: Call ahead for instructions
Reservations: Yes, Preferred **Credit Cards:** Visa/MC
Discounts: None
Pets: Welcome, Dog Walk Area **Handicap Access:** Yes, Heads

Lankford Bay Marina

23002 McKinleyville Road; Rock Hall, MD 21661

Tel: (410) 778-1414 **VHF: Monitor** 16 **Talk** 71
Fax: (410) 639-2547 **Alternate Tel:** n/a
Email: lankford@intercom.net **Web:** www.chesapeake-bay.com/lankford
Nearest Town: Rock Hall *(5 mi.)* **Tourist Info:** (410) 639-7611

Marina Services and Boat Supplies
Services - Docking Assistance, Trash Pick-Up, Dock Carts **Communication -** Mail & Package Hold, Phone Messages, Fax in/out *($1)*, FedEx, UPS, Express Mail **Supplies - OnSite:** Ice *(Block, Cube)*, Ships' Store, Bait/Tackle **3+ mi:** West Marine *(639-9959, 5 mi.)*, Propane *(Village Hardware 639-7014, 5 mi.)*, CNG *(Sailing Emporium 778-1342, 5 mi.)*

Boatyard Services
OnSite: Travelift *(40T)*, Engine mechanic *(gas, diesel)*, Bottom Cleaning, Brightwork, Compound, Wash & Wax, Interior Cleaning **OnCall:** Electrical Repairs *(Hyland Marine 810-1979)*, Electronics Repairs, Hull Repairs, Rigger *(Atlantic Spears 269-6042)*, Sail Loft *(Meade Breese 639-2646)*, Canvas Work, Air Conditioning *(Miller Marine 778-5951)*, Refrigeration, Divers *(Ricks Marine 639-7367)*, Propeller Repairs, Woodworking, Inflatable Repairs *(Inflatable Boat Repair 701-3386)*, Life Raft Service, Metal Fabrication, **Near:** Launching Ramp. **Member:** ABBRA, ABYC **Yard Rates:** $60/hr., Haul & Launch $13/ft. *(blocking incl.)*, Power Wash Incl.

Restaurants and Accommodations
Near: Restaurant *(Jesse's Steak and Pub)*, Seafood Shack *(J&J Seafood)*, Pizzeria *(Pasta Plus 639-7916)* **3+ mi:** Restaurant *(P.E. Pruitt 639-7454, D $10-25, 5 mi.)*, *(Bay Wolf 639-2000, L $7-9, D $17-20, 5 mi.)*, *(Swan Point Inn 639-2500, 5 mi.)*, *(Chessie's Restaurant 639-7727, L $7-10, D $8-18, 5 mi., specialty is pizza)*, *(Old Wharf Inn 778-3566, L $6-10, D $8-20, 5 mi., seafood platter highly recommended)*, Seafood Shack *(Ford's Seafood 639-2032, 5 mi.)*, Inn/B&B *(Black Duck Inn 639-2478, $98-120, 5 mi.)*, *(Tallulah's On Main 639-2596, 5 mi.)*, *(Carriage House B&B 639-2855, $125, 5 mi.)*

Recreation and Entertainment
OnSite: Pool, Beach, Picnic Area, Grills *(charcoal)*, Playground, Jogging Paths, Roller Blade/Bike Paths **3+ mi:** Tennis Courts *(5 mi.)*, Boat Rentals *(5 mi.)*, Fishing Charter *(5 mi.)*, Park *(5 mi.)*, Museum *(Rock Hall Museum, weekends 11am-3pm, 5 mi.)*, Cultural Attract *(The Mainstay, 5 mi.)*, Galleries *(Reuben Rodney 639-2494, 5 mi.)*

Provisioning and General Services
OnSite: Crabs/Waterman **3+ mi:** Convenience Store *(Shore Stop 639-7441, 4 mi.)*, Supermarket *(Bayside Foods 639-2552 7am-10pm 7 days, 4 mi.)*, Liquor Store *(Rock Hall Liquors 639-2177, 4 mi.)*, Bakery *(5 mi.)*, Bank/ATM *(5 mi.)*, Post Office *(5 mi.)*, Protestant Church *(5 mi.)*, Library *(Rock Hall 639-7162, 5 mi.)*, Dry Cleaners *(5 mi.)*, Pharmacy *(Harry's Drug Store 639-9140, 5 mi.)*, Hardware Store *(Ace Hardware Store 639-7014, 4 mi.)*, Retail Shops *(5 mi.)*

Transportation
OnSite: Bikes **OnCall:** Rental Car *(Enterprise 810-0971, or Geno's 778-0131, 12 mi.)*, Local Bus *(Rock Hall Trolley 639-7996 $3/1-day or $5 round-trip)* **3+ mi:** Taxi *(45 mi.)*
Airport: Baltimore-Washington Int'l./Bay Bridge *(70 mi./45 mi.)*

Medical Services
911 Service **OnCall:** Ambulance **3+ mi:** Doctor *(Rock Hall Medical 639-2221, 5 mi.)*, Dentist *(Fallowfield 639-7987, 4 mi.)*, Veterinarian *(Kent County Veterinary 639-7084, 4 mi.)*
Hospital: Kent & Queen Anne's 778-3300 *(16 mi.)*

Setting -- At the nexus of Davis and Lankford Creeks, 105 slips and 23 moorings beckon boaters to this picturesque, quiet country setting accompanied by appropriately low-key, well-managed and intelligently designed resort-style facilities. Anchoring the main dock is the blue-gray barn-roofed main building, trimmed with white and accented with a deep red door, colorful banners, and a plethora of flowers. The views from the slips, the picnic areas, the small hexagonal pool and the "tone-setting" hammocks are wide open and pristine. On "C" dock, there's a comfortable bench to watch the boats come in.

Marina Notes -- *Closed on weekends in the off-season. Built in 1949, owned and operated by the same service-oriented family for over 50 years. Second-generation of Edwards' are at the helm. All the docks, except the one main dock that goes straight out from the office building, have full-length finger piers. An extremely well-equipped ships' store with bins and bins of all kinds of screws, nuts and bolts is on-site. One of the large work sheds is also a boathouse. Extensive on-the-hard storage. Dedicated pumpout dock. Mooring field launch. Staff will arrange people or food deliveries when the trolley's not running, so this bucolic environment does not mean a lack of contact with civilization. Accommodates group cruises. Lovely heads have their own separate bathhouse.

Notable -- On a nicely landscaped rise, a small hexagonal, terraced pool overlooks the marina; it's edged with ocean-liner-style railings and has magnificent vistas out to the Creek - especially at sunset. A new pavilion is being built to take advantage of the same views. Nearby are a shaded picnic area with charcoal grills, a "porch" swing, and a play gym. Along the grassed bulkhead that fronts the basin is another picnic area. A tiny sand beach encourages wading.

PHOTOS ON CD-ROM: 16

Kennersley Point Marina

223 Marina Lane; Church Hill, MD 21623

Tel: (410) 758-2394 **VHF: Monitor** n/a **Talk** n/a
Fax: (410) 556-6446 **Alternate Tel:** n/a
Email: kenpoint@dmv.com **Web:** n/a
Nearest Town: Chestertown *(11 mi.)* **Tourist Info:** (410) 810-2968

Navigational Information

Lat: 39°09.080' **Long:** 076°02.230' **Tide:** 2 ft. **Current:** 1 kt. **Chart:** 12272
Rep. Depths (*MLW*): Entry 3 ft. **Fuel Dock** n/a **Max Slip/Moor** 6 ft./4 ft.
Access: Chester River to Red "2", east to Island Creek on starboard

Marina Facilities *(In Season/Off Season)*

Fuel: No
Slips: 75 Total, 4 Transient **Max LOA:** 60 ft. **Max Beam:** n/a
Rate *(per ft.)*: **Day** $1.00 **Week** n/a **Month** n/a
Power: 30 amp $3, **50 amp** $5, **100 amp** n/a, **200 amp** n/a
Cable TV: No **Dockside Phone:** Yes
Dock Type: Fixed, Short Fingers, Pilings, Wood
Moorings: 0 Total, 0 Transient **Launch:** n/a
Rate: Day n/a **Week** n/a **Month** n/a
Heads: 4 Toilet(s), 4 Shower(s) *(with dressing rooms)*
Laundry: 1 Washer(s), 2 Dryer(s), Book Exchange **Pay Phones:** No
Pump-Out: 1 Central **Fee:** $5 **Closed Heads:** Yes

Marina Operations

Owner/Manager: Philip Donahue **Dockmaster:** Same
In-Season: Year-Round **Off-Season:** n/a
After-Hours Arrival: Call ahead
Reservations: Yes, Required **Credit Cards:** Visa/MC
Discounts: None
Pets: Welcome **Handicap Access:** No

Marina Services and Boat Supplies

Services - Docking Assistance, Concierge, Security *(24 hrs.)*, Trash Pick-Up, Dock Carts **Communication -** Mail & Package Hold, Phone Messages, Fax in/out **Supplies - OnSite:** Ice *(Block, Cube)*, Ships' Store **3+ mi:** Propane *(Suburban Propane 758-1200, 10 mi.)*

Boatyard Services

OnSite: Travelift *(25T)*, Launching Ramp, Engine mechanic *(gas, diesel)*, Electrical Repairs, Hull Repairs, Rigger, Bottom Cleaning, Brightwork **OnCall:** Air Conditioning, Refrigeration, Compound, Wash & Wax, Interior Cleaning, Propeller Repairs **Dealer for:** Electric Launch Company (ELCO). **Yard Rates:** $50/hr., Haul & Launch $4/ft. *(blocking $1.50/ft.)*, Power Wash $1.50/ft.

Restaurants and Accommodations

1-3 mi: Inn/B&B *(Courtyard Inn 778-2755, $55-95), (Claddaugh Farm B&B 778-4894, $95-110)* **3+ mi:** Restaurant *(Joe Dave's Restaurant 778-3354, 11 mi.), (Ellen's Family Restaurant 810-1992, 5 mi.), (Chessie's Restaurant 639-7727, L $7-10, D $8-18, 11 mi.), (Bay Wolf 639-2000, L $7-9, D $17-20, 11 mi.), (Old Wharf Inn 778-3566, L $6-10, D $8-20, 11 mi., seafood platter highly recommended), (Andy's 778-6779, 11 mi.)*, Lite Fare *(Ethel's Sub Shop 556-6388, 5 mi.)*, Pizzeria *(Roma Pizza 810-3331, 9 mi.)*, Hotel *(Imperial Hotel 778-5000, $125-200, 5 mi.)*

Recreation and Entertainment

OnSite: Pool, Beach, Picnic Area, Grills, Playground *(and horseshoes)* **3+ mi:** Fitness Center *(Curves for Women 810-1011, 11 mi.)*, Movie Theater *(Chester 5 Theatres 778-2227, 12 mi.)*, Video Rental *(Video Shop 758-2935, 10 mi.)*

Provisioning and General Services

OnSite: Convenience Store *(snacks, sodas, boat supplies)* **1-3 mi:** Bank/ATM, Post Office **3+ mi:** Supermarket *(Acme 778-5641, 11 mi.)*, Delicatessen *(C-Town Deli 778-3119, 11 mi.)*, Health Food *(Chestertown Natural Foods 778-1677, 11 mi.)*, Liquor Store *(C-Town Liquors 778-2988, 12 mi.)*, Market *(Rhodes Store 556-6355, 5 mi.)*, Library *(Chestertown 778-3636, 11 mi.)*, Pharmacy *(Chestertown 778-2575, 11 mi.)*, Hardware Store *(JBK True Value 778-9600, 12 mi.)*

Transportation

OnSite: Courtesy Car/Van *(No charge)* **OnCall:** Rental Car *(Enterprise 810-0971)*, Taxi *(Country Sedan 810-0139)*, Airport Limo *(Prince 778-4860)*
Airport: Baltimore-Washington Int'l./Bay Bridge *(50 mi./30 mi.)*

Medical Services

911 Service **3+ mi:** Doctor *(Bay River Medical 758-3103, 10 mi.)*, Chiropractor *(Chesapeake Chiropractic Clinic 556-6377, 4 mi.)*, Holistic Services *(Chester River Massage 778-6735 R 11 mi., 11 mi.)*, Veterinarian *(Eastern Shore 778-1200, 8 mi.)*
Hospital: Kent & Queen Anne's 778-3300 *(10 mi.)*

Setting -- Down-home and casual, Kennersely Point has a comfy club atmosphere in a beautiful spot tucked up Island Creek, just off the Chester River. Ten quiet, rural acres provide a land-base for the 75 slips on two docks that line a boardwalk parallel to the shoreline. The environment is natural - well maintained but not manicured - and feels just right. The paths are edged with impatiens backed by shrubs and some perennial borders. Wildlife abounds.

Marina Notes -- Owners live onsite. The office, which has basic boat supplies, sodas, and snacks, is right off the main dock; it's "managed" by a delightful quartet of friendly canines. Extensive grounds for storage on-the-hard; many boats, on poppets or trailers, are tucked in here and there. If you need marine services, KPM can likely help. A washer and dryer are in the clubhouse next to the office. The heated and air-conditioned bathhouse is adjacent to the rustic picnic pavilion; two private shower rooms with dressing rooms and doors, two heads, two sinks. It's linoleum and Formica, but it's still inviting.

Notable -- A large pool is furnished with recent umbrella-topped tables and blue and white chairs and chaises. Scattered around the property, picnic tables and an occasional bench invite a quiet moment as do horseshoe pits, a small playground, and a huge vegetable garden. The docks are based on a wharf that was part of an early 18th C. estate. This is a place for a quiet respite - bring your books, stretch out, and enjoy the completely unspoiled creek. Eat aboard, swim in the lovely pool, or stroll the grounds. By land, it's a very long way to anywhere; but take a walk down tree-lined Kennersley Farm Lane for spectacular views of acres of fenced fields with crops and horses.

PHOTOS ON CD-ROM: 15

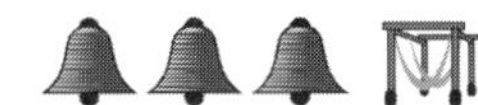

Navigational Information
Lat: 39°10.433' **Long:** 076°02.233' **Tide:** 4 ft. **Current:** 3 kt. **Chart:** 12272
Rep. Depths (*MLW*): Entry 23 ft. **Fuel Dock** 11 ft. **Max Slip/Moor** 12 ft./15 ft.
Access: Chester River north to Buoy 35

Marina Facilities *(In Season/Off Season)*
Fuel: Gasoline, Diesel, High-Speed Pumps
Slips: 40 Total, 15 Transient **Max LOA:** 50 ft. **Max Beam:** 15 ft.
Rate *(per ft.)*: **Day** $1.50 **Week** n/a **Month** n/a
Power: 30 amp $5, **50 amp** $10, **100 amp** n/a, **200 amp** n/a
Cable TV: No **Dockside Phone:** No
Dock Type: Fixed, Short Fingers, Pilings, Wood
Moorings: 10 Total, 8 Transient **Launch:** No, Dinghy Dock (None)
Rate: Day $1.50 **Week** n/a **Month** n/a
Heads: 6 Toilet(s), 4 Shower(s) *(with dressing rooms)*
Laundry: 2 Washer(s), 2 Dryer(s) **Pay Phones:** No
Pump-Out: Self Service, 1 Central **Fee:** $5 **Closed Heads:** Yes

Marina Operations
Owner/Manager: Chip Dreibelbis **Dockmaster:** Same
In-Season: May-Oct, 8am-5pm* **Off-Season:** Nov-Apr, Closed
After-Hours Arrival: Tie-up and report to office next morning
Reservations: Required **Credit Cards:** Visa/MC, Dscvr, Amex
Discounts: None
Pets: Welcome, Dog Walk Area **Handicap Access:** Yes

Rolph's Wharf Marina

1008 Rolph's Wharf Road; Chestertown, MD 21620

Tel: (410) 778-6389; (800) 894-6347 **VHF: Monitor** 16 **Talk** 68
Fax: (410) 778-1757 **Alternate Tel:** n/a
Email: rolphs@aol.com **Web:** www.rolphswharf.com
Nearest Town: Chestertown *(4 mi.)* **Tourist Info:** (410) 810-2968

Marina Services and Boat Supplies
Services - Docking Assistance, Security *(24 hrs., Live on premises)*, Trash Pick-Up, Dock Carts **Communication -** Mail & Package Hold, Phone Messages, FedEx, UPS, Express Mail **Supplies - OnSite:** Ice *(Block, Cube)*, Ships' Store, Bait/Tackle, Live Bait *(bloodworms, nitecrawlers)* **1-3 mi:** Propane *(Kingstown Tractor)*

Boatyard Services
OnSite: Travelift *(25T)*, Launching Ramp, Engine mechanic *(gas, diesel)*, Hull Repairs, Bottom Cleaning, Brightwork, Compound, Wash & Wax, Interior Cleaning, Propeller Repairs, Metal Fabrication, Painting **OnCall:** Electrical Repairs, Electronics Repairs, Air Conditioning, Refrigeration, Divers **Near:** Rigger. **Dealer for:** Mercury. **Yard Rates:** $55/hr., Haul & Launch $5/ft. *(blocking $45)*, Bottom Paint $10/ft. *(paint incl.)* **Storage:** In-Water $19/ft.

Restaurants and Accommodations
OnSite: Snack Bar *(Sandbar 778-6389, L $2-7, D $2-7, Thu 5-10pm, Fri 5pm-1am, Sat-Sun Noon-11pm - sandwiches & baskets)*, Lite Fare *(River Inn 778-6389, B Complimentary)*, Inn/B&B *(The River Inn 800-894-6347, $105-125)* **OnCall:** Pizzeria *(Domino's 810-3811)* **1-3 mi:** Restaurant *(Louisa's Café 778-5360, L $6-14, D $7-25)*, Inn/B&B *(Claddaugh Farm B&B 778-4894)*, *(Courtyard Inn 778-2755)* **3+ mi:** Restaurant *(Hillside Steak & Crab House 758-1300, 5 mi.)*, *(Old Wharf Inn 778-3566, L $6-10, D $8-20, 5 mi.)*, Fast Food *(McDonald's, Taco Bell, Dunkin Donuts 5 mi.)*, Hotel *(Imperial Hotel 778-5000, $125-200, 5 mi.)*

Recreation and Entertainment
OnSite: Pool, Beach, Picnic Area, Grills, Boat Rentals *(Canoes $40/day, Skiffs $100/day, Pontoon boats $200-225/day)*, Special Events *(Tea Party Weekend - Mem Day; Jul 4th fireworks)* **Near:** Playground **1-3 mi:** Tennis Courts, Jogging Paths, Bowling *(Queen Anne's Bowling 778-5800)*, Cultural Attract *(Church Hill Theater)*, Sightseeing *(Sultana Shipyard)* **3+ mi:** Fitness Center *(Curves 810-1011, 5 mi.)*, Horseback Riding *(Crimson Stables 778-7304, 5 mi.)*, Movie Theater *(Chester 778-2227, 5 mi.)*, Video Rental

Provisioning and General Services
Under 1 mi: Beauty Salon **1-3 mi:** Supermarket *(Acme 778-5641)*, Wine/Beer, Bakery, Green Grocer, Fishmonger, Bank/ATM, Post Office, Catholic Church, Protestant Church, Dry Cleaners, Florist, Department Store *(Peebles)* **3+ mi:** Delicatessen *(C-Town 778-3119, 5 mi.)*, Health Food *(Chestertown Natural Foods 778-1677, 5 mi.)*, Liquor Store *(C-Town 778-2988, 4 mi.)*, Library *(Chestertown 778-3636, 5 mi.)*, Bookstore *(Compleat Bookseller 778-1480, 5 mi.)*, Pharmacy *(Chestertown 778-2575, 5 mi.)*, Hardware Store *(Chestertown Lumber 810-9080, 5 mi.)*

Transportation
OnSite: Courtesy Car/Van *(free limo to town and restaurants)*
OnCall: Rental Car *(Enterprise 810-0971)*, Taxi *(Country Sedan 810-0139)*, Airport Limo *(Prince 778-4860)*
Airport: Baltimore-Washington Int'l./Bay Bridge *(50 mi./30 mi.)*

Medical Services
911 Service **OnCall:** Ambulance **Under 1 mi:** Veterinarian *(Eastern Shore 778-1200)* **3+ mi:** Doctor *(Chestertown 778-0300, 5 mi.)*, Dentist *(Jones 758-0286, 4 mi.)*, Chiropractor *(Advanced Chiro 778-1225, 5 mi.)*
Hospital: Kent & Queen Anne's 778-3300 *(5 mi.)*

Setting -- On the eastern side of the Chester River, Rolph's Wharf's six acres range from the casual, beachy riverfront to the manicured upland grounds of the charming River Inn B&B -- a nicely restored 1830's Victorian farmhouse. Stretched along the waterfront are 2 main piers hosting 40 slips, a dockhouse, picnic tables and grills, a hefty travlift and bay, backed by a lovely pool surrounded by attractive white picket fencing; adjacent is the fun and funky Sandbar.

Marina Notes -- *In season open 'til 7pm on weekends. Family owned and operated since 1991. Boat & Breakfast - complimentary breakfast at the River Inn for everyone on the boat!! (Thu-Sun there is a "to-go" alternative at the Sandbar) Three real limos will provide courtesy transport to Chestertown for dinner - which also makes this a viable club cruise or rendezvous destination. Two main docks, the short one hosts the fuel station at the end - very short finger piers. Full boatyard services. The laundry room has a coin-operated washer and dryer - attached to the back of the inn. Brand new bathhouse in '05 - men's and women's each have two showers with dressing rooms, three heads, three sinks.

Notable -- The Sandbar, a very casual open air pavilion built right on the sand beach, features an old bay boat as its bar. The assorted picnic tables and wrought iron table & chairs spill out onto the beach (sandwiches and baskets - from $1.50 for a hot dog, to $7 for a fried oyster or shrimp sandwich - beer, wine & soft drinks). The pet and child-friendly Inn features six rooms with en-suite baths. It's miles by road to anywhere. Some weekend days the schooner Sultana will sail by from her part-time base in Chestertown - she's a full-scale reproduction of the ship that cruised colonial America collecting British tea taxes.

PHOTOS ON CD-ROM: 13

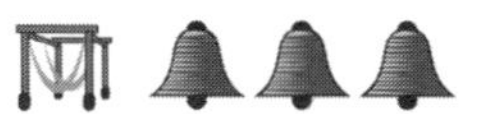

Chestertown Marina

PO Box 7; 211 S. Front Street; Chestertown, MD 21620

Tel: (410) 778-3616 **VHF: Monitor** 16 **Talk** 73
Fax: (410) 778-5381 **Alternate Tel:** -
Email: n/a **Web:** www.chestertown.com/chestertownmarina
Nearest Town: Chestertown **Tourist Info:** (410) 810-2968

Navigational Information
Lat: 39°12.365' **Long:** 076°03.829' **Tide:** 3 ft. **Current:** 1 kt. **Chart:** 12272
Rep. Depths (*MLW*): Entry 12 ft. **Fuel Dock** 12 ft. **Max Slip/Moor** 12 ft./-
Access: 18 miles up Chester River from Kent Narrows

Marina Facilities *(In Season/Off Season)*
Fuel: Gasoline, Diesel
Slips: 60 Total, 18 Transient **Max LOA:** 100 ft. **Max Beam:** 20 ft.
Rate *(per ft.)*: **Day** $1.50/1.00 **Week** $0.30 **Month** $0.25
Power: 30 amp $5, **50 amp** $10, **100 amp** n/a, **200 amp** n/a
Cable TV: No **Dockside Phone:** No
Dock Type: Fixed, Long Fingers, Short Fingers, Wood
Moorings: 0 Total, 0 Transient **Launch:** n/a, Dinghy Dock
Rate: Day n/a **Week** n/a **Month** n/a
Heads: 2 Toilet(s), 2 Shower(s) *(with dressing rooms)*
Laundry: 1 Washer(s), 1 Dryer(s) **Pay Phones:** No
Pump-Out: OnCall **Fee:** $5 **Closed Heads:** Yes

Marina Operations
Owner/Manager: Danny Stuber **Dockmaster:** Ben Dernis
In-Season: Apr-Nov, 8am-5pm **Off-Season:** Dec-Mar, 8am-5pm
After-Hours Arrival: Call ahead
Reservations: Yes, Preferred **Credit Cards:** Visa/MC, Dscvr, Amex
Discounts: None
Pets: Welcome, Dog Walk Area **Handicap Access:** Yes, Docks

Marina Services and Boat Supplies
Services - Docking Assistance, Dock Carts **Communication -** Mail & Package Hold, Phone Messages, Fax in/out, FedEx, UPS, Express Mail **Supplies - OnSite:** Ice *(Block, Cube)*, Ships' Store **Under 1 mi:** Propane *(Synergy Gas 778-0787)* **1-3 mi:** Bait/Tackle *(Chester River Marine Services 778-2240)* **3+ mi:** West Marine *(639-9959, 12 mi.)*

Boatyard Services
OnSite: Travelift *(25T)*, Launching Ramp, Engine mechanic *(gas, diesel)*, Electrical Repairs, Bottom Cleaning, Compound, Wash & Wax, Yacht Broker *(Yachts Unlimited)* **Yard Rates:** $45-52.50/hr., Haul & Launch $3/ft. + lab. **Storage:** In-Water $13/ft., On-Land $19/ft. incl haul, block & launch

Restaurants and Accommodations
OnSite: Restaurant *(Old Wharf Inn 778-3566, L $6-9, D $6-20, Sun brunch $4-8)* **OnCall:** Pizzeria *(Domino's 810-3811)* **Near:** Restaurant *(La Ruota Ristorante 778-9989, L $6-12, D $15-25)*, *(Andy's 778-6797, L $4-12, D $4-12)*, *(Blue Heron 778-0188, L $7-12, D $17-22)*, *(Imperial Hotel 778-5000, D $17-28)*, *(Kettledrum Tea Room 810-1497, L $8-11, D $16-24, Mon 11am-4pm, Thu 11am-8pm, Fri-Sat 11am-9pm, Sun 11am-7:30pm)*, Coffee Shop *(Dunkin' Donuts)*, Lite Fare *(Feast of Reason 778-3828, carryout)*, Hotel *(Imperial 778-5000, $125-200)*, Inn/B&B *(Hill's Inn 778-1926, $100-120)*, *(Parker House 778-9041, $125-150)*, *(White Swan 778-2300, $120-200)*, *(Widow's Walk 778-6864, $75-125)* **Under 1 mi:** Fast Food *(Subway)*, Hotel *(Comfort Suites 810-0555, $75-150)*

Recreation and Entertainment
Near: Park *(Philip G. Wilmer)*, Museum *(Geddes-Piper House 778-3499, self-guided tours Wed-Fri 10am-4pm)*, Cultural Attract *(Prince Theatre 810-2060, movies & shows)*, Sightseeing *(Historic Walking Tour; The Sultana)*, Galleries, Special Events *(Candlelight Walking Tour - mid-Sep 778-3499; Crazy Days - last wknd Jul - festive sidewalk sales)* **Under 1 mi:** Fitness Center *(Kent Athletic Club 778-3148)*, Movie Theater *(Chester 778-2227)*, Video Rental *(Video Scene 778-7900)* **1-3 mi:** Horseback Riding *(Crimson Stables 778-7304)*, Bowling *(Queen Anne's 778-5800)*

Provisioning and General Services
Near: Convenience Store *(Royal Farms)*, Health Food *(C-Town Natural Foods 778-1677)*, Wine/Beer, Bakery, Farmers' Market *(Sat from 9am at Fountain Park 639-7217)*, Bank/ATM, Post Office, Catholic Church, Protestant Church, Barber Shop *(Old Town 778-4771)*, Dry Cleaners, Laundry, Bookstore *(Compleat Bookseller 778-1480)*, Pharmacy *(Stam Drug 778-3030)* **Under 1 mi:** Delicatessen *(C-Town Deli 778-3119)*, Liquor Store *(C-Town 778-2988)*, Library *(778-3636)*, Beauty Salon *(Rendezvous 778-0540)*, Hardware Store *(Chestertown Lumber 810-9080)*, Florist, Copies Etc. *(Mail Boxes 778-9446)* **1-3 mi:** Supermarket *(Acme 778-5641)*

Transportation
OnCall: Rental Car *(Enterprise 810-0971)*, Airport Limo *(Prince 778-4860)*
Near: Bikes *(Bike Works)*, Local Bus *(Rock Hall Trolley $5/RT)*
Airport: Baltimore-Washington Int'l./Bay Bridge *(53 mi./32 mi.)*

Medical Services
911 Service **OnCall:** Ambulance **Near:** Dentist *(Wyman 810-3110)* **Under 1 mi:** Doctor, Chiropractor *(Schreppler 778-4696)* **1-3 mi:** Veterin--arian *(Buckel 778-4979)* **Hospital:** Kent & Queen Anne's 778-3300 *(1 mi.)*

Setting -- A block from exquisite colonial Chestertown, three main piers lie perpendicular to the Chester River, hosting 48 slips and alongside dockage -- all anchored by a small, single-story building: the well-stocked ships' store and office, with chairs along its dock-side front porch. A brick riverfront promenade runs from the marina past the adjacent, recently rebuilt, Old Wharf Restaurant to the Town Dock. Directly upland is tree shaded High Street that passes brick Georgian mansions and ends at Cross Street and Fountain Park - the town center.

Marina Notes -- 25T travelift and a remarkable amount of on-the-hard storage for an in-town location. When in port, the reproduction 1768 schooner Sultana is docked due east of Chestertown's Pier 1. Built by Chestertown shipwrights & volunteers, the vessel invites boardings, 2-hr. tours and overnight cruises. Echo Hill Outdoor School's '57 Buy Boat "Annie D" & '01 skipjack Elsworth also berth here. On the office's east side is the laundry room and dedicated, locked men's and ladies' room - decent, all-tile complete bathrooms. FYI: Scott's Point next door has been sold; condos are being built on the property.

Notable -- Founded in 1706, Chestertown is today as vibrant and pretty as ever - well worth the trip up the river. The historic district has a tantalizing mix of unique shops, galleries, eateries, tea parlors, and perfectly preserved homes - Georgian mansions to Federal-style, Italianate and Queen Anne Victorians set back from brick sidewalks. Pick up a copy of the 24-stop Walking Tour. No supermarkets are within walking distance (and no taxis), but there are quite a few casual fine-dining restaurants and a Saturday farmers' market. Former train depot, Stepney Station houses more shops and services and classic trains.

PHOTOS ON CD-ROM: 15

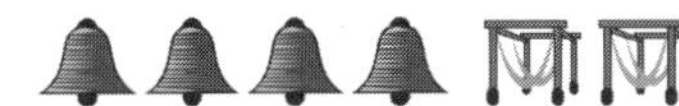

Bay Bridge Marina

357 Pier One Road; Stevensville, MD 21666

Tel: (410) 643-3162 **VHF: Monitor** 16 **Talk** 68
Fax: (410) 643-3154 **Alternate Tel:** n/a
Email: office@baybridgemarina.com **Web:** www.baybridgemarina.com
Nearest Town: Stevensville *(2 mi.)* **Tourist Info:** (410) 604-6420

Navigational Information

Lat: 38°58.770' **Long:** 076°20.110' **Tide:** 1 ft. **Current:** n/a **Chart:** 12270
Rep. Depths (*MLW*): Entry 6 ft. **Fuel Dock** 9 ft. **Max Slip/Moor** 9 ft./-
Access: Just south of the Chesapeake Bay Bridge

Marina Facilities *(In Season/Off Season)*

Fuel: *Amoco* - Gasoline, Diesel, High-Speed Pumps
Slips: 325 Total, 15 Transient **Max LOA:** 100 ft. **Max Beam:** n/a
Rate *(per ft.)*: **Day** $3.00 **Week** Inq. **Month** Inq.
Power: 30 amp Incl., **50 amp** Incl., **100 amp** n/a, **200 amp** n/a
Cable TV: Yes **Dockside Phone:** No
Dock Type: Floating, Long Fingers, Alongside, Wood
Moorings: 0 Total, 0 Transient **Launch:** n/a
Rate: Day n/a **Week** n/a **Month** n/a
Heads: 26 Toilet(s), 25 Shower(s) *(with dressing rooms)*
Laundry: 4 Washer(s), 3 Dryer(s), Book Exchange **Pay Phones:** Yes, 3
Pump-Out: OnSite **Fee:** n/a **Closed Heads:** Yes

Marina Operations

Owner/Manager: Tom McCary, Manager **Dockmaster:** Karen Smith
In-Season: Jun-Aug, 8am-6pm **Off-Season:** Sep-May, 8am-5pm
After-Hours Arrival: Call in advance
Reservations: Yes **Credit Cards:** Visa/MC, Dscvr, Amex, Amoco
Discounts: None
Pets: Welcome, Dog Walk Area **Handicap Access:** Yes, Heads, Docks

Marina Services and Boat Supplies

Services - Docking Assistance, Concierge, Dock Carts **Communication -** Mail & Package Hold, Phone Messages, Fax in/out, Data Ports *(Wi-Fi)*, FedEx, UPS, Express Mail *(Sat Del)* **Supplies - OnSite:** Ice *(Block, Cube)*, Ships' Store **1-3 mi:** West Marine *(604-1752)*, Boater's World *(604-2613)*, Bait/Tackle *(Big Mouth 643-0158)*, Propane *(Kent Island Mobil 643-5277)*

Boatyard Services

OnSite: Travelift *(25 & 70T)*, Forklift, Engine mechanic *(gas, diesel)*, Electrical Repairs, Electronics Repairs, Hull Repairs, Canvas Work, Bottom Cleaning, Brightwork, Compound, Wash & Wax, Interior Cleaning, Propeller Repairs, Woodworking, Painting, Awlgrip, Yacht Broker **Near:** Launching Ramp, Rigger. **Yard Rates:** $75/hr., Haul & Launch $9-13.50/ft. *(blocking incl.)*, Power Wash $3-5.50/ft. **Storage:** On-Land $4-5.50/ft./mo.

Restaurants and Accommodations

OnSite: Restaurant *(Hemingway's 643-2722, L $8-13, D $20-28, 7 days)*, Snack Bar *(Dockside Café 643-3601, B $4-10, L $4-11, D $9-16, 9am-8pm, closed Mon; B all day, L after 12pm, D after 4pm)*, Lite Fare *(Lola's Tropical Grill 643-2722, D $4-14, Thu-Fri 5-11pm, Sat-Sun noon-mid; Caribbean lite and steamed crabs)* **Near:** Crab House *(Stevensville Crab Shack 604-2722)*, Pizzeria *(Carini 604-2501)*, Inn/B&B *(Kent Manor 643-5757, $135-215)*, *(Island Inn 643-2466)* **Under 1 mi:** Restaurant *(Matapeake 643-5330)*, *(Seagrapes 643-6460)*, Fast Food **1-3 mi:** Lite Fare *(Beanos Coffee & Bagel 643-7700)* **3+ mi:** Motel *(Comfort Inn 827-6767, 5 mi.)*

Recreation and Entertainment

OnSite: Pool, Beach, Picnic Area, Fitness Center, Jogging Paths, Fishing Charter, Special Events *(Bay Bridge Boat Show - late Apr)* **Near:** Dive Shop, Roller Blade/Bike Paths, Video Rental *(Blockbuster 643-8400)*, Sightseeing **Under 1 mi:** Park *(Terrapin Beach Nature Park - walking trails)*, Museum *(Cray House, Stevensville Train Depot)* **1-3 mi:** Tennis Courts, Group Fishing Boat **3+ mi:** Golf Course *(Blue Heron 643-5721, 6 mi.)*

Provisioning and General Services

OnSite: Convenience Store, Wine/Beer **Under 1 mi:** Delicatessen *(Lovepoint 604-2447)*, Liquor Store *(Lovepoint Deli Wine & Spirits 604-2447)*, Bakery *(Piece of Cake 604-0355)*, Post Office, Beauty Salon *(Clipper Ship 643-5600)*, Bookstore *(Book Warehouse 827-8474)*, Pharmacy *(Rite Aid 604-2337)* **1-3 mi:** Provisioning Service, Supermarket *(Food Lion 643-9687, Safeway 643-4929)*, Gourmet Shop, Fishmonger *(Mr B's Seafoods 643-5536)*, Bank/ATM, Catholic Church, Protestant Church, Library, Barber Shop, Dry Cleaners *(Thompson Creek 643-4864)*, Laundry, Hardware Store *(Rommel's Ace 643-7702)*, Florist, Department Store *(Kmart 643-9600)*

Transportation

OnCall: Rental Car *(Enterprise 604-6154, Total Car 604-2529)*, Taxi *(Kent Island 604-0486)*, Airport Limo *(Above & Beyond 827-8835)* **Near:** Local Bus **1-3 mi:** InterCity Bus *(Greyhound 643-6584)*
Airport: Baltimore-Washington Int'l./Bay Bridge *(50 mi./0.25 mi.)*

Medical Services

911 Service **OnCall:** Ambulance, Veterinarian *(Mobile Vet 643-7565)* **Under 1 mi:** Dentist *(Bayside Dental 643-8110)* **1-3 mi:** Doctor, Chiropractor *(Fish 604-0900)* **Hospital:** Anne Arundel 267-1000 *(15 mi.)*

Setting -- Forty-six acre Bay Bridge Marina bills itself as "simply superb" - and it really is. Immediately south of the Bay Bridge, 325 high-end slips sit in a very secure basin surrounded by finely tuned services and amenities. Nicely sited plantings soften the neo-modern gray clapboard buildings with "port-hole" dormers, an occasional teak bench interrupts the paver-stone boardwalk that rims the marina basin, and attention to detail reinforces the resort feel.

Marina Notes -- DCM. Formerly called Pier 1 Marina. New owner and huge renovation in 1995 - a professionally-designed and managed operation. Floating docks trimmed with canvas have full finger piers and wider inserts. The boat yard, dry storage, work shed and travelift areas are completely separated from the marina, divided by tall evergreens. New 17,000 square ft. maintenance building, accommodates to 80 ft. LOA. Eight brokers on site selling over 22 lines of new boats. Three bathhouses - two are standard, nicely done, group configurations (Corian vanities but no private dressing rooms); preferable one is at the pool & fitness center - 4 lovely all tile full bathrooms with sinks, toilets, hair dryers and glass-doored showers. The single laundry room is at the head of the basin.

Notable -- Cornered by two buildings with striped awnings, a comfortable pool overlooks the docks; the deck is furnished with chaises interspersed with three tiki huts - each with a wrought iron table and chairs. Dockside Café, now in Bldg. 2, has glass tables and rattan chairs - service poolside and to the tiki huts as well. A small but well-equipped fitness center overlooks the docks and pool. Near the bridge, Hemingway's chef "Poncho" Ledezma promises a bit of Key West, Spain & Cuba plus spectacular views - especially sunsets. On the lower level, seasonal Lola's Tropical Grill serves steamed crabs with live entertainment.

PHOTOS ON CD-ROM: 15

Kentmorr Harbour Marina

910 Kentmorr Road; Stevensville, MD 21666

Tel: (410) 643-0029 **VHF: Monitor** 9 **Talk** 73
Fax: (410) 643-1593 **Alternate Tel:** n/a
Email: n/a **Web:** www.kentmorrharbourmarina .com
Nearest Town: Stevensville *(6 mi.)* **Tourist Info:** (410) 604-6420

Navigational Information

Lat: 38°54.900' **Long:** 076°21.820' **Tide:** 2 ft. **Current:** n/a **Chart:** 12273
Rep. Depths (*MLW*): Entry 4 ft. **Fuel Dock** 6 ft. **Max Slip/Moor** 6 ft./-
Access: Five miles south of Bay Bridge, steer East to Channel entrance

Marina Facilities *(In Season/Off Season)*

Fuel: *Unbranded* - Gasoline, Diesel
Slips: 105 Total, 20+ Transient **Max LOA:** 55 ft. **Max Beam:** n/a
Rate *(per ft.)*: **Day** $1.50/1.25 **Week** $8.75 **Month** $10
Power: 30 amp $5, **50 amp** $8, **100 amp** n/a, **200 amp** n/a
Cable TV: No **Dockside Phone:** No
Dock Type: Fixed, Short Fingers, Pilings
Moorings: 0 Total, 0 Transient **Launch:** n/a
Rate: Day n/a **Week** n/a **Month** n/a
Heads: 4 Toilet(s), 4 Shower(s)
Laundry: None, Book Exchange **Pay Phones:** No
Pump-Out: OnSite, Full Service, 1 Central **Fee:** $10 **Closed Heads:** Yes

Marina Operations

Owner/Manager: Paul Lippold **Dockmaster:** Same
In-Season: May-Nov, 8am-7pm **Off-Season:** Nov-May, 9am-5pm
After-Hours Arrival: Dock at restaurant register in morning
Reservations: Yes, Preferred **Credit Cards:** Visa/MC, Dscvr
Discounts: None
Pets: Welcome, Dog Walk Area **Handicap Access:** No

Marina Services and Boat Supplies

Services - Docking Assistance, Boaters' Lounge, Security *(24 hrs., Manager on site)*, Trash Pick-Up, Dock Carts **Communication -** Mail & Package Hold, Phone Messages **Supplies - OnSite:** Ice *(Block, Cube)* **3+ mi:** West Marine *(604-1752, 9 mi.)*, Boater's World *(604-2613, 6 mi.)*, Bait/Tackle *(Big Mouth Lures 643-0158, 6 mi.)*, Propane *(Kent Island Mobil 643-5277, 8 mi.)*

Boatyard Services

OnSite: Travelift *(40T)*, Hydraulic Trailer, Engine mechanic *(gas, diesel)*, Electrical Repairs, Electronics Repairs, Hull Repairs, Rigger, Bottom Cleaning, Brightwork, Air Conditioning, Refrigeration, Compound, Wash & Wax, Interior Cleaning, Propeller Repairs, Woodworking, Painting, Awlgrip, Total Refits **OnCall:** Divers **1-3 mi:** Launching Ramp. **3+ mi:** Sail Loft *(5 mi.)*, Canvas Work *(5 mi.)*, Life Raft Service *(5 mi.)*.

Restaurants and Accommodations

OnSite: Restaurant *(Kentmorr Restaurant and Crab House 643-2263, L $6-25, D $6-25, 7 days 11:30am-9pm, inside & porch dining, kids' $4)*, Seafood Shack *(Pincer's Crab Deck)* **OnCall:** Pizzeria *(Domino's 643-3002)*, *(Short Stop 643-7220)* **1-3 mi:** Restaurant *(Queen Anne 643-2021, L $5-20, D $5-20)* **3+ mi:** Restaurant *(Kent Manor Inn 643-7716, 6 mi.)*, *(Stevensville Crab Shack 604-2722, 6 mi.)*, *(Hemingway's 643-2722, L $8-13, D $20-28, 6 mi.)*, *(Dockside Café 643-3601, 6 mi.)*, Fast Food *(Hardee's, Burger King, Subway 8 mi.)*, Hotel *(Holiday Inn Express 827-4454, 10 mi.)*, Inn/B&B *(Kent Manor Inn 643-5757, $135-215, 6 mi.)*, *(Island Inn 643-2466, 7 mi.)*

Recreation and Entertainment

OnSite: Pool, Beach, Picnic Area, Grills, Fishing Charter *(large fleet - Pink Hooker 289-4396, Chesapeake Lady 643-0734)*, Group Fishing Boat, Volleyball **Under 1 mi:** Golf Course *(Blue Heron 643-5721)* **1-3 mi:** Park *(Matapeake State Park: 900 ft. fishing pier, bo at ramp, picnic area)* **3+ mi:** Playground *(4 mi.)*, Tennis Courts *(4 mi.)*, Fitness Center *(Curves 6 604-2997,8 mi.)*, Video Rental *(Movie King 643-8365, 8 mi.)*

Provisioning and General Services

OnSite: Bank/ATM **1-3 mi:** Farmers' Market **3+ mi:** Convenience Store *(6 mi.)*, Supermarket *(Food Lion 643-9687, Safeway 643-4929, 8 mi.)*, Delicatessen *(Lovepoint Deli Wine & Spirits 604-2447, 6 mi.)*, Wine/Beer *(Thompson Creek 604-3440, 8 mi.)*, Liquor Store *(Jinx's Liquor Store 643-5437, 8 mi.)*, Bakery *(6 mi.)*, Fishmonger *(L&L Seafood 604-0338, 8 mi.)*, Catholic Church *(8 mi.)*, Library *(Stevensville 643-8161, 8 mi.)*, Beauty Salon *(Clipper Ship 643-5600, 6 mi.)*, Barber Shop *(8 mi.)*, Dry Cleaners *(Thompson Creek 643-4864, 8 mi.)*, Bookstore *(Book Warehouse 827-8474, 8 mi.)*, Pharmacy *(Happy Harry's 643-5119, 8 mi.)*, Hardware Store *(American 643-3500, 8 mi.)*, Department Store *(Kmart 643-9600, 8 mi.)*

Transportation

OnCall: Rental Car *(Enterprise 604-6154)*, Taxi *(Kent Island 604-0486)*, Airport Limo *(Associated Sedan 643-1500)*
Airport: Baltimore-Washington Int'l./Bay Bridge / Kentmorr *(50 mi./6 mi.)*

Medical Services

911 Service **OnCall:** Ambulance **1-3 mi:** Dentist *(Olmstead 643-7367)*, Holistic Services *(Mid-Shore Massage 643-9910)*, Veterinarian *(Kent Island 643-4204)* **3+ mi:** Doctor *(Queen Anne's 643-6205, 3 mi.)*, Chiropractor *(Jennings 643-7100, 3 mi.)* **Hospital:** Anne Arundel 267-1000 *(19 mi.)*

Setting -- Jetties edge the private channel leading from the Bay into Kentmorr's protected harbor; flanking the entrance are two wide sand beaches. Passing the pool, which overlooks the entrance to the basin, the attractive restaurant complex comes into view. Dominating the landside is a cream-colored Tidewater-style structure - its brick-red metal roof supporting a charming faux lighthouse. Docks rim the basin with three additional piers - one of them covered.

Marina Notes -- Fuel dock closes fifteen minutes before the office. Marina has undergone major reservation - new piers and an upgraded service yard. On site Brickhouse Yacht Yard is a completely separate operation in a leased facility. The central part of the basin is a set of covered slips that radiate from the far side of the land and the Brickhouse yard. Slips 1 to 9 are for the restaurant only, dock-and-dine. Fish cleaning station, fishing tournament weigh station. Heads and showers are cinderblock with cement floors, freshly painted and in good condition: two showers with little dressing rooms, three heads, two sinks.

Notable -- Kentmorr Harbor Restaurant has a variety of inviting eating venues - vinyl clothed tables with banquet-style chairs furnish the simple inside dining room. Long picnic tables with benches - designed to be covered with brown paper for crab feasts - are out on the screened porch - Pincer's Crab Deck along with Pincer's Dock Bar; additional tables are outside along the docks. They cater crab feasts & buffets for groups of 50 or more - up to 150 can be accommodated under the tent for a sit-down, and up to 250 for a cocktail reception. The larger, northern beach sports picnic tables and a volleyball net. Kentmorr Air Park, a unique private community airstrip with 2800 foot grass runway, is a quarter mile up the road.

PHOTOS ON CD-ROM: 14

Navigational Information
Lat: 38°53.933' **Long:** 076°21.916' **Tide:** n/a **Current:** n/a **Chart:** 12273
Rep. Depths (*MLW*): Entry 7 ft. **Fuel Dock** 6 ft. **Max Slip/Moor** 6 ft./-
Access: Directly off the Bay; at Prices Creek 6 mi. south of the Bay Bridge

Marina Facilities *(In Season/Off Season)*
Fuel: Gasoline, Diesel
Slips: 107 Total, 20 Transient **Max LOA:** 50 ft. **Max Beam:** 20 ft.
Rate *(per ft.)*: **Day** $1.50 **Week** n/a **Month** 12.00
Power: 30 amp Inq., **50 amp** Inq., **100 amp** n/a, **200 amp** n/a
Cable TV: Yes, Inc **Dockside Phone:** Yes
Dock Type: Floating, Long Fingers
Moorings: 0 Total, 0 Transient **Launch:** n/a
Rate: Day n/a **Week** n/a **Month** n/a
Heads: 4 Toilet(s)
Laundry: None **Pay Phones:** No
Pump-Out: OnSite, Full Service, 1 Port **Fee:** $5 **Closed Heads:** Yes

Marina Operations
Owner/Manager: Patrick Tracy **Dockmaster:** Same
In-Season: Year-Round, 7:30am-4pm **Off-Season:** n/a
After-Hours Arrival: Key card entry
Reservations: Yes **Credit Cards:** Visa/MC, Dscvr, Amex
Discounts: 10% ship's store **Dockage:** n/a **Fuel:** n/a **Repair:** n/a
Pets: Welcome **Handicap Access:** Yes, Heads, Docks

Queen Anne Marina

412 Congressional Drive; Stevensville, MD 21666-3

Tel: (410) 643-2021; (866) 643-2021 **VHF: Monitor** 16 **Talk** n/a
Fax: (410) 643-0153 **Alternate Tel:** n/a
Email: qamarina@verizon.net **Web:** www.queenannemarina.com
Nearest Town: Stevensville *(8 mi.)* **Tourist Info:** (410) 604-6420

Marina Services and Boat Supplies
Services - Docking Assistance, Security *(24 hrs., key card entry)* **Communication -** Mail & Package Hold, Phone Messages, Fax in/out *($0.50)*, Data Ports *(At Slip)*, FedEx, UPS, Express Mail **Supplies - OnSite:** Ships' Store **3+ mi:** West Marine *(604-1752, 9 mi.)*, Boater's World *(604-2613, 6 mi.)*, Propane *(Kent Island Mobil 643-5277, 9 mi.)*

Boatyard Services
OnSite: Travelift *((30T))*, Bottom Cleaning **OnCall:** Engine mechanic *(gas, diesel)*, Electrical Repairs, Electronics Repairs, Air Conditioning, Refrigeration **Near:** Brightwork, Divers, Compound, Wash & Wax, Interior Cleaning, Propeller Repairs, Woodworking, Inflatable Repairs, Upholstery, Yacht Interiors, Painting, Awlgrip. **1-3 mi:** Launching Ramp.
Yard Rates: Haul & Launch $4.50/ft., Power Wash $1.50/ft., black/$2.00/ft.

Restaurants and Accommodations
OnSite: Restaurant *(Queen Anne Restaurant 643-2021, L $5-20, D $5-20, Sun breakfast 11am-2pm)* **OnCall:** Pizzeria *(Domino's 643-3002)*, *(Short Stop 643-7220)* **1-3 mi:** Restaurant *(Kentmorr 643-2263)* **3+ mi:** Restaurant *(Kent Manor 643-7716, 5 mi.)*, *(Hemingway's 643-2722, L $8-13, D $20-28, 5 mi.)*, *(Dockside Café 643-3601, L $3-8, D $13-23, 5 mi.)*, Seafood Shack *(Stevensville Crab Shack 604-2722, 5 mi.)*, Fast Food *(Burger King, Hardee's 8 mi.)*, Motel *(Comfort Inn 827-6767, 10 mi.)*, Inn/B&B *(Kent Manor Inn 643-5757, $135-215, 5 mi.)*, *(Island Inn 643-2466, 6 mi.)*

Recreation and Entertainment
OnSite: Beach, Picnic Area, Grills *(charcoal)*, Fishing Charter, Group Fishing Boat **Under 1 mi:** Golf Course *(Blue Heron Golf Course 643-5721)*, Jogging Paths, Roller Blade/Bike Paths **1-3 mi:** Park *(Matapeake State Park: 900 ft. fishing pier, boat ramp, picnic area)* **3+ mi:** Playground *(3 mi.)*, Tennis Courts *(3 mi.)*, Fitness Center *(Curves 604-2997, 8 mi.)*, Video Rental *(Blockbuster 643-8400, 8 mi.)*

Provisioning and General Services
OnSite: Convenience Store *(Mon-Sun 7:30am-6pm)* **1-3 mi:** Green Grocer *(Farmer John's)* **3+ mi:** Supermarket *(Food Lion 643-9687, Safeway 643-4929, 8 mi.)*, Delicatessen *(6 mi.)*, Liquor Store *(Lovepoint Deli Wine & Spirits 604-2447, 6 mi.)*, Fishmonger *(L&L Seafood 604-0338, 8 mi.)*, Bank/ATM *(5 mi.)*, Library *(Stevensville 643-8161, 8 mi.)*, Beauty Salon *(Clipper Ship 643-5600, 6 mi.)*, Dry Cleaners *(Thompson Creek 643-4864, 8 mi.)*, Bookstore *(Book Warehouse 827-8474, 8 mi.)*, Pharmacy *(Happy Harry's 643-5119, 8 mi.)*, Hardware Store *(American 643-3500, 5 mi.)*, Department Store *(Kmart 643-9600, 8 mi.)*

Transportation
OnCall: Rental Car *(Enterprise 604-6154)*, Taxi *(Kent Island 604-0486)*, Airport Limo *(Associated Sedan 643-1500)* **3+ mi:** Local Bus *(Park & Ride, 6 mi.)* **Airport:** Baltimore-Washington International/Bay Bridge *(50 mi./ 6 mi.)*

Medical Services
911 Service **OnCall:** Ambulance, Veterinarian *(Mobile Vet 643-7565)* **3+ mi:** Doctor *(Chester Reginal Medical 643-7141, 8 mi.)*, Dentist *(Bayside Dental 643-8110, 8 mi.)*, Chiropractor *(Fish Chiropractic 604-0900, 8 mi.)*, Holistic Services *(New Possibilities Acupuncture 643-3700, 8 mi.)*
Hospital: Anne Arundel 267-1000 *(20 mi.)*

Setting -- Six miles south of the Bay Bridge, Queen Anne is tucked into Prices Creek, directly off the Bay. A low brick and clapboard building is home to the Queen Anne restaurant. Just beyond is the protected, dock-filled basin. Picnic tables and charcoal grills line the grassy strip by the docks; an attractive deck overlooks the water -- more picnic tables, topped by beige market umbrellas, provide a venue for a drink, an ice cream, or watching the sunset over panoramic views of the Chesapeake Bay Bridge and Annapolis across the Bay.

Marina Notes -- Dredged in '04 to six feet for "A" and "B" dock and five feet at "C" dock. All the stationary docks were ripped out and replaced with floating ones for the '05 season. A new marina office has just been built. The convenience store has an ice cream parlor, drinks, lots of pantry staples, and takeout. The heads are now shared with the restaurant and there is no longer a boaters' bathhouse or showers.

Notable -- The Queen Anne Restaurant (formerly the upscale Silver Swan) was renovated with a new pub-like theme - all freshly painted in light blue. The new iteration offers a more casual, relaxed and upbeat tempo; tanks and shorts are welcomed. Local specialties include blackened rockfish and burgers as well as wholesome meaty reubens with a variety of side dishes. Live entertainment is featured on Fridays (6-10pm) with monthly radio station visits and a personable bartender. Prices Creek demands a bit of exploring, so if there are kayaks aboard, consider heading further upstream.

PHOTOS ON CD-ROM: 9

Boaters' Notes

Add Your Ratings and Reviews at www.AtlanticCruisingClub.com

AtlanticCruisingClub.com provides updated Marina Reports, Destination and Harbor Articles, a Boaters' Forum and much more — including an option within each on-line Marina Report for Boaters to add their ratings and comments regarding that facility. Please log on frequently to share your experiences — and to read other boaters' comments.

On the website, boaters may rate marinas on one or more of the following categories — on a scale of 1 (basic) to 5 (world class) — and also enter additional commentary.

- **Facilities & Services** (Fuel, Reservations, Concierge Services and General Helpfulness):
- **Amenities** (Pool, Beach, Internet Access, including Wi-Fi, Picnic/Grill area, Boaters' Lounge):
- **Setting** (Views, Design, Landscaping, Maintenance, Ship-Shapeness, Overall Ambiance):
- **Convenience** (Access — including delivery services — to Supermarkets, other provisioning sources, Shops, Services. Attractions, Entertainment, Sightseeing, Recreation, including Golf and Sport Fishing & Medical Services):
- **Restaurants/Eateries/Lodgings** (Availability of Fine Dining, Snack Bars, Lite Fare, On Call food service, and Lodgings ashore):
- **Transportation** (Courtesy Car/Vans, Buses, Water Taxis, Bikes, Taxis, Rental Cars, Airports, Amtrak, Commuter Trains):
- **Please Add Any Additional Comments**

7. Eastern Shore: St Michaels & Tilghman Island

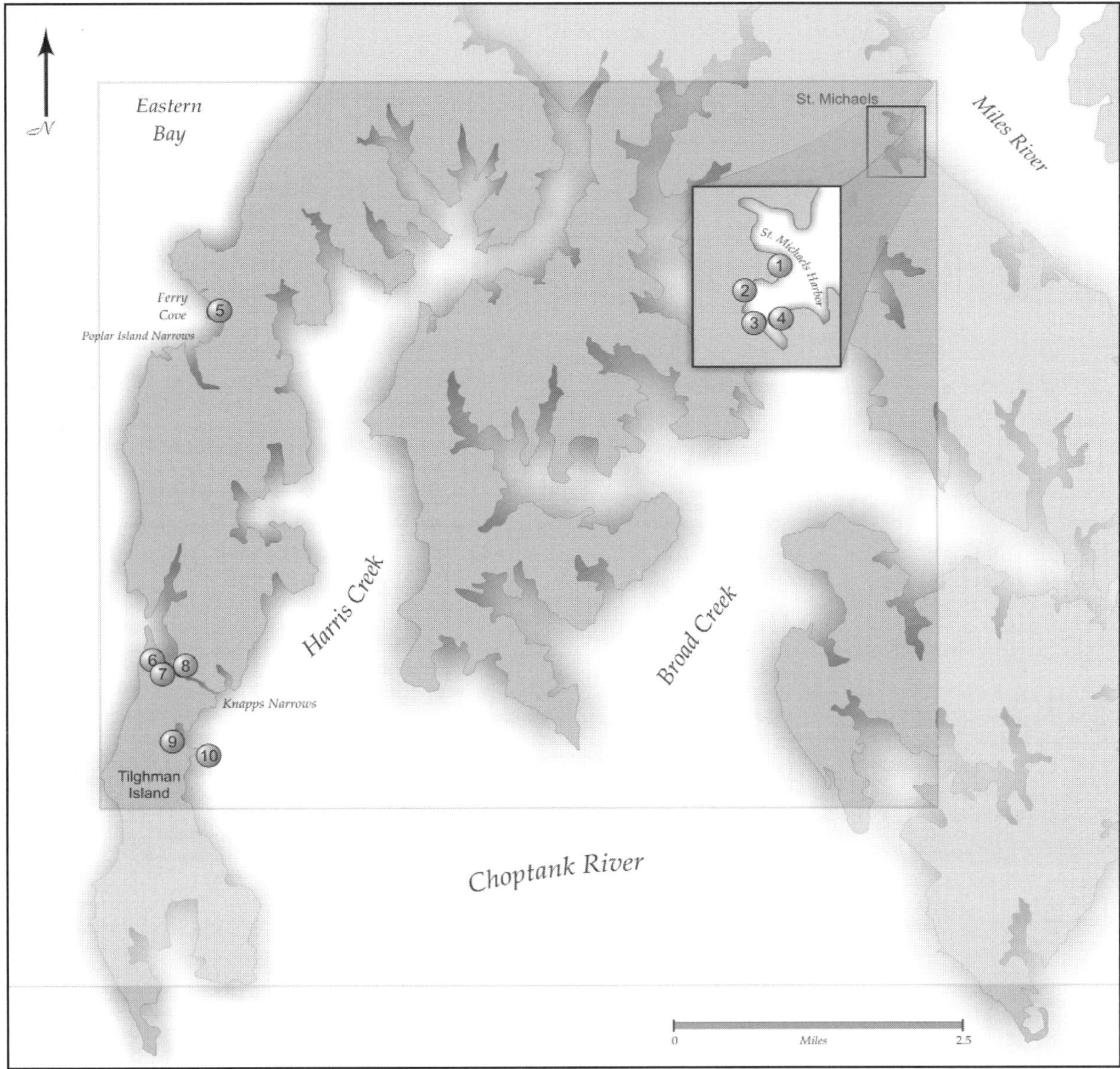

MAP	MARINA	HARBOR	PAGE
1	**Chesapeake Bay Maritime Museum**	*Miles R./St. Michaels Harbor*	138
2	**Higgins Yacht Yard**	*Miles R./St. Michaels Harbor*	139
3	**St. Michaels Marina**	*Miles R./St. Michaels Harbor*	140
4	**St. Michaels Harbour Inn & Marina**	*Miles R./St. Michaels Harbor*	141
5	**Lowes Wharf Marina Inn**	*Ferry Cove*	142
6	**Tilghman Island Marina**	*Knapp's Narrows*	143
7	**The Tilghman Island Inn & Marina**	*Knapp's Narrows*	144
8	**Knapp's Narrows Marina & Inn**	*Knapp's Narrows*	145
9	**Harrison's Chesapeake House**	*Dogwood Harbor*	146
10	**Tilghman on Chesapeake**	*Dogwood Harbor*	147

- **A "DCM" symbol in Marina Notes means Designated Clean Marina** — This is a coveted state-level award given to marinas that meet stringent, environmentally supportive requirements (see page 307). *For a list of DCM's & pump-out facilities, see page 308.*
- **Ratings & Reviews** — An explanation of the Atlantic Cruising Club's rating system, and a detailed explanation of what is in each section of the Marina Report is on pages 6 – 11. *The Data-Gathering Process is detailed on page 322.*
- **Marina Report Updates** — Updates to Marina Reports (from readers, ACC reviewers, and marinas) are posted regularly on *www.AtlanticCruisingClub.com.*

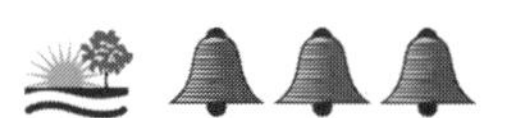

Chesapeake Bay Museum

PO Box 636; Mill Street; Saint Michaels, MD 21663

Tel: (410) 745-2916 **VHF: Monitor** 16 & 9 **Talk** 68
Fax: (410) 745-6088 **Alternate Tel:** (410) 745-2916
Email: rnewberg@cbmm.org **Web:** www.cbmm.org
Nearest Town: St. Michaels **Tourist Info:** (410) 822-4653

Navigational Information

Lat: 38°47.273' **Long:** 076°13.154' **Tide:** 2 ft. **Current:** n/a **Chart:** 12270
Rep. Depths (*MLW*): Entry 10 ft. **Fuel Dock** n/a **Max Slip/Moor** 10 ft./-
Access: Eastern Bay to Miles River, starboard side

Marina Facilities *(In Season/Off Season)*

Fuel: No
Slips: 35 Total, 35 Transient **Max LOA:** 200 ft. **Max Beam:** n/a
Rate *(per ft.)*: **Day** $1.50* **Week** n/a **Month** n/a
Power: 30 amp $5, **50 amp** $5, **100 amp** n/a, **200 amp** n/a
Cable TV: No **Dockside Phone:** No
Dock Type: Fixed, Short Fingers, Pilings, Alongside, Wood
Moorings: 0 Total, 0 Transient **Launch:** n/a, Dinghy Dock
Rate: Day n/a **Week** n/a **Month** n/a
Heads: 6 Toilet(s), 6 Shower(s) *(with dressing rooms)*
Laundry: None **Pay Phones:** Yes, 2
Pump-Out: Self Service, 1 Central **Fee:** $5 **Closed Heads:** Yes

Marina Operations

Owner/Manager: John Ford **Dockmaster:** Robin Newberg
In-Season: May-Oct, 9am-6pm **Off-Season:** Nov-Apr, 9am-4pm
After-Hours Arrival: Must be museum member; check in next morning
Reservations: Yes, Preferred, $10 **Credit Cards:** Visa/MC, Dscvr, Amex
Discounts: None
Pets: Welcome, Dog Walk Area **Handicap Access:** Yes, Heads, Docks

Marina Services and Boat Supplies

Services - Docking Assistance, Security *(After museum hours)* **Supplies - OnSite:** Ice *(Block, Cube)* **OnCall:** Boat/US **Near:** Ships' Store, Bait/Tackle *(Oak Creek 745-9102)*, CNG *(Higgins)* **Under 1 mi:** Propane *(United Propane 745-5051)* **3+ mi:** West Marine *(770-3080, 12 mi.)*

Boatyard Services

OnCall: Engine mechanic *(gas, diesel)*, Electrical Repairs, Air Conditioning, Refrigeration, Divers **Near:** Travelift *(20T)*, Electronics Repairs, Hull Repairs, Rigger, Bottom Cleaning, Brightwork, Compound, Wash & Wax, Interior Cleaning, Propeller Repairs, Woodworking, Painting, Awlgrip, Total Refits. **Nearest Yard:** Higgins Yacht Yard (410) 745-9303

Restaurants and Accommodations

Near: Restaurant *(208 Talbot 745-3838, inside & deck)*, *(Carpenter Street Poppi's 745-5111)*, Seafood Shack *(The Crab Claw 745-2900, L $5-25, D $5-25, kids' $7 - 11am-10pm)*, *(Big Al's 745-3838, D $21-26)*, Coffee Shop *(Blue Crab Coffee 745-4155)*, Pizzeria *(Rusticana 745-3434)*, Hotel *(St. Michaels Harbour Inn 745-9001)*, Inn/B&B *(Parsonage 745-5519)*, *(Barrett's 745-3322)* **Under 1 mi:** Restaurant *(Poppi's 745-3158)*, *(Morsels 745-2911, Chesapeake Cove)*, *(Inn at Perry Cabin - Sherwood's Landing 745-2200, B $7-12, L $10-25, D $30-40, chef's tasting menu)*, *(Foxy's 745-4340, L $7-22, D $7-22)*, *(Mezzaluna 745-2911)*, Seafood Shack *(Chesapeake Landing 745-9600, D $9-17)*, Motel *(Best Western 745-3333)*, Inn/B&B *(Inn at Perry Cabin $250-550, Conde-Nast Gold List)*

Recreation and Entertainment

OnSite: Picnic Area, Park, Museum *(CBMM + nearby Historical Costumes 745-5154 & St. Mary's Square 745-9561)* **Near:** Galleries **Under 1 mi:** Playground, Video Rental *(Bay Country 745-5988)* **1-3 mi:** Golf Course *(Harbortown 745-9066)*, Fitness Center *(Fit Stop 745-5592)* **3+ mi:** Bowling *(Easton 822-3426, 10 mi.)*, Movie Theater *(Avon 822-5566, 10 mi.)*

Provisioning and General Services

OnSite: Bookstore *(Museum Store 745-2098)* **Near:** Supermarket *(Acme 745-9819)*, Delicatessen, Wine/Beer *(Acme)*, Bank/ATM, Library *(St. Michaels 745-5877)*, Laundry *(Village Laundry 745-9293)*, Pharmacy *(Medicine Shoppe 745-6700)*, Newsstand, Florist, Clothing Store, Retail Shops **Under 1 mi:** Gourmet Shop *(Gourmet by the Bay 745-6260)*, Liquor Store *(Village Shoppe 745-9300)*, Bakery, Farmers' Market *(Willow & Green St. Sat 8:30am-12pm 745-3457)*, Fishmonger, Market *(Clark's 745-3537)*, Post Office, Protestant Church, Beauty Salon *(Helen's 745-2688)*, Barber Shop, Dry Cleaners *(Admiral 745-4272)*, Hardware Store *(Lumber Yard 820-7090)*, Copies Etc. *(Poore House 745-3200)* **1-3 mi:** Convenience Store, Catholic Church **3+ mi:** Department Store *(Peebles 822-8010, 10 mi.)*

Transportation

OnCall: Water Taxi *(Harbor Shuttle Ch.71)*, Rental Car *(Enterprise 822-3260)*, Taxi *(770-9030)*, Airport Limo *(Spectrum 820-0038)* **Near:** Bikes *(St. Michaels Marina)* **3+ mi:** Ferry Service *(Bellevue/Oxford, 6 mi.)*
Airport: Baltimore-Washington Int'l./Easton *(60 mi./12 mi.)*

Medical Services

911 Service **OnCall:** Ambulance **Under 1 mi:** Doctor *(Family Practice 745-5000)*, Dentist *(Family Dentistry 745-9200)* **1-3 mi:** Veterinarian *(St Michaels Vet 745-5275)* **Hospital:** Easton Memorial 822-1000 *(10 mi.)*

Setting -- Head for the museum's Hooper Straight Lighthouse - the visual anchor for this sprawling 18-acre waterside campus. Thirty-five buildings connected by brick paths dot the landscape. 85 Chesapeake Bay watercraft jam the sheds or annotate the lawn - the 6 largest float at the docks. Visiting pleasure craft mingle with the bug-eyed "Edna E. Lockwood," the replica buyboat "Mister Jim and the Skipjacks' "Lady Katie," "H.M.Krentz" and "Thomas Clyde." Bigger boat dockage edges the waterfront, and smaller boat slips fill Fogg's Cove in the shadow of the oystering exhibit.

Marina Notes -- *Overnight dockage is available only to CBMM members at contributor level or higher - under 80' $1.50/ft., over 80' $2/ft. DCM. Reserve for an additional $10. Day dockage: boat fee + admission fee for all non-members on board; must cast off by 4pm. Call 745-2916 ext. 106 or Ch.9 for slip assignment. Membership: "Contributor" level $75 - includes free admission for household members (spouse & children under 18) and 2 additional guests, privilege of paying for dockage, plus the bathhouse combination. Pump-out free to "Contributor Plus" members, $5 for others. Hours: Spring & Fall, 9am-5pm, Summer 'til 6pm. The rustic bathhouse has three cinderblock showers with dressing rooms and floor mats - accessible by keycode to boaters 24 hours.

Notable -- Founded in 1965. Ten of the buildings house exhibits; the newest one, "At Play on the Bay," opened in June '05 in a dedicated 2-story natural wood and glass building, with a steeply-pitched red metal roof, located right on the River. The Crab Claw Restaurant is adjacent, and the charming town of St. Michaels, with B&Bs, eateries galore, and unique, upscale shops, is a short walk out to Talbot Street.

PHOTOS ON CD-ROM: 17

Navigational Information
Lat: 38°47.196' **Long:** 076°13.280' **Tide:** 2 ft. **Current:** n/a **Chart:** 12270
Rep. Depths (*MLW*): Entry 10 ft. **Fuel Dock** 10 ft. **Max Slip/Moor** 9 ft./-
Access: Miles River, off Eastern Bay

Marina Facilities *(In Season/Off Season)*
Fuel: No
Slips: 40 Total, 5-15 Transient **Max LOA:** 70 ft. **Max Beam:** n/a
Rate *(per ft.)*: **Day** $2.00/1.50* **Week** n/a **Month** Inq.
Power: 30 amp $5, **50 amp** $10, **100 amp** n/a, **200 amp** n/a
Cable TV: No **Dockside Phone:** No
Dock Type: Fixed, Short Fingers, Alongside, Wood
Moorings: 0 Total, 0 Transient **Launch:** n/a
Rate: Day n/a **Week** n/a **Month** n/a
Heads: 2 Toilet(s), 2 Shower(s)
Laundry: None **Pay Phones:** No
Pump-Out: OnSite **Fee:** n/a **Closed Heads:** Yes

Marina Operations
Owner/Manager: Cathy Stinchcomb **Dockmaster:** Tad Du Pont/Byron Reillie
In-Season: Apr-Oct, 8am-5pm **Off-Season:** n/a
After-Hours Arrival: Tie up and register in the morning
Reservations: Preferred **Credit Cards:** Visa/MC
Discounts: None
Pets: Welcome, Dog Walk Area **Handicap Access:** No

Higgins Yacht Yard

PO Box 727; 203 Carpenter Street; St. Michaels, MD 21663

Tel: (410) 745-9303 **VHF: Monitor** n/a **Talk** n/a
Fax: (410) 745-5613 **Alternate Tel:** (443) 786-0513
Email: www.twoswaninn@friendly.net **Web:** www.twoswaninn.com
Nearest Town: St. Michaels *(0.1 mi.)* **Tourist Info:** (410) 822-4653

Marina Services and Boat Supplies
Services - Docking Assistance, Dock Carts **Communication -** Fax in/out, FedEx, DHL, UPS, Express Mail **Supplies - OnSite:** Ice *(Cube)*, Ships' Store, CNG **Near:** Bait/Tackle *(Oak Creek 745-9102)*, Propane *(United Propane 745-5051)* **3+ mi:** West Marine *(770-3080, 12 mi.)*

Boatyard Services
OnSite: Travelift *(30T)*, Hull Repairs, Rigger, Bottom Cleaning, Brightwork, Compound, Wash & Wax, Interior Cleaning, Woodworking, Painting **OnCall:** Electronics Repairs, Canvas Work, Divers, Propeller Repairs, Upholstery, Yacht Interiors, Metal Fabrication, Yacht Building, Total Refits **Near:** Launching Ramp, Engine mechanic *(gas, diesel)*, Electrical Repairs, Sail Loft, Refrigeration, Yacht Broker. **Yard Rates:** Upon request

Restaurants and Accommodations
OnSite: Inn/B&B *(Two Swan Inn 745-2929, $419, wknd and Two Swan Cottages $375-400, wknd for two)* **Near:** Restaurant *(Poppi's 745-3158)*, *(Bistro St. Michaels 745-9111)*, *(Foxy's 745-4340, L $7-22, D $7-22, most under $13)*, *(St. Michael's Crab & Steakhouse 745-3737, L $6-21, D $6-21)*, Seafood Shack *(Crab Claw 745-2900, L $5-25, D $5-25, kids' $7 - not crab, Hrs 11am-10pm)*, *(208 Talbot 745-3838, D $27-34, Bar Menu $11-18)*, (Big Al's *745-3151)*, Pizzeria *(Rusticana 745-3434)*, Inn/B&B *(Dr. Dodson House 45-3691)*, *(Barrett's 745-3322)* **Under 1 mi:** Motel *(Best Western 745-3333)*, Inn/B&B *(Inn at Perry Cabin 745-2200, $250-550)*

Recreation and Entertainment
Near: Picnic Area, Playground, Jogging Paths, Boat Rentals, Fishing Charter, Park *(Hollis Park)*, Museum *(Ches Bay Maritime 745-2916, Museum of Historical Costumes 745-5154, St. Mary's Square 745-9561)*, Cultural Attract, Sightseeing *(Walking Tours 886-2643)*, Galleries, Special Events **Under 1 mi:** Fitness Center *(Fit Stop 745-5592)*, Horseback Riding **1-3 mi:** Golf Course *(Harbortown Golf 745-9066)*, Video Rental *(Bay Country 745-5988)* **3+ mi:** Bowling *(Easton Bowling Center 822-3426, 10 mi.)*

Provisioning and General Services
Near: Supermarket *(Acme 745-9819)*, Gourmet Shop *(Gourmet by the Bay 745-6260)*, Delicatessen, Liquor Store *(Village Shoppe 745-9300)*, Bakery, Farmers' Market *(Willow & Green St. Sat 8:30am-12pm 745-3457)*, Fishmonger, Market *(Clark's 745-3537)*, Bank/ATM, Post Office, Catholic Church, Library *(745-5877)*, Beauty Salon *(Helen's 745-2688)*, Barber Shop, Dry Cleaners *(Admiral 745-4272)*, Laundry *(Village 745-9293)*, Bookstore *(Salty Dog770-5982)*, Pharmacy *(Medicine Shoppe 745-6700)* **Under 1 mi:** Hardware Store *(Lumber Yard 820-7090)*, Florist, Copies Etc. *(Poore House 745-3200)*

Transportation
OnCall: Water Taxi *(Ch.71)*, Rental Car *(Enterprise 822-3260)*, Taxi *(770-9030)*, Airport Limo *(Eastern Shore 800-453-2023)* **Near:** Courtesy Car/Van *(Dockside Express)*, Bikes *(St. Michaels Marina)* **3+ mi:** Ferry Service *(Bellevue/Oxford 886-2643)* **Airport:** Baltimore-Washington Int'l./Easton *(60 mi./12 mi.)*

Medical Services
911 Service **OnCall:** Ambulance **Under 1 mi:** Doctor *(745-5000)*, Dentist *(745-9200)*, Veterinarian *(St. Michaels 745-5275)* **Hospital:** Easton Memorial 822-1000 *(10 mi.)*

Setting -- Just past the sprawling, red, two-story Crab Claw Restaurant is Higgins' classic, well kept Eastern Shore yacht yard - an eloquent reminder of St. Michael's roots. It's a relief to return to this spiffy, elegant little town and find that Higgins is still there - untouched, just a little unkempt, but freshly painted and utterly charming. Two main docks host twenty open slips and six covered ones; sixteen smaller boat slips edge the sweep of lawn - dotted with Adirondack chairs - in front of Two Swan Inn. Two blocks inland - down a sweet little lane lined with Higgins' restored buildings - is the village center.

Marina Notes -- *30/ft min. First night $2/ft., additional nights $1.75/ft. Established in 1790, current owners at the helm since 1979. Only full-service yacht yard in St. Michaels. Recent power upgrade - full service 30/50 amp set on the pilings. Bay Hundred custom yachts and restorations. Accommodating staff makes this a good place to leave the boat. Inquire about off-season rates. Wednesday night sailboat races. Heads are a step above standard boatyard - perfectly serviceable, well-maintained and inviting - freshly painted cinderblock walls and cement floors. Internet Access: Pixel, Print & Post, 606 Talbot St.

Notable -- Higgins' Two Swan Inn & Cottages is onsite and includes The Sailshed and several other quaintly restored cottages (Roberts, Cygnet & Sunset) that front two-block long Carpenter Street. The oldest house in Talbot County was moved there, brick by brick, as well. A short walk around the shore is Hollis Park, with picnic tables and grills on a nice stretch of lawn; past it is The Crab Claw. Three inside dining rooms - overlooking the harbor or the Chesapeake Bay Maritime Museum - complete with waterside decks laden with umbrella-topped picnic tables. The 18-acre museum grounds are "out the back door."

PHOTOS ON CD-ROM: 14

St. Michaels Marina

PO Box 398; 305 Mulberry Street; St. Michaels, MD 21663

Tel: (410) 745-2400; (800) 678-8980 **VHF: Monitor** 16 **Talk** n/a
Fax: (410) 745-2808 **Alternate Tel:** n/a
Email: lynsey@harborinn.com **Web:** www.stmichaelsmarina.com
Nearest Town: St. Michaels **Tourist Info:** (410) 822-4653

Navigational Information

Lat: 38°47.103' **Long:** 076°13.229' **Tide:** 1.2 ft. **Current:** n/a **Chart:** 12270
Rep. Depths (*MLW*): Entry 12 ft. **Fuel Dock** 9 ft. **Max Slip/Moor** 9 ft./-
Access: On Miles River, off Eastern Bay, between Marker 2 & 3

Marina Facilities *(In Season/Off Season)*

Fuel: Gasoline, Diesel, High-Speed Pumps
Slips: 50 Total, 50 Transient **Max LOA:** 165 ft. **Max Beam:** n/a
Rate *(per ft.)*: **Day** $2.25/1.50-2* **Week** n/a **Month** n/a
Power: 30 amp $6, **50 amp** $12, **100 amp** $25, **200 amp** n/a
Cable TV: Yes Incl. **Dockside Phone:** No
Dock Type: Fixed, Long Fingers, Pilings, Alongside, Wood
Moorings: 0 Total, 0 Transient **Launch:** n/a
Rate: Day n/a **Week** n/a **Month** n/a
Heads: 4 Toilet(s), 4 Shower(s), Hair Dryers, Wireless Internet
Laundry: 2 Washer(s), 2 Dryer(s) **Pay Phones:** Yes, 3
Pump-Out: OnSite, Full Service **Fee:** $5-10 **Closed Heads:** Yes

Marina Operations

Owner/Manager: F. A. Morgan **Dockmaster:** A. Barysdale
In-Season: May15-Oct15, 8am-Dusk **Off-Season:** Oct16-May14, 8am-5pm
After-Hours Arrival: Call ahead
Reservations: Recommended **Credit Cards:** Visa/MC, Dscvr, Amex
Discounts: None
Pets: Welcome **Handicap Access:** Yes, Heads, Docks

Marina Services and Boat Supplies

Services - Docking Assistance, Concierge, Dock Carts **Communication -** Mail & Package Hold, Phone Messages, Fax in/out *($1-4)*, Data Ports *(Wi-Fi, Free)*, FedEx, UPS, Express Mail **Supplies - OnSite:** Ice *(Block, Cube)*, Ships' Store **Near:** Propane *(United Propane 745-5051)*, CNG *(Higgins)* **Under 1 mi:** Bait/Tackle, Live Bait **3+ mi:** West Marine *(770-3080, 12 mi.)*

Boatyard Services

OnCall: Engine mechanic *(gas, diesel)*, Electrical Repairs, Electronics Repairs, Hull Repairs, Rigger, Canvas Work, Bottom Cleaning, Brightwork, Refrigeration, Divers, Compound, Wash & Wax, Interior Cleaning, Propeller Repairs, Woodworking, Inflatable Repairs, Yacht Interiors **Near:** Travelift, Launching Ramp, Yacht Building. **Under 1 mi:** Sail Loft. **1-3 mi:** Yacht Broker. **Nearest Yard:** Higgins Yacht Yard (410) 745-9303

Restaurants and Accommodations

OnSite: Restaurant *(Rork's Town Dock 745-5577, L $8-15, D $10-27, inside and dockside deck)*, *(St. Michaels Crab & Steak House 745-3737, L $6-21, D $6-21, Mon-Thu 11am-9pm, Fri-Sun 11am-10pm)*, *(Foxy's Marina Bar 745-4340, L $7-22, D $7-22, 12pm-Mid)* **Near:** Restaurant *(Poppi's 745-3158)*, *(Characters 745-6206)*, *(208 Talbot 745-3838, D $27-34)*, *(Bistro St. Michaels 745-9111, D $9-30, Thu-Mon)*, *(Mezzaluna 745-2911)*, Seafood Shack *(Crab Claw 745-2900, L & D $5-25, Kids $7, not crab)*, *(Big Al's 745-3151)*, Coffee Shop *(Blue Crab Coffee 745-4155)*, Pizzeria *(Rusticana)*, Hotel *(St. Michaels Harbour Inn 745-9001)*, Inn/B&B *(Barrett's 745-3322)*

Recreation and Entertainment

OnSite: Pool, Sightseeing *(Sirius Catamaran Tour - 2 hrs. $30)* **Near:** Picnic Area, Grills, Playground, Tennis Courts, Jogging Paths, Fishing Charter, Park *(Muskrat/Church Cove - at the end of the docks)*, Museum *(Ches Bay Maritime 745-2916, Museum of Historical Costumes 745-5154, St. Mary's Square 745-9561)*, Cultural Attract, Special Events **Under 1 mi:** Fitness Center *(Fit Stop 745-5592)* **1-3 mi:** Golf Course *(Harbortown Golf 745-9066)*, Video Rental *(Bay Country Video 745-5988)*

Provisioning and General Services

Near: Convenience Store, Supermarket *(Acme 745-9819)*, Gourmet Shop *(Gourmet by the Bay 745-8200)*, Delicatessen *(Village Shop)*, Wine/Beer *(Acme)*, Liquor Store *(Village Shoppe 745-9300)*, Farmers' Market *(Willow & Green St. Sat 8:30am-12pm 745-3457)*, Meat Market, Market *(Clark's 745-3537)*, Bank/ATM, Post Office, Catholic Church, Library *(St. Michaels 745-5877)*, Beauty Salon *(Helen's 745-2688)*, Barber Shop, Dry Cleaners *(Admiral 745-4272)*, Laundry *(Village Laundry 745-9293)*, Bookstore *(Salty Dog Books & Music 770-5982)*, Pharmacy, Newsstand, Florist, Clothing Store, Retail Shops *(Shaw Bay Classics, Annabelle)* **Under 1 mi:** Hardware Store *(Lumber Yard 820-7090)*, Copies Etc. *(Poore House 745-3200)*

Transportation

OnSite: Bikes *($4/hr, $16/day)*, Rental Car, Taxi **OnCall:** Water Taxi *(Ch.71)*, Airport Limo *(Eastern Shore 800-453-2023)* **3+ mi:** Ferry Service *(6 mi.)* **Airport:** Baltimore-Washington Int'l./Easton *(60 mi./12 mi.)*

Medical Services

911 Service **OnCall:** Ambulance **Under 1 mi:** Doctor *(Family Practice 745-5000)*, Dentist *(Family Dentistry 745-9200)*, Veterinarian *(St Michaels Vet 745-5275)* **Hospital:** Easton Memorial 822-1000 *(10 mi.)*

Setting -- St. Michael's Marina is in the center of the waterfront action; a popular small pool with an attractively furnished deck and two expansive eateries are directly dockside. Forty-eight hospitable slips radiate from the undulating bulkhead and the two main piers. Two mocha clapboard restaurants with chocolate brown trim dominate the landside - the picnic tables on the Crab & Steak House's patio seem to spill onto the docks and adjacent pool. All the shops and services of charming, historic St. Michaels are an easy walk.

Marina Notes -- *$2.25/ft. (min. $67); Saturday & holiday weekends $3.25/ft. (min. $97). Hourly $10/hr. 4-14 days 10% disc, 15+ days 20% disc. DCM. Established in 1860, family owned and operated since 1982. Formerly called St. Michael's Town Dock. The long, easy-access fuel dock is along the outside of the eastern-most dock.Fax charge $1/pg. in, $4/pg. out. The small but complete bathhouse is behind a gate marked "Private" (walk along the side of the restaurant up a cement path); it sports tile floors and tile shower stalls - no private dressing rooms, but hair dryers and a vanity sink.

Notable -- Overlooking the slips are casual Crab & Steak House (inside dining, pub, or a patio with brick-red metal picnic tables under colorful umbrellas) and more upscale Michael Rork's Town Dock Restaurant and Foxy's Bar. For outside dining sit on the dockside deck at tables topped by camel-colored umbrellas or in a cozy picnic area. Inside are 3 air-conditioned, white-tableclothed dining areas: the Porch, the Gazebo and the main Greenhouse. Foxy's (Noon-Midnight) is literally "on the docks" - appetizers, snacks, steamed and grilled light fare. Don't forget to pay homage at Captain Frank's Weather Stone.

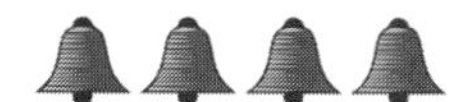

Navigational Information
Lat: 38°47.104' **Long:** 076°13.158' **Tide:** 2 ft. **Current:** n/a **Chart:** 12270
Rep. Depths (*MLW*): Entry 6 ft. **Fuel Dock** n/a **Max Slip/Moor** 11 ft./-
Access: Eastern Bay to Miles River

Marina Facilities *(In Season/Off Season)*
Fuel: No
Slips: 50 Total, 50 Transient **Max LOA:** 220 ft. **Max Beam:** n/a
Rate *(per ft.)*: **Day** $2.00/1.00* **Week** Inq. **Month** Inq.
Power: 30 amp $5, **50 amp** $10, **100 amp** $30, **200 amp** n/a
Cable TV: Yes, Free **Dockside Phone:** No
Dock Type: Fixed, Long Fingers, Pilings
Moorings: 0 Total, 0 Transient **Launch:** n/a
Rate: Day n/a **Week** n/a **Month** n/a
Heads: 5 Toilet(s), 4 Shower(s), Hair Dryers
Laundry: 2 Washer(s), 2 Dryer(s), Iron, Iron Board **Pay Phones:** Yes, 1
Pump-Out: OnSite, Full Service, 1 Central **Fee:** n/a **Closed Heads:** Yes

Marina Operations
Owner/Manager: Todd Mathias **Dockmaster:** Same
In-Season: May 1-Oct 19, 7am-8pm **Off-Season:** Jan-Apr, 9am-5pm
After-Hours Arrival: Hail on Ch. 16
Reservations: Recommended **Credit Cards:** Visa/MC, Dscvr, Din, Amex
Discounts: None
Pets: Welcome, Dog Walk Area **Handicap Access:** Yes, Heads, Docks

St. Michaels Harbour Inn Marina

101 North Harbor Road; St. Michaels, MD 21663

Tel: (410) 745-9001; (800) 955-9001 **VHF: Monitor** 16 **Talk** 74
Fax: (410) 745-9150 **Alternate Tel:** n/a
Email: rooms@harbourinn.com **Web:** www.harbourinn.com
Nearest Town: St. Michaels *(0.5 mi.)* **Tourist Info:** (410) 822-4653

Marina Services and Boat Supplies
Services - Docking Assistance, Concierge, Room Service to the Boat, Trash Pick-Up, Dock Carts, Megayacht Facilities **Communication -** Mail & Package Hold, Phone Messages, Fax in/out, Data Ports *(Front desk + Wi-Fi)*, FedEx, DHL, UPS, Express Mail **Supplies - OnSite:** Ice *(Cube)*, Ships' Store **Under 1 mi:** Bait/Tackle, Propane *(United Propane 745-5051)*, CNG *(Higgins Yacht Yard 745-9303)* **3+ mi:** West Marine *(770-3080, 12 mi.)*

Boatyard Services
Near: Launching Ramp, Electrical Repairs, Electronics Repairs, Hull Repairs, Rigger, Canvas Work, Divers, Propeller Repairs, Yacht Design, Yacht Broker. **Nearest Yard:** Higgins Yacht Yard, nearby (410) 745-9303

Restaurants and Accommodations
OnSite: Restaurant *(Shore Restaurant 924-4769, D $21-32, dinner 6-10pm)*, Lite Fare *(Shore Lounge L $8-16, D $8-28, two specials $26-28, Sun brunch 10am-2pm)*, Hotel *(St. Michaels Harbour Inn 745-9001, $189-525, 46 water-front suites)* **Near:** Restaurant *(Carpenter Street Salon 745-5111)*, *(St. Michaels' Crab & Steakhouse 745-3737, L $6-21, D $6-21, L 11:30am-2:30pm, D 3:30-11pm)*, Seafood Shack *(Crab Claw 745-2400, L $5-25, D $5-25, dinghy)*, Coffee Shop *(Blue Crab Coffee 745-4155)*, Pizzeria *(Rusticana 745-3434)*, Hotel *(Inn at Perry Cabin 745-2200)*, Inn/B&B *(Barrett's B&B 7453322)*, *(Mount Misery B&B 745-6811)*
3+ mi: Restaurant *(Bistro StMichaels 745-9111, D $9-30, Thu-Mon)*

Recreation and Entertainment
OnSite: Pool *(8am-8pm)*, Spa, Picnic Area, Grills, Fitness Center, Boat Rentals *(kayaks, canoes, paddle boats)* **Near:** Tennis Courts, Horseback Riding, Park, Museum *(Chesapeake Bay Maritime 745-2916, Museum of Historical Costumes 745-5154, St. Mary's Square 745-9561)*, Cultural Attract, Sightseeing **1-3 mi:** Golf Course *(Harbortown Golf 745-9066)*, Video Rental *(Bay Country Video 745-5988)*

Provisioning and General Services
OnSite: Convenience Store *(Ship's Locker - clothing, sundries, wine & beer)* **Near:** Supermarket *(Acme 745-9819)*, Gourmet Shop *(Gourmet by the Bay 745-8200)*, Delicatessen *(Village Market 745-9300 - groceries, deli, butcher)*, Wine/Beer *(Acme)*, Liquor Store *(Graul's)*, Farmers' Market *(Muskrat Park Sat 8:30am-12pm 745-3457)*, Fishmonger, Meat Market, Bank/ATM, Post Office, Catholic Church, Protestant Church, Beauty Salon *(St. Michaels Salon 745-4181)*, Dry Cleaners *(Admiral 745-4272)*, Laundry, Newsstand, Florist, Retail Shops **Under 1 mi:** Market *(Clark's 745-3537)*, Library *(St. Michaels 745-5877)*, Bookstore *(Salty Dog 770-5982)*, Pharmacy *(Reeser's 745-2207)*, Hardware Store *(Lumber Yard 820-7090)*

Transportation
OnSite: Courtesy Car/Van, Bikes *(complimentary)*, Rental Car **OnCall:** Water Taxi *(Harbor Shuttle Ch.71)*, Taxi *(Scotty's 822-1475)*, Airport Limo *(Eastern Shore 800-453-2023)* **3+ mi:** Ferry Service *(Bellevue/Oxford, 6 mi.)* **Airport:** Baltimore-Washington Int'l./Easton *(60 mi./12 mi.)*

Medical Services
911 Service **OnSite:** Holistic Services *(full service spa; treatments $30-200, massage $100/60 min.)* **Under 1 mi:** Doctor *(St Michaels745-5000)*, Dentist *(Family 745-9200, Schulman 886-2293)*, Ambulance **1-3 mi:** Veterinarian *(St Michaels 745-5275)* **Hospital:** Easton Memorial 822-1000 *(10 mi.)*

Setting -- A bit out of the hubbub of the well-touristed historic and shopping district, St. Michaels Inn is on the "quiet side" of the harbor. The attractive three-story gray contemporary hotel wraps two sides of the waterfront. One wing looks north, over a large rectangle of docks hosting 40 slips, to the active harbor and the Maritime Museum beyond. The other wing looks west over 12 slips, with long finger piers, that hug the bulkhead.

Marina Notes -- *In season Sun-Thu $2/ft. ($60 min.), Fri, Sat & hols $3/ft. $80 min.); off-season Sun-Fri $1.00, Sat $1.50. DCM. A guest of the marina is a guest of the resort, and all facilities are available, including room service to the boat and concierge services. Complimentary cable, coffee, newspaper and bicycles. Canoes, kayaks, Aqua bikes available for rental as well. A three-year, half-million dollar dock renovation completed May '05. Excellent, designer-tile heads and showers with dressing rooms and gleaming stainless steel dividers - hair dryers, large mirror, vanity. A washer/dryer set in each.

Notable -- Most of the 46 luxurious suites and rooms overlook the water and many have furnished balconies. As part of the renovation, the former Harborlights and Pascal eateries were replaced by contemporary, casual Shore Restaurant (upstairs - a window wall provides an extraordinary view of the harbor) and Shore Lounge (downstairs & poolside) -- both under the baton of Jim & Sidney Trond of Gourmet by the Bay. The full-service spa has four treatment rooms, a relaxation room and couples massage room. A delightful four-block walk through a lovely residential area of small, antique houses in various stages of restoration leads to Talbot Street, which is the beginning of the charming, historic "town that fooled the British."

Lowes Wharf Marina Inn

PO Box 12; 21651 Lowes Wharf Road; Sherwood, MD 21665

Tel: (410) 745-6684; (888) 484-9267 **VHF: Monitor** 16 **Talk** n/a
Fax: (410) 745-5085 **Alternate Tel:** n/a
Email: info@loweswharf.com **Web:** www.loweswharf.com
Nearest Town: Tilghman Island *(3 mi.)* **Tourist Info:** (410) 770-8000

Navigational Information

Lat: 38°45.984' **Long:** 076°19.632' **Tide:** 2 ft. **Current:** 0 kt. **Chart:** 12276
Rep. Depths (*MLW*): Entry 5 ft. **Fuel Dock** 5 ft. **Max Slip/Moor** 5 ft./5 ft.
Access: 2 mi east of Poplar Island

Marina Facilities *(In Season/Off Season)*

Fuel: Gasoline, Diesel
Slips: 22 Total, 6 Transient **Max LOA:** 60 ft. **Max Beam:** 15 ft.
Rate *(per ft.)*: **Day** $1.00* **Week** n/a **Month** n/a
Power: 30 amp $5, **50 amp** n/a, **100 amp** n/a, **200 amp** n/a
Cable TV: No **Dockside Phone:** No
Dock Type: Fixed, Long Fingers, Pilings, Wood
Moorings: 0 Total, 0 Transient **Launch:** n/a
Rate: Day n/a **Week** n/a **Month** n/a
Heads: 2 Toilet(s), 1 Shower(s)
Laundry: 1 Washer(s), 1 Dryer(s), Iron, Iron Board **Pay Phones:** No
Pump-Out: Self Service, 1 Central, 1 Port **Fee:** Free **Closed Heads:** Yes

Marina Operations

Owner/Manager: Paul Zelinske **Dockmaster:** Same
In-Season: Apr-Oct, 8:30am-6pm **Off-Season:** Nov-Mar, 8:30am-5pm
After-Hours Arrival: Check in at bar
Reservations: Preferred **Credit Cards:** Visa/MC, Dscvr
Discounts: None
Pets: Welcome **Handicap Access:** No

Marina Services and Boat Supplies

Services - Docking Assistance, Boaters' Lounge **Communication -** Phone Messages, Fax in/out, FedEx, UPS, Express Mail **Supplies - OnSite:** Ice *(Block, Cube)*, Ships' Store, Bait/Tackle, Live Bait, Propane

Boatyard Services

OnSite: Launching Ramp **Near:** Divers. **1-3 mi:** Travelift, Engine mechanic *(gas, diesel)*. **Nearest Yard:** Knapp's Narrows, 4 mi. (410) 886-2720

Restaurants and Accommodations

OnSite: Lite Fare *(Wharf Tavern 745-0119, L $4-11, D $4-19, kids' menu, Mon-Fri 4-9pm, Sat-Sun 12-10pm, live entertainment; free continental breakfast weekends)*, Motel *(Lowes Wharf Marina Inn 745-6684, $80-180)* **1-3 mi:** Restaurant *(Bridge Restaurant 886-2320, D $14-20)*, *(Harrison's Chesapeake House 886-2121, B $3-11, L $4-15, D $12-25, picks up)*, *(Bay Hundred 886-2126, L $5-13, D $15-22)*, *(Tilghman Island Inn 886-2141, L $8-12, D $17-35, closed Wed, Mon-Thu casual menu $8-13, 5-course prix-fix $60/pp, Sun brunch buffet $19)*, Inn/B&B *(Tilghman Island Inn 886-2141, $100-300, weekends 2nt./min)*

Recreation and Entertainment

OnSite: Beach, Picnic Area, Playground, Fitness Center, Boat Rentals *(kayaks, single $12.50/hr., double $15/hr., $50/day)*, Fishing Charter *(Miss Tracey day trips $525, half-days $375; Sea Ducking Oct & Nov $325-600, hunting licenses on-site, or "Cast-n-Blast" on the same day $600)*, Volleyball **Near:** Jogging Paths, Roller Blade/Bike Paths **1-3 mi:** Park *(Back Creek Park)*

Provisioning and General Services

OnSite: Crabs/Waterman, Oysterman **Under 1 mi:** Post Office *(886-2634)* **1-3 mi:** Market *(Island Market 886-2817, Corner Market 886-9033)*, Library *(Tilghman Branch 886-9816)*, Bookstore *(Crawfords Nautical Books 886-2230)*

Transportation

OnSite: Bikes *($4.50/hr., $16/day)*, Rental Car *(Easton Enterprise 822-3260 20 mi., Hertz 822-1676)* **OnCall:** Airport Limo *(Eastern Shore 800-453-2023)* **Airport:** Baltimore-Washington Int'l./Easton *(70 mi./20 mi.)*

Medical Services

911 Service **OnCall:** Ambulance **1-3 mi:** Doctor *(St Michaels Family Practice 745-5000)*, Dentist *(Family 745-9200)*
Hospital: Easton Memorial 822-1000 *(20 mi.)*

Setting -- The contemporary gray-clapboard Lowes Wharf Inn sits in the center of a small bulkheaded peninsula that juts out into the Bay. Slips line one side, The Wharf eatery - with an open air bar - looks out across the point and, on the opposite side, picnic tables, a volleyball court and a row of Adirondack chairs enjoy wide open views of the Bay and the sunset.

Marina Notes -- *$30 min. Family owned and operated since 1995. All facilities are available to marina guests (lodgings, bar, restaurant, bike & kayak rentals, fishing). Six dedicated transient slips have new power posts and short finger piers. Most boats dock stern-to. Free pump-out, and free continental breakfast on the weekends. In the main building is a small fitness room with three pieces of exercise equipment, a conveniently sited washer & dryer and an adjacent shower. The actual heads are shared with the restaurant, but are key-coded to give dockage patrons 24-hour access. Another small building houses the ships' store, bait and tackle shop, and breakfast room.

Notable -- The inn consists of six fresh, modern motel-style rooms (2 suites) that overlook the water across the volleyball court - all brand new as a result of Isabel. At the end of the Inn, directly on the waterfront, The Wharf eatery offers three very casual seating areas: outside at picnic tables or around the bar, inside at tables or in the bar area near the pool table - all serve the same menu. Crabbing and fishing are reportedly good right off the bulkhead - bring your chicken necks. Lowes Wharf is very secluded - out of the hububb of this busy peninsula - 7 mi. east to St. Michaels and 3-4 mi. west to Tilghman Island.

PHOTOS ON CD-ROM: 11

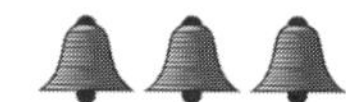

Navigational Information
Lat: 38°43.273' **Long:** 076°20.237' **Tide:** 1 ft. **Current:** 3 kt. **Chart:** 12276
Rep. Depths (*MLW*): Entry 12 ft. **Fuel Dock** n/a **Max Slip/Moor** 9 ft./-
Access: Chesapeake Bay to Knapps Narrows

Marina Facilities *(In Season/Off Season)*
Fuel: No
Slips: 31 Total, 20 Transient **Max LOA:** 85 ft. **Max Beam:** n/a
Rate *(per ft.)*: **Day** $1.75 **Week** Inq. **Month** n/a
Power: 30 amp Incl., **50 amp** Incl., **100 amp** n/a, **200 amp** n/a
Cable TV: No **Dockside Phone:** No
Dock Type: n/a
Moorings: 0 Total, 0 Transient **Launch:** n/a
Rate: Day n/a **Week** n/a **Month** n/a
Heads: 4 Toilet(s), 4 Shower(s)
Laundry: None **Pay Phones:** No
Pump-Out: OnSite **Fee:** Free **Closed Heads:** Yes

Marina Operations
Owner/Manager: Ron and Nancy Cicero **Dockmaster:** Same
In-Season: LabDay-MemDay, 8am-8pm **Off-Season:** MemDay-Lab-Day, Inq
After-Hours Arrival: Call ahead
Reservations: No **Credit Cards:** Visa/MC
Discounts: None
Pets: Welcome **Handicap Access:** No

Tilghman Island Marina

PO Box 31; 6140 Mariners Court; Tilghman, MD 21671
Tel: (410) 886-2500 **VHF: Monitor** 16 **Talk** 72
Fax: (410) 886-2979 **Alternate Tel:** n/a
Email: captain@tilghmanmarina.com **Web:** tilghmanmarina.com
Nearest Town: St. Michaels *(12 mi.)* **Tourist Info:** (410) 770-8000

Marina Services and Boat Supplies
Services - Security *(24 hrs., owners live on premises)* **Communication -** FedEx, UPS, Express Mail **Supplies - OnSite:** Ice *(Cube)* **Near:** Ships' Store, Bait/Tackle *(Fairbank Tackle 886-9807)*, Propane

Boatyard Services
Near: Travelift, Engine mechanic *(gas, diesel)*, Electronics Repairs, Hull Repairs, Rigger, Sail Loft, Bottom Cleaning, Propeller Repairs, Painting.
Nearest Yard: Knapp's Narrows Marina (410) 886-2720

Restaurants and Accommodations
Near: Restaurant *(Bay Hundred 886-2126, L $5-13, D $15-22, kids' $5)*, *(Bridge Restaurant 886-2330, D $14-20)*, *(Tilghman Island Inn 886-2141, L $8-12, D $17-35, closed Wed, Mon-Thu casual menu $8-13, 5-course prix-fix $60/pp, Sun brunch buffet $19)*, Hotel *(Knapps Narrows 886-2720, $80-275)*, Inn/B&B *(Tilghman Island Inn 886-2141, $200-300)*
Under 1 mi: Restaurant *(Harrison's Chesapeake House 886-2121, B $3-11, L $4-15, D $12-25 picks up)*, Lite Fare *(So Neat Café & Bakery 886-2143)*, *Inn/B&B (Lazy Jack886-2215)*, *(Sinclair House 886-2147)*, *(Chesapeake Wood Duck 886-2070)* **1-3 mi:** Inn/B&B *(Black Walnut Point Inn 886-2452)*

Recreation and Entertainment
OnSite: Pool *(10am-7pm)*, Boat Rentals *(double kayaks $35/hr., $50/2 hrs., $75/half-day; Wave Runners, pontoons, sailboats, canoes, fishing skiffs, crabbing and fishing equipment)*, Fishing Charter *(Huntress 886-2971 - 35 ft. Custom Markley)* **Near:** Playground, Jogging Paths, Roller Blade/Bike Paths, Park *(Back Creek Park for kayaking)*, Sightseeing *(Chesapeake Bay Skipjack Charters 886-2176, Dockside Express Cruises & Tours 886-2643; Lady Patty 45 ft. Bay ketch 886-2215 $30/20)*, Galleries, Special Events *(Tilghman Island Day - 3rd week Oct)*

Provisioning and General Services
Near: Convenience Store, Green Grocer *(Dogwood Harbor)*, Market *(Island Market 886-2817, Corner Market 886-9033)* **Under 1 mi:** Wine/Beer, Fishmonger *(Chesapeake Landing 410-820-0113)*, Bank/ATM, Post Office *(886-2444)*, Protestant Church, Library *(Tilghman Branch 886-9816)*, Beauty Salon *(Judy's Beauty Shoppe 886-2188)*, Barber Shop, Bookstore *(Crawfords Nautical Books 886-2230)*

Transportation
OnSite: Bikes *($5/hr.,$15/half-day, $20/day; also scooters & mopeds)*
OnCall: Airport Limo **3+ mi:** Rental Car *(Easton Enterprise 822-3260, Hertz 822-1676, 23 mi.)*
Airport: Baltimore-Washington Int'l./Easton *(73mi./3 mi.)*

Medical Services
911 Service **OnSite:** Holistic Services **OnCall:** Ambulance **1-3 mi:** Dentist *(Shulman 886-2293)* **3+ mi:** Doctor *(St. Michael's Family Medical 745-5000, 9mi.)* **Hospital:** Easton Memorial 822-1000 *(23 mi.)*

Setting -- This very protected rectangular basin is edged with 31 slips along 3 sides, a 9-foot pier head; and 60 feet of alongside bulkhead - all surrounded by Tilghman Island Quay, a quite nice Cape Cod-style townhouse complex set on acres of rolling lawn. A crushed shell path borders the docks and nearby are a small kidney-shaped pool and a canvas-topped decked filled with picnic tables for corn & crab feasts. Lots of activities and water toys are available on-site.

Marina Notes -- Tilghman Island Marina is a small, but buttoned-up facility - the marina is the focus of the business. Club cruises are encouraged - can handle up to 27 boats, 30 with rafting, and up to 70 people for an onshore event. The physical landside amenities are limited but more than compensated by the many recreational options: crabbing & fishing equipment, bikes, scooters, mopeds, small fishing boats, canoes, wave-runners, pontoon boats and 14 sit-a-top kayaks - all available for rental. The individual bathrooms have wood paneled walls and indoor-outdoor carpeted floors.

Notable -- If you want to play - on water or land - TIM has the equipment or excursion available. They also offer powerboat and sailing lessons. Most restaurants are either dinghyable or walkable, except for Harrison's - and they'll send a van out for pickup. The elegant Tilghman Island Inn is right down the road. Nearby is the water entrance to Back Creek Park, a wildlife refuge with a designated kayaking trail. 4-hour excursions also take paddlers and kayaks 2.5 miles to the Popular Islands on a pontoon boat - tour the 4 islands to observe the wildlife and the restoration projects. Hour and a half sunset drifts on the pontoon boat are $25. Right up the block, the Island Market is a nicely supplied convenience store; a produce stand is less than 0.25 mile at Dogwood Harbor.

PHOTOS ON CD-ROM: 10

Tilghman Island Inn & Marina

21384 Coopertown Road; Tilghman, MD 21671

Tel: (410) 886-2141; (800) 886-2141 **VHF: Monitor** 16 **Talk** 68
Fax: (410) 886-2216 **Alternate Tel:** n/a
Email: info@tilghmanislandinn.com **Web:** www.tilghmanislandinn.com
Nearest Town: St. Michaels *(12 mi.)* **Tourist Info:** (410) 770-8000

Navigational Information

Lat: 38°43.235' **Long:** 076°20.175' **Tide:** 1 ft. **Current:** 3 kt. **Chart:** 12276
Rep. Depths (*MLW*): Entry 11 ft. **Fuel Dock** n/a **Max Slip/Moor** 4 ft./4 ft.
Access: Chesapeake Bay to Knapps Narrows #1 FG. FLR

Marina Facilities *(In Season/Off Season)*

Fuel: No
Slips: 21 Total, 11 Transient **Max LOA:** 40 ft. **Max Beam:** 15 ft.
Rate *(per ft.)*: **Day** $1.50* **Week** n/a **Month** n/a
Power: 30 amp Incl., **50 amp** $5, **100 amp** n/a, **200 amp** n/a
Cable TV: No **Dockside Phone:** Yes
Dock Type: Fixed, Short Fingers, Pilings, Alongside, Wood
Moorings: 0 Total, 0 Transient **Launch:** n/a, Dinghy Dock
Rate: Day n/a **Week** n/a **Month** n/a
Heads: 2 Toilet(s), 1 Shower(s) *(with dressing rooms)*, Hair Dryers
Laundry: None, Book Exchange **Pay Phones:** No
Pump-Out: OnSite, Self Service, 1 Central **Fee:** Free **Closed Heads:** Yes

Marina Operations

Owner/Manager: Jack Redmon **Dockmaster:** Thom Sevco
In-Season: Feb-Dec, 8am-8pm **Off-Season:** n/a, Closed
After-Hours Arrival: Locate slip - see dockmaster in the morning
Reservations: Yes, Preferred **Credit Cards:** Visa/MC, Dscvr, Amex
Discounts: None
Pets: Welcome, Dog Walk Area **Handicap Access:** Yes, Heads, Docks

Marina Services and Boat Supplies

Services - Docking Assistance, Concierge, Room Service to the Boat, Boaters' Lounge, Crew Lounge, Trash Pick-Up, Dock Carts **Communication -** Mail & Package Hold, Phone Messages, Fax in/out *($1)*, FedEx, DHL, UPS, Express Mail *(Sat Del)* **Supplies - OnSite:** Ice *(Block, Cube)* **Near:** Ships' Store, Bait/Tackle *(Fairbank Tackle 886-9807)*, Live Bait, Propane **3+ mi:** West Marine *(22 mi.)*, Boat/US *(22 mi.)*

Boatyard Services

Near: Travelift, Railway, Crane, Launching Ramp, Engine mechanic *(gas, diesel)*, Electrical Repairs, Electronics Repairs, Hull Repairs, Rigger, Bottom Cleaning, Brightwork, Air Conditioning, Refrigeration, Divers, Metal Fabrication, Painting. **Nearest Yard:** Knapps Narrows (410) 886-2720

Restaurants and Accommodations

OnSite: Restaurant *(Tilghman Island Inn's Main Dining Rooms 886-2141, L $8-12, D $17-35, Mon-Thu casual menu $8-13, 5-course prix-fix $60/pp, Sun brunch buffet $19, closed Wed)*, Lite Fare *(Tilghman Island Inn's Fireside Lounge D $7-12, light entrees or starters from dinner menu)*, Inn/B&B *(Tilghman Island Inn 886-2141, $100-300, weekends 2 night min.)* **Near:** Restaurant *(Bay Hundred 886-2126, L $5-13, D $15-22)*, *(Bridge Restaurant 886-2330, D $14-20)*, Inn/B&B *(Chesapeake Wood Duck Inn)*, 886-2070) *(Harrison's Chesapeake House 886-2121)* **Under 1 mi:** Lite Fare *(So Neat Café & Bakery 886-2143)*, Inn/B&B *(Sinclair House 886-2147)*

Recreation and Entertainment

OnSite: Pool, Picnic Area, Grills, Tennis Courts, Boat Rentals *(Deep Reef 886-2545 - row, motor & sailboats)*, Fishing Charter, Special Events *(St. Michaels Food & Wine Fest - 1st of May,)* **Near:** Playground, Jogging Paths, Roller Blade/Bike Paths, Group Fishing Boat, Park *(Back Creek Park, kayaking)*, Sightseeing *(Chesapeake Bay Skipjack Charters 886-2176, Dockside Express Cruises & Tours 886-2643)*, Galleries *(Tilghman Island Day - Oct)*

Provisioning and General Services

OnSite: Wine/Beer **Near:** Green Grocer *(Dogwood Farm produce stand)*, Fishmonger, Market *(Island Market 886-2817, Corner Market 886-9033)*, Bank/ATM **Under 1 mi:** Convenience Store, Liquor Store, Bakery, Post Office *(886-2444)*, Protestant Church, Library *(Tilghman Branch 886-9816)*, Beauty Salon *(Judy's Beauty Shoppe 886-2188)*, Barber Shop, Bookstore *(Crawfords Nautical Books 886-2230)* **3+ mi:** Pharmacy *(13 mi.)*, Hardware Store *(10 mi.)*, Retail Shops *(13 mi.)*, Department Store *(Peebles, 25 mi.)*, Copies Etc. *(13 mi.)*

Transportation

OnCall: Water Taxi, Airport Limo **3+ mi:** Rental Car *(Easton Enterprise, on call 23 mi., 822-3260, Hertz in Easton 822-1676, 23 mi.)*
Airport: Baltimore-Washington Int'l./Easton *(73 mi./23 mi.)*

Medical Services

911 Service **OnSite:** Holistic Services **OnCall:** Ambulance **Under 1 mi:** Dentist *(Shulman 886-2293)* **3+ mi:** Doctor *(St. Michael's Family Medical 745-5000, 9 mi.)* **Hospital:** Easton Memorial 822-1000 *(23 mi.)*

Setting -- The views from the rooms and docks of the intimate, sophisticated, two-story, red-roofed Tilghman Island Inn are of Knapps Narrows and the pristine, ever-changing salt marsh beyond. A row of painted Adirondack chairs lines the waterfront - a garden away from the Inn's charming rooms; the bulkhead in front is edged with slips. Five waterfront acres, seemingly one large, well-tended perennial garden, also host a pool, tennis court, outdoor sculptures, a water garden, an awning-topped dining deck, and a flock of wrought-iron chairs and tables interspersed with natural-colored market umbrellas.

Marina Notes -- *$0.50/ft. up to 33 ft., $1.50/ft. over 33 ft. Closed Jan. Present owners have managed the inn, restaurant, and boat slips since 1990. Weekday & weekend hotel packages including some meals available. Pet friendly (even in the rooms!). Limited dockage discourages club cruises, but up to 50 can accommodated for events and more for parties - including once-a-month weddings. The upscale rooms of the inn are stylishly decorated in a variety of motifs with superb amenities; well-chosen antiques intermingled with contemporary pieces furnish the elegant public rooms. Alas, only 1 shower for boaters.

Notable -- The highlight of a visit is, no doubt, dinner. Chef David McCallum's creative American cuisine, served in 2 stunning waterfront dining rooms - Isabel & Baywatch - and in the more casual Fireside Lounge, is complimented by a world-class wine cellar - featured in Gourmet Magazine, Southern Living, and Wine Spectator, (which gives their "Award of Excellence" virtually every year). The dishes are innovative riffs on Eastern Shore classics, featuring local produce and seafood. B 8-10am; L Noon-3/4pm; D: Mon, Tue, Thu 6-9pm, Fri & Sat 6-10pm, Sun 5-9:30pm, Sun brunch Noon-3pm. The Lounge Sun-Tue & Thu 4-9pm.

7. ES: ST MICHAELS & TILGHMAN IS
PHOTOS ON CD-ROM: 13

Navigational Information
Lat: 38°43.207' **Long:** 076°20.003' **Tide:** 3 ft. **Current:** n/a **Chart:** 12276
Rep. Depths (*MLW*): Entry 7 ft. **Fuel Dock** 7 ft. **Max Slip/Moor** 7 ft./-
Access: Chesapeake Bay to Knapp's Narrows

Marina Facilities *(In Season/Off Season)*
Fuel: *Texaco 7am-6pm* - Gasoline, Diesel
Slips: 130 Total, 25 Transient **Max LOA:** 50 ft. **Max Beam:** n/a
Rate *(per ft.)*: **Day** $1.85/1.00 **Week** Inq. **Month** Inq.
Power: 30 amp $5, **50 amp** $10, **100 amp** Inq., **200 amp** Inq.
Cable TV: No **Dockside Phone:** No
Dock Type: Fixed, Floating
Moorings: 0 Total, 0 Transient **Launch:** n/a
Rate: Day n/a **Week** n/a **Month** n/a
Heads: 2 Toilet(s), 2 Shower(s)
Laundry: 1 Washer(s), 1 Dryer(s), Book Exchange **Pay Phones:** Yes, 1
Pump-Out: OnSite **Fee:** $5 **Closed Heads:** Yes

Marina Operations
Owner/Manager: Mark Julan **Dockmaster:** Derek Abbott
In-Season: May-Oct, 7:30am-7pm **Off-Season:** Nov-Apr, 7:30am-4pm
After-Hours Arrival: Call ahead
Reservations: Preferred **Credit Cards:** Visa/MC, Dscvr
Discounts: None
Pets: Welcome **Handicap Access:** No

Knapp's Narrows Marina & Inn

PO Box 277; 6176 Tilghman Road; Tilghman Island, MD 21671

Tel: (410) 886-2720; (800) 322-5181 **VHF: Monitor** 16 **Talk** n/a
Fax: (410) 886-2716 **Alternate Tel:** n/a
Email: knappsnarrows@bluecrab.org **Web:** knappsnarrowsmarina.com
Nearest Town: St. Michael's *(11 mi.)* **Tourist Info:** (410) 770-8000

Marina Services and Boat Supplies
Services - Docking Assistance, Boaters' Lounge, Dock Carts **Communication -** Mail & Package Hold, Phone Messages, Fax in/out, Data Ports, FedEx, UPS, Express Mail **Supplies - OnSite:** Ice *(Block, Cube)*, Ships' Store **Near:** Bait/Tackle *(Fairbank Tackle 886-9807)*, Live Bait

Boatyard Services
OnSite: Travelift *(35T)*, Forklift, Engine mechanic *(gas, diesel)*, Electrical Repairs, Electronics Repairs, Hull Repairs, Rigger, Sail Loft, Bottom Cleaning, Interior Cleaning, Propeller Repairs, Woodworking, Upholstery, Painting, Awlgrip, Total Refits **Yard Rates:** $58-75/hr, Haul & Launch $8/ft. *(blocking incl.)*, Power Wash Incl., Bottom Paint sailboats $12.50/ft., powerboat $14/ft. *(paint incl.)* **Storage:** In-Water yes

Restaurants and Accommodations
OnSite: Restaurant *(Bay Hundred 886-2126, L $5-13, D $15-22, kids' menu $5, Free dock 'n' dine)*, Hotel *(The Inn at Knapps Narrows 886-2720, $120-275, daily $120-275, weekly $720-1650)* **Near:** Restaurant *(Bridge Restaurant 886-2330, D $14-20)*, *(Tilghman Island Inn 886-2141, L $8-12, D $17-35, Mon-Thu casual menu $8-13, 5-course prix-fix $60/pp, Sun brunch buffet $19, closed Wed)*, Inn/B&B *(Tilghman Island Inn 886-2141, $100-300)* **Under 1 mi:** Crab House *(Harrison's 886-2121, B $3-11, L $4-15, D $12-25, picks up)*, Lite Fare *(So Neat Café & Bakery 886-2143)*, Inn/B&B *(Lazyjack Inn 886-2215, $109-269)*, *(Chesapeake Wood Duck Inn 886-2070)* **1-3 mi:** Inn/B&B *(Black Walnut Point 886-2452, $120-135)*

Recreation and Entertainment
OnSite: Pool *(25 ft.x 60 ft.)*, Picnic Area, Grills *(charcoal)*, Playground, Fishing Charter *(Chesapeake Lady II, J-B Charters, Lady Patty Sailing Charters)* **Near:** Boat Rentals *(kayaks, wave runners at Tilghman Island Marina)*, Park *(Back Creek Park, kayaking)*, Sightseeing *(Chesapeake Bay Skipjack Charters 886-2176, Dockside Express Cruises & Tours 886-2643; Chesapeake Lights Lighthouse tours 886-2215)*, Special Events *(Tilghman Island Seafood Fest - late Jun, Tilghman Days - Oct)*

Provisioning and General Services
Near: Green Grocer *(Dogwood Farm produce stand)*, Market *(Island Market 886-2817, Corner Market 886-9033)* **Under 1 mi:** Wine/Beer, Bank/ATM, Post Office *(886-2444)*, Library *(Tilghman Branch 886-9816)*, Beauty Salon *(Judy's Beauty Shoppe 886-2188)*, Bookstore *(Crawfords Nautical Books 886-2230)* **1-3 mi:** Catholic Church, Protestant Church

Transportation
OnSite: Bikes **OnCall:** Taxi, Airport Limo **3+ mi:** Rental Car *(Easton Enterprise 822-3260 23 mi., Hertz in Easton 822-1676, 23 mi.)*
Airport: Baltimore-Washington Int'l./Easton *(73 mi./23 mi.)*

Medical Services
911 Service **OnCall:** Ambulance **Under 1 mi:** Dentist *(Shulman 886-2115)* **3+ mi:** Doctor *(St. Michael's Family Medical 745-5000, 9 mi.)*
Hospital: Easton Memorial 822-1000 *(23 mi.)*

Setting -- Bayside of the famous Swing Bridge, right off Knapps Narrows, this sheltered rectangular basin is lined with slips - with a core of docks down the center and a travelift well at the end. A 1,000 foot long floating pier with alongside dockage on both sides lines the Narrows. Rising above the basin's western edge, the sparkling new 3-story, 20-room gray-sided contemporary Knapp's Narrows Inn has expansive vistas of the channel, the Bay and the bridge. A large pool and cabana with upper deck are tucked at the head of the basin, and a shaded picnic area with grills overlooks the waterway. Groups are welcome.

Marina Notes -- DCM. Passage dredged to 11 feet in 1996. Transients tend to be mostly at the alongside slips. The quite new main docks inside the basin are stationary with half-length fingers and power boxes on posts. A 24-hour full service boatyard with fuel is on-site. Complimentary breakfast is served in the nautically-inspired boaters' lounge, decorated in white wicker and navy striped cushions; it's just delightful, and available during the day and early evening. Two plugs provide Internet access (with an 800 number or a local access code) - a couple of comfortable chairs invite you to plug in your laptop. Two conference rooms available. Workboats tie up along the bulkhead (a good place to look for soft crabs). Two bathhouses are on either side of the basin.

Notable -- The favorably reviewed Bay Hundred Restaurant sits right on the Narrows and features local seafood and "fusion" cuisine. Inside it's tablecloths and quiet; outside it's umbrella-topped tables and bustling boat traffic. Right across the waterway is The Bridge Restaurant; Fair Bait & Tackle, which has a small convenience store and gas station, is just beyond. A produce stand is just a short way up the road and The Tilghman Island Inn is an easy walk.

PHOTOS ON CD-ROM: 17

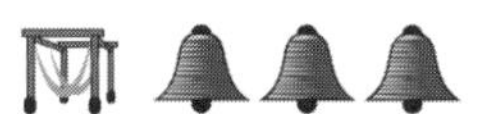

Harrison's Chesapeake House

21551 Chesapeake House Dr.; Tilghman Is., MD 21671

Tel: (410) 886-2121 **VHF: Monitor** 16 **Talk** 18
Fax: (410) 886-2599 **Alternate Tel:** n/a
Email: cheshse@goeaston.net **Web:** www.chesapeakehouse.com
Nearest Town: St. Michael's *(12 mi.)* **Tourist Info:** (410) 770-8000

Navigational Information

Lat: 38°42.647' **Long:** 076°20.098' **Tide:** 1 ft. **Current:** n/a **Chart:** 12276
Rep. Depths (*MLW*): Entry 8 ft. **Fuel Dock** 7 ft. **Max Slip/Moor** 6 ft./-
Access: Knapp's Narrows to Dogwood Harbor

Marina Facilities *(In Season/Off Season)*

Fuel: No
Slips: 30 Total, 20 Transient **Max LOA:** 100 ft. **Max Beam:** 18 ft.
Rate *(per ft.)*: **Day** $50.00* **Week** Inq. **Month** Inq.
Power: 30 amp Incl., **50 amp** $6, **100 amp** n/a, **200 amp** n/a
Cable TV: No **Dockside Phone:** Yes
Dock Type: Fixed, Short Fingers, Alongside, Wood
Moorings: 0 Total, 0 Transient **Launch:** n/a
Rate: Day n/a **Week** n/a **Month** n/a
Heads: 1 Toilet(s), 1 Shower(s)
Laundry: None **Pay Phones:** Yes, 3
Pump-Out: OnSite, Self Service, 1 Central **Fee:** n/a **Closed Heads:** Yes

Marina Operations

Owner/Manager: Buddy Harrison **Dockmaster:** Same
In-Season: Year-Round, 6am-Mid **Off-Season:** n/a
After-Hours Arrival: Call ahead
Reservations: No **Credit Cards:** Visa/MC
Discounts: None
Pets: Welcome, Dog Walk Area **Handicap Access:** No

Marina Services and Boat Supplies

Services - Docking Assistance, Concierge, Crew Lounge **Communication -** Mail & Package Hold, Phone Messages, Fax in/out, FedEx, UPS, Express Mail **Supplies - OnSite:** Ice *(Block, Cube)*, Ships' Store, Bait/Tackle **OnCall:** Live Bait, Propane **Near:** Ice *(Shaved)*

Boatyard Services

OnSite: Travelift *(15T)*, Divers, Compound, Wash & Wax, Woodworking, Painting **OnCall:** Crane, Forklift, Engine mechanic *(gas, diesel)*, Electrical Repairs, Electronics Repairs, Hull Repairs, Rigger, Canvas Work, Bottom Cleaning, Brightwork, Refrigeration, Interior Cleaning, Propeller Repairs, Upholstery, Yacht Interiors, Metal Fabrication, Yacht Design, Yacht Building, Total Refits, Yacht Broker **Near:** Launching Ramp. **Yard Rates:** $2.50/ft., Haul & Launch $4/ft. *(blocking $10/ft.)*, Power Wash $30 **Storage:** On-Land $5/ft./mo.

Restaurants and Accommodations

OnSite: Restaurant *(Chesapeake House B $3-11, L $4-15, D $12-25, kids' menu $3-9)*, Inn/B&B *(Harrison's Chesapeake House Country Inn $115-130, 60 rooms, winter 2 night MAP $250/for 2)* **Near:** Lite Fare *(So Neat Café & Bakery 886-2143)*, Hotel *(The Inn at Knapps Narrows 886-2720, $120-275)*, Inn/B&B *(Lazyjack Inn 886-2215, $130-205)*, *(Chesapeake Wood Duck Inn 886-2070, $125-155)* **Under 1 mi:** Restaurant *(Bridge Restaurant 886-2330, D $14-20)*, *(Tilghman Island Inn 886-2141, L $8-12, D $17-35, Mon-Thu casual menu $8-13, 5-course prix-fix $60/pp, Sun brunch buffet $19, closed Wed)*, *(Bay Hundred 886-2126, L $5-13, D $15-22)*, Inn/B&B *(Tilghman Island Inn 886-2141, $100-300)*

Recreation and Entertainment

OnSite: Pool, Picnic Area, Fishing Charter *(20 boats, 7 days Apr-Nov: "Beaudacious," "Brooks Hooks" & other boats: $750/day for up to 6, $75 add'l. person; "Buddy Plan," with Capt. Buddy Harrison, $1000/day, $112 add'l. person)*, Group Fishing Boat, Volleyball, Video Arcade, Sightseeing *(Cruises)*, Special Events **Near:** Playground, Jogging Paths, Roller Blade/Bike Paths, Video Rental, Park, Museum

Provisioning and General Services

OnSite: Provisioning Service, Convenience Store, Fishmonger, Lobster Pound, Bank/ATM, Laundry, Clothing Store *(Island Treasures Gift Shop)*, Retail Shops, Copies Etc. **OnCall:** Gourmet Shop, Florist **Near:** Delicatessen, Wine/Beer, Bakery, Market *(Island Market 886-2817, Corner Market 886-9033)*, Post Office *(886-2444)*, Protestant Church, Library *(Tilghman Branch 886-9816)*, Beauty Salon *(Judy's Beauty Shoppe 886-2188)*, Barber Shop, Bookstore *(Crawfords Nautical Books 886-2230)*, Newsstand **Under 1 mi:** Green Grocer *(Dogwood produce stand)*

Transportation

OnSite: Courtesy Car/Van, Bikes *(Island Treasureds 886-2058)* **OnCall:** Water Taxi, Rental Car *(Easton Enterprise 822-3260, Hertz 822-1676)*, Airport Limo **Airport:** Baltimore-Washington International / Easton *(73* **Airport:** Baltimore-Washington Int'l./Easton *(73 mi./25 mi.)*

Medical Services

911 Service **OnCall:** Ambulance **Under 1 mi:** Dentist *(Shulman 886-2115)* **3+ mi:** Doctor *(St. Michael's Family Medical 745-5000, 10mi.)*
Hospital: Easton Memorial 822-1000 *(25 mi.)*

Setting -- Harrison's is authentic, old-time Tilghman Island. This famous sport-fishing center and un-gussied up restaurant and crab house were originally built in 1856 and have retained much of the early country appeal. The meandering main building - a three story white clapboard colonial with wings, the motel annex, a large gift shop and a casual pool sprawl across the come-as-you-are grounds. All overlook the single main dock that hosts commercial fishing boats on one side and pleasure craft (seasonal and transient) on the other.

Marina Notes -- *Flat rate plus $10 for water & power. Original business started in 1899, family owned and operated ever since - 3rd, 4th & 5th generations at the helm. Short but fairly wide finger piers, the power is on the posts. The old-fashioned inn and motel rooms are simple, more than adequate, but with little in the way of luxury. This is a roll-up-your-sleeves kind of place that attracts lots of families and lots of sportsmen. Pull up to the dock and charter one of the 20 sport fish boats for 7am the next day, or, in the fall, for duck hunting. Capt. Buddy Harrison heads up the Bay's largest privately owned sport fishing fleet.

Notable -- "Family style" meals are served dockside at the 150 seat deck bar (with a family picnic atmosphere), in the 300 seat main dining rooms overlooking the water (with tablecloths unless it's a crab feast), and at tables in the lounge area. Breakfast from 6-11am, lunch 11am-5pm, and dinner menu from Noon to 9:30pm. They also do large parties and weddings. The charming wicker-furnished porch is a well-known spot for relaxing and swapping fish stories at the end of the day. And the large Island Treasures gift shop features nautically-inspired clothing and gifts in a stylish, well merchandised environment.

7. ES: ST MICHAELS & TILGHMAN IS
PHOTOS ON CD-ROM: 15

Navigational Information

Lat: 38°42.517' **Long:** 076°19.795' **Tide:** 1 ft. **Current:** n/a **Chart:** 12276
Rep. Depths (*MLW*): Entry 6 ft. **Fuel Dock** n/a **Max Slip/Moor** 6 ft./-
Access: Knapps Narrows to 3 Green; starboard to marina

Marina Facilities *(In Season/Off Season)*

Fuel: No
Slips: 55 Total, 10 Transient **Max LOA:** 70 ft. **Max Beam:** 20 ft.
Rate *(per ft.)*: **Day** $1.50/$1.00 **Week** Inq. **Month** Inq.
Power: 30 amp $4, **50 amp** $6, **100 amp** n/a, **200 amp** n/a
Cable TV: No **Dockside Phone:** No
Dock Type: Floating
Moorings: 0 Total, 0 Transient **Launch:** n/a
Rate: Day n/a **Week** n/a **Month** n/a
Heads: 4 Toilet(s), 3 Shower(s) *(with dressing rooms)*
Laundry: 2 Washer(s), 2 Dryer(s), Book Exchange **Pay Phones:** Yes
Pump-Out: OnSite, Full Service **Fee:** n/a **Closed Heads:** Yes

Marina Operations

Owner/Manager: Paul Davis **Dockmaster:** Same
In-Season: Year-Round, 9am-5pm **Off-Season:** n/a
After-Hours Arrival: By arrangement, call ahead
Reservations: Yes **Credit Cards:** Visa/MC
Discounts: None
Pets: Welcome, Dog Walk Area **Handicap Access:** No

Tilghman on Chesapeake

21610 Island Club; Tilghman, MD 21617

Tel: (410) 886-2389; (800) REL-AXED **VHF: Monitor** 16 **Talk** 71
Fax: (410) 886-2118 **Alternate Tel:** n/a
Email: toc@bluecrab.org **Web:** www.tochesapeake.com
Nearest Town: Tilghman *(1 mi.)* **Tourist Info:** (410) 770-8000

Marina Services and Boat Supplies

Services - Docking Assistance, Dock Carts **Communication -** Mail & Package Hold, Phone Messages, Fax in/out, Express Mail **Supplies - OnSite:** Ice *(Block, Cube)* **Near:** Ships' Store **Under 1 mi:** Bait/Tackle *(Fairbank Tackle 886-9807)*, Propane

Boatyard Services

Near: Launching Ramp. **Under 1 mi:** Travelift *(35T)*, Engine mechanic *(gas, diesel)*, Electrical Repairs, Hull Repairs, Rigger, Bottom Cleaning, Brightwork, Divers, Compound, Wash & Wax, Interior Cleaning, Woodworking, Painting, Awlgrip. **Nearest Yard:** Knapps Narrows Marina (410) 886-2720

Restaurants and Accommodations

Near: Restaurant *(Harrison's Chesapeake House 886-2121, B $3-11, L $4-15, D $12-25, picks up)*, Lite Fare *(So Neat Café & Bakery 886-2143)*, Inn/B&B *(Harrison's Chesapeake House Country Inn 886-2121, $115-130, 60 rooms, winter 2 night MAP $250/for 2)*, *(Lazyjack Inn 886-2215)*, *(Chesapeake Wood Duck Inn 886-2070, $125-155)*, *(Sinclair House 886-2147)* **Under 1 mi:** Restaurant *(Bridge Restaurant 886-2330, D $14-20)*, *(Tilghman Island Inn 886-2141, L $8-12, D $17-35, closed Wed; Mon-Thu casual menu $8-13, 5-course prix-fix $60/pp, Sun brunch buffet $19)*, *(Bay Hundred 886-2126, L $5-13, D $15-22)*

Recreation and Entertainment

OnSite: Pool, Picnic Area, Grills **OnCall:** Fishing Charter **Near:** Group Fishing Boat, Sightseeing *(Chesapeake Bay Skipjack Charters 886-2176, Dockside Express Cruises & Tours 886-2643)*, Special Events *(Tilghman Island Day - Oct; Tilghman Island Seafood Festival - late Jun; Water Fowl Fest - early Nov)* **Under 1 mi:** Park

Provisioning and General Services

Near: Wine/Beer, Bakery, Post Office *(886-2444)*, Protestant Church, Library *(Tilghman Branch 886-9816)*, Bookstore *(Crawfords Nautical Books 886-2230)* **Under 1 mi:** Convenience Store, Green Grocer *(Dogwood)*, Market *(Island Market 886-2817, Corner Market 886-9033)*, Bank/ATM, Beauty Salon *(Judy's Beauty Shoppe 886-2188)*

Transportation

OnCall: Rental Car *(Easton Enterprise 822-3260, Hertz in Easton 822-1676)*, Airport Limo
Airport: Baltimore-Washington Int'l./Easton *(75 mi./26 mi.)*

Medical Services

911 Service **OnCall:** Ambulance **Under 1 mi:** Dentist *(Shulman 886-2115)* **3+ mi:** Doctor *(St. Michael's Family Medical 745-5000, 11 mi.)*
Hospital: Easton Memorial 822-1000 *(26 mi.)*

Setting -- At the southern edge of Dogwood Harbor, this upscale marina sits on a two-acre island attached to the mainland by a narrow causeway. A dramatic 2-story, postmodern shingled clubhouse rises from the center, topped by a cupola. Blue awnings shade the first floor wraparound porch. Open decks surround the second floor, overlooking the sparkling, immaculate waterside pool and pool house.

Marina Notes -- This man-made island was originally built in 1897. Three main docks with floating slips are anchored by the causeway, and a fourth pier, adjacent to the island, has alongside dockage. Vinyl-edged docks have full finger piers and high-end pedestals. Security is very tight and access to the causeway is by key card. The locker-room/bathhouse is very well done and most inviting: the tile floor and tile walls are highlighted with fish and lighthouse designer motifs; fresh navy and white striped curtains create privacy.

Notable -- Tilghman on Chesapeake is a sharp counterpoint to the quiet, laid-back watermen's village of Tilghman Island. Brick circular driveways and artful, carefully maintained landscaping set the tone. The pool, with views of the water, is surrounded by a wood deck, pristine white fencing and furnished with white strap chaises. A small raised pavilion at the end hosts a table and chairs. On the upper floor a portion of the open veranda is topped with a blue awning that also shades a group of tables and chairs. On the mainland, Tilghman On Chesapeake is a planned waterfront community of 73 homesites on 186 acres that is moving into its final development phase. St. Michaels is 12 miles away and Easton is about 25 miles.

Boaters' Notes

Add Your Ratings and Reviews at www.AtlanticCruisingClub.com

AtlanticCruisingClub.com provides updated Marina Reports, Destination and Harbor Articles, a Boaters' Forum and much more — including an option within each on-line Marina Report for Boaters to add their ratings and comments regarding that facility. Please log on frequently to share your experiences — and to read other boaters' comments.

On the website, boaters may rate marinas on one or more of the following categories — on a scale of 1 (basic) to 5 (world class) — and also enter additional commentary.

- **Facilities & Services** (Fuel, Reservations, Concierge Services and General Helpfulness):
- **Amenities** (Pool, Beach, Internet Access, including Wi-Fi, Picnic/Grill area, Boaters' Lounge):
- **Setting** (Views, Design, Landscaping, Maintenance, Ship-Shapeness, Overall Ambiance):
- **Convenience** (Access — including delivery services — to Supermarkets, other provisioning sources, Shops, Services. Attractions, Entertainment, Sightseeing, Recreation, including Golf and Sport Fishing & Medical Services):
- **Restaurants/Eateries/Lodgings** (Availability of Fine Dining, Snack Bars, Lite Fare, On Call food service, and Lodgings ashore):
- **Transportation** (Courtesy Car/Vans, Buses, Water Taxis, Bikes, Taxis, Rental Cars, Airports, Amtrak, Commuter Trains):
- **Please Add Any Additional Comments**

8. Western Shore: West River To Jerome Creek

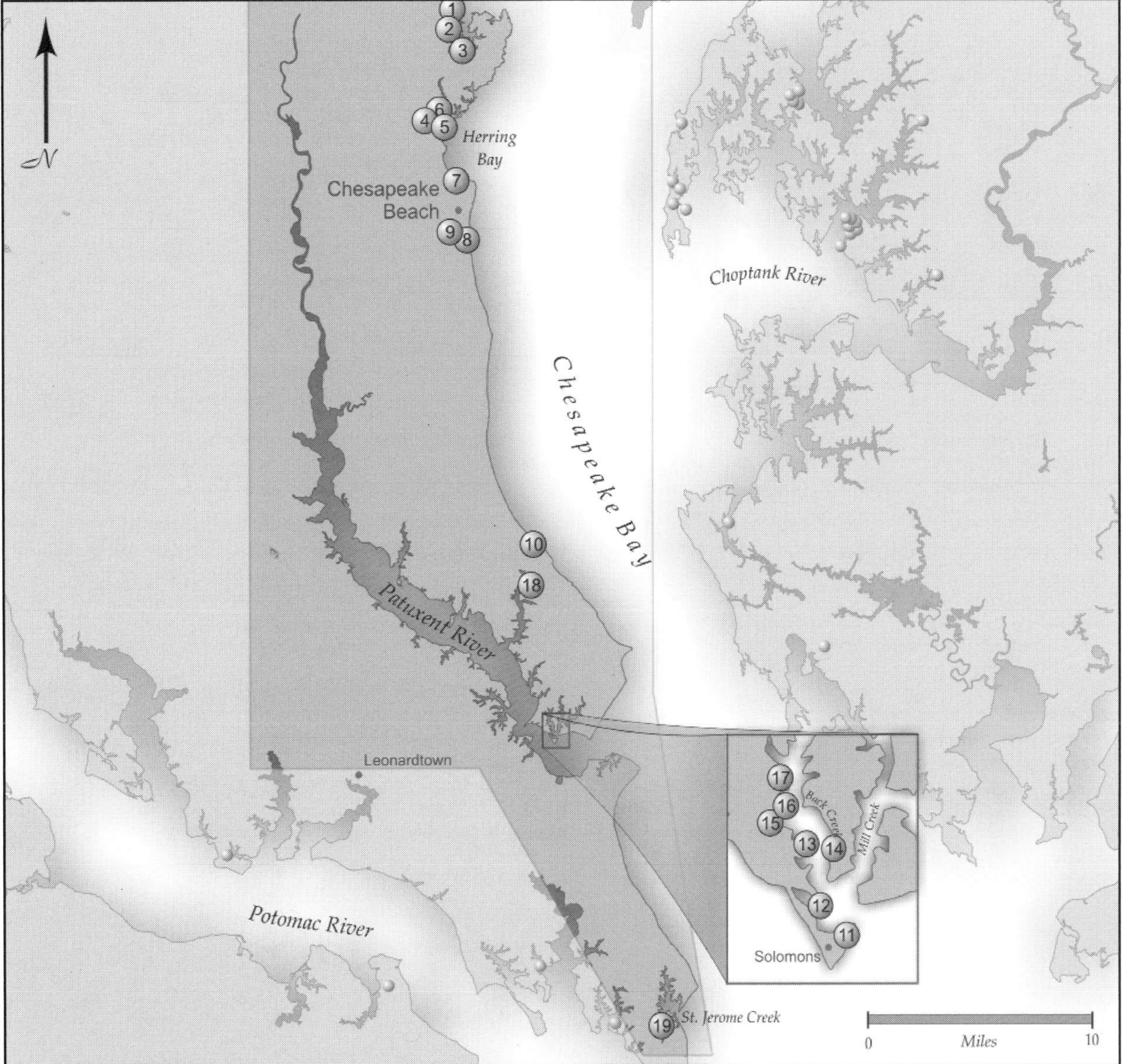

MAP	MARINA	HARBOR	PAGE	MAP	MARINA	HARBOR	PAGE
1	**West River Fuel Dock**	*West River*	150	11	**Harbor Island**	*Patuxent R./Solomons Hbr*	160
2	**Pirates Cove Marina & Restaurant**	*West River*	151	12	**Solomon's Yachting Center**	*Patuxent R./Back Creek*	161
3	**Hartge Yacht Yard**	*West River*	152	13	**Zahniser's Yachting Center**	*Patuxent R./Back Creek*	162
4	**Herrington Harbour North Marina**	*Herring Bay/Tracey's Creek*	153	14	**Calvert Marina**	*Patuxent R./Back Creek*	163
5	**Shipwright Harbor Marina**	*Herring Bay/Rockhold Creek*	154	15	**Beacon Marina**	*Patuxent R./Back Creek*	164
6	**Rockhold Creek Marina**	*Herring Bay/Rockhold Creek*	155	16	**Spring Cove Marina**	*Patuxent R./Back Creek*	165
7	**Herrington Harbour South**	*Herring Bay*	156	17	**Hospitality Harbor Marina**	*Patuxent R./Back Creek*	166
8	**Rod & Reel Docks**	*Fishing Creek*	157	18	**Vera's White Sands Marina**	*Patuxent R./St. Leonard Cr*	167
9	**Fishing Creek Landings Marina**	*Fishing Creek*	158	19	**Drury's Marina**	*St. Jerome Creek*	168
10	**Flag Harbor Yacht Haven**	*Flag Harbor*	159				

- **A "DCM" symbol in Marina Notes means Designated Clean Marina** — This is a coveted state-level award given to marinas that meet stringent, environmentally supportive requirements (see page 307). *For a list of DCM's & pump-out facilities, see page 308.*
- **Ratings & Reviews** — An explanation of the Atlantic Cruising Club's rating system, and a detailed explanation of what is in each section of the Marina Report is on pages 6 – 11. *The Data-Gathering Process is detailed on page 322.*
- **Marina Report Updates** — Updates to Marina Reports (from readers, ACC reviewers, and marinas) are posted regularly on *www.AtlanticCruisingClub.com.*

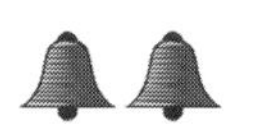

West River Fuel Dock

PO Box 321; 4801 Riverside Drive; Galesville, MD 20765

Tel: (410) 867-1444 **VHF: Monitor** 16 **Talk** n/a
Fax: (410) 867-1450 **Alternate Tel:** (410) 320-3489
Email: n/a **Web:** n/a
Nearest Town: Galesville *(0.5 mi.)* **Tourist Info:** (410) 867-3129

Navigational Information
Lat: 38°50.588' **Long:** 076°32.255' **Tide:** n/a **Current:** n/a **Chart:** 12270
Rep. Depths (*MLW*): Entry 13 ft. **Fuel Dock** 10 ft. **Max Slip/Moor** 10 ft./-
Access: Chesapeake Bay to West River

Marina Facilities *(In Season/Off Season)*
Fuel: Gasoline, Diesel, High-Speed Pumps
Slips: 4 Total, 2 Transient **Max LOA:** n/a **Max Beam:** n/a
Rate *(per ft.)*: **Day** $1.50 **Week** n/a **Month** n/a
Power: 30 amp $5, **50 amp** n/a, **100 amp** n/a, **200 amp** n/a
Cable TV: No **Dockside Phone:** No
Dock Type: n/a
Moorings: 0 Total, 0 Transient **Launch:** n/a
Rate: Day n/a **Week** n/a **Month** n/a
Heads: 6 Toilet(s), 6 Shower(s) *(with dressing rooms)*
Laundry: None **Pay Phones:** No
Pump-Out: OnSite, 1 Central **Fee:** $5 **Closed Heads:** Yes

Marina Operations
Owner/Manager: Howard Baldwin **Dockmaster:** Bill Locke
In-Season: Year-Round, 8am-5pm **Off-Season:** Oct 15-Mar 15, closed Tue &
After-Hours Arrival: Call ahead
Reservations: Yes **Credit Cards:** Visa/MC, Dscvr
Discounts: None
Pets: Welcome **Handicap Access:** No

Marina Services and Boat Supplies
Services - Boaters' Lounge, Trash Pick-Up, Dock Carts **Communication -** Data Ports *(Business center)*, FedEx, UPS, Express Mail *(Sat Del)*
Supplies - OnSite: Ice *(Block, Cube)*, Ships' Store **Near:** Bait/Tackle *(West River Market)* **Under 1 mi:** CNG *(Hartge Yacht Yard)* **3+ mi:** West Marine *(889-0004, 8 mi.)*, Propane *(Loch Haven Amoco 798-4668, 6 mi.)*

Boatyard Services
OnSite: Launching Ramp, Engine mechanic *(gas, diesel)* **Nearest Yard:**
Nearest Yard: Hartge Yacht Yard (410) 867-2188

Restaurants and Accommodations
OnCall: Pizzeria *(Domino's 867-3003, L & D $5-10)* **Near:** Restaurant *(Top Side Inn 867-1321, Sun "Jazz" brunch with live performances)*, *(Thursday's Steak & Crab House 867-7200, L $6-10, D $12-20, at Steamboat Landing)*, *(Pirate's Cove 867-2300, L $7-13, D $15-25, next door)*, Lite Fare *(West River Market umbrella-topped picnic tables out back)*, Inn/B&B *(Pirate's Cove Inn 269-1345, $45-85)*, *(Topside Inn 867-1321)*

Recreation and Entertainment
OnSite: Pool *(Mon 12-8pm, Closed Tue, 12-8pm Wed & Fri, 11am-8pm Sat-Sun)*, Picnic Area, Grills **Near:** Tennis Courts, Boat Rentals *(kayaks - West River Market)*, Museum *(Galesville Heritage Museum 867-9499, Hartge Nautical)*, Galleries *(River Gallery 867-0954)* **Under 1 mi:** Park
3+ mi: Golf Course *(Atlantic Golf 956-3310, 8 mi.)*, Fitness Center *(Body Shapers 867-3006, 6 mi.)*, Video Rental *(Deale Video 867-2972, 6 mi.)*

Provisioning and General Services
Near: Delicatessen, Wine/Beer *(Topside 867-1321)*, Liquor Store, Market *(West River Market 867-4844, 7am-7pm, 7 days)*, Bank/ATM, Post Office
Under 1 mi: Convenience Store *(High's 956-8388)*, Fishmonger, Crabs/Waterman *(Buck's Crab & Fish - outside Hartge's gate)*
3+ mi: Supermarket *(IGA 867-1510, 6 mi.)*, Dry Cleaners *(Riley 867-3449, 6 mi.)*, Pharmacy *(Friendly 301-889-0014, 6 mi.)*, Hardware Store *(Wheeler's True Value 867-2277, 6 mi.)*

Transportation
OnCall: Rental Car *(Enterprise 268-7751, Hertz 224-1414)*, Airport Limo *(Deale Limo 301-855-7175)* **Near:** Bikes *(community bikes)*
Airport: Baltimore-Washington Int'l./Easton *(35 mi.)*

Medical Services
911 Service **OnCall:** Ambulance **1-3 mi:** Doctor *(Owensville Medical 867-4700)* **3+ mi:** Veterinarian *(Muddy Creek 867-0770, 4 mi.)*
Hospital: Anne Arundel 267-1000 *(13 mi.)*

Setting -- Just past Councilors' Point, the little cream-colored, red-roofed fuel dockhouse welcomes boaters to Galesville. The sign above says "West River Yacht Harbor." 185 slips are divided among two main open docks and a slightly shorter covered dock. The environment tends toward boatyard, and the amenities skirt the edges of the parking lot. Galesville still has a touch of "old Western Shore" about it - it's laid back, casual and blissfully undeveloped.

Marina Notes -- The West River Fuel Dock manages the transient slips for West River Yacht Harbor - sign in at the fuel dockhouse (8am-5pm). All the amenities for West River Yacht Harbor are available to transients, so if you're in a slip, you've got the heads, the showers, the pool, and the gazebos. Bathhouses are all tile and have cushioned changing benches - each have two showers, (no dressing rooms), two sinks and two toilets. Another set of heads is at the pool - cinderblock walls and cement floors - bring your flip-flops - two showers with dressing rooms, two toilets two sinks for each.

Notable -- A pool surrounded by a cement patio and chain-link fence perches half way up the hill with expansive, long views of the river; there's a small kiddie pool as well. Little picnic spots are sprinkled about overlooking the water; 2 gazebos, Oyster and Crab, provide sheltered eating spots with grills outside. The pool's open 12-8pm on Mon, Wed, & Fri, 11am-8pm Sat, Sun, and holidays (closed Tues & Thurs). Right next door, Pirate's Cove offers a variety of pleasant venues and a bit farther along, Thursday's Steak and Crab House sits right over the water with a couple dozen dock 'n' dine slips. Once known as Brownton Plantation, 350-year-old Galesville was one of the original Colonial-era Ports of Entry; its 660 acres still maintain much of their rural character.

Navigational Information
Lat: 38°50.565' **Long:** 076°32.311' **Tide:** n/a **Current:** n/a **Chart:** 12270
Rep. Depths (*MLW*): Entry 13 ft. **Fuel Dock** n/a **Max Slip/Moor** 10 ft./-
Access: Chesapeake Bay to West River

Marina Facilities *(In Season/Off Season)*
Fuel: Gasoline, Diesel
Slips: 80 Total, 4 Transient **Max LOA:** 60 ft. **Max Beam:** 15 ft.
Rate *(per ft.)*: **Day** $36.00* **Week** n/a **Month** n/a
Power: 30 amp Incl., **50 amp** n/a, **100 amp** n/a, **200 amp** n/a
Cable TV: No **Dockside Phone:** No
Dock Type: Fixed, Short Fingers, Pilings, Alongside, Wood
Moorings: 0 Total, 0 Transient **Launch:** n/a
Rate: Day n/a **Week** n/a **Month** n/a
Heads: 4 Toilet(s), 4 Shower(s) *(with dressing rooms)*
Laundry: 1 Washer(s), 1 Dryer(s) **Pay Phones:** No
Pump-Out: OnSite **Fee:** $5 **Closed Heads:** Yes

Marina Operations
Owner/Manager: Bob Platt **Dockmaster:** Same
In-Season: Year-Round, 9am-7pm **Off-Season:** n/a
After-Hours Arrival: Call ahead
Reservations: Not accepted **Credit Cards:** Visa/MC, Amex
Discounts: None
Pets: No **Handicap Access:** No

Pirates Cove Marina

P.O.Box 140; 4817 Riverside Drive; Galesville, MD 20765

Tel: (410) 867-2300 **VHF: Monitor** 16 **Talk** 14
Fax: (410) 867-1861 **Alternate Tel:** (410) 867-2301
Email: n/a **Web:** www.piratescovemd.com
Nearest Town: Galesville *(0.5 mi.)* **Tourist Info:** (410) 867-3129

Marina Services and Boat Supplies
Services - Docking Assistance, Dock Carts **Communication -** FedEx, UPS, Express Mail **Supplies - Near:** Ice *(Block, Cube)*, Ships' Store, Bait/Tackle *(West River Market)* **3+ mi:** West Marine *(889-0004, 8 mi.)*, Propane *(Loch Haven Amoco 798-4668, 6 mi.)*

Boatyard Services
Near: Travelift, Forklift, Engine mechanic *(gas, diesel)*, Electrical Repairs, Hull Repairs, Rigger, Canvas Work, Bottom Cleaning, Brightwork, Air Conditioning, Refrigeration, Divers. **Nearest Yard:** Galesville Yacht Yard (410) 867-7517

Restaurants and Accommodations
OnSite: Restaurant *(Pirates Cove 867-2300, L $7-13, D $15-25, kid's $4-9, Monthly features $13, Skippers' Lite Fare 4-6:30pm $9-16, Sun brunch $7-12)*, Lite Fare *(Big Mary's Dock Bar L $3-10, D $3-10, appetizers, baskets, soups, desserts & frozen drinks)*, Motel *(Pirates Cove Inn 867-2300, $45-83)* **OnCall:** Pizzeria *(Domino's 867-3003, L & D $5-10)* **Near:** Restaurant *(Topside Inn 867-1321)*, *(Thursday's Steak & Crab House 867-7200, L $6-10, D $12-20)*, Inn/B&B *(Topside Inn 867-1321)*

Recreation and Entertainment
Near: Picnic Area, Grills, Tennis Courts, Boat Rentals *(kayaks at West River Market)*, Fishing Charter, Museum *(Galesville Heritage Museum 867-9499, Hartge Nautical)*, Galleries *(River Gallery 867-0954)* **3+ mi:** Golf Course *(Atlantic Golf 956-3310, 8 mi.)*, Fitness Center *(Body Shapers 867-3006, 6 mi.)*, Video Rental *(Deale Video 867-2972, 6 mi.)*

Provisioning and General Services
OnSite: Gourmet Shop *(meals & platters to go)*, Wine/Beer *(on-site or at Topside 867-1321)*, Liquor Store, Bank/ATM, Retail Shops *(Gift Shop)* **Near:** Delicatessen, Market *(West River Market 867-4844 7am-7pm, 7 days)*, Post Office **Under 1 mi:** Convenience Store *(High's 956-8388)*, Crabs/Waterman *(Buck's Crab & Fish - just before Hartge's)* **3+ mi:** Supermarket *(IGA 867-1510, 6 mi.)*, Dry Cleaners *(Riley 867-3449, 6 mi.)*, Pharmacy *(Friendly 301-889-0014, 6 mi.)*, Hardware Store *(Wheeler's True Value 867-2277, 6 mi.)*

Transportation
OnSite: Bikes *(Town Bikes Free)* **OnCall:** Airport Limo *(Deale Limousine 301-855-7175)* **3+ mi:** Rental Car *(Enterprise 268-7751, Hertz 224-1414, 13 mi.)* **Airport:** Baltimore-Washington Int'l. *(35 mi.)*

Medical Services
911 Service **OnCall:** Ambulance **1-3 mi:** Doctor *(Owensville Medical 867-4700)* **3+ mi:** Veterinarian *(Muddy Creek 867-0770, 4 mi.)*
Hospital: Anne Arundel 267-1000 *(13 mi.)*

Setting -- One long dock with a very wide, slip-filled T-head hosts over 80 boats. The dock ends, conveniently, right at the restaurant's outdoor umbrella-topped dining deck. Pirates Cove's sandstone-washed stucco exterior with wooden shake roof has a vaguely southwestern flair. Most of its dining areas have wide views of the river and the boats themselves. Out the back door is laid-back, pretty and unpretentious Galesville.

Marina Notes -- *Dockage is flat fee. Sailboat races Wed 6pm, catamaran races Tue 6pm. The stationary docks have fairly long finger piers and power on the pilings. Ships' store has beer, wine, liquor, sodas, giftwear, meals and take-out platters. Groups accommodated in the restaurant. On the north side of Mary's Bar is a "slip holders only" bathhouse. There's a washer and dryer, and 2 private bathrooms with toilet, sink, and a glass-doored shower. Attached to the restaurant, and shared with its patrons, is a men's & ladies' room - 3 more heads and a shower in each (we assume that the shower is for slip holders only!)

Notable -- Pirates Cove Restaurant, which specializes in seafood, has 5 different dining areas - most with views of the docks and river - inside, outside under umbrellas, outside under the covered porch, inside in the all-glass porch - deep red walls patterned with antique sailboats, honey colored chairs and white tablecloths - or in the cozy wood-paneled bar. Lunch Mon-Sat 11:30am-4pm, Dinner Mon-Thu 4-10pm, Fri & Sat 'til 10:30pm, Sun 11am-10pm, Sun Brunch 11am-2pm. Big Mary's Dock Bar is a warm weather thing - open weekends-only in May and Wed, Fri, Sat & Sun Jun-Sep. For sleeping ashore, five guest rooms, with phones & cable, are on the second floor just above Big Mary's open patio. In the Lounge, there's live entertainment and dancing Fri & Sat 8pm-Mid.

PHOTOS ON CD-ROM: 10

Hartge Yacht Yard

PO Box 248; 4880 Church Lane; Galesville, MD 20765

Tel: (410) 867-2188 **VHF: Monitor** 16 **Talk** n/a
Fax: (410) 261-9273 **Alternate Tel:** n/a
Email: hartgeyard@aol.com **Web:** www.hartgeyard.com
Nearest Town: Galesville *(0.5 mi.)* **Tourist Info:** (410) 867-3129

Navigational Information

Lat: 38°50.250' **Long:** 076°32.591' **Tide:** n/a **Current:** n/a **Chart:** 12270
Rep. Depths (*MLW*): Entry 9 ft. **Fuel Dock** 9 ft. **Max Slip/Moor** 9 ft./8 ft.
Access: Chesapeake Bay to West River

Marina Facilities *(In Season/Off Season)*

Fuel: Gasoline, Diesel
Slips: 250 Total, 2 Transient **Max LOA:** 80 ft. **Max Beam:** n/a
Rate *(per ft.)*: **Day** $1.00 **Week** $5.00 **Month** $14.00
Power: 30 amp Incl., **50 amp** Incl., **100 amp** n/a, **200 amp** n/a
Cable TV: No **Dockside Phone:** No
Dock Type: Fixed, Wood
Moorings: 70 Total, 2 Transient **Launch:** n/a, Dinghy Dock
Rate: Day $0.50/ft. **Week** $2.50/ft. **Month** $7/ft.
Heads: 10 Toilet(s), 6 Shower(s)
Laundry: None **Pay Phones:** No
Pump-Out: OnSite, Full Service **Fee:** n/a **Closed Heads:** Yes

Marina Operations

Owner/Manager: Alex Schlegel **Dockmaster:** Same
In-Season: Year-Round, 7am-5pm **Off-Season:** n/a
After-Hours Arrival: Call ahead
Reservations: Yes **Credit Cards:** Visa/MC, Amoco
Discounts: None
Pets: Welcome, Dog Walk Area **Handicap Access:** No

Marina Services and Boat Supplies

Services - Docking Assistance, Dock Carts **Communication -** Mail & Package Hold, Phone Messages, Fax in/out, FedEx, UPS, Express Mail **Supplies - OnSite:** Ice *(Block, Cube)*, Ships' Store *(7:30am-4:30pm Mon-Fri, 8am-6pm Sat)*, CNG **Under 1 mi:** Bait/Tackle *(West River Market)* **3+ mi:** West Marine *(889-0004, 8 mi.)*, Propane *(Loch Haven Amoco 798-4668, 6 mi.)*

Boatyard Services

OnSite: Travelift *(25&30T)*, Railway *(40&70T- up to 20 ft. beam)*, Crane, Engine mechanic *(gas, diesel)*, Electrical Repairs, Electronics Repairs, Hull Repairs, Rigger, Bottom Cleaning, Brightwork, Air Conditioning, Refrigeration, Compound, Wash & Wax, Interior Cleaning, Woodworking, Metal Fabrication, Painting, Awlgrip, Total Refits, Yacht Broker **OnCall:** Divers, Propeller Repairs **Near:** Canvas Work. **Dealer for:** Westerbeke, Universal, Harken, Navtec, Yanmar, Onan, Sea Frost, Grunert, Marine Air, Awlgrip, Raymarine, Simrad, Adler-Barbour, etc.. **Member:** ABBRA - 4 Certified Tech(s), ABYC - 4 Certified Tech(s), Other Certifications: various OEM's **Yard Rates:** $54-64/hr., Haul & Launch $5-7/ft. *(blocking $2/ft.)*, Power Wash Incl., Bottom Paint $10-20/ft. based on size *(paint incl.)* **Storage:** In-Water $1920-3480 yr. slips / $720-1560 moorings, On-Land $18-20/ft.

Restaurants and Accommodations

OnCall: Pizzeria *(Domino's 867-3003, L & D $5-10)* **Near:** Restaurant *(Thursday's Steak and Crab House 867-7200, L $6-10, D $12-20)*, *(Top Side Inn 867-1321)* **Under 1 mi:** Restaurant *(Pirates Cove 867-2300, L $7-13, D $15-25)*, Motel *(Pirates Cove 867-2300)*, Inn/B&B *(Topside Inn 867-1321)*

Recreation and Entertainment

OnSite: Picnic Area, Grills, Boat Rentals *(Hartge Ches Charters - sail 25-40+; also Kayaks from West River Market)*, Museum *(Hartge Nautical, plus Galesville Heritage Museum 867-9499, nearby)* **Near:** Tennis Courts *(public courts)*, Park **Under 1 mi:** Playground, Sightseeing *(two privately-owned buildings: 1750 Tulip Hill, a Georgian brick mansion, and 1652 Cedar Park - Lord Baltimore's hunting lodge)*, Galleries *(River Gallery 867-0954)* **3+ mi:** Golf Course *(Atlantic Golf 956-3310, 8 mi.)*, Fitness Center *(Body Shapers 867-3006, 6 mi.)*, Video Rental *(Deale Video 867-2972, 6 mi.)*

Provisioning and General Services

Near: Wine/Beer *(The Wine Store)*, Liquor Store *(Topside 867-1321)*, Fishmonger *(Buck's Crab & Fish)*, Post Office, Catholic Church, Protestant Church, Newsstand **Under 1 mi:** Convenience Store *(High's 956-8388)*, Delicatessen, Market *(West River Market 867-4844, 7am-7pm, 7 days)*, Bank/ATM **3+ mi:** Supermarket *(IGA 867-1510, 6 mi.)*, Dry Cleaners *(Riley 867-3449, 6 mi.)*, Pharmacy *(Friendly 301-889-0014, 6 mi.)*, Hardware Store *(Wheeler's True Value 867-2277, 6 mi.)*

Transportation

OnSite: Courtesy Car/Van, Bikes *(community bicycles)* **OnCall:** Rental Car *(Enterprise 268-7751, Hertz 224-1414)*, Airport Limo *(Deale Limousine 301-855-7175)* **Airport:** Baltimore-Washington Int'l. *(35 mi.)*

Medical Services

911 Service **OnCall:** Ambulance **1-3 mi:** Doctor *(Owensville Medical Center 867-4700)* **3+ mi:** Veterinarian *(Muddy Creek 867-0770, 4 mi.)* **Hospital:** Anne Arundel 267-1000 *(13 mi.)*

Setting -- Hartge occupies a 17-acre peninsula known as White Stake Point, bound on one side by the West River and on the other by Lerch Creek. Eight sets of docks radiate from the point and along the very protected creek side - interrupted by white boatyard sheds and haul-out bays. The yard is crowded with an assortment of work sheds and offices and the grassy point is populated by lovely Adirondack chairs, rope swings and picnic tables, inviting a quiet respite.

Marina Notes -- DCM. The oldest working yard on the bay, owned and operated by the Hartge family since 1865. Emile Alexander Hartge started building boats in nearby Shady Side, and moved to this site in 1878, building log canoes and later bateaus. Today, they specialize in sailboats, particularly refitting ocean cruisers. Their reputation extends up and down the East Coast making this a destination for sailors - but they certainly welcome powerboats. The easily accessible fuel dock has three pumps (7:30am-4:30pm Mon-Fri, 8am-6pm Sat & Sun). Slips 1-13 have views up or down West River to Galesville. The bathhouses are adequate with tiled floors and walls, two showers with dressing rooms and three toilets each.

Notable -- The Hartge Nautical Museum, located in Emile Hartge's original 1878 home - a quaint 2-story white farmhouse with covered porch - tells the story of shipbuilding on the river with models of many of the boats built here. A "sign-posted" Walking Tour of the Yard begins here. Walk into "town" for a light meal or a full-course dinner at 3 well-regarded eateries. West River Market is abundantly supplied and has a small deli. Historic Galesville is a diverse, unspoiled, rural village. Look for "Buck's Crab and Fish" a few houses down from Hartge's - ask Norman "Buck" Scotten to steam a dozen large - they're the best.

8. WS: WEST R TO ST JEROME CREEK

PHOTOS ON CD-ROM: 11

Navigational Information
Lat: 38°46.378' **Long:** 076°33.858' **Tide:** 2 ft. **Current:** n/a **Chart:** 12270
Rep. Depths (*MLW*): Entry 7 ft. **Fuel Dock** 7 ft. **Max Slip/Moor** 7 ft./-
Access: Herrington Bay to Rockhold Creek

Marina Facilities *(In Season/Off Season)*
Fuel: No
Slips: 580 Total, 40 Transient **Max LOA:** 110 ft. **Max Beam:** 35 ft.
Rate *(per ft.)*: **Day** $1.50/Inq. **Week** 10.50 **Month** Inq.
Power: 30 amp $5, **50 amp** $10, **100 amp** $25, **200 amp** n/a
Cable TV: No **Dockside Phone:** No
Dock Type: Fixed, Long Fingers, Pilings, Alongside, Wood
Moorings: 0 Total, 0 Transient **Launch:** n/a
Rate: Day n/a **Week** n/a **Month** n/a
Heads: 18 Toilet(s), 12 Shower(s) *(with dressing rooms)*
Laundry: 2 Washer(s), 2 Dryer(s), Book Exchange **Pay Phones:** Yes, 2
Pump-Out: OnSite, Self Service, 12 Central **Fee:** $5 **Closed Heads:** Yes

Marina Operations
Owner/Manager: Tom Wilhelm **Dockmaster:** Same
In-Season: Year-Round, 9am-5pm **Off-Season:** n/a
After-Hours Arrival: See security guard
Reservations: Preferred **Credit Cards:** Visa/MC, Amex
Discounts: None
Pets: Welcome, Dog Walk Area, Kennel **Handicap Access:** No

Herrington Harbour North

PO Box 40; 389 Deale Road; Tracy's Landing, MD 20779

Tel: (410) 867-4343; (800) 297-1930 **VHF: Monitor** 16, 9 **Talk** 68
Fax: (410) 867-2435 **Alternate Tel:** (410) 867-4343
Email: hhn@chesapeake.net **Web:** www.herringtonharbour.com
Nearest Town: Deale *(1.5 mi.)* **Tourist Info:** (410) 867-3129

Marina Services and Boat Supplies
Services - Docking Assistance, Boaters' Lounge, Security, Trash Pick-Up, Dock Carts, Megayacht Facilities **Communication -** Mail & Package Hold, Phone Messages, Fax in/out *(Free)*, Data Ports *(Laundry room)*, FedEx, DHL, UPS, Express Mail *(Sat Del)* **Supplies - OnSite:** Ice *(Block, Cube)*, West Marine *(301-889-0004)* **Near:** Bait/Tackle *(JJ's Tackle 867-4515)*, Live Bait, Propane

Boatyard Services
OnSite: Travelift *(30/35/70T)*, Crane, Forklift, Hydraulic Trailer *(35T)*, Engine mechanic *(gas, diesel)*, Electrical Repairs, Electronics Repairs, Hull Repairs, Rigger, Sail Loft, Canvas Work, Bottom Cleaning, Brightwork, Air Conditioning, Refrigeration, Compound, Wash & Wax, Interior Cleaning, Propeller Repairs, Woodworking, Upholstery, Yacht Interiors, Metal Fabrication, Painting, Awlgrip, Total Refits, Yacht Broker **OnCall:** Inflatable Repairs, Life Raft Service **Member:** ABBRA - 10 Certified Tech(s), ABYC - 10 Certified Tech(s) **Yard Rates:** Haul & Launch $10.50/ft. *(blocking $2/ft.)*, Power Wash $2.25 **Storage:** On-Land $4.50/ft./mo., $90 min.

Restaurants and Accommodations
OnSite: Restaurant *(Calypso Bay 867-9787, L $6-17, D $6-17, D specials)* **OnCall:** Pizzeria *(Domino's 867-3013)* **Near:** Restaurant *(Happy Harbor Inn 867-0949, B $3-8, L $4-9, D $8-25, mostly teens, kids' $3)*, *(Skipper's Pier 867-7110, L $8-15, D $13-25, kids' $3-4; dinghy)*, *(Pier 44 867-2392)*, Inn/B&B *(Happy Harbor Inn 867-0949)* **Under 1 mi:** Lite Fare *(Shirley's Carry Out 867-0692)*, Pizzeria *(Deal 867-1133)*, *(Happy House 867-1133)* **1-3 mi:** Coffee Shop *(Deale Cup & Cone 867-3919)*, Fast Food *(Subway)*, Inn/B&B *(Inn at Deale 867-1202)*, *(Herrington Inn 741-5100)*

Recreation and Entertainment
OnSite: Heated Pool *(kiddie pool, too)*, Spa, Picnic Area, Grills *(charcoal)*, Jogging Paths, Fishing Charter, Special Events *(Festivals)* **Near:** Beach, Playground, Tennis Courts, Volleyball, Park *(People Park)* **Under 1 mi:** Fitness Center *(Body Shapers 867-3006)* **1-3 mi:** Video Rental *(Blockbuster 867-9520)* **3+ mi:** Golf Course *(Twin Shields 301-855-8228, 10 mi.)*

Provisioning and General Services
OnSite: Wine/Beer, Liquor Store **OnCall:** Provisioning Service **Near:** Crabs/Waterman, Bank/ATM, Catholic Church, Protestant Church *(St. Mark's Episcopal, near entrance)*, Dry Cleaners, Bookstore, Florist **Under 1 mi:** Delicatessen, Farmers' Market *(Thu 3-6pm, Cedar Grove Methodist parking lot 301-261-5727)*, Fishmonger *(Bayside 301-261-5751)*, Post Office *(867-4858)*, Library *(South County 867-4164)*, Beauty Salon *(Hair Harbor 867-6990)*, Hardware Store *(Wheeler's 867-2277)*, Copies Etc. *(Zancan 301-261-5903)* **1-3 mi:** Supermarket *(IGA 867-1510)*, Pharmacy *(Friendly 301-867-2500)* **3+ mi:** Department Store *(Kmart 301-855-1612, 10 mi.)*

Transportation
OnSite: Courtesy Car/Van *(rental cars)* **OnCall:** Water Taxi *(ch.68, Free in season)*, Rental Car *(Enterprise 301-627-0181)*, Taxi *(Carl's 257-2849)*, Airport Limo *(Dreamride Limos 286-3137)* **Airport:** Reagan Nat'l. *(32 mi.)*

Medical Services
911 Service **OnCall:** Ambulance **Under 1 mi:** Doctor *(South County 301-889-0854)*, Dentist *(Curl 301-261-5252)* **1-3 mi:** Veterinarian *(Stott 812-0315)* **Hospital:** Anne Arundel 267-1000 *(19 mi.)*

Setting -- Near the entrance to Herring Bay, enormous, upscale Herrington Harbor North delivers an 18-dock facility with a full-service boatyard and acres of gravel-topped dry storage - wrapped in an appealing country setting. Docks run along the channel and up Tracey's Creek to the Rt. 256 bridge. A lovely pool, surrounded by gated gardens and flanked by 3 Colonial brick outbuildings, overlooks the creek. Views across the creek are down a fairway - between docks.

Marina Notes -- DCM. Family-owned & operated since 1983. Many new docks since Isabel. Three travelift bays; pump-out is right near the entrance channel. On-site independent operations include Phipp's Boatworks, Osprey Marine Composites, Conlyn Marine Services, Cook's Marine, Tradewinds Diesel, Digital Prop Shop, yacht brokers and a full-size West Marine. Ancient oaks and weeping willows shade pretty waterside picnic areas. The laundry room, one washer and dryer, is conveniently located adjacent to the pool area. Three bath houses - tile, formica and Corian - each "side" has 3 toilets, 2 sinks, and 2 showers with private dressing rooms.

Notable -- The elegant pool area is an oasis in the midst of the marsh and gravel and it's very gracefully executed. Navy strap chaises and matching umbrella-topped tables dot the wide brick and concrete patio. A pavilion with teak furnishings provides a bit of shade. Adjacent to R dock, the Calypso Bay Restaurant & Dock Bar's indoor and outdoor dining manage a real Caribbean feeling (sports bar, too). Acres of dry storage are as tidy and pleasant as possible; paved roads wind around the parking area and little signs identify the rows. Herrington Harbour South is just two miles away by boat.

PHOTOS ON CD-ROM: 15

Shipwright Harbor Marina

PO Box 510; 6047-57 Herring Bay Road; Deale, MD 20751

Tel: (410) 867-7686 **VHF: Monitor** n/a **Talk** n/a
Fax: (410) 867-3247 **Alternate Tel:** n/a
Email: See Marina Notes **Web:** shipwrightharbormarina.com
Nearest Town: Deale *(2 mi.)* **Tourist Info:** (410) 867-3129

Navigational Information
Lat: 38°46.573' **Long:** 076°33.711' **Tide:** 2 ft. **Current:** n/a **Chart:** 12270
Rep. Depths (*MLW*): Entry 7 ft. **Fuel Dock** n/a **Max Slip/Moor** 7 ft./-
Access: Chesapeake Bay

Marina Facilities *(In Season/Off Season)*
Fuel: No
Slips: 250 Total, 12 Transient **Max LOA:** 45 ft. **Max Beam:** n/a
Rate *(per ft.)*: **Day** $1.50 **Week** Inq. **Month** $125-525 based on slip size
Power: 30 amp $5, **50 amp** n/a, **100 amp** n/a, **200 amp** n/a
Cable TV: No **Dockside Phone:** No
Dock Type: Fixed, Short Fingers, Pilings, Wood
Moorings: 0 Total, 0 Transient **Launch:** n/a, Dinghy Dock
Rate: Day n/a **Week** n/a **Month** n/a
Heads: 10 Toilet(s), 4 Shower(s)
Laundry: 2 Washer(s), 2 Dryer(s), Book Exchange **Pay Phones:** Yes
Pump-Out: OnSite, Full Service **Fee:** $5 **Closed Heads:** Yes

Marina Operations
Owner/Manager: Brant Rodey **Dockmaster:** Same
In-Season: Year-Round, 9am-5pm **Off-Season:** n/a
After-Hours Arrival: Call ahead
Reservations: Recommended **Credit Cards:** Visa/MC, Dscvr
Discounts: None
Pets: Welcome, Dog Walk Area **Handicap Access:** Yes, Heads, Docks

Marina Services and Boat Supplies
Services - Docking Assistance, Security, Dock Carts **Communication -** Mail & Package Hold, Phone Messages, Fax in/out, FedEx, DHL, UPS, Express Mail *(Sat Del)* **Supplies - OnSite:** Ice *(Block, Cube)* **Near:** Ships' Store, West Marine *(301-889-0004)*, Bait/Tackle *(JJ's 867-4515)*, Live Bait

Boatyard Services
OnSite: Travelift *(15T)*, Crane, Electrical Repairs, Electronics Repairs, Hull Repairs, Bottom Cleaning, Brightwork, Refrigeration, Compound, Wash & Wax, Woodworking, Painting, Awlgrip **OnCall:** Divers *(Charley Gillis)*, Interior Cleaning, Propeller Repairs **Near:** Railway, Forklift, Hydraulic Trailer, Launching Ramp *(Deale Marina)*, Engine mechanic *(gas, diesel)*, Rigger *(Alpha 867-6755)*, Canvas Work *(Canvas Connection)*, Air Conditioning, Inflatable Repairs *(Outfitters USA 410-626-1122)*, Yacht Interiors, Yacht Design, Yacht Building, Yacht Broker *(Wilson Yachts 867-4328)*. **1-3 mi:** Metal Fabrication *(Max Metals 301-261-5060)*.
Yard Rates: $65/hr., Haul & Launch $7-8.50/ft. *(blocking incl.)*, Power Wash $8/ft., Bottom Paint $65/hr. **Storage:** On-Land $100/mo.

Restaurants and Accommodations
OnCall: Pizzeria *(Domino's 867-3013, L & D $5-10)* **Near:** Restaurant *(Happy Harbor Inn 867-0949, B $3-8, L $4-9, D $8-25, most entrees in "teens," kids' menu $3)*, *(Calypso Bay 867-9787, L $6-13, D $10-17, specials more)*, *(Skipper's Pier 867-7110, L $8-15, D $13-25, kids' menu $3-4 - dinghy)*, Motel *(Happy Harbor Inn 867-0949)*, Inn/B&B *(Herrington Harbor 867-0949)* **Under 1 mi:** Lite Fare *(Shirley's Carry Out 867-0692)*, Pizzeria *(Deale 867-1133)*, *(Happy House 867-1133)* **1-3 mi:** Inn/B&B *(Inn at Deale 867-1202)*, *(Creekside B&B 301-261-9438)*

Recreation and Entertainment
OnSite: Pool, Picnic Area, Grills **Near:** Playground, Dive Shop, Tennis Courts, Jogging Paths, Roller Blade/Bike Paths, Fishing Charter *(Lynn Marine 766-0194, Ebb Tide 867-2639)*, Group Fishing Boat, Park *(People Park)*, Cultural Attract **Under 1 mi:** Fitness Center *(Body Shapers 867-3006)* **1-3 mi:** Video Rental *(Blockbuster 867-9520)* **3+ mi:** Golf Course *(Twin Shields Golf Club 301-855-8228, 10 mi.)*

Provisioning and General Services
Near: Fishmonger *(Bayside 301-261-5751)*, Bank/ATM, Catholic Church, Protestant Church, Barber Shop, Dry Cleaners, Laundry, Newsstand, Hardware Store *(Wheelers 867-2277)*, Florist **Under 1 mi:** Post Office *(867-4858)*, Library *(South County 867-4164)*, Beauty Salon *(Hair Harbor 867-6990)*, Copies Etc. *(Zancan 301-261-5903)* **1-3 mi:** Convenience Store *(7-Eleven)*, Supermarket *(IGA 867-1510)*, Delicatessen, Liquor Store *(Park's 867-4577)*, Farmers' Market *(Thu 3-6pm, Cedar Grove Methodist parking lot 301-261-5727)*, Meat Market *(Food Rite)*, Pharmacy *(Friendly 301-867-2500)* **3+ mi:** Department Store *(Kmart 301-855-1612, 10 mi.)*

Transportation
OnCall: Water Taxi *(Free in season Ch.68)*, Rental Car *(Enterprise 301-627-0181)*, Taxi *(Carl's Cab 257-2849)*, Airport Limo *(Dreamride Limos 286-3137)* **Airport:** Reagan Nat'l *(32 mi.)*

Medical Services
911 Service **OnCall:** Ambulance **Under 1 mi:** Doctor *(South County 301-889-0854)*, Dentist *(Curl 301-261-5252)* **1-3 mi:** Veterinarian *(Stott 812-0315)* **Hospital:** Anne Arundel 267-1000 *(19 mi.)*

Setting -- A peninsula bound by Tracey's Creek and Rockhold Creek hosts Shipwright Harbor's attractively sited 250 slips. "F" dock runs along Tracey's Creek with views across to Herrington Harbor, and an extensive network of docks pushes out into Rockhold Creek. Several yards out from the grassy banks, a boardwalk anchors most of the docks contributing to an unstructured country feel. A pool sits in the center and delightful "People Park" is on the point.

Marina Notes -- DCM. A complete yacht maintenance and repair facility including engine repairs, rigging, painting, fiberglass and woodworking and a do-it-yourself yard. Head mechanic Robert Kidd won Best of Bay. Very service-oriented - will provision, do boat laundry, clean the interior, etc. On the Rockhold side, "B" and "E" docks hug the shore, "C" and "D" parallel them farther into the creek, and "A" is perpendicular. Stainless steel fish-cleaning table at the corner of "C" Dock. A laundry with two washers & dryers plus a lending library are adjacent to the pool as is the fully tiled bathhouse - four toilets and two showers share a dressing room. (Email: shipwrightharbor@mindspring.com)

Notable -- Overlooking the docks and creeks, the nicely planted park on the peninsula's point is an appealing spot. Picnic tables, grills, painted Adirondack chairs, and a well-appointed rectangular gazebo with wrought iron tables and chairs fence enhance the setting. Inland a bit, a chain-link fenced pool is sited on a little rise, affording views of the docks on both sides. In three corners are umbrella-topped tables and chairs; the fourth has a canvas-topped pavilion with larger tables and chairs. Scattered about the property are two other picnic areas and a smaller gazebo. Complimentary Sunday brunch is served in the large gazebo.

Navigational Information
Lat: 38°46.674' **Long:** 076°33.601' **Tide:** 3 ft. **Current:** 1 kt. **Chart:** 12270
Rep. Depths (*MLW*): Entry 10 ft. **Fuel Dock** 8 ft. **Max Slip/Moor** 8 ft./-
Access: Herring Bay to Rockhold Creek. West of Buoy 83

Marina Facilities *(In Season/Off Season)*
Fuel: No
Slips: 50 Total, 4 Transient **Max LOA:** 65 ft. **Max Beam:** 20 ft.
Rate *(per ft.)*: **Day** $1.00 **Week** $5.00 **Month** $10
Power: 30 amp $5, **50 amp** $8, **100 amp** n/a, **200 amp** n/a
Cable TV: No **Dockside Phone:** No
Dock Type: Fixed, Short Fingers, Pilings, Wood
Moorings: 0 Total, 0 Transient **Launch:** n/a, Dinghy Dock
Rate: Day n/a **Week** n/a **Month** n/a
Heads: 3 Toilet(s), 2 Shower(s) *(with dressing rooms)*
Laundry: None, Book Exchange **Pay Phones:** No
Pump-Out: Full Service, 1 Central, 1 Port **Fee:** $5 **Closed Heads:** Yes

Marina Operations
Owner/Manager: Jon Sheller **Dockmaster:** Kathy Dixon
In-Season: Apr-Dec 24, 9am-5pm **Off-Season:** Jan 10-Mar, 10am-4pm
After-Hours Arrival: Tie-up at empty dock; leave note at office mailbox
Reservations: Yes, Preferred **Credit Cards:** Visa/MC
Discounts: None
Pets: Welcome, Dog Walk Area **Handicap Access:** Yes, Docks

Rockhold Creek Marina

PO Box 610; 453 Deale Road; Deale, MD 20751

Tel: (410) 867-7919 **VHF: Monitor** n/a **Talk** n/a
Fax: (301) 261-9885 **Alternate Tel:** (410) 867-2524
Email: sasha2011@aol.com **Web:** n/a
Nearest Town: Deale *(1 mi.)* **Tourist Info:** (410) 867-3129

Marina Services and Boat Supplies
Services - Docking Assistance, Security *(Lights)*, Dock Carts
Communication - Mail & Package Hold, Phone Messages, Fax in/out, Data Ports *(Office)*, FedEx, UPS *(Sat Del)* **Supplies - OnSite:** Ice *(Cube)*
OnCall: Ice *(Block)* **Near:** Ships' Store, West Marine *(301-889-0004)*, Bait/Tackle *(JJ's Tackle 867-4515)*, Live Bait

Boatyard Services
OnSite: Travelift *(20T)*, Crane *(9000 lbs.)*, Forklift *(7500 lbs.)*, Engine mechanic *(gas, diesel)*, Electrical Repairs, Electronics Repairs, Hull Repairs, Rigger, Bottom Cleaning, Air Conditioning, Compound, Wash & Wax, Woodworking, Painting, Yacht Broker **OnCall:** Canvas Work, Refrigeration, Upholstery **Near:** Launching Ramp, Propeller Repairs, Metal Fabrication.
Dealer for: Yanmar, Westerbake, Crusader, Perkins, Cat, Nextgen.
Member: ABBRA - 1 Certified Tech(s), ABYC - 2 Certified Tech(s), Other Certifications: Sams Surveyor **Yard Rates:** $45-72/hr., Haul & Launch $5.50-8.50/ft. *(blocking $2.50/ft.or incl.)*, Power Wash $2/ft. or Incl., Bottom Paint $11/ft. **Storage:** In-Water $3/ft./mo., On-Land $3/ft/mo.

Restaurants and Accommodations
OnCall: Pizzeria *(Domino's 867-3013)* **Near:** Restaurant *(Skipper's Pier 867-7110, L $8-15, D $13-25, kids' $3-4; dinghy)*, *(Calypso Bay 867-9787, L $8-13, D $10-24)*, *(Happy Harbor Inn 867-0949, B $3-8, L $4-9, D $8-25, most in teens)*, Lite Fare *(Shirley's Carry-Out 867-0692)*, Inn/B&B *(Happy Harbor 867-0949)*, *(Herrington Harbor 867-4343)* **Under 1 mi:** Pizzeria *(Deal Pizzaria 867-1133)* **1-3 mi:** Restaurant *(Happy House 867-6116)*, Coffee Shop *(Deale Cup & Cone 867-3919)*, Fast Food *(Subway)*, Pizzeria *(Papa Johns 867-9518)*, Inn/B&B *(Inn at Deale 867-1202)*

Recreation and Entertainment
OnSite: Picnic Area, Grills **Near:** Pool, Jogging Paths, Fishing Charter *(Jill Carrie 867-4944)*, Group Fishing Boat, Park *(People Park)*
Under 1 mi: Playground, Tennis Courts, Roller Blade/Bike Paths
1-3 mi: Fitness Center *(Body Shapers 867-3006)*, Video Rental *(Blockbuster 867-9520)* **3+ mi:** Golf Course *(Twin Shields 301-855-8228, 10 mi.)*

Provisioning and General Services
Near: Protestant Church, Hardware Store *(Wheeler's True Value 867-2277)*
Under 1 mi: Convenience Store *(7-11)*, Bank/ATM, Post Office *(867-4858)*, Catholic Church, Library *(South County 867-4164)*, Beauty Salon *(Hair Harbor 867-6990)*, Florist, Copies Etc. *(Zancan 301-261-5903)*
1-3 mi: Supermarket *(IGA 867-1510)*, Liquor Store *(Parks 867-4577)*, Crabs/Waterman *(Bayside 301-261-5751)*, Meat Market, Dry Cleaners, Laundry, Pharmacy *(Friendly Pharmacy 301-867-2500)* **3+ mi:** Synagogue *(14 mi.)*, Department Store *(Kmart 301-855-1612, 10 mi.)*

Transportation
OnSite: Courtesy Car/Van, Bikes **OnCall:** Water Taxi *(ch. 68 Free)*, Rental Car *(Enterprise 301-627-0181)*, Airport Limo *(Dreamride Limos 286-3137)*
3+ mi: Taxi *(Carl's Cab 257-2849, 10 mi.)* **Airport:** Reagan Nat'l. *(32 mi.)*

Medical Services
911 Service **OnCall:** Ambulance **Under 1 mi:** Doctor *(South County 301-889-0854)*, Dentist *(Curl 301-261-5252)* **1-3 mi:** Veterinarian *(Stott 812-0315)* **Hospital:** Anne Arundel 267-1000 *(19 mi.)*

Setting -- On the west side of Rockhold Creek, just past Shipwright Harbor, Wilson's Yachts, and Bay Harbor Boatyard, this small, casual, friendly marina offers two docks with 50 slips. Views are across and down the pretty boat-filled creek. Landside, a deck overlooks the waterway and hosts grills and gray and white striped umbrellas shading wooden picnic tables. More picnic tables dot the adjacent grassy bulkhead and an attractive yellow single-story building houses the office.

Marina Notes -- DCM. Established in 1990, current owner since 1999. Stationary docks with power on the short finger pier pilings. On-site 20-ton travelift, a crane, and a multitude of boatyard services. The staff takes pride in providing personal attention to customers' needs. The inviting tiled-floor bathhouse features an attractive baker's rack with a lending library, wood-based vanities, and fresh navy and white printed shower curtains for the shower and dressing room.

Notable -- The free harbor taxi makes several restaurants easily accessible, including Skippers Pier at the mouth of the creek. It's also an easy dinghy or "big boat" ride -- they offer dock 'n' dine if you want to come over for lunch or stop on your way up the creek (but not for overnight). An easy walk is Calypso Bay, right across the Rt. 256 bridge at Herrington Harbor or, closer - up the road right on the creek is Happy Harbor Inn - which serves three meals a day, has lunch and dinner specials and also books charter fishing boats.

PHOTOS ON CD-ROM: 9

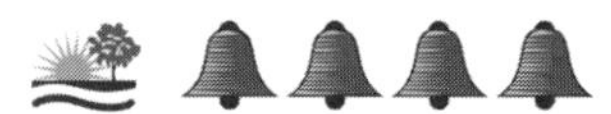

Herrington Harbour South

PO Box 150; Rose Haven on Bay; Friendship, MD 20758

Tel: (301) 855-8399; (800) 213-9438 **VHF: Monitor** 9 **Talk** 73
Fax: (301) 855-6819 **Alternate Tel:** (410) 741-5100
Email: hhs@chesapeake.net **Web:** www.herringtonharbour.com
Nearest Town: Chesapeake Beach *(3 mi.)* **Tourist Info:** (410) 280-0045

Navigational Information

Lat: 38°43.583' **Long:** 076°32.531' **Tide:** 1.5 ft. **Current:** 0 kt. **Chart:** 12270
Rep. Depths (*MLW*): Entry 8 ft. **Fuel Dock** 8 ft. **Max Slip/Moor** 8 ft./-
Access: Right off Chesapeake Bay - Private channel

Marina Facilities *(In Season/Off Season)*

Fuel: *BP* - Gasoline, Diesel, On Call Delivery
Slips: 620 Total, 50 Transient **Max LOA:** 200 ft. **Max Beam:** 35 ft.
Rate *(per ft.)*: **Day** $2.50/2.00* **Week** Inq. **Month** Inq.
Power: 30 amp $5, **50 amp** $10, **100 amp** n/a, **200 amp** n/a
Cable TV: Yes, $5.00 **Dockside Phone:** Yes Seasonal
Dock Type: Fixed, Long Fingers, Short Fingers, Pilings, Alongside, Wood
Moorings: 0 Total, 0 Transient **Launch:** n/a
Rate: Day n/a **Week** n/a **Month** n/a
Heads: 26 Toilet(s), 30 Shower(s) *(with dressing rooms)*
Laundry: 5 Washer(s), 5 Dryer(s), Iron, Iron Board **Pay Phones:** Yes, 3
Pump-Out: Full Service, 2 Central, 1 Port **Fee:** $5 **Closed Heads:** Yes

Marina Operations

Owner/Manager: Jed Dickman **Dockmaster:** Alex Persons
In-Season: Jun-Sep, 8am-6pm **Off-Season:** Oct-May, 9am-5pm
After-Hours Arrival: Check in at inn office
Reservations: Recommended **Credit Cards:** Visa/MC, Amex
Discounts: Boat/US **Dockage:** 40% off season **Fuel:** $0.10 **Repair:** n/a
Pets: Welcome, Dog Walk Area **Handicap Access:** Yes, Heads, Docks

Marina Services and Boat Supplies

Services - Docking Assistance, Concierge, Security *(24 hrs., On-site management)*, Trash Pick-Up, Dock Carts **Communication -** Mail & Package Hold, Phone Messages, Fax in/out *($1)*, Data Ports *(Wi-Fi & Office)*, FedEx, DHL, UPS, Express Mail *(Sat Del)* **Supplies - OnSite:** Ice *(Block, Cube)* **Near:** Ships' Store, Bait/Tackle **1-3 mi:** West Marine *(301-889-0004)*, Live Bait, Propane, CNG

Boatyard Services

OnSite: Yacht Broker **OnCall:** Engine mechanic *(gas, diesel)*, Electrical Repairs, Electronics Repairs, Hull Repairs, Rigger, Sail Loft, Canvas Work, Brightwork, Air Conditioning, Refrigeration, Divers, Compound, Wash & Wax, Interior Cleaning, Propeller Repairs, Woodworking, Inflatable Repairs, Life Raft Service, Upholstery, Yacht Interiors, Metal Fabrication, Painting, Awlgrip, Yacht Design, Total Refits **1-3 mi:** Travelift, Crane, Forklift, Hydraulic Trailer, Launching Ramp, Yacht Building.
Nearest Yard: Herrington Harbor North (800) 247-1930

Restaurants and Accommodations

OnSite: Restaurant *(Mango's Bar & Grill 257-0095, L $7-12, D $13-23, kids' menu $4-6, Lite Fare $10-13, Sun brunch, specials nightly)*, Lite Fare *(Bayside Market B $2-5, L $3-8)*, *(Herington on the Bay 741-5100, catering service)*, Motel *(Herrington Inn $60-160)* **1-3 mi:** Restaurant *(Thursday's Bar & Grill 286-8695)*, *(Bay Harbor Marina 867-2392)*, *(Westlawn Inn 257-7000)*, Snack Bar *(Tastee Freez 301-855-0585)*, Pizzeria *(Jerry's Subs & Pizza 257-9480, L $4-10, D $6-10)*, Inn/B&B *(Bay Views 410-257-1000)* **3+ mi:** Hotel *(Chesapeake Beach Hotel & Spa 410-257-5596, 4 mi.)*

Recreation and Entertainment

OnSite: Pool, Spa, Beach *(with tiki umbrellas)*, Picnic Area, Grills *(charcoal)*, Playground, Tennis Courts, Fitness Center, Jogging Paths, Boat Rentals *(kayaks & paddle boats)*, Fishing Charter *("Lucky Duck" 410-257-2927; "My Decision II" 410-886-2705)*, Volleyball, Video Arcade, Special Events
Near: Park *(North Beach Park)* **1-3 mi:** Golf Course *(Twin Shields 855-8228)*, 855-8228), Video Rental *(Blockbuster 867-9520)*, Museum

Provisioning and General Services

OnSite: Convenience Store, Delicatessen, Wine/Beer, Liquor Store, Market *(Bayside Market & Deli 301-855-3663)*, Bank/ATM, Beauty Salon *(La Mer 410-257-9838)*, Retail Shops *(Gecko Gifts)* **1-3 mi:** Supermarket *(Safeway 301-855-3765, Giant 301-855-9349)*, Gourmet Shop, Bakery, Farmers' Market, Fishmonger *(Neptune 410-257-7899)*, Meat Market, Post Office, Catholic Church, Protestant Church, Library *(Calvert County 410-257-2101)*, Barber Shop, Dry Cleaners *(Fastop Laundry & Cleaners 410-257-0982)*, Pharmacy *(CVS 410-326-6731)*, Florist, Department Store *(KMart 301-855-1612)* **3+ mi:** Hardware Store *(Sneade's Ace 410-257-2963, 4 mi.)*

Transportation

OnSite: Courtesy Car/Van *(Courtesy Car)*, Rental Car **OnCall:** Taxi *(Carl's Cab 257-2849)*, Airport Limo *(Deale Limo 301-855-7175)* **3+ mi:** Rail *(New Carrolton, 23 mi.)* **Airport:** Reagan Nat'l. *(32 mi.)*

Medical Services

911 Service **Under 1 mi:** Dentist *(Curl 301-855-8812)* **1-3 mi:** Doctor *(Calvert Family 301-855-1513)*, Chiropractor, Veterinarian *(Calvert Animal 301-855-8525)* **Hospital:** Calvert Memorial 301-855-1012 *(3 mi.)*

Setting -- A true marina resort with a Bahamian flair, Herrington Harbour's picturesque peach buildings trimmed with verandas and white lattice line a long protected basin chock-a-block with quality dockage. Brick paths, lush plantings and palm trees--including nearly 1000 banana palm trees--enhance the tropical ambiance. The huge Olympic pool and nearby kiddie pool are ringed with peach strap chaises and thatched umbrellas. Adjacent is Mango's bar and al fresco dining deck - white tables topped with hunter green umbrellas overlook the pool and the docks beyond. Two wide sand beaches flank the jettied entrance.

Marina Notes -- *40% Boat/US discount LabDay-MemDay. Family owned. Over 800 ft. of alongside dockage. Docks are divided into east and west - all of the amenities are on the east side and every effort is made to put transients there. Anna Chaney's Herrington on the Bay (741-5101) caters events in two large tents near the beach and at the yacht club. Two laundry rooms - the main one has a folding table, reading material and a small seating area right outside. Five inviting bathhouses - two types - beige and tan tiled individual bathrooms or rows of toilets, showers with dressing rooms & sinks.

Notable -- Mike & Jennifer Brown's upscale Mangos' dining room features a two to three-piece band Wed, Fri and Sat (and outside after 9pm), and a single acoustic guitar on the deck Sat and Sun from 3 to 7pm. Two tennis courts, a sauna, volleyball, playground, picnic areas, exercise room, boat rentals, courtesy car, shuffleboard, a hair stylist, small market, a gift shop and lodgings complete the amenities. The Beachfront Inn, really a single-story motel, has nicely decorated, well-equipped rooms - refrigerators, microwaves, coffeemakers, hair dryers, and hot tubs (cocktails in the afternoon, breakfast in the am).

8. WS: WEST R TO ST JEROME CREEK
PHOTOS ON CD-ROM: 16

Rod & Reel Docks

Route 261 & Mears Avenue; Chesapeake Beach, MD 20732

Tel: (301) 855-8450; (800) 233-2080 **VHF: Monitor** 88A **Talk** n/a
Fax: (301) 855-5350 **Alternate Tel:** n/a
Email: FID@rodnreelinginc.com **Web:** www.rodnreelinc.com
Nearest Town: Chesapeake Beach **Tourist Info:** (410) 257-2230

Navigational Information
Lat: 38°41.463' **Long:** 076°31.987' **Tide:** 2 ft. **Current:** n/a **Chart:** 12264
Rep. Depths (*MLW*): Entry 6 ft. **Fuel Dock** 6 ft. **Max Slip/Moor** 6 ft./-
Access: Chesapeake Bay to flashing green "1" - Private Channel into Fishing

Marina Facilities *(In Season/Off Season)*
Fuel: *Citgo* - Gasoline, Diesel
Slips: 125 Total, 10 Transient **Max LOA:** 60 ft. **Max Beam:** n/a
Rate *(per ft.)*: **Day** $1.50 **Week** Inq. **Month** Inq.
Power: 30 amp Incl., **50 amp** Incl., **100 amp** n/a, **200 amp** n/a
Cable TV: No **Dockside Phone:** No
Dock Type: Fixed, Wood
Moorings: 0 Total, 0 Transient **Launch:** n/a
Rate: Day n/a **Week** n/a **Month** n/a
Heads: 2 Toilet(s), 1 Shower(s)
Laundry: None **Pay Phones:** Yes
Pump-Out: OnSite, Self Service, 1 Central **Fee:** n/a **Closed Heads:** Yes

Marina Operations
Owner/Manager: Freddie Donovan **Dockmaster:** Same
In-Season: Spr-Sum-Fall, 5am-8pm **Off-Season:** Winter, 8am-5pm
After-Hours Arrival: Check in at restaurant
Reservations: Yes **Credit Cards:** Visa/MC
Discounts: Boat/US **Dockage:** 10% **Fuel:** n/a **Repair:** n/a
Pets: Welcome, Dog Walk Area **Handicap Access:** Yes, Heads, Docks

Marina Services and Boat Supplies
Services - Docking Assistance, Security, Dock Carts **Communication -** Mail & Package Hold, Phone Messages, Fax in/out, Data Ports *(Office, Free)*, FedEx, DHL, UPS, Express Mail **Supplies - OnSite:** Ice *(Cube)*, Bait/Tackle **Near:** Ships' Store, Live Bait, Propane

Boatyard Services
Near: Launching Ramp, Engine mechanic *(gas)*, Electrical Repairs, Hull Repairs. **Nearest Yard:** Fishing Creek Landings (301) 855-3572

Restaurants and Accommodations
OnSite: Restaurant *(Smokey Joe's 257-2427, B $3-7, L $6-19, D $6-19, 7am-10pm M-F 5am-10pm; S&S, sandwiches to entrees, BBQ, steaks, ribs, seafood, kids' menu $3-6)*, *(Rod & Reel 855-8450, L $5-19, D $16-28)*, Seafood Shack *(Buckmaster Seafood 257-7310, picnic tables or take-out - live or cooked)*, Hotel *(Chesapeake Beach Hotel & Spa 257-5596, $110-290)* **Near:** Restaurant *(Italia by the Bay 257-1601, L $7-$12, D $14-17)*, *(Trader's Seafood Steak and Ale 855-0766)*, *(Little Panda 855-8068)*, *(Chaney's on the Beach 855-2323)*, Seafood Shack *(Abner's 257-3689, L $3-21, D $3-21, dock)*, Snack Bar *(Scoops by the Bay)*, Pizzeria *(Domino's 257-0087)* **Under 1 mi:** Fast Food, Pizzeria *(Papa John's 257-1700)* **1-3 mi:** Hotel *(Herrington Harbor 741-5100)*, Inn/B&B *(Bay Views 257-1000)*

Recreation and Entertainment
OnSite: Beach *(or walk 0.6 mi. south to Brownie's at Bay Front Park)*, Picnic Area, Boat Rentals *(Bay Paddlers 286-3663)*, Fishing Charter *(7 6-packs $400 6hrs., $550 8hrs.; 17 larger boats - same rates, then $60/pp over 6)*, Group Fishing Boat *(Lady Hooker & Tom Hooker $40/pp, rod rental $5, 8am-3pm or 6pm-Mid - M-F kids $3 less)*, Museum *(Railway Museum 257-3892 1-4pm, Free)*, Special Events *(Bluefish Tournament - May; Rockfish Tournament - Apr)* **Near:** Pool *(Water Park 11am-8pm)*, Playground, Fitness Center *(Curves 286-5500)*, Volleyball, Video Arcade *(Lucky Star Bingo)*, Park *(Water Park 855-3803, Breezy Point Beach)*, Sightseeing, Galleries *(One of a Kind)* **Under 1 mi:** Video Rental *(Blockbuster 286-0764)* **3+ mi:** Golf Course *(Twin Shields 855-8228, 9 mi.)*

Provisioning and General Services
OnSite: Crabs/Waterman *(Buckmaster Seafood)*, Beauty Salon *(CB Salon - hair & nails $15-115 - cut & style $40)* **Near:** Convenience Store, Liquor Store, Bakery, Fishmonger *(Tyler's Crab House 257-6610)*, Bank/ATM, Post Office, Library *(Twin Beaches 257-2411)*, Dry Cleaners *(Fastop Laundry & Dry Cleaners 257-0982)* **Under 1 mi:** Market *(Twin Beach 855-2851)*, Catholic Church, Pharmacy *(Chesapeake Drug 855-7400)*, Department Store *(Kmart 855-1612)* **1-3 mi:** Supermarket *(Roland's 257-0187)*, Delicatessen *(Bayside Market & Deli 855-3663)*, Hardware Store *(Ace 855-8120)*

Transportation
OnSite: Bikes *(two courtesy)* **OnCall:** Taxi *(Carl's Cab 257-2849)*, Airport Limo *(Bayside 855-6630)* **3+ mi:** Rental Car *(Enterprise 414-2500, 12 mi.)*
Airport: Reagan Natl. *(35 mi.)*

Medical Services
911 Service **OnSite:** Holistic Services *(CB Spa, services $45-110; 60 min massage $75)* **OnCall:** Ambulance **1-3 mi:** Doctor *(Twin Beaches 257-7279)*, Dentist *(Frazer 855-1053)*, Chiropractor *(Carver 257-0466)*
Hospital: Calvert Memorial 855-1012 *(15 mi.)*

Setting -- This bay-front destination resort offers a compelling selection of waterfront activities. The new 4-story contemporary, islands-style hotel and spa seriously upscales the old Rod & Reel marina. Three waterfront eateries, a major sportfish operation and the railroad museum add to the experience. Right on the Bay, 2 long transient docks - protected by two stone jetties and a wave fence - are anchored by a boardwalk that connects the restaurants and the hotel. The charter boats, fuel dock, and a 3rd restaurant are along Fishing Creek, the channel that edges the northern perimeter of the complex.

Marina Notes -- In season, the fuel dock is open daily 5am-8pm. Boat/US discounts. The charter boats line Fishing Creek, with the two big party boats (accommodating up to 80 anglers) docked at the entrance followed by about two dozen sportfish vessels - 7 charters can take up to 6 anglers and 17 can handle over 6. Fishing season is Apr 16th to Dec 15th. Smokey Joe's opens up right onto the docks and the large bait & tackle shop is there as well. The reasonable showers are in the B&T shop and can be accessed either during their open hours (5am- 8pm, 7 days) - or through Smokey Joe's until 2am.

Notable -- The updated Rod & Reel eatery has attractive, natural Windsor chairs & tables tiered on two levels, to take advantage of the huge window wall that overlooks the bay. On the second floor a quasi-banquet room could work for large groups. The Chesapeake Beach Hotel & Spa, opened in '04, features 72 fresh, stylishly furnished, well-equipped waterfront rooms - most with balconies, some with fireplaces & whirlpools, plus a fitness center, bay-front indoor pool, business center and full-service spa and salon. A walk through the nearby condo complex leads to a boardwalk and Brownie's powdery sand beach.

PHOTOS ON CD-ROM: 16

Fishing Creek Landings Marina

PO Box 1150; 4055 Gordon Stinnett Ave; Chesapeake Beach, MD

Tel: (301) 855-3572 **VHF: Monitor** 9 **Talk** 9, 68
Fax: (410) 257-6216 **Alternate Tel:** n/a
Email: n/a **Web:** www.fishingcreekmarina.com
Nearest Town: Chesapeake Beach **Tourist Info:** (410) 257-2230

Navigational Information

Lat: 38°41.458' **Long:** 076°32.199' **Tide:** 3 ft. **Current:** n/a **Chart:** 12264
Rep. Depths (*MLW*): Entry 5 ft. **Fuel Dock** 5 ft. **Max Slip/Moor** 5 ft./-
Access: From the Bay west into channel entrance at Green #1 daymarker

Marina Facilities *(In Season/Off Season)*

Fuel: Gasoline
Slips: 180 Total, 5 Transient **Max LOA:** 40 ft. **Max Beam:** 12 ft.
Rate *(per ft.)*: **Day** $1.25 **Week** n/a **Month** n/a
Power: 30 amp $3, **50 amp** n/a, **100 amp** n/a, **200 amp** n/a
Cable TV: No **Dockside Phone:** No
Dock Type: Fixed, Short Fingers
Moorings: 0 Total, 0 Transient **Launch:** n/a
Rate: Day n/a **Week** n/a **Month** n/a
Heads: 4 Toilet(s), 3 Shower(s)
Laundry: None **Pay Phones:** No
Pump-Out: OnCall, Self Service **Fee:** $1 **Closed Heads:** Yes

Marina Operations

Owner/Manager: Pamela Sisson **Dockmaster:** Tom Cody
In-Season: Apr-Nov, 7am-7pm **Off-Season:** Dec-Mar, 8am-4pm
After-Hours Arrival: Take preassigned slip, settle up in am
Reservations: Yes, Required **Credit Cards:** Visa/MC, Dscvr, Amex
Discounts: Boat/US **Dockage:** 25% **Fuel:** n/a **Repair:** n/a
Pets: Welcome **Handicap Access:** Yes, Heads

Marina Services and Boat Supplies

Services - Dock Carts **Communication -** FedEx, UPS, Express Mail
Supplies - OnSite: Ice *(Block, Cube, Shaved)*, Ships' Store, Bait/Tackle, Live Bait *(bloodworms)* **Near:** Propane *(Fastop Gas Station)*

Boatyard Services

OnSite: Travelift *(12T)*, Hydraulic Trailer, Launching Ramp, Interior Cleaning, Propeller Repairs **Near:** Engine mechanic *(gas)*.
Yard Rates: $38/hr., Haul & Launch $7/ft. *(blocking incl.)*, Power Wash $2.50/ft., Bottom Paint $20.20-$26.50/ft. *(paint incl.)*

Restaurants and Accommodations

OnCall: Pizzeria *(Domino's 257-0087)*, *(Papa John's 257-1700)*
Near: Restaurant *(Italia by the Bay 257-1601, L $7-12, D $14-17)*, *(Rod & Reel 855-8450, L $5-19, D $16-28)*, *(Smokey Joe's 257-2427, B $3-7, L $6-19, D$6-19)*, *(Chaney's on the Beach 855-2323)*, *(Little Panda 855-8068)*, Seafood Shack *(Abner's Crab House 257-3689, L $3-21, D $3-21, dock)*, *(Buckmasters' Crabs 257-7310, take-out available)*, Fast Food *(Subway)*, Lite Fare *(Scoops 50's Style Ice Cream Parlor)*, Hotel *(Chesapeake Beach Hotel & Spa 257-5596, $110-290)* **1-3 mi:** Hotel *(Herrington Harbor 741-5100, $60-160)*, Inn/B&B *(Bay Views 257-1000)*

Recreation and Entertainment

OnSite: Picnic Area, Grills, Boat Rentals *(Bay Paddlers 286-3663 rentals $35-45/4 hrs, instruction, tours $25-75)* **Near:** Pool *(Chesapeake Beach Water Park 257-1404 11am-8pm, 7 days MemDay-LabDay $17.50/15.50, discount for county residents)*, Dive Shop, Fitness Center *(Northeast Community Center)*, Fishing Charter *(at Rod & Reel)*, Group Fishing Boat, Video Rental *(Blockbuster 286-0764)*, Park *(Water Park 855-3803, Breezy Point Beach)*, Museum *(Railway Museum 257-3892 1-4pm, Free)*, Galleries **Under 1 mi:** Beach *(Brownie's at Bay Front Park - 0.6 mi.)* **1-3 mi:** Special Events *(Bay Fest - last weekend Aug - North Beach)* **3+ mi:** Golf Course *(Twin Shields 855-8228, 9 mi.)*

Provisioning and General Services

Near: Convenience Store, Wine/Beer, Liquor Store, Fishmonger *(Buckmaster Seafood 257-7310)*, Crabs/Waterman *(Tyler's Crab House 257-6610)*, Bank/ATM, Post Office, Library *(Twin Beaches 257-2411)*, Beauty Salon *(Chesapeake Beach Salon)*, Dry Cleaners *(Fastop Laundry & Dry Cleaners 257-0982)*, Laundry *(at the Citgo)*, Pharmacy *(Chesapeake Drug 855-7400, CVS)*, Newsstand, Florist **Under 1 mi:** Market *(Twin Beach Market 855-2851)*, Catholic Church, Department Store *(Kmart 855-1612)* **1-3 mi:** Supermarket *(Roland's 257-0187)*, Delicatessen *(Bayside Market & Deli 855-3663)*, Hardware Store *(Sneade's Ace 855-8120)*

Transportation

OnCall: Taxi *(Carl's Cab 257-2849)*, Airport Limo *(Bayside 855-6630)* Rental Car *(Enterprise 414-2500, 12 mi.)* **Airport:** Reagan Nat'l. *(35 mi.)*

Medical Services

911 Service **OnCall:** Ambulance **Near:** Holistic Services *(Chesapeake Beach Hotel & Spa)* **Under 1 mi:** Veterinarian *(Calvert 855-8525)* **1-3 mi:** Doctor *(Twin Beaches 257-7279)*, Dentist *(Frazer 855-1053)*, Chiropractor *(Carver 257-0466)* **Hospital:** Calvert Memorial 855-1012 *(15 mi.)*

Setting -- Past the Rod & Reel sport fish charter boat docks, and under the 10-foot fixed Route 261 bridge, Fishing Creek Landings' slips flank both sides of the waterway and extend into a long rectangular basin. The conveniently located docks are surrounded by parking lots, on-the-hard storage and sit in the shadow of the Northeast Community Center and the Chesapeake Beach Water Park. Almost everything is within a few blocks, including restaurants.

Marina Notes -- DCM. About 30 of the slips are covered and these are first-come first-served. Significant boatel and trailer boat launch operation. The management prides itself on customer care and personal service. The ships' store has a full line of tackle, fuel, ice, boating supplies, snacks, and fairly recent comfortably large heads with showers. In '05 the entire south side was closed for condo construction. It is anticipated that full service will be restored by '06 - Call for details. Harborvista Condos and Yacht Club are being developed adjacent to the marina, with a first phase target of 2006.

Notable -- Everything is within a five-block radius. Practically dockside is the Community Center, which hosts exercise classes; behind it is Bay Paddlers Kayak Rentals and excusions, and just north, the municipal Chesapeake Waterpark - with 8 water slides, a kids' activity pool, fountains, waterfalls, a slow tubing river, a lagoon and water volleyball. Directly across Route 261 are the Rod & Reel Docks at the new Chesapeake Beach Hotel & Spa, with 4 eateries, the largest sport fishing operation on the Bay, and the on-site C.B. Railway Museum. Housed in the original depot, it memorializes Otto Mear's abandoned railroad that ran from D.C. to C.B. from 1900-1935, making this a very chic summer destination in its 1920's heyday. Brownie's Beach is great for fossil hunting.

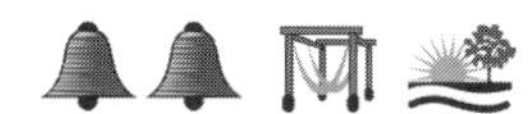

Navigational Information
Lat: 38°27.825' **Long:** 076°28.334' **Tide:** 1.5 ft. **Current:** 0.5 kt. **Chart:** 1226
Rep. Depths (*MLW*): Entry 7 ft. **Fuel Dock** 8 ft. **Max Slip/Moor** 8 ft./-
Access: Chesapeake Bay to private channel

Marina Facilities *(In Season/Off Season)*
Fuel: Gasoline
Slips: 168 Total, 2 Transient **Max LOA:** 40 ft. **Max Beam:** 14 ft.
Rate *(per ft.)*: **Day** $1.00 **Week** n/a **Month** n/a
Power: 30 amp Incl., **50 amp** n/a, **100 amp** n/a, **200 amp** n/a
Cable TV: No **Dockside Phone:** No
Dock Type: Fixed, Wood
Moorings: 0 Total, 0 Transient **Launch:** n/a
Rate: Day n/a **Week** n/a **Month** n/a
Heads: 6 Toilet(s), 5 Shower(s)
Laundry: None **Pay Phones:** No
Pump-Out: OnSite **Fee:** n/a **Closed Heads:** Yes

Marina Operations
Owner/Manager: John Little **Dockmaster:** Same
In-Season: Year-Round, 9am-5pm **Off-Season:** n/a
After-Hours Arrival: Call ahead
Reservations: Yes, Preferred **Credit Cards:** n/a
Discounts: Boat/US **Dockage:** Inq. **Fuel:** $0.10/gal **Repair:** n/a
Pets: Welcome **Handicap Access:** No

Flag Harbor Yacht Haven

PO Box 91; 1565 Flag Harbor Blvd.; Saint Leonard, MD 20685

Tel: (410) 586-0070 **VHF: Monitor** n/a **Talk** n/a
Fax: (410) 586-0070 **Alternate Tel:** (410) 586-1915
Email: fbca@flagharbor.com **Web:** www.flagharbor.com
Nearest Town: St. Leonard *(2 mi.)* **Tourist Info:** (410) 257-2230

Marina Services and Boat Supplies
Services - Dock Carts **Communication -** FedEx, UPS, Express Mail
Supplies - OnSite: Ice *(Block)* **1-3 mi:** Bait/Tackle, Live Bait, Propane *(United 386-0222)* **3+ mi:** West Marine *(326-6006, 15 mi.)*

Boatyard Services
OnSite: Travelift *(20T)*, Launching Ramp *(Breezy Point 535-6259, Slomons Public Ramp)*, Engine mechanic *(gas, diesel)*, Electrical Repairs, Electronics Repairs, Hull Repairs, Rigger, Bottom Cleaning, Brightwork, Compound, Wash & Wax, Interior Cleaning, Woodworking, Painting, Awlgrip, Yacht Broker *(Clipper Bay)* **OnCall:** Sail Loft, Canvas Work, Air Conditioning, Refrigeration, Divers, Propeller Repairs, Inflatable Repairs, Life Raft Service, Upholstery, Yacht Interiors, Metal Fabrication

Restaurants and Accommodations
Under 1 mi: Condo/Cottage *(Mataaka Beach Cabins 586-0260), (Chesapeake Bay Rentals 495-8674)* **1-3 mi:** Restaurant *(C & L Seafood Restaurant Carryout 586-3700), (The Tavern 586-2225), (Gateway 586-1870)*, Pizzeria *(S & P's 495-7880, L $4-10, D $4-10, subs and pizza)*, Motel *(Cliffs Motor Inn 586-1514)* **3+ mi:** Restaurant *(Italia by the Bay 257-1601, L $7-12, D $14-17, 16 mi., pizza, sandwiches, & Italian food), (Cerro Grande Mexican Restaurant 862-3901, L $5-15, D $5-15, 13 mi., authentic Mexican food)*, Motel *(Super 8 535-8668, 9 mi.)*, Inn/B&B *(The Cliff House 535-4837, 7 mi.)*

Recreation and Entertainment
OnSite: Pool, Beach, Picnic Area, Grills **3+ mi:** Playground *(Calvert Cliffs State Park, 7 mi.)*, Tennis Courts *(Hollowing Point 535-1295, 10 mi.)*, Golf Course *(Chesapeake Hills 326-4653, 7 mi.)*, Fitness Center *(World Gym 414-9001, 7 mi.)*, Horseback Riding *(Pardners' Farm 414-2171, 8 mi.)*, Bowling *(Lord Calvert Bowl 535-3560, 9 mi.)*, Movie Theater *(Apex Cinemas 535-0776, 7 mi.)*, Video Rental *(Blockbuster 535-2424, 7 mi.)*, Park *(Flag Ponds 586-1477, Calvert Cliffs, 5-7 mi.)*

Provisioning and General Services
1-3 mi: Convenience Store, Delicatessen *(Fastop 586-8300)*, Wine/Beer, Liquor Store *(Wemyss 586-9626)*, Bank/ATM, Post Office, Newsstand, Florist **3+ mi:** Supermarket *(Safeway 414-7400, Food Lion 394-6236, 9 mi.)*, Green Grocer *(4 mi.)*, Market *(Britton's 586-0600, 7 mi.)*, Catholic Church *(7 mi.)*, Protestant Church *(Methodist, Episcopal, Baptist, 7 mi.)*, Library *(Calvert 326-5289, 11 mi.)*, Beauty Salon *(Shear Elegance 586-1300, 7 mi.)*, Laundry *(Dunn Clean Laundryette 535-9274, 9 mi.)*, Pharmacy *(Safeway 414-7404, 9 mi.)*, Hardware Store *(Ace 326-3222, 10 mi.)*, Department Store *(Peebles 7 mi., Wal-Mart 535-5552, 9 mi.)*, Buying Club *(BJ's, 15 mi.)*

Transportation
OnCall: Rental Car *(Enterprise 414-2500)*, Taxi *(Calvert 535-6272)*, Airport Limo *(Parran Limo 586-2424)* **Airport:** Reagan/Baltimore-Washington Int'l. *(52 mi./59 mi.)*

Medical Services
911 Service **OnCall:** Ambulance **1-3 mi:** Chiropractor *(Boehm 586-3937)* **3+ mi:** Doctor *(Bell Family Practice 286-8606, 10 mi.)*, Dentist *(Yazdan 326-4078, 9 mi.)*, Veterinarian *(St. Leonard Animal Hospital 586-8700, 7 mi.)*
Hospital: Calvert Memorial 535-4000 *(11 mi.)*

Setting -- A welcome sight in the long stretch of looming Calvert Cliffs, Flag Harbor's 600 foot channel, flanked by rock jetties, leads into a long, rectangular, well-protected placid basin. Slips rim the edges anchored by a boardwalk that surrounds the basin. A long, freestanding dock with slips on either side sits right in the center. A few private houses are tucked behind trees above the basin's terraced banks. At the head, an attractive, contemporary gray clubhouse with French blue trim sits atop a grassy knoll with a commanding view of the whole basin.

Marina Notes -- DCM. A condominium marina that also offers seasonal and, generally, transient dockage. Flag Harbor Marine Service is the on-site boat yard with a 20 ton lift and sheds for Awlgrip. The yard is on the level above the basin and the bows of the dry-stored boats peek over the edge. Do-it-yourself is permitted - ample water and 15 amp service provided throughout the yard for that purpose. The bathhouse is in the ground floor of the main office building.

Notable -- The terraced lawn is well cared for and sprinkled with flowering perennials. An attached open-air picnic pavilion with grills is advantageously sited to provide the same expansive views as those of the main clubhouse office building - across the basin and out to the Bay. An inviting pool, with a small number of white strap chaises, neighbors the clubhouse and shares some of its views. Stroll out to the mouth of the basin and enjoy a two-mile stretch of sand beach heading north that promises good fossil hunting as well. Situated between Calvert Beach and Long Beach, Flag Harbor is about two miles from St. Leonard's town center - where there are groceries and boat supplies. The basin acts as a harbor of refuge.

Harbor Island Marina

PO Box 85; 105 Charles Street; Solomons, MD 20688

Tel: (410) 326-3441 **VHF: Monitor** 16 **Talk** 68
Fax: (410) 326-5221 **Alternate Tel:** (410) 321-8002
Email: him@radix.net **Web:** www.harborislandmarina.com
Nearest Town: Lexington Park **Tourist Info:** (410) 326-6027

Navigational Information

Lat: 38°19.167' **Long:** 076°272167' **Tide:** 2 ft. **Current:** 0 kt. **Chart:** 12264
Rep. Depths (*MLW*): Entry 20 ft. **Fuel Dock** 12 ft. **Max Slip/Moor** 12 ft./-
Access: A few hundred feet past Harbor Entrance on Port side

Marina Facilities *(In Season/Off Season)*

Fuel: Gasoline, Diesel
Slips: 96 Total, 20 Transient **Max LOA:** 250 ft. **Max Beam:** n/a
Rate *(per ft.)*: **Day** $1.30 **Week** $6.50/ft. **Month** $8/ft.
Power: 30 amp $3, **50 amp** $6, **100 amp** n/a, **200 amp** n/a
Cable TV: No **Dockside Phone:** No
Dock Type: Fixed, Long Fingers, Short Fingers, Pilings, Wood
Moorings: 0 Total, 0 Transient **Launch:** n/a, Dinghy Dock
Rate: Day n/a **Week** n/a **Month** n/a
Heads: 4 Toilet(s), 2 Shower(s)
Laundry: None **Pay Phones:** No
Pump-Out: Onsite *(first 50 gals.)*, Full Service **Fee:** $5 **Closed Heads:** Yes

Marina Operations

Owner/Manager: Leonard Schultz **Dockmaster:** Same
In-Season: Year-Round, 8am-Dusk **Off-Season:** n/a
After-Hours Arrival: Call ahead
Reservations: preferred **Credit Cards:** Visa/MC, Dscvr, Amex
Discounts: None
Pets: Welcome **Handicap Access:** No

Marina Services and Boat Supplies

Services - Docking Assistance, Trash Pick-Up, Dock Carts **Communication -** Mail & Package Hold, Phone Messages, FedEx, DHL, UPS, Express Mail *(Sat Del)* **Supplies - OnSite:** Ice *(Block, Cube)*, Ships' Store **Under 1 mi:** Bait/Tackle *(Bunky's 326-3241)*, CNG **1-3 mi:** West Marine *(326-6006)*, Boater's World *(394-6007)*, Propane *(Mobil 326-6537)*

Boatyard Services

OnSite: Travelift *(25T & 12T)*, Engine mechanic *(gas, diesel)*, Electrical Repairs, Hull Repairs, Bottom Cleaning, Brightwork, Compound, Wash & Wax, Interior Cleaning, Woodworking, Metal Fabrication, Painting, Awlgrip, Yacht Broker **OnCall:** Divers **Under 1 mi:** Launching Ramp, Rigger, Sail Loft, Canvas Work, Propeller Repairs, Life Raft Service, Upholstery. **Dealer for:** Volvo Penta, Mercruiser and OMC stern drives. **Yard Rates:** $40-65/hr., Haul & Launch $4.50-5.50/ft. *(blocking $2/ft.)*, Power Wash $1.50/ft., Bottom Paint $17/ft. *(paint incl.)* **Storage:** On-Land $3.10/ft./mo.

Restaurants and Accommodations

OnSite: Restaurant *(Captain George's 326-2270, replaced Harbor Sounds in '05)* **OnCall:** Pizzeria *(Domino's 394-0600)* **Near:** Restaurant *(Lighthouse Inn 326-2444, L $7-20, D $7-27)*, *(77 Charles St. 326-4852)*, *(Catamarans 326-8399)*, Inn/B&B *(Locust Inn 326-9817)*, *(Ireland Manor 326-2022)*, *(Victorian 326-4811)* **Under 1 mi:** Restaurant *(Zahniser's Dry Dock Restaurant 326-4817, D $18-30)*, *(China Harbour 326-6888)*, Seafood Shack *(Stoney's Kingfishers Seafood 394-0236, L $8-30, D $8-30)*, *(Solomons Crabhouse 326-2800)*, Snack Bar *(Annie's Ice Cream)*, Motel *(Comfort Inn)*

Recreation and Entertainment

Near: Cultural Attract *(Ches. Biological Laboratory 326-4281)*, Galleries *(local art weekends at visitors' center)* **Under 1 mi:** Video Rental *(Videos 'n More 326-2116)*, Park *(Annmarie sSculpture Garden 326-4640)*, Museum *(Marine Museum 326-2042)* **1-3 mi:** Dive Shop *(Sea Dive & Cycle 326-4386)*, Boat Rentals *(Patuxent Adventure 394-2770, kayaks)*, Sightseeing *(cruises)* **3+ mi:** Golf Course *(Chesapeake Hills 326-4653, 5 mi.)*

Provisioning and General Services

Near: Beauty Salon *(Julia & Co. 394-1222)* **Under 1 mi:** Fishmonger *(Digiovanni's 394-6400)*, Bank/ATM, Post Office, Catholic Church, Protestant Church, Laundry *(Wash n' Fold 535-WASH)* **1-3 mi:** Supermarket *(Food Lion 394-6236)*, Liquor Store *(Port of Call 326-2525)*, Bakery, Green Grocer, Market *(Woodburn's 326-3284)*, Library *(Calvert 326-5289)*, Dry Cleaners *(Royal 326-4010)*, Pharmacy *(CVS 326-6731)*, Hardware Store *(True Value 326-1000)*, Copies Etc. *(K&R 326-6659)* **3+ mi:** Bookstore *(Bay Books 862-1424, 6 mi.)*, Department Store *(Kmart 737-3585, 6 mi.)*

Transportation

OnCall: Courtesy Car/Van *(courtesy drive into town)*, Water Taxi, Rental Car *(Enterprise 737-0100/Hertz 863-0033, 6 mi.)*, Taxi *(B&C 326-8200)*, Airport Limo *(Goldstar 373-4444)* **1-3 mi:** Bikes *(Patuxent Adventure 394-2770)* **Airport:** Reagan Nat'l. *(65 mi.)*

Medical Services

911 Service **OnCall:** Ambulance **Under 1 mi:** Dentist *(Sachs 326-0010)*, Chiropractor *(Alexander 394-1000)* **1-3 mi:** Doctor *(Urgent Care 394-2800)*, Veterinarian *(Solomons 326-4300)* **Hospital:** Calvert 855-1012 *(20 mi.)*

Setting -- The first pleasure craft facility on your port side, a few hundred feet after you enter Solomons Harbor, it's just across from Ma Leg Island. The small French blue dockhouse with a big sign atop is hard to miss. Behind it, the 2-two story funky Captain George's sports dining porches on each floor. Two main docks host most of the slips near one of the travelift bays. Additional docks neatly line the bulkhead west of the restaurant. In the middle, a boardwalk leads to the fuel dock which also provides alongside transient tie-ups. Owner Leonard Schultz's office is in the building across the road - along with an antique shop.

Marina Notes -- Most transients are on the 300 foot, 6 pump fuel dock (daily 8am-Sundown), or on T-heads. The active boatyard is right off the docks (Mon-Fri 8am-5pm, Sat by appt). Full service or do-it-yourself yard. Many boats on-the-hard. Transients are given priority for repair service. Two full bathrooms on the second floor of the restaurant (a door at the back of Capt. George's leads up the stairs) are also used by the restaurant, so learn the cleaning schedule.

Notable -- This classic old-time marina is the only boating facility actually on Solomons Island. In 1870, a 550 foot causeway was built to connect the island to the mainland. Thanks to centuries of oyster shells, the new bridge is only 23 feet long. On-site Captain George's restaurant replaced Harbor Sounds in '05. The atmosphere is very much the same - casual food (baskets and platters) and music - 11am-10pm, 7 days. Entertainment begins about 9:30: DJs Thu & Fri, live band on Sat. For more nightlife, Island Manor Motel's Tiki Bar seems to be the place. Right on the point is the world class Chesapeake Biological Lab. The small Visitors' Center (Tue-Sun, 10am-4pm) includes a video and a series of exhibits on the Bay's ecology. 90 minute tours Wed & Fri at 2pm.

Navigational Information
Lat: 38°19.350' **Long:** 076°27.377' **Tide:** 2 ft. **Current:** n/a **Chart:** 12264
Rep. Depths (*MLW*): Entry 12 ft. **Fuel Dock** 12 ft. **Max Slip/Moor** 25 ft./-
Access: Patuxent River to mouth of Back Creek

Marina Facilities *(In Season/Off Season)*
Fuel: Gasoline, Diesel, High-Speed Pumps
Slips: 100 Total, 15 Transient **Max LOA:** 140 ft. **Max Beam:** n/a
Rate *(per ft.)*: **Day** $1.90/1.40 **Week** 8.00 **Month** 15.00
Power: 30 amp $4, **50 amp** $6, **100 amp** $12, **200 amp** n/a
Cable TV: Yes, $5 some slips **Dockside Phone:** No
Dock Type: Fixed, Floating, Long Fingers, Alongside, Wood, Aluminum
Moorings: 0 Total, 0 Transient **Launch:** n/a, Dinghy Dock ($5/pp shower)
Rate: Day n/a **Week** n/a **Month** n/a
Heads: 4 Toilet(s), 4 Shower(s), 7 ind. bathroom suites
Laundry: 3 Washer(s), 3 Dryer(s), Iron, Iron Board **Pay Phones:** Yes, 1
Pump-Out: OnSite, Full Service, 2 Central **Fee:** $5 **Closed Heads:** Yes

Marina Operations
Owner/Manager: Suzanne Butler **Dockmaster:** Same
In-Season: Sum, 7am-8pm **Off-Season:** Fall-Win-Spr, 8am-5pm
After-Hours Arrival: Please call ahead
Reservations: Yes, Preferred **Credit Cards:** Visa/MC
Discounts: AAA **Dockage:** n/a **Fuel:** n/a **Repair:** n/a
Pets: Welcome, Dog Walk Area **Handicap Access:** No

Solomon's Yachting Center

PO Box 367; 255 Alexander Lane; Solomons, MD 20688

Tel: (410) 326-2401 **VHF: Monitor** 16 **Talk** 68
Fax: (410) 326-3202 **Alternate Tel:** n/a
Email: solomonsyachtingcenter@att.net **Web:** solomonsyachtingcenter.com
Nearest Town: Solomons *(0.5 mi.)* **Tourist Info:** (410) 326-6027

Marina Services and Boat Supplies
Services - Docking Assistance, Concierge, Boaters' Lounge, Dock Carts, Megayacht Facilities **Communication -** Mail & Package Hold, Phone Messages, Fax in/out *($2)*, Data Ports *(Wi-Fi Lounge, Free)*, FedEx, UPS **Supplies - OnSite:** Ice *(Block, Cube)*, Ships' Store **Near:** Bait/Tackle *(Bunky's 326-3241)*, CNG *(Zahnisers 326-2166)* **Under 1 mi:** West Marine *(326-6006)*, Propane *(Mobil 326-6537)* **1-3 mi:** Boater's World *(394-6007)*

Boatyard Services
OnSite: Travelift *(50T)*, Forklift, Bottom Cleaning, Divers, Compound, Wash & Wax, Yacht Broker **OnCall:** Engine mechanic *(gas, diesel)* **Near:** Launching Ramp, Electrical Repairs, Sail Loft, Canvas Work, Air Conditioning, Refrigeration, Interior Cleaning, Propeller Repairs, Upholstery, Metal Fabrication, Painting, Awlgrip. **Dealer for:** Interlux / Pettit. Other Certifications: do-it-yourself yard **Yard Rates:** $50/hr., Haul & Launch $7/ft. *(blocking $2/ft.)*, Power Wash $2/ft., Bottom Paint $37/hr.
Storage: In-Water $15/ft./mo. 40' min, On-Land $4.50/ft./mo.

Restaurants and Accommodations
OnCall: Pizzeria *(Domino's 394-0600)* **Near:** Restaurant *(China Harbour 326-6888)*, *(Solomons Crabhouse 326-2800)*, *(Catamarans 326-8399)*, *(Dry Dock 326-4817, D $18-30)*, Seafood Shack *(Stoney's Kingfishers Seafood 394-0236, L $8-30, D $8-30, kids' $4, best crabcakes)*, Fast Food *(Roy Rogers)*, Motel *(Comfort Inn Beacon Marina 326-6303)*, Inn/B&B *(By The-Bay B&B 326-3428, $90-125)*, *(Back Creek Inn 326-2022, $95-145)*
Under 1 mi: Restaurant *(CD Café 326-3877)*, *(Lighthouse Inn 326-2444, D $7-27, kids' $5-7)*, *(Jethro's BBQ 394-6700)*, Lite Fare *(Tiki Bar 326-4075)*, Pizzeria *(Papa John's 394-1200)*, Hotel *(Holiday Inn 326-6311, $130)*

Recreation and Entertainment
OnSite: Pool, Picnic Area, Grills **Near:** Boat Rentals *(Patuxent Adventure 394-2770)*, Fishing Charter, Video Rental *(Videos 'n More 326-2116)*, Galleries *(Carmen's)*, Special Events *(Tiki Bar)* **Under 1 mi:** Park *(Annmarie Sculpture Garden 326-4640)*, Museum *(Calvert Marine 326-2042 $7/2 10am-5pm, 7 days)*, Sightseeing *(cruises from museum: harbor, daily $7/4; 1828 Cove Pt. Lighthouse, 1:30pm & 11am wkends)* **1-3 mi:** Dive Shop *(Sea Dive & Cycle 326-4386)* **3+ mi:** Golf Course *(Ches. Hills 326-4653, 5 mi.)*, Fitness Center *(Curves 394-6600, 5 mi.)*

Provisioning and General Services
OnSite: Convenience Store *(Soda/beer/ice cream)*, Wine/Beer
Near: Delicatessen *(Woodburn's)*, Fishmonger *(Stoney's 394-0236)*, Catholic Church, Protestant Church, Beauty Salon *(Julia & Co. 394-1222)*
Under 1 mi: Supermarket *(Woodburn's 326-3284)*, Liquor Store *(Port of Call 326-2525)*, Bank/ATM, Post Office, Florist **1-3 mi:** Library *(Calvert 326-5289)*, Dry Cleaners *(Royal 326-4010)*, Pharmacy *(CVS 326-6731)*, Hardware Store *(True Value 326-1000)*, Copies Etc. *(K&R 326-6659)*
3+ mi: Department Store *(Target 862-5003, 6 mi.)*

Transportation
OnSite: Bikes *(free)* **OnCall:** Water Taxi *(free)*, Rental Car *(Enterprise 737-0100 or Hertz 863-0033, 6 mi.)*, Taxi *(B&C 326-8200)*, Airport Limo *(Goldstar 373-4444)* **Airport:** Reagan Nat'l. *(65 mi.)*

Medical Services
911 Service **OnCall:** Ambulance **Near:** Dentist **Under 1 mi:** Doctor *(Solomons Urgent Care 394-2800)* **Hospital:** Calvert 855-1012 *(20 mi.)*

Setting -- Sparkling new Solomon's Yachting Center sits on a narrow peninsula that separates Solomons Harbor from Back Creek - dead ahead after passing Ma Leg Island. A dozen gorgeous high-end IPE floating docks surround the peninsula hosting a hundred slips with 40 foot finger piers. A long fuel dock, across the peninsula's point, is backed by a newly renovated yellow 2-story office. Behind that are grassy picnic areas, a new pool, and a yellow brick clubhouse.

Marina Notes -- On the site of the old Town Center Marina, acquired in 2002 by Underhill Properties. Manager Suzanne Butler and her family live on-site. The original Town Center structure on the point has been totally redone - on the 2nd floor, a comfortably furnished boaters' lounge has a bar, cable TV and complimentary broadband Internet. Bring your laptop or use theirs. Below is a ships' store with B&T and provisions. Floating IPE (Brazilian hardwood) docks. Beyond the clubhouse is a full-service boatyard - do-it-yourself allowed. 50-ton travelift and dry storage area. The clubhouse has seven impeccable, individual full bathroom suites and a new laundry room. Improved landscaping, a pool deck, and more - promised soon.

Notable -- From SYC, it's a reasonable walk to many of Solomon's restaurants and sights. Complimentary bikes and water taxi makes most of the area accessible. The must-visit Calvert Marine Museum also has a dinghy dock; fun things for kids include climbing through the hatch of the 1883 screw-pile Drum Point Lighthouse to see how keepers and their families lived; a 15-tank estuarium includes funny river otters. Cruises also start at the museum: relive Solomon's oyster-packing days onboard the Wm. B. Tennison, an historic Chesapeake Bay bugeye "buy-boat."

PHOTOS ON CD-ROM: 12

Zahniser's Yachting Center

PO Box 760; 245 C Street; Solomons, MD 20688

Tel: (410) 326-2166 **VHF: Monitor** 09,16 **Talk** 69
Fax: (410) 326-4099 **Alternate Tel:** (410) 326-2166
Email: marina@zahnisers.com **Web:** www.zahnisers.com
Nearest Town: Solomons **Tourist Info:** (410) 326-8410

Navigational Information

Lat: 38°19.738' **Long:** 076°27.502' **Tide:** 1.5 ft. **Current:** 0 kt. **Chart:** 12264
Rep. Depths (*MLW*): Entry 13 ft. **Fuel Dock** n/a **Max Slip/Moor** 13 ft./14 ft.
Access: Chesapeake Bay - Solomons Harbor

Marina Facilities *(In Season/Off Season)*

Fuel: No
Slips: 275 Total, 30 Transient **Max LOA:** 150 ft. **Max Beam:** 30 ft.
Rate *(per ft.)*: **Day** $1.90/1.50 **Week** $10.50/ft **Month** $15/ft
Power: 30 amp $4, **50 amp** $8, **100 amp** n/a, **200 amp** n/a
Cable TV: No **Dockside Phone:** No
Dock Type: Fixed, Long Fingers, Short Fingers, Pilings, Alongside, Wood
Moorings: 0 Total, 0 Transient **Launch:** n/a, Dinghy Dock ($1 trash/$2 heads
Rate: Day n/a **Week** n/a **Month** n/a
Heads: 20 Toilet(s), 18 Shower(s) *(with dressing rooms)*
Laundry: 3 Washer(s), 3 Dryer(s), Iron, Iron Board **Pay Phones:** Yes, 1
Pump-Out: OnSite, Full Service, 1 Central **Fee:** $5 **Closed Heads:** Yes

Marina Operations

Owner/Manager: Skip & Ellen Zahniser **Dockmaster:** Jim Sharkey
In-Season: Apr-Nov, 8am-5pm **Off-Season:** Nov-Mar, 8am-4:30pm
After-Hours Arrival: Radio dock personnel
Reservations: Yes, Preferred **Credit Cards:** Visa/MC
Discounts: None
Pets: Welcome, Dog Walk Area **Handicap Access:** Yes, Heads, Docks

Marina Services and Boat Supplies

Services - Docking Assistance, Concierge, Security *(24 hrs.)*, Trash Pick-Up, Dock Carts **Communication -** Mail & Package Hold, Phone Messages, Fax in/out, Data Ports *(Dial-Up, Free)*, FedEx, UPS *(Sat Del)* **Supplies - OnSite:** Ice *(Block, Cube)*, Ships' Store *(Dry Dock Supply)*, CNG **Near:** Bait/Tackle *(Bunky's 326-3241)* **Under 1 mi:** West Marine *(326-6006)*, Boater's World *(394-6007)*, Propane *(Mobil 326-6537)*

Boatyard Services

OnSite: Travelift *(30T)*, Railway *(70T)*, Crane *(15T)*, Hydraulic Trailer *(30T)*, Launching Ramp, Engine mechanic *(gas, diesel)*, Electrical Repairs, Electronics Repairs, Hull Repairs, Rigger, Sail Loft, Canvas Work, Bottom Cleaning, Brightwork, Air Conditioning, Refrigeration, Compound, Wash & Wax, Interior Cleaning, Woodworking, Upholstery, Metal Fabrication, Painting, Awlgrip, Yacht Broker **OnCall:** Divers, Propeller Repairs **Dealer for:** Awlgrip, Yanmar, Perkins, Caterpillar, Autohelm, Datamarine, Volvo, Universal, Westerbeke, C-Frost, Balmar, Farymann, Marine Air, Cruise Air, LuneAir, Sparcraft, Tops "N" Quality, Adler-Barbour, Lewmar, Staylock, Norseman, Furlex, Furuno, Harken, Racor, Sealand, Onan, Perko, Rolls Batteries, Prevailer, Raytheon, Groco. **Member:** ABBRA - 4 Certified Tech (s), ABYC - 6 Certified Tech(s), Other Certifications: electrical/fiberglass
Yard Rates: $45-85/hr., Haul & Launch $45/hr., Bottom Paint $45/hr.

Restaurants and Accommodations

OnSite: Restaurant *(Dry Dock 326-4817, D $18-30, Sun Brunch $10-16)*, Snack Bar *(Patio Bar & Grill 326-2829, L $3-7, D $3-7)* **Near:** Restaurant *(Captain's Table 326-2772)*, *(Lighthouse Inn 326-2444, D $7-27)*, Seafood Shack *(Stoney's 394-0236)*, *(Solomons Crabhouse 326-2800)*, Motel *(Comfort Inn 326-6303)*, Inn/B&B *(By-the-Bay 326-3428)*, *(Back Creek Inn 326-2022)* **Under 1 mi:** Pizzeria *(Jerry's Subs & Pizza 326-4820, $5-10)*

Recreation and Entertainment

OnSite: Pool, Picnic Area, Grills, Playground, Volleyball, Special Events *(Concerts, Wed night races, Screwpile Race Week)* **Near:** Boat Rentals *(Patuxent Adven. 394-2770, kayaks)*, Park *(Annmarie Sculpture Garden 326-4640)*, Museum *(Calvert Marine 326-2042 & J.C. Lore Oyster House)* **Under 1 mi:** Dive Shop *(Sea Dive & Cycle 326-4386)*, Video Rental *(Blair's 326-9667)* **3+ mi:** Golf Course *(Chesapeake Hills 326-4653, 4 mi.)*

Provisioning and General Services

OnSite: Retail Shops, Copies Etc. **Near:** Convenience Store, Supermarket *(Woodburn's 326-3284, Food Lion 394-6236 2 mi.)*, Fishmonger *(Capt. Smith 326-1134)*, Bank/ATM, Post Office, Beauty Salon *(Hair Port 326-4553)*, Barber Shop, Newsstand **Under 1 mi:** Liquor Store *(Port of Call 326-2525)*, Bakery, Library *(326-5289)*, Pharmacy *(CVS 326-6731)*, Florist **1-3 mi:** Dry Cleaners *(Royal 326-4010)*, Hardware Store *(True Value 326-1000)*

Transportation

OnSite: Courtesy Car/Van, Bikes *(free)* **OnCall:** Rental Car *(Enterprise 737-0100)*, Taxi *(B&C Cab 326-8200)*, Local Bus *(Smart Ride)*, InterCity Bus, Airport Limo *(Goldstar 373-4444)* **Airport:** Reagan/BWI *(65 mi./71 mi.)*

Medical Services

911 Service **Near:** Doctor *(Solomons Urg. Care 394-2800)*, Dentist *(Sachs 326-0010)*, Chiropractor *(Alexander 394-1000)* **Under 1 mi:** Veterinarian *(Solomons 326-4300)* **Hospital:** Calvert Mem 855-1012 *(20 mi.)*

Setting -- On the southern shore of Back Creek, Zahniser's always full docks surround a peninsula of services and amenities housed in multiple flawlessly maintained charcoal gray buildings with fresh white trim. A pool complex is the recreational center of this relaxed family facility. Towering maples shade picnic tables scattered about the well-clipped lawns; flowering trees and bushes add to the parklike village ambiance. Historic Solomons is a short walk.

Marina Notes -- DCM. Established in 1960 - owned and managed by the Zahniser family ever since. Complimentary bikes & courtesy car. Professional staff manages 300 slips on 11 docks. Complete hi-tech marine services are isolated at the eastern end - 22 full-time service staff meet most needs. Dry storage for 120 boats. Free dial-up internet access. Power outlets generally on pilings/posts - some full pedestals. Clubs and rendezvous welcomed - tents and recreation areas provided and catering easily arranged. 3 bath houses feature inviting individual full tiled bathrooms with shower/tubs.

Notable -- Overlooing the docks is a large pool with cement surround furnished with white chaises and hunter green umbrella-topped tables. The pool bar serves lunch and cocktails poolside or at the pavilion under the striped awning. The intimate second floor of the Dry Dock Restaurant offers innovative cuisine, focused on steak & seafood, and a view of the marina (Sun-Thu 5-9pm, Fri&Sat 5-9:30pm, Sun Brunch 10am-1pm). Dry Dock Supply has gifts & books, sportswear, foul-weather gear, boat supplies & hardware. Zahniser's hosts the Screwpile Sailing Regatta (3rd weekend in July) - 200 boats compete and it's wild. A short walk finds the fun and enlightening Calvert Marine Museum and Riverwalk - which runs from Waterman's Mem. Park to Solomons Pier Restaurant.

Navigational Information
Lat: 38°19.737' **Long:** 076°27.317' **Tide:** 2 ft. **Current:** n/a **Chart:** 12264
Rep. Depths (*MLW*): Entry 14 ft. **Fuel Dock** 14 ft. **Max Slip/Moor** 14 ft./-
Access: Patuxent River to Back Creek

Marina Facilities *(In Season/Off Season)*
Fuel: Gasoline, Diesel
Slips: 450 Total, 20 Transient **Max LOA:** 150 ft. **Max Beam:** n/a
Rate *(per ft.)*: **Day** $1.50/.50 **Week** Inq. **Month** 10
Power: 30 amp $3, **50 amp** $6, **100 amp** n/a, **200 amp** n/a
Cable TV: No **Dockside Phone:** No
Dock Type: Fixed, Pilings, Alongside, Wood
Moorings: 12 Total, 12 Transient **Launch:** n/a, Dinghy Dock
Rate: Day n/a **Week** n/a **Month** n/a
Heads: 1 Toilet(s), 1 Shower(s)
Laundry: 2 Washer(s), 2 Dryer(s), Book Exchange **Pay Phones:** No
Pump-Out: OnSite, Self Service **Fee:** $5 **Closed Heads:** Yes

Marina Operations
Owner/Manager: Matt Gambrill **Dockmaster:** Same
In-Season: Year-Round, 8am-6pm **Off-Season:** n/a
After-Hours Arrival: Call ahead
Reservations: Yes **Credit Cards:** Visa/MC, Dscvr, Amex
Discounts: Boat/US **Dockage:** 25% **Fuel:** $0.10 **Repair:** n/a
Pets: Welcome, Dog Walk Area **Handicap Access:** Yes, Heads, Docks

Calvert Marina

14485 Dowell Road; Dowell, MD 20629

Tel: (410) 326-4251 **VHF: Monitor** 16 **Talk** 68
Fax: (410) 326-1035 **Alternate Tel:** (410) 394-6823
Email: n/a **Web:** n/a
Nearest Town: Solomons **Tourist Info:** (410) 326-6027

Marina Services and Boat Supplies
Services - Docking Assistance, Dock Carts **Communication -** Mail & Package Hold, Phone Messages, Fax in/out, Data Ports *(Office)*, FedEx, UPS **Supplies - OnSite:** Ice *(Block, Cube)*, Ships' Store **Near:** Boat/US, Marine Discount Store, Bait/Tackle, Live Bait, Propane, CNG **Under 1 mi:** West Marine *(326-6006)*

Boatyard Services
OnSite: Yacht Broker *(Solo, Selene & Island Gypsy trawlers)* **Near:** Travelift *(30T)*, Railway *(70T)*, Crane, Forklift, Engine mechanic *(gas, diesel)*, Electrical Repairs, Electronics Repairs, Hull Repairs, Canvas Work, Bottom Cleaning, Brightwork, Air Conditioning, Refrigeration, Divers, Compound, Wash & Wax, Interior Cleaning, Propeller Repairs, Woodworking, Metal Fabrication, Painting, Awlgrip, Total Refits. **Under 1 mi:** Launching Ramp, Rigger, Sail Loft. **Nearest Yard:** Washburns 300' away (410) 326-6701

Restaurants and Accommodations
OnSite: Restaurant *(Riverside - Private catered events only)*, Seafood Shack *(Dockside Diner 394-1697, B $5-11, L $3-12, D $8-22, Mon-Fri 11am-9pm, Sat-Sun 7am-9pm, kids menu $4-7)* **OnCall:** Pizzeria *(Domino's 394-0600)* **Under 1 mi:** Restaurant *(Dynasty Chinese Resturant 394-1185)* **1-3 mi:** Restaurant *(Solomon's Pier 326-2424)*, *(Isaac's 326-6311, L $7-24, D $10-28, previously "Maryland Way", at Holiday Inn)*, *(Boomerangs Original Ribs 326-6050)*, *(Dry Dock 326-4817, D $18-30)*, Pizzeria *(Jerry's Subs & Pizza 326-4820, L $5-10, D $5-10)*, Motel *(Comfort Inn Beacon Marina 326-6303, $70-140)*, Hotel *(Holiday Inn Select 326-6311, $130)*, Inn/B&B *(By The-Bay 326-3428, $90-125)*, *(Back Creek 326-2022, $95-145)*

Recreation and Entertainment
OnSite: Pool, Picnic Area, Grills, Tennis Courts, Jogging Paths, Boat Rentals *(Calvert Charters)*, Fishing Charter, Special Events *(TrawlerFest - early Oct)* **Near:** Dive Shop, Cultural Attract *(Annmarie Garden 326-4640 10-4, Free)* **1-3 mi:** Video Rental *(Videos N More 326-2116)*, Museum *(Calvert Marine Museum 326-2042 10am-5pm, $7/2; cruises daily)*, Galleries **3+ mi:** Golf Course *(Chesapeake Hills 326-4653, 5 mi.)*

Provisioning and General Services
OnSite: Wine/Beer **Near:** Post Office **Under 1 mi:** Convenience Store *(Citgo 326-6537)* **1-3 mi:** Supermarket *(Food Lion 394-6236)*, Delicatessen, Liquor Store *(Port of Call 326-3535)*, Fishmonger *(Capt. Smith's 326-1134)*, Market *(Woodburn's 326-3284)*, Bank/ATM, Catholic Church, Protestant Church, Library *(Calvert 326-5289)*, Beauty Salon *(Hair Solomons 394-2930)*, Barber Shop, Dry Cleaners *(Royal 326-4010)*, Laundry, Pharmacy *(CVS 326-3461)*, Newsstand, Hardware Store *(True Value 326-1000)*, Florist **3+ mi:** Department Store *(Kmart 737-3585, 7 mi.)*

Transportation
OnCall: Rental Car *(Enterprise 737-0100 or Hertz 863-0033, 6 mi.)*, Taxi *(B&C 326-8200)*, Airport Limo *(Goldstar 373-4444)* **1-3 mi:** Bikes
Airport: Reagan Nat'l./Baltimore-Washington Int'l. *(65 mi./71 mi.)*

Medical Services
911 Service **OnCall:** Ambulance **1-3 mi:** Doctor *(Urgent Care 394-2800)*, Dentist *(Gaylord 326-0800)*, Chiropractor *(Alexander 394-1000)*, Veterinarian *(Solomons 326-4300)* **Hospital:** Calvert Memorial 855-1012 *(20 mi.)*

Setting -- On a peninsula flanked by Back & Mill Creeks, a 120-acre sprawling, untamed campus hosts 450 slips, a new 1,000-foot floating transient dock, and the marina's amenities. An easy-access fuel dock dominates the tip and a gazebo and a few picnic tables perch above on the grassy bank. Farther inland, on a rise overlooking the entire harbor, is a casual pool and beyond a similarly maintained tennis. Docks radiate from the natural shoreline all along Back Creek ending at Washburn Boatyard. Pretty stands of trees shade more redwood picnic tables.

Marina Notes -- Mailing Address: PO Box 157; Solomons, MD 20688. This former Naval amphibious base trained 68,000 officers before closing in 1947. Owned and operated by the Gambrill family since 1981. Boat/US discounts. Windward Harbor at Solomons, a townhouse community, is being developed on this site. The facility's level of maintenance suggests that it is in a holding pattern during the construction process. The heads are tile but could use attention. Washburn's Boatyard is 300 ft. up the creek and provides extensive marine services. Home of the South Maryland Sailing Association and Lord Calvert YC.

Notable -- The laid-back Dockside Diner sits among the docks a short way up Back Creek (Mon-Fri 11am-9pm, Sat & Sun 7am-9pm). Farther up Dowell Road, dramatic ceramic walls and iron gates open into 30-acre Annemarie Garden on St. John. Paths wind through the wilderness stopping at a variety of outdoor sculptures. Watch for the Solomon Sea Horses. It's a short dinghy ride across Back Creek to "downtown" Solomons and all services - there's a dinghy dock at the Calvert Marine Museum near the lighthouse (10am-5pm) and another at Hospitality Harbor ($1/day).

PHOTOS ON CD-ROM: 12

Beacon Marina

PO Box 869; 255 Lore Road; Solomons, MD 20688

Tel: (410) 326-6303 **VHF: Monitor** 16 **Talk** n/a
Fax: (410) 326-6303 **Alternate Tel:** n/a
Email: n/a **Web:** n/a
Nearest Town: Solomons **Tourist Info:** (410) 326-6303

Navigational Information

Lat: 38°19.905' **Long:** 076°27.743' **Tide:** 1.5 ft. **Current:** Slight **Chart:** 1226
Rep. Depths (*MLW*): Entry 6 ft. **Fuel Dock** n/a **Max Slip/Moor** 10 ft./-
Access: Chesapeake Bay to Patuxent River to Back Creek

Marina Facilities *(In Season/Off Season)*

Fuel: No
Slips: 186 Total, 60 Transient **Max LOA:** 100 ft. **Max Beam:** n/a
Rate *(per ft.)*: **Day** $1.00 **Week** $4 **Month** $6
Power: 30 amp $6*, **50 amp** $6*, **100 amp** n/a, **200 amp** n/a
Cable TV: No **Dockside Phone:** Yes
Dock Type: Fixed
Moorings: 0 Total, 0 Transient **Launch:** n/a
Rate: Day n/a **Week** n/a **Month** n/a
Heads: 4 Toilet(s), 4 Shower(s)
Laundry: 1 Washer(s), 1 Dryer(s), Iron, Iron Board **Pay Phones:** Yes
Pump-Out: OnSite **Fee:** n/a **Closed Heads:** Yes

Marina Operations

Owner/Manager: Humphrey Hospitality **Dockmaster:** Jamie Pfeiffer
In-Season: Year-Round, 24 hrs. **Off-Season:** n/a
After-Hours Arrival: Call ahead
Reservations: No **Credit Cards:** Visa/MC, Dscvr, Din, Amex
Discounts: None
Pets: Welcome, Dog Walk Area **Handicap Access:** No

Marina Services and Boat Supplies

Services - Docking Assistance, Dock Carts **Communication -** Mail & Package Hold, Phone Messages, Fax in/out, Data Ports *(front desk)*, FedEx, DHL, UPS, Express Mail *(Sat Del)* **Supplies - OnSite:** Ice *(Cube)* **Near:** West Marine *(326-6006)*, Propane *(Mobil 326-6537)*, CNG *(Zahniser's)* **Under 1 mi:** Boater's World *(394-6007)*, Bait/Tackle *(Bunky's 326-3241)*

Boatyard Services

Near: Launching Ramp, Electrical Repairs, Electronics Repairs, Hull Repairs, Rigger, Canvas Work, Bottom Cleaning, Brightwork, Refrigeration. **Nearest Yard:** Zahniser's Yachting (410) 326-2166

Restaurants and Accommodations

OnSite: Restaurant *(Captain's Table 326-2772, B $5-13, L $5-12, D $5-26, kids' menu $3-4,)*, Motel *(Comfort Inn Beacon Marina 326-6303, $70-140)* **Near:** Restaurant *(Boomerangs Original Ribs 326-6050)*, *(Navarros Mexican Restaurant 394-1115)*, *(Dry Dock 326-4817, D $18-30)*, *(Naughty Gull 326-4855, L $5-12, D $8-25)*, *(Isaac's 326-6311, L $7-24, D $10-28, previously "Maryland Way", at Holiday Inn)*, Fast Food *(Burger King)*, Lite Fare *(CD Café 326-3877)*, Pizzeria *(Jerry's Subs & Pizza 326-4820, L $5-10, D $5-10)*, *(Papa John's 394-1700)*, Hotel *(Holiday Inn Select 326-6311, $76-123)*, Inn/B&B *(By The-Bay B&B 326-3428)*, *(Back Creek 326-2022, $95-145)* **Under 1 mi:** Lite Fare *(Spyro's Bagels 394-6565)*

Recreation and Entertainment

OnSite: Pool, Picnic Area, Grills, Special Events *(Spring Fling - mid-May)* **Near:** Playground, Dive Shop *(Sea Dive & Cycle 326-4386)*, Boat Rentals *(Patuxent Adventure 394-2770, kayaks)*, Roller Blade/Bike Paths, Fishing Charter *(Lucky Strike behind DiGiovanni's Rest 326-0444 $520/day)*, Video Rental *(Blair's 326-9667)*, Museum *(Calvert Marine Museum 326-2042 10-5 $7/2)*, Cultural Attract, Sightseeing *(Tennison harbor cruises Wed-Sun at 2pm, weekends 12:30, 2 & 3:10pm, $7/4 kids)* **Under 1 mi:** Park *(Annmarie Sculpture Garden 326-4640)* **3+ mi:** Golf Course *(Chesapeake Hills 326-4653, 4 mi.)*

Provisioning and General Services

OnCall: Dry Cleaners **Near:** Convenience Store, Supermarket *(Woodburn's 326-3284-delivers; 1 mi. Food Lion 394-6236)*, Green Grocer, Fishmonger *(Capt. Smith's 326-1134)*, Bank/ATM *(Cedar Point Federal)*, Post Office, Catholic Church, Library *(Calvert County 326-5289)*, Beauty Salon *(Hair Port 326-4553)*, Pharmacy *(CVS 326-6731)*, Newsstand, Florist **Under 1 mi:** Delicatessen, Liquor Store *(Southern 394-6889)*, Hardware Store *(True Value 326-1000)*, Copies Etc. *(K&R Copy 326-6659)* **3+ mi:** Bookstore *(Bay Books 862-1424, 5 mi.)*, Department Store *(Target 862-5003, 5 mi.)*

Transportation

OnSite: Bikes **OnCall:** Rental Car *(Enterprise 737-0100 or Hertz 863-0033, 6 mi.)*, Airport Limo *(Goldstar 373-4444)* **Near:** Water Taxi, Taxi *(B&C 326-8200)* **Airport:** Reagan Nat'l./BWI *(65 mi./71 mi.)*

Medical Services

911 Service **Near:** Doctor *(Solomons Urgent Care 394-2800)*, Ambulance **Under 1 mi:** Dentist *(Zanardelli 394-6690)*, Chiropractor *(Alexander Chiropractic Center 394-1000)*, Veterinarian *(Solomons Veterinary Clinic 326-4300)* **3+ mi:** Holistic Services *(Hanson John Licensed Acupuncturist 737-0662, 5 mi.)* **Hospital:** Calvert Memorial 855-1012 *(20 mi.)*

Setting -- A "Beacon Marina" sign atop the first covered shed welcomes boaters to this facility. Docks are anchored by a grassy bulkhead along the western shore of Back Creek. Landside, a gravel parking lot connects the gray shingle colonial-style Comfort Inn, a small matching dockhouse and the vine-covered Captain's Table eatery. Adjacent to the dockhouse, a small pool with hot tub overlooks the docks - separated by an attractive white wrought iron fence. Hunter green and white strap chaises and a handful of striped umbrella-topped tables furnish the surrounding concrete patio.

Marina Notes -- *Power is a one-time fee. Owned and operated by Humphrey Hospitality. 40 of the 186 slips are covered. 10% discount on Comfort Inn motel rooms based on availability. Updated in 2001, this two-story 60-room motel features simple, contemporary rooms with new baths & windows, a fax center, and meeting rooms. Pets are no longer permitted in the motel. Basic marina bathhouse with fiberglass shower stalls (no dressing rooms).

Notable -- On-site Captain's Table is a casual dining spot featuring Maryland seafood; a perfect "summer porch" affords diners sparkling views of Back Creek framed in greenery. The cozy dining room's window wall shares the view (Sun-Thu 7am-9pm, Fri & Sat 7am-10pm). A block or so away is the must-see Calvert Marine Museum. Well-executed exhibits and a kids' discovery room interpret the palentology of the Calvert Cliffs and the biology of the Pautuxent River - elucidated in a 15-tank "estuarium." Kids love the river otters. On the campus is the restored 1833 screwpile Drum Point Lighthouse and the "Wm. B. Tennison," an 1899 bugeye (buyboat) that used to buy oysters from the dredgers and now tours the harbor at 2pm daily. Nearby is the Lore Oyster House (326-2878).

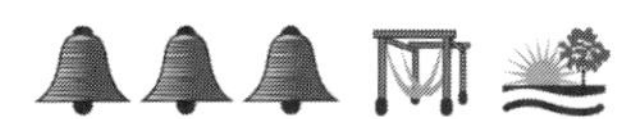

Navigational Information
Lat: 38°20.016' **Long:** 076°27.727' **Tide:** 2 ft. **Current:** n/a **Chart:** 12264
Rep. Depths (*MLW*): Entry 12 ft. **Fuel Dock** 12 ft. **Max Slip/Moor** 12 ft./-
Access: Patuxent River to Back Creek

Marina Facilities *(In Season/Off Season)*
Fuel: Gasoline, Diesel
Slips: 248 Total, 20 Transient **Max LOA:** 100 ft. **Max Beam:** n/a
Rate *(per ft.)*: **Day** $1.85/1.40* **Week** Inq. **Month** Inq.
Power: 30 amp $4, **50 amp** $8, **100 amp** n/a, **200 amp** n/a
Cable TV: No **Dockside Phone:** No
Dock Type: Fixed, Short Fingers, Pilings, Alongside, Wood
Moorings: 0 Total, 0 Transient **Launch:** n/a
Rate: Day n/a **Week** n/a **Month** n/a
Heads: 13 Toilet(s), 13 Shower(s)
Laundry: 3 Washer(s), 3 Dryer(s), Book Exchange **Pay Phones:** Yes, 1
Pump-Out: Self Service, 2 Central, 50 InSlip **Fee:** Free **Closed Heads:** Yes

Marina Operations
Owner/Manager: Trevor Richards **Dockmaster:** Same
In-Season: Sum, 8am-6pm **Off-Season:** Fall-Spr, 8am-5pm
After-Hours Arrival: Call during hours or tie up at fuel dock
Reservations: Yes, Recommended **Credit Cards:** Visa/MC, Dscvr, Amex
Discounts: None
Pets: Welcome, Dog Walk Area **Handicap Access:** Yes, Heads, Docks

Spring Cove Marina

PO Box 160; 455 Lore Road; Solomons, MD 20688

Tel: (410) 326-2161 **VHF: Monitor** 16 **Talk** 68
Fax: (410) 326-4187 **Alternate Tel:** n/a
Email: scm@tgci.net **Web:** www.springcovemarina.com
Nearest Town: Solomons *(0.25 mi.)* **Tourist Info:** (410) 326-6027

Marina Services and Boat Supplies
Services - Docking Assistance, Concierge, Boaters' Lounge, Security *(24 hrs., Cameras and Gate)*, Dock Carts **Communication -** Mail & Package Hold, Phone Messages, Fax in/out *($1)*, Data Ports *(Dial-up in Lobby; Wi-Fi at docks, Free)*, FedEx, DHL, UPS, Express Mail **Supplies - OnSite:** Ice *(Block, Cube)*, Ships' Store *(marine supplies, gifts, snacks)* **Near:** West Marine *(326-6006)*, Propane *(Mobil 326-6537)* **Under 1 mi:** Boater's World *(394-6007)*, Bait/Tackle *(Bunky's 326-3241)*, CNG *(Zahniser's 326-2166)*

Boatyard Services
OnSite: Travelift *(35T)*, Crane, Engine mechanic *(gas, diesel)*, Electrical Repairs, Hull Repairs, Bottom Cleaning, Air Conditioning, Refrigeration, Compound, Wash & Wax, Yacht Broker **OnCall:** Propeller Repairs, Woodworking **Near:** Launching Ramp, Electronics Repairs, Rigger, Metal Fabrication, Painting, Awlgrip. **Member:** ABYC **Yard Rates:** $46-80/hr., Haul & Launch $9.50-13.50/ft. *(blocking incl.)*, Power Wash Incl., Bottom Paint $10/ft.+ *(paint incl.)* **Storage:** In-Water Inq., On-Land $4.50/ft./mo.

Restaurants and Accommodations
OnSite: Restaurant *(Naughty Gull 326-4855, L $5-12, D $8-25, Mon-Thu 11am-9pm, Fri-Sat to 9:30pm, Sun 9am-8pm - brunch til 1:30pm, kids' $3-7 lite fare $4-17)* **OnCall:** Pizzeria *(Domino's 394-0600)* **Near:** Restaurant *(Dry Dock 326-4817, D $18-30)*, *(Isaac's 326-6311, L $7-24, D $10-28)*, *(Captain's Table 326-2772)*, *(Jethro's BBQ 394-6700)*, *(Boomerangs Original Ribs 326-6050)*, Snack Bar *(Annie's Ice Cream)*, Fast Food *(Burger King, Subway)*, Lite Fare *(CD Café 326-3877)*, *(After Deck)*, Pizzeria *(Papa John's 394-1700)*, Motel *(Comfort Inn 326-6303, $70-140)*, Hotel *(Holiday Inn 326-6311, $76-123)*, Inn/B&B *(Back Creek 326-2022, $90-125)*

Recreation and Entertainment
OnSite: Heated Pool *(75 ft.)*, Picnic Area, Grills, Playground, Video Rental **Near:** Dive Shop *(Sea Dive & Cycle 326-4386)*, Tennis Courts, Jogging Paths, Boat Rentals *(Patuxent Adventure 394-2770)*, Museum *(Calvert Marine 326-2042)*, Sightseeing *(harbor cruises Wed-Sun 2pm, weekends 12:30, 2 & 3:10pm, $7/4 kids)*, Special Events *(Patuxent River Discovery Day)* **Under 1 mi:** Park *(Annmarie sculpture garden 326-4640)* **3+ mi:** Golf Course *(Ches. Hills 326-4653, 4 mi.)*, Fitness Center *(Curves 394-6600)*

Provisioning and General Services
OnSite: Convenience Store, Retail Shops *(Emporium)* **Near:** Fishmonger *(Capt. Smith's 326-1134)*, Bank/ATM, Post Office, Catholic Church, Protestant Church, Library *(326-5289)*, Beauty Salon *(Hair Solomons 394-2930)*, Pharmacy *(CVS 326-6731)* **Under 1 mi:** Supermarket *(Woodburn's 326-3284, Food Lion 394-6236)*, Liquor Store *(Southern 394-6889)*, Dry Cleaners *(Royal 326-4010)*, Hardware Store *(True Value 326-1000)*, Copies Etc. *(K&R 326-6659)* **3+ mi:** Bookstore *(Bay Books 862-1424, 5 mi.)*, Department Store *(Target 862-5003, 5 mi.)*

Transportation
OnSite: Bikes *($3/hr., $6/half-day, $12/day)* **OnCall:** Rental Car *(Enterprise 737-0100 or Hertz 863-0033, 6 mi.)*, Airport Limo *(Goldstar 373-4444)*
Airport: Reagan Nat'l./Baltimore-Washington Int'l *(65 mi./71 mi.)*

Medical Services
911 Service **OnCall:** Ambulance **Near:** Doctor *(Solomons Medical 394-2800)* **Under 1 mi:** Dentist *(Zanardelli 394-6690)*, Chiropractor *(Alexander 394-1000)*, Veterinarian **Hospital:** Calvert 855-1012 *(20 mi.)*

Setting -- 10-acre Spring Cove has an Adirondack ambiance: on a rise above the docks, picnic tables and charcoal grills scatter among the hickories, evergreens and oaks, pine needles under foot. The sparkling competition-length pool is on a promentory jutting into the creek - a gazebo, chaises, umbrella-topped tables and a slate-blue poolhouse populate the patio. Docks radiate from the shore along both sides. Boardwalks line the well-tended waterfront.

Marina Notes -- *MemDay-LabDay: $1.85, weekends $2.05/ft.; May & Sep $1.65, Off-Season $1.40/ft. DCM. Established in the '60s, part owners Trevor & Liz Richards have been providing personal attention since 1988. Full service boatyard, large dry storage area (do-it-yourself, too), and 3-pump fuel dock. Higher letter slips are more secluded, lower letters closer to the pool. Free dockside Wi-Fi. Convenient, free central vaccum pump-out - plug in at your slip! A 2-story slate-blue building with covered porch houses a lavishly stocked gift shop, local memorabilia, clothing, groceries, a wall of marine supplies, plus coffee, tea, snacks and drinks. Upstairs is lending library and lounge. Perfect full bathrooms, in two-tone tile, sport glass shower doors, nautical borders and artwork.

Notable -- Nestled above "H" dock (the most wooded one) cozy Naughty Gull's restaurant & pub features sturdy natural Stickley-style chairs and windowed & mirrored walls. Kitchen hours: Mon-Thu 11am-9pm, Fri- Sat to 9:30pm, Sun 9am-8pm; bar is open to 1am or later. Happy Hour Mon-Fri 3-7pm. Right next door, the Holiday Inn has 2 eateries, After Deck and Isaac's, and just beyond is Solomons Medical Center. The Calvert Marine Museum is a block away, a bit farther is Putuxent Plaza for shopping, & West Marine. J.C. Lore Oyster Processing House, founded 1888, explains much of Solomon's past; 1-4:30pm (326-2878).

PHOTOS ON CD-ROM: 17

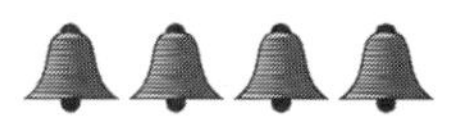

Hospitality Harbor Marina

PO Box 382; 205 Holiday Drive; Solomons, MD 20688

Tel: (410) 326-1052 **VHF: Monitor** 16 **Talk** 69
Fax: (410) 326-1052 **Alternate Tel:** n/a
Email: hospharbor@chesapeake.net **Web:** chesapeake.net/~hospharbor
Nearest Town: Solomons *(0.25 mi.)* **Tourist Info:** (410) 326-6027

Navigational Information

Lat: 38°20.187' **Long:** 076°27.726' **Tide:** 2 ft. **Current:** .3 kt. **Chart:** 12264
Rep. Depths (*MLW*): Entry 10 ft. **Fuel Dock** n/a **Max Slip/Moor** 9 ft./-
Access: Patuxent River to Back Creek

Marina Facilities *(In Season/Off Season)*

Fuel: No
Slips: 80 Total, 30 Transient **Max LOA:** 100 ft. **Max Beam:** n/a
Rate *(per ft.)*: **Day** $1.60/1.00* **Week** Inq. **Month** Inq.
Power: 30 amp $5, **50 amp** $10, **100 amp** n/a, **200 amp** n/a
Cable TV: Yes **Dockside Phone:** Yes, Free Limited
Dock Type: Fixed, Long Fingers, Pilings, Alongside, Wood
Moorings: 0 Total, 0 Transient **Launch:** n/a, Dinghy Dock ($2/day)
Rate: Day n/a **Week** n/a **Month** n/a
Heads: 5 Toilet(s), 4 Shower(s)
Laundry: 2 Washer(s), 2 Dryer(s), Book Exchange **Pay Phones:** Yes, 4
Pump-Out: OnSite, Self Service, 1 Central **Fee:** $5 **Closed Heads:** Yes

Marina Operations

Owner/Manager: John Simpson **Dockmaster:** Bill Glascock
In-Season: May-Oct, 8am-7pm **Off-Season:** Oct-Dec, Mar-Apr, 9am-5pm
After-Hours Arrival: Find a slip and pay in the morning
Reservations: Yes, Preferred **Credit Cards:** Visa/MC
Discounts: None
Pets: Welcome, Dog Walk Area **Handicap Access:** No

Marina Services and Boat Supplies

Services - Docking Assistance, Concierge, Dock Carts **Communication -** Mail & Package Hold, Phone Messages, Fax in/out *($1)*, Data Ports *(Office)*, FedEx, UPS, Express Mail **Supplies - OnSite:** Ice *(Block, Cube)* **Near:** West Marine *(326-6006)*, Propane *(Mobil 326-6537)*, CNG *(Zahnisers)* **Under 1 mi:** Boater's World *(394-6007)*, Bait/Tackle *(Bunky's 326-3241)*

Boatyard Services

OnSite: Divers, Yacht Broker **OnCall:** Engine mechanic *(gas, diesel)*, Electrical Repairs, Electronics Repairs, Compound, Wash & Wax, Interior Cleaning **Near:** Travelift, Launching Ramp, Hull Repairs, Rigger, Bottom Cleaning, Brightwork, Air Conditioning, Refrigeration. **Under 1 mi:** Railway, Sail Loft, Canvas Work. **Nearest Yard:** Spring Cove Marina (Adjacent)

Restaurants and Accommodations

OnSite: Restaurant *(Isaac's 326-6311, L $7-24, D $10-28, previously Maryland Way)*, Lite Fare *(Mallard's Café 326-1052)*, *(After Deck poolside)*, Hotel *(Holiday Inn Select 326-6311, $76-123)* **OnCall:** Pizzeria *(Domino's 394-0600)* **Near:** Restaurant *(Boomerangs Original Ribs 326-6050)*, *(Naughty Gull 326-8455, L $5-12, D $8-25)*, *(Lighthouse Inn 326-2444, D $7-27)*, *(Capt. Smith's Seafood 326-1134)*, *(China Harbour 326-6888)*, *(Jethro's Barbecue 394-6700)*, Motel *(Comfort Inn Beacon Marina 326-6303)*, Inn/B&B *(By The-Bay B & B 326-3428)*, *(Back Creek 326-2022)* **Under 1 mi:** Lite Fare *(Spyro's Bagels 394-6565)*

Recreation and Entertainment

OnSite: Pool, Picnic Area, Grills, Tennis Courts, Fitness Center, Boat Rentals *(Patuxent Adventure 394-2770, kayaks)* **Near:** Dive Shop *(Sea Dive & Cycle 326-4386)*, Jogging Paths, Park *(Annmarie Sculpture Garden 326-4640)*, Museum *(Calvert Marine Museum 326-2042)*, Special Events *(Sharkfest - July; Solomons Is. Fest Early Sep)* **Under 1 mi:** Video Rental *(Blair's 326-9667)* **3+ mi:** Golf Course *(Chesapeake Hills 326-4653, 4 mi.)*

Provisioning and General Services

OnSite: Retail Shops *(Sandpiper Gifts)* **Near:** Convenience Store *(7-Eleven)*, Liquor Store *(Port of Call 326-2525)*, Green Grocer, Fishmonger *(Capt. Smith's 326-1134)*, Market *(Woodburn's 326-3284)*, Bank/ATM, Post Office, Catholic Church, Library *(Calvert County 326-5289)*, Beauty Salon *(Hair Port 326-4553)*, Laundry *(Wash n' Fold 535-WASH)*, Pharmacy *(CVS 326-3461)*, Florist **Under 1 mi:** Supermarket *(Food Lion 394-6236)*, Protestant Church, Dry Cleaners *(Royal 326-4010)*, Hardware Store *(True Value 326-1000)* **3+ mi:** Bookstore *(Bay Books 862-1424, 5 mi.)*

Transportation

OnSite: Bikes **OnCall:** Water Taxi, Rental Car *(Enterprise 737-0100)*, Taxi *(B&C Cab 326-8200)*, Airport Limo *(Goldstar 373-4444)* **Near:** Local Bus *(County Public)* **Airport:** Reagan Nat'l./Baltimore-Washington International *65 mi./71 mi.)*

Medical Services

911 Service **OnCall:** Ambulance **Near:** Doctor *(Urgent Care 394-2800)*, Holistic Services *(Yoga 326-4421 $15)* **Under 1 mi:** Dentist *(Zanardelli 394-6690)*, Chiropractor *(Alexander Chiro 394-1000)*, Veterinarian *(Solomons 326-4300)* **Hospital:** Calvert Memorial 855-1012 *(14 mi.)*

Setting -- Sequestered among towering pines and maples, the 5-story tan brick Holiday Inn rises above the docks. The south wing anchors "D" & "C" docks and north wing "B" & "A" docks. Waterfront is the After Deck open-air bar, and behind it is a courtyard with a sprightly fountain and Mallard's Café patio. The junior Olympic-size pool has a brick surround with chaises and tables. Boardwalks with rope railings wind through the 9-acre grounds leading to the amenties.

Marina Notes -- *Discounts 3rd and 5th night. Monthly rates. Founded 1988, family-owned and operated. New 90 foot T-head can handle up to 100'+ with 9 ft. at MLW. The pool, fitness center & tennis courts available to marina guests. Phone messages for emergency only; brief e-mail hookups at off-peak hours. Complete business center - Faxes: $1 first page, $0.50 each add'l. $1/day for use of dinghy dock. On the ground level of the north wing, directly accessible, are superb all-tile heads and showers, 2 toilets, 2 showers, 3 sinks in a granite vanity (toiletries provided) plus a sauna, fitness center and laundry. Another laundry is on the 2nd floor of the south wing. 16,000 sq. ft. of flexible function space, including two ballrooms, make this an interesting cruise destination.

Notable -- In addition to the After Deck Outdoor Lounge and Mallard's Café is the full-service Isaac's - housed in a bright, airy waterfront dining room with a curved window-wall that takes full advantage of the views. The Sandpiper Shop has gifts and clothing. Many of the 326 well-appointed guest rooms feature upscale decor and views across the docks and up the creek; 50 have kitchenettes, Jacuzzis and balconies. Spring Marina's Naughty Gull Restaurant is close by. A little farther is the Calvert Marine Museum - its bugeye "Wm. B. Tennison," the oldest passenger-carrying boat in the country, which tours the harbor.

Navigational Information
Lat: 38°25.268' **Long:** 076°29.236' **Tide:** 2 ft. **Current:** n/a **Chart:** 12264
Rep. Depths (*MLW*): Entry 15 ft. **Fuel Dock** 12 ft. **Max Slip/Moor** 12 ft./-
Access: Patuxent River to St. Leonard Creek

Marina Facilities *(In Season/Off Season)*
Fuel: *Texaco* - Gasoline, Diesel
Slips: 135 Total, 84 Transient **Max LOA:** 120 ft. **Max Beam:** n/a
Rate *(per ft.)*: **Day** $1.00 **Week** Inq. **Month** Inq.
Power: 30 amp Incl., **50 amp** Incl., **100 amp** n/a, **200 amp** n/a
Cable TV: No **Dockside Phone:** No
Dock Type: Fixed, Short Fingers
Moorings: 0 Total, 0 Transient **Launch:** n/a
Rate: Day n/a **Week** n/a **Month** n/a
Heads: 2 Toilet(s), 3 Shower(s)
Laundry: None **Pay Phones:** No
Pump-Out: OnSite **Fee:** n/a **Closed Heads:** Yes

Marina Operations
Owner/Manager: Vera Freeman **Dockmaster:** Dr. Selvin Kumar
In-Season: May-Oct, 7am-11pm* **Off-Season:** Oct-Dec, 5am-9pm
After-Hours Arrival: Call 410-586-1182
Reservations: Yes **Credit Cards:** Visa/MC, Dscvr, Din
Discounts: None
Pets: Welcome **Handicap Access:** No

Vera's White Sands Marina

PO Box 355; 1200 White Sands Drive; Lusby, MD 20657

Tel: (410) 586-1182 **VHF: Monitor** n/a **Talk** n/a
Fax: (410) 586-3896 **Alternate Tel:** n/a
Email: verasrestaurant@hotmail.com **Web:** www.veraswhitesands.com
Nearest Town: Solomons *(6 mi.)* **Tourist Info:** (410) 326-6027

Marina Services and Boat Supplies
Services - Docking Assistance, Dock Carts **Communication -** FedEx, UPS, Express Mail *(Sat Del)* **Supplies - OnSite:** Ice *(Block)*, Ships' Store **3+ mi:** West Marine *(326-6006, 10 mi.)*, Propane *(Bowen Gas 586-0222, 6 mi.)*

Boatyard Services
Nearest Yard: Spring Cove (410) 326-2161

Restaurants and Accommodations
OnSite: Restaurant *(Vera's White Sands Polynesian 586-1182, L $5-11, D $14-27, Plus a $33 three-course Luau, Tue-Fri 5-9, Sat & Sun Noon-9pm)* **OnCall:** Pizzeria *(Guido's 326-0040)* **3+ mi:** Restaurant *(C & L Seafood Carryout 586-3700, 6 mi.)*, *(Frying Pan 326-1125, 6 mi.)*, *(Isaac's 326-6311, L $7-24, D $10-28, 5 mi., previously "Maryland Way")*, Pizzeria *(S & P's 495-7880, L $4-10, D $4-10, 4 mi.)*, *(CJ's Pizza & Carry Out 326-4077, 6 mi.)*, Motel *(Cliff's Motor Inn 586-1514, 6 mi.)*, Hotel *(Holiday Inn 326-6311, 9 mi.)*, Inn/B&B *(Gatehouse B & B 280-0024, 7 mi.)*

Recreation and Entertainment
OnSite: Pool **Near:** Sightseeing **1-3 mi:** Park *(Flags Pond Nature Park)* **3+ mi:** Golf Course *(Chesapeake Hills Golf Club 326-4653, 6 mi.)*, Fitness Center *(Curves 394-6600, 6 mi.)*, Video Rental *(Blair's 326-9667, 9 mi.)*, Museum *(Calvert Marine Museum 326-2042, 9 mi.)*, Cultural Attract *(by water - 90-acre 1717 Sotterly Plantation 373-2280 - a bit further up the Patuxent, this living history, Nat'l Hist Landmark Tue-Sat 10-4, Sun 12-4 Tours $7/5, Grounds only $2. - call to confirm access to the Sotterly Creek Wharf, 5 mi.)*

Provisioning and General Services
1-3 mi: Gourmet Shop **3+ mi:** Supermarket *(Food Lion 394-6236, 9 mi.)*, Wine/Beer *(Lusby Liquors 394-6737, 6 mi.)*, Liquor Store *(Southern Liquor 394-6889, 7 mi.)*, Market *(Woodburn's 326-3284, 9 mi.)*, Bank/ATM *(5 mi.)*, Post Office *(326-4406, 6 mi.)*, Library *(Calvert 326-5289, 6 mi.)*, Pharmacy *(Whitesell, 6 mi.)*, Hardware Store *(Sneade's Ace 326-3222, 7 mi.)*

Transportation
OnCall: Airport Limo *(Parran Limo 586-2424)* **3+ mi:** Rental Car *(Hertz 301-863-0033, 15 mi.)*, Taxi *(B & C Cab 326-8200, 8 mi.)*
Airport: Reagan Nat'l./Baltimore-Washington Int'l. *(60 mi./65 mi.)*

Medical Services
911 Service **OnCall:** Ambulance **3+ mi:** Doctor *(Bennet 326-4398, 6 mi.)*, Dentist *(Ursic 326-4078, 6 mi.)*, Chiropractor *(Alexander Chiropractic 394-1000, 8 mi.)*, Veterinarian *(St. Leonard 586-8700, 6 mi.)*
Hospital: Calvert Memorial 535-4000 *(14 mi.)*

Setting -- About 2.5 miles upstream from the Patuxent at the confluence of St. Leonard and St. John's Creeks, a large Easter Island-like statue, backed by the low-slung pink stucco Vera's White Sands Restaurant, is perched high on a cliff. Fun, kitschy, funky and fascinating, Vera's is a trip. The bamboo-lined dining rooms with shell chandeliers and leopard print everywhere are stopped-in-time tropical fantasies - but the pristine view down the creek is very real.

Marina Notes -- *Closed Mondays. Transient dockage only in summer. Opened in 1960 as the members-only White Sands Yacht Club, it was converted to a public marina and restaurant in the late '70s by Vera and her now-deceased husband, real estate developer & Hollywood optometrist Effus Freeman. Two long, aging docks anchored by the peninsula host 135 slips in 12 feet of water -- one is angled west and one south, the latter's long T-head hosts a fuel pump and pump-out. Peeling white paint covers the piers and superstructure. Power is on the pilings. The tile-floored bathhouse is basic at best.

Notable -- Vera Freeman's extensive collection of authentic artifacts from her world travels is a key part of the restaurant's exotic decor. The Polynesian Islands motif doesn't extend entirely to the menu which includes mainly international & southern Maryland dishes. There's good live music in the Piano Bar and Miss Vera greets her guests between 6 and 7pm each evening in her trademark fantastical, flowing old Hollywood-style garb - her white tresses wrapped in pearls or rhinestones. Vera's bio has been formalized in a recent book by manager Selvin Kumar. Cruise events for up to 200 can be managed by combining three rooms - Bamboo Hall, The Atrium and Palm Palm room. A little-used teardrop shaped pool with a tired thatched hut rests behind the restaurant.

PHOTOS ON CD-ROM: 14

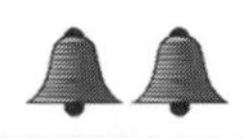

Drury's Marina

49599 Airedale Road; Ridge, MD 20680

Tel: (301) 872-4480 **VHF: Monitor** 16 **Talk** 71
Fax: (301) 872-9067 **Alternate Tel:** (301) 872-4480
Email: n/a **Web:** n/a
Nearest Town: Lexington Park *(11 mi.)* **Tourist Info:** (260) 111-2551

Navigational Information

Lat: 38°06.857' **Long:** 076°21.297' **Tide:** 1.5 ft. **Current:** 0 kt. **Chart:** 12233
Rep. Depths (*MLW*): Entry 4 ft. **Fuel Dock** 4 ft. **Max Slip/Moor** 4 ft./-
Access: Follow Markers to #11, 255 M to #1 in North Prong - ahead to port

Marina Facilities *(In Season/Off Season)*

Fuel: Gasoline, Diesel
Slips: 25 Total, 2 Transient **Max LOA:** 55 ft. **Max Beam:** 14 ft.
Rate *(per ft.)*: **Day** $0.50/0.50* **Week** n/a **Month** n/a
Power: 30 amp $2*, **50 amp** n/a, **100 amp** n/a, **200 amp** n/a
Cable TV: No **Dockside Phone:** No
Dock Type: Fixed, Wood
Moorings: 0 Total, 0 Transient **Launch:** n/a
Rate: Day n/a **Week** n/a **Month** n/a
Heads: 2 Toilet(s), 2 Shower(s)
Laundry: None **Pay Phones:** Yes, 1
Pump-Out: OnSite, Self Service, 1 Central **Fee:** Free **Closed Heads:** No

Marina Operations

Owner/Manager: Drury Family **Dockmaster:** Ruth Drury
In-Season: Year-Round, Dawn-Dusk **Off-Season:** n/a
After-Hours Arrival: Call on PA system.
Reservations: No **Credit Cards:** n/a
Discounts: None
Pets: Welcome **Handicap Access:** Yes, Heads

Marina Services and Boat Supplies

Services - Docking Assistance, Dock Carts **Communication -** Phone Messages, FedEx, UPS, Express Mail **Supplies - OnSite:** Ice *(Block, Cube)*, Live Bait **Under 1 mi:** Ships' Store *(Ridge Marina 872-5886)*, Bait/Tackle *(Ridge Marina 872-5886, or Ricks Marine 872-5156 2 mi.)* **3+ mi:** Propane *(Badens, 7 mi.)*

Boatyard Services

OnSite: Launching Ramp *(double-ramp $5.00 fee)* **Nearest Yard:** Point Lookout Marina - 12 mi. (301) 872-9000

Restaurants and Accommodations

OnCall: Pizzeria *(Domino's 863-2700)* **Under 1 mi:** Restaurant *(Deano's 872-5445, L $6-8, D $8-19)* **1-3 mi:** Restaurant *(Courtney's Restaurant & Seafood 872-4403, L $3-8, D $10-15)*, Crab House *(American Soft Shell Crab 872-4444)* **3+ mi:** Restaurant *(Scheible's 872-0028, L $4-10, D $13-24, 3 mi., closed Mon)*, *(Spinnakers At Pt. Lookout Marina 872-4340, 3 mi.)*, *(Seaside View 872-4141, 3 mi.)*, Motel *(Scheibel's Motel 872-5285, 3 mi.)*, *(Hampton Inn 863-3200, 15 mi.)*, Hotel *(Days Inn 863-6666, 15 mi.)*, *(Fairfield Inn 863-0203, 15 mi.)*, Inn/B&B *(Creekside Inn 872-5792, 3 mi.)*

Recreation and Entertainment

OnSite: Fishing Charter *(reservations required)*, Group Fishing Boat *(reservations required)* **Near:** Cultural Attract *(Circle "C" Oyster Ranch 872-5126)* **1-3 mi:** Tennis Courts, Volleyball *(Cardinal Park)* **3+ mi:** Movie Theater *(Sony Lexington 862-5000, 13 mi.)*, Museum *(St Mary's City Museum 862-3785, 10 mi.)*

Provisioning and General Services

Under 1 mi: Supermarket *(Raley's Town & Country Market 872-5121-delivers)*, Delicatessen *(Raley's)*, Wine/Beer, Liquor Store *(Raley's)*, Farmers' Market *(Trossbacks)*, Bank/ATM *(Cedar Point Federal)*, Post Office *(872-5864)*, Hardware Store *(Ridge Hardware 872-0444, True Value)*, Copies Etc. *(Post office)* **1-3 mi:** Catholic Church, Beauty Salon **3+ mi:** Library *(St. Mary's PL 863-8188, 14 mi.)*, Laundry *(Badens, 7 mi.)*, Pharmacy *(CVS 863-5992, 14 mi.)*, Department Store *(Wal-Mart 705-7070, JC Penney, 13 mi.)*

Transportation

OnCall: Rental Car *(Enterprise 737-0100, Avis 863-7373, 14 mi.)*, Airport Limo *(EJ's Mirage Express 866-7640)* **3+ mi:** Taxi *(Courtesy Cab 866-9600, 13 mi.)* **Airport:** Reagan Nat'l. *(15 mi.)*

Medical Services

911 Service **OnCall:** Ambulance **3+ mi:** Doctor *(Bennett 863-5835, 15 mi.)*, Dentist *(Munns Family Dentistry 737-1660, 13 mi.)*, Chiropractor *(Henry Chiropractic 737-0662, 14 mi.)*, Veterinarian *(St Mary's Veterinary Hops. 862-2441, 13 mi.)* **Hospital:** St. Mary's 475-8981 *(20 mi.)*

Setting -- Right off the Bay, south of the Patuxent, sprawling St. Jerome's Creek pierces the shoreline. Drury's two docks, protected by a wave attenuator, offer access to a world that has all but disappeared. It is down-home and classically rustic in the very best sense of those words. The wide open creek vistas are sylvan and untouched - the developers, it appears, have not gotten in here quite yet. The main dock, with a fuel pump and pump-out, ends at the white, low-slung shed roofed office; mostly working vessels base here with an occasional slip for transients. The second dock is off to the side and hosts much smaller boats. Landside, RVs are scattered in and around the dry-stored boats, just back from the docks.

Marina Notes -- *Also $2 for 15 amp electric. Established in 1950 as Trossbacks. Purchased by the Drury family in 1987; family-owned and operated ever since. Personal service - owners are always available either on the premises or by phone. Storage rates: In Water $15/ft./mo.; On Land $25/mo. A bright yellow very basic cinderblock bathhouse - deftly painted with sprigs of green ivy - has 2 full bathrooms.

Notable -- St. Jerome's Creek - the only safe harbor between the Patuxent River and Point Lookout - is home to many charter boats and watermen. Nearby is the Circle C Oyster Ranch, a state-of-the-art aquaculture facility that raises LIneback Oysters. This is rural farm country. Beyond the marina one will find little except cornfields and modest houses, and the occasional more-than-modest house that's waterfront. A half-mile west on Airdele Road is a very small shopping center with Raley's Mart - a good-size, locally-owned supermarket with a deli and liquor store plus a post office, a True Value hardware store and a Star ATM.

9. Eastern Shore: Choptank & Tred Avon Rivers

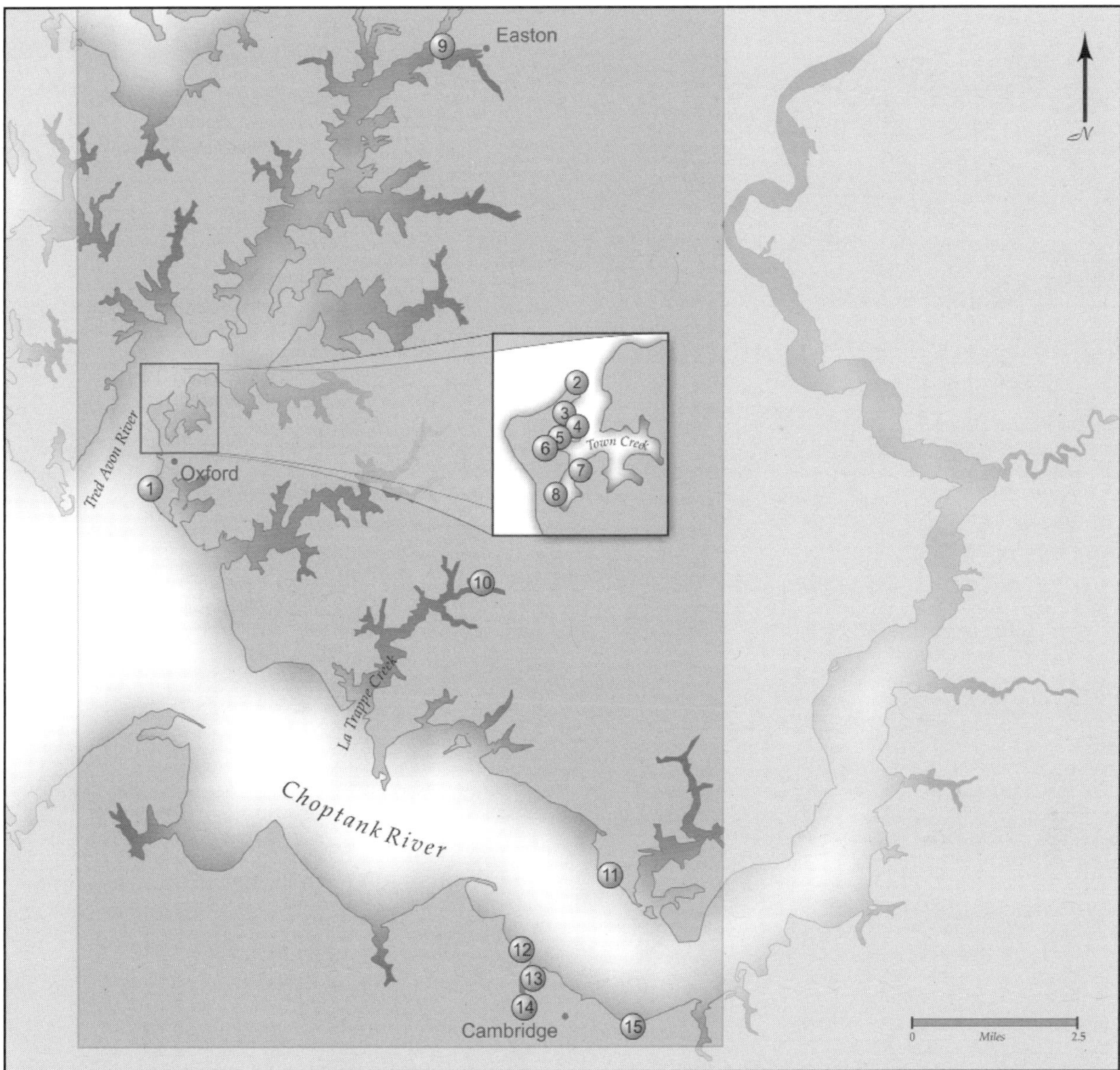

MAP	MARINA	HARBOR	PAGE	MAP	MARINA	HARBOR	PAGE
1	**Campbell's Bachelor Point**	*Tred Avon/Bachelors Harbor*	170	9	**Easton Point Marina**	*Tred Avon River*	178
2	**Mears Yacht Haven**	*Tred Avon River/Town Creek*	171	10	**Oxford Yacht Agency at Dickerson**	*La Trappe Creek*	179
3	**Oxford Boatyard**	*Tred Avon River/Town Creek*	172	11	**Gateway Marina & Ships Store**	*Choptank River*	180
4	**Schooners Landing**	*Tred Avon River/Town Creek*	173	12	**Cambridge Municipal Yacht Basin**	*Cambridge Creek*	181
5	**Cutts & Case**	*Tred Avon River/Town Creek*	174	13	**Yacht Maintenance Co.**	*Cambridge Creek*	182
6	**Hinckley Yacht Services**	*Tred Avon River/Town Creek*	175	14	**Generation III Marina**	*Cambridge Creek*	183
7	**Campbell's Boatyard**	*Tred Avon River/Town Creek*	176	15	**River Marsh Marina**	*Choptank River*	184
8	**Oxford Yacht Agency**	*Tred Avon River/Town Creek*	177				

- **A "DCM" symbol in Marina Notes means Designated Clean Marina** — This is a coveted state-level award given to marinas that meet stringent, environmentally supportive requirements (see page 307). *For a list of DCM's & pump-out facilities, see page 308.*
- **Ratings & Reviews** — An explanation of the Atlantic Cruising Club's rating system, and a detailed explanation of what is in each section of the Marina Report is on pages 6 – 11. *The Data-Gathering Process is detailed on page 322.*
- **Marina Report Updates** — Updates to Marina Reports (from readers, ACC reviewers, and marinas) are posted regularly on *www.AtlanticCruisingClub.com.*

Campbell's Bachelor Point Yacht

26106 Bachelors Harbor Drive; Oxford, MD 21654

Tel: (410) 226-5592 **VHF: Monitor** 16 **Talk** 68
Fax: (410) 226-5489 **Alternate Tel:** n/a
Email: campbells@goeaston.net **Web:** www.campbellsboatyard.com
Nearest Town: Oxford *(1.5 mi.)* **Tourist Info:** (410) 226-5730

Navigational Information

Lat: 38°40.545' **Long:** 076°10.590' **Tide:** 3 ft. **Current:** 1 kt. **Chart:** 12263
Rep. Depths (*MLW*): Entry 11 ft. **Fuel Dock** n/a **Max Slip/Moor** 11 ft./-
Access: Choptank River to Mouth of Tred Avon River

Marina Facilities *(In Season/Off Season)*

Fuel: No
Slips: 80 Total, 3 Transient **Max LOA:** 120 ft. **Max Beam:** 25 ft.
Rate *(per ft.)*: **Day** $1.50/1.00 **Week** Inq. **Month** Inq.
Power: 30 amp Incl., **50 amp** Incl., **100 amp** n/a, **200 amp** n/a
Cable TV: No **Dockside Phone:** No
Dock Type: Fixed, Long Fingers, Wood
Moorings: 0 Total, 0 Transient **Launch:** n/a
Rate: Day n/a **Week** n/a **Month** n/a
Heads: 4 Toilet(s), 4 Shower(s)
Laundry: 2 Washer(s), 2 Dryer(s), Book Exchange **Pay Phones:** Yes, 1
Pump-Out: OnSite, Self Service **Fee:** $5 **Closed Heads:** Yes

Marina Operations

Owner/Manager: Mark Stein **Dockmaster:** Sarah Bradbury
In-Season: Year-Round **Off-Season:** 7:30am-4:30pm
After-Hours Arrival: Call ahead
Reservations: Preferred **Credit Cards:** Visa/MC
Discounts: None
Pets: Welcome, Dog Walk Area **Handicap Access:** No

Marina Services and Boat Supplies

Services - Docking Assistance, Dock Carts **Communication -** Mail & Package Hold, FedEx, DHL, UPS, Express Mail *(Sat Del)* **Supplies - OnSite:** Ice *(Block, Cube)*, Ships' Store **1-3 mi:** Bait/Tackle *(Oxford Market 226-0015)*

Boatyard Services

OnSite: Travelift *(70T)*, Crane, Forklift, Hydraulic Trailer, Engine mechanic *(gas, diesel)*, Electrical Repairs, Electronics Repairs, Hull Repairs, Rigger, Bottom Cleaning, Brightwork, Air Conditioning, Refrigeration, Compound, Wash & Wax, Interior Cleaning, Propeller Repairs, Woodworking, Metal Fabrication, Painting, Awlgrip, Yacht Design, Yacht Building, Total Refits, Yacht Broker *(Bollard Yachts)* **OnCall:** Sail Loft, Canvas Work, Divers, Inflatable Repairs, Life Raft Service, Upholstery **Under 1 mi:** Launching Ramp. **Dealer for:** Cummins Engines. **Member:** ABBRA, ABYC, Other Certifications: Cummins **Yard Rates:** $44-60/hr, Haul & Launch $6/ft. *(blocking $1.50/ft.)*, Power Wash $2/ft., Bottom Paint T+M
Storage: On-Land $18/foot Nov-Mar

Restaurants and Accommodations

Under 1 mi: Restaurant *(Masthead at Pier Street 226-5171, L $6-12, D $13-24)* **1-3 mi:** Restaurant *(Lattitude 38 226-3303, D $20-27, Bar - smaller portions, 1/2 price; Shuttle)*, *(Schooner's Landing 226-0160, L $5-15, D $10-25)*, *(Robert Morris Inn 226-5111, B $7-15, L $11-17, D $17-35)*, *(Pope's at Oxford Inn 226-5220, D $20-30)*, Inn/B&B *(Oxford Inn 226-5220, $90-160)*, *(Robert Morris 226-5111, $90-260)*, *(1876 House 226-5496, $90-160)*

Recreation and Entertainment

OnSite: Pool, Beach, Picnic Area, Grills, Boat Rentals *(Eastern Shore Electric Boats)*, Park **Under 1 mi:** Playground, Tennis Courts *(Causeway Park)*, Fishing Charter, Video Rental, Cultural Attract *(Tred Avon Players at Community Cntr. 226-0061)* **1-3 mi:** Golf Course *(Easton Club)*, Museum *(Oxford Museum 226-0191)*

Provisioning and General Services

OnCall: Provisioning Service **Under 1 mi:** Convenience Store, Bank/ATM, Protestant Church, Library *(Oxford 226-5727)*, Barber Shop **1-3 mi:** Liquor Store *(Oxford 226-0002)*, Farmers' Market *(Wed 4-7 Comm Center)*, Post Office *(226-5629)*, Beauty Salon *(On The Park 226-5079)*, Florist *(Fabulous Flowers 770-5720)* **3+ mi:** Supermarket *(Safeway 822-5055 or Food Lion 819-3234, 12 mi.)*, Fishmonger *(Gay's 822-5019, 11 mi.)*, Bookstore *(Unicorn 476-3838, 11 mi.)*, Pharmacy *(Hill's 822-2666, 11 mi.)*, Hardware Store *(Easton 822-0910, 12 mi.)*, Department Store *(Wal-Mart 819-0140, 13 mi.)*

Transportation

OnSite: Bikes *(complimentary)* **OnCall:** Rental Car *(Enterprise 822-3260)*, Taxi *(Bay Country 770-9030)*, Airport Limo *(Eastern Shore 820-8431, 24 hrs.)* **1-3 mi:** Ferry Service *(Oxford Bellevue 745-9023)*
Airport: Baltimore-Washington Int'l./Bay Bridge *(63 mi./41 mi.)*

Medical Services

911 Service **OnCall:** Ambulance **Under 1 mi:** Doctor *(Adams 226-5964)*
1-3 mi: Dentist *(Holston 226-5184)*, Veterinarian *(Parkes 226-5457)*
3+ mi: Holistic Services *(Evergreen Cove Holistic 819-3395, 11 mi.)*
Hospital: Easton Memorial 822-1000 *(*

PHOTOS ON CD-ROM: 12

Setting -- The first marina up the Tred Avon, Campbell's 3 sets of docks are on the port side of an 8-acre man-made basin - protected by twin jetties. The travelift bay flanks 2 sets of pilgrim gray buildings with starched white trim that give the facility a crisp look. Half-round palladium windows in the peaks of the 2-story New England-style structures add a nice touch of polish. New plantings soften the boatyard atmosphere and a chain-link fence encloses a small pool.

Marina Notes -- DCM. Specializes in large refits, custom design and boat-building. 70T travelift, 6,000 sq. feet of work shed space (including Awlgrip bays) and 1.5 acres of dry storage. One of three Campbell boatyard and marina facilities in Oxford. Home to Eastern Shore Electric Boats & Bollard Yachts. FYI: the new floating docks on the starboard side of the basin belong to the condo complex on the shore. Pool hours: 9am to 7pm. Picnic area, sandy beach and courtesy bikes. Laundry room has two washers and two dryers, a phone, a folding table and a lending library. Very nice bathhouse with functional and inviting heads - tile floors, standard wall-hung sinks and tiled shower stalls with dressing rooms.

Notable -- On the outskirts of Oxford, Cambell's Bachelor Point sits on two acres of land surrounded by a twelve-acre wildlife sanctuary. "A" dock has great views of unspoiled marsh and the surrounding sanctuary. It's just a mile to Masthead at Pier Street Marina, a bustling, casual seafood eatery on the water with courtesy dock 'n' dine slips - an easy dinghy ride, too (try for sunset). About a mile-and-a-half bike ride is stopped-in-time Oxford's Morris Street with the well-supplied Oxford Market (7am-8pm), the Oxford Museum and a handful of gift shops and galleries.

Navigational Information
Lat: 38°41.664' **Long:** 076°10.152' **Tide:** 2 ft. **Current:** n/a **Chart:** 12263
Rep. Depths (*MLW*): Entry 10 ft. **Fuel Dock** 8 ft. **Max Slip/Moor** 8 ft./-
Access: Choptank River to Tred Avon River to Town Creek

Marina Facilities *(In Season/Off Season)*
Fuel: Gasoline, Diesel
Slips: 95 Total, 30 Transient **Max LOA:** 150 ft. **Max Beam:** n/a
Rate *(per ft.)*: **Day** $1.10/1.50 **Week** Inq. **Month** Inq.
Power: 30 amp $5, **50 amp** $10, **100 amp** n/a, **200 amp** n/a
Cable TV: Yes All slips **Dockside Phone:** No
Dock Type: Fixed, Long Fingers, Pilings, Alongside, Wood
Moorings: 0 Total, 0 Transient **Launch:** n/a, Dinghy Dock
Rate: Day n/a **Week** n/a **Month** n/a
Heads: 4 Toilet(s), 4 Shower(s)
Laundry: 2 Washer(s), 2 Dryer(s), Book Exchange **Pay Phones:** Yes, 1
Pump-Out: OnSite, Full Service, 2 Central **Fee:** $5 **Closed Heads:** Yes

Marina Operations
Owner/Manager: Tom Gannon **Dockmaster:** Same
In-Season: Sum, 8am-Dusk **Off-Season:** Fall-Win-Sprg, 8am-5pm
After-Hours Arrival: Channel 16 or Fuel Dock
Reservations: Yes **Credit Cards:** Visa/MC, Dscvr, Amex
Discounts: None
Pets: Welcome, Dog Walk Area **Handicap Access:** Yes, Heads, Docks

Mears Yacht Haven

PO Box 130; 502 E. Strand; Oxford, MD 21654

Tel: (410) 226-5450 **VHF: Monitor** 16 **Talk** 73
Fax: (410) 226-5450 **Alternate Tel:** n/a
Email: CPM@erols.com **Web:** www.coastalproperties.com
Nearest Town: Oxford *(0.5 mi.)* **Tourist Info:** (410) 226-5730

Marina Services and Boat Supplies
Services - Docking Assistance, Concierge, Boaters' Lounge, Security, Trash Pick-Up, Dock Carts **Communication -** Mail & Package Hold, Phone Messages, Fax in/out, Data Ports *(Office)*, FedEx, DHL, UPS, Express Mail *(Sat Del)* **Supplies - OnSite:** Ice *(Block, Cube)*, Ships' Store
OnCall: Boat/US *(delivery)* **Near:** Bait/Tackle *(Oxford Market 226-0015)*, Propane, CNG *(Crockett Bros. 226-5113)* **Under 1 mi:** Live Bait

Boatyard Services
OnCall: Divers, Interior Cleaning, Inflatable Repairs, Life Raft Service, Upholstery, Yacht Interiors **Near:** Travelift, Forklift, Launching Ramp, Engine mechanic *(gas, diesel)*, Electrical Repairs, Electronics Repairs, Hull Repairs, Rigger, Sail Loft, Canvas Work, Bottom Cleaning, Brightwork, Air Conditioning, Refrigeration, Compound, Wash & Wax, Propeller Repairs, Painting, Awlgrip. **Nearest Yard:** Oxford Boatyard (410) 226-5101

Restaurants and Accommodations
Near: Restaurant *(Robert Morris Inn 226-5111, B $7-15, L $11-17, D $17-35, best crabcakes)*, Seafood Shack *(Schooners Landing 226-0160, L $5-15, D $10-25)*, Inn/B&B *(Robert Morris 226-5111, $90-260)* **Under 1 mi:** *Rest-*Restaurant *(Pope's at Oxford Inn 226-5220, D $20-30)*, *(Masthead at Pier Street 226-5171, L $6-12, D $13-24)*, Inn/B&B *(Oxford Inn 226-5220, $90-160)* **1-3 mi:** Restaurant *(Latitude 38 226-5303, D $20-27, Shuttle)*

Recreation and Entertainment
OnSite: Pool *(sundeck)*, Picnic Area, Grills *(charcoal)*, Fishing Charter
Near: Beach *(The Strand)*, Boat Rentals, Video Rental, Park *(Morris Street)*, Museum *(Oxford Customs House - wk-ends; Oxford Museum 226-0191)* **Under 1 mi:** Tennis Courts *(Town Park)*, Volleyball, Galleries **1-3 mi:** Cultural Attract *(Tred Avon Players 226-0061)* **3+ mi:** Golf Course *(Easton Club 820-9017, 8 mi.)*, Movie Theater *(Easton 822-9950, 11 mi.)*

Provisioning and General Services
Near: Liquor Store *(Oxford Spirits 226-0002)*, Market *(Oxford 226-0015)*, Bank/ATM, Post Office *(226-5629)*, Catholic Church, Protestant Church, Library *(226-5727)*, Beauty Salon *(On The Park 226-5079)*, Retail Shops **Under 1 mi:** Florist *(Fabulous Flowers 770-5720)* **1-3 mi:** Farmers' Market *(Wed 4-7 Comm. Center)* **3+ mi:** Supermarket *(Safeway 822-5055 or Food Lion 819-3234, 11 mi.)*, Gourmet Shop *(Gourmet & More 763-7077, 11 mi.)*, Bakery *(Sweet Nina's 763-9272, 11 mi.)*, Fishmonger *(Captain's Ketch 820-7177, 11 mi.)*, Bookstore *(Unicorn 476-3838, 10 mi.)*, Pharmacy *(Hill's 822-2666, 10 mi.)*, Hardware Store *(Easton 822-0910, 11 mi.)*, Department Store *(Wal-Mart 819-0140, 12 mi.)*

Transportation
OnSite: Bikes *($3/hr., $10/half-day, $15/day w/ helmets & baskets)* **OnCall:** Rental Car *(Enterprise 822-3260)*, Taxi *(Bay Country 770-9030)*, Airport Limo *(820-8431)* **Near:** Ferry Service *(Bellevue 745-9023 M-F 7am-8:30pm, S&S 9am-8:30pm $2/pp)* **Airport:** Baltimore-Washington Int'l *(62 mi.)*

Medical Services
911 Service **Under 1 mi:** Doctor *(Adams 226-5964)*, Veterinarian *(Parkes 226-5457)* **1-3 mi:** Dentist *(Holston 226-5184)*
Hospital: Easton 822-1000 *(10 mi.)*

Setting -- Right off the Tred Avon, around the point at the entrance to Town Creek - past the replica screwpile lighthouse, spiffy Mears takes full advantage of its stunning location. The office, fuel dock, and the amenities building sit on a small peninsula, with docks along both sides. A total of 7 main piers - 6 fairways - host nearly a hundred slips. Near the fuel dock, a covered pavilion furnished with tables and chairs provides a perfect venue for watching boats arrive.

Marina Notes -- DCM. Built in the early '70s on the site of an old oyster processing plant, family-owned and operated until '93 - when it was acquired by Coastal Properties. Complimentary continental breakfast on weekends, coffee always. Adjacent to the pavilion, the ships' store features a wicker-furnished lounge area with lending library. Inland, a small, nicely treed, grass & wood-chip picnic area sports four charcoal grills. The Oxford Yacht Club makes its home here and Oxford Boatyard is next door. The bathhouse arrangement is a little different but quite serviceable - sinks and toilets in men's/women's rooms, plus a narrow shed-roofed corridor with 4 unisex showers - tile & fiberglass, each with a wood-grate floored dressing room with bench - plus the laundry.

Notable -- The good-sized, sparkling pool and surrounding sundeck are populated with strap chairs and chaises; five steps up is a generous second sundeck which affords a truly spectacular view of the harbor and the boat traffic on the river and creek. Just up the road, stretched along The Strand, is the town beach. Some of the boats anchored in the harbor beach their dinghies here; others launch their kayaks. Sweet, charming, affluent Oxford village is about half-mile along North Morris Street.

PHOTOS ON CD-ROM: 12

Oxford Boatyard

Oxford Boatyard

PO Box 340; 402 E. Strand; Oxford, MD 21654

Tel: (410) 226-5101 **VHF: Monitor** 16 **Talk** 68
Fax: (410) 226-5116 **Alternate Tel:** n/a
Email: oby@goeaston.com **Web:** n/a
Nearest Town: Oxford *(0.4 mi.)* **Tourist Info:** (410) 226-5730

Navigational Information
Lat: 38°41.629' **Long:** 076°10.189' **Tide:** 2 ft. **Current:** n/a **Chart:** 12263
Rep. Depths (*MLW*): Entry 9 ft. **Fuel Dock** n/a **Max Slip/Moor** 10 ft./-
Access: Choptank River to Tred Avon River to Town Creek

Marina Facilities *(In Season/Off Season)*
Fuel: No
Slips: 112 Total, 30 Transient **Max LOA:** 150 ft. **Max Beam:** 24 ft.
Rate *(per ft.)*: **Day** $1.25 **Week** $4.00 **Month** $10
Power: 30 amp $2, **50 amp** $4, **100 amp** n/a, **200 amp** n/a
Cable TV: No **Dockside Phone:** No
Dock Type: Fixed, Long Fingers, Pilings, Alongside, Wood
Moorings: 0 Total, 0 Transient **Launch:** n/a
Rate: Day n/a **Week** n/a **Month** n/a
Heads: 4 Toilet(s), 4 Shower(s) *(with dressing rooms)*
Laundry: 2 Washer(s), 2 Dryer(s), Book Exchange **Pay Phones:** Yes
Pump-Out: OnSite, Full Service, 1 Central **Fee:** n/a **Closed Heads:** Yes

Marina Operations
Owner/Manager: Branton Strueber **Dockmaster:** Jimmy Taylor
In-Season: Sum, 8am-6pm **Off-Season:** Fall-Win-Sprg, 8am-4:30pm
After-Hours Arrival: T-dock
Reservations: Recommended **Credit Cards:** Visa/MC, Dscvr, Din, Amex
Discounts: None
Pets: Welcome, Dog Walk Area **Handicap Access:** Yes, Heads, Docks

Marina Services and Boat Supplies
Services - Docking Assistance, Security, Dock Carts **Communication -** Mail & Package Hold, Phone Messages, Fax in/out, FedEx, DHL, UPS, Express Mail **Supplies - OnSite:** Ice *(Block, Cube)*, Ships' Store **Near:** CNG *(Crockett Bros 228-5113)* **Under 1 mi:** Bait/Tackle *(Oxford Market 226-0015)*, Live Bait, Propane

Boatyard Services
OnSite: Travelift *(75T, 20' beam)*, Crane *(10T)*, Forklift, Hydraulic Trailer *(35T)*, Engine mechanic *(gas, diesel)*, Electrical Repairs, Electronics Repairs, Hull Repairs, Rigger, Bottom Cleaning, Brightwork, Air Conditioning, Refrigeration, Compound, Wash & Wax, Interior Cleaning, Woodworking, Yacht Interiors, Metal Fabrication, Painting, Awlgrip, Yacht Building, Total Refits, Yacht Broker **OnCall:** Sail Loft, Canvas Work, Divers, Propeller Repairs, Life Raft Service **Member:** ABBRA, ABYC **Yard Rates:** $42-61/hr., Haul & Launch $9.50/ft. *(blocking incl.)*, Power Wash Incl.

Restaurants and Accommodations
Near: Restaurant *(Robert Morris Inn 226-5111, B $7-15, L $11-17, D $17-35, lite fare 3-9pm $11-17)*, *(Masthead at Pier Street 226-5171, L $6-12, D $13-24)*, *(Schooners Landing 226-0160, L $5-15, D $10-25)*, Inn/B&B *(Robert Morris Inn 226-5111, $90-290)* **Under 1 mi:** Restaurant *(Pope's Tavern at Oxford Inn 226-5220, D $20-30)*, Inn/B&B *(Oxford Inn 226-5220, $90-160)* **1-3 mi:** Restaurant *(Latitude 38 226-5303, D $20-27, Shuttle)*

Recreation and Entertainment
OnSite: Picnic Area, Grills **OnCall:** Fishing Charter **Near:** Beach *(The Strand)*, Playground, Museum *(Oxford 226-0191, Customs House)* **Under 1 mi:** Pool, Tennis Courts *(Town Park)*, Jogging Paths, Boat Rentals, Video Rental, Cultural Attract *(Tred Avon Players 226-0061)* **3+ mi:** Golf Course *(Easton Club 820-9017, 8 mi.)*, Fitness Center *(YMCA 822-0566, 8 mi.)*, Bowling *(Easton 822-3426, 10 mi.)*, Movie Theater *(Easton 822-9950)*

Provisioning and General Services
Near: Delicatessen, Crabs/Waterman, Market *(Oxford Market & Deli 226-0015)* **Under 1 mi:** Liquor Store *(Oxford Spirits 226-0002)*, Bank/ATM, Post Office *(226-5629)*, Protestant Church, Library *(Oxford 226-5727)*, Beauty Salon *(On The Park 226-5079)*, Florist *(Fabulous Flowers 770-5720)* **1-3 mi:** Farmers' Market *(Wed 4-7pm Comm Center)* **3+ mi:** Supermarket *(Safeway 822-5055 or Food Lion 819-3234, 11 mi.)*, Gourmet Shop *(Gourmet & More 763-7077, 11 mi.)*, Bakery *(Sweet Nina's 763-9272, 11 mi.)*, Dry Cleaners *(McCord's Laundry & Cleaners 822-0800, 10 mi.)*, Bookstore *(Unicorn Book Shop 476-3838, 10 mi.)*, Pharmacy *(Hill's 822-2666, 10 mi.)*, Hardware Store *(Easton 822-0910, 11 mi.)*, Department Store *(Wal-Mart 819-0140, 12 mi.)*

Transportation
OnCall: Rental Car *(Enterprise 822-3260)*, Taxi *(Bay Country 770-9030)*, Airport Limo *(Eastern Shore 820-8431, 24 hrs.)* **Near:** Bikes *(Mears 226-5440)* **Under 1 mi:** Ferry Service *(Oxford Bellevue 745-9023)*
Airport: Baltimore-Washington Int'l./Bay Bridge *(62 mi./40 mi.)*

Medical Services
911 Service **OnCall:** Ambulance **Under 1 mi:** Doctor *(Adams 226-5964)*, Dentist *(Bishop 226-0011)*, Veterinarian *(Parkes 226-5457)*
Hospital: Easton Memorial 822-1000 *(10 mi.)*

Setting -- Quintessential Oxford, the Boatyard embodies the village's quiet, peaceful, historic zeitgeist. This is pure boatyard and proud of it. Two main docks poke into Town Creek from the boatyard grounds - one is all new with new pedestals, and one is not. There is a third set of docks with slips that line the outer bulkhead that forms the perimeter of the basin, which is right next to Schooners Landing.

Marina Notes -- Over 200 years old and in its current incarnation since 1840. Extraordinarily well-supplied ships' store, comprehensive yard services (or do-it-yourself with pro assist). Heated facilities, inside spray building. Certified mechanics. No attempt has been made to soften the boatyard atmosphere; judging by the upscale boats, that's fine with the residents. Just north of the travelift is all-new "A"-dock, with slips, "B" is alongside. "C" has a few slips and "D" runs all along the perimeter of the basin. A small white clapboard house with red shutters is the all-tile bathhouse; showers have a separate dressing room.

Notable -- Utterly charming, moneyed Oxford, a one-time fishing village that has been through controlled gentrification, is frequently described as the Eastern Shore's "Mayberry." It's boaty and less touristed than most of this region. Browse the shops and galleries along Morris Street and then follow the water tower back to the Boatyard. Right outside the entrance is The Strand, a long crescent town beach fronting the Tred Avon; at the far end of the beach, near the Tred Avon Y.C., is the Gibson Family's renowned Robert Morris Inn & Restaurant. The golden yellow 1720 Inn's elegant crystal chandeliered dining room, with murals made from 1860 wallpaper samples, regency chairs, and a fireplace, serves crab cakes that are solid backfin with barely a hint of filler - baked or fried.

PHOTOS ON CD-ROM: 12

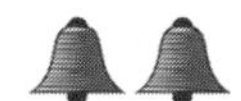

Schooners Landing

314 Tilghman Street; Oxford, MD 21654

Tel: (410) 226-0160 **VHF: Monitor** n/a **Talk** n/a
Fax: (410) 226-0162 **Alternate Tel:** n/a
Email: n/a **Web:** n/a
Nearest Town: Oxford *(0.3 mi.)* **Tourist Info:** (410) 226-5730

Navigational Information
Lat: 38°41.567' **Long:** 076°10.100' **Tide:** 2 ft. **Current:** n/a **Chart:** 12263
Rep. Depths (*MLW*): Entry 13 ft. **Fuel Dock** n/a **Max Slip/Moor** 11 ft./-
Access: Choptank to Tred Avon to Town Creek

Marina Facilities *(In Season/Off Season)*
Fuel: No
Slips: 22 Total, 6 Transient **Max LOA:** 120 ft. **Max Beam:** n/a
Rate *(per ft.)*: **Day** $5.00 **Week** n/a **Month** n/a
Power: 30 amp $5, **50 amp** $8, **100 amp** n/a, **200 amp** n/a
Cable TV: No **Dockside Phone:** No
Dock Type: n/a
Moorings: 0 Total, 0 Transient **Launch:** n/a
Rate: Day n/a **Week** n/a **Month** n/a
Heads: None
Laundry: None **Pay Phones:** No
Pump-Out: No **Fee:** n/a **Closed Heads:** Yes

Marina Operations
Owner/Manager: Don Smith **Dockmaster:** Same
In-Season: Year-Round, 11:30am-8pm **Off-Season:** n/a
After-Hours Arrival: Call ahead
Reservations: Required **Credit Cards:** Visa/MC, Amex
Discounts: None
Pets: Welcome **Handicap Access:** No

Marina Services and Boat Supplies
Communication - FedEx, UPS, Express Mail **Supplies - Near:** Ice *(Block, Cube)*, Bait/Tackle *(Oxford Market 226-0015)*, Live Bait, Propane, CNG
3+ mi: West Marine *(770-3080, 12 mi.)*

Boatyard Services
Nearest Yard: Oxford Boatyard (410) 226-5101

Restaurants and Accommodations
OnSite: Restaurant *(Schooners Landing L $5-15, D $10-25)*
Near: Restaurant *(Robert Morris Inn 226-5111, B $7-15, L $11-17, D $17-35)*, nn/B&B *(Robert Morris Inn 226-5111, $90-260)*
Under 1 mi: Restaurant *(Masthead at Pier Street Marina & Restaurant 226-5171, L $6-12, D $13-24)*, *(Pope's Tavern at Oxford Inn 226-5220, D $20-30)*, Inn/B&B *(Oxford Inn 226-5220, $90-160)*
1-3 mi: Restaurant *(Latitude 38 226-5303, D $20-27, shuttle)*

Recreation and Entertainment
OnSite: Video Arcade **Near:** Museum *(Oxford Museum 226-0191)*, Sightseeing, Galleries **Under 1 mi:** Beach *(The Strand)*, Playground, Tennis Courts *(Easton Club 820-9017)*, Jogging Paths, Video Rental, Park
3+ mi: Golf Course *(Hog Neck Golf Course 822-6079, 9 mi.)*, Fitness Center *(YMCA 822-0566, 8 mi.)*, Bowling *(Easton Bowling 822-3426, 10 mi.)*, Movie Theater *(Easton 822-9950, 11 mi.)*

Provisioning and General Services
Near: Convenience Store, Delicatessen, Wine/Beer, Market *(Oxford Market 226-0015)*, Bank/ATM, Post Office *(226-5629)*, Library *(Oxford Library 226-5727)*, Beauty Salon *(On The Park Hair Studio 226-5079)* **Under 1 mi:** Supermarket *(Safeway 822-5055 or Food Lion 819-3234)*, Florist *(Fabulous Flowers 770-5720)* **1-3 mi:** Farmers' Market *(Wed 4-7pm Community Center, Oxford Market 226-0015)* **3+ mi:** Liquor Store *(Oxford Spirits 226-0002, 11 mi.)*, Bakery *(Sweet Nina's 763-9272, 11 mi.)*, Fishmonger *(Captains Ketch Seafood Market 820-7177, 11 mi.)*, Dry Cleaners *(McCord's Laundry & Cleaners 822-0800, 10 mi.)*, Bookstore *(Unicorn Book Shop 476-3838, 10 mi.)*, Pharmacy *(Hill's 822-2666, 10 mi.)*, Hardware Store *(Easton Hardware 822-0910, 11 mi.)*, Buying Club *(Wal-Mart 819-0140, 12 mi.)*

Transportation
OnCall: Rental Car *(Enterprise 822-3260)*, Taxi *(Bay Country Taxi 770-9030)*, Airport Limo *(Deelegance Luxury Limousine 822-5432)*
Near: Ferry Service *(Oxford Bellevue 745-9023)*
Airport: Baltimore-Washington Int'l./Bay Bridge *(63 mi./41 mi.)*

Medical Services
911 Service **OnCall:** Ambulance **Under 1 mi:** Doctor *(Adams 226-5964)*, Dentist *(Bishop 226-0011)*, Veterinarian *(Parkes 226-5457)* **3+ mi:** Chiropractor *(Brooks 820-7705, 10 mi.)*, Holistic Services *(Evergreen Cove 819-3395, 10 mi.)* **Hospital:** Easton Memorial 822-1000 *(10 mi.)*

Setting -- On the starboard shore of Town Creek, just past Oxford Boatyard, Schooner Landing's gray boathouse restaurant and barn-red dining pavilion back a single full-service dock. The eatery sits directly on the water surrounded by decks that open onto the dock. A short stroll out the "back door" is idyllic Oxford.

Marina Notes -- Transient slips are on the docks or on the face of the restaurant bulkhead; the slips along the side are for permanent slip holders. Fairly good-sized short finger piers with power on pilings. A couple of very wide, cat-size slips. Can manage banquets for up to 250; with adjacent Oxford Boatyard, there would appear to be room for a fleet. Access to the boats is 24 hours a day even when the restaurant's closed. No showers; heads are shared with restaurant patrons.

Notable -- Schooners offers three eating venues: outside on the deck at wooden picnic tables or round tables under large umbrella-style awnings; inside around the waterview bar; or in the all-window dining room where Windsor chairs surround vinyl-clothed tables. A wood-paneled game room adjacent to the bar features two Rush Rock Atari video games, a South Park pinball machine and a pool table. Several blocks straight down Tilghman Street is "downtown" Oxford. Along North Morris is the well-supplied Oxford Market, storefront Oxford Museum (Mon, Wed, Fri, Sat 10am-4pm, Sun 12-4pm), five shops including the Oxford Mews Emporium, which has a selection of tchotchkes, art, and clothing, and the Americana Antique Shop. An expansive riverfront park features a wide swath of lawn, sweeping water views plus a playground - a swing set, a climb-aboard locomotive, slides -- three picnic tables, and a handful of waterside benches.

PHOTOS ON CD-ROM: 9

Cutts & Case

PO Box 9; 306 Tilghman Street.; Oxford, MD 21654

Tel: (410) 226-5416 **VHF: Monitor** n/a **Talk** n/a
Fax: (410) 226-5035 **Alternate Tel:** n/a
Email: n/a **Web:** n/a
Nearest Town: Oxford *(0.2 mi.)* **Tourist Info:** (410) 226-5730

Navigational Information

Lat: 38°41.490' **Long:** 076°10.164' **Tide:** 2 ft. **Current:** .3 kt. **Chart:** 12263
Rep. Depths (*MLW*): Entry 10 ft. **Fuel Dock** n/a **Max Slip/Moor** 10 ft./-
Access: Choptank River to Tred Avon River to Town Creek

Marina Facilities *(In Season/Off Season)*

Fuel: No
Slips: 30 Total, 2 Transient **Max LOA:** 100 ft. **Max Beam:** 14 ft.
Rate *(per ft.)*: **Day** $1.00 **Week** n/a **Month** n/a
Power: 30 amp 15Amp, **50 amp** n/a, **100 amp** n/a, **200 amp** n/a
Cable TV: No **Dockside Phone:** No
Dock Type: Fixed, Long Fingers, Pilings, Wood
Moorings: 0 Total, 0 Transient **Launch:** n/a
Rate: Day n/a **Week** n/a **Month** n/a
Heads: 2 Toilet(s), 1 Shower(s)
Laundry: None **Pay Phones:** No
Pump-Out: No **Fee:** n/a **Closed Heads:** Yes

Marina Operations

Owner/Manager: Edmund Cutts Jr. **Dockmaster:** Same
In-Season: Year-Round, 8am-4:30pm* **Off-Season:** n/a
After-Hours Arrival: Call in advance
Reservations: Yes, Preferred **Credit Cards:** Cash or checks
Discounts: None
Pets: Welcome, Dog Walk Area **Handicap Access:** No

Marina Services and Boat Supplies

Services - Security *(2 live on premises)*, Dock Carts **Communication -** Mail & Package Hold, FedEx, DHL, UPS **Supplies - Near:** Ice *(Block, Cube)*, Ships' Store, Bait/Tackle *(Oxford Market 226-0015)*, Live Bait, Propane, CNG **3+ mi:** West Marine *(770-3080, 12 mi.)*

Boatyard Services

OnSite: Railway *(30T)*, Crane, Forklift, Engine mechanic *(gas, diesel)*, Electrical Repairs, Hull Repairs, Rigger, Bottom Cleaning, Brightwork, Compound, Wash & Wax, Interior Cleaning, Woodworking, Metal Fabrication, Painting, Awlgrip, Yacht Design, Yacht Building, Total Refits, Yacht Broker *(Cutts & Case, Inc.)* **OnCall:** Electronics Repairs, Air Conditioning, Refrigeration, Divers, Upholstery, Yacht Interiors
Near: Launching Ramp. **Yard Rates:** $50/hr., Haul & Launch $3/ft.

Restaurants and Accommodations

Near: Restaurant *(Schooners Landing 226-0160, L $5-15, D $10-25)*, *(Masthead at Pier Street 226-5411, L $6-12, D $13-24)*, *(Pope's Tavern - Oxford Inn 226-5220, D $20-30)*, *(Robert Morris Inn 226-5111, B $7-15, L $11-17, D $17-35)*, Inn/B&B *(1876 House 226-5496, $110-145)*, *(Robert Morris Inn 226-5111, $90-260)* **1-3 mi:** Restaurant *(Latitude 38 226-5303, D $20-27, bar menu - smaller portions, 1/2 price; Shuttle)*

Recreation and Entertainment

OnSite: Picnic Area, Jogging Paths **Near:** Playground, Fishing Charter, Museum *(Oxford Museum 226-0191)*, Cultural Attract *(1668 "Byeberry" & "Calico" - a private Tudor cottage)*, Galleries **Under 1 mi:** Tennis Courts *(Town Park)*, Video Rental *(Oxford Market)*, Park **3+ mi:** Golf Course *(Easton Club 820-9017, 8 mi.)*, Fitness Center *(YMCA 822-0566, 8 mi.)*, Movie Theater *(Easton 822-9950, 11 mi.)*

Provisioning and General Services

Near: Convenience Store, Delicatessen, Wine/Beer, Liquor Store *(Oxford Spirits 226-0002)*, Market *(Oxford 226-0015)*, Bank/ATM, Post Office *(226-5629)*, Library *(Oxford 226-5727)*, Beauty Salon *(On The Park Hair Studio 226-5079)*, Newsstand **Under 1 mi:** Florist *(Fabulous Flowers 770-5720)* **1-3 mi:** Farmers' Market *(Wed 4-7pm Community Center)*, Lobster Pound **3+ mi:** Supermarket *(Safeway 822-5055 or Food Lion 819-3234, 11 mi.)*, Gourmet Shop *(Gourmet & More 763-7077, 11 mi.)*, Bakery *(Sweet Nina's 763-9272, 11 mi.)*, Fishmonger *(Captains Ketch's 820-7177, 11 mi.)*, Dry Cleaners *(McCord's Laundry & Cleaners 822-0800, 10 mi.)*, Bookstore *(Unicorn Book Shop 476-3838, 10 mi.)*, Pharmacy *(Hill's 822-2666, 10 mi.)*, Hardware Store *(Easton Hardware 822-0910, 11 mi.)*, Department Store *(Wal-Mart 819-0140, 12 mi.)*

Transportation

OnCall: Rental Car *(Enterprise 822-3260)*, Taxi *(Bay Country 770-9030)*, Airport Limo *(Eastern Shore 820-8431, 24hrs)*
Near: Ferry Service *(Oxford Bellevue 745-9023 $1.25)*
Airport: Baltimore-Washington Int'l./Bay Bridge *(62 mi./40 mi.)*

Medical Services

911 Service **OnCall:** Ambulance **Under 1 mi:** Doctor *(Adams 226-5964)*, Veterinarian *(Parkes 226-5457)* **1-3 mi:** Dentist *(Holston 226-5184)* **3+ mi:** Chiropractor *(Brooks Chiro. 820-7705, 10 mi.)*, Holistic Services *(Evergreen Cove 819-3395, 10 mi.)* **Hospital:** Easton 822-1000 *(10 mi.)*

Setting -- Snuggled into a cove, 3 basic docks host classic boats - from small skiffs to good-size yachts - backed by barn-red work sheds. In a nod to boater amenities, charming 1668 "Byeberry", the oldest house in Oxford, is surrounded by a collection of anchors, a small cannon, a bench & picnic table and flowers - a sweet tableau overlooking the docks. A white gravel path steers transients to the road, neatly bypassing the expected detritus of an old-time boatyard.

Marina Notes -- *Closed on Sundays. T-head takes up to 100 ft. with 12 ft. of water. In business since 1927, this design & build firm has an obvious passion for beautiful boats in all sizes and shapes. Specializes in classic woodwork, repairs, refits, and one-offs using state of the art composite construction (very high strength to weight ratios) which matches the work of 19th C. artisans while using technologically innovative structural engineering. Gorgeous vessels in various stages of recovery populate the yard and docks. Power pedestals appear a bit ad hoc. The perfectly nice, wood-paneled full bathroom has a dressing bench.

Notable -- A magnificent street-side display window features the original "Foto" boat used by renowned maritime photographer Morris Rosenfeld and his sons to document the heyday of American yachting. Her first venture was Thomas Lipton's Challenge; she served the Rosenfelds for 50 years. Now more than 75, sporting her original engines, she's in exquisite condition - a testament to this yard. A couple of blocks away, Oxford's main drag, North Morris St. dead-ends at the 1836 Oxford-Bellevue ferry, the oldest private ferry in the country. Crossings are every 25 min., with a popular Sunset Ride (RT $2). The replica Customs House next to the terminal opens weekends. Celebrated Robert Morris Inn serves 3 meals daily (except Tue) in the formal Dining Room and casual Tavern.

Navigational Information
Lat: 38°41.457' **Long:** 076°10.276' **Tide:** 2 ft. **Current:** n/a **Chart:** 12263
Rep. Depths (*MLW*): Entry 7 ft. **Fuel Dock** n/a **Max Slip/Moor** 7 ft./-
Access: Choptank River to Tred Avon River to Town Creek

Marina Facilities *(In Season/Off Season)*
Fuel: No
Slips: 76 Total, 20+ Transient **Max LOA:** 55 ft. **Max Beam:** 20 ft.
Rate *(per ft.)*: **Day** $1.95 **Week** n/a **Month** $30
Power: 30 amp Incl., **50 amp** Incl., **100 amp** n/a, **200 amp** n/a
Cable TV: No **Dockside Phone:** No
Dock Type: Fixed, Floating, Long Fingers, Short Fingers, Alongside, Wood
Moorings: 0 Total, 0 Transient **Launch:** n/a, Dinghy Dock
Rate: Day n/a **Week** n/a **Month** n/a
Heads: 4 Toilet(s), 4 Shower(s)
Laundry: 3 Washer(s), 3 Dryer(s) **Pay Phones:** Yes, 1
Pump-Out: OnSite, Self Service, 1 Central **Fee:** n/a **Closed Heads:** Yes

Marina Operations
Owner/Manager: Ben Sheets **Dockmaster:** Jim Robinson
In-Season: Year-Round, 7:30am-5pm **Off-Season:** n/a
After-Hours Arrival: Call ahead
Reservations: Preferred **Credit Cards:** Visa/MC, Dscvr, Amex
Discounts: None
Pets: Welcome, Dog Walk Area **Handicap Access:** Yes, Heads

Hinckley Yacht Services

PO Box 369; 202 Banks Street; Oxford, MD 21654

Tel: (410) 226-5113 **VHF: Monitor** 16 **Talk** n/a
Fax: (410) 226-5602 **Alternate Tel:** n/a
Email: bsheets@hinckleyyachts.com **Web:** www.hinckleyyachts.com
Nearest Town: Oxford *(0.1 mi.)* **Tourist Info:** (410) 226-5730

Marina Services and Boat Supplies
Services - Docking Assistance, Trash Pick-Up, Dock Carts
Communication - Mail & Package Hold, Phone Messages, Fax in/out *(Inq.)*, Data Ports *(Ships' Store)*, FedEx, DHL, UPS, Express Mail *(Sat Del)*
Supplies - OnSite: Ice *(Block, Cube)*, Ships' Store, Propane, CNG
Under 1 mi: Bait/Tackle *(Oxford Market)* **1-3 mi:** West Marine *(770-3080)*

Boatyard Services
OnSite: Travelift *(30T)*, Crane, Forklift *(5T)*, Hydraulic Trailer *(35T)*, Engine mechanic *(gas, diesel)*, Electrical Repairs, Electronics Repairs, Hull Repairs, Rigger, Bottom Cleaning, Brightwork, Air Conditioning *(Installation)*, Refrigeration *(Installation)*, Divers, Compound, Wash & Wax, Interior Cleaning, Propeller Repairs, Woodworking, Metal Fabrication, Painting, Awlgrip, Total Refits, Yacht Broker **Near:** Launching Ramp. **Dealer for:** Yanmar, Seafrost, Marine Air, Caterpillar, Detroit Diesel, Grunert, Hamilton, Sea Recovery, Max-Prop, Perkins, Spurs, Westerbeke, Edson, Forespar, Lewmar, Navtec, Samson, Ronstan, Schaeffer etc. **Member:** ABBRA - 10 Certified Tech(s), ABYC - 10 Certified Tech(s), Other Certifications: Fiberglass **Yard Rates:** $67.50/hr., Haul & Launch $8/ft. *(blocking $1.50/ft.)*, Power Wash $1.50/ft. **Storage:** On-Land $25/ft.*

Restaurants and Accommodations
Near: Restaurant *(Schooner's Landing 226-0160, L $5-15, D $10-25)*, *(Robert Morris Inn 226-5111, B $7-15, L $11-17, D $17-35)*, *(Pope's Tavern at Oxford Inn 226-5220, D $20-30)*, *(Masthead at Pier St. 226-5171, L $6-12, D $13-24, steamed crabs!)*, Inn/B&B *(Robert Morris Inn 226-5111, $90-260)*, *(Oxford Inn 226-5220, $90-160)*, *(1876 226-5496, $100-145)*
1-3 mi: Restaurant *(Latitude 38 226-5303, D $20-27, Shuttle)*

Recreation and Entertainment
OnSite: Pool, Picnic Area *(umbrellas)*, Grills **Near:** Beach, Playground, Jogging Paths, Video Rental, Park, Museum *(Oxford Museum 226-0191)*, Sightseeing, Special Events *(Cardboard Boat Race - late Jun; Oxford Day, late Apr)* **Under 1 mi:** Tennis Courts *(Causeway Park)* **1-3 mi:** Cultural Attract *(Tred Avon Players)* **3+ mi:** Golf Course *(Easton 20-9017, 8 mi.)*

Provisioning and General Services
OnSite: Clothing Store **Near:** Convenience Store, Liquor Store *(Oxford Spirits 226-0002)*, Market *(Oxford Market & Deli 226-0015)*, Bank/ATM, Post Office *(226-5629)*, Library *(226-5727)*, Beauty Salon *(On The Park 226-5079)*, Newsstand, Retail Shops **Under 1 mi:** Protestant Church
1-3 mi: Farmers' Market *(Wed 4-7 Comm Center)* **3+ mi:** Supermarket *(Safeway 822-5055 or Food Lion 819-3234, 11 mi.)*, Fishmonger *(Captains Ketch 827177, 11 mi.)*, Bookstore *(Unicorn 476-3838, 10 mi.)*, Pharmacy *(Hill's 822-2666, 10 mi.)*, Hardware Store *(Easton 822-0910, 11 mi.)*, Department Store *(Wal-Mart 819-0140, 12 mi.)*

Transportation
OnSite: Bikes **OnCall:** Courtesy Car/Van, Rental Car *(Enterprise 822-3260)*, Taxi *(Gotta Go 822-1475)*, Airport Limo *(Eastern Shore 820-8431)*
Under 1 mi: Ferry Service *(to Bellevue 745-9023; RiverRunner to Easton 822-2206)* **Airport:** Baltimore-Washington Int'l./Bay Bridge *(62 mi./40 mi.)*

Medical Services
911 Service **OnCall:** Ambulance **Near:** Veterinarian *(Parkes 226-5457)*
Under 1 mi: Doctor *(Adams 226-5964)*
Hospital: Easton Memorial 822-1000 *(10 mi.)*

Setting -- Past Cutts & Case, in a long, narrow basin carved deeper into the cove, Hinckley's putty-colored clapboard two-story buildings and big white vinyl work shed rise above the docks. A mix of sleek, downeast-style sail and power vessels, many labeled Hinckley, populate the slips. Picnic tables with navy blue market umbrellas are sprinkled along the bulkhead and a nicely appointed dockside pool is tucked between two structures.

Marina Notes -- *Storage rate if work being done: to 35 ft. $5, 36-45' $11, 46-55' $18. DCM. Formerly Crockett's Boatyard. Now one of 6 Hinckley yards, they service practically every piece of equipment found on a sail or powerboat. The nicely merchandised ships' store has boating supplies, seasonal clothing and Hinckley logo products. Pool hours Mon-Fri 8am-5pm, Sat-Sun 9am-5pm. The poolside bathhouse has Tuscan tile floors and cinderblock walls; shower stalls with tile and brightly-colored shower curtains; laundry is adjacent. An additional single head is in the ships' store.

Notable -- The closest docks to charming "downtown" Oxford - North Morris Street is just two blocks away. The well-supplied Oxford Market & Deli shares the street with old fashioned Oxford Mews Emporium, a few gift shops, galleries, a diminutive museum (moving soon) and a peaceful riverfront park. Founded around 1694, this stopped-in-time, affluent colonial town was once one of two ports of entry for all of Maryland and a center of the region's oyster industry. The Oxford Museum's exhibits focus on the town's 18th and 19th C. history (Fri-Sun, 2-5pm) and Skipper Marquess' walking tour explores the perfectly restored edifices that line the nearby streets, including the house sporting the oldest grapevine in the US and the 1710 Robert Morris Inn.

PHOTOS ON CD-ROM: 14

Campbell's Boatyard at Jack's Pt.

PO Box; 106 Richardson Street; Oxford, MD 21654

Tel: (410) 226-5105 **VHF: Monitor** 16 **Talk** n/a
Fax: (410) 226-5962 **Alternate Tel:** (410) 226-5105
Email: info@campbellsboatyard.com **Web:** www.campbellsboatyard.com
Nearest Town: Oxford *(0.8 mi.)* **Tourist Info:** (410) 226-5730

Navigational Information

Lat: 38°41.340' **Long:** 076°10.080' **Tide:** 2 ft. **Current:** n/a **Chart:** 12263
Rep. Depths (*MLW*): Entry 6 ft. **Fuel Dock** 7 ft. **Max Slip/Moor** -/7 ft.
Access: Choptank River to Tred Avon to Town Creek

Marina Facilities *(In Season/Off Season)*

Fuel: Gasoline, Diesel, High-Speed Pumps
Slips: 54 Total, 5 Transient **Max LOA:** 60 ft. **Max Beam:** 25 ft.
Rate *(per ft.)*: **Day** $1.50 **Week** Inq. **Month** Inq.
Power: 30 amp Incl., **50 amp** Incl., **100 amp** n/a, **200 amp** n/a
Cable TV: No **Dockside Phone:** No
Dock Type: Fixed, Long Fingers, Short Fingers, Pilings, Alongside, Wood
Moorings: 0 Total, 0 Transient **Launch:** n/a, Dinghy Dock
Rate: Day n/a **Week** n/a **Month** n/a
Heads: 2 Toilet(s), 4 Shower(s)
Laundry: None, Book Exchange **Pay Phones:** No
Pump-Out: OnSite **Fee:** $5 **Closed Heads:** Yes

Marina Operations

Owner/Manager: Daryl Frey **Dockmaster:** Same
In-Season: May-Sept, 8am-6pm **Off-Season:** Oct-Apr, 7:30am-4pm
After-Hours Arrival: Call ahead
Reservations: Yes, Required **Credit Cards:** Visa/MC
Discounts: MTOA **Dockage:** n/a **Fuel:** n/a **Repair:** n/a
Pets: Welcome, Dog Walk Area **Handicap Access:** Yes, Heads, Docks

Marina Services and Boat Supplies

Services - Docking Assistance, Dock Carts **Communication -** FedEx, DHL, UPS, Express Mail **Supplies - OnSite:** Ice *(Block, Cube)* **Near:** Propane, CNG **Under 1 mi:** Ships' Store, Bait/Tackle *(Oxford Market 226-0015)*, Live Bait **3+ mi:** West Marine *(770-3080, 12 mi.)*

Boatyard Services

OnSite: Travelift *(20T)*, Hydraulic Trailer, Engine mechanic *(gas, diesel)*, Electrical Repairs, Hull Repairs, Rigger, Bottom Cleaning, Brightwork, Compound, Wash & Wax, Interior Cleaning, Woodworking, Metal Fabrication, Painting, Awlgrip, Yacht Design, Yacht Building, Total Refits **OnCall:** Electronics Repairs, Sail Loft, Canvas Work, Refrigeration, Propeller Repairs, Inflatable Repairs, Upholstery, Yacht Interiors **Near:** Crane. **Under 1 mi:** Launching Ramp. **Dealer for:** Cummins. **Member:** ABBRA, ABYC - 1 Certified Tech(s) **Yard Rates:** $44/hr., Haul & Launch $4/ft. *(blocking $1.50/ft.)*, Power Wash $2/ft., Bottom Paint $14, up to 32/ft. **Storage:** On-Land $5/ft./mo.

Restaurants and Accommodations

Under 1 mi: Restaurant *(Schooner's Landing 226-0160, L $5-15, D $10-25)*, *(Oxford Inn 226-5220, D $20-30)*, *(Robert Morris Inn 226-5111, B $7-15, L $11-17, D $17-35)*, *(Masthead at Pier St. 226-5411)*, Hotel *(Nichols House 226-5799)*, Inn/B&B *(Oxford Inn 226-5220)*, *(Robert Morris Inn 226-5111, $100-120)* **1-3 mi:** Restaurant *(Latitude 38 226-5303, D $20-27)*

Recreation and Entertainment

OnSite: Picnic Area **Near:** Grills, Playground, Jogging Paths, Roller Blade/Bike Paths *(Causeway Park)*, Video Rental, Cultural Attract *(Tred Avon Players 226-0061)* **Under 1 mi:** Beach, Tennis Courts *(Causeway Park)*, Boat Rentals, Park, Museum *(Oxford Museum 226-0191)*, Sightseeing, Special Events **1-3 mi:** Horseback Riding, Fishing Charter **3+ mi:** Golf Course *(Easton Club 820-9017, 8 mi.)*, Fitness Center *(YMCA 822-0566, 8 mi.)*, Movie Theater *(Easton 822-9950, 11 mi.)*

Provisioning and General Services

Near: Farmers' Market *(Wed 4-7pm Comm. Center)*, Bank/ATM, Protestant Church, Synagogue, Retail Shops **Under 1 mi:** Convenience Store, Liquor Store *(Oxford Spirits 226-0002)*, Market *(Oxford Market & Deli 226-0015)*, Post Office *(226-5629)*, Library *(Oxford 226-5727)*, Beauty Salon *(On The Park 226-5079)* **3+ mi:** Supermarket *(Safeway 822-5055, Food Lion 819-3234, 11 mi.)*, Fishmonger *(Captains Ketch 820-7177, 11 mi.)*, Dry Cleaners *(McCord's Laundry & Cleaners 822-0800, 10 mi.)*, Bookstore *(Unicorn 476-3838, 10 mi.)*, Pharmacy *(Hill's 822-2666, 10 mi.)*, Hardware Store *(Easton 822-0910, 11 mi.)*, Department Store *(Wal-Mart 819-0140, 12 mi.)*

Transportation

OnSite: Bikes **OnCall:** Rental Car *(Enterprise 822-3260)*, Taxi *(Bay Country Taxi 770-9030)*, Airport Limo *(Eastern Shore 820-8431, 24hrs.)* **Under 1 mi:** Ferry Service *(Oxford Bellevue 745-9023)* **Airport:** Baltimore-Washington Int'l./Bay Bridge *(62 mi./40 mi.)*

Medical Services

911 Service **OnCall:** Ambulance **Under 1 mi:** Doctor *(Adams 226-5964)*, Dentist *(Bishop 226-0011)* **3+ mi:** Chiropractor *(Brooks Chiropractic 820-7705, 10 mi.)*, Holistic Services *(Evergreen Cove Holistic 819-3395, 10 mi.)* **Hospital:** Easton Memorial 822-1000 *(10 mi.)*

PHOTOS ON CD-ROM: 10

Setting -- On the port side of Town Creek, Campbell's big hunter-green work shed marks the beginning of its docks. Open "D" dock is first followed by the covered "C" docks - with some great classic boats. Long "B" dock, hosting the bulk of the slips, parallels the covered slips and "A" heads straight out from the butter-yellow office. Picnic tables sit on a grassy stretch near the bike shed, overlooking the docks and creek.

Marina Notes -- Formerly Bates Marina - changed ownership March 2003. Upgraded pumps and several refaced docks. One of three Campbell's Boatyards in Oxford. The one at Bachelor's Point also takes transients, but the one at the head of Town Creek does not. Both Town Creek facilities have full boatyard services: construction, repairs, repowers and maintenance projects - with carpenters, mechanics and varnishers on staff. Inside the butter-yellow bathhouse are quite nice heads: cinderblock walls, tile floor and shower stalls with a little separate dressing room and bright, fresh curtains.

Notable -- Jack's Point is on the opposite side of Town Creek from Oxford's Morris Street services. It's known as the "quiet side," but nothing is very far from any place in pocket-sized Oxford. For instance, it's about 0.8 miles to the Oxford Market & Deli (Richardson St. to Bonfield Ave. to Oxford Rd. to Morris St.); a short 0.4 mile walk to the Community Center, home to the well-regarded Tred Avon Players (which presents about five musicals and plays a year) and the Wednesday Farmers' Market. A bit farther is Causeway Park - with tennis and basketball courts, a playground, sports field, and an in-line skating pad. It's just 0.7 miles to Masthead's Pier Street Restaurant, which offers lunch and dinner (including steamed crabs).

Navigational Information
Lat: 38°41.222' **Long:** 076°10.247' **Tide:** 2 ft. **Current:** n/a **Chart:** 12263
Rep. Depths (*MLW*): Entry 6 ft. **Fuel Dock** n/a **Max Slip/Moor** 6 ft./-
Access: Choptank to Tred Avon to head of Town Creek

Marina Facilities *(In Season/Off Season)*
Fuel: *nearby* - On Call Delivery
Slips: 20 Total, 5 Transient **Max LOA:** 49 ft. **Max Beam:** 15 ft.
Rate *(per ft.)*: **Day** $1.25 **Week** Inq. **Month** Inq.
Power: 30 amp Incl., **50 amp** n/a, **100 amp** n/a, **200 amp** n/a
Cable TV: No **Dockside Phone:** No
Dock Type: Fixed, Short Fingers, Pilings, Wood
Moorings: 0 Total, 0 Transient **Launch:** n/a
Rate: Day n/a **Week** n/a **Month** n/a
Heads: 2 Toilet(s), 2 Shower(s)
Laundry: 1 Washer(s), 1 Dryer(s) **Pay Phones:** No
Pump-Out: No **Fee:** n/a **Closed Heads:** Yes

Marina Operations
Owner/Manager: John Shannaman **Dockmaster:** Same
In-Season: Year-Round, 8am-5pm **Off-Season:** n/a
After-Hours Arrival: Call ahead
Reservations: Preferred **Credit Cards:** Visa/MC
Discounts: None
Pets: Welcome **Handicap Access:** No

Oxford Yacht Agency

PO Box 190; 317 South Morris Street; Oxford, MD 21654

Tel: (410) 226-5454 **VHF: Monitor** n/a **Talk** n/a
Fax: (410) 226-5244 **Alternate Tel:** n/a
Email: oya@dmv.com **Web:** www.oya.com
Nearest Town: Oxford *(0.3 mi.)* **Tourist Info:** (410) 226-5730

Marina Services and Boat Supplies
Services - Docking Assistance, Trash Pick-Up **Communication -** Mail & Package Hold, Phone Messages, Fax in/out, FedEx, UPS, Express Mail
Supplies - Near: Ice *(Block, Cube)*, Ships' Store, Propane, CNG
Under 1 mi: Bait/Tackle *(Oxford Market 226-0015)*, Live Bait
3+ mi: West Marine *(770-3080, 11 mi.)*

Boatyard Services
OnCall: Engine mechanic *(gas, diesel)*, Electrical Repairs, Electronics Repairs, Hull Repairs, Rigger, Sail Loft, Canvas Work, Bottom Cleaning, Brightwork, Air Conditioning, Refrigeration, Divers, Compound, Wash & Wax, Interior Cleaning, Propeller Repairs, Woodworking, Inflatable Repairs, Life Raft Service, Upholstery, Yacht Interiors, Metal Fabrication, Painting, Awlgrip, Total Refits **Near:** Launching Ramp. **1-3 mi:** Travelift.
Nearest Yard: Campbell's Boatyard (410) 226-5730

Restaurants and Accommodations
Near: Restaurant *(Robert Morris Inn 226-5111, B $7-15, L $11-17, D $17-35)*, *(Pope's Tavern at Oxford Inn 226-5220, D $20-30)*, *(Masthead at Pier St. 226-5171, L $6-12, D $13-24)*, *(Schooner's Landing 226-0160, L $5-15, D $10-25)*, Inn/B&B *(Oxford Inn 226-5220, $90-160)*, *(Nichols House 226-5799)*, *(Robert Morris Inn 226-5111, $90-260)* **1-3 mi:** Restaurant *(Latitude 38 226-5303, D $20-27, Shuttle)*

Recreation and Entertainment
Near: Beach, Picnic Area, Grills, Playground, Tennis Courts *(Town Park)*, Video Rental, Museum *(Oxford 226-0191)*, Sightseeing *(Skipper Marguess' Walking Tour 226-0191)* **3+ mi:** Golf Course *(Easton Club 820-9017, 8 mi.)*, Fitness Center *(YMCA 822-0566, 8 mi.)*, Bowling *(Easton Bowling Center 822-3426, 10 mi.)*, Movie Theater *(Easton Premier Cinema 822-9950, 11 mi.)*

Provisioning and General Services
Near: Convenience Store, Catholic Church, Protestant Church, Library *(Oxford Library 226-5727)*, Clothing Store **Under 1 mi:** Delicatessen, Liquor Store *(Oxford Spirits 226-0002)*, Farmers' Market *(Wed 4-7pm Comm. Center)*, Market *(Oxford 226-0015)*, Bank/ATM, Post Office *(226-5629)*, Beauty Salon *(On The Park Hair Studio 226-5079)* **3+ mi:** Supermarket *(Safeway 822-5055 or Food Lion 819-3234, 11 mi.)*, Gourmet Shop *(Gourmet & More 763-7077, 11 mi.)*, Bakery *(Sweet Nina's 763-9272, 11 mi.)*, Fishmonger *(Captains Ketch's 820-7177, 11 mi.)*, Bookstore *(Unicorn 476-3838, 10 mi.)*, Pharmacy *(Hill's 822-2666, 10 mi.)*, Hardware Store *(Easton 822-0910, 11 mi.)*, Department Store *(Wal-Mart 819-0140, 12 mi.)*

Transportation
OnCall: Rental Car *(Enterprise 822-3260)*, Taxi *(Bay Country 770-9030)*, Airport Limo *(Eastern Shore 820-8431, 24 hrs.)*
Near: Ferry Service *(Oxford Bellevue 745-9023)*
Airport: Baltimore-Washington Int'l./Bay Bridge *(62 mi./40 mi.)*

Medical Services
911 Service **OnCall:** Ambulance **Near:** Dentist *(Bishop 226-0011)* **Under 1 mi:** Doctor **1-3 mi:** Veterinarian *(Parkes 226-5457)* **3+ mi:** Chiropractor *(Brooks Chiropractic 820-7705, 10 mi.)*, Holistic Services *(Evergreen Cove Holistic 819-3395, 10 mi.)* **Hospital:** Easton Memorial 822-1000 *(10 mi.)*

Setting -- Almost to the head of Town Creek on the starboard side, Oxford Yacht Agency is trawler heaven. The barn-red outbuilding and weathered shingle main office flavor the environment with Downeast salt. A variety of spiffy Grand Banks yachts populate the two main docks and a third that edges the marine railway. A narrow front porch furnished with an assortment of chairs invites sitting and watching the passing scene.

Marina Notes -- Family-owned & operated - acquired 1975. OYA seems to specialize in new and vintage Grand Banks and Holby skiffs and utility boats. OYA is also now producing their own 32 foot Downeast lobster boat built on a Jarvis Newman hull. Most yard work is handled at their Dickerson Harbor yard on Trappe Creek - specialized in retrofits and rebuilds. Transient power options vary - some is on the pilings.

Notable -- Oxford yacht Agency is well situated to take advantage of Oxford's two parks - a few blocks north, pretty riverfront Town Park has picnic tables, a playground, and waterside benches surrounded by Oxford's shopping district. Oxford Market is "action central," a source of to-go meals and the latest local info; little Oxford Museum's walking tour led by Skipper Marguess, describes many of the surrounding historic houses. A block south, Causeway Park has two well-maintained tennis courts, play gym equipment, a basketball court, playing field and an in-line skate space. Across the street from Causeway Park is the Oxford Inn - a B&B with Pope's Tavern and Pope's Treasures, Gifts & Books. Oxford has lots of green spaces - at the end of every road there seems to be a bench for sitting and watching the river.

PHOTOS ON CD-ROM: 10

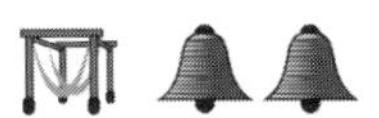

Easton Point Marina

Easton Point Marina

PO Box 2877; 975 Port Street; Easton, MD 21601

Tel: (410) 822-1201 **VHF: Monitor** 18 **Talk** n/a
Fax: (410) 822-1202 **Alternate Tel:** n/a
Email: epm@goeaston.net **Web:** www.eastonpointmarina.com
Nearest Town: Easton *(1.2 mi.)* **Tourist Info:** (410) 822-4653

Navigational Information
Lat: 38°46.095' **Long:** 076°05.672' **Tide:** n/a **Current:** n/a **Chart:** 12266
Rep. Depths (*MLW*): Entry 6 ft. **Fuel Dock** 6 ft. **Max Slip/Moor** 6 ft./-
Access: Chop Tank to Tred Avon to the beginning of North Fork

Marina Facilities *(In Season/Off Season)*
Fuel: Slip-Side Fueling, Gasoline, Diesel
Slips: 25 Total, 6 Transient **Max LOA:** 45 ft. **Max Beam:** n/a
Rate *(per ft.)*: **Day** $2.50 **Week** $14/ft/wk **Month** $60/ft/mo
Power: 30 amp Incl., **50 amp** Incl., **100 amp** n/a, **200 amp** n/a
Cable TV: No **Dockside Phone:** No
Dock Type: Fixed, Short Fingers, Wood
Moorings: 0 Total, 0 Transient **Launch:** n/a
Rate: Day n/a **Week** n/a **Month** n/a
Heads: 2 Toilet(s), 2 Shower(s)
Laundry: None **Pay Phones:** No
Pump-Out: OnSite, Full Service, 1 Port **Fee:** $25 **Closed Heads:** Yes

Marina Operations
Owner/Manager: Victor Michael **Dockmaster:** Same
In-Season: Apr-Oct, 7am-6pm **Off-Season:** Nov-Mar, 9am-4pm
After-Hours Arrival: Call ahead
Reservations: Preferred **Credit Cards:** Visa/MC
Discounts: None
Pets: Welcome, Dog Walk Area **Handicap Access:** No

Marina Services and Boat Supplies
Services - Docking Assistance, Security **Communication -** FedEx, DHL, UPS, Express Mail **Supplies - OnSite:** Ships' Store *(Ship's Galley)*, Bait/Tackle, Live Bait **1-3 mi:** West Marine *(770-3080)*

Boatyard Services
OnSite: Travelift *(25T)*, Launching Ramp, Bottom Cleaning, Compound, Wash & Wax

Restaurants and Accommodations
OnSite: Lite Fare *(Ship's Galley)* **OnCall:** Pizzeria *(Domino's 820-8330)* **Under 1 mi:** Restaurant *(Kendall's 822-9898, L $5-10, D $11-24, early bird/bar dinner $10; happy hour 5-7pm)*, *(Columbia 770-5172, D $28-35)*, *(Chez Lafitte 770-8868, French; live piano Thu & Sat)*, Lite Fare *(Washington Street Pub 822-9011)* **1-3 mi:** Restaurant *(Rustic Inn 820-8212, D $11-29, lite fare at the Tavern, dinner cruises)*, *(Inn at Easton 822-4910, D $65-85, 4-6 course prix fixe)*, *(Hunter's Tavern 822-1300, Sun brunch)*, *(Out of the Fire Café & Wine Bar 770-4777, L $9-12, D $12-23, closed Sun; wine bar from 4pm, D 6-10pm)*, Motel *(Comfort Inn 800-221-2222)*, *(Holiday Inn 819-6500)*, Inn/B&B *(Inn at Easton 822-4910, $175-395)*, *(Bishop's House 800-223-7290)*

Recreation and Entertainment
OnSite: Boat Rentals *(kayaks, jet skis)*, Fishing Charter *(Giant Fishing Charter 822-1010 - Luhrs 40 ft.)*, Group Fishing Boat *(River Runner 822-1201)* **Near:** Playground **Under 1 mi:** Fitness Center *(YMCA 822-0566)*, Jogging Paths, Park, Sightseeing *(Historical Soc. Walking Tours 822-0773)*, Galleries *(1st Friday 10 Gallery Walk 5-9pm)* **1-3 mi:** Tennis Courts *(Cross Court Athletic Club 822-1515)*, Golf Course *(Hog Neck 822-6079, $45-55; Easton Club 820-9800)*, Movie Theater, Video Rental *(Blockbuster 820-0016)*, Museum *(Academy Art Museum 822-2787, $2/1)*, Cultural Attract *(Avalon Performing Arts 822-0345)*, Special Events *(Plein Air Arts Fest - early Jul; Chamber Music Fest - Jun; Water Fowl Fest - Nov)*

Provisioning and General Services
OnSite: Delicatessen *(Carry Out Deli 822-1201)*, Wine/Beer **Under 1 mi:** Gourmet Shop *(Mason's 822-3204, lunch to go)*, Health Food, Liquor Store *(TJ's 822-1433)*, Bakery, Bank/ATM, Catholic Church, Protestant Church,Beauty Salon *(Fay Hair Care 822-8080)*, Barber Shop *(Outlaws 820-8674)*, Dry Cleaners *(McCord's 822-0800)*, Florist **1-3 mi:** Supermarket *(Safeway 822-5055, Food Lion 819-3234)*, Farmers' Market *(Talbot Shop. Ctr. Sat 8am-1pm 819-0444)*, Post Office, Library *(820-8217)*, Bookstore *(Rainy Day 819-5988)*, Pharmacy *(Hill's 822-2666)*, Hardware Store *(Easton 822-0910)*, Department Store *(Wal-Mart 819-0140)*

Transportation
OnSite: Ferry Service *(River Runner 822-2206 to Oxford Ferry Dock)*
OnCall: Rental Car *(Enterprise 822-3260)*, Taxi, Airport Limo
1-3 mi: InterCity Bus *(Greyhound 822-3333)*
Airport: Baltimore-Washington Int'l./Easton *(52 mi./5 mi.)*

Medical Services
911 Service **OnCall:** Ambulance **Near:** Holistic Services *(Evergreen Cove 819-3395)* **Under 1 mi:** Dentist *(Knudsen 820-0230)* **1-3 mi:** Doctor *(E. Shore Emergency 763-7040)*, Chiropractor *(Brooks 820-7705)*, Veterinarian *(Animal Clinic 822-2922)* **Hospital:** Easton Memorial 822-1000 *(2 mi.)*

PHOTOS ON CD-ROM: 11

Setting -- Seven miles past Oxford toward the head of the Tred Avon is Easton Point. A single-story gray shingled building sits at the headwaters just before the North Fork. Docks line a boardwalk that travels along the bulkhead. Upland is a large work and storage shed and graveled dry storage area serviced by a 25 ton travelift. Right next door is the town launch ramp and large, square, wooden town landing which permits two-hour tie-ups.

Marina Notes -- Recent docks and newish pedestals. A small, well-stocked ships' store also carries bait and tackle and live bait; its cozy wood stove is welcome on damp spring and fall days. The Ship's Galley, the on-site carryout deli, has sundries, sodas, beer. Two very spacious full bathrooms with stand-alone showers - one for men and one for women - are in the gray modular building near the storage shed.

Notable -- This is the closest landing to the engaging, historic town of Easton, 1.2 miles straight east - the Eastern Shore's commercial center. An on-site taxi service makes access easy - many walk one way and cab the other. Beautifully maintained, colonial Easton has received multiple citations for its historic preservation-based revitalization under the National Trust's Main Street program. It has a bit of a movie-set look and was recently named the 8th best small town in America. The pretty downtown offers an impressive choice of restaurants, a plethora of historic sites, museums, and galleries, wonderful strolling opportunities - including walking tours - plus lots of good shopping with many unique local emporia.

Navigational Information

Lat: 38°39.267' **Long:** 076°05.033' **Tide:** 2 ft. **Current:** n/a **Chart:** 12263
Rep. Depths (*MLW*): Entry 7 ft. **Fuel Dock** n/a **Max Slip/Moor** 4 ft./-
Access: Choptank River then turn left at 18A into La Trappe Creek

Marina Facilities *(In Season/Off Season)*

Fuel: No
Slips: 50 Total, 3 Transient **Max LOA:** 75 ft. **Max Beam:** 18 ft.
Rate *(per ft.)*: **Day** $1.00 **Week** n/a **Month** n/a
Power: 30 amp Incl., **50 amp** $5, **100 amp** $10, **200 amp** n/a
Cable TV: No **Dockside Phone:** No
Dock Type: Fixed, Pilings, Wood
Moorings: 0 Total, 0 Transient **Launch:** n/a
Rate: Day n/a **Week** n/a **Month** n/a
Heads: 4 Toilet(s), 3 Shower(s) *(with dressing rooms)*
Laundry: None **Pay Phones:** No
Pump-Out: No **Fee:** n/a **Closed Heads:** Yes

Marina Operations

Owner/Manager: John Shanahaw **Dockmaster:** Same
In-Season: Year-Round, 8am-4:30pm **Off-Season:** n/a
After-Hours Arrival: Call ahead
Reservations: Yes, Preferred **Credit Cards:** Visa/MC
Discounts: None
Pets: Welcome **Handicap Access:** No

Oxford Yacht at Dickerson Harbor

3831 Trappe Landing Road; Trappe, MD 21673

Tel: (410) 822-8556 **VHF: Monitor** n/a **Talk** n/a
Fax: (410) 822-2769 **Alternate Tel:** n/a
Email: willy@oya.com **Web:** www.oya.com/dickerson
Nearest Town: Trappe **Tourist Info:** (410) 822-4653

Marina Services and Boat Supplies

Communication - Mail & Package Hold, Phone Messages, FedEx, UPS, Express Mail *(Sat Del)* **Supplies - 3+ mi:** Ships' Store *(Gateway Marina 476-3304, 7 mi.)*, West Marine *(770-3080, 10 mi.)*, Propane *(Pep-Up 376-0011, 9 mi.)*

Boatyard Services

OnSite: Travelift *(50T)*, Engine mechanic *(gas, diesel)*, Rigger, Sail Loft, Bottom Cleaning, Brightwork, Air Conditioning, Compound, Wash & Wax, Interior Cleaning, Woodworking, Metal Fabrication, Painting, Awlgrip, Yacht Design, Yacht Building, Total Refits, Yacht Broker *(Oxford Yacht Agency)* **3+ mi:** Electronic Sales *(Mid-Shore Electronics 228-7335, 9 mi.)*, Canvas Work *(Cambridge Canvas & Sail Loft 228-7414, 10 mi.)*.

Restaurants and Accommodations

3+ mi: Restaurant *(Neal's Italian Café 820-0005, 8 mi.)*, *(Ocean Odyssey 228-8633, L $6-10, D $12-23, 7 mi.)*, *(Kendall's Restaurant & Catering 822-9898, L $5-10, D $11-24, 8 mi.)*, *(Plaza Tapatia 770-8550, L $5-10, D $7-15, 7 mi. 7.4 mi.)*, *(House of Hunan 820-4015, 8 mi.)*, Coffee Shop *(Coffee East 819-6711, 8 mi.)*, Pizzeria *(Rusticana 228-1515, L $5-15, D $5-15, 7 mi.)*, Motel *(Comfort Inn 820-8333, 11 mi.)*, *(Talbot Landing 476-3189, 6 mi.)*, Hotel *(Holiday Inn 819-6500, 11 mi.)*, *(Hyatt 901-6301, 10 mi.)*, Inn/B&B *(Combs Berry 226-5353, 7 mi.)*, *(Robert Morris 226-5111, 7 mi.)*

Recreation and Entertainment

3+ mi: Tennis Courts *(Bay Country Racquet Club 228-9311, 11 mi.)*, Golf Course *(Easton Club 800- 277-9800, 8 mi.)*, Fitness Center *(YMCA 822-0566, 8 mi.)*, Bowling *(Easton Bowling Center 822-3426, 8 mi.)*, Movie Theater *(Premiere Cinema 221-8688, 10 mi.)*, Video Rental *(Blockbuster 221-0600, 10 mi.)*, Museum *(Richardson Maritime Museum 221-1871, 11 mi.)*, Cultural Attract *(Oxford Museum 226-0191, 8 mi.)*

Provisioning and General Services

1-3 mi: Beauty Salon *(Craig's Place 476-4644)*, Barber Shop *(That Hair Place 476-3898)*, Bookstore *(Unicorn 476-3838)* **3+ mi:** Convenience Store *(Wawa 901-9794, 9 mi.)*, Supermarket *(Safeway 822-5055, 10 mi.)*, Delicatessen *(Choptank Market 221-8032, 10 mi.)*, Liquor Store *(Wishing Well 822-2272, 9 mi.)*, Fishmonger *(TL Morris Seafood 476-4811, 7 mi.)*, Crabs/Waterman *(Soft Crabs Direct 226-0566, 8 mi.)*, Market *(Oxford 226-0015, 8 mi.)*, Bank/ATM *(7 mi.)*, Post Office *(Oxford 226-5629, 9 mi.)*, Library *(Oxford 226-5727, 8 mi.)*, Dry Cleaners *(McCord's Laundry & Cleaners 822-0800, 10 mi.)*, Pharmacy *(Rite Aid 228-8601, 10 mi.)*, Hardware Store *(Rommel's 228-9391, 10 mi.)*, Florist *(Seasonal Flowers 476-3255, 5 mi.)*, Clothing Store *(J C Penney 770-5198, 10 mi.)*, Department Store *(Wal-Mart 221-0388, 10 mi.)*

Transportation

OnCall: Rental Car *(Enterprise 822-3260)*, Taxi *(Bay Country 770-9030)*, Airport Limo *(Eastern Shore 800-453-2023)* **3+ mi:** Rail *(Amtrak 672-6167, 64 mi.)* **Airport:** Baltimore-Washington Int'l./Easton *(60 mi./12 mi.)*

Medical Services

911 Service **OnCall:** Ambulance **1-3 mi:** Doctor *(Farkas 476-5236)*, Dentist *(Haley 476-4823)* **3+ mi:** Chiropractor *(Anderson Chiropractic 901-2903, 9 9 mi.)*, Veterinarian *(Parkes 226-5457, 8 mi.)*
Hospital: Dorchester General 476-3771 *(9 mi.)*

Setting -- Tucked way up at the navigable head of serene La Trappe Creek at Trappe Landing, a conglomeration of large work sheds dominates the shoreline above an oval basin. A set of docks hosting larger vessels - mostly trawlers - sits on either side of the basin's mouth; slips for smaller boats ring the basin. Some additional alongside dockage supplements both. In marked contrast to this working yard is the peaceful, pristine surrounding shoreline.

Marina Notes -- This is the boatyard half of the Oxford Yacht Agency in downtown Oxford. Inside storage summer & winter for vessels to 65'. All types of repair on trawlers & lobster yachts with 30 years of history working on Grand Banks (an Authorized Repair Center). OYA. Also mail orders some standard upgrades and tackles any kind of retrofit, customization, rebuild or Awlgrip job. On-site staff includes mechanics, carpenters, electricians, fiberglass technicians and detailers. A new storage building can house over 40 boats. Outside are 8 acres dry storage. Dickerson Boat Building originally occupied this site. Nearby is a county launch and fishing pier.

Notable -- The cruise up La Trappe Creek is lovely - overhanging trees and well-spaced quiet estates, some reaching back to the 18th century. Trappe Landing has been a shipping point for produce since Colonial days. There is a planned pump-out at Trappe Landing which is being developed into an 11-slip marina. Nearby LaTrappe Landing Farm & Native Sanctuary - a 34-acre sustainable landscaping effort - occasionally welcomes the public to tour the grounds.

PHOTOS ON CD-ROM: 8

Gateway Marina & Ships Store

1606 Marina Drive; Trappe, MD 21673

Tel: (410) 476-3304 **VHF: Monitor** 16 **Talk** 68
Fax: (410) 476-5360 **Alternate Tel:** n/a
Email: gatewaymarina@bluecrab.org **Web:** www.gatewaymarina.com
Nearest Town: Cambridge *(2 mi.)* **Tourist Info:** (410) 228-3575

Navigational Information

Lat: 38°35.581' **Long:** 076°02.983' **Tide:** 2 ft. **Current:** n/a **Chart:** 12263
Rep. Depths (*MLW*): Entry 4 ft. **Fuel Dock** 4.5 ft. **Max Slip/Moor** 5 ft./-
Access: Choptank River on the portside, almost to the Rt.50 Bridge

Marina Facilities *(In Season/Off Season)*

Fuel: *Shell* - Gasoline, Diesel
Slips: 112 Total, 4 Transient **Max LOA:** 50 ft. **Max Beam:** 16 ft.
Rate *(per ft.)*: **Day** $40.00* **Week** $50 **Month** $165
Power: 30 amp Incl., **50 amp** Inq., **100 amp** Inq., **200 amp** n/a
Cable TV: No **Dockside Phone:** No
Dock Type: Fixed, Short Fingers, Alongside, Wood
Moorings: 0 Total, 0 Transient **Launch:** n/a
Rate: Day n/a **Week** n/a **Month** n/a
Heads: 1 Toilet(s), 1 Shower(s) *(with dressing rooms)*
Laundry: None, Book Exchange **Pay Phones:** No
Pump-Out: OnSite, Full Service, 1 Central **Fee:** $5 **Closed Heads:** Yes

Marina Operations

Owner/Manager: Jack & Sharon Morrison **Dockmaster:** n/a
In-Season: May-Nov, 8am-5pm **Off-Season:** Dec-Apr, 8am-4pm
After-Hours Arrival: Call ahead
Reservations: No **Credit Cards:** Visa/MC, Dscvr, CFN
Discounts: None
Pets: Welcome, Dog Walk Area **Handicap Access:** No

Marina Services and Boat Supplies

Communication - Phone Messages, Fax in/out *($1.50)*, FedEx, UPS, Express Mail **Supplies - OnSite:** Ice *(Block, Cube)*, Ships' Store, Marine Discount Store, Bait/Tackle, Live Bait *(bloodworms, squid, etc.)* **1-3 mi:** Propane *(Pep-Up 376-0011)*

Boatyard Services

OnSite: Travelift *(25T)*, Engine mechanic *(gas, diesel)*, Electrical Repairs, Hull Repairs, Rigger, Bottom Cleaning, Brightwork, Compound, Wash & Wax, Interior Cleaning, Propeller Repairs, Woodworking, Painting, Awlgrip **Near:** Air Conditioning, Refrigeration. **Under 1 mi:** Launching Ramp, Upholstery. **Dealer for:** Interlux Volvo Penta, Pettit. **Yard Rates:** $53/hr., Haul & Launch $5/ft. *(blocking $30)*, Power Wash $50, Bottom Paint $16/ft. *(paint incl.)* **Storage:** In-Water $1.65/ft/mo., On-Land $3/ft./mo.

Restaurants and Accommodations

OnSite: Seafood Shack *(T.L. Morris Crab Shack)* **OnCall:** Pizzeria *(Pizza City 221-7500)*, *(Rusticana 228-1515, L $5-15, D $5-15)* **1-3 mi:** Restaurant *(Snappers Waterfront Café 228-0112, L $6-8, D $13-22)*, *(Great Wall 228-0332)*, *(Town & Country Deli & Café 901-6000, L $4-9, D $9-14)*, Seafood Shack *(Creek Side Seafood & Produce 221-1611, L $5-10, D $9-18)*, Fast Food *(McD's, BK, Hardee's)*, Lite Fare *(Moody John 901-2720, pool tables)*, *(Café On the Square 758-0471)*, *(Point Break Beach Bar 221-7850)*, Hotel *(Holiday Inn 221-9900)*, *(Hyatt 901-6301)*, Inn/B&B *(Cambridge House 221-7700)*

Recreation and Entertainment

OnSite: Beach, Picnic Area, Fishing Charter **1-3 mi:** Playground, Tennis Courts *(Bay Country 228-9311)*, Fitness Center *(Cambridge 228-6710)*, Movie Theater *(Premiere 221-8688)*, Video Rental *(Blockbuster 221-0600)*, Park *(Monument Park)*, Museum *(Dorchester Hist. Society 228-7953)*, Galleries *(Joie de Vivre 228-7000)* **3+ mi:** Golf Course *(Cambridge CC 221-0521, 4 mi.)*, Bowling *(Cambridge 228-6823, 4 mi.)*

Provisioning and General Services

OnSite: Wine/Beer **1-3 mi:** Supermarket *(Food Lion 228-8328)*, Gourmet Shop *(A Few of My Favorite Things 221-1960)*, Delicatessen *(Choptank Mkt & Deli 221-8032)*, Bakery *(Bay Country 228-9111)*, Farmers' Market *(Sailwinds Tue, Fri 8-Noon)*, Fishmonger *(Van Dyke's 228-9000)*, Market *(Center Market 228-4313)*, Bank/ATM, Post Office *(228-1484)*, Catholic Church, Protestant Church, Library *(901-2880)*, Beauty Salon *(Tresses 228-4996)*, Barber Shop *(Mike's 221-0077)*, Dry Cleaners *(Skip Jack 221-1101)*, Laundry *(Cambridge Plaza 221-0513)*, Bookstore *(Cambridge Books 901-9950)*, Pharmacy *(Craig's 228-3322)*, Hardware Store *(Ace 228-9391)*, Department Store *(Wal-Mart 221-0292)*

Transportation

OnCall: Rental Car *(Enterprise 901-2978)*, Taxi *(Moxeys 221-0698)*, Airport Limo *(Eastern Shore Limo 800-453-2023)* **3+ mi:** Rail *(Amtrak 672-6167, 63 mi.)* **Airport:** Baltimore-Washington Int'l. *(63 mi.)*

Medical Services

911 Service **1-3 mi:** Doctor *(Black Water 228-1068)*, Dentist *(Taylor 228-2980)*, Chiropractor *(Cambridge Chiro 221-0781)*, Ambulance, Veterinarian *(Choptank 221-0444)* **Hospital:** Dorchester General 228-5511 *(2.3 mi.)*

PHOTOS ON CD-ROM: 13

Setting -- Just west of the Rt. 50 bridge on the north side, Gateway is easy to spot as you're coming up the Choptank. Look for the big red crab on the top of the T.L. Morris Crab Shack; it sits right at the entrance into this completely protected harbor. Slips ring the perimeter of the big, rectangular basin and a single dock runs down the middle. A few casual umbrella-topped picnic tables overlook the river with a nice stretch of sandy beach nearby.

Marina Notes -- *Transient rates are flat, not by the foot. DCM. Family-owned for the last 18 years, it serves both working boats and pleasure craft. Volvo Penta parts and service. Land transport of boats. Well-equipped ships' store - if they don't have it, it can likely be delivered overnight. The management prides itself on locating parts no one else can find, so challenge them with your requests. Two travelifts and 3.2 acres of on-the-hard storage. A derelict multi-story vessel, once a club, dominates the bridge end of the marina. There's a basic cinderblock full bathroom.

Notable -- T.L. Morris Seafood is right on-site, which is wonderfully convenient and worth the trip. At the last visit, #1 male crabs were $50 per half bushel or $90 per bushel, females $28 for a half, $50 for a bushel - or by the dozen; steaming extra. They also have soft shell crabs - with peeler sheds right on-site, when they say soft crabs, they really mean it. Local corn, tomatoes, cucumbers, lemons, local oysters, Gulf shrimp and a few other necessities are also available. The convenience store carries cold beer to go with the crabs. Casual but convenient picnic tables sit right at the waters' edge inviting an immediate feast. Nearby, a 25-acre park has a fishing pier (remains of the old bridge) and walking paths wind along the River and Bolingbroke Creek.

Navigational Information
Lat: 38°34.633' **Long:** 076°04.417' **Tide:** 2 ft. **Current:** n/a **Chart:** 12263
Rep. Depths (*MLW*): Entry 10 ft. **Fuel Dock** n/a **Max Slip/Moor** 12 ft./-
Access: Choptank River to Red Nun #2 into private channel

Marina Facilities *(In Season/Off Season)*
Fuel: No
Slips: 186 Total, 20 Transient **Max LOA:** 100 ft. **Max Beam:** 20 ft.
Rate *(per ft.)*: **Day** $1.25/1.00 **Week** $5.00 **Month** $9.00/$2.85
Power: 30 amp $5, **50 amp** $5, **100 amp** n/a, **200 amp** n/a
Cable TV: No **Dockside Phone:** No
Dock Type: Fixed, Short Fingers, Alongside, Concrete, Wood, Vinyl
Moorings: 0 Total, 0 Transient **Launch:** n/a
Rate: Day n/a **Week** n/a **Month** n/a
Heads: 4 Toilet(s), 6 Shower(s) *(with dressing rooms)*
Laundry: 1 Washer(s), 1 Dryer(s), Book Exchange **Pay Phones:** Yes, 6
Pump-Out: OnSite, Self Service, 1 Central **Fee:** Free **Closed Heads:** Yes

Marina Operations
Owner/Manager: Scott Fitzhugh **Dockmaster:** Same
In-Season: May-Sept, 8am-6pm **Off-Season:** Oct-Apr
After-Hours Arrival: Pull into slips marked with "visitor" signs
Reservations: Yes, Preferred **Credit Cards:** Visa/MC, Dscvr
Discounts: None
Pets: Welcome, Dog Walk Area **Handicap Access:** Yes, Heads

Cambridge Municipal Yacht

PO Box 255; 2 Yacht Club Drive.; Cambridge, MD 21613

Tel: (410) 228-4031 **VHF: Monitor** 16 **Talk** 68
Fax: (410) 228-1474 **Alternate Tel:** (410) 330-2856
Email: dockmaster@ci.cambridge.md.us **Web:** www.ci.cambridge.md.us
Nearest Town: Cambridge *(0 mi.)* **Tourist Info:** (410) 228-3575

Marina Services and Boat Supplies
Services - Docking Assistance, Security *(24 hrs., City Police Dept.)*, Trash Pick-Up, Dock Carts **Communication -** Mail & Package Hold, Fax in/out, Data Ports *(Library, Free)*, FedEx, UPS, Express Mail *(Sat Del)* **Supplies - OnSite:** Ice *(Block, Cube)* **OnCall:** Ships' Store **Under 1 mi:** Marine Discount Store *(R & D 228-0674)*, Propane

Boatyard Services
OnCall: Bottom Cleaning, Divers, Compound, Wash & Wax
Near: Launching Ramp, Sail Loft *(Cambridge Canvas & Sail Loft 228-7414)*, Inflatable Repairs. **Under 1 mi:** Travelift *(Cambridge Marine 228-4820)*, Railway *(Yacht Maintenance 228-8878)*, Engine mechanic *(gas, diesel)*, Electrical Repairs, Hull Repairs, Air Conditioning, Propeller Repairs.
Nearest Yard: Cambridge Marine Yacht (410) 228-4020

Restaurants and Accommodations
OnSite: Restaurant *(Cambridge Y.C. 228-2141, L Tue-Sun 12-2pm, D Wed-Sat 6-8:30pm)* **OnCall:** Pizzeria *(Pizza City 221-7500)*, *(Rusticana 228-1515, L $5-15, D $5-15)* **Near:** Restaurant *(Snappers 228-0112, L $6-8, D $13-22)*, *(Canvas Back 221-7888)*, *(Doris May's B $5-10)*, Seafood Shack *(Creek Side 221-1611, L $5-10, D $9-18)*, Lite Fare *(Café on the Square 758-0471)*, Inn/B&B *(Cambridge House 221-7700, $120, 24-room mansion)* **Under 1 mi:** Restaurant *(Great Wall 228-0332)*, Snack Bar *(Point Break Beach Bar 221-7850)*, Motel *(Holiday Inn 221-9900)*, Inn/B&B *(Glasgow B&B 228-0575)* **1-3 mi:** Fast Food, Hotel *(Days Inn 228-4444)*

Recreation and Entertainment
OnSite: Picnic Area, Grills, Cultural Attract *(Nathan of Dorchester 228-7141, $20/5)* **Near:** Park *(Long Wharf & Great Marsh)*, Museum *(Richardson Maritime 221-1871, Wed & Sun 1-4pm, Sat 10am-4pm; Harriet Tubman 228-0401)*, Sightseeing *(Walking Tours, Cambridge Lady 221-0776)*, Galleries *(Dorchester Arts 228-7782)*, Special Events *(Seafood Fest, APBA Power Boat Races, Eagle Man Triathlon)* **Under 1 mi:** Playground, Tennis Courts *(Bay Country 228-9311)*, Fitness Center *(Cambridge 228-6710)*, Video Rental *(Videoland 228-3648)* **1-3 mi:** Beach, Golf Course *(River Marsh)*

Provisioning and General Services
Near: Convenience Store *(Zipmart 228-1234)*, Farmers' Market *(Sailwinds Tue & Fri 8-12)*, Bank/ATM, Post Office *(228-1484)*, Beauty Salon *(Hair Perfection 228-2800)* **Under 1 mi:** Gourmet Shop *(A Few of My Favorite Things 221-1960)*, Delicatessen *(Choptank Mkt & Deli 221-8032, plus beer & wine)*, Fishmonger *(Creek Side Seafood & Produce 221-1611)*, Library *(901-2880)*, Bookstore *(Cambridge 901-9950)*, Pharmacy *(Craig's 228-3322)*
1-3 mi: Supermarket *(Food Lion 228-8328)*, Health Food, Liquor Store *(Jinx's 643-5437)*, Catholic Church, Protestant Church, Dry Cleaners *(Skip Jack 221-1101)*, Hardware Store *(Ace 228-9391)*, Department Store *(Kmart 228-0809)*

Transportation
OnSite: Bikes *(complimentary)* **OnCall:** Rental Car *(Enterprise 901-2978)*, Taxi *(Moxeys 221-0698, $3.50/2people)* **Near:** Local Bus *(Community Trolley at Long Wharf)* **Airport:** Baltimore-Washington Int'l.*(66 mi.)*

Medical Services
911 Service **OnCall:** Ambulance **Under 1 mi:** Doctor *(Black Water 228-1068)*, Dentist *(Harbor 228-5445)* **Hospital:** Dorchester 228-5511 *(1 mi.)*

Setting -- On the southern shore of the Choptank just west of the entrance to Cambridge Creek, this large, nicely executed municipal facility fills a protected man-made basin. The outer docks have sweeping vistas of the river and Rt. 50 bridge. 4-acre Marina Park, a wide swath of lawn, is studded with flowering bushes, shade trees and picnic tables. Just beyond it the city's historic district begins. Adjacent is Long Wharf - a public park with dock and fishing pier.

Marina Notes -- Founded in the 1920's for skipjacks, always owned by the City of Cambridge. Closed Dec-Feb. Fuel since in '04. Divided into two sections by the entrance channel, with four main docks on each side and very generous fairways. Outer bulkhead acts as a wave attenuator and hosts a pavilion. Marina guests have use of Cambridge Yacht Club facilities, including their Dining Room; club cruises welcome. No license required to fish from Long Wharf. Propane & charcoal grills, complete with utensils. The inviting bathhouse has quarry tile floors, private dressing rooms, off-white tile walls, stainless steel enclosures.

Notable -- The 1994 replica skipjack "Nathan of Dorchester" docks at Long Wharf (once the ferry terminal) and sails on Saturdays May-October - 2 hr. cruise, family rates available. The marina office has copies of the Visitors' Center's Cycling Trails and fascinating Historic District Walking Tour - wander the several square blocks of lovely brick-paved streets lined with more than 70 grand, restored late 19th and early 20th C houses and commercial structures. One of the buildings is the expanding Dorchester Arts Center (Mon-Sat 10am-2pm) featuring exhibits, workshops and performances. The Community Trolley picks up at Long Wharf Mon-Fri, 6:30am-6:30pm, Sat 8:30am-5:30pm at 50 minutes past the hour.

PHOTOS ON CD-ROM: 14

Yacht Maintenance Co.

Yacht Maintenance Co.

101 Hayward Street; Cambridge, MD 21613

Tel: (410) 228-8878 **VHF: Monitor** FM 10 **Talk** 68
Fax: (410) 228-4216 **Alternate Tel:** n/a
Email: charlie@yachtmaintenanceco.com **Web:** yachtmaintenanceco.com
Nearest Town: Cambridge **Tourist Info:** (410) 228-3575

Navigational Information

Lat: 38°34.300' **Long:** 076°04.300' **Tide:** 3 ft. **Current:** n/a **Chart:** 12263
Rep. Depths (*MLW*): Entry 15 ft. **Fuel Dock** n/a **Max Slip/Moor** 12 ft./-
Access: Choptank River to Cambridge Creek

Marina Facilities *(In Season/Off Season)*

Fuel: No
Slips: 30 Total, 12 Transient **Max LOA:** 120 ft. **Max Beam:** 30 ft.
Rate *(per ft.)*: **Day** $1.00 **Week** n/a **Month** n/a
Power: 30 amp Incl., **50 amp** Incl., **100 amp** Inq., **200 amp** Inq.
Cable TV: No **Dockside Phone:** No
Dock Type: Fixed, Alongside
Moorings: 0 Total, 0 Transient **Launch:** n/a, Dinghy Dock
Rate: Day n/a **Week** n/a **Month** n/a
Heads: None
Laundry: None **Pay Phones:** No
Pump-Out: OnSite, Self Service **Fee:** $5 **Closed Heads:** Yes

Marina Operations

Owner/Manager: Charles R. Smith **Dockmaster:** Same
In-Season: Year-Round, 7am-4pm **Off-Season:** n/a
After-Hours Arrival: Call ahead
Reservations: Yes **Credit Cards:** Visa/MC, Dscvr, Amex
Discounts: None
Pets: No **Handicap Access:** No

Marina Services and Boat Supplies

Services - Docking Assistance, Megayacht Facilities, 300 amps **Communication -** FedEx, UPS, Express Mail **Supplies - OnSite:** Ships' Store **Near:** Ice *(Block, Cube)* **Under 1 mi:** Ice *(Shaved)*, Marine Discount Store *(R & D 228-0674)*, Bait/Tackle *(Pintail Pt. Outfitters 228-8353)*, Propane **3+ mi:** West Marine *(770-3080, 15 mi.)*

Boatyard Services

OnSite: Travelift *(68T)*, Railway *(400T)*, Engine mechanic *(gas, diesel)*, Electrical Repairs, Hull Repairs, Rigger, Bottom Cleaning, Brightwork, Air Conditioning, Refrigeration, Compound, Wash & Wax, Interior Cleaning, Propeller Repairs, Woodworking, Upholstery, Yacht Interiors, Metal Fabrication, Yacht Design, Yacht Building **OnCall:** Inflatable Repairs **Under 1 mi:** Sail Loft, Canvas Work, Life Raft Service. **Dealer for:** Onan, Caterpillar, Westerkeke Universal, Northern Lights, Yanmar, FlowScan, Perkins, Spurs, Tides Marine **Yard Rates:** $47/hr.

Restaurants and Accommodations

OnCall: Pizzeria *(Rusticana 228-1515, L $5-15, D $5-15)*, *(Pizza City 221-7500)* **Near:** Restaurant *(Great Wall 228-0332)*, *(Portside 228-9007)*, Seafood Shack *(Creek Side Seafood & Produce 221-1611, L $5-10, D $9-18, kids' $3-7, Tues-Thurs crab feast $22/7)* **Under 1 mi:** Restaurant *(Snappers Waterfront Café 228-0112, L $6-8, D $13-22)*, *(American Classics 901-6000)*, Lite Fare *(Moody John 901-2720, pool tables)*, *(Café on the Square 758-0471)*, *(Point Break Beach Bar 221-7850)*, Motel *(Holiday Inn 221-9900)*, Hotel *(Hyatt 901-6301)*, Inn/B&B *(Cambridge House 221-7700)*

Recreation and Entertainment

Near: Museum *(Richardson Maritime 221-1871, Wed & Sun 1-4pm, Sat 10am-4pm)*, Cultural Attract *(Sailwinds Park 228-7245)*, Sightseeing *(Historic Ghost Walk 228-7782, Thu-Sat 7 & 8pm; Harriet Tubman Walking tour)*, Special Events *(Seafood Feast - Aug; Choptank R. Beer & Wine Fest - Fall)* **Under 1 mi:** Tennis Courts *(Bay Country 228-9311)*, Fitness Center *(Cambridge 228-6710)*, Galleries *(High St. Gallery 221-9961)* **1-3 mi:** Golf Course *(Cambridge CC 221-0521)*, Bowling *(Cambridge 228-6823)*, Movie Theater *(Premiere 221-8688)*, Video Rental *(Videoland 228-3648)*

Provisioning and General Services

Near: Convenience Store *(Wawa 901-9794)*, Gourmet Shop *(A Few of My Favorite Things 221-1960)*, Farmers' Market *(Sailwinds Tue & Fri 8-12)*, Fishmonger *(Van Dyke's 228-9000)* **Under 1 mi:** Supermarket *(Food Lion 228-8328)*, Delicatessen *(221-8032)*, Bank/ATM, Post Office, Catholic Church, Library *(901-2880)*, Dry Cleaners, Bookstore *(Cambridge 901-9950)*, Hardware Store *(Ace 228-9391)* **1-3 mi:** Liquor Store *(Jinx's 643-5437)*, Laundry *(228-0779)*, Pharmacy *(Craig's 228-3322)*, Department Store *(Kmart 228-0809)*

Transportation

OnCall: Rental Car *(Enterprise 901-2978)*, Taxi *(Moxeys 221-0698)*, Airport Limo *(Eastern Shore 800-453-2023)* **Airport:** BWI *(65 mi.)*

Medical Services

911 Service **Near:** Doctor *(Black Water 228-1068)*, Chiropractor *(Cambridge 221-0781)* **Under 1 mi:** Dentist *(Harbor 228-5445)*, Veterinarian *(Choptank 221-0444)* **Hospital:** Dorchester 228-5511 *(W/in 1 mi)*

Setting -- Entering Cambridge Creek, the first building to port - cream-colored with a turquoise roof - is Governor's Hall at Sailwinds Park. Next is the back of a gray boat shed emblazoned with a large red "Yacht Maintenance Company Inc" and a half-hull. The boatyard's docks run in front of their 4 red brick work buildings with views of the creek and an attractive condominium complex. This is a significant working shipyard and purports to be nothing else.

Marina Notes -- Since 1980; extensive maintenance facility and shipyard serving commercial and pleasure vessels - wood, fiberglass, aluminum or steel. Imron, Awlgrip, TBT paint applications, Osmotic Blister repairs. 68-ton travelift and 400-ton railway. Several huge work sheds with accompanying work slips. YMC also offers good quality transient dockage - in slips on one long dock and also alongside dockage in two other areas, with virtually no amenities. Plus on-the-hard storage. No dedicated heads and no showers; the head in the office is available during business hours.

Notable -- Sail sculptures soar above adjacent 35-acre Sailwinds Park - home to the Visitors' Center (with exhibits about Dorchester), 14,000 sq. ft. Governor's Hall - a large performance venue which hosts a variety of events, festivals, and a popular concert series - plus a boardwalk leading to the fishing pier and Everybody's Playspace. In the planning stage is a 300-room hotel, a marina, playground, wetlands interpretive center, and a public beach. Ground has also been broken for the new $10 million Richardson Maritime Heritage Center to open in 2008 along Cambridge Creek. It will initially occupy 3 buildings, linked by catwalks, that combine the collections of both the Brannock and Richardson Maritime Museums, celebrating Cambridge's 250 years of shipbuilding tradition.

PHOTOS ON CD-ROM: 10

Navigational Information
Lat: 38°33.950' **Long:** 076°04.400' **Tide:** 1 ft. **Current:** n/a **Chart:** 12263
Rep. Depths (*MLW*): Entry 7 ft. **Fuel Dock** n/a **Max Slip/Moor** 10 ft./-
Access: Choptank River to the head of Cambridge Creek

Marina Facilities *(In Season/Off Season)*
Fuel: No
Slips: 50 Total, 5 Transient **Max LOA:** 120 ft. **Max Beam:** n/a
Rate *(per ft.)*: **Day** $1.00 **Week** Inq. **Month** Inq.
Power: 30 amp $3, **50 amp** $5, **100 amp** n/a, **200 amp** n/a
Cable TV: No **Dockside Phone:** No
Dock Type: Fixed, Pilings, Wood
Moorings: 0 Total, 0 Transient **Launch:** n/a
Rate: Day n/a **Week** n/a **Month** n/a
Heads: 2 Toilet(s), 2 Shower(s)
Laundry: None **Pay Phones:** No
Pump-Out: Full Service, 50 InSlip **Fee:** n/a **Closed Heads:** Yes

Marina Operations
Owner/Manager: Eddie Wheatley **Dockmaster:** Same
In-Season: Year-Round*, 7:30am-5pm **Off-Season:** n/a
After-Hours Arrival: Call in Advance
Reservations: Yes **Credit Cards:** Visa/MC
Discounts: Boat/US; West Marine **Dockage:** 25% **Fuel:** n/a **Repair:** 10%
Pets: Welcome **Handicap Access:** No

Generation III Marina

205 Cedar Street; Cambridge, MD 21613

Tel: (410) 228-2520 **VHF: Monitor** 16 **Talk** 29
Fax: (410) 228-5906 **Alternate Tel:** n/a
Email: n/a **Web:** n/a
Nearest Town: Cambridge **Tourist Info:** (410) 228-3575

Marina Services and Boat Supplies
Services - Docking Assistance, Concierge **Communication -** Mail & Package Hold, Phone Messages, Fax in/out, FedEx, UPS, Express Mail **Supplies - Near:** Ice *(Block, Cube)*, Ships' Store, Bait/Tackle *(Pintail Point Outfitters 228-8353)*, Propane *(Pep-Up 376-0011)* **Under 1 mi:** Marine Discount Store *(West Marine)*

Boatyard Services
OnSite: Travelift *(50T)*, Crane, Hydraulic Trailer, Engine mechanic *(gas, diesel)*, Electrical Repairs, Electronics Repairs, Hull Repairs, Rigger, Bottom Cleaning, Brightwork, Compound, Wash & Wax, Interior Cleaning, Woodworking, Yacht Interiors, Metal Fabrication, Painting, Awlgrip, Yacht Design, Yacht Building, Total Refits **OnCall:** Canvas Work, Air Conditioning, Refrigeration, Propeller Repairs, Inflatable Repairs, Life Raft Service, Upholstery **Near:** Launching Ramp, Sail Loft *(Cambridge Canvas & Sail 228-7414)*. **Member:** ABYC **Yard Rates:** $50-60/hr., Haul & Launch $6.50-8.50/ft. **Storage:** In-Water annual rates, On-Land $20-23/ft.

Restaurants and Accommodations
OnCall: Pizzeria *(Pizza City 221-7500)*, *(Rusticana 228-1515, L $5-15, D $5-15)* **Near:** Restaurant *(Portside 228-9007)*, *(Great Wall 228-0332)*, Seafood Shack *(Creek Side Seafood & Produce 221-1611, L $5-10, D $9-18, kids' $3-7, Tue-Thur crab feast $22/7)*, Hotel *(Hyatt 901-6301)* **Under 1 mi:** Restaurant *(Snappers 228-0112, L $6-8, D 13-22)*, *(American Classics 901-6000)*, *(Canvasback 221-5177, casual, fine-dining; Pub 11am-11pm $5-11)*, *(Spicer's Seafood 221-0222)*, Lite Fare *(Café On the Square 758-0471)*, *(Moody John 901-2720, pool tables)*, *(Point Break Beach Bar 221-7850)*, Motel *(Holiday Inn 221-9900)*, Inn/B&B *(Cambridge House 221-7700)*

Recreation and Entertainment
OnCall: Cultural Attract *(Blackwater Refuge Bird Sanctuary, tours available)* **Near:** Pool, Picnic Area, Grills, Playground *(Everybody's Playspace at Sailwind)*, Tennis Courts, Boat Rentals, Bowling *(Cambridge 228-6823)*, Park *(Harriet Tubman Mem. Garden)*, Museum *(Richardson Maritime 221-1871)*, Sightseeing *(Cambridge Lady tours - historic Cambridge $15, Michner's Chesapeake Tours $22, 221-0776)*, Special Events *(Sailwind)* **Under 1 mi:** Golf Course *(Cambridge CC 221-0521; River Marsh 901-1234)*, Video Rental *(Videoland 228-3648)*, Galleries *(High Street)*

Provisioning and General Services
Near: Wine/Beer, Bakery *(Bay Country Bakery 228-9111)*, Fishmonger *(Van Dyke's 228-9000)*, Bank/ATM, Post Office, Catholic Church, Protestant Church, Library *(901-2880)*, Dry Cleaners, Pharmacy *(Craig's 228-3322)* **Under 1 mi:** Convenience Store *(Wawa 901-9794)*, Supermarket *(Food Lion 228-8328)*, Liquor Store *(Jinx's 643-5437)*, Farmers' Market *(Sailwinds Tue & Fri 8am-noon)*, Laundry *(The Laundromat 228-0779)*, Hardware Store *(Ace 228-9391)*, Department Store *(KMart 228-0809)*

Transportation
OnSite: Courtesy Car/Van **OnCall:** Rental Car *(Enterprise 901-2978)*, Taxi *(Moxeys 221-0698)*, Airport Limo *(Eastern Shore 800-453-2023)*
Near: Bikes **Airport:** Baltimore-Washington Int'l./Dorchester *(65 mi./2 mi.)*

Medical Services
911 Service **OnCall:** Ambulance **Under 1 mi:** Doctor *(Black Water Medical 228-1068)*, Dentist *(Taylor 228-2980)*, Chiropractor *(Cambridge Chiro 221-0781)*, Veterinarian **Hospital:** Dorchester General 228-5511 *(1 mi.)*

Setting -- At the navigable head of mile-long Cambridge Creek, on the far side of the drawbridge, Generation III's docks line the shore. The creek is deep and narrow and the marina's slips are very protected. An attractive contemporary farmhouse-style two-story gray sided main office, which fronts a large storage shed, is trimmed in charcoal and carefully landscaped with annuals and perennial groundcover. The rest of the facility is neatly graveled.

Marina Notes -- *Closed Sat & Sun. Caters to sport fishing boats. Individual pump-out at every slip, also available to public Mon-Fri- 7:30am-4:30pm. Specializes in custom fabrication, interior redesigning, canvas repairs, deck repairs and replacement, fiberglass work, bottom and topside spray painting. Boat/US cooperating marina. Two complete, perfectly adequate, bathrooms have wallpapered walls and linoleum floors. Drawbridge is manned 24 hrs. Nearby Snapper's Restaurant offers overnight dockage if you eat at the restaurant ($1.50/ft. otherwise) and has a function room that can accommodate 40.

Notable -- Once a "town in transition," which for years "experienced no significant growth," Cambridge is now a jubilant Phoenix rising from the ashes. New investments, the arrival of the Hyatt, and an energetic and visionary citizenry have conspired to reinvigorate this early shipbuilding center to its moneyed glory days - then fueled by lumber and flour mills and oyster packing. Where skipjacks and schooners once jammed the shores of the creek, condo complexes and restaurants are now sprouting - replacing stagnant land and boatyard detritus. Downtown is an easy walk and the storefronts are gradually filling with upscale shops and eateries. The large Historic District invites a stroll, walking tour in hand - stop at the Dorchester Arts Center and Richardson Maritime Museum.

PHOTOS ON CD-ROM: 9

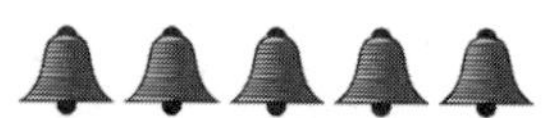

River Marsh Marina

100 Heron Boulevard; Cambridge, MD 21613

Tel: (410) 901-6383 **VHF: Monitor** 09 **Talk** 72
Fax: (410) 901-6619 **Alternate Tel:** (410) 901-1234
Email: jharper@chesapo.hyatt.com **Web:** chesapeakebay.hyatt.com
Nearest Town: Cambridge *(2 mi.)* **Tourist Info:** (410) 228-3575

Navigational Information

Lat: 38°33.698' **Long:** 076°02.531' **Tide:** 3 ft. **Current:** n/a **Chart:** 12263
Rep. Depths (*MLW*): Entry 10 ft. **Fuel Dock** 10 ft. **Max Slip/Moor** 10 ft./-
Access: 16 mi. from mouth of Choptank, past Rt. 50 bridge on starbord side

Marina Facilities *(In Season/Off Season)*

Fuel: Gasoline, Diesel
Slips: 150 Total, 150 Transient **Max LOA:** 200 ft. **Max Beam:** 25 ft.
Rate *(per ft.)*: **Day** $3.00/Inq.* **Week** $10 **Month** Inq.
Power: 30 amp $6, **50 amp** $12, **100 amp** $24, **200 amp** n/a
Cable TV: Yes Free **Dockside Phone:** No
Dock Type: Fixed, Floating, Long Fingers, Alongside, Concrete, Wood
Moorings: 0 Total, 0 Transient **Launch:** n/a, Dinghy Dock
Rate: Day n/a **Week** n/a **Month** n/a
Heads: 10 Toilet(s), 10 Shower(s), Hair Dryers
Laundry: 2 Washer(s), 2 Dryer(s) **Pay Phones:** Yes
Pump-Out: OnSite, 1 Central **Fee:** $5 **Closed Heads:** Yes

Marina Operations

Owner/Manager: John Harper **Dockmaster:** Eddy Shorter
In-Season: Apr 15-Oct 15, 8am-8pm **Off-Season:** Oct 16-Apr 14, 8am-5pm
After-Hours Arrival: Call 410-901-1234 for assistance
Reservations: Yes, Required **Credit Cards:** Visa/MC, Dscvr, Din, Amex
Discounts: Marinalife **Dockage:** F&S 10% **Fuel:** F&S 10% **Repair:** n/a
Pets: Welcome, Dog Walk Area **Handicap Access:** Yes, Heads, Docks

Marina Services and Boat Supplies

Services - Docking Assistance, Concierge, Security *(24 hrs., Hotel security)*, Trash Pick-Up, Dock Carts, Megayacht Facilities **Communication -** Mail & Package Hold, Fax in/out *($2)*, Data Ports *(T-Mobile Hotspots)*, FedEx, DHL, UPS, Express Mail *(Sat Del)* **Supplies - OnSite:** Ice *(Block, Cube)*, Ships' Store *(The Quarterdeck)* **Near:** Bait/Tackle *(Pintail Pt. Outfitters 228-8353)* **Under 1 mi:** Marine Discount Store *(R & D Boat Supply 228-0674)* **1-3 mi:** Propane *(Pep-Up 376-0011)* **3+ mi:** West Marine *(770-3080, 15 mi.)*

Boatyard Services

Nearest Yard: Yacht Maintenance Co. (410) 228-8878

Restaurants and Accommodations

OnSite: Restaurant *(Water's Edge 901-6383, L $10-15, D $22-30, at Hyatt Resort)*, *(Blue Point Provision Co. 901-6383, at the marina, opens at 5pm)*, Coffee Shop *(Bay Country Market Starbucks 901-6383)*, Lite Fare *(Dock's Poolside 901-6383)*, *(Eagle's Nest 901-6383)*, *(Michner Library 901-6383, entertainment Fri & Sat 8pm-Mid)*, Hotel *(Hyatt Regency 901-6301, $89-450)* **OnCall:** Pizzeria *(Pizza City 221-7500)* **Near:** Restaurant *(Spicer's Seafood 221-0222)*, Motel *(Holiday Inn 221-9900)* **Under 1 mi:** Restaurant *(Town & Country Café & Deli 901-6000, L $4-9, D $9-14)*, Lite Fare *(Moody John 901-2720, L $4-10, D $12-25, pool tables)* **1-3 mi:** Inn/B&B *(Cambridge House 221-7700, $129)*

Recreation and Entertainment

OnSite: Heated Pool *(4)*, Spa, Beach *(2)*, Picnic Area, Playground *(1,000 sq. ft. Pirates Cove)*, Tennis Courts *(4 lighted)*, Golf Course *(18-hole, par-71, Keith Foster design - $45-108, mini-golf too)*, Fitness Center, Boat Rentals *(Kayaks & canoes; Sailing lessons)*, Roller Blade/Bike Paths, Fishing Charter *(Orvis Fly Fishing)*, Group Fishing Boat, Volleyball, Video Arcade **OnCall:** Sightseeing *(Blackwater Refuge Bird Sanctuary, tours available)* **Near:** Bowling *(Cambridge Bowling 228-6823)* **Under 1 mi:** Movie Theater *(Premiere 221-8688)* **1-3 mi:** Video Rental *(Videoland 228-3648)*, Park, Museum *(Richardson Maritime 221-1871, Wed & Sun 1-4pm, Sat 10-4pm)*

Provisioning and General Services

OnSite: Convenience Store *(or Wawa 901-9794, w/in 1 mi.)*, Liquor Store *(or Jinx's 643-5437, 2 mi.)*, Bank/ATM, Beauty Salon *(Stillwater Spa)*, Newsstand, Clothing Store, Retail Shops **Under 1 mi:** Supermarket *(Food Lion 228-8328)*, Bakery *(Bay Country 228-9111)* **1-3 mi:** Gourmet Shop *(A Few of My Favorite Things 221-1960)*, Farmers' Market *(Sailwinds Tue & Fri 8-noon)*, Fishmonger *(Van Dyke's 228-9000)*, Post Office, Catholic Church, Protestant Church, Synagogue, Library *(901-2880)*, Dry Cleaners *(Skip Jack 221-1101)*, Bookstore *(Cambridge 901-9950)*, Pharmacy *(Craig's 228-3322)*, Hardware Store *(Ace 228-9391)*, Department Store *(Kmart 228-0809)*

Transportation

OnCall: Rental Car *(Enterprise 901-2978)*, Taxi *(Moxeys 221-0698)*, Airport Limo *(Eastern Shore 800-453-2023)* **1-3 mi:** Local Bus **3+ mi:** Rail *(Amtrak 672-6167, 66 mi.)* **Airport:** Baltimore/Washington Int'l. *(66 mi.)*

Medical Services

911 Service **OnSite:** Holistic Services *(Stillwater Spa - 60 min. massage $115, $20/pp to use facilies w/out treatment)* **OnCall:** Ambulance **Near:** Veterinarian *(Bayside 228-1479)* **Under 1 mi:** Chiropractor *(Cambridge 221-0781)* **Hospital:** Dorchester General 228-5511 *(2 mi.)*

PHOTOS ON CD-ROM: 16

Setting -- A half-mile past the 50 ft. Rt. 50 bridge, River Marsh Marina and the majestic 342 acre Hyatt Regency's Chesapeake Bay Resort sprawl along the starboard side. Before arriving at the 150-slip marina, boaters pass the 18-hole golf course, two beaches and the 6-story 400-room hotel with Raven's View cupola & 2-story glass-enclosed Wintergarden pool - surrounded by lushly landscaped grounds. Three sets of floating docks are protected by a breakwater.

Marina Notes -- *$1.50/ft. Sun-Thu, $3/ft. Fri, Sat, Hol. & special events. Special rates for hotel guests. Well-supplied ships' store. One of 5 eateries, Blue Point Provision is dockside. 24 hr. valet transport around the resort. Marina guests are full-fledged guests of the Resort - follow the shell path to four pools, Jacuzzi, tennis courts, miniature golf, activities room, health club, volleyball, and concierge services. Fees for the Stillwater Spa, the River Marsh Golf Club, beach rentals and Camp Hyatt at Pirates Cove (ages 4-12 - half/full day $30-55/child). 42,000 square feet of flexible indoor/outdoor event space. A surprisingly basic bathhouse features 10 individual bathrooms (albeit with hairdryers). A nicer one is off the pool. Pets only permitted in marina & 11 pet-friendly rooms.

Notable -- Creative touches abound, raising this destination far above the ordinary. The Wintergarden pool's eastern wall lifts to open it to the outside; the hot tub straddles inside/outside. Sat nights movies are projected above the pool; watch from the water. The fire pit hosts nightly "s'more roasts." Flyfish with an Orvis guide in Shoal Creek. Take a guided hike through 8-acre Blue Heron Preserve or tour the Blackwater Wildlife Refuge. Cushioned chaises surround pools with slides and fountains. 500' of beach features water toys and anchored islands. Cozy fireplaced nooks for reading or billiards surround the Michner Library.

10. Eastern Shore: Choptank To Cape Charles

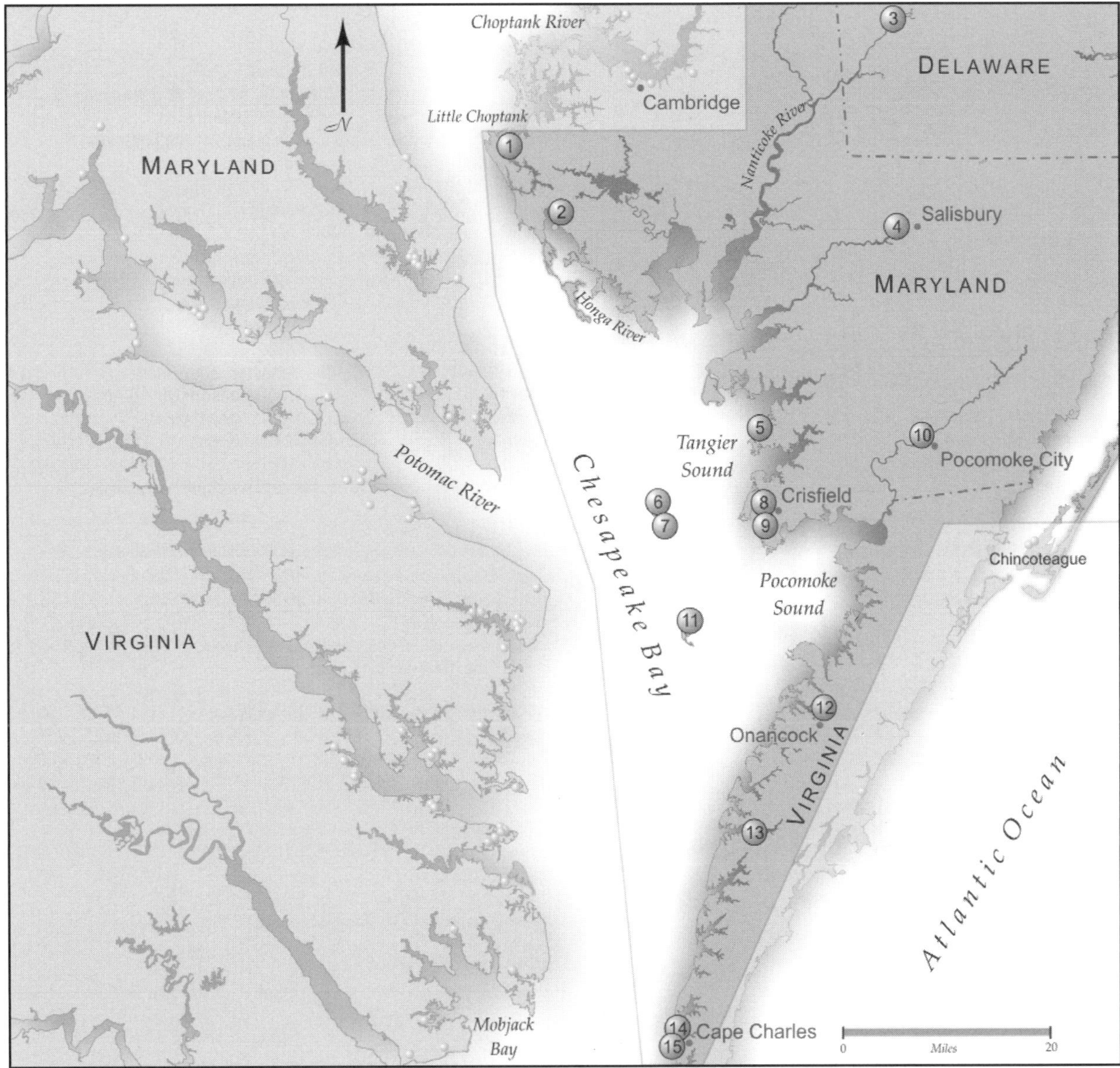

MAP	MARINA	HARBOR	PAGE	MAP	MARINA	HARBOR	PAGE
1	**Taylors Island Marina**	*Little Choptank/Slaughter Cr.*	186	9	**Somers Cove Marina**	*Little Annemessex River*	194
2	**Gootee's Marine**	*Honga River*	187	10	**Downtown Riverwalk Marina**	*Pocomoke River*	195
3	**Nanticoke River Marine Park**	*Nanticoke River*	188	11	**Parks' Marina**	*Tangier Channel*	196
4	**Port of Salisbury Marina**	*Wicomico River*	189	12	**Onancock Wharf**	*Onancock Creek*	197
5	**Goose Creek Marina**	*Manokin River/Goose Creek*	190	13	**Davis Wharf Marine Services**	*Occohannock River*	198
6	**Smith Island Marina**	*Big Thorofare/Smith Island Ch.*	191	14	**Bay Creek Marina & Resort**	*King's Creek*	199
7	**Tylerton County Dock**	*Tyler Ditch*	192	15	**Cape Charles Town Harbor**	*Cape Charles Harbor*	200
8	**Seamark Marine**	*Little Annemessex River*	193				

- **A "DCM" symbol in Marina Notes means Designated Clean Marina** — This is a coveted state-level award given to marinas that meet stringent, environmentally supportive requirements (see page 307). *For a list of DCM's & pump-out facilities, see page 308.*
- **Ratings & Reviews** — An explanation of the Atlantic Cruising Club's rating system, and a detailed explanation of what is in each section of the Marina Report is on pages 6 – 11. *The Data-Gathering Process is detailed on page 322.*
- **Marina Report Updates** — Updates to Marina Reports (from readers, ACC reviewers, and marinas) are posted regularly on *www.AtlanticCruisingClub.com.*

Taylors Island Marina

PO Box 188; Route 16; Taylors Island, MD 21669

Tel: (410) 397-3454 **VHF: Monitor** 16 **Talk** 68
Fax: n/a **Alternate Tel:** (410) 463-1846
Email: n/a **Web:** www.timarina.com
Nearest Town: Cambridge *(16 mi.)* **Tourist Info:** (410) 228-1000

Navigational Information

Lat: 38°28.567' **Long:** 076°17.150' **Tide:** 2 ft. **Current:** n/a **Chart:** 12263
Rep. Depths (*MLW*): Entry 6 ft. **Fuel Dock** n/a **Max Slip/Moor** -/-
Access: Little Choptank to Slaughter Creek

Marina Facilities *(In Season/Off Season)*

Fuel: *Shell* - Gasoline, Diesel, High-Speed Pumps
Slips: 110 Total, 50 Transient **Max LOA:** 60 ft. **Max Beam:** n/a
Rate *(per ft.)*: **Day** $45.00* **Week** n/a **Month** n/a
Power: 30 amp Incl., **50 amp** Incl., **100 amp** n/a, **200 amp** n/a
Cable TV: No **Dockside Phone:** No
Dock Type: Floating
Moorings: 0 Total, 15 Transient **Launch:** n/a
Rate: Day n/a **Week** n/a **Month** n/a
Heads: 2 Toilet(s), 2 Shower(s)
Laundry: 1 Washer(s), 1 Dryer(s) **Pay Phones:** No
Pump-Out: OnSite **Fee:** $5 **Closed Heads:** Yes

Marina Operations

Owner/Manager: Ken Smith **Dockmaster:** Same
In-Season: Mar-Dec, 8am-5pm **Off-Season:** Jan-Feb, Closed
After-Hours Arrival: Empty slips posted on store front door; pay next am
Reservations: No **Credit Cards:** Visa/MC, Dscvr
Discounts: None
Pets: Welcome, Dog Walk Area **Handicap Access:** No

Marina Services and Boat Supplies

Services - Trash Pick-Up, Dock Carts **Communication -** FedEx, UPS, Express Mail **Supplies - OnSite:** Ice *(Block, Cube)*, Ships' Store, West Marine, Bait/Tackle

Boatyard Services

OnSite: Travelift *(25T - new)*, Launching Ramp, Engine mechanic *(gas, diesel)*, Bottom Cleaning

Restaurants and Accommodations

OnSite: Restaurant *(Dockside Bar and Grill 397-3454, L $3-8, D $7-17, Dinner baskets $6-8. Pig Roast $15. closed Mon & Tues)* **3+ mi:** Restaurant *(Snappers Waterfront Café 228-0112, L $6-8, D $13-22, 17 mi.)*, *(Creek Side Seafood and Produce 221-1611, 17 mi.)*, *(Snappers Waterfront Cafe 228-0112, L $6-8, D $13-22, 15 mi.)*, Pizzeria *(Rusticana 228-1515, L $5-15, D $5-15, 17 mi.)*, Motel *(Days Inn 228-4444, 17 mi.)*, Hotel *(Holiday Inn 221-9900, 17 mi.)*, *(Hyatt 901-6301, 17 mi.)*

Recreation and Entertainment

OnSite: Pool, Beach, Picnic Area, Boat Rentals *(rowboats - with or without motors)*, Fishing Charter *(Miss Pritch - Merle (Jack) Samakow 221-1205 or Charles Thompson 901-2172)*, Sightseeing *(Taylors Island Wildlife Management Area)* **Under 1 mi:** Museum *(Taylors Island Museum 221-1207)* **3+ mi:** Tennis Courts *(Cambridge 228-6710, 17 mi.)*

Provisioning and General Services

OnSite: Wine/Beer, Crabs/Waterman, Hardware Store **Under 1 mi:** Market *(Taylor's Island General Store 221-2911)* **1-3 mi:** Post Office *(221-8570)*, Catholic Church, Protestant Church **3+ mi:** Supermarket *(Food Lion 228-8328, 17 mi.)*, Delicatessen *(Super Stop Deli 228-7301, 17 mi.)*, Pharmacy *(CVS 228-9030, 17 mi.)*

Transportation

OnSite: Bikes **3+ mi:** Rental Car *(Enterprise 901-2978, 17 mi.)*
Airport: Baltimore-Washington Int'l./Easton *(83 mi./63 mi.)*

Medical Services

911 Service **OnCall:** Ambulance **Hospital:** Dorchester General 228-5511 *(17 mi.)*

Setting -- Past Jame's Island, into the Little Choptank and up Slaughter Creek, Taylors Island Marina sits on a solid piece of upland with views of the open creek and a peaceful, pristine tidal marsh dotted with small groups of loblolly pine and cedar. Three docks host a combination of commercial and pleasure boats, and a basin is filled with the working boats of the nearby watermen's community. A very attractive pool sports a petite pool house spilling marigolds out of its window box. Quarry tile coping sets off the concrete patio furnished with new blue-green and white strap chaises. The floating Dockside restaurant is moored at the head of the docks. There's a small beach on the creek side of the marina.

Marina Notes -- *Dockage is flat rate. DCM. Founded in 1955; owned by present owner since 1970. Can handle large cruise groups and has an average of 50 transient slips. New 25-ton travelift. The fairly basic heads with key coded entry have faux tile walls with cement floors and gratings in the showers.

Notable -- All services are 17 miles away in Cambridge. The floating Dockside Bar and Grill's eleven tables seat over sixty. Closed Mon & Tue; Wed & Sun Noon-10pm, Thu-Sat Noon-2am. Kitchen closes every night at 9pm. Lunch includes sandwiches, burgers, salads, baskets and pizzas. At dinner, there are baskets, pizzas and platters -- the seafood platters are roughly $17. All kinds of special events, including pig roasts and fishing tournaments, are sponsored by Dockside. A dinghy is perfect for exploring the 1100 acre Taylors Island and the surrounding tidal marsh in search of wildlife (or rent rowboats from the marina). Raccoons, muskrats, river otters, white tailed and sika deer, Delmarva fox squirrels, ospreys, herons, egrets, ducks, and bald eagles can be spotted.

PHOTOS ON CD-ROM: 11

Gootee's Marine

1439 Hoopers Island Road; Church Creek, MD 21622

Tel: (410) 397-3122; (800) 792-0082 **VHF: Monitor** 19 **Talk** n/a
Fax: (410) 397-3183 **Alternate Tel:** n/a
Email: sales@gootees.com **Web:** www.gootees.com
Nearest Town: Cambridge *(17 mi.)* **Tourist Info:** (410) 228-1000

Navigational Information
Lat: 38°23.183' **Long:** 076°11.783' **Tide:** 4 ft. **Current:** n/a **Chart:** 12263
Rep. Depths (*MLW*): Entry 5 ft. **Fuel Dock** 5 ft. **Max Slip/Moor** -/6 ft.
Access: At the head of the Honga River

Marina Facilities *(In Season/Off Season)*
Fuel: *Shell* - Slip-Side Fueling, Gasoline, Diesel
Slips: 50 Total, 5 Transient **Max LOA:** 48 ft. **Max Beam:** 14 ft.
Rate *(per ft.)*: **Day** $40.00* **Week** $40 **Month** $100
Power: 30 amp n/a, **50 amp** n/a, **100 amp** n/a, **200 amp** n/a
Cable TV: No **Dockside Phone:** No
Dock Type: n/a
Moorings: 0 Total, 0 Transient **Launch:** n/a
Rate: Day n/a **Week** n/a **Month** n/a
Heads: 1 Toilet(s)
Laundry: None **Pay Phones:** Yes, 1
Pump-Out: Onsite *(7:30am-5pm)*, Self Service **Fee:** $5 **Closed Heads:** Yes

Marina Operations
Owner/Manager: Gootee Family **Dockmaster:** Same
In-Season: Year-Round, 7:30am-5pm** **Off-Season:** n/a
After-Hours Arrival: Call ahead
Reservations: Required **Credit Cards:** Visa/MC
Discounts: None
Pets: Welcome **Handicap Access:** No

Marina Services and Boat Supplies
Communication - UPS, Express Mail **Supplies - OnSite:** Ice *(Block)*
3+ mi: Bait/Tackle *(8 mi.)*

Boatyard Services
OnSite: Travelift *(25T)*, Launching Ramp, Rigger, Bottom Cleaning, Brightwork, Compound, Wash & Wax **OnCall:** Sail Loft, Canvas Work, Interior Cleaning, Metal Fabrication, Painting, Awlgrip **Near:** Yacht Design. **Dealer for:** Hydra-Sports, Yamaha, Load-Rite, May-Craft, . Other Certifications: Yamaha Outboards

Restaurants and Accommodations
Near: Restaurant *(J-Bird's Church Creek Cafe' 228-1900, L $2-7, D $8-16)* **3+ mi:** Restaurant *(Snappers Waterfront Café 228-0112, L $6-8, D $13-22, 17 mi.)*, *(Creek Side Seafood and Produce 221-1611, L $5-10, D $9-18, 17 mi.)*, Pizzeria *(Rusticana 228-1515, L $5-15, D $5-15, 17 mi.)*, Motel *(Holiday Inn 221-9900, 17 mi.)*, Inn/B&B *(Hyatt 901-1234, 17 mi.)*

Recreation and Entertainment
OnSite: Fishing Charter, Group Fishing Boat *(Striker& Fish Magnet 46-ft., 20 passengers Capts. Philip & Henry Gootee 397-3851 $600/day for 8, $55/pp thereafter up to 20)* **3+ mi:** Golf Course *(Cambridge 228-6710, 17 mi.)*, Sightseeing *(Blackwater National Wildlife Refuge 228-2677 $3 for vehicle, $1 bicycle Mon-Fri 8am-4pm, Sat-Sun 9am-5pm. Two wildlife drives 3.5 & 6.5 mi. plus walking trails, 5 mi.)*

Provisioning and General Services
1-3 mi: Market *(King's Pride Grocery 397-3123)* **3+ mi:** Convenience Store *(10 mi.)*, Supermarket *(17 mi.)*, Wine/Beer *(8 mi.)*, Liquor Store *(8 mi.)*, Green Grocer *(12 mi.)*, Bank/ATM *(15 mi.)*, Post Office *(10 mi.)*, Catholic Church *(5 mi.)*, Library *(Cambridge 901-2880, 17 mi.)*, Pharmacy *(CVS 228-9030, 17 mi.)*, Hardware Store *(Ace 228-9391, 17 mi.)*, Department Store *(Wal-Mart 221-0704, 17 mi.)*

Transportation
OnCall: Rental Car *(Enterprise 901-2978, 17 mi.)*
Airport: Baltimore/Washington Int'l./Easton *(83 mi./75 mi.)*

Medical Services
911 Service **OnCall:** Ambulance
Hospital: Dorchester General 228-5511 *(17 mi.)*

Setting -- Five miles up the Honga River, under two 65' bridges, Gootee's is just before Hoopers Island. The docks of this immaculate operation emanate from the paved parking lot on the port side of narrow on Wallace Creek. The starboard side is densely wooded and undeveloped.

Marina Notes -- *Dockage is flat rate. Daily & weekly rates the same. **Open Mon-Fri 7:30am-5pm, Sat 7:30am-2pm. Advanced reservations key. Family-owned and operated since 1955. Focus is on boats to 33 feet, but can accommodate boats into the high 40s. The Honga is shallow and was dredged to 5 ft. MLW in 2004. Attractive, well-merchandised store with one of the largest inventories of boating supplies on the Delmarva Peninsula also has snacks, sundries and drinks. The marina, fuel dock and store keep the same hours. Members of the Gootee family were instrumental in the original design and development of the May-Craft line of boats in the early 1990s and can assist with customizations. No showers; heads are in the store - open during store hours.

Notable -- Gootees makes a good tie-up after a leisurely cruise up the river. Wildlife viewing is improving along the Honga. A colony of more than 7,500 once-endangered brown pelicans has nested on Barren Island and bird watchers report sightings of bald eagles and a variety of unexpected species. About 5 miles away, the 23,000-acre Blackwater National Wildlife Refuge was established in 1933 as a refuge for migratory birds. It's one of the main wintering areas for birds using the Atlantic Flyway - including about 35,000 Canada geese and 15,000 ducks - and also a haven for bald eagles, peregrine falcons, and the Delmarva fox squirrels. At the intersection of Routes 335 & 336 in Golden Hill, Gootee's is 17 miles from central Cambridge.

PHOTOS ON CD-ROM: 9

Nanticoke River Marine Park

26 North Market Street; Blades, DE 19973

Tel: (302) 628-8600 **VHF: Monitor** 16 **Talk** n/a
Fax: (302) 628-8014 **Alternate Tel:** (302) 629-8683
Email: NanticokeRiverMarina@msn.com **Web:** *(see marina notes)
Nearest Town: Seaford *(0.1 mi.)* **Tourist Info:** (302) 739-4271

Navigational Information
Lat: 38°38.267' **Long:** 075°36.617' **Tide:** 3.3 ft. **Current:** 3 kt. **Chart:** 12261
Rep. Depths (*MLW*): Entry 6 ft. **Fuel Dock** 6 ft. **Max Slip/Moor** 6 ft./-
Access: 35 miles up the Nanticoke River

Marina Facilities *(In Season/Off Season)*
Fuel: Slip-Side Fueling, Gasoline, Diesel
Slips: 87 Total, 30 Transient **Max LOA:** 60 ft. **Max Beam:** 20 ft.
Rate *(per ft.)*: **Day** $1.50* **Week** $3.00 **Month** $6.00
Power: 30 amp $3, **50 amp** $5, **100 amp** n/a, **200 amp** n/a
Cable TV: No **Dockside Phone:** No
Dock Type: Floating, Long Fingers, Concrete
Moorings: 0 Total, 0 Transient **Launch:** yes
Rate: Day n/a **Week** n/a **Month** n/a
Heads: 2 Toilet(s), 2 Shower(s)
Laundry: 1 Washer(s), 1 Dryer(s) **Pay Phones:** No
Pump-Out: OnCall **Fee:** Free **Closed Heads:** Yes

Marina Operations
Owner/Manager: B.E.D.C.O. **Dockmaster:** Roland Downes
In-Season: May 1-Oct 31, 8am-5pm **Off-Season:** Nov 1-Apr 30, as needed
After-Hours Arrival: Call in advance
Reservations: Yes, Preferred **Credit Cards:** Visa/MC
Discounts: None
Pets: Welcome **Handicap Access:** Yes, Heads, Docks

Marina Services and Boat Supplies
Services - Docking Assistance, Boaters' Lounge, Crew Lounge, Security *(partial fenced property)*, Trash Pick-Up, Dock Carts **Communication -** Fax in/out *(Free)*, FedEx, UPS, Express Mail **Supplies - OnSite:** Ice *(Block)* **OnCall:** Propane *(Peninsuca Oil)* **1-3 mi:** Bait/Tackle *(Taylored 629-9017)*

Boatyard Services
OnSite: Travelift *(20T)*, Launching Ramp, Engine mechanic *(gas, diesel)*, Hull Repairs, Bottom Cleaning, Brightwork, Air Conditioning, Refrigeration, Compound, Wash & Wax **OnCall:** Electrical Repairs, Electronic Sales, Electronics Repairs, Sail Loft, Canvas Work, Divers, Interior Cleaning, Propeller Repairs ABYC - 1 Certified Tech(s) **Yard Rates:** $55/hr., Haul & Launch $6/ft. *(blocking $2/ft.)*, Power Wash $2/ft., Bottom Paint $8/ft.

Restaurants and Accommodations
OnSite: Restaurant *(Skipjacks 628-8600, B $2-6, L $5-9, D $11-23, kids' breakfast $2-3, Sun brunch)* **OnCall:** Pizzeria *(Domino's 628-5000)* **Near:** Restaurant *(Bon Appetit 629-3700)*, Coffee Shop *(Autumn Bay 628-5282)*,Lite Fare *(Truitts Sub Shop 629-7970, L $6-9, D $6-9)* **Under 1 mi:**Restaurant *(Dugout 629-8149)*, *(Hong Kong 629-5101)*, *(Café Milano 629-9403)*, Fast Food *(Hardee's, Arby's)*, Pizzeria *Pizza King 629-6003)*, Motel *(Best Western 629-8385)*, Hotel *(Hampton Inn 629-4500)*, *(Holiday Inn 629-2000)*

Recreation and Entertainment
Near: Playground, Park, Museum *(Seaford Museum, Gov. Boss Mansion)*, Sightseeing *(Seaford City Hall Annex antique fire engines)* **Under 1 mi:** Fitness Center, Video Rental *(Blockbuster 628-9302)* **1-3 mi:** Pool, Tennis Courts *(Seaford Racquetball and Nautilus Fitness Center 629-9100)*, Golf Course *(Woodland 628-9700)*, Bowling *(Seaford Bowling Lanes 629-9778)*

Provisioning and General Services
Near: Convenience Store *(Uncle Willy's - Blade 629-9321, Royal Farms - Seaford 628-4620)*, Bakery *(Elegante 628-8090)*, Market *(Jars Spanish-American 28-3935)*, Bank/ATM, Beauty Salon *(Ray Adkins 629-5213)*, Barber Shop *(Dick's 629-2073)*, Florist **Under 1 mi:** Health Food *(Open Cupboard 629-6147)*, Wine/Beer, Liquor Store, Fishmonger *(Harbor House 629-0444)*, Catholic Church, Protestant Church, Library *(Seaford 629-2524)*, Dry Cleaners **1-3 mi:** Supermarket *(Food Lion 629-6309, Shore Stop 629-3100)*, Delicatessen *(Truitts Sub Shop 629-7970)*, Meat Market, Post Office, Pharmacy *(Eckerd 628-1297)*, Hardware Store *(Burton Brothers 629-8595)*, Clothing Store, Retail Shops *(Browsery-Amish & other Antique Shops)*, Department Store *(Wal-Mart 628-1668)*, Copies Etc.

Transportation
OnCall: Rental Car *(Enterprise 528-2931, Nanticoke Auto)*, Taxi *(City Cab 628-2588)*, Airport Limo *(Nylon Capital 629-9548)*
Airport: Salisbury, MD *(14 mi.)*

Medical Services
911 Service **OnCall:** Ambulance **Near:** Holistic Services *(Serenityville Massage; Jessica's Body Shop 628-4283)* **1-3 mi:** Doctor *(Aguillon 629-6664)*, Dentist *(Seaford Dental 629-3008)*, Chiropractor *(Seaford Chiropractic 629-4710)* **Hospital:** Nanticoke Memorial Medical Center *(1 mi.)*

Setting -- Thirty-five miles up the heavily forested Nanticoke River, past two 50-foot fixed bridges and a cable ferry crossing, are the twin towns of Seaford and Blades - so far up that it's Delaware. On the Blades side, recent vinyl-edged, floating cement docks lie just off the river in a round, peaceful basin presided over by a contemporary gray colonial with white trim. A pavilion shelters a half dozen picnic tables and charcoal grills. The Nanticoke River Yacht Club is onsite, a well-reviewed eatery is next door and, a very short walk across the bridge, the town of Seaford's triangular town green and small park welcomes visitors.

Marina Notes -- *$3/ft. weekend, holidays, special events, Sun-Thu $1.50/ft. The railroad bridge is open to marine traffic from Mar 15-Nov 15, 5am-11pm, or by calling (717) 541-2121 (allowing 2.5 hours' notice). A poured-pan concrete Unideck dock system, with full-length finger piers and hi-ghend pedestals, follows the curved edge of the basin. On-site 20-ton travelift and launching ramp for haul out. The new key coded heads and showers are in the gray Colonial main building. *(Website soon to be available: www.nanticokerivermarina.com)

Notable -- Adjacent Skipjack Restaurant, featuring seafood and barbecue, has a 2nd floor eating deck with a partial view of the docks and an indoor dining room open Tue-Sun (lunch 11am-4pm, dinner Tue-Fri 4-9pm, wknds to 10pm, Sun brunch, too). The Nanticoke is unique among Chesapeake tributaries because of the extensive unbroken forests that line its shore. 38% of the watershed is forest, the largest on the Delmarva; it's renowned as a waterfowl habitat. Anglers find a wide variety of species, especially tournament-quality largemouth bass - plus the river supports a commercial crab fishery as well.

Navigational Information

Lat: 38°21.867' **Long:** 075°36.433' **Tide:** 4 ft. **Current:** n/a **Chart:** 12261
Rep. Depths (*MLW*): Entry 40 ft. **Fuel Dock** 15 ft. **Max Slip/Moor** 17 ft./-
Access: 18 miles up the Wicomico River

Marina Facilities *(In Season/Off Season)*

Fuel: Gasoline, Diesel
Slips: 86 Total, 10 Transient **Max LOA:** 100 ft. **Max Beam:** 35 ft.
Rate *(per ft.)*: **Day** $1.00/1.00 **Week** n/a **Month** $4.00/2.50
Power: 30 amp Incl., **50 amp** Incl., **100 amp** n/a, **200 amp** n/a
Cable TV: No **Dockside Phone:** No
Dock Type: Fixed
Moorings: 0 Total, 0 Transient **Launch:** No
Rate: Day n/a **Week** n/a **Month** n/a
Heads: 4 Toilet(s), 4 Shower(s)
Laundry: None **Pay Phones:** No
Pump-Out: Self Service, 1 Central **Fee:** $5 **Closed Heads:** Yes

Marina Operations

Owner/Manager: Paul Lewis **Dockmaster:** Same
In-Season: May-Oct, 8am-8pm **Off-Season:** Nov-Apr, 10am-5pm
After-Hours Arrival: Call ahead
Reservations: No **Credit Cards:** Visa/MC
Discounts: None
Pets: Welcome, Dog Walk Area **Handicap Access:** Yes

Port of Salisbury Marina

506 West Main Street; Salisbury, MD 21801

Tel: (410) 548-3176 **VHF: Monitor** 16 **Talk** 16
Fax: (410) 548-3176 **Alternate Tel:** (410) 572-2060
Email: n/a **Web:** www.coastalproperties.com
Nearest Town: Salisbury *(0.1 mi.)* **Tourist Info:** (410) 651-2968

Marina Services and Boat Supplies

Communication - FedEx, UPS, Express Mail **Supplies - OnSite:** Ice *(Block, Cube)* **Under 1 mi:** Bait/Tackle *(Salisbury Fly Shop 435-8359)*, Propane *(Sharp Energy 749-4147)* **1-3 mi:** Boater's World *(548-3493)*, Live Bait *(Cast & Hook Bait & Tackle Shop 749-1882)*

Restaurants and Accommodations

OnSite: Restaurant *(Brew River Restaurant & Bar 677-6757, L $6-11, D $9-23, kids' $4-6, Sun brunch $5-10)* **OnCall:** Pizzeria *(Lombardi's Italian 749-0522)*, *(Pizza City 546-3800)* **Near:** Restaurant *(City Bistro 341-0606)*, *(Chesapeake Treasures 860-1488, L $3-17, D $8-17)*, *(Market St. Inn 742-4145, L $5-12, D $16-22, award-winning wine list)*, Lite Fare *(Downtown Deli 749-0611)* **Under 1 mi:** Restaurant *(Cajun Café at Flannery's 546-2570)*, *(Grill Kabob Halal 341-6767)*, Coffee Shop *(Tyme For Tea 677-4766)*, Motel *(Towne House 742-5135)*, Hotel *(Ramada 546-4400)* **1-3 mi:** Motel *(Economy Inn 749-6178)*, *(Temple Hill 742-3284)*, Hotel *(Best Western 546-1300)*

Recreation and Entertainment

OnSite: Picnic Area, Sightseeing *(Capt. Cole's Wicomico R. Cruises 546-1753 $10/5 - to Shed Pt.)* **Near:** Fitness Center *(Eastern Shore 742-7697)*, Fishing Charter *(Captain Cole's 546-1753)*, Galleries *(Art Institute & Gallery 546-4748)*, Special Events *(Pemberton Park Colonial Fair - late Sep)* **Under 1 mi:** Golf Course *(Nutters Crossing 860-4653)*, Cultural Attract *(Salisbury Zoo 548-3165 Free; Delmarva Shorebirds, Class A minor league team at Purdue Stadium)* **1-3 mi:** Boat Rentals *(Survival Products 543-1244)*, Bowling *(Cherokee Lanes 742-3030)*, Movie Theater *(Regal 10 543-0902)*, Video Rental *(Blockbuster 548-1200)*, Park *(Pemberton Park 860-2447)*, Museum *(Ward Museum Of Wildfowl Art 742-4988 - bird carvings, decoys)*

Provisioning and General Services

Near: Delicatessen *(Pop's 543-4320)*, Farmers' Market *(Court House 713-2022 Sat 8-1, Wed 3-6)*, Meat Market *(Cornish's 749-6132)*, Bank/ATM, Library *(749-3612)*, Beauty Salon *(L A Hair 341-0021)*, Bookstore *(Market St. Books 219-3210)*, Pharmacy *(Riverside 742-1188)* **Under 1 mi:** Convenience Store *(Wawa 677-0384)*, Liquor Store *(Beverage Barn 749-0626)*, Bakery *(Schmidt 742-3121)*, Market *(Caribbean Express 860-0448)*, Post Office *(742-9261)*, Catholic Church, Protestant Church, Synagogue, Barber Shop *(Clark's 749-3010)*, Laundry *(Camden Heights 860-9800)*, Hardware Store *(True Value 548-2000)*, Florist *(Springer's Bouquet 742-6600)*, Department Store *(JC Penney 742-3269, Kmart 749-1145)*
1-3 mi: Supermarket *(Super Giant 742-1343)*, Health Food *(Healthful Habits 749-1997)*, Fishmonger *(Skipjack's 543-1644)*, Dry Cleaners *(Salisbury 546-0030)*, Copies Etc. *(Kinko's 546-199)* **3+ mi:** Green Grocer *(How Sweet It Is Produce 742-8600, 6 mi.)*, Buying Club *(Sam's 546-1031, 4 mi.)*

Transportation

OnCall: Taxi *(Bailey's 546-4025)*, Airport Limo *(Yellow Cab 749-3500)*
3+ mi: Rail *(Amtrak BWI 672-6167, 95 mi.)*
Airport: Baltimore-Washington Int'l./Wicomico County *(95 mi./6 mi.)*

Medical Services

911 Service **OnCall:** Ambulance **Near:** Doctor *(Reilly & Associates 543-9916)*, Dentist *(Salisbury Dental 749-7873)* **Under 1 mi:** Chiropractor *(Salisbury Chiro 749-6672)*, Veterinarian *(Salisbury Animal 749-4393)*
Hospital: Peninsula Regional 546-6400 *(0.4 mi.)*

Setting -- The deep, verdant Wicomico, well-maintained as a shipping channel, sees pleasure craft along with tugs and fishing barges. At the headwaters, an 18-mile run upriver, is Port of Salisbury Marina - a nicely developed municipal facility with stationary docks surrounding a small grassy peninsula dotted with picnic tables and charcoal grills. A pale gray two-story dockmaster's office, which houses the amenities, and the onsite Brew River restaurant complex both overlook the docks and tranquil river. The town center is an easy walk.

Marina Notes -- Three-quarter length finger piers and full-race pedestals. In the marina office is a laundry and four full bathrooms - basic, cinderblock municipal heads, but well-maintained and quite usable. Note: 2 cable ferries cross the river.

Notable -- The cupola and bell tower make it easy to spot the large, contemporary 2-story Brew River Restaurant & Bar (11am-11pm); it has an indoor window-walled dining room, deck seating, an outdoor bar area overlooking the marina and dock 'n' dine docks. Wicomico River Cruises' small but elegantly outfitted "Cheryl Ann" - leather seats, handmade pillows and throws - tours the river. Across the street is the main entrance to Perdue's Processing Plant. Within walking distance is a charming 2-block brick promenade landscaped with potted shrubs and flowers and lined with restored buildings. Professional offices, the City Bistro, Downtown Deli, plus several boutiques attract a loyal following of bay boaters. Sunday mornings, municipal parking lot No.10 hosts a flea market. Less than 1 mi. away, one of the best small zoos in the US, Salisbury Zoological Park, fronts the river (8am-7:30pm, MemDay-LabDay, to 4:30pm other times).

PHOTOS ON CD-ROM: 13

Goose Creek Marina

25763 Rumbley Road; Westover, MD 21871

Tel: (410) 651-1193 **VHF: Monitor** 16 **Talk** 66
Fax: (410) 651-1193 **Alternate Tel:** n/a
Email: felserfamilty@comcast.net **Web:** n/a
Nearest Town: Crisfield *(9 mi. by water)* **Tourist Info:** (410) 651-2968

Navigational Information
Lat: 38°05.550' **Long:** 075°51.667' **Tide:** n/a **Current:** n/a **Chart:** 12228
Rep. Depths (*MLW*): Entry 8 ft. **Fuel Dock** n/a **Max Slip/Moor** 6 ft./-
Access: Tangier Sound to Manokin River to Goose Creek

Marina Facilities *(In Season/Off Season)*
Fuel: Gasoline, Diesel
Slips: 70 Total, 8 Transient **Max LOA:** 45 ft. **Max Beam:** 18 ft.
Rate *(per ft.)*: **Day** $2.00 **Week** n/a **Month** n/a
Power: 30 amp Incl., **50 amp** n/a, **100 amp** n/a, **200 amp** n/a
Cable TV: No **Dockside Phone:** No
Dock Type: Fixed, Wood
Moorings: 0 Total, 0 Transient **Launch:** n/a
Rate: Day n/a **Week** n/a **Month** n/a
Heads: 2 Toilet(s), 2 Shower(s)
Laundry: None **Pay Phones:** No
Pump-Out: OnSite **Fee:** Inq. **Closed Heads:** Yes

Marina Operations
Owner/Manager: Adams Dannenfelser **Dockmaster:** Same
In-Season: Year-Round, 8am-4pm **Off-Season:** n/a
After-Hours Arrival: Call ahead
Reservations: No **Credit Cards:** Out-of-town checks
Discounts: None
Pets: Welcome **Handicap Access:** Yes

Marina Services and Boat Supplies
Services - Security *(owner on-site)* **Communication -** FedEx, UPS, Express Mail **Supplies - OnSite:** Ships' Store, Bait/Tackle, Live Bait **3+ mi:** Marine Discount Store *(Riverside Marine 651-1500, 15 mi.)*, Propane *(Mrohs Gas 968-0252, 23 mi.)*

Boatyard Services
OnSite: Travelift *(30T)*, Engine mechanic *(gas, diesel)*, Electrical Repairs, Electronics Repairs, Hull Repairs, Bottom Cleaning, Propeller Repairs

Restaurants and Accommodations
OnSite: Seafood Shack *(Goose Creek Crab House 651-1193, L $12-25, D $12-25, Fri-Sun only)* **3+ mi:** Seafood Shack *(Linton's Seafood 968-0127, L $8-$15, D $8-15, 21 mi.)*, Lite Fare *(Mom's Diner 651-0905, 16 mi.)*, *(BBQ Junction 651-2900, 13 mi.)*, *(Main Street Café 621-0301, L $4-8, D $8-13, 16 mi.)*, Pizzeria *(Pizza Hut 651-3454, 15 mi.)*, Motel *(Econo Lodge 651-9400, $48-119, 14 mi.)*, Hotel *(Washington Hotel 651-2525, 16 mi.)*

Recreation and Entertainment
OnSite: Boat Rentals *(kayaks)* **3+ mi:** Golf Course *(Great Hope Golf Course 651-5900, 10 mi.)*

Provisioning and General Services
OnSite: Crabs/Waterman *(Goose Creek Seafood)* **3+ mi:** Convenience Store *(413 Mini Mart 623-2247, 15 mi.)*, Supermarket *(Food Lion 651-1508, 17 mi.)*, Liquor Store *(Price Cutters 651-5500, 16 mi.)*, Fishmonger *(Linton's Seafood 968-0127, 21 mi.)*, Market *(King's Creek Market 651-3557, 14 mi.)*, Post Office *(800-275-8777, 5 mi.)*, Beauty Salon *(Pat's Beauty Salon 623-2044, 17 mi.)*, Pharmacy *(Karemore Pharmacy 651-3980, 17 mi.)*, Hardware Store *(Harris Ace Hardware 651-0422, 16 mi.)*

Transportation
OnCall: Rental Car *(Enterprise 957-3472)* **Airport:** Norfolk 855-7772/ Crisfield & Somerset County 968-3062 *(120 mi./20 mi.)*

Medical Services
911 Service **OnCall:** Ambulance **3+ mi:** Doctor *(Gill 651-0717, 9 mi.)*, Dentist *(Lustig 651-1498, 16 mi.)*, Veterinarian *(Somerset Animal Hospital 651-1044, 16 mi.)* **Hospital:** McCready Memorial 968-1801 *(23 mi.)*

Setting -- Just off the Manokin River in bucolic Goose Creek, this small, down-home, full-service facility caters to both pleasure craft and the local working vessels. The wide views are mostly vast stretches of unspoiled marsh, with an occasional car glinting in the distance. Just up the road is the village of Rumbley, a traditional waterman's community. On the distant shore, a few upscale dwellings suggest the inevitable encroachment of development.

Marina Notes -- Established in the mid-fifties. Current owner Adam Dannenfelser summered in Deale as a child and moved here from Baltimore in '03. He plans improvements over time. An easily accessible fuel dock also has a relatively new pumpout system. Thirty-ton lift and significant yard services. Modest services on the docks, some limited electrical. The small ships' store has a large parts department and sells boat supplies, cold drinks, beer, snacks, tackle and a good variety of bait. Thirteen commercial vessels dock here. The adjacent campground has 14 riverfront sites; many units appear quite permanent. The wallpapered, nicely maintained bathhouse has four rooms - two with toilets and two with showers.

Notable -- The marina management also owns the seafood company across the road and will steam crabs on request. An outdoor crab house specializing in local seafood premiered in August '05. Open Friday to Sunday, they seat 30 on the screened-in covered porch and another 30 on the two 15-foot decks. There are really no other services of any kind in Rumbley. Goose Creek promises a quiet, Eastern Shore experience, gorgeous pristine views and, perhaps, some steamed crabs ashore or on the boat. The closest services are in Crisfield, which is nine miles by water and twenty minutes by land.

PHOTOS ON CD-ROM: 11

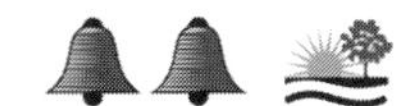

Navigational Information
Lat: 37°59.756' **Long:** 076°01.993' **Tide:** 2 ft. **Current:** n/a **Chart:** 12231
Rep. Depths (*MLW*): Entry 6 ft. **Fuel Dock** 6 ft. **Max Slip/Moor** 5 ft./-
Access: Follow "Big Thoroughfare" into Smith Is. Harbor

Marina Facilities *(In Season/Off Season)*
Fuel: *Smith Is. Oil Co. 8am-1pm, 4-5pm* - Gasoline, Diesel
Slips: 6 Total, 6 Transient **Max LOA:** 60 ft. **Max Beam:** n/a
Rate *(per ft.)*: **Day** $1.00* **Week** n/a **Month** n/a
Power: 30 amp Incl., **50 amp** Incl., **100 amp** n/a, **200 amp** n/a
Cable TV: No **Dockside Phone:** No
Dock Type: Fixed, Short Fingers, Wood
Moorings: 0 Total, 0 Transient **Launch:** n/a
Rate: Day n/a **Week** n/a **Month** n/a
Heads: 2 Toilet(s), 2 Shower(s)
Laundry: None **Pay Phones:** No
Pump-Out: OnSite, Self Service **Fee:** $5 **Closed Heads:** Yes

Marina Operations
Owner/Manager: Capt. Steve Eades **Dockmaster:** Same
In-Season: Apr-Oct, 8am-7pm **Off-Season:** Nov-Mar, Closed
After-Hours Arrival: Call ahead
Reservations: Yes **Credit Cards:** Visa/MC, Dscvr, Amex
Discounts: None
Pets: Welcome **Handicap Access:** No

Smith Island Marina

PO Box 54; Ewell, Smith Island, MD 21824

Tel: (410) 425-4220 **VHF: Monitor** 16 **Talk** 78
Fax: (410) 425-4110 **Alternate Tel:** (410) 425-2111
Email: paulizk@earthlink.net **Web:** www.smithisland.net
Nearest Town: Crisfield *(18 mi.)* **Tourist Info:** (410) 651-2968

Marina Services and Boat Supplies
Services - Boaters' Lounge, Security *(manager onsite)* **Communication -** UPS

Boatyard Services
Under 1 mi: Railway, Hull Repairs, Yacht Building.
Nearest Yard: L. Marsh & Sons Boatyard (410) 425-4211

Restaurants and Accommodations
Near: Restaurant *(Bayside Inn 425-2771, L $6-21, MemDay-MidOct 11am-4pm - baskets, "Baywiches" & main entrées)*, Seafood Shack *(Rukes General Store & Seafood Deck 425-2311, L $2-7, D $11-19, May-Oct - subs, sandwiches, burgers, steaks, chicken, shrimp, crab cakes, soft shells)*, Lite Fare *(Harbor Side Grocery 968-9090, L $2-7, D $2-7)*, Inn/B&B *(Chesapeake Sunrise B&B 425-4220, owned by the marina)*, *(Ewell Tide Inn 425-2141, $50-95)* **1-3 mi:** Inn/B&B *(Inn of Silent Music 425-3541, $105-125, in Tylerton)*, Condo/Cottage *(Smith Island Bayside Cottage 968-3086, $500/wk., at Rhodes Point - opened Summer '05 - 2 bedroom, 1 bath)*

Recreation and Entertainment
OnSite: Boat Rentals *(Kayak - no charge for guests)*, Fishing Charter *(Capt Eades "Sunrise" 425-4220; Capt. Terry Laird 425-5931)*, Sightseeing *(Sunrise Nature Tours 425-4220; Smith Island Cruises-Tyler 425-2771)* **Near:** Playground *(at Elementary School)*, Jogging Paths, Roller Blade/Bike Paths, Park *(Martin National Wildlife Refuge - northern half of Smith Is. - tidal creeks meander through salt marsh - exhibits located in the Middleton House)*, Museum *(Smith Island Center 425-3351 - 7 days, Apr-Oct 12-4pm $2/0)*, Cultural Attract *(Workshops with local artist Pauli Zmolek)*, Galleries *(Smith Island Gallery, Chart's Antiques)*, Special Events *(Ruke's Pig Fest; Camp Meeting Week at Wilson-Butler Tabernacle)*

Provisioning and General Services
OnCall: Hardware Store *(Call & they'll put your order on the ferry: L. Forbush & Sons 968-0220; J.P. Tawes Bros. 968-1066; Clarence Sterling & Son 968-1222)* **Near:** Convenience Store *(Ruke's Grocery Store 425-2311)*, Supermarket *(Harbour Side Grocery 968-9090)*, Post Office, Protestant Church *(Ewell United Methodist -spiritual and physical center of each village)*, Beauty Salon *(Island Styles)*, Retail Shops *(J.W. Gifts; Bayside Gifts)* **1-3 mi:** Crabs/Waterman *(Smith Island Crabmeat Cooperative 968-1344)*, Market *(Drum Point Market 425-2108)* **3+ mi:** Liquor Store *(Crisfield - Smith Island is dry but BYO is accepted, 12 mi.)*

Transportation
OnSite: Bikes *(No charge for guests - $3 for 1/2hr., $5 for 1hr., $10 for 2 1/2hrs., $18 for 5hrs.; everything has to be back by 4pm)*, Water Taxi *(Sunrise charter boat - 425-4220 $75/hr.; Capt. Terry Laird 425-5931or 422-0620)*, Rental Car *(golf cart rentals: $10/.5 hr., $15/1 hr., $28/2.5 hrs.)* **Near:** Ferry Service *(to Crisfield: Capt. Jason I & II 425-5931; Capt. Tyler II 425-2771; Island Belle II - mailboat 968-1118; to Pt. Lookout: Spirit of Chesapeake 804-453-3430)* **Airport:** Crisfield *(18 mi.)*

Medical Services
No 911 Service **OnCall:** Ambulance *(Ewell Volunteer Fire Department 425-5521)* **Near:** Doctor *(Weekly Visiting Nurse)* **Hospital:** McCready Memorial 968-1200 in Crisfield - via "Jason II" Ferry to the hospital dock or Medevac to Peninsula Regional in Salisbury *(11 mi.)*

Setting -- Eight miles offshore, the Smith Island archipelago rises above the Bay - weathered clapboard houses and acres of salt marsh line winding roads. Smith Island Marina's six transient slips edge the bulkhead on the approach to the village of Ewell. A small white dockhouse hosts a lovely wood-paneled boaters' lounge - furnished with wicker and wrought iron. The strikingly handsome nearby Smith Island Center offers a perfect place to begin a tour.

Marina Notes -- *$5/2hrs., $10/4hrs. New docks & pedestals. Transport by foot, bicycle or golf cart. Ferries are delivery trucks, ambulances, school buses and commuter trains. Boatyard services across the island at L. Marsh in Rhodes Pt. Gorgeous varnished beadboard full bathrooms. Next door, bright and spacious Bayside Inn serves lunch. Down-home, rustic Rukes General Store has an inside snack bar, a screened crab deck, and transient slips after 2pm.

Notable -- First discovered by Capt. John Smith, the island was settled in early 1700's. Today, many of the 300 residents trace their ancestry back 12 generations and still speak with a hint of Elizabethan dialect - muted by Satellite TV and ferry-loads of tourists. Three towns, Ewell, Rhodes Pt. & Tylerton, occupy the only high ground. "Soft crabs" are the primary business. Award-winning Smith Island Center is a single-story contemporary take on a traditional island house. Sharply pitched clerestory windows rise from the low-slung roof; rockers furnish the wraparound covered porch. In the summer, the cultural center welcomes about 5,000 tourists - exhibits interpret the history and lifestyles of the Island as does the superb 20-minute film "Land and Water, People and Time." Resident artist Reuben Becker's vibrant 30-foot mural dominates one wall. The gift shop sells crafts & books. In winter, this is the islanders' Social Hall.

Tylerton County Dock

Tylerton, Smith Island, MD

Tel: n/a **VHF: Monitor** n/a **Talk** n/a
Fax: n/a **Alternate Tel:** n/a
Email: n/a **Web:** www.smithisland.com
Nearest Town: Crisfield *(18 mi. by water)* **Tourist Info:** (410) 651-2968

Navigational Information
Lat: 37°58.163' **Long:** 076°01.381' **Tide:** n/a **Current:** n/a **Chart:** 12231
Rep. Depths (*MLW*): Entry 6 ft. **Fuel Dock** n/a **Max Slip/Moor** 6 ft./-
Access: Up Tyler Creek or via Ewell through the ferry channel

Marina Facilities *(In Season/Off Season)*
Fuel: No
Slips: 7 Total, 7 Transient **Max LOA:** 50 ft. **Max Beam:** n/a
Rate *(per ft.)*: **Day** Free* **Week** n/a **Month** n/a
Power: 30 amp n/a, **50 amp** n/a, **100 amp** n/a, **200 amp** n/a
Cable TV: No **Dockside Phone:** No
Dock Type: Fixed, Alongside, Wood
Moorings: 0 Total, 0 Transient **Launch:** n/a
Rate: Day n/a **Week** n/a **Month** n/a
Heads: None
Laundry: None **Pay Phones:** No
Pump-Out: No **Fee:** n/a **Closed Heads:** Yes

Marina Operations
Owner/Manager: The Town of Tylerton **Dockmaster:** n/a
In-Season: Year-Round, Daylight **Off-Season:** n/a
After-Hours Arrival: n/a
Reservations: No **Credit Cards:** n/a
Discounts: None
Pets: Welcome **Handicap Access:** No

Marina Services and Boat Supplies
Communication - UPS **Supplies - Near:** Ice *(Cube)*

Boatyard Services
1-3 mi: Railway, Engine mechanic *(gas, diesel)*, Hull Repairs.
Nearest Yard: L. Marsh & Sons at Rhodes Pt. (410) 425-4211

Restaurants and Accommodations
Near: Restaurant *(Inn of Silent Music 425-3541, D $20pp, there is sometimes an extra place or two for their famous seafood dinners; call in advance and hope!)*, Inn/B&B *(Inn of Silent Music 425-3541, $105-125, flags fly from this waterfront white clapboard farmhouse colonial with powder blue shutters - Apr-Nov - 3 charmingly appointed upscale rooms w/ private baths, refrigerators and scrumptious gourmet breakfast)*, *(Chesapeake fishing Adventures 968-0175, 2 rooms in waterfront fishing lodge - long natural clapboard building)* **1-3 mi:** Restaurant *(Bayside Inn 425-2771, L $6-18, MemDay-MidOct 11am-4pm - baskets, "Baywiches," to 3-course meal)*, Seafood Shack *(Rukes General Store & Seafood Deck 425-2311, L $2-7, D $11-19)*, Motel *(Smith Island Motel 425-4441)*, Inn/B&B *(Ewell Tide Inn 425-2141)*

Recreation and Entertainment
Near: Boat Rentals *(For kayaks, inquire at Inn of Silent Music or Chesapeake Fishing Adventures)*, Fishing Charter *(Chesapeake Fishing Adventures 968-0175)*, Sightseeing *(Smith Island Crabmeat Cooperative 968-1344 - founded in '93 by 15 Tylerton women who raised $236,000 to build this "crab-picking" facility in '96 - 2 large viewing windows. A bushel of crabs = 8-9 lbs of picked crab meat in 2-3 hours!)*

Provisioning and General Services
OnCall: Hardware Store *(Call & they'll put your order on the ferry: L. Forbush & Sons 968-0220; J.P. Tawes Bros. 968-1066; Clarence Sterling & Son 968-1222)* **Near:** Fishmonger *(Smith Island Crabmeat Cooperative 968-1344 - Call in advance to have your order prepared)*, Crabs/Waterman, Market *(Drum Point Market 425-2108 - the local hangout; famous 10-layer Smith Island Cakes come in all flavors)*, Post Office *(425-4181)*, Protestant Church *(Union Methodist - the true spiritual center of all island life - one minister travels to each Smith Is. town every Sunday)* **1-3 mi:** Supermarket *(Harbour Side Grocery 968-9090 - small supermarket)*, Beauty Salon *(Island Styles)*

Transportation
OnCall: Water Taxi *(Sunrise charter boat - 425-4220 $75/hr.; Capt. Terry Laird 425-5931or 422-0620)*, Ferry Service *(Cap't Jason II departs Crisfield for Tylerton 12:30 & 5pm, $20/pp RT 425-5931or 425-4471)* **Near:** Bikes *(Inq. at Inn of Silent Music)* **Airport:** Crisfield & Somerset County *(18 mi.)*

Medical Services
No 911 Service **Near:** Doctor *(weekly nurse's visit)*, Ambulance *(Tylerton Fire & Rescue 425-2420)* **Hospital:** McCready Memorial 968-1200 in Crisfield - via "Jason II" Ferry to the hospital dock or by Medevac helicopter to Peninsula Regional in Salisbury *(11 mi.)*

Setting -- The Tylerton Dock is the only public access to the remote, untouristed village of Tylerton, the smallest of the three Smith Island towns. Set on its own peaceful island, separated from the others by water, its 60 residents cherish their insular, self-sufficient lifestyle. The dock is easy to spot among the rows of wharfs poking into the water - a crane and small red building sit on a wide boardwalk that leads from the dock to the bulkhead.

Marina Notes -- *Dockage is free. The community dock is about two hundred feet long. The center section belongs to the 42 ft. "Jason II" - the Crisfield-via-Ewell ferry, but any other spot is available to transients. There's 75 feet on each side on the outside plus the same on the inside - netting three hundred linear feet of transient dockage. A couple of peeler sheds and other commercial crabbing apparatus sit on the boardwalk. There are no services of any kind - this is an "on your own" dock. Note: the engines rev at dawn; watermen crab from sunup to 1 or 2 in the afternoon. Perhaps the night to tie up and move ashore.

Notable -- Just to starboard is the delightful waterfront Inn of Silent Music. Innkeepers Sharryl Lindberg & LeRoy Friesen, erudite interpreters of island life, have created a beautifully appointed, tranquil oasis affording a unique opportunity to experience this special, other-worldly place. Their "sunset" porch hosts lively conversation and wonderful meals; a secret tree house offers more solitude. To port, author Tom Horton's maroon-shuttered brick house was home for three years while he wrote the acclaimed "An Island Out of Time." Smith Island watermen specialize in delicate, pricey soft shell crabs. The about-to-shed crabs are kept in peeler shanties until they molt into prized "soft crabs." Every morning, the "Jason II" hauls dozens of carefully labeled boxes into Crisfield.

PHOTOS ON CD-ROM: 17

Navigational Information
Lat: 37°58.839' **Long:** 075°51.552' **Tide:** n/a **Current:** n/a **Chart:** 12228
Rep. Depths (*MLW*): Entry 5 ft. **Fuel Dock** n/a **Max Slip/Moor** 5 ft./-
Access: Little Annemessex River, turn to starboard at G11

Marina Facilities *(In Season/Off Season)*
Fuel: No
Slips: 30 Total, 3 Transient **Max LOA:** 60 ft. **Max Beam:** n/a
Rate *(per ft.)*: **Day** $1.00 **Week** $5 **Month** $10
Power: 30 amp Incl., **50 amp** Incl., **100 amp** n/a, **200 amp** n/a
Cable TV: No **Dockside Phone:** No
Dock Type: Fixed, Short Fingers, Wood
Moorings: 0 Total, 0 Transient **Launch:** n/a
Rate: Day n/a **Week** n/a **Month** n/a
Heads: 1 Toilet(s)
Laundry: None **Pay Phones:** No
Pump-Out: OnSite, Self Service **Fee:** $5 **Closed Heads:** Yes

Marina Operations
Owner/Manager: Mark Good **Dockmaster:** Same
In-Season: Year Round, 8am-5pm **Off-Season:** n/a
After-Hours Arrival: Call ahead
Reservations: Yes **Credit Cards:** Visa/MC, Amex
Discounts: None
Pets: Welcome **Handicap Access:** No

Seamark Marine

822 West Main Street; Crisfield, MD 21817

Tel: (410) 968-0800 **VHF: Monitor** n/a **Talk** n/a
Fax: (410) 968-2048 **Alternate Tel:** n/a
Email: n/a **Web:** www.crisfield.com/seamark
Nearest Town: Crisfield **Tourist Info:** (800) 782-3913

Marina Services and Boat Supplies
Services - Docking Assistance **Communication -** Mail & Package Hold, FedEx, UPS, Express Mail **Supplies - OnSite:** Ships' Store *(;arge ships' store)* **Near:** Ice *(Block, Cube)*, Propane *(Mrohs Gas 968-0252)* **Under 1 mi:** Marine Discount Store *(Sterling Clarence & Son 968-1222)*, Bait/Tackle *(Crisfield Bait and Tackle 968-9440)*

Boatyard Services
OnSite: Travelift *(50T)*, Engine mechanic *(gas, diesel)*, Electrical Repairs, Electronics Repairs, Hull Repairs, Bottom Cleaning, Brightwork, Compound, Wash & Wax, Propeller Repairs, Woodworking, Painting, Awlgrip
Near: Canvas Work *(Dave Pruitt's Boat Canvas)*.

Restaurants and Accommodations
Near: Restaurant *(The Cove 968-9532, L $6-14, D $9-30, kids' $3-4, L 11am-4pm; D 4pm-9pm)*, *(Harborside Lighthouse 968-9730)*, *(Circle Inn 698-1969, B $2-5, L $3-7, D $6-13, kids' $4)*, *(Studio Lookout 968-3622, L $6-10,D $6-20)*, *(Oriental Jade 968-3888)*, *(Watermen's Inn 968-2119, D $8-14,fine dining)*, *(Dockside 968-2800)*, Seafood Shack *(Captain's Carry Out 968-1305, delivers)*, *(Side St. Seafood Market 968-2442)*, Pizzeria (Luigi's 968-9089), Motel *(The Cove 425-2771)*, *(Paddlewheel 968-2220)*, Inn/B&B *(MyFair Lady 968-0352, $110-255)* **Under 1 mi:** Restaurant *(Mi Pueblito Grill 968-9984, delivers)*, Pizzeria *(Pizza Shoppe 968-0333, delivers)*, Motel *(Pines 968-0900)*, Inn/B&B *(Bea's B&B 968-0423, $80-90)*

Recreation and Entertainment
Near: Beach *(Brick Kilm)*, Picnic Area *(Somers Cove)*, Grills, Playground, Tennis Courts, Jogging Paths, Fishing Charter *(Barbara Ann II & III 957-2562)*, Group Fishing Boat *(Prime Time II 800-791-1470)*, Museum *(Tawes Historical 968-2501; Tawes Library)*, Sightseeing *(Tangier Is. Cruise 968-2338 $20/10 12:30pm; Smith Is. Cruise 425-2771)*, Special Events *(Soft Shell Fair - last Sun May, Crab & Clam Bake - 3rd Wed Jul, Crab Derby LabDay, Oyster & Bull Roast - 3rd wk. Oct)* **Under 1 mi:** Boat Rentals *(Tangier Outfitters; Croaker Motorboat 968-3644)*, Galleries *(Crabtown 968-1535)* **3+ mi:** Golf Course *(Great Hope 651-5900, 12 mi.)*, Park *(2900 acre Janes Is. State Park 968-1565 - camping, trails, small boat marina, 5 mi.)*

Provisioning and General Services
Near: Convenience Store *(Big Willey's 968-9010)*, Supermarket *(Meatland 968-9834)*, Liquor Store *(Somerset 968-0646)*, Fishmonger *(Walston & Tyler 968-1398)*, Crabs/Waterman *(Southern Connection 968-3678)*, Bank/ATM, Post Office *(968-1550)*, Protestant Church, Library *(968-0955)*, Beauty Salon *(Michelle's 968-3030)*, Hardware Store *(Forbush 968-0220)*, Other *(Family Dollar 968-3141)* **Under 1 mi:** Market *(Riggin's 968-0484)*, Laundry *(Extra Touch 290-7709)*, Pharmacy *(Crisfield 968-1660)*, Retail Shops *(Carvel Hall Factory Store)* **1-3 mi:** Delicatessen *(Puff's Place 968-3218)*

Transportation
OnCall: Rental Car *(Enterprise 957-3472)* **Near:** Bikes *(rentals - Side St. Seafood Mkt.)*, Local Bus *(Crisfield Trolley 968-2501- wave)*, InterCity Bus *(to Ocean City/Salisbury)*, Ferry Service *(Smith & Tangier Is.)*
Airport: Norfolk/Crisfield *(122 mi./4 mi.)*

Medical Services
911 Service **OnCall:** Ambulance **Hospital:** McCready 968-1200 *(2 mi.)*

Setting -- Approaching the Crisfield Town Wharf and the two-story observation tower on its end, bear to port and head farther up the Little Annemessex. Just past G11, a hard turn to starboard leads into Seamark's very sheltered basin. The first dock is mostly transient. On shore is an active working boatyard backed by an attractive three-story pale yellow barn-roofed office and shop.

Marina Notes -- Established in 1959; family-owned and operated. Stationary docks with short finger piers. Large, well-supplied ships' store. Very extensive boatyard services catering to both commercial and pleasure craft - including the famous Deale Island Chesapeake Bay Skipjacks which are painted and repaired here. Customization is a specialty - repairing and rigging. Under the brand Crisfield Propeller, they make and repair propellers right on-site. Plus propulsion specialists, machine shop, aluminum welding, fiberglass repair, carpentry work, Imron/Awlgrip painting, repair & sales of gas and diesel engines.

Notable -- A block away, the J. W. Tawes/Crisfield Historical Museum memorializes the "town the oyster built," One exhibit helps sort out Tangier Sound's historic boats - the differences among a skipjack, bugeye, Hooper Island Draketail, Chesapeake Buy boat, Chesapeake Deadrise workboat or a Pungy Schooner. An outbuilding teaches the life cycles of the blue crab - and how to catch them. Another section focuses on the evolution of decoy carving, including the famous Lem & Steve Ford collection. A wall chart shows a 20,000 year history of Chesapeake Bay. A Trolley Tour of Crisfield leaves at 1pm and a walking tour at 10am ($2.50/free). Janes' Island's perimeter Kayak Trail passes the marina's entrance through Daugherty Creek Canal.

PHOTOS ON CD-ROM: 16

Somers Cove Marina

PO Box 67; 715 Broadway; Crisfield, MD 21817

Tel: (410) 968-0925; (800) 967-3474 **VHF: Monitor** 16 **Talk** 9
Fax: (410) 968-1408 **Alternate Tel:** n/a
Email: somers-cove@dnr.state.md.us **Web:** dnr.state.md.us/publiclands
Nearest Town: Crisfield **Tourist Info:** (800) 782-3913

Navigational Information

Lat: 37°58.684' **Long:** 075°51.445' **Tide:** 2 ft. **Current:** n/a **Chart:** 12228
Rep. Depths (*MLW*): Entry 10 ft. **Fuel Dock** 10 ft. **Max Slip/Moor** 10 ft./10 ft.
Access: Little Annemessex River

Marina Facilities *(In Season/Off Season)*

Fuel: Gasoline, Diesel
Slips: 485 Total, 100 Transient **Max LOA:** 150 ft. **Max Beam:** 40 ft.
Rate *(per ft.)*: **Day** $1.75* **Week** n/a **Month** $18/ft
Power: 30 amp $5, **50 amp** $8, **100 amp** $16, **200 amp** n/a
Cable TV: No **Dockside Phone:** Yes Annual slips only
Dock Type: Fixed, Floating, Long Fingers, Short Fingers, Pilings, Wood
Moorings: 0 Total, 0 Transient **Launch:** n/a, Dinghy Dock
Rate: Day n/a **Week** n/a **Month** n/a
Heads: 27 Toilet(s), 15 Shower(s), AC in heads
Laundry: 5 Washer(s), 5 Dryer(s), Book Exchange **Pay Phones:** Yes, 8
Pump-Out: OnSite, Full Service, 2 Central **Fee:** Free **Closed Heads:** Yes

Marina Operations

Owner/Manager: Dennis Smith **Dockmaster:** n/a
In-Season: May-Sep, 7am-9pm **Off-Season:** Oct-Apr, 8am-5pm
After-Hours Arrival: Call ahead and check in with security
Reservations: Yes **Credit Cards:** Visa/MC, Dscvr, Amex
Discounts: Boat/US **Dockage:** n/a **Fuel:** n/a **Repair:** n/a
Pets: Welcome, Dog Walk Area **Handicap Access:** Yes, Heads, Docks

Marina Services and Boat Supplies

Services - Docking Assistance, Concierge, Security *(24 hrs.)*, Dock Carts, Megayacht Facilities **Communication -** Mail & Package Hold, Phone Messages, Fax in/out, Data Ports *(Office, Phone)*, FedEx, DHL, UPS, Express Mail *(Sat Del)* **Supplies - OnSite:** Ice *(Block, Cube)* **Near:** Ships' Store *(Seamark 968-0800)*, Marine Discount Store *(Sterling 968-1222)*, Bait/Tackle *(Crisfield B&T 968-9440)*, Propane *(Mrohs Gas 968-0252)*

Boatyard Services

OnSite: Launching Ramp *($8/lauch or $35/season)* **Near:** Travelift, Railway, Crane, Forklift, Engine mechanic *(gas, diesel)*, Electrical Repairs, Electronics Repairs, Hull Repairs, Rigger, Sail Loft, Canvas Work, Bottom Cleaning, Brightwork, Air Conditioning, Refrigeration, Divers, Compound, Wash & Wax, Interior Cleaning, Propeller Repairs, Woodworking, Inflatable Repairs, Life Raft Service, Upholstery, Yacht Interiors, Metal Fabrication, Painting. **Nearest Yard:** Seamark Marine - 1/2 mile (410) 968-0800

Restaurants and Accommodations

OnSite: Restaurant *(The Cove 968-9532, L $6-14, D $9-30, Kids' $3-4)*, Motel *(Somers Cove Best Value 968-1900)* **Near:** Restaurant *(Circle Inn 968-1969, L $7-12, D $7-12)*, *(Mi Peublo Grill 968-9984, B $3-4, L $5-15, D $5-15, kids' $3-4.50, delivers)*, *(Waterman's Inn 968-2119, D $8-14, fine dining)*, *(Captain's Carryout 968-1305, delivers)*, Seafood Shack *(Studio Lookout 968-3622, adjacent)*, Snack Bar *(Ice Cream Gallery 968-2881)*, Fast Food *(Subway 968-3000)*, Lite Fare *(Café at the Pottery 968-9040, B $1-3, L $5-7)*, Pizzeria *(The Pizza Shoppe 968-0333, delivers)*, Motel *(Paddlewheel 968-2220)*, Inn/B&B *(My Fair Lady 968-0352, $110-255)* **Under 1 mi:** Motel *(Pines Motel 968-0900)*, Inn/B&B *(Bea's B&B 968-0423, $80-90)*

Recreation and Entertainment

OnSite: Pool, Picnic Area, Grills, Playground, Jogging Paths, Boat Rentals *(968-3644)*, Fishing Charter *(Barbara Ann II & III; Miss H.B. Good II, Carol Jane, Carolyn D. II, Capt Rocky, Prime Time II, Lady Anna, Skipper II)*, Group Fishing Boat *(Prime Time II 800-791-1470; Steppin' Stone, 651-5311; Bay Eagle 968-2545)*, Volleyball, Museum *(Millard 968-2501)*, Special Events **Near:** Beach, Tennis Courts, Video Rental, Sightseeing *(Tangier Island Cruises 968-2338; Eco-Tours 968-9870 $18/10)* **Under 1 mi:** Galleries *(Crabtown Gallery 968-1535)* **1-3 mi:** Park *(Janes Isl.State Park 968-1565)* **3+ mi:** Golf Course *(Great Hope 651-5900, 12 mi.)*

Provisioning and General Services

OnSite: Provisioning Service **Near:** Convenience Store *(Big Willey's 968-9010)*, Supermarket *(Meatland 968-9834)*, Liquor Store *(Brew Thru 968-2211)*, Fishmonger *(Walston & Tyler 968-1398)*, Crabs/Waterman *(Southern Connection 968-3678)*, Oysterman, Bank/ATM, Post Office *(968-1550)*, Barber Shop *(Salon One 968-3449)*, Hardware Store *(L Forbush & Sons 968-0220)* **Under 1 mi:** Market *(Riggin's 968-0484)*, Library *(968-0955)*, Laundry *(Extra Touch 290-7709)*, Pharmacy *(Crisfield 968-1660)* **1-3 mi:** Delicatessen *(Puff's Place 968-3218)*, Catholic Church, Protestant Church

Transportation

OnSite: Bikes, Local Bus *(Trolley 968-2501)*, Ferry Service *(to Smith & Tangier Islands)* **OnCall:** Rental Car *(Enterprise 957-3472)*, Taxi **Airport:** Norfolk 757-857-3200/Crisfield 968-3062 *(122 mi./2 mi.)*

Medical Services

911 Service **OnCall:** Ambulance **Hospital:** McCready 968-1200 *(1 mi.)*

Setting -- Just past the Crisfield town wharf and Captain Quarters condominium is the expansive, protected Somers Cove harbor. Pleasure craft docks, separated by generous fairways, line two sides of the basin edged by long bulkheads. A large tan and brown stucco contemporary houses the office; a pool, picnic pavilion, playground and small bathhouses dot the nicely maintained grounds. Across the basin, the Charterboat Fishing Center homes commercial craft. On the northern edge, docks fronting the Crisfield Museum & Visitor Center host excursion boats to the Islands.

Marina Notes -- *Sun-Thu 1.50/night; Holidays $2/night. Built in 1984. DCM. Operated by MD Dept. of Natural Resources - considering privatizing management. Caters to sport fishing boats and megayachts. A cement deck, furnished with cushioned chaises, surrounds a large pool. The bike shed is adjacent. Somers Cove Y.C. occupies the area around "J" dock with an office and screened picnic area. Four quite nice, all-tiled bathhouses dot the edges of the basin; each with three toilets, four showers and private dressing rooms (one roll-in). In a state of emergency, all boats are welcome & dockage is free.

Notable -- Tents and pavilions available for groups. The Visitors' Center and "must see" museum are perfect places to begin. Crisfield's shops, restaurants, and ferry landing are a short walk. In Crisfield, the "Crab Capital of the World," every restaurant specializes in the crustacean, and some processors at the north end of town will sell direct (in quantity). On-site excursion boats to Smith & Tangier Islands - both worth a visit. Alternative transport are the ferries that leave from the city dock; the lifelines to the islands (and the "school bus"), they provide a unique, fascinating experience.

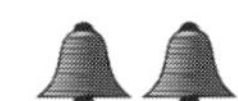

Downtown Riverwalk Marina

PO Box 29; 101 Clark Avenue; Pocomoke City, MD 21851

Tel: (410) 957-1333 **VHF: Monitor** n/a **Talk** n/a
Fax: (410) 957-0939 **Alternate Tel:** n/a
Email: paula@cityofpocomoke.com **Web:** www.cityofpocomoke.com
Nearest Town: Pocomoke City **Tourist Info:** (410) 957-1919

Navigational Information

Lat: 38°04.653' **Long:** 075°34.224' **Tide:** 2-3 ft. **Current:** n/a **Chart:** 12230
Rep. Depths (*MLW*): Entry 7 ft. **Fuel Dock** n/a **Max Slip/Moor** 10 ft./-
Access: Tangier Sound, through The Muds, up Pocomoke River

Marina Facilities *(In Season/Off Season)*

Fuel: On Call Delivery
Slips: 50 Total, 35 Transient **Max LOA:** 75 ft. **Max Beam:** 20 ft.
Rate *(per ft.)*: **Day** $15.00* **Week** Inq. **Month** $150
Power: 30 amp n/a, **50 amp** n/a, **100 amp** n/a, **200 amp** n/a
Cable TV: No **Dockside Phone:** No
Dock Type: Fixed, Alongside, Concrete
Moorings: 0 Total, 0 Transient **Launch:** n/a
Rate: Day n/a **Week** n/a **Month** n/a
Heads: 2 Toilet(s), 2 Shower(s)
Laundry: None **Pay Phones:** Yes, 1
Pump-Out: OnCall **Fee:** n/a **Closed Heads:** Yes

Marina Operations

Owner/Manager: Russell W. Blake **Dockmaster:** Same
In-Season: Year-Round, 9am-5pm **Off-Season:** n/a
After-Hours Arrival: Call next day or walk to City Hall
Reservations: No **Credit Cards:** Visa/MC
Discounts: None
Pets: Welcome, Dog Walk Area **Handicap Access:** Yes, Heads

Marina Services and Boat Supplies

Services - Security *(City Police)*, Trash Pick-Up, 3 Phase **Communication -** FedEx, UPS, Express Mail *(Sat Del)* **Supplies - Near:** Ice *(Block)*, Propane *(Riverview Market)* **1-3 mi:** Ships' Store, Boater's World, Bait/Tackle

Boatyard Services

Near: Launching Ramp, Engine mechanic *(gas, diesel)*. **1-3 mi:** Compound, Wash & Wax, Interior Cleaning, Woodworking. **Nearest Yard:** Seamark, Crisfield, MD (410) 968-0800

Restaurants and Accommodations

Near: Hotel *(Holiday Inn 957-6444)*, Inn/B&B *(Littleton's B&B 957-1645)* **Under 1 mi:** Restaurant *(Ruby Tuesday L $7-10, D $9-15)*, *(Trader's Fried Chicken 957-1682, L $6-15, D $6-15)*, Motel *(Quality Inn 957-1300)* **1-3 mi:** Restaurant *(Don's Seafood 957-0177, L $5-10, D $13-24)*, *(Upper Deck 957-3166, L $5-9, D $7-19)*

Recreation and Entertainment

OnSite: Picnic Area, Grills, Playground, Tennis Courts, Jogging Paths, Roller Blade/Bike Paths, Park *(Cypress)*, Sightseeing *(P.C. Nature & Exercise Trail 957-1333; Cruise further up the Pocomoke)*, Special Events *(Cypress Fest Fathers' Day, Downtown Block Party - midSep)* **Near:** Cultural Attract *(Mar-Va Theatre 957-2752 - a beautifully restored 1927 Art Deco 700 seat theater)* **Under 1 mi:** Golf Course *(Winter Quarters 957-1171, Riverfront 9 hole, Par 70, club rentals)*, Fitness Center *(YMCA)*, Boat Rentals *(Sea Hawk Sport Center 957-0198)*, Museum *(Costen House 957-3110, a Victorian Italianate home on the National Register - Wed & Sat afternoons; Sturgis One Room School 957-1913 -local African-American history)* **1-3 mi:** Pool *(YMCA 957-9622)*, Heated Pool, Spa, Bowling *(Eastern Shore Lanes 957-0775)*, Video Rental **3+ mi:** Beach *(Assateague, VA, 20 mi.)*, Fishing Charter *(Chincoteague, VA, 20 mi.)*

Provisioning and General Services

Near: Convenience Store, Delicatessen, Wine/Beer, Liquor Store, Farmers' Market *(Market St. at Front St., Sat 7am-2pm 957-1333)*, Protestant Church *(Episcopal, Methodist, Presbyterian)*, Synagogue, Library *(Pocomoke Public Library 957-0878)*, Beauty Salon, Barber Shop, Newsstand, Hardware Store, Clothing Store, Retail Shops, Copies Etc. *(Copy machine at library)* **Under 1 mi:** Supermarket, Bank/ATM, Dry Cleaners, Pharmacy, Department Store *(Wal-Mart, Peebles)* **1-3 mi:** Catholic Church, Laundry, Bookstore, Florist *(Pocomoke Flower Shop 957-0811)*

Transportation

OnCall: Rental Car *(Enterprise 957-3472)* **1-3 mi:** Taxi, Local Bus
Airport: Salisbury, MD *(25 mi.)*

Medical Services

911 Service **OnCall:** Ambulance **Near:** Doctor *(Everest Medical)*, Dentist
Hospital: Salisbury, MD *(25 mi.)*

Setting -- The city docks line both sides of the tanin-colored Pockomoke between the bridges. Most transients congregate on the Cypress Park side where the alongside docks are separated from the park's natural shoreline by luxurious masses of water lilies. The Park's amenities include lighted tennis courts, picnic tables and pavilions, a ball field, a brightly painted playground, an exercise trail and pretty wood bridges and benches. Downtown is a very brief walk.

Marina Notes -- *First 2 nites free, $15 each add'l nite. Share the "bank-to-bank" channel with barges headed for the plywood mill. Swing bridge operates 6am-10pm on request. "Pocomoke" means dark water. Pocomoke City's Nature & Exercise Trail winds 4 miles through 8-acre Stevenson's Pond over floating boarwalks to Greenway Ave. to Winter Quarters Landing; it passes exercise stations, a pedestrian bridge, 260 foot fishing pier and a canoe launch site. There's also a 1.5 mile loop. In '06 the Delmarva Discovery Center - museum & restaurant - will open on-site (957-1919) with interpretive exhibits on coastal and river ecology & the shipbuilding that sustained the area in the late 19th century.Tull Shipyards built 200 vessels - luxury oceangoing schooners to steamships.

Notable -- The Pocomoke River, stained dark brown by the tannin from the Cypress swamps through which it meanders, is remarkable for the diverse number of species on its shores - recent sightings include two dozen mammals, 30 reptiles, a dozen amphibians, and 175 species of birds - including pileated wood-peckers and bald eagles. Designated a wild and scenic river by the state, it offers myriad opportunities for nature lovers, including kayaking the upper reaches beyond Shad Landing (accessible by either private or excursion boat from Snow Hill). Anglers fish for perch, gar, catfish, pickerel, herring, & large

PHOTOS ON CD-ROM: 11

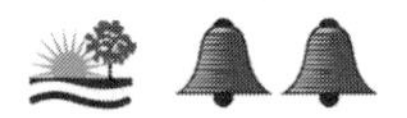

Parks' Marina

PO Box 162; 16070 Parks Marina Lane; Tangier, VA 23440

Tel: (757) 891-2567 **VHF: Monitor** 16 **Talk** 72
Fax: n/a **Alternate Tel:** (757) 891-2567
Email: n/a **Web:** n/a
Nearest Town: Crisfield, MD *(12 mi.)* **Tourist Info:** (757) 331-2304

Navigational Information

Lat: 37°49.790' **Long:** 075°59.621' **Tide:** 2 ft. **Current:** 3 kt. **Chart:** 12228
Rep. Depths (*MLW*): Entry 8 ft. **Fuel Dock** n/a **Max Slip/Moor** 7 ft./12 ft.
Access: West - Chesapeake Bay Entrance; East - Tangier Sound

Marina Facilities *(In Season/Off Season)*

Fuel: *Tangier Oil & Gas* - Gasoline, Diesel
Slips: 30 Total, 30 Transient **Max LOA:** 65 ft. **Max Beam:** 15 ft.
Rate *(per ft.)*: **Day** $25.00* **Week** n/a **Month** n/a
Power: 30 amp $5, **50 amp** $5, **100 amp** n/a, **200 amp** n/a
Cable TV: No **Dockside Phone:** No
Dock Type: Fixed, Short Fingers, Pilings, Wood
Moorings: 6 Total, 6 Transient **Launch:** n/a
Rate: Day n/a **Week** n/a **Month** n/a
Heads: 2 Toilet(s), 2 Shower(s)
Laundry: None **Pay Phones:** No
Pump-Out: No **Fee:** n/a **Closed Heads:** Yes

Marina Operations

Owner/Manager: Milton Parks **Dockmaster:** Same
In-Season: Year-Round, 8am-8pm **Off-Season:** n/a
After-Hours Arrival: Tie-up anywhere available
Reservations: No **Credit Cards:** Cash or checks
Discounts: None
Pets: Welcome **Handicap Access:** No

Marina Services and Boat Supplies

Services - Docking Assistance, Trash Pick-Up, Dock Carts
Communication - FedEx, UPS, Express Mail **Supplies - Near:** Ice *(Cube, Shaved)*, Propane

Boatyard Services

Near: Railway, Crane, Forklift, Engine mechanic *(gas, diesel)*.
Yard Rates: $25.00/hr. engine service

Restaurants and Accommodations

Near: Restaurant *(Fisherman's Corner 891-2900, Mon-Sat 10am-7pm, Sun 12:30-5pm)*, *(Waterfront 891-2248, L $5-10, D $5-12, Mon-Sat 10am-4pm, Sun 1-4pm)*, Seafood Shack *(Hilda Crockett's Chesapeake House 891-2331, B $7, L $19, D $19, family-style, all-you-can-eat buffet, 6:30am-6pm prix fixe)*, *(Channel Marker 891-2220, L $6-25, D $6-25, kids' menu $3-5)*, Snack Bar *(Spanky's Place 891-2514, 1950's ice-cream parlor with music)*, Lite Fare *(Bay View Inn 891-2396)*, Motel *(Sunset Inn 891-2535, $95, A/C, private bath, breakfast; cottages, too)*, Inn/B&B *(Shirley's Bay View Inn 891-2396, $110-125, Wallace Pruitt was born here - perfectly maintained 1806 flower-bedecked white clapboard Victorian with red trim with 9 cottages - A/C, cable & breakfast)*, *(Chesapeake House 891-2331, $100-120, opened in 1940, 8 lovely well appointed rooms, breakfast & dinner or lunch)*, *(Jolly Jim's Inn 891-2535)*

Recreation and Entertainment

Near: Beach *(3-mi. beach at the end of Hog Ridge Road)*, Playground *(at the 120-student school - which boasts Virginia's highest percentage of graduates headed to college)*, Fishing Charter *("Elizabeth Thomas" - 46 ft. Chesapeake deadrise 891-2240)*, Museum *(Tangier Gift Shop & Museum)*, Sightseeing *(Guided Golf Cart Tours $4/pp; plus bird watching)*

Provisioning and General Services

OnSite: Crabs/Waterman *(Runboats headed to Crisfield with the community's catch tie up at the marina - watermen will often sell direct to boaters)* **Near:** Market *(Daley-Son Grocery 891-2469, 8am-5pm Mon-Sat; Island Market 891-2453)*, Post Office, Protestant Church *(2 - Swain Memorial United Methodist & New Testament)*, Library, Barber Shop, Retail Shops *(Robin's Whatnot, Jim's Gift Shop, Wanda's Gift Shop, Sandy's Gift Shop)*

Transportation

Near: Bikes *(Waterfront Restaurant $5/day, RB's Rentals 891-2240, or Wanda's Gift Shop)*, Water Taxi *("Courtney Thomas" Mailboat to Crisfield 891-2240 8am; David Crockett's "My Tangier" 4pm)*, Ferry Service *(Tangier Island excursions to Crisfield 410-968-2338 4pm, to Onancock 891-2240 2pm, to Reedville 804-453-2628 $22/11 RT)*
Airport: Crisfield & Somerset County *(13 mi.)*

Medical Services

No 911 Service **Near:** Doctor *(Gladstone Memorial Health Center, twice weekly physician visits)*, Dentist *(monthly visits)*, Ambulance *(Helicopter service)*, Optician *(monthly visits)* **Hospital:** McCready Memorial, Crisfield 968-1801- by ferry or water taxi to their dock or Medivac to Peninsula Regional in Salisbury *(15 mi.)*

Setting -- The spiffiest, most touristed of the Islands, Tangier is 3.5 miles long by 1.5 miles wide. Three fingers of solid upland are surrounded by breathtaking tidal marsh carved by narrow creeks. Crabbing and tourism support the 700 members of this tight-knit community. Watermen's shanties flank the main channel - inside these little islands-on-stilts, the day's catch is sorted and out back shedding pens hold crabs ready to molt. Park's Marina is on the channel's south shore. Just past the little white dockhouse, emblazoned "Parks," a long boardwalk parallels the shore hosting 32 fairly new docks with good pedestals.

Marina Notes -- *Flat rate. Brief stay $5; overnight transients - to 30 ft. $25, over 30 ft. $30. Charming septuagenarian Milton Parks tools around on his shiny white motor scooter tending his cats and his professionally-run marina. He's gracious and informative - as are most islanders. Well-maintained wood-paneled full bathrooms. Beware - current can run strong at right angles to slips. Bring insect repellent, alcholic beverages and cash - Tangiers is dry & credit-card free.

Notable -- About 90% of the men earn their living from the water (mostly crabs) and many of the women from tourism. It's red alert when the excursion boats arrive creating a bit of a carnival atmosphere. One of the joys of arriving by private vessel is the opportunity to experience the real Tangier - when the boatloads of tourists leave. Three miles of roads are lined with well-maintained vintage houses and hundreds of stacks of crab traps. Some of the eateries serve "family-style" at long vinyl topped tables and most close early - when the boats leave. Amazingly, this small island supports 4 gift shops (plus unofficial craft & recipe stands), 3 B&Bs, 6 eateries, 2 churches, 2 grocery stores, 2 cemeteries, a recreation center, small airport, health center, post office and K-12 school.

PHOTOS ON CD-ROM: 17

Navigational Information
Lat: 37°42.693' **Long:** 075°45.293' **Tide:** 2.5 ft. **Current:** n/a **Chart:** 12228
Rep. Depths (*MLW*): Entry 9 ft. **Fuel Dock** 9 ft. **Max Slip/Moor** 6 ft./-
Access: n/a

Marina Facilities *(In Season/Off Season)*
Fuel: Gasoline, Diesel
Slips: 15 Total, 12 Transient **Max LOA:** 90 ft. **Max Beam:** n/a
Rate *(per ft.)*: **Day** $1.00 **Week** n/a **Month** n/a
Power: 30 amp $3, **50 amp** $5, **100 amp** n/a, **200 amp** n/a
Cable TV: No **Dockside Phone:** No
Dock Type: Fixed, Pilings, Alongside
Moorings: 0 Total, 0 Transient **Launch:** n/a, Dinghy Dock
Rate: Day n/a **Week** n/a **Month** n/a
Heads: 2 Toilet(s), 2 Shower(s)
Laundry: None **Pay Phones:** Yes
Pump-Out: OnSite, 1 Central **Fee:** $5 **Closed Heads:** Yes

Marina Operations
Owner/Manager: Isaac Annis, Harbormaster **Dockmaster:** n/a
In-Season: May-Sep, 8am-6pm **Off-Season:** Mar-Apr, Oct-Nov15, 8am-5pm
After-Hours Arrival: Call ahead
Reservations: Yes, Prefered **Credit Cards:** Visa/MC, Cash/Checks
Discounts: None
Pets: Welcome, Dog Walk Area **Handicap Access:** Yes, Heads

Onancock Wharf

15 North Street; Onancock, VA 23417

Tel: (757) 787-7911 **VHF: Monitor** 16 **Talk** 9
Fax: (757) 787-3309 **Alternate Tel:** n/a
Email: onancock@esva.net **Web:** www.onancock.com
Nearest Town: Onancock *(0.1 mi.)* **Tourist Info:** (757) 331-2304

Marina Services and Boat Supplies
Services - Docking Assistance, Trash Pick-Up **Communication -** FedEx, UPS, Express Mail **Supplies - OnSite:** Ice *(Block, Cube)*
Near: Bait/Tackle *(House of Deals 787-8213)* **3+ mi:** Propane

Boatyard Services
OnSite: Launching Ramp *($5)*

Restaurants and Accommodations
OnSite: Restaurant *(Mallards At The Wharf 787-8558, L $13-20, D $13-20)*
Near: Restaurant *(Charlotte Inn 787-7400, D $19-27, B Sat & Sun 8am-10pm, L Wed-Sat 11:30am-1:30pm, D Wed-Sun)*, *(Sandpiper Family Restaurant 302-0333)*, Lite Fare *(Bizzotto's Deli 787-4330, L $1.25-8, D $1.25-8, gallery & cafe in an historic storefront)*, *(Stella's Second Story 789-7770)*, *(The Blarney Stone Pub 302-0300)*, Hotel *(Charlotte 787-7400, $120+)*, Inn/B&B *(76 Market St. B&B 787-7600, $95-110)*, *(Creekside B&B 787-7578, $130-175)*, *(Colonial Manor Inn 787-3521, $65-165)*
Under 1 mi: Restaurant *(Peppers 787-3457)*, *(Armando's 787-8044)*
1-3 mi: Fast Food*(Subway, Wendy's)*

Recreation and Entertainment
Near: Picnic Area, Fishing Charter *(Tuna Hunter 787-3611, James Gang 787-1226, Fish n' Finn 787-3399)*, Movie Theater *(Roseland Movie Theater, Fri-Sun 787-2010)*, Park *(Ingleside Town Park)*, Museum *(1799 Kerr Place 787-8012 Tue-Sat 10am-4pm, $5/free; Manor House Museum, Outlaw Blacksmith Museum)*, Cultural Attract *(North Street Playhouse 787-2050)*, Galleries

Provisioning and General Services
Near: Gourmet Shop *(North Street Market 787-8805)*, Liquor Store *(Stella's 789-7770)*, Bakery *(The Corner Bakery 787-4520)*, Green Grocer *(Marker 29 Produce 787-1000)*, Bank/ATM *(Sun Trust)*, Post Office *(787-3923)*, Protestant Church *(Cokesbury Church, 1854; Onancock Baptist; Market Street United Methodist)*, Beauty Salon *(Tangela's Hair Creations 787-8133)*, Bookstore *(Vineyard Bookstore 302-0322)*, Hardware Store *(House of Deals Trustworthy Hardware 787-8213)*, Florist *(Alisa's Flowers & More 787-8104)*
Under 1 mi: Convenience Store *(Corner Mart 787-4352)*, Laundry *(coin-op)*
1-3 mi: Supermarket *(Fresh Pride 787-2876)*, Delicatessen *(Onancock Laundry & Deli 787-7191)*, Barber Shop, Pharmacy *(CVS 787-5608)*

Transportation
OnSite: Ferry Service *(Capt Eulice to Tangier Island 453-4434, MemDay-Oct 15, Tue-Sun, 10am $24/12 RT)* **Airport:** Norfolk *(72 mi.)*

Medical Services
911 Service **OnCall:** Ambulance **Near:** Doctor *(Onancock Medical 787-9212)* **1-3 mi:** Dentist *(Fosque 787-2565)* **3+ mi:** Chiropractor *(Accomack Chiropractic 787-4500, 3 mi.)*, Veterinarian *(Accomack Animal Hosp. 787-3112, 3 mi.)* **Hospital:** Shore Memorial 414-8000 *(20 mi.)*

Setting -- Four miles up beautiful, meandering Onancock Creek is the town of Onancock and its municipal marina. After passing the Bagwell Oil marine fuel tanks on the starboard side, the historic Hopkins Brothers General Store is straight ahead with Onancock Wharf just to the right annotated by a pale gray dockhouse with French-blue trim. Two slips are to the left of the launching ramp and the remainder follow the curving bulkhead back to the small bridge.

Marina Notes -- The harbormaster's office is right on the docks and in the back of that building is the more than adequate bathhouse - one shower, three heads each. Plenty of water and lots of sailboats. Sport fish charters and the Capt. Eulice boat to Tangiers berth next door at Hopkins (which does not take transients.) Owned by the Association for the Preservations of Virginia Antiquities, Hopkins is leased to concessionaires who operate the marina & general store. (At press time the Association was seeking a new lessee, so call ahead). Bagwell Oil provides marine fuel with new tanks and a new system.

Notable -- It's about 2 blocks to the charming historic village of Onancock, with leafy lanes lined with perfectly maintained Colonial, Queen Anne and late-Victorian houses and beautiful old churches. (A number of those houses are actually B&Bs and most will pick up from the Wharf.) It's all very elegant in a perfect low-key manner. Right up the road from the Wharf is the 1854 Cokesbury Church. Just beyond is the town square with a gazebo, picnic tables, and statues. Across the street from the church, a narrow path to an historic cemetery offers an interesting detour. The village has quite a few restaurants, a '50s-style movie theater, most key services, some provisioning and not-to-be-missed Kerr Place, a 1799 mansion with exhibits depicting the region's history.

Davis Wharf Marine Services

11498 Davis Wharf Drive; Belle Haven, VA 23345

Tel: (757) 442-9242 **VHF: Monitor** 9 **Talk** 9
Fax: (757) 442-5492 **Alternate Tel:** n/a
Email: n/a **Web:** n/a
Nearest Town: Belle Haven *(3 mi.)* **Tourist Info:** (757) 787-2460

Navigational Information

Lat: 37°33.002' **Long:** 075°52.650' **Tide:** 2 ft. **Current:** 0.5 kt. **Chart:** 12224
Rep. Depths (*MLW*): Entry 5.5 ft. **Fuel Dock** 6 ft. **Max Slip/Moor** 7 ft./-
Access: 3.5 mi. from Bay on Occohannock River

Marina Facilities *(In Season/Off Season)*

Fuel: Gasoline, Diesel
Slips: 15 Total, 2 Transient **Max LOA:** 50 ft. **Max Beam:** 15 ft.
Rate *(per ft.)*: **Day** $1.00 **Week** n/a **Month** n/a
Power: 30 amp Incl., **50 amp** n/a, **100 amp** n/a, **200 amp** n/a
Cable TV: No **Dockside Phone:** No
Dock Type: Fixed, Short Fingers, Wood
Moorings: 0 Total, 0 Transient **Launch:** n/a, Dinghy Dock
Rate: Day n/a **Week** n/a **Month** n/a
Heads: None
Laundry: None **Pay Phones:** No
Pump-Out: OnSite, 1 Port **Fee:** $10 **Closed Heads:** Yes

Marina Operations

Owner/Manager: Bob White or Dennis Melsov **Dockmaster:** Same
In-Season: Year-Round, 8am-4pm **Off-Season:** n/a
After-Hours Arrival: Call in advance
Reservations: Yes **Credit Cards:** Visa/MC
Discounts: None
Pets: Welcome **Handicap Access:** No

Marina Services and Boat Supplies

Services - Docking Assistance **Communication -** Phone Messages, Fax in/out, FedEx, DHL, UPS, Express Mail *(Sat Del)* **Supplies - OnSite:** Ice *(Shaved)*, Ships' Store, Bait/Tackle, Live Bait *(frozen & live)* **3+ mi:** Propane *(Sharp Energy 442-4328, 6 mi.)*

Boatyard Services

OnSite: Travelift *(25T)*, Electronics Repairs *(minor repairs)*, Hull Repairs, Bottom Cleaning, Brightwork, Compound, Wash & Wax, Woodworking, Metal Fabrication, Painting, Total Refits **OnCall:** Engine mechanic *(gas, diesel)*, Divers, Interior Cleaning, Propeller Repairs **Yard Rates:** $40/hr., Haul & Launch $4/ft., Power Wash $1/ft.

Restaurants and Accommodations

OnSite: Snack Bar *(Davis Wharf)* **1-3 mi:** Inn/B&B *(Bayview Waterfront 442-6963, $115, or 0.5 mile by water - beautiful 18thC. Colonial on 140-acres overlooking Occohannock Creek - deep water dock)*
3+ mi: Restaurant *(The Trawler 442-2092, L $6-9, D $7-23, 7 mi.)*, *(China Wok 442-3300, L $5-10, D $8-10, 8 mi.)*, *(El Maguey Mexican 442-2900, L $5-10,D $7-12, 8 mi.)*, Fast Food *(Subway, Burger King, McDonalds 8 mi.)*, Motel*(Best Western 442-7378, 8 mi.)*, Inn/B&B *(Martha's Inn 442-4641, 7 mi.)*, *(Gladstone House 442-4616, $100-185, 7 mi.)*

Recreation and Entertainment

3+ mi: Golf Course *(Back 9 Golf 414-0159, 7 mi.)*, Fitness Center *(Healthy Lifestyles 442-2010, 6 mi.)*, Movie Theater *(Idle Hour Theatre 442-9192, 6 mi.)*

Provisioning and General Services

OnSite: Crabs/Waterman *(Direct from the boats or from Davis Wharf's peeler sheds or freezer)* **1-3 mi:** Bank/ATM **3+ mi:** Supermarket *(Food Lion 442-6803, 8 mi.)*, Liquor Store *(Exmore 414-0752, 7 mi.)*, Market *(Shoreway Market 442-5003, 8 mi.)*, Library *(Northampton Free Library 442-2839, 11 mi.)*, Beauty Salon *(Hair Harbour 442-7404, 7 mi.)*, Dry Cleaners *(Poulson's Cleaners 442-6061, 8 mi.)*, Pharmacy *(Rite Aid 442-8542, 8 mi.)*, Hardware Store *(Ace 442-4900, 8 mi.)*

Transportation

Airport: Norfolk 857-3200 *(70 mi.)*

Medical Services

911 Service **OnCall:** Ambulance **3+ mi:** Doctor *(Eastern Shore 442-6600, 7 mi.)*, Dentist *(Coastal Dental 442-4436, 7 mi.)*, Chiropractor *(Eastern Shore Chiro 442-3444, 7 mi.)*, Veterinarian *(Johnson 442-4600, 7 mi.)*
Hospital: Shore Memorial 414-8000 *(*

PHOTOS ON CD-ROM: 9

Setting -- Quiet, laid back Davis Wharf is about 3.5 miles from the Bay on the Occohannock River, a truly bucolic deep water creek. Around the marina there's little development and the views of the distant, untouched shore are spectacular - especially at sunset. A long, recently updated dock parallels the shore, hosting most of the slips. Flags fly from the small white cinderblock dockhouse and a deck, populated with chairs and tables, is cantilevered over the water.

Marina Notes -- New owner, Bob White, took over in early '04. Only fuel between Onancock and Cape Charles. Well-supplied ships' store. No heads or showers at present because of permitting restrictions but there are plans for a bathhouse by '06 (call to inquire). In the meantime, there's a porta-potty. Full boatyard services, including a 25 ton travelift, and overnight delivery of parts. Two dedicated transient slips and more as available. The accommodating staff of four are all cruisers (Bob White owned a boatyard in the Caribbean), so they really cater to their transient guests and will often drive them for provisions or other critical needs.

Notable -- Workboats also berth at Davis Wharf, so if it's crab season - and sometime between 2:30 and 4pm - crabs will likely be available directly form the watermen. Bob also has a peeler shed and fresh and frozen soft shells will generally be available. In '05 a deck was built out over the water with a few tables and chairs for sandwiches and other lite fare. The beautiful and historic Bayview Waterfront B&B is 1.8 miles by road or 0.5 miles by water. It's about 5.5 miles to a small grocery store and 6 miles to Route 13 with a Fresh Pride, a bank, a dollar store and the Trawler and Maguay Restaurants.

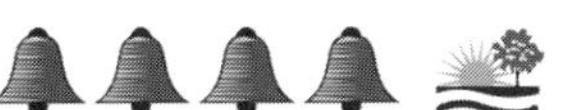

Navigational Information
Lat: 37°16.733' **Long:** 076°00.667' **Tide:** 3 ft. **Current:** n/a **Chart:** 12224
Rep. Depths (*MLW*): Entry 7 ft. **Fuel Dock** 7 ft. **Max Slip/Moor** 7 ft./7 ft.
Access: Chesapeake Bay to King's Creek

Marina Facilities *(In Season/Off Season)*
Fuel: *Shell* - Gasoline, Diesel, High-Speed Pumps
Slips: 226 Total, 50 Transient **Max LOA:** 150 ft. **Max Beam:** n/a
Rate *(per ft.)*: **Day** $2.00 **Week** n/a **Month** n/a
Power: 30 amp $5, **50 amp** $8, **100 amp** $20, **200 amp** n/a
Cable TV: Yes, Incl. **Dockside Phone:** Yes
Dock Type: Floating, Long Fingers, Alongside, Wood
Moorings: 0 Total, 0 Transient **Launch:** n/a, Dinghy Dock
Rate: Day n/a **Week** n/a **Month** n/a
Heads: 12 Toilet(s), 6 Shower(s) *(with dressing rooms)*, Hair Dryers
Laundry: 1 Washer(s), 1 Dryer(s), Iron, Iron Board **Pay Phones:** No
Pump-Out: OnSite, Full Service, 1 Central **Fee:** Free **Closed Heads:** Yes

Marina Operations
Owner/Manager: Joseph Habel **Dockmaster:** Same
In-Season: Year-Round, 7am-6pm Sun-Thu, 7am-8pm, F&S **Off-Season:** n/a
After-Hours Arrival: Call ahead or self dock
Reservations: Preferred **Credit Cards:** Visa/MC, Dscvr, Amex, Checks
Discounts: Boat/US; Marina Life **Dockage:** n/a **Fuel:** yes **Repair:** n/a
Pets: Welcome **Handicap Access:** Yes, Heads, Docks

Bay Creek Marina & Resort

1 Marina Village Circle; Cape Charles, VA 23310

Tel: (757) 331-8640 **VHF: Monitor** 16/09 **Talk** n/a
Fax: (757) 331-8659 **Alternate Tel:** n/a
Email: jhabel@baycreek.net **Web:** www.baycreek.net
Nearest Town: Cape Charles *(1 mi.)* **Tourist Info:** (757) 331-2304

Marina Services and Boat Supplies
Services - Docking Assistance, Concierge, Room Service to the Boat, Boaters' Lounge, Security *(24 hrs., cameras)*, Dock Carts, Megayacht Facilities **Communication -** Mail & Package Hold, Fax in/out *(Free)*, Data Ports *(Wi-Fi, Free)*, FedEx, UPS, Express Mail **Supplies - OnSite:** Ice *(Cube)*, Ships' Store *(The Complete Angler 331-8648 - also clothing, drinks, snacks, beer)*, Bait/Tackle **Near:** Propane *(Bottle Gas 331-2297, Ewells)*

Boatyard Services
OnSite: Yacht Broker *(Pete Horst Yacht Sales 331-3008)* **Under 1 mi:** Engine mechanic *(gas, diesel)*, Electrical Repairs, Electronics Repairs, Hull Repairs *(Low-Sea Co. 710-1233)*, Rigger, Sail Loft, Canvas Work, Bottom Cleaning *(Bill's Dive Service 331-3105)*, Divers *(Mark Sanford 331-1153)*.
Nearest Yard: Davis Wharf (757) 442-9242

Restaurants and Accommodations
OnSite: Restaurant *(Aqua D $23-30, Mon-Thu 5-9pm, Fri & Sat 'til 10)*, Lite Fare *(Cabana Bar L $8-21, D $8-21, 11am-10pm M-Th, 'til 11 Fri & Sat, seafood, raw-bar)*, *(Fish Heads Café B $5, L $5, 8am-6pm: cold cuts, gourmet items, sandwiches, salads)*, Inn/B&B *(Bimini Flats 331-8601, $250-350)*, Condo/Cottage *(Dockside Townhouses)* **Under 1 mi:** Restaurant *(Coach House Tavern at the Golf Club)*, *(Mariah's 331-1700)*, *(Chesapeake 331-3123)*, *(Harbor Grille 331-3005, L $5-10, D $13-28)*, Coffee Shop *(Cape Charles Coffee Co. 331-1880)*, Pizzeria *(Veneto's 331-2275, L $4-20, D $4-20)*, Inn/B&B *(Cape Charles House 331-4920)*, *(Chesapeake Charm 331-2676, $95-150)*, *(Tower Hill Inn 331-1700)*, *(Sterling House 331-2483, $110-135)* **1-3 mi:** Restaurant *(Eastville Inn 678-5745, L $5-14, D $14-22, local seafood specialties include crab cakes & fried oysters)*

Recreation and Entertainment
OnSite: Beach, Picnic Area, Boat Rentals *(pedal boats $5-8/hr., kayaks $15-20/hr., $45-50/day)*, Fishing Charter, Galleries *(Veranda 331-8680)* **Near:** Sightseeing *(65' Schooner Serenity 710-1233, $30/pp)* **Under 1 mi:** Heated Pool, Playground, Tennis Courts, Golf Course *($20 discount for transient boaters)*, Park *(Cape Kids, Central Park)*, Museum *(Cape Charles 331-1008, Barrier Islands Ctr.)*, Cultural Attract *(Arts Enter Cape Charles 331-2787 - performing arts & gallery)* **1-3 mi:** Video Rental *(Movie Gallery 331-4742)*

Provisioning and General Services
OnSite: Wine/Beer, Retail Shops *(Bahama Breeze - clothing; Veranda - gifts & collectibles; Purple Pelican - gifts & kids items)* **Under 1 mi:** Convenience Store *(B&B 331-2282)*, Green Grocer *(Mason Ave Sat 10am-4pm)*, Bank/ATM, Post Office *(331-4927)*, Catholic Church *(St. Charles)*, Protestant Church, Library *(Cape Charles 331-1300)*, Beauty Salon *(Bay Style 331-4330)*, Barber Shop *(Samples 331-3808)*, Pharmacy *(Rayfield's 331-1212)*, Hardware Store *(Watson's 331-3979)*, Copies Etc. *(Sullivan's 331-3180)*
1-3 mi: Supermarket *(Food Lion 331-2340)*, Liquor Store *(ABC)*

Transportation
OnSite: Courtesy Car/Van *(free, within the limits of Cape Charles - eateries, markets, golf, etc.)*, Bikes *($5/hr, $35/day; golf carts also)* **1-3 mi:** Local Bus *(STARR 665-1994)* **Airport:** Norfolk/Accomac Regional *(40 mi.)*

Medical Services
911 Service **OnCall:** Ambulance **Under 1 mi:** Doctor *(Cape Charles Medical 331-1422)*, Dentist *(Selph 331-1589)*, Chiropractor *(Banks Chiropractic 331-1190)* **Hospital:** Shore Memorial 331-1200 *(19 mi.)*

Setting -- High-end Bay Creek Marina is a sherbet-colored fusion of Tide Water & Carribean styles tucked into protected Kings Creek. It has wide open Bay views, miles of untamed natural wetlands and is part of a developing 1,729-acre well-reviewed planned community with 6.5 miles of waterfront in two separate tracts - Marina and Golf Course - anchored by the sweet little town of Cape charles that is gentrifying at warp speed to meet its new residents' needs.

Marina Notes -- Opened in spring '04 on the site of King's Creek Marina. Lime pavilions dot the walkways that connect the floating IPE docks edged with canvas fire hose. In the lemon-lime Pier House are: The Complete Angler (Sun-Thu 7am-6pm, Fri &Sat 'til 8pm), a well-stocked ships' store with a large tackle shop, some quality clothing, drinks, & snacks, elegant Bimini Flats with 1-2 Bedroom bay/harbor view suites, and the luxurious, spa-like bath house where polished stone vanities with hairdryers hover above slate tile floors; commodious showers are polished stone & granite.

Notable -- An on-demand courtesy van connects the 182-acre northern marina tract (with nearly a mile of Bay frontage and a mile on King's Creek) and the 1,547-acre southern golf-centered tract (with another mile of Bay frontage and 3.5 miles on Plantation Creek). On-site the all window Asian-inspired Aqua restaurant features back-lit white onyx, brown leather, rattan, turquoise columns and decks. Upstairs the Cabana Bar repeats the motif adding a fireplace & glass cathedral ceiling. A rasberry-colored arcade hosts a few upscale shops and a deli/coffee shop. At the southern tract are two intersecting consistently "top ten" 18-hole golf courses designed by Jack Nicklaus & Arnold Palmer, a community activity center with a Jr. Olympic pool, tennis courts and fitness center.

Cape Charles Town Harbor Docks

2 Plum Street; Cape Charles, VA 23310

Tel: (757) 331-2357 **VHF: Monitor** 16 **Talk** 14
Fax: n/a **Alternate Tel:** n/a
Email: n/a **Web:** n/a
Nearest Town: Cape Charles *(0.3 mi.)* **Tourist Info:** (757) 331-2304

Navigational Information

Lat: 37°16.000' **Long:** 076°01.000' **Tide:** 3 ft. **Current:** n/a **Chart:** 12224
Rep. Depths (*MLW*): Entry 7 ft. **Fuel Dock** 7 ft. **Max Slip/Moor** 6 ft./-
Access: Chesapeake Bay to Cape Charles Harbor

Marina Facilities *(In Season/Off Season)*

Fuel: Gasoline, Diesel
Slips: 51 Total, 7 Transient **Max LOA:** 60 ft. **Max Beam:** 20 ft.
Rate *(per ft.)*: **Day** $0.75 **Week** $4.48 **Month** $18
Power: 30 amp $5, **50 amp** $10, **100 amp** n/a, **200 amp** n/a
Cable TV: No **Dockside Phone:** No
Dock Type: Fixed, Short Fingers
Moorings: 0 Total, 0 Transient **Launch:** n/a
Rate: Day n/a **Week** n/a **Month** n/a
Heads: None
Laundry: None **Pay Phones:** No
Pump-Out: OnSite **Fee:** $5 **Closed Heads:** Yes

Marina Operations

Owner/Manager: Town of Cape Charles **Dockmaster:** William Dize
In-Season: Apr 1-Dec 1, 9am-5pm **Off-Season:** Dec 2-Mar 31, varies
After-Hours Arrival: Call in advance, pay in morning
Reservations: Preferred **Credit Cards:** Visa/MC
Discounts: None
Pets: Welcome **Handicap Access:** No

Marina Services and Boat Supplies

Services - Docking Assistance, Concierge **Communication -** Data Ports *(Library)*, FedEx, DHL, UPS, Express Mail **Supplies - OnSite:** Ice *(Cube)* **Near:** Bait/Tackle *(Bailey's 331-1982)*, Propane *(Bottle Gas 331-2297)* **Under 1 mi:** Ships' Store *(The Complete Angler 331-8648 at Bay Creek)*

Boatyard Services

OnSite: Launching Ramp **Nearest Yard:** Davis Wharf (757) 442-9242

Restaurants and Accommodations

Near: Restaurant *(Rebecca's)*, *(Garden Café)*, *(Chesapeake Seafood Bistro & Wine Bar 331-3123, D $11-34, 5:30-9pm)*, *(Harbor Grille 331-3005, L $5-10, D $13-28, Sun brunch)*, *(Peppers 787-3457, L $3-7, D $3-7)*, Coffee Shop *(Cape Charles Coffee Co. 331-1880)*, Lite Fare *(Rayfield's Pharmacy's Fountain & Grill 331-1212, sandwiches at 50's prices)*, Pizzeria *(Veneto's 331-2275, L $3-20, D $3-20)*, Inn/B&B *(Sea Gate 331-2206, $85-95)*, *(Cape Charles House 331-4920, $95-150)*, *(Wilson-Lee House 331-1954)*, *(Chesapeake Charm 331-2676, $95-150, sweet '20s vintage, helpful innkeeper; 2 blocks from beach)*, *(Sterling House 331-2483, $100-140, near town beach pavilion)* **1-3 mi:** Restaurant *(Mariah's at Tower Hill 18th C. Mansion on King's Creek)*, *(Shore Break 331-4447)*, Motel *(Rittenhouse 331-2768)* **3+ mi:** Restaurant *(Sting Rays 331-1541, B $3-6, L $3-10, D $3-10, 7 mi., gourmet platters, fab wines in a renovated Exxon station)*, Motel *(Days Inn 331-1000, 6 mi.)*

Recreation and Entertainment

OnSite: Fishing Charter *(Capt. Paul Rogers, 331-3012 24' Carolina Skiff)* **Near:** Movie Theater *(Palace Theater)*, Park, Cultural Attract *(Arts Enter Cape Charles 331-2787 - performing arts & gallery)*, Sightseeing *(Historic Cape Charles Walking Tour; Haunted Cape Charles Walking Tours 331-2274 $10/7; vintage brick houses on Bay Ave.)*, Special Events *(Applaud the Sun Harbor Party - 1st wknd Jul, Aug & Sep; Eastern Shore VA Blue Crab Music Fest - End July)* **Under 1 mi:** Beach *(pristine & gorgeous)*, Playground *(Community Center)*, Tennis Courts *(Community Center)*, Golf Course *(Bay Creek 331-9000)*, Museum *(Cape Charles Museum & Welcome Ctr. 331-1008)* **1-3 mi:** Video Rental *(Movie Gallery 331-4742)*

Provisioning and General Services

Near: Convenience Store *(B&B Quick Mart 331-2282)*, Liquor Store *(Wendell 331-2472)*, Bakery, Post Office *(331-4927)*, Catholic Church, Library *(Cape Charles 331-1300, Internet access)*, Beauty Salon *(Bay Style Salon 331-4330)*, Barber Shop *(Samples Barber Shop 331-3808)*, Pharmacy *(Rayfield's 442-2111)*, Newsstand, Hardware Store *(Watson's 331-3979; Hubbard's Home Ctr.)* **Under 1 mi:** Bank/ATM *(Bank of America)*, Protestant Church, Laundry *(Laundry Basket)* **1-3 mi:** Supermarket *(Food Lion 331-2340)*

Transportation

OnCall: Rental Car *(Enterprise)*, Taxi *(Bicycle rickshaws - 331-2274 $5 for 10 minutes, 0.50 each add'l min.; tokens at Rayfield's; also delivers to boats)* **1-3 mi:** Local Bus *(STARR 665-1994)* **Airport:** Norfolk *(40 mi.)*

Medical Services

911 Service **OnCall:** Ambulance **Near:** Doctor *(Cape Charles Medical 331-1422)*, Dentist *(Selph 331-1589)*, Chiropractor *(Banks 331-1190)*
Hospital: Shore Memorial 331-1200 *(19 mi.)*

PHOTOS ON CD-ROM: 10

Setting -- The entrance to Cape Charles Town Harbor is flanked by a gravel yard with a large crane and an active railroad yard. Straight ahead, wedged between the two, a slightly more picturesque harbor is softened by greenery and a treed shoreline. The protected basin boasts relatively recent docks which host an even mix of working vessels and pleasure craft. The emerging and increasingly interesting and compelling historic downtown is a short walk away.

Marina Notes -- Harbor of Refuge. Municipal facility. Stationary wood docks with short finger piers and very nice pedestals. Note: Workboats leave at 5am, and they can be loud. New bulkhead at the head of the harbor. Rebuilding fuel dock, the office, and putting in heads and showers (now two porta-potties).

Notable -- Cape Charles Town Harbor offers an interesting, textured experience - meeting the waterman in the adjacent slip can be very enlightening. It's an easy 0.3 mile to town - a gravel path leads west paralleling, then crossing the RR tracks, and weaving onto Mason Avenue right across from the well-reviewed Harbor Grill and Bank of America. Intriguing shops, galleries, museums, and restaurants line the street. The whole town is on the National Historic Register, with one of the East Coast's largest concentrations of late-Victorian, colonial-revival and neo-classic buildings - 500 structures from 1884-1920 (5 are now B&Bs). All are remnants of the period when Cape Charles was a headquarters and terminus for the Pennsylvania RR from New York. Currently, the Eastern Shore RR operates a 26-mile barge ferry to Norfolk. Bicycle rickshaws offer a unique transportation and sightseeing option; and the 50's soda fountain at Rayfield's Pharmacy (a bit farther out) where the rickshaws are based is fun.

11. Western Shore: Lower Potomac River

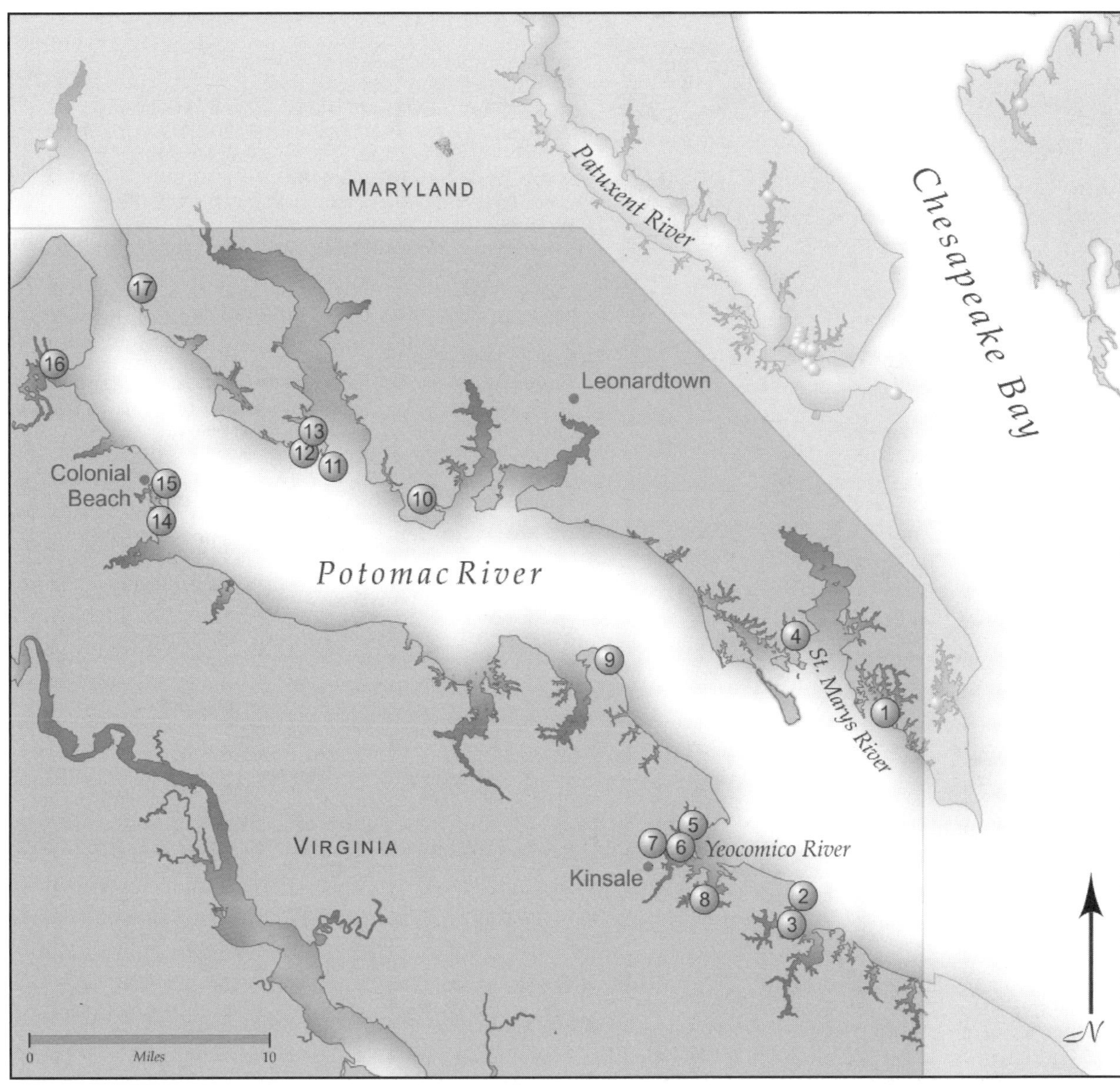

MAP	MARINA	HARBOR	PAGE	MAP	MARINA	HARBOR	PAGE
1	**Point Lookout Marina**	*Smith Creek*	*202*	*10*	**Colton's Point**	*St. Clement's Bay*	*211*
2	**Lewisetta Marina**	*Coan River*	*203*	*11*	**Pirate's Den Marina**	*Wicomico R./Neale Sound*	*212*
3	**Coan River Marina**	*Coan River*	*204*	*12*	**Shymansky's River Restaurant**	*Wicomico R./Neale Sound*	*213*
4	**Dennis Point Marina**	*St. Marys R./Carthegena Cr.*	*205*	*13*	**Captain John's Crabhouse & Marina**	*Wicomico R./Neale Sound*	*214*
5	**White Point Marina**	*Yeocomico River*	*206*	*14*	**Colonial Beach Yacht Center**	*Monroe Bay*	*215*
6	**Port Kinsale Marina**	*Yeocomico River*	*207*	*15*	**Nightingale Motel & Marina**	*Monroe Bay*	*216*
7	**Kinsale Harbour Yacht Club**	*Yeocomico River*	*208*	*16*	**Dahlgren Marine Works**	*Upper Machodoc Creek*	*217*
8	**Olverson's Lodge Creek Marina**	*Yeocomico River*	*209*	*17*	**Aqua-land Marina**	*Potomac River*	*218*
9	**Cole's Point Plantation Marina**	*Potomac River*	*210*				

- **A "DCM" symbol in Marina Notes means Designated Clean Marina** — This is a coveted state-level award given to marinas that meet stringent, environmentally supportive requirements (see page 307). *For a list of DCM's & pump-out facilities, see page 308.*
- **Ratings & Reviews** — An explanation of the Atlantic Cruising Club's rating system, and a detailed explanation of what is in each section of the Marina Report is on pages 6 – 11. *The Data-Gathering Process is detailed on page 322.*
- **Marina Report Updates** — Updates to Marina Reports (from readers, ACC reviewers, and marinas) are posted regularly on *www.AtlanticCruisingClub.com.*

Point Lookout Marina

16244 Miller's Wharf Road; Ridge, MD 20680

Tel: (301) 872-5000; (877) 384-9723 **VHF: Monitor** 16 **Talk** 68
Fax: (301) 872-4033 **Alternate Tel:** (301) 872-5000
Email: on website **Web:** www.pointlookoutmarina.com
Nearest Town: Ridge *(3 mi.)* **Tourist Info:** (301) 475-4200

Navigational Information

Lat: 38°06.880' **Long:** 076°24.040' **Tide:** 2 ft. **Current:** n/a **Chart:** 12285
Rep. Depths (*MLW*): Entry 9 ft. **Fuel Dock** 15 ft. **Max Slip/Moor** 20 ft./-
Access: 5.5 mi. from Pt. Lookout mouth of Potomac River to Smith's Creek

Marina Facilities *(In Season/Off Season)*

Fuel: Gasoline, Diesel, High-Speed Pumps
Slips: 160 Total, 30 Transient **Max LOA:** 200 ft. **Max Beam:** n/a
Rate *(per ft.)*: **Day** $1.00/$0.75 **Week** $4.00/3.00 **Month** $8.00/6.00
Power: 30 amp $4, **50 amp** $8, **100 amp** n/a, **200 amp** n/a
Cable TV: No **Dockside Phone:** No
Dock Type: Fixed, Long Fingers, Short Fingers, Pilings, Alongside, Wood
Moorings: 0 Total, 0 Transient **Launch:** n/a
Rate: Day n/a **Week** n/a **Month** n/a
Heads: 8 Toilet(s), 8 Shower(s)
Laundry: 2 Washer(s), 2 Dryer(s), Book Exchange **Pay Phones:** Yes, 1
Pump-Out: Full Service, 1 Central, 1 Port **Fee:** $5 **Closed Heads:** Yes

Marina Operations

Owner/Manager: Cindy Salvo & Joseph Salvo **Dockmaster:** Samantha Irwin
In-Season: May-LabDay, 8am-8pm **Off-Season:** LabDay-Apr 30, 8am-Dusk
After-Hours Arrival: Call on VHF 16
Reservations: Yes, Preferred. **Credit Cards:** Visa/MC, Dscvr
Discounts: Over 100 gal. **Dockage:** n/a **Fuel:** $0.10 **Repair:** n/a
Pets: Welcome, Dog Walk Area **Handicap Access:** Yes, Heads, Docks

Marina Services and Boat Supplies

Services - Docking Assistance, Concierge, Boaters' Lounge, Crew Lounge, Security *(24 hrs., Lives on-site)*, Trash Pick-Up, Dock Carts **Communication -** Mail & Package Hold, Phone Messages, Fax in/out, Data Ports *(Marina office)*, FedEx, DHL, UPS, Express Mail *(Sat Del)* **Supplies - OnSite:** Ice *(Block, Cube)*, Ships' Store **Near:** Bait/Tackle **1-3 mi:** Live Bait, Propane

Boatyard Services

OnSite: Travelift *(35T)*, Railway *(85T)*, Crane, Engine mechanic *(gas, diesel)*, Electrical Repairs, Hull Repairs, Bottom Cleaning, Brightwork, Air Conditioning, Refrigeration, Compound, Wash & Wax, Propeller Repairs, Woodworking, Painting, Awlgrip, Yacht Broker **OnCall:** Electronics Repairs, Rigger, Sail Loft, Canvas Work, Divers, Interior Cleaning, Metal Fabrication **3+ mi:** Launching Ramp *(10 mi.)*. **Dealer for:** Volvo, Yanmar, Crusader. **Member:** ABYC - 1 Certified Tech(s) **Yard Rates:** $49-60/hr. **Storage**: In-Water $3/ft./mo. Nov - Mar, On-Land $2.20 /ft./mo.

Restaurants and Accommodations

OnSite: Restaurant *(Spinnakers at Point Lookout Marina 872-4340, D $9-19)*, Inn/B&B *(The Creekside Inn 872-5792, $115-135)* **OnCall:** Pizzeria *(Domino's 863-2700)* **Near:** Restaurant *(Scheible's 872-4600, L $4-10, D $13-24, Tue-Sat 6am-9pm, Sun 'til 8pm)*, Motel *(Scheible's 872-5185)*, Inn/B&B *(Pratt's 872-5989, $65)*, *(St. Michael's Manor 872-4025)* **Under 1 mi:** Restaurant *(Courtney's 872-4403, L $3-8, D $10-15)* **1-3 mi:** Restaurant *(Deano's 872-5445, L $6-8, D $8-19)* **3+ mi:** Hotel *(Days Inn 863-6666, $75, 10 mi.)*

Recreation and Entertainment

OnSite: Pool, Picnic Area, Grills, Playground, Fishing Charter *(Marcia II 872-5506 & Hurricane)*, Park **Near:** Group Fishing Boat **1-3 mi:** Video Rental **3+ mi:** Movie Theater *(Sony Lexington 862-5000, 13 mi.)*, Museum *(St. Mary's City Museum 862-3785, 10 mi.)*, Cultural Attract *(Point Lookout State Park, 8 mi.)*

Provisioning and General Services

OnSite: Newsstand **1-3 mi:** Convenience Store, Supermarket *(Raley's Town & Country Market 872-5121 delivers, or Food Lion 863-5445, 13 mi.)*, Gourmet Shop, Delicatessen *(Raley's)*, Wine/Beer, Liquor Store *(Raley's)*, Bakery, Farmers' Market, Fishmonger, Lobster Pound, Meat Market, Market *(Ben's Bar & Grocery 872-9340)*, Bank/ATM *(Raley's Town & Country 872-5121)*, Post Office *(872-5864)*, Catholic Church, Protestant Church, Hardware Store *(Ridge Hardware 872-0444)* **3+ mi:** Library *(St. Mary's PL 863-8188, 13 mi.)*, Laundry *(Lore's 737-0560, 13 mi.)*, Pharmacy *(CVS 863-5992, 13 mi.)*, Department Store *(Wal-Mart 705-7070, Kmart, 10 mi.)*

Transportation

OnSite: Courtesy Car/Van *(to nearest town)*, Bikes **OnCall:** Rental Car *(Enterprise 737-0100)*, Airport Limo *(Goldstar Limo 373-4444* **3+ mi:** Taxi *(Courtesy 866-9600, 10 mi.)* **Airport:** Reagan Nat'l. *(77 mi.)*

Medical Services

911 Service **OnCall:** Ambulance **1-3 mi:** Doctor **3+ mi:** Dentist *(12 mi.)*, Chiropractor *(Henry Chiropractic 737-0662, 13 mi.)*, Veterinarian *(Park Veterinary 863-9222, 13 mi.)* **Hospital:** St. Mary's 475-8981 *(20 mi.)*

Setting -- On Jutland Creek, the marina is snugged into a protected cove just around the point from the on-site, low-country-style Spinnaker's Restaurant. Beyond the fuel dock are two open docks and two short and one long shed dock. The nicely maintained grounds - punctuated by glorious perennial beds - spread across 24 rural acres. An expansive recreation area sits on a rise above the docks with peek-a-boo views of the creek and boats. The picnic area is sheltered by a stand of pines; nearby is a playground and pool - protected by chain link fence nicely obfuscated by a garden featuring Black-eyed Susans.

Marina Notes -- DCM. The name can be confusing - the marina is about 7 miles from Point Lookout, at the mouth of the Potomac. 85 ton railway. Courtesy car and bicycles. Boat/US Towboats. Complimentary newspapers and coffee. 5th, 6th, 7th nights dockage free. Cute little shop behind the marina office - with bait refrigerator, too. Accommodates club cruises with up to 30 boats and 100 in the restaurant; the elegant Creekside Inn, with two waterfront rooms, can manage up to 25 for a meeting/event. Two sets of heads - new ones near the restaurant and another set near the big blue boat shed past the pool are tile and Formica with two showers with a dressing room.

Notable -- The whole area is bucolic - little traffic on land or water promises glorious stars at night. Spinnaker's Restaurant was completely rebuilt in late '04 thanks to Isabel - the mostly windowed, raised gray clapboard with mansard roof is surrounded by white railed decks. Broad, breathtaking views across the juncture of the creeks are practically devoid of civilization. Inside and on the deck is casual but distinctive dining. Light is fare down at the Cabana Bar.

Navigational Information
Lat: 37°59.825' **Long:** 076°27.855' **Tide:** 2 ft. **Current:** 1 kt. **Chart:** 12285
Rep. Depths (*MLW*): Entry 12 ft. **Fuel Dock** 9 ft. **Max Slip/Moor** 7 ft./-
Access: Potomac to Coan River to Kinscote Creek

Marina Facilities *(In Season/Off Season)*
Fuel: Gasoline, Diesel, High-Speed Pumps
Slips: 25 Total, 1 Transient **Max LOA:** 47 ft. **Max Beam:** 14.5 ft.
Rate *(per ft.)*: **Day** $1.00 **Week** n/a **Month** n/a
Power: 30 amp $5, **50 amp** n/a, **100 amp** n/a, **200 amp** n/a
Cable TV: No **Dockside Phone:** No
Dock Type: Fixed, Long Fingers, Short Fingers, Alongside
Moorings: 0 Total, 0 Transient **Launch:** n/a
Rate: Day n/a **Week** n/a **Month** n/a
Heads: 2 Toilet(s), 2 Shower(s)
Laundry: 1 Washer(s), 1 Dryer(s) **Pay Phones:** No
Pump-Out: OnSite, 1 Central **Fee:** $5 **Closed Heads:** Yes

Marina Operations
Owner/Manager: Helen & Mark Scerbo **Dockmaster:** Mark Scerbo
In-Season: Mar-Nov, 7am-7pm **Off-Season:** Dec-Feb, 9am-5pm
After-Hours Arrival: Call ahead
Reservations: No **Credit Cards:** Visa/MC
Discounts: None
Pets: Welcome, Dog Walk Area **Handicap Access:** No

Lewisetta Marina

369 Church Lane; Lottsburg, VA 22511

Tel: (804) 529-7299 **VHF: Monitor** n/a **Talk** n/a
Fax: (804) 529-7800 **Alternate Tel:** n/a
Email: n/a **Web:** n/a
Nearest Town: Callao *(7 mi.)* **Tourist Info:** (804) 333-1919

Marina Services and Boat Supplies
Services - Docking Assistance **Communication -** FedEx, UPS, Express Mail **Supplies - OnSite:** Ice *(Cube)*, Ships' Store, Bait/Tackle, Live Bait

Boatyard Services
OnSite: Travelift *(two 25T - one open, one closed)*, Launching Ramp, Engine mechanic *(gas, diesel)*, Hull Repairs, Bottom Cleaning, Brightwork, Compound, Wash & Wax, Interior Cleaning, Propeller Repairs, Painting, Yacht Design **Yard Rates:** $52/hr., Haul & Launch $2/ft. *(blocking $3/ft.)*, Power Wash $2/ft., Bottom Paint $15.50/ft. *(paint incl.)* **Storage:** In-Water Inq., On-Land $2/ft./mo.

Restaurants and Accommodations
3+ mi: Restaurant *(Lottsburg Cafe 529-5300, L $5-10, D $5-10, 8 mi.)*, *(Cafe Lotte & Marty Smokehouse 529-5938, L $5-9, 8 mi., lunch only)*, *(Nino's Pizza & Subs 529-7548, L $3-7, D $6-9, 8 mi.)*, Motel *(Heathsville Country Inn 580-2157, 11 mi.)*, *(Northumberland 529-6370, $60-65, 7 mi.)*

Recreation and Entertainment
OnSite: Beach *(sand)* **3+ mi:** Golf Course *(Quinton Oaks Golf Course 529-5367, 10 mi.)*, Video Rental *(Movie Gallery 529-5079, 8 mi.)*

Provisioning and General Services
OnSite: Convenience Store *(7am-7pm)*, Delicatessen, Wine/Beer
1-3 mi: Green Grocer *(O' Brien's Produce, Mellville Farms)* **3+ mi:** Supermarket *(Callao Supermarket 529-7251, 7 mi.)*, Liquor Store *(Callao 529-7125, 7 mi.)*, Fishmonger *(Pride of VA Seafood 453-6191, 7 mi.)*, Bank/ATM *(9 mi.)*, Post Office *(529-7936, 6 mi.)*, Protestant Church *(6 mi.)*, Beauty Salon *(LA Images 529-5836, 7 mi.)*, Dry Cleaners *(Northern Neck 529-6280, 8 mi.)*, Pharmacy *(Rite Aide 529-6230, 7 mi.)*, Hardware Store *(Allison's Ace 529-7578, 7 mi.)*

Transportation
Airport: Richmond *(70 mi.)*

Medical Services
911 Service **OnCall:** Ambulance **3+ mi:** Doctor *(Lottsburg Family Practice 529-9996, 8 mi.)*, Dentist *(Suter 529-7339, 7 mi.)*, Veterinarian *(Hundley 580-6555, 10 mi.)* **Hospital:** Riverside Tappahannock 804-443-6090 *(25 mi.)*

Setting -- Right off of the Potomac, on the Coan River at the mouth of Kinscote Creek, Lewisetta offers two main dockage areas backed by a two story, gray clapboard historic general store with a green metal porch roof. One long pier ends at the fuel dock on the T-head, and the other docking area is a combination of covered and open slips that line a gravel peninsula poking into the creek. Transient slips are seaward of the covered slips. A nice sandy beach is nearby, sharing with the docks wide views of a pastoral waterscape.

Marina Notes -- A small, service-oriented, owner-operated marina and boatyard. Generally quick help with dock lines and fuel pump. Two travelifts service seven acres of on-the-hard storage that can - and often does - host up to 100 boats. Most boatyard services are available, including fiberglass and gel coat repairs and painting. The slips on the fuel dock have full finger piers but no power. Some of the other slips have either short finger piers or no finger piers; they're stern to. Basic power is on the pilings along with the water. Adjacent, integrated into the marina, is a small RV park. Lewisetta was hit hard by Isabel but is now fully recovered.

Notable -- The on-site general store, euphemistically referred to as downtown Lewisetta, is well over 150 years old and also serves as the marina office. Open 7 days from 7am to 7pm, it's well stocked with convenience-store style provisions, a full-service deli, boat supplies, bait, tackle, chum and most anything else you might need. Home to Virginia Marine Patrol boats - which adds to the security.

PHOTOS ON CD-ROM: 9

Coan River Marina

3170 Lake Road; Lottsburg, VA 22511

Tel: (804) 529-6767 **VHF: Monitor** 16 **Talk** any
Fax: (804) 529-7300 **Alternate Tel:** n/a
Email: crm@sylvaninfo.net **Web:** www.b-a-y.com
Nearest Town: Callao *(5 mi.)* **Tourist Info:** (804) 333-1919

Navigational Information

Lat: 37°58.933' **Long:** 076°28.283' **Tide:** 1.5 ft **Current:** n/a **Chart:** 12285
Rep. Depths (*MLW*): Entry 12 ft. **Fuel Dock** 7 ft. **Max Slip/Moor** 12 ft./12 ft.
Access: Potomac to Coan River jetty to private channel

Marina Facilities *(In Season/Off Season)*

Fuel: *Shell* - Gasoline, Diesel, High-Speed Pumps
Slips: 48 Total, 5 Transient **Max LOA:** 65 ft. **Max Beam:** 20 ft.
Rate *(per ft.)*: **Day** $1.00* **Week** $4.25 **Month** n/a
Power: 30 amp Incl., **50 amp** Incl., **100 amp** n/a, **200 amp** n/a
Cable TV: No **Dockside Phone:** No
Dock Type: Fixed, Short Fingers, Wood
Moorings: 0 Total, 0 Transient **Launch:** n/a, Dinghy Dock (none)
Rate: Day n/a **Week** n/a **Month** n/a
Heads: 4 Toilet(s), 2 Shower(s) *(with dressing rooms)*
Laundry: 1 Washer(s), 1 Dryer(s), Book Exchange **Pay Phones:** Yes, 1
Pump-Out: OnSite, Full Service, 1 Central **Fee:** $5 **Closed Heads:** Yes

Marina Operations

Owner/Manager: John Hornby **Dockmaster:** Same
In-Season: Year-Round, 8am-5pm **Off-Season:** n/a
After-Hours Arrival: find a slip and see Dockmaster in morning
Reservations: Yes, Preferred **Credit Cards:** Visa/MC, Tex
Discounts: None
Pets: Welcome, Dog Walk Area **Handicap Access:** Yes, Heads, Docks

Marina Services and Boat Supplies

Services - Docking Assistance, Trash Pick-Up, Dock Carts, European Voltage **Communication -** Mail & Package Hold, Data Ports *(Fuel dock)*, FedEx, UPS, Express Mail **Supplies - OnSite:** Ice *(Block, Cube, Shaved)* **3+ mi:** Bait/Tackle *(RW's Sport Shop 529-5634, 5 mi.)*

Boatyard Services

OnSite: Travelift *(25T)*, Launching Ramp, Electrical Repairs, Hull Repairs, Rigger, Bottom Cleaning, Brightwork, Divers, Compound, Wash & Wax, Interior Cleaning, Woodworking, Painting, Awlgrip, Total Refits **OnCall:** Engine mechanic *(gas, diesel)* **1-3 mi:** Metal Fabrication **Dealer for:** Yanmar. **Yard Rates:** $40/hr., Haul & Launch $3/ft. *(blocking $3/ft.)*, Power Wash $1/ft., Bottom Paint $5.75/ft. **Storage:** On-Land $2/ft./mo.

Restaurants and Accommodations

1-3 mi: Restaurant *(The Town Tavern)*, *(Keyser Bros. Crab House 529-6837)* **3+ mi:** Restaurant *(Marty's Smokehouse 529-5938, L $5-9, 4 mi., eat-in or carryout, 11am-6pm, lunch only)*, *(Lottsburg Cafe 529-5300, L $5-10, D $5-10, 4 mi.)*, *(Nino's Pizza & Subs 529-7548, L $3-7, D $6-9, 6 mi.)*, Motel *(Northumberland Motel 529-6370, 6 mi.)*, Inn/B&B *(Heathsville Country Inn 580-2157, 9 mi.)*

Recreation and Entertainment

OnSite: Picnic Area, Grills **OnCall:** Group Fishing Boat *(Bay Quest 43 ft. 15-25 passengers 529-6725)* **3+ mi:** Golf Course *(Quinton Oaks Golf Course 529-5367, 8 mi.)*, Video Rental *(Movie Gallery 529-5079, 6 mi.)*

Provisioning and General Services

OnSite: Crabs/Waterman **1-3 mi:** Convenience Store, Barber Shop **3+ 3+ mi:** Supermarket *(Callao Supermarket 529-7251, 5 mi.)*, Liquor Store (Callao *529-7125, 6 mi.)*, Green Grocer *(O' Brien's Produce, Mellville Farms, 4 mi.)*, Fishmonger *(Pride of VA Seafood 453-6191, 6 mi.)*, Bank/ATM *(8 mi.)*, Post Office *(529-7936, 4 mi.)*, Protestant Church *(4 mi.)*, Beauty Salon *(Lisa's Hair Fashion 529-6070, 6 mi.)*, Dry Cleaners *(Northern Neck Cleaners 529-6280, 6 mi.)*, Pharmacy *(Rite Aid 529-6230, 6 mi.)*, Hardware Store *(Allison's Ace 529-7578, 4 mi.)*

Transportation

OnSite: Courtesy Car/Van **Airport:** Richmond *(70 mi.)*

Medical Services

911 Service **OnCall:** Ambulance **3+ mi:** Doctor *(Lottsburg Family Practice 529-9996, 6 mi.)*, Dentist *(Suter 529-7339, 6 mi.)*, Veterinarian *(Hundley 580-6555, 8 mi.)* **Hospital:** Riverside Tappahannock 804-443-6090 *(25 mi.)*

Setting -- Just past the Coan River jetty, nestled between two small seafood packing plants, Coan River Marina is accessed by its own private channel. A low-slung blue clapboard building with a small deck overlooks the two recently rebuilt pleasure craft piers with slips on either side and T-heads at the end. A small fleet of working boats berth near the travelift. Landside are 6 acres of dry storage and a tree-shaded picnic area with grills.

Marina Notes -- *$1/ft. first day, $0.75/ft. 2nd day, $ 0.50/ft. thereafter. DCM. Everything is neat, clean and shipshape. Good pedestals and very recent docks. Primarily sailboats with a power boat or two sprinkled in. Wide half-length finger piers. 25 ton travelift. Barnacle Bill, the sailor dog (Barney, for short) insists on at least one round of fetch the ball - this is a requirement. On-site ships' store can get parts overnight. Marina manages winterization and commissioning but also permits do-it-yourself. A washer and dryer are perched on an open porch overlooking the docks. The bathhouse is in the blue building - peach walls and tile floors. Each has two sinks set into a vanity, two toilets and a private, completely tiled shower with a comfortable dressing room.

Notable -- Crabs can frequently be purchased live from the watermen at the marina - and one of them will also cook the crabs in the marina office. The work boats seem to arrive around 1pm, so that's a good time to check on the availability. The Town Tavern in Heathsville and Keyser Bros Crab House are doable. Anything else is many miles away, but a courtesy car and truck dramatically minimize the distance issues. Two farm stands, Mellville Farms and O' Brien's Produce, are within half a mile of the intersection of Lake Avenue and Route 360.

Navigational Information
Lat: 38°09.334' **Long:** 076°28.088' **Tide:** 2 ft. **Current:** n/a **Chart:** n/a
Rep. Depths (*MLW*): Entry 10 ft. **Fuel Dock** 10 ft. **Max Slip/Moor** 10 ft./-
Access: Potomac to St. Mary's River to Carthegen Creek

Marina Facilities *(In Season/Off Season)*
Fuel: Gasoline, Diesel, On Call Delivery
Slips: 116 Total, 25 Transient **Max LOA:** 120 ft. **Max Beam:** 28 ft.
Rate *(per ft.)*: **Day** $1.50/1.00 **Week** $7.00 **Month** $5.60 annual
Power: 30 amp Inq., **50 amp** $7, **100 amp** n/a, **200 amp** n/a
Cable TV: No **Dockside Phone:** No
Dock Type: Fixed, Short Fingers, Pilings, Alongside, Wood
Moorings: 1 Total, 1 Transient **Launch:** n/a
Rate: Day n/a **Week** n/a **Month** n/a
Heads: 1 Toilet(s), 4 Shower(s) *(with dressing rooms)*
Laundry: 1 Washer(s), 1 Dryer(s), Book Exchange **Pay Phones:** Yes, 1
Pump-Out: Full Service, 1 Central, 1 Port **Fee:** $5 **Closed Heads:** Yes

Marina Operations
Owner/Manager: Nancy Gardiner **Dockmaster:** Doug Gardiner
In-Season: Apr-Oct, 8am-9pm **Off-Season:** Nov-Mar, 8:30am-5pm
After-Hours Arrival: Call ahead
Reservations: Preferred **Credit Cards:** Visa/MC, Amex
Discounts: Boat/US **Dockage:** n/a **Fuel:** 10% **Repair:** n/a
Pets: Welcome, Dog Walk Area **Handicap Access:** No

Dennis Point Marina

46555 Dennis Point Way; Drayden, MD 20630

Tel: (301) 994-2288; (800) 974-2288 **VHF: Monitor** 16 **Talk** 68
Fax: (301) 994-2253 **Alternate Tel:** (301) 994-1077
Email: dennispoint@eorls.com **Web:** www.dennispointmarina.com
Nearest Town: Lexington Park *(12 mi.)* **Tourist Info:** (301) 475-4200

Marina Services and Boat Supplies
Services - Docking Assistance, Boaters' Lounge, Crew Lounge, Security *(On property manager)*, Trash Pick-Up, Dock Carts **Communication -** Mail & Package Hold, Phone Messages, Fax in/out *($1/p)*, FedEx, DHL, UPS, Express Mail *(Sat Del)* **Supplies - OnSite:** Ice *(Block, Cube)*, Ships' Store *(minimal)*, Propane

Boatyard Services
OnSite: Travelift *(25T/75T)*, Crane *(5T)*, Forklift *(8,000 lb.)*, Launching Ramp, Engine mechanic *(gas, diesel)*, Electrical Repairs, Electronic Sales, Hull Repairs, Bottom Cleaning, Brightwork, Air Conditioning, Refrigeration, Compound, Wash & Wax, Interior Cleaning, Painting, Awlgrip, Total Refits **OnCall:** Electronics Repairs, Rigger, Sail Loft, Canvas Work, Divers, Propeller Repairs, Woodworking, Inflatable Repairs, Life Raft Service, Upholstery, Metal Fabrication **Yard Rates:** $60, Haul & Launch $4.60/ft + labor *(blocking $50 + labor)*, Power Wash $50 + labor, Bottom Paint $22/ft *(paint incl.)* **Storage:** In-Water $4.60/ft, On-Land $4.60/ft

Restaurants and Accommodations
OnSite: Restaurant *(Still Anchors 994-2288, B $8*, L $8-16, D $15-29, Thu-Sat L 12-3pm, D 4-9pm, Sun 1-8pm ; Sun breakfast buffet 8am-Noon $8; kids half-price)* **Under 1 mi:** Restaurant *(Brome-Howard Inn 866-0656, by water - dinner only - can accommodate 75 for an event)*, Inn/B&B *(Brome-Howard Inn 866-0656, $125-185, by water - within Historic St. Mary's City - Mid-week special $99-125 includes picnic lunch and museum entrance)* **1-3 mi:** Restaurant *(Bear Creek 994-1030, L $5-12, D $5-12)* **3+ mi:** Restaurant *(Outback Steakhouse 863-5530, D $7-24, 14 mi., serves dinner only)*, Fast Food *(KFC, Subway, Arby's 10 mi.)*, Motel *(Days Inn 863-6666, 10 mi.)*, *(Fairfield Inn 863-0203, 10 mi.)*, *(Hampton Inn 863-3200, 10 mi.)*

Recreation and Entertainment
OnSite: Pool, Picnic Area *(overlooking the water)*, Grills, Playground, Fitness Center, Jogging Paths, Volleyball **Near:** Fishing Charter, Group Fishing Boat **Under 1 mi:** Museum *(St. Mary's restored 1676 State House - also available for events)*, Sightseeing *(by water - Historic St. Mary's City 895-4990 $7.50/3.50 Wed-Sun 10am-5pm - including the Godiah Spray Plantation, Smith's Ordinary, 1676 State House, "Dove," and a woodland Indian hamlet)* **1-3 mi:** Boat Rentals **3+ mi:** Golf Course *(Breton Bay 475-2300, 15 mi.)*, Movie Theater *(Sony Lexington Park 862-5000, 11 mi.)*

Provisioning and General Services
Under 1 mi: Fishmonger *(Maryland Seafood 994-1525)*, Crabs/Waterman **1-3 mi:** Market **3+ mi:** Supermarket *(Food Lion 863-5445, 12 mi.)*, Liquor Store *(International Beverage 862-9000, 9 mi.)*, Bank/ATM *(10 mi.)*, Post Office *(10 mi.)*, Library *(St. Mary's 863-8188, 10 mi.)*, Newsstand *(Eckerd 862-5590, 12 mi.)*, Hardware Store *(Dyson's 994-0084, 8 mi.)*, Department Store *(Target 862-5003, Wal-Mart 705-7070, 12 mi.)*

Transportation
OnCall: Rental Car *(Enterprise 737-0100, or American Car Rental 862-5300, 12 mi.)*, Taxi *(Friendly Cab 301-863-8141)* **Airport:** Reagan *(73 mi.)*

Medical Services
911 Service **OnCall:** Ambulance **3+ mi:** Doctor *(Shah 863-5835, 12 mi.)*, Chiropractor *(Grimsley 737-0662, 12 mi.)* **Hospital:** St. Mary's 475-8981 *(13 mi.)*

Setting -- Sequestered behind Josh Point on Carthegena Creek off the St. Mary's, 40-acre Dennis Point is the only visible commercial entity along the quiet, wooded shore. Covered and open slips line the waterfront on two sides of a peninsula. On a short rise above the docks, recreation facilities surround the small inviting restaurant and office - a good-sized pool, lovely picnic grove and playground all overlook the creek.

Marina Notes -- Family owned & operated since 1970. Two open-ended travelifts; 25/75T. Easily accessible one-pump fuel dock. Three main uncovered docks, a large U-shaped basin lined with covered slips - home to some very large sport fish boats and trawlers - plus an additional open dock area for stern-to. A T-head accomodates up to a 100 footer. On the dock (basement) level of the marina office/restaurant building is a very basic bathhouse; painted cinderblock stalls are divided by colorful curtains. A washer & dryer share an anteroom with restaurant equipment. Trees hide the adjacent campground and RV park.

Notable -- Family operated "Still Anchors" restaurant has several nicely appointed dining options: A lovely glassed-in porch, presided over by Pete, a blue and gold Macaw and Lucy, a yellow Amazon, has views of the docks and creek. Inside a cozy room features a large window and bar area. Beyond is an outdoor tiki bar and poolside deck with tables, chairs and chaises. A bit further up the St. Mary's, historic St. Mary's City - Maryland's first colony (1634-1695) - is now an 800 acre living history museum with costumed docents. The 65 ft. "Dove," a replica of the 17th C. ship that brought the colonists from England, docks just below the rebuilt 1676 State House. St. Mary's College's 275 ft. dock may have short stay space or anchor and dinghy to the beach near the "Dove."

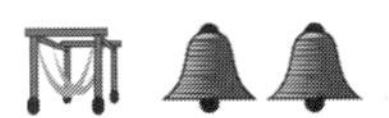

White Point Marina

175 Marina Drive; Kinsale, VA 22488

Tel: (804) 472-2977 **VHF: Monitor** 16 **Talk** 68
Fax: (804) 472-4161 **Alternate Tel:** (804) 472-3396
Email: whitept@crosslink.net **Web:** www.whitepointmarina.com
Nearest Town: Kinsale *(1.5 mi.)* **Tourist Info:** (804) 333-1919

Navigational Information

Lat: 38°02.454' **Long:** 076°33.135' **Tide:** 2 ft. **Current:** 1 kt. **Chart:** 12285
Rep. Depths (*MLW*): Entry 10 ft. **Fuel Dock** 8 ft. **Max Slip/Moor** 8 ft./-
Access: Yeocomico River NW Shannon Branch to White Point Creek

Marina Facilities *(In Season/Off Season)*

Fuel: Gasoline, Diesel, On Call Delivery
Slips: 50 Total, 15 Transient **Max LOA:** 110 ft. **Max Beam:** n/a
Rate *(per ft.)*: **Day** $1.50 **Week** Inq. **Month** Inq.
Power: 30 amp $4, **50 amp** $8, **100 amp** n/a, **200 amp** n/a
Cable TV: No **Dockside Phone:** No
Dock Type: Fixed, Long Fingers, Alongside, Wood
Moorings: 0 Total, 0 Transient **Launch:** n/a
Rate: Day n/a **Week** n/a **Month** n/a
Heads: 5 Toilet(s), 4 Shower(s) *(with dressing rooms)*, Hair Dryers, A/C
Laundry: None, Book Exchange **Pay Phones:** No
Pump-Out: Full Service, 1 Central **Fee:** $5 **Closed Heads:** Yes

Marina Operations

Owner/Manager: Rob Redfearn **Dockmaster:** Same
In-Season: Year-Round, 7:30am-5pm **Off-Season:** n/a
After-Hours Arrival: Take available slip or dockspace, check-in following am
Reservations: Yes, Preferred **Credit Cards:** Visa/MC, Dscvr
Discounts: 200+ gals. diesel **Dockage:** n/a **Fuel:** $0.10 **Repair:** n/a
Pets: Welcome, Dog Walk Area **Handicap Access:** Yes, Docks

Marina Services and Boat Supplies

Services - Docking Assistance, Security *(24 hrs., Dockmaster lives on-site)*, Dock Carts **Communication -** Mail & Package Hold, Phone Messages, Fax in/out, Data Ports *(Office)*, FedEx, DHL, UPS, Express Mail *(Sat Del)* **Supplies - OnSite:** Ice *(Block, Cube)* **Near:** Ships' Store, Bait/Tackle, Propane *(Port Kinsale Marina)*

Boatyard Services

OnSite: Railway *(40T)*, Engine mechanic *(gas, diesel)*, Electrical Repairs, Electronic Sales, Hull Repairs, Bottom Cleaning, Brightwork, Compound, Wash & Wax, Interior Cleaning, Woodworking, Painting, Awlgrip, Total Refits, Yacht Broker *(White Point Marina)* **OnCall:** Rigger, Air Conditioning, Refrigeration, Propeller Repairs, Inflatable Repairs, Life Raft Service, Upholstery, Yacht Interiors **Under 1 mi:** Launching Ramp. **1-3 mi:** Canvas Work. **Yard Rates:** $35-65/hr.

Restaurants and Accommodations

Under 1 mi: Restaurant *(The Mooring 472-3636, L $7-10, D $10-20)*, Inn/B&B *(Skipjack Inn 472-2044, $95-125)* **1-3 mi:** Restaurant *(Kinsale Harbour 472-5484, L $3-19, D $3-19)*, Motel *(Tin Lodge Inn 472-4851)*, Inn/B&B *(Tarry-A-Bit)* **3+ mi:** Restaurant *(Good Eats Café 472-4385, D $10-20, 4 mi.)*, Pizzeria *(Nino's Pizza & Subs 529-7548, L $3-7, D $6-9, 8 mi.)*, Motel *(Northumberland Motel 529-6370, 8 mi.)*

Recreation and Entertainment

OnSite: Pool, Beach, Picnic Area, Grills *(propane)*, Playground, Tennis Courts *(basketball also)*, Jogging Paths **OnCall:** Fishing Charter *(Capt. D. Scott Moss 472-2358)* **1-3 mi:** Museum *(Kinsale Museum 472-3001)* **3+ mi:** Golf Course *(Quinton Oaks Golf Course 529-5367, 10 mi.)*, Video Rental *(Movie Gallery 529-5079, 8 mi.)*

Provisioning and General Services

OnSite: Newsstand *(daily for guests)* **1-3 mi:** Post Office **3+ mi:** Convenience Store *(Handy Store 472-4628, 3 mi.)*, Supermarket *(Callao Supermarket 529-7251, 8 mi.)*, Liquor Store *(Callao Liquor 529-7125, 8 mi.)*, Green Grocer *(O' Brien's Produce, Mellville Farms, 8 mi.)*, Fishmonger *(Pride of VA Seafood 453-6191, 8 mi.)*, Bank/ATM *(8 mi.)*, Protestant Church *(Methodist, Episcopal, 4 mi.)*, Library *(Hague Branch 472-3820, 7 mi.)*, Dry Cleaners *(Northern Neck Cleaners 529-6280, 8 mi.)*, Pharmacy *(Rite Aid 529-6230, 8 mi.)*, Hardware Store *(Allison's Ace 529-7578, 8 mi.)*

Transportation

OnSite: Courtesy Car/Van *(Available for local trips at no charge with valid drivers permit; sightseeing arranged for a fee)* **OnCall:** Rental Car *(Enterprise 443-5666)* **Airport:** Richmond *(70 mi.)*

Medical Services

911 Service **OnCall:** Ambulance *(472-2637)* **3+ mi:** Doctor *(Callao Family Health 529-6141, 8 mi.)*, Dentist *(Suter 529-7339, 8 mi.)*
Hospital: Riverside Tappahannock 804-443-6090 *(24 mi.)*

Setting -- This very neat, tidy and buttoned-up marina sits on three rural, tree-shaded acres on the northwest branch of the Yeocomico River - about a half mile past the White Point packing plant on White Point Creek. Tennis courts, a basketball hoop, a lovely pool, a picnic deck and impeccably restored classic vessels tied up under covered sheds all add to the ambiance.

Marina Notes -- Marina established in the '50s. Owned and managed by the Redfearn Family since 1966. Accommodating owners permit use of their office line for Internet and telephone access; courtesy car as well. 50 ton railway leads into a large work shed. Major refits on larger craft a specialty; the experienced staff serves mostly pleasure vessels and some commercial. A black Lab and brown & white Spaniel escort guests about the property. The well-done bathhouse is cinderblock -- immaculate, seriously painted cinderblock. The showers - with nice new shower heads - have small dressing areas.

Notable -- On a grassy hillock above the docks, the pretty, sparkling pool with palladium-style curved ends is surrounded by a concrete deck nicely furnished with strap chaises and tables & chairs - with vistas across the wide waterway to the treed shoreline. A few steps above the pool, the picnic deck with wooden tables and propane grills shares the same views. Behind the picnic area is the screened porch of the main office and amenities building. The Mooring and Skipjack restaurants are within a mile and the village of Kinsale is about a mile and a half away.

PHOTOS ON CD-ROM: 14

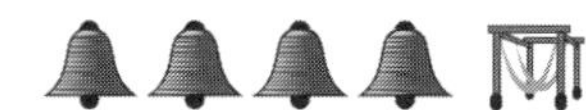

Navigational Information
Lat: 38°01.876' **Long:** 076°33.418' **Tide:** 2 ft. **Current:** 1 kt. **Chart:** 12285
Rep. Depths (*MLW*): Entry 10 ft. **Fuel Dock** 8 ft. **Max Slip/Moor** 10 ft./-
Access: Yeocomico River, Green 3 to port-honor day marks, due west

Marina Facilities *(In Season/Off Season)*
Fuel: *Texaco* - Gasoline, Diesel, On Call Delivery
Slips: 0 Total, 20 Transient **Max LOA:** 75 ft. **Max Beam:** 20 ft.
Rate *(per ft.)*: **Day** $1.50 **Week** $7.50 **Month** n/a
Power: 30 amp $4, **50 amp** $8, **100 amp** n/a, **200 amp** n/a
Cable TV: No **Dockside Phone:** No
Dock Type: Fixed, Short Fingers, Pilings, Alongside
Moorings: 0 Total, 0 Transient **Launch:** n/a
Rate: Day n/a **Week** n/a **Month** n/a
Heads: 10 Toilet(s), 7 Shower(s) *(with dressing rooms)*
Laundry: 2 Washer(s), 2 Dryer(s), Iron, Iron Board **Pay Phones:** Yes, 1
Pump-Out: Full Service, 2 Central **Fee:** $5 **Closed Heads:** Yes

Marina Operations
Owner/Manager: Weston Owens **Dockmaster:** Kathy Morse
In-Season: Apr-Oct, 8am-5pm* **Off-Season:** Oct-Apr, Mon-Fri, 8am-4:30pm
After-Hours Arrival: Take any available slip and register in the morning
Reservations: Preferred **Credit Cards:** Visa/MC, Dscvr, Amex
Discounts: Boat/US **Dockage:** 25% **Fuel:** n/a **Repair:** n/a
Pets: Welcome, Dog Walk Area **Handicap Access:** No

Port Kinsale Marina & Resort

PO Box 280; 347 Allen Point Lane; Kinsale, VA 22488

Tel: (804) 472-2044 **VHF: Monitor** 16 **Talk** 68
Fax: (804) 472-2942 **Alternate Tel:** n/a
Email: pkinsale@crosslink.net **Web:** www.portkinsale.com
Nearest Town: Kinsale *(1 mi.)* **Tourist Info:** (804) 333-1919

Marina Services and Boat Supplies
Services - Docking Assistance, Room Service to the Boat, Boaters' Lounge, Dock Carts **Communication -** Mail & Package Hold, Phone Messages, Fax in/out *($2.50)*, Data Ports *(Wi-Fi, $9.95)*, FedEx, DHL, UPS, Express Mail **Supplies - OnSite:** Ice *(Cube)*, Ships' Store, Bait/Tackle *(squid, shrimp)*, Live Bait *(bloodworms, night crawlers)*, Propane **1-3 mi:** Ice *(Block)*

Boatyard Services
OnSite: Travelift *(30T)*, Launching Ramp, Engine mechanic *(gas, diesel)*, Electrical Repairs, Electronics Repairs, Hull Repairs, Rigger, Bottom Cleaning, Brightwork, Air Conditioning, Refrigeration, Divers, Compound, Wash & Wax, Interior Cleaning, Woodworking, Painting, Yacht Broker *(Kathy Morse)* **OnCall:** Propeller Repairs **1-3 mi:** Railway. **3+ mi:** Canvas Work *(10 mi.)*, Metal Fabrication *(10 mi.)*. **Yard Rates:** $45/hr., Haul & Launch $2/ft. *(blocking $2/ft.)*, Power Wash $2/ft., Bottom Paint $7.25/ft. **Storage:** In-Water $1.50/ft./day, On-Land $3/ft./mo. or $10/day 1st & last days free

Restaurants and Accommodations
OnSite: Restaurant *(The Mooring 472-3636, L $6-9, D $9-16, Mon-Fri 5-10pm, Sat 9am-10pm, Sun 9am-9pm, Sun brunch 9am-2pm, kids' menu)*, Inn/B&B *(Skipjack Inn 472-2044, $95-125, 1912 waterfront famhouse, three rooms)*, Condo/Cottage *(Oyster Reef Cottage 472-2044, $400-900, weekend min., contemporary, waterfront sleeps four)* **Under 1 mi:** Restaurant *(Cajun Grill 472-9305)* **1-3 mi:** Restaurant *(Tarry-A-Bit)*, *(Kinsale Harbour 472-5484, L $3-19, D $3-19)*, Inn/B&B *(Tarry-A-Bit)* **3+ mi:** Restaurant *(Good Eats Café 472-4385, D $10-20, 4 mi.)*, Pizzeria *(Nino's Pizza & Subs 529-7548, L $3-7, D $6-9, 9 mi.)*, Motel *(Northumberland 529-6370, 8 mi.)*

Recreation and Entertainment
OnSite: Pool, Beach, Picnic Area, Grills *(charcoal & propane)*, Playground, Jogging Paths, Roller Blade/Bike Paths, Fishing Charter *(Capt. Scottie Moss' "Subek" 472-2358 - 40 ft. Deltaville Deadrise)*, Group Fishing Boat, Volleyball *(horseshoes, basketball, too - "stuff" in office)*, Video Arcade, Special Events *(Oyster Roast - late Oct)* **1-3 mi:** Museum *(Kinsale Museum 472-3001)* **3+ mi:** Golf Course *(Quinton Oaks 529-5367, 10 mi.)*, Video Rental *(Movie Gallery 529-5079, 8 mi.)*, Galleries *(Left Bank Gallery 472-4408, 6 mi.)*

Provisioning and General Services
OnSite: Convenience Store *(or Handy Store 472-4628, 3 mi.)*, Wine/Beer, Newsstand, Clothing Store, Retail Shops, Copies Etc. **Under 1 mi:** Post Office **3+ mi:** Supermarket *(Callao Supermarket 529-7251, 8 mi.)*, Liquor Store *(Callao Liquor 529-7125, 8 mi.)*, Green Grocer *(O'Brien's Produce, Mellville Farms, 8 mi.)*, Fishmonger *(Pride of VA Seafood 453-6191, 8 mi.)*, Bank/ATM *(Bank of Lancaster, 8 mi.)*, Library *(Hague Branch 472-3820, 7 mi.)*, Dry Cleaners *(Northern Neck Cleaners 529-6280, 8 mi.)*, Pharmacy *(Rite Aid 529-6230, 8 mi.)*, Hardware Store *(Allison's Ace 529-7578, 8 mi.)*, Florist *(10 mi.)*

Transportation
OnSite: Courtesy Car/Van *(golf carts for rent)*, Bikes *(courtesy)* **OnCall:** Rental Car *(Enterprise 443-5666)* **Airport:** Richmond *(70 mi.)*

Medical Services
911 Service **OnCall:** Ambulance **3+ mi:** Doctor *(Callao Family Health 529-6141, 8 mi.)*, Dentist *(Suter 529-7339, 8 mi.)*, Veterinarian *(15 mi.)* **Hospital:** Riverside Tappahannock 804-443-6090 *(24 mi.)*

Setting -- A well-clipped lawn rolls down from the Mooring Restaurant to a picnic grove, playground and 4 sets of docks that fill the picturesque protected cove. Directly adjacent is a seasonal RV and mobile home park that hosts the inviting pool backed by a screened picnic pavilion. A path leads around the cove to the Skipjack Inn and Port Kinsale Maritime Museum with access to one of the docks. All have wonderful views of the cove and West Yeocomico beyond.

Marina Notes -- *In season open Sun-Thu 8am-5pm, Fri & Sat to 6:30pm. A large storage/work shed is on the port side adjacent to the 30 ton open-ended travelift. Extensive dry storage. Boat supplies, tackle and convenience store. The fuel dock has a big, umbrellaed picnic table and pumpout; another pump out is on the first dock's T-head. Wi-Fi $9.95 a day, $15.95 weekend. The marina owns the on-site waterfront, elegant Skipjack Inn and the Oyster Reef Cottage. At the head of "C"-dock, just under the pool, basic but brightly painted blue cinderblock bathhouses have cement floors - each with three toilets, two sinks, and shower stalls with a dressing room area. Additional heads are next to the office and behind Skipjack Inn. Laundry and arcade in campgrounds.

Notable -- The Mooring Restaurant's new chef Charlie Santangelo features local seafood and produce in his eclectic menu. It's served in a spectacular, cathedral-ceilinged dining room with all-glass walls "papered" with gorgeous cove and river views (proper attire requested), in a second room that provides a cosier ambiance, on the country porch or out on the deck. The Mooring is known for its crabcakes and we assume that will continue: eight ounces of 100% jumbo lump crab meat (no filler) with a hint of Old Bay and a dusting of crust makes it one of the best on the Bay - rivals Oxford and Broome Island.

PHOTOS ON CD-ROM: 14

Kinsale Harbour Marina

PO Box 203; 285 Highway 203; Kinsale, VA 22488

Tel: (804) 472-2514 **VHF: Monitor** 16 **Talk** 68
Fax: (804) 472-2514 **Alternate Tel:** n/a
Email: n/a **Web:** n/a
Nearest Town: Callao *(4 mi.)* **Tourist Info:** (804) 333-1919

Navigational Information
Lat: 38°01.867' **Long:** 076°34.617' **Tide:** n/a **Current:** n/a **Chart:** 12285
Rep. Depths (*MLW*): Entry n/a **Fuel Dock** n/a **Max Slip/Moor** 12 ft./-
Access: Potomac River to Yeocomico River to Northwest branch

Marina Facilities *(In Season/Off Season)*
Fuel: No
Slips: 92 Total, 10 Transient **Max LOA:** 46 ft. **Max Beam:** 10 ft.
Rate *(per ft.)*: **Day** $35.00* **Week** n/a **Month** $100/ft.
Power: 30 amp Incl., **50 amp** n/a, **100 amp** n/a, **200 amp** n/a
Cable TV: No **Dockside Phone:** No
Dock Type: Fixed, Long Fingers, Short Fingers, Wood
Moorings: 0 Total, 0 Transient **Launch:** n/a, Dinghy Dock (Free)
Rate: Day n/a **Week** n/a **Month** n/a
Heads: 6 Toilet(s), 6 Shower(s) *(with dressing rooms)*
Laundry: 1 Washer(s), 1 Dryer(s), Book Exchange **Pay Phones:** Yes
Pump-Out: OnSite, 1 Central **Fee:** $8 **Closed Heads:** Yes

Marina Operations
Owner/Manager: William Marshall **Dockmaster:** Same
In-Season: Feb 3-Dec 15, 9am-9pm **Off-Season:** Jan, 10am-2pm
After-Hours Arrival: Call ahead
Reservations: No **Credit Cards:** Visa/MC, Cash
Discounts: None
Pets: Welcome, Dog Walk Area **Handicap Access:** Yes, Heads, Docks

Marina Services and Boat Supplies
Services - Docking Assistance, Trash Pick-Up, Dock Carts **Communication -** Mail & Package Hold, Phone Messages, Fax in/out *($3)*, FedEx, UPS, Express Mail *(Sat Del)* **Supplies - 1-3 mi:** Ships' Store, Bait/Tackle, Propane *(Post Kinsale Marina)*

Boatyard Services
Nearest Yard: Port Kinsale Marina (804) 472-2044

Restaurants and Accommodations
OnSite: Restaurant *(Kinsale Harbour 472-2514, L $3-19, D $3-19)* **1-3 mi:** Restaurant *(Good Eats Café 472-4385, D $10-20)*, *(The Mooring 472-3636, L $7-10, D $10-20)*, Inn/B&B *(Skipjack Inn 472-9366, $95-125)*, *(Tin Lodge Inn 472-4851)*, *(Tarry-A-Bit)* **3+ mi:** Pizzeria *(Nino's Pizza & Subs 529-7548, L $3-7, D $6-9, 8 mi.)*, Motel *(Northumberland Motel 529-6370, 8 mi.)*

Recreation and Entertainment
OnSite: Pool, Grills *(propane)* **Near:** Park *(town square)*, Museum *(Kinsale Museum 472-3001 Fri & Sat 10-5, Sun 2-5)*, Sightseeing *(Village Walking Tour)* **Under 1 mi:** Fishing Charter **3+ mi:** Golf Course *(Quinton Oaks Golf Course 529-5367, 10 mi.)*, Video Rental *(Movie Gallery 529-5079, 8 mi.)*

Provisioning and General Services
OnSite: Delicatessen, Wine/Beer **Near:** Post Office **3+ mi:** Convenience Store *(Handy Store 472-4628, 3 mi.)*, Supermarket *(Callao Supermarket 529-7251, 8 mi.)*, Liquor Store *(Callao Liquor 529-7125, 8 mi.)*, Green Grocer *(O' Brien's Produce, Mellville Farms, 8 mi.)*, Fishmonger *(Pride of VA Seafood 453-6191, 8 mi.)*, Bank/ATM *(8 mi.)*, Library *(Hague Branch 472-3820, 6 mi.)*, Dry Cleaners *(Northern Neck Cleaners 529-6280, 8 mi.)*, Pharmacy *(Rite Aid 529-6230, 8 mi.)*, Hardware Store *(Allison's Ace 529-7578, 8 mi.)*

Transportation
OnCall: Rental Car *(Enterprise 443-5666)* **Airport:** Richmond *(70 mi.)*

Medical Services
911 Service **OnCall:** Ambulance **3+ mi:** Doctor *(Callao Family Health 529-6141, 8 mi.)*, Dentist *(Suter 529-7339, 8 mi.)* **Hospital:** Riverside Tappahannock 804-443-6090 *(24 mi.)*

Setting -- At the navigable head of the west Yeocomico, in the shadow of an imposing Perdue grain elevator, is the lovely Kinsale Harbor Restaurant's modified "A" frame with second floor covered tiki bar. Hunter green market umbrellas top tables and chairs that line the bulkhead. A small pool sits an easy six steps up from the dock-level dining deck which gives it a nice view across the docks; trees block the view of the grain elevators and provide some privacy.

Marina Notes -- *Flat fee - $35/night transient fee includes water, power. An "E" shaped dock parallels the bridge with the long, bridge-side offering along-side dockage; an additional long single pier is adjacent to the grain elevators - and the only one affected by the dust. (Note: The grain elevators are only active in the early fall when the fans are working; other than that, the only consequence is the view.) The heads are quite nice - each bathhouse has three toilets with varnished wood dividers, a wood-fronted Formica vanity with three sinks, and three aluminum shower stalls with fiberglass pans - two with private dressing rooms.

Notable -- The restaurant has a modest dining room, an inviting dockside deck and Carribean music on the top deck overlooking the river. Beer and wine are generally available. An 8 foot bridge limits traffic farther up the river. A half mile walk is the Kinsale Museum, an 18th C. pub, which celebrates the history of this oldest town on the Viginia Potomac. The steamboat era, when it was was an active seaport and ship building center is the focus of many of the exhibits. A village walking tour is also available at the museum. The nearest store is 2 miles away.

Navigational Information
Lat: 37°59.833' **Long:** 076°32.433' **Tide:** n/a **Current:** n/a **Chart:** 12285
Rep. Depths (*MLW*): Entry 10 ft. **Fuel Dock** 8 ft. **Max Slip/Moor** -/-
Access: Potomac to Yeocomico's S. E. branch to Lodge Creek

Marina Facilities *(In Season/Off Season)*
Fuel: Yes
Slips: 15 Total, 15 Transient **Max LOA:** 110 ft. **Max Beam:** 24 ft.
Rate *(per ft.)*: **Day** $1.50 **Week** n/a **Month** $130
Power: 30 amp Incl., **50 amp** Incl., **100 amp** n/a, **200 amp** n/a
Cable TV: No **Dockside Phone:** No
Dock Type: Short Fingers
Moorings: 0 Total, 0 Transient **Launch:** n/a
Rate: Day n/a **Week** n/a **Month** n/a
Heads: 5 Toilet(s), 5 Shower(s)
Laundry: 2 Washer(s), 2 Dryer(s) **Pay Phones:** Yes, 2
Pump-Out: OnSite, 1 Central **Fee:** $5 **Closed Heads:** Yes

Marina Operations
Owner/Manager: Fred Olverson **Dockmaster:** same
In-Season: Year-Round, 9am-5pm **Off-Season:** n/a
After-Hours Arrival: check in the am
Reservations: No **Credit Cards:** Visa/MC
Discounts: Boat/US **Dockage:** n/a **Fuel:** n/a **Repair:** n/a
Pets: Welcome, Dog Walk Area **Handicap Access:** Yes, Heads

Olverson's Lodge Creek Marina

PO Box; 1161 Melrose Road; Callao, VA 22435

Tel: (804) 529-6868; (800) 529-5071 **VHF: Monitor** 16 **Talk** 68
Fax: (804) 529-7951 **Alternate Tel:** n/a
Email: marina@olversonsmarina.com **Web:** www.olversonsmarina.com
Nearest Town: Lottsburg *(4 mi.)* **Tourist Info:** (804) 333-1919

Marina Services and Boat Supplies
Services - Boaters' Lounge **Communication -** FedEx, DHL, UPS, Express Mail *(Sat Del)* **Supplies - OnSite:** Ice *(Cube)* **3+ mi:** Bait/Tackle *(RW's Sport Shop 529-5634, 3 mi.)*, Propane *(U-Haul 529-9381, 4 mi.)*

Boatyard Services
Nearest Yard: Port Kinsale Marina (804) 472-2044

Restaurants and Accommodations
OnSite: Inn/B&B *(Banana Wind Boat & Breakfast 445-3005, $70-80, stateroom on 65 ft. motorsailer)*, Condo/Cottage *(Olverson's Farmhouse weekly)* **3+ mi:** Restaurant *(Tavern on the Green 529-9200, 6 mi.)*, *(Cafe Lotte & Marty's Smokehouse 529-5938, L $5-9, 4 mi., lunch only)*, *(Bambery's 580-8181, L $6-12, D $18-22, 6 mi.)*, *(Lottsburg Café 529-5300, L $5-10, D $5-10, 4 mi.)*, Lite Fare *(Callao Dairy Freeze 529-6881, 4 mi.)*, Pizzeria *(Nino's Pizza & Subs 529-7548, L $3-7, D $6-9, 4 mi.)*, Motel *(Northumberland Motel 529-6370, 6 mi.)*, Hotel *(Best Western 333-1700, 15 mi.)*

Recreation and Entertainment
OnSite: Pool, Beach, Picnic Area, Fishing Charter *(Sea Sarah 529-9303)* **3+ mi:** Golf Course *(Quinton Oaks Golf Course 529-5367, 6 mi.)*, Video Rental *(Movie Gallery 529-5079, 5 mi.)*

Provisioning and General Services
3+ mi: Supermarket *(Callao Supermarket 529-7251, 5 mi.)*, Liquor Store *(ABC, 6 mi.)*, Green Grocer *(O' Brien's Produce, Mellville Farms, 4 mi.)*, Fishmonger *(Pride of VA Seafood 453-6191, 6 mi.)*, Bank/ATM *(6 mi.)*, Post Office *(529-7936, 4 mi.)*, Beauty Salon *(LA Images 529-5836, 4 mi.)*, Dry Cleaners *(Northern Neck Cleaners 529-6280, 5 mi.)*, Pharmacy *(Rite Aid 529-6230, 6 mi.)*, Hardware Store *(Allison's Ace 529-7578, 5 mi.)*

Transportation
OnSite: Courtesy Car/Van, Bikes *(complimentary)* **OnCall:** Rental Car *(Enterprise Car Rental)* **Airport:** Richmond *(70 mi.)*

Medical Services
911 Service **3+ mi:** Doctor *(Lottsburg Family Practice 529-9996, 4 mi.)*, Dentist *(Cottrell 529-7339, 5 mi.)* **Hospital:** Riverside Tappahannock 443-6090 *(25 mi.)*

Setting -- About 5 miles up the Yeocomico's southeastern branch, Olverson's sprawls along a peninsula fronting Lodge Creek. The ambiance is relaxed and peaceful - a bit of old, unfussy Northern Neck. To reinforce that theme, right next to the dockside office, a circle of white Adirondack chairs and rockers invite casual conversation - with soda machines and ice chests at hand. A heated pool (84 degrees) sits up on the hill with sweeping views of the docks and creek. Nearby is a play gym and classic white clapboard Virginia farmhouse. Perpendicular to the shore five docks - the first is open, the others are half covered - feature covered walkways with raised power lines and 110 foot T-heads.

Marina Notes -- Built in the '60's by the Olverson family. Several 24 foot wide multi-hull slips. The fuel dock is inboard to the new transient T-dock, signaled by a little lighthouse and flag. The Club House, a covered pavillion (with plastic sides for inclement weather), holds over 150 for a group function - complimented by lots of transient dock space. The creek is a hurricane hole. Steps from the T-dock, a small, brightly furnished boaters' lounge has a TV and kitchen. Adjacent is a basic cinderblock bathhouse, and an additional, preferable, single full handicap bathroom is next to the laundry room with new washers & dryers.

Notable -- A small "beach" on the other side of a grassy spit from the docks has a gradual bottom and is part of a local conservation group's sea grass renourishment project. The picturesque white farmhouse on the hill, once owned by the late Albert Olverson, is available for weekly rental. A courtesy car and complementary bikes make the towns of Calleo and Lottsburg - 5 minute drives - accessible to transients. Just beyond is well-reviewed Bambery's Restaurant.

PHOTOS ON CD-ROM: 11

Cole's Point Plantation Marina

PO Box 77; Route 728; Coles Point, VA 22442

Tel: (804) 472-3955 **VHF: Monitor** 16 **Talk** 68
Fax: (804) 472-4488 **Alternate Tel:** n/a
Email: cpplantation@hotmail.com **Web:** www.colespoint.com
Nearest Town: Coles Point *(0.5 mi.)* **Tourist Info:** (804) 333-1919

Navigational Information
Lat: 38°08.599' **Long:** 076°36.823' **Tide:** 2 ft. **Current:** n/a **Chart:** 12285
Rep. Depths (*MLW*): Entry 6 ft. **Fuel Dock** 8 ft. **Max Slip/Moor** 8 ft./-
Access: Potomac River to Coles Point via private marked channel

Marina Facilities *(In Season/Off Season)*
Fuel: *Exxon* - Gasoline, Diesel
Slips: 151 Total, 25 Transient **Max LOA:** 90 ft. **Max Beam:** n/a
Rate *(per ft.)*: **Day** $1.25* **Week** $6.30 **Month** Inq.
Power: 30 amp $5, **50 amp** $10, **100 amp** n/a, **200 amp** n/a
Cable TV: Yes limited slips **Dockside Phone:** No
Dock Type: Fixed, Floating, Long Fingers, Pilings, Alongside
Moorings: 0 Total, 0 Transient **Launch:** n/a
Rate: Day n/a **Week** n/a **Month** n/a
Heads: 8 Toilet(s), 4 Shower(s)
Laundry: 3 Washer(s), 3 Dryer(s), Book Exchange **Pay Phones:** Yes
Pump-Out: OnSite, Self Service **Fee:** $5 **Closed Heads:** Yes

Marina Operations
Owner/Manager: Capt. Clark Demyen **Dockmaster:** Same
In-Season: May-Aug, 8am-4pm **Off-Season:** Sept-Apr, 8:30am-5pm
After-Hours Arrival: See restaurant manager or call on VHF 16
Reservations: Yes **Credit Cards:** Visa/MC, Dscvr, Amex
Discounts: None
Pets: Welcome, Dog Walk Area **Handicap Access:** No

Marina Services and Boat Supplies
Services - Docking Assistance, Dock Carts **Communication -** Mail & Package Hold, Phone Messages, Fax in/out, Data Ports *(Restaurant)*, FedEx, DHL, UPS, Express Mail **Supplies - OnSite:** Ice *(Block, Cube)*, Ships' Store *(souveniers and fishing supplies)*, Bait/Tackle, Live Bait, Propane

Boatyard Services
OnSite: Travelift *(30T)*, Forklift *(6T)*, Launching Ramp, Electrical Repairs, Hull Repairs, Rigger, Bottom Cleaning, Painting **OnCall:** Engine mechanic *(gas, diesel)*, Air Conditioning, Refrigeration, Divers, Compound, Wash & Wax, Interior Cleaning **Near:** Railway, Electronics Repairs, Brightwork. **1-3 mi:** Canvas Work, Woodworking, Metal Fabrication **Yard Rates:** $40/hr., Haul & Launch $6.50/ft. sail, $6/ft. power, Power Wash $1/ft., Bottom Paint $9.50/ft. Interlux ATC *(paint incl.)* **Storage:** On-Land $9/ft./mo./jack stand

Restaurants and Accommodations
OnSite: Restaurant *(Pilots Wharf 472-4761, B B $5-12, L $7-9, D $15-27, open daily 11:30am-10pm, Sat & Sun breakfast & brunch - call for hours.)*, Condo/Cottage *(4 Units 5-bedroom lodge: $610 weekend/$1650 week. 3-bedroom cottage: $395 weekend/$750 week)* **1-3 mi:** Restaurant *(AC Café & Grill 472-5528, L $5-15, D $5-25)*, *(Driftwood 472-3892, L $5-14, D $18-25, closed Mon)* **3+ mi:** Motel *(Washington & Lee Motel 493-8093, 18 mi.)*, Inn/B&B *(Inn at Montross 493-0573, 18 mi., Mt. Holly Steamboat Inn, 472-9070, 10 mi.)*

Recreation and Entertainment
OnSite: Pool, Beach, Picnic Area, Grills, Playground, Jogging Paths, Roller Blade/Bike Paths, Volleyball, Video Rental **Near:** Tennis Courts **3+ mi:** Golf Course *(Millers Glen 472-2602, 13 mi.)*, Sightseeing *(Stafford Hall, Winery, Berry Farm; Courtesy van to local sites/sights, 30 mi.)*

Provisioning and General Services
OnSite: Wine/Beer, Newsstand, Copies Etc. **Under 1 mi:** Fishmonger *(Allen's Oyster House 472-2931)*, Post Office **1-3 mi:** Liquor Store, Market *(Oyster House Mart 472-2154)*, Protestant Church **3+ mi:** Supermarket *(Montross Food Lion, 5 mi.)*, Catholic Church *(5 mi.)*, Library *(Hague Branch 472-3820, 5 mi.)*, Pharmacy *(Rite Aid 493-9505, 18 mi.)*

Transportation
OnSite: Courtesy Car/Van *(Courtesy van and golf cart)*, Bikes, Airport Limo
Airport: Richmond *(65 mi.)*

Medical Services
911 Service **OnCall:** Ambulance **3+ mi:** Doctor *(Sisson 472-2657, 6 mi.)*
Hospital: Riverside Tappahannock 804-443-6090 *(28 mi.)*

PHOTOS ON CD-ROM: 15

Setting -- A jetty marks the private channel into Coles Point - right off the Potomac. A small riverside cove hosts smaller transient vessels. Behind the Pilot's Wharf Restaurant, four large docks - open and covered - and a full-service boatyard fill a very large basin. Surrounding this core are 340 acres of wildlife, a freshwater bass-stocked pond, five miles of trout streams, and a campground. Pine shaded picnic tables, grills and a play gym dot the riverfront behind a half-mile of sandy beach; the covered pool, horseshoe pits and volleyball courts lie inland.

Marina Notes -- *$2/ft. covered. Cole's Point is a work in progress, constantly in transition, with enormous potential. Over time the basin will be carved and dredged to double its current size (courtesy of a 15-year-old permit, the last issued on the river) to a total of 400 slips. Older slips are stationary and the newer ones floating. Small, but well-stocked convenience & ships' store. A full-service boat yard occupies the western side of the basin. Campground and cabin/lodge accommodations. Courtesy car or a golf cart. The bathhouse is being renovated.

Notable -- Pilot's Wharf, the well-rated waterfront restaurant, now under new management - with 2 new chefs and all new venues, an attractive inside dining room. A lovely covered deck with a Tiki Bar has spectacular views of the river and of the 500 ft. fishing pier. The giant smoker providessome regional specialties; plus they'll smoke your catch as well! Four rental cabins; two are near the shore and two in the adjacent RV park (which is quite invisible to the docks). There are monthly special events, call for listing. In historic Virginia near George Washington's birthplace, home of two other presidents and Robert E.

Navigational Information

Lat: 38°14.373' **Long:** 076°45.775' **Tide:** 3 ft. **Current:** 2 kt. **Chart:** 12285
Rep. Depths (*MLW*): Entry 5 ft. **Fuel Dock** 5 ft. **Max Slip/Moor** 8 ft./-
Access: Potomac River to St. Clement's Bay to St. Patrick Creek

Marina Facilities *(In Season/Off Season)*

Fuel: Gasoline, Diesel
Slips: 125 Total, 5 Transient **Max LOA:** 65 ft. **Max Beam:** 17 ft.
Rate *(per ft.)*: **Day** $0.50 **Week** n/a **Month** n/a
Power: 30 amp $5, **50 amp** $5, **100 amp** $5, **200 amp** $5
Cable TV: Yes **Dockside Phone:** No
Dock Type: Fixed
Moorings: 0 Total, 0 Transient **Launch:** n/a
Rate: Day n/a **Week** n/a **Month** n/a
Heads: 6 Toilet(s), 2 Shower(s) *(with dressing rooms)*
Laundry: 1 Washer(s), 1 Dryer(s) **Pay Phones:** No
Pump-Out: OnSite **Fee:** n/a **Closed Heads:** Yes

Marina Operations

Owner/Manager: Clark Lutz **Dockmaster:** Same
In-Season: Year-Round, 8:30am-4pm **Off-Season:** n/a
After-Hours Arrival: Call ahead
Reservations: Yes, Preferred **Credit Cards:** Visa/MC
Discounts: None
Pets: Welcome **Handicap Access:** Yes, Heads, Docks

Colton's Point Marina

PO Box 69; 38000 Kopels Road; Coltons Point, MD 20626

Tel: (301) 769-3121 **VHF: Monitor** 16 **Talk** 68
Fax: (301) 769-2547 **Alternate Tel:** n/a
Email: cpmarina1@starpower.net **Web:** www.coltonspointmarina.com
Nearest Town: Leonardtown *(14 mi.)* **Tourist Info:** (301) 475-4200

Marina Services and Boat Supplies

Services - Dock Carts, 300 amps, 3 Phase **Communication -** FedEx, DHL, UPS, Express Mail *(Sat Del)* **Supplies - OnSite:** Ice *(Block, Cube)*, Ships' Store, Bait/Tackle **Near:** Propane

Boatyard Services

OnSite: Travelift *(40T)*, Forklift, Engine mechanic *(gas)*, Electrical Repairs, Electronics Repairs, Hull Repairs, Rigger, Bottom Cleaning, Brightwork, Air Conditioning, Refrigeration, Compound, Wash & Wax, Interior Cleaning, Woodworking, Painting **OnCall:** Propeller Repairs, Inflatable Repairs, Life Raft Service **Dealer for:** Wellcraft. **Member:** ABBRA, ABYC, Other Certifications: Yamaha, Mercury, Mercruiser **Yard Rates:** $45/hr., Haul & Launch $4/ft. *(blocking $2/ft.)*, Power Wash $2.50/ft., Bottom Paint $8.50/ft.

Restaurants and Accommodations

1-3 mi: Inn/B&B *(Enfield's B&B 769-4755)* **3+ mi:** Restaurant *(Abell's 769-4010, L $5-15, 7 mi.)*, *(Shymansky's 259-2221, L $5-12, D $14-25, 6 mi.)*, *(Morris Point Restaurant 769-2500, L $10-22, D $10-22, 4 mi.)*, Fast Food *(McDonalds, KFC, Taco Bell 13 mi.)*, Motel *(Relax Inn 475-3011, 15 mi.)*, Inn/B&B *(Pin Cushion's B&B 475-8952, 12 mi.)*

Recreation and Entertainment

OnSite: Picnic Area, Grills, Playground **Near:** Beach **Under 1 mi:** Museum *(St. Clements Island Potomac River Museum 769-2222, $1, Mon-Fri 9am-5pm, weekends 12-5pm, incl. 1820 Little Red Schoolhouse & two Potomac Dory Boats)*, Cultural Attract *(Lord Proprietor's Players - historical re-enactments)*, Sightseeing *("The Tolerance" Water Taxi Tours to Historic St. Clements Island 769-2222, $5/3 Sat & Sun 12:30 & 2:30)*, Special Events *(Jazz & Seafood Fest 2nd Sat July; Bleesing of Fleet 1st weekend of Oct)* **1-3 mi:** Tennis Courts, Jogging Paths, Boat Rentals, Roller Blade/Bike Paths **3+ mi:** Golf Course *(Wicomico Shores 884-4601, 11 mi.)*

Provisioning and General Services

Under 1 mi: Fishmonger *(Shop Cove Seafood 69-4300)*, Catholic Church **1-3 mi:** Wine/Beer, Market *(Murphy's Town & Country 769-3131)*, Protestant Church **3+ mi:** Supermarket *(Food Lion 475-9104, McKay's Food & Drug 862-7702, 13 mi.)*, Health Food *(Good Earth Natural Foods 475-1630, 13 mi.)*, Beauty Salon *(Janie's Beauty Salon 769-3400, 4 mi.)*, Pharmacy *(Rite Aid 475-7212, 12 mi.)*, Hardware Store *(Leonardtown True Value 862-7702, 13 mi.)*

Transportation

Under 1 mi: Water Taxi *(to St. Clement's Island, Sat & Sun in season, $5/$3 kids 12 and under)* **3+ mi:** Rental Car *(Hertz 863-0033, 23 mi.)*, Taxi *(Leonardtown Cab 475-9157, 13 mi.)* **Airport:** Reagan Nat'l *(55 mi.)*

Medical Services

911 Service **OnCall:** Ambulance **3+ mi:** Doctor *(Shah Associates 475-8885, 12 mi.)* **Hospital:** St. Mary's 475-8981 *(13 mi.)*

Setting -- Securely tucked up pretty St. Patrick's Creek off St. Clement's Bay, neat and tidy Colton's Point has three main docks - two covered - and a large inland boatyard. An attractive picnic pavilion is perched above the docks, inviting crab feasts. The views from the docks are of picturesque, rural shorelines.

Marina Notes -- DCM. Established in 1961 as Kopel's Marina. The Lutz family has been at the helm since 1999 and is completing an extensive renovation program. Docks are in very good condition. The full-service yard with a large indoor shop and shed (for up to 4 cruisers) has a long history as a wooden boat specialist - now repowering & fiberglass are among the services. Good sized ships' store. All tile, nicely done bathhouse has separate showers with dressing rooms. Cather Marine, on the port side across from St. Patrick Campground, may also have an occasional transient slip.

Notable -- St. Clements Island, a 1/2 mile off Colton's Point, is a do-not-miss. Gov. Leonard Calvert & the Maryland colonists first landed here in 1634 and it played a key role in our early wars. About a mile walk from the marina, the fascinating St. Clements Island Potomac River Museum has a pretty riverfront picnic grove and a large pier. Home to the water taxi, which offers 1 hr. 45 min. tours on weekends. Private dinghies and most "big boats" can land right at the island's docks as well: a short pier for smaller boats is on the south side (near the 40-ft. memorial cross) and a longer pier for deeper draft craft on the north -- generally plenty of water. Overnight stays require a permit issued only by Point Lookout State Park - so this is really a day trip. Picnic pavilions and groves with charcoal grills and fresh water. The island has been protected since 1943 when it passed to public hands. The shorelines have, sadly, eroded from 400 acres to 40.

PHOTOS ON CD-ROM: 12

Pirate's Den Marina

PO Box 279; 12364 Neale Sound Dr.; Cobb Island, MD 20625

Tel: (301) 259-2879 **VHF: Monitor** 16 **Talk** 68
Fax: (301) 259-4896 **Alternate Tel:** (301) 259-2879
Email: blackbeard@piratesdenmarina.com **Web:** piratesdenmarina.com
Nearest Town: La Plata *(25 mi.)* **Tourist Info:** (301) 475-4200

Navigational Information

Lat: 38°15.841' **Long:** 076°50.850' **Tide:** 4 ft. **Current:** 7 kt. **Chart:** 12285
Rep. Depths (*MLW*): Entry 14 ft. **Fuel Dock** 17 ft. **Max Slip/Moor** 17 ft./-
Access: Potomic R. to Wicomico R. RGN (WR) to Neale Sound

Marina Facilities *(In Season/Off Season)*

Fuel: *Texaco* - Gasoline, Diesel
Slips: 100 Total, 20 Transient **Max LOA:** 50 ft. **Max Beam:** 15 ft.
Rate *(per ft.)*: **Day** $1.25 **Week** n/a **Month** $140
Power: 30 amp $6, **50 amp** $10, **100 amp** n/a, **200 amp** n/a
Cable TV: No **Dockside Phone:** No
Dock Type: Fixed, Long Fingers, Alongside, Wood, Composition
Moorings: 0 Total, 0 Transient **Launch:** n/a
Rate: Day n/a **Week** n/a **Month** n/a
Heads: 6 Toilet(s), 2 Shower(s) *(with dressing rooms)*
Laundry: 1 Washer(s), 1 Dryer(s), Iron **Pay Phones:** Yes, 1
Pump-Out: Self Service, 1 Central, 1 Port **Fee:** $5 **Closed Heads:** Yes

Marina Operations

Owner/Manager: See Marina Notes **Dockmaster:** D.Bradshaw
In-Season: Apr-Sep, 7am-7pm **Off-Season:** Oct-Dec, Sat & Sun, 8am-5pm
After-Hours Arrival: Leave msg. on machine or check-in at restaurant.
Reservations: Yes, Preferred **Credit Cards:** Visa/MC, Dscvr, Amex
Discounts: None
Pets: Welcome, Dog Walk Area **Handicap Access:** No

Marina Services and Boat Supplies

Services - Docking Assistance, Boaters' Lounge, Dock Carts **Communication -** Fax in/out *($2)*, FedEx, DHL, UPS, Express Mail *(Sat Del)* **Supplies - OnSite:** Ice *(Cube)*, Ships' Store **Near:** Ice *(Block)*, Marine Discount Store, Bait/Tackle, Live Bait, Propane *(Shymansky's Marina)*

Boatyard Services

OnSite: Travelift, Engine mechanic *(gas, diesel)*, Electrical Repairs, Bottom Cleaning, Compound, Wash & Wax, Interior Cleaning, Painting **Near:** Railway, Crane, Forklift, Hydraulic Trailer, Launching Ramp, Electronics Repairs, Hull Repairs, Rigger, Sail Loft, Canvas Work, Brightwork, Air Conditioning, Refrigeration, Divers, Woodworking, Inflatable Repairs, Life Raft Service, Upholstery, Yacht Interiors, Metal Fabrication, Awlgrip. **Yard Rates:** Haul & Launch $6/ft. *(blocking $3/ft.)*, Power Wash $2.50/ft., Bottom Paint $20/ft.H&L Incl. **Storage:** In-Water $140, On-Land $140

Restaurants and Accommodations

OnSite: Restaurant *(Pirate's Den 259-4990, L $6-24, D $6-25, pizzas $7-19, delivery available; outdoor tiki bar, Mon-Fri 3pm-mid, Sat & Sun Noon-Mid)* **Near:** Restaurant *(Fish Tales 259-2600, L $4-7, D $7-15, Karaoke Fri, live music Sat)*, *(Capt. John's 259-2315, B $4-7, L $7-15, D $11-39, most entrees $13-17; same menu all day; Sunday breakfast buffet $6)*, *(Shymansky's 259-2221, B $4-7, L $5-12, D $14-25, most entrees $13-17, Sunday breakfast buffet $7)*, Seafood Shack *(Norris Seafood 259-2434)* **3+ mi:** Motel *(White House 932-2990, 11 mi.)*

Recreation and Entertainment

OnSite: Picnic Area, Grills, Playground **Near:** Boat Rentals, Video Rental, Park, Sightseeing *(stroll the lanes of quaint Cobb Island - a haven for birdwatchers - osprey nests)*, Special Events *(Cobb Island Days - early Jun & July 4th)* **3+ mi:** Golf Course *(Swan Point Yacht & Country Club 259-0042, 7 mi.)*, Movie Theater *(30 mi.)*, Museum *(by boat - St. Clements Island Potomac River Museum 769-2222, $1, 9am-5pm, 12-5pm weekends incl. 1820 Little Red Schoolhouse & 2 Potomac Dory Boats, 4 mi.)*, Cultural Attract *(by boat - St. Clements Island State Park - land at one of two docks - site of original 1634 Maryland Settlement, 4 mi.)*

Provisioning and General Services

Near: Convenience Store, Wine/Beer *(Cobb Island Market)*, Liquor Store *(Shymansky's)*, Crabs/Waterman, Market *(Cobb Island Market 259-2465)*, Bank/ATM, Post Office *(259-4159)*, Copies Etc. **Under 1 mi:** Protestant Church, Newsstand, Florist **1-3 mi:** Catholic Church **3+ mi:** Library *(30 mi.)*, Beauty Salon *(25mi.)*, Barber Shop *(25 mi.)*, Dry Cleaners *(25 mi.)*, Laundry *(25 mi.)*, Bookstore *(30 mi.)*, Pharmacy *(25 mi.)*, Hardware Store *(11 mi.)*, Retail Shops *(25 mi.)*, Department Store *(30 mi.)*, Buying Club *(30 mi.)*

Transportation

OnSite: Bikes *(complimentary)* **OnCall:** Taxi, Airport Limo *(Call-A-Ride 301-609-9112)* **Airport:** Reagan Nat'l. *(55 mi.)*

Medical Services

911 Service **OnCall:** Ambulance *(local VFD)* **Under 1 mi:** Dentist *(Armstrong 259-0454)* **Hospital:** St. Mary's 475-8981 *(35 mi.)*

Setting -- At the mouth of the Wicomico River, three marinas are nestled into Neal Sound. Pirate's Den Marina is on the Cobb Island side - at the entrance to the island. Two long piers plus a travelift bay end at a grassy slope topped by a low-slung white stucco office and restaurant with slate blue trim. Cantilevered over the hill is an open air tiki bar. Hunter green strap chairs surround bright blue umbrella-topped tables on a new brick deck. A few picnic tables populate the lawn.

Marina Notes -- Closed Dec-Mar. Established in 1975 as Cobb Island Marina; current owners (J. Houghrigh, R. Sterling & A. Jollife) took over in October '03. Loaner bikes available. A bright orange open-ended travelift is pulled by a truck. Coming soon is a ships' and convenience store. The quite nice all-tile key coded heads and showers (with a vanity for the women) are at the back of the main building.

Notable -- The airy, casual Priate's Den restaurant is lined with water-view windows and furnished with new, bright blue bentwood chairs and white table cloths; it also features a new varnished wood bar. Two menus - Italian and American - offer pasta, steaks, shrimp, crab cakes, homemade bread, sandwiches and special salads plus hand-tossed pizzas and party platters (delivery to the boat). The kitchen is open every night 'til midnight - Mon-Fri from 3pm, Sat & Sun from Noon. Karaoke Friday nights and live entertainment Saturdays. Just up the road is a wonderfully creative, good-sized playground. A block farther is the small, modestly supplied Cobb Island Market (cold beer, bait, groceries, fresh meats), post office, and ATM.

PHOTOS ON CD-ROM: 9

Navigational Information

Lat: 38°15.978' **Long:** 076°50.966' **Tide:** 3 ft. **Current:** n/a **Chart:** 12285
Rep. Depths (*MLW*): Entry 6 ft. **Fuel Dock** 6 ft. **Max Slip/Moor** 7 ft./-
Access: Potomac to Wicomico River to Neale Sound

Marina Facilities *(In Season/Off Season)*

Fuel: Yes
Slips: 75 Total, 20 Transient **Max LOA:** 40 ft. **Max Beam:** 14 ft.
Rate *(per ft.)*: **Day** $1.00 **Week** n/a **Month** n/a
Power: 30 amp Inq., **50 amp** Inq., **100 amp** n/a, **200 amp** n/a
Cable TV: No **Dockside Phone:** No
Dock Type: Fixed, Short Fingers
Moorings: 0 Total, 0 Transient **Launch:** n/a
Rate: Day n/a **Week** n/a **Month** n/a
Heads: 4 Toilet(s), 2 Shower(s)
Laundry: None **Pay Phones:** No
Pump-Out: No **Fee:** n/a **Closed Heads:** Yes

Marina Operations

Owner/Manager: Robert Shymansky **Dockmaster:** Same
In-Season: Summer, 6am-11pm **Off-Season:** Fall-Spring, 8am-9pm
After-Hours Arrival: Call ahead
Reservations: Preferred **Credit Cards:** Visa/MC, Dscvr, Amex
Discounts: None
Pets: No **Handicap Access:** Yes

Shymansky's River Marina

PO Box 449; 16320 Cobb Island Road; Cobb Island, MD 20625

Tel: (301) 259-2221 **VHF: Monitor** 16 **Talk** n/a
Fax: (301) 259-0145 **Alternate Tel:** (301) 259-0300
Email: n/a **Web:** n/a
Nearest Town: La Plata *(20 mi.)* **Tourist Info:** (301) 475-4200

Marina Services and Boat Supplies

Services - Docking Assistance, Trash Pick-Up, Dock Carts **Communication -** Phone Messages, Fax in/out *($2)*, FedEx, DHL, UPS, Express Mail **Supplies - OnSite:** Ice *(Cube)*, Ships' Store, Bait/Tackle, Live Bait, Propane

Boatyard Services

OnSite: Travelift *(15T)*, Launching Ramp, Engine mechanic *(gas)*, Electrical Repairs, Hull Repairs, Bottom Cleaning, Divers, Compound, Wash & Wax **Yard Rates:** $38/hr., Haul & Launch $8.50/ft. *(blocking incl.)*, Power Wash Inq.

Restaurants and Accommodations

OnSite: Restaurant *(Shymansky's 259-2221, B $7, L $5-12, D $14-25, most entrees $13-17; Sunday all-you-can-eat breakfast buffet $7, unbeatable cream of crab soup)* **Near:** Restaurant *(Captain John's Crab House 259-2315, B $4-7, L $7-15, D $11-39, same menu all day, Sunday breakfast buffet $6)*, *(Pirate's Den 259-4990, L $6-25, D $6-25, Mon-Fri 3pm-mid, Sat & Sun Noon-Mid)*, *(Fish Tales Bar & Grill 259-2600, L $4-7, D $7-15)* **3+ mi:** Motel *(White House Motel 932-2990, 11 mi.)*

Recreation and Entertainment

OnSite: Picnic Area, Boat Rentals *(runabouts)*, Fishing Charter **Near:** Playground, Park, Special Events *(Cobb Island Days - early June)* **3+ mi:** Golf Course *(Swan Point Yacht & Country Club 259-0042, 7 mi.)*, Museum *(by boat - on the mainland - St. Clements Island Potomac River 769-2222, $1, 9am-5pm, 12-5pm weekends incl. 1820 Little Red Schoolhouse & 2 Potomac Dory Boats, 4 mi.)*, Sightseeing *(by boat - St. Clements Island State Park - land at one of two docks - site of original 1634 Maryland Settlement, 4 mi.)*

Provisioning and General Services

OnSite: Convenience Store, Wine/Beer, Liquor Store **Near:** Bakery, Farmers' Market, Fishmonger, Bank/ATM, Post Office *(259-4159)*, Newsstand, Hardware Store, Florist **Under 1 mi:** Market *(Cobb Island Market 259-2465)* **1-3 mi:** Catholic Church

Transportation

OnCall: Airport Limo *(Call-A-Ride 609-9112)* **Airport:** Reagan *(55 mi.)*

Medical Services

911 Service **OnCall:** Ambulance **Under 1 mi:** Dentist *(Armstrong 259-0454)* **Hospital:** St. Mary's 475-8981 *(35 mi.)*

Setting -- Shymansky's is on a little peninsula just on the north side of the 18-foot fixed Cobb Island Bridge. Neale Sound is on the west side and a deep river inlet is on the east side. Right in the middle is the large, well-known seafood restaurant surrounded by dockage. Three main piers are on the east side of the bridge (across from Pirate's Den); additional dockage and the fuel dock are on the shallower west side across the road from the restaurant entrance.

Marina Notes -- Restaurant and marina owned by the Shymansky Family since 1950. The large, extremely well-equipped store - which also serves as the marina office - has marine supplies, bait-and-tackle (including live bait), liquor, and convenience items; it opens at 6am on weekdays and 5:30am weekends. Pets are not welcomed at this marina. 15 ton travelift. The local fireboat makes its home here - big, red and quite spectacular - often joined by marine police boats and towboats. Bright blue cinderblock bathhouses are basic.

Notable -- Shymansky's River Restaurant has three eating areas. To the left is the main dining room; to the right is the bar. On the far side of the bar is the "deck" - which is really a large all-window room - and where most people tend to gather. White tables and chairs topped with green umbrellas are scattered on the lawn. The whole menu is available all day. Most of the fish is right off local boats including the rockfish. Steamers, hard crabs, oysters, and steamed shrimp are also available. The famous crab feasts depend on availability. Sandwiches range from $3-9, baskets $7-12, and entrées $14-25. While you're waiting there's Keno. Right across the Cobb Island bridge is a great playground and a block farther inland is the post office and a well-equipped market with an ATM.

PHOTOS ON CD-ROM: 12

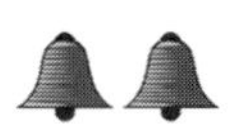

Captain John's Crabhouse

PO Box 288; 16215 Cobb Island Road; Cobb Island, MD 20625

Tel: (301) 259-2315 **VHF: Monitor** n/a **Talk** n/a
Fax: (301) 259-2471 **Alternate Tel:** n/a
Email: cjcrab@comcast.net **Web:** www.cjcrab.com
Nearest Town: Cobb Island *(0.5 mi.)* **Tourist Info:** (301) 475-4200

Navigational Information

Lat: 38°16.067' **Long:** 076°51.169' **Tide:** 3 ft. **Current:** n/a **Chart:** 12285
Rep. Depths (*MLW*): Entry 6 ft. **Fuel Dock** n/a **Max Slip/Moor** 7 ft./-
Access: Potomac to Wicomico River to Neale Sound

Marina Facilities *(In Season/Off Season)*

Fuel: Gasoline
Slips: 40 Total, 10 Transient **Max LOA:** 45 ft. **Max Beam:** n/a
Rate *(per ft.)*: **Day** Free* **Week** n/a **Month** $55-95
Power: 30 amp Incl, **50 amp** n/a, **100 amp** n/a, **200 amp** n/a
Cable TV: No **Dockside Phone:** No
Dock Type: Fixed, Short Fingers, Pilings, Alongside, Wood
Moorings: 0 Total, 0 Transient **Launch:** n/a
Rate: Day n/a **Week** n/a **Month** n/a
Heads: 6 Toilet(s)
Laundry: None **Pay Phones:** No
Pump-Out: OnSite, Full Service, 1 Central **Fee:** $5 **Closed Heads:** Yes

Marina Operations

Owner/Manager: Bob Magorian **Dockmaster:** Jack Yates
In-Season: Year-Round, 5am-10pm **Off-Season:** n/a
After-Hours Arrival: Call in advance
Reservations: Yes, Preferred **Credit Cards:** Visa/MC, Dscvr, Amex
Discounts: None
Pets: Welcome **Handicap Access:** Yes, Heads, Docks

Marina Services and Boat Supplies

Communication - FedEx, UPS, Express Mail **Supplies - OnSite:** Ice *(Cube)*, Ships' Store, Bait/Tackle, Live Bait *(worms)*

Boatyard Services

OnSite: Launching Ramp *($5)* **Near:** Travelift, Engine mechanic *(gas)*.
Nearest Yard: Shymansky's Marina (301) 259-2221

Restaurants and Accommodations

OnSite: Restaurant *(Capt. John's 259-2315, B $4-7, L $7-15, D $11-39, Mon-Thu 11:30am-9pm, Sat 11:30am-10:30pm, Sun 8:30am-9pm; Sun breakfast buffet $6)* **Near:** Restaurant *(Fish Tales Bar & Grill 259-2600, L $4-7, D $7-15)*, *(Shymansky's 259-2331, B $7, L $5-12, D $14-25)*, *(Pirate's Den 259-4990, L $6-25, D $6-25, Lunch weekends only, entreés mostly mid-teens)*, Seafood Shack *(Norris Seafood 259-2434)* **3+ mi:** Motel *(White House Motel 932-2990, 11 mi.)*

Recreation and Entertainment

OnSite: Boat Rentals *(runabouts $70/day)* **Near:** Sightseeing *(Cobb Island)*, Special Events *(Cobb Island Days - early June)* **Under 1 mi:** Park **3+ mi:** Golf Course *(Swan Point Yacht & Country Club 259-0042, 7 mi.)* Museum*(by boat - on the mainland by boat - St. Clements Island Potomac River 769-2222, $1, 9am-5pm, 12-5pm weekends incl. 1820 Little Red Schoolhouse & 2 Potomac Dory Boats, 4 mi.)*, Cultural Attract *(St. Clements Island - land at one of the two docks - picnic, grills, history, 4 mi.)*

Provisioning and General Services

OnSite: Wine/Beer, Fishmonger *(steamed shrimp, fish, crab legs, fresh crabmeat & oysters)* **Near:** Liquor Store, Market *(Cobb Island Market 259-2465)* **Under 1 mi:** Convenience Store, Bakery, Bank/ATM, Post Office *(259-4159)*, Protestant Church **3+ mi:** Catholic Church *(5 mi.)*

Transportation

OnCall: Airport Limo *(Call-A-Ride 609-9112)*
Airport: Reagan Nat'l. *(55 mi.)*

Medical Services

911 Service **Under 1 mi:** Dentist *(Armstrong 259-0454)*
Hospital: St. Mary's 475-8981 *(35 mi.)*

Setting -- Just west of Shymansky's on Neal Sound, about halfway from each river entrance, Captain John's network of docks is populated by an even mix of pleasure craft and working vessels spread out directly in front of the restaurant. The attractive two-story beige clapboard contemporary restaurant with brown trim sports large expanses of windows and a variety of indoor and outdoor eating options. Burgundy umbrellas shade benches line the waterfront.

Marina Notes -- *Free overnight dockage for diners. Docks are being replaced in Feb '06 and there may be a charge after that. This is a very popular restaurant with docks and the restaurant takes priority. On-site are boat and fishing supplies. Power consists of plugs on pilings. New pump-out. The restaurant heads (with a baby changing table) are also the boaters' heads- no showers.

Notable -- The bright, casual, carpeted, pine paneled main dining room is mostly windows and furnished with turquoise chairs and booths. The narrow waterside eating deck has a single row of umbrella-topped tables accented with potted plants. The restaurant is open 7 days all year - also offer carryout. At the last visit, steamed crabs were $25 per dozen for medium, $31 for large, and $45 for jumbo. (Call main # and press extension #5 for today's prices- usually M-F specials). Same menu all day. Light fare and baskets $7-14, sandwiches $3-9. Shore and seafood dinners range from $9-18, surf and turf is $27, topped by the huge $30 seafood special. Upstairs event rooms accomodate guests from 20-60. Next door at Shymansky's is liquor and more supplies, and across the Cobb Island Bridge is a well-supplied market, post office, playground and ATM.

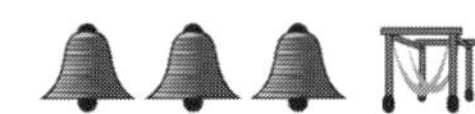

Navigational Information
Lat: 38°13.855' **Long:** 076°57.780' **Tide:** 3 ft. **Current:** n/a **Chart:** 12285
Rep. Depths (*MLW*): Entry 9 ft. **Fuel Dock** 10 ft. **Max Slip/Moor** 6 ft./6 ft.
Access: 40 miles up the Potomac at the mouth of Monroe Bay

Marina Facilities *(In Season/Off Season)*
Fuel: *Texaco* - Gasoline, Diesel
Slips: 90 Total, 20 Transient **Max LOA:** 120 ft. **Max Beam:** 22 ft.
Rate *(per ft.)*: **Day** $1.25 **Week** $6.25/6.25 **Month** $275/275.00
Power: 30 amp $5, **50 amp** $5, **100 amp** n/a, **200 amp** n/a
Cable TV: Yes **Dockside Phone:** No
Dock Type: Fixed, Short Fingers, Pilings, Alongside, Wood
Moorings: 0 Total, 0 Transient **Launch:** n/a
Rate: Day n/a **Week** n/a **Month** n/a
Heads: 4 Toilet(s), 4 Shower(s)
Laundry: None, Book Exchange **Pay Phones:** No
Pump-Out: Self Service, 1 Central, 2 Port **Fee:** $5 **Closed Heads:** Yes

Marina Operations
Owner/Manager: Kyle & Relda Schick **Dockmaster:** Ben Theis
In-Season: Year-Round, 9am-5pm **Off-Season:** n/a
After-Hours Arrival: Check in at restaurant
Reservations: Preferred **Credit Cards:** Visa/MC, Dscvr, Din, Amex, Tex
Discounts: None
Pets: Welcome, Dog Walk Area **Handicap Access:** No

Colonial Beach Yacht Center

PO Box 400; 1787 Castlewood Drive; Colonial Beach, VA 22443
Tel: (804) 224-7230 **VHF: Monitor** 16 **Talk** 68
Fax: (804) 224-7232 **Alternate Tel:** n/a
Email: n/a **Web:** www.colonialbeachyachtcenter.com
Nearest Town: Colonial Beach *(1 mi.)* **Tourist Info:** (804) 224-8145

Marina Services and Boat Supplies
Services - Docking Assistance, Concierge, Boaters' Lounge, Security *(24 hr.)*, Trash Pick-Up, Dock Carts **Communication -** Mail & Package Hold, Phone Messages, Fax in/out, Data Ports, FedEx, DHL, UPS, Express Mail **Supplies - OnSite:** Ice *(Block, Cube)*, Ships' Store, Bait/Tackle, Live Bait **1-3 mi:** Propane *(D & D Gas 224-2552)*

Boatyard Services
OnSite: Travelift *(two 30T)*, Hydraulic Trailer, Launching Ramp, Engine mechanic *(gas, diesel)*, Electrical Repairs, Electronics Repairs, Hull Repairs, Bottom Cleaning, Brightwork, Compound, Wash & Wax, Interior Cleaning, Propeller Repairs, Woodworking, Painting, Yacht Broker **OnCall:** Canvas Work, Air Conditioning, Refrigeration, Divers, Upholstery, Metal Fabrication, Awlgrip **Member:** ABBRA, ABYC **Yard Rates:** $45/hr., Haul & Launch $4/ft. *(blocking $1/ft.)*, Power Wash $35, Bottom Paint $10/ft. *(paint incl.)* **Storage:** In-Water $5/day, On-Land $10/day

Restaurants and Accommodations
OnSite: Restaurant *(Dockside 224-8726, L $6-10, D $13-32, kids' $4-7, brunch Sat & Sun)* **OnCall:** Pizzeria *(Domino's 224-2334)* **Near:** Motel *(Wakefield 224-7311, $60)* **Under 1 mi:** Motel *(Doc's 224-7840)*, *(Nightingales 224-7956, $49-55)*, Inn/B&B *(Bell House 224-7000, $100-140, Alexander Graham Bell's elegant riverfront home - breakfast plus wine & cheese)* **1-3 mi:** Restaurant *(Wilkerson's Seafood 224-7117, L $5-10, D $11-23, kids' $1/year)*, *(South Bay Café L $5-7, D $10-17, kids' $2-4)*, (The *Lighthouse 224-8282, L $6-15, D $15-25, kids' $4)*, *(Margaritas 214-9990, L $3-6, D $5-16)*, *(Hunan Dinner 224-8754, L $6-13, D $6-13, whole duck $20)*, Snack Bar *(Sand Castles Ice Cream & Deli 224-0600)*

Recreation and Entertainment
OnSite: Beach, Picnic Area, Grills, Playground, Boat Rentals *(Rattle & Hum 214-9003)*, Volleyball **Under 1 mi:** Park *(Westmoreland State 224-7311)*, Museum *(Colonial Beach 224-3379)*, Cultural Attract *(Colonial Beach Pier)*, Special Events *(River Fest - Jun)* **1-3 mi:** Video Rental *(Movie Gallery 224-1156)* **3+ mi:** Golf Course *(Cameron Hills 540-775-4653, 11 mi.)*

Provisioning and General Services
OnSite: Wine/Beer **Under 1 mi:** Beauty Salon *(Linda's 224-7330)* **1-3 mi:** Convenience Store *(7-Eleven 224-7660)*, Supermarket *(Food Lion 224-2064)*, Delicatessen *(Hall's 224-9310)*, Liquor Store, Green Grocer *(Winter Harbor Seafood & Produce 224-7779)*, Fishmonger *(Shady Lane 224-7878)*, Oysterman *(L L Curley 224-7544)*, Market *(Colonial Beach 224-1857)*, Bank/ATM, Post Office *(214-9636)*, Protestant Church, Library *(224-0921)*, Laundry *(Maybush 224-6900)*, Pharmacy *(Rite Aide 224-2318)*, Newsstand *(Westmoreland 493-8096)*, Hardware Store *(Rankin's 224-8996)*, Florist *(Four Seasons 224-9020)*

Transportation
OnSite: Local Bus *(Trolley 804-224-0175)* **OnCall:** Rental Car *(Enterprise 540-663-2244)*, Airport Limo *(Fredericksburg 888-565-3262)* **Under 1 mi:** Bikes *(Metro Golf Carts & Scooters 804-224-2278)* **1-3 mi:** InterCity Bus **Airport:** Reagan Nat'l.*(67 mi.)*

Medical Services
911 Service **OnCall:** Ambulance **1-3 mi:** Doctor *(Dominion Medical 224-7196)*, Dentist *(Gares 224-0727)* **3+ mi:** Veterinarian *(Twin Rivers 224-0011, 9 mi.)* **Hospital:** Mary Washington 800-722-2788 *(32 mi.)*

Setting -- Right at the entrance to Monroe Bay, just past the thatched umbrellas outboard of Dockside's tiki bar, play gym and picnic grove, is CBYC's convenient fuel dock - backed by two white tanks. Around the bend, tucked behind Gum Bar Point, its extensive network of superb new docks edges the curving shore. At the far end, next to the travelift bay, a series of slips are covered by bright blue vinyl covered steel hoops.

Marina Notes -- Family owned/operated since 1988, completely rebuilt after two disasters: a fire in '02 followed by Isabel in '03. Brand new stationary docks with short, wide finger piers and brand new pedestals. Covered slips topped with fireproof and UV resistant vinyl. Full BY operation with 2 lifts and well-supplied marine store. Fish cleaning station. Fishing licenses. Shelly and Shiloh, two sweet little black & white pups, greet arriving boats. The green-sided bathhouse with teal trim has tile floors and faux tile walls (heat & A/C). Fiberglass shower stalls with dressing rooms plus 3 sinks set into a Formica vanity & good mirrors.

Notable -- The casual Dockside Restaurant, once an oyster packing plant, sits in the midst of the 9-acre point - with a venue and menu for every mood: main dining room, cozy Blue Heron English Pub (with fireplace), open air screened porch (designed for crabs) and outdoor deck and tiki huts - overlooking the Potomac. A wide sandy beach lies across the entrance road. Touring reemerging, leafy Colonial Beach is easy - a seasonal trolley loops hourly and golf carts (rentals delivered) are the rage. The charming, Nat'l. Register riverfront 1883 Bell House B&B is half a mile. Another mile to the Town Pier and concrete beachside boardwalk. A half mile farther is the Food Lion shopping center. Eateries and local shops are sprinkled among the gentrifying neighborhoods.

PHOTOS ON CD-ROM: 17

Nightingale Motel & Marina

101 Monroe Bay Avenue; Colonial Beach, VA 22443

Tel: (804) 224-7956 **VHF: Monitor** n/a **Talk** n/a
Fax: n/a **Alternate Tel:** n/a
Email: n/a **Web:** n/a
Nearest Town: Colonial Beach *(0.5 mi.)* **Tourist Info:** (804) 224-8145

Navigational Information

Lat: 38°14.888' **Long:** 076°57.914' **Tide:** n/a **Current:** n/a **Chart:** 12285
Rep. Depths (*MLW*): Entry 5 ft. **Fuel Dock** 5 ft. **Max Slip/Moor** 5 ft./5 ft.
Access: Potomac River to Monroe Bay; 1.5 mi. west

Marina Facilities *(In Season/Off Season)*

Fuel: No
Slips: 34 Total, 8 Transient **Max LOA:** 40 ft. **Max Beam:** n/a
Rate *(per ft.)*: **Day** $1.00 **Week** n/a **Month** n/a
Power: 30 amp $5, **50 amp** n/a, **100 amp** n/a, **200 amp** n/a
Cable TV: No **Dockside Phone:** No
Dock Type: Fixed
Moorings: 0 Total, 0 Transient **Launch:** n/a
Rate: Day n/a **Week** n/a **Month** n/a
Heads: 2 Toilet(s), 2 Shower(s)
Laundry: None **Pay Phones:** No
Pump-Out: OnSite **Fee:** Free **Closed Heads:** Yes

Marina Operations

Owner/Manager: Janice Swink **Dockmaster:** Same
In-Season: Apr-Nov, 24 hrs. **Off-Season:** Dec-Mar, closed
After-Hours Arrival: Tie-up in empty slip and plug in; check in next day
Reservations: No **Credit Cards:** Visa/MC, Amex
Discounts: None
Pets: Welcome, Dog Walk Area **Handicap Access:** Yes

Marina Services and Boat Supplies

Services - Docking Assistance, Dock Carts **Communication -** Phone Messages, FedEx, UPS, Express Mail **Supplies - Near:** Ice *(Cube)*, Ships' Store, West Marine, Boat/US, Marine Discount Store, Bait/Tackle *(DJ's Place)*, Live Bait **Under 1 mi:** Propane *(D & D Gas Services 224-2552)*

Boatyard Services

Near: Travelift, Railway, Crane, Forklift, Launching Ramp, Engine mechanic *(gas, diesel)*, Electrical Repairs, Hull Repairs, Bottom Cleaning, Divers, Propeller Repairs, Woodworking, Yacht Interiors, Metal Fabrication, Painting. **Nearest Yard:** Stanford's Marine Railway (804) 224-7644

Restaurants and Accommodations

OnSite: Motel *(Nightingales 224-7956, $49-55)* **Near:** Restaurant *(Hunan Diner 224-8754)*, *(Ola's Country Kitchen 224-9050)*, Seafood Shack *(The Lighthouse 224-8282, L $6-15, D $15-25)*, Snack Bar *(Tropical Delights)*, *(Sand Castles Ice Cream & Deli 224-0600)*, Lite Fare *(Margaritas 214-9990, L $5-16, D $5-16, Peruvian & Latin American)*, *(Lenny's Bagel 224-9675, B $4, L $5)*, Pizzeria *(Domino's 224-2334)*, Motel *(Doc's Motor Court 224-7840)*, Hotel *(River View Inn 224-0006)* **Under 1 mi:** Restaurant *(The Riverboat 224-7055, B $3-7, L $3-8, D $13-24, kids' $3-4)*, Motel *(Days Inn 224-0404, $75)*, Inn/B&B *(Bell House B&B 224-7000, $100-140)* **1-3 mi:** Restaurant *(Wilkerson's Seafood 224-7117, L $5-10, D $11-23, all-you-can-eat snow crab legs & spiced shrimp $32)*, *(Dockside 224-8726, L $6-10, D $13-32, kids' $4-7, Sat & Sun brunch)*

Recreation and Entertainment

OnSite: Picnic Area, Grills, Fishing Charter **Near:** Beach, Playground, Group Fishing Boat *(Potomac River Charters 224-1400 3-4 hrs. $20/pp 9am)*, Park *(Westmoreland State Park 224-7311)*, Museum *(Colonial Beach 224-3379)*, Cultural Attract *(Colonial Beach Municipal Pier)* **Under 1 mi:** Video Rental *(Movie Gallery 224-1156)* **1-3 mi:** Boat Rentals *(Rattle & Hum 214-9003)* **3+ mi:** Golf Course *(Cameron Hills 540-775-4653, 10 mi.)*

Provisioning and General Services

Near: Health Food, Wine/Beer, Liquor Store, Bakery, Oysterman *(L L Curley 224-7544)*, Bank/ATM, Catholic Church, Protestant Church, Synagogue, Beauty Salon *(Linda's 224-7330)*, Barber Shop, Laundry *(Maybush Laundry 224-6900)*, Bookstore, Newsstand *(Westmoreland News 493-8096)*, Florist *(Four Seasons 224-9020)* **Under 1 mi:** Convenience Store *(7-Eleven 224-7660)*, Supermarket *(Food Lion 224-2064)*, Market *(Colonial Beach 224-1857)*, Post Office *(214-9636)*, Library *(224-0921)*, Pharmacy *(Rite Aid 224-2318)* **1-3 mi:** Delicatessen *(Hall's Super Market 224-9310)*, Green Grocer *(Winter Harbor Seafood & Produce 224-7779)*, Crabs/Waterman *(Shady Lane Seafood Carry-Out 224-7878)*, Hardware Store *(Rankin's 224-8996)*

Transportation

OnSite: Bikes *(free)*, Local Bus *(Trolley 504-224-0175)* **OnCall:** Rental Car *(Enterprise 540-663-2244)*, Airport Limo *(Fredericksburg 888-565-3262)* **3+ mi:** Rail *(Amtrak 906-3104, 65 mi.)* **Airport:** Reagan Nat'l. *(66 mi.)*

Medical Services

911 Service **OnCall:** Ambulance, Optician *(Dr. Gilchrest)* **Near:** Dentist *(Gares 224-0727)* **Under 1 mi:** Doctor *(Colonial Beach 224-6322)*
Hospital: Mary Washington 800-722-2788 *(31 mi.)*

Setting -- Tucked about a mile and a half deep into Monroe Bay, Nightingale's Motel and Marina offers 8 transient slips at its wide single dock. Shoreside is an attractive, pale yellow single-story motel, a boat house, several picnic tables with grills - nicely sited among the well-tended foliage, a fleet of bikes, a bathhouse and a welcome hammock. The gorgeous sunsets streak across the placid bay to the docks; five resident swans visit twice a day.

Marina Notes -- Gizmo is the Shih Tzu in charge. Stationary docks with short tapered finger piers. 30-amp power and water are attached to the pilings. A new Sani-Sailor pump-out too. Motel has 5 nicely appointed rooms. Two new, very comfortable full bathrooms have fiberglass shower stalls and cement floors. Nearby, venerable Stanford's Boat Railway provides most boatyard services, and may in '06 again offer transient dockage.

Notable -- Nightingale is the closest marina to the Town Pier, which makes it a perfect base for discovering revitalized, tree-shaded, Victorian Colonial Beach. The seasonal trolley stops at the door, and Metro Golf Carts is four blocks away. Two doors down is the Lantern Restaurant. The Town Pier sits between two wide swaths of sugary sand backed by some casual eateries. The concrete boardwalk, a remnant of this historic town's glory days, heads north ending at the rebuilt Riverboat II's pier - it's actually in Maryland - where gaming laws are more lenient. Colonial Beach invites passion - near the Town Pier, a whole block, anchored by the perfectly restored yellow & blue art deco Riverview Inn and Tropical Delights, has been reclaimed by Michael Wardman of the famous D.C. construction company. Gentrification is aggressively underway. A half mile farther the Food Lion shopping center meets more prosaic needs.

11. WS: LOWER POTOMAC RIVER

PHOTOS ON CD-ROM: 13

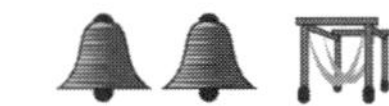

Navigational Information
Lat: 38°19.350' **Long:** 077°02.950' **Tide:** 2 ft. **Current:** n/a **Chart:** 12285
Rep. Depths (*MLW*): Entry 7 ft. **Fuel Dock** 6 ft. **Max Slip/Moor** 7 ft./-
Access: Potomac River Bell #29 to Upper Machodok Creek

Marina Facilities *(In Season/Off Season)*
Fuel: *Texaco* - Gasoline, Diesel
Slips: 62 Total, 2 Transient **Max LOA:** 60 ft. **Max Beam:** 18 ft.
Rate *(per ft.)*: **Day** $1.25* **Week** $60 **Month** $240
Power: 30 amp Inq., **50 amp** Inq., **100 amp** Inq., **200 amp** n/a
Cable TV: No **Dockside Phone:** No
Dock Type: Fixed, Short Fingers, Pilings, Alongside, Wood
Moorings: 0 Total, 0 Transient **Launch:** n/a
Rate: Day n/a **Week** n/a **Month** n/a
Heads: 2 Toilet(s), 2 Shower(s) *(with dressing rooms)*
Laundry: 1 Washer(s), 1 Dryer(s) **Pay Phones:** Yes, 1
Pump-Out: OnSite, Full Service, 1 Central **Fee:** $25 **Closed Heads:** Yes

Marina Operations
Owner/Manager: Don Paul **Dockmaster:** Same
In-Season: Apr-Oct, 9am-6pm **Off-Season:** Nov-Mar, 9am-5pm
After-Hours Arrival: Call ahead
Reservations: Preferred **Credit Cards:** Visa/MC
Discounts: None
Pets: Welcome, Dog Walk Area **Handicap Access:** Yes, Heads, Docks

Dahlgren Marine Works

17088 Ferry Dock Road; Dahlgren, VA 22448

Tel: (540) 663-2741 **VHF: Monitor** 16&68 **Talk** 68
Fax: n/a **Alternate Tel:** n/a
Email: n/a **Web:** n/a
Nearest Town: King George *(2 mi.)* **Tourist Info:** (804) 333-1919

Marina Services and Boat Supplies
Services - Trash Pick-Up **Communication -** FedEx, UPS **Supplies - OnSite:** Ice *(Cube)*, Ships' Store **3+ mi:** Propane *(Big Timber Campground 775-9630, 9 mi.)*

Boatyard Services
OnSite: Travelift *(6T)*, Launching Ramp, Bottom Cleaning, Compound, Wash & Wax, Painting **OnCall:** Engine mechanic *(gas, diesel)*, Electrical Repairs, Hull Repairs, Brightwork, Air Conditioning, Refrigeration, Divers, Propeller Repairs, Woodworking, Awlgrip **Dealer for:** Volvo Penta parts.
Yard Rates: $45/hr., Haul & Launch $5/ft., Power Wash $1.50/ft., Bottom Paint $14/ft. *(paint incl.)* **Storage:** On-Land $50/mo.

Restaurants and Accommodations
Under 1 mi: Restaurant *(Hunan Cafe 663-4354, L $4-7, D $7-11)*, *(Marathon 663-3218)*, *(China Garden 663-2993, L $4-6, D $7-10)*, *(Roma Pizza 663-2200, L $6-10, D $6-10, delivers)*, Snack Bar *(Normand's)*, Pizzeria *(Domino's 644-1414, delivers)*, *(Pizza Hut 663-2575)* **1-3 mi:** Restaurant *(Polar Bear 663-9900)*, *(Avanti 644-8904)*, Seafood Shack *(Crabby Oyster 644-8804)*, Fast Food *(McDonalds, Burger King, KFC)*, Motel *(Comfort Inn 663-3060)*, *(Holiday Inn Express 644-1500)*, *(Hillcrest 663-3100)*

Recreation and Entertainment
Under 1 mi: Beach *(dinghy)* **1-3 mi:** Picnic Area, Playground, Tennis Courts, Park *(Barnesfield)* **3+ mi:** Golf Course *(Cameron Hills 775-4653, 17 mi.)*, Video Rental *(Movie Gallery 804-224-1156, 14 mi.)*

Provisioning and General Services
Under 1 mi: Delicatessen *(Clubhouse Deli 663-2802, Olympus Deli, 644-1199)*, Post Office *(663-3230)*, Protestant Church, Beauty Salon *(Finesse Hair Gallery 644-9400)*, Barber Shop *(Jeff's Barber Shop)*, Dry Cleaners *(JB's Dry Cleaners 663-3670)* **1-3 mi:** Convenience Store *(7-Eleven)*, Supermarket *(Food Lion 663-2959)*, Wine/Beer, Liquor Store *(ABC 663-0021)*, Bank/ATM, Pharmacy *(King George 663-2665)*, Florist
3+ mi: Fishmonger *(Roy's Seafood 775-2384, 8 mi.)*, Library *(Colonial Beach Branch 804-224-0921, 14 mi.)*, Hardware Store *(Rankin's True Value 804-224-8996, 13 mi.)*

Transportation
OnCall: Rental Car *(Enterprise 663-2244)*, Airport Limo *(Call-A-Ride 301-609-9112)* **Airport:** Fredericksburg/Reagan Nat'l. *(30 mi./70 mi.)*

Medical Services
911 Service **OnCall:** Ambulance **1-3 mi:** Doctor *(King George Family Medicine 663-2188)*, Dentist *(Donahue/Lunceford 663-2221)*, Chiropractor *(King George 663-2833)* **3+ mi:** Veterinarian *(Potomac Ridge 775-2980, 10 mi.)* **Hospital:** Mary Washington 800-722-2788 *(30 mi.)*

Setting -- Upper Machodoc Creek is home to the active Dahlgren Naval Weapons Station and two marinas on the north shore. The first is the military-only Dalgren Yacht Club. A quarter mile further are Dahlgren Marine Works' two new piers backed by a modest boatyard operation. The views across the creek are bucolic, disturbed only by the occasional discrete dwelling, and the more frequent test firings.

Marina Notes -- *Off-season rates available. Open to all boaters. The larger pier hosts mostly open slips interrupted by a corrugated steel shed roof (which, remarkably, survived Isabel) that protects about a dozen slips. A 6 ton, closed-end travel lift pulled by a tractor. New power is safely at shoulder height on new pilings that support new docks. Totally recovered from Isabel by summer '05; farther up the creek proved to be an excellent hurricane hole - where most of the local boats safely rode out the storm. Animals rule! Sarah the dog and Tiger, one of three cats, provide security. Basic, old-time, cinderblock and cement floor heads. Contact Dahlgren Range Control on the VHF to inquire about test-firing schedules.

Notable -- When the Navy is standing down, Upper Machodoc Creek promises peace and quiet and an almost unspoiled southern shoreline with a few beaches. About 0.8 miles out on Route 614 is a small gaggle of eateries and services and then, another mile farther, is a Food Lion and a larger shopping area. One of Dahlgren's claims to fame is that it is on John Wilkes Booth's escape route after he assassinated Abraham Lincoln. Booth and a co-conspirator fled Maryland, crossed the Potomac and landed just past the marina in Gambo Creek. Three days later, he was captured by Union soldiers and killed.

Aqua-land Marina

9700 Orland Park Road; Newburg, MD 20664

Tel: (301) 259-0572 **VHF: Monitor** n/a **Talk** n/a
Fax: (301) 259-0512 **Alternate Tel:** n/a
Email: n/a **Web:** n/a
Nearest Town: La Plata *(12 mi.)* **Tourist Info:** (301) 475-4200

Navigational Information

Lat: 38°21.967' **Long:** 076°58.933' **Tide:** n/a **Current:** n/a **Chart:** 12285
Rep. Depths (*MLW*): Entry 4 ft. **Fuel Dock** n/a **Max Slip/Moor** -/-
Access: West of the 301 Potomac Bridge on the Maryland side

Marina Facilities *(In Season/Off Season)*

Fuel: Gasoline, Diesel
Slips: 160 Total, 76 Transient **Max LOA:** 40 ft. **Max Beam:** 13 ft.
Rate *(per ft.)*: **Day** $1.75 **Week** n/a **Month** n/a
Power: 30 amp Incl., **50 amp** n/a, **100 amp** n/a, **200 amp** n/a
Cable TV: No **Dockside Phone:** No
Dock Type: Short Fingers
Moorings: 0 Total, 0 Transient **Launch:** n/a
Rate: Day n/a **Week** n/a **Month** n/a
Heads: 2 Toilet(s), 1 Shower(s)
Laundry: None **Pay Phones:** No
Pump-Out: 1 Central **Fee:** $10/$5 Boat-US **Closed Heads:** Yes

Marina Operations

Owner/Manager: Mel Brigitte **Dockmaster:** Linda Wedding
In-Season: Year-Round, 7am-Dusk* **Off-Season:** Nov & Dec, weekends only
After-Hours Arrival: Call ahead
Reservations: No **Credit Cards:** Visa/MC, Amex
Discounts: Boat/US **Dockage:** 20% **Fuel:** $0.10 **Repair:** Store 10%
Pets: Welcome **Handicap Access:** No

Marina Services and Boat Supplies

Communication - FedEx, UPS, Express Mail *(Sat Del)* **Supplies - OnSite:** Ice *(Cube)*, Ships' Store *(Mon-Fri 8am-Dusk, Sat & Sun 7am-Dusk)*, Live Bait *(bloodworms, crawlers, etc.)* **Near:** Propane *(Suburban Propane/AQ Campground)*

Boatyard Services

OnSite: Travelift *(20T)*, Launching Ramp, Engine mechanic *(gas, diesel)*, Electrical Repairs, Hull Repairs, Bottom Cleaning, Brightwork, Compound, Wash & Wax, Propeller Repairs, Woodworking, Metal Fabrication, Painting, Awlgrip, Total Refits **OnCall:** Electronic Sales, Air Conditioning, Refrigeration, Divers, Upholstery, Yacht Interiors **Dealer for:** Custom Trailers, Inc.. **Yard Rates:** $70/hr., Haul & Launch $3.50/ft. *(blocking $40)*, Power Wash $2.75/ft., Bottom Paint $17/ft.

Restaurants and Accommodations

OnSite: Seafood Shack *(Crab Shack 751-5435, Fri -Sun, opens at Noon; steamed shrimp, steamed crabs, fish sandwiches)*, Snack Bar *(L $2-7, D $2-7, crab cakes, hot dogs, barbecue)* **3+ mi:** Restaurant *(Capt. John's 259-2315, B $4-7, L $7-15, D $11-39, 8 mi.)*, *(China Garden 540-663-2993, 6 mi.)*, *(Capt. Billy's Crabhouse 932-4323, L $7-39, D $7-39, 5 mi.)*, *(Robertson's 259-0545, L $15-30, D $15-30, 5 mi.)*, Seafood Shack *(Gilligan's Pier 259-4514, 5 mi.)*, Fast Food *(Burger King, Subway 5 mi.)*, Pizzeria *(Pizza Hut 540-663-2575, 6 mi.)*, Motel *(White House Motel 932-2990, 4 mi.)*, *(Comfort Inn 540-663-3060, 6 mi.)*, *(Holiday Inn 866-270-5110, 6 mi.)*

Recreation and Entertainment

OnSite: Beach, Picnic Area, Boat Rentals, Group Fishing Boat **3+ mi:** Golf Course *(Swan Point 259-0042, 12 mi.)*, Fitness Center *(The Little Gym 932-9770, 13 mi.)*, Movie Theater *(Port Tobacco Players 938-6813, 13 mi.)*, Video Rental *(Movie Gallery 804-224-1156, 18 mi.)*

Provisioning and General Services

OnSite: Convenience Store *(drinks, coffee, hot dogs, ice cream)*, Wine/Beer, Crabs/Waterman *(shrimp, crabs by the bushel or the dozen - $20-30 per dozen)* **Near:** Laundry **1-3 mi:** Liquor Store *(Hardesty's Liquor 259-4114)*, Market *(Dan's Store 259-2314)*, Post Office *(259-2527)*, Hardware Store *(Walgren's True Value 259-2540)* **3+ mi:** Supermarket *(Food Lion 934-6429, 13 mi.)*, Bank/ATM *(6 mi.)*, Library *(La Plata PL 934-9001, 13 mi.)*, Beauty Salon *(Hairstyling By Joan 540-663-2300, 6 mi.)*, Dry Cleaners *(Mimi's Dry Cleaning 609-7597, 13 mi.)*, Pharmacy *(King George 540-663-2665, 6 mi.)*

Transportation

OnCall: Rental Car *(Enterprise 540-663-2244)*, Airport Limo *(Gio's Limo Service 934-6283)* **Near:** Local Bus **Airport:** Reagan Nat'l. *(43 mi.)*

Medical Services

911 Service **OnCall:** Ambulance **3+ mi:** Doctor *(Harrington 540-644-8200, 6 mi.)*, Dentist *(Dedmond & Donahue 540-663-2221, 7 mi.)*, Chiropractor *(Dahlgren Chiropractic 703-644-1119 across bridge, 6 mi.)*, Veterinarian *(Animal Clinic of La Plata 609-8387, 12 mi.)* **Hospital:** Civista Medical Center La Plata 609-4150 *(12 mi.)*

Setting -- On the Maryland side, just west of the 301 Potomac Bridge, an almost invisible cut is marked with a large "Aqua-land Marina" sign. The weathered red-roofed Crab Shack with large screened porch sits right at the marina entrance. Inside the fairly protected basin, docks line the western shore and next to the travelift a single pier, hosting open and covered slips, marches down the center. Working vessels tie up on the far, eastern, shore. Two candy-striped smoke stacks loom above the docks behind the bridge.

Marina Notes -- Flat Fee $30/day. The convenience store/snack bar/tackle shop also has live and frozen bait, ice cream and cold beer and is open Monday-Friday 7am-Dusk, and Saturday & Sunday from 6am, weekends only in Nov & Dec 8am-6pm. Short finger piers with power on the pilings. Extensive on-the-hard storage serviced by a 20 ton tractor-pulled closed-end lift. The heads are in a trailer -- there's a sink, toilet and shower in each full bathroom.

Notable -- The Crab Shack makes this a destination. The basin's even mix of watermen's vessels and pleasure craft adds to the working port ambiance. Rows of picnic tables sit in the large screened porch just waiting for crabs. At the last visit, the price for steamed crabs was: medium - $20/dozen; large - $25/dozen; jumbos - $30/dozen. Plus: $3 fish sandwiches, $7 crab cake sandwiches; steam spiced shrimp, $12/pound; king crab legs, $10/pound. The short curve of untended gravelly sand private beach is open to the public for a fee ($3.75 car & driver, $1.50 each additional person). La Plata, the Charles County seat, is about 15 miles north.

12. Western Shore: Upper Potomac River

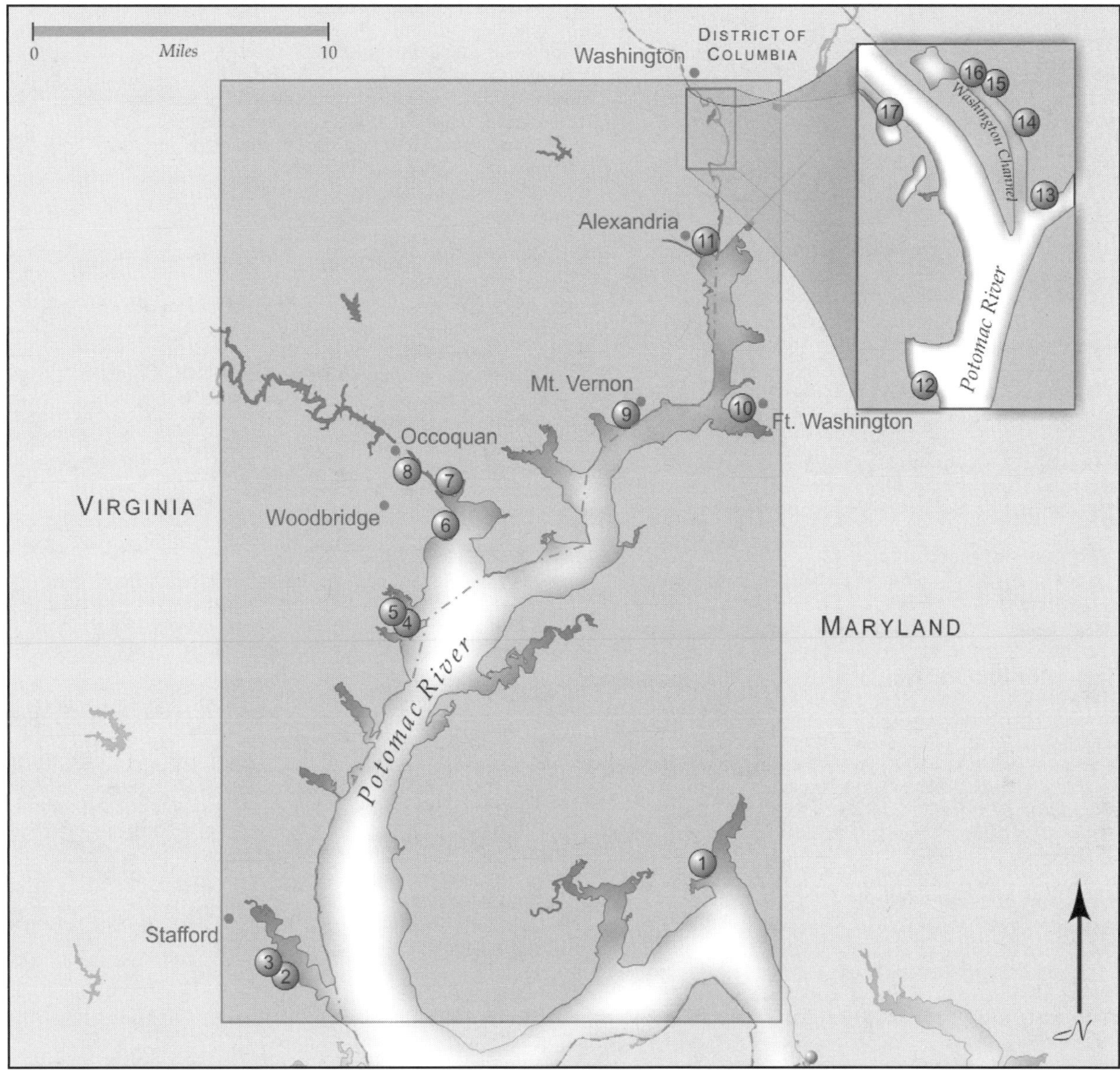

MAP	MARINA	HARBOR	PAGE
1	**Goose Bay Marina**	*Goose Creek*	220
2	**Aquia Bay Marina**	*Aquia Creek*	221
3	**Hope Springs Marina**	*Aquia Creek*	222
4	**EZ Cruz Marina**	*Neabsco Creek*	223
5	**Hamptons Landing**	*Neabsco Creek*	224
6	**Belmont Bay Harbor**	*Occoquan River*	225
7	**Occoquan Harbour Marina**	*Occoquan River*	226
8	**Occoquan Village Docks**	*Occoquan River*	227
9	**Mount Vernon Docks**	*Potomac River*	228
10	**Fort Washington Marina**	*Piscataway Creek*	229
11	**Alexandria City Marina**	*Potomac River*	230
12	**Washington Sailing Marina**	*Potomac River*	231
13	**James Creek Marina**	*Anacostia River*	232
14	**Gangplank Marina**	*Washington Channel*	233
15	**Capital Yacht Club**	*Washington Channel*	234
16	**Washington Marina**	*Washington Channel*	235
17	**Columbia Island Powerboat Marina**	*Potomac River*	236

- **A "DCM" symbol in Marina Notes means Designated Clean Marina** — This is a coveted state-level award given to marinas that meet stringent, environmentally supportive requirements (see page 307). *For a list of DCM's & pump-out facilities, see page 308.*
- **Ratings & Reviews** — An explanation of the Atlantic Cruising Club's rating system, and a detailed explanation of what is in each section of the Marina Report is on pages 6 – 11. *The Data-Gathering Process is detailed on page 322.*
- **Marina Report Updates** — Updates to Marina Reports (from readers, ACC-reviewers, and marinas) are posted regularly on *www.AtlanticCruisingClub.com.*

Goose Bay Marina

PO Box 58; 9365 Goosebay Lane; Welcome, MD 20693

Tel: (301) 933-0885 **VHF: Monitor** 16 **Talk** 68
Fax: (301) 934-0063 **Alternate Tel:** n/a
Email: goosebay@olg.com **Web:** www.goosebaymarina.com
Nearest Town: La Plata *(9 mi.)* **Tourist Info:** (301) 475-4200

Navigational Information

Lat: 38°27.233' **Long:** 077°03.166' **Tide:** 2 ft. **Current:** n/a **Chart:** 12285
Rep. Depths (*MLW*): Entry 7 ft. **Fuel Dock** 5 ft. **Max Slip/Moor** 7 ft./-
Access: From Potomac 1st marina on left as you enter Port Tobacco River

Marina Facilities *(In Season/Off Season)*

Fuel: Gasoline, Diesel
Slips: 290 Total, 20 Transient **Max LOA:** 60 ft. **Max Beam:** 15 ft.
Rate *(per ft.)*: **Day** $1.00 **Week** n/a **Month** n/a
Power: 30 amp $5, **50 amp** $5, **100 amp** n/a, **200 amp** n/a
Cable TV: No **Dockside Phone:** No
Dock Type: Fixed, Floating, Wood
Moorings: 0 Total, 0 Transient **Launch:** n/a
Rate: Day n/a **Week** n/a **Month** n/a
Heads: 3 Toilet(s), 3 Shower(s) *(with dressing rooms)*
Laundry: None **Pay Phones:** No
Pump-Out: OnSite, Self Service **Fee:** $5 **Closed Heads:** Yes

Marina Operations

Owner/Manager: Sharon Hile **Dockmaster:** n/a
In-Season: Apr-Oct, 9am-8pm **Off-Season:** Nov-Mar, 9am-5pm
After-Hours Arrival: Find empty slip or site, check in next morning
Reservations: Yes, Preferred **Credit Cards:** Visa/MC
Discounts: None
Pets: Welcome **Handicap Access:** No

Marina Services and Boat Supplies

Services - Docking Assistance **Communication -** Mail & Package Hold, Phone Messages, Fax in/out *(no)*, FedEx, DHL, UPS, Express Mail *(Sat Del)* **Supplies - OnSite:** Ice *(Cube)*, Ships' Store, Bait/Tackle, Live Bait, Propane

Boatyard Services

OnSite: Travelift *(20T)*, Launching Ramp *(3)*, Engine mechanic *(gas)*, Electrical Repairs, Hull Repairs, Canvas Work, Bottom Cleaning, Air Conditioning, Compound, Wash & Wax, Interior Cleaning, Yacht Broker *(Goose Bay Boat Sales)* **Dealer for:** Mercury Mercruiser. Other Certifications: Mercury Mercruiser **Yard Rates:** $68/hr., Haul & Launch $2.50/ft. *(blocking $2/ft.)*, Bottom Paint $13.50/ft. *(paint incl.)*
Storage: On-Land Inq.

Restaurants and Accommodations

OnCall: Restaurant *(Domino's 932-0333)* **1-3 mi:** Restaurant *(Capt. Billy's Crabhouse 932-4323, L $7-39, D $7-39, by boat)*, *(Robertson's Crab House 259-0545, L $14-28, D $14-28, by boat)*, Seafood Shack *(Gilligan's Pier 259-4514, L $6-10, D $11-25, by boat - tiki bar, beach volleyball)* **3+ mi:** Restaurant *(Gustavo's Italian 934-6200, 10 mi.)*, *(The Crossing at Casey Jones 932-6226, 10 mi.)*, *(Amarillo Steak House & Buffett 392-9044, 10 mi.)*, *(Goodies Restaurant & Carryout 870-1549, 10 mi.)*, Seafood Shack *(Crab Shack 934-9282, 5 mi.)*, Lite Fare *(Scott's Carry-out 934-3292, 4 mi.)*, Motel *(Bel Alton Motel 934-9505, 12 mi.)*, *(Best Western 934-4900, 10 mi.)*, *(Super 8 934-3465, 10 mi.)*

Recreation and Entertainment

OnSite: Pool, Picnic Area, Grills, Playground, Fishing Charter, Special Events *(Campground every Friday night.)* **3+ mi:** Golf Course *(White Plains Park & Golf Course 843-2947, 15 mi.)*, Fitness Center *(The Little Gym 932-9770, 9 mi.)*, Cultural Attract *(Port Tobacco Players 938-6813, 9 mi.)*

Provisioning and General Services

OnSite: Convenience Store **Near:** Catholic Church **3+ mi:** Supermarket *(Safeway 934-8176, 10 mi.)*, Wine/Beer *(LaPlata Liquors 934-2800, 10 mi.)*, Liquor Store *(Colonial Liquors 934-9515, 10 mi.)*, Market *(Murphy's Grocery 934-4544, 7 mi.)*, Bank/ATM *(8 mi.)*, Post Office *(934-3052, 4 mi.)*, Library *(LaPlata PL 934-9001, 10 mi.)*, Dry Cleaners *(LaPlata Cleaners 934-3346, 9 mi.)*, Laundry *(LaPlata Laundromat 934-8299, 10 mi.)*, Pharmacy *(CVS 934-9564, 10 mi.)*, Hardware Store *(True Value 934-6066, 10 mi.)*

Transportation

OnCall: Rental Car *(Enterprise 540-663-2244)*, Airport Limo *(Gio's Limo Service 934-6283)* **Airport:** Reagan Nat'l. *(40 mi.)*

Medical Services

911 Service **OnCall:** Ambulance **3+ mi:** Doctor *(Family Health Care 870-3322, 10 mi.)*, Dentist *(Family Dental 932-2121, 10 mi.)*, Chiropractor *(LaPlata Family Chiropractic 932-2100, 10 mi.)* **Hospital:** St. Mary's 290-1499 *(20 mi.)*

PHOTOS ON CD-ROM: 12

Setting -- Off Port Tobacco River, five very long main piers stretch along the northern shore of broad Goose Bay, offering nearly 300 slips. On the shore is a convenience store with a casual outdoor "boaters' lounge" and tucked in among thick stands of trees are 90 waterfront campsites. Inland from the campground is a small recreation area with a pool, a play gym, and covered picnic pavilion. With the exception of this nicely tempered bit of civilization, most of Goose Bay is completely untouched; the sweeping views from the outer docks are of pristine marsh and densely wooded shoreline.

Marina Notes -- A recent high quality floating dock with full length, wide finger piers joins 4 fairly new stationary docks with short finger piers. High-end pedestals - bigger ones are on the farther out slips. Full service boatyard with 2 lifts plus acres of dry storage, trailered boats and RVs. The tree shaded RV park has some long term transients. The ships' store stocks light basics and sports a pool table. A rustic open-air pavilion shelters a handful of cushioned redwood chairs and some tables with chairs. Well-maintained painted cinderblock bathhouse with tile floors and fresh shower curtains. Port Tobacco Marina (870-3133) at the head of Port Tobacco Creek is mostly a dry stack storage operation but has a few wet slips with 30 amp power and an occasional transient one.

Notable -- The small fenced pool is edged with quarry tile and surrounded by a cement patio furnished with chaises. Directly adjacent is a picnic pavilion with views of trailered boats. Outside the entrance, it's a mile past well-tended farms and cornfields to the main road, which is more of the same. Most services are about 10 miles away in LaPlata (Enterprise delivers). About 3 miles southeast by boat, three restaurants with docks cluster around Popes Creek.

Navigational Information

Lat: 38°25.123' **Long:** 077°21.127' **Tide:** 2 ft. **Current:** n/a **Chart:** 12285
Rep. Depths (*MLW*): Entry 5 ft. **Fuel Dock** 4.5 ft. **Max Slip/Moor** 10 ft./-
Access: Potomac River 2.25 miles up Aquia Creek to a well marked channel

Marina Facilities *(In Season/Off Season)*

Fuel: Gasoline
Slips: 134 Total, 3 Transient **Max LOA:** 50 ft. **Max Beam:** 16 ft.
Rate *(per ft.)*: **Day** $1.25/1.00 **Week** 8.75 **Month** n/a
Power: 30 amp Incl., **50 amp** n/a, **100 amp** n/a, **200 amp** n/a
Cable TV: No **Dockside Phone:** No
Dock Type: Fixed, Floating, Long Fingers, Short Fingers, Concrete, Wood
Moorings: 0 Total, 0 Transient **Launch:** n/a
Rate: Day n/a **Week** n/a **Month** n/a
Heads: 8 Toilet(s), 8 Shower(s) *(with dressing rooms)*
Laundry: 1 Washer(s), 1 Dryer(s), Book Exchange **Pay Phones:** No
Pump-Out: OnSite, Full Service, 1 Central **Fee:** n/a **Closed Heads:** Yes

Marina Operations

Owner/Manager: Scott Willis **Dockmaster:** Same
In-Season: Jun-Sep, 9am-6pm **Off-Season:** Oct-May, Sat & Sun 10am-5pm
After-Hours Arrival: Call ahead
Reservations: Yes, Preferred **Credit Cards:** Visa/MC, Dscvr, Amex
Discounts: None
Pets: Welcome, Dog Walk Area **Handicap Access:** Yes, Heads, Docks

Aquia Bay Marina

432 Aquia Creek Road; Stafford, VA 22554

Tel: (540) 720-7437 **VHF: Monitor** 16 **Talk** 68
Fax: (540) 720-6412 **Alternate Tel:** n/a
Email: n/a **Web:** n/a
Nearest Town: Stafford *(5 mi.)* **Tourist Info:** (540) 658-8681

Marina Services and Boat Supplies

Services - Boaters' Lounge **Communication -** FedEx, UPS, Express Mail
Supplies - OnSite: Ice *(Cube)*, Ships' Store **3+ mi:** Propane *(Wal-Mart 720-7323, 12 mi.)*

Boatyard Services

OnSite: Travelift *(35T)*, Launching Ramp, Engine mechanic *(gas, diesel)*, Electrical Repairs, Hull Repairs, Canvas Work, Bottom Cleaning, Brightwork, Air Conditioning, Compound, Wash & Wax, Interior Cleaning, Propeller Repairs, Woodworking, Upholstery, Painting **Yard Rates:** $75/hr., Haul & Launch $6/ft., Power Wash $4/ft., Bottom Paint $17/ft.

Restaurants and Accommodations

OnCall: Restaurant *(Shunxing Chinese 657-2600)*, Pizzeria *(Domino's 657-5858)* **1-3 mi:** Inn/B&B *(Courthouse Road B&B 720-3785, $75-200, 4 rooms & a suite)* **3+ mi:** Restaurant *(Dougherty's Tavern 657-8985, 6 mi.)*, *(Durango's Steak House 720-6315, 6 mi.)*, *(Brock's American Grill 657-4300, L $6-18, D $8-31, 5 mi.)*, *(Southern Flavor Fish & Chips 288-8868, L $5-10, D $9-18, 6 mi.)*, Pizzeria *(Sam's Pizza & Subs 720-9797, L $5-10, D $8-11, 5 mi.)*, Motel *(Days Inn 659-0022, 8 mi.)*, *(Hampton Inn 657-0999, 8 mi.)*

Recreation and Entertainment

OnSite: Beach, Picnic Area, Grills **Near:** Park *(Aquia Landing Beach Park 658-5019)* **3+ mi:** Golf Course *(Augustine Golf Club 720-7374, 10 mi.)*, Fitness Center *(Gold's Gym 720-7043, 9 mi.)*, Movie Theater *(Regal Cinemas 659-3200, 9 mi.)*, Video Rental *(Blockbuster 659-7080, 10 mi.)*, Museum *(Fredericksburg, 13 mi.)*

Provisioning and General Services

3+ mi: Supermarket *(Food Lion 720-6512, or Giant 657-5006, 8 mi., 5 mi.)*, Delicatessen *(Chicas Deli Market 657-5500, 9 mi.)*, Wine/Beer *(5 mi.)*, Liquor Store *(ABC 657-0672, 8 mi.)*, Bank/ATM *(899-3355, 6 mi.)*, Library *(John Porter Memorial 659-4909, 11 mi.)*, Laundry *(Aquia Laundry 659-9274, 9 mi.)*, Pharmacy *(CVS 657-4593, 7 mi.)*, Hardware Store *(Home Depot 657-6478, 11 mi.)*, Department Store *(Wal-Mart 720-0055, Kohl's 866-887-8884, Target 658-9901, 12 mi.)*

Transportation

OnCall: Rental Car *(Enterprise 657-9315 or Avis 288-2764, 8 mi.)*, Taxi *(Yellow Cab 659-1200, Brenda's Taxi 659-3295, Red Top)*, Airport Limo *(Fredericksburg Limousine 659-1759)* **1-3 mi:** Rail *(Virginia Rail Express - Brooke $7.85 to D.C. 684-0400)* **Airport:** Reagan Nat'l./Stafford Regional *(42 mi./5 mi.)*

Medical Services

911 Service **OnCall:** Ambulance **3+ mi:** Doctor *(Aquia Family Medical 657-9191, 7 mi.)*, Dentist *(Coast Dental 288-9212, 8 mi.)*, Chiropractor *(Aquia Family Chiropractor 720-5256, 9 mi.)*, Veterinarian *(Stafford Animal Hosp. 659-3811, 12 mi.)* **Hospital:** Mary Washington 741-1100 *(14 mi.)*

Setting -- About 2.25 miles deep into Aquia Creek, on the Virginia side, Aquia Bay Marina's three main piers line the southwestern shore. At the end of the central dock, a bright blue and white shelter with a red roof provides a covered sitting area and an easy marker for boaters. Landside is a big white shed with bright blue garage door. The creek is wide and the eye can travel quite a way before settling on a building - providing quiet, verdant vistas from the slips.

Marina Notes -- DCM. Aquia Creek's only marina on the Potomac side of the fixed 26 foot railroad bridge and the 36 foot power lines - about a third of the seasonal boats are sail. Many recent docks. Yard services by East Coast Marine. Dockside pump-out. Modest ships' store. Commercial filtration system provides quality water. A lovely, glass-walled boaters' lounge has four sofas, tables & chairs, satellite TV, a pool table, stereo and a kitchen. On the deck in front are sparkling white picnic tables and grills. Brightly painted bathhouse has linoleum floors and signature white walls with bright blue trim. Each has toilet stalls with accordion doors, 3 fiberglass showers, dressing rooms with double shower curtains and two sinks. A washer, dryer and laundry tub are in the anteroom.

Notable -- The trip up the wide, deep creek to the marina provides a very pleasant interlude - rolling lawns interspersed with long stands of trees and very few dwellings. For a night off the boat, a couple of miles down the road is elegant Courthouse Road B&B - built in the style of Mount Vernon. Virginia Rail Express is 1.5 miles with service to D.C.'s Union Station. Back at the entrance to the creek (by land at the end of Brooke Rd.), Stafford County's Aquia Landing Beach Park offers picnicking, fishing, volleyball, concession stands and lifeguard protected swimming areas (MemDay-LabDay, 10am-6pm 7 days $6/4.50).

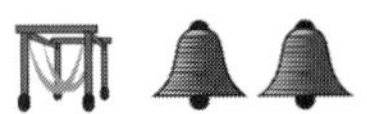

Hope Springs Marina

4 Hope Springs Lane; Stafford, VA 22554

Tel: (540) 659-1128 **VHF: Monitor** 16 **Talk** 16
Fax: (540) 659-7209 **Alternate Tel:** (540) 842-4201
Email: n/a **Web:** www.hopespringsmarina.com
Nearest Town: Stafford *(3.5 mi.)* **Tourist Info:** (540) 658-8681

Navigational Information

Lat: 38°25.338' **Long:** 077°21.421' **Tide:** 2 ft. **Current:** 2 kt. **Chart:** 12285
Rep. Depths (*MLW*): Entry 6 ft. **Fuel Dock** 6 ft. **Max Slip/Moor** 6 ft./-
Access: Potomic River to Aquia Creek, channel to Train Bridge

Marina Facilities *(In Season/Off Season)*

Fuel: *24 hrs.* - Gasoline, Diesel
Slips: 190 Total, 6 Transient **Max LOA:** 60 ft. **Max Beam:** 20 ft.
Rate *(per ft.)*: **Day** $1.25 **Week** n/a **Month** n/a
Power: 30 amp $5, **50 amp** n/a, **100 amp** n/a, **200 amp** n/a
Cable TV: No **Dockside Phone:** No
Dock Type: Fixed, Short Fingers, Alongside
Moorings: 0 Total, 0 Transient **Launch:** n/a
Rate: Day n/a **Week** n/a **Month** n/a
Heads: 6 Toilet(s), 5 Shower(s) *(with dressing rooms)*
Laundry: 2 Washer(s), 2 Dryer(s), Iron, Iron Board **Pay Phones:** No
Pump-Out: OnSite, Self Service, 1 Central **Fee:** $5 **Closed Heads:** Yes

Marina Operations

Owner/Manager: Jimmy Franklin **Dockmaster:** Same
In-Season: May-Aug, 9am-7pm **Off-Season:** Sep-Dec15, 10am-6pm
After-Hours Arrival: Call ahead for slip assignment
Reservations: Yes, Preferred **Credit Cards:** Visa/MC, Dscvr, Amex
Discounts: Boat/US **Dockage:** 25% **Fuel:** n/a **Repair:** n/a
Pets: Welcome, Dog Walk Area **Handicap Access:** Yes, Heads, Docks

Marina Services and Boat Supplies

Services - Dock Carts **Communication -** FedEx, UPS, Express Mail **Supplies - OnSite:** Ice *(Block)*, Ships' Store *(One Stop Boat Shop 659-6940)*, Bait/Tackle, Live Bait *(night crawlers)* **3+ mi:** West Marine *(15 mi.)*, Propane *(Wal-Mart 720-7323, 7 mi.)*

Boatyard Services

OnSite: Forklift *(11T)*, Launching Ramp, Engine mechanic *(gas)*, Electrical Repairs, Bottom Cleaning, Compound, Wash & Wax **OnCall:** Electronics Repairs, Hull Repairs, Canvas Work, Air Conditioning, Refrigeration, Divers, Interior Cleaning, Propeller Repairs **Yard Rates:** $80/hr., Haul & Launch $3.50/ft *(blocking $2/ft)*, Power Wash $3.50/ft, Bottom Paint $28/ft. *(paint incl.)*

Restaurants and Accommodations

OnCall: Restaurant *(Shunxing Chinese 657-2600)*, Pizzeria *(Domino's 657-5858)*, *(Tony's Pizza & Subs 659-2553, L $4-8, D $4-8)* **3+ mi:** Restaurant *(Applebee's 658-0717, L $7-10, D $9-15, 7 mi.)*, *(Ruby Tuesday's 659-6911, L $7-10, D $8-15, 5 mi.)*, *(Chili's 288-1212, L $7-10, D $8-15, 8 mi.)*, *(Southern Flavor Fish & Chips 288-8868, 5 mi.)*, *(Durango's Steak House 720-6315, 5 mi.)*, *(Dougherty's Tavern 657-8985, 4 mi.)*, *(Brock's American Grill 657-4300, L $6-18, D $8-31, 3 mi.)*, Lite Fare *(Botta Bing Bagel & Deli 720-8777, 7 mi.)*, Pizzeria *(Sam's Pizza & Subs 720-9797, L $5-10, D $8-11, 3 mi.)*, Motel *(Days Inn 659-0011, 6 mi.)*, *(Comfort Inn 663-3060, 10 mi.)*, *(Wytestone Suites 10 mi.)*

Recreation and Entertainment

OnSite: Beach *(700 ft. sand)*, Picnic Area, Grills *(charcoal)* **3+ mi:** Golf Course *(Augustine Golf Club 720-7374, 9 mi.)*, Fitness Center *(Gold's Gym 720-7043, 8 mi.)*, Movie Theater *(Regal Cinemas 659-3200, 6 mi.)*, Video Rental *(Blockbuster 659-7080, 7 mi.)*, Museum *(Fredericksburg, 13 mi.)*, Sightseeing *(Historic Aquia Episcopal Church, 6 mi.)*

Provisioning and General Services

OnSite: Convenience Store *(or 7-Eleven 659-7172)* **Near:** Post Office **1-3 mi:** Supermarket *(Food Lion 720-6512)*, Wine/Beer *(Food Lion)*, Beauty Salon *(Judith's 659-3450)*, Barber Shop *(Brothers Barber 657-2401)*, Pharmacy *(CVS 657-4593)*, Florist *(Anita's 720-5040)* **3+ mi:** Delicatessen *(Chicas 657-5500, 8 mi.)*, Liquor Store *(ABC 659-1176, 11 mi.)*, Bank/ATM *(899-3355, 5 mi.)*, Library *(John Porter Memorial 659-4909, 9 mi.)*, Laundry *(Aquia 659-9274, 6 mi.)*, Hardware Store *(Home Depot 657-6478, 8 mi.)*, Department Store *(Wal-Mart 720-0055, Kohl's 866-887-8884, Target 658-9901, 8 mi.)*

Transportation

OnCall: Rental Car *(Enterprise 657-9315 or Avis 288-2764, 7 mi.)*, Taxi *(Yellow Cab 659-1200, Brenda's Taxi 659-3295 - 24 hrs.)*, Airport Limo *(Fredericksburg Limousine 659-1759)* **3+ mi:** Rail *(Virginia Rail Express in Brooke $7.85 to D.C. 684-0400, 8 mi.)* **Airport:** Reagan Nat'l./Stafford Regional *(42 mi./5 mi.)*

Medical Services

911 Service **OnCall:** Ambulance **3+ mi:** Doctor *(Aquia Family Medical 657-9191, 5 mi.)*, Dentist *(Coast Dental 288-9212, 7 mi.)*, Chiropractor *(Aquia Family Chiropractor 720-5256, 6 mi.)*, Veterinarian *(Stafford Animal Hosp. 659-3811, 10 mi.)* **Hospital:** Mary Washington 741-1100 *(12 mi.)*

Setting -- Just above the 26 foot fixed railroad bridge, 3.5 miles from the Potomac, two enormous new tan, white and charcoal sheds dominate the shoreline and offer dry stack storage for 300 boats. Three protected, gated piers line the shore with the gas dock on the first T-head. A 700 foot sandy swimming beach with a float and water swings is inboard of the docks; the picnic area with charcoal grills and horseshoe pit sits on a nicely landscaped rise.

Marina Notes -- One Stop Boat Shop (659-6940), an independent on-site repair facility, is open daily from Memorial Day to Labor Day. Forklift can haul up to 35 ft. boat, 22,000 lb. Docks can manage to 60 ft. A raft of WaveRunners home here. Stationary docks, half-length finger piers, full race lighthouse pedestals. The railroad bridge trestles act as a wave attenuator - virtually no damage from Isabel - making this a bit of a hurricane hole. New '04 $160,000 fueling system at the easy access dock - fuel 24 hrs. a day with a credit card - includes receipt (for retrieving the 17.5% VA gas tax). Well-stocked ships' & convenience store for basic boating and provisioning needs. Brand new heads & showers built summer of '05, although the older cinderblock ones were quite adequate.

Notable -- It's about 6 miles to Stafford's supermarkets and restaurants. A tour of upper Aquia Creek can make for a pleasant afternoon. About a mile northeast of Hope Springs, the creek narrows considerably, becoming a meandering little waterway with switchbacks, high banks, stands of colorful water plants and unexpected vistas - albeit with a safe 40 foot wide channel dredged to 5 feet of water. The creek ends about two miles later at Aquia Harbour Marina (659-4232), part of a 2,000-acre planned community, where a transient slip may be available.

PHOTOS ON CD-ROM: 12

Navigational Information
Lat: 38°35.966' **Long:** 077°15.531' **Tide:** 2 ft. **Current:** 2 kt. **Chart:** 12285
Rep. Depths (*MLW*): Entry 6 ft. **Fuel Dock** 5 ft. **Max Slip/Moor** 10 ft./-
Access: Potomac Rvr. to Buoy 47, thru railroad bridge -1st marina on left

Marina Facilities *(In Season/Off Season)*
Fuel: *24hrs* - Gasoline
Slips: 190 Total, 10 Transient **Max LOA:** 45 ft. **Max Beam:** 15 ft.
Rate *(per ft.)*: **Day** $2.00/1.50 **Week** Inq. **Month** Inq.
Power: 30 amp Incl., **50 amp** Incl., **100 amp** n/a, **200 amp** n/a
Cable TV: No **Dockside Phone:** No
Dock Type: Fixed, Short Fingers
Moorings: 0 Total, 0 Transient **Launch:** Yes
Rate: Day n/a **Week** n/a **Month** n/a
Heads: 6 Toilet(s), 2 Shower(s)
Laundry: 2 Washer(s), 2 Dryer(s) **Pay Phones:** Yes
Pump-Out: No **Fee:** n/a **Closed Heads:** Yes

Marina Operations
Owner/Manager: Michael Hart **Dockmaster:** n/a
In-Season: Year-Round, 9am-6pm **Off-Season:** n/a
After-Hours Arrival: Call ahead
Reservations: Preferred **Credit Cards:** Visa/MC, Dscvr, Amex
Discounts: None
Pets: Welcome **Handicap Access:** No

EZ Cruz Marina

16245 Neabsco Road; Woodbridge, VA 22191

Tel: (703) 670-8111; (888) 670-8111 **VHF: Monitor** 16 **Talk** 68
Fax: (703) 680-9262 **Alternate Tel:** n/a
Email: robert@ezcruz.com **Web:** www.ezcruz.com
Nearest Town: Woodbridge *(4 mi.)* **Tourist Info:** (703) 590-5000

Marina Services and Boat Supplies
Services - Dock Carts **Communication -** FedEx, UPS, Express Mail
Supplies - OnSite: Ice *(Cube)* **Near:** Ships' Store, Bait/Tackle *(Hamptons Landing)*, Live Bait **3+ mi:** West Marine *(492-6225, 7 mi.)*, Boater's World *(680-0743, 5 mi.)*, Boat/US *(492-6225, 7 mi.)*, Propane *(Prince William Trailer Village 221-2474, 7 mi.)*

Boatyard Services
OnSite: Travelift *(two 12T)*, Launching Ramp, Engine mechanic *(gas)*, Electrical Repairs, Electronics Repairs, Hull Repairs, Bottom Cleaning, Compound, Wash & Wax **Yard Rates:** $85/hr., Power Wash $3/ft., Bottom Paint $20/ft.

Restaurants and Accommodations
OnCall: Pizzeria *(Geno's Pizza & Subs 491-0565, L $5-7, D $5-7, salads, turnovers, beer - pizzas $7-14)*, *(Pizza Gourmet 490-6798)* **1-3 mi:** Restaurant *(Philly Subs and Pizza 780-7501, L $6-10, D $6-10)* **3+ mi:** Restaurant *(Osprey's Landing 494-1935, D $12-20, 4 mi, .)*, *(Hunan D'Lite 490-1688, L $3-20, D $6-20, 4 mi.)*, *(Dale Seafood 583-7788, 4 mi.)*, *(Sakura 492-8464, 5 mi.)*, *(El Charro 680-0484, 5 mi.)*, *(Thomas' Pizza and Subs 497-8681, 4 mi.)*, *(China House 490-2750, 4 mi.)*, *(Woodbridge Crab & Seafood 492-1239, 4 mi.)*, *(Pollo Loco 490-4200, 4 mi.)*, *(Seven Seas 491-2112, 4 mi.)*, Lite Fare *(Gina's Carry-Out 491-1172, 4 mi.)*, Motel *(Best Western 494-4433, 4 mi.)*, *(Holiday Inn 576-1600, 4 mi.)*, *(Fairfield Inn 800-228-2800, 5 mi.)*, *(Sleep Inn 580-9200, 5 mi.)*

Recreation and Entertainment
Under 1 mi: Beach *(Leesylvania St. Park)*, Playground, Roller Blade/Bike Paths, Park *(Leesylvania St. Park 670-0372)* **3+ mi:** Tennis Courts *(Veteran's Memorial Park 491-2183, 5 mi.)*, Golf Course *(Belmont Bay 497-1384, 6 mi.)*, Fitness Center *(Fitness Equation 897-0200, 4 mi.)*, Bowling *(AMF Dale City 670-2111, 5 mi.)*, Movie Theater *(AMC Potomac Mills 490-5151, 6 mi.)*, Video Rental *(MVC 494-9856, 4 mi.)*, Museum *(Weems Botts Museum 221-2218, 6 mi.)*

Provisioning and General Services
Near: Beauty Salon *(Sandra's Hair Gallery 897-1679)* **1-3 mi:** Convenience Store, Bank/ATM, Protestant Church, Barber Shop, Dry Cleaners *(Summit Cleaners 583-8738)* **3+ mi:** Supermarket *(Food Lion 492-0244, 4 mi.)*, Health Food *(Natural Grocer 494-7287, 6 mi.)*, Liquor Store *(ABC 494-7108, 4 mi.)*, Crabs/Waterman *(J&T Seafood 490-1450, 4 mi.)*, Post Office *(494-6427, 4 mi.)*, Library *(Dumfries 792-5678, 4 mi.)*, Bookstore *(Borders 897-8100, 6 mi.)*, Pharmacy *(Medicine Shoppe 491-7883, 4 mi.)*, Hardware Store *(Home Depot 670-3699, 6 mi.)*, Department Store *(Kmart 670-3186, 5 mi.)*, Buying Club *(Sam's 491-2662, 7 mi.)*, Copies Etc. *(Staples 491-0947, 4 mi.)*

Transportation
OnCall: Rental Car *(Enterprise 490-0566, Thrifty 494-0101 4 mi.)*, Taxi *(Yellow Cab 491-2222)*, Airport Limo *(Airport Sedan 580-8877)* **3+ mi:** Rail *(Amtrak 684-1001, 6 mi.)* **Airport:** Reagan Nat'l. *(25 mi.)*

Medical Services
911 Service **OnCall:** Ambulance **3+ mi:** Doctor *(Potomac Family Health 680-3084, 4 mi.)*, Dentist *(Mostofi 494-9171, 4 mi.)*, Chiropractor *(Jefferson 499-8840, 4 mi.)*, Veterinarian *(River Oaks 441-0900, 4 mi.)*
Hospital: Potomac Hospital 583-3000 *(5 mi.)*

Setting -- Just north of Freestone Point, past the 33 foot fixed railroad bridge, EZ Cruz's five recent docks, hosting over 200 slips, line the southwestern shore of Neabsco Creek. Landside the facility is anchored by a two-story gray vertical-sided office and bathhouse with an outdoor railed walkway and a boatyard. Waterside a few picnic tables sit among the boatyard detritus. The views from the outer docks are of masses of lily pads and marsh backed by forest.

Marina Notes -- The original 24-hour credit card operated fuel stop on the Potomac (gas only). Welcome is provided by Charlie, a Golden Retriever who's always on his way in or out of the creek. Pump-out and full boatyard services with two travelifts. Mostly smaller boats, many appearing to have been here for a long time, berth at the inner stationary docks with small new lighthouse pedestals and half-length finger piers. But the outer slips and T-head have full-size pedestals and can accommodate larger boats to 40 foot. A very nice, carefully maintained and painted cinderblock bathhouse has tile floors, tile shower stalls, benches and molded sinks. Adjacent Pilot House Marina no longer accepts transients. "The Pilot House" restaurant, closed by Isabel, has not been replaced.

Notable -- A tenth of a mile from the marinas is the beginning of Leesylvania State Park, the birthplace of Gen Robert E. Lee's father - Henry Lee III (Light Horse Harry). The Freestone Point peninsula, formed by the Potomac, Neabsco Creek and Powell's Creek, hosts the 508-acre former Colonial plantation. The amenities include a half-mile sand beach (no swimming allowed) plus expansive picnic areas, boat launches, concession stands, 6 miles of hiking trails, plus guided canoe, historic, and nature walks. Note: It's another 1/2 miles to the formal park entrance, then a couple more miles to the actual facilities and services.

PHOTOS ON CD-ROM: 9

Hamptons Landing

16205 Neabsco Road; Woodbridge, VA 22191

Tel: (703) 221-4915 **VHF: Monitor** 16 /06 **Talk** 06
Fax: (703) 580-0105 **Alternate Tel:** (703) 906-9700
Email: hamptonsinfo@comcast.net **Web:** www.hamptonslandingmarina.com
Nearest Town: Woodbridge **Tourist Info:** (703) 590-5000

Navigational Information

Lat: 38°36.008' **Long:** 077°15.631' **Tide:** 2 ft. **Current:** 2 kt. **Chart:** 12285
Rep. Depths (*MLW*): Entry 5 ft. **Fuel Dock** 5 ft. **Max Slip/Moor** 5 ft./5 ft.
Access: Potomac to Buoy 49 to Daymark #2, Neabsco Creek

Marina Facilities *(In Season/Off Season)*

Fuel: Gasoline, Diesel
Slips: 140 Total, 5 Transient **Max LOA:** 50 ft. **Max Beam:** 17 ft.
Rate *(per ft.)*: **Day** $1.00* **Week** n/a **Month** n/a
Power: 30 amp $5, **50 amp** $5, **100 amp** n/a, **200 amp** n/a
Cable TV: Yes Slip holders only **Dockside Phone:** No
Dock Type: Fixed, Short Fingers, Pilings, Wood
Moorings: 0 Total, 0 Transient **Launch:** n/a
Rate: Day n/a **Week** n/a **Month** n/a
Heads: 6 Toilet(s), 4 Shower(s)
Laundry: None **Pay Phones:** Yes
Pump-Out: OnSite, Full Service, 1 Central **Fee:** $5 **Closed Heads:** Yes

Marina Operations

Owner/Manager: Terry Hill **Dockmaster:** Same
In-Season: Mar-Oct, 8am-5pm **Off-Season:** Nov-Feb, 9am-5pm**
After-Hours Arrival: Call ahead
Reservations: Required **Credit Cards:** Visa/MC
Discounts: Boat/US **Dockage:** 25% **Fuel:** $0.10 **Repair:** n/a
Pets: Welcome, Dog Walk Area **Handicap Access:** Yes, Heads, Docks

Marina Services and Boat Supplies

Services - Docking Assistance, Dock Carts **Communication -** FedEx, UPS, Express Mail **Supplies - OnSite:** Ice *(Cube)*, Ships' Store, Bait/Tackle, Live Bait *(worms)* **3+ mi:** West Marine *(492-6225, 7 mi.)*, Boater's World *(680-0743, 5 mi.)*, Boat/US *(492-6225, 7 mi.)*, Propane *(Prince William Trailer Village 221-2474, 7 mi.)*

Boatyard Services

OnSite: Travelift *(30T)*, Forklift, Launching Ramp *($4-5/ft.)*, Canvas Work *(Potomac Canvas 670-2265)*, Divers **OnCall:** Air Conditioning, Refrigeration, Compound, Wash & Wax, Interior Cleaning, Propeller Repairs, Metal Fabrication **Near:** Engine mechanic *(gas, diesel)*, Electrical Repairs, Bottom Cleaning, Yacht Interiors. **Dealer for:** MerCruiser, Volvo Penta, OMC, and Quicksilver. **Yard Rates:** $65/hr., Haul & Launch $4-5/ft., Power Wash $4/ft. **Storage:** In-Water $300/season, On-Land $35/ft.

Restaurants and Accommodations

OnCall: Pizzeria *(Domino's 491-1716)*, *(Pizza Gourmet 490-6798)*
3+ mi: Restaurant *(Bob Evans 491-7633, B $5-10, L $7-15, D $8-13, 6 mi.)*, *(Woodbridge Crab & Seafood 492-1239, 4 mi.)*, *(China Garden 494-2621, 4 mi.)*, *(Dak's Grill 680-5788, L $7-10, D $10-20, 6 mi.)*, Seafood Shack *(Tim's Rivershore 441-1375, 5 mi.)*, Fast Food *(McDonald's, Burger King 4 mi.)*, Lite Fare *(Dumfries Café 441-1465, B $4-9, L $6-10, 6 mi.)*, Hotel *(Best Western 494-4433, $70, 4 mi.)*, *(Holiday Inn 490-2300, $80, 4 mi.)*

Recreation and Entertainment

OnSite: Picnic Area *(patio overlooking the docks)*, Grills *(propane)*
Under 1 mi: Beach *(Leesylvania St. Park)*, Playground, Jogging Paths, Roller Blade/Bike Paths, Park *(Leesylvania St. Park 670-0372)* **3+ mi:** Tennis Courts *(Veteran's Memorial Park 491-2183, 5 mi.)*, Golf Course *(Belmont Bay 497-1384, 6 mi.)*, Bowling *(AMF 670-2111, 5 mi.)*, Movie Theater *(AMC 490-5151, 6 mi.)*, Video Rental *(Blockbuster 491-2911, 5 mi.)*, Museum *(Weems Botts 221-2218, 6 mi.)*

Provisioning and General Services

OnSite: Convenience Store *(or 3 mi. to Wawa 583-3558)* **Near:** Beauty Salon *(Sandra's Hair Gallery 897-1679)* **1-3 mi:** Protestant Church, Barber Shop **3+ mi:** Supermarket *(Safeway 643-0764, 4 mi.)*, Health Food *(Natural Grocer 494-7287, 6 mi.)*, Liquor Store *(ABC 494-7108, 4 mi.)*, Crabs/Waterman *(J&T Seafood 490-1450, 4 mi.)*, Bank/ATM *(Bank of America, 4 mi.)*, Post Office *(494-6427, 4 mi.)*, Catholic Church *(494-2444, 10 mi.)*, Synagogue *(Ner Shalom 878-6904, 10 mi.)*, Library *(Dumfries 792-5678, 4 mi.)*, Dry Cleaners *(Bob's 490-3374, 4 mi.)*, Bookstore *(Borders 897-8100, 6 mi.)*, Pharmacy *(Safeway 497-2028, 4 mi.)*, Hardware Store *(Home Depot 670-3699, 7 mi.)*, Retail Shops *(Potomac Mills Outlet Mall 490-3459, 5 mi.)*, Copies Etc. *(Staples 491-0947, 4 mi.)*

Transportation

OnCall: Rental Car *(Enterprise 490-0566, Alamo 497-0752, 4 mi.)*, Taxi *(Yellow Cab 491-2222)*, Airport Limo *(Airport Sedan 580-8877)* **1-3 mi:** Local Bus **3+ mi:** Rail *(Amtrak 684-1001, 6 mi.)* **Airport:** Reagan Nat'l. *(25 mi.)*

Medical Services

911 Service **OnCall:** Ambulance **3+ mi:** Doctor *(Potomac Family Health 680-3084, 4 mi.)*, Dentist *(Mostofi 494-9171, 4 mi.)*, Chiropractor *(Jefferson 499-8840, 4 mi.)* **Hospital:** Potomac Hospital 583-3000 *(5 mi.)*

Setting -- The tone for this exceedingly ship-shape, nicely landscaped facility is set by an attractive white clapboard tidewater-style two-story main building topped by a cupola - highlighted by green trim and a matching metal roof. Two levels of white-railed decks encircle the building; in front of the store entrance, a small deck hosts tables & chairs topped by dark green market umbrellas that overlook the 3 docks - 2 sets of open slips and 1 set of slips coved by dark green flame-retardant vinyl hooped domes.

Marina Notes -- *$25 min. **Off-season closed on Sun. In business since 1950. Today, the founder's son, Butch Hampton & Capt. Terry Hill co-manage the facility. The renovations began in 2000 with the covered slips (avail. to trans.) Careful maintenance has kept everything looking fresh and new. The inviting ships' store is nicely merchandised and sports an aquarium and some basics. Fuel dock is the middle dock T-head. Stationary docks with short finger piers and full-size lighthouse pedestals. Large area for on-the-hard storage across the street. Special covered slip houses the fireboat "Firestorm" and TowBoat/US bases here as well. A nice handicapped-accessible full bathroom plus separate all-tile bathhouses with showers, molded sinks, wooden benches and dividers.

Notable -- Al fresco picnic spots abound. Square picnic tables topped by large vinyl market umbrellas and chaises populate a dockside concrete patio set off by stands of sea oats and perennial beds. A built-in brick propane grill and a large portable stainless steel grill are adjacent. A picnic dock pokes into the creek next to the covered slips. And on the 2nd floor of the marina building, a deck overlooking the docks has teak tables and chairs topped by dark green umbrellas.

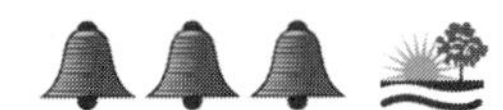

Navigational Information
Lat: 38°39.078' **Long:** 077°13.645' **Tide:** 2 ft. **Current:** n/a **Chart:** 12285
Rep. Depths (*MLW*): Entry 15 ft. **Fuel Dock** 15 ft. **Max Slip/Moor** 8 ft./-
Access: Belmont Bay to Occoquan River, 150 yards SE of Marker R10

Marina Facilities *(In Season/Off Season)*
Fuel: *93 oct* - Gasoline, Diesel
Slips: 160 Total, 5 Transient **Max LOA:** 60 ft. **Max Beam:** 18 ft.
Rate *(per ft.)*: **Day** $1.00 **Week** $7.50 **Month** $15
Power: 30 amp $3, **50 amp** $5, **100 amp** n/a, **200 amp** n/a
Cable TV: Yes Hook up w/Comp **Dockside Phone:** Yes Hook up w/ Comp
Dock Type: Floating, Long Fingers, Wood
Moorings: 0 Total, 0 Transient **Launch:** n/a
Rate: Day n/a **Week** n/a **Month** n/a
Heads: Toilet(s), 3 Shower(s) *(with dressing rooms)*, Hair Dryers
Laundry: 2 Washer(s), 2 Dryer(s), Book Exchange **Pay Phones:** Yes
Pump-Out: OnSite **Fee:** n/a **Closed Heads:** Yes

Marina Operations
Owner/Manager: Tammy Ritchie **Dockmaster:** Johnny Phelps
In-Season: Mar-Nov, 8:30am-5pm **Off-Season:** Dec-Feb, 8:30am-5:30pm*
After-Hours Arrival: Call ahead
Reservations: Required **Credit Cards:** Visa/MC
Discounts: None
Pets: Welcome, Dog Walk Area **Handicap Access:** Yes, Heads

Belmont Bay Harbor

570 Harbor Side Street; Woodbridge, VA 22191

Tel: (703) 490-5088 **VHF: Monitor** 16 **Talk** 68
Fax: (703) 490-5188 **Alternate Tel:** (571) 238-5273
Email: bbharbor@erols.com **Web:** www.belmontbay.com
Nearest Town: Woodbridge **Tourist Info:** (703) 590-5000

Marina Services and Boat Supplies
Services - Docking Assistance, Trash Pick-Up, Dock Carts
Communication - FedEx, UPS, Express Mail **Supplies - OnSite:** Ice *(Cube)*, Ships' Store **Under 1 mi:** West Marine *(492-6225)* **1-3 mi:** Boater's World *(680-0743)*, Boat/US *(492-6225)*, Bait/Tackle, Live Bait, Propane

Boatyard Services
OnSite: Yacht Broker *(North Atlantic Marine Group)* **Yard Rates:** Haul & Launch $10/ft. *(blocking $10/ft.)*, Bottom Paint $10/ft.

Restaurants and Accommodations
OnSite: Restaurant *(Osprey's Landing 494-1935, L $7-15, D $12-20, in the Clubhouse)* **OnCall:** Restaurant *(Dixie Bones BBQ 492-2205)*, *(Hunan D'Lite 490-1688, L $3-20, D $6-20)*, Pizzeria *(Joe's Pizza & Subs 491-8498)*, *(Geno's 491-0565, $5-7, Pizzas $7-14)* **Under 1 mi:** Restaurant *(Oasis On the Occoquan 494-5000, L $7-20, D $7-20)*, Pizzeria *(Astoria Pizza 491-5044)*, Motel *(Hampton Inn 490-2300)*, *(Econo Lodge 491-5196)* **1-3 mi:** Restaurant *(Kow Loon 490-5515)*, *(Taco Place 491-8535)*, Lite Fare *(Ann's Wings & Things 490-5397)*, *(USA Subs & Deli 491-9955)*, Motel *(Quality Inn 494-0300)*, *(Roadway Inn 494-4144)*

Recreation and Entertainment
OnSite: Picnic Area, Golf Course *(BBH's Ospreys G.C. 10% discount)*, Jogging Paths, Cultural Attract *(Science Museum of Virginia - ground breaking '05 - next to marina)* **Under 1 mi:** Pool, Tennis Courts *(Sport & Health Clubs 491-4126)*, Fitness Center, Video Rental *(Blockbuster 491-2911)*, Park **1-3 mi:** Bowling *(Bowl America 494-9191)*, Galleries **3+ mi:** Movie Theater *(AMC Potomac Mills 490-5151, 5 mi.)*, Museum *(Occoquan Mill House Museum 491-7525, 4 mi.)*

Provisioning and General Services
OnSite: Retail Shops *(clothing, snacks, ice cream)* **Under 1 mi:** Convenience Store *(Food Mart)*, Supermarket *(Food Lion 492-0244)*, Liquor Store *(ABC 494-7108)*, Bakery *(Teddy's Fresh Baked 497-0572)*, Bank/ATM, Beauty Salon *(Station Beauty 494-4497)*, Barber Shop, Pharmacy *(CVS 494-9781)*, Newsstand, Florist **1-3 mi:** Delicatessen *(Big Mamas Deli 418-8738)*, Catholic Church, Protestant Church, Dry Cleaners *(VIP Cleaners 491-8186)*, Department Store *(Kmart 491-7089)*, Copies Etc. *(Mailbox Junction 492-7200)* **3+ mi:** Health Food *(The Natural Grocer 494-7287, 5 mi.)*, Post Office *(494-6427, 4 mi.)*, Library *(Occoquan 494-8126, 4 mi.)*, Bookstore *(Books-A-Million 490-6272, 5 mi.)*, Hardware Store *(Home Depot 670-3699, 6 mi.)*

Transportation
OnCall: Rental Car *(Enterprise 490-0566, Thrifty 494-0101, 4 mi.)*, Taxi *(Yellow Cab 491-2222)*, Airport Limo *(Airport Sedan 580-8877)*
3+ mi: Rail *(Woodbridge Commuter Rail/Amtrak 493-8168, 1 mi./ 6 mi.)*
Airport: Reagan Nat'l. *(20 mi.)*

Medical Services
911 Service **OnCall:** Ambulance **1-3 mi:** Doctor *(Occoquan Medical Care 499-9939)*, Dentist *(Mazin 491-1115)*, Chiropractor *(Prymak 494-9922)*, Veterinarian *(Gill 550-3970)* **Hospital:** Potomac Hospital 583-3000 *(4 mi.)*

Setting -- Tucked into a large square basin on the Occoquan River off Belmont Bay, this handsome high-end marina is a centerpiece of 300-acre Belmont Harbor - a large, growing community of townhouses, condominiums, and private homes. Slips ring the basin, two main piers run down the center, and a fuel dock that functions as a wave attenuator nearly closes the entrance. A Georgian-style pavilion overlooks the water and a distant surprisingly green shoreline.

Marina Notes -- *Off-Season open Mon-Fri 8:30am-5:30pm, Sat 8:30am-1pm, closed on Sun. DCM. Managed by Coastal Properties. Long, easy-access fuel dock is right along the river's edge. IPE floating docks have vinyl-edged full finger piers and full-size lighthouse pedestals. Small ships' store with ice cream, beverages, and insigniaed Belmont Bay Harbor memorabilia. Most services deliver, but the very accommodating manager may lend his truck or the marina's golf cart. The bathhouses are in a brick building at the head of "A" dock. Each has a tile floor, sinks set into faux granite counter tops and three fiberglass shower stalls with dressing rooms. Adjacent is a washer/dryer and folding tables.

Notable -- A path, punctuated by gazebos and benches, edges the marina. It passes in front of the waterside condos and townhouses, interspersed with mews, along the shoreline, into a wooded area ending at the original Manor House. Belmont Harbor's Ospreys 18-hole Golf Course is within the community and will deliver a golf cart to the marina so boaters can load up dockside. A new clubhouse restaurant, Osprey's Landing, recently opened and serves lunch & dinner. Most other services are out on Route 1, about a mile hike through this newly developed community and past the Woodbridge Commuter Rail Station.

PHOTOS ON CD-ROM: 16

Occoquan Harbour Marina

13180 Marina Way; Woodbridge, VA 22191

Tel: (703) 494-3600 **VHF: Monitor** 16 **Talk** 68
Fax: (703) 494-3096 **Alternate Tel:** n/a
Email: ohmboats@comcast.net **Web:** www.occoquanharbourmarina.com
Nearest Town: Woodbridge **Tourist Info:** (703) 491-4045

Navigational Information

Lat: 38°40.111' **Long:** 077°14.564' **Tide:** 3 ft. **Current:** n/a **Chart:** 12285
Rep. Depths (*MLW*): Entry 10 ft. **Fuel Dock** 8 ft. **Max Slip/Moor** 10 ft./9 ft.
Access: Potomac River to G51 to Occoquan River

Marina Facilities *(In Season/Off Season)*

Fuel: Gasoline, Diesel, High-Speed Pumps
Slips: 215 Total, 10 Transient **Max LOA:** 65 ft. **Max Beam:** n/a
Rate *(per ft.)*: **Day** $1.50/lnq. **Week** 7 **Month** 30
Power: 30 amp $5, **50 amp** metered, **100 amp** metered, **200 amp** metered
Cable TV: Yes Comcast **Dockside Phone:** Yes
Dock Type: Floating, Long Fingers, Wood
Moorings: 0 Total, 0 Transient **Launch:** n/a
Rate: Day n/a **Week** n/a **Month** n/a
Heads: 4 Toilet(s), 4 Shower(s) *(with dressing rooms)*
Laundry: None, Book Exchange **Pay Phones:** No
Pump-Out: OnCall, Full Service, 1 Central **Fee:** $5 **Closed Heads:** Yes

Marina Operations

Owner/Manager: Richard Lynn **Dockmaster:** Same
In-Season: May-Oct, 9am-6pm **Off-Season:** Oct-May, 9am-5pm*
After-Hours Arrival: Call ahead
Reservations: Yes, Preferred **Credit Cards:** Visa/MC, Dscvr, Amex
Discounts: None
Pets: Welcome **Handicap Access:** Yes, Heads, Docks

Marina Services and Boat Supplies

Services - Docking Assistance, Security *(8, 7 days a week)*, Trash Pick-Up, Dock Carts **Communication -** FedEx, UPS, Express Mail **Supplies - OnSite:** Ice *(Cube)*, Ships' Store **Under 1 mi:** West Marine *(492-6225)*, Marine Discount Store, Bait/Tackle, Live Bait, Propane **1-3 mi:** Boater's World *(680-0743)*, Boat/US *(492-6225)*

Boatyard Services

OnSite: Travelift *(25T)*, Launching Ramp, Engine mechanic *(gas, diesel)*, Electrical Repairs, Hull Repairs, Bottom Cleaning, Compound, Wash & Wax, Inflatable Repairs, Life Raft Service, Painting, Awlgrip **OnCall:** Air Conditioning, Refrigeration, Divers, Interior Cleaning, Propeller Repairs, Upholstery, Yacht Interiors, Metal Fabrication **1-3 mi:** Electronics Repairs.

Restaurants and Accommodations

OnSite: Restaurant *(Oasis On the Occoquan 494-5000, L $6-9, D $6-16, kids' $5, sandwiches all day; indoor, deck, and tiki bar)* **OnCall:** Pizzeria *(Domino's 490-4500)*, *(Brothers 491-1185, salads, subs, pasta $6-9, pizza $10-17)* **Near:** Restaurant *(Lum's Family Restaurant 491-1970)*, Fast Food *(Taco Bell, Subway)*, Motel *(Quality Inn 494-0300)*, *(Econol Lodge 491-5196)*, *(Hampton Inn 490-2300)*, *(Inns of Virginia)* **Under 1 mi:** Restaurant *(Pulgarcito Grill 490-9800)*, *(Dixie Bones BBQ 492-2205)*, *(Occoquan Inn 491-1888, D $16-25)*, *(Virginia Grill 491-1888, L $7-15, D $7-15)*, *(Osprey's Landing 494-1935)*, Lite Fare *(Xela Super Deli & Kabob 492-4600)*, *(Ann's Wings & Things 490-5397)*

Recreation and Entertainment

OnSite: Picnic Area, Grills *(charcoal)*, Video Arcade *(& pool tables)* **Near:** Tennis Courts *(Sport & Health Clubs 491-4126)*, Golf Course *(Belmont Bay 497-1384)*, Fitness Center **Under 1 mi:** Bowling *(Bowl America 494-9191)*, Video Rental *(Blockbuster 491-2911)*, Galleries **1-3 mi:** Park, Museum *(Occoquan Mill House 491-7525)*, Sightseeing *(Occoquan Village)* **3+ mi:** Movie Theater *(AMC Potomac Mills 490-5151, 5 mi.)*

Provisioning and General Services

OnSite: Bank/ATM **Near:** Dry Cleaners *(Bridge 494-8677)* **Under 1 mi:** Convenience Store, Supermarket *(Food Lion 492-0244, Giant 494-4550)*, Wine/Beer, Liquor Store *(ABC 494-7108)*, Bakery *(Teddy's 497-0572)*, Market *(Aldi 's)*, Protestant Church, Beauty Salon *(Villalta's 491-7400)*, Barber Shop, Laundry, Pharmacy *(CVS 494-9781)*, Newsstand, Florist, Department Store *(Kmart 491-7089)*, Copies Etc. *(Mailbox Junction 492-7200)* **1-3 mi:** Delicatessen *(Big Mamas 418-8738)*, Post Office *(494-6427)* **3+ mi:** Health Food *(Natural Grocer 494-7287, 5 mi.)*, Library *(Occoquan 494-8126, 4 mi.)*, Bookstore *(Borders 897-8100, 5 mi.)*, Hardware Store *(Home Depot 670-3699, 5 mi.)*

Transportation

OnCall: Rental Car *(Enterprise 490-0566, Alamo 497-0752, 4 mi.)*, Taxi *(Yellow Cab 491-2222)*, Airport Limo *(Airport Sedan 580-8877)* **3+ mi:** Rail *(Amtrak 493-8168, 6 mi.)* **Airport:** Reagan Nat'l. *(20 mi.)*

Medical Services

911 Service **OnCall:** Ambulance **Under 1 mi:** Dentist *(Mazin 491-1115)*, Chiropractor *(Prymak 494-9922)* **1-3 mi:** Doctor *(Occoquan Medical Care 499-9939)* **Hospital:** Potomac Hospital 583-3000 *(4 mi.)*

Setting -- On the north side of the 65 foot railroad bridge, Occoquan Harbor Marina's seven upscale docks sprawl along the western shore of narrow Occoquan River. Abundant mature shade trees - magnolias, willows, maples - provide the bones for this very pretty, nicely groomed facility. Small perennial beds and borders are tucked in among established evergreens - even the travelift bay is beautifully planted - and each area is defined by rope fences.

Marina Notes -- *Off-season closed Sundays. Easy access fuel is on the T-head at the end of "B" dock. Vinyl-edged, diagonally-laid, screwed wood floating docks with full-length finger piers. Power varies by dock - from full-size pedestals to plugs embedded in the piers. Full BY services - 25T lift. Full Tilt Marine is an on-site, independent marine services company focused on smaller boats. Extensive and landscaped on-the-hard storage across the street. Attractive, well-merchandised ships' store, decorated with pine paneling and exposed brick. All-tiled thoughtfully-conceived bathhouses - each has two toilets, a vanity with two molded sinks and a separate shower room with two glass-doored shower stalls, a joint dressing room plus a vanity with hair dryer plugs and big mirrors.

Notable -- A dark green canvas and a white awning shelters waterfront picnic decks with chairs and tables plus charcoal and propane grills. A couple of grassy areas and raised open picnic decks all overlook the docks and river. The expansive Oasis restaurant shares the marina building. Dining venues include an outdoor riverfront deck with tables under a pavilion, in the open or flanking the tiki bar. Inside, overlooking the deck, the pool room features five regulation tables; an adjacent bamboo-themed room has a dance floor, bandstand and a wall of TVs. An all-window waterview room can also serve private functions.

PHOTOS ON CD-ROM: 15

Navigational Information
Lat: 38°41.027' **Long:** 077°15.568' **Tide:** 2 ft. **Current:** n/a **Chart:** 12285
Rep. Depths (*MLW*): Entry 6 ft. **Fuel Dock** n/a **Max Slip/Moor** 6 ft./6 ft.
Access: Up Occoquan River on the left past the Rt. 123 bridge

Marina Facilities *(In Season/Off Season)*
Fuel: No
Slips: 4 Total, 4 Transient **Max LOA:** 40 ft. **Max Beam:** n/a
Rate *(per ft.)*: **Day** $1.00* **Week** n/a **Month** n/a
Power: 30 amp $5, **50 amp** n/a, **100 amp** n/a, **200 amp** n/a
Cable TV: No **Dockside Phone:** No
Dock Type: Fixed, Wood
Moorings: 0 Total, 0 Transient **Launch:** n/a
Rate: Day n/a **Week** n/a **Month** n/a
Heads: None
Laundry: None **Pay Phones:** No
Pump-Out: No **Fee:** n/a **Closed Heads:** Yes

Marina Operations
Owner/Manager: Village of Occoquan **Dockmaster:** n/a
In-Season: n/a **Off-Season:** n/a
After-Hours Arrival: First come, first served
Reservations: No **Credit Cards:** Cash or checks
Discounts: None
Pets: Welcome **Handicap Access:** No

Occoquan Village Docks

PO Box 195; 314 Mill Street; Occoquan, VA 22125

Tel: (703) 491-1918 **VHF: Monitor** n/a **Talk** n/a
Fax: (703) 491-4962 **Alternate Tel:** n/a
Email: occoquantownhall@aol.com **Web:** www.occoquan.org
Nearest Town: Occoquan *(0 mi.)* **Tourist Info:** (703) 491-4045

Marina Services and Boat Supplies
Communication - FedEx, UPS, Express Mail **Supplies - 1-3 mi:** West Marine *(492-6225)*, Boat/US *(492-6225)*, Bait/Tackle **3+ mi:** Boater's World *(680-0743, 4 mi.)*

Boatyard Services
Nearest Yard: Occoquan Harbor (703) 494-3600

Restaurants and Accommodations
OnCall: Pizzeria *(Domino's 491-1716)* **Near:** Restaurant *(Tobys Café 494-1317)*, *(Pizzeria Chicago 490-4883)*, *(Bistro Belgique Gourmande 494-1180, Dinner Fri, Sat, Sun; Sun B & L)*, *(Sea Sea & Co. 690-2004, L $7-13, D $15-23, kids' $6-8; indoor or out, tiki bar - live bands, dancing on weekends, billiards club)*, *(Occoquan Inn 491-1888, D $16-25, Sun champagne brunch 11am-2pm $15)*, *(Virginia Grill 491-1888, B $6-9, L $7-9, D $7-16, 7am-10pm)*, Lite Fare *(Down Under Tavern 490-0904, at Occoquan Inn)*, *(Garden Kitchen Café 494-2848, B $3-5, L $4-5, terraced garden)*, *(Coffee House 492-8976, $3-5, 8:30am-5pm)*, *(DeRubeen's Pastry 494-4777, 8am-6pm, Sun 12-6pm)*, *(Maxl's Snack Shop 490-3540, $2-4, 10:30am-4pm)*, *(Mom's Apple Pie 497-7437, take-out only)*, *(Blue Arbor Café 494-1317, $7-8, 11am-5pm)*, *(Pink Bicycle Tea Room 491-1317, $8-19, 11am-4:30pm, complete tea)* **1-3 mi:** Motel *(Quality Inn 494-0300)*, *(The Inns of Viginia 490-3400)*, *(Econo Lodge 491-5196)*, Inn/B&B *(Cockrell Hill 497-7994)*

Recreation and Entertainment
Near: Playground, Jogging Paths, Park *(River Walk - Mamie Davis)*, Museum *(Mill House Museum 491-7525 11am-4pm daily)*, Sightseeing *(Walking History & Ghost Tours 571-334-7357 or follow the map from the tourist center)*, Galleries *(Many)*, Special Events *(Craft Fairs)* **Under 1 mi:** Fitness Center *(Curves 497-4244)*, Roller Blade/Bike Paths **1-3 mi:** Tennis Courts *(Sport & Health Clubs 491-4126)*, Bowling *(Bowl America 494-9191)*, Video Rental **3+ mi:** Golf Course *(Belmont Bay 497-1384, 4 mi.)*, Movie Theater *(AMC Potomac Mills 490-5151, 5 mi.)*

Provisioning and General Services
Near: Supermarket *(Safeway 497-2227)*, Gourmet Shop, Delicatessen, Wine/Beer *(Olde Dominion Wine Shoppe 494-1622)*, Bakery *(Mom's Apple Pie 497-7437)*, Bank/ATM, Post Office *(491-2062)*, Library *(Occoquan 494-8126)*, Beauty Salon *(Hair Studio 492-1461)*, Barber Shop, Bookstore *(The Eclectic Ram 492-1221)*, Retail Shops *(dozens)* **Under 1 mi:** Convenience Store, Dry Cleaners *(Betty Brite 491-7778)*, Pharmacy *(Opt Care 499-9440)*, Florist **1-3 mi:** Fishmonger, Laundry *(Spincycle Coin 492-9622)* **3+ mi:** Hardware Store *(Home Depot 670-3699, 6 mi.)*

Transportation
OnCall: Rental Car *(Enterprise 490-0566)*, Taxi *(Yellow Cab 491-2222)*, Airport Limo *(Airport Sedan 580-8877)* **3+ mi:** Rail *(Amtrak 493-8168, 8 mi.)* **Airport:** Reagan Nat'l. *(20 mi.)*

Medical Services
911 Service **OnCall:** Ambulance **Near:** Chiropractor *(Occoquan Family Chiropractic 492-4144)*, Holistic Services *(Acupuncture Healing Arts 494-1212)* **Under 1 mi:** Doctor *(Occoquan Medical Care 499-9939)*, Dentist *(Occoquan Family Dentistry 490-9094)* **Hospital:** Potomac Hospital 583-3000 *(6 mi.)*

Setting -- At the navigational head of the Occoquan River is the delightful, historic village of Occoquan - the Dogue Indian word for "at the end of the river." The new Riverwalk & Town Pier is located in front of Mamie Davis Park on the site of the Occoquan Wharves - right in the center of town. The stationary wood pier, built over the original jetty, provides alongside dockage with good pedestals. At the top of the ramp a brick path leads through the sweet pocket park, with a Victorian gazebo and benches, out to Mill Street. The boardwalk, with benches and picnic tables, runs along the river to Riverwalk Mall.

Marina Notes -- *Day-only dockage is free. Honor system - envelopes provided, leave money in the box. Current Rt.123 bridge clearance 27 feet; new bridge by '07 with clearance of 44 feet. Current depths 5 foot with a max of 50 foot boat. 130 feet of alongside dockage now (4 slips) with 24 floating docks (to 40 feet) to be added soon; 230 feet additional alongside after bridge completion when the 12 foot wide boardwalk will extend under the bridge. The 100-ft channel will be dredged to 9 feet. Included will be the restoration of the "historic rocks" that were navigational aids implanted by the Corps of Engineers in the 1890's. Their removal in 1973 as part of rebuilding the bridge created extensive silting. New heads & showers slated for '06. Meanwhile, boaters are welcome at Sea Sea or the Visitors' Bureau. Note: the floating docks in front of Sea Sea are private and only for restaurant guests.

Notable -- An historic mill town (circa 1734) turned arts-oriented community, engaging Occoquan offers much to do; the Tourist Center on Mill St. provides a helpful guide. About 8 square blocks host unique shops. Mill House Museum is located in the original Merchant's Mill, the first automated grist mill in the US.

PHOTOS ON CD-ROM: 12

Mount Vernon Docks

3200 George Washington Mem'l Pkwy.; Mount Vernon, VA 22121

Tel: (703) 799-8678 **VHF: Monitor** 16 **Talk** 13
Fax: (703) 799-8609 **Alternate Tel:** (703) 780-2000
Email: n/a **Web:** www.mountvernon.org
Nearest Town: Mount Vernon **Tourist Info:** (703) 780-2000

Navigational Information

Lat: 38°42.396' **Long:** 077°05.075' **Tide:** n/a **Current:** n/a **Chart:** 12285
Rep. Depths (*MLW*): Entry 15 ft. **Fuel Dock** n/a **Max Slip/Moor** 9 ft./-
Access: Private Channel off the Potomac

Marina Facilities *(In Season/Off Season)*

Fuel: No
Slips: 4 Total, 4 Transient **Max LOA:** 100 ft. **Max Beam:** n/a
Rate *(per ft.)*: **Day** Free **Week** n/a **Month** n/a
Power: 30 amp n/a, **50 amp** n/a, **100 amp** n/a, **200 amp** n/a
Cable TV: No **Dockside Phone:** No
Dock Type: Fixed, Alongside, Wood
Moorings: 0 Total, 0 Transient **Launch:** n/a
Rate: Day n/a **Week** n/a **Month** n/a
Heads: None
Laundry: None **Pay Phones:** No
Pump-Out: No **Fee:** n/a **Closed Heads:** Yes

Marina Operations

Owner/Manager: Mount Vernon Ladies Assoc. **Dockmaster:** Daniel Frogett
In-Season: Apr-Oct, 8am-5:15pm **Off-Season:** Nov-Mar, 9am-4pm
After-Hours Arrival: Not permitted
Reservations: First come, first served* **Credit Cards:** n/a
Discounts: None
Pets: Welcome **Handicap Access:** No

Marina Services and Boat Supplies

Services - Security *(Guard dogs roam the Plantation after 6 pm)*

Boatyard Services

Under 1 mi: Travelift. **Nearest Yard:** Fort Washington Marina (301) 292-7700

Restaurants and Accommodations

OnSite: Restaurant *(Mount Vernon Inn Restaurant 780-0011, L $6-11, D $15-30, wharf to restaurant Shuttle; L 11am-3:30pm, D 5-9pm - Note: dinner not possible for boaters)*, Lite Fare *(Federal City Deli L $5-7)*, *(Café Lafayette B $2-5, L $2-5)*, *(Red Devon Grill L $3-7)*, *(Pizza Hot L $5-7)*

Recreation and Entertainment

OnSite: Museum *(George Washington's Mount Vernon 780-2000. Pay security guard at wharf: $11.00 p/p, under 5 Free - Plan for 3 hrs., begin at the new $85 million Ford Orientation Center & Reynolds Museum & Education Center (slated for '06). Mansion hours: Apr-Aug, 8am-5pm, Mar, Sep, Oct 9am-5pm; Nov-Feb 9am-4pm.)*, Cultural Attract *(Pioneer Farmer Site: Four-acre Working Farm with 8 cultivated fields and horses in a 16-sided treading barn demonstrates Washington's advanced farming practices - lots of heritage animals. Included in entrance fee.)*, Sightseeing *(a 20-stop audio tour, $4 at main gate; A narrated 30-min excursion on Potomac aboard Potomac Spirit or Miss Christin Tues-Sun, 10:30, 11:30, 12:30, 2 & 3 $8/4)*, Special Events *(a constantly changing schedule of special activities and programs - call)*

Provisioning and General Services

OnSite: Bookstore, Retail Shops *(A large three-room gift shop at the main entrance, and a smaller one near the Mansion)*

Transportation

OnSite: Ferry Service *(Potomac Spirit 202-554-8000 Mar-Oct - tours between Mount Vernon & D.C.)*

Medical Services

911 Service **OnCall:** Ambulance **Hospital:** Northern Virginia Community 671-1200 *(9 mi.)*

Setting -- Arriving at Mount Vernon by water is a unique opportunity to step into the shoes of George Washington's visitors. At the end of the wharf is an octagonal, deep red-shingled pavilion with cupola. Beyond it is alongside transient day-only dockage on the 80-foot "cat walks" that flank the pier. Immediately to port is a working farm and a five-minute walk up the brick path leads to the mansion and 45 acres of beautiful gardens, outbuildings and wooded grounds.

Marina Notes -- Dockmaster 799-8678, Lorenzo in Control Room 799-8056. Since 9/11, overnight transient dockage has not been permitted but boaters may tie up 8am-5:15pm. Pay entrance fees to the security guard at the wharf. First priority are two tour boats. The 80-foot "up-river" catwalk is available all day. "Miss Christin" occupies the down-river catwalk from Noon-4pm, making it available to boaters 8am-noon. (*Reservations not accepted for the catwalks, but radio dockmaster 1-2 hrs. ahead to determine availability) The 150 foot "Potomac Spirit" lies against the pilings across the front of the pavilion from 10am-1:30pm; that spot is available in the afternoon for large vessels capable of docking there (reservations possible for this spot). After 5:15pm, boaters move to an anchorage - just off either side of the wharf or on the opposite side of the main channel. If docks are full, then anchor and dinghy - dinghy dock is rarely full.

Notable -- The Georgian Mansion, beveled pine to replicate stone, is on 300 acres deeded to the Washington family in 1674 and surrounded by an extraordinary living history museum. Kids' Adventure Map encourages sightseeing to solve nine puzzles. Two eating options: the elegant Inn at Mount Vernon with authentic Colonial atmosphere and costumed wait staff or the food court with five kiosks and a spacious cathedral ceiling glass pavilion and outdoor patio.

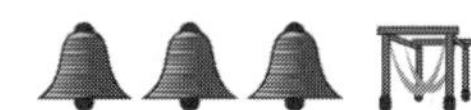

Navigational Information
Lat: 38°42.120' **Long:** 077°01.500' **Tide:** 3 ft. **Current:** 1 kt. **Chart:** 12285
Rep. Depths (*MLW*): Entry 7 ft. **Fuel Dock** 6 ft. **Max Slip/Moor** 6 ft./-
Access: Chesapeake Bay to Potomac River to Piscataway Creek

Marina Facilities *(In Season/Off Season)*
Fuel: Gasoline, Diesel
Slips: 296 Total, 40 Transient **Max LOA:** 50 ft. **Max Beam:** 17 ft.
Rate *(per ft.)*: **Day** $1.00 **Week** $7.00 **Month** $240
Power: 30 amp $3, **50 amp** $4, **100 amp** n/a, **200 amp** n/a
Cable TV: No **Dockside Phone:** No
Dock Type: Fixed, Floating, Long Fingers, Pilings, Wood
Moorings: 0 Total, 0 Transient **Launch:** n/a
Rate: Day n/a **Week** n/a **Month** n/a
Heads: 12 Toilet(s), 10 Shower(s) *(with dressing rooms)*
Laundry: 2 Washer(s), 2 Dryer(s) **Pay Phones:** Yes, 1
Pump-Out: OnSite, Self Service, 2 Central **Fee:** $5 **Closed Heads:** Yes

Marina Operations
Owner/Manager: Tim Newell **Dockmaster:** Same
In-Season: Apr-Oct, 8:30am-5pm **Off-Season:** Nov-Mar, 8:30am-4:30pm
After-Hours Arrival: Call ahead
Reservations: Yes **Credit Cards:** Visa/MC
Discounts: AAA **Dockage:** n/a **Fuel:** n/a **Repair:** n/a
Pets: Welcome, Dog Walk Area **Handicap Access:** Yes, Heads, Docks

Fort Washington Marina

13600 King Charles Terrace; Fort Washington, MD 20744

Tel: (301) 292-7700 **VHF: Monitor** 16 **Talk** 68
Fax: (301) 292-9577 **Alternate Tel:** n/a
Email: *See Below **Web:** coastal-properties/public/html/ftwashington.html
Nearest Town: Ft. Washington *(3 mi.)* **Tourist Info:** (301) 475-4200

Marina Services and Boat Supplies
Services - Security *(key-coded access to docks)*, Dock Carts **Communication -** FedEx, DHL, UPS, Express Mail **Supplies - OnSite:** Ice *(Cube)* **3+ mi:** Propane *(Campbell's 292-9013, 4 mi.)*

Boatyard Services
OnSite: Travelift *(35T)*, Launching Ramp, Electrical Repairs, Electronics Repairs, Hull Repairs, Bottom Cleaning, Brightwork **OnCall:** Crane, Forklift, Engine mechanic *(gas, diesel)*, Interior Cleaning, Woodworking, Upholstery, Metal Fabrication, Painting **1-3 mi:** Rigger, Propeller Repairs.
Yard Rates: Haul & Launch $6/ft. *(blocking $1.75/ft.)*, Power Wash $1.75/ft.

Restaurants and Accommodations
OnSite: Restaurant *(Proud Mary 292-5521, L $8-28, D $8-28, good buzz on their jumbo lump crab cakes)* **1-3 mi:** Restaurant *(Hong Kong Express 203-8888)*, *(Charlie's Pizzeria and Carry-Out 292-0655, L $3-16, D $3-16)*, Fast Food *(McDonalds, Wendy's)*, Pizzeria *(Pizza Hut 292-0990)* **3+ mi:** Restaurant *(Steak in the Sack 292-4494, L $5-10, D $5-10, 4 mi.)*, *(Pizza Subs & Pasta 248-9780, 5 mi.)*, *(Silesia Carry Out 292-2180, 4 mi.)*, Pizzeria *(Papa John's 203-5000, 4 mi.)*, Motel *(Red Roof Inn 567-8030, 9 mi.)*, *(Best Western Potomac View 749-9400, 8 mi.)*

Recreation and Entertainment
OnSite: Pool *(Fort Washington Pool Club, $5/day)*, Picnic Area, Grills, Tennis Courts *(Fort Washington Pool Club)*, Boat Rentals *(Atlantic Kayak 292-6455 - tours, rental, sales, instruction: Apr, May, Sep, Oct Sat & Sun 10am-5pm; Jun-Aug Fri, Sat, Sun, 9am-noon or 1-4pm $54)*, Special Events *(Ft. Washington Boating Assoc)* **Near:** Playground **Under 1 mi:** Park *(Fort Washington Nat'l. Park 763-4600, Year-round - picnic areas, hiking & biking trails, 9-5 $3)* **1-3 mi:** Video Rental *(Blockbuster 292-5456)*, Museum *(George Washington's Mount Vernon - by water $11/9, Dockmaster 703-799-8678, Plantation 703-780-2000)* **3+ mi:** Golf Course *(Henson Creek 567-4646, 8 mi.)*, Fitness Center *(YMCA 203-2302, 4 mi.)*

Provisioning and General Services
Near: Convenience Store **1-3 mi:** Supermarket *(Safeway 965-6012 or Food Lion 292-9234, 4 mi.)*, Delicatessen, Wine/Beer, Liquor Store *(Silesia Liquors 292-1542)*, Crabs/Waterman, Bank/ATM, Post Office *(292-3658)*, Catholic Church, Protestant Church, Newsstand, Florist, Copies Etc. *(UPS Store 203-9120)* **3+ mi:** Bakery *(North Star Bakery 248-4101, 5 mi.)*, Fishmonger *(Seafood Shanty 248-1705, 5 mi.)*, Library *(Accokeek Memorial 283-2521, 8 mi.)*, Dry Cleaners *(Michael's Cleaners 248-4495, 4 mi.)*, Pharmacy *(CVS 292-3600, 4 mi.)*, Hardware Store *(South Potomac 292-0518, 4 mi.)*, Department Store *(Kmart 839-0550, 9 mi.)*

Transportation
OnCall: Rental Car *(Enterprise 292-9700 or Budget 248-3949, 5 mi.)*, Taxi *(Bluebird Cab 864-7700)*, Airport Limo *(M & R Limousine 292-8218)* **3+ mi:** Rail *(Amtrak (Alexandria) 703-836-4339, 15 mi.)* **Airport:** Reagan *(23 mi.)*

Medical Services
911 Service **OnCall:** Ambulance **Under 1 mi:** Dentist *(Droter 292-2408)* **1-3 mi:** Doctor *(Family Medical 292-1590)* **3+ mi:** Veterinarian *(Accokeek Animal Hospital 292-4000, 5 mi.)*
Hospital: Howard University Hosp. 686-0100 *(10 mi.)*

Setting -- The 19th C. stone fortification, Fort Washington, sits above the Potomac at the entrance to Piscataway Creek, marked by a miniature lighthouse. About a mile up the creek, ten-acre Fort Washington Marina's seven keycoded docks offer more up-to-date facilities along with an attractive 2-story gray and white contemporary office, restaurant and optional pool membership. A grassy area has a trio of wooden picnic tables and a full-service kayak center.

Marina Notes -- DCM. E-mail: cpm@erols.com. Established in the 1950's and rebuilt in late 80's by the MD Department of Natural Resources. Managed by Coastal Properties since '92. Extensive dockage dedicated for dock 'n' dine and for flotillas and other cruising groups. Mostly vinyl-edged floating docks, showing a bit of age, with good lighthouse pedestals. U-shaped fuel dock has 8 pumps. Temporary membership in the casual Ft. Washington Pool Club, right up hill from the docks, is $5/per person per day (pool, kids' pool & tennis). Full boatyard services and 35 ton travelift. Two sections of dedicated on-the-hard storage discreetly away from the marina - one section near the travelift and another shielded by evergreens above the docks. Key-coded all-tile bathhouses with raspberry dividers, 5 sinks and 5 quite nice tile shower stalls with dressing rooms. Laundry room has 2 washers, 2 dryers, and a large folding table.

Notable -- Proud Mary, the restaurant and tiki bar, plans a major expansion that will double the capacity of their tropically-inspired, white tablecloth indoor dining room to 90 - with a glass-walled room that overlooks the river - and will add a gazebo to the large outdoor, canvas-topped deck. Mount Vernon is across the Potomac from the mouth of Piscataway Creek so these docks may be a welcome alternative to anchoring in the river after a day at the plantation.

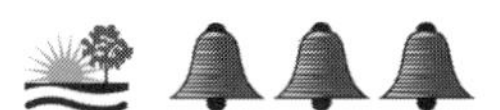

Alexandria City Marina

'O' Cameron Street; Alexandria, VA 22314

Tel: (703) 838-4265 **VHF: Monitor** 16 **Talk** 68
Fax: (703) 838-6344 **Alternate Tel:** (703) 838-4843
Email: ***See Below **Web:** ci.alexandria.va.us/recreation/marina/marina.htm
Nearest Town: Alexandria **Tourist Info:** (703) 838-5005

Navigational Information

Lat: 38°48.305' **Long:** 077°02.316' **Tide:** 3 ft. **Current:** 3 kt. **Chart:** 12285
Rep. Depths (*MLW*): Entry 20 ft. **Fuel Dock** n/a **Max Slip/Moor** 10 ft./-
Access: Upper Potomac River approx. 92 miles from Ches. Bay

Marina Facilities *(In Season/Off Season)*

Fuel: No
Slips: 60 Total, 20 Transient **Max LOA:** 200 ft. **Max Beam:** n/a
Rate *(per ft.)*: **Day** $1.00* **Week** n/a **Month** n/a
Power: 30 amp $2, **50 amp** $2, **100 amp** $5, **200 amp** n/a
Cable TV: No **Dockside Phone:** No
Dock Type: Fixed, Composition
Moorings: 0 Total, 0 Transient **Launch:** n/a
Rate: Day n/a **Week** n/a **Month** n/a
Heads: 5 Toilet(s), 4 Shower(s)
Laundry: None **Pay Phones:** Yes, 5
Pump-Out: OnCall, 1 Central **Fee:** n/a **Closed Heads:** Yes

Marina Operations

Owner/Manager: City of Alexandria **Dockmaster:** n/a
In-Season: Apr-Oct, 10am-9pm** **Off-Season:** Nov-Mar, 10am-5pm
After-Hours Arrival: Reservation only
Reservations: Yes **Credit Cards:** Cash/checks only
Discounts: None
Pets: Welcome, Dog Walk Area **Handicap Access:** No

Marina Services and Boat Supplies

Services - Docking Assistance, Security *(8 hrs.)*, Megayacht Facilities **Communication -** Mail & Package Hold, Phone Messages, Data Ports *(Wi-Fi)*, FedEx, UPS, Express Mail **Supplies - Near:** Ice *(Cube)*, Bait/Tackle *(Trophy Room 837-8215)* **Under 1 mi:** West Marine *(549-7020)* **1-3 mi:** Propane *(Quarles 550-8000)* **3+ mi:** Boat/US *(461-2850, 5 mi.)*

Restaurants and Accommodations

OnSite: Restaurant *(Chart House 684-5080, L $9-19, D $17-30, Sun brunch $14-23)*, Lite Fare *(Food Court coffee, espresso, global deli, dragon eatery, california wraps, etc.)* **Near:** Restaurant *(Gadsby's Tavern 548-1288, L $8-12, D $17-26)*, *(Elysium 838-8000, D $75, 7-course prix fixe, B&L, too)*, *(The Warehouse 683-6868, L $8-15, D $10-29)*, *(Mai Thai 548-0600, L $6-9, D $10-17)*, *(219 Fish House 549-1141, L $7-12, D $15-25)*, *(Landini Bros 836-8404, D $14-29)*, *(The Wharf 836-2836, D $15-22)*, Fast Food *(Popeye's/Subway)*, Hotel *(Holiday Inn 86-627-0511, $170-210, Colonial ambiance,)*, Inn/B&B *(Princely B&B 800-470-5588, $90-250, 30 private "Old Town" houses)* **Under 1 mi:** Hotel *(Morrison House 838-8000, $150-300, Relais & Chateau)*, *(Radisson 683-6000, $150-180)*

Recreation and Entertainment

OnSite: Picnic Area *(and Dog Park)*, Boat Rentals *(Seaport Foundation 549-7078; Atlantic Kayak 838-9072)*, Park *(Founders Park)*, Sightseeing *(Potomac Riverboat 548-9000 - "Matthew Hayes/Miss Mallory" Monuments - Alexandria to Georgetown $20/10RT, $12/6 1/way; "Miss Christin" to Mt. Vernon $30/17)*, Galleries *(Torpedo Factory Art Center 549-9550)* **Near:** Video Rental *(Blockbuster 549-4681)*, Museum *(Carlyle House, Gadsby's Tavern & Stabler-Leadbeater Apothecary 549-2997 All 3 -$9/5/Free; 1773 Christ Church 549-1450; Waterfront Mus. 838-4288; Black History Ctr. 838-4356)*, Cultural Attract *(Ramsay House 838-4200, Noon $8; on-site: Seaport Foundation 9am-5pm, Free)*, Special Events *(Cherry Blossoms, Garden/House Tour - Apr; Waterfront Fest - Jun; Alexandria's B'day - Jul; Art Fest - Sep)* **Under 1 mi:** Fitness Center *(Jungle's Gym 838-9838)* **1-3 mi:** Tennis Courts *(Sport & Health Clubs 416-4900)*, Movie Theater *(Hoyts 739-4040)* **3+ mi:** Golf Course *(Greendale 971-6170; Haines Pt. 202-554-7660, 5 mi.)*

Provisioning and General Services

OnSite: Bank/ATM **Near:** Convenience Store *(Old Town Mkt. 836-5509)*, Delicatessen *(Picca 683-4441; Jack's B&L)*, Bakery *(Firehook 519-8020)*, Farmers' Market *(838-5006, Sat 5-10:30am - 300 King)*, Catholic Church, Protestant Church, Dry Cleaners *(Beverly 549-1330)*, Bookstore *(Olsson's 684-0077)*, Pharmacy *(CVS 548-8043)* **Under 1 mi:** Supermarket *(Safeway 836-0380)*, Gourmet Shop *(Trader Joe's 548-0611; Sutton Place 549-6611)*, Health Food *(Cash Grocer 549-9544)*, Wine/Beer *(Michael's 548-9463)*, Fishmonger *(Old Town 684-0090)*, Post Office *(684-7168)*, Beauty Salon *(Aveda Circe Spa 519-8528)* **1-3 mi:** Library *(768-6700)*, Laundry *(Norge 549-5027)*

Transportation

OnCall: Rental Car *(Enterprise 960-6900)*, Taxi *(Yellow Cab 549-2500)*, Airport Limo *(Airport Car 971-4200)* **Near:** Bikes, Local Bus *(weekend shuttle from Metro to Market Sq.)*, InterCity Bus **Under 1 mi:** Rail *(Metro & Amtrak 836-4339)* **Airport:** Reagan Nat'l. *(5 mi.)*

Medical Services

911 Service **OnCall:** Ambulance **Hospital:** Northern VA 671-1200 *(6 mi.)*

Setting -- Just north of the Woodrow Wilson bridge (a 50 foot drawbridge), the Alexandria City Marina's three main piers line up along the charming, vibrant Old Town's waterfront. The first of the three, in front of the Torpedo Arts Center and the Chart House Restaurant, has just been rebuilt. The second pier shares a dock with the Alexandria Seaport Foundation - the rustic little floating wood-sided building with metal roof. The final pier, just beyond the Foundation, lands in Founder's Park - one of a string of several Alexandria waterfront parks. A promenade stretches along the leafy riverfront.

Marina Notes -- *72 hours max, 1-4 hrs. $5. **Sat 8am-10pm, Sun 8am-9pm (Free Wi-Fi). ***E-Mail: city.marina@alexandria.gov. Stationary composite docks with short finger piers (many new '04-'05) accommodate to 40 foot LOA. Vessels up to 200 feet tie up on the T-heads and at the end of the gazebos. Authentic paddle wheeler "Cherry Blossom" berths here. Standard cinderblock municipal bathhouses with live hyacinths! - 3 sinks, 3 heads, 2 fiberglass shower stalls with a joint, private dressing room. Directly south, Old Dominion Yacht Club - the nation's first boating club - welcomes members with reciprocity.

Notable -- A history, art or food buff's dream stop - the docks are right in the heart of 1749 Old Town. More than 2,000 carefully restored buildings line the brick sidewalks - now occupied by galleries, restaurants (100+), hotels, boutiques, superb museums, services and, on the side streets, private residences. The Old Torpedo Factory Arts Center, at the head of the docks, hosts 85 studios - open 10am-5pm, 7 days - and 165 artists. Adjacent is the Food Pavilion and the upscale Chart House restaurant. Tour boats to Mount Vernon, D.C. and Georgetown base along the main wharf. The Visitors' Center is next to Market Square.

Navigational Information
Lat: 38°49.950' **Long:** 077°02.517' **Tide:** n/a **Current:** n/a **Chart:** 12285
Rep. Depths (*MLW*): Entry 7 ft. **Fuel Dock** n/a **Max Slip/Moor** 9 ft./-
Access: R "14" then "16" into basin

Marina Facilities *(In Season/Off Season)*
Fuel: No
Slips: 200 Total, 6 Transient **Max LOA:** 40 ft. **Max Beam:** n/a
Rate *(per ft.)*: **Day** $2.00 **Week** n/a **Month** n/a
Power: 30 amp $10, **50 amp** $10, **100 amp** n/a, **200 amp** n/a
Cable TV: No **Dockside Phone:** No
Dock Type: Floating, Long Fingers, Composition
Moorings: 0 Total, 0 Transient **Launch:** n/a
Rate: Day n/a **Week** n/a **Month** n/a
Heads: 4 Toilet(s), 4 Shower(s) *(with dressing rooms)*
Laundry: None **Pay Phones:** No
Pump-Out: OnSite, 1 Central **Fee:** $5 **Closed Heads:** Yes

Marina Operations
Owner/Manager: Frederick Razafindrainise **Dockmaster:** Brian Paulik
In-Season: May-Oct, 9am-6pm **Off-Season:** Nov-Apr, 10am-5pm
After-Hours Arrival: Go to guard shed
Reservations: Yes **Credit Cards:** Visa/MC, Dscvr
Discounts: None
Pets: Welcome **Handicap Access:** No

Washington Sailing Marina

1 Marina Drive; Alexandria, VA 22314

Tel: (703) 548-9027 **VHF: Monitor** 16 **Talk** 69
Fax: (703) 684-5903 **Alternate Tel:** n/a
Email: wsm@guestservices.com **Web:** www.washingtonsailingmarina.com
Nearest Town: Alexandria *(1 mi.)* **Tourist Info:** (703) 549-1000

Marina Services and Boat Supplies
Services - Security *(24 hrs.)* **Communication -** FedEx, DHL, UPS, Express Mail **Supplies - OnSite:** Ice *(Block, Cube)*, Ships' Store *(Spinnaker 'n Spoke)* **1-3 mi:** West Marine *(549-7020)*, Bait/Tackle *(Trophy Room 837-8215)*, Propane *(Quarles 550-8000)* **3+ mi:** Boat/US *(461-2850, 7 mi.)*

Boatyard Services
OnSite: Travelift *(15T)*, Crane *(31T)*, Launching Ramp, Engine mechanic *(gas, diesel)*, Electrical Repairs, Rigger, Bottom Cleaning **Yard Rates:** $50/hr., Haul & Launch $6/ft., Power Wash $2/ft., Bottom Paint $10/ft.

Restaurants and Accommodations
OnSite: Restaurant *(Potowmack Landing 548-0001, L $8-15, D $11-29, Champagne Sun brunch $20, Jazz Thur night)*, Lite Fare *(Afterdeck Café L $2-5)* **OnCall:** Pizzeria *(Domino's 548-3030)* **Under 1 mi:** Pizzeria *(Monterey's Gourmet Pizza 683-9400)*, Inn/B&B *(Executive Club Suites 739-2582, $190-220)* **1-3 mi:** Restaurant *(Le Refuge 548-4661)*, *(Tokyo Japanese Steakhouse 683-8878)*, *(La Bergerie 683-1007, L $10-19, D $14-33)*, *(Afghan Restaurant 548-0022, L $9-15, D $9-15, lunch buffet $9pp)*, Pizzeria *(Marino's Pizza & Subs 548-8544)*, Motel *(Old Colony Inn 739-2478)*, Hotel *(Sheraton Suites 836-4700)*, *(Radisson Hotel Old Town 683-6000, $150-180)*, Inn/B&B *(Holiday Inn 548-6300, $149-179)*

Recreation and Entertainment
OnSite: Picnic Area, Grills, Jogging Paths, Boat Rentals *(Sailboats - 14' Sunfish $10/hr., 17' Island $17/hr. 19' Flying Scot $19/hr.)*, Roller Blade/Bike Paths *(Mount Vernon Bike Trail)* **1-3 mi:** Tennis Courts *(Sport & Health)*, Fitness Center *(Sport & Health Clubs 416-4900)*, Movie Theater *(Hoyts 739-4040)*, Video Rental *(Blockbuster 820-8822)*, Museum *(Alexandria Archaeology Museum 838-4399)*, Galleries *(Del Ray Artisans 838-4827)* **3+ mi:** Golf Course *(Greendale 971-6170, 7 mi.)*

Provisioning and General Services
Under 1 mi: Convenience Store *(Lee's Market)*, Delicatessen *(Towngate Deli 683-3360)*, Beauty Salon *(Julia's Beauté 683-4021)*, Dry Cleaners *(Sam's 548-2833)* **1-3 mi:** Supermarket *(Giant 549-8149)*, Gourmet Shop *(Sutton Place 549-6611)*, Health Food *(My Organic Market 535-5980)*, Wine/Beer *(Vinotopia 549-3444)*, Bakery *(Gold Crust 549-0420)*, Farmers' Market *(838-5006, Sat 5-10:30am at 300 King St.)*, Green Grocer *(Cash Grocer 549-9544)*, Fishmonger *(Old Town 684-0090)*, Bank/ATM, Post Office *(684-7821)*, Library *(838-4566)*, Barber Shop *(Barber Shop 971-6000)*, Laundry *(Norge 549-5027)*, Bookstore *(Olsson's 347-3686)*, Pharmacy *(CVS 683-4433)*, Florist *(Conklyn's 243-6660)*, Department Store *(J C Penney 971-1091)*, Copies Etc. *(Mail Boxes, Etc 739-9100)*

Transportation
OnSite: Bikes *($4-6/hr. $16.50-22/day)* **OnCall:** Taxi *(Diamond 543-6200)*, Airport Limo *(Airport Car 971-4200)* **1-3 mi:** Rail *(Amtrak 836-4339)*
Airport: Reagan Nat'l. *(2 mi.)*

Medical Services
911 Service **OnCall:** Ambulance **1-3 mi:** Doctor *(Heron 549-2626)*, Dentist *(Alexandria Old Town 549-1331)*, Chiropractor *(Chrysalis 535-7881)*, Veterinarian *(Banfield Pet Hosp. 518-8492)*, Optician *(Advanced Eye Care 313-8001)* **3+ mi:** Holistic Services *(Moksa Yoga & Holistic Health 317-0060, 4 mi.)* **Hospital:** Northern VA 671-1200 *(8 mi.)*

Setting -- Tucked into a long basin on Daingerfield Island, this buttoned-up sailboat-only marina is an oasis of green tranquility on the edge of bustling Washington. Seven piers line the eastern shore, each hosting new floating composite docks and a T-head for larger vessels. At the head of the docks is a large, well-landscaped park and an upscale gray contemporary restaurant and amenities complex with decks and vast windowed rooms. The far shore is densely treed; Washington Memorial Parkway peeks through the trees, but for the most part it is a green view.

Marina Notes -- Opened in 1948. Managed by Guest Services. Owned by National Park Service which restricts it to sailboats only - even for dock 'n' dine. Nicely equipped Spinnaker 'n' Spoke ships' store specializes in sailing hardware, basic boating needs, gifts and sailing & cycling gear. On-the-hard storage for over 400 trailered boats. Home to many one-design fleets - racing almost every day. Modestly priced sailing classes - weekends for adults. Inviting all-tile bathhouses are way above municipal issue; heads are open to the public, but the tile showers with private dressing rooms are key-coded for boaters only.

Notable -- Two eateries share views of the dock-filled basin and a wide-open expanse of the Potomac and DC skyline: the fine-dining Potomac Landing Restaurant (10am-8pm, a "Contemporary American Fish House") has 4 indoor dining areas, all tiered for best views, and 2 outdoor dining areas. There's also a large function room. Very casual Afterdeck Café (10:30am-5pm) has inside and outside seating. Easy access to Reagan National, but the planes take off right overhead. The 18.5 mile Mt. Vernon Bike Path, also a great jogging trail, runs along the river - 13 miles to Mount Vernon, one mile to Alexandria's Old Town.

James Creek Marina

200 V Street, SW; Washington, DC 20024

Tel: (202) 554-8844; (866) 554-8844 **VHF: Monitor** 16 **Talk** 68
Fax: (202) 488-4758 **Alternate Tel:** n/a
Email: info@jamescreek.com **Web:** www.jamescreek.com
Nearest Town: Washington, D.C. **Tourist Info:** (202) 347-7201

Navigational Information
Lat: 38°51.800' **Long:** 077°00.900' **Tide:** 6 ft. **Current:** n/a **Chart:** 12285
Rep. Depths (*MLW*): Entry 15 ft. **Fuel Dock** 12 ft. **Max Slip/Moor** 12 ft./-
Access: Potomac River at the mouth of Anacostia River

Marina Facilities *(In Season/Off Season)*
Fuel: *Citgo* - Gasoline, Diesel
Slips: 205 Total, 50 Transient **Max LOA:** 100 ft. **Max Beam:** n/a
Rate *(per ft.)*: **Day** $1.00/$0.75 **Week** $3.50 **Month** $7
Power: 30 amp $3, **50 amp** $5, **100 amp** n/a, **200 amp** n/a
Cable TV: No **Dockside Phone:** Yes
Dock Type: Floating, Long Fingers, Short Fingers, Pilings
Moorings: 0 Total, 0 Transient **Launch:** None
Rate: Day n/a **Week** n/a **Month** n/a
Heads: 4 Toilet(s), 1 Shower(s) *(with dressing rooms)*, Hair Dryers
Laundry: None **Pay Phones:** No
Pump-Out: OnSite, Full Service **Fee:** $5 **Closed Heads:** Yes

Marina Operations
Owner/Manager: Greg Smith **Dockmaster:** Jeremy Heckler
In-Season: Year-Round, 9am-5pm **Off-Season:** n/a
After-Hours Arrival: Call ahead
Reservations: Yes, Preferred **Credit Cards:** Visa/MC, Dscvr, Amex, Checks
Discounts: None
Pets: Welcome, Dog Walk Area **Handicap Access:** Yes, Heads, Docks

Marina Services and Boat Supplies
Services - Docking Assistance, Security, Trash Pick-Up, Dock Carts **Communication -** Mail & Package Hold, Fax in/out, FedEx, UPS, Express Mail *(Sat Del)* **Supplies - OnSite:** Ice *(Block)*, Marine Discount Store **1-3 mi:** Propane *(Frager's Hardware 543-6157)* **3+ mi:** West Marine *(703-549-7020, 8 mi.)*

Boatyard Services
OnCall: Engine mechanic *(gas, diesel)*, Electrical Repairs, Electronics Repairs, Canvas Work, Brightwork, Air Conditioning, Refrigeration, Divers, Compound, Wash & Wax, Interior Cleaning, Upholstery

Restaurants and Accommodations
OnSite: Lite Fare *(Market Place 488-8100, 7am-3pm daily in summer)* **Under 1 mi:** Restaurant *(Ziegfeld's 554-5141)*, *(Zanzibar On The Waterfront 554-9100)*, *(Pier 7 554-2500, at Channel Inn)*, *(Jenny's Chinese)*, *(Jenny's Asian Fusion 554-2202, L $7-17, D $10-32)*, Snack Bar *(BJ's Cantina & Marina Café 554-8396, D $8-17, by water - at Gangplank Marina Sun-Thu 11:30am-10pm, Fri-Sat until 11pm)*, Pizzeria *(Pizza Hut 488-8309)*, Hotel *(Best Western 488-7500)*, *(Channel Inn 554-2400, $115-145)* **1-3 mi:** Coffee Shop *(Olympic Espresso 554-7035)*, Hotel *(Mandarin Oriental 554-8588)*, *(Greenhouse 484-1000)*, Inn/B&B *(Maison Orleans 544-3694)*

Recreation and Entertainment
OnSite: Grills, Volleyball **Under 1 mi:** Fitness Center *(Waterside Fitness & Swim Club 488-3701)*, Boat Rentals *(Tidal Basin Boat House 484-0206)*, Roller Blade/Bike Paths, Fishing Charter, Video Rental *(In & Out Video 554-3669)* **1-3 mi:** Tennis Courts *(East Potomac Tennis Center 554-5962)*, Golf Course *(East Potomac Park 554-7660)*, Movie Theater *(Gallery Place 393-2121)*, Museum *(Smithsonian Institute 357-2700)*

Provisioning and General Services
Near: Bakery *(Lyon's 484-2100)*, Catholic Church, Protestant Church, Library *(724-4752)* **Under 1 mi:** Convenience Store *(Potomac Place 488-9403)*, Supermarket *(Safeway 554-9155)*, Liquor Store *(Harry's 783-4200)*, Fishmonger *(Phillips 488-8515)*, Bank/ATM, Post Office *(800-275-8777)*, Laundry *(863-0689)*, Pharmacy *(CVS 554-2144)* **1-3 mi:** Delicatessen *(L'Enfant 554-1345)*, Health Food *(Good Health 543-2266)*, Farmers' Market *(Fri 10am-2pm 800-384-8704)*, Crabs/Waterman *(The Wharf 314-5759)*, Beauty Salon *(L'Enfant 484-8830)*, Barber Shop *(Metro Barber 554-2891)*, Dry Cleaners *(Cosmo 554-4880)*, Bookstore *(Olsson's 347-3686)*, Hardware Store *(Frager's 543-6157)*, Florist *(L'Enfant 554-3480)*, Department Store *(Wal-Mart 842-3742)*, Copies Etc. *(Best Copy 488-5300)*

Transportation
OnSite: Taxi *(Lincoln Cab 484-2222)*, InterCity Bus **OnCall:** Rental Car *(Enterprise 332-1716, Thrifty 3 mi.)* **Under 1 mi:** Airport Limo *(Admiral Limousine 638-3006)* **3+ mi:** Rail **Airport:** Reagan Nat'l *(5 mi.)*

Medical Services
911 Service **Near:** Doctor *(Cohen 488-8556)* **Under 1 mi:** Dentist *(Anderson 554-5800)*, Ambulance **1-3 mi:** Chiropractor *(Capitol Hill 544-6035)*, Holistic Services *(Shovlin 547-4234)*, Veterinarian *(Capitol Hill 546-1972)* **Hospital:** Medlink Hospital At Capital Hill 546-5700 *(3 mi.)*

Setting -- On the Anacostia River, just past Washington Channel and Greenleaf Point, the four James Creek floating docks are tucked into a small alcove adjacent to the Army War College at Fort McNair. A lunch cart snack bar has a roped off patio and a couple of nice, bright blue picnic tables. The shed-roofed, cedar-sided little office sports a small patio with benches topped by a pergola. Picnic tables with charcoal grills are sprinkled across a large swath of well clipped grass, populated by small trees and bushes, overlooking the docks and river. Across the river is the Anacostia Naval Station.

Marina Notes -- Owned by the National Park Service. Discounts Tuesday. Good vinyl-edged wooden floating docks with full length finger piers and Lighthouse pedestals. Larger yachts accommodated alongside or on T-heads. The fuel dock has four pumps and is right at the entrance to the marina. Shore side services are limited to the cute little office building - with discounted boat supplies - and the delightful cinderblock bathhouse. It features tile floor, carefully painted walls, 3 sinks in a skirted marble vanity with a wall-size mirror, and a fiberglass shower stall with dressing room - fairly recently refurbished.

Notable -- This is an industrial area that's a bit off the beaten path - "Tourist D.C."made accessible by the G-71 bus that stops on the corner during rush hour, or by the metro; the Waterfront station is under a mile (a walk perhaps not comfortable at night); next to the stop is the Waterside Mall. The US Coast Guard Headquarters is on one side of the marina and the Army War College at Fort McNair on the other. At bit farther up the Anacostia, Buzzard's Point Yacht Club, also on National Park Service land, tends to have smaller boats and a nice little picnic area (the land directly adjacent called Buzzard Point Marina is for sale).

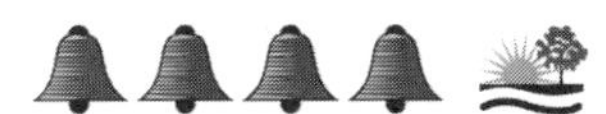

Navigational Information
Lat: 38°52.518' **Long:** 077°01.298' **Tide:** 3 ft. **Current:** 2 kt. **Chart:** 12285
Rep. Depths (*MLW*): Entry 16 ft. **Fuel Dock** n/a **Max Slip/Moor** 16 ft./-
Access: 75 miles up the Potomac River from the Chesapeake Bay

Marina Facilities *(In Season/Off Season)*
Fuel: No
Slips: 306 Total, 25 Transient **Max LOA:** 130 ft. **Max Beam:** n/a
Rate *(per ft.)*: **Day** $1.25 **Week** $7.50 **Month** $12.60
Power: 30 amp $5 (need adapter), **50 amp** $5, **100 amp** $10, **200 amp** n/a
Cable TV: Yes, $35 Per month **Dockside Phone:** No
Dock Type: Floating, Long Fingers, Concrete, Wood
Moorings: 0 Total, 0 Transient **Launch:** None, Dinghy Dock ($10)
Rate: Day n/a **Week** n/a **Month** n/a
Heads: 4 Toilet(s), 4 Shower(s) *(with dressing rooms)*
Laundry: 4 Washer(s), 4 Dryer(s), Book Exchange **Pay Phones:** Yes, 4
Pump-Out: Onsite *(dockside)*, Full Service **Fee:** $12 **Closed Heads:** Yes

Marina Operations
Owner/Manager: Dave Goshman **Dockmaster:** Mark Bergeran
In-Season: Year-Round, 24 hrs. **Off-Season:** n/a
After-Hours Arrival: Call ahead, dock office open 24 hrs.
Reservations: Required **Credit Cards:** Visa/MC, Dscvr, Amex
Discounts: None
Pets: Welcome, Dog Walk Area **Handicap Access:** Yes, Heads, Docks

Gangplank Marina

600 Water Street SW; Washington, D.C. 20024

Tel: (202) 554-5000 **VHF: Monitor** 16 **Talk** 68
Fax: (202) 863-1945 **Alternate Tel:** (202) 554-5000
Email: gangplankmarina@juno.com **Web:** www.gangplank.com
Nearest Town: Washington, DC **Tourist Info:** (202) 347-7201

Marina Services and Boat Supplies
Services - Docking Assistance, Concierge, Boaters' Lounge, Crew Lounge, Security *(24 hrs., guards, key-code)*, Trash Pick-Up, Dock Carts, Megayacht Facilities **Communication -** Mail & Package Hold, Phone Messages, Fax in/out, Data Ports, FedEx, DHL, UPS, Express Mail *(Sat Del)* **Supplies - OnSite:** Ice *(Block, Cube)* **Near:** Ships' Store *(Washington Marina)* **1-3 mi:** Bait/Tackle *(G & S 546-8163)*, Propane *(Frager's 543-6157)*

Boatyard Services
OnCall: Engine mechanic *(gas, diesel)*, Electrical Repairs, Hull Repairs, Bottom Cleaning, Air Conditioning, Refrigeration, Divers, Compound, Wash & Wax, Interior Cleaning, Propeller Repairs, Woodworking, Inflatable Repairs **Nearest Yard:** Ft. Washington (301) 292-7700

Restaurants and Accommodations
OnSite: Restaurant *(BJ's Cantina Marina Café 554-8396, D $8-17, Sun-Thu 11:30am-10pm , Fri-Sat 'til 11pm - Tex-Mex meets the Keys)* **OnCall:** Pizzeria *(Domino's 484-3030)* **Near:** Restaurant *(Hogates 484-6300)*, *(Jenny's Asian Fusion 554-2202, L $7-17, D $10-32)*, *(Le Rivage)*, *(Zanzibar On The Waterfront 554-9100)*, *(Pier 7 554-2500, at Channel Inn)*, Seafood Shack *(Phillips Flagship 488-8515, L $15-30, D $15-30)*, Hotel *(Channel Inn 554-2400, $115-145)* **Under 1 mi:** Seafood Shack *(Captain White's Seafood City 484-2722)*, Coffee Shop *(Olympic Espresso 554-7035)*, Lite Fare *(Atrium Café 863-7590)*, Hotel *(Best Western 488-7500)*, *(Holiday Inn 86-627-0511)*, *(Mandarin Oriental 554-8588)*

Recreation and Entertainment
OnSite: Picnic Area, Grills, Sightseeing *(The Spirit of Washington II, Odyssey Dinner Cruises; w/in 1 mi. U.S. Capitol, etc.)*, Special Events *(Fleet Blessing 3rd wknd May)* **Near:** Pool *(East Potomac)*, Fitness Center *(Waterside 488-3701)*, Park *(across channel - East Potomac Park)*, Cultural Attract *(Arena Stage 488-3300; w/in 1 mi. Kennedy Ctr. 467-4600)* **Under 1 mi:** Boat Rentals *(Tidal Basin 484-0206)*, Video Rental *(In & Out Video 554-3669)*, Museum *(Natl. Museum of the American Indian 357-1300; 9 of 14 Smithsonian Museums)* **1-3 mi:** Golf Course *(East Potomac 554-7660)*

Provisioning and General Services
Near: Supermarket *(Safeway 554-9155)*, Liquor Store *(Harry's 783-4200)*, Fishmonger *(Phillips 488-8515)*, Bank/ATM, Catholic Church, Library *(724-4752)*, Pharmacy *(CVS 554-2144)*, Newsstand **Under 1 mi:** Delicatessen *(L'Enfant Gourmet 554-1345)*, Farmers' Market *(800-384-8704 Fri 10am-2pm)*, Crabs/Waterman *(The Wharf 314-5759)*, Post Office *(800-275-8777)*, Beauty Salon *(L'Enfant Hairsalon 484-8830)*, Dry Cleaners *(Cosmo 554-4880)*, Copies Etc. *(Best Copy & Printing 488-5300)* **1-3 mi:** Gourmet Shop *(Lawson's Gourmet 789-1440)*, Health Food *(Good Health 543-2266)*, Bookstore *(Olsson's 347-3686)*, Hardware Store *(Frager's 543-6157)*, Department Store *(Wal-Mart 842-3742)*

Transportation
OnCall: Water Taxi *(Harbouritaville 554-0677)*, Taxi *(Executive 863-1136)* **Near:** Local Bus *(Metro)* **Under 1 mi:** Airport Limo *(Capital City 484-0200)* **1-3 mi:** Rail *(Amtrak 906-3104)* **Airport:** Reagan Nat'l. *(3 mi.)*

Medical Services
911 Service **OnCall:** Ambulance **Near:** Doctor *(Cohen 488-8556)* **Under 1 mi:** Dentist *(Anderson 554-5800)* **Hospital:** Medlink 546-5700 *(3 mi.)*

Setting -- Enormous Gangplank dominates the eastern shore of Washington Channel. Ten main piers, hosting over 300 docks, are generously spaced along the Water Street promenade - deep slips and wide thorofares ease maneuvering for the larger craft that berth here. A stilt house and floating office houses the management and amenities and, at the southern end, lively BJ's Cantina Marina Café overlooks the "Sequoia" and the docks. To the north the Washington Monument peeks above the new Mandarin Oriental Hotel; across the channel, past the popular anchorage, is leafy 300 acre East Potomac Park.

Marina Notes -- In business since 1975. Tagged "DC's Downtown Marina," with one of the largest live aboard populations in the East - about a third of the slips (including the GM, politicians, & an IT company). A blend of vinyl-edged wood and concrete floating docks with full-size Lighthouse pedestals are showing some age. Security is tight - the dockmaster's office is at the marina's key-coded entrance. Adjacent is the linoleum-floored, tidy, but basic, bathhouse and laundry room - 2 of each including 2 fiberglass shower stalls with dressing rooms and fresh shower curtains plus 4 washers, 4 dryers and a nice folding table.

Notable -- Tall ships visit and several charter boats berth at the south end - including a 104-ft. 1925 Trumpy, the beautifully restored former presidential yacht "Sequoia" ($10,000/4 hrs.). The next docks down host the "Spirit of Washington" and "Potomac Spirit" to Mount Vernon. The marina is part of Maine Avenue redevelopment, which boasts Hogate's, the storied seafood restaurant, a host of other eateries, and the Maine Ave. Fish Market - which is really a "trip." The Arena Stage is across the street and many of the monuments are walking distance; for all the other D.C. sites and sights, the Metro stop is about 2 blocks.

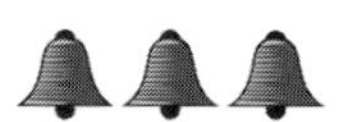

Capital Yacht Club

1000 Water Street SW; Washington, DC 20024

Tel: (202) 488-8110 **VHF: Monitor** 9 **Talk** 68
Fax: (202) 488-1429 **Alternate Tel:** (202) 488-8110
Email: cyc.office@verizon.net **Web:** www.capitalyachtclub.net
Nearest Town: Washington **Tourist Info:** (202) 347-7201

Navigational Information
Lat: 38°52.787' **Long:** 770°1..565' **Tide:** 3 ft. **Current:** 2 kt. **Chart:** 12285
Rep. Depths (*MLW*): Entry 30 ft. **Fuel Dock** n/a **Max Slip/Moor** 20 ft./-
Access: Chesapeake Bay to Potomac River to Washington Channel

Marina Facilities *(In Season/Off Season)*
Fuel: No
Slips: 89 Total, 10 Transient **Max LOA:** 200 ft. **Max Beam:** n/a
Rate *(per ft.)*: **Day** $1.25* **Week** 7.87 **Month** 33.75
Power: 30 amp $5, **50 amp** $12, **100 amp** 0.15/kwh, **200 amp** n/a
Cable TV: Yes **Dockside Phone:** Yes
Dock Type: Fixed, Floating, Long Fingers
Moorings: 0 Total, 0 Transient **Launch:** n/a, Dinghy Dock
Rate: Day n/a **Week** n/a **Month** n/a
Heads: 6 Toilet(s), 6 Shower(s)
Laundry: 4 Washer(s), 4 Dryer(s), Book Exchange **Pay Phones:** Yes
Pump-Out: OnSite **Fee:** $10 **Closed Heads:** Yes

Marina Operations
Owner/Manager: Kelvin J.Lee **Dockmaster:** Same
In-Season: Year-Round, 8am-6pm **Off-Season:** n/a
After-Hours Arrival: Call in advance
Reservations: Yes, Required **Credit Cards:** Visa/MC, Amex, Tex
Discounts: None
Pets: Welcome, Dog Walk Area **Handicap Access:** No

Marina Services and Boat Supplies
Services - Docking Assistance, Boaters' Lounge, Security, Trash Pick-Up, Dock Carts, Megayacht Facilities **Communication -** Mail & Package Hold, Phone Messages, Fax in/out, Data Ports *(Conf. Room)*, FedEx, DHL, UPS, Express Mail *(Sat Del)* **Supplies - OnSite:** Ice *(Block, Cube)* **Near:** Ships' Store *(Washington Marina 554-0222)* **1-3 mi:** Bait/Tackle *(G & S 546-8163)*, Propane *(Frager's 543-6157)* **3+ mi:** West Marine *(703-549-7020, 7 mi.)*

Boatyard Services
OnSite: Electrical Repairs, Electronics Repairs, Brightwork, Refrigeration **Near:** Divers, Compound, Wash & Wax, Interior Cleaning, Propeller Repairs, Woodworking. **1-3 mi:** Launching Ramp.

Restaurants and Accommodations
OnSite: Seafood Shack *(Phillips Flagship 488-8515, L $15-30, D $15-30)* **OnCall:** Pizzeria *(Domino's 484-3030)* **Near:** Restaurant *(Zanzibar On The Waterfront 554-9100)*, *(Pier 7 554-2500, at Channel Inn)*, *(Talay Thai Restaurant 546-5100)*, Snack Bar *(BJ's Cantina and Marina Café 554-8396, D $8-17, Sun-Thu 11:30am-10pm, Fri-Sat 'til 11pm)* **Under 1 mi:** Seafood Shack *(Captain White's 484-2722)*, Lite Fare *(Olympic Espresso 554-7035)*, Pizzeria *(Pizza Hut 488-8309)*, Motel *(Holiday Inn 479-4000, $179-255)*, Hotel *(Mandarin Oriental 554-8588)*, *(Channel Inn 554-2400)*, *(Greenhouse 484-1000)*

Recreation and Entertainment
OnSite: Special Events *(Fleet Blessing - 3rd wknd May)* **Near:** Fitness Center *(Waterside Fitness & Swim Club 488-3701)*, Park, Cultural Attract *(Arena Stage 488-3300; Kennedy Ctr. 467-4600 w/in 1 mi.)*, Sightseeing *(D.C. Monuments)* **Under 1 mi:** Pool, Picnic Area, Grills, Playground, Boat Rentals *(Tidal Basin 484-0206)*, Video Rental *(In & Out 554-3669)*, Museum *(9 Smithsonian Museums 357-2700)* **1-3 mi:** Golf Course *(East Potomac 554-7660)*, Galleries *(Artists' Museum 638-7001)*

Provisioning and General Services
OnSite: Newsstand **Near:** Supermarket *(Safeway 554-9155)*, Liquor Store *(Harry's 783-4200)*, Green Grocer, Fishmonger *(Main Ave. Fish Mkt.)*, Bank/ATM, Catholic Church, Protestant Church, Synagogue, Library *(724-4752)*, Pharmacy *(CVS 554-2144)* **Under 1 mi:** Delicatessen *(L'Enfant Gourmet 554-1345)*, Bakery *(Tropical Desserts 488-4647)*, Farmers' Market *(800-384-8704 Fri 10am-2pm)*, Crabs/Waterman *(The Wharf 314-5759)*, Post Office *(800-275-8777)*, Beauty Salon *(L'Enfant Hairsalon 484-8830)*, Barber Shop *(Metro Barber 554-2891)*, Dry Cleaners *(Cosmo 554-4880)*, Laundry *(Wash 863-0689)*, Copies Etc. *(Best Copy & Printing 488-5300)* **1-3 mi:** Gourmet Shop *(Lawson's Gourmet 789-1440)*, Health Food *(Good Health 543-2266)*, Bookstore *(Olsson's 347-3686)*, Hardware Store *(Frager's 543-6157)*, Department Store *(Wal-Mart 842-3742)*

Transportation
OnSite: Local Bus *(& 2 blocks to Metro)* **Near:** Bikes, Taxi *(Mayflower 783-1111)* **Under 1 mi:** Airport Limo *(Admiral 554-1000)* **1-3 mi:** Rail *(Amtrak 906-3104)* **Airport:** Reagan Nat'l. *(3 mi.)*

Medical Services
911 Service **OnCall:** Ambulance **Near:** Doctor *(Cohen 488-8556)* **Under 1 mi:** Dentist *(Anderson 554-5800)* **1-3 mi:** Veterinarian *(Capitol Hill 546-1972)* **Hospital:** Medlink 546-5700 *(3 mi.)*

Setting -- Just past Gangplank, the hospitable Capital Yacht Club's 90 slips are the next 4 piers. At the head of the docks is the modern two-story Dutch hip-roofed cement and pale brick clubhouse. An awning and gaff-rigged flagpole makes it easy to spot. Directly south, the kelly green Phillips Flagship restaurant sports a green and white striped awning above its outdoor deck. Across the narrow Washington Channel is the tree-lined shore of East Potomac Park.

Marina Notes -- *Up to 65'; over 65' $2.50/ft. Pumpout add'l over 65'. Founded in 1892; welcomes all boaters. A comfortable lounge furnished with leather captain's chairs, a polished mahagony bar and TV is available to guests and members. Bar is open 5-10pm weekdays, Fri & Sat 'til 11pm. Food is not served, but boaters are encouraged to take out from neaby seafood provisioners and eat there. The adjacent conference room features wired and Wi-Fi Internet, plus a computer with dedicated DSL line. Several courtesy phones. The two outer docks ("A"&"D") are stationary; "B"&"C" are floating both with long finger piers. Aging docks & pedestals are in good working order. Dinghy dock for anchored boats - facilities available for $15 fee. Very nice, fully equipped tiled "bathhouse" reflects a private club ambiance - fiberglass showers with private dressing rooms, vanities, hair dryers, complimentary toiletries. Excellent laundry.

Notable -- In front of CYC, redwood picnic tables flanked by flower pots overlook the docks; on the 2nd floor, Jenny's Asian Fusion Seafood offers expansive views of the Channel. Immediately adjacent is tourist-packed Phillips, with all-you-can-eat buffets. Directly north are the docks of the famous Maine Ave. Fish Market - a bustling seafood marketplace. The Mall, the Washington Monument and many historic sights are within walking distance, as are a few Metro stops.

PHOTOS ON CD-ROM: 15

Navigational Information
Lat: 38°52.893' **Long:** 077°01.763' **Tide:** 3 ft. **Current:** 2 kt. **Chart:** 12285
Rep. Depths (*MLW*): Entry 15 ft. **Fuel Dock** n/a **Max Slip/Moor** 10 ft./-
Access: Washington Channel under fixed bridge to head of navigation

Marina Facilities *(In Season/Off Season)*
Fuel: No
Slips: 125 Total, 20 Transient **Max LOA:** 100 ft. **Max Beam:** n/a
Rate *(per ft.)*: **Day** $2.00 **Week** 12 **Month** 18
Power: 30 amp Incl., **50 amp** Inq., **100 amp** Inq., **200 amp** n/a
Cable TV: No **Dockside Phone:** No
Dock Type: Floating, Short Fingers, Alongside, Composition

Moorings: 0 Total, 0 Transient **Launch:** n/a
Rate: Day n/a **Week** n/a **Month** n/a
Heads: 2 Toilet(s), 2 Shower(s)
Laundry: None **Pay Phones:** No
Pump-Out: OnSite, Self Service, 34 InSlip **Fee:** Free **Closed Heads:** Yes

Marina Operations
Owner/Manager: Robert L.Stickell **Dockmaster:** Same
In-Season: Year-Round, 8am-6pm* **Off-Season:** n/a
After-Hours Arrival: Must be pre-arranged
Reservations: Yes, Required **Credit Cards:** Visa/MC
Discounts: None
Pets: Welcome, Dog Walk Area **Handicap Access:** Yes, Heads

Washington Marina

1300 Maine Avenue SW; Washington, DC 20024

Tel: (202) 554-0222 **VHF: Monitor** n/a **Talk** n/a
Fax: (202) 484-1950 **Alternate Tel:** n/a
Email: sales@washingtonmarina.com **Web:** washingtonmarina.com
Nearest Town: Washington, D.C. **Tourist Info:** (202) 347-7201

Marina Services and Boat Supplies
Services - Security *(24 hrs., key-card)*, Dock Carts, Megayacht Facilities **Communication -** FedEx, UPS, Express Mail **Supplies - OnSite:** Ice *(Cube)*, Ships' Store **1-3 mi:** Propane *(Frager's 543-6157)* **3+ mi:** West Marine *(703-549-7020, 7 mi.)*

Restaurants and Accommodations
Near: Restaurant *(Phillips Flagship 488-8515, L $15-30, D $15-30, sushi bar, plus all-you-can-eat seafood buffet L Mon-Fri $15)*, *(Pier 7 554-2400)*, *(Jenny's Asian Fusion 554-2202, L $7-17, D $10-32, delivery)*, *(H2O at Hogates 484-6300)*, *(Zanzabar on the Waterfront 554-9100)*, Seafood Shack *(Jessie's Cooked Seafood 554-4173, L $5-6, D $6-10, to go)*, *(Custis & Brown Seafood 484-0168, to go)*, *(Captain White's Seafood City 484-2722, to go - 12 clams/$6; 12 oysters/$8, sandwiches $5-$6, D $6-10)*, Coffee Shop *(Olympic Espresso 554-7035)*, Lite Fare *(Giovannis Gourmet Deli 554-7452)*, Hotel *(Mandarin Oriental 554-8588, 5-star hotel)*, *(Greenhouse 484-1000)* **Under 1 mi:** Pizzeria *(Roma Pizza 554-0977, L $6-10, D $6-10)*, Hotel *(Channel Inn 554-2400, $115-145)* **1-3 mi:** Hotel *(Holiday Inn 479-4000)*, Inn/B&B *(B&B Victoria & Maxwell 483-4079)*, *(Maison Orleans B&B 544-3694)*, *(Independence House B&B 544-6011)*

Recreation and Entertainment
OnSite: Special Events *(Fleet Blessing 3rd wknd May)* **Near:** Fitness Center *(Waterside Fitness & Swim Club 488-3701)*, Boat Rentals *(Tidal Basin Boat House 484-0206)*, Cultural Attract *(Arena Stage 488-3300; w/in 1 mi. Kennedy Ctr. 467-4600)*, Sightseeing *(Jefferson Memorial & Other Monuments)* **Under 1 mi:** Tennis Courts *(East Potomac Tennis 554-5962)*, Video Rental *(In & Out Video 554-3669)*, Museum *(9 Smithsonian Museums 357-2700)* **1-3 mi:** Golf Course *(East Potomac Park 554-7660)*, Movie Theater *(Gallery Place 393-2121)*, Galleries *(Artists' Museum 638-7001)*

Provisioning and General Services
Near: Farmers' Market *(800-384-8704 Fri 10am-2pm)*, Green Grocer *(part of Jessie's Cooked Seafood)*, Fishmonger *(Custis and Brown 484-0168, Pruitt)*, Crabs/Waterman *(The Wharf 314-5759; Capt. White's - Steamed Crabs)*, Library *(724-4752)*, Beauty Salon *(L'Enfant Hairsalon 484-8830)*, Barber Shop, Dry Cleaners *(Elite 863-9003)*, Florist *(L'Enfant Florist 554-3480)* **Under 1 mi:** Convenience Store *(Potomac Place 88-9403)*, Supermarket *(Safeway 554-9155)*, Delicatessen *(Irene's Deli 488-5555)*, Liquor Store *(Bernstein's 484-3389)*, Bakery *(The Wishbone 479-1005)*, Post Office *(800-275-8777)*, Laundry *(Wash 863-0689)*, Bookstore *(Olsson's 347-3686)*, Pharmacy *(CVS 554-2144)* **1-3 mi:** Gourmet Shop *(Lawson's 789-1440)*, Health Food *(Good Health 543-2266)*, Bank/ATM, Hardware Store *(Frager's Hardware 543-6157)*, Department Store *(Wal-Mart 842-3742)*

Transportation
OnCall: Water Taxi *(Harbouritaville, Washington's first on-call Water Taxi 554-0677)* **Near:** Local Bus *(& Metro)* **1-3 mi:** Taxi *(Inet-Taxi 488-3952)*, Rail *(Union Station)*, Airport Limo *(ABC 941-4900)* **Airport:** Reagan *(3 mi.)*

Medical Services
911 Service **OnCall:** Ambulance **Near:** Doctor *(Cohen 488-8556)*, Dentist *(Anderson 554-5800)* **1-3 mi:** Chiropractor *(Capitol Hill Chiropractic Center 544-6035)*, Holistic Services *(Marjorie Shovlin & Associates 547-4234)*, Veterinarian *(Capitol Hill Veterinary Clinic 546-1972)*
Hospital: Medlink Hospital At Cap

Setting -- Just north of the fixed 37 foot I-395 bridge, venerable Washington Marina is tucked into the top end of the Washington Channel before the Tidal Basin. The original historic brick marina building anchors a dozen main piers hosting over 150 floating composite slips. Shoreside views are of the East Potomac Park, the bridge, and the Mandarin Oriental Hotel with the Washington Monument in the background.

Marina Notes -- *Closed Sun. Cancellations require 48 hrs. notice (4 days on hols). Created by Franklin Roosevelt as part of the WPA & designed by Charles Channey in 1939; Yacht Basin One opened in '41. In 1951, C.M. Stickell took over, changing the name. Today the third generation is at the helm. The wharf itself is original, but the beautiful, vinyl-edged floating composite docks, with full-size Lighthouse pedestals, are new and a welcome upgrade. Dedicated transient docks are hard by and under the bridge infrastructure. Lighting all long the walkways. Good security with electronic-carded dock access. The large, very well-supplied ships' store maintains over 30,000 parts. Very small dry stack storage. On the docket is a renovation of the heads and showers as soon as approvals are obtained. In the meantime, aging cement floor, tiled wall full bathrooms are right on the dock 24/7. Additional bathrooms inside the ships' store.

Notable -- Directly south are the Fish Market docks - famous Pruitt Seafood, Curtis & Brown Seafood, Jessie's Cooked Seafood and Capt. White's. A huge assortment of fresh seafood, freshly shucked clams & oysters, plus steamed and fried. A footbridge over the roadway at the end of the parking lot leads to the Mandarin Oriental. Then, it's under a quarter-mile to the Jefferson Memorial and about a mile to the White House, to the Capitol and to the Reflecting Pool.

Columbia Island Marina

George Washington Parkway; South Arlington, VA 22202

Tel: (202) 347-0173 **VHF: Monitor** 16 **Talk** 68
Fax: (202) 347-3196 **Alternate Tel:** n/a
Email: cim@guestservices.com **Web:** www.columbiaisland.com
Nearest Town: Washington, D.C. *(1 mi.)* **Tourist Info:** (202) 347-7201

Navigational Information

Lat: 38°52.300' **Long:** 077°02.550' **Tide:** 5 ft. **Current:** n/a **Chart:** 12285
Rep. Depths (*MLW*): Entry 6 ft. **Fuel Dock** 6 ft. **Max Slip/Moor** 6 ft./-
Access: Just N of 14th St. Bridge, entrance through small bridge

Marina Facilities *(In Season/Off Season)*

Fuel: Gasoline, High-Speed Pumps
Slips: 384 Total, 4 Transient **Max LOA:** 55 ft. **Max Beam:** 20 ft.
Rate *(per ft.)*: **Day** $1.00/Inq. **Week** Inq. **Month** Inq.
Power: 30 amp Incl., **50 amp** Incl., **100 amp** n/a, **200 amp** n/a
Cable TV: No **Dockside Phone:** No
Dock Type: Fixed, Floating, Long Fingers, Short Fingers, Composition
Moorings: 0 Total, 0 Transient **Launch:** n/a
Rate: Day n/a **Week** n/a **Month** n/a
Heads: 2 Toilet(s), 2 Shower(s)
Laundry: None **Pay Phones:** No
Pump-Out: OnSite, Self Service **Fee:** $5 **Closed Heads:** Yes

Marina Operations

Owner/Manager: Renee J.P. Sanders **Dockmaster:** Same
In-Season: Apr-Oct, 8:30am-7pm **Off-Season:** Nov-Mar, 6am-5pm
After-Hours Arrival: See nightwatchman
Reservations: Yes, Preferred **Credit Cards:** Visa/MC, Dscvr, Amex
Discounts: Boat/US **Dockage:** 50% **Fuel:** n/a **Repair:** n/a
Pets: Welcome, Dog Walk Area **Handicap Access:** Yes, Heads, Docks

Marina Services and Boat Supplies

Services - Room Service to the Boat, Security, Trash Pick-Up, Dock Carts **Communication -** FedEx, UPS, Express Mail **Supplies - OnSite:** Ice *(Cube)* **1-3 mi:** Marine Discount Store *(Washington Marina)*, Bait/Tackle *(G & S Bait Shop 546-8163)*

Boatyard Services

OnSite: Launching Ramp **OnCall:** Engine mechanic *(gas, diesel)*

Restaurants and Accommodations

OnSite: Lite Fare *(Columbia Island Café 347-0174, L $3-5, D $3-5, 9am-7pm, will deliver to boat w/ 24 hr. notice)* **OnCall:** Pizzeria *(Domino's 484-3030)* **1-3 mi:** Restaurant *(Phillips Flagship Restaurant 488-8515, L $15-30, D $15-30)*, *(Jenny's Asian Fusion 554-2202, L $7-17, D $10-32)*, *(Georgia Browns 393-4499, D $11-20)*, Seafood Shack *(DC Coast Restaurant 216-5988)*, Fast Food *(McDonald's)*, Pizzeria *(Pizza Amore 546-9512)*, Inn/B&B *(B&B Victoria & Maxwell 483-4079)* **3+ mi:** Hotel *(Hotel George 347-4200, $295, 4 mi.)*

Recreation and Entertainment

OnSite: Picnic Area, Volleyball, Park **OnCall:** Jogging Paths, Boat Rentals, Roller Blade/Bike Paths, Cultural Attract, Sightseeing, Special Events **1-3 mi:** Tennis Courts *(East Potomac Tennis Center 554-5962)*, Fitness Center *(Results Gym 518-0001)*, Bowling *(Fort Myers Bowling 528-4766)*, Movie Theater *(DC Playback Theater Co. 328-0412)*, Video Rental *(Video 2000 232-6801)*, Museum *(Corcoran Gallery of Art - Museum 639-1790)* **3+ mi:** Golf Course *(National Park Service - Golf Course 554-7660, 4 mi.)*, Horseback Riding *(Rock Creek Park Horse Centre 362-0117, 9 mi.)*

Provisioning and General Services

OnSite: Wine/Beer **Under 1 mi:** Bank/ATM, Post Office, Beauty Salon, Barber Shop **1-3 mi:** Convenience Store, Supermarket *(A K Market 462-7333 R 4 mi.)*, Gourmet Shop *(Lawson's Gourmet Provisions 789-0800)*, Delicatessen *(Plaza Deli 682-1869)*, Health Food *(Natural Health Options 289-8802)*, Liquor Store *(Pan Mar Wine & Liquors 659-2645)*, Fishmonger, Meat Market, Bookstore *(Olsson's 638-7610)*, Pharmacy *(Dunbarton 338-1020)*, Newsstand, Hardware Store *(Dean Home Center 638-3886)*, Florist, Clothing Store, Retail Shops, Department Store, Copies Etc. *(A Plus 332-4290)* **3+ mi:** Bakery, Farmers' Market, Green Grocer, Lobster Pound, Catholic Church, Protestant Church, Synagogue, Dry Cleaners

Transportation

OnCall: Taxi *(Red Top Cab 703-522-3333)* **Near:** Local Bus *(Metro & Subway)* **1-3 mi:** Rail, Airport Limo *(Airport Car 388-5466)*
Airport: Reagan Nat'l. *(2 mi.)*

Medical Services

911 Service **OnCall:** Ambulance, Veterinarian *(Acacia Mobile Veterinary Clinic 244-8595)* **Under 1 mi:** Holistic Services **1-3 mi:** Dentist *(Greater Wash Dental 726-2447)*, Chiropractor *(Absolute Chiropractic 548-6000)* **3+ mi:** Doctor *(Joshi /Sobhani 296-4897, 4 mi.)*
Hospital: George Washington University 715-4833 *(3 mi)*

Setting -- On the Georgetown Channel, between the Memorial and the 14th Street (George Mason) Bridge, 11 piers hosting 370 slips rim the north side of the snug, dipper-shaped Pentagon Lagoon - across from the Tidal Basin entrance. It's on the Virginia side, down the hill from the Pentagon and across from Lady Bird Johnson Park, with a view of the Washington Monument. Wide swaths of lawn populated by mature trees and picnic tables surround the docks.

Marina Notes -- Owned by the National Park Service and run by Guest Services. Powerboats only - transients welcome, but no live-aboards. Two fixed 18-foot bridges limit boat size. Gated, floating, vinyl-trimmed composite docks with full-length finger piers, dock boxes and full Lighthouse pedestals - 30 and 50-amp service. C dock hosts pump-out and gas pumps - but no diesel - dial 10 for assistance. A small, single-story brick building houses a cafe and ships' store. Very nice, gray and white tiled recent full bathrooms are near "C" dock.

Notable -- The Columbia Island Café is open daily 9am-7pm, 7 days during the season, for sandwiches, barbecue pork, burgers, daily specials and ice cream. Casual café-style seating indoors at contemporary, polished chrome and wood chairs and tables or outdoors in a heated, tented pavilion with picnic tables (which can also be rented, making this is a possible group cruise destination). The DC Duck, which originates at Union Station, goes into the water here. Regan National's runways begin one mile south - the docks are frequently in the flight path. Two miles northwest is Georgetown, a once major port and now fashionable neighborhood with abundant restaurants and lively nightlife. It can be a magnificent cruise; dockage at Washington Harbour from 6am-Midnight.

PHOTOS ON CD-ROM: 11

13. Western Shore: Wicomicoes To Windmill Point

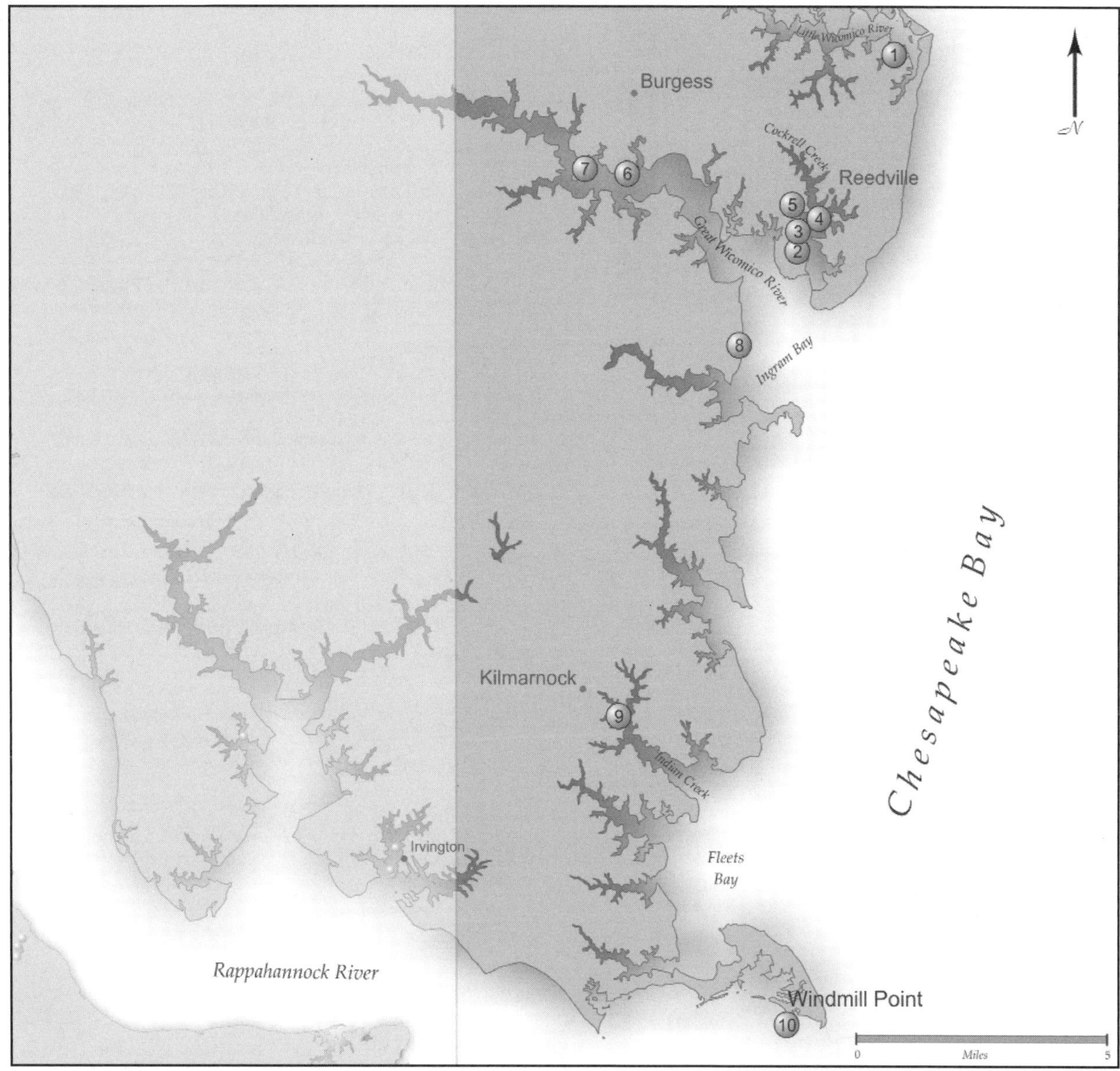

MAP	MARINA	HARBOR	PAGE	MAP	MARINA	HARBOR	PAGE
1	**Smith Point Marina**	*Little Wicomico River*	238	6	**Great Wicomico River Marina**	*Great Wicomico River*	243
2	**Jennings Boatyard**	*Ingram Bay/Cockrell Creek*	239	7	**Tiffany Yachts**	*Great Wicomico River*	244
3	**Fairport Marina & Restaurant**	*Ingram Bay/Cockrell Creek*	240	8	**Ingram Bay Marina**	*Great Wicomico River*	245
4	**Reedville Marina**	*Ingram Bay/Cockrell Creek*	241	9	**Chesapeake Boat Basin**	*Fleets Bay/Indian Creek*	246
5	**Buzzard's Point Marina**	*Ingram Bay/Cockrell Creek*	242	10	**Windmill Point Marine Resort**	*Windmill Point*	247

- **A "DCM" symbol in Marina Notes means Designated Clean Marina** — This is a coveted state-level award given to marinas that meet stringent, environmentally supportive requirements (see page 307). *For a list of DCM's & pump-out facilities, see page 308.*
- **Ratings & Reviews** — An explanation of the Atlantic Cruising Club's rating system, and a detailed explanation of what is in each section of the Marina Report is on pages 6 – 11. *The Data-Gathering Process is detailed on page 322.*
- **Marina Report Updates** — Updates to Marina Reports (from readers, ACC reviewers, and marinas) are posted regularly on *www.AtlanticCruisingClub.com.*

Smith Point Marina

989 Smith Point Road; Reedville, VA 22539

Tel: (804) 453-4077 **VHF: Monitor** 16 **Talk** 69
Fax: (804) 453-4077 **Alternate Tel:** (804) 453-4077
Email: smithpt@crosslink.net **Web:** www.crosslink.net/~smithpt
Nearest Town: Reedville *(4 mi.)* **Tourist Info:** (804) 333-1919

Navigational Information
Lat: 37°53.000' **Long:** 076°15.080' **Tide:** 1.5 ft. **Current:** n/a **Chart:** 12285
Rep. Depths (*MLW*): Entry 5 ft. **Fuel Dock** 6 ft. **Max Slip/Moor** 6 ft./6 ft.
Access: LIttle Wicomico River to Slough Creek

Marina Facilities *(In Season/Off Season)*
Fuel: *Marine* - Gasoline, Diesel
Slips: 92 Total, 10 Transient **Max LOA:** 55 ft. **Max Beam:** 20 ft.
Rate *(per ft.)*: **Day** $1.10 **Week** Inq. **Month** Inq.
Power: 30 amp $3, **50 amp** $6, **100 amp** n/a, **200 amp** n/a
Cable TV: No **Dockside Phone:** No
Dock Type: Fixed, Floating, Long Fingers, Pilings, Alongside, Wood
Moorings: 0 Total, 0 Transient **Launch:** n/a
Rate: Day n/a **Week** n/a **Month** n/a
Heads: 5 Toilet(s), 4 Shower(s) *(with dressing rooms)*
Laundry: 1 Washer(s), 1 Dryer(s), Book Exchange **Pay Phones:** Yes, 1
Pump-Out: OnSite, Full Service, 1 Central **Fee:** $10 **Closed Heads:** Yes

Marina Operations
Owner/Manager: Dan & Jeanne Hickey **Dockmaster:** Dan Hickey
In-Season: Apr-Dec, 6am-6pm **Off-Season:** Jan-Mar, 8am-5pm
After-Hours Arrival: Ring bell on store at gas pumps
Reservations: No **Credit Cards:** Visa/MC, Dscvr, Amex
Discounts: Boat/US; Pump-out 50% **Dockage:** 25% **Fuel:** n/a **Repair:** n/a
Pets: Welcome, Dog Walk Area **Handicap Access:** Yes, Heads, Docks

Marina Services and Boat Supplies
Services - Docking Assistance, Security *(24 hrs., Owner lives on the premises)*, Trash Pick-Up, Dock Carts **Communication -** Mail & Package Hold, Phone Messages, Fax in/out, Data Ports *(Office)*, FedEx, DHL, UPS, Express Mail **Supplies - OnSite:** Ice *(Cube)*, Ships' Store, Bait/Tackle *(or Chesapeake Bait 453-5003, 5 mi.)*, Propane **OnCall:** Marine Discount Store *(Overnight delivery)*

Boatyard Services
OnSite: Travelift *(12T)*, Forklift *(3T)*, Launching Ramp, Electrical Repairs, Electronics Repairs, Hull Repairs, Bottom Cleaning, Brightwork, Divers, Compound, Wash & Wax, Interior Cleaning, Painting **OnCall:** Engine mechanic *(gas, diesel)*, Rigger, Sail Loft, Canvas Work, Air Conditioning, Refrigeration, Propeller Repairs, Woodworking, Upholstery, Yacht Interiors, Metal Fabrication, Awlgrip **Member:** ABYC - 1 Certified Tech(s), Other Certifications: Virginia Clean Marina **Yard Rates:** $44/hr., Haul & Launch $2.40/ft. *(blocking $1.50/ft.)*, Power Wash $1.60/ft. **Storage:** On-Land $72/mo.

Restaurants and Accommodations
Near: Condo/Cottage *(KOA Kamping Kabins 800-KOA-0795, weekly)*
3+ mi: Restaurant *(Tommy's 453-4666, D $8-24, 4 mi.)*, *(Crazy Crab 453-6789, L $8-13, D $9-25, 4 mi., recommends the "Captain's Platter")*, *(Lewis Seafood 453-3373, 7 mi.)*, *(Cockrell's Creek Seafood & Deli 453-6326, L $7-14, 5 mi., Mon-Sat 10am-5pm , Sun 11am-3pm)*, *(Italian Garden Café 453-5800, 6 mi.)*, Motel *(Bay Motel 453-5171, 5 mi.)*, Inn/B&B *(Fleeton Fields B&B 453-5014, $135-175, 7 mi., charming waterfront suites - picks up from* marinas), (Gables B&B *453-5228, 5 mi.)*

Recreation and Entertainment
OnSite: Picnic Area, Grills, Fishing Charter *(Sea Dragon 540-825-2804; Midnight Sun 453-5812; Jeannie C 453-4021)*, Special Events *(Bluefish Derby - Jun, Rockfish Bay-wide Tournament - Nov)* **Near:** Beach *(Smith Pt. Beach)*, Boat Rentals *(Canoes at KOA Campground)*, Sightseeing *(Smith Island Cruise 453-3430 $24.50/pp includes island bus tour)* **1-3 mi:** Park
3+ mi: Golf Course *(Village Green Golf Club 529-6332, 4 mi.)*, Fitness Center *(Beafit 453-7411, 4 mi.)*, Video Rental *(B & D Video 453-5802, 6 mi.)*, Museum *(Reedville Fisherman's Museum 453-6529 - daily May-Oct, 10:30am-4:30pm, $5/Free, 4 mi.)*

Provisioning and General Services
OnSite: Wine/Beer **Near:** Crabs/Waterman **3+ mi:** Convenience Store *(5 mi.)*, Fishmonger *(Jett Fish Dock 453-5302, 3 mi.)*, Lobster Pound *(5 mi.)*, Market *(Little River Market 453-6076, 8 mi.)*, Bank/ATM *(4 mi.)*, Post Office *(4 mi.)*, Protestant Church *(Baptist, Methodist, 7th Day Adventist, Episcopal, 4 mi.)*, Library *(Northumberland 580-5051, 15 mi.)*, Pharmacy *(CVS 435-0329, 18 mi.)*, Hardware Store *(Jetts Hardware 453-5325, 4 mi.)*

Transportation
OnSite: Courtesy Car/Van *(Courtesy car to Reedville $5)*
Airport: Richmond *(85 mi.)*

Medical Services
911 Service **OnCall:** Ambulance **3+ mi:** Doctor *(Lewis Clinic 453-3777, 4 mi.)*, Dentist *(Hurt 453-3101, 9 mi.)*, Veterinarian *(Marston 453-3524, 7 mi.)*
Hospital: Rapahannock General 435-8000 *(20 mi.)*

Setting -- About a mile up Little Wicomico River on Slough Creek, a large gray, blue-roofed work shed - perched on a hill - overlooks the the Smith Point docks. The approach is dominated by a white boatshed with 55 foot open slips on its creek side. To port, the fuel dock is on the "T" of a long dock hosting large sport fish boats; along the bulkhead, smaller boats rest under a low-slung shelter. The peaceful creek is lined with salt marsh backed by brush and trees.

Marina Notes -- DCM. Established in 1955, purchased by the Hickley family in 1998. Full yard services to all vessels, haulout only to 12 ton. The owners will take boaters to restaurants or a grocery store for $5 (the restaurants can deliver boaters home). Very helpful seasonal tenants. Boat/US discount for dockage, haul & pump-out. Smith Point Sea rescue. In summer '05, a new two-story building overlooking the covered docks was built to house a larger store and the offices. Previously, a houseboat moored on the fuel docks featured useful boating togs, ice cream & sundries - plus Fishin' Nuts, their signature peanuts. 10 RV-sites. Bathhouses have oversized, tile shower stalls with a shared dressing room and colorful shower curtains. Everything is hand painted, including the green, yellow and purple picket fence stall doors - dripping in fish net. The men's room is a little more subdued, but just as fun.

Notable -- Across the creek is a KOA campground; "Capt. Evans," a 150-passenger excursion boat to Smith Island leaves the dock at 10am - dinghy over; it's an alternative for those who want to visit the archipelago but are not comfortable cruising the 13.5 miles there. The boat docks at Ewell, the largest of 3 towns. Start at the S.I. Center, stroll the island, lunch at Bayside Inn. Back on the mainland, the Fisherman's Museum in Historic Reedville is 4 miles.

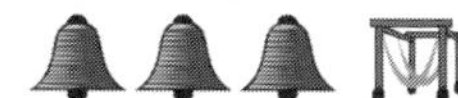

Navigational Information
Lat: 37°49.922' **Long:** 076°17.196' **Tide:** 2 ft. **Current:** n/a **Chart:** 12235
Rep. Depths (*MLW*): Entry 15 ft. **Fuel Dock** n/a **Max Slip/Moor** 9 ft./-
Access: Wicomico River to Cockrell Creek

Marina Facilities *(In Season/Off Season)*
Fuel: No
Slips: 30 Total, 3 Transient **Max LOA:** 50 ft. **Max Beam:** 18 ft.
Rate *(per ft.)*: **Day** $20.00* **Week** n/a **Month** $22/ft
Power: 30 amp Incl., **50 amp** n/a, **100 amp** n/a, **200 amp** n/a
Cable TV: No **Dockside Phone:** No
Dock Type: Fixed, Short Fingers, Pilings
Moorings: 0 Total, 0 Transient **Launch:** n/a
Rate: Day n/a **Week** n/a **Month** n/a
Heads: 2 Toilet(s), 2 Shower(s)
Laundry: None **Pay Phones:** No
Pump-Out: No **Fee:** n/a **Closed Heads:** Yes

Marina Operations
Owner/Manager: Larry Jennings **Dockmaster:** Same
In-Season: Year-Round, 7am-5pm **Off-Season:** n/a
After-Hours Arrival: Call ahead
Reservations: No **Credit Cards:** n/a
Discounts: Boat/US **Dockage:** Inq. **Fuel:** n/a **Repair:** n/a
Pets: Welcome, Dog Walk Area **Handicap Access:** No

Jennings Boatyard

169 Boatyard Road; Reedville, VA 22539

Tel: (804) 453-7181 **VHF: Monitor** n/a **Talk** n/a
Fax: (804) 453-4497 **Alternate Tel:** (804) 453-4497
Email: n/a **Web:** n/a
Nearest Town: Reedville *(5 mi.)* **Tourist Info:** (804) 435-6092

Marina Services and Boat Supplies
Services - Trash Pick-Up **Communication -** Mail & Package Hold, UPS, Express Mail **Supplies - Near:** Ships' Store **1-3 mi:** Propane **3+ mi:** Bait/Tackle *(Chesapeake Bait 453-5003, 6 mi.)*

Boatyard Services
OnSite: Travelift *(20T)*, Railway, Hull Repairs, Bottom Cleaning, Divers, Propeller Repairs, Painting

Restaurants and Accommodations
Near: Seafood Shack *(Cockrells Creek Seafood 453-6326, L $7-14, lunch only), (Fairport Marina 453-5002, L $3-6, D $9-20, everyday for lunch, dinner on Thu, Fri, Sat)* **3+ mi:** Restaurant *(Italian Garden Café 453-5800, D $8-17, 7 mi., dinner only), (Reedville Steamboat Wharf 453-5186, 6 mi., or by boat), (Crazy Crab 453-6789, L $8-13, D $9-25, 6 mi.), (Lewis Seafood453-3373, 7 mi.), (T&T's 453-4990, 7 mi., includes seafood deli)*, Fast Food *(Burgess Drive Inn 7 mi.)*, Motel *(Bay Motel 453-5171, 5 mi.)*, Inn/B&B *(Grandview 453-3890, 6 mi.), (Gables B&B 453-5228, $90-155, 6 mi.)*

Recreation and Entertainment
Under 1 mi: Sightseeing *(Tangier-Rappahannock Cruises 453-2628)* **1-3 mi:** Fitness Center *(Beafit 453-7411)* **3+ mi:** Golf Course *(Village Green Golf Club 529-6332, 5 mi.)*, Video Rental *(B & D Video 453-5802, 5 mi.)*, Museum *(Reedville Fisherman's Museum 453-6529 - or around the bend by water to their dock, 5 mi.)*

Provisioning and General Services
Near: Wine/Beer *(Fairpoint Marina)*, Crabs/Waterman *(Fairport)* **Under 1 mi:** Fishmonger *(Cockerell Creek Seafood 453-6326 - by water to cove just past the brick smokestack or Reedville Steamboat Wharf, 10am-Noon)* **1-3 mi:** Convenience Store, Health Food, Bank/ATM, Catholic Church, Protestant Church, Beauty Salon *(Bonnie's 453-3500)*, Hardware Store *(Jetts Hardware 453-5325)* **3+ mi:** Supermarket *(Food Lion 580-7326, 12 mi.)*, Delicatessen *(Little River Market, 5 mi.)*, Green Grocer *(Olin-Fox Farms 453-4125, 3 mi.)*, Market *(Little River Market & Deli 453-5092, 5 mi.)*, Post Office *(453-7503, 5 mi.)*, Pharmacy *(Heathsville 580-7400, 10 mi.)*

Transportation
OnCall: Local Bus **Under 1 mi:** Bikes *(at Reedville Fisherman's Museum - by water)* **1-3 mi:** Ferry Service *(to Tangier Island)*
Airport: Richmond *(90 mi.)*

Medical Services
911 Service **1-3 mi:** Doctor *(Lewis Clinic 453-3777)* **3+ mi:** Dentist *(Radcliffe 453-4361, 7 mi.)*, Holistic Services *(Claire Michie 453-4488, 6 mi.)*, Veterinarian *(Marston 453-3524, 6 mi.)*
Hospital: Rappahannock General 435-8000 *(19 mi.)*

Setting -- Off the Wicomico River, past Cockrell Creek's last remaining menhaden processing plant with its 100-foot motherships and small purse boats, Jenning's is the next facility to port. Three stationary piers offer alongside dockage; a boardwalk leads to a 4th, newer pier that parallels the shore with slips on both sides. Mostly seasonal vessels berth here. Landside the old-time boatyard, surrounded by decades of detritus, has a thriving build and repair business.

Marina Notes -- *Dockage is flat rate. Family owned and operated - Larry Jennings, John Jennings and Jason Jennings. Recent stationary docks have short finger piers, power on the pilings. Additional alongside dockage is perpendicular to the shore. The boatyard operation serves recreational craft but the bulk of its business is fueled by commercial fishermen from Tangier Island and the Northern Neck. They build as well as repair. If the folks at the nearby $17 million Omega Protein menhaden plant - the 2nd largest in the US - are "cooking," check the wind direction before settling in for the night.

Notable -- By land most everything is a long way - and transportation is limited. But until the mid-20th Century, all transport in the region was by water, and that is still possible today. It's 6 miles to Reedville by land and less than a mile by water. Dinghy or big boat around Tim Point and head farther up the creek to this once wealthy port village made famous by 15 menhaden processing plants and dozens of ships. The Reedville Marina has dockage as does the well-done Fisherman's Museum on the west side of the peninsula - with a small fleet of traditional Chesapeake watercraft. Mile-long Main Street, on the National Register of Historic Districts, is dotted with restored sea captains' mansions and former homes of fish processing tycoons - a short stretch is called Millionaires' Row.

PHOTOS ON CD-ROM: 11

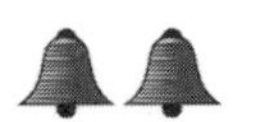

Fairport Marina & Restaurant

252 Polly Cove Road; Reedville, VA 22539

Tel: (804) 453-5002 **VHF: Monitor** 72 **Talk** n/a
Fax: (804) 453-9061 **Alternate Tel:** n/a
Email: fairport@crosslink.net **Web:** n/a
Nearest Town: Reedville *(4 mi.)* **Tourist Info:** (804) 435-6092

Navigational Information

Lat: 37°49.985' **Long:** 076°17.168' **Tide:** 2 ft. **Current:** n/a **Chart:** 12235
Rep. Depths (*MLW*): Entry 25 ft. **Fuel Dock** 12 ft. **Max Slip/Moor** 15 ft./-
Access: Wicomico River to Cockrell Creek

Marina Facilities *(In Season/Off Season)*

Fuel: *BP* - Slip-Side Fueling, Gasoline, Diesel
Slips: 49 Total, 12 Transient **Max LOA:** 150 ft. **Max Beam:** n/a
Rate *(per ft.)*: **Day** $0.70 **Week** n/a **Month** n/a
Power: 30 amp $5, **50 amp** $5, **100 amp** n/a, **200 amp** n/a
Cable TV: No **Dockside Phone:** No
Dock Type: Fixed, Floating, Short Fingers, Pilings, Alongside, Wood
Moorings: 0 Total, 0 Transient **Launch:** n/a
Rate: Day n/a **Week** n/a **Month** n/a
Heads: 2 Toilet(s)
Laundry: None **Pay Phones:** No
Pump-Out: OnSite, Self Service **Fee:** $5 **Closed Heads:** Yes

Marina Operations

Owner/Manager: Paige Headley **Dockmaster:** Mary Rittenhouse
In-Season: Year-Round, 9am-6pm **Off-Season:** Winter, 9am-5pm
After-Hours Arrival: See dockmaster in the morning
Reservations: No **Credit Cards:** Visa/MC
Discounts: None
Pets: Welcome, Dog Walk Area **Handicap Access:** No

Marina Services and Boat Supplies

Services - Boaters' Lounge, Security *(owners live onsite)* **Communication -** Mail & Package Hold, Phone Messages, Fax in/out *(Free)*, FedEx, UPS, Express Mail **Supplies - OnSite:** Ice *(Block, Cube, Shaved)* **1-3 mi:** Ships' Store, Propane **3+ mi:** Bait/Tackle *(Chesapeake Bait 453-5003, 6 mi.)*

Boatyard Services

OnSite: Launching Ramp **OnCall:** Crane, Engine mechanic *(gas, diesel)*, Electrical Repairs, Electronics Repairs **Near:** Travelift, Railway, Hull Repairs, Bottom Cleaning. **Under 1 mi:** Forklift. **Nearest Yard:** Jennings Boatyard (804) 453-4497

Restaurants and Accommodations

OnSite: Restaurant *(Fairport 453-5002, L $3-7, D $6-18, everyday for lunch, dinner on Thu, Fri, Sat)* **Under 1 mi:** Restaurant *(Crazy Crab 453-6789, L $8-13, D $9-25, by water)*, *(Cockrell's Creek 453-6326, L $7-14, D $7-14, 10am-4pm, 10am-9pm Thu, Fri, Sat - by water)* **3+ mi:** Restaurant *(Tommy's 453-4666, D $7-19, 5 mi.)*, *(T&T's 453-4990, L $3-8, D $6-20, 7 mi., includes seafood deli)*, Fast Food *(Burgess Drive Inn 7 mi.)*, Pizzeria *(Italian Garden Café 453-5800, D $8-17, 5 mi., dinner only)*, Motel *(Bay Motel 453-5171, 5 mi.)*, Inn/B&B *(Fleeton Fields 453-5014, $135-175, 7 mi.)*, *(Gables B&B 453-5228, 6 mi.)*, *(Grandview B&B 453-3890, 6 mi.)*

Recreation and Entertainment

OnSite: Special Events *(Reedville Bluefishing Derby - 2nd weekend Jun)* **OnCall:** Group Fishing Boat *(Bay Quest 43 ft. 15-25 passengers 529-6725)* **Under 1 mi:** Fishing Charter, Museum *(Reedville Fishermens Museum 453-6529 or 5 mi. by land)*, Sightseeing *(Tangier-Rappahannock Cruises 453-2628)* **1-3 mi:** Fitness Center *(Beafit 453-7411)* **3+ mi:** Golf Course *(Village Green Golf Club 529-6332, 5 mi.)*, Video Rental *(B & D Video 453-5802, 5 mi.)*

Provisioning and General Services

OnSite: Wine/Beer, Crabs/Waterman *(peeler sheds)*, Copies Etc. **Near:** Protestant Church **Under 1 mi:** Fishmonger *(Cockrell Creek Seafood 453-6326 - by water - cove just past the brick smokestack or Reedville Steamboat Wharf 10am-Noon)* **1-3 mi:** Convenience Store, Bank/ATM, Catholic Church, Beauty Salon *(Bonnie's 453-3500)*, Hardware Store *(Jetts Hardware 453-5325)* **3+ mi:** Supermarket *(Food Lion 580-7326, 12 mi.)*, Delicatessen *(Little River Market, 5 mi.)*, Green Grocer *(Olin-Fox Farms 453-4125, 3 mi.)*, Market *(Little River Market & Deli 453-5092, 5 mi.)*, Post Office *(453-7503, 5 mi.)*, Pharmacy *(Heathsville 580-7400, 10 mi.)*

Transportation

OnSite: Courtesy Car/Van **1-3 mi:** Ferry Service *(to Tangier Island)* **Airport:** Richmond, 90 mi./ Middle Peninsua Regional, 60 mi. *(3+ mi)*

Medical Services

911 Service **OnCall:** Ambulance **1-3 mi:** Doctor *(Lewis Clinic 453-3777)* **3+ mi:** Dentist *(Hurt 453-3101, 7 mi.)*, Holistic Services *(Claire Michie 453-4488, 6 mi.)*, Veterinarian *(Marston 453-3524, 6 mi.)* **Hospital:** Rappahannook General 435-8000 *(19 mi.)*

Setting -- Straight past the $17 million Omega Protein menhaden plant, 3 long piers with T-heads welcome a wide range of cruising vessels to pretty Cockrell Creek. At the head of "A" dock, also the fuel dock, a low, dark gray mostly-window building houses the popular Fairport seafood eatery with its screened crab deck and peeler sheds. The owners' house sits above "B" & "C" docks, which have new decking and pedestals. Right across the cove is Jenning's Boatyard.

Marina Notes -- Established in 1985 as a family owned and managed business; the owners live onsite and are generous with their car and van for provisioning and sightseeing. The good, stationary docks have wide, half-length finger piers. Three long T-heads provide plenty of room for cats or large vessels and "A" dock devotes one side to alongside tie-ups. The marina and the docks are open year-round, but the restaurant closes from Dec-Apr. The restaurant shares the heads with the docks; there are no showers - the marina is below the slip limit at which the State of Virginia requires showers.

Notable -- The Fairport has indoor seating with sage green vinyl booths and stand-alone tables, or outside at well-scrubbed picnic tables on the crab deck - both overlook the docks. The on-site peeler sheds are active all summer until September - the soft-shells they serve in the restaurant are fresh from those sheds. In the fall, when the crabs are big and fat they have all-you-can-eat crab feasts - usually on Sundays. Open May through November, for lunch from 11am-4pm, plus dinner until 9pm on Thursday, Friday and Saturday. Seafood buffet Friday and Saturday nights ($19); Thursday nights all-you-can-eat chilled, steamed shrimp ($14). If the menhaden processing plant's working, it's obvious. Historic Reedville, a do not miss, is less than a mile by water or 5 miles by land.

Navigational Information
Lat: 37°50.283' **Long:** 076°16.767' **Tide:** 2 ft **Current:** n/a **Chart:** 12235
Rep. Depths (*MLW*): Entry 15 ft. **Fuel Dock** n/a **Max Slip/Moor** 14 ft./-
Access: Past smoke stack, straight ahead to the foot of Reedville peninsula

Marina Facilities *(In Season/Off Season)*
Fuel: Gasoline, Diesel
Slips: 16 Total, 6 Transient **Max LOA:** 200 ft. **Max Beam:** n/a
Rate *(per ft.)*: **Day** $1.00 **Week** n/a **Month** $90
Power: 30 amp $3, **50 amp** $6, **100 amp** n/a, **200 amp** n/a
Cable TV: No **Dockside Phone:** No
Dock Type: Fixed, Short Fingers, Pilings, Alongside, Wood
Moorings: 0 Total, 0 Transient **Launch:** n/a
Rate: Day n/a **Week** n/a **Month** n/a
Heads: 2 Toilet(s), 2 Shower(s)
Laundry: None **Pay Phones:** No
Pump-Out: OnSite, Self Service **Fee:** $5 **Closed Heads:** Yes

Marina Operations
Owner/Manager: Olivia & Charles Williams **Dockmaster:** Charles Williams
In-Season: Mar-Dec, Tue-Sun 10am-9pm **Off-Season:** Jan-Feb, Closed
After-Hours Arrival: Call ahead
Reservations: Preferred **Credit Cards:** Visa/MC
Discounts: Boat/US **Dockage:** n/a **Fuel:** $0.10 **Repair:** n/a
Pets: Welcome **Handicap Access:** No

Reedville Marina

P.O.Box 369; 902 Main Street; Reedville, VA 22539

Tel: (804) 453-6789 **VHF: Monitor** 16 **Talk** n/a
Fax: (804) 453-7447 **Alternate Tel:** n/a
Email: n/a **Web:** n/a
Nearest Town: Reedville **Tourist Info:** (804) 635-6092

Marina Services and Boat Supplies
Services - Docking Assistance **Communication -** UPS, Express Mail **Supplies - OnSite:** Ice *(Cube)*, Ships' Store, Bait/Tackle, Live Bait *(Seasonal)* **Under 1 mi:** Propane

Boatyard Services
Under 1 mi: Railway, Engine mechanic *(gas)*. **1-3 mi:** Travelift, Launching Ramp, Engine mechanic *(diesel)*, Hull Repairs, Bottom Cleaning, Divers, Propeller Repairs. **3+ mi:** Upholstery *(10 mi.)*, Yacht Interiors *(10 mi.)*. **Nearest Yard:** Jennings Boatyard (804) 453-7181

Restaurants and Accommodations
OnSite: Restaurant *(Crazy Crab 453-6789, L $4.50-13, D $9-25, kids' menu $3-6, Tue-Sun 12-9pm, Mar-Apr, Fri-Sun)*, Snack Bar *(Peppermints 453-6468, ice cream)* **Near:** Restaurant *(Tommy's 453-4666, D $7-19, Wed-Sun 5:30-9pm; in restored Reedville Market, wonderful ambiance, formerly Elijah's)*, Seafood Shack *(Cockrells Creek 453-6326, L $4-15, by water; Mon-Sat 10am-5pm, Sun 11am-3pm)*, Snack Bar *(Chitterchats Gossip Parlor - ice cream)*, Inn/B&B *(Gables B&B 453-5228, $90-155, Victorian mansion & carriage house)*, *(Grandview 453-3890)*, *(Morris 453-7016, $70-170)* **Under 1 mi:** Restaurant *(Fairport 453-5002, L $3-7, D $6-18, by water)* **1-3 mi:** Motel *(Bay Motel 453-5171)* **3+ mi:** Restaurant *(T&T's 453-4990, L $3-8, D $6-20, 7 mi.)*, Fast Food *(Burgess Drive Inn 8 mi.)*, Pizzeria *(Italian GardenCafé 453-5800, D $8-17, 7 mi., dinner only)*, Inn/B&B *(Fleeton Fields 453-5014, $135-175, 4 mi., Lovely, peaceful gorgeously landscaped waterfront colonial - 3 suites - picks up from the marinas)*

Recreation and Entertainment
OnSite: Fishing Charter *(Rock 'n Robin 453-4265)* **Near:** Museum *(Reedville Fishermens Museum 453-6529)*, Cultural Attract *(Skipjack "Claud W. Somers" 453-6529 - $25, sails every other Sat 10am, May-Oct)*, Sightseeing *(Walking Tour of Historic Reedville)*, Special Events *(Oyster Roast - 2nd Sat in Nov)* **1-3 mi:** Fitness Center *(Beafit 453-7411)*, Jogging Paths **3+ mi:** Golf Course *(Village Green Golf Club 529-6332, 4 mi.)*, Video Rental *(B & D Video 453-5802, 6 mi.)*

Provisioning and General Services
OnSite: Wine/Beer, Fishmonger *(Reedville Steamboat Wharf 453-5186)*, Crabs/Waterman *(Sea Products)*, Bank/ATM **Near:** Convenience Store *(Reed Square)*, Post Office *(453-7503)*, Protestant Church **Under 1 mi:** Delicatessen **1-3 mi:** Market *(Little River Market & Deli 453-5092)*, Beauty Salon *(Virginia's Hair Salon 453-9008)*, Hardware Store *(Jetts 453-5325)* **3+ mi:** Supermarket *(Food Lion 580-7326, 12 mi.)*, Green Grocer *(Olin-Fox Farms 453-4125, 3 mi.)*, Pharmacy *(Heathsville 580-7400, 9 mi.)*

Transportation
3+ mi: Ferry Service *(Passenger ferry to Tangier Island, 5 mi.)*
Airport: Richmond / Middle Peninsula Regional *(90 mi./61 mi.)*

Medical Services
911 Service **OnCall:** Ambulance **Near:** Holistic Services *(Claire Michie 453-4488 - acupuncture & Chinese herbs)* **1-3 mi:** Doctor *(Lewis Clinic 453-3777)* **3+ mi:** Dentist *(Hurt 453-3101, 8 mi.)*, Veterinarian *(Marston 453-3524, 7 mi.)* **Hospital:** Rappahannook General 435-8000 *(20 mi.)*

Setting -- At the tip of the narrow Reedville peninsula on Cockrell Creek, a single pier is backed by the Crazy Crab - a one-story tan building with deep red metal roof. Alongside dockage, for larger boats, edges the fenced wood dining deck sprinkled with umbrella-topped tables. Commercial fishing businesses surround the marina which sits at the foot of the mile-long Main Street Historic District. A Reedville to Crisfield, MD auto ferry is anticipated for 2007.

Marina Notes -- Established May 1999. Formerly the old "Huff and Puff" fish canning factory. Can accommodate up to 200' LOA with 12-14' depth. Currently 50 amp max. Stationary wood docks with short finger piers and small lighthouse pedestals flank the single pier; caters to a mix of power, sail, charter and sport fishing boats. A gift shop has local crafts, souvenirs and some clothing and a modest ships' store also offers beer, wine and soda. A single very basic, cement floored boaters' bathroom with an open shower stall is in a small cinderblock building; nicer heads are in the Crazy Crab.

Notable -- Overlooking the creek, popular, well-reviewed Crazy Crab offers fish "right off the boat" in a casual dining room; an outdoor alternative is dockside. "Reedville: A Walking, Biking & Driving Tour" describes two dozen sights on Main Street and then a 12-mile & 24-mile loop of the region. Built by the menhaden fishing industry, Reedville once had the highest per-capita income in the country, and the National Historic District's "Millionaires' Row" is lined with sea captains' mansions. The superb Fisherman's Museum describes the menhaden industry, Reedville's history, and displays a number of traditional bay vessels, including the still active 1922 Buy-Boat "Elva-C," and the Skipjack "Claud W. Somers." Nearby Festival Halle (453-4311) can accommodate 200 for a special event.

PHOTOS ON CD-ROM: 11

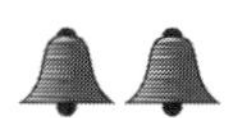

Buzzard's Point Marina

468 Buzzard Point Road (Route 1); Reedville, VA 22539

Tel: (804) 453-3545 **VHF: Monitor** 16 **Talk** n/a
Fax: (804) 453-3018 **Alternate Tel:** (804) 453-2628
Email: n/a **Web:** n/a
Nearest Town: Reedville *(5 mi.)* **Tourist Info:** (804) 435-6092

Navigational Information

Lat: 37°50.510' **Long:** 076°17.187' **Tide:** 2 ft. **Current:** n/a **Chart:** 12235
Rep. Depths (*MLW*): Entry 10 ft. **Fuel Dock** 7 ft. **Max Slip/Moor** 10 ft./-
Access: Wicomico River to Cockrells Creek

Marina Facilities *(In Season/Off Season)*

Fuel: *Shell* - Gasoline, Diesel
Slips: 50 Total, 20 Transient **Max LOA:** 50 ft. **Max Beam:** n/a
Rate *(per ft.)*: **Day** $0.50 **Week** Inq. **Month** $60
Power: 30 amp Incl., **50 amp** Incl., **100 amp** n/a, **200 amp** n/a
Cable TV: No **Dockside Phone:** No
Dock Type: Fixed, Short Fingers, Pilings, Alongside, Wood
Moorings: 0 Total, 0 Transient **Launch:** n/a
Rate: Day n/a **Week** n/a **Month** n/a
Heads: 3 Toilet(s), 2 Shower(s) *(with dressing rooms)*
Laundry: None **Pay Phones:** No
Pump-Out: OnSite, Full Service **Fee:** n/a **Closed Heads:** Yes

Marina Operations

Owner/Manager: Linwood Bowis **Dockmaster:** Justin Bowis
In-Season: Mar 6-Dec 19, 8am-5pm **Off-Season:** Dec 20-Mar 5, closed
After-Hours Arrival: Call ahead
Reservations: Yes **Credit Cards:** Visa/MC
Discounts: None
Pets: Welcome **Handicap Access:** No

Marina Services and Boat Supplies

Services - Docking Assistance **Communication -** Phone Messages, UPS, Express Mail **Supplies - OnSite:** Ice *(Cube)* **Near:** Ships' Store, Bait/Tackle, Propane

Boatyard Services

OnSite: Forklift *(to 27 ft.)*, Launching Ramp, Engine mechanic *(gas, diesel)*, Electrical Repairs, Hull Repairs, Bottom Cleaning *(pressure wash $35/ft.)*, Brightwork, Refrigeration, Compound, Wash & Wax *($4/ft.)*, Interior Cleaning, Painting **1-3 mi:** Electronics Repairs. **Yard Rates:** Inq., Power Wash Inq., Bottom Paint $10/ft. **Storage:** In-Water $60/mo., On-Land $3/ft. inside, $2.50/ft. outside

Restaurants and Accommodations

OnSite: Snack Bar *(snacks, ice cream, coffee, sodas)* **Under 1 mi:** Restaurant *(Crazy Crab 453-6789, L $8-13, D $9-25, by water or 5 mi. by land)*, Seafood Shack *(Cockrells Creek 453-6326, L $7-14, D $7-14, by water)*, Motel *(Bay Motel 453-5171)* **1-3 mi:** Restaurant *(Fairport 453-5002, L $3-7, D $6-18, by water)* **3+ mi:** Restaurant *(Tommy's 453-4666, D $15-29, 6 mi.)*, *(T&T's 453-4990, L $3-8, D $6-20, 6 mi.)*, *(Italian Garden Café 453-5800, D $8-17, 6 mi., dinner only)*, Fast Food *(Burgess Drive Inn 6 mi.)*, Inn/B&B *(Morris House 453-7016, $70-170, 5 mi.)*, *(Fleeton Fields 453-5014, $135-175, 7 mi.)*, *(Gables 453-5228, $90-155, 5 mi., or by water to dock; Victorian mansion & Cariage house)*, *(Grandview B&B 453-3890, 5 mi.)*

Recreation and Entertainment

OnSite: Picnic Area, Grills, Fishing Charter *(Seatoy)*, Group Fishing Boat, Sightseeing *("Chesapeake Breeze" to Tangier Island 453-2628 $24/13 10am, returns 3:30pm - also possible to spend the night or take another boat to Crisfield or Onancock)* **Under 1 mi:** Museum *(Reedville Fishermens Museum 453-6529 $3 - or 5 mi. by land)*, Cultural Attract *(Reedville Historic District - or 5 mi. by land)* **1-3 mi:** Pool **3+ mi:** Golf Course *(Village Green Golf Club 529-6332, 5 mi.)*, Fitness Center *(Beafit 453-7411, 6 mi.)*, Video Rental *(B & D Video 453-5802, 5 mi.)*

Provisioning and General Services

Under 1 mi: Fishmonger *(Reedville Steamboat Wharf 453-5186 - right off the boats - by water)*, Catholic Church **1-3 mi:** Convenience Store, Delicatessen, Green Grocer *(Olin-Fox Farms 453-4125)*, Bank/ATM, Hardware Store *(Jetts Hardware 453-5325)* **3+ mi:** Supermarket *(Food Lion 580-7326, 12 mi.)*, Market *(Little River Market & Deli 453-5092, 4 mi.)*, Post Office *(453-7503, 4 mi.)*, Pharmacy *(Heathsville 580-7400, 9 mi.)*

Transportation

OnSite: Courtesy Car/Van, Ferry Service *(to Tangier Island)*
Airport: Richmond *(90 mi.)*

Medical Services

911 Service **OnCall:** Ambulance **Under 1 mi:** Doctor *(Lewis Clinic 453-3777)* **3+ mi:** Dentist *(Radcliffe 453-4361, 7 mi.)*, Holistic Services *(Claire Michie 453-4488, 5 mi.)*, Veterinarian *(Marston 453-3524, 5 mi.)*
Hospital: Rappahannook General 435-8000 *(*

Setting -- Tucked deeply into a peaceful and remote arm of Cockrell Creek, Buzzard Point's docks edge the grassy banks of a broad peninsula. At the top of a short rise, two picnic pavilions and a large pale-blue storage shed overlook the pretty creek. The single pier with T-head hosts slips with short finger piers; a long stretch of stern-to dockage lines the bulkhead interrupted by a wharf that berths the 100-foot "Chesapeake Breeze" excursion boat to Tangier Island.

Marina Notes -- Formerly known as Walnut Point; acquired by the Bowis Family in 1973. In the season, coffee, sodas, snacks, ice cream are available at the little snack stand next to the ferry terminal. Dry storage shed for up to 10 boats inside and 40 on racks outside. Basic cinderblock bathhouse with cement floors is next to the Tangier Island ticket office (and shared with the passengers) - each is clean and newly painted with 3 heads, 3 sinks and 2 showers stalls with fiberglass shower pans and dressing rooms. When the enormous menhaden processing plant operates, a distinct fragrance wafts over the marina.

Notable -- The daylong cruise to Tangier Island is an alternative to taking one's own boat, and dockage is complimentary while on the cruise. Purchased from Native Americans for two overcoats, this "soft crab capital of the world" has a population of 700, largely descendents of the original settlers. The incursion of tourism and satellite TV has moved the island into the new millennium with proliferating B&Bs and eateries - but underneath, it is still home to independent watermen's families determined to maintain a fragile way of life. Reedville Marina's Crazy Crab has a dinghy dock; stroll Reedville's Main Street and visit the Fisherman's Museum. Or dinghy to Cockrell's Seafood for prepared fresh fish, or turn to starboard at the white house and head to Fairport Marina.

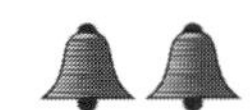

Great Wicomico River Marina

PO Box 10; Route 10, Horn Harbor Road; Burgess, VA 22432

Tel: (804) 453-3351 **VHF: Monitor** n/a **Talk** n/a
Fax: (804) 453-3516 **Alternate Tel:** n/a
Email: n/a **Web:** n/a
Nearest Town: Burgess *(2 mi.)* **Tourist Info:** (804) 435-6092

Navigational Information
Lat: 37°51.060' **Long:** 076°20.880' **Tide:** 2 ft. **Current:** 0 kt. **Chart:** 12235
Rep. Depths (*MLW*): Entry 10 ft. **Fuel Dock** 7 ft. **Max Slip/Moor** 15 ft./-
Access: Great Wicomico River to mouth of Horn Harbor Creek

Marina Facilities *(In Season/Off Season)*
Fuel: *Texaco* - Gasoline
Slips: 35 Total, 3 Transient **Max LOA:** 60 ft. **Max Beam:** n/a
Rate *(per ft.)*: **Day** $15.00* **Week** Inq. **Month** Inq.
Power: 30 amp Incl., **50 amp** n/a, **100 amp** n/a, **200 amp** n/a
Cable TV: No **Dockside Phone:** No
Dock Type: Fixed
Moorings: 0 Total, 0 Transient **Launch:** n/a
Rate: Day n/a **Week** n/a **Month** n/a
Heads: 2 Toilet(s), 2 Shower(s) *(with dressing rooms)*
Laundry: 1 Washer(s), 1 Dryer(s) **Pay Phones:** No
Pump-Out: OnSite **Fee:** $5 **Closed Heads:** Yes

Marina Operations
Owner/Manager: n/a **Dockmaster:** Jamie Knighton
In-Season: Mar-Nov, 7am-6pm **Off-Season:** Dec-Feb, Closed
After-Hours Arrival: Check in at front desk of restaurant
Reservations: No **Credit Cards:** n/a
Discounts: None
Pets: Welcome, Dog Walk Area **Handicap Access:** No

Marina Services and Boat Supplies
Services - Docking Assistance, Dock Carts **Communication -** Phone Messages, UPS, Express Mail **Supplies - OnSite:** Ice *(Cube)*, Ships' Store, Bait/Tackle, Propane

Boatyard Services
OnSite: Launching Ramp **OnCall:** Electrical Repairs, Electronics Repairs, Hull Repairs, Rigger, Canvas Work, Bottom Cleaning, Brightwork, Refrigeration **Nearest Yard:** Tiffany Yachts (804) 453-3351

Restaurants and Accommodations
OnSite: Restaurant *(Horn Harbor House D $5-29, kids' $6, Fri-Sat 5-10pm, Sun 4-9pm - sandwiches $5 -6, entrées $10-16, lobster $22/29, pizza $6+)*, Lite Fare *(Boathouse Bar)* **Near:** Fast Food *(Burgess Drive Inn)*
1-3 mi: Seafood Shack *(T & T's 453-4990, L $3-8, D $6-20)*, Pizzeria *(Italian Garden Café 453-5800, D $8-17, dinner only)*, Inn/B&B *(The Pointe 453-4174, $100-135)* **3+ mi:** Motel *(Bay Motel 453-5171, 7 mi.)*, Inn/B&B *(Gables B&B 453-5228, 8 mi.)*

Recreation and Entertainment
OnSite: Beach, Picnic Area **1-3 mi:** Video Rental *(B & D Video 453-5802)*
3+ mi: Golf Course *(Village Green Golf Club 529-6332, 5 mi.)*, Fitness Center *(Beafit 453-7411, 4 mi.)*, Museum *(Reedville Fishermen's Museum 453-6529, 9 mi.)*

Provisioning and General Services
1-3 mi: Convenience Store, Delicatessen *(Little River Market & Deli 453-6076)*, Bank/ATM, Post Office *(453-3772)*, Catholic Church **3+ mi:** Green Grocer *(Olin-Fox Farms 453-4125, 6 mi.)*, Market *(Little River Market & Deli 453-6076, 4 mi.)*, Library *(Northumberland 580-5051, 10 mi.)*, Pharmacy *(Heathsville 580-7400, 9 mi.)*, Hardware Store *(Lilian Lumber Co 453-4911, 4 mi.)*

Transportation
OnCall: Taxi *(Howard's 24 Hours Taxi 435-9348)*
Airport: Richmond *(82 mi.)*

Medical Services
911 Service **OnCall:** Ambulance **1-3 mi:** Doctor *(Bay Harbor Medical 453-5466)*, Dentist *(Hurt 453-3101)*, Veterinarian *(Marston 453-3524)*
3+ mi: Holistic Services *(Claire Michie 453-4488, 8 mi.)*
Hospital: Rappahannook General 435-8000 *(15 mi.)*

Setting -- Up the Great Wicomico, about 2.5 miles from Ingram Bay, the Great Wicomico River Campgrounds and Marina lie along the northern shore just past the entrance to Horn Harbor (reputed to be a perfect hurricane hole). The popular, weekend-only restaurant's numerous eating areas overlook the single, long offset pier and adjacent fuel dock - and the very peaceful river. Along the wooded shore of the campground, well-established seasonal RVs are tucked among the trees. Two picnic tables sit under a shelter overlooking the docks.

Marina Notes -- *Dockage is Flat Rate. Dry storage. Stationary wood docks with short finger piers flank both sides of the main dock which makes a couple of jogs as it angles into the river. Power varies from a 30 amp plug on the post to more sophisticated versions. A small gift shop is open during the same hours as the restaurant. Many rules and lots of signs. The cinderblock bathhouse has unfinished wood-paneled walls and tile floors; each includes 2 sinks - inset into a laminate vanity, one toilet, and a fiberglass shower stall with a private dressing area; $3 per person for a hot shower, payable in advance.

Notable -- The attractive natural cedar sided and roofed Horn Harbor House Seafood Restaurant, with a red, white and blue awning, offers inside and outside dining. The covered deck offers a clever arrangement of high and low benches, to give all diners unobstructed views of the marina and river. The inviting indoor windowed dining room overlooks the docks as well. Then there's the Boathouse Lounge for cocktails, raw bar, a quick food menu and a casual dining section out on the pier. Note: Hours are Friday and Saturday, 5-10pm and Sunday 4-9pm. (It's closed Monday through Thursday.)

PHOTOS ON CD-ROM: 9

Tiffany Yachts

2355 Jessie Dupont Highway; Burgess, VA 22432

Tel: (804) 453-3464 **VHF: Monitor** n/a **Talk** n/a
Fax: (804) 453-3837 **Alternate Tel:** n/a
Email: n/a **Web:** www.tiffanyyachts.com
Nearest Town: Burgess *(3 mi.)* **Tourist Info:** (804) 435-6092

Navigational Information

Lat: 37°51.138' **Long:** 076°21.820' **Tide:** 2 ft. **Current:** 1 kt. **Chart:** 12235
Rep. Depths (*MLW*): Entry 15 ft. **Fuel Dock** 12 ft. **Max Slip/Moor** 12 ft./-
Access: Great Wicomico River to bridge - Tiffany Yachts to right of Bridge

Marina Facilities *(In Season/Off Season)*

Fuel: *Texaco* - Gasoline, Diesel
Slips: 21 Total, 5 Transient **Max LOA:** 80 ft. **Max Beam:** 30 ft.
Rate *(per ft.)*: **Day** $0.75 **Week** Inq. **Month** Inq.
Power: 30 amp $5, **50 amp** $10, **100 amp** n/a, **200 amp** n/a
Cable TV: No **Dockside Phone:** No
Dock Type: Fixed, Floating, Alongside, Wood
Moorings: 0 Total, 0 Transient **Launch:** n/a
Rate: Day n/a **Week** n/a **Month** n/a
Heads: 3 Toilet(s), 1 Shower(s) *(with dressing rooms)*
Laundry: None **Pay Phones:** No
Pump-Out: OnSite, Full Service, 1 Port **Fee:** n/a **Closed Heads:** Yes

Marina Operations

Owner/Manager: Randy Cockrell **Dockmaster:** Gary Bryant
In-Season: Year-Round, 7am-5pm **Off-Season:** n/a
After-Hours Arrival: Tie up
Reservations: No **Credit Cards:** Visa/MC, Dscvr, Amex
Discounts: None
Pets: Welcome, Dog Walk Area **Handicap Access:** No

Marina Services and Boat Supplies

Services - Docking Assistance, Boaters' Lounge, Trash Pick-Up **Communication -** Phone Messages, Fax in/out *($2)*, UPS **Supplies - OnSite:** Ice *(Cube)*, Ships' Store **1-3 mi:** Bait/Tackle, Propane *(Great Wicomico River Marina)*

Boatyard Services

OnSite: Travelift *(60T)*, Railway *(2)*, Forklift, Engine mechanic *(gas, diesel)*, Electrical Repairs, Electronics Repairs, Hull Repairs, Canvas Work, Bottom Cleaning, Brightwork, Air Conditioning, Refrigeration, Compound, Wash & Wax, Interior Cleaning, Woodworking, Upholstery, Yacht Interiors *(Tiffany's Custom Interiors)*, Metal Fabrication, Painting, Awlgrip, Yacht Design, Yacht Building, Total Refits **OnCall:** Rigger, Sail Loft, Divers, Propeller Repairs, Inflatable Repairs, Life Raft Service **Member:** ABYC - 1 Certified Tech(s), Other Certifications: HVACR **Yard Rates:** $55/hr. **Storage:** In-Water $2.50/ft./mo., On-Land $2.50/ft./mo.

Restaurants and Accommodations

Under 1 mi: Inn/B&B *(The Pointe 453-4174, $100-135)* **1-3 mi:** Restaurant *(Crazy Crab 453-6789, L $8-13, D $9-25)*, *(Italian Garden Café 453-5800, D $8-17)*, *(T & T's 453-4990, L $3-8, D $6-20)* **3+ mi:** Restaurant *(Tommy's 453-4666, D $15-29, 5 mi., Chesapeake regional cuisine, dinner only)*, *(Horn Harbor 453-3351, D $6-16, 4 mi., dinner only)*, Motel *(Bay Motel 453-5171, 7 mi.)*, Inn/B&B *(Grandview B&B 453-3890, 8 mi.)*, *(Gables 453-5228, 9 mi.)*

Recreation and Entertainment

3+ mi: Golf Course *(Village Green Golf Club 529-6332, 7 mi.)*, Fitness Center *(Beafit 453-7411, 5 mi.)*, Movie Theater *(Lancaster Players Playhouse 435-3776, 18 mi.)*, Video Rental *(B & D Video 453-5802, 12 mi.)*, Museum *(Reedville Fishermen's Museum 453-6529, 11 mi.)*

Provisioning and General Services

1-3 mi: Convenience Store, Wine/Beer, Farmers' Market, Bank/ATM, Post Office, Protestant Church, Beauty Salon, Barber Shop, Dry Cleaners **3+ mi:** Delicatessen *(Little River, 5 mi.)*, Market *(Little River Market & Deli 453-6076, 5 mi.)*, Library *(Northumberland 580-5051, 10 mi.)*, Pharmacy *(Heathsville 580-7400, 10 mi.)*, Hardware Store *(Lilian Lumber Co 453-4911, 5 mi.)*

Transportation

OnCall: Taxi *(Howard's 24 Hours Taxi 435-9348)*
Airport: Richmond *(75 mi.)*

Medical Services

911 Service **OnCall:** Ambulance **1-3 mi:** Doctor *(Bay Harbor Medical 453-5466)*, Dentist *(Hurt 453-3101)*, Veterinarian *(Marston 453-3524)*
Hospital: Rappahannook General 435-8000 *(15 mi.)*

Setting -- On the Great Wicomico River near Glebe Point, just north of the bridge, this high-end boat builder offers a few slips and full boatyard services to cruising boaters. An enormous sage green work shed looms along the shoreline. All manner of yachts are docked here for service - from its own high-end custom vessels to an assortment of impeccably maintained historic wooden craft.

Marina Notes -- Established in 1934 by Tiffany Cockrell and his father to build commercial Chesapeake deadrise vessels. Turned to custom pleasure craft after WW II in 1945; has built over 150 one-of-a-kind sport fish vessels since - most in the 40-70 foot range. Most transient slips are either alongside - on 3 piers with T-heads, or stern to. But there's power - whatever you need. On-site, in addition to the large travelift, are two marine railways, a full-service yard, a large, well-stocked marine store and a full service canvas and upholstery shop - Tiffany's Yacht Interiors. At the back of the property a white clapboard building with red trim houses the customer lounge with a single, fully tiled bathroom with tub and shower.

Notable -- Tiffany Yachts' specialty is sophisticated state-of-the-art sport fish hull designs coupled with extraordinary woodworking and exquisite interior finishes - but it also attracts a wide variety of other vessels in need of meticulous attention. Poking into these sheds is fun for anyone with a passion for boats. Fascinating Reedville, once the fish-processing capital of the world, is 5 miles by land (closer by water) and promises 2 excellent restaurants, charming, upscale B&Bs, an historic district lined with Victorian houses that's made the National Register, and the superb, ever-growing Fishermen's Museum.

Navigational Information

Lat: 37°48.196' **Long:** 076°18.574' **Tide:** 2 ft. **Current:** 1 kt. **Chart:** 12235
Rep. Depths (*MLW*): Entry 10 ft. **Fuel Dock** 6 ft. **Max Slip/Moor** 7 ft./-
Access: Great Wicomico Light, 255° heading 1.5 NM to 2MC, chan. to stbd.

Marina Facilities *(In Season/Off Season)*

Fuel: *Shell* - Gasoline, Diesel, High-Speed Pumps
Slips: 52 Total, 6 Transient **Max LOA:** 65 ft. **Max Beam:** 18 ft.
Rate *(per ft.)*: **Day** $1.25 **Week** n/a **Month** n/a
Power: 30 amp $5, **50 amp** $7.50, **100 amp** n/a, **200 amp** n/a
Cable TV: No **Dockside Phone:** No
Dock Type: Fixed, Floating, Long Fingers, Short Fingers, Alongside, Wood
Moorings: 0 Total, 0 Transient **Launch:** n/a, Dinghy Dock ($3/pp showers)
Rate: Day n/a **Week** n/a **Month** n/a
Heads: 4 Toilet(s), 4 Shower(s)
Laundry: 1 Washer(s), 1 Dryer(s), Book Exchange **Pay Phones:** Yes, 1
Pump-Out: Full Service, 1 Central, 1 Port **Fee:** $5 **Closed Heads:** Yes

Marina Operations

Owner/Manager: Bill Pipkin **Dockmaster:** Mary Pipkin
In-Season: May-Dec, 7am-9pm **Off-Season:** Jan-Apr, 9am-4pm
After-Hours Arrival: Tie up at gas dock
Reservations: Preferred **Credit Cards:** Visa/MC, Shell
Discounts: Boat/US **Dockage:** 25% **Fuel:** $0.10/gal **Repair:** n/a
Pets: Welcome, Dog Walk Area **Handicap Access:** Yes, Heads, Docks

Ingram Bay Marina

545 Harveys Neck Road; Heathsville, VA 22473

Tel: (804) 580-7292 **VHF: Monitor** 16 **Talk** 9
Fax: (804) 580-2139 **Alternate Tel:** (804) 580-7292
Email: captbill@crosslink.net **Web:** www.captbillyscharters.com/marina
Nearest Town: Wicomico Church *(4 mi.)* **Tourist Info:** (804) 333-1919

Marina Services and Boat Supplies

Services - Docking Assistance, Security *(Owner lives on-site)*, Trash Pick-Up, Dock Carts **Communication -** Mail & Package Hold, Phone Messages, Fax in/out *($2)*, Data Ports *(Office, Inq.)*, FedEx, DHL, UPS **Supplies - OnSite:** Ice *(Block, Cube)*, Ships' Store, Bait/Tackle, Live Bait *(minnows, squid, worms, chum, menhaden)* **1-3 mi:** Propane

Boatyard Services

OnSite: Launching Ramp, Interior Cleaning **OnCall:** Crane, Engine mechanic *(gas, diesel)*, Electrical Repairs, Electronics Repairs *(on call)*, Sail Loft, Canvas Work, Bottom Cleaning, Air Conditioning, Refrigeration, Divers, Compound, Wash & Wax, Propeller Repairs, Metal Fabrication
1-3 mi: Travelift, Railway. **Nearest Yard:** Tiffany Yachts (804) 453-3464

Restaurants and Accommodations

1-3 mi: Restaurant *(Fairport Marina 453-5002, L $3-6, D $9-20)* **3+ mi:** Restaurant *(Tommy's 435-4666, D $15-29, 4 mi.)*, *(Crazy Crab 453-6789, L $8-13, D $9-25, 4 mi.)*, *(Hughlett's Tavern & Ranger Arms Pub 580-7900, 5 mi., authentically restored 18thC. tavern; Wed-Sat 11am-2:30pm & 5:30-9pm, Sun brunch 11am-2:30pm)*, Inn/B&B *(The Inn At Levelfields 435-6887, 11 mi.)*, *(Crab Point Manor 436-1200, 13 mi.)*

Recreation and Entertainment

OnSite: Beach, Picnic Area, Grills *(charcoal)*, Playground, Boat Rentals *(Rental canoes and small outboard boats available for 'creek peek' tours into unexplored areas)*, Fishing Charter *(Liquid Assets II; Fishes Up 580-4337; Jimmick Jr. III 580-7744; Captain Bulldog)*, Group Fishing Boat, Volleyball, Sightseeing *(River cruises to waterfront dining)* **3+ mi:** Golf Course *(Village Green Golf Club 529-6332, 13 mi.)*, Fitness Center *(Ben's Gym 436-0202, 12 mi.)*, Video Rental *(B & D Video 453-5802, 9 mi.)*, Museum *(Reedville Fishermens Museum 453-6529, 16 mi.)*, Cultural Attract *(Rice's Hotel/Hughlett's Tavern 580-3377 - 18th C. courthouse tavern, 5 mi.)*

Provisioning and General Services

OnSite: Fishmonger **OnCall:** Provisioning Service *(contact dockmaster)*
Under 1 mi: Dry Cleaners **1-3 mi:** Convenience Store, Delicatessen, Wine/Beer, Crabs/Waterman *(Great Wicomico Oyster Company)*, Newsstand **3+ mi:** Supermarket *(Tri-Star Supermarket 435-3800, 13 mi.)*, Farmers' Market *(Heathsville Farmers Market 580-3377 once a month, 4 mi.)*, Bank/ATM *(10 mi.)*, Post Office *(580-2409, 4 mi.)*, Library *(Lancaster Community Library 435-1729, 13 mi.)*, Beauty Salon *(Wicomico Hair Design 580-2777, 4 mi.)*, Pharmacy *(CVS 435-6834, 12 mi.)*, Hardware Store *(Jetts Hardware 453-5325, 10 mi.)*, Retail Shops *(8 mi.)*

Transportation

OnSite: Courtesy Car/Van, Bikes *($2)* **OnCall:** Local Bus *(on call bus)*
1-3 mi: Ferry Service *(passenger ferry to Tangier Island)* **3+ mi:** Rail *(Richmond, 80 mi.)* **Airport:** Richmond *(80 mi.)*

Medical Services

911 Service **OnCall:** Ambulance **3+ mi:** Doctor *(Chesapeake Medical Group 435-2651, 13 mi.)*, Dentist *(Johnston 435-2110, 13 mi.)*, Veterinarian *(Heathsville 435-6320, 13 mi.)*
Hospital: Rappahannock General 435-8000*(14 mi.)*

Setting -- Right off Ingram Bay, the 53 well-protected slips line the south shore of pretty Towles Creek - the open slips are followed by a long stretch of very tidy high gray covered sheds. The 18-acre marina has extensive on-the-hard storage and seriously caters to fishermen as well as families. Dockside, a couple of umbrella-topped picnic tables overlook the creek and a well-tended garden; three more picnic tables and two charcoal grills are sheltered by an old maple tree. Right outside the entrance is a sand beach. The surrounding area is quiet - mostly farm land and undeveloped space abundant with wildlife.

Marina Notes -- Est. 1969, bought by the Pipkins in 1985 who have managed and lived on-site since. 3 new transient slips with new power and water, plus 2 new alongside for a total of 7 dedicated transient slips that can accommodate 50 & 60 foot boats. Launching ramp, full covered storage, and 2 pump-out stations. Large covered fish cleaning station. Pavilion and pool planned for '06 season. The narrow entrance to the creek reportedly makes this a safe hurricane hole. Cinderblock bathhouse with cement floors has been significantly stepped-up with wallpaper borders, window curtains, a park bench and a basket of toiletries. Sinks are set into a vanity, shower stalls have wooden slatted floors, shower curtains and a shared dressing room. Laundry $3/load honor system.

Notable -- Several charter sport fish boats are on-site including owner Capt. Bill Pipkin's Markley 46, "Liquid Assets II." On the Bay is a neat little sand beach, owned by the marina, that is only accessible by dinghy. It's many miles back to town, and little is there - except the wonderful, restored 18th C. Rice's Hotel/Hughlett's Tavern; the marina's courtesy car makes the trip possible. The Great Wicomico Oyster Co. is on the way for fresh or steamed seafood.

PHOTOS ON CD-ROM: 10

Chesapeake Boat Basin

1686 Waverly Avenue; Kilmarnock, VA 22482

Tel: (804) 435-3110; (877) 482-4287 **VHF: Monitor** 16 **Talk** 9
Fax: (804) 435-3059 **Alternate Tel:** n/a
Email: boatbasin@verizon.net **Web:** www.chesapeakeboatbasin.com
Nearest Town: Kilmarnock *(1.5 mi.)* **Tourist Info:** (804) 333-1919

Navigational Information

Lat: 37°42.016' **Long:** 076°21.083' **Tide:** n/a **Current:** n/a **Chart:** 12235
Rep. Depths (*MLW*): Entry 12 ft. **Fuel Dock** 12 ft. **Max Slip/Moor** 12 ft./-
Access: Just N of Windmill Pt Light follow markers, port side at granary

Marina Facilities *(In Season/Off Season)*

Fuel: Gasoline, Diesel
Slips: 50 Total, 4 Transient **Max LOA:** 50 ft. **Max Beam:** n/a
Rate *(per ft.)*: **Day** $1.25 **Week** n/a **Month** $20
Power: 30 amp Incl., **50 amp** Incl., **100 amp** n/a, **200 amp** n/a
Cable TV: No **Dockside Phone:** No
Dock Type: Fixed, Long Fingers, Wood
Moorings: 0 Total, 0 Transient **Launch:** n/a
Rate: Day n/a **Week** n/a **Month** n/a
Heads: 4 Toilet(s), 4 Shower(s) *(with dressing rooms)*, Hair Dryers
Laundry: None **Pay Phones:** No
Pump-Out: OnSite **Fee:** $5 **Closed Heads:** Yes

Marina Operations

Owner/Manager: Clay Holcomb **Dockmaster:** Bruce Kuykendall
In-Season: Apr-Oct, 8am-5pm, Sun 'til 2pm **Off-Season:** Nov-Mar, 9am-5pm*
After-Hours Arrival: Call ahead
Reservations: Yes **Credit Cards:** Visa/MC, Personal checks
Discounts: Boat/US **Dockage:** $1/ft. **Fuel:** n/a **Repair:** 10%
Pets: Welcome **Handicap Access:** No

Marina Services and Boat Supplies

Services - Docking Assistance, Boaters' Lounge, Dock Carts **Communication -** UPS, Express Mail **Supplies - OnSite:** Ice *(Cube)*, Ships' Store, Bait/Tackle **1-3 mi:** Propane *(Exxon 435-1126)*

Boatyard Services

OnSite: Hydraulic Trailer *(up to 32' power only)*, Engine mechanic *(gas)*, Electrical Repairs, Electronic Sales, Electronics Repairs, Bottom Cleaning, Divers, Compound, Wash & Wax, Propeller Repairs *(sent out)*, Painting, Yacht Broker *(Lisa Holcomb)* **Dealer for:** Suzuki, Triton Boats. **Yard Rates:** Haul & Launch Inq., Power Wash Inq., Bottom Paint Inq.

Restaurants and Accommodations

Under 1 mi: Pizzeria *(Sal's Pizza 435-6770, L $4-10, D $4-10, pizza, Italian dishes, subs)* **1-3 mi:** Restaurant *(Lee's 435-1255)*, *(Alley Café 436-1100)*, *(Rappahannock Seafood 435-1605)*, *(Thai Pot 436-8424, L $7-10, D $10-16, take-out menu)*, *(Great Fortune 435-6333)*, Crab House *(Rose's Crab House & Raw Bar 436-8439, Sunday a la carte brunch)*, Lite Fare *(Dixie Deli 435-6745)*, Pizzeria *(Pizza Hut 435-3551, L $5-10, D $5-10, no longer delivers)*, Motel *(Holiday Inn 436-1500)*, Inn/B&B *(Crab Point Manor 436-1200)*, *(The Inn At Levelfields 435-6887)*, *(Flowering Fields 435-6238)* **3+ mi:** Motel *(Whispering Pines 435-1101, 5 mi.)*

Recreation and Entertainment

OnSite: Picnic Area, Grills *(propane)* **Under 1 mi:** Jogging Paths **1-3 mi:** Fitness Center *(Ben's Gym 436-0202)*, Bowling *(Evans Bowling Center 435-3950)*, Video Rental *(Movie Gallery 435-1504)*, Museum *(Kilmarnock Museum 436-9100)*, Cultural Attract *(Center for the Arts)*, Galleries *(Two antique malls & two art galleries)*, Special Events *(Firemen's Fest - last week Jul - 9 days; Rivah Fest - MemDay, Scottish Days - Oct)* **3+ mi:** Golf Course *(Golden Eagle Golf Course 438-5501, 6 mi.)*, Movie Theater *(Lancaster Players Playhouse 435-3776, 6 mi.)*

Provisioning and General Services

Under 1 mi: Post Office *(642-4121)* **1-3 mi:** Convenience Store, Supermarket *(Tri-Star 435-3800)*, Gourmet Shop *(Kelsick Gardens 435-1500)*, Health Food *(Higher Health Foods)*, Liquor Store *(ABC 435-7628)*, Fishmonger, Bank/ATM *(Chesapeake Bank)*, Catholic Church, Protestant Church *(United Methodist)*, Library *(Lancaster Community Library 435-1729)*, Beauty Salon *(Peridot 435-2285)*, Barber Shop *(Terry's 435-9552)*, Dry Cleaners *(Henderson Cleaners 435-1249)*, Laundry *(Speedwash 436-1300)*, Bookstore *(Book Nook 435-3355)*, Pharmacy *(CVS 435-6834; Anchor)*, Hardware Store, Florist *(Bonner)*, Clothing Store *(6)*, Retail Shops *(15 local gift shops, many nautical items and a doll shop)*, Copies Etc.

Transportation

OnSite: Bikes **OnCall:** Rental Car *(Enterprise 435-1851)* **Near:** Local Bus *(Bay Transit weekdays only 8-5)* **3+ mi:** Rail *(Richmond, 67 mi.)*
Airport: Richmond *(70 mi.)*

Medical Services

911 Service **OnCall:** Ambulance **1-3 mi:** Doctor *(Chesapeake 435-2651)*, Dentist *(Harperon 435-3041)*, Chiropractor *(Northern Neck Chiropractic Acupuncture 435-3333)*, Veterinarian *(Heathsville 435-6320)*
Hospital: Rappahannock General 435-8000 *(3 mi.)*

Setting -- A mile and a half off Fleets Bay on Indian Creek, nicely run Chesapeake Boat Basin sits on the end of Kilmarnock Wharf - which it shares with an assortment of Perdue Grain elevators. Two main piers poke into the creek with another one parallel to the shore. Along the bulkhead and adjacent to it are covered boathouses sheltering additional rows of slips. The views out to the creek are leafy and green.

Marina Notes -- *Off-season closed Sun & Mon. Neat, well-supplied 16,000 square foot ships' store with supplies, bait & tackle. Good quality stationary wood piers have slips on both sides and about three-quarter length finger piers with upgraded power - post Isabel. Upgrades continue annually. Note: the grain elevator fans only run in the fall - and then they run all night. Three propane grills are available for slip holders and transients, and three picnic tables sit on the front porch, overlooking the docks. The nicely done tile-floor boaters' lounge has upholstered wicker furniture, a large screen TV, stereo, a fireplace, games, lending library, and magazines. Lovely bathhouse has a composite floor, fiberglass shower stalls with dressing rooms and brightly patterned curtains, benches, toiletries, vanity sinks and hair dryers.

Notable -- It's a 1.5 mile straight shot down Waverly Avenue from the marina to the newly renovated South Main Street in Kilmarnock - which runs about 4 blocks and hosts a nice assortment of services, 2 well-known antique malls, 3 smaller shops, 2 art galleries, an assortment of unique clothing and gift shops, and more than 20 eateries. Historic cross-shaped Christ Church, recognized as the finest Colonial church in the US, was built in 1735 by Robert "King" Carter.

PHOTOS ON CD-ROM: 11

Navigational Information
Lat: 37°36.930' **Long:** 076°17.580' **Tide:** 2 ft. **Current:** 2 kt. **Chart:** 12235
Rep. Depths (*MLW*): Entry 6 ft. **Fuel Dock** 7 ft. **Max Slip/Moor** 8 ft./-
Access: Mouth of the Rappahannock

Marina Facilities *(In Season/Off Season)*
Fuel: *Exxon* - Gasoline, Diesel, High-Speed Pumps
Slips: 150 Total, 24 Transient **Max LOA:** 100 ft. **Max Beam:** n/a
Rate *(per ft.)*: **Day** $1.35/1.10 **Week** n/a **Month** Inq.
Power: 30 amp $6, **50 amp** $8, **100 amp** $15, **200 amp** n/a
Cable TV: Yes **Dockside Phone:** No
Dock Type: Fixed, Long Fingers, Pilings, Wood
Moorings: 0 Total, 0 Transient **Launch:** n/a
Rate: Day n/a **Week** n/a **Month** n/a
Heads: 8 Toilet(s), 8 Shower(s), Hair Dryers
Laundry: 3 Washer(s), 3 Dryer(s), Iron, Iron Board **Pay Phones:** Yes, 3
Pump-Out: OnSite, 1 Central **Fee:** $8 **Closed Heads:** Yes

Marina Operations
Owner/Manager: Unknown **Dockmaster:** Unknown
In-Season: Apr-Oct, 7am-11pm **Off-Season:** Nov-Mar, 7am-6pm
After-Hours Arrival: Call in advance
Reservations: Yes, Preferred **Credit Cards:** Visa/MC, Amex
Discounts: None
Pets: Welcome, Dog Walk Area **Handicap Access:** No

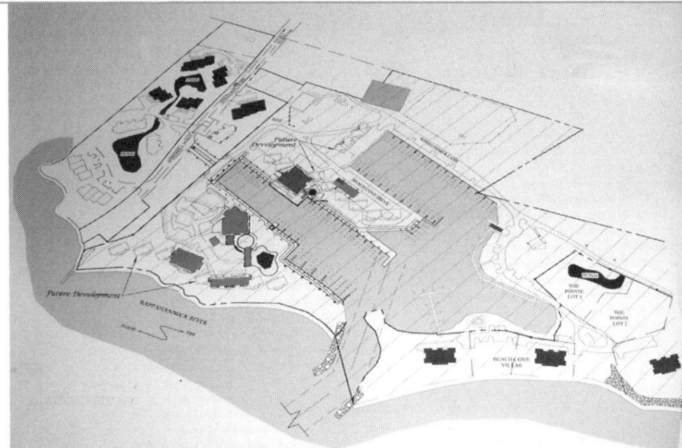

Windmill Point Marina Resort

PO Box 368; 32 Windjammer Lane; White Stone, VA 22578

Tel: (804) 435-1166; (800) 520-8439 **VHF: Monitor** 16 **Talk** 68
Fax: (804) 435-0789 **Alternate Tel:** (804) 435-1166
Email: n/a **Web:** www.windmillpointresort.com
Nearest Town: White Stone *(7 mi.)* **Tourist Info:** (804) 333-1919

Marina Services and Boat Supplies
Services - Docking Assistance, Room Service to the Boat, Boaters' Lounge, Security *(11pm-7am)*, Trash Pick-Up, Megayacht Facilities **Communication -** Mail & Package Hold, Phone Messages, Fax in/out, Data Ports *(Wi-Fi)*, FedEx, DHL, UPS, Express Mail *(Sat Del)* **Supplies - OnSite:** Ice *(Block, Cube)*, Ships' Store, Bait/Tackle **Near:** Propane

Boatyard Services
OnSite: Launching Ramp **OnCall:** Engine mechanic *(gas, diesel)*, Electrical Repairs, Bottom Cleaning, Compound, Wash & Wax, Yacht Interiors **Near:** Electronics Repairs, Brightwork. **Nearest Yard:** Walden's Marina (804) 776-9440

Restaurants and Accommodations
OnSite: Restaurant *(Aqua 435-1166, in the original redevelopment plan)*, Lite Fare *(Harborside Grille 435-1166, also in the plan)*, Inn/B&B *(52 room beachfront inn planned)*, Condo/Cottage *(17 condos planned)* **1-3 mi:** Restaurant *(Rice's Inn 435-3550)*, Inn/B&B *(Flowering Fields 435-6238)* **3+ mi:** Restaurant *(Rappahannock Seafood Co 435-1605, 4 mi.)*, *(Northside Grille 435-3100, 4 mi.)*, Crab House *(Rose's Crab House & Raw Bar 436-8439, 4 mi.)*, Pizzeria *(Pizza Hut 435-3551, L $5-10, D $5-10, 5 mi.)*, Motel *(Holiday Inn Express 436-1500, 4 mi.)*, Inn/B&B *(Crab Point Manor 436-1200, 4 mi.)*

Recreation and Entertainment
OnSite: Pool, Beach *(mile-long stretch of sand)*, Picnic Area, Playground, Tennis Courts *(3 planned)*, Jogging Paths, Volleyball **Near:** Fitness Center, Boat Rentals, Park **1-3 mi:** Golf Course *(Golden Eagle Golf Course 438-5501 - on-site 9-hole course planned)*, Movie Theater *(Lancaster Players Playhouse 435-3776)* **3+ mi:** Bowling *(Evans Bowling Center 435-3950, 5 mi.)*, Video Rental *(Movie Gallery 435-1504, 4 mi.)*, Museum *(Kilmarnock Museum 436-9100, Steam Boat Museum 438-6888, 5 mi.)*

Provisioning and General Services
OnSite: Post Office, Copies Etc. **1-3 mi:** Oysterman *(Pride of Virginia Bait & Oyster 435-6740)*, Market *(River Market 435-1725)* **3+ mi:** Convenience Store *(3 mi.)*, Supermarket *(Tri-Star Supermarket 435-3800, 5 mi.)*, Liquor Store *(ABC 435-7628, 5 mi.)*, Farmers' Market *(Seasonal, 8 mi.)*, Crabs/Waterman *(8 mi.)*, Meat Market *(8 mi.)*, Bank/ATM *(4 mi.)*, Catholic Church *(12 mi.)*, Protestant Church *(4 mi.)*, Library *(Lancaster Community Library 435-1729, 5 mi.)*, Beauty Salon *(Amy's Braids 435-0100, 3 mi.)*, Dry Cleaners *(Henderson Cleaners 435-1249, 4 mi.)*, Bookstore *(Book Nook 435-3355, 4 mi.)*, Pharmacy *(White Stone Pharmacy 435-1051, 4 mi.)*, Hardware Store *(Lamberth 435-1695, 4 mi.)*, Retail Shops *(5 mi.)*

Transportation
OnSite: Courtesy Car/Van *(shuttle service to town, golf, sighseeing & shopping - planned)*, Bikes **OnCall:** Rental Car *(Enterprise 435-1851)*
Airport: Richmond *(66 mi.)*

Medical Services
911 Service **OnCall:** Ambulance **3+ mi:** Doctor *(Bagnall 435-3133, 9 mi.)*, Dentist *(Westbrook 438-1000, 10 mi.)*
Hospital: Rappahannock General 435-8000 *(12 mi.)*

Setting -- One of the few marinas directly off the Bay, Windmill Point is just north of the mouth of the Rappahannock and occupies 45 acres that surround a protected basin behind a mile-long sand beach. Anticipated on this site is a large redevelopment with a high-end, full service 160 slip marina, two pools, a 9-hole golf course, 3 tennis courts, two eateries, an inn - all wrapped in a condo community.

Marina Notes -- NOTE: As of November 2005, Windmill Point was a project in limbo. All of the original resort buildings had been razed and bits and pieces of the new ones had been constructed - including parts of the marina. But the developers ran into trouble, and all work stopped. Right now it is a ghost town. All presumptions in this Report are based on the original redevelopment plan. A new developer may make some changes - but many of the basic facts - the marina basin, the acreage, the beach, the location - cannot be altered. So, of course, call ahead and also check the ACC Website for updates. As progress is made, the information will be posted. This facility will be rated when it re-opens.

Notable -- The site is so superb that it is inconceivable that this or another developer will not complete the project in a reasonable time frame; by including this Report, the author and editors are obviously convinced of that fact. It may be ready in Spring '06 as promised, but more likely it will stretch well beyond that. Most bystanders believe that the marina will be the first piece completed since it can generate immediate income. Stay tuned!

PHOTOS ON CD-ROM: 1

Boaters' Notes

Add Your Ratings and Reviews at www.AtlanticCruisingClub.com

AtlanticCruisingClub.com provides updated Marina Reports, Destination and Harbor Articles, a Boaters' Forum and much more — including an option within each on-line Marina Report for Boaters to add their ratings and comments regarding that facility. Please log on frequently to share your experiences — and to read other boaters' comments.

On the website, boaters may rate marinas on one or more of the following categories — on a scale of 1 (basic) to 5 (world class) — and also enter additional commentary.

- **Facilities & Services** (Fuel, Reservations, Concierge Services and General Helpfulness):
- **Amenities** (Pool, Beach, Internet Access, including Wi-Fi, Picnic/Grill area, Boaters' Lounge):
- **Setting** (Views, Design, Landscaping, Maintenance, Ship-Shapeness, Overall Ambiance):
- **Convenience** (Access — including delivery services — to Supermarkets, other provisioning sources, Shops, Services. Attractions, Entertainment, Sightseeing, Recreation, including Golf and Sport Fishing & Medical Services):
- **Restaurants/Eateries/Lodgings** (Availability of Fine Dining, Snack Bars, Lite Fare, On Call food service, and Lodgings ashore):
- **Transportation** (Courtesy Car/Vans, Buses, Water Taxis, Bikes, Taxis, Rental Cars, Airports, Amtrak, Commuter Trains):
- **Please Add Any Additional Comments**

14. Western Shore: Rappahannock River

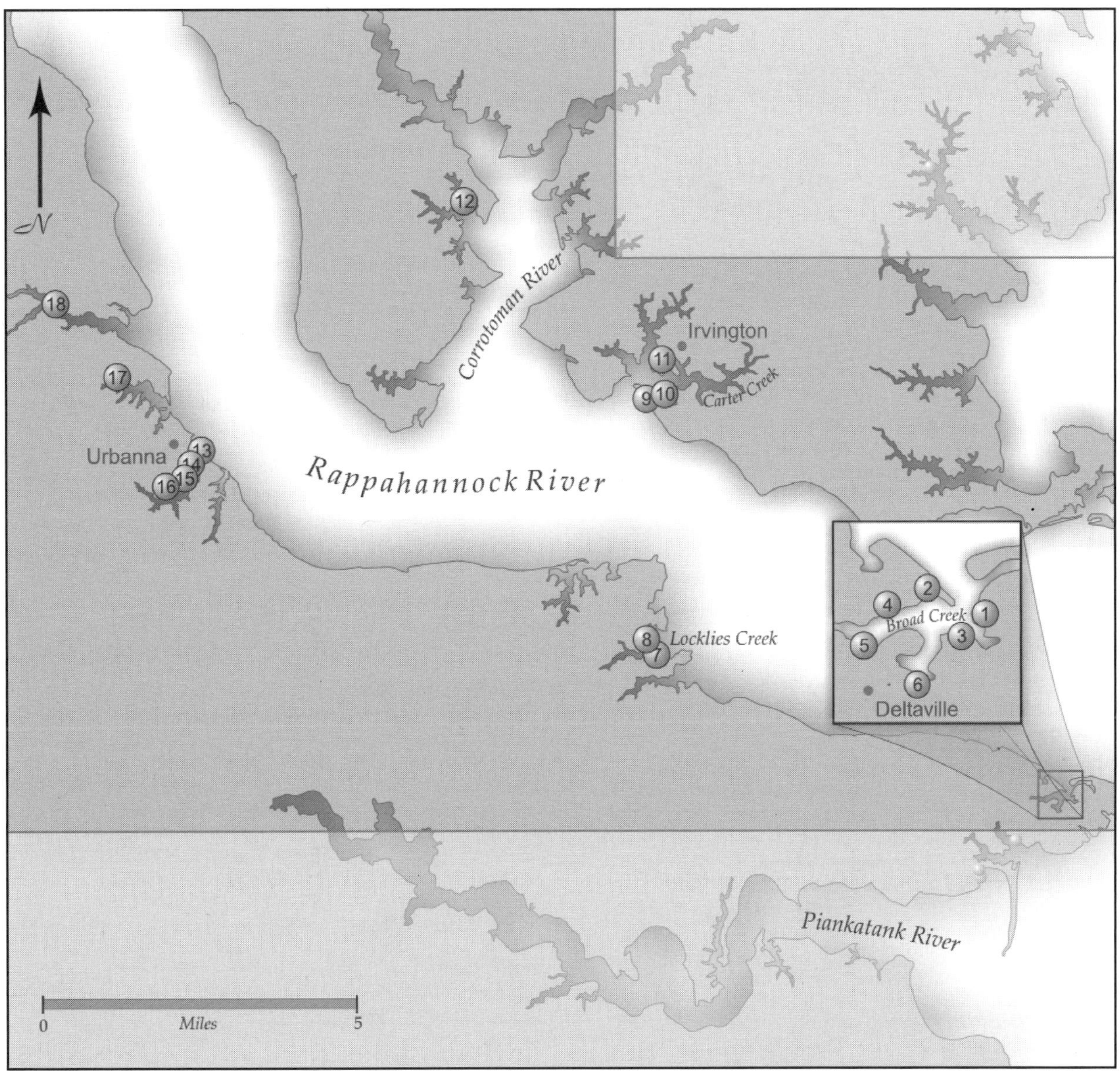

MAP	MARINA	HARBOR	PAGE	MAP	MARINA	HARBOR	PAGE
1	**Dozier's Regatta Point Yacht Club**	*Broad Creek*	*250*	*10*	**Irvington Marina**	*Carter Creek*	*259*
2	**Walden's Marina**	*Broad Creek*	*251*	*11*	**The Tides Marinas**	*Carter Creek*	*260*
3	**Norview Marina**	*Broad Creek*	*252*	*12*	**Yankee Point Sailboat Marina**	*Corrotomon River/Myer Creek*	*261*
4	**Norton's Yacht Sales**	*Broad Creek*	*253*	*13*	**Urbana Town Marina**	*Urbanna Creek*	*262*
5	**Chesapeake Cove Marina**	*Broad Creek*	*254*	*14*	**Dozier's Port Urbanna Yachting Ctr.**	*Urbanna Creek*	*263*
6	**Deltaville Yachting Center**	*Broad Creek*	*255*	*15*	**Urbanna Yachting Center**	*Urbanna Creek*	*264*
7	**Regent Point Marina**	*Locklies Creek*	*256*	*16*	**Urbanna Bridge Marina**	*Urbanna Creek*	*265*
8	**Locklies Marina**	*Locklies Creek*	*257*	*17*	**Burrell's Marine**	*Robinson Creek*	*266*
9	**Rappahannock Yachts**	*Carter Creek*	*258*	*18*	**Remlik Marina**	*La Grange Creek*	*267*

- **A "DCM" symbol in Marina Notes means Designated Clean Marina** — This is a coveted state-level award given to marinas that meet stringent, environmentally supportive requirements (see page 307). *For a list of DCM's & pump-out facilities, see page 308.*
- **Ratings & Reviews** — An explanation of the Atlantic Cruising Club's rating system, and a detailed explanation of what is in each section of the Marina Report is on pages 6 – 11. *The Data-Gathering Process is detailed on page 322.*
- **Marina Report Updates** — Updates to Marina Reports (from readers, ACC reviewers, and marinas) are posted regularly on *www.AtlanticCruisingClub.com.*

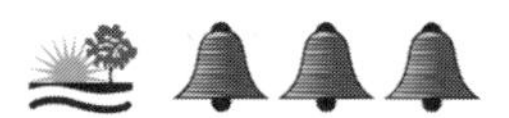

Dozier's Regatta Point Yacht Club

Regatta Point Yacht Club

PO Box 1188; 137 Neptune Lane; Deltaville, VA 23043

Tel: (804) 776-6711; (800) REG-ATTA **VHF: Monitor** 16 **Talk** 72
Fax: (804) 776-0672 **Alternate Tel:** (804) 776-6999
Email: jdozier@waterwayguide.com **Web:** www.doziermarine.com
Nearest Town: Deltaville *(1 mi.)* **Tourist Info:** (804) 725-9029

Navigational Information

Lat: 37°33.550' **Long:** 076°18.770' **Tide:** 2 ft. **Current:** 1 kt. **Chart:** 12235
Rep. Depths (*MLW*): Entry 8 ft. **Fuel Dock** 8 ft. **Max Slip/Moor** 8 ft./-
Access: Mouth of Rappahannock, S Shore, enter Broad Creek. 1st on left

Marina Facilities *(In Season/Off Season)*

Fuel: *Texaco* - Slip-Side Fueling, Gasoline, Diesel, High-Speed Pumps
Slips: 105 Total, 20 Transient **Max LOA:** 120 ft. **Max Beam:** 25 ft.
Rate *(per ft.)*: **Day** $1.50 **Week** $5.00 **Month** $14
Power: 30 amp $5, **50 amp** $8, **100 amp** $12, **200 amp** n/a
Cable TV: Yes satellite in captain's lounge **Dockside Phone:** No
Dock Type: Fixed, Floating, Long Fingers, Alongside, Wood
Moorings: 0 Total, 0 Transient **Launch:** n/a, Dinghy Dock
Rate: Day n/a **Week** n/a **Month** n/a
Heads: 6 Toilet(s), 6 Shower(s) *(with dressing rooms)*, Hair Dryers
Laundry: 1 Washer(s), 1 Dryer(s), Iron, Iron Board **Pay Phones:** No
Pump-Out: OnSite, Self Service, 1 Central **Fee:** $5 **Closed Heads:** Yes

Marina Operations

Owner/Manager: Jack Dozier **Dockmaster:** Margie Moore
In-Season: Apr-Oct, 8am-5pm **Off-Season:** Nov-Mar, 8am-4:30pm
After-Hours Arrival: Tie up at any floating dock check-in in am
Reservations: Preferred **Credit Cards:** Visa/MC, Dscvr, Amex
Discounts: Boat/US **Dockage:** 10% **Fuel:** 5% **Repair:** n/a
Pets: Welcome, Dog Walk Area **Handicap Access:** Yes, Heads, Docks

Marina Services and Boat Supplies

Services - Docking Assistance, Boaters' Lounge, Trash Pick-Up, Dock Carts, Megayacht Facilities **Communication -** Mail & Package Hold, Phone Messages, Fax in/out, Data Ports *(DSL & Wi-Fi, free)*, FedEx, UPS, Express Mail *(Sat Del)* **Supplies - OnSite:** Ice *(Block, Cube)*, Ships' Store **Under 1 mi:** Bait/Tackle *(J&W Seafood)* **1-3 mi:** West Marine *(776-0400)*, Boat/US *(776-8583)*, Live Bait, Propane *(Revere Gas 776-9724)*

Boatyard Services

OnSite: Engine mechanic *(gas, diesel)*, Electrical Repairs, Hull Repairs, Rigger, Compound, Wash & Wax, Interior Cleaning **OnCall:** Bottom Cleaning, Air Conditioning, Refrigeration, Divers, Propeller Repairs, Inflatable Repairs, Life Raft Service **Near:** Travelift, Launching Ramp, Electronics Repairs, Brightwork, Woodworking, Painting, Awlgrip, Total Refits. **Under 1 mi:** Sail Loft, Canvas Work, Yacht Interiors, Metal Fabrication. **Nearest Yard:** Deltaville Yacht Yard (804) 776-7500

Restaurants and Accommodations

Under 1 mi: Hotel *(Dockside Inn 776-9224)*, Inn/B&B *(River Place 776-9153, $95-175)* **1-3 mi:** Restaurant *(Boat House Café 776-8882, picks up)*, *(Galley 776-6040, L $5, D $12, picks up)*, *(Taylor's 776-9611, B $2-5, L $5-8, D $10-20, picks up)*, *(Steamboat 776-6516)*, *(Toby's 776-6913, L $5-10, D $8-18, picks up)*, Lite Fare *(Sweet Shop B $2-4, L $3-6)*, Pizzeria *(Sal's 776-7611)*, Inn/B&B *(Sanderling House B&B 776-0970, $95-150)*, *(Rivers Rise B&B 776-7521)*, Condo/Cottage *(Fishing Bay 776-9153)*

Recreation and Entertainment

OnSite: Pool, Beach, Picnic Area, Grills, Jogging Paths **Near:** Boat Rentals, Roller Blade/Bike Paths, Fishing Charter, Group Fishing Boat, Special Events *(July 4th)* **Under 1 mi:** Playground, Tennis Courts, Video Rental *(Hollywood Video 776-7715)*, Park **1-3 mi:** Museum *(Deltaville Maritime Museum 776-7200)*, Galleries *(Yates House 776-8505)* **3+ mi:** Golf Course *(Piankatank River GC 776-6516, 6 mi.)*

Provisioning and General Services

OnCall: Market *(Sandy Bottom Market 776-8803 min. $25, p/u & returns boaters)*, Dry Cleaners **Under 1 mi:** Convenience Store *(Little Sue 776-9600)*, Wine/Beer, Fishmonger *(J&W Seafood 776-6400)*, Bank/ATM, Post Office *(776-9750)*, Protestant Church, Library *(Deltaville 776-7362)*, Hardware Store *(Hurds 776-9241)*, Clothing Store, Copies Etc. **1-3 mi:** Farmers' Market *(Yates House Fine Art Sat 9am-1pm)*, Beauty Salon *(Hair by Sarah 776-0061)*, Barber Shop *(Sully's 776-0052)*, Florist **3+ mi:** Supermarket *(Deltaville Town & Country Market 776-6131 Mon-Fri & Sun 7am-8:30pm, Fri & Sat 'til 9:30pm, 4 mi.)*, Catholic Church *(7 mi.)*, Pharmacy *(Medicine Shoppe 776-9990, 5 mi.)*

Transportation

OnSite: Courtesy Car/Van, Bikes *(complimentary)* **OnCall:** Rental Car *(Enterprise 694-8226)*, Airport Limo *(Tri-County 693-3475)* **Under 1 mi:** Local Bus *(Bay Transit 693-6977 - reservations)* **Airport:** Newport News/Richmond *(45 mi./65 mi.)*

Medical Services

911 Service **OnCall:** Ambulance **1-3 mi:** Doctor *(Chesapeake Medical Grp. 776-9221)*, Dentist *(Lennon 776-9484)*, Veterinarian *(Hartfield Animal Hosp. 776-9219)* **Hospital:** Riverside Walter Reed 693-6368 *(22 mi.)*

Setting -- Just past the entrance to Stingray Point, RPYC's new high-end floating docks sprawl along the eastern edge of Broad Creek. Beyond, a network of tall natural cedar-sided boat sheds host an impressive collection of vessels. On shore the elegant pale yellow tidewater clubhouse topped with a sea green steel roof sports a long front porch with views out to the river. Boardwalks wander through carefully preserved natural vegetation punctuated by large stands of sea oats. Behind the clubhouse, a small sparkling pool and nicely furnished patio overlook the new docks and creek; a fountain feng shuis the entrance.

Marina Notes -- Family-owned & operated since 1975. Corporate office of Waterway Guides. Reverse osmosis water system. Boat sheds have uncovered walkways creating alongside dockage - perfect for cats. Cement floating docks with wood finger piers covered in non-skid with vinyl edging. Cruising clubs accommodated; party and meeting rooms available. Plans for a waterfront restaurant and tennis courts. Basic yard services, no haulout. This is where the big boats live, including some exquisitely restored yachts. Courtesy car goes only as far as West Marine. Complimentary Wi-Fi & bikes, too. 2 full bathrooms feature Corian vanities, tile floor & shower stalls with bright curtains and hair dryers. The laundry has an iron and ironing board.

Notable -- Sixteen high-backed Kennedyesque white rocking chairs (with green cushions) march down the wonderful wide porch - each with spectacular views of the boat traffic. Inside, the handsome boaters' lounge is furnished with an L-shaped sofa, comfortable, plantation-style upholstered wicker, oriental rugs, a campaign desk and a big screen TV with video. Boater-oriented Deltaville - with restaurants, a maritime museum and key services - is an easy bike ride.

PHOTOS ON CD-ROM: 15

Walden's Marina

PO Box 300A; 1224 Timberneck Rd; Deltaville, VA 23043

Tel: (804) 776-9440 **VHF: Monitor** 16 **Talk** n/a
Fax: (804) 776-9440 **Alternate Tel:** n/a
Email: n/a **Web:** www.waldensmarina.com
Nearest Town: Deltaville *(1 mi.)* **Tourist Info:** (804) 725-9029

Navigational Information

Lat: 37°33.617' **Long:** 076°18.936' **Tide:** 2 ft. **Current:** n/a **Chart:** 12235
Rep. Depths (*MLW*): Entry 7 ft. **Fuel Dock** 6 ft. **Max Slip/Moor** 6 ft./-
Access: On Broad Creek, west of Sting Ray Point

Marina Facilities *(In Season/Off Season)*

Fuel: Gasoline, Diesel
Slips: 50 Total, 7 Transient **Max LOA:** 55 ft. **Max Beam:** n/a
Rate *(per ft.)*: **Day** $0.50 **Week** n/a **Month** Open $85/Covered $145-175
Power: 30 amp $3, **50 amp** $6, **100 amp** n/a, **200 amp** n/a
Cable TV: No **Dockside Phone:** No
Dock Type: Fixed, Long Fingers
Moorings: 75 Total, 4 Transient **Launch:** n/a
Rate: Day $0.75/ft. **Week** $3/ft. **Month** $145-175
Heads: 3 Toilet(s), 2 Shower(s)
Laundry: None **Pay Phones:** Yes
Pump-Out: OnSite, Full Service **Fee:** $5 **Closed Heads:** Yes

Marina Operations

Owner/Manager: Costa Plakas **Dockmaster:** Same
In-Season: Apr-Dec, 8am-6pm **Off-Season:** Jan-Mar, 8am-4:30pm
After-Hours Arrival: Tie up at T-dock, check-in next morning
Reservations: No **Credit Cards:** Visa/MC
Discounts: None
Pets: Welcome, Dog Walk Area **Handicap Access:** No

Marina Services and Boat Supplies

Services - Docking Assistance, Dock Carts **Communication -** Mail & Package Hold, Phone Messages, Fax in/out, FedEx, DHL, UPS, Express Mail **Supplies - OnSite:** Ice *(Block, Cube)*, Ships' Store, Bait/Tackle **Near:** Live Bait **1-3 mi:** West Marine *(776-0400)*, Boat/US *(776-8583)*, Propane *(Revere Gas 776-9724)*

Boatyard Services

OnSite: Travelift *(40T)*, Railway *(to 60 ft.)*, Crane *(masts up to 40 ft)*, Engine mechanic *(gas, diesel)*, Hull Repairs, Bottom Cleaning, Brightwork, Compound, Wash & Wax, Interior Cleaning, Woodworking, Painting **OnCall:** Electrical Repairs, Electronics Repairs, Rigger, Canvas Work, Air Conditioning, Refrigeration, Divers **Near:** Propeller Repairs. **Under 1 mi:** Launching Ramp, Sail Loft, Upholstery, Yacht Broker. **Dealer for:** Westerbeke, Tohatsu & Segal outboards, Mercruiser, Chrysler, Crusader & Universal. **Yard Rates:** $45/hr., Haul & Launch $5-6.50/ft. *(blocking incl.)*, Power Wash Incl., Bottom Paint $11/ft. *(paint incl.)* **Storage:** In-Water cvrd $145-175, uncvrd $100-170, On-Land $60-80/mo.

Restaurants and Accommodations

OnCall: Pizzeria *(Dano's 776-8031)* **Near:** Restaurant *(Boat House Café 776-8882, D Tue-Sun 4:30-10pm, Sat & Sun brunch 11am-3pm; closed Mon)* **Under 1 mi:** Restaurant *(Taylor's 776-9611, B $2-5, L $5-8, D $10-20, picks up)*, *(The Galley 776-6040, picks up)*, Inn/B&B *(Sanderling House B&B 776-0970, $90-170)*, *(Up the Creek 776-9621)* **1-3 mi:** Restaurant *(Toby's 776-6913, L $5-10, D $8-18, picks up)*, Lite Fare *(Sweet Shop 776-7021, B $2-4, L $3-6)*, Hotel *(Dockside Inn 776-9224)*, Inn/B&B *(Rivers Rise B&B 776-7521)*

Recreation and Entertainment

OnSite: Picnic Area *(landscaping under construction)*, Grills *(under construction)*, Boat Rentals **OnCall:** Fishing Charter **Near:** Galleries *(Nauti Nell's 776-9811)* **1-3 mi:** Pool, Tennis Courts, Video Rental *(Hollywood Video 776-7715)*, Museum *(Deltaville Maritime Museum 776-7200)* **3+ mi:** Golf Course *(Piankatank River Golf Club 776-6516, 6 mi.)*

Provisioning and General Services

OnCall: Market *(Sandy Bottom Market 776-8803 picks up & returns boaters - min. order $25)* **Under 1 mi:** Beauty Salon *(Cacky's Cut & Curl 776-6775)*, Hardware Store *(Hurds Hardware 776-9241)* **1-3 mi:** Convenience Store, Supermarket *(Deltaville Town & Country Market 776-6131)*, Wine/Beer *(Sandy Bottom)*, Bakery *(Sweet Shop)*, Farmers' Market *(Yates House Fine Art, Sat 9am-1pm)*, Fishmonger *(J&W Seafood 776-6400)*, Bank/ATM, Post Office *(776-9750)*, Catholic Church, Protestant Church, Library *(Deltaville Library 776-7362)*, Barber Shop *(Sully's Barber Shop 776-0052)*, Pharmacy *(Medicine Shoppe 776-9990)*, Florist

Transportation

OnSite: Courtesy Car/Van *(courtesy drop-off by staff)*, Bikes *(courtesy)* **OnCall:** Rental Car *(Enterprise 694-8226)*, Airport Limo *(Tri-County 693-3475)* **1-3 mi:** Local Bus *(Bay Transit 693-6977 - reservations)* **Airport:** Newport News/Richmond *(45 mi./65 mi.)*

Medical Services

911 Service **1-3 mi:** Doctor *(Chesapeake Medical Group 776-9221)*, Dentist *(Lennon 776-9484)*, Veterinarian *(Hartfield Animal Hosp. 776-9219)* **Hospital:** Riverside Walter Reed 693-6368 *(23 mi.)*

Setting -- The first slips on the starboard side at the entrance to Broad Creek, Walden's pair of main docks poke almost into the channel. The north (first) is a bit longer and edges an extended, narrow sand spit planted with scrub and pines that dutifully shelter the docks. The outer half are open slips and the inner are covered docks. The south docks are almost all under covered sheds with a handful of open slips at the end. A travelift bay and railway anchor the west end. Between the docks, the rustic landside facilities include a single-story white building with green shingle shed roof that houses a large ships' & parts store.

Marina Notes -- Founded in 1940's by Alvin and Moody Walden. Owned by Chris & Costa Plakas since 1982. An old-time boatyard with docks, it sports the only marine railway in Broad Creek. Machine shop with a large & jumbled parts department - likely the largest ships' store in Deltaville, with shelves and shelves of parts, findings and fittings. A counterpoint, the sheds and the docks are neat and tidy. Courtesy phone. Dry storage. The accommodating Walden staff and the residents of Deltaville are generous with rides - and most of the restaurants provide pick-up and return. Basic bathhouse has three toilets and two showers.

Notable -- Walden's is an echo of Deltaville's impressive past - once the wooden boatbuilding capital of the Chesapeake with more than 20 boat yards - today the town caters mostly to pleasure craft. Its year-round population is about 800, yet there are over 2,000 seasonally-berthed vessels in its marinas plus a steady flow of transients. Bikes are perfect - the distances are not overwhelming and the terrain is flat. The Boathouse Café (776-8882), between Walden's Marina and Norton's, is open for dinner Tuesday through Sunday 4:30-10pm, brunch Saturday and Sunday 11am-3pm, closed Mondays.

PHOTOS ON CD-ROM: 8

Norview Marina

PO Box 219; 18691 General Puller Highway; Deltaville, VA 23043

Tel: (804) 776-6463 **VHF: Monitor** 16 **Talk** 78
Fax: (804) 776-7606 **Alternate Tel:** (804) 776-6463
Email: n/a **Web:** www.norviewmarina.com
Nearest Town: Deltaville **Tourist Info:** (800) 527-6360

Navigational Information

Lat: 37°33.483' **Long:** 076°18.870' **Tide:** 2 ft. **Current:** 3 kt. **Chart:** 12235
Rep. Depths (*MLW*): Entry 6 ft. **Fuel Dock** 6 ft. **Max Slip/Moor** 6 ft./-
Access: Rappahanock River to southern shore to Broad Creek

Marina Facilities *(In Season/Off Season)*

Fuel: Gasoline, Diesel
Slips: 110 Total, 8 Transient **Max LOA:** 175 ft. **Max Beam:** n/a
Rate *(per ft.)*: **Day** $1.50 **Week** Inq. **Month** Inq.
Power: 30 amp $5, **50 amp** $8, **100 amp** n/a, **200 amp** n/a
Cable TV: Yes **Dockside Phone:** No
Dock Type: Fixed, Floating, Long Fingers, Short Fingers, Alongside, Wood
Moorings: 0 Total, 0 Transient **Launch:** n/a, Dinghy Dock
Rate: Day n/a **Week** n/a **Month** n/a
Heads: 9 Toilet(s), 8 Shower(s) *(with dressing rooms)*
Laundry: 1 Washer(s), 1 Dryer(s), Book Exchange **Pay Phones:** No
Pump-Out: OnSite, Full Service **Fee:** $10 **Closed Heads:** Yes

Marina Operations

Owner/Manager: Barnes & Respress **Dockmaster:** Wes Hunley
In-Season: Apr-Dec, 7:30am-4:30pm **Off-Season:** Jan-Mar, 7:30am-4:30pm
After-Hours Arrival: Call ahead
Reservations: Preferred **Credit Cards:** Visa/MC
Discounts: Boat/US **Dockage:** $1.00 **Fuel:** $0.10 **Repair:** No
Pets: Welcome, Dog Walk Area **Handicap Access:** No

Marina Services and Boat Supplies

Services - Docking Assistance, Boaters' Lounge, Security *(24 hrs.)*, Trash Pick-Up, Dock Carts **Communication -** Mail & Package Hold, Phone Messages, Fax in/out, Data Ports *(Lounge)*, FedEx, UPS, Express Mail *(Sat Del)* **Supplies - OnSite:** Ice *(Block, Cube)*, Ships' Store, Bait/Tackle **OnCall:** Live Bait **Near:** CNG *(Texaco)* **Under 1 mi:** West Marine *(776-0400)*, Boat/US *(776-8583)* **3+ mi:** Propane *(Revere 776-9724, 4 mi.)*

Boatyard Services

OnSite: Travelift *(30T)*, Forklift *(10T, 36 ft.)*, Launching Ramp, Engine mechanic *(gas, diesel)*, Hull Repairs, Bottom Cleaning, Divers, Compound, Wash & Wax, Interior Cleaning, Yacht Broker *(Delta Boat Sales, Bud Bowen, 776-7447)* **OnCall:** Crane, Hydraulic Trailer, Woodworking, Life Raft Service, Metal Fabrication **Near:** Electrical Repairs, Electronics Repairs. **Under 1 mi:** Sail Loft, Canvas Work, Air Conditioning, Refrigeration, Propeller Repairs, Yacht Interiors, Painting, Awlgrip. **Dealer for:** Yamaha, Mercruiser, Cummins, Volvo, OMC, Johnson/Evinrude, Westerbeke, Onan, Cruisar, Cruisader . **Yard Rates:** $55/hr., Haul & Launch $6.50/ft. *(blocking incl.)*, Bottom Paint $22.50/ft. **Storage:** On-Land $95/mo.

Restaurants and Accommodations

OnCall: Pizzeria *(Dano's 776-8031)* **1-3 mi:** Restaurant *(Toby's 776-6913, L $5-10, D $8-18, picks up)*, *(Galley 776-6040, D $6-20, picks up)*, *(Taylor's 776-9611, B $2-5, L $5-8, D $10-20, picks up)*, *(Boat House Café 776-8882, L $5-10, D $6-23, kids' $5-6; Sun brunch 11am-4pm $15/6; picks up)*, *(Steamboat 776-6516)*, Inn/B&B *(Rivers Rise 776-7521)*, *(Sanderling House B&B 776-0970, $95-150)*, *(Up the Creek B&B 776-9621)*

Recreation and Entertainment

OnSite: Pool, Picnic Area, Grills *(propane)*, Volleyball *(and horseshoe pit)* **Under 1 mi:** Video Rental *(Hollywood Video 776-7715)*, Video Arcade, Park **1-3 mi:** Playground, Tennis Courts, Galleries *(Yates House 776-8505)* **3+ mi:** Golf Course *(Piankatank River Golf Club 776-6516, 6 mi.)*, Museum *(Deltaville Maritime Museum 776-7200, 4 mi.)*

Provisioning and General Services

OnSite: Retail Shops *(Market on A Dock - clothing, snacks, sodas, beer, ice cream)* **OnCall:** Supermarket *(Deltaville Market 776-6131)*, Market *(Sandy Bottom Market 776-8803 - min order $25)*, Florist **Near:** Convenience Store *(Little Sue 776-9600)*, Bank/ATM **Under 1 mi:** Hardware Store *(Hurds Hardware 776-9241)* **1-3 mi:** Wine/Beer, Bakery, Farmers' Market *(Sat 9am-1pm at Yates House Fine Art)*, Fishmonger *(J&W Seafood 776-6400)*, Post Office *(776-9750)*, Protestant Church, Library *(Deltaville 776-7362)*, Beauty Salon *(Hair By Sarah 776-0061)*, Barber Shop *(Sully's 776-0052)*, Pharmacy *(Medicine Shoppe 776-9990)*

Transportation

OnCall: Rental Car *(Enterprise 694-8226)*, Airport Limo *(Tri-County 693-3475)* **Under 1 mi:** Local Bus *(Bay Transit 693-6977 - reservations)* **Airport:** Newport News/Richmond *(45 mi./65 mi.)*

Medical Services

911 Service **OnCall:** Ambulance **Under 1 mi:** Doctor *(Ransone 776-8000)* **1-3 mi:** Dentist *(Lennon 776-9484)*, Veterinarian *(Hartfield Animal Hosp. 776-9219)* **3+ mi:** Chiropractor *(Merithew 725-9376, 9 mi.)* **Hospital:** Riverside Walter Reed 693-6368 *(21 mi.)*

Setting -- Stretched along the southeast shore of Broad Creek, Norview's signature brick-red metal roofs top well-maintained pale gray boathouses, sheds and facilities buildings. The unique congregation of red roofs intersecting at various angles serves as beacon to guide boaters. At the end of the each covered shed are open slips served by broad boardwalks. 38 tidy acres house a pool, picnic areas, extensive dry storage, work sheds, a lounge and a ships' store.

Marina Notes -- Built in early '70s; acquired by current owners in '86. Formerly Rappahanock Yacht Haven. Transients mostly on "B" &"C". 24-hr. fueling at easily-accessed "A" dock, pump-out on "C". Dry stack storage for 200 boats. Full-service yard and extensive ships' store (Mon-Fri 7:30am-4:30pm). The boaters' lounge sits right near the docks with comfortable sofa and chairs, a TV, table and chairs, a microwave and a phone jack for laptops. "The Market on 'A' Dock" (Mon-Thu 7:30am-4:30pm, Fri 'til 6, Sat 7am-7pm, Sun 7am-5:30pm) has sundries. In the covered sheds, "customization" by residents evokes an old fishing-lodge feel. The bathhouses have been upgraded - tile floors, wallpapered walls, large mirrors, vanity sinks, laminate dividers and fiberglass showers; laundromat on the back side.

Notable -- An attractive small kidney-shaped pool (10am-10pm) is set in a fenced, grassy area surrounded by a concrete patio dotted with white chaises and cement tables and benches. Redwood picnic tables sit under a red & white striped awning, and 3 propane grills stand at the ready nearby. Views are of the boats stored on-the-hard. Adjacent is a volleyball net and a horseshoe pit. Additional cement tables and benches populate a second picnic area.

PHOTOS ON CD-ROM: 12

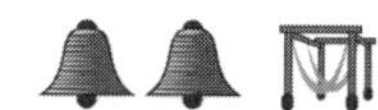

Navigational Information
Lat: 37°33.545' **Long:** 076°19.143' **Tide:** 2 ft. **Current:** n/a **Chart:** 12235
Rep. Depths (*MLW*): Entry 6 ft. **Fuel Dock** 8 ft. **Max Slip/Moor** 8 ft./-
Access: Broad Creek to north fork port side

Marina Facilities *(In Season/Off Season)*
Fuel: Gasoline, Diesel, On Call Delivery
Slips: 30 Total, 4-6 Transient **Max LOA:** 50 ft. **Max Beam:** 15 ft.
Rate *(per ft.)*: **Day** $1.00 **Week** $7 **Month** n/a
Power: 30 amp Incl., **50 amp** n/a, **100 amp** n/a, **200 amp** n/a
Cable TV: No **Dockside Phone:** No
Dock Type: Fixed, Short Fingers, Wood
Moorings: 0 Total, 0 Transient **Launch:** n/a
Rate: Day n/a **Week** n/a **Month** n/a
Heads: 2 Toilet(s), 2 Shower(s) *(with dressing rooms)*
Laundry: None **Pay Phones:** No
Pump-Out: OnSite, Full Service, 1 Central **Fee:** $10 **Closed Heads:** Yes

Marina Operations
Owner/Manager: Carolyn & Ken Schmalenberger **Dockmaster:** Staff
In-Season: Jan 2-Dec 20, 8am-4:30pm **Off-Season:** Dec 21-Jan 1, closed
After-Hours Arrival: Tie up at dock
Reservations: Preferred **Credit Cards:** Visa/MC
Discounts: None
Pets: Welcome, Dog Walk Area **Handicap Access:** Yes, Heads, Docks

Norton's Yacht Sales

PO Box 100; 97 Marina Road; Deltaville, VA 23043

Tel: (804) 776-9211; (888) 720-4306 **VHF: Monitor** 16 **Talk** n/a
Fax: (804) 776-9044 **Alternate Tel:** n/a
Email: yachts@nortonyachts.com **Web:** www.nortonyachts.com
Nearest Town: Deltaville *(1.5 mi.)* **Tourist Info:** (804) 725-9029

Marina Services and Boat Supplies
Services - Docking Assistance, Dock Carts **Communication -** FedEx, DHL, UPS, Express Mail **Supplies - OnSite:** Ice *(Block, Cube)* **Near:** Ships' Store, Bait/Tackle *(J&W Seafood 776-6400)*, Live Bait **1-3 mi:** West Marine *(776-0400)*, Boat/US *(776-8583)*, Propane *(Revere Gas 776-9724)*

Boatyard Services
OnSite: Travelift *(35T)*, Crane, Engine mechanic *(gas, diesel)*, Electrical Repairs, Hull Repairs, Rigger, Bottom Cleaning, Compound, Wash & Wax, Woodworking, Painting, Yacht Broker **Near:** Launching Ramp, Electronics Repairs, Sail Loft, Canvas Work, Air Conditioning, Refrigeration, Divers, Interior Cleaning, Propeller Repairs, Inflatable Repairs, Life Raft Service, Yacht Interiors, Metal Fabrication, Awlgrip, Yacht Building, Total Refits. **Dealer for:** Hunter, Jeanneau. **Yard Rates:** $60/hr., Haul & Launch $7/ft. *(blocking $25/hr.)*, Power Wash $25, Bottom Paint $14/hr. *(paint incl.)*

Restaurants and Accommodations
OnCall: Pizzeria *(Dano's 776-8031)* **Near:** Seafood Shack *(Boat House Café 776-8882, D Tue-Sun 4:30-10pm, Sat & Sun brunch 11am-3pm; closed Mon; picks up)*, Inn/B&B *(Edentide Inn B&B 776-6915)*, *(Sanderling House 776-0970, $95-150)* **Under 1 mi:** Restaurant *(Taylor's 776-9611, B $2-5, L $5-8, D $10-20, picks up)*, *(Toby's 776-6913, L $5-10, D $8-18, picks up)*, Lite Fare *(Sweet Shop 776-7021)*, Inn/B&B *(Rivers Rise B&B 776-7521)* **1-3 mi:** Restaurant *(Galley 776-6040, L $6-10, D $6-10, picks up)*, Inn/B&B *(Dockside Inn 776-9224)*

Recreation and Entertainment
OnSite: Picnic Area, Grills *(propane)*, Boat Rentals *(Norton Yacht Charters - Hunter 310 $1300/wk, 340 $1600/wk - shorter times possible)* **Near:** Playground, Jogging Paths, Roller Blade/Bike Paths, Fishing Charter, Movie Theater, Park *(Holly Point)*, Cultural Attract, Sightseeing *(Gwynn Island)* **Under 1 mi:** Video Rental *(Hollywood Video 776-7715)*, Museum *(Deltaville Maritime Museum 776-7200 - call for hours)*, Galleries *(Yates House 776-8505)*, Special Events *(Holly Point Art & Seafood Fest - Oct)* **3+ mi:** Golf Course *(Piankatank River 776-6516, 6 mi.)*

Provisioning and General Services
Near: Convenience Store, Bank/ATM, Catholic Church, Protestant Church, Dry Cleaners, Laundry, Bookstore, Florist, Clothing Store, Copies Etc. **Under 1 mi:** Bakery, Farmers' Market *(Sat 9am-1pm at Yates House Fine Art)*, Fishmonger *(J&W Seafood 776-6400)*, Post Office *(776-9750)*, Library *(Deltaville 776-7362)*, Beauty Salon *(Cacky's Cut & Curl 776-6775)*, Pharmacy *(Medicine Shoppe 776-9990)*, Hardware Store *(Hurds 776-9241)* **1-3 mi:** Supermarket *(Deltaville Market 776-6131 Mon-Fri & Sun 7am-8:30pm, 'til 9:30pm Fri & Sat)*, Wine/Beer, Market *(Sandy Bottom Market 776-8803)*, Barber Shop *(Sully's 776-0052)*

Transportation
OnCall: Rental Car *(Enterprise 694-8226)*, Airport Limo *(Tri-County 693-3475)* **Near:** Local Bus *(Bay Transit 693-6977 - reservations)* **Airport:** Newport News/Richmond *(45 mi./65 mi.)*

Medical Services
911 Service **OnCall:** Ambulance **Under 1 mi:** Doctor *(Chesapeake Medical Group 776-9221)* **1-3 mi:** Dentist *(Lennon 776-9484)*, Veterinarian *(Hartfield 776-9219)* **Hospital:** Walter Reed 693-6368 *(22 mi.)*

Setting -- On the north branch side of Broad Creek, the pale, creamy yellow sides and brown shingle roofs identify Nortons two-sided docks. The first one is divided equally between a covered shed and open slips; the second is virtually all covered dockage with a fuel dock at the end. A third set of open slips rests on the far side of the travelift bay. Landside is basically a boat brokerage and boat yard.

Marina Notes -- Established in 1948 and still run by the Norton family. A major boat brokerage specializing in Tartan and Hunter Yachts - top 5 in sales for over 20 years and voted #1 in service for 12. All stationary wood docks with short finger piers. On the covered docks, power is attached to the posts high above the water. Fish cleaning station on the "C" dock T-head. Price's is no longer part of the facility; Norton's now provides complete yard services to its resident fleet and to guests - 35 ton travelift and large work shed. Norton's ASA-sanctioned Sailing School offers sailing, navigation and cruising courses - and bareboat charters. Pleasant tile floor bathhouses - each has 2 molded sinks, 2 wood toilet stalls and one tiled shower stall with glass door dressing room.

Notable -- Just down the road The Boathouse Café is open for dinner Tue-Sun 4:30-10pm, brunch Sat & Sun 11am-3pm, closed Mon. Less than a mile away, on the grounds of the Holly Point Nature Park, the Deltaville Maritime Museum has exhibits on the early years of wooden boatbuilding, identifying more than 75 builders. Other exhibits include the Art of the Watermen; and "The Callis Store" which recreates a general store from the era. Outside are several classic bay vessels. Right across the street is the Deltaville Convenience Center and The Galley restaurant. The commercial strip is along General Puller Highway.

PHOTOS ON CD-ROM: 8

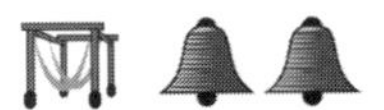

Chesapeake Cove Marina

Chesapeake Cove Marina

PO Box 369; Route 110 Broad Creek; Deltaville, VA 23043

Tel: (804) 776-6855 **VHF: Monitor** 16 **Talk** 68
Fax: (804) 776-7194 **Alternate Tel:** (804) 776-6855
Email: n/a **Web:** n/a
Nearest Town: Deltaville *(1 mi.)* **Tourist Info:** (804) 843-4499

Navigational Information

Lat: 37°33.453' **Long:** 076°18.910' **Tide:** 2 ft. **Current:** .5 kt. **Chart:** 12235
Rep. Depths (*MLW*): Entry 6 ft. **Fuel Dock** 5 ft. **Max Slip/Moor** 5 ft./6 ft.
Access: Rappahannock to Broad Creek, North Branch

Marina Facilities *(In Season/Off Season)*

Fuel: *B/P* - Gasoline, Diesel
Slips: 40 Total, 2 Transient **Max LOA:** 50 ft. **Max Beam:** 18 ft.
Rate *(per ft.)*: **Day** $1.00 **Week** n/a **Month** n/a
Power: 30 amp $5, **50 amp** $10, **100 amp** n/a, **200 amp** n/a
Cable TV: No **Dockside Phone:** No
Dock Type: Fixed, Long Fingers, Short Fingers, Pilings, Wood
Moorings: 0 Total, 0 Transient **Launch:** n/a
Rate: Day n/a **Week** n/a **Month** n/a
Heads: 6 Toilet(s), 2 Shower(s) *(with dressing rooms)*
Laundry: 1 Washer(s), 1 Dryer(s) **Pay Phones:** No
Pump-Out: OnSite, Full Service, 1 Central **Fee:** $5 **Closed Heads:** Yes

Marina Operations

Owner/Manager: Bob & Pam Reiner **Dockmaster:** Same
In-Season: Apr-Oct, 7:30am-5:30pm **Off-Season:** Nov-Apr, 7:30am-5pm
After-Hours Arrival: Tie up to fuel dock
Reservations: Preferred **Credit Cards:** Visa/MC, Dscvr, Amex, B/P
Discounts: None
Pets: Welcome, Dog Walk Area **Handicap Access:** No

Marina Services and Boat Supplies

Services - Docking Assistance, Security *(24 hrs.)* **Communication -** Phone Messages, Fax in/out, FedEx, DHL, UPS, Express Mail **Supplies - OnSite:** Ice *(Block, Cube)*, Ships' Store **Near:** Propane **1-3 mi:** West Marine *(776-0400)*, Boat/US *(776-8583)*, Bait/Tackle *(J&W Seafood 776-6400)*

Boatyard Services

OnSite: Travelift *(30T)*, Crane *(15T)*, Engine mechanic *(gas, diesel)*, Electrical Repairs, Hull Repairs, Bottom Cleaning, Brightwork, Compound, Wash & Wax, Interior Cleaning, Propeller Repairs, Woodworking, Metal Fabrication, Painting, Awlgrip **OnCall:** Electronics Repairs, Rigger, Divers, Life Raft Service, Upholstery **Near:** Air Conditioning, Refrigeration, Yacht Interiors, Yacht Building, Yacht Broker *(Bill Thacker, Jess Saunders)*. **Under 1 mi:** Launching Ramp, Sail Loft, Canvas Work. **Dealer for:** Mercruiser, Volvo Penta gas+ diesel, Yanmar, Kohler, Nesterbeice, OMC, Crusader,Transmissions.. **Member:** ABBRA, ABYC - 2 Certified Tech(s) **Yard Rates:** $65/hr., Haul & Launch $3.50/ft. *(blocking $3.50/ft.)*, Power Wash $2.75/ft., Bottom Paint $20/ft. *(paint incl.)* **Storage:** In-Water $6.25/ft./mo., On-Land $3.75/ft./mo.

Restaurants and Accommodations

OnCall: Pizzeria *(Dano's 776-8031)* **Near:** Inn/B&B *(Sanderling House B&B 776-0970, $95-150)* **Under 1 mi:** Restaurant *(Boat House Café 776-8882, picks up)*, *(Taylor's 776-9611, B $2-5, L $5-8, D $10-20, picks up)*, Motel *(Up the Creek 776-9621)*, Inn/B&B *(Rivers Rise B&B 776-7521)* **1-3 mi:** Restaurant *(Galley 776-6040, L $6-10, D $6-20, picks up)*, *(Toby's 776-6913, L $5-10, D $8-18, picks up)*, *(Steamboat 776-6516)*, Lite Fare *(Sweet Shop 776-7021, B $2-4, L $3-6)*, Hotel *(Dockside Inn 776-9224)*

Recreation and Entertainment

OnSite: Fishing Charter **Under 1 mi:** Galleries *(Pat's for maritime art & Jerry's for local artists)* **1-3 mi:** Group Fishing Boat, Video Rental *(Hollywood Video 776-7715)*, Park *(Holly Point)*, Museum *(Maritime Museum 776-7200)* **3+ mi:** Golf Course *(Piankatank 776-6516, 5 mi.)*

Provisioning and General Services

OnCall: Market *(Sandy Bottom Market 776-8803 picks up & returns boaters - min order $25)*, Dry Cleaners **Near:** Convenience Store *(Texaco Food Mart)*, Wine/Beer **1-3 mi:** Supermarket *(Deltaville Town & Country Market 776-6131 Mon-Fri & Sun 7am-8:30pm, 'til 9:30pm Fri & Sat)*, Gourmet Shop *(Latitudes)*, Bakery *(Sweet Shop)*, Farmers' Market *(Sat 9am-1pm at Yates House Fine Art)*, Fishmonger *(J&W Seafood 776-6400 Mon-Thu 5:30am-5:30pm, Fri & Sat to 6pm, Sun 6am-2pm)*, Lobster Pound, Bank/ATM, Post Office *(776-9750)*, Synagogue, Library *(Deltaville 776-7362)*, Beauty Salon *(Hair By Sarah 776-0061)*, Barber Shop *(Sully's Barber Shop 776-0052)*, Pharmacy *(Medicine Shoppe 776-9990)*, Hardware Store *(Hurds Hardware 776-9241)*, Florist, Retail Shops, Copies Etc.

Transportation

OnCall: Rental Car *(Enterprise 694-8226)*, Airport Limo *(Tri-County 693-3475)* **Under 1 mi:** Local Bus *(Bay Transit 693-6977 - reservations)* **Airport:** Newport News/Richmond *(45 mi./65 mi.)*

Medical Services

911 Service **OnCall:** Ambulance **1-3 mi:** Doctor *(RGH Medical Center 776-9221)*, Dentist *(Lennon 776-9484)*, Veterinarian *(Hartfield Animal Hosp. 776-9219)* **Hospital:** Riverside Walter Reed 693-6368 *(22 mi.)*

Setting -- Tucked deep into protected Broad Creek's north fork, Chesapeake Cove is near the head of the narrowing waterway on the southern shore - with a quiet, leafy "working harbor" ambiance. The useful color-coding in this crowded harbor continues. Here gray siding is accented with deep brick red trim and topped with unpainted steel roofs. A beautiful new boathouse was completed in late '04 adding 12 new 40 foot covered slips to this full service boatyard.

Marina Notes -- Founded in the 1950s as the R.S. Green Boatyard - Robert Green Sr. and his son built traditional Chesapeake Bay deadrise workboats for watermen. Since 1983, Owned and operated by Bob & Pam Reiner - commercial fishing and boatbuilding gave way to a contemporary marina and boatyard for pleasure craft; commercial fishing vessels still head here for work. Full-length piers, power up on the posts. Boatyard is capable of handling some large vessel and has been cited in surveys for its engine repairs. On-site are the Chesapeake Electric Company, propeller sales and service, and a Mercruiser, Yanmar, and Volvo dealer. Basic cinderblock bathhouse, with a single cinderblock shower stall (dressing area separated by a shower curtain). Three brightly-colored shower curtains replace toilet stall doors. Note: the washer and dryer are in the women's bathhouse.

Notable -- Deltaville is totally boating oriented and caters to cruisers. Most the of the restaurants pick up and deliver back to the marinas. The Deltaville Maritime Museum, located in Holly Point Nature Park, tells the story of the region's tenure as the Wooden Boat Building Capital of the Chesapeake. The commercial strip along Route 33 has craft & gift shops, restaurants, and provisioning resources; J&W Seafood includes a big bait and tackle department.

PHOTOS ON CD-ROM: 9

Navigational Information

Lat: 37°33.344' **Long:** 076°19.033' **Tide:** 1 ft. **Current:** n/a **Chart:** 12235
Rep. Depths (*MLW*): Entry 8 ft. **Fuel Dock** n/a **Max Slip/Moor** 7 ft./-
Access: Broad Creek to South Branch to G 13

Marina Facilities *(In Season/Off Season)*

Fuel: *Texaco* - Slip-Side Fueling, Gasoline
Slips: 76 Total, 10 Transient **Max LOA:** 55 ft. **Max Beam:** 20 ft.
Rate *(per ft.)*: **Day** $1.33 **Week** n/a **Month** n/a
Power: 30 amp $4, **50 amp** $8, **100 amp** n/a, **200 amp** n/a
Cable TV: Yes long term only **Dockside Phone:** No
Dock Type: Fixed, Long Fingers, Pilings, Alongside, Wood
Moorings: 0 Total, 0 Transient **Launch:** n/a, Dinghy Dock
Rate: Day n/a **Week** n/a **Month** n/a
Heads: 10 Toilet(s), 8 Shower(s) *(with dressing rooms)*
Laundry: None, Book Exchange **Pay Phones:** No
Pump-Out: Full Service, 2 Central **Fee:** $5 **Closed Heads:** Yes

Marina Operations

Owner/Manager: Lew & Onna Grimm **Dockmaster:** Mary Howell
In-Season: Year-Round, 8am-4:30pm **Off-Season:** n/a
After-Hours Arrival: Call ahead or tie up at any T-head, check-in in am
Reservations: Preferred **Credit Cards:** Visa/MC
Discounts: Boat/US **Dockage:** 25% **Fuel:** $0.10/gal **Repair:** No
Pets: Welcome, Dog Walk Area **Handicap Access:** Yes, Heads, Docks

Deltaville Yachting Center

PO Box 388; 18355 Puller Hwy; Deltaville, VA 23043

Tel: (804) 776-9898; (800) 296-2628 **VHF: Monitor** 16 **Talk** 72
Fax: (804) 776-6998 **Alternate Tel:** (804) 776-9898
Email: info@dycboat.com **Web:** www.dycboat.com
Nearest Town: Deltaville *(1 mi.)* **Tourist Info:** (804) 725-9029

Marina Services and Boat Supplies

Services - Docking Assistance, Concierge, Boaters' Lounge, Security *(12 hrs.)*, Trash Pick-Up, Dock Carts **Communication -** Mail & Package Hold, Phone Messages, Fax in/out, Data Ports *(Office, Free)*, FedEx, DHL, UPS, Express Mail **Supplies - OnSite:** Ice *(Block, Cube)*, Ships' Store **Under 1 mi:** West Marine *(776-0400)*, Boat/US *(776-8583)*, Bait/Tackle *(J&W Seafood)*, Live Bait **3+ mi:** Propane *(Revere Gas, 4 mi.)*

Boatyard Services

OnSite: Travelift *(50T)*, Forklift, Hydraulic Trailer, Engine mechanic *(gas, diesel)*, Electrical Repairs, Electronics Repairs, Hull Repairs, Rigger, Bottom Cleaning, Brightwork, Compound, Wash & Wax, Interior Cleaning, Propeller Repairs, Woodworking, Painting, Awlgrip, Total Refits, Yacht Broker *(Chesapeake Yacht Sales - Catalina, Carolina Classic & Albin)* **OnCall:** Crane, Divers, Inflatable Repairs **Near:** Launch Ramp, Upholstery. **1-3 mi:** Sail Loft, Air Conditioning, Refrigeration. **Dealer for:** Catalina, Albin, Albin, Carolina Classic. **Member:** ABBRA - 10 Certified Tech(s), ABYC **Yard Rates:** $55/hr., Haul & Launch $6.50-7.50/ft. *(blocking incl.)*, Power Wash *(incl. with H&L)*, Bottom Paint $12-14/ft. *(paint incl.)*

Restaurants and Accommodations

OnCall: Pizzeria *(Dano's 776-8031)* **Near:** Inn/B&B *(Dockside Inn 776-9224)* **1-3 mi:** Restaurant *(Galley 776-6040, L $6-10, D $6-10, picks up)*, *(Taylor's 776-9611, B $2-5, L $5-8, D $6-20, picks up)*, *(Steamboat 776-6516)*, *(Toby's 776-6913, L $5-10, D $8-18, picks up)*, Snack Bar *(Sweet Shop 776-7021, B $2-4, L $3-6)*, Pizzeria *(Sal's 776-7611)*, Inn/B&B *(Rivers Rise B&B 776-7521)*, *(River Place 776-9153, $95-175)*, *(Edentide Inn 776-6915)*, *(Sanderling House B&B 776-0970, $95-150)*

Recreation and Entertainment

OnSite: Pool, Beach, Picnic Area, Grills *(charcoal)* **Near:** Jogging Paths, Roller Blade/Bike Paths **Under 1 mi:** Fishing Charter, Video Rental *(Hollywood Video 776-7715)*, Museum *(Deltaville Maritime Museum 776-7200)*, Cultural Attract, Special Events *(Firemen's Crab Feast - Aug)* **1-3 mi:** Playground, Tennis Courts, Boat Rentals, Galleries *(Yates House 776-8505)* **3+ mi:** Golf Course *(Piankatank River 776-6516, 5 mi.)*

Provisioning and General Services

OnSite: Copies Etc. **OnCall:** Market *(Sandy Bottom Market 776-8803 - min order $25)*, Dry Cleaners **Under 1 mi:** Convenience Store *(Little Sue 776-9600)*, Fishmonger *(J&W Seafood 776-6400)*, Bank/ATM, Post Office *(776-9750)*, Protestant Church, Library *(776-7362)*, Beauty Salon *(Hair By Sarah 776-0061)*, Barber Shop *(Sully's 776-0052)*, Bookstore, Hardware Store *(Hurds 776-9241)* **1-3 mi:** Supermarket *(Deltaville Town & Country Market 776-6131)*, Wine/Beer, Farmers' Market *(Sat 9am-1pm at Yates House Fine Art)*, Florist **3+ mi:** Pharmacy *(Medicine Shoppe 776-9990, 5 mi.)*

Transportation

OnCall: Rental Car *(Enterprise 694-8226)*, Airport Limo *(Tri-County 693-3475, Temp James 695-7070)* **Under 1 mi:** Local Bus *(Bay Transit 693-6977 - reservations)* **Airport:** Newport News/Richmond *(45 mi./65 mi.)*

Medical Services

911 Service **OnCall:** Ambulance **Under 1 mi:** Doctor *(RGH Medical 776-9221)*, Dentist *(Lennon 776-9484)* **1-3 mi:** Veterinarian *(Hartfield Animal Hosp. 776-9219)* **3+ mi:** Chiropractor *(Merithew 725-9376, 9 mi.)*
Hospital: Walter Reed 693-6368 *(22 mi.)*

Setting -- On the southern branch of Broad Creek, DYC's 76 slips, a mix of covered and open docks, are backed by a thoughtful selection of eco-friendly amenities - from a large sparkling pool to a gracious clubhouse to a major boatyard operation. The carefully-tended natural landscaping - native grasses, shrubs and trees - creates a habitat that attracts wildlife and integrates the buildings, obsfucating the view of the service centers from the recreation areas.

Marina Notes -- DCM. Founded in 1973 as Dozier's Deltaville Yachting Center. Family-owned & operated by Lew & Onna Grimm since 2001. Gas only, Diesel nearby; ships' store (Mon-Fri 8:30am-4:30pm, Sat 9am-4pm). Pets not allowed in buildings. Professional technicians man the full service yard; do-it-yourself also permitted. Boatel space for 150. Brand new 13-slip boathouse due to be completed by spring '06. Small power pedestals. Fish cleaning station. Sailing Lessons. Tiled-floor bathhouses have molded vanity sinks, fiberglass shower stalls with curtains and green laminate dressing room doors and laminate-covered stall doors, plus full length mirrors, skylights for natural light and designated hair dryer sockets.

Notable -- The patio surrounding the large "L" shaped pool is furnished with chaises and umbrella-topped tables & chairs - one side has views out to the docks, two sides are densely planted, and the clubhouse is on the fourth side. A separate sundeck is off the pool. The cathedral-ceiling boaters' lounge sports wide glass sliding doors out to the deck and pool, a black & white checkerboard floor, 2 comfortable wicker seating groups, 2 tables with chairs, a full kitchen and an upright piano - the Foggy Bottom Yacht Club bases here as well. At the foot of one of the wider fairways another picnic area has creek views.

PHOTOS ON CD-ROM: 12

Regent Point Marina

Regent Point Marina

317 Regent Point Drive; Topping, VA 23169

Tel: (804) 758-4457 **VHF: Monitor** 16 **Talk** n/a
Fax: (804) 758-5080 **Alternate Tel:** (804) 436-1051
Email: dockmaster@regent-point.com **Web:** www.regent-point.com
Nearest Town: Whitestone *(8 mi.)* **Tourist Info:** (804) 843-4499

Navigational Information

Lat: 37°35.426' **Long:** 076°26.063' **Tide:** 2 ft. **Current:** 3 kt. **Chart:** 12235
Rep. Depths (*MLW*): Entry 7 ft. **Fuel Dock** n/a **Max Slip/Moor** 9 ft./9 ft.
Access: 2 mi. from White Stone Bridge to south side of River, Locklies Creek

Marina Facilities *(In Season/Off Season)*

Fuel: No
Slips: 130 Total, 3 Transient **Max LOA:** 46 ft. **Max Beam:** 19 ft.
Rate *(per ft.)*: **Day** $2.00 **Week** n/a **Month** n/a
Power: 30 amp Incl., **50 amp** n/a, **100 amp** n/a, **200 amp** n/a
Cable TV: No **Dockside Phone:** No
Dock Type: Fixed, Wood
Moorings: 0 Total, 0 Transient **Launch:** n/a, Dinghy Dock (Free)
Rate: Day n/a **Week** n/a **Month** n/a
Heads: 6 Toilet(s), 4 Shower(s)
Laundry: 1 Washer(s), 1 Dryer(s) **Pay Phones:** No
Pump-Out: OnSite **Fee:** Free **Closed Heads:** Yes

Marina Operations

Owner/Manager: Jim Wagner **Dockmaster:** Same
In-Season: Mar15-Nov14, 8am-6pm **Off-Season:** Nov15-Mar14, 9am-4pm
After-Hours Arrival: Call 804-436-1051
Reservations: Required **Credit Cards:** Visa/MC, Checks
Discounts: None
Pets: Welcome **Handicap Access:** Yes, Heads, Docks

Marina Services and Boat Supplies

Services - Docking Assistance, Dock Carts **Communication -** Phone Messages, Fax in/out *($1)*, FedEx, UPS, Express Mail *(Sat Del)* **Supplies - OnSite:** Ice *(Block, Cube)* **Under 1 mi:** Live Bait **3+ mi:** Ships' Store *(6 mi.)*, West Marine *(776-0400, 13 mi.)*, Boat/US *(776-8583, 13 mi.)*, Propane *(Revere Gas, 4 mi.)*

Boatyard Services

OnSite: Travelift *(6T)*, Launching Ramp, Engine mechanic *(gas, diesel)*, Electrical Repairs, Hull Repairs, Rigger, Bottom Cleaning, Brightwork, Air Conditioning, Refrigeration, Compound, Wash & Wax, Interior Cleaning, Propeller Repairs, Woodworking, Painting, Total Refits, Yacht Broker *(Regent Point Marina)* **OnCall:** Divers **Dealer for:** Tartan. ABBRA - 2 Certified Tech(s), ABYC - 2 Certified Tech(s)

Restaurants and Accommodations

OnCall: Pizzeria *(Rudy's Pizza & Deli 758-0605, L $4-10, D $4-10)*
1-3 mi: Restaurant *(Eckhard's 758-4060)*, Motel *(Beacon 758-2262)*
3+ mi: Restaurant *(Trick Dog 438-1055, D $25, 8 mi.)*, *(Sandpiper 435-6176, D $20,6 mi.)*, *(David's Last Chance 758-9611, 5 mi.)*, *(Abbott Brothers 438-5273, 8 mi.)*, Hotel *(Tides Inn 436-8000, $195-850, 8 mi.)*, Inn/B&B *(Hope & Glory 438-6053, $175-300, 8 mi.)*

Recreation and Entertainment

OnSite: Beach, Picnic Area, Grills, Playground, Fitness Center **Near:** Cultural Attract *(Kauffman Aquacultural Center)* **Under 1 mi:** Group Fishing Boat **1-3 mi:** Jogging Paths, Video Rental *(Vanity Video 758-9604)*, Video Arcade, Park **3+ mi:** Tennis Courts *(6 mi.)*, Golf Course *(Piankatank River Golf Club 776-6589, 6 mi.)*, Bowling *(Evans Bowling Center 435-3950, 10 mi.)*, Movie Theater *(Lancaster Players Playhouse 435-3776, 6 mi.)*, Museum *(Steam Boat Museum 438-6888, 8 mi.)*, Special Events *(Urbanna Oyster Festival - Nov, 10 mi.)*

Provisioning and General Services

1-3 mi: Convenience Store, Green Grocer *(Taylor's Fresh Vegetable Stand)*, Post Office *(Topping)*, Catholic Church, Protestant Church, Hardware Store **3+ mi:** Supermarket *(Food Lion 435-1163/Tri-Star 435-3800, 10 mi.)*, Gourmet Shop *(River Market, 6 mi.)*, Health Food *(Higher Health Foods 436-0011, 11 mi.)*, Wine/Beer *(6 mi.)*, Liquor Store *(11 mi.)*, Farmers' Market *(Irvington 1st Sat of month, 8 mi.)*, Fishmonger *(Captain's Choice Seafood 435-6750, 6 mi.)*, Market *(River Market 435-1725, 6 mi.)*, Bank/ATM *(Bank of Lancaster/South Side Bank, 5 mi.)*, Library *(Lancaster Community Library 435-1729, 10 mi.)*, Beauty Salon *(Cheryl's Hair Salon 435-2230, 6 mi.)*, Dry Cleaners *(Henderson Cleaners 435-1249, 11 mi.)*, Bookstore *(Book Nook 435-3355, 10 mi.)*, Pharmacy *(Medicine Shoppe 776-9990, 6 mi.)*

Transportation

OnSite: Bikes *(Free)* **OnCall:** Rental Car *(Enterprise 435-1851)*
Airport: Newport News/Richmond *(45 mi./57 mi.)*

Medical Services

911 Service **OnCall:** Ambulance **3+ mi:** Doctor *(White Stone Family Practice 435-3133, 7 mi.)*, Dentist *(Antonio 435-6466, 7 mi.)*, Chiropractor *(Pure N'Simple 435-2273, 10 mi.)*, Veterinarian *(Bayside Animal Hospital 435-2896, 7 mi.)* **Hospital:** Rappahannock General 435-8000 *(9 mi.)*

Setting -- On the south side of deep Locklies Creek, six piers - hosting over 130 sailboats - march along the forested shore. Regent Point's carefully maintained, pretty upland, actually a peninsula, is reminiscent of the Adirondacks - a floor of pine needles shaded by towering evergreens, with swaths of well-clipped lawn stretched along the sunny shore. Nestled in the pines are two pyramidal-roofed picnic pavilions, a basketball hoop above a shuffleboard court, a wooden swing and slide set, and a couple of perfectly placed hammocks inviting parents to laze while the kids play.

Marina Notes -- Sold in December 2004 to current owners. Primarily a sailboat marina. The office is in a small single story structure with signature pyramidal roof. Plenty of depth right at the mouth of the creek. 30 amp service on the posts at the dock. Token-operated pumpout - offered since 1978! Extensive, very neat on-the-hard storage, partially graveled and partially grassed, is a few steps up - discreetly separated by stone-walled terracing. A washer & dryer are located in the open air locker building. The inviting climate controlled bathhouse is in an attractive two-story greige building.

Notable -- Right outside the entrance to Regent Point is the $1.4 million William and Mary Kauffman Aquaculture Center. Dedicated in April '04, it is part of the Virginia Institute of Marine Science and College of William and Mary. VIMS is considered one of the top ocean and coastal sciences research centers. Much of the work being done at its Aquaculture Genetics and Breeding Technology Center at Gloucester Point is being extended to Kauffman - including studies on native and Asian oysters (Crassostrea Virginica and the non-native oyster C. Ariakensis) which are quarantined in the lab.

PHOTOS ON CD-ROM: 11

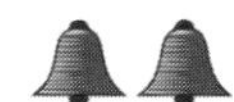

Navigational Information
Lat: 37°35.610' **Long:** 076°26.193' **Tide:** 2 ft. **Current:** 3 kt. **Chart:** 12235
Rep. Depths (*MLW*): Entry 7 ft. **Fuel Dock** n/a **Max Slip/Moor** 6 ft./-
Access: Buoy #9, White Stone Bridge, to Locklies Creek on south side

Marina Facilities *(In Season/Off Season)*
Fuel: Gasoline, Diesel
Slips: 58 Total, 17 Transient **Max LOA:** 45 ft. **Max Beam:** 16 ft.
Rate *(per ft.)*: **Day** $25.00 **Week** $100 **Month** $300
Power: 30 amp TBD**, **50 amp** TBD**, **100 amp** n/a, **200 amp** n/a
Cable TV: No **Dockside Phone:** No
Dock Type: Fixed, Short Fingers, Pilings
Moorings: 0 Total, 0 Transient **Launch:** n/a
Rate: Day n/a **Week** n/a **Month** n/a
Heads: 2 Toilet(s), 1 Shower(s)
Laundry: None **Pay Phones:** No
Pump-Out: OnSite, Full Service, 1 Central **Fee:** $10 **Closed Heads:** Yes

Marina Operations
Owner/Manager: Jack Mazmanian **Dockmaster:** Same
In-Season: Mar-Dec, Dusk-Dawn **Off-Season:** Jan-Feb, Closed
After-Hours Arrival: Call ahead
Reservations: Yes, Preferred **Credit Cards:** Visa/MC, Dscvr
Discounts: Boat/US **Dockage:** n/a **Fuel:** $0.10/gal **Repair:** n/a
Pets: Welcome **Handicap Access:** No

Locklies Marina

PO Box 517; 784 Locklies Creek Road; Topping, VA 23169

Tel: (804) 758-2871; (888) 860-1014 **VHF: Monitor** All **Talk** 68
Fax: (804) 758-0232 **Alternate Tel:** n/a
Email: lockliesmarina@aol.com **Web:** www.lockliesmarina.com
Nearest Town: Topping *(1 mi.)* **Tourist Info:** (804) 843-4499

Marina Services and Boat Supplies
Communication - FedEx, UPS, Express Mail **Supplies - OnSite:** Ice *(Block, Cube)*, Ships' Store, Bait/Tackle, Live Bait **Under 1 mi:** Propane **3+ mi:** West Marine *(776-0400, 12 mi.)*

Boatyard Services
OnSite: Launching Ramp *(2)*, Yacht Broker *(22-32 ft. power)* **OnCall:** Engine mechanic *(gas, diesel)* **Near:** Travelift *(30T)*, Electronic Sales & Repairs, Hull Repairs, Rigger, Sail Loft, Canvas Work, Bottom Cleaning, Brightwork, Air Conditioning, Refrigeration, Divers, Compound, Wash & Wax, Interior Cleaning, Propeller Repairs, Woodworking, Inflatable Repairs, Life Raft Service, Yacht Interiors, Metal Fabrication, Painting, Awlgrip. **Nearest Yard:** Regent Point (804) 758-4457

Restaurants and Accommodations
Under 1 mi: Restaurant *(Rudy's Pizza & Deli 758-0605, L $4-10, D $4-10, dinners, pizza and deli)* **1-3 mi:** Restaurant *(Eckhard's 758-4060, Daily specials, prime rib Fri & Sat)*, Motel *(Beacon 758-2262)* **3+ mi:** Restaurant *(Sandpiper 435-6176, 6 mi.)*, *(Rice's Inn 435-3550, 8 mi.)*, *(Galley 776-6040, L $6-10, D $6-10, 6 mi.)*, *(Taylor's 776-9611, B $2-5, L $5-8, D $6-20, 7 mi.)*, *(Toby's 776-6913, L $5-10, D $8-18, 6 mi.)*, Snack Bar *(Sweet Shoppe 776-7021, B $2-4, L $3-6, 6 mi.)*, Motel *(St. Andrews Motel 435-1101, 6 mi.)*, Inn/B&B *(Inn at Woodstock 776-9877, 7 mi.)*

Recreation and Entertainment
OnSite: Picnic Area, Grills, Boat Rentals, Fishing Charter *(largest fleet in Virginia)*, Special Events *(Live Bands & Crab Feasts, Blessing of the Fleet, Northern Neck Anglers Club Tournament Series, Southern Chesapeake Leukemia Cup Poker Run)* **1-3 mi:** Jogging Paths, Video Rental *(Vanity Video 758-9604)*, Park **3+ mi:** Golf Course *(Piankatank River Golf Club 776-6589, 6 mi.)*, Bowling *(Evans Bowling Center 435-3950, 10 mi.)*, Movie Theater *(Lancaster Players Playhouse 435-3776, 6 mi.)*, Museum *(Steam Boat Museum 438-6888, 8 mi.)*

Provisioning and General Services
OnSite: Oysterman *(Chesapeake Bay Oyster Farms)* **Under 1 mi:** Green Grocer *(Taylor's Fresh Vegetable Stand)*, Catholic Church, Beauty Salon *(Majestic Nails 758-1999)*, Retail Shops *(Two Bees A Buzzin Gift Shop)* **1-3 mi:** Delicatessen *(East Pizza & Deli 758-0605)*, Bank/ATM, Post Office *(758-4100)* **3+ mi:** Health Food *(Higher Health Foods 436-0011, 10 mi.)*, Fishmonger *(Captain's Choice Seafood 435-6750, 5 mi.)*, Market *(Town & Country 776-6131, River Market 435-1725, 8 mi.)*, Library *(Lancaster Community Library 435-1729, 10 mi.)*, Dry Cleaners *(Henderson Cleaners 435-1249, 10 mi.)*, Bookstore *(Book Nook 435-3355, 10 mi.)*, Pharmacy *(Medicine Shoppe 776-9990, 8 mi.)*, Hardware Store *(Hurd's 776-9241, 8 mi.)*

Transportation
OnCall: Bikes, Water Taxi, Rental Car *(Enterprise 435-1851)*
Airport: Newport News/Richmond *(45 mi./57 mi.)*

Medical Services
911 Service **OnCall:** Ambulance **1-3 mi:** Dentist *(Smithea 758-2573)* **3+ mi:** Doctor *(Chesapeake Medical 776-9221, 8 mi.)*, Chiropractor *(Pure 'N' Simple 435-2273, 10 mi.)* **Hospital:** Rappahannock General 435-8000 *(8 mi.)*

Setting -- On the northern shore of Locklies Creek is rural, down-home Locklies Marina. The sweet peachy-pink store with bright blue trim is the base of operations. A tumble of chairs and potted plants line the front porch under a pergola arbor inviting boaters to sit a while, chat and watch the creek and dock traffic. Stern-to docks line the bulkhead and a large L-shaped pier embraces the basin. Several more piers poke into the creek as well.

Marina Notes -- *Flat fees for dockage. **Anticipate power to be installed before '06 season - inquire. Helpful management. Oldest marina in Virginia, it's known for oysters and crabbers. Casual shop has tackle, bait, drinks, chips and basic sundries. Some docks are stern-to with no finger piers and others have very short finger piers. Mix of pleasure and working craft. USCG courtesy inspections. Devastated by Isabel in '03, the marina is slowly recovering. Part of that is the installation of a new wave attenuator outboard of the docks. The rustic bathhouse has two heads and two sinks and a new shower.

Notable -- Locklies promises great local color and a newly arrived fleet of wooden Chesapeake Deadrisers. A downeast-style weathered clapboard building headquarters Chesapeake Bay Oyster Farms; their hatchery is in and around the docks. Locklies is also using some of the pilings left from Isabel for its own oyster beds. And across the creek, the new Kauffman Aquaculture Center is experimenting with new oyster breeds. A little less than a mile is Hummel Field, a local private plane airstrip; Hummel Aviation rents airplanes and gives lessons. A bit further is Rappahannock Crossing strip mall with Two Bees a Buzzin' gift shop, Rudy's Pizza and Deli, Movie Time, Majestic Nails & Tanning and, across the street, Taylor's Fresh Vegetable Stand. Everything else is 7 miles or more.

PHOTOS ON CD-ROM: 7

Rappahannock Yachts

Rappahannock Yachts

PO Box 64; 70 Rappahannock Road; Irvington, VA 22480

Tel: (804) 438-5353 **VHF: Monitor** 16 **Talk** 16
Fax: (804) 438-6907 **Alternate Tel:** n/a
Email: info@rappyachts.com **Web:** www.rappyachts.com
Nearest Town: Irvington *(0.5 mi.)* **Tourist Info:** (804) 435-6092

Navigational Information

Lat: 37°39.426' **Long:** 076°26.057' **Tide:** 1 ft. **Current:** 1 kt. **Chart:** 12235
Rep. Depths (*MLW*): Entry 12 ft. **Fuel Dock** n/a **Max Slip/Moor** 10 ft./-
Access: N. Shore Rappahannock River to Carter Creek, just west of bridge

Marina Facilities *(In Season/Off Season)*

Fuel: No
Slips: 40 Total, 2 Transient **Max LOA:** 50 ft. **Max Beam:** 17 1/2 ft.
Rate *(per ft.)*: **Day** $25.00* **Week** n/a **Month** n/a
Power: 30 amp Incl., **50 amp** n/a, **100 amp** n/a, **200 amp** n/a
Cable TV: No **Dockside Phone:** No
Dock Type: Fixed, Short Fingers, Pilings, Alongside, Wood
Moorings: 0 Total, 0 Transient **Launch:** n/a
Rate: Day n/a **Week** n/a **Month** n/a
Heads: 2 Toilet(s), 2 Shower(s)
Laundry: None **Pay Phones:** No
Pump-Out: No **Fee:** n/a **Closed Heads:** Yes

Marina Operations

Owner/Manager: Bruce Sanders **Dockmaster:** Patsy Panis
In-Season: Year-Round, 8-5pm **Off-Season:** Dec 20-Mar 1, closed wkends.
After-Hours Arrival: Call in advance
Reservations: Required **Credit Cards:** Visa/MC
Discounts: None
Pets: Welcome **Handicap Access:** No

Marina Services and Boat Supplies

Services - Docking Assistance, Trash Pick-Up, Dock Carts **Communication -** Mail & Package Hold, Phone Messages, Fax in/out, FedEx, UPS, Express Mail **Supplies - OnSite:** Ships' Store **Near:** Ice *(Cube)*, Bait/Tackle, Live Bait

Boatyard Services

OnSite: Travelift *(30T)*, Engine mechanic *(gas, diesel)*, Electrical Repairs, Electronics Repairs, Hull Repairs, Rigger, Brightwork, Compound, Wash & Wax, Interior Cleaning, Woodworking, Painting, Awlgrip, Yacht Design, Yacht Building **OnCall:** Sail Loft, Canvas Work, Bottom Cleaning, Air Conditioning, Refrigeration, Divers, Propeller Repairs, Life Raft Service, Upholstery, Metal Fabrication **Near:** Launching Ramp. **Member:** ABYC - 2 Certified Tech(s), Other Certifications: Diesel **Yard Rates:** $45.50/hr., Haul & Launch $6/ft. *(blocking incl.)*, Power Wash Incl., Bottom Paint $10/ft. *(paint incl.)* **Storage:** In-Water $200/mo., On-Land $2/ft/mo.

Restaurants and Accommodations

OnCall: Pizzeria *(Pizza Hut 435-3551)* **Under 1 mi:** Restaurant *(Trick Dog Café 438-1055, L $9-12, D $17-25)*, *(Chesapeake Club 438-4427, L $8-14, D $16-28, at the Tides plus 3 other eateries)*, Coffee Shop *(Roundtable 438-5884)*, *(The Local 438-9356, B $2-4, L $6-8, Mon-Thu 7:30am-3pm, Fri & Sat 7:30am-5pm, Sun 7:30-11am; Wi-Fi)*, Hotel *(Tides Inn 438-5000, $200-550)*, Inn/B&B *(Hope & Glory 438-6953, $160-280, T&L's 30 Great Inns)* **1-3 mi:** Restaurant *(Sand Piper 438-6176)*, Hotel *(Holiday Inn 438-1500)*

Recreation and Entertainment

OnSite: Sightseeing *("Deja Vu" a 1935 Elco Cruisette - 1.5 hrs. 438-1212; or stroll the streets with Irvington Bus. Assoc's village map)* **Near:** Pool, Beach, Picnic Area, Grills, Jogging Paths, Fishing Charter, Galleries *(Old Post Office)* **Under 1 mi:** Tennis Courts, Museum *(Steam Boat 438-6888)*, Cultural Attract *(White Fences Vineyard)* **1-3 mi:** Golf Course *(Golden Eagle 438-9063)*, Movie Theater *(Lancaster Players 435-3776)*

Provisioning and General Services

Near: Convenience Store *(Mom & Pops 438-6958)*, Meat Market, Newsstand **Under 1 mi:** Farmers' Market *(Irvington Farmers' Market - 1st Sat of month, 8am-noon, Irvington Commons 438-5447)*, Bank/ATM, Post Office *(438-5033)*, Catholic Church, Protestant Church, Florist, Clothing Store *(Dandelion Gifts & Clothes, Khaki's, Avalon)* **1-3 mi:** Wine/Beer, Liquor Store, Fishmonger *(Captain's Choice 435-6750)*, Market *(River Market 435-1725)*, Beauty Salon *(Anjel's Hare 438-9346)*, Barber Shop, Copies Etc. **3+ mi:** Supermarket *(Tri-Star 435-3800, 5 mi.)*, Library *(Lancaster 435-1729, 6 mi.)*, Pharmacy *(White Stone 435-1051, 4 mi.)*, Hardware Store *(Lamberth 435-1695, 6 mi.)*

Transportation

OnCall: Rental Car *(Enterprise 435-1851)*, Taxi *(Howards 24 hr. 435-9348)* **Airport:** Newport News/Richmond *(52 mi./65 mi.)*

Medical Services

911 Service **OnCall:** Ambulance **Under 1 mi:** Dentist *(Westbrook 438-1000)* **3+ mi:** Doctor *(White Stone 435-3133, 4 mi.)*, Veterinarian *(Kilmarnock 435-6320, 6 mi.)* **Hospital:** Rappahannock 435-8000 *(6 mi.)*

Setting -- Just past the Rappahannock Yacht Club on the east side of Carter Creek, Rappahannock Yachts' buttoned-up boatyard backs a small network of stationary docks hosting a seasonal fleet of upscale vessels - many of them impeccably restored vintage craft. The two-story charcoal and white main office building is surrounded by a well-tended graveled yard for dry storage. A simple dockhouse sits at the end of the main pier.

Marina Notes -- *Flat rate. Primarily a boatyard with seasonal slips. Transient dockage is on a T-head - usually 2 spots available with solid power boxes up on the pilings. The yard has specialized in yacht restoration since the early 1970s and can provide most services. Extensive on-the-hard storage. Travelift bay for 30 ton lift. C. Scott Vail Yacht Brokerage is located on the 2nd floor. Simple, but clean and neat cement-floored cinderblock bathhouse has wallpaper borders just below the ceiling, fish swimming on the walls, and fresh new shower curtains. (The Rappahannock Y.C. may have a slip for reciprocal members.)

Notable -- An easy walk is the pitch-perfect little village of Irvington. With the mid-century development of The Tides resorts, the FFVs and many others headed to this quaint bend in the "Rivah" for the summer. Over time, their presence encouraged a handful of unique, chic, upscale shops, restaurants and lodgings. A half mile up the road, whimsical, eccentric Hope & Glory Inn, a remodeled 1800s schoolhouse, has garnered extraordinary international press. And a bit farther, the now-famous Trick Dog Café lends a bit of urban cachet to this tiny, touristed town - Choose bar, white tablecloth or outside dining. For Internet access, grab a coffee at The Local - then browse the shops that surround it or head to the spectacularly renovated Tides for a casual meal or formal dinner.

Navigational Information
Lat: 37°39.464' **Long:** 076°26.070' **Tide:** 2 ft. **Current:** 1 kt. **Chart:** 12235
Rep. Depths (*MLW*): Entry 12 ft. **Fuel Dock** 12 ft. **Max Slip/Moor** 12 ft./12 ft.
Access: 4 mi. up Rappahannock from bridge, right into Carter Creek

Marina Facilities *(In Season/Off Season)*
Fuel: *Chevron* - Gasoline, Diesel
Slips: 50 Total, 4 Transient **Max LOA:** 40 ft. **Max Beam:** n/a
Rate *(per ft.)*: **Day** $1.00 **Week** n/a **Month** n/a
Power: 30 amp Incl., **50 amp** n/a, **100 amp** n/a, **200 amp** n/a
Cable TV: Yes **Dockside Phone:** No
Dock Type: Fixed, Concrete, Wood
Moorings: 0 Total, 0 Transient **Launch:** n/a, Dinghy Dock
Rate: Day n/a **Week** n/a **Month** n/a
Heads: 2 Toilet(s), 2 Shower(s)
Laundry: None, Book Exchange **Pay Phones:** No
Pump-Out: OnSite, Full Service, 1 Central **Fee:** $20 **Closed Heads:** Yes

Marina Operations
Owner/Manager: Andy Wylie, Sr. **Dockmaster:** Same
In-Season: Year-Round, 8am-5pm **Off-Season:** n/a
After-Hours Arrival: Make fast and call dockmaster
Reservations: Yes, Preferred **Credit Cards:** Visa/MC
Discounts: None
Pets: Welcome, Dog Walk Area **Handicap Access:** No

Irvington Marina

PO Box 189; 201 Carters Creek Road; Irvington, VA 22480

Tel: (804) 438-5113 **VHF: Monitor** n/a **Talk** n/a
Fax: (804) 438-5113 **Alternate Tel:** n/a
Email: n/a **Web:** n/a
Nearest Town: Irvington *(0.5 mi.)* **Tourist Info:** (804) 435-6092

Marina Services and Boat Supplies
Services - Docking Assistance, Dock Carts **Communication -** Mail & Package Hold, Phone Messages, Fax in/out, Data Ports *(at The Local)*, FedEx, UPS, Express Mail **Supplies - OnSite:** Ice *(Cube)*, Ships' Store **1-3 mi:** Bait/Tackle *(Captain's Choice)*, Propane

Boatyard Services
OnSite: Engine mechanic *(gas, diesel)*, Electrical Repairs, Electronics Repairs, Hull Repairs, Rigger, Canvas Work, Bottom Cleaning, Metal Fabrication **3+ mi:** Travelift *(25T)*. **Yard Rates:** $30/hr., Haul & Launch $4/ft.

Restaurants and Accommodations
Under 1 mi: Restaurant *(Chesapeake Club L $8-14, D $16-28, at the Tides)*, *(Trick Dog Café 438-1055, L $9-12, D $17-25)*, Coffee Shop *(The Local 438-9356, B $2-4, L $6-8, Mon-Thu 7:30am-3pm, Fri & Sat 7:30am-5pm, Sun 7:30-11am; Wi-Fi)*, *(Roundtable 438-5884)*, Hotel *(Tides Inn 538-4000, $200-550, Check phone)*, Inn/B&B *(Hope and Glory Inn 438-6053, $160-280, T&L's 30 top inns)* **1-3 mi:** Restaurant *(Rice's Inn 435-4550)*, *(Willaby's Café 435-0044)*, Inn/B&B *(Kendall Hall Inn 438-6927)* **3+ mi:** Pizzeria *(Pizza Hut 435-3551, 6 mi.)*, Motel *(Whispering Pines 435-1101, $60-85, 3 mi.)*, *(St. Andrews 435-1101, 4 mi.)*

Recreation and Entertainment
Near: Sightseeing *("Deja Vu," a 1935 Elco Cruisette - 1.5 hrs. 438-1212; or stroll the streets with Irvington Business Assoc.'s village map)*
Under 1 mi: Playground, Museum *(Steam Boat 438-6888)*, Cultural Attract *(White Fences Vineyard)*, Galleries *(Old Post Office)*
1-3 mi: Golf Course *(Golden Eagle 438-9063)*, Movie Theater *(Lancaster Players Playhouse 435-3776)* **3+ mi:** Bowling *(Evans 435-3950, 6 mi.)*, Video Rental *(B&D Video 435-1504, 4 mi.)*

Provisioning and General Services
Near: Convenience Store *(Chris Mart III 438-5605; Mom & Pops 438-6958)*, Farmers' Market *(Irvington Farmers' Market - 1st Sat of mon, 8am-noon, Irvington Commons 438-5447)*, Protestant Church *(Baptist, Methodist)*
Under 1 mi: Bank/ATM *(Chesapeake Bank)*, Post Office *(438-5033)*, Clothing Store *(The Dandelion, Khaki's, Avalon, Maybebaby)*, Retail Shops *(River Lifestyle, Time to Cook, Duncan & Drake, Village Needlepoint)* **1-3 mi:** Wine/Beer, Fishmonger *(Captain's Choice Seafood 435-6750)*, Market *(River Market 435-1725)*, Beauty Salon, Barber Shop **3+ mi:** Supermarket *(Tri-Star Supermarket 435-3800, 5 mi.)*, Delicatessen *(Bay Breeze Deli 435-7796, 6 mi.)*, Health Food *(Higher Health Foods 436-0011, 7 mi.)*, Library *(Lancaster Community Library 435-1729, 6 mi.)*, Dry Cleaners *(6 mi.)*, Bookstore *(Book Nook 435-3355, 6 mi.)*, Pharmacy *(White Stone 435-1051, 5 mi.)*, Hardware Store *(Lamberth 435-1695, 6 mi.)*

Transportation
OnCall: Rental Car *(Enterprise 435-1851)*, Taxi *(Howards 24 hrs. 435-9348)* **Airport:** Newport News/Richmond *(52 mi./65 mi.)*

Medical Services
911 Service **OnCall:** Ambulance **Under 1 mi:** Dentist *(Westbrook 438-1000)* **3+ mi:** Doctor *(White Stone 435-3133, 4 mi.)*, Chiropractor *(Northern Neck Chiropractic Acupuncture 435-3333, 6 mi.)*, Veterinarian *(Kilmarnock 435-6320, 6 mi.)* **Hospital:** Rappahannock General 435-8000 *(6 mi.)*

Setting -- On the eastern shore of Carter Creek, just past Rappahannock Yachts, Irvington Marina is a bit of an anachronism in this sleepy, upscale and tidy community. It is a work in progress, as it gradually evolves from an almost derelict old-time boatyard to a convenient, easily accessible pleasure craft marina - like a phoenix rising from the ashes. Landside, its location is equally ideal - within an easy walk of the enchanting little village of Irvington.

Marina Notes -- A hurricane in '03, followed by a tornado in '04 only complicated the acres of boatyard detritus that had been escalating for decades. 3 new piers will be going in over time - first 30, 60 and then another 30 slips to accommodate up to 40' on the T-head - with nine feet of draft. Two new transient docks are already in with satellite TV and power. It's the beginning of the process. New power on the docks and 3 new filter systems on the fuel dock. New pumpout. 3 mechanics, 2 electricians, 4 carpenters. There's also an aluminum foundry, specializing in die casting and sand casting. Primary product is hand wheels for big valves, but they will cast anything needed - mast trucks, boom goosenecks, or other critical, no-longer-made parts.

Notable -- Irvington, also referred to as Carter Creek, was a bustling steamboat stop and oyster capital from the late 19th C. through the mid-thirties. A fire in 1917 and the end of the steamboat era two decades later conspired to close down the town. Then in 1947, The Tides Inn resort was built and it once again became a destination. Many original buildings have been restored - as B&B's (the renowned Hope & Glory, for instance) or restaurants (Trick Dog's reputation is bicoastal) or delightful shops featuring high-end clothing, housewares and specialty foods. Today Irvington claims the priciest real estate in the region.

PHOTOS ON CD-ROM: 8

The Tides Inn & Marina

PO Box 480; 480 King Carter Drive; Irvington, VA 22480

Tel: (804) 438-5000; (800) 843-3746 **VHF: Monitor** 9 **Talk** 69
Fax: (804) 438-5222 **Alternate Tel:** (804) 438-5000
Email: info@tidesinn.com **Web:** www.tidesinn.com
Nearest Town: Irvington *(0.5 mi.)* **Tourist Info:** (804) 435-6092

Navigational Information

Lat: 37°39.827' **Long:** 076°25.967' **Tide:** 2 ft. **Current:** n/a **Chart:** 12235
Rep. Depths (*MLW*): Entry 9 ft. **Fuel Dock** 6 ft. **Max Slip/Moor** 9 ft./-
Access: North side of river to Carter Creek

Marina Facilities *(In Season/Off Season)*

Fuel: Gasoline, Diesel
Slips: 60 Total, 60 Transient **Max LOA:** 125 ft. **Max Beam:** n/a
Rate *(per ft.)*: **Day** $1.95/$1.50* **Week** Inq. **Month** Inq.
Power: 30 amp $5, **50 amp** $10, **100 amp** $20, **200 amp** n/a
Cable TV: Yes **Dockside Phone:** Yes, Switchboard per call
Dock Type: Fixed, Long Fingers, Short Fingers, Pilings
Moorings: 0 Total, 0 Transient **Launch:** n/a
Rate: Day n/a **Week** n/a **Month** n/a
Heads: 10 Toilet(s), 8 Shower(s) *(with dressing rooms)*, Hair Dryers, Towels
Laundry: 2 Washer(s), 2 Dryer(s), Iron, Iron Board **Pay Phones:** No
Pump-Out: OnSite, Full Service, 18 InSlip **Fee:** $5 **Closed Heads:** Yes

Marina Operations

Owner/Manager: John Paulette **Dockmaster:** Same
In-Season: Mem-LabDay, 8am-6pm **Off-Season:** Lab-MemDay, 8:30am-5pm
After-Hours Arrival: Front desk registration
Reservations: Yes, Preferred **Credit Cards:** Visa/MC, Dscvr, Din, Amex
Discounts: None **Dockage:** n/a **Fuel:** $0.10/gal+200 **Repair:** n/a
Pets: Welcome, Dog Walk Area **Handicap Access:** Yes, Heads, Docks

Marina Services and Boat Supplies

Services - Docking Assistance, Concierge, Room Service to the Boat, Security, Trash Pick-Up, Dock Carts, Megayacht Facilities **Communication -** Mail & Package Hold, Phone Messages, Fax in/out *($1/p)*, Data Ports *(View Sitting Room - Wi-Fi or Cat-5)*, FedEx, DHL, UPS **Supplies - OnSite:** Ice *(Cube)*, Ships' Store *(limited)* **3+ mi:** Bait/Tackle *(Pride of VA 435-6740, 4 mi.)*

Boatyard Services

OnCall: Divers, Compound, Wash & Wax, Interior Cleaning **Under 1 mi:** Travelift *(30T)*. **Nearest Yard:** Rappahannock Yachts (804) 438-5353

Restaurants and Accommodations

OnSite: Restaurant *(Cap'n B's L & D $7-11, at the golf club, New Orleans-style)*, *(Chesapeake Club L $8-18, D $13-28, L 11am-5pm, D 5-10pm - smart casual)*, *(Commodores 438-5000, L $7-14, D $$10-21, pool-side; L daily; D Fri & Sat 5:30-9:30pm; casual)*, *(The Dinning Room B $8-15, D $20-35, B 6:30-10:30am, D 5:30-9:30pm; res. required; jackets after 5pm)*, Hotel *(Tides Inn 438-5000, $195-850)* **Under 1 mi:** Inn/B&B *(Hope and Glory 438-6053)* **1-3 mi:** Restaurant *(Trick Dog Café 438-1055, L $9-12, D $17-25)*, Coffee Shop *(The Local 438-9356, B $2-4, L $6-8)* **3+ mi:** *Fast Food (6 mi.)*, Pizzeria *(Pizza Hut 435-3551, 6 mi.)*, Motel *(Whispering Pines 435-1101, $60-85, 3 mi.)*

Recreation and Entertainment

OnSite: Pool, Spa, Beach, Picnic Area, Grills, Playground, Tennis Courts, Golf Course *(Golden Eagle $57-85/round, incl. cart)*, Fitness Center *(circuit training, treadmills, etc. complimentary)*, Jogging Paths, Boat Rentals *(Duffy electric boat, 8am-6pm, $60/hr.; complimentary kayaks, canoes & paddle boats)*, Volleyball, Video Rental **OnCall:** Fishing Charter
Under 1 mi: Museum *(Steam Boat Museum 438-6888)*
1-3 mi: Sightseeing *(White Fences Vineyard and Winery)*

Provisioning and General Services

OnSite: Dry Cleaners, Laundry *(hotel service)*, Newsstand, Clothing Store, Retail Shops, Copies Etc. **Near:** Convenience Store *(Mom & Pops 438-6958)*, Bank/ATM **Under 1 mi:** Post Office *(438-5033)* **1-3 mi:** Wine/Beer, Fishmonger *(Captain's Choice 435-6750)*, Market *(River Market 435-1725)*, Catholic Church, Protestant Church, Pharmacy *(White Stone 435-3784)*, Florist **3+ mi:** Supermarket *(Tri-Star 435-3800, 5 mi.)*, Delicatessen *(Bay Breeze 435-7796, 6 mi.)*, Library *(Lancaster Community Library 435-1729, 6 mi.)*, Bookstore *(Book Nook 435-3355, 6 mi.)*, Hardware Store *(Lamberth Building Materials 435-1695, 4 mi.)*

Transportation

OnSite: Courtesy Car/Van *(van trips into town: 10:30, 2:30, 6:30 & 9:30, last 2 for restaurants)*, Bikes *(complimentary - kids bikes, too - 8am-7pm/dark)*, Water Taxi **OnCall:** Rental Car *(Local Dodge dealer or Enterprise 435-1851 from Gloucester 10% disc.)*, Taxi *(Howards 24 hr. 435-9348)*, Airport Limo
Airport: Newport News/Richmond *(52 mi./65 mi.)*

Medical Services

911 Service **OnSite:** Holistic Services *(full-service spa; The Tides Inn 9am-7pm - 60 min massage $105 - overlooks the water garden & creek)* **OnCall:** Ambulance **Under 1 mi:** Dentist *(Westbrook 438-1000)* **3+ mi:** Doctor *(White Stone 435-3133, 4 mi.)* **Hospital:** Rappahannock 435-8000 *(6 mi.)*

Setting -- Perched on a bluff above the single main pier, The Tides Inn's simple three-story white buildings with brick red roofs are strung along the shore - with magnificent views of Carter Creek. Brick paths wind up the terraced hillside amid azaleas, magnolias and carefully tended gardens. A wide sand beach, large heated pool, 4 eateries, full-service marina, serious spa, 27-hole golf course, and 106-room hotel all benefited from a recent multi-million dollar renovation.

Marina Notes -- *MemDay-LabDay: Sun-Thu $1.95/ft., Fri-Sat $2.25/ft., $65 min. Holidays 2-night min, July 4th $3/ft. 3 nites or $100 min. Low seas $1.50/ft. (No minimum for lodging guests). An '01 facelift by new owner, Sedona Resorts, turned elegant bones and a fabulous location into a Leading Small Hotel of the World. A guest of the marina is a guest of the resort. New pedestals with cable & phone to main switchboard. Across the creek, there are 45 more transient slips - a little water taxi zips over and back - perfect for club cruises. Special rates/transport for golf. Crab Net Kids Club $45/day, $25-30/half day. British Colonial-style rooms & suites have balconies, water views and gorgeous marble baths. All-tile boaters' bathhouse has fiberglass showers, dressing rooms & hotel amenities, including towels and hair dryers. Complimentary laundry room with folding table.

Notable -- Cruises on the "Rivah" aboard the newly refurbished 125-foot 1926 yacht "Miss Ann" is The Tides' signature experience. A boardwalk skirts the sand beach and a few steps up is the pool surrounded by chaises and umbrellas. Nautically-themed, casual Commodores has director's chairs and natural

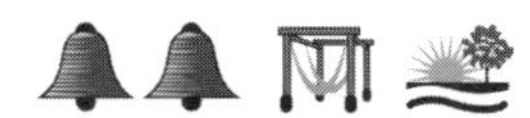

Navigational Information
Lat: 37°41.647' **Long:** 076°29.386' **Tide:** 2 ft. **Current:** .2 kt. **Chart:** 12235
Rep. Depths (*MLW*): Entry 8 ft. **Fuel Dock** 8 ft. **Max Slip/Moor** 8 ft./12 ft.
Access: Rappahannock to Corrotoman River to Myer Creek

Marina Facilities *(In Season/Off Season)*
Fuel: Gasoline, Diesel
Slips: 105 Total, 10 Transient **Max LOA:** 127 ft. **Max Beam:** 20 ft.
Rate *(per ft.)*: **Day** $1.00 **Week** $60 **Month** $185
Power: 30 amp $3.50, **50 amp** n/a, **100 amp** n/a, **200 amp** n/a
Cable TV: Yes **Dockside Phone:** Yes
Dock Type: Fixed, Pilings, Alongside, Wood
Moorings: 0 Total, 0 Transient **Launch:** n/a, Dinghy Dock
Rate: Day n/a **Week** n/a **Month** n/a
Heads: 6 Toilet(s), 4 Shower(s) *(with dressing rooms)*
Laundry: 1 Washer(s), 1 Dryer(s), Book Exchange **Pay Phones:** Yes, 1
Pump-Out: OnSite, Self Service, 1 Central **Fee:** Free **Closed Heads:** Yes

Marina Operations
Owner/Manager: Ken Knull **Dockmaster:** Karen Knull
In-Season: Apr-Oct, 9am-4:30pm **Off-Season:** Nov-Mar, 8am-4:30pm
After-Hours Arrival: Take any available slip
Reservations: Preferred **Credit Cards:** Visa/MC, Dscvr
Discounts: Boat/US **Dockage:** Inq. **Fuel:** n/a **Repair:** n/a
Pets: Welcome, Dog Walk Area **Handicap Access:** Yes, Heads

Yankee Point Sailboat Marina

1303 Oak Hill Road; Lancaster, VA 22503

Tel: (804) 462-7018 **VHF: Monitor** 16 **Talk** 68
Fax: (804) 462-6225 **Alternate Tel:** (804) 462-9836
Email: ken@yankeepointmarina.com **Web:** www.yankeepointmarina.com
Nearest Town: Kilmarnock *(16 mi.)* **Tourist Info:** (804) 435-6092

Marina Services and Boat Supplies
Services - Docking Assistance, Boaters' Lounge, Trash Pick-Up, Dock Carts **Communication -** Mail & Package Hold, Phone Messages, Fax in/out, Data Ports *(In office, 56K)*, FedEx, DHL, UPS *(Sat Del)* **Supplies - OnSite:** Ice *(Block, Cube)*, Ships' Store **Under 1 mi:** Propane *(Village Center)* **1-3 mi:** Bait/Tackle **3+ mi:** Live Bait *(5 mi.)*

Boatyard Services
OnSite: Travelift *(40T)*, Launching Ramp, Engine mechanic *(gas, diesel)*, Electrical Repairs, Electronics Repairs, Hull Repairs, Rigger, Sail Loft, Canvas Work, Bottom Cleaning, Brightwork, Air Conditioning, Refrigeration, Divers, Compound, Wash & Wax, Interior Cleaning, Propeller Repairs, Woodworking, Inflatable Repairs, Life Raft Service, Upholstery, Yacht Interiors, Metal Fabrication, Painting, Awlgrip, Yacht Building, Total Refits, Yacht Broker *(Yankee Point Marina Service Association)* **Dealer for:** Yanmar, Quantum Sails, Vanguard. **Member:** ABBRA - 1 Certified Tech(s), ABYC - 3 Certified Tech(s), Other Certifications: 1 Cummins, CAT, ISUZU **Yard Rates:** $35-55/hr., Haul & Launch $6/ft. (min. $180.00) *(blocking incl.)*, Power Wash Incl., Bottom Paint $14/ft. *(paint incl.)* **Storage:** In-Water $4.50/ft., On-Land $2.50/ft. (min. $62.50)

Restaurants and Accommodations
OnSite: Snack Bar, Condo/Cottage *(Inn at Yankee Point 462-7018, $150, 2 br cottage with dock)* **3+ mi:** Restaurant *(Thai Pot 436-8424, L $7-10, D$10-16, 6 mi., has take out)*, *(Trick Dog Cafe 438-1055, B $8-10, D $18-27, 5 mi, Sunday brunch 11am-2pm, no lunch)*, Coffee Shop *(Something Different 758-8000, L $4-10, D $4-10, 5 mi, on the other side of the river - roasts coffee beans on premises)*, Inn/B&B *(Inn at Levelfields 435-6887, $60-110, 14 mi.)*

Recreation and Entertainment
OnSite: Beach, Picnic Area, Grills, Playground, Boat Rentals *(Sunfish, canoes)*, Special Events *(Turkey shoot regatta - Oct, Non Profit Boat Auction - May)* **1-3 mi:** Video Rental, Park **3+ mi:** Golf Course *(Tides the Golden Eagle 438-5501, 24 mi.)*, Museum *(Mary Ball Washington Museum & Library 462-7280, 12 mi.)*

Provisioning and General Services
OnSite: Wine/Beer **Near:** Green Grocer **1-3 mi:** Crabs/Waterman, Bank/ATM, Post Office, Protestant Church *(Baptist, Episcopal)*, Laundry **3+ mi:** Convenience Store *(Village Center 462-7676, 5 mi.)*, Fishmonger *(Cap'n Tom's Seafood 462-5507, 6 mi.)*, Shrimper *(Doggett Seafood 462-7112, 5 mi.)*, Market *(R&K Country Inn 462-7404, 5 mi.)*, Beauty Salon *(Millenium 462-0433, 5 mi.)*, Dry Cleaners *(Jr's 462-9075, 6 mi.)*

Transportation
OnSite: Courtesy Car/Van *(loaner car)*, Bikes *(tandem bikes for rent)* **OnCall:** Rental Car *(Enterprise 435-1851)*, Taxi, Local Bus *(Bay Area Transit - pick-up and return to marina)* **1-3 mi:** Ferry Service *(Merry Point - Lancaster)* **Airport:** Williamsburg/Middle Peninsula *(73 / 55 mi.)*

Medical Services
911 Service **OnCall:** Ambulance **3+ mi:** Doctor *(Holden 462-6258, 5 mi.)*, Dentist *(Gilesn 462-5419, 7 mi.)* **Hospital:** Rappahannock General 435-8000 *(22 mi.)*

Setting -- Up the bucolic Corrotoman, Yankee Point's broad peninsula pokes into the river at the mouth of Myer Creek. Five main piers, hosting over 100 slips, radiate from the shore A little farther around the point a travelift well is marked by a faux lighthouse. A large fenced picnic deck on the bluff above the docks sports wooden tables, grills and a hammock with breathtaking views straight down the river. Behind it is the office in a pale yellow two-story Victorian farmhouse with green metal roof surrounded by dry storage and work sheds. Another pretty picnic area is riverside, sheltered by ancient trees.

Marina Notes -- DCM. Marina has been here since 1975, boat yard since the late '80s. Family-owned and operated since 1999. There are a surprising number of powerboats in this sailboat marina now; "A"&" B" docks are completely new with new pedestals, screwed-down decking and full-width, short finger piers. New TV and telephone hook-ups installed; new fuel dock and pumps in '04. The full service yard is best known for classic sailboat restorations, blue water preparations and premium paint service. Cottage available for weekend or week/month rental during service. Two full bathrooms - men's and ladies' - tile floor, fiberglass shower stall, wood-paneled walls, sink, toilet and a bench.

Notable -- The only commercial marina on the Corrotoman River; the surroundings are simply beautiful - untouched shorelines with dense foliage pierced by the occasional lovely large house. Yankee Point Yacht Club also makes its home here, on the second floor of the building right at the foot of B Dock; potentially a reciprocal agreement with members of other yacht clubs - but not really available to transients. The nearest major town, Kilmarnock, is 16 miles away.

PHOTOS ON CD-ROM: 13

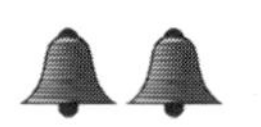

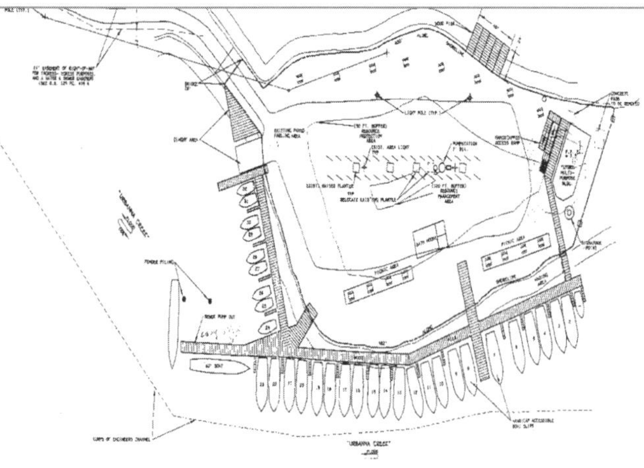

Urbanna Town Marina

PO Box 179; 200 Oyster Road / 45 Cross St; Urbanna, VA 23175

Tel: (804) 758-2613 **VHF: Monitor** 16 **Talk** 68
Fax: (804) 758-0389 **Alternate Tel:** (804) 758-2613
Email: urbannatownmarina@cablefirst.net **Web:** www.visiturbanna.com
Nearest Town: Urbanna *(0.3 mi.)* **Tourist Info:** (804) 758-8181

Navigational Information
Lat: 37°38.264' **Long:** 076°34.223' **Tide:** 4 ft. **Current:** n/a **Chart:** 12237
Rep. Depths (*MLW*): Entry 6 ft. **Fuel Dock** n/a **Max Slip/Moor** 6 ft./-
Access: Rappahannock River to Urbanna Creek, to marker 7

Marina Facilities *(In Season/Off Season)*
Fuel: No
Slips: 32 Total, 16 Transient **Max LOA:** 60 ft. **Max Beam:** 20 ft.
Rate *(per ft.)*: **Day** $1.50 **Week** n/a **Month** $300
Power: 30 amp Incl., **50 amp** Incl., **100 amp** n/a, **200 amp** n/a
Cable TV: Yes **Dockside Phone:** No
Dock Type: Fixed, Long Fingers, Wood
Moorings: 0 Total, 0 Transient **Launch:** n/a, Dinghy Dock
Rate: Day n/a **Week** n/a **Month** n/a
Heads: 4 Toilet(s), 4 Shower(s)
Laundry: 2 Washer(s), 2 Dryer(s) **Pay Phones:** No
Pump-Out: OnSite **Fee:** $5 **Closed Heads:** Yes

Marina Operations
Owner/Manager: Dianne Franck **Dockmaster:** Same
In-Season: Year-Round, 9am-6pm **Off-Season:** n/a
After-Hours Arrival: Check in advance with dockmaster
Reservations: Yes, Preferred **Credit Cards:** Visa/MC
Discounts: None
Pets: Welcome, Dog Walk Area **Handicap Access:** Yes, Heads, Docks

Marina Services and Boat Supplies
Services - Docking Assistance, Security *(24 hrs.)* **Communication -** Mail & Package Hold, Data Ports, FedEx, UPS, Express Mail **Supplies - OnSite:** Ice *(Block, Cube)* **Under 1 mi:** Propane *(Urbanna Auto & Marine 758-5300)* **3+ mi:** West Marine *(Deltaville 776-0400, 16 mi.)*

Restaurants and Accommodations
Near: Restaurant *(Boat House Café 758-0080, L $8-12, D $13-25, fresh fish specials)*, *(Virginia Street Café 758-3798, L $6-8, D $9-16, B too)*, Seafood Shack *(Shuckers 758-1034, Tue & Wed, 4pm-9pm, Thu-Sat 11am-'til, closed Mon)*, Snack Bar *(Moo's River's Edge Eatery 758-1447, ice cream)*, Lite Fare *(Marshall's Drug 758-5344, B $2-4, L $1.50-3.00)*, *(Café MoJo's 758-4141, L $6-15, Sun brunch 11am-3pm)*, Pizzeria *(Colonial Pizza 758-4079, L $3-10, D $7-13, Mon-Fri 11am-10pm)*, Inn/B&B *(Atherston Hall B&B 758-2809, $110-125, 4 rooms in historic district - home of Capt. James H. Bohannon, commander of schooner "Legonia," comp. bikes)* **Under 1 mi:** Hotel *(Inn At Urbana Creek 758-4661, $85-145)*, Inn/B&B *(Magnolia Inn 758-1011)*

Recreation and Entertainment
OnSite: Beach, Picnic Area, Grills, Special Events *(Oyster Festival, 1st week in Nov; Art on the Half Shell - mid May.)* **Near:** Sightseeing *(16 Historic Sites walking tour)*, Galleries *(Nimcock Gallery 758-2602)* **Under 1 mi:** Pool *(town pool located at Tabor Park; Tue-Thu 12-6pm, Fri-Sat 12-8pm, Sun 1-6pm, $3 non-residents)*, Playground, Tennis Courts, Video Rental, Park *(Tabor Park)* **1-3 mi:** Fitness Center *(YMCA 758-9622)* **3+ mi:** Golf Course *(Riverview 758-9495, 6 mi.)*, Museum *(Middlesex County Museum 758-3663, 6 mi.)*

Provisioning and General Services
Near: Health Food *(Natures Store 758-9864)*, Wine/Beer *(The Grape and the Goat)*, Liquor Store *(ABC 758-9774 Mon-Sat 11am to 6pm)*, Crabs/Waterman *(Payne's Crab House 758-5301 6am-1pm in season: hard shell, soft shell, or soft-shelled steamed; crab meat by the pound)*, Market *(Urbanna Market IGA 758-2250)*, Bank/ATM, Post Office *(758-5355)*, Protestant Church *(Methodist, Baptist)*, Library *(Middlesex 758-5910)*, Beauty Salon *(Hair Port 758-2334)*, Barber Shop *(Urbanna Barber Shop 758-3542)*, Dry Cleaners *(Village Cleaners 758-2385)*, Laundry *(Urbanna Laundromat)*, Pharmacy *(Marshalls Drug Store 758-5344)*, Hardware Store *(Taylor Hardware 758-2301)* **Under 1 mi:** Fishmonger *(Shore & Ruark Seafood 758-5640)*, Clothing Store *(Urbanna Republic, Cyndy's Bynn, Fashion Exchange)*, Retail Shops *(Dollar General; R.S. Bistrow - gift shop - original artifacts from historic interior preserved)* **1-3 mi:** Florist *(Cup & Petal 758-4443)* **3+ mi:** Supermarket *(Food Lion 758-2257, 7 mi.)*

Transportation
OnCall: Rental Car *(Enterprise 694-8226)* **Near:** Local Bus *(The Pearl Trolley MemDay-LabDay)* **3+ mi:** Taxi *(Tri County 693-3475, 20 mi.)*, Rail *(Amtrak Williamsburg 757-229-8750, 45 mi.)*, Airport Limo *(Classy Limousine 642-1770, 20 mi.)* **Airport:** Middle Peninsula Regional/Richmond *(16 mi./55 mi.)*

Medical Services
911 Service **1-3 mi:** Doctor *(Urbanna Family Practice 758-2110)*, Dentist *(Miller 758-1103)* **3+ mi:** Chiropractor *(Family Chiropractic of Saluda 758-1800, 6 mi.)*, Veterinarian *(Saluda Veterinary Clinic 443-2878, 4 mi.)*
Hospital: Riverside Walter Reed Hospital 693-8800 *(20 mi.)*

PHOTOS ON CD-ROM: 11

Setting -- First set of docks on Urbanna Creek, immediately after Marker 7, belongs to all-new 36-slip Upton Municipal Marina located on a small peninsula that pokes into the creek and is backed by Jamison Cove. Riverside are 2 long pavilions hosting 8 picnic tables, and a bathhouse. Nine more picnic tables are scattered along the cove side. A parking lot occupies the center. Adjacent is a new waterfront shops and motel complex, just past Payne's Crab House.

Marina Notes -- Slated to re-open Summer '06, the new municipal marina is being completely rebuilt after Hurricane Isabel. Along the creekfront, 23 40 foot slips edge the wood boardwalk - with pumpout at the end and space for two 60-footers. The boardwalk makes a sharp turn inland with slips for 9 smaller vessels. The new riverfront complex to the south, being built by the David A. Nice Company, will have shops on the first floor, motel units on the second, and event spaces for parties & weddings at each end. Historically, $300 slip reservations for the Oyster Fest open July 1, and are completely booked by Noon.

Notable -- Follow the road around from Upton Point and just up the hill, then it's another block to the heart of "downtown" Urbanna. Designated an official tobacco port in 1680, seven buildings have been in continuous use ever since - the center section of the village has been placed on the National Register of Historic Places. Marshall's Drug Store is a do-not-miss - with the original soda fountain, it's the hottest breakfast spot in town. The Urbanna Oyster Festival - Virginia's official Oyster Fest - is Friday and Saturday of the first weekend in November. It is without doubt the biggest event of the year, held since 1958 - with over 75,000 attending. Over 50 food vendors and lots of contests. The Fireman's Parade is Friday night and the Oyster Fest Parade is Saturday afternoon.

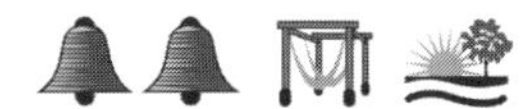

Navigational Information
Lat: 37°38.126' **Long:** 076°34.327' **Tide:** 2 ft. **Current:** 2 kt. **Chart:** 12237
Rep. Depths (*MLW*): Entry 9 ft. **Fuel Dock** n/a **Max Slip/Moor** 9 ft./-
Access: Rappahannock to Urbanna; south side of Creek

Marina Facilities *(In Season/Off Season)*
Fuel: On Call Delivery
Slips: 50 Total, 3 Transient **Max LOA:** 110 ft. **Max Beam:** 25 ft.
Rate *(per ft.)*: **Day** $1.50 **Week** Inq. **Month** Inq.
Power: 30 amp $3, **50 amp** $6, **100 amp** $10, **200 amp** n/a
Cable TV: Yes **Dockside Phone:** Yes
Dock Type: Fixed, Long Fingers, Alongside, Wood
Moorings: 0 Total, 0 Transient **Launch:** n/a
Rate: Day n/a **Week** n/a **Month** n/a
Heads: 4 Toilet(s), 4 Shower(s) *(with dressing rooms)*, Hair Dryers
Laundry: 1 Washer(s), 1 Dryer(s), Book Exchange **Pay Phones:** Yes
Pump-Out: OnSite, Self Service **Fee:** $5 **Closed Heads:** Yes

Marina Operations
Owner/Manager: Jack Dozier **Dockmaster:** Diana Allison
In-Season: Apr-Oct, 8am-5pm **Off-Season:** Oct-Apr, 8am-4:30pm
After-Hours Arrival: Tie up at T-head check in am.
Reservations: Yes, Preferred **Credit Cards:** Visa/MC, Dscvr
Discounts: Boat/US **Dockage:** inq **Fuel:** n/a **Repair:** n/a
Pets: Welcome, Dog Walk Area **Handicap Access:** Yes, Heads, Docks

Dozier's Port Urbanna Yachting

PO Box 388; 1 Waterfront Street; Urbanna, VA 23175

Tel: (804) 758-0000; (800) 734-2882 **VHF: Monitor** 16 **Talk** 72
Fax: (804) 758-2332 **Alternate Tel:** (804) 758-2331
Email: information@doziermarine.com **Web:** www.doziermarine.com
Nearest Town: Urbanna *(0.1 mi.)* **Tourist Info:** (804) 758-8181

Marina Services and Boat Supplies
Services - Docking Assistance, Boaters' Lounge, Crew Lounge, Trash Pick-Up, Dock Carts, Megayacht Facilities **Communication -** Mail & Package Hold, Phone Messages, Fax in/out, Data Ports *(Office)*, FedEx, DHL, UPS, Express Mail **Supplies - OnSite:** Ships' Store **Near:** Ice *(Cube)*

Boatyard Services
OnSite: Travelift *(40T)*, Crane, Engine mechanic *(gas, diesel)*, Electrical Repairs, Electronics Repairs, Hull Repairs, Rigger, Canvas Work, Bottom Cleaning, Brightwork, Air Conditioning, Refrigeration, Compound, Wash & Wax, Interior Cleaning, Woodworking, Metal Fabrication, Painting, Awlgrip, Yacht Design, Yacht Building, Total Refits, Yacht Broker *(Jack Dozier)* **OnCall:** Propeller Repairs, Inflatable Repairs, Life Raft Service, Upholstery, Yacht Interiors **Near:** Sail Loft. **Yard Rates:** $55/hr., Haul & Launch $7/ft. *(blocking $1/ft.)*, Bottom Paint $12-15/ft. *(paint incl.)* **Storage:** On-Land $125/mo.

Restaurants and Accommodations
OnSite: Restaurant *(Boat House Café 758-0080)* **Near:** Restaurant *(Café Mojo 758-4141, D $8-28)*, Seafood Shack *(Shuckers 758-1034, L $3-10, D $10-15)*, Pizzeria *(Colonial Pizza and Restaurant 758-4079, L $3-10, D $7-13)*, Motel *(Atherston Hall 758-2809, $110-125)*, Inn/B&B *(Inn at Urbanna Creek 758-4661, $85-145)* **1-3 mi:** Hotel *(Hewick Plantation 758-4214, $120-170, 66 acres, 2 rooms)*, Inn/B&B *(The Inn 758-4852)*

Recreation and Entertainment
OnSite: Picnic Area, Grills, Fitness Center, Special Events *(Oyster Fest - 1st weekend of Nov)* **Near:** Beach, Sightseeing *(Walking tour)*, Galleries *(Nimcock Gallery 758-2602)* **Under 1 mi:** Pool *(town pool located at Tabor Park, $3 non-residents; open Tue-Thu 12p-6pm, Fri-Sat 12-8pm, Sun 1-6pm)*, Playground, Jogging Paths, Video Rental, Park *(Tabor Park)* **3+ mi:** Golf Course *(Riverview 758-9495, 6 mi.)*

Provisioning and General Services
Near: Wine/Beer, Liquor Store *(ABC 758-2207)*, Fishmonger *(Shore & Ruark Seafood 758-5640)*, Crabs/Waterman *(Payne's Crab House 758-5301 6am-1pm in season)*, Market *(Urbanna Market IGA 758-2250)*, Bank/ATM, Post Office *(758-5355)*, Catholic Church, Protestant Church, Library *(Middlesex 758-5910)*, Beauty Salon *(Hair Port 758-2334)*, Barber Shop, Dry Cleaners *(Village Cleaners 758-2385)*, Laundry *(Urbanna Laundromat)*, Pharmacy *(Marshalls Drug Store 758-5344)*, Hardware Store *(Taylor 758-2301)*, Clothing Store *(Urbanna Republic, Cyndy's Bynn, Fashion Exchange)*, Retail Shops *(Dollar General; R.S. Bistrow - gifts)*, Copies Etc. **Under 1 mi:** Health Food *(Natures Store 758-9864)* **3+ mi:** Convenience Store *(Little Sue 776-7038, 4 mi.)*, Supermarket *(Food Lion 758-2257, 7 mi.)*

Transportation
OnCall: Rental Car *(Enterprise 804-6948226)*, Airport Limo *(Glassy Limousine Service 642-1770)* **Near:** Local Bus *(Pearl Trolley MemDay-LabDay)* **Airport:** Middle Peninsula Regional/Richmond *(16 mi./55 mi.)*

Medical Services
911 Service **OnCall:** Ambulance **Near:** Dentist *(Miller 758-1103)*
1-3 mi: Doctor *(Carrizales/Robusto 758-2110)*
Hospital: Riverside Walter Reed 693-8800 *(20 mi.)*

Setting -- The second marina on Urbanna Creek, carefully landscaped Dozier's is certainly the most elegant. Signature lattice work accents the large covered boat sheds and the 2nd floor boaters' lounge built at the creek end of the main pier. At the head of the fairway, the low-slung Boat House Café fronts the larger repair and boat building sheds. Three sets of well-maintained covered slips and a handful of open slips welcome large power & sail boats, even megayachts.

Marina Notes -- Formerly Southside Marine, founded 1947. Acquired and refurbished by the Doziers in 1995. Part-time on-site staff - so call far ahead. A small on-site fitness center hosts flexible work-out equipment and also opens out onto a deck. The lovely second floor knotty-pine boaters' lounge is furnished with comfortable, rugged sofas and easy chairs, a table and chairs, a small bar, large television, stereo, and piano; large windows and French doors open onto the decks. Outdoor chairs offer spectacular views up and down the creek. Lovely full baths are off the boaters lounge. Cambrook Boatyard Inc, a marine service center, Cat-Man Catamarans, and Jackson's Smoked Salmon.

Notable -- The Boat House Café sits at the head of the docks with open views to the creek. It looks deceptively low-key from the outside - a slightly pitched roof tops casual picnic tables on the waterside deck. But inside, it's all fieldstone and stained glass with multiple levels providing views through enormous windows. A copper topped bandstand is near the bar. (L 11am-3:30pm, D 5 -10pm). Right up the hill is the Old Tobacco Warehouse - now the Visitors' Center; pick up their 16-site walking tour map. A bit farther is the delightful, historic village of Urbanna -- with more eateries and a variety of unique local shops.

PHOTOS ON CD-ROM: 13

Urbanna Yachting Center

PO Box 397; 15 Watling Street; Urbanna, VA 23175

Tel: (804) 758-2342 **VHF: Monitor** 16 **Talk** 9
Fax: (804) 758-2344 **Alternate Tel:** n/a
Email: urbannayachts@oonl.com **Web:** www.urbannayachts.com
Nearest Town: Urbanna *(0.25 mi.)* **Tourist Info:** (804) 758-8181

Navigational Information

Lat: 37°38.015' **Long:** 076°34.289' **Tide:** 2 ft. **Current:** n/a **Chart:** 12237
Rep. Depths (*MLW*): Entry 10 ft. **Fuel Dock** 8 ft. **Max Slip/Moor** 8 ft./-
Access: Rappahannock River to Urbanna Creek

Marina Facilities *(In Season/Off Season)*

Fuel: *Shell* - Gasoline, Diesel
Slips: 90 Total, 5 Transient **Max LOA:** 65 ft. **Max Beam:** n/a
Rate *(per ft.)*: **Day** $1.25 **Week** $6.50 **Month** $12
Power: 30 amp $4, **50 amp** $8, **100 amp** n/a, **200 amp** n/a
Cable TV: No **Dockside Phone:** No
Dock Type: Fixed, Wood
Moorings: 0 Total, 0 Transient **Launch:** n/a
Rate: Day n/a **Week** n/a **Month** n/a
Heads: 4 Toilet(s), 6 Shower(s)
Laundry: None **Pay Phones:** No
Pump-Out: OnSite **Fee:** $10 **Closed Heads:** No

Marina Operations

Owner/Manager: Jim Scott **Dockmaster:** Same
In-Season: May-Sep, 8:30am-5pm **Off-Season:** Oct-Apr, 9am-4:30pm
After-Hours Arrival: Call in advance.
Reservations: Yes **Credit Cards:** Visa/MC
Discounts: None
Pets: Welcome, Dog Walk Area **Handicap Access:** No

Marina Services and Boat Supplies

Services - Docking Assistance, Boaters' Lounge, Dock Carts **Communication -** Mail & Package Hold, Phone Messages, Fax in/out, Data Ports *(Office)*, FedEx, DHL, UPS, Express Mail **Supplies - OnSite:** Ice *(Block, Cube)*, Ships' Store **Under 1 mi:** Propane *(Urbanna Marine 758-5300)* **3+ mi:** West Marine *(Deltaville 776-0400, 16 mi.)*

Boatyard Services

OnSite: Travelift, Electrical Repairs, Hull Repairs, Rigger, Sail Loft *(Scott Sail Makers)*, Canvas Work, Bottom Cleaning, Brightwork, Compound, Wash & Wax, Interior Cleaning, Woodworking, Painting, Awlgrip, Yacht Broker **Near:** Divers. **Yard Rates:** $50/hr., Haul & Launch $7/ft. *(blocking incl.)*, Power Wash $1/ft.,$30min., Bottom Paint Inq.

Restaurants and Accommodations

Near: Restaurant *(Boat House Café 758-0080, L $8-12, D $13-25, fresh fish specials)*, *(Café MoJo's 758-4141, D $8-28, Sun brunch 11am-3pm)*, *(Virginia Street Café 758-3798, L $6-8, D $9-16, B, too)*, Seafood Shack *(Shuckers 758-1034, L $3-10, D $10-15, closed Mon)*, Snack Bar *(Moo's River's Edge Eatery 758-1447, ice cream, sandwiches)*, Lite Fare *(Marshall's Drug 758-5344, B $1.50-3, L $1.50-3, B 8am)*, Pizzeria *(Colonial Pizza 758-4079, L $3-10, D $7-13, Mon-Fri 11am-10pm)*, Inn/B&B *(Atherston Hall B&B 758-2809, $110-125, home of Capt. James Bohannon, commander of schooner "Legonia")* **Under 1 mi:** Inn/B&B *(Magnolia Inn 758-1011)*

Recreation and Entertainment

OnSite: Picnic Area, Grills **Near:** Tennis Courts, Video Rental, Special Events *(Oyster Fest, 1st wk Nov)* **Under 1 mi:** Pool *(Tabor Park, $3; Tue-Thu 12-6pm, Fri-Sat 12-8pm, Sun 1-6pm)*, Park *(Tabor)*, Galleries *(Nimcock 758-2602)* **1-3 mi:** Fitness Center *(YMCA 758-9622)* **3+ mi:** Golf Course *(Riverview 758-9495, 6 mi.)*, Museum *(Middlesex County 758-3663, 5 mi.)*

Provisioning and General Services

Near: Delicatessen, Wine/Beer *(The Grape & the Goat)*, Liquor Store *(ABC 758-9774 Mon-Sat 11am-6pm)*, Bank/ATM, Post Office *(758-5355)*, Catholic Church, Protestant Church, Library *(Middlesex 758-5910)*, Beauty Salon *(Hair Port 758-2334; Portside Nail Salon)*, Laundry, Pharmacy *(Marshalls 758-5344)*, Hardware Store *(Taylor 758-2301)* **Under 1 mi:** Health Food *(Nature's Store 758-9864)*, Crabs/Waterman *(Payne's 758-5301)*, Market *(Urbanna IGA 758-2250)*, Barber Shop *(Urbanna 758-3542)*, Dry Cleaners *(Village 758-2385)*, Clothing Store *(Fashion Exchange 758-8393)*, Retail Shops *(Cyndy's Bynn 758-3756, Dollar General)* **1-3 mi:** Fishmonger *(Shore & Ruark 758-5640)*, Florist *(Cup & Petal 758-4443)* **3+ mi:** Supermarket *(Food Lion 758-2257, 7 mi.)*

Transportation

OnCall: Rental Car *(Enterprise 694-8226)* **Near:** Local Bus *(Pearl Trolley MemDay-LabDay)* **3+ mi:** Rail *(Amtrak Williamsburg 757-229-8750, 45 mi.)*, Airport Limo *(Classy Limo 642-1770, 19 mi.)*
Airport: Middle Peninsula Regional/Richmond *(16 mi./55 mi.)*

Medical Services

911 Service **OnCall:** Ambulance **1-3 mi:** Doctor *(Family Practice 758-2110)*, Dentist *(Miller 758-1103)* **3+ mi:** Chiropractor *(Family Chiro. 758-1800, 5 mi.)* **Hospital:** Riverside Walter Reed 693-8800 *(20 mi.)*

PHOTOS ON CD-ROM: 12

Setting -- The third marina on quiet Urbanna Creek, UYC's whitewashed 2-story building has a silver metal roof topped by a red sign. An extensive network of open and covered docks stretches along the creek, reaching far into the waterway near the bridge. Picnic tables sit on a dockside grassy plot, and dry storage occupies the area in front of the office. In the main boat house, a rustic boaters' lounge, furnished with a comfortable rattan set, evokes a fishing lodge feel.

Marina Notes -- Current owner at the helm since 1989. UYC is the largest facility in Urbanna: it begins with one set of covered sheds for smaller boats, followed by a long pier with dockage on both sides, another stretch of pier with bulkhead dockage, another large pier with slips on both sides, then an L-shaped covered boathouse for larger yachts, and then, outboard of that, a covered boathouse has a pier with slips on either side. Power is on the pilings. Extensive onsite repair services. Scott Sail Makers is also on-site. Two bathhouses: one has tiled showers with dressing rooms and sinks set in a tiled vanity. In the boathouse, next to the boaters' lounge, is another set of heads and with fiberglass shower stalls.

Notable -- The charming village of Urbanna, with many 18th C. buildings, begins four blocks up the hill. Along the way are two hairdressers and Colonial Pizza - which overlooks the marina. With each visit Urbanna becomes more delightful and interesting. The nearby Visitors' Center in the restored Old Tobacco Warehouse has a fascinating 16-site walking tour. Many of the unique antique shops, gift, clothing and specialty shops are housed in period buildings, as well. Six eateries offer a wide range of options. The famous Oyster Festival is the first weekend in November.

Urbanna Bridge Marina

PO Box 358; Foot of Watling Street; Urbanna, VA 23175

Tel: (804) 740-1813 **VHF: Monitor** n/a **Talk** n/a
Fax: (804) 758-8503 **Alternate Tel:** (804) 758-8503
Email: n/a **Web:** n/a
Nearest Town: Urbanna *(0.1 mi.)* **Tourist Info:** (804) 758-8181

Navigational Information

Lat: 37°37.987' **Long:** 076°34.341' **Tide:** 2 ft. **Current:** n/a **Chart:** 12237
Rep. Depths (*MLW*): Entry 10 ft. **Fuel Dock** n/a **Max Slip/Moor** 10 ft./-
Access: Urbanna Creek almost to the bridge just past G "11"

Marina Facilities *(In Season/Off Season)*

Fuel: No
Slips: 46 Total, 6 Transient **Max LOA:** 40 ft. **Max Beam:** n/a
Rate *(per ft.)*: **Day** $1.25 **Week** n/a **Month** n/a
Power: 30 amp Incl., **50 amp** n/a, **100 amp** n/a, **200 amp** n/a
Cable TV: No **Dockside Phone:** No
Dock Type: n/a
Moorings: 0 Total, 0 Transient **Launch:** n/a
Rate: Day n/a **Week** n/a **Month** n/a
Heads: 3 Toilet(s), 1 Shower(s)
Laundry: None **Pay Phones:** No
Pump-Out: No **Fee:** n/a **Closed Heads:** No

Marina Operations

Owner/Manager: Jim Thompson **Dockmaster:** Same
In-Season: Apr-Dec, 6am-6pm **Off-Season:** Jan-Mar, closed
After-Hours Arrival: Call cell 804-740-1813
Reservations: Yes **Credit Cards:** Cash only
Discounts: None
Pets: Welcome **Handicap Access:** No

Marina Services and Boat Supplies

Services - Trash Pick-Up, Dock Carts **Communication -** UPS, Express Mail **Supplies - Near:** Ice *(Block, Cube, Shaved)*, Ships' Store, Bait/Tackle, Live Bait **Under 1 mi:** Propane *(Urbanna Auto & Marine 758-5300)* **3+ mi:** West Marine *(Deltaville 776-0400, 16 mi.)*

Boatyard Services

OnSite: Yacht Broker *(Jim Thompson 758-8503)* **Near:** Travelift, Railway, Crane, Forklift, Engine mechanic *(gas, diesel)*, Electrical Repairs, Electronics Repairs, Hull Repairs, Sail Loft, Canvas Work, Bottom Cleaning, Brightwork, Air Conditioning, Refrigeration, Divers, Compound, Wash & Wax, Interior Cleaning, Propeller Repairs, Woodworking, Upholstery, Metal Fabrication, Awlgrip. **Nearest Yard:** Urbanna Yachting Center (804) 758-2342

Restaurants and Accommodations

Near: Restaurant *(Boat House Café 758-0080, L $8-12, D $13-25, fresh fish specials)*, *(Virginia Street Café 758-3798, L $6-8, D $9-16, B, too)*, *(Colonial 758-4079, L $3-10, D $7-13, Italian & Greek; closed Mon)*, Seafood Shack *(Shuckers 758-1034, Tue-Sun)*, Snack Bar *(Moo's River's Edge 758-1447, sandwiches)*, Lite Fare *(Café MoJo's 758-4141, L $6-15, Sun brunch 11am-3pm)*, *(Marshall's Drug 758-5344, B $1.50-3, L $1.50-3, great spot for breakfast)*, Inn/B&B *(Atherston Hall 758-2809)* **Under 1 mi:** Hotel *(Inn At Urbana Creek 758-4661, $85-145)*, Inn/B&B *(Magnolia Inn 758-1011)*

Recreation and Entertainment

Near: Spa, Beach, Picnic Area, Grills, Playground, Tennis Courts, Jogging Paths, Boat Rentals, Fishing Charter **Under 1 mi:** Pool *(town pool - Tabor Park $3; Tue-Thu 12-6pm, Fri-Sat 12-8pm, Sun 1-6pm)*, Park *(Tabor)*, Galleries *(Nimcock 758-2602)*, Special Events *(Oyster Festival, 1st week in Nov)* **1-3 mi:** Fitness Center *(YMCA 758-9622)* **3+ mi:** Golf Course *(Riverview 758-9495, 6 mi.)*, Museum *(Middlesex 758-3663, 5 mi.)*

Provisioning and General Services

Near: Delicatessen *(Something Different)*, Wine/Beer *(The Grape and the Goat)*, Liquor Store *(ABC 758-9774)*, Bank/ATM, Post Office *(758-5355)*, Catholic Church, Protestant Church, Library *(Middlesex 758-5910)*, Beauty Salon *(Hair Port 758-2334)*, Barber Shop *(Urbanna Barber Shop 758-3542)*, Dry Cleaners *(Village Cleaners 758-2385)*, Pharmacy *(Marshalls Drug Store 758-5344)*, Hardware Store *(Taylor 758-2301)*, Clothing Store *(Fashion Exchange 758-8393)*, Retail Shops *(Cyndy's Bynn 758-3756, Dollar General)* **Under 1 mi:** Health Food *(Natures Store 758-9864)*, Crabs/Waterman *(Payne's 758-5301)*, Market *(Urbanna Market IGA 758-2250)* **1-3 mi:** Fishmonger *(Shore & Ruark Seafood 758-5640)*, Florist *(Cup & Petal 758-4443)* **3+ mi:** Supermarket *(Food Lion 758-2257, 7 mi.)*

Transportation

OnCall: Rental Car *(Enterprise 694-8226)*, Airport Limo *(Classy Limousine 642-1770)* **Near:** Local Bus *(Pearl Trolley MemDay-LabDay)* **3+ mi:** Taxi *(Tri-County 693-3475, 20 mi.)*, Rail *(Amtrak Williamsburg 757-229-8750, 45 mi.)* **Airport:** Middle Peninsula/Richmond *(16 mi./55 mi.)*

Medical Services

911 Service **1-3 mi:** Doctor *(Family Practice 758-2110)*, Dentist *(Miller 758-1103)* **3+ mi:** Chiropractor *(Family Chiro. 758-1800, 5 mi.)*, Veterinarian *(Saluda 443-2878, 4 mi.)* **Hospital:** Walter Reed 693-8800 *(20 mi.)*

Setting -- Hard by the Route 227 Bridge, two docks poke into the creek backed by a two-story building. The bulk of the open slips are on the first pier, to which a very recent extension has been added - it is just lightly offset from the original pier. The second, shorter pier has alongside dockage. Delightful Urbanna is three blocks up the hill.

Marina Notes -- In business since 1985. Closed January-March. No permanant dockmaster on-site so this requires a telephone call in advance. Short finger piers, 30 amp power on the piling at the end of the pier. The main pier takes a quick jog at the end onto the new docks. The bathhouse is in the two-story building at the head of the dock and has three heads and a single shower.

Notable -- Right up the hill - Watling Street - past the 1875 Palmer-Chowning House, Haywood's Store, and a couple hairdressers - is Angelo's Colonial Pizza Restaurant on the left. Turn right for the rest of quaint, real, downtown Urbanna. The center of this 18th century village, founded in 1680, is on the National Historic Register and many of the restaurants and shops are in restored buildings. Bristow House is a fascinating shop that has retained all of the original artifacts and decor. Marshall's Drug Store has a '50s soda fountain and is packed every morning at 8am for breakfast. For an off-the-boat respite Atherston Hall, an 1880 white Charles Palmer house with green roof and burgundy shutters, is also a sweet B&B. Stop by the Visitors' Center in the restored 17th C. Old Tobacco Warehouse - they offer a 16-site walking tour.

PHOTOS ON CD-ROM: 9

Burrell's Marine

PO Box 842; 792 Burrell Marina Road; Urbanna, VA 23175

Tel: (804) 758-5016 **VHF: Monitor** n/a **Talk** n/a
Fax: n/a **Alternate Tel:** n/a
Email: n/a **Web:** n/a
Nearest Town: Urbanna *(3 mi.)* **Tourist Info:** (804) 758-8181

Navigational Information

Lat: 37°39.233' **Long:** 076°35.450' **Tide:** 2 ft. **Current:** n/a **Chart:** 12237
Rep. Depths (*MLW*): Entry 6 ft. **Fuel Dock** n/a **Max Slip/Moor** 8 ft./-
Access: Rappahannock River to Robinson Creek

Marina Facilities *(In Season/Off Season)*

Fuel: No
Slips: 25 Total, 4 Transient **Max LOA:** 42 ft. **Max Beam:** n/a
Rate *(per ft.)*: **Day** $15.00* **Week** $25 **Month** $100
Power: 30 amp Incl., **50 amp** n/a, **100 amp** n/a, **200 amp** n/a
Cable TV: Yes **Dockside Phone:** No
Dock Type: Fixed, Wood
Moorings: 0 Total, 0 Transient **Launch:** Yes
Rate: Day n/a **Week** n/a **Month** n/a
Heads: 2 Toilet(s), 2 Shower(s) *(with dressing rooms)*
Laundry: None **Pay Phones:** No
Pump-Out: Self Service, 1 Port, 1 InSlip **Fee:** $25 **Closed Heads:** Yes

Marina Operations

Owner/Manager: Willis Braxton Jr. **Dockmaster:** Same
In-Season: Apr-Oct, 7am-4pm **Off-Season:** Nov-Mar, Closed
After-Hours Arrival: Call in advance
Reservations: Yes, Preferred **Credit Cards:** Cash or Checks
Discounts: None
Pets: Welcome **Handicap Access:** No

Marina Services and Boat Supplies

Services - Docking Assistance, Security *(police checks)*, Trash Pick-Up, Dock Carts **Communication -** Express Mail *(Sat Del)* **Supplies - OnSite:** Ice *(Cube)*, Bait/Tackle **1-3 mi:** Marine Discount Store *(Lancaster 462-7635)*, Propane *(Revere Gas 776-9724)* **3+ mi:** West Marine *(Deltaville 776-0400)*, Boat/US *(776-8583)*

Boatyard Services

OnSite: Launching Ramp, Hull Repairs, Bottom Cleaning, Interior Cleaning, Painting **OnCall:** Compound, Wash & Wax **1-3 mi:** Engine mechanic *(gas)*, Electrical Repairs, Brightwork. **Yard Rates:** Haul & Launch $6/ft., Power Wash $4/ft., Bottom Paint $4/ft. **Storage:** In-Water $100/mo., On-Land $50/mo.

Restaurants and Accommodations

1-3 mi: Restaurant *(Café MoJo's 758-4141, D $8-28, Sun brunch)*, *(Colonial 758-4079, L $3-10, D $7-13)*, *(Shuckers 758-1043, L $3-10, D $10-15)*, *(Boathouse Café 758-0080, L $7-12, D $13-25, fresh fish specials)*, *(Virginia Street Café 758-3798, L $6-8, D $9-16, recommends soft-shell crabs)*, Fast Food *(Hardee's 758-4931)*, Lite Fare *(Something Different 758-8000, L $4-10, take-out; smokes meats & roasts coffee beans on premises)*, Inn/B&B *(Inn at Urbanna Creek 758-4661, $85-145)*, *(Atherston Hall B&B 758-2809, $110-125)*, *(Magnolia Inn 758-1011)*

Recreation and Entertainment

OnSite: Picnic Area, Playground, Tennis Courts, Special Events *(fishing / pool tournaments)* **Under 1 mi:** Boat Rentals *(Recreation Rental 642-1888)*, Video Arcade *(Topping)* **1-3 mi:** Fitness Center *(YMCA 758-9622)*, Roller Blade/Bike Paths, Video Rental *(Urbanna)*, Museum *(Urbanna, Saluda)* **3+ mi:** Pool *(town pool - Tabor Park $3; Tue-Thu 12-6pm, Fri-Sat 12-8pm, Sun 1-6pm, 5 mi.)*

Provisioning and General Services

Near: Dry Cleaners *(642-2880)*, Laundry, Newsstand **Under 1 mi:** Hardware Store *(Taylor's 758-2501)*, Florist *(River Birch 758-3522)* **1-3 mi:** Gourmet Shop *(Something Different 758-8000)*, Delicatessen, Health Food *(Nature's Store 758-9864)*, Liquor Store *(ABC 758-2207)*, Fishmonger *(Shore & Ruark Seafood 758-5640)*, Crabs/Waterman *(Payne's Crab House 758-5301)*, Market *(Urbanna Market 758-2250)*, Bank/ATM *(Southside Bank)*, Library *(Middlesex 758-5910)*, Beauty Salon *(758-9542)*, Barber Shop *(Urbanna Barber Shop 758-3542)*, Pharmacy *(Marshalls 758-5344)*, Retail Shops *(Cyndy's Bynn 758-3756, Dollar General)* **3+ mi:** Supermarket *(Food Lion 758-2257, 7 mi.)*

Transportation

OnCall: Rental Car *(Enterprise 694-8226)*, Airport Limo *(Classy Limousine 642-1770)* **3+ mi:** Rail *(Amtrak Williamsburg 757-229-8750, 45 mi.)*
Airport: Middle Peninsula/Richmond *(16 mi./54 mi.)*

Medical Services

911 Service **OnSite:** Holistic Services **OnCall:** Ambulance **Near:** Doctor *(Robusto 758-2110)* **1-3 mi:** Dentist *(Miller 758-1103)* **3+ mi:** Chiropractor *(Family Chiro. 758-1800, 6 mi.)*, Veterinarian *(Saluda 443-2878, 5 mi.)*
Hospital: Walter Reed 693-8800 *(20 mi.)*

Setting -- Just west of the mouth of Urbanna Creek is sylvan Robinson Creek. At the head of the creek, a beautiful new pale-cream two-story tidewater Colonial with red metal roof and a lovely screened veranda overlooks the small network of docks tucked into a small cove. The clubhouse's first floor veranda hosts a row of chairs with views out to the dock and a couple of long tables and chairs. The second floor veranda has a bowed porch with a double set of stairs leading down to the pretty lawn.

Marina Notes -- *Transient fee is flat rate. Founded by the Burrell's many years ago. Now owned by Betty Christian. Rebuilt in 1997. Bait and tackle. A party room with full-size kitchen for servicing special events. Stationary docks, short finger piers with electric on the pilling. Launching ramp and marine railway. A combination of working vessels and recreational boats. A 42-footer fits here quite comfortably; they don't want anything bigger than that. Very nice bathhouse with a sink set into a Formica vanity, 2 toilets with an asphalt tile floor, and comfortable fiberglass shower stalls with dressing area.

Notable -- The spacious grounds are naturally landscaped and nicely maintained. A row of picnic tables sits below the second floor veranda with views out to the creek. A small snack bar is also on-site. Upstairs is a pool room with two good regulations-size tables and a big party room that takes advantage of the second floor veranda and sweeping views of the creek. A tennis court is nearby. Little is within walking distance but "Something Different" takeout barbecue and smokehouse is about 2 miles and Urbanna's village is about 3 miles.

PHOTOS ON CD-ROM: 10

Navigational Information
Lat: 37°40.333' **Long:** 076°36.483' **Tide:** 2 ft. **Current:** n/a **Chart:** 12237
Rep. Depths (*MLW*): Entry 6 ft. **Fuel Dock** n/a **Max Slip/Moor** 5 ft./-
Access: Rappahannock to La Grange Creek

Marina Facilities *(In Season/Off Season)*
Fuel: Gasoline, Diesel, On Call Delivery
Slips: 81 Total, 6 Transient **Max LOA:** 40 ft. **Max Beam:** 13 ft.
Rate *(per ft.)*: **Day** $1.50 **Week** n/a **Month** n/a
Power: 30 amp Incl., **50 amp** Incl., **100 amp** n/a, **200 amp** n/a
Cable TV: No **Dockside Phone:** No
Dock Type: Fixed
Moorings: 0 Total, 0 Transient **Launch:** n/a
Rate: Day n/a **Week** n/a **Month** n/a
Heads: 4 Toilet(s), 4 Shower(s) *(with dressing rooms)*
Laundry: None **Pay Phones:** No
Pump-Out: No **Fee:** n/a **Closed Heads:** No

Marina Operations
Owner/Manager: Mike Terrier **Dockmaster:** Same
In-Season: Apr-Nov, 8am-5pm **Off-Season:** Dec-Mar, Closed
After-Hours Arrival: Call (804)758-4321
Reservations: Yes, Preferred **Credit Cards:** no
Discounts: None
Pets: Welcome **Handicap Access:** Yes

Remlik Marina

PO Box ; 485 Burch Road; Urbanna, VA 23175

Tel: (804) 758-5450 **VHF: Monitor** 16 **Talk** 67
Fax: (804) 758-3015 **Alternate Tel:** (804) 758-4321
Email: rterr14329@aol.com **Web:** n/a
Nearest Town: Urbanna *(5 mi.)* **Tourist Info:** (804) 758-8181

Marina Services and Boat Supplies
Services - Docking Assistance, Security *(24 hrs.)*, Dock Carts **Communication -** FedEx, UPS, Express Mail **Supplies - OnSite:** Ice *(Block)*, Ships' Store, Live Bait **3+ mi:** Propane *(Urbanna Auto & Marine 758-5300, 4 mi.)*

Boatyard Services
OnSite: Travelift *(35T)*, Launching Ramp, Engine mechanic *(gas)*, Electrical Repairs, Hull Repairs, Bottom Cleaning, Brightwork, Life Raft Service, Painting, Yacht Broker *(Mike's Marine Services)* **OnCall:** Refrigeration, Divers, Upholstery, Yacht Interiors, Metal Fabrication, Yacht Design, Yacht Building **Yard Rates:** $60/hr., Haul & Launch $2.50/ft., Power Wash $2/ft., Bottom Paint $12.50/ft. *(paint incl.)* **Storage:** In-Water $170-235/mo.

Restaurants and Accommodations
Under 1 mi: Inn/B&B *(Edentide Inn 77-669-15 , $90-145)* **1-3 mi:** Restaurant *(Boathouse Café 758-0080, L $7-12, D $13-25, fresh fish specials)*, Seafood Shack *(Shuckers 758-1034, L $3-10, D $10-15)*, Pizzeria *(Colonial Pizza and Restaurant 758-4079, L $3-7, D $8-11)*, Inn/B&B *(Sanderling 77-609-70 , $90-170)* **3+ mi:** Coffee Shop *(Something Different 758-8000, L $4-10, 2 mi., smokes meats & roasts coffee beans on premises)*

Recreation and Entertainment
OnSite: Pool, Picnic Area, Grills, Group Fishing Boat **Under 1 mi:** Jogging Paths **1-3 mi:** Video Rental **3+ mi:** Fitness Center *(YMCA 758-9622, 5 mi.)*, Sightseeing *(Urbanna walking tour, 6 mi.)*, Special Events *(Oyster Festival, 1st week in Nov, 6 mi.)*

Provisioning and General Services
1-3 mi: Convenience Store, Wine/Beer, Bakery, Green Grocer, Bank/ATM, Post Office, Catholic Church, Florist, Clothing Store **3+ mi:** Supermarket *(Food Lion 758-2257, 8 mi.)*, Gourmet Shop *(Something Different, 6 mi.)*, Health Food *(Natures Store 758-9864, 6 mi.)*, Liquor Store *(ABC 758-2207, 6 mi.)*, Fishmonger *(Shore & Ruark Seafood 758-5640, 4 mi.)*, Crabs/ Waterman *(Payne's Crab House 758-5301, 6 mi.)*, Library *(Middlesex 758-5910, 6 mi.)*, Beauty Salon *(Hair Port 758-2334, 6 mi.)*, Barber Shop *(Urbanna Barber Shop 758-3542, 6 mi.)*, Dry Cleaners *(Village Cleaners 758-2385, 6 mi.)*, Pharmacy *(Marshalls Drug Store 758-5344, 6 mi.)*, Hardware Store *(Taylor Hardware 758-2301, 6 mi.)*, Retail Shops *(Dollar General; R.S. Bristow - gifts, 6 mi.)*

Transportation
OnCall: Rental Car *(Enterprise 694-8226)*, Airport Limo *(Classy Limousine 642-1770)* **3+ mi:** Rail *(Amtrak Williamsburg 757-229-8750, 45 mi.)*
Airport: Middle Peninsula/Richmond *(16 mi./54 mi.)*

Medical Services
911 Service **OnCall:** Ambulance **3+ mi:** Doctor *(Urbanna Family Practice 758-2110, 5 mi.)*, Dentist *(Miller 758-1103, 5 mi.)*
Hospital: Walter Reed 693-8800 *(20 mi.)*

Setting -- On quiet La Grange Creek are Remlik's three sets of covered slips (a single and two doubles) plus an open pier with slips on both sides. At the top of a nicely terraced, grassy slope is an inviting pool decorated with pots of sea oats and a light cream stucco bathhouse with pyramidal roof. They both have spectacular views down the creek along the open fairway between the boat sheds.

Marina Notes -- Originally built in 1994. In September '04, Mike's Marine, which ran the boatyard part of the facility, took over the whole operation. Full finger piers in the sheds, power up on the uprights. All of the docks are very new and in excellent condition. The amenities are a little tired. A variety of craft from classic bay boats to houseboats to ski boats to restored and not-so-restored classics. Full boatyard services with a 35 ton travelift. Fish cleaning station at the end of the dock. There are heads for men and women, plus two full bathrooms with shower, toilet, and sink at either end of the bathhouse.

Notable -- Remlik's is in the town of Remlik, even though the address is Urbanna - and it's quite far from most everything. In downtown Remlik, there is a market, and about two miles away is the contemporary 'Something Different' smokehouse, barbecue and coffee shop which specializes in the Virginia Sandwich and a variety of specialty smoking and curing processes.

PHOTOS ON CD-ROM: 8

Boaters' Notes

Add Your Ratings and Reviews at www.AtlanticCruisingClub.com

AtlanticCruisingClub.com provides updated Marina Reports, Destination and Harbor Articles, a Boaters' Forum and much more — including an option within each on-line Marina Report for Boaters to add their ratings and comments regarding that facility. Please log on frequently to share your experiences — and to read other boaters' comments.

On the website, boaters may rate marinas on one or more of the following categories — on a scale of 1 (basic) to 5 (world class) — and also enter additional commentary.

- **Facilities & Services** (Fuel, Reservations, Concierge Services and General Helpfulness):
- **Amenities** (Pool, Beach, Internet Access, including Wi-Fi, Picnic/Grill area, Boaters' Lounge):
- **Setting** (Views, Design, Landscaping, Maintenance, Ship-Shapeness, Overall Ambiance):
- **Convenience** (Access — including delivery services — to Supermarkets, other provisioning sources, Shops, Services. Attractions, Entertainment, Sightseeing, Recreation, including Golf and Sport Fishing & Medical Services):
- **Restaurants/Eateries/Lodgings** (Availability of Fine Dining, Snack Bars, Lite Fare, On Call food service, and Lodgings ashore):
- **Transportation** (Courtesy Car/Vans, Buses, Water Taxis, Bikes, Taxis, Rental Cars, Airports, Amtrak, Commuter Trains):
- **Please Add Any Additional Comments**

15. Western Shore: Piankatank River To Salt Ponds

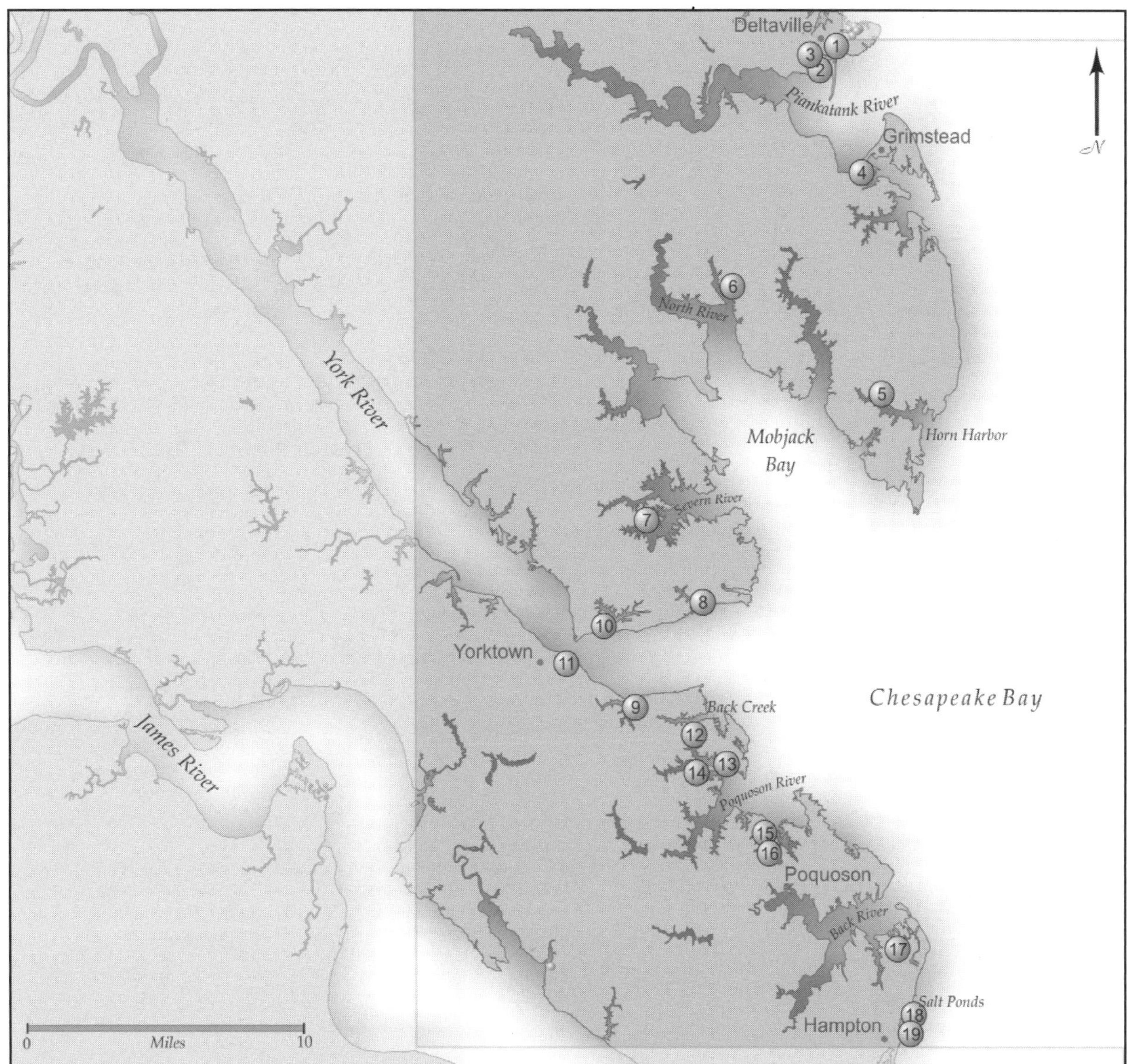

MAP	MARINA	HARBOR	PAGE	MAP	MARINA	HARBOR	PAGE
1	**Deltaville Marina**	*Piankatank River/Jackson Cr.*	270	11	**Riverwalk Landing**	*York River*	280
2	**Ruark Marina**	*Piankatank River/Fishing Bay*	271	12	**Mills Marina**	*York River/Back Creek*	281
3	**Fishing Bay Harbor Marina**	*Piankatank River/Fishing Bay*	272	13	**Seaford Aqua Marina**	*Poquoson River/Chisman Cr.*	282
4	**Narrows Marina**	*Piankatank River*	273	14	**Dare Marina**	*Poquoson River/Chisman Cr.*	283
5	**Horn Harbor Marina**	*Horn Harbor*	274	15	**York Haven Marina**	*Poquoson R./White House Cove*	284
6	**Mobjack Bay Marina**	*Mobjack Bay/North River*	275	16	**Poquoson Marina**	*Poquoson R./White House Cove*	285
7	**Severn River Marina**	*Mobjack Bay/Severn River*	276	17	**Bell Isle Marina**	*Back River*	286
8	**Crown Pointe Marina**	*York River/Perrin River*	277	18	**Southall Landings Marina**	*Salt Ponds*	287
9	**Wormley Creek Marina**	*York River/Wormley Creek*	278	19	**Salt Ponds Marina**	*Salt Ponds*	288
10	**York River Yacht Haven**	*York River/Sarah Creek*	279				

- **A "DCM" symbol in Marina Notes means Designated Clean Marina** — This is a coveted state-level award given to marinas that meet stringent, environmentally supportive requirements (see page 307). *For a list of DCM's & pump-out facilities, see page 308.*
- **Ratings & Reviews** — An explanation of the Atlantic Cruising Club's rating system, and a detailed explanation of what is in each section of the Marina Report is on pages 6 – 11. *The Data-Gathering Process is detailed on page 322.*
- **Marina Report Updates** — Updates to Marina Reports (from readers, ACC reviewers, and marinas) are posted regularly on *www.AtlanticCruisingClub.com.*

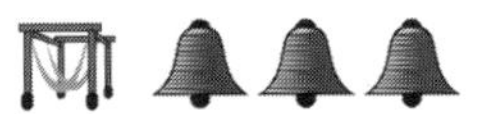

Deltaville Marina

PO Box 497; Route 683, Bucksview Lane; Deltaville, VA 23043

Tel: (804) 776-9812; (888) 741-9812 **VHF: Monitor** 16 **Talk** 69
Fax: (804) 776-9125 **Alternate Tel:** n/a
Email: reservations@deltavillemarina.com **Web:** www.deltavillemarina.com
Nearest Town: Deltaville *(0.5 mi.)* **Tourist Info:** (804) 725-9029

Navigational Information

Lat: 37°32.963' **Long:** 076°19.754' **Tide:** 2 ft. **Current:** 0.5 kt. **Chart:** 12235
Rep. Depths (*MLW*): Entry 9 ft. **Fuel Dock** 9 ft. **Max Slip/Moor** 9 ft./-
Access: Piankatank River due north to Jackson Creek

Marina Facilities *(In Season/Off Season)*

Fuel: *Independent* - Slip-Side Fueling, Gasoline, Diesel
Slips: 77 Total, 10 Transient **Max LOA:** 110 ft. **Max Beam:** 15 ft.
Rate *(per ft.)*: **Day** $1.00/Inq. **Week** $5 **Month** Inq.
Power: 30 amp $3, **50 amp** $5, **100 amp** n/a, **200 amp** n/a
Cable TV: Yes **Dockside Phone:** No
Dock Type: Fixed, Long Fingers, Pilings, Wood
Moorings: 0 Total, 0 Transient **Launch:** n/a, Dinghy Dock ($10/pp)
Rate: Day n/a **Week** n/a **Month** n/a
Heads: 5 Toilet(s), 6 Shower(s) *(with dressing rooms)*
Laundry: 1 Washer(s), 1 Dryer(s), Iron, Iron Board **Pay Phones:** No
Pump-Out: OnSite, Full Service, 1 Central **Fee:** $7.50 **Closed Heads:** Yes

Marina Operations

Owner/Manager: Jacqui Ruse **Dockmaster:** n/a
In-Season: Apr-Dec 31, 8am-5pm **Off-Season:** Jan 1-Mar 31, 8am-4pm
After-Hours Arrival: Tie up to fuel dock, check-in am
Reservations: Required **Credit Cards:** Visa/MC, Amex
Discounts: None
Pets: Welcome, Dog Walk Area **Handicap Access:** Yes, Heads

Marina Services and Boat Supplies

Services - Docking Assistance, Boaters' Lounge, Trash Pick-Up, Dock Carts **Communication -** Mail & Package Hold, Phone Messages, Fax in/out *(Yes)*, Data Ports *(Dial-up)*, FedEx, DHL, UPS, Express Mail **Supplies - OnSite:** Ice *(Block, Cube)*, Ships' Store **Under 1 mi:** Bait/Tackle *(J&W Seafood)* **1-3 mi:** West Marine *(776-0400)*, Boat/US *(776-8583)*, Live Bait, Propane *(Revere Gas 776-9724)*

Boatyard Services

OnSite: Travelift *(35T)*, Crane, Engine mechanic *(gas, diesel)*, Electrical Repairs, Electronics Repairs, Hull Repairs, Rigger, Sail Loft, Bottom Cleaning, Brightwork, Air Conditioning, Refrigeration, Compound, Wash & Wax, Interior Cleaning, Propeller Repairs, Woodworking, Yacht Interiors, Metal Fabrication, Painting, Awlgrip, Yacht Design, Total Refits, Yacht Broker **OnCall:** Canvas Work **Dealer for:** Yanmar. **Member:** ABBRA - 1 Certified Tech(s), ABYC - 13 Certified Tech(s), Other Certifications: ABYC cert. electricians, Diesel mechanics, standards accredited
Yard Rates: $50/hr., Haul & Launch $4/ft., Bottom Paint $9/ft.
Storage: On-Land $3/ft./mo.

Restaurants and Accommodations

OnSite: Condo/Cottage *(efficiency apt, weekly)* **OnCall:** Pizzeria *(Dano's 776-8031)* **Near:** Restaurant *(The Galley 776-6040, L $5-10, D $8-21, picks up)*, *(Toby's 776-6713, L $5-10, D $8-18, picks up)* **Under 1 mi:** Restaurant *(Taylor's 776-9611, B $2-5, L $5-8, D $10-20, picks up)*, Lite Fare *(Sweet Shoppe 776-7021, B $2-4, L $3-6)*, Inn/B&B *(River Place 776-9153, $95-175)*, *(Dockside Inn 776-9224)*, *(Sanderling House B&B 776-0970)* **1-3 mi:** Restaurant *(Boat House Café 776-8882, picks up)*

Recreation and Entertainment

OnSite: Pool, Picnic Area, Grills **Near:** Museum *(Deltaville Maritime Museum 776-7200)* **Under 1 mi:** Playground, Tennis Courts, Fitness Center *(YMCA 776-8846)*, Park **1-3 mi:** Golf Course *(Piankatank River Golf Club 776-6516)*, Boat Rentals, Video Rental *(Hollywood Video 776-7715)*

Provisioning and General Services

OnCall: Market *(Deltaville Market 776-6131; Sandy Bottom Market 776-8803 picks up & returns boaters - min. order $25)*, Dry Cleaners **Near:** Convenience Store *(Little Sue 776-9600)*, Wine/Beer, Meat Market **Under 1 mi:** Fishmonger *(J&W Seafood 776-6400)*, Bank/ATM, Post Office *(776-9750)*, Catholic Church, Protestant Church, Library *(Deltaville Library 776-7362)*, Hardware Store *(Hurds 776-9241)* **1-3 mi:** Supermarket *(Deltaville Town & Country 776-6131, Mon-Thu & Sun 7am-8:30pm, Fri & Sat 'til 9:30pm)*, Delicatessen, Farmers' Market *(Sat 9am-1pm at Yates House Fine Art)*, Beauty Salon *(Hair By Sarah 776-0061)*, Barber Shop *(Sully's 776-0052)*, Pharmacy *(Medicine Shoppe 776-9990)*, Florist *(Wilton Cottage)*

Transportation

OnSite: Bikes *(complimentary)* **OnCall:** Rental Car *(Enterprise 694-8226)*, Airport Limo *(Tri County 693-3475)* **Under 1 mi:** Local Bus
Airport: Newport News/Richmond *(45 mi./65 mi.)*

Medical Services

911 Service **Under 1 mi:** Doctor *(Fishing Bay 776-8000)* **1-3 mi:** Dentist *(Lennon 776-9484 4 mi.)*, Veterinarian *(Hartfield 776-9219)*
Hospital: Riverside Walter Reed 693-6368 *(21 mi.)*

Setting -- Near the mouth of tranquil Jackson Creek off the Piankatank, are full-service Deltaville Marina's 3 open docks and a large covered shed. The landside is dominated by a white 2-story base building topped by a green metal roof; recent plantings are punctuated by stands of sea oats. Attractive white railings enclose a rectangular pool and deck overlooking the docks and creek. Picnic areas are in the white canvas pavilion and new screened picnic porch.

Marina Notes -- All new docks and pedestals post-Isabel. Cats off T's & alongside - no extra charge. New water filtration system. Adjacent Deltaville Boatyard hauled every boat in the marina before the last hurricane - all did very well. On the first floor of the main building, next to the office, is an attractive boaters' lounge - a cherry table and chairs, comfortable sofas and easy chairs, dial-up Internet, TV, and book corner. Upstairs, the VIP Room, a new efficiency apartment with views of the docks, is available for nightly rental - double bed, living room area, and a kitchenette. The excellent bathhouse, green and cream checkerboard tile floor, features a vanity with 2 sinks, hair dryer plugs, big mirrors (full-length, too), 3 toilets, 3 fiberglass shower stalls, commodious dressing rooms and a roll-in shower. Laundry room has a big folding table and ironing board. Anchored boats can use facilities for $10/pp/day, $50/pp/week.

Notable -- The Deltaville Maritime Museum, in Holly Point Nature Park, is close by - with exhibits on original local wooden-boat builders, an Art of the Watermen exhibit, and a re-creation of the Callis Store. Outside are classic Bay vessels: a buy boat, small skipjacks, several deadrise workboats and a sora skiff. The Galley restaurant is across the street. Complimentary bicycles make for a quick trip out to the main road. Next to West Marine is the Deltaville Market.

PHOTOS ON CD-ROM: 12

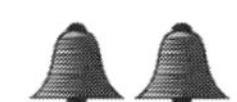

Navigational Information
Lat: 37°32.526' **Long:** 076°20.394' **Tide:** 2.5 ft. **Current:** n/a **Chart:** 12235
Rep. Depths (*MLW*): Entry 18 ft. **Fuel Dock** n/a **Max Slip/Moor** 12 ft./-
Access: Piankatank River to Fishing Bay-Porpoise Cove

Marina Facilities *(In Season/Off Season)*
Fuel: No
Slips: 85 Total, 4 Transient **Max LOA:** 70 ft. **Max Beam:** n/a
Rate *(per ft.)*: **Day** $1.00 **Week** n/a **Month** n/a
Power: 30 amp Incl., **50 amp** Incl., **100 amp** n/a, **200 amp** n/a
Cable TV: No **Dockside Phone:** No
Dock Type: Fixed, Long Fingers, Pilings, Alongside, Wood
Moorings: 0 Total, 0 Transient **Launch:** n/a
Rate: Day n/a **Week** n/a **Month** n/a
Heads: 4 Toilet(s), 4 Shower(s)
Laundry: None **Pay Phones:** No
Pump-Out: OnSite **Fee:** $50* **Closed Heads:** Yes

Marina Operations
Owner/Manager: Gene A. Ruark **Dockmaster:** Mrs. Huston
In-Season: Year-Round, 10am-5pm **Off-Season:** n/a
After-Hours Arrival: Tie up, check-in am
Reservations: No **Credit Cards:** Cash or Check
Discounts: None
Pets: Welcome, Dog Walk Area **Handicap Access:** No

Ruark Marina

PO Box ; 1102 Fishing Bay Road; Deltaville, VA 23043

Tel: (804) 776-9776 **VHF: Monitor** n/a **Talk** n/a
Fax: (804) 776-6780 **Alternate Tel:** (804) 337-7913
Email: n/a **Web:** n/a
Nearest Town: Deltaville *(1.5 mi.)* **Tourist Info:** (804) 725-9029

Marina Services and Boat Supplies
Services - Trash Pick-Up, Dock Carts **Supplies - OnSite:** Ice *(Block, Cube)* **1-3 mi:** West Marine *(776-0400)*, Boat/US *(776-8583)*, Bait/Tackle *(J&W Seafood 776-6400)*, Propane *(Revere Gas 776-9724)*

Boatyard Services
Nearest Yard: Deagle (804) 776-9741

Restaurants and Accommodations
OnCall: Pizzeria *(Dano's 776-8031)* **Under 1 mi:** Restaurant *(Toby's 776-6913, L $5-10, D $8-18, picks up)*, Inn/B&B *(Fishing Bay 776-9153)* **1-3 mi:**Restaurant *(Galley 776-6040, L $5-10, D $8-21, picks up)*, *(Taylor's 776-9611, B $2-5, L $5-8, D $10-20, picks up)*, Lite Fare *(The Sweet Shop 776-7021, B $2-4, L $3-6, deli)*, *(Boat House Café 776-8882, picks up)*, Inn/B&B *(Dockside Inn 776-9224)*, *(River Place 776-9153, $95-175)*, *(Rivers Rise 776-7521)*

Recreation and Entertainment
OnSite: Beach, Picnic Area *(charcoal & propane)*, Grills **Under 1 mi:** Fitness Center *(YMCA 776-8846)* **1-3 mi:** Tennis Courts *(2 courts in village of Deltaville)*, Golf Course *(Piankatank River Golf Club 776-6516)*, Park *(Holly Point)*, Museum *(Deltaville Maritime Museum 776-7200)*

Provisioning and General Services
OnCall: Market *(Sandy Bottom Market 776-8803 picks up & returns boaters - min. order $25)* **Near:** Bank/ATM, Post Office *(776-9750)* **Under 1 mi:** Convenience Store *(Little Sue 776-9600)*, Protestant Church, Hardware Store *(Hurds Hardware 776-9241)*, Retail Shops, Copies Etc. **1-3 mi:** Supermarket *(Deltaville Town & Country Market 776-6131 Mon-Thu & Sun 7am-8:30pm, Fri & Sat 'til 9:30pm)*, Farmers' Market *(Sat 9am-1pm at Yates House Fine Art)*, Fishmonger *(J&W Seafood 776-6400)*, Library *(Deltaville Library 776-7362)*, Beauty Salon *(Hair By Sarah 776-0061)* **3+ mi:** Catholic Church *(6 mi.)*, Barber Shop *(Sully's 776-0052, 5 mi.)*, Pharmacy *(Medicine Shoppe 776-9990, 5 mi.)*

Transportation
OnSite: Bikes **OnCall:** Rental Car *(Enterprise 694-8226)*, Airport Limo (Tri-*County 693-3475)* **Under 1 mi:** Local Bus
Airport: Newport News/Richmond *(45 mi./65 mi.)*

Medical Services
911 Service **Under 1 mi:** Doctor *(Fishing Bay Family Practice 776-8000)*
1-3 mi: Dentist, Veterinarian *(Hartfield Animal Hosp. 776-9219)*
Hospital: Riverside Walter Reed 693-6368 *(21 mi.)*

Setting -- Tucked up into a small arm on Fishing Bay, Ruark's and Fishing Bay Harbor Marina sit side-by-side. First are Ruark's two long piers anchored by a small two-story natural shingled building that houses the offices and bathhouse. On a stretch of lawn along the bulkhead are a nicely appointed gazebo and a small picnic area with charcoal and gas grills overlooking the docks

Marina Notes -- Founded in 1940 as a boatyard by Eugene Ruark; in late 50's became a marina. Two main piers - one with alongside dockage on two sides, and one with alongside dockage on one side and finger pier slips on the other side, plus an additional two piers that parallel the shore with generous, angled, half-length finger piers. Power is on the pilings. All-tile bathhouse features large tile showers with glass sliding doors plus two heads, three sinks in each. An obvious effort has been made to make it as nice as possible - with hair dryer plugs, a book swap, and a cute little vanity made from a sewing trestle.

Notable -- Deltaville is a boater-oriented town; they expect transients to be on foot and accommodate that - most of the restaurants pick up and deliver boating diners), as do the markets. A little over half a mile is Toby's Restaurant (walking one way and getting a ride back is just about right). Near it is handy Little Sue's convenience store. The all-new, very well supplied Deltaville Country Market has re-opened after a fire (Mon-Thu 7am-8:30pm, Fri & Sat 'til 9:30pm, Sun 7:30am-8:30pm) and is adjacent to West Marine. The Deltaville Maritime Museum makes a good biking destination - check out the skipjacks and Chesapeake deadrises on their lawn even if the museum is closed.

PHOTOS ON CD-ROM: 8

Fishing Bay Harbor Marina

PO Box 340; 519 Deagle's Road; Deltaville, VA 23043

Tel: (804) 776-6800 **VHF: Monitor** 16 **Talk** 72
Fax: (804) 776-7658 **Alternate Tel:** n/a
Email: info@fishingbay.com **Web:** www.fishingbay.com
Nearest Town: Deltaville *(1 mi.)* **Tourist Info:** (804) 725-9029

Navigational Information

Lat: 37°32.500' **Long:** 076°20.364' **Tide:** 2.5 ft. **Current:** n/a **Chart:** 12235
Rep. Depths (*MLW*): Entry 16 ft. **Fuel Dock** 12 ft. **Max Slip/Moor** 12 ft./-
Access: Piankatank River to Fishing Bay

Marina Facilities *(In Season/Off Season)*

Fuel: *ValvTect* - Gasoline, Diesel, High-Speed Pumps
Slips: 120 Total, 10 Transient **Max LOA:** 150 ft. **Max Beam:** n/a
Rate *(per ft.)*: **Day** $1.25/1.00 **Week** $4.75 **Month** $8.00
Power: 30 amp $4, **50 amp** $7, **100 amp** n/a, **200 amp** n/a
Cable TV: Yes Incl. **Dockside Phone:** No
Dock Type: Fixed, Long Fingers, Short Fingers, Pilings, Alongside
Moorings: 0 Total, 0 Transient **Launch:** n/a, Dinghy Dock ($3)
Rate: Day n/a **Week** n/a **Month** n/a
Heads: 5 Toilet(s), 6 Shower(s) *(with dressing rooms)*
Laundry: 1 Washer(s), 1 Dryer(s), Iron Board **Pay Phones:** No
Pump-Out: Full Service, 1 Central **Fee:** $5/Free-guests **Closed Heads:** Yes

Marina Operations

Owner/Manager: Ron Hall **Dockmaster:** Andy Moser
In-Season: Apr-Dec, 8am-5pm **Off-Season:** Jan-Mar, Wed-Sun, 8am-5pm
After-Hours Arrival: Call in advance or tie up at transient dock
Reservations: Preferred **Credit Cards:** Visa/MC
Discounts: Boat/US; Marina Life **Dockage:** 20% **Fuel:** $0.10 **Repair:** n/a
Pets: Welcome, Dog Walk Area **Handicap Access:** Yes, Heads, Docks

Marina Services and Boat Supplies

Services - Docking Assistance, Boaters' Lounge, Trash Pick-Up, Dock Carts **Communication -** Phone Messages, Fax in/out *($1.50)*, Data Ports *(Hi-Speed Wi-Fi by iDock.com)*, FedEx, DHL, UPS, Express Mail **Supplies - OnSite:** Ice *(Block, Cube)*, Ships' Store **1-3 mi:** West Marine *(776-0400)*, Boat/US *(776-8583)*, Bait/Tackle *(J&W Seafood 776-6400)*, Live Bait, Propane *(Revere Gas 776-9724)*

Boatyard Services

OnCall: Engine mechanic *(gas, diesel)*, Electrical Repairs, Electronics Repairs, Rigger, Sail Loft, Canvas Work, Bottom Cleaning, Brightwork, Air Conditioning, Refrigeration, Divers, Compound, Wash & Wax, Interior Cleaning, Woodworking, Upholstery **Near:** Travelift *(50T)*, Railway, Crane, Forklift, Hull Repairs, Propeller Repairs, Inflatable Repairs, Yacht Interiors, Painting, Awlgrip, Yacht Design, Yacht Building, Total Refits, Yacht Broker. **Nearest Yard:** Deagles - next door (804) 776-9741

Restaurants and Accommodations

OnCall: Pizzeria *(Dano's 776-8031, Delivers Tue-Sun)* **Under 1 mi:** Restaurant *(Toby's 776-6913, L $5-10, D $8-18, diners picked up from marina)* **1-3 mi:** Restaurant *(Galley 776-6040, L $5-10, D $8-21, pick-up)*, *(Taylor's 776-9611, B $2-5, L $5-8, D $10-20, picks up)*, Lite Fare *(Sweet Shop 776-7021, B $2-4, L $3-6)*, Inn/B&B *(River Place-At-Deltaville 776-9153, $95-175)*, *(Sanderling House B & B 776-0970)*, *(Up the Creek B & B 776-9621)*, *(Dockside Inn 776-9224)*

Recreation and Entertainment

OnSite: Pool *(25-meter with waterfall)*, Picnic Area, Grills, Volleyball **Near:** Roller Blade/Bike Paths **Under 1 mi:** Tennis Courts, Boat Rentals, Sightseeing **1-3 mi:** Beach, Golf Course *(Piankatank River 776-6516)*, Fitness Center *(YMCA 776-8846)*, Fishing Charter, Group Fishing Boat, Park *(Holly Point Nature Park)*, Museum *(Maritime Museum 776-7200)*

Provisioning and General Services

OnSite: Copies Etc. **OnCall:** Market *(Sandy Bottom Market 776-8803 picks up & returns boaters - min order $25)* **Near:** Pharmacy *(Medicine Shoppe 776-9990)*, Retail Shops **Under 1 mi:** Bank/ATM, Post Office *(776-9750)*, Protestant Church, Newsstand **1-3 mi:** Convenience Store *(Little Sue 776-9600)*, Supermarket *(Deltaville Town & Country Market 776-6131 Mon-Thu & Sun 7am-8:30pm, Fri & Sat 'til 9:30pm)*, Delicatessen *(Sandy Bottom Market 776-8803)*, Wine/Beer, Bakery, Farmers' Market *(Sat 9am-1pm at Yates House Fine Art)*, Fishmonger *(J&W Seafood 776-6400)*, Catholic Church, Library *(Deltaville Library 776-7362)*, Beauty Salon *(Hair By Sarah 776-0061)*, Barber Shop *(Sully's Barber Shop 776-0052)*, Dry Cleaners, Laundry, Hardware Store *(Hurds Hardware 776-9241)*, Florist

Transportation

OnSite: Bikes *(Complimentary)* **OnCall:** Rental Car *(Enterprise 694-8226)*, Local Bus *(will come to marina when called)*, Airport Limo *(Tri County 693-3475)* **Airport:** Newport News/Richmond *(45 mi./65 mi.)*

Medical Services

911 Service **Under 1 mi:** Doctor *(Fishing Bay Family Practice 776-8000)*, Ambulance **1-3 mi:** Dentist *(Lennon 776-9484)*, Veterinarian *(Hartfield Animal Hosp. 776-9219)* **Hospital:** Walter Reed 693-6368 *(21 mi.)*

Setting -- Fishing Harbor's signature 2-story white octagonal building with bright blue metal roof and little cupola anchors an extensive network of good docks and high-end, thoughtful amenities. An L-shaped main pier stretches into the harbor capped by an easy-access fuel dock. A long narrow basin cuts into the upland with a row of covered docks along the south side and open slips along the north. An inviting recreation center is farther inland by the covered docks.

Marina Notes -- DCM. Formerly Club on Fishing Bay. Family-owned & operated since 1997. Boat/US & Marina Life discounts. Special pricing for 5 or more vessels. Adjacent Deagles Marine Railway, with a 50 ton travelift and railway, specializes in classic wooden craft. Stationary wood docks with wide 3/4 length finger piers, Lighthouse pedestals. The Fishing Bay Harbor "B" dock (north) is adjacent to Ruark's Marina with separate land access. Free Wi-Fi throughout the marina. Attractive, well-supplied ships' store with snacks, gifts and sundries. Two very nice all-tile bathhouses and laundries (2nd one is on "B" dock). Tile and fiberglass showers with good-size dressing rooms (one roll-in) plus 2 sinks, 3 toilets, a separate, large vanity, and a pull-down ironing board.

Notable -- A wide, cascading waterfall enhances the mosaic tiled Olympic-size pool. The adjacent white building with bright blue trim has a covered porch with tables & chairs and houses a snack bar, boaters' lounge and bathhouse/laundry room complex. The patio surround has views across the covered docks to the basin and bay beyond. The very pleasant boaters' lounge is furnished with sturdy, yet attractive, upholstered pieces, tables and chairs, a TV, small stereo, an assortment of games, books and magazines, and a Wi-Fi hot spot. "Downtown" Deltaville sprawls along Route 33; about a mile-long bike ride away.

PHOTOS ON CD-ROM: 13

Navigational Information
Lat: 37°29.343' **Long:** 076°18.735' **Tide:** 2.5 ft. **Current:** 3 kt. **Chart:** 12235
Rep. Depths (*MLW*): Entry 10 ft. **Fuel Dock** 9 ft. **Max Slip/Moor** 7 ft./-
Access: Piankatank River to Milford Haven

Marina Facilities *(In Season/Off Season)*
Fuel: *Exxon* - Gasoline, Diesel, High-Speed Pumps
Slips: 105 Total, 20 Transient **Max LOA:** 110 ft. **Max Beam:** 18 ft.
Rate *(per ft.)*: **Day** $1.25 **Week** 7th day free **Month** Inq.
Power: 30 amp Incl., **50 amp** $7, **100 amp** n/a, **200 amp** n/a
Cable TV: Yes, Free **Dockside Phone:** No
Dock Type: Fixed, Long Fingers, Pilings
Moorings: 0 Total, 0 Transient **Launch:** n/a
Rate: Day n/a **Week** n/a **Month** n/a
Heads: 4 Toilet(s), 4 Shower(s)
Laundry: 2 Washer(s), 2 Dryer(s) **Pay Phones:** Yes
Pump-Out: Onsite *($5)* **Fee:** n/a **Closed Heads:** Yes

Marina Operations
Owner/Manager: Preston C. Jenkins **Dockmaster:** Same
In-Season: Year-Round, 24 hrs. **Off-Season:** n/a
After-Hours Arrival: Call ahead
Reservations: Yes **Credit Cards:** Visa/MC, Dscvr
Discounts: None
Pets: Welcome, Dog Walk Area **Handicap Access:** No

Narrows Marina

PO Box 340; Old Ferry Road; Grimstead, VA 23064

Tel: (804) 725-2151 **VHF: Monitor** n/a **Talk** n/a
Fax: n/a **Alternate Tel:** (804) 815-8897
Email: islander@inna.net **Web:** n/a
Nearest Town: Mathews *(7 mi.)* **Tourist Info:** (804) 725-9009

Marina Services and Boat Supplies
Services - Docking Assistance **Communication -** Mail & Package Hold, Phone Messages, FedEx, DHL, UPS *(Sat Del)* **Supplies - OnSite:** Ice *(Cube)*, Ships' Store **Near:** Marine Discount Store *(Pulley's Marine 725-3814)* **3+ mi:** West Marine *(Deltaville - 776-0400, 18 mi.)*, Boat/US *(Deltaville - 776-8583, 19 mi.)*, Bait/Tackle *(Captain Kirk's Bait & Tackle 725-1700, 6 mi.)*, Propane *(Phillips Oil & Gas 725-9020, 5 mi.)*

Boatyard Services
OnSite: Travelift *(40T)*, Engine mechanic *(gas, diesel)*, Electrical Repairs, Hull Repairs, Bottom Cleaning, Brightwork, Air Conditioning, Compound, Wash & Wax, Woodworking, Painting **OnCall:** Electronics Repairs, Rigger, Canvas Work, Refrigeration, Divers **Near:** Launching Ramp.

Restaurants and Accommodations
Near: Restaurant *(Seabreeze 725-4000, L $3-7, D $8-14)*
3+ mi: Restaurant *(Andy's Barbecue & Ribs 725-9320, 7 mi.)*, *(Lynne's Family Restaurant 725-9996, L $4-7, D $4-18, 7 mi., prime rib, fried oysters, steamed shrimp)*, *(Southwind Café 725-2766, 6 mi.)*, Coffee Shop (Bradley & *Bartlett's Café 725-4900, 7 mi.)*, Pizzeria *(Sal's Pizza 725-9301, L $2-5, D $2-5, 6 mi.)*, Inn/B&B *(Buckley Hall Inn 725-1900, 6 mi.)*, (Ravenwood Inn *725-7272, 7 mi.)*

Recreation and Entertainment
OnSite: Beach, Picnic Area, Grills **1-3 mi:** Museum *(Gwynn's Island Museum 725-2656)*, Sightseeing *(exquisite 1776 Matthews Baptist Church)* **3+ mi:** Golf Course *(Piankatank River Golf Club 776-6589, 16 mi)*, Fitness Center *(Mathews Family YMCA 725-1488, 7 mi.)*, Movie Theater *(Hillside Cinema 693-7766, 17 mi.)*, Video Rental *(Vanity Video 725-9614, 7 mi.)*, Park *(Bethel Beach Nature Sanctuary, 7 mi.)*, Cultural Attract *(Mathews County Visitor & Information Center 725-4229, 6 mi.)*, Galleries *(Mathews Art Gallery 725-3326, 7 mi.)*

Provisioning and General Services
Near: Convenience Store *(Island Market & Deli 725-4153)*, Bank/ATM, Post Office *(725-7618)* **Under 1 mi:** Fishmonger *(Island Seafood Co 725-4962)*, Market *(Zooms)*, Protestant Church, Beauty Salon *(M&J Beauty Boutique 725-3074)* **1-3 mi:** Barber Shop *(Country Cuts 725-7588)* **3+ mi:** Supermarket *(Food Lion 725-1240, 7 mi.)*, Liquor Store *(ABC 725-4353, 7 mi.)*, Oysterman *(Middle Peninsula Aquaculture 725-0159, 7 mi.)*, Library *(Mathews 725-0808, 6 mi.)*, Dry Cleaners *(Village Cleaners 725-5400, 6 mi.)*, Pharmacy *(Hudgins 725-2222, 6 mi.)*, Hardware Store *(Moughon's 725-2600, 7 mi.)*, Florist *(Flowers from the Heart 725-3020, 7 mi.)*, Clothing Store *(Country Casuals 725-4050, 7 mi.)*

Transportation
OnCall: Rental Car *(Enterprise 694-8226 20 mi.)*
3+ mi: Rail (Amtrak - *Newport News 757-245-3589, 48 mi.)*
Airport: Newport News/Williamsburg Int'l. *(42 mi.)*

Medical Services
911 Service **3+ mi:** Doctor *(Riverside Health System 725-5005, 7 mi.)*, Dentist *(Lennon 725-9485, 6 mi.)*, Chiropractor *(Merithew Layton 725-9376, 7 mi.)*, Veterinarian *(Mathews Veterinary Services 725-4123, 6 mi.)*
Hospital: Riverside Walter Reed 693-8800 *(21 mi.)*

Setting -- On historic Gwynn's Island, just west of the swing bridge, convenient Narrows Marina is in a spectacular but otherworldly location. Set along the bulkheads of a protected basin, the docks are surrounded by the remains of the Islander Motel & Restaurant. Already deep in decline, the nearly 10-acre complex was devastated by Hurricane Isabel. Open dockage lines the port side of the channel - as one approaches - leading to two covered boat sheds.

Marina Notes -- A 24-hour fuel dock is on the premises. Clearly a facility in transition. Very helpful manager certainly mitigates some of the environment. Cable TV hook-ups at 60 slips. The docks damaged by Isabel were repaired by summer '05. Many annual and seasonal tenants, but transient space is always available. A few work boats berth here as well, which augers well for provisions. The facility has apparently been for sale for some time. Basic bathhouse has two toilets, two showers, two sinks and newly repaired quarry tile floors.

Notable -- At the tip of the peninsula, a really lovely white sand beach - backed by a once-lovely pool - sprawls in front of the concrete shells of the old restaurant and motel. Tufts of beach grass add to the stopped-in-time feeling. A few blocks' walk, just on the other side of the entrance to the bridge, small, casual Sea Breeze restaurant is literally on the water's edge, with dock-and-dine. Across the bridge, on the mainland, is the Coast Guard Station. The area around the marina has developed very nicely with many lovely homes. A "Zooms" at the Citgo at Buckley Hall & Cricket Hill Roads provides some basics. Biking distance is Gwynn's Island Museum - Indian and Colonial artifacts, plus the Island's history to the present. Most services are seven miles away in Mathews.

PHOTOS ON CD-ROM: 10

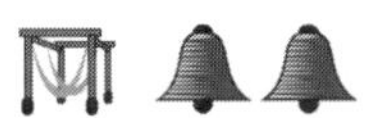

Horn Harbor Marina

308 Railway Road; Port Haywood, VA 23138

Tel: (804) 725-3223 **VHF: Monitor** n/a **Talk** n/a
Fax: n/a **Alternate Tel:** (804) 725-3223
Email: n/a **Web:** n/a
Nearest Town: Mathews *(6 mi.)* **Tourist Info:** (804) 725-9009

Navigational Information

Lat: 37°22.183' **Long:** 076°18.016' **Tide:** 2 ft. **Current:** n/a **Chart:** 12238
Rep. Depths (*MLW*): Entry 6 ft. **Fuel Dock** n/a **Max Slip/Moor** 8 ft./-
Access: Chesapeake to Horn Harbor

Marina Facilities *(In Season/Off Season)*

Fuel: *Texaco* - Gasoline, Diesel, High-Speed Pumps
Slips: 65 Total, 7 Transient **Max LOA:** 50 ft. **Max Beam:** 17 ft.
Rate *(per ft.)*: **Day** $1.25 **Week** n/a **Month** $7/ft
Power: 30 amp $5, **50 amp** n/a, **100 amp** n/a, **200 amp** n/a
Cable TV: No **Dockside Phone:** No
Dock Type: Fixed, Floating, Short Fingers, Pilings, Alongside
Moorings: 0 Total, 0 Transient **Launch:** n/a
Rate: Day n/a **Week** n/a **Month** n/a
Heads: 5 Toilet(s), 4 Shower(s)
Laundry: None, Book Exchange **Pay Phones:** No
Pump-Out: Full Service, 1 Central **Fee:** $10 **Closed Heads:** Yes

Marina Operations

Owner/Manager: Norm Turner **Dockmaster:** Same
In-Season: Apr-Dec, 8am-4:30pm **Off-Season:** Jan-Mar, 8am-noon
After-Hours Arrival: Take a slip, check in the am
Reservations: No **Credit Cards:** Visa/MC
Discounts: None
Pets: Welcome **Handicap Access:** Yes, Heads, Docks

Marina Services and Boat Supplies

Services - Boaters' Lounge, Trash Pick-Up, Dock Carts **Supplies - OnSite:** Ice *(Block, Cube)*, Ships' Store **3+ mi:** Bait/Tackle *(Queens Creek Outfitters 725-3889, 10 mi.)*, Propane *(Phillips Oil & Gas 725-9020, 5 mi.)*

Boatyard Services

OnSite: Travelift *(15T/40T)*, Railway, Electrical Repairs, Bottom Cleaning, Woodworking, Painting **OnCall:** Divers **3+ mi:** Electronics Repairs *(20 mi.)*, Hull Repairs *(20 mi.)*, Rigger *(20 mi.)*, Sail Loft *(20 mi.)*, Canvas Work *(20 mi.)*. **Yard Rates:** $50/hr., Haul & Launch $5/ft. *(blocking $2/ft.)*, Power Wash $2/ft.

Restaurants and Accommodations

1-3 mi: Inn/B&B *(Inn at Tabb's Creek Landing 725-5136)* **3+ mi:** Restaurant *(Shun Xing 725-4682, 6 mi.)*, *(Main Street Cottage 725-7900, L $5-8, D $8-20, 6 mi., lunch only on Saturdays, rest of week, dinner only)*, Coffee Shop *(Bradley & Bartlett's Cafe 725-4900, 6 mi.)*, Lite Fare *(Southwind Cafe 725-2766, 6 mi.)*, Pizzeria *(Sal's Pizza 725-9301, L $2-5, D $2-5, 6 mi.)*, Inn/B&B *(Buckley Hall Inn 725-1900, 6 mi.)*

Recreation and Entertainment

OnSite: Pool, Picnic Area **OnCall:** Group Fishing Boat *(Bay Quest 43 ft. 15-25 passengers 529-6725)* **3+ mi:** Beach *(5 mi.)*, Tennis Courts *(6 mi.)*, Golf Course *(Gloucester Country Club 693-2662, 22 mi.)*, Fitness Center *(Mathews Family YMCA 725-1488, 6 mi.)*, Movie Theater *(Donk's Theater 725-7760, 8 mi.)*, Museum *(Gwynn Island Museum 725-2656, 12 mi.)*, Cultural Attract *(Donk's - Virginia's Li'l Ole Opry 725-7760 , 6 mi.)*, Galleries *(Mathews Art Gallery 725-3326, 6 mi.)*

Provisioning and General Services

Under 1 mi: Convenience Store *(JR's Convenient Store 725-0742)* **1-3 mi:** Fishmonger *(Davis Creek Marina & Seafood 725-2452)*, Post Office *(725-2943)* **3+ mi:** Supermarket *(Best Value Supermarket 725-7647, 6 mi.)*, Oysterman *(Middle Peninsula Aquaculture 725-0159, 6 mi.)*, Bank/ATM *(6 mi.)*, Library *(Friends of Mathews Memorial Library 725-0808, 6 mi.)*, Beauty Salon *(Hair Creations, 6 mi.)*, Barber Shop *(Deb's Haircuts 725-4100, 6 mi.)*, Dry Cleaners *(Village Cleaners 725-5400, 6 mi.)*, Pharmacy *(Medicine Shoppe 725-2556, 6 mi.)*, Hardware Store *(Moughon's 725-2600, 6 mi.)*, Florist *(Country Flower Shop 725-5222, 6 mi.)*, Clothing Store *(Country Casuals 725-4050, 6 mi.)*

Transportation

OnCall: Rental Car *(Enterprise 694-8226,21 mi.)*
3+ mi: Rail *(Amtrak Newport News 757-245-3589, 50 mi.)*
Airport: Newport News/ Williamsburg Int'l. *(44 mi.)*

Medical Services

911 Service **3+ mi:** Doctor *(Riverside Health System 725-5005, 6 mi.)*, Dentist *(David Helsel 725-7500, 6 mi.)*, Chiropractor *(Dicesaro Spine & Sport 412-299-3824, 7 mi.)*, Veterinarian *(Mathews Veterinary Services 725-4123, 10 mi.)* **Hospital:** Riverside Walter Reed 693-8800 *(24 mi.)*

Setting -- Tucked up into shallow Horn Harbor, this very neat and tidy, well-tended marina offers open and covered dockage on a very quiet, almost bucolic stretch of water. Boardwalks edged with rope railings connect the boatyard-area docks with office and pool-area docks. The covered slips are very nicely done with a clapboard exterior and a metal roof.

Marina Notes -- The fuel dock is on the end of the boatyard pier. There are two sections of covered docks and one section of open docks (anchored by the boatyard) plus the floating, vinyl-edged open slips on the far side of the boat sheds. For the open docks, power and water are on short little posts. The boatyard offers limited services, an aging travelift and serious railway. The white building with bright blue trim, near the pool, has ice and soft drink machines and a comfortable bathhouse with asphalt tile floor, wood dividers, fiberglass shower stalls with dressing rooms, and bright, fresh shower curtains. Sinks are set into a long vanity with a little skirt. An effort was made to make this a pleasant place.

Notable -- An inviting pool with chaises and umbrella-topped picnic tables overlooks the covered docks. A few more picnic tables are scattered on the grass outside with propane grills tucked under cover. In the building adjacent to the pool, which also houses the heads, the Horn Harbor Association's very nice boaters' lounge has tables and chairs, a television, a microwave, and small kitchen. A mile away is JR's Convenient Store (725-0742) and a post office - everything else is in Mathews, 6 miles away.

Navigational Information
Lat: 37°25.600' **Long:** 076°24.016' **Tide:** 2 ft. **Current:** n/a **Chart:** 12238
Rep. Depths (*MLW*): Entry 8 ft. **Fuel Dock** 8 ft. **Max Slip/Moor** 8 ft./8 ft.
Access: Mobjack Bay to North River

Marina Facilities *(In Season/Off Season)*
Fuel: *Texaco* - Gasoline, Diesel
Slips: 108 Total, 3 Transient **Max LOA:** 50 ft. **Max Beam:** n/a
Rate *(per ft.)*: **Day** $20.00* **Week** n/a **Month** n/a
Power: 30 amp Incl., **50 amp** n/a, **100 amp** n/a, **200 amp** n/a
Cable TV: No **Dockside Phone:** No
Dock Type: Fixed, Long Fingers, Short Fingers, Pilings, Wood
Moorings: 0 Total, 0 Transient **Launch:** n/a
Rate: Day n/a **Week** n/a **Month** n/a
Heads: 5 Toilet(s), 4 Shower(s)
Laundry: None, Book Exchange **Pay Phones:** No
Pump-Out: Full Service, 1 Central, 1 Port **Fee:** n/a **Closed Heads:** Yes

Marina Operations
Owner/Manager: Kay Dorlene Talbott **Dockmaster:** Same
In-Season: May-Nov, 8am-5pm **Off-Season:** Dec-Apr, 9am-4pm
After-Hours Arrival: Call ahead
Reservations: Preferred **Credit Cards:** Cash or checks
Discounts: None
Pets: Welcome, Dog Walk Area **Handicap Access:** No

Mobjack Bay Marina

PO Box 547; 454 Marina Drive; North, VA 23128

Tel: (804) 725-7245 **VHF: Monitor** n/a **Talk** n/a
Fax: (804) 725-7245 **Alternate Tel:** (804) 725-9021
Email: mobjack@visit.net **Web:** n/a
Nearest Town: Mathews *(8 mi.)* **Tourist Info:** (804) 725-9009

Marina Services and Boat Supplies
Services - Docking Assistance, Security *(24 hrs., owner lives onsite)*, Dock Carts **Supplies - OnSite:** Ice *(Cube)*, Ships' Store **3+ mi:** Bait/Tackle *(Captain Kirk's 725-1700, 7 mi.)*, Propane *(Phillips 725-9020, 8 mi.)*

Boatyard Services
OnSite: Travelift *(20T)*, Railway, Launching Ramp, Engine mechanic *(gas, diesel)*, Hull Repairs, Rigger, Sail Loft, Canvas Work, Bottom Cleaning, Compound, Wash & Wax, Interior Cleaning, Propeller Repairs, Woodworking, Inflatable Repairs, Painting **OnCall:** Divers **Near:** Yacht Building, Total Refits. **Yard Rates:** Inq., Haul & Launch $2.50/ft *(blocking $1.25/ft)*, Power Wash $1.25/ft, Bottom Paint $13.50/ft *(paint incl.)*
Storage: On-Land $85/mo

Restaurants and Accommodations
Near: Restaurant *(Southwind 725-2766, D $15, Tue-Sat 11am-3pm & 5-9pm; take out available; beer & wine)*, *(Linda's Diner 725-7070, B $3-5, L $2-13, D $2-13)*, *(Main Street Cottage 725-7900, L $5-8, D $8-20, Lunch on Saturdays, rest of the week dinner only)*, Condo/Cottage *(Ladybug Cottage 725-7560, $75/nite, 2 nite min.)* **3+ mi:** Restaurant *(The Irish Cottage 725-7900, 8 mi., Lunch daily, Dinner Tue-Sat only)*, *(Lynne's Family Restaurant 725-9996, L $4-7, D $4-18, 8 mi., Mon-Sat 7am-8pm, kids menu; take out also)*, Inn/B&B *(Buckley Hall B&B 725-1900, $75-120, 8 mi., bikes provided)*, Condo/Cottage *(Mobjack Bay Cottage 725-2513, 4 mi., 1800-sq. ft. waterfront cottage; $1000 weekly, $350-450/2-nt. weekend)*

Recreation and Entertainment
OnSite: Picnic Area, Grills **Near:** Galleries *(plus Mathews galleries, antique & pottery shops 725-3326)* **1-3 mi:** Sightseeing *(biking trils, kayaking)* **3+ mi:** Golf Course *(Gloucester Country Club 693-2662, 11 mi.)*, Fitness Center *(Mathews Family YMCA 725-1488, 8 mi.)*, Movie Theater *(Hillside Cinema 693-2770, 10 mi.)*, Video Rental *(Vanity Video 725-9614, 8 mi.)*, Park *(Beavers Dam Park, Williams Wharf)*, Cultural Attract *(Donk's Theatre - Virginia's Li'l Ole Opry - live country music 725-7760 , 9 mi.)*, Special Events *(Mathews Market Days - Sat & Sun after Labor Day, 8 mi.)*

Provisioning and General Services
Near: Convenience Store *(North Star Market 725-0708)*, Post Office **1-3 mi:** Bank/ATM **3+ mi:** Supermarket *(Food Lion 725-1240, 8 mi.)*, Health Food *(Kelsick Gardens 804-693-6500, 10 mi.)*, Liquor Store *(ABC 693-3973, 10 mi.)*, Fishmonger *(Mobjack Bay Seafood 693-0044, 11 mi.)*, Catholic Church *(3+ mi.)*, Protestant Church *(3+ mi.)*, Library *(Mathews 725-5747, wireless Internet, 8 mi.)*, Dry Cleaners *(Village Cleaners 725-5400, 8 mi.)*, Pharmacy *(Hudgins 725-2222, 8 mi.)*, Hardware Store *(Home Depot 695-9037, 11 mi.)*, Department Store *(Peebles, Wal-Mart 693-8916, 12 mi.)*, Copies Etc. *(Gloucester Office Supply 693-4155, 12 mi.)*

Transportation
OnSite: Bikes *(Inq.)* **OnCall:** Rental Car *(Enterprise 694-8226)*
3+ mi: Rail*(Amtrak - Newport News 757-245-3589, 36 mi.)*
Airport: Newport News/Williamsburg Int'l. *(35 mi.)*

Medical Services
911 Service **OnCall:** Ambulance **Near:** Doctor *(Stewart 725-4115)*, Dentist *(Lennon 725-9485)* **Hospital:** Riverside Walter Reed 693-8800 *(11 mi.)*

Setting -- Off the North River at the mouth of Greenmansion Cove, rural, small-town Mobjack Bay Marina's blissful location invites peace and quiet and breathing space without sacrificing buttoned-up, which it certainly seems to be. Primarily a sailboat marina, the wide, recent docks are in good shape with full-size pedestals. Most of the facility is devoted to a full-service boatyard operation with extensive on-the-hard storage.

Marina Notes -- *Nightly transient dockage is flat rate. Owner lives on premises in the lovely Tidewater Colonial - providing good security. The boatyard provides an extensive array of onsite services. A small ships' store supplies basic boating needs. Small covered slips for the handful of powerboats that make their home here. The fuel pumps are to starboard. A stationary dock outboard of the small boathouse near the Quonset hut work sheds can accommodate a catamaran. An attractive clapboard building houses a fairly basic, although neat, clean, bathhouse. An effort has been made to spruce it up with some tile walls and floors and pretty shower curtains.

Notable -- On the far side of the Cove is its namesake Greenmansion Plantation - a three story Tidewater Colonial topped with many sets of chimmneys that hint at its glorious past. A small one bedroom cottage on the plantation is available for $75 a night, two night minimum. The quiet rural area invites kayak or dinghy exploration. Surrounding rural Mathews County offers some fascinating touring as well as galleries, antique shops and Donk's--Virginia's Li'l Ole Opry. It's a bit of a bike, but also a pretty flat route.

PHOTOS ON CD-ROM: 10

Severn River Marina

PO Box 1228; 3398 Stonewall Road; Hayes, VA 23072

Tel: (804) 642-6969 **VHF: Monitor** 16 **Talk** 69
Fax: (804) 642-0073 **Alternate Tel:** n/a
Email: severnrivermarina@msn.com **Web:** www.severnrivermarina.com
Nearest Town: Gloucester **Tourist Info:** (804) 693-0014

Navigational Information

Lat: 37°18.283' **Long:** 076°27.233' **Tide:** 2 ft **Current:** 2 kt. **Chart:** 12238
Rep. Depths (*MLW*): Entry 6 ft. **Fuel Dock** 6 ft. **Max Slip/Moor** 6 ft./6 ft.
Access: Mobjock Bay, 1 mile up Severn River

Marina Facilities *(In Season/Off Season)*

Fuel: Yes
Slips: 52 Total, 5 Transient **Max LOA:** 120 ft. **Max Beam:** 22 ft.
Rate *(per ft.)*: **Day** $1.15* **Week** Inq. **Month** $210
Power: 30 amp $6, **50 amp** $8, **100 amp** n/a, **200 amp** n/a
Cable TV: No **Dockside Phone:** No
Dock Type: Fixed, Short Fingers, Pilings, Wood
Moorings: 0 Total, 0 Transient **Launch:** n/a
Rate: Day n/a **Week** n/a **Month** n/a
Heads: 6 Toilet(s), 4 Shower(s)
Laundry: None, Book Exchange **Pay Phones:** No
Pump-Out: Onsite *(In slip 52)* **Fee:** n/a **Closed Heads:** Yes

Marina Operations

Owner/Manager: Dan Camp **Dockmaster:** Tom Reule
In-Season: Year Round, 8am-5pm **Off-Season:** n/a
After-Hours Arrival: Call ahead
Reservations: Yes, Preferred **Credit Cards:** Visa/MC, Dscvr
Discounts: Boat/US **Dockage:** 10% **Fuel:** $0.05 **Repair:** 10% ($400 max)
Pets: Welcome, Dog Walk Area **Handicap Access:** Yes, Heads, Docks

Marina Services and Boat Supplies

Services - Dock Carts **Communication -** Mail & Package Hold, Fax in/out, FedEx, UPS **Supplies - OnSite:** Ice *(Block, Cube)*, Ships' Store, Bait/Tackle *(or Regensburg 642-9112, 2mi.)*, Live Bait *(squid and shrimp)* **3+ mi:** West Marine *(642-3470, 6 mi.)*, Propane *(Phillips 642-2166, 6 mi.)*

Boatyard Services

OnSite: Travelift *(75T)*, Engine mechanic *(gas, diesel)*, Electrical Repairs, Electronics Repairs, Hull Repairs, Rigger, Canvas Work, Bottom Cleaning, Brightwork, Air Conditioning, Refrigeration, Divers, Compound, Wash & Wax, Interior Cleaning, Propeller Repairs, Woodworking, Yacht Interiors, Metal Fabrication, Painting, Awlgrip, Total Refits **OnCall:** Inflatable Repairs, Life Raft Service **3+ mi:** Sail Loft *(Hayes Sails)*. **Yard Rates:** $65/hr., Haul & Launch $6/ft., Bottom Paint $60/hr. **Storage:** On-Land $4.00/ft./mo.

Restaurants and Accommodations

OnCall: Pizzeria *(Pizza Hut 642-4620)* **1-3 mi:** Restaurant *(Seawall's Ordinary 642-3635, D $10-17, picks up & delivers boaters)* **3+ mi:** Restaurant *(River's Inn 642-9942, L $9-14, D $20-25, 8 mi.)*, *(Carolina BBQ 684-2450, L $6-9, D $8-12, 6 mi.)*, *(Goodfellas 693-5950, 6 mi.)*, *(Dolphin Cove 684-2222, 6 mi.)*, *(King's Seafood 642-2605, 8 mi.)*, Snack Bar *(Scoops 684-2744, L $5-10, 5 mi.)*, Coffee Shop *(Java Joint 684-2606, 6 mi.)*, Pizzeria *(Sal's Sicilian 642-6470, 6 mi.)*, Motel *(Duke of York 757-898-3232, 9 mi.)*, *(Comfort Inn 695-1900, $75-100, 10 mi.)*, *(Gloucester Inn 642-3337, 6 mi.)*, Inn/B&B *(York River 757-887-8800, 8 mi.)*

Recreation and Entertainment

OnSite: Picnic Area, Grills **3+ mi:** Beach *(Gloucester Pt., 8 mi.)*, Golf Course *(Gloucester 693-2662, 10 mi.)*, Fitness Center *(Curves 684-0877, 5 mi.)*, Fishing Charter *(Erin Kay 642-5076, 5 mi.)*, Movie Theater *(Regal 642-1097, 5 mi.)*, Park *(Colonial Nat'l Historical Park Archeology 757-886-5341, 9 mi.)*, Museum *(Watermen's Museum 757-887-2641, 9 mi.)*, Cultural Attract *(VA Institute of Marine Science 684-7000 9am-4:30pm, 7 mi.)*

Provisioning and General Services

1-3 mi: Post Office *(Bena 642-6311)* **3+ mi:** Convenience Store *(Little Sue 642-2285, 4 mi.)*, Supermarket *(Farm Fresh 642-6101/Food Lion 580-7326, 4 mi.)*, Health Food *(Healthy Solutions 693-2450, 5 mi.)*, Liquor Store *(ABC 642-9084, 5 mi.)*, Green Grocer *(Mon-Sat 8am-4pm, 5 mi.)*, Crabs/Waterman *(Shackelford Seafood 642-2022, Abby Dog 642-2323, 6 mi.)*, Bank/ATM *(5 mi.)*, Protestant Church *(5 mi.)*, Library *(642-9790, 7 mi.)*, Beauty Salon *(Jana Kay's 642-4280, 5 mi.)*, Dry Cleaners *(Boulevard 684-2333, 6 mi.)*, Laundry *(U-Do-It 642-2497, 6 mi.)*, Bookstore *(That Book Place 642-3800, 6 mi.)*, Pharmacy *(Rite Aid 642-1292, 5 mi.)*, Hardware Store *(Ace 642-5300, 5 mi.)*, Department Store *(Wal-Mart 694-0110, 10 mi.)*

Transportation

OnSite: Courtesy Car/Van *(Free to trans - fill gas tank)* **OnCall:** Rental Car *(Enterprise 694-8226)*, Taxi *(Yorktown 757-890-2840)*, Airport Limo *(Associated Cabs 757-887-3412)* **3+ mi:** Rail *(Amtrak Williamsburg 757-229-8750, 22 mi.)* **Airport:** Newport News/Williamsburg Int'l. *(19 mi./18 mi.)*

Medical Services

911 Service **3+ mi:** Doctor *(Gloucester Convenient Care 684-2060, 5 mi.)*, Chiropractor *(Gloucester 642-6106, 5 mi.)* **Hospital:** Sentara Williamsburg Community Hospital 684-2000/Walter Reed 693-8800 *(5 mi./12 mi.)*

Setting -- About one mile off Mobjack Bay, this ship-shape marina stretches along the starboard side of Severn River's Southwest Branch. At this wide spot of water, the vista is almost 180 degrees of pristine shoreline. Landside, an L-shaped single story white office and large travelift are backed by a tall work shed. The cement patio outside the office serves as a crab deck with grills and wooden picnic tables; fiberglass picnic tables line the grassy bulkhead.

Marina Notes -- DCM. *50 ft. + $325/mo. Pump-out at every slip! Wide, recent stationary docks with step-down tapered finger piers. Lighthouse pedestals. Roomy slips - several catamarans berth here. Fish cleaning station. Fuel dock is the one closest to the office. Ships' store with most everything a boater might need - including recycling bins. The yard, with a 75 ton travelift, is one of the prime attractions - even manages some large tour boats. Extensive on-the-hard storage. All-tile bathhouses have quarry tile floors, molded Corian sinks and two shower stalls each; a laundry room is adjacent. FYI: Across the river, in Rowes Creek, small, rustic Holiday Marina (642-2528) berths mostly working vessels (think crabs!) but has an occasional transient slip.

Notable -- Walking outside the marina or cruising this section of the water, the location has a "beyond forever" sense of isolation - that encourages relaxation. Yet about 2.5 miles (at the crossroads of Route 17 & Brays Point Rd.) is a small strip mall and historic Seawell's Ordinary Restaurant - elegant dining in an authentic Colonial atmosphere; their Tavern & Courtyard offers a lighter menu, Saturday & Sunday brunch, and live entertainment Friday & Saturday nights. Farm Fresh supermarket is 4 miles and historic Yorktown is 8 miles.

Navigational Information

Lat: 76°25.297' **Long:** 037°16.080' **Tide:** 3 ft. **Current:** 2 kt. **Chart:** 12238
Rep. Depths (*MLW*): Entry 7 ft. **Fuel Dock** 6 ft. **Max Slip/Moor** 7 ft./7 ft.
Access: On the Perrin River at the mouth of the York River

Marina Facilities *(In Season/Off Season)*

Fuel: Gasoline, Diesel
Slips: 235 Total, 25 Transient **Max LOA:** 50 ft. **Max Beam:** 16 ft.
Rate *(per ft.)*: **Day** $1.00 **Week** Inq. **Month** Inq.
Power: 30 amp $5, **50 amp** $5, **100 amp** n/a, **200 amp** n/a
Cable TV: Yes -currently being installed **Dockside Phone:** No
Dock Type: Fixed, Short Fingers, Pilings, Alongside, Wood
Moorings: 0 Total, 0 Transient **Launch:** n/a, Dinghy Dock
Rate: Day n/a **Week** n/a **Month** n/a
Heads: 10 Toilet(s), 10 Shower(s), Hair Dryers, A/C
Laundry: 2 Washer(s), 2 Dryer(s), Iron, Iron Board **Pay Phones:** No
Pump-Out: OnSite, Full Service, 1 Central **Fee:** Free **Closed Heads:** Yes

Marina Operations

Owner/Manager: Ralph Beckman **Dockmaster:** Nelson Mowry
In-Season: Year-Round, 8:30am-5pm **Off-Season:** n/a
After-Hours Arrival: Call in advance
Reservations: Preferred **Credit Cards:** Visa/MC, Dscvr, Din, Amex, JCB
Discounts: Boat/US; 5% retail **Dockage:** 10% **Fuel:** .10/gal **Repair:** n/a
Pets: Welcome, Dog Walk Area **Handicap Access:** Yes, Heads, Docks

Crown Pointe Marina

PO Box ; 9397 Cook's Landing; Hayes, VA 23072

Tel: (804) 642-6177 **VHF: Monitor** 16 **Talk** 68
Fax: (804) 642-6050 **Alternate Tel:** n/a
Email: n/a **Web:** www.crownpointemarina.com
Nearest Town: Hayes *(5 mi.)* **Tourist Info:** (804) 693-0014

Marina Services and Boat Supplies

Services - Docking Assistance, Concierge, Security *(on-site)*, Dock Carts **Communication -** Mail & Package Hold, Phone Messages, Fax in/out, Data Ports *(Office, DSL)*, FedEx, UPS, Express Mail **Supplies - OnSite:** Ice *(Block, Cube)*, Ships' Store **3+ mi:** West Marine *(642-3470, 6 mi.)*, Bait/Tackle *(A&S 642-4940, 7 mi.)*, Propane *(Phillips 642-2166, 7 mi.)*

Boatyard Services

OnSite: Travelift *(30T)*, Launching Ramp, Engine mechanic *(gas, diesel)*, Electrical Repairs, Electronics Repairs, Hull Repairs, Rigger, Bottom Cleaning, Compound, Wash & Wax, Interior Cleaning, Woodworking, Painting, Awlgrip, Total Refits **OnCall:** Sail Loft, Canvas Work, Brightwork, Air Conditioning, Refrigeration, Divers, Propeller Repairs, Life Raft Service, Yacht Interiors, Metal Fabrication **Dealer for:** C&C, Romarine, Tartan, MacGregor, Mirage, Newport, Irwin, Hinterhoeller, Soverel.
Yard Rates: $45/hr., Haul & Launch $4.50/ft. *(blocking $40/ft.)*, Power Wash $1.25/ft., Bottom Paint $3.50/ft. **Storage:** On-Land $5/day flat rate

Restaurants and Accommodations

OnSite: Snack Bar **OnCall:** Pizzeria *(Domino's 642-9995)*, *(Pizza Hut 642-4620)* **Under 1 mi:** Restaurant *(King's Seafood 642-2605)* **1-3 mi:** Seafood Shack *(Bay Water Oyster Co. 642-4094)*, Fast Food *(Taco Bell/KFC/Hardee's)* **3+ mi:** Restaurant *(Rivers Inn 642-9942, L $9-14, D $20-25,* 8 mi.), *(Smokin Joe's BBQ 875-7774, L $4-15, D $5-17, 5 mi.)*, *(Olivia's at the Point 684-2234, L $5-8, D $8-20, 7 mi.)*, Pizzeria *(Sal's 642-6470, 5 mi.)*, Motel *(Comfort Inn 695-1900, $89, 10 mi., special rate available)*, *(Gloucester Inn 642-3337, 6 mi.)*, Inn/B&B *(Duke of York 757-898-3232, 9 mi.)*

Recreation and Entertainment

OnSite: Pool *(2)*, Picnic Area, Grills *($10 fee)*, Boat Rentals *(kayaks)*, Fishing Charter, Volleyball **1-3 mi:** Beach *(near Coleman Bridge)* **3+ mi:** Golf Course *(Gloucester 693-2662, 15 mi.)*, Movie Theater *(York River 692-5999, 5 mi.)*, Park *(4 mi.)*, Museum *(Watermen's Museum 757-887-2641, Yorktown Battlefields & Victory Center, 9 mi.)*, Cultural Attract *(VA Institute of Marine Science - aquarium, tours, family programs 684-7000, 7 mi.)*

Provisioning and General Services

OnSite: Wine/Beer *(Beer)* **1-3 mi:** Farmers' Market, Fishmonger *(Shackelford 642-2022)*, Market *(Achilles 642-4234)*, Post Office *(642-9908)*, Newsstand **3+ mi:** Supermarket *(Farm Fresh 642-6101, 6 mi.)*, Liquor Store *(ABC 642-1516, 6 mi.)*, Bank/ATM *(4 mi.)*, Library *(642-9790, 6 mi.)*, Beauty Salon *(Hair Statements 642-0283, 6 mi.)*, Dry Cleaners *(Boulevard 684-2333, 5 mi.)*, Bookstore *(That Book Place 642-3800, 6 mi.)*, Pharmacy *(Rite Aid 642-1292, 5 mi.)*, Hardware Store *(Ace 642-5300, 7 mi.)*, Retail Shops *(Dollar 684-9917, 6 mi.)*, Department Store *(Wal-Mart 693-8916, 14 mi.)*

Transportation

OnSite: Courtesy Car/Van, Bikes *(rentals on-site)* **OnCall:** Rental Car *(Enterprise 694-8226)*, Taxi *(Yorktown 757-890-2840)*, Airport Limo *(Associated 757-887-3412)* **3+ mi:** Rail *(Amtrak Williamsburg 757-229-8750, 20 mi.)* **Airport:** Newport News/Williamsburg Int'l. *(19 mi.)*

Medical Services

911 Service **OnCall:** Ambulance **3+ mi:** Doctor *(Convenient Care 684-2060, 5 mi.)*, Dentist *(Dukart 642-6594, 6 mi.)*
Hospital: Sentara Comm. 684-2000/Walter Reed 693-8800 *(5 mi./16 mi.)*

Setting -- Close to the mouth, off York River's north shore, nine piers hosting 235 slips sprawl along quiet Perrin River. A few houses dot the shoreline and a local watermen's dock with a fish packing plant is nearby. Eleven acres of upland are home to an extensive boatyard and brokerage operation, two pools and a yacht club. The office and a small luncheonette with a screened porch are in the low two-tone blue building.

Marina Notes -- Formerly known as Cook's Landing Marina. New owners Joe Heyman & Martha Heric took the helm in August '04 and are updating this long neglected but ideally located facility. Managed by Lane Hospitality. Easy access fuel dock. Picnics and modest provisioning can be ordered with 48 hrs. notice. Home of the Colonial Yacht Club. Boatyard with full-time mechanic, totally overhauled 30 ton lift in early '05. Do-it-yourself area available. Complimentary hi-speed Internet at front desk. Notary on staff. Book exchange (free) & DVD rentals ($2). Lovely climate-controlled all-tile bathhouses feature hand-painted borders: each has 2 sinks set in vanities, 2 toilets and 2 fully tiled showers with private dressing rooms and colorful shower curtains.

Notable -- The upgrade is being tackled with gusto - detritus that's both on the hard and under the slips has been carted off and it's quickly morphing into a buttoned-up, maintenance-oriented facility. The two pools - one extending from the Colonial Yacht Club's party room and the other next to the office - have been cleaned and the patio surrounds furnished with sparkling chaises and tables and chairs topped by new umbrellas. A large canvas covered picnic shelter is between "B" & "C" docks with a propane grill ($10 fee). Additional picnic tables and new Phillipine mahogany benches dot the grassy bulkhead.

PHOTOS ON CD-ROM: 11

Wormley Creek Marina

1221 Waterview Road; Yorktown, VA 23692

Tel: (757) 898-5060 **VHF: Monitor** 16 **Talk** 8
Fax: (757) 898-3561 **Alternate Tel:** (757) 898-8062
Email: dtruston@msn.com **Web:** www.wormleycreekmarina.com
Nearest Town: Yorktown **Tourist Info:** (757) 766-2000

Navigational Information

Lat: 37°12.866' **Long:** 076°28.045' **Tide:** 3 ft. **Current:** .5 kt. **Chart:** 12238
Rep. Depths (*MLW*): Entry 7 ft. **Fuel Dock** 7 ft. **Max Slip/Moor** 7 ft./7 ft.
Access: Southern shore of York River

Marina Facilities *(In Season/Off Season)*

Fuel: Gasoline, Diesel
Slips: 92 Total, 0 Transient **Max LOA:** 70 ft. **Max Beam:** 15 ft.
Rate *(per ft.)*: **Day** $1.00 **Week** Inq. **Month** Inq.
Power: 30 amp $5, **50 amp** $10, **100 amp** n/a, **200 amp** n/a
Cable TV: No **Dockside Phone:** No
Dock Type: Fixed
Moorings: 0 Total, 0 Transient **Launch:** n/a
Rate: Day n/a **Week** n/a **Month** n/a
Heads: 3 Toilet(s), 2 Shower(s)
Laundry: None **Pay Phones:** No
Pump-Out: OnSite, Self Service **Fee:** n/a **Closed Heads:** Yes

Marina Operations

Owner/Manager: Doug Truston **Dockmaster:** Jim Taylor
In-Season: Year-Round, 8am-5pm **Off-Season:** n/a
After-Hours Arrival: Notify office next day or call ahead
Reservations: Preferred **Credit Cards:** Visa/MC, Dscvr, Amex
Discounts: None **Dockage:** n/a **Fuel:** $.10/gal. **Repair:** n/a
Pets: Welcome, Dog Walk Area **Handicap Access:** No

Marina Services and Boat Supplies

Services - Docking Assistance, Dock Carts **Communication -** Mail & Package Hold, Phone Messages, Fax in/out, Data Ports, FedEx, DHL, UPS, Express Mail **Supplies - OnSite:** Ice *(Block, Cube)*, Ships' Store **3+ mi:** West Marine *(804-642-3470, 8 mi.)*, Bait/Tackle *(Grafton Fishing Supply 890-2100, 4 mi.)*, Propane *(Little Big Store 804-642-4663, 8 mi.)*

Boatyard Services

OnSite: Travelift *(37T)*, Crane, Forklift, Engine mechanic *(diesel)*, Electrical Repairs, Hull Repairs, Bottom Cleaning, Brightwork, Compound, Wash & Wax, Interior Cleaning, Woodworking, Metal Fabrication, Painting, Awlgrip, Total Refits **OnCall:** Engine mechanic *(gas)*, Air Conditioning **Yard Rates:** $48/hr., Haul & Launch $4/ft. *(blocking $1/ft.)*, Power Wash $0.50, BottomPaint $23/ft. *(paint incl.)* **Storage:** On-Land $3.50/ft./mo.

Restaurants and Accommodations

OnCall: Pizzeria *(Domino's 898-3003)*, *(Pizza Hut 898-3100)* **1-3 mi:** Rest-aurant *(Billy Seafood 898-4903, L $5-8, D $10-25)*, *(China Ocean 833-3899, L $3-5, D $6-9)*, *(Beachcomber 874-9420)*, Motel *(Crown Inn 898-5436)* **3+ mi:** Restaurant *(Seaford Scallop 898-8512, 4 mi.)*, *(Main Moon Chinese 874-8986, 4 mi.)*, *(Nick's Riverwalk 875-1522, L $8.50-15, D $18-35, 7 mi., or by water)*, *(Smokin Joe's BBQ 875-7774, L $4-15, D $5-17, 4 mi.)*, Lite Fare *(The Rivah Café at Riverwalk L $6-15, D $6-15, 7 mi., or by water)*, Motel *(Yorktown Motor Lodge 898-5451, 4 mi.)*, *(Travelodge 874-4100, 5 mi.)*, *(Duke of York 898-3232, $74-85, 7 mi.)*

Recreation and Entertainment

OnSite: Picnic Area **OnCall:** Group Fishing Boat *(Miss Yorktown, Sea Spray - eves 868-6220)* **1-3 mi:** Beach, Fitness Center *(Fyzique 283-5303)* **3+ mi:** Golf Course *(Kiln Creek 874-2600, 10 mi.)*, Bowling *(York Lanes 890-0495, 5 mi.)*, Movie Theater *(Regal 989-5200, 8 mi.)*, Video Rental *(Blockbuster 872-7022, 7 mi.)*, Museum *(Watermen's Mus. 887-2641, 7 mi. or by water)*, Cultural Attract *(Historic Yorktown, 7 mi. or by water)*

Provisioning and General Services

1-3 mi: Convenience Store *(Terrace Grocery 833-7815)*, Supermarket *(Food Lion 890-2655)*, Delicatessen, Catholic Church, Protestant Church, Beauty Salon *(Hair Designs 898-5348)*, Dry Cleaners *(Boulevard 898-4588)*, Pharmacy *(Rite Aid 898-5466)*, Retail Shops **3+ mi:** Health Food *(Food Herbs & More 898-0100, 4 mi.)*, Liquor Store *(ABC 886-2846, 7 mi.)*, Bakery *(Merita Bread 595-8673, 7 mi.)*, Fishmonger *(Tran's Seafood 874-0157, 9 mi.)*, Bank/ATM *(7 mi.)*, Post Office *(898-4401, 7 mi.)*, Library *(890-5100, 7 mi.)*, Barber Shop *(Hair Cuttery 898-8790, 4 mi.)*, Laundry *(Washington Sq. 898-0637, 5 mi.)*, Bookstore *(Chelsea's 898-7208, 4 mi.)*, Hardware Store *(True Value 898-3040, 5 mi.)*, Department Store *(JC Penney, Patrick Henry Mall 249-1090, 9 mi.)*, Buying Club *(Sam's Club 875-0243, 8 mi.)*

Transportation

OnCall: Rental Car *(Enterprise 872-9536)*, Taxi *(Yorktown Shuttle 890-2840)*, Airport Limo *(Associated 887-3412)* **3+ mi:** Rail *(Amtrak 245-3589, 15 mi.)* **Airport:** Newport News/Williamsburg Int'l. *(8 mi.)*

Medical Services

911 Service **OnCall:** Ambulance **1-3 mi:** Dentist *(Cabaniss 898-6761)* **3+ mi:** Doctor *(Tidewater 898-7261, 4 mi.)*, Chiropractor *(York County 989-5393, 4 mi.)* **Hospital:** Mary Immaculate 886-6000 *(6 mi.)*

Setting -- Slipped in between the Coast Guard Reserve Training Station and the Yorktown Amoco Refinery, on the lower shore of the York, lies pretty Wormley Creek. Just past the jetty, the marina's network of well-protected docks is on the port side flanking a travelift bay. An unassuming low tan building houses the ships' store and office. Ancient trees line the shore, with the refinery stacks in the distance. An inviting deck, furnished with wrought-iron tables & chairs is nestled beneath a towering beech tree with views across the docks and river beyond.

Marina Notes -- DCM. Managed by the Trustons since 1999. Recent, good stationary docks with wide, half-length finger piers have Lighthouse pedestals. Mostly sailboats, except in the small covered shed. Sailors' inventory in the ships' store. Extensive yard service, 37 ton lift, unique powerwash recycling system. Dry storage area is 16 ft. above MLW. Easy access fuel dock. Designated fish cleaning area. Trustons also run the water taxi used by Amoco for crew changes and for ship refueling. Basic tile-floor cinderblock bathhouse has a sink, toilet and shower in each - the showers appear to be antique relics.

Notable -- Landside, the marina is literally at the end of the road and little is accessible by foot. But the new Riverwalk Landing, a short cruise upriver, offers 4-hour dockage for dinghies or big boats for $5 - providing easy access to the historic sights and services of Yorktown. Alternatively, the Yorktown Shuttle is a taxi/van service that will provide transport to the Food Lion ($8-10) or to the Yorktown historic sites ($12) or to wherever. Once in Yorktown, the Trolley loops through 9 sites every 20 minutes. A 4-site package - Yorktown Battlefield, Victory Center, Waterman's Museum & a short narrated River Cruise $30.75/$15.50.

PHOTOS ON CD-ROM: 11

Navigational Information
Lat: 37°15.421' **Long:** 076°28.792' **Tide:** 3 ft. **Current:** n/a **Chart:** 12238
Rep. Depths (*MLW*): Entry 8 ft. **Fuel Dock** 7 ft. **Max Slip/Moor** 7 ft./-
Access: York River to Sarah Creek

Marina Facilities *(In Season/Off Season)*
Fuel: *Phillips Energy* - Gasoline, Diesel, High-Speed Pumps, On Call Delivery
Slips: 324 Total, 20 Transient **Max LOA:** 130 ft. **Max Beam:** n/a
Rate *(per ft.)*: **Day** $1.25 **Week** Inq. **Month** Inq.
Power: 30 amp $4, **50 amp** $8, **100 amp** $20, **200 amp** n/a
Cable TV: Yes **Dockside Phone:** Yes By contract
Dock Type: Fixed, Floating, Alongside, Wood, Composition
Moorings: 0 Total, 0 Transient **Launch:** n/a, Dinghy Dock
Rate: Day n/a **Week** n/a **Month** n/a
Heads: 11 Toilet(s), 11 Shower(s)
Laundry: 3 Washer(s), 3 Dryer(s), Iron, Iron Board **Pay Phones:** No
Pump-Out: OnSite, Self Service **Fee:** $5 **Closed Heads:** Yes

Marina Operations
Owner/Manager: Dan Bacot **Dockmaster:** Chuck Lantis
In-Season: Mar-Nov, 8am-6pm **Off-Season:** Nov-Mar, 8am-5pm
After-Hours Arrival: Call in advance, personnel on site 24 hrs.
Reservations: Preferred **Credit Cards:** Visa/MC, Dscvr, Amex
Discounts: None
Pets: Welcome, Dog Walk Area **Handicap Access:** Yes, Heads, Docks

York River Yacht Haven

PO Box 1070; 8109 Yacht Haven Road; Gloucester Pt., VA 23062

Tel: (804) 642-2156 **VHF: Monitor** 16 **Talk** 68
Fax: (804) 642-4766 **Alternate Tel:** (804) 642-2156
Email: marina@yryh.com **Web:** www.yryh.com
Nearest Town: Yorktown *(3 mi.)* **Tourist Info:** (757) 766-2000

Marina Services and Boat Supplies
Services - Docking Assistance, Concierge, Boaters' Lounge, Security *(24 hrs., on-site personnel)*, Trash Pick-Up, Dock Carts, Megayacht Facilities **Communication -** Mail & Package Hold, Phone Messages, Fax in/out *($2/pp)*, Data Ports *(Lounge)*, FedEx, UPS, Express Mail **Supplies - OnSite:** Ice *(Block, Cube)*, Ships' Store, Bait/Tackle *(Severn Wharf 642-0404)* **OnCall:** Ice *(Shaved)*, CNG **Under 1 mi:** Live Bait **1-3 mi:** West Marine *(642-3470)*, Propane *(Phillips 642-2166)*

Boatyard Services
OnSite: Travelift *(35T/60T)*, Crane, Forklift, Hydraulic Trailer, Engine mechanic *(gas, diesel)*, Electrical Repairs, Hull Repairs, Rigger, Bottom Cleaning, Brightwork, Air Conditioning, Compound, Wash & Wax, Interior Cleaning, Woodworking, Painting, Awlgrip, Total Refits, Yacht Broker *(Common Wealth Yachts)* **OnCall:** Electronics Repairs, Sail Loft, Canvas Work, Refrigeration, Divers, Propeller Repairs, Yacht Interiors, Metal Fabrication **Yard Rates:** $35-62, Haul & Launch $7/ft. *(blocking incl.)*, Power Wash Incl., Bottom Paint $12 **Storage:** On-Land $7/ft./mo.

Restaurants and Accommodations
OnSite: Restaurant *(River's Inn 642-9942, L $8-14, D $22-28, kids' $7-10, Sun brunch $10-15)*, Seafood Shack *(Crab Deck L $8-16, D $6-16, kids' $5-7; local crabs MemDay-LabDay)* **OnCall:** Pizzeria *(Domino's 642-9995)* **1-3 mi:** Restaurant *(Olivia's at the Point 684-2234, L $5-8, D $8-20)*, *(Nick's 785-6300)*, Seafood Shack *(Shuckers 684-9196, L $3-10, D $10-15)*, Lite Fare *(Cruisers Sports Bar & Gril 693-6246)*, Motel *(Duke of York Motor Hotel 757-898-3232, $74-85)*, *(Gloucester Inn 642-6564)*, *(Tidewater 642-6604)*, Inn/B&B *(York River Inn B&B 75-887-8800)*, *(Marl Inn 757-898-3859)*

Recreation and Entertainment
OnSite: Pool, Beach, Picnic Area, Grills *(propane/charcoal)*, Jogging Paths, Video Rental **OnCall:** Dive Shop, Group Fishing Boat *(Miss Yorktown, Sea Spray 868-6220)* **1-3 mi:** Boat Rentals, Movie Theater *(Regal 642-1097)*, Park, Sightseeing *(Dinner Cruise; Yorktown - or across the river)* **3+ mi:** Golf Course *(Gloucester 693-2662, 12 mi.)*, Fitness Center *(Fyzique 757-283-5303, 6 mi.)*, Museum *(Fifes & Drums 757-898-9418, 4 mi.)*

Provisioning and General Services
OnCall: Crabs/Waterman **Under 1 mi:** Convenience Store *(7-11 769-3410)*, Supermarket *(Food Lion 642-9736, dinghy)*, Fishmonger *(Abby Dog Seafood 642-2323)*, Bank/ATM, Post Office *(642-4968)*, Protestant Church **1-3 mi:** Liquor Store *(ABC 642-1516)*, Library *(757-890-5100)*, Barber Shop *(Gloucester Pt. 642-8818)*, Dry Cleaners *(Boulevard 684-2333)*, Bookstore *(Imperial Outpost 642-1556)*, Pharmacy *(Eckerd 642-9834)*, Clothing Store *(Styles & Fashions 642-0187)*, Department Store *(Dollar General 684-9917)* **3+ mi:** Hardware Store *(Ace 642-5300, 5 mi.)*

Transportation
OnSite: Courtesy Car/Van *(1 hour limit)*, Ferry Service *(Yorktown Lady)* **OnCall:** Rental Car *(Enterprise 800-736-8222)*, Taxi *(Yorktown Cab 757-890-2840)* **Under 1 mi:** Local Bus **3+ mi:** Rail *(Amtrak 757-229-8750, 16 mi.)* **Airport:** Newport News/Williamsburg Int'l. *(13 mi.)*

Medical Services
911 Service **OnCall:** Ambulance **1-3 mi:** Doctor *(Convenient Care 684-2060)*, Dentist *(Luckham 642-2120)*, Veterinarian *(Abingdon Animal Clinic 642-2181)* **Hospital:** Mary Immaculate 757-886-6868 *(11 mi.)*

Setting -- Right across from Yorktown, just inside Sarah's Creek, buttoned-up YRYH sits on a long, narrow peninsula literally surrounded by docks. The striking gray clapboard home of River's Inn Restaurant and Crab Deck occupies the point - with brightly colored umbrella-topped tables dockside. Inland, a large pool and boaters' lounge sit between the attractive gray clapboard, covered docks and parking lot, backed by the two-story office. The boat sheds, which line the entire north side, are nicely camouflaged with mature, well-clipped hedges. Picnic tables and charcoal grills are sheltered by an enormous magnolia.

Marina Notes -- DCM. The main dock and the covered sheds are stationary, almost all the rest are floating - new sections with environmentally-neutral, vinyl-edged composite decking float in front of the restaurant, anchored by 12-foot steel pilings with new Lighthouse pedestals. Do-it-yourself & full-service yard - with 35 & 60 ton lifts. (Hauled 72 boats in 72 hours before Isabel.) Separate dry storage area. Some working boats berth here, too. Standard issue heads and showers; tile floors & walls, metal dividers, Formica vanities and glass-doored shower stalls. Laundry room with folding table & book exchange.

Notable -- YRYH's aqua-culture program combines species restoration with water quality improvement. Under the floating docks, 25-gallon oyster-filled containers each filter 50 gals. of water a day. Nautically-inspired River's Inn serves lunch 11:30am-3pm, dinner 5:30-9pm, (closed Mon & Tue, Oct-Mar) and steamed crabs on the deck. Possible to dinghy a mile up the creek to York Crossing shopping center (Food Lion) at mid-tide or higher (ask for map) or across the River to Riverwalk Landing in Yorktown (4 hr. tie-up $5). Staff will arrange transportation to Yorktown, Jamestown, Williamsburg, Busch Gardens, etc.

PHOTOS ON CD-ROM: 14

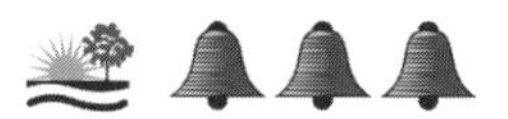

Riverwalk Landing

Riverwalk Landing

425 Water Street; Yorktown, VA

Tel: (757) 890-3370 **VHF: Monitor** 16 **Talk** 9
Fax: (757) 890-3371 **Alternate Tel:** n/a
Email: dockmaster@yorkcounty.gov **Web:** riverwalklanding.com
Nearest Town: Yorktown **Tourist Info:** (757) 766-2000

Navigational Information

Lat: 37°14.294' **Long:** 076°30.434' **Tide:** 3 ft. **Current:** n/a **Chart:** 12238
Rep. Depths (*MLW*): Entry 87 ft. **Fuel Dock** n/a **Max Slip/Moor** 50 ft./-
Access: South shore York River, just before Coleman Bridge

Marina Facilities *(In Season/Off Season)*

Fuel: No
Slips: 100 Total, 35** Transient **Max LOA:** 395 ft. **Max Beam:** n/a
Rate *(per ft.)*: **Day** $1.75* **Week** n/a **Month** n/a
Power: 30 amp Incl., **50 amp** Incl., **100 amp** n/a, **200 amp** n/a
Cable TV: No **Dockside Phone:** No
Dock Type: Floating, Alongside, Concrete
Moorings: 9 Total, 9 Transient **Launch:** n/a
Rate: Day $25 **Week** n/a **Month** n/a
Heads: 8 Toilet(s), 2 Shower(s)
Laundry: None **Pay Phones:** Yes
Pump-Out: OnSite, 2 Central **Fee:** $10 **Closed Heads:** Yes

Marina Operations

Owner/Manager: Coastal Properties **Dockmaster:** Dennis Nate
In-Season: Year-Round, 8:30am-5pm **Off-Season:** n/a
After-Hours Arrival: Call ahead (757) 570-4140
Reservations: Preferred **Credit Cards:** Visa/MC
Discounts: None
Pets: Welcome **Handicap Access:** Yes, Docks

Marina Services and Boat Supplies

Services - Docking Assistance, Dock Carts **Communication -** FedEx, DHL, UPS, Express Mail **Supplies - OnSite:** Ships' Store *(Hospitality & Ticket Center 890-3003, 10am-9pm)* **1-3 mi:** West Marine *(642-3470)*, Bait/Tackle *(A&S 804-642-4940)*, Propane *(Little Big Store 804-642-4663)*

Boatyard Services

Nearest Yard: York River Yacht Haven (804) 642-2156

Restaurants and Accommodations

OnSite: Restaurant *(Nick's Riverwalk 875-1522, L $9-15, D $18-35, kids' $6-8 - dishes from a variety of coastal regions; L 11:30am-3pm, D 5:30-10pm)*, Snack Bar *(Ben & Jerry's, Green Moutain Coffee 10am-10pm, Fri-Sun 'til 11pm)*, Lite Fare *(The Rivah Café at Riverwalk L $6-15, D $6-15, Casual, w/outdoor courtyard; 11:30am-10pm)* **OnCall:** Pizzeria *(Domino's 642-9995)*, *(Pizza Hut 642-4620)* **Near:** Restaurant *(Yorktown Pub 886-9964, L $3-8, D $3-17, waterview)*, *(Waterstreet Landing 886-5890, L $5-10, D $8-23, every seat has a waterview!)*, *(Duke of York 898-5270)*, Lite Fare (Carrot *Tree 246-9559, 8am-4pm)*, Motel *(Duke of York 898-3232, $80-130)*, Inn/B&B *(Marl Inn 898-3859, $80-175)*, *(York River Inn 887-8800, $110-130)* **Under 1 mi:** Coffee Shop *(Mark's Coffee 642-5009)* **1-3 mi:** Restaurant *(Olivia's at the Point 684-2234, L $5-8, D $8-20, surf-and-turf)*, Motel *(Gloucester Inn 804-642-6564)*, *(Travelers Motel 898-3565)*

Recreation and Entertainment

OnSite: Beach *(Yorktown Beach)*, Sightseeing *(The Yorktown Lady 229-6244 narrated river cruises $13.50/10.50; Haunting Tour Land & Sea $19.50/13.50)* **OnCall:** Group Fishing Boat *(Miss Yorktown - Sea Spray, eve. 868-6220)* **Near:** Picnic Area *(east of Yorktown Pier)*, Park *(Yorktown Waterfront; Yorktown Battlefield)*, Museum *(Watermen's 887-2641)*, Cultural Attract *(Yorktown 890-3003, Williamsburg 229-1000 $34-48/ $15-21, Jamestown 253-4838 $17/8.25)*, Galleries *(Nancy Thomas 898-3665)* **3+ mi:** Golf Course *(Kiln Creek 874-2600, 14 mi.)*, Fitness Center *(Fyzique 283-5303, 4 mi.)*, Movie Theater *(Regal 804-642-1097, 4 mi.)*

Provisioning and General Services

OnSite: Convenience Store *(Yorktown Hospitality)* **Near:** Bank/ATM, Post Office *(898-4401)*, Clothing Store *(Swan Song 898-7023)* **Under 1 mi:** Fishmonger *(Abby Dog 804-642-2323)* **1-3 mi:** Delicatessen *(Community Deli 888-9980)*, Beauty Salon *(Beautiful Hair 887-1239)*, Bookstore *(Imperial Outpost 804-642-1556)* **3+ mi:** Supermarket *(Food Lion 890-2655, 4 mi.)*, Liquor Store *(ABC 804-642-9084, 4 mi.)*, Library *(804-642-9790, 5 mi.)*, Dry Cleaners *(Boulevard 804-684-2333, 4 mi.)*, Pharmacy *(Rite Aid 804-642-8747, 4 mi.)*, Hardware Store *(Ace 804-642-5300, 5 mi.)*

Transportation

OnSite: Local Bus *(Free Trolley MemDay-LabDay Apr-May 10am-6pm, Sep-Oct Sat & Sun 10am-6pm & Historic Triangle Shuttle MemDay-LabDay)* **OnCall:** Rental Car *(Enterprise 872-9536)*, Taxi *(Yorktown Cab 890-2840)*, Airport Limo *(Associated Cabs 887-3412)* **3+ mi:** Rail *(Amtrak 229-8750, 13 mi.)* **Airport:** Newport News/ Williamsburg Int'l. *(11 mi.)*

Medical Services

911 Service **OnCall:** Ambulance **Near:** Dentist *(Sotack 820-0870)*
3+ mi: Doctor *(Gloucester Convenient Care 804-684-2060, 5 mi.)*
Hospital: Mary Immaculate 886-6868 *(9 mi.)*

Setting -- On the south shore, just before the Coleman Bridge, this exciting new $12.5 million complex's two main docking areas - a 395 foot main pier and a smaller boat marina - are backed by an attractive "village" with a large restaurant, a dozen retail shops, and the restored "Freight Shed." The brick Riverwalk stretches along a sand beach. Upland is charming, historic Yorktown's beautifully restored 18th C. Main Street and its three outstanding museums.

Marina Notes -- **No slips, alongside. *Under 4 hrs. $5; after 24 hrs., under 12 hrs., half rate. Opened in Summer '05. The 395 x 20 ft. pier provides over 1,000 feet of dockage for tall ships, excursion boats and pleasure craft. The concrete floating docks have power & water. Hospitality Center sells marine supplies, souvenirs, refreshments & tickets to local attractions. On-site, Nick's Riverwalk Restaurant features the bounty of all 50 states. River-view Landing banquet room accommodates 70 for club cruises; The Freight Shed (814-1633) is also available for events. Two restrooms dedicated to boaters, each with a toilet and two showers, and six additional restrooms with 2-4 toilets in each - the set near the dock master's office has an outdoor shower for beach goers.

Notable -- An ideal base for touring the Historic Triangle. To start, the Yorktown Trolley loops 9 key sites every 20 minutes; a 4-site package - the Battlefield, Victory Center, Waterman's Museum & a cruise $30.75/$15.50. For farther travel, the Historic Triangle Shuttle leaves both Yorktown Battlefield and Victory Center every hour on the half, 9:30am to 5:30pm. Buses also leave from Williamsburg to Jamestown every hour (back from Williamsburg to Yorktown on the hour 9am-3pm). A Jamestown area trolley runs from 9am-5pm every 20 minutes MemDay-LabDay. All are free with tickets to the attractions.

PHOTOS ON CD-ROM: 14

Navigational Information
Lat: 37°12.150' **Long:** 076°25.517' **Tide:** 3 ft **Current:** n/a **Chart:** 12238
Rep. Depths (*MLW*): Entry 7 ft. **Fuel Dock** n/a **Max Slip/Moor** 7 ft./7 ft.
Access: Bay or York River to Thorofare Channel to Back Creek

Marina Facilities *(In Season/Off Season)*
Fuel: *Marine* - Gasoline, Diesel
Slips: 60 Total, 10 Transient **Max LOA:** 75 ft. **Max Beam:** n/a
Rate *(per ft.)*: **Day** $2.00 **Week** Inq. **Month** Inq.
Power: 30 amp $5, **50 amp** $10, **100 amp** n/a, **200 amp** n/a
Cable TV: Yes, Free **Dockside Phone:** No
Dock Type: Fixed, Long Fingers, Short Fingers, Pilings, Wood
Moorings: 0 Total, 0 Transient **Launch:** n/a
Rate: Day n/a **Week** n/a **Month** n/a
Heads: 2 Toilet(s), 1 Shower(s)
Laundry: None **Pay Phones:** No
Pump-Out: No **Fee:** n/a **Closed Heads:** Yes

Marina Operations
Owner/Manager: John Wydur **Dockmaster:** Same
In-Season: Jun-Oct, 8am-4:30pm **Off-Season:** Nov-May, 9am-3pm
After-Hours Arrival: Owners on premises, knock on door or call 898-4411
Reservations: Preferred **Credit Cards:** n/a
Discounts: None
Pets: Welcome **Handicap Access:** No

Mills Marina

PO Box 215; 1742 Back Creek Road; Seaford, VA 23696

Tel: (757) 898-4411 **VHF: Monitor** n/a **Talk** n/a
Fax: (757) 898-4461 **Alternate Tel:** (757) 898-4411
Email: jwydur99@aol.com **Web:** www.millsmarina.com
Nearest Town: Seaford *(5 mi.)* **Tourist Info:** (757) 766-2000

Marina Services and Boat Supplies
Services - Docking Assistance, Security *(24/7)*, Trash Pick-Up, Dock Carts
Communication - Data Ports *(Wi-Fi - Verizon or Cox, longer term)*
Supplies - OnSite: Ice *(Block, Cube)*, Ships' Store **3+ mi:** West Marine *(804-642-3470, 10 mi.)*, Bait/Tackle *(Grafton Fishing Supply & Seafood 890-2100, 4 mi.)*, Propane *(Little Big Store 804-642-4663, 10 mi.)*

Boatyard Services
OnSite: Launching Ramp **Near:** Metal Fabrication. **Under 1 mi:** Engine mechanic *(gas)*. **Nearest Yard:** Wormley Creek, 4 mi. (757) 898-5060

Restaurants and Accommodations
Near: Restaurant *(Byrds by the Bay coming '06- maybe!)* **3+ mi:** Restaurant *(Cinco de Mayo 872-0061, L $3-7, D $17-22, 5 mi.)*, *(Pop's 898-6870, B $4-7, L $4-7, 4 mi., Packed local hangout famous for breakfast)*, *(George's Family 875-0039, 5 mi.)*, *(Smokin' Joe's BBQ 875-7774, L $4-15, D $5-17, 5 mi.)*, *(Main Moon Chinese 874-8986, 4 mi.)*, *(Madison 898-1044, L $9-16, D $10-22, 5 mi.)*, Seafood Shack *(Captain Bill's 898-4908, 5 mi.)*, Pizzeria (Joe & *Mimma's 898-6612, 5 mi.)*, *(The Pizza Shop 898-4301, L $4-8, D $11-20, 5mi.)*, Motel *(Crown Inn 898-5436, 5 mi.)*, *(Yorktown Motor Lodge 898-5451, $55-75, 5 mi.)*, *(Travelers 898-3565, 5 mi.)*

Recreation and Entertainment
OnCall: Group Fishing Boat *(Sea Spray, eves 868-6220)* **Near:** Playground *(Back Creek Park)*, Tennis Courts *(Back Creek Park - dinghy)*, Park *(Back Creek Park across the creek - dinghy)* **3+ mi:** Spa *(Victoria's Day Spa, 5 mi.)*, Beach *(Yorktown Beach, 8 mi.)*, Golf Course *(Kiln Creek 874-2600, 10 mi.)*, Bowling *(York Lanes 890-0495, 6 mi.)*, Movie Theater *(Regal Kiln Creek 989-5200, 9 mi.)*, Video Rental *(Blockbuster 872-7022, 7 mi.)*, Museum *(Fifes & Drums of Yorktown 898-9418, 8 mi.)*, Cultural Attract *(Virginia Living 595-1900, 13 mi.)*, Sightseeing *(Yorktown, Williamsburg, 15 mi.)*

Provisioning and General Services
Under 1 mi: Wine/Beer, Market *(Seaford Country Market 898-5721)*, Post Office *(898-7471)* **1-3 mi:** Protestant Church *(Methodist, Baptist)* **3+ mi:** Convenience Store *(Uppy's 874-3388, 5 mi.)*, Supermarket *(Food Lion 898-5023, 5 mi.)*, Health Food *(Food Herbs & More 898-0100, 5 mi.)*, Liquor Store *(ABC 886-2846, 8 mi.)*, Bakery *(Merita Bread 595-8673, 8 mi.)*, Fishmonger *(Tran's Seafood 874-0157, 10 mi.)*, Bank/ATM *(5 mi.)*, Library *(York County 890-5100, 4 mi.)*, Beauty Salon *(Hair Designs Salon & Spa 898-5348, 4 mi.)*, Barber Shop *(Hair Cuttery 898-8790, 5 mi.)*, Dry Cleaners *(Boulevard Cleaners 898-4588, 4 mi.)*, Laundry *(Washington Square 898-0637, 5 mi.)*, Bookstore *(Chelsea's Books 898-7208, 4 mi.)*, Pharmacy *(Eckerd 989-0734, 4 mi.)*, Hardware Store *(True Value 898-3040, 6 mi.)*, Florist *(Floral Designs II 877-0998, 4 mi.)*, Department Store *(Patrick Henry Mall 249-0200, 10 mi.)*, Buying Club *(Costco 448-5020, 10 mi.)*

Transportation
OnCall: Rental Car *(Enterprise 873-3003)*, Taxi *(Yorktown Cab 890-2840)*, Airport Limo *(Associated Cabs 887-3412)* **3+ mi:** Rail *(Amtrak - Newport News 245-3589, 15 mi.)* **Airport:** Newport News/Williamsburg Int'l. *(9 mi.)*

Medical Services
911 Service **OnCall:** Ambulance **3+ mi:** Doctor *(Tidewater Physicians 898-7261, 5 mi.)*, Dentist *(General Dental Care 838-3400, 6 mi.)*, Veterinarian *(Seaford 833-6440, 4 mi.)* **Hospital:** Mary Immaculate 886-6000 *(7 mi.)*

Setting -- The Thorofare Channel, just south of the mouth of York River, connects the Bay to the York and both to beautiful, quiet Back Creek. On the waterway's south shore, past the Seaford/Wells scallop plant, this small "mom and pop" marina offers basic, protected dockage at two main piers.

Marina Notes -- Established in 1930, expanded in 1968. The current, service-oriented owners, have been at the helm since 1975 - the Wydurs live on the premises providing personal attention and good security. Despite four feet of water in the ships' store, in the office, and over the docks, not one of their resident boats was lost in Hurricane Isabel. New fuel tanks have been installed. Many improvements are on the way including handicapped access and bicycles in '06. Owners are very helpful in getting boaters where they need to go. Two individual bathrooms with showers.

Notable -- Dinghy farther up the creek to 26-acre Back Creek Park on the north shore - picnic area, playground, tennis courts and floating docks. Most services are out on Route 17 - four miles away, but Seaford Country Market is 0.7 mile (and sells Seaford's local Wells scallops). The elegant yellow and white colonial-style Byrd's by the Bay facility, directly adjacent to Mills, is a charmingly renovated former crab house. According to existing plans, it will open in '06 as a restaurant with dock 'n' dine facilities (but no overnight transients). Their recent very wide, beautiful long single pier accommodates 27 alongside boats and features a charming hip roofed pavilion and a pergola arbor. The dock is anchored by an alfresco bar area that leads into the main dining room. (Check with the marina to confirm that their next door neighbor actually opened - there is considerable uncertainty.)

PHOTOS ON CD-ROM: 10

Seaford Aqua Marina

512 Wildey Road; Seaford, VA 23696

Tel: (757) 890-6200 **VHF: Monitor** 16 **Talk** n/a
Fax: (757) 890-8025 **Alternate Tel:** n/a
Email: aquamarine@aol.com **Web:** n/a
Nearest Town: Seaford *(1.5 mi.)* **Tourist Info:** (757) 766-2000

Navigational Information

Lat: 37°10.933' **Long:** 076°24.483' **Tide:** 3 ft. **Current:** 1 kt. **Chart:** 12238
Rep. Depths (*MLW*): Entry 6 ft. **Fuel Dock** n/a **Max Slip/Moor** 6 ft./-
Access: Poquoson to Chisman Creek

Marina Facilities *(In Season/Off Season)*

Fuel: No
Slips: 26 Total, 3 Transient **Max LOA:** 60 ft. **Max Beam:** 15 ft.
Rate *(per ft.)*: **Day** $1.50 **Week** n/a **Month** $4.00
Power: 30 amp $4, **50 amp** n/a, **100 amp** n/a, **200 amp** n/a
Cable TV: No **Dockside Phone:** No
Dock Type: Floating, Long Fingers, Short Fingers, Pilings, Wood
Moorings: 0 Total, 0 Transient **Launch:** n/a
Rate: Day n/a **Week** n/a **Month** n/a
Heads: 2 Toilet(s)
Laundry: None **Pay Phones:** No
Pump-Out: OnCall **Fee:** n/a **Closed Heads:** Yes

Marina Operations

Owner/Manager: Capt. Jim Vaughn **Dockmaster:** Jim Strong
In-Season: Year-Round, 8am-5pm **Off-Season:** n/a
After-Hours Arrival: Tie up to main pier
Reservations: Yes, Preferred **Credit Cards:** Visa/MC
Discounts: None
Pets: Welcome **Handicap Access:** No

Marina Services and Boat Supplies

Services - Docking Assistance, Trash Pick-Up, Dock Carts **Communication -** Mail & Package Hold, Phone Messages, Fax in/out *($2/pp)*, FedEx, DHL, UPS, Express Mail *(Sat Del)* **Supplies - OnSite:** Ice *(Block, Cube)*, Ships' Store **1-3 mi:** Propane *(Seaford Country Market 898-5721)* **3+ mi:** West Marine *(825-4900, 15 mi.)*, Boat/US *(827-1613, 15 mi.)*, Bait/Tackle *(Grafton Fishing Supply 890-2100, 6 mi.)*

Boatyard Services

OnSite: Travelift, Railway *(60T)*, Engine mechanic *(gas, diesel)*, Electronics Repairs, Hull Repairs, Bottom Cleaning, Brightwork, Compound, Wash & Wax, Interior Cleaning, Propeller Repairs, Woodworking, Yacht Building, Yacht Broker *(Aqua Marine)* **1-3 mi:** Launching Ramp. **Yard Rates:** $45/hr., Haul & Launch $7/ft. *(blocking incl.)*, Power Wash $2/ft.

Restaurants and Accommodations

3+ mi: Restaurant *(Madison's 898-7044, L $9-16, D $10-22, 6 mi.)*, *(Cactus 5 mi.)*, *(Pattaya Thai 833-3790, 7 mi.)*, *(Bangkok City 886-8500, L $5-8, D $7-11, 7 mi.)*, *(New Garden Buffet 825-8777, L $6, D $8, 11 mi., L/D buffet, 11am-10pm daily)*, Seafood Shack *(Bill's Seafood 898-4903, 5 mi.)*, Lite Fare *(Pop's 898-6870, B $4-7, L $4-7, 5 mi.)*, *(Steven's European Bakery 877-6668, L $2-6, D $5-10, 7 mi.)*, Motel *(Courtyard 874-9000, 10 mi.)*, *(Comfort Inn 249-0200, 10 mi.)*, *(Yorktown Motor Lodge 898-5451, 7 mi.)*, *(Crown Inn 898-5436, 7 mi.)*

Recreation and Entertainment

OnCall: Group Fishing Boat *(Miss Yorktown - Sea Spray, Evenings 868-6220)* **1-3 mi:** Jogging Paths **3+ mi:** Golf Course *(Kiln Creek 874-2600, 12 mi.)*, Fitness Center *(Curves 898-8308, 6 mi.)*, Bowling *(York Lanes 890-0495, 5 mi.)*, Video Rental *(House of Video 867-8266, 6 mi.)*, Museum *(Watermen's Museum 887-2641, VA Living Museum 595-1900, 10 mi.)*

Provisioning and General Services

1-3 mi: Convenience Store, Market *(Seaford Country Market 898-5721)*, Bank/ATM, Post Office, Catholic Church, Protestant Church, Florist **3+ mi:** Supermarket *(Food Lion 898-5023, 6 mi.)*, Gourmet Shop *(4 mi.)*, Delicatessen *(4 mi.)*, Liquor Store *(ABC 890-3104, 10 mi.)*, Library *(York County 890-3376, 15 mi.)*, Beauty Salon *(Hair Designs Salon & Spa 898-5348, 5 mi.)*, Dry Cleaners *(Boulevard Cleaners 898-4588, 5 mi.)*, Laundry *(Washington Square 898-0637, 5 mi.)*, Bookstore *(Waldenbooks 249-2191, 10 mi.)*, Pharmacy *(Rite Aid 898-5466, 6 mi.)*, Hardware Store *(Grafton True Value 898-3040, 7 mi.)*, Department Store *(Patrick Henry Mall, 10 mi.)*

Transportation

OnCall: Rental Car *(Enterprise 873-3003)*, Taxi *(Yorktown Cab 890-2840)*, Airport Limo *(Associated Cabs 887-3412)*
Airport: Newport News/Williamsburg Int'l. *(10 mi.)*

Medical Services

911 Service **OnCall:** Ambulance **3+ mi:** Doctor *(5 mi.)*, Dentist *(5 mi.)*, Chiropractor *(Gunderman Chiropractic & Wellness Center 874-5666, 7 mi.)*, Veterinarian *(Grafton Animal Hospital 898-8433, 6 mi.)*
Hospital: Mary Immaculate 886-6000 *(11 mi.)*

Setting -- Located on quiet Chisman Creek off the Poquoson, this very small marina and boatyard has one primary floating dock and two side docks, each containing slips with half-length, floating finger piers. A large boathouse workshed is directly dockside for float-in service and a marine railway occupies the remainder of the waterfront.

Marina Notes -- Formerly Wildey Marina, purchased July 1999 by Aqua Marine, which upgraded with new slips/floating docks and changed the name to Seaford in 2004. Owner Capt. Jim Vaughn was also, at one time, one of the owners of Poquoson Marine. Power at the docks is somewhat adhoc at present. A small railway can haul some decent size boats and a storage work shed is right on the water. There are 2 heads (one each), that appear to be barely operational, and no showers.

Notable -- The surrounding area is a pleasant, rural community with lovely neighborhoods. Very little is nearby, but cabs are readily available and Enterprise delivers here. Most services are out on Route 17 (George Washington Memorial Highway) which is about 5.5 miles away. At the crossroads is Pop's, the local hangout where regulars stand on line outside to get a table for their famous breakfast - one is hard pressed to spend more than $5. About another mile is the nearest Food Lion and in between are most services and a handful of eateries.

Navigational Information
Lat: 37°10.936' **Long:** 076°25.501' **Tide:** n/a **Current:** n/a **Chart:** 12238
Rep. Depths (*MLW*): Entry 8 ft. **Fuel Dock** 6 ft. **Max Slip/Moor** 6 ft./-
Access: Poquoson River starboard after R10 to Chisman Creek

Marina Facilities *(In Season/Off Season)*
Fuel: *89* - Gasoline, Diesel
Slips: 54 Total, 4 Transient **Max LOA:** 65 ft. **Max Beam:** 16 ft.
Rate *(per ft.)*: **Day** $1.00 **Week** $6 **Month** n/a
Power: 30 amp $5, **50 amp** $5, **100 amp** n/a, **200 amp** n/a
Cable TV: No **Dockside Phone:** No
Dock Type: Fixed, Floating, Wood, Composition
Moorings: 0 Total, 0 Transient **Launch:** n/a
Rate: Day n/a **Week** n/a **Month** n/a
Heads: 3 Toilet(s), 2 Shower(s)
Laundry: None **Pay Phones:** No
Pump-Out: OnSite **Fee:** $5 **Closed Heads:** Yes

Marina Operations
Owner/Manager: Michael P. Hanna **Dockmaster:** Same
In-Season: Summer, 7am-7pm **Off-Season:** Winter, 9am-4:30pm
After-Hours Arrival: Fuel dock or floating docks
Reservations: Yes **Credit Cards:** Visa/MC, Amex
Discounts: Boat/US **Dockage:** n/a **Fuel:** n/a **Repair:** n/a
Pets: Welcome **Handicap Access:** Yes, Heads, Docks

Dare Marina

821 Railway Road; Yorktown, VA 23692

Tel: (757) 898-3000 **VHF: Monitor** 16 **Talk** 14
Fax: (757) 898-1923 **Alternate Tel:** n/a
Email: info@daremarina.com **Web:** www.daremarina.com
Nearest Town: Yorktown *(3 mi.)* **Tourist Info:** (757) 766-2000

Marina Services and Boat Supplies
Services - Docking Assistance, Dock Carts **Communication -** Mail & Package Hold, Phone Messages, FedEx, DHL, UPS, Express Mail *(Sat Del)* **Supplies - OnSite:** Ice *(Cube)*, Ships' Store, Bait/Tackle, Live Bait *(Squid)* **3+ mi:** West Marine *(825-4900, 13 mi.)*, Boat/US *(827-1613, 13 mi.)*, Propane *(Dixie Gas 249-4110, 9 mi.)*

Boatyard Services
OnSite: Forklift *(2,000-lbs.)*, Engine mechanic *(gas)*, Electrical Repairs, Hull Repairs, Bottom Cleaning, Compound, Wash & Wax, Interior Cleaning, Propeller Repairs, Yacht Broker *(Dare Marine Yacht Broker, Michael P Hanna)* **OnCall:** Canvas Work, Divers, Inflatable Repairs, Upholstery **Dealer for:** Mercury, Mercruiser, Volvo, Yamaha, Glacier Bay Boats. **Yard Rates:** Inq., Power Wash $3/ft.

Restaurants and Accommodations
OnCall: Pizzeria *(Papa John's 898-6789)*, *(Domino's 898-3003)* **1-3 mi:** Restaurant *(Cinco de Mayo 872-0061, L $3-7, D $17-22)*, *(George's Family Restaurant 875-0039)*, *(Sakura Japanese 988-1988)*, *(Smokin Joe's BBQ 875-7774, L $4-15, D $5-17)*, *(Joe & Mimma's 898-6612, L $5, D $10-15)*, Fast Food *(Taco Bell, Wendy's, Burger King)* **3+ mi:** Restaurant *(Country Grill 591-0600, D $10-15, 6 mi.)*, Motel *(Yorktown Motor Lodge 898-5451, 6 mi.)*, *(Crown Inn 898-5436, 5 mi.)*, Hotel *(Candlewood Suites 866-270-5110, 6 mi.)*, *(Courtyard 874-9000, 6 mi.)*

Recreation and Entertainment
OnSite: Picnic Area, Grills, Fishing Charter **3+ mi:** Golf Course *(Kiln Creek 874-2600, 7 mi.)*, Fitness Center *(Fyzique Fitness 283-5303, 5 mi.)*, Bowling *(York Lanes 890-0495, 4 mi.)*, Movie Theater *(Regal Kiln Creek 989-5200, 7 mi.)*, Video Rental *(Blockbuster 872-7022, 7 mi.)*, Museum *(VA Living Museum 595-1900, 10 mi.)*, Galleries *(Iris Art Studio 868-4205, 9 mi.)*

Provisioning and General Services
OnSite: Wine/Beer **Near:** Market *(Sheena's)* **1-3 mi:** Convenience Store *(Gino's Kwik Pik 898-1656)*, Delicatessen *(Kelsie's 874-2776)*, Health Food *(Naturally Healthy 657-7202)*, Bank/ATM, Post Office *(898-5435)*, Catholic Church, Beauty Salon *(Salon de Chae 890-1399)*, Barber Shop *(Clippers 877-9893)*, Dry Cleaners *(Boulevard 898-4588)*, Pharmacy *(Rite Aid 898-5466)*, Florist *(Jeff's 898-5600)* **3+ mi:** Supermarket *(Food Lion 898-5023, 4 mi.)*, Liquor Store *(ABC 886-2846, 7 mi.)*, Bakery *(Mary Jane 596-1443, 7 mi.)*, Fishmonger *(Tran's Seafood 874-0157, 9 mi.)*, Library *(890-5100, 4 mi.)*, Laundry *(Washington Square 898-0637, 4 mi.)*, Bookstore *(Chelsea's Books 898-7208, 4 mi.)*, Hardware Store *(True Value 898-3040, 4 mi.)*, Clothing Store *(Ann's Fashion 898-4343, 4 mi.)*, Department Store *(Kmart 874-0170, 7 mi.)*, Buying Club *(Costco 448-5020, 8 mi.)*

Transportation
OnCall: Rental Car *(Enterprise 873-3003)*, Taxi *(Yorktown Cab 890-2840)*, Airport Limo *(Associated Cabs 887-3412)* **3+ mi:** Rail *(Amtrak - Newport News 245-3589, 13 mi.)* **Airport:** Newport News/Williamsburg Int'l. *(9 mi.)*

Medical Services
911 Service **OnCall:** Ambulance **1-3 mi:** Doctor *(Glass 898-6118)*, Chiropractor *(York County Chiropractic 989-5393)* **3+ mi:** Dentist *(General Dental Care 838-3400, 4 mi.)*, Veterinarian *(Grafton Animal Hospital 898-8433, 4 mi.)* **Hospital:** Mary Immaculate 886-6000 *(7 mi.)*

Setting -- Off the Poquoson River, on the south side of Chisman Creek, a tall white storage shed wrapped with a red stripe announces Dare Marina. The signature copper-roofed gazebo sits right at the head of the main dock of this small ship-shape facility. The shoreline of the creek is fairly built up, but trees seem to soften some of the development so there's still a feeling of quiet, and, every once in a while, the eye rests on a spot where there is still nothing.

Marina Notes -- Easy-access fuel dock The main dock is stationary and the others floating; all are composite and in excellent condition - with half-length, wide finger piers and a variety of pedestals. Large new and used boat brokerage business, including extensive customization program for Glacier Bay and Pioneer. The gazebo is good for sitting and watching the docks -- or, more important, for washing your dog, apparently an additional service of the marina. All tile, freshly painted bathhouses, each with two toilets, two sinks, a fiberglass shower stall and wallpaper borders.

Notable -- Brightly-colored, poison green and bright sea-blue tables (topped by umbrellas in good weather) and matching benches populate a large raised deck that looks out over the water. There's a propane grill and a fish cleaning station, so this is a good spot to picnic or watch the boats coming in from the river. A half-mile away is Sheena's - a little market. About three and a half miles out on Route 17 is Heritage Square strip mall with a laundry, several fast food eateries, a pharmacy and small services. Just beyond is York Lanes and half-mile farther is the Food Lion supermarket. Cabs are readily available and Enterprise delivers here.

PHOTOS ON CD-ROM: 8

York Haven Marina

100 Mingee St.; Poquoson, VA 23662

Tel: (757) 868-4532 **VHF: Monitor** n/a **Talk** n/a
Fax: n/a **Alternate Tel:** n/a
Email: yorkhavenmarina@yahoo.com **Web:** n/a
Nearest Town: Poquoson *(1 mi.)* **Tourist Info:** (757) 262-2000

Navigational Information

Lat: 37°08.749' **Long:** 076°22.529' **Tide:** 3 ft. **Current:** 3 kt. **Chart:** 12238
Rep. Depths (*MLW*): Entry 10 ft. **Fuel Dock** n/a **Max Slip/Moor** 8 ft./-
Access: Poquoson, starboard at R10 to Bennett Creek to White House Cove

Marina Facilities *(In Season/Off Season)*

Fuel: *adjacent Owens Marina* - Gasoline, Diesel
Slips: 70 Total, 5 Transient **Max LOA:** 65 ft. **Max Beam:** 17 ft.
Rate *(per ft.)*: **Day** $1.00 **Week** n/a **Month** $75-120
Power: 30 amp Inq., **50 amp** n/a, **100 amp** n/a, **200 amp** n/a
Cable TV: No **Dockside Phone:** No
Dock Type: Fixed, Short Fingers, Pilings
Moorings: 0 Total, 0 Transient **Launch:** n/a
Rate: Day n/a **Week** n/a **Month** n/a
Heads: 3 Toilet(s), 1 Shower(s) *(with dressing rooms)*
Laundry: None **Pay Phones:** Yes
Pump-Out: OnSite **Fee:** n/a **Closed Heads:** Yes

Marina Operations

Owner/Manager: Jamie Moore **Dockmaster:** Same
In-Season: Year-Round, 8:30am-5:30pm **Off-Season:** n/a
After-Hours Arrival: Call ahead
Reservations: No **Credit Cards:** n/a
Discounts: None
Pets: Welcome **Handicap Access:** No

Marina Services and Boat Supplies

Services - Docking Assistance, Security *(on-site)*, Trash Pick-Up
Communication - Mail & Package Hold, FedEx, UPS, Express Mail
Supplies - OnSite: Ships' Store **Near:** Ice *(Cube)* **1-3 mi:** Bait/Tackle *(Weekender Boating 868-4072)* **3+ mi:** West Marine *(825-4900, 9 mi.)*, Propane *(Dixie Gas 249-4110, 9 mi.)*

Boatyard Services

OnSite: Travelift *(50T)*, Engine mechanic *(gas, diesel)*, Hull Repairs, Bottom Cleaning, Divers, Compound, Wash & Wax, Woodworking, Painting, Awlgrip, Yacht Design, Yacht Building, Total Refits **OnCall:** Rigger, Sail Loft, Canvas Work, Air Conditioning, Refrigeration, Interior Cleaning, Propeller Repairs, Life Raft Service, Upholstery **Near:** Launching Ramp. **1-3 mi:** Inflatable Repairs, Metal Fabrication. **Yard Rates:** $35/hr., Haul & Launch $4.50-5.50/ft. *(blocking $25)*, Bottom Paint $5.50/ft.
Storage: In-Water $75-100, On-Land $100-120

Restaurants and Accommodations

OnCall: Pizzeria *(Domino's 868-7666)* **Near:** Restaurant *(Owens Marina Restaurant 868-8407, B $2-6, L $2-8, D $6-14, Mon-Sat 6:30am-10pm, Sun 'til 9pm - dock 'n' dine)* **1-3 mi:** Restaurant *(East Wok 868-1200)*, *(George's 868-7955)*, *(El Zarape 868-0057)*, Seafood Shack *(Poquoson Seafood House 868-7333, L $7-10, D $10-15)*, Pizzeria *(Mr C's Pizza & Subs 868-7082)*, Inn/B&B *(Martin-Wilson House 868-7070)* **3+ mi:** Restaurant *(Bubba's Ships Galley 868-4219, L $4-8, D $7-15, 4 mi., lunch specials)*, *(The Crabcake House 868-8598, L $5-18, D $5-18, 4 mi., lunch & dinner specials)*, Motel *(Arrow Inn & Efficiencies 865-0300, 4 mi.)*, Hotel *(Towne Place Suites 800-257-3000, 5 mi.)*

Recreation and Entertainment

OnSite: Fishing Charter, Group Fishing Boat **1-3 mi:** Pool, Beach, Picnic Area, Grills, Playground, Jogging Paths, Horseback Riding, Roller Blade/Bike Paths, Video Rental *(Blockbuster 868-4006)*, Video Arcade, Park *(Plum Tree Island National Wildlife Refuge 721-2412)* **3+ mi:** Golf Course *(The Hamptons 766-9148, 8 mi.)*, Fitness Center *(New Vision 867-9099, 5 mi.)*, Movie Theater *(Regal Kiln Creek 989-5200, 7 mi.)*

Provisioning and General Services

Under 1 mi: Convenience Store *(Geno's Kwik Pik 868-8336)*
1-3 mi: Supermarket *(Food Lion 868-8029)*, Delicatessen, Health Food *(Nutrition Store 868-6158)*, Wine/Beer, Fishmonger *(Bubba's 868-4219)*, Crabs/Waterman *(Capt Harrell's 868-9909)*, Bank/ATM, Post Office *(868-3428)*, Catholic Church, Library *(868-3060)*, Beauty Salon *(Colonial 868-6111)*, Dry Cleaners *(Poquoson 868-8254)*, Pharmacy *(Poquoson 868-7114)*, Hardware Store *(Islander 868-8467)* **3+ mi:** Liquor Store *(ABC 825-7906, 8 mi.)*, Laundry *(Chin's 865-7235, 4 mi.)*

Transportation

OnSite: Bikes, Water Taxi **OnCall:** Rental Car *(Enterprise 873-3003)*, Taxi *(Tidewater 868-0477)*, Airport Limo *(A-1 591-0486)* **3+ mi:** Rail *(Amtrak 245-3589, 12 mi.)* **Airport:** Newport News/Williamsburg Int'l. *(10 mi.)*

Medical Services

911 Service **OnCall:** Ambulance **Under 1 mi:** Doctor *(Palmer 868-8221)*
1-3 mi: Dentist *(Taylor 868-9334)*, Chiropractor *(Svihla 868-9499)*, Veterinarian *(Poquoson)* **Hospital:** Sentara Careplex 736-1000 *(8 mi.)*

PHOTOS ON CD-ROM: 9

Setting -- Up Bennett Creek from the Poquoson, down home York Haven is securely tucked into the north side of White House Cove. An egalitarian mix of working vessels and pleasure craft berth at its docks. The distinguishing shore-side features are a mint green, barn-roofed building - home to Jim Vaughn Marine on the first floor and a private residence on the second - and the three story, tri-color structure which houses the offices. The surroundings may be old-time boatyard rustic, but the elegant shear of a fleet of watermen's boats is for many the best view around.

Marina Notes -- Fuel is next door at Owens, not onsite. Stationary docks have short finger piers and ad hoc electric - no pedestals, occasional plugs on posts. Provides serious boatyard services in a cluttered environment and houses a number of wooden vessels, some on the water, some on the hard - in various stages of restoration, renovation or decay. The bathhouse restoration was in some doubt at last visit, so call ahead.

Notable -- Owens Marina Restaurant (dock 'n' dine only) is right next door, open seemingly all the time. There's a sweet but casual dining room and a picnic deck; the dock is lighted at night and the owners' gorgeous deadrise is usually at the dock. A short way back down Bennett Creek is Plum Tree Island National Wildlife Refuge with about 3,450 acres of salt marsh, shrub-scrub and wooded habitat. About half way on the Atlantic Flyway, it is well known for bird watching and wildlife viewing. On Plum Tree Point is the last surviving tower used by the Army Air Force; until the '50's, this was a bombing range for Langley. A trove of recently discovered unexploded bombs, probably churned up by Isabel, has closed the refuge to the public. However, ospreys still nest here.

Navigational Information

Lat: 37°08.491' **Long:** 076°22.537' **Tide:** 3 ft. **Current:** 3 kt. **Chart:** 12238
Rep. Depths (*MLW*): **Entry** 8 ft. **Fuel Dock** 8 ft. **Max Slip/Moor** 12 ft./-
Access: Poquoson River to Bennett Creek to White House Cove

Marina Facilities *(In Season/Off Season)*

Fuel: No
Slips: 150 Total, 7 Transient **Max LOA:** 157 ft. **Max Beam:** 10 ft.
Rate *(per ft.)*: **Day** $1.00 **Week** n/a **Month** $10/ft
Power: 30 amp Incl., **50 amp** Incl., **100 amp** n/a, **200 amp** n/a
Cable TV: No **Dockside Phone:** Yes
Dock Type: Fixed, Concrete, Wood
Moorings: 0 Total, 0 Transient **Launch:** n/a
Rate: Day n/a **Week** n/a **Month** n/a
Heads: 4 Toilet(s), 2 Shower(s) *(with dressing rooms)*
Laundry: 1 Washer(s), 1 Dryer(s) **Pay Phones:** Yes
Pump-Out: OnSite, 1 Central **Fee:** n/a **Closed Heads:** Yes

Marina Operations

Owner/Manager: Craig Brown **Dockmaster:** Same
In-Season: Year-Round, 9am-5pm **Off-Season:** n/a
After-Hours Arrival: Call ahead
Reservations: Yes, Preferred **Credit Cards:** n/a
Discounts: None
Pets: Welcome **Handicap Access:** No

Poquoson Marina

105 Rens Road; Poquoson, VA 23696

Tel: (757) 868-6171 **VHF: Monitor** 16 **Talk** n/a
Fax: (757) 808-2602 **Alternate Tel:** n/a
Email: craigbrown@robertbrownassociates.com **Web:** *see marina notes
Nearest Town: Poquoson *(1.5 mi.)* **Tourist Info:** (757) 766-2000

Marina Services and Boat Supplies

Services - Docking Assistance, Trash Pick-Up, Dock Carts **Communication -** Mail & Package Hold, Phone Messages, Fax in/out *($2/pp)*, FedEx, UPS **Supplies - Under 1 mi:** Ice *(Block, Cube, Shaved)* **1-3 mi:** Bait/Tackle *(Back River Market 868-4130)*, Live Bait, Propane *(Shefield's 868-0014)* **3+ mi:** West Marine *(825-4900, 9 mi.)*

Boatyard Services

OnSite: Launching Ramp *(two)*, Divers **Yard Rates:** $45/hr., Haul & Launch $7/ft., Power Wash $2/ft.

Restaurants and Accommodations

OnSite: Restaurant *(Bubba's Ships Galley 868-4219, B $2-8, L $2-7, D $3-16, eat in or take-out, kids' breakfast $3.50, lunch & dinner $2-7)* **OnCall:** Pizzeria *(Anna's 868-8006)* **Near:** Restaurant *(Owen's Marina Restaurant B $2-6, L $2-8, D $6-14, dock 'n' dine right across the creek)* **1-3 mi:** Restaurant *(East Wok 868-1200)*, *(El Zarape 868-0057, Mexican)*, *(Victor's Steakhouse L $3-6, D $7-14)*, Seafood Shack *(Poquoson Seafood House 868-7333, L $7-10, D $10-15* , Crab House *(The Crabcake House 868-8598,L $3-7, D $12-18, Mon-Sat 11am-8:30pm, Closed Sun; daily specials)*, Snack Bar *(Briar Patch Tea Room 868-6843)*, Fast Food *(Subway, McDonald's)*, Pizzeria *(Mr C's Pizza & Subs 868-7082)*, Inn/B&B *(Martin-Wilson House 868-7070)* **3+ mi:** Motel *(Courtyard 874-9000, 6 mi.)*, *(Hilton Garden Inn 947-1080, 7 mi.)*, *(Holiday Inn 596-6417, 7 mi.)*

Recreation and Entertainment

Under 1 mi: Park **1-3 mi:** Playground, Fitness Center *(Curves 868-1488)*, Jogging Paths, Video Rental *(Blockbuster 868-4006)*, Galleries *(Iris 868-4205, Peedles by the Bay 868-6546)* **3+ mi:** Golf Course *(Heath Tres 766-7550, 8 mi.)*, Bowling *(AMF York Lanes 890-0495, 7 mi.)*, Movie Theater *(Regal Kiln Creek 989-5200, 7 mi.)*, Museum *(Watermans Museum in Yorktown 887-2641, Jamestown Settlement 888-6537, Virginia War Museum 247-8523, VA Virginia Air & Space Center 727-0800, 9 mi.)*

Provisioning and General Services

OnSite: Beauty Salon, Barber Shop, Newsstand **Near:** Fishmonger *(Ferguson Seafood 868-8959 or Capt. Harrell's 868-9909, 3 mi.)* **Under 1 mi:** Convenience Store, Wine/Beer, Bank/ATM, Catholic Church **1-3 mi:** Supermarket *(Food Lion 868-8029)*, Delicatessen *(Poquoson Deli 868-0044)*,Liquor Store, Market *(Sheffield's 868-0014, Back River Market 868-4130)*, Post Office *(868-3428)*, Protestant Church, Dry Cleaners *(Poquoson Cleaners 868-8254)*, Laundry, Pharmacy *(Poquoson Pharmacy 868-7114, Eckerd 868-0297)*, Hardware Store *(Islander Hardware & Sporting Goods 868-8467)*, Florist **3+ mi:** Library *(Newport News 890-3376, 8 mi.)*, Bookstore *(Barnes & Noble 249-2488, 9 mi.)*, Department Store *(Kmart 874-0170, 9 mi.)*

Transportation

OnCall: Rental Car *(Enterprise 873-3003; or Auto Rent 272-0030, 8 mi.)*, Taxi *(Porter Cab 244-3838)*, Airport Limo *(Airport Taxi 877-0279)* **Airport:** Newport News/Williamsburg Int'l. *(10 mi.)*

Medical Services

911 Service **OnCall:** Ambulance **1-3 mi:** Doctor, Dentist *(Taylor 868-9334)*, Chiropractor *(Poquoson Chiropractic 868-7709)*, Veterinarian *(Poquoson 868-8532)* **Hospital:** Sentara Careplex 736-1000 *(8 mi.)*

Setting -- On the south side of White House Cove, off Bennett Creek, Poquoson's is tucked behind a stretch of marsh. The main pier is covered with a shingle shake roof providing unique protection to the inhabitants of the sailboats berthed there. A "U" shaped set of covered docks line a long and narrow basin cut into the upland. The ambiance is rustic and funky, with a community feel. The detritus of the boating life seems to spill out onto most surfaces. At the head of the docks is an aging, though nicely maintained, mobile home community and a variety of RVs.

Marina Notes -- *www.robertbrownassociates.com/poquosonmarina - Fuel is across the creek at Owens Marina Restaurant. Five main docks - all but one are stationary, concrete, with step down short finger piers and a mix of power pedestals. The dock that leads out from Bubba's is wood. Large, expansive dry storage area holds many vessels on the hard, some of which look like they may have been here for quite some time. Quite a number of live-aboards with their own mailboxes. The town pier is next door with a pump-out. Two all-tile full bathrooms - one each, could use some sprucing up.

Notable -- The fun looking Bubba's Family Restaurant is built in the shape of a bright blue tubby boat. Inside, the motif continues and some tables are tucked into the bow. The atmosphere is casual and convivial. Bubba's serves 3 meals a day, 6am to 8pm, Thu-Sat 'til 9pm. Huge breakfasts, sandwiches and salads for lunch, and a variety of seafood and steaks for dinner. Across the cove, Owen's also serves 3 meals a day in a casual atmosphere - with a deck when the weather's good; a beautiful deadrise at the docks adds to the ambiance. More eateries and services are along Wythe Creek Rd (Rt. 172) about 2 miles away.

PHOTOS ON CD-ROM: 10

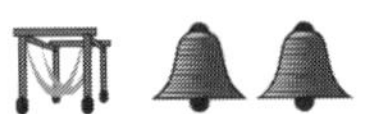

Bell Isle Marina

Two Bells Island Drive; Hampton, VA 23664

Tel: (757) 850-0466 **VHF: Monitor** n/a **Talk** n/a
Fax: (757) 851-2879 **Alternate Tel:** n/a
Email: info@bellislemarina.com **Web:** www.bellislemarina.com
Nearest Town: Hampton *(4 mi.)* **Tourist Info:** (757) 262-2000

Navigational Information

Lat: 37°05.849' **Long:** 076°17.618' **Tide:** 3 ft. **Current:** n/a **Chart:** 12238
Rep. Depths (*MLW*): Entry 6 ft. **Fuel Dock** n/a **Max Slip/Moor** 6 ft./-
Access: Back River to Wallace Creek

Marina Facilities *(In Season/Off Season)*

Fuel: *Amoco* - Gasoline, Diesel
Slips: 100 Total, 12 Transient **Max LOA:** 50 ft. **Max Beam:** n/a
Rate *(per ft.)*: **Day** $1.50* **Week** Inq. **Month** Inq.
Power: 30 amp Incl., **50 amp** n/a, **100 amp** n/a, **200 amp** n/a
Cable TV: No **Dockside Phone:** No
Dock Type: Fixed, Floating, Long Fingers, Pilings
Moorings: 0 Total, 0 Transient **Launch:** n/a
Rate: Day n/a **Week** n/a **Month** n/a
Heads: 2 Toilet(s), 2 Shower(s)
Laundry: None **Pay Phones:** Yes, 1
Pump-Out: OnSite **Fee:** n/a **Closed Heads:** Yes

Marina Operations

Owner/Manager: Charles Frazier **Dockmaster:** Same
In-Season: Year-Round, 8am-5pm **Off-Season:** n/a
After-Hours Arrival: Call in advance
Reservations: Yes **Credit Cards:** Visa/MC
Discounts: None
Pets: Welcome, Dog Walk Area **Handicap Access:** No

Marina Services and Boat Supplies

Services - Docking Assistance, Security, Dock Carts **Communication -** Phone Messages, Fax in/out, FedEx, UPS, Express Mail **Supplies - OnSite:** Ice *(Cube)*, Ships' Store **Near:** Propane *(or James River Welding 827-1453, 10 mi.)* **Under 1 mi:** Bait/Tackle *(Wallace B&T 851-5451)* **3+ mi:** West Marine *(825-4900, 9 mi.)*, Boater's World *(827-1613, 9 mi.)*

Boatyard Services

OnSite: Travelift *(30T, 20' beam)*, Forklift *(7.5T)*, Hull Repairs, Bottom Cleaning, Brightwork, Compound, Wash & Wax, Interior Cleaning, Painting **OnCall:** Engine mechanic *(gas, diesel)*, Electrical Repairs, Electronics Repairs, Rigger, Canvas Work, Air Conditioning, Refrigeration, Divers, Propeller Repairs, Woodworking, Upholstery, Yacht Broker **Yard Rates:** $55/hr. Lift 80/hr., Haul & Launch $10/ft. *(blocking incl.)*, Power Wash Incl., Bottom Paint $6/ft. **Storage:** In-Water $125/mo., On-Land $120/mo.

Restaurants and Accommodations

OnCall: Pizzeria *(Anna's Pizza 723-3593)* **1-3 mi:** Seafood Shack *(Fish Tales 850-2474)* **3+ mi:** Restaurant *(Grants 245-2200, 4 mi.)*, *(Michael James 265-2304, 4 mi.)*, *(Good Fortune 851-6888, 4 mi.)*, *(Win Wok Buffet 851-8089, 4 mi.)*, *(Number 1 Kitchen 851-3388, 4 mi.)*, *(Brass Lantern 850-4586, 4 mi.)*, Seafood Shack *(Buckroe Beach Grille 850-6500, 5 mi.)*, Fast Food *(Subway 850-0286, 4 mi.)*, Lite Fare *(May Way Grill 850-9200, 4 mi.)*, Motel *(Sans Souci 851-9300, 5 mi.)*, *(Golden Sands 851-8551, 5 mi.)*, *(Buckroe 722-7611, 4 mi.)*, Inn/B&B *(Lady Neptune 850-6060, 5 mi.)*

Recreation and Entertainment

OnCall: Fishing Charter **Near:** Beach **1-3 mi:** Special Events *(Bay Days - Sep; Hampton Oyster Festival - Oct)* **3+ mi:** Picnic Area *(Gosnold's Hope Park, 5 mi.)*, Grills *(5 mi.)*, Playground *(5 mi.)*, Golf Course *(The Woodlands 727-1195, 6 mi.)*, Jogging Paths *(5 mi.)*, Bowling *(Century Lanes 722-2551, 5 mi.)*, Movie Theater *(AMC Hampton 24 896-2330, 11 mi.)*, Video Rental *(Blockbuster 850-9298, 4 mi.)*, Park *(5 mi.)*, Museum *(VA Air & Space 727-0900, 7 mi.)*, Galleries *(Eden Gallery 723-6600, 7 mi.)*

Provisioning and General Services

OnSite: Wine/Beer **1-3 mi:** Convenience Store *(Zooms 851-7869)*, Bank/ATM, Beauty Salon *(Rhonda's 851-1479)* **3+ mi:** Supermarket *(Save-A-Lot 723-3645, 4 mi.)*, Gourmet Shop *(Medik's Market 262-0711, 5 mi.)*, Delicatessen *(Jason's Deli 825-1501, 8 mi.)*, Liquor Store *(ABC 850-0869, 4 mi.)*, Fishmonger *(Buckroe 850-4166, Henry's Seafood 722-2563, 4 mi./ 6 mi.)*, Crabs/Waterman *(Cod N Crab 723-6505, 7 mi.)*, Market *(Buckroe Beach 848-0562, 4 mi.)*, Post Office *(851-3914, 4 mi.)*, Library *(850-5114, 4 mi.)*, Dry Cleaners *(Boulevard 851-8110, 4 mi.)*, Laundry *(Soap-N-Suds 722-3250, 6 mi.)*, Pharmacy *(Rite Aid 851-9260, 4 mi.)*, Hardware Store *(Home Depot 827-5121, 8 mi.)*, Department Store *(Coliseum Mall 838-1505, 8 mi.)*

Transportation

OnCall: Rental Car *(Enterprise 865-7201)*, Taxi *(Harvest Taxicab 723-7922)*, Airport Limo *(A-1 Executive 591-0486, 24 hrs.)* **3+ mi:** Rail *(Amtrak 245-3589, 12 mi.)* **Airport:** Newport News/Williamsburg Int'l. *(18 mi.)*

Medical Services

911 Service **1-3 mi:** Dentist *(Behm 851-4155)*, Ambulance **3+ mi:** Doctor *(Lakes Family Health 850-1311, 4 mi.)*, Veterinarian *(Pembroke 722-2883, 5 mi.)* **Hospital:** Sentara Careplex 736-1000 *(9 mi.)*

Setting -- An attractive, three-story gray shingled tidewater colonial guides boaters from Back River through Wallace Creek. Vinyl-edged, floating alongside dockage lines the grassy bank and makes a sharp turn to port, following the shoreline into the marina's main basin. Free standing porch swings and picnic tables march along the bulkhead above the docks. A large travelift bay is backed by acres of dry storage - together, they visually dominate the string of long piers that host stationary slips. The sunsets are spectacular from the wooden pavilion that cantilevers above the docks.

Marina Notes -- *$15 min. Nav aids on Wallace Creek have been upgraded, but drafts over six feet should exercise caution. A casual, friendly atmosphere prevails among a can-do staff. Ships' store sells drinks, ice, beer, marine accessories. Wide range of boatyard services on-site or available. Mostly stationary docks in generally good condition. with a step down to a half-length, tapered finger pier. Alongside dockage is floating. One very large and very nice tiled bathroom with large Italian soft green tiles with a picture inset, big roll-in shower, separate small toilet area, and sink. There's one full bathroom, and one with two toilets and a shower. While it's not all fully tiled, it's certainly attractively painted cinderblock.

Notable -- Once rustic, very protected Bell Isle's landscape is moving in the direction of "park-like." Out of the hub-bub of Hampton, it is still close enough for provisioning (4 miles) and access to Hampton's many maritime supplies and services as well as the museums and sightseeing (7 miles). Note that the flight pattern from nearby Langley Air Force Base is sometimes right over head.

PHOTOS ON CD-ROM: 9

Navigational Information
Lat: 37°03.518' **Long:** 076°17.146' **Tide:** 3 ft. **Current:** n/a **Chart:** 12222
Rep. Depths (*MLW*): Entry 7 ft. **Fuel Dock** n/a **Max Slip/Moor** 7 ft./-
Access: Bay to Salt Ponds, docks along western shore

Marina Facilities *(In Season/Off Season)*
Fuel: No
Slips: 200 Total, 30 Transient **Max LOA:** 50 ft. **Max Beam:** 24 ft.
Rate *(per ft.)*: **Day** $1.25 **Week** Inq. **Month** $5.50
Power: 30 amp $4.50, **50 amp** $5.50, **100 amp** n/a, **200 amp** n/a
Cable TV: No **Dockside Phone:** No
Dock Type: Fixed, Short Fingers, Pilings, Wood
Moorings: 0 Total, 0 Transient **Launch:** n/a, Dinghy Dock
Rate: Day n/a **Week** n/a **Month** n/a
Heads: 8 Toilet(s), 6 Shower(s) *(with dressing rooms)*
Laundry: None, Book Exchange **Pay Phones:** No
Pump-Out: OnSite **Fee:** Free **Closed Heads:** Yes

Marina Operations
Owner/Manager: Jerry Powell **Dockmaster:** Same
In-Season: Apr-Sep, 7am-6pm **Off-Season:** Oct-Mar, 8:30am-5pm
After-Hours Arrival: Call ahead
Reservations: No **Credit Cards:** Visa/MC
Discounts: Boat/US **Dockage:** 20% **Fuel:** n/a **Repair:** n/a
Pets: Welcome, Dog Walk Area **Handicap Access:** No

Southall Landings Marina

333 Mainsail Drive; Hampton, VA 23664

Tel: (757) 850-9929 **VHF: Monitor** 16 **Talk** 9
Fax: (757) 850-7622 **Alternate Tel:** (757) 850-9939
Email: southallmarina@aol.com **Web:** www.southalllandingmarina.com
Nearest Town: Hampton **Tourist Info:** (757) 262-2000

Marina Services and Boat Supplies
Services - Docking Assistance, Boaters' Lounge, Security *(24 hrs., Gated community)*, Trash Pick-Up, Dock Carts **Communication -** Mail & Package Hold, Phone Messages, Fax in/out, Data Ports *(Office)*, FedEx, DHL, UPS, Express Mail *(Sat Del)* **Supplies - OnSite:** Ice *(Block, Cube)*, Ships' Store **Under 1 mi:** Bait/Tackle *(Buckroe Bait & Tackle 850-4166)* **1-3 mi:** Propane *(A-Helium Service 723-5422)* **3+ mi:** West Marine *(825-4900, 7 mi.)*, Boater's World *(827-1613, 7 mi.)*

Boatyard Services
OnSite: Engine mechanic *(gas, diesel)*, Electrical Repairs *(Tidewater Marine)*, Electronics Repairs, Hull Repairs, Rigger, Sail Loft, Canvas Work, Bottom Cleaning, Brightwork, Divers, Compound, Wash & Wax **OnCall:** Interior Cleaning, Propeller Repairs, Woodworking, Inflatable Repairs **Near:** Launching Ramp. **1-3 mi:** Travelift, Forklift.

Restaurants and Accommodations
OnCall: Pizzeria *(Anna's 723-3593)*, *(Pizza Hut 723-8000)* **1-3 mi:** Restaurant *(Capri 850-4355, delivers)*, *(Brass Lantern 850-4586)*, *(Grants 245-2200)*, *(Blue Marlin 723-8003)*, Seafood Shack *(Fish Tales 850-2474)*, *(Buckroe Beach Grille 850-6500, L $4-8, D $10-23, Sun brunch)*, Lite Fare *(Mona Lisa's 851-5621)*, *(May Way Grill & Subs 850-9200)*, Motel *(Buckroe 722-7611)*, *(Golden Sands 851-8551)*, *(Sans Souci 851-9300)*, Inn/B&B *(Lady Neptune 850-6060)*, Condo/Cottage *(Todds Cottages 851-7700)* **3+ mi:** Restaurant *(The Grill at Woodlands G.C. 722-2488, 4 mi.)*

Recreation and Entertainment
OnSite: Pool *(open 7am-10pm)*, Spa *(Sauna)*, Picnic Area, Grills, Tennis Courts, Jogging Paths **OnCall:** Fishing Charter *(Capt. Hogg's 723-3200)* **Under 1 mi:** Beach, Playground **1-3 mi:** Bowling *(Century Lanes 722-2551)*, Video Rental *(Blockbuster 850-9298)*, Park *(Buckroe Park)* **3+ mi:** Golf Course *(The Woodlands 727-1195, 4 mi.)*, Fitness Center *(XtremeMuscle 723-0537, 5 mi.)*, Movie Theater *(AMC 896-2330, 9 mi.)*, Museum *(Hampton History M. 727-1610, 5 mi.)*

Provisioning and General Services
Under 1 mi: Delicatessen, Bank/ATM, Post Office *(851-3914)* **1-3 mi:** Convenience Store *(Buckroe Beach 848-0562)*, Supermarket *(Save-A-Lot 723-3645)*, Gourmet Shop *(Medik's 262-0711)*, Liquor Store *(ABC 850-1342)*, Market *(Beach 850-3502)*, Catholic Church, Protestant Church, Library *(850-5114)*, Beauty Salon *(Rhonda's 851-1479)*, Barber Shop *(Hair Cuttery 850-9349)*, Dry Cleaners *(Boulevard 851-8110)*, Bookstore *(Lord Byron 851-3921)*, Pharmacy *(Eckerd 723-0152)*, Hardware Store *(Beach 723-8644)* **3+ mi:** Fishmonger *(Henry's 722-2563, 4 mi.)*, Laundry *(Soaps-N-Suds 722-1414, 4 mi.)*, Department Store *(Wal-Mart 825-1181, 6 mi.)*

Transportation
OnSite: Courtesy Car/Van, Water Taxi, InterCity Bus **OnCall:** Rental Car *(Enterprise 723-7997)*, Taxi *(Harvest 723-7922)*, Airport Limo *(Diamond 851-1090)* **Near:** Local Bus **3+ mi:** Rail *(Newport News 245-3589, 10 mi.)*
Airport: Newport News/Williamsburg Int'l. *(16 mi.)*

Medical Services
911 Service **OnCall:** Ambulance **1-3 mi:** Doctor *(Lakes Family Health 850-1311)*, Dentist *(Pearlman 723-6565)*, Chiropractor *(Peninsula 723-3893)*, Veterinarian *(Pembroke 722-2883)* **Hospital:** Sentara 736-1000 *(7 mi.)*

Setting -- The entrance jetty into deep, slender Salt Ponds is clearly marked by double flashing beacons. Just inside, a long network of well-outfitted docks stretches along the starboard side of the salt marsh. A raised boardwalk, paralleling the shore, anchors the docks and two boardwalks lead through the swaying grasses to the upland. On shore is the carefully-tended Southall Landing Community - naturally landscaped neighborhoods of appealing townhouses and private homes - with good amenities that are shared with boaters.

Marina Notes -- The helpful hands-on marina staff manages to get boaters what they need and where they need to be - restaurants, the supermarket, etc. Dedicated transient slips - stationary docks have one-step down half-length tapered finger piers. Optional dry storage area for dinghies. Dataports in the office, WiFi in process. Cable is not possible, so satellite service on the transient docks is also in the works (check on progress). Fish cleaning station. Heavy-duty carts for hauling over the boardwalks. This is the quiet side of Salt Ponds and a great place to leave the boat. All services and facilities available to transients. Attractive tiled bathhouses have fiberglass shower stalls and a good-sized sauna in each. No laundry, but a service picks up and delivers - all folded.

Notable -- The office and most of the amenities are in the 2-story contemporary gray club house. A small, inviting pool, cloistered behind white picket fencing outboard of the bathhouses, is surrounded by quality strap chaises and tables and chairs. On the 2nd floor is an expansive wrap-around sun deck with views across the undulating marsh. A half flight up is a second deck with even more impressive views of the harbor. Two well-maintained tennis courts are nearby.

PHOTOS ON CD-ROM: 12

Salt Ponds Marina

One Ivory Gull Crescent; Hampton, VA 23664

Tel: (757) 850-4300; (888) 881-0897 **VHF: Monitor** 16 **Talk** 9
Fax: (757) 850-4893 **Alternate Tel:** n/a
Email: spm@verizon.net **Web:** www.saltpondsmarinaresort.com
Nearest Town: Hampton **Tourist Info:** (757) 262-2000

Navigational Information

Lat: 37°03.243' **Long:** 076°17.154' **Tide:** 2 ft. **Current:** n/a **Chart:** 12222
Rep. Depths (*MLW*): Entry 8 ft. **Fuel Dock** 10 ft. **Max Slip/Moor** 10 ft./-
Access: Between Thimble Shoals and Back River, eastern shore of Salt Pond

Marina Facilities *(In Season/Off Season)*

Fuel: *Texaco* - Gasoline, Diesel
Slips: 254 Total, 50 Transient **Max LOA:** 110 ft. **Max Beam:** n/a
Rate *(per ft.)*: **Day** $1.35 **Week** $6.75 **Month** Inq.
Power: 30 amp $3, **50 amp** $5, **100 amp** n/a, **200 amp** n/a
Cable TV: Yes, $3 /nt., limited **Dockside Phone:** Yes & courtesy phone
Dock Type: Floating, Long Fingers, Pilings, Wood
Moorings: 0 Total, 0 Transient **Launch:** n/a
Rate: Day n/a **Week** n/a **Month** n/a
Heads: 10 Toilet(s), 10 Shower(s)
Laundry: 4 Washer(s), 4 Dryer(s), Book Exchange **Pay Phones:** No
Pump-Out: OnSite, Full Service, 1 Central **Fee:** n/a **Closed Heads:** Yes

Marina Operations

Owner/Manager: Cindy Hawkins **Dockmaster:** Same
In-Season: May-Oct, 7am-7pm **Off-Season:** Nov-Apr, 7:30am-5pm
After-Hours Arrival: Check in at opening the following day
Reservations: Recommended **Credit Cards:** Visa/MC, Amex
Discounts: None
Pets: Welcome, Dog Walk Area **Handicap Access:** No

Marina Services and Boat Supplies

Services - Docking Assistance, Security, Trash Pick-Up, Dock Carts **Communication -** Mail & Package Hold, Phone Messages, Fax in/out *(Free)*, Data Ports *(Beacon Wi-Fi)*, FedEx, DHL, UPS, Express Mail *(Sat Del)* **Supplies - OnSite:** Ice *(Block, Cube)*, Ships' Store **1-3 mi:** Bait/Tackle *(Buckroe B&T 850-4166)*, Live Bait, Propane *(A-Helium Service 723-5422)* **3+ mi:** West Marine *(825-4900, 8 mi.)*, Boater's World *(827-1613, 8 mi.)*

Boatyard Services

OnSite: Engine mechanic *(gas, diesel)*, Electrical Repairs, Bottom Cleaning, Brightwork, Propeller Repairs, Painting, Yacht Broker *(Paradise Pt. Yacht Sales)* **OnCall:** Electronics Repairs, Hull Repairs, Rigger, Canvas Work, Air Conditioning, Refrigeration, Divers, Compound, Wash & Wax, Interior Cleaning, Upholstery **1-3 mi:** Travelift, Launching Ramp. **Nearest Yard:** Dandy Haven Marina (3 mi.) (757) 851-1573

Restaurants and Accommodations

OnSite: Restaurant *(Buckroe Beach Grille 850-6500, L $4-8, D $10-23, Sun brunch $3-8)*, Lite Fare *(Cabana Bar L $6-16, D $6-16, plus raw bar; lunch Sat & Sun only)* **OnCall:** Pizzeria *(Anna's 723-3593)* **1-3 mi:** Restaurant *(Grants 245-2200)*, *(Brass Lantern 850-4586)*, *(Blue Marlin 723-8003)*, Lite Fare *(Mona Lisa's 851-5621)*, *(May Way Grill & Subs 850-9200)*, Motel *(Sans Souci 851-9300)*, *(Buckroe 722-7611)*, Inn/B&B *(Lady Neptune 850-6060)* **3+ mi:** Hotel *(Radisson 727-9700, $89-125, 5 mi.)*

Recreation and Entertainment

OnSite: Pool *(2)*, Picnic Area, Grills, Tennis Courts, Fishing Charter *(three boats)* **Near:** Beach, Playground **Under 1 mi:** Boat Rentals, Park *(8 acre Buckroe Park)*, Cultural Attract *(Buckroe Beach - Sunday eve. concerts)* **1-3 mi:** Bowling *(Century 722-2551)*, Video Rental *(Blockbuster 850-9298)* **3+ mi:** Golf Course *(The Woodlands 727-1195, 4 mi.)*, Fitness Center *(Xtreme Muscle 723-0537, 5 mi.)*, Museum *(Hampton History, 5 mi.)*

Provisioning and General Services

OnSite: Wine/Beer, Newsstand **Under 1 mi:** Bank/ATM, Post Office *(851-3914)*, Catholic Church, Protestant Church, Pharmacy *(Eckerd 723-0152)* **1-3 mi:** Convenience Store *(Buckroe Beach Market 848-0562)*, Supermarket *(Save-A-Lot 723-3645)*, Gourmet Shop *(Medik's Market 262-0711)*, Liquor Store *(ABC 850-1342)*, Market *(Beach Market 850-3502)*, Library *(850-5114)*, Beauty Salon *(Kartrez 848-1448)*, Barber Shop *(Hair Cuttery 850-9349)*, Dry Cleaners *(Boulevard 851-8110)*, Bookstore *(Benders Books 723-3741)*, Hardware Store *(Beach 723-8644)*, Retail Shops **3+ mi:** Bakery *(Flowers 723-7668, 4 mi.)*, Fishmonger *(Henry's 722-2563, 4 mi.)*, Department Store *(Wal-Mart 825-1181, 6 mi.)*

Transportation

OnSite: Courtesy Car/Van, Bikes *(complimentary)* **OnCall:** Rental Car *(Enterprise & Triangle - discounts)*, Taxi *(Harvest 723-7922)*, Airport Limo *(Diamond 851-1090)* **Near:** Local Bus **3+ mi:** Rail *(Amtrak, 10 mi.)* **Airport:** Newport News/Williamsburg Int'l. *(16 mi.)*

Medical Services

911 Service **OnCall:** Ambulance **1-3 mi:** Doctor *(Lakes Family Health 850-1311)*, Dentist *(Pearlman 723-6565)*, Chiropractor *(Peninsula 723-3893)*, Veterinarian *(Pembroke 722-2883)* **Hospital:** Sentara 736-1000 *(7 mi.)*

Setting -- Partway past Southall, the Salt Pond Marina's boardwalk begins. Edged by pristine marsh, it anchors 17 main floating piers with over 250 slips. Overlooking the central basin is a lovely, flower-shaped pool with a well-furnished sun deck backed by the marina office, store and a brace of tennis courts. The Buckroe Grille occupies the signature gray two-story octagonal building, surrounded by decks, and topped by a lighthouse cupola -- all carefully landscaped.

Marina Notes -- DCM. The accommodating staff manages the marina by golf cart and happily picks up boaters en route. Group rates. Small ships' store has some clothing and other critical items. Fuel dock fronts the restaurants. Dockominium with many transient places (but not enough to continue staging the cruising rallies). Long-time manager now lives on-site for even better oversight. Excellent maintenance includes annual cleaning of the dock decking - it shows. Vinyl-edged floating docks with full-length wide finger piers. Cats occupy most T-heads. Two bathhouses are at "C" & "O" docks, laundry at "O."

Notable -- The 2nd floor octagonal Buckroe Beach Grille serves lunch, dinner and Sun brunch - modestly priced menu, strong on seafood in a fabulous setting (Mon-Thu 11am-11pm, Fri & Sat 11am-mid, Sun 9am-9pm; shorter hours off-season). Dine in the casual windowed dining room or outside on the covered deck at white wrought iron tables & chairs, with expansive views across the marsh and harbor. The first floor Cabana Bar surrounds a little pool with a net, available for anyone so inspired - which creates a party atmosphere; a consideration when choosing a slip. (Wed & Thu 5pm on, Fri-Sun, 11am on). Same menu as the Grille - different ambiance. A walkway runs from the boardwalk at "O" dock to the public access beach. A mile away is larger Buckroe Beach Park.

16. Western Shore: Hampton & James Rivers

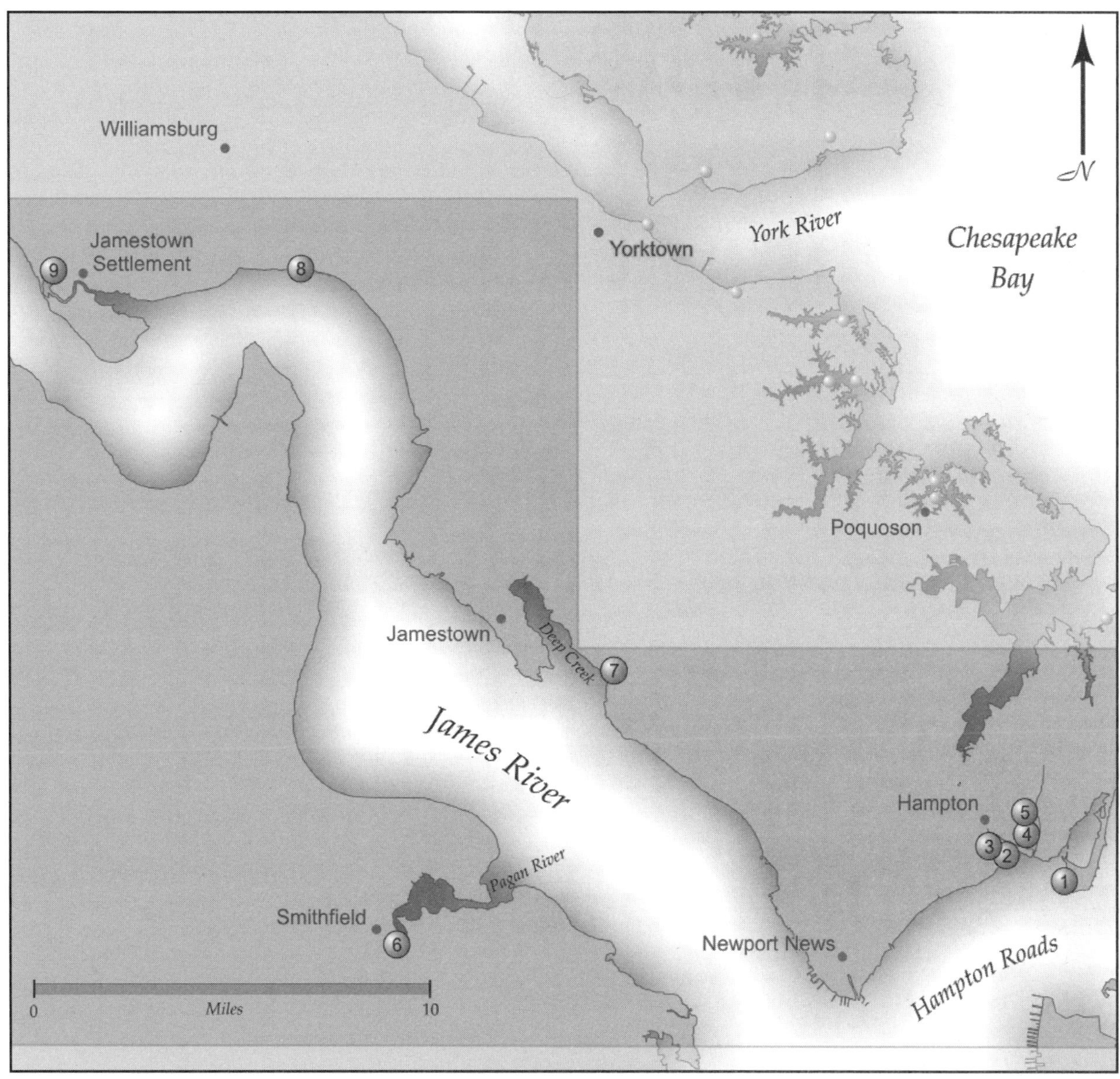

MAP	MARINA	HARBOR	PAGE	MAP	MARINA	HARBOR	PAGE
1	**Old Point Comfort Marina**	*Hampton Roads*	290	6	**Smithfield Station**	*James River/Pagan River*	295
2	**Bluewater Yachting Center**	*Hampton River/Sunset Creek*	291	7	**James River Marina**	*James River/Deep Creek*	296
3	**Sunset Boating Center**	*Hampton River/Sunset Creek*	292	8	**Kingsmill Marina**	*James River*	297
4	**Customs House Marina**	*Hampton River*	293	9	**Jamestown Yacht Basin**	*James River/Powhatan Creek*	298
5	**Downtown Hampton Public Piers**	*Hampton River*	294				

- **A "DCM" symbol in Marina Notes means Designated Clean Marina** — This is a coveted state-level award given to marinas that meet stringent, environmentally supportive requirements (see page 307). *For a list of DCM's & pump-out facilities, see page 308.*
- **Ratings & Reviews** — An explanation of the Atlantic Cruising Club's rating system, and a detailed explanation of what is in each section of the Marina Report is on pages 6 – 11. *The Data-Gathering Process is detailed on page 322.*
- **Marina Report Updates** — Updates to Marina Reports (from readers, ACC reviewers, and marinas) are posted regularly on *www.AtlanticCruisingClub.com.*

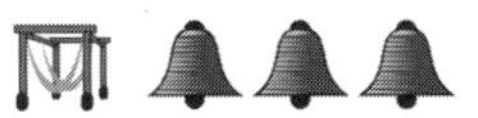

Old Point Comfort Marina

PO Box ; 207 McNair Road; Fort Monroe, VA 23651

Tel: (757) 788-4308 **VHF: Monitor** 16 **Talk** 68
Fax: (757) 788-4354 **Alternate Tel:** (757) 788-4308
Email: grogant@monroe.army.mil **Web:** www.monroemwr.com/marina.htm
Nearest Town: Hampton *(1 mi.)* **Tourist Info:** (757) 262-2000

Navigational Information

Lat: 37°00.265' **Long:** 076°18.844' **Tide:** 3 ft. **Current:** 7 kt. **Chart:** 12222
Rep. Depths (*MLW*): Entry 20 ft. **Fuel Dock** 20 ft. **Max Slip/Moor** 24 ft./-
Access: Hampton Roads Bridge Tunnel to western shore of Ft. Monroe

Marina Facilities *(In Season/Off Season)*

Fuel: Gasoline, Diesel, High-Speed Pumps
Slips: 314 Total, 10 Transient **Max LOA:** 52 ft. **Max Beam:** 15 ft.
Rate *(per ft.)*: **Day** $1.00/Inq. **Week** Inq. **Month** Inq.
Power: 30 amp Incl., **50 amp** Incl., **100 amp** n/a, **200 amp** n/a
Cable TV: No **Dockside Phone:** No
Dock Type: Floating, Long Fingers, Short Fingers, Pilings, Wood
Moorings: 0 Total, 0 Transient **Launch:** n/a, Dinghy Dock
Rate: Day n/a **Week** n/a **Month** n/a
Heads: 7 Toilet(s), 7 Shower(s) *(with dressing rooms)*
Laundry: 2 Washer(s), 2 Dryer(s), Iron, Iron Board **Pay Phones:** No
Pump-Out: OnSite, Self Service, 1 Central **Fee:** $5 **Closed Heads:** Yes

Marina Operations

Owner/Manager: Theresa I. Grogan **Dockmaster:** Same
In-Season: MemDay-LabDay, 8am-6pm **Off-Season:** Sept-Dec, 8am-5pm
After-Hours Arrival: Call ahead
Reservations: Preferred **Credit Cards:** Visa/MC
Discounts: Boat/US **Dockage:** no **Fuel:** $0.10/gal **Repair:** n/a
Pets: Welcome, Dog Walk Area **Handicap Access:** Yes, Heads, Docks

Marina Services and Boat Supplies

Services - Docking Assistance, Security *(24 hrs., Military Police)*, Dock Carts **Communication -** Mail & Package Hold, Fax in/out **Supplies - OnSite:** Ice *(Cube)*, Ships' Store *(next-day special orders)*, Bait/Tackle, Live Bait *(minnows, night crawlers, worms, squid, etc.)* **1-3 mi:** Ice *(Block, Shaved)* **3+ mi:** West Marine *(825-4900, 7 mi.)*, Propane *(4 mi.)*

Boatyard Services

OnSite: Travelift *(6T)*, Launching Ramp, Bottom Cleaning **OnCall:** Engine mechanic *(gas, diesel)*, Hull Repairs, Canvas Work, Air Conditioning, Refrigeration, Divers, Propeller Repairs, Upholstery **Under 1 mi:** Yacht Design, Yacht Building. **Yard Rates:** $40/hr., Haul & Launch $2-3/ft., Power Wash $2-3/ft., Bottom Paint $40/hr.

Restaurants and Accommodations

OnSite: Lite Fare *(Thumper's on the Bay 788-4680, B $3-5, L $4-8, B & L Mon-Fri)* **OnCall:** Pizzeria *(Anna's Italian Pizza 723-3593)*, *(Domino's 728-0033)* **Near:** Restaurant *(Chamberlin Resort 723-6511)*, Hotel *(Chamberlin Resort 723-6511)* **Under 1 mi:** Restaurant *(Sam's Seafood 723-3709)*, *(Wanchese Fish Co. 722-1443)*, *(Keith's Dockside 723-1781)*
1-3 mi: Restaurant *(Paul's 723-9063)*, *(Sarah's Irish Pub 722-2373, B $2-4, L $3-8, D $3-8)*, *(Golden City 728-9782)*, Lite Fare *(Signals 727-9700, L $6-9D $9-16, 11am-Mid)*, Hotel *(Radisson 727-9700, $90-125)*

Recreation and Entertainment

OnSite: Playground, Jogging Paths, Boat Rentals, Park *(Continental)*, Museum *(Casement M. daily 10:30am-4:30pm, Free - plan on 90 min.; Chapel of the Centurion; Old Point Comfort Lighthouse)*, Cultural Attract *(Fort Monroe, part of VA Civil War Trail)*, Special Events *(July 4th @ the Fort, Seafood Fling)* **Near:** Horseback Riding *(D & P Stables 838-2931)*
Under 1 mi: Pool, Beach, Tennis Courts **1-3 mi:** Picnic Area, Golf Course *(The Woodlands 727-1195)*, Bowling *(Century Lanes 722-2551)*, Fishing Charter *(Captain Hoggs 723-3200)*, Video Rental *(Treasure Chest 722-9870)*, Galleries *(Harbor 723-6400)*

Provisioning and General Services

OnSite: Wine/Beer, Market *(PX for military only)* **Near:** Catholic Church
Under 1 mi: Post Office *(722-9621)*, Protestant Church, Dry Cleaners *(Berkeley 726-0008)*, Florist *(Smith 723-6006)* **1-3 mi:** Convenience Store *(Benthall Market 723-8462)*, Supermarket *(Save-A-Lot 723-3645, Food Lion 723-8802)*, Liquor Store *(La Bodega 722-8466)*, Green Grocer *(Wood's Orchards 722-2873)*, Fishmonger *(Henry's 722-2563)*, Bank/ATM, Synagogue, Library *(727-1149)*, Beauty Salon *(Liz's 723-9327)*, Laundry *(Clear Water 722-2300)*, Bookstore *(Benders 723-3741)*, Pharmacy *(Rite Aid 728-9538)*, Hardware Store *(Beach 723-8644)*

Transportation

OnCall: Rental Car *(Enterprise 723-7997)*, Taxi *(Yellow 727-7777)*, Airport Limo *(Airport Express 622-2227)* **1-3 mi:** Local Bus *(HRT 222-6100)*
3+ mi: Rail *(Amtrak 245-3589, 10 mi.)* **Airport:** Norfolk International *(15 mi.)*

Medical Services

911 Service **1-3 mi:** Doctor *(Old Hampton 726-5000)*, Dentist *(Familant 722-5316)*, Chiropractor *(Bayview 723-1496)*, Veterinarian *(Pembroke 722-2883)* **Hospital:** Sentara Careplex 736-1000 *(7 mi.)*

Setting -- The ten main piers of Old Point Comfort sprawl along the protected western shore of Fort Monroe. A wave attenuator made of pilings runs the full length of the marina, with entrances opposite F and K docks. Inside are recent floating docks with half-length finger piers and fairly recent pedestals. The shore is well treed, with views of the famous Chamberlain Hotel and the Fort. Picnic decks front the restaurant building, and a walking/jogging path rims the island.

Marina Notes -- DCM. Dockage restricted to military, retired military, DOD & local Fed employees. With 24 hrs. notice, a guest boat may accompany the authorized boat. The dinghy dock is open to all boats in the anchorage for access to the Fort. Maximum stay is three weeks. Frozen and live bait. 24-hour security cameras throughout, monitored by both the military police and the marina staff. Second floor Thumper's Restaurant, a very casual eatery patronized mostly by the local military, serves breakfast, lunch and dinner (cash or check only). Across from "H" are six pleasant air-conditioned full bathrooms with cement floors and fiberglass shower stalls, including a handicapped-accessible. Additional head is at "A" dock, behind the office next to the laundry.

Notable -- A large gazebo centers the beautifully manicured waterfront. Continental Park is bordered by lovely old turn-of-the-century Tidewater homes--residences of the base's senior officers. Just past the fishing pier is the beginning of the moat which surrounds the largest stone fort in the U.S. Several entrances lead under the embankment into the Fort. Fascinating Casement Museum chronicles the history of the Fort and the Coast Artillery Corps; exhibits snake through the low arches of the rooms, all with original herringbone brick floors. Highlights are Jefferson Davis' cell and Freedom's Fortress.

PHOTOS ON CD-ROM: 15

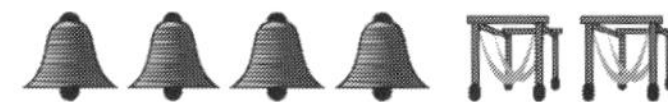

Bluewater Yachting Center

15 Marina Road; Hampton, VA 23669

Tel: (757) 723-6774 **VHF: Monitor** 16 **Talk** 72
Fax: (757) 227-6688 **Alternate Tel:** (757) 723-0793
Email: ian@bluewateryachtingcenter.com **Web:** bluewateryachtsales.com
Nearest Town: Hampton **Tourist Info:** (800) 487-8778

Navigational Information
Lat: 37°00.968' **Long:** 076°20.607' **Tide:** 3 ft. **Current:** 1 kt. **Chart:** 12222
Rep. Depths (*MLW*): Entry 12 ft. **Fuel Dock** 12 ft. **Max Slip/Moor** 10 ft./-
Access: Hampton Roads to Hampton River

Marina Facilities *(In Season/Off Season)*
Fuel: Gasoline, Diesel, High-Speed Pumps
Slips: 208 Total, 50 Transient **Max LOA:** 230 ft. **Max Beam:** n/a
Rate *(per ft.)*: **Day** $1.50 **Week** Inq. **Month** $10
Power: 30 amp $3, **50 amp** $6, **100 amp** $15, **200 amp** n/a
Cable TV: No **Dockside Phone:** No
Dock Type: Fixed, Floating, Long Fingers, Alongside, Wood
Moorings: 0 Total, 0 Transient **Launch:** n/a
Rate: Day n/a **Week** n/a **Month** n/a
Heads: 5 Toilet(s), 4 Shower(s)
Laundry: 2 Washer(s), 2 Dryer(s), Book Exchange **Pay Phones:** Yes, 1
Pump-Out: OnSite, Full Service **Fee:** $5 **Closed Heads:** Yes

Marina Operations
Owner/Manager: Ian L. Bates **Dockmaster:** Same
In-Season: May-Oct, 7am-7pm **Off-Season:** Nov-Apr, 8am-5pm
After-Hours Arrival: Call ahead
Reservations: Yes **Credit Cards:** Visa/MC, Amex
Discounts: None
Pets: Welcome, Dog Walk Area **Handicap Access:** Yes, Heads, Docks

Marina Services and Boat Supplies
Services - Docking Assistance, Security *(8 hrs., 9pm-5am)*, Trash Pick-Up, Dock Carts, Megayacht Facilities **Communication -** Mail & Package Hold, Phone Messages, Fax in/out, Data Ports *(office or Wi-Fi)*, FedEx, DHL, UPS, Express Mail *(Sat Del)* **Supplies - OnSite:** Ice *(Cube)*, Ships' Store **Near:** West Marine *(825-4900)*, Bait/Tackle *(Captain Hoggs)*

Boatyard Services
OnSite: Travelift *(37T & 100T)*, Engine mechanic *(gas, diesel)*, Electrical Repairs, Electronics Repairs, Hull Repairs, Rigger, Canvas Work, Bottom Cleaning, Brightwork, Air Conditioning, Refrigeration, Compound, Wash & Wax, Interior Cleaning, Propeller Repairs, Woodworking, Yacht Interiors, Metal Fabrication, Painting, Awlgrip, Yacht Building, Total Refits, Yacht Broker **OnCall:** Crane, Divers, Inflatable Repairs, Life Raft Service **Near:** Launching Ramp, Sail Loft. **Dealer for:** Viking Yachts, Regulator, Fountain. **Yard Rates:** Haul & Launch $4.50/ft. + labor *(blocking incl.)*

Restaurants and Accommodations
OnSite: Restaurant *(Surfrider 723-9366, L $4-8, D $4-19, plus Steamer Bar)* **OnCall:** Pizzeria *(Vancostas 725-1800)*, *(Domino's 728-0033)* **Near:** Restaurant *(Magnolia House 722-6881)*, Seafood Shack *(Hampton Roads723-4936)* **Under 1 mi:** Restaurant *(Pier 21 Shuttle)*, *(Signals Sports Bar Shuttle)*, *(American Grill 827-1044, Shuttle)*, Hotel *(Radisson 727-9700, $90-125)*, Inn/B&B *(Little England 722-0985)*, *(Victoria 722-2658)*

Recreation and Entertainment
OnSite: Pool **Near:** Playground, Fishing Charter *(Captain Hoggs 723-3200)*, Special Events *(Bay Days Fest - Sep; Blackbeard's Fest - Jun)* **Under 1 mi:** Volleyball, Video Rental *(Moviescene 723-1625)*, Park, Museum *(Air & Space Center 727-0900; Hampton History Museum - learn about Crab Town)*, Cultural Attract *(Walk Downtown Hampton)*, Galleries *(Harbor 723-6400)* **1-3 mi:** Dive Shop, Golf Course *(Woodlands 727-1195 - $50-60 for 2 incl. cart & $10 cert.- see dockmaster)*, Fitness Center *(YMCA 722-9044)*, Bowling *(Century Lanes 722-2551)*

Provisioning and General Services
Near: Bank/ATM **Under 1 mi:** Convenience Store *(7-Eleven)*, Supermarket *(Food Lion 723-8802)*, Health Food *(Healthy Connection)*, Wine/Beer *(La Bodega, ABC 727-4852)*, Fishmonger *(Hampton 723-8542)*, Market *(Swami 722-1164)*, Catholic Church, Protestant Church, Library *(727-1312)*, Laundry *(Econo 722-2359)*, Pharmacy *(Medicine Shoppe 722-6359)*, Newsstand, Retail Shops *(Family Dollar 728-0444)* **1-3 mi:** Bakery *(Flowers 723-7668)*, Green Grocer *(Hampton Oriental 723-3003)*, Post Office *(722-9961)*, Dry Cleaners *(Kecoughtan 723-0703)*, Bookstore *(Bender's 723-3741)*, Hardware Store *(Patrick's 722-2866)*, Department Store *(Target 827-7637)*

Transportation
OnSite: Water Taxi **OnCall:** Rental Car *(Enterprise 723-7997)*, Taxi *(Yellow Cab 727-7777)*, Airport Limo *(Puddin's 722-9700)* **Near:** Local Bus *(HRT 222-6100)*, InterCity Bus **3+ mi:** Rail *(Amtrak 245-3589, 8 mi.)* **Airport:** Norfolk Int'l. *(15 mi.)*

Medical Services
911 Service **OnCall:** Ambulance **Under 1 mi:** Doctor *(Sentara 726-5000)*, Dentist *(Steele 723-5225)*, Chiropractor *(Bridge Street 722-5151)*, Holistic Services *(Salters Creek 723-1899)* **Hospital:** Sentara 736-1000 *(3 mi.)*

Setting -- Gorgeous, high-end, relatively new Bluewater sits at the junction of the Hampton River and Sunset Creek just past the fishing fleet; docks run along the river, around the corner and up the creek. Pretty Tidewater-style buildings are sided with light tan clapboard, trimmed in white with blue steel roofs. Sea oats punctuate the immaculate grounds and soften the gravel. Views are of the Hampton skyline and the surrounding quiet, nicely done townhouse development.

Marina Notes -- DCM. Formerly Hampton Road Marina, completely rebuilt and reopened Aug '02. Very professional operation; caters to megayachts. Over 200 state-of-the-art floating slips plus 1,500 feet of alongside dockage - IPE-decked. Up to 100A, 240V service. Very long fuel dock with 3 hi-speed pumps. Pumpout. Wi-Fi. Two boatyards with 37 & 100 ton lifts - the second yard, catering to over 50-footers, is farther up the creek. Emergency transient repairs. 2,000 square feet of meeting space - group cruise friendly. Very nice blue and white all-tiled bathhouses - each features molded 3 Corian sinks, 3 heads, 2 private showers with commodious dressing rooms and a baby-changing table. Laundry room has 2 washers & 2 dryers with a small folding table.

Notable -- A large, lovely pool, with views of the docks, is sheltered in an arm of the main building. Upscale white strap chaises plus tables and chairs populate the IPE decking. Surfrider Restaurant, famous for its crabcakes (a hint of cracker crumbs, lightly broiled) is open daily, Sun-Thu 11am-9pm, Fri & Sat 'til 10. Same menu all day, plus lunch and dinner specials. A delightful screened porch literally rests on the docks with open views of the water. Easy 0.4 mile to a big, new Food Lion surrounded by a very useful shopping center. Complimentary water taxi makes downtown Hampton a stone's throw away.

Sunset Boating Center

800 S. Armistead Avenue; Hampton, VA 23669

Tel: (757) 722-3325 **VHF: Monitor** 16 **Talk** n/a
Fax: (757) 722-8464 **Alternate Tel:** (757) 722-3325
Email: n/a **Web:** n/a
Nearest Town: Hampton **Tourist Info:** (757) 262-2000

Navigational Information

Lat: 37°01.069' **Long:** 076°20.991' **Tide:** 4 ft. **Current:** n/a **Chart:** 12222
Rep. Depths (*MLW*): Entry 10 ft. **Fuel Dock** 10 ft. **Max Slip/Moor** 15 ft./-
Access: Chesapeake Bay to Hampton River, west into Sunset Creek

Marina Facilities *(In Season/Off Season)*

Fuel: Gasoline, Diesel, High-Speed Pumps
Slips: 550 Total, 50 Transient **Max LOA:** 60 ft. **Max Beam:** 18 ft.
Rate *(per ft.)*: **Day** $1.25 **Week** Inq. **Month** Inq.
Power: 30 amp Incl., **50 amp** Incl., **100 amp** n/a, **200 amp** n/a
Cable TV: No **Dockside Phone:** No
Dock Type: Floating, Long Fingers, Short Fingers, Pilings, Wood, Vinyl
Moorings: 0 Total, 0 Transient **Launch:** n/a, Dinghy Dock
Rate: Day n/a **Week** n/a **Month** n/a
Heads: 6 Toilet(s), 2 Shower(s) *(with dressing rooms)*
Laundry: 2 Washer(s), 2 Dryer(s) **Pay Phones:** Yes, 2
Pump-Out: Full Service, 2 Central **Fee:** $5 **Closed Heads:** Yes

Marina Operations

Owner/Manager: Rick Schlegel **Dockmaster:** Cindy Lafferty
In-Season: Apr-Oct, 7am-7pm **Off-Season:** Nov-Mar, 8am-5pm
After-Hours Arrival: Call ahead
Reservations: Yes, Preferred **Credit Cards:** Visa/MC, Dscvr, Amex
Discounts: Boat/US **Dockage:** 25% **Fuel:** 10% **Repair:** n/a
Pets: Welcome, Dog Walk Area **Handicap Access:** Yes, Heads, Docks

Marina Services and Boat Supplies

Services - Docking Assistance, Boaters' Lounge, Security *(24 hrs., Uniformed guard)*, Trash Pick-Up, Dock Carts **Communication -** Mail & Package Hold, Phone Messages, Fax in/out, Data Ports *(Office)*, FedEx, DHL, UPS, Express Mail *(Sat Del)* **Supplies - OnSite:** Ice *(Block, Cube, Shaved)*, Ships' Store, Bait/Tackle *(Captain Hoggs)*, Live Bait **3+ mi:** West Marine *(825-4900, 4 mi.)*, Propane *(James River Welding 827-1453, 5 mi.)*

Boatyard Services

OnSite: Forklift *(10T)*, Engine mechanic *(gas, diesel)*, Electrical Repairs, Electronics Repairs, Hull Repairs, Rigger, Canvas Work, Bottom Cleaning, Brightwork, Compound, Wash & Wax, Interior Cleaning, Painting, Awlgrip **OnCall:** Air Conditioning, Refrigeration, Divers, Propeller Repairs, Woodworking, Inflatable Repairs, Life Raft Service, Yacht Interiors, Metal Fabrication **Near:** Launching Ramp. **Dealer for:** Mercury, Evenrude, Yanmar, Yamaha, Honda, Volvo Penta . **Yard Rates:** Haul & Launch $5/ft., Power Wash $1.75/ft., Bottom Paint Inq. **Storage:** On-Land $8.50/ft./mo.

Restaurants and Accommodations

OnCall: Pizzeria *(Domino's 728-0033)* **Near:** Restaurant *(Magnolia House 722-6881)*, Seafood Shack *(Hampton Roads Seafoods Ltd. 723-3363)*, *(Old Hampton Seafood Kitchen 723-4936)*, Hotel *(Victoria House 722-2658)*, Inn/B&B *(Little England Inn 722-0985)* **Under 1 mi:** Restaurant *(Goodfellas 723-4979)*, *(Surf Rider 723-9366, L $4-8, D $4-19)*, *(Anna's Italian 727-7707)*, *(Musasi Japanese 728-0298)*, *(Pier 21 727-9700)*, *(Real Bread Company Bistro 727-9738)*, *(American Grill 827-1044)*, Coffee Shop *(Coffee Connection 722-6300)*, Hotel *(Radisson 727-9700, $90-125)* **1-3 mi:** Motel *(Hampton Manor 723-0727)*, *(Super 8 723-2888)*

Recreation and Entertainment

OnSite: Picnic Area, Grills, Fishing Charter *(Captain Hoggs 723-3200)* **Near:** Playground **Under 1 mi:** Video Rental *(Moviescene 723-1625)*, Park, Museum *(VA Air & Space Center 727-0900)*, Cultural Attract *(Downtown Hampton)*, Galleries *(Harbor 723-6400)* **1-3 mi:** Beach, Golf Course *(The Woodlands 727-1195)*, Fitness Center *(YMCA 722-9044)*, Bowling *(Century 722-2551)* **3+ mi:** Movie Theater *(YRC 825-3999, 4 mi.)*

Provisioning and General Services

Near: Library *(727-1312)*, Laundry *(Econo Wash 722-2359)* **Under 1 mi:** Convenience Store *(7-Eleven 723-2195)*, Supermarket *(Food Lion 723-8802)*, Liquor Store *(ABC 727-4852)*, Fishmonger *(Hampton Seafood 723-8542)*, Market *(Swami Food Store 722-1164)*, Bank/ATM, Catholic Church, Beauty Salon *(Final Touch Hair Salon 722-4511)*, Barber Shop *(Dan's 723-9486)*, Pharmacy *(The Medicine Shoppe 722-6359)*, Hardware Store *(Patrick's 722-2866)*, Retail Shops *(Family Dollar Store 728-0444)* **1-3 mi:** Health Food *(Healthy Connection 826-6404)*, Post Office *(722-9961)*, Bookstore *(Bender's 723-3741)*, Department Store *(Target 827-7637)*

Transportation

OnCall: Rental Car *(Enterprise 723-7997)*, Taxi *(Harvest 723-7922)*, Airport Limo *(Puddin's 722-9700)* **3+ mi:** Rail *(Amtrak 245-3589, 8 mi.)*
Airport: Norfolk International *(15 mi.)*

Medical Services

911 Service **OnCall:** Ambulance **Near:** Dentist *(Steele 723-5225)*
Under 1 mi: Doctor *(Sentara Medical 726-5000)*, Chiropractor *(Bridge Street 722-5151)* **Hospital:** Sentara Careplex 736-1000 *(3 mi.)*

PHOTOS ON CD-ROM: 9

Setting -- At the head of Sunset Creek, past Bluewater Yachting's portside docks and some absolutely lovely, classic, turn-of-the-century and Georgian-period homes to starboard, the four big gray, blue-trimmed, Sunset dry-stack sheds anchor the north side. A set of new floating wet slips lie in front of the last building and just past the last dock, and a small picnic deck looks out over the boats and water.

Marina Notes -- Primarily a dry-stack storage operation with room for over five hundred boats inside the sheds; overnight transient dockage is available on quite new floating docks with vinyl-edged full-length finger piers. There are no pedestals, but they can provide power. Totally quiet, secure place to leave the boat for a longer period of time. On-site is Hampton River Bait and Tackle - live and frozen bait, as well as a small convenience store with various items and sundries. Johnson Family Boating is also on-site, (722-BOAT), selling parts and accessories for smaller fishing boats. There are four sets of "heads" scattered around on the first and second floors -- a full bathroom with a sink outside, and then another smaller room that contains a toilet and a shower, then a single toilet on the first floor.

Notable -- The HRT route, Hampton Rapid Transit, runs right by the door; it interchanges with several other lines permitting boaters to easily access the greater Hampton area. About a quarter of a mile away is a dentist and a full-service laundromat, and a bit further is the new Food Lion shopping center which includes a Radio Shack. The marina can arrange a package to Colonial Williamsburg, Jamestown & Busch Gardens.

Navigational Information
Lat: 37°01.462' **Long:** 076°20.549' **Tide:** 3 ft. **Current:** 1 kt. **Chart:** 12222
Rep. Depths (*MLW*): Entry 13 ft. **Fuel Dock** n/a **Max Slip/Moor** 10 ft./-
Access: Hampton Roads to Hampton River

Marina Facilities *(In Season/Off Season)*
Fuel: No
Slips: 60 Total, 5 Transient **Max LOA:** 100 ft. **Max Beam:** n/a
Rate *(per ft.)*: **Day** $1.00 **Week** n/a **Month** Inq.
Power: 30 amp $3.50, **50 amp** $7, **100 amp** n/a, **200 amp** n/a
Cable TV: No **Dockside Phone:** No
Dock Type: Fixed, Long Fingers
Moorings: 0 Total, 0 Transient **Launch:** n/a
Rate: Day n/a **Week** n/a **Month** n/a
Heads: 7 Toilet(s), 5 Shower(s)
Laundry: None **Pay Phones:** Yes
Pump-Out: OnSite **Fee:** n/a **Closed Heads:** Yes

Marina Operations
Owner/Manager: Lynn Turnage **Dockmaster:** Same
In-Season: May-Oct, 9am-5pm **Off-Season:** Nov-Apr, on-call
After-Hours Arrival: Call in advance
Reservations: yes **Credit Cards:** n/a
Discounts: None
Pets: Welcome, Dog Walk Area **Handicap Access:** No

Customs House Marina

PO Box 344; 714 Settlers Landing Road; Hampton, VA 23669

Tel: (757) 636-7772 **VHF: Monitor** n/a **Talk** n/a
Fax: n/a **Alternate Tel:** (757) 868-9375
Email: n/a **Web:** n/a
Nearest Town: Hampton **Tourist Info:** (757) 262-2000

Marina Services and Boat Supplies
Services - Docking Assistance **Communication -** Mail & Package Hold, Phone Messages, FedEx, UPS **Supplies - OnSite:** Ice *(Cube)* **Under 1 mi:** Bait/Tackle *(Capt. Hoggs 723-3200)*, Live Bait **1-3 mi:** Propane (A-*Helium 723-5422)* **3+ mi:** West Marine *(825-4900)*

Boatyard Services
OnCall: Electrical Repairs, Electronics Repairs, Hull Repairs, Rigger, Canvas Work, Bottom Cleaning, Brightwork, Refrigeration
Nearest Yard: Bluewater Yacht Center (757) 723-0793

Restaurants and Accommodations
OnSite: Restaurant *(Pier 21 727-9700, L $6-13, D $12-16, placemats at lunchtime, white tablecloths at dinner)*, Lite Fare *(Signals 727-9700, L $9-16, D $9-16, 11am to Midnight everyday, pizza too)*, *(Oyster Alley L $6-9, D $6-13, Fri & Sat 11am-11pm, Sun & Thu 11am-3pm)* **Near:** Restaurant *(Bobby's Americana 727-0545)*, *(Musasi Japanese 728-0298)*, *(Bahir Dar 723-0100, L $7-14, D $7-14, Ethiopian, 11am-11pm)*, Lite Fare *(Goodfellas 723-4979, pick-up or delivery)*, *(Rooney's Downtown Café 726-2614)*, Pizzeria *(Anna's Italian 727-7707)*, Hotel *(Radisson 727-9700, $90-125)* **Under 1 mi:** Inn/B&B *(Little England Inn 722-0985)*, *(Victoria House 722-2658)* **1-3 mi:** Motel *(Super 8 723-2888)*, *(Buckroe 722-7611)*

Recreation and Entertainment
OnSite: Museum *(VA Air & Space 727-0900, Cousteau Society, nearby - Hampton History Museum)* **Near:** Park *(Millpoint Park)*, Cultural Attract *(American Theater in Phoebus, a 1908 Vaudeville house - HRT Rte 117)*, Sightseeing, Galleries *(Art by Gerome 723-6700)* **Under 1 mi:** Fishing Charter *(Captain Hoggs 723-3200)* **1-3 mi:** Beach *(Buckroe HRT Rte. 115)*, Golf Course *(Hamptons & Woodlands 727-1195)*, Fitness Center *(YMCA 722-9044)*, Bowling *(Century 722-2551)*, Video Rental *(Treasure Chest)*

Provisioning and General Services
Near: Wine/Beer *(La Bodega 722-8466)*, Fishmonger *(Amerie's Seafood - behind the carousel)*, Bank/ATM, Post Office *(722-9961)*, Catholic Church, Protestant Church, Beauty Salon *(Studio 762 722-4330)*, Barber Shop *(Barry's 728-9636)*, Bookstore *(Books Ahoy 723-5300)*, Retail Shops *(Odyssey Books & Old Village Boot Blue Skies Gallery 727-0028 - gifts)* **Under 1 mi:** Convenience Store *(7-Eleven)*, Bakery *(Flowers 723-7668)*, Library *(727-1154)*, Laundry *(Clear Water 722-2300)*, Pharmacy *(Rite Aid 726-0340)*, Hardware Store *(Patrick's 722-2866)* **1-3 mi:** Supermarket *(Farm Fresh 723-0771)*, Gourmet Shop *(Medik's 262-0711)*, Delicatessen *(EZ Food Mart & Deli 722-5300)*, Health Food *(Healthy Connection 851-0321)*, Liquor Store *(ABC 727-4852)*, Green Grocer *(Oriental Market 723-3003)*, Market *(W&W Market 723-3038)*, Dry Cleaners *(Ames 722-4301)*

Transportation
OnCall: Rental Car *(Enterprise 723-7997)*, Taxi *(Yellow Cab 722-1111)*, Airport Limo *(Puddin's 722-9700)* **Near:** Local Bus *(HRT 222-6100)*, InterCity Bus *(HRT to Virginia Beach, Newport News)* **3+ mi:** Rail *(Amtrak 245-3589, 8 mi.)* **Airport:** Norfolk Int'l. *(14 mi.)*

Medical Services
911 Service **OnCall:** Ambulance **Near:** Doctor *(Bowers 728-1100)*, Chiropractor *(Salters Creek 723-1899)*, Holistic Services *(Massage Ochranek 723-1899)* **Hospital:** Sentara 736-1000 *(3 mi.)*

Setting -- About a quarter-mile up the Hampton River, the Customs House docks are backed by the nine-story, mostly glass Radisson Hotel and the soft green pyramidal roof of the Cousteau Society's two-story octagon. A tree-lined brick promenade separates the docks from the Radisson's alfresco eateries - sheltered under a green awning. To the south is a 1920s carousel and the Air & Space Museum, and, to the west ,delightful downtown Hampton.

Marina Notes -- No on-site dockmaster or supervision. Telephone for reservations. Stationary docks with short, tapered finger piers. Adjacent is the American headquarters of the Cousteau Society with a public gallery. The dockside Radisson's eateries - Oyster Alley, Pier One and Signals Sports Grill - have views of the river, as do the hotel rooms' panoramic windows and the large event & banquet rooms - club cruise friendly. Slip holders share the Hampton Public Pier's bathhouse facilities. The one in the dockmaster's building has single, cinderblock bathrooms with tile floors, a sink and a fiberglass shower. The bathhouses in the Cousteau Society have three toilets and sinks open to the public and key-coded tile showers with commodious dressing areas.

Notable -- The juxtaposition of pleasure craft, fishing trawlers, carousel, museums, hotel and eateries delivers a richly textured ambiance - plus the trawlers' downlights create a fabulous other-worldly glow at night. The soaring Air and Space Museum has a glass-walled elevator; go to the top and walk down through a century of flying machines suspended in the gallery. Don't miss the DC-3 flight simulator. A very easy walking tour through downtown Hampton is guided by signposts that lead from one site to the next, including the new Hampton History Museum (which also now houses the Visitor's Center).

PHOTOS ON CD-ROM: 16

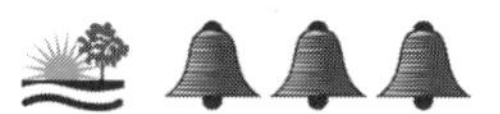

Downtown Hampton Public Piers

756 Settlers Landing Road; Hampton, VA 23669

Tel: (757) 727-1276; (866) 556-9631 **VHF: Monitor** 16 **Talk** 9
Fax: (757) 727-1255 **Alternate Tel:** (757) 727-1276
Email: info@downtownhampton.com **Web:** www.downtownhampton.com
Nearest Town: Hampton **Tourist Info:** (757) 262-2000

Navigational Information

Lat: 37°01.501' **Long:** 076°20.471' **Tide:** 3 ft. **Current:** 1 kt. **Chart:** 12222
Rep. Depths (*MLW*): Entry 12 ft. **Fuel Dock** n/a **Max Slip/Moor** 12 ft./-
Access: West of Old Point Comfort in the Hampton River

Marina Facilities *(In Season/Off Season)*

Fuel: No
Slips: 26 Total, 26 Transient **Max LOA:** 110 ft. **Max Beam:** n/a
Rate *(per ft.)*: **Day** $1.25 **Week** n/a **Month** Inq.
Power: 30 amp $3, **50 amp** $6, **100 amp** n/a, **200 amp** n/a
Cable TV: No **Dockside Phone:** No
Dock Type: Fixed, Floating, Long Fingers, Alongside, Concrete
Moorings: 0 Total, 0 Transient **Launch:** n/a, Dinghy Dock (Showers $1)
Rate: Day n/a **Week** n/a **Month** n/a
Heads: 7 Toilet(s), 6 Shower(s)
Laundry: None, Book Exchange **Pay Phones:** Yes, 5
Pump-Out: OnSite, Self Service **Fee:** $5 **Closed Heads:** Yes

Marina Operations

Owner/Manager: City of Hampton **Dockmaster:** Renie Martin
In-Season: May-Oct, 8am-8pm **Off-Season:** Nov-Apr, 8:30am-5:30pm
After-Hours Arrival: Tie up and call to leave message; check-in in morning
Reservations: Required on weekends **Credit Cards:** Visa/MC, Amex
Discounts: None
Pets: Welcome, Dog Walk Area **Handicap Access:** Yes, Heads, Docks

Marina Services and Boat Supplies

Services - Docking Assistance, Concierge, Dock Carts **Communication -** Mail & Package Hold, Phone Messages, Fax in/out *(Yes)*, Data Ports *(Office)*, FedEx, DHL, UPS, Express Mail *(Sat Del)* **Supplies - OnSite:** Ice *(Block, Cube)* **Near:** Ships' Store **Under 1 mi:** Bait/Tackle *(Captain Hoggs 723-3200)* **1-3 mi:** Propane *(A-2 Helium)*

Boatyard Services

OnCall: Engine mechanic *(gas, diesel)*, Electrical Repairs, Electronics Repairs, Hull Repairs, Rigger, Canvas Work, Bottom Cleaning, Air Conditioning, Refrigeration, Divers, Interior Cleaning, Propeller Repairs, Woodworking, Inflatable Repairs, Life Raft Service, Upholstery, Yacht Interiors, Metal Fabrication, Painting, Awlgrip **Near:** Sail Loft, Brightwork, Yacht Broker. **Nearest Yard:** Bluewater Yachting Center (757) 723-6774

Restaurants and Accommodations

OnSite: Restaurant *(Pier 21 727-9700, L $8, D $12-16, placemats at lunch, white tablecloths at dinner)*, Lite Fare *(Signals 727-9700, L $9-16, D $9-16, 7days 11am-mid)*, *(Oyster Alley L $6-13, D $6-13, L Mon-Fri, L&D Sat-Sun)*, *(Coffee Connection 722-6300)* **Near:** Restaurant *(Goodfellas 723-4979, pick-up or delivery)*, *(Bahir Dar 723-0100, D $7-14, Ethiopian 11am-11pm)*, Hotel *(Radisson 727-9700, $90-125)* **Under 1 mi:** Inn/B&B *(Little England Inn 722-0985)*, *(Victoria House 722-2658)* **1-3 mi:** Seafood Shack *(Seafood Market & Restaurant 722-8168)*

Recreation and Entertainment

OnSite: Pool, Fishing Charter, Group Fishing Boat, Museum *(Cousteau Society, Free; Air & Space Center 727-0900 $8.75/6.75, with Imax $13.75/10.75)* **Near:** Park *(Millpoint)*, Sightseeing *(Hampton Walking Tour)*, Galleries *(Art Market - outdoor on Queen's Way)* **1-3 mi:** Beach *(Buckroe Beach - Sun night band concerts)*, Golf Course *(Hamptons & Woodlands 727-1195 - see dockmaster - 2/$50-60 incl. cart & $10 cert.)*, Fitness Center *(YMCA 722-9044)*, Bowling *(Century 722-2551)*, Video Rental *(Treasure Chest 722-9870)*, Cultural Attract *(American Theater - Phoebus)*

Provisioning and General Services

OnSite: Newsstand **Near:** Liquor Store *(La Bodega 722-8466)*, Bank/ATM, Post Office *(722-9961)*, Catholic Church, Bookstore *(Books Ahoy 723-5300)*, Retail Shops *(Odyssey Books; Old Village Boot Blue Skies Gallery 727-0028 - gifts)*, Department Store *(Family Dollar 728-0444)* **Under 1 mi:** Convenience Store *(7-Eleven 723-1141)*, Bakery *(Flowers 723-7668)*, Fishmonger *(Hampton Seafood 723-8542)*, Library *(727-1154)*, Laundry *(Clear Water 722-2300)*, Pharmacy *(Rite Aid 726-0340)*, Hardware Store *(Patrick's 722-2866)* **1-3 mi:** Supermarket *(Farm Fresh 723-0771)*, Delicatessen *(EZ Mart 722-5300)*, Dry Cleaners *(Ames 722-4301)*

Transportation

OnSite: Bikes **OnCall:** Rental Car *(Enterprise 723-7997)*, Taxi *(Yellow Cab 722-1111)*, Airport Limo *(Puddin's 722-9700)* **Near:** Water Taxi, Local Bus *(HRT 222-6100)*, InterCity Bus **3+ mi:** Rail *(Amtrak 245-3589, 8 mi.)*
Airport: Norfolk Int'l. *(14 mi.)*

Medical Services

911 Service **OnCall:** Ambulance **Near:** Doctor *(Bowers 728-1100)*, Chiropractor *(Salters Creek 723-1899)* **3+ mi:** Veterinarian *(Armistead Avenue Vet 723-5118 1 mi., 8 mi.)* **Hospital:** Sentara 736-1000 *(3 mi.)*

Setting -- Just past the 9-story Radisson Hotel and the octagonal Cousteau Society, DHPP's 26 new floating slips stretch along the waterfront. Alongside dockage, for yachts to 110 feet, flanks the east and north side of the Cousteau pier and more dockage lies along the south side of the basin adjacent to the restored, hand-carved 1920 carousel. On-site are four eateries. The Virginia Air & Space Center and pretty, vibrant downtown Hampton are both a short walk.

Marina Notes -- Superb new floating cement docks with vinyl-edged finger piers have high-end pedestals, new July '04. Ice is right next to the heads and showers. Internet access in a little room off the dockmaster's office; bring your laptop and dial-up. Helpful, knowledgeable staff assists with boat services, recreational and entertainment suggestions. The pool at Radisson can be made available to guests. For group cruises, event facilities at the Radisson and at the Air & Space Center are available. Bathhouse near dockmaster's office has single, cinderblock bathrooms with tile floors, composite molded sinks and fiberglass showers. The ones in the Cousteau Society have 3 toilets/sinks open to the public and commodious key-coded all tiled showers for boaters.

Notable -- Hampton is a boaters' town; a wag once called it the "Swiss Army Knife" of ports. Every service is accessible by foot or by bus. The new American headquarters of Cousteau Society has a first floor education exhibit & retail shop. The exciting, recently renovated Air & Space Center ($8.9 million total) is directly adjacent - open MemDay-LabDay Mon-Wed 10am-5pm, Thu-Sun 10am-7pm, Off-season 10am-5pm. Four eateries are dockside: upscale Pier 21, alfresco Oyster Alley, Signals Sports Bar, and the Coffee Connection. For a night ashore, the Radisson rooms promise breathtaking panoramas.

Navigational Information
Lat: 36°58.933' **Long:** 076°37.333' **Tide:** 3 ft. **Current:** 3 kt. **Chart:** 12248
Rep. Depths (*MLW*): Entry 13 ft. **Fuel Dock** n/a **Max Slip/Moor** 13 ft./13 ft.
Access: Through high rise at James River Bridge, channel entrance to port

Marina Facilities *(In Season/Off Season)*
Fuel: No
Slips: 75 Total, 20 Transient **Max LOA:** 120 ft. **Max Beam:** 18 ft.
Rate *(per ft.)*: **Day** $1.25* **Week** n/a **Month** $6
Power: 30 amp Incl., **50 amp** $5, **100 amp** n/a, **200 amp** n/a
Cable TV: Yes **Dockside Phone:** No
Dock Type: Floating, Wood
Moorings: 0 Total, 0 Transient **Launch:** n/a, Dinghy Dock (n/c)
Rate: Day n/a **Week** n/a **Month** n/a
Heads: 6 Toilet(s), 4 Shower(s)
Laundry: 1 Washer(s), 1 Dryer(s) **Pay Phones:** No
Pump-Out: OnSite, Full Service, 1 Central **Fee:** $5 **Closed Heads:** Yes

Marina Operations
Owner/Manager: Randy Pack **Dockmaster:** Same
In-Season: Year-Round, 24/7 **Off-Season:** n/a
After-Hours Arrival: Hail on VHF 16
Reservations: Preferred **Credit Cards:** Visa/MC, Dscvr, Din, Amex
Discounts: None
Pets: Welcome, Dog Walk Area **Handicap Access:** Yes, Heads, Docks

Smithfield Station

PO Box 468; 415 S. Church St.; Smithfield, VA 23430

Tel: (757) 357-7700 **VHF: Monitor** 16 **Talk** 68
Fax: (757) 357-4638 **Alternate Tel:** n/a
Email: smithfieldstation@smithfieldstation.com **Web:** smithfieldstation.com
Nearest Town: Smithfield *(0.5 mi.)* **Tourist Info:** (757) 357-5182

Marina Services and Boat Supplies
Services - Docking Assistance, Concierge, Room Service to the Boat, Boaters' Lounge, Security *(24 hrs., patrolled)*, Trash Pick-Up, Dock Carts **Communication -** Mail & Package Hold, Phone Messages, Fax in/out *($1.00)*, Data Ports *(Lounge, Dial-Up)*, FedEx, UPS, Express Mail *(Sat Del)* **Supplies - OnSite:** Ice *(Cube)* **Under 1 mi:** Propane *(True Value 357-8705)* **1-3 mi:** Ships' Store, Bait/Tackle

Boatyard Services
OnSite: Yacht Broker *(Smithfield Yacht Sales)* **OnCall:** Engine mechanic *(gas, diesel)*, Electrical Repairs, Air Conditioning, Refrigeration, Divers, Compound, Wash & Wax, Interior Cleaning, Woodworking, Yacht Interiors

Restaurants and Accommodations
OnSite: Restaurant *(Smithfield Station 357-7700, B $7-11, L $7-15, D $11-24, kids $4-7; B Sat only; Sun brunch $10/6)*, Lite Fare *(IBX Bar & Grille)*, Hotel *(Smithfield Station 357-7700, $79-225)* **OnCall:** Pizzeria *(Domino's 357-6710)* **Near:** Restaurant *(Smithfield Inn & Tavern 357-1752, L $7-13, D $17-29, lite fare $7-11)*, Lite Fare *(Smithfield Confectionary & Ice Cream Parlor 357-6166)*, *(Twins Old Towne Inn 357-3031, Mon-Fri B & L, Sat B only)*, *(Painted Garden & Beehive 357-9377)*, Inn/B&B *(Mansion on Main 357-0006, $100-110)*, *(Smithfield Inn 357-1752, $85-145)*
Under 1 mi: Inn/B&B *(Church Street Inn 357-3176, $90-180)*
1-3 mi: Restaurant *(Angelo's Seafood & Steak 365-9235)*, *(Battery* Park Grill 357-1747), Fast Food *(Subway, Burger King)*

Recreation and Entertainment
OnSite: Pool, Picnic Area, Grills **Near:** Playground, Jogging Paths, Museum *(Isle of Wight Museum 357-7459, Tue-Sat 10am-4pm, Sun 1-5pm, Free; Old Courthouse of 1750, Free Thu-Sat 10am-4pm Sun,Tue & Wed 1-4pm)*, Cultural Attract *(Little Theater)*, Sightseeing *(44-site Walking tour - Hattie Drummond Visitors' Center or rent an audio tour)*, Galleries *(Cultural Arts Center 357-7707 Free, Tue-Sun - resident artists studios open)*, Special Events *(outdoor concerts, Fri 8pm, MemDay-LabDay, Smithfield Times lawn)* **Under 1 mi:** Tennis Courts *(YMCA - free)*, Golf Course *(Cypress Creek 365-0495)*, Fitness Center *(YMCA 365-4060)*

Provisioning and General Services
OnSite: Retail Shops *(Smithfield Antique Ctr 357-0223)* **Near:** Convenience Store *(Food Mart)*, Gourmet Shop *(Ham Shoppe 357-1798)*, Bakery *(Gourmet 357-0045)*, Farmers' Market *(Jul & Aug Sat 9am-Noon, 357-3502, 115 Main St; Fall special markets)*, Market *(Little's 357-4685)*, Bank/ATM, Post Office, Library *(357-3244)*, Beauty Salon *(Cindy & Sandy's 357-4553)*, Pharmacy *(Simpson's 357-4361)* **Under 1 mi:** Dry Cleaners *(Boothe Cleaner 357-3936)* **1-3 mi:** Supermarket *(Food Lion 357-0200, Farm Fresh 357-2138)*, Wine/Beer *(Bon Vivant 365-0932)*, Catholic Church, Hardware Store *(True Value 357-8705)*, Department Store *(Peebles 357-3241)*

Transportation
OnCall: Courtesy Car/Van *(to Golf Course)*, Rental Car *(Enterprise 357-9711)*, Taxi *(Better Way 357-7266)* **3+ mi:** Rail *(12 mi.)*, Ferry Service *(Williamsburg, 20 mi.)* **Airport:** Newport News/Norfolk Int'l. *(25 mi./35 mi.)*

Medical Services
911 Service **OnCall:** Ambulance **Near:** Doctor, Dentist, Chiropractor
1-3 mi: Veterinarian *(Roger's Veterinary Hospital)* **Hospital:** *(15 mi.)*

Setting -- Cut into the James' south shore, the serpentine Pagan River weaves past marshlands and old estates. About four NMs upriver, a faux screwpile lighthouse welcomes boaters to the elegant Smithfield Station Inn. A compact basin hosts floating docks that stretch from "The Light" to the large 3-story gray clapboard Tidewater contemporary Inn topped by a striking widow's walk. Picnic tables, a small pool and charming cottages stretch along the boardwalk.

Marina Notes -- *$30 min. Family-owned and operated since 1987. The main pier, which runs from The Light to the Inn, has floating weathered docks with gray vinyl-edged half-length finger piers. Another set of docks lies in front of the restaurant, and vinyl-edged alongside dockage is also adjacent to the boardwalk - directly outboard of the pool and cottages. The accommodating staff at the front desk helps when transportation is necessary. Pleasant bathhouses each feature tile floors, fiberglass composite walls, 2 toilets, 2 sinks with well-lighted mirrors, and 2 fiberglass shower stalls with private dressing rooms.

Notable -- Cantilevered over the water, the Inn houses a large, inviting knotty-pine paneled restaurant featuring 3 dining rooms plus a deck - with sylvan views across the panorama of the river and marsh. On the second and third floors are lovely rooms with waterfront decks. Dockside, the small, nicely furnished pool, suffers slightly from the traffic noise from the Route 10/258 bridge. Waterfront cottages line the boardwalk and two suites are actually in "The Light." The sweet, restored historic district invites a stroll. Wonderful, restored houses and unique local shops line the brick sidewalks. Town merchants provide old-fashioned red wagons for boaters (to haul home their loot). Smithfield hams can be purchased in town and the processing plants are a couple miles up the road.

PHOTOS ON CD-ROM: 14

Navigational Information

Lat: 37°04.783' **Long:** 076°31.367' **Tide:** 3 ft. **Current:** 0 kt. **Chart:** 12248
Rep. Depths (*MLW*): Entry 9 ft. **Fuel Dock** 8 ft. **Max Slip/Moor** 8 ft./-
Access: Hampton Roads to James River, 5 mi. W of James River Bridge

Marina Facilities *(In Season/Off Season)*

Fuel: Gasoline
Slips: 28 Total, 4 Transient **Max LOA:** 50 ft. **Max Beam:** 17 ft.
Rate *(per ft.)*: **Day** $1.00 **Week** n/a **Month** n/a
Power: 30 amp Incl., **50 amp** n/a, **100 amp** n/a, **200 amp** n/a
Cable TV: No **Dockside Phone:** No
Dock Type: Fixed, Short Fingers, Pilings, Alongside, Wood
Moorings: 0 Total, 0 Transient **Launch:** n/a
Rate: Day n/a **Week** n/a **Month** n/a
Heads: 3 Toilet(s), 2 Shower(s) *(with dressing rooms)*
Laundry: None **Pay Phones:** No
Pump-Out: OnSite **Fee:** n/a **Closed Heads:** Yes

James River Marina

665 Deep Creek Road; Newport News, VA 23606

Tel: (757) 930-1909 **VHF: Monitor** n/a **Talk** n/a
Fax: (757) 930-3200 **Alternate Tel:** n/a
Email: n/a **Web:** n/a
Nearest Town: Newport News **Tourist Info:** (757) 262-2000

Marina Operations

Owner/Manager: Marty Moliken **Dockmaster:** Same
In-Season: Apr-Sep, 8am-6pm **Off-Season:** Oct-Mar, 8am-5pm
After-Hours Arrival: Find empty slip, check in next morning
Reservations: Preferred **Credit Cards:** Visa/MC, Amex
Discounts: None
Pets: Welcome **Handicap Access:** Yes, Docks

Marina Services and Boat Supplies

Services - Docking Assistance, Dock Carts **Communication -** Phone Messages, FedEx, UPS *(Sat Del)* **Supplies - OnSite:** Ice *(Cube)*, Ships' Store, Bait/Tackle, Live Bait *(squid, mullet)* **1-3 mi:** Propane *(Harris Teeter 695-6000)* **3+ mi:** West Marine *(825-4900, 10 mi.)*

Boatyard Services

OnSite: Forklift *(15,000 lbs.)*, Engine mechanic *(gas, diesel)*, Electrical Repairs, Electronic Sales, Electronics Repairs, Hull Repairs, Bottom Cleaning, Brightwork, Air Conditioning, Refrigeration, Divers, Compound, Wash & Wax, Interior Cleaning, Woodworking, Metal Fabrication, Painting **OnCall:** Propeller Repairs **Yard Rates:** Haul & Launch $6.50/ft., Bottom Paint $19.50/ft. **Storage:** In-Water $115/mo.

Restaurants and Accommodations

OnSite: Restaurant *(Herman's Harbor House 930-1000)* **OnCall:** Pizzeria *(Domino's 595-3030)* **Under 1 mi:** Restaurant *(Mama Lina's 930-1800)*, *(So Ya Hibachi 930-0156)*, Seafood Shack *(Dearia's Seafood 930-3474, mostly fried baskets & platters; priced by the pound plus $3.50/per order to cook)* **1-3 mi:** Restaurant *(Bone Fish Grill 269-0002)*, *(Hong Kong 882-8777)*, *(Kapo Nara 249-5395)*, *(Savannah 596-5180)*, *(Plaza Azteca 599-6727)*, Coffee Shop *(Port City Java)* **3+ mi:** Motel *(Days Inn 873-6700, 4 mi.)*, *(Comfort Inn 249-0200, 4 mi.)*, Hotel *(Omni 873-6664, $160, 5 mi.)*

Recreation and Entertainment

OnSite: Picnic Area, Grills **Under 1 mi:** Playground **1-3 mi:** Fitness Center *(Bally 249-1315)*, Jogging Paths, Bowling *(AMF 595-2221)*, Video Rental *(Blockbuster 249-9010)*, Cultural Attract *(Christopher Newport Univ.)* **3+ mi:** Golf Course *(Kiln Creek 874-2600, 7 mi.)*, Movie Theater *(Regal 989-5200, 6 mi.)*, Park *(Mariners/Deer Park, 5 mi.)*, Museum *(Mariners Museum 596-2222, $6/4 10am-5pm daily, VA Living Museum 595-1900, $7/5 + $3 for planetarium Mon-Sat 9am-5pm, Sun 12-5pm, 5.5 mi.)*, Sightseeing *(Busch Gardens, 12 mi.)*, Special Events *(Bay Days 2nd week Sep, 8 mi.)*

Provisioning and General Services

1-3 mi: Convenience Store *(7-Eleven)*, Supermarket *(Harris Teeter 596-6000)*, Gourmet Shop *(Wine & Cheese 599-3985)*, Liquor Store *(ABC 594-7165)*, Fishmonger *(Demaria's Seafood 930-3474 - sushi grade tuna)*, Bank/ATM *(Suntrust)*, Post Office, Beauty Salon *(Lady & Lads 595-2259)*, Barber Shop, Dry Cleaners *(Boulevard 595-0545)*, Laundry *(Wash Land 833-6622)*, Pharmacy *(Hidenwood 595-1151)*, Hardware Store *(Ace 594-9890)*, Florist *(Mercer's 596-6364)* **3+ mi:** Delicatessen *(Danny's 595-0252, 4 mi.)*, Catholic Church *(Mt. Carmel 595-0385, 4 mi.)*, Synagogue *(Temple Sinai 596-8352, 4 mi.)*, Library *(591-4858, 5 mi.)*, Bookstore *(B&N 896-0500, 5 mi.)*, Department Store *(Patrick Henry Mall, 5 mi.)*, Buying Club *(Costco 448-5020, 4 mi.)*, Copies Etc. *(Kinko's 249-8480, 5 mi.)*

Transportation

OnCall: Rental Car *(Enterprise 595-7880)*, Taxi *(Yellow Cab 855-1111)* **Under 1 mi:** Local Bus *(HRT)* **3+ mi:** Rail *(Amtrak 245-3589, 6 mi.)*
Airport: Newport News/Norfolk Int'l. *(7 mi./27 mi.)*

Medical Services

911 Service **OnCall:** Ambulance **1-3 mi:** Dentist *(Goodwin 930-3744)*, Chiropractor *(Tidewater 890-2030)* **3+ mi:** Doctor *(Sentora Urgent Care 599-6117, 4 mi.)* **Hospital:** Riverside 594-2000 *(3 mi.)*

Setting -- Just inside the mouth of Deep Creek, off the north shore of the James River, a single dock, where pleasure craft share slips with an occasional working vessel, is tucked into the quiet cove - some call it a hurricane hole. Adjacent is the town dock, which will soon be under the management of James River Marina, as well.

Marina Notes -- Founded in 1970. With their new acquisition, the current 28 slips will expand to 50 floating slips, many dedicated to transients currently. The T-head can easily take a 50 foot boat . A bright blue shed has dry storage for 200 boats. Boat yard services - Mercruiser Certified Repair facility. 15,000 lbs forklift. The upscale Herman's Harbor House eatery is on-site. Quite nice, fully-tiled individual baths - sparkling white tiles trimmed with sage green, and fun "ducky" shower curtains. (Beware: if you rent a car, Deep Creek Road is max 25 mph; the local constabulary lines the town coffers here).

Notable -- Two fabulous, world-class museums are within a few miles - take a cab or rent a car (delivery & special rates with Enterprise). The new Virginia Living Museum is a native wildlife park-size museum, aquarium, botanical preserve and planetarium, with a 62,000 square foot exhibition building. The Mariner's Museum, an easy 5.5 miles, is one of the most comprehensive in the world, with 35,000 items (remarkably, no water access). A special center focuses on the iron-clad USS Monitor - as artifacts are recovered, they are stored in special tanks. Galleries cover an exquisite miniature ship collection, exhibits on Chesapeake watermen, early shipbuilding, gloriously restored vintage Chris Crafts, early whalers' scrimshaw and an aircraft carrier's ready room.

Navigational Information
Lat: 37°13.366' **Long:** 076°39.766' **Tide:** 3 ft. **Current:** 2 kt. **Chart:** 12248
Rep. Depths (*MLW*): Entry 10 ft. **Fuel Dock** 6 ft. **Max Slip/Moor** 6 ft./-
Access: Hampton roads, Marker 40, then 35 mi. up the James River

Marina Facilities *(In Season/Off Season)*
Fuel: *Dockside* - Gasoline, Diesel
Slips: 75 Total, 15 Transient **Max LOA:** 60 ft. **Max Beam:** 17 ft.
Rate *(per ft.)*: **Day** $100.00* **Week** $700 **Month** $3,000
Power: 30 amp Incl., **50 amp** Incl., **100 amp** n/a, **200 amp** n/a
Cable TV: No **Dockside Phone:** No
Dock Type: Floating, Concrete
Moorings: 0 Total, 0 Transient **Launch:** n/a, Dinghy Dock
Rate: Day n/a **Week** n/a **Month** n/a
Heads: 4 Toilet(s), 2 Shower(s)
Laundry: None **Pay Phones:** Yes
Pump-Out: OnSite, OnCall, 1 Central **Fee:** $5 **Closed Heads:** Yes

Marina Operations
Owner/Manager: Wayne Nooe **Dockmaster:** David H. Martin
In-Season: Jun-Sep 5, 8am-8pm **Off-Season:** Sep 6-May, 8am-4pm
After-Hours Arrival: Call ahead; see dockmaster next morning
Reservations: Yes, Required **Credit Cards:** Visa/MC, Dscvr, Din, Amex
Discounts: None
Pets: Welcome, Dog Walk Area **Handicap Access:** Yes, Heads, Docks

Kingsmill Marina

1010 Kingsmill Road; Williamsburg, VA 23185

Tel: (757) 253-1703; (800) 832-5665 **VHF: Monitor** 16 **Talk** 9
Fax: n/a **Alternate Tel:** (757) 253-8237
Email: David.Martin@kingsmill.com **Web:** www.kingsmill.com
Nearest Town: Williamsburg *(5 mi.)* **Tourist Info:** (757) 253-0192

Marina Services and Boat Supplies
Services - Docking Assistance, Concierge, Room Service to the Boat, Boaters' Lounge, Security *(24 hrs.)*, Dock Carts **Communication -** Mail & Package Hold, Phone Messages, Data Ports *(Resort Center)*, FedEx, DHL, UPS, Express Mail *(Sat Del)* **Supplies - OnSite:** Ice *(Cube)*, Ships' Store *(fishing supplies too)*, Bait/Tackle **1-3 mi:** Propane *(Suburban 229-5777)*

Boatyard Services
Nearest Yard: Deep Creek Landing Marina (757) 877-9555

Restaurants and Accommodations
OnSite: Restaurant *(Eagles 253-3902, D $19-34, steak & chophouse at the Golf Club - 3 meals)*, *(Regattas' Café & Marketplace 253-8203, L $8-25, D $8-25, Italian - at the Sports Club, 11am-11pm)*, *(Bray Bistro 253-1510, B $14, L $18, D $28-45, Contemporary American, Breakfast & Lunch Buffets, Sun Brunch $20 & Sun Seafood Buffet $25)*, *(Moody's Tavern 253-1394, Sports Bar - weekend only; TVs, darts, billiards, video games)*, Coffee Shop *(Bray Landing coffee, drinks and snacks)*, Lite Fare *(Marina Bar & Grille 253-1434, D $7-19, lite fare and live entertainment - also group events)*, Hotel *(Kingsmill Resort 253-1703, $160-1020, single room to a 3-bed. suite)* **OnCall:** Pizzeria *(College Deli & Pizza 229-6627, delivery 10:30am-2pm)* **Near:** Hotel *(Marriott 800-228-9290)* **Under 1 mi:** Restaurant *(Tequila Rose 258-8634)*, *(Maurizio's 229-0337)*, Motel *(Quality Inn 220-1100)*

Recreation and Entertainment
OnSite: Heated Pool, Beach *(sand)*, Picnic Area, Grills, Playground, Tennis Courts *(253-3945 15-courts, 6 Hydro-courts, 2 lighted $10-16/day, teens $5-8)*, Golf Course *(3 18-hole courses plus Bray Links, a 9 hole par 3; golf school)*, Fitness Center, Jogging Paths *(4 mi. loop - map)*, Boat Rentals *(canoes & kayaks)*, Fishing Charter, Video Arcade, Special Events *(Michelob Ultra Open - May, Jamestown Day - May)* **Under 1 mi:** Galleries *(Art & Glass Studio 259-9222)* **1-3 mi:** Video Rental *(Movie Time 253-2008)*, Park *(Quarterpath Park 259-3760)*, Cultural Attract *(Busch Gardens 253-3350 $37/30 & Water Country 229-9300 $28/20.50)* **3+ mi:** Bowling *(Williamsburg Lanes 565-3311, 10 mi.)*, Museum *(Colonial Williamsburg 220-7645 $35/day, add'l. days $5, Kids $18/wk, under 6 free, 4 mi.)*

Provisioning and General Services
OnSite: Gourmet Shop *(Regatta's Market - gourmet, to-go & convenience products)*, Bank/ATM, Post Office, Copies Etc. **Under 1 mi:** Convenience Store *(Food Mart 253-0968)* **1-3 mi:** Liquor Store *(ABC 253-4825)*, Pharmacy *(Eckerd 229-4200)*, Retail Shops *(Prime Outlets 565-0702)* **3+ mi:** Supermarket *(Fresh Market 565-1661; Food Lion 229-2010, 8 mi.)*, Fishmonger *(TNT 258-7757, 4 mi.)*, Library *(259-4040, 6 mi.)*, Hardware Store *(Ace 229-1901, 4 mi.)*, Department Store *(Kmart 220-2200, 5 mi.)*

Transportation
OnSite: Courtesy Car/Van *(hourly shuttle to Busch Gardens, Water Country & Colonial Williamsburg)*, Bikes *(rentals)* **OnCall:** Rental Car *(Enterprise 220-1900)*, Taxi *(Colonial 380-8333)*, Airport Limo *(Town & Country 564-4450)* **3+ mi:** Rail *(Amtrak 229-8750, 4 mi.)*
Airport: Williamsburg-Jamestown/Newport News *(6 mi./20 mi.)*

Medical Services
911 Service **OnSite:** Holistic Services *(Kingsmill Spa, 50 min. massage $90)* **OnCall:** Ambulance **Hospital:** Williamsburg 259-6000 *(10 mi.)*

Setting -- 35 miles from Hampton, Kingsmill Resort lies along the storied James River's north shore. Woven through 2,900 acres of lush landscaping are 63 holes of championship golf, 425 suites or villas, a world-class spa, 6 eateries, a spectacular pool and fitness complex, a tennis center and brand new marina.

Marina Notes -- *Flat Rate. Protected by a wave attenuator, the marina - rebuilt & reopened in '05 - features floating concrete docks. Marina guests have use of an extensive fitness center, indoor/outdoor swimming pools, sauna and steam rooms, bath facilities (in addition to those dockside) as well as complimentary Bray Links par-3 golf course (clubs available). Major resort renovation in '03. A shuttle helps navigate the vast facility. Concierge assists with car rentals/ taxis 253-1390. Owned by adjacent 360-acre Busch Gardens (Kingsmill's guests can enter an hour before park opens). Kids Camp 5-12 yrs, Mon-Sat 9am-3:30pm, $45, 2nd 50% off. Event facilities for group cruises. Integrated into the resort are upscale communities of private homes, townhouses & condos.

Notable -- The Deck at the Marina features casual fare in an upscale, alfresco environment centered around a blue-tiled outdoor fireplace. The Sports Club, a shuttle ride away, includes more than 30 fitness machines, an indoor lap pool with whirlpool, outdoor pool with kids pool, daily classes, steam rooms, saunas, locker rooms, racquetball courts and a game room with billiards, table tennis, video & board games. Plus a state-of-the-art European-style spa and salon. Kingsmill's signature dining experience is cold-smoked meat, poultry & seafood over Budweiser-bathed beech wood chips. In '05, a multi-million dollar renovation prepared the Pete Dye-designed River golf course for the next LPGA's annual Michelob Ultra Open. Williamsburg is minutes away via shuttle.

PHOTOS ON CD-ROM: 17

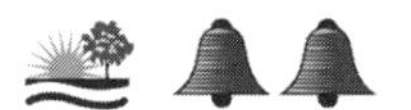

Jamestown Yacht Basin

2080 Jamestown Road; Williamsburg, VA 23185

Tel: (757) 229-8309 **VHF: Monitor** 16 **Talk** 68
Fax: (757) 564-9530 **Alternate Tel:** n/a
Email: n/a **Web:** www.jamestownyachtbasin.com
Nearest Town: Williamsburg **Tourist Info:** (757) 253-0192

Navigational Information

Lat: 37°13.522' **Long:** 076°46.627' **Tide:** n/a **Current:** n/a **Chart:** 12251
Rep. Depths (*MLW*): Entry 6 ft. **Fuel Dock** n/a **Max Slip/Moor** 8 ft./-
Access: James River to Powhatan Creek - beyond 11.5 ft. fixed bridge

Marina Facilities *(In Season/Off Season)*

Fuel: No
Slips: 80 Total, 10 Transient **Max LOA:** 40 ft. **Max Beam:** n/a
Rate *(per ft.)*: **Day** $25.00* **Week** n/a **Month** n/a
Power: 30 amp $5, **50 amp** n/a, **100 amp** n/a, **200 amp** n/a
Cable TV: No **Dockside Phone:** No
Dock Type: Floating, Wood
Moorings: 0 Total, 0 Transient **Launch:** n/a
Rate: Day n/a **Week** n/a **Month** n/a
Heads: 2 Toilet(s), 2 Shower(s)
Laundry: None **Pay Phones:** No
Pump-Out: No **Fee:** n/a **Closed Heads:** Yes

Marina Operations

Owner/Manager: Trust for Public Lands **Dockmaster:** Same
In-Season: Year-Round, 8:30am-5pm **Off-Season:** n/a
After-Hours Arrival: To be determined
Reservations: To be determined **Credit Cards:** n/a
Discounts: None
Pets: Welcome **Handicap Access:** No

Marina Services and Boat Supplies

Supplies - OnSite: Ice *(Cube)*, Live Bait **1-3 mi:** Bait/Tackle *(Hooker Bair & Tackle 229-6609)*, Propane *(Peninsula Gas 566-9090)*

Boatyard Services

Nearest Yard: Deep Creek Marina (757) 877-9555

Restaurants and Accommodations

OnSite: Lite Fare *(Jamestown Cafe 253-2571, L $2-6, in the Interpretive Center, 9-5, 7 days, grill from 11am)* **Near:** Restaurant *(Jamestown Grill 220-8823)* **1-3 mi:** Restaurant *(Garden Cafe 221-7330)*, *(Little Maurizio's Italian American Grill 258-5300)*, *(Cities Grille Williamsburg 564-3955)*, *(Chownings Tavern 229-2141)*, Pizzeria *(Two Sisters 258-1600)* **3+ mi:** Motel *(Travelodge 800-544-7774, 5 mi.)*, *(Best Western Williamsburg 229-9540, 5 mi.)*, Hotel *(Sheraton Four Points 800-325-3535, 5 mi.)*

Recreation and Entertainment

OnSite: Cultural Attract *(Jamestown Settlement 253-4838 $10.25/5.75; Daily 9am-5pm - comb. tix w/ Yorktown Victory Ctr. $14/6.75)*, Sightseeing *(Circumnavigate the island by dinghy or kayak)* **Near:** Museum *(Jamestown Island's 22-acre National Historic Site 898-2410 $5/free for 7 days, Audio Tours $2, Visitors Center 8:30am-5pm, Park 8:30am-dusk -comb. tix w/ Yorktown Battlefield $7/Free. An audio tour ($2) leads visitors through the foundations of 17th C. "James Cittie" &1907 re-creation of Memorial Church.)* **1-3 mi:** Golf Course *(Williamsburg National 258-9642)*, Fitness Center *(Curves 221-0330)*, Video Rental *(Blockbuster 259-1680)*, Galleries

Provisioning and General Services

OnSite: Bookstore *(devoted to the history of the region)*, Retail Shops *(very large gift shop)* **1-3 mi:** Convenience Store *(Zooms 220-3244)*, Supermarket *(Winn Dixie 564-8850)*, Delicatessen *(Short Stop Deli 229-1388)*, Bank/ATM, Post Office, Catholic Church, Protestant Church, Beauty Salon *(European Day Spa 220-4959)*, Barber Shop, Laundry, Pharmacy *(Winn Dixie 564-8549, Jamestown Pharmacy 565-7570)*, Hardware Store *(Ace Peninsula 229-1900)*, Florist **3+ mi:** Library *(259-4040, 6 mi.)*, Department Store *(Target 258-9794, Kmart 220-2200, 6 mi.)*

Transportation

OnSite: Local Bus *(Jamestown Area Shuttle - loops the various sites every 20 min. Free 9am-5pm - Summer only)*, InterCity Bus *(Historic Triangle Shuttle to Williamsburg 898-2410, 9:30. 11:30am, 1:30 & 5pm, Free with attraction ticket - returns at 9am, 11am & 1pm - Summer only - also goes to Yorktown)* **OnCall:** Rental Car *(Enterprise 220-1900)*, Taxi *(Williamsburg Taxi 221-0004)*, Airport Limo *(Dynasty 220-8600)* **Near:** Ferry Service *(Jamestown-Scotland Ferry)*
Airport: Williamsburg-Jamestown/Newport News *(5 mi./21 mi.)*

Medical Services

911 Service **OnCall:** Ambulance **1-3 mi:** Doctor *(First Care of Williamsburg 229-4141)*, Dentist *(Piascik 229-8920)*, Holistic Services *(Acupuncture Chiropractic Care 565-6464)* **Hospital:** Williamsburg 259-6000 *(7 mi.)*

PHOTOS ON CD-ROM: 13

Setting -- Off Powhatan Creek, under the 11.5 foot fixed bridge, is rustic 198-acre Jamestown Campsites and Yacht Basin - in the process of being acquired by the Trust for Public Land. Dockage in the nearly land-locked basin consists of two main docks covered with blue & white steel roofs, and additional stern-to floating dockage along the main bulkhead. Landside is a large work shed and storage. Adjacent is the Jamestown Settlement Living History Museum.

Marina Notes -- *Flat Rate: Bulkhead $15, Open slip $25, Covered $35, with power $40. The TPL announced its commitment to complete the purchase of the Yacht Basin site by December '06, as part of the 2007 commemoration of the 400th anniversary of the founding of Jamestown - the first permanent settlement in the Americas. The intention is to enhance the marina and maintain public boating access while conserving 65 acres of marshland. The Jamestown Explorer Adventure and the Jamestown Island Cruise will continue to berth here. Currently, very rustic bathhouses, with mosaic quarry-tile floors, are enhanced by the plethora of plants hanging in each - creating a charming environment.

Notable -- On Jamestown Island, "Historic Jamestown" - site of the original colony - is administered by the APVA, which owns the "Olde Towne" archeological dig; the National Park Service operates "New Town." On the mainland, the spectacular Visitors' Center adjacent to the marina offers a 15-min. film "Jamestown: The Beginning" on the settlement's founding. Costumed interpreters depict life in the colony against a backdrop of recreations of a Powhatan Indian village, James Fort, and full-size replicas of the 3 ships - Discovery, the Susan Constant and, in '06, a new Goodspeed - that carried 104 men and boys here in 1607.

ATLANTIC CRUISING CLUB'S

GUIDE TO
CHESAPEAKE BAY MARINAS

ADDENDA

Suggested Reading List

SPECIFIC REGIONAL CRUISING GUIDES

The Embassy Guide's Chesapeake Bay to Florida by Maptech
A well-researched cruising guide that covers Cape May and Delaware Bay to Fernandina on the Florida/Georgia border. It's a welcome expansion of the Chesapeake Bay edition and corresponds to Maptech's Chartkit Regions 4 & 6.

Reed's Nautical Almanac — East Coast by Carl Herzog
Nova Scotia to Florida & the Gulf Coast – coastal pilot info, lights, beacons & buoys, communications and tides & currents and major waypoints for anchorages and harbors.

Waterway Guide Mid-Atlantic: Chesapeake Bay and the ICW to Florida by Waterway Publishing
This annually updated guide gives information for cruising the Chesapeake Bay through the ICW in Georgia. It has become more thorough and easier to use in the last few years — with impressive harbor aerials.

Cruising the Chesapeake: A Gunkholer's Guide by William H. Shellenberger
This edition includes coverage of the Atlantic coasts of New Jersey, Delaware, and Maryland, including Delaware Bay. It also includes a cruise planner for long or short trips, as well as a catalog of GPS coordinates. A favorite for many decades.

Cruising Guide to Chesapeake Bay by Chesapeake Bay Magazine
More than 300 ports of call, both secluded and popularly known, are covered with helpful insights and local knowledge.

Discovering the Tidal Potomac: A Cruising Guide and Boating Reference, 2nd ed. by Rick Rhodes
A detailed guide to cruising the Potomac River from Washington, DC to the Chesapeake Bay. Included are Potomac River marinas, restaurants, museums, and places of interest — and dock diagrams.

Chesapeake Bay — Ports of Call and Anchorages by Tom Henschel
Gorgeous aerial color photographs of Chesapeake Bay from Chesapeake City, Maryland to Norfolk, Virginia. The author recommends specific anchorages, navigational dangers, entrance and exit routes, and places of interest.

Exploring the Chesapeake in Small Boats by John Page Williams, William S. Portlock (Photographer)
Guidebook for sailing the Chesapeake region in runabouts, one-designs, and kayaks. Good, useful information applicable to big boats as well as dinghy trips.

Sea Kayaking Maryland's Chesapeake Bay: Day Trips on the Tidal Tributaries and Coastlines of the Western and Eastern Shore by Michael Savario, Andrea Nolan
A sea-kayaking manual to the Maryland part of the Bay with plans for 30 unique trips — most of which are great dinghy itineraries as well.

Sea Kayaking Virginia — A Paddler's Guide to Day Trips from Georgetown to Chincoteague by Andrea Nolan
30 trips designed for sea kayaks that would be, in most cases, equally interesting in a dinghy — or even the big boat.

GENERAL CRUISING GUIDES

World Cruising Handbook by Jimmy Cornell
A reference for offshore cruisers covering all 185 maritime countries with up-to-date information on language, currency, customs and quarantine regulations, cruising permits, visas, port and medical facilities, and much more.

Advanced Blue Water Cruising by Hal Sutphen
What the prospective offshore sailor needs to know. Learn the pros and cons of every major equipment choice, trouble shooting systems, weather considerations, and much more.

Comfortable Cruising Around North and Central America by Liza & Andy Copeland
A cruising guide to destinations that don't require ocean crossings; the sections on the North American seaboard will be of particular interest.

Voyager's Handbook: The Essential Guide to Blue Water Cruising by Beth Leonard
Lots of really useful information even if you're just planning a coastal cruise.

Nigel Calder's Cruising Handbook by Nigel Calder
From the basics for a coastal cruise to readying for an offshore passage, this is a good place to start.

Cruising for Cowards, 2nd ed. by Liza & Andy Copeland
A terrific "how-to" guide to cruising anywhere; it's funny and filled with details and great information.

Voyaging Under Power by Robert Beebe
A little dated, but it's still filled with important and useful info.

Stapleton's Powerboat Bible: The Complete Guide to Selection, Seamanship, and Cruising by Sid Stapleton
Comprehensive and current, it's written for larger, cruising powerboats.

Advice to the Sealorn by Herb Payson
In 50 delightful, informative chapters, the author covers virtually every subject of concern to cruising sailors, from what it's really like out there, to different rigs, to repairs on board.

Sensible Cruising — The Thoreau Approach: A Philosophic and Practical Approach to Cruising by Don Casey & Lew Hackler
A popular guide, both practical and philosophical, to cruising in a commonsense, "make-do-with-what-you-have" fashion. This book is full of sound, but gently humorous advice.

The Essentials of Living Aboard a Boat by Mark Nicholas
Mark Nicholas has combined his experience of life aboard with the advice of other live aboards, marina owners, technicians, boat manufacturers and advocates in order to detail the challenges and offer real advice for success.

Capable Cruiser by Lin & Larry Pardey
A classic manual for hands-on sailors. Discusses what every cruising sailor needs to know: preparation, maintenance at sea, safety aloft, seamanship, and staying healthy.

Sail Book of Common Sense Cruising by Patience Wales
A collection of interesting articles from Sail Magazine.

Seagoing Hitchhiker's Handbook by Greg Becker
Practical, well-researched guide to roaming the globe on other people's yachts: how to hitch a ride, where to do it, being a good crew member, along with valuable tables listing most cruised routes, distances, and storm and sailing seasons for those routes.

All in the Same Boat by Tom Neale
For cruisers who want to go offshore with their families for exploration and adventure but need to know how to provide for such things as home schooling, earning a living, staying in contact with home, provisioning, and more.

The Perfect First Mate: A Woman's Guide to Recreational Boating by Joy Smith
How to manage provisioning and organizing for comfort afloat along with the less than glamorous aspects of boating from packing and planning to performing first mate duties on deck.

Bluewater Checklist by Rory & Sandra Burke
A comprehensive portfolio of vital checklists covering every aspect of bluewater cruising: shopping lists & equipment inventories to safety procedures, going ashore and abandoning ship.

The Best Tips from Women Aboard by Maria Russell
Loaded with "tried-and-true" tips on organizing, storage, provisioning; bringing along guests, kids, or pets; cruising; maintenance, etc.

PROVISIONING GUIDES

Chesapeake Bay Cooking by John Shields
Describes the history of the region and its fare, and shares cooking techniques indigenous to the Chesapeake Bay.

The Flavor of the Chesapeake Bay Cookbook by Whitey Schmidt
Cookbook specializes in meals native to the Chesapeake region, especially blue crab.

Eat, Drink, and Be Merry in Maryland by Frederick P. Stieff
A collection of hundreds of traditional recipes found in Maryland, even has a chapter that specializes in oyster recipes.

The Cruisers Handbook of Fishing
by Scott Bannerot & Wendy Bannerot
The complete guide to finding, catching, processing, and cooking fish from the decks of a slow-moving cruising sail or powerboat.

Provisioning by Dottie Haynes
Far more than a galley guide, a complete discussion of provisioning as well as an introduction to cruising basics and living aboard for those new to cruising. Includes proven menus, advice on health, safety, seasickness, and more.

The Cruising Chef Cookbook by Michael Greenwald
Thorough and practical for a weeklong cruise or an ocean voyage.

Cruising Cuisine: Fresh Food from the Galley
by Kay Pastorius, Hal Pastorius (Illustrator)
Lots of really good recipes.

Dining on Deck: Fine Foods for Sailing & Boating
by Linda Vail, Loretta Braren (Illustrator)
Encourages a little style and panache at anchor.

Feasts Afloat: 150 Recipes for Great Meals from Small Spaces
by Jennifer Trainer Thompson, Elizabeth Wheeler
An earlier version was called The Yachting Cookbook *and it was a longtime favorite of many cruisers.*

The Care and Feeding of Sailing Crew
by Lin Pardey and Larry Pardey (Editor)
A true classic that tells you "everything." Practical, current information on all facets of bluewater galley provisioning, rough weather cooking, coping with differing dietary needs, seasickness, trash disposal, healthful eating, and much more.

Cooking Under Pressure by Lorna J. Sass
Teaches the basics and the sophisticated possibilities of pressure cooking — one of the best methods of cooking under-way. Using pressure cookers in the galley saves fuel, keeps everything safely "in the pot", and turns out delicious, healthful meals.

Guilt Free Gourmet and **Guilt Free Gourmet 2** by Sam Miles
Over 1200 low-fat recipes in each of two easily-stowable volumes — get the 70 Days of Menus, too — great for master lists and long-term cruise menu planning.

Boat Cuisine: The All-Weather Cookbook by June Raper
This book features tasty, tested-at-sea recipes from basic ingredients. It is packed with information on cooking safely afloat, cooking in heavy weather, and quick meals.

Cooks Afloat: Gourmet Cooking on the Move
by David Hoar & Noreen Rudd
An exquisite cookbook that helps the epicurean boater prepare gourmet meals using only a limited galley pantry and plenty of fresh-caught seafood. Includes salad alternatives, bread making, tips for canning, sprouting, and harvesting shellfish.

Cooking the One-Burner Way by Melissa Gray and Buck Tilton
More than 170 elaborate to simple recipes all tailored for the one-burner stove. Emphasis is on low-fat, high carbohydrate meals and snacks. Includes good advice on utensils, storage, and campsite or, more appropriately, galley hygiene.

Cruising Cook by Shirley Herd Deal
The author covers how to buy, stow and prepare food for a month or more at sea. Loose-leaf pages protected by an oversize plastic three-ring binder to take abuse aboard.

From the Galleys of Women Aboard edited by Maria Russell
This is a lively collection of proven seagoing recipes from the Sea Sisters of Women Aboard. Everything from salads to cookies.

Natural Gourmet by Annemarie Colbin
Healthy cooking and provisioning concepts that are easily applicable to the galley. Easy to follow recipes that'll change the way you cruise.

Living Off the Sea by Charlie White
Charlie White offers wisdom from a master at living off the shoreline harvest. Includes chapters on survival, living off the beach. Also includes info on red tides, exotic seafoods.

Food and Healing — 10th Anniversary by Annemarie Colbin
Not a cookbook, but an indispensable guide to natural healing using natural remedies, many of which are stowed in most galleys.

CHESAPEAKE REGION TRAVEL GUIDES

Longstreet Highroad Guide to the Chesapeake Bay (Longstreet Highroad Coastal Series) by Deane Winegar, Garvey Winegar
This guide offers meticulous details on geological data, historic landmarks, beaches, lodging, and restaurants.

The Chesapeake Bay Book, 5th ed. (A Great Destinations Guide) by Allison Blake
This guide reviews places to stay, dining, culture, & recreation. It is organized regionally to help boaters plan more easily.

Maryland: An Explorer's Guide, 1st ed. by Leonard M. Adkins
This book explores the history and culture of Maryland, as well as recommending places of interest — with restaurant commentary and recommendations.

Maryland and Delaware Off the Beaten Path: A Guide to Unique Places, 6th ed. by Judy Colbert
An original guide to often "missed" and one-of-a-kind coastal destinations.

Virginia Off the Beaten Path: A Guide to Unique Places, 7th ed. by Judy Colbert
Offers travelers a unique lens to view the back roads of Virginia.

Fodor's Virginia and Maryland: The Guide for All Budgets, Where to Stay, Eat, and Explore On and Off the Beaten Path, 7th ed.
A guide with in-depth coverage of Virginia and Maryland.

Frommer's Maryland & Delaware by Mary K. Tilghman
Introduces readers to a variety of special locations and activities in Maryland and Delaware, for first-time travelers and even residents.

Frommer's Virginia by Bill Goodwin
This book includes special highlights such as Jefferson's Monticello, Arlington National Cemetery, Colonial Williamsburg, Shenandoah National Park, Virginia Beach, and Civil War battlefields.

Lonely Planet Virginia & the Capital Region by Randy Peffer, J. Williams, K. Stann
Covers the Capital Region, from educational DC to history-saturated Jamestown to good eats on the Eastern Shore.

Adventuring in the Chesapeake Bay Area, 2nd ed. by John Bowen
Gives a variety of activities and adventures for those exploring the Chesapeake region.

National Geographic Guide to 100 Easy Hikes: Washington DC, Virginia, Maryland, Delaware by Barbara A. Noe
Hikes within three hours of Washington, DC. Nature hikes and urban hikes to explore the region's history — many reachable from marinas.

Tidewater Virginia with Children: Where to Go and What to Do in Williamsburg, Jamestown, Yorktown, Newport News, and Hampton by Barbara M. Wohlford, Mary L. Eley
A guide to Virginia recreation for the whole family.

Hiking, Cycling, and Canoeing in Maryland: A Family Guide by Bryan MacKay
"Well-written, the book includes excellent maps, line drawings, and numerous sidebars on the wonders of wandering in the state." — Paul Sullivan, Fredericksberg Free Lance-Star

Walks & Rambles on the Delmarva Peninsula by Jay Abercrombie
Some good ideas when it's time to stretch those cockpit-cramped legs and see the world from the ground.

Breaking Away to Virginia and Maryland Wineries by Elisabeth Frater
Part of a "Washington Weekends series" with details on the up-and-coming wine industry in Virginia and Maryland, reviewing numerous wineries and places of interest.

25 Bicycle Tours on Delmarva: Cycllng the Chesapeake Bay Country by John R. Wennersten, Stewart M. Wennersten
A reference guide for bicycling on the Delmarva coast.

Chesapeake Country by Lucian Niemeyer, Eugene L. Meyer
A gracefully photographed guide to a region rich in national history and natural beauty.

CHESAPEAKE HISTORY, CULTURE and ECOLOGY

Chesapeake by James A. Michener
Michener tells his story over 400 years, from Colonial times through today, utilizing the Chesapeake's Eastern Shore as a setting, and shaping the tale around the Steed family.

Life in the Chesapeake Bay by Alice Jane Lippson, Robert L. Lippson
"This is the best-written and best-illustrated guide ever about a North American tidal estuary. It is the model for all future coastal nature guides." — Whole Earth Review

Beautiful Swimmers: Watermen, Crabs and the Chesapeake Bay by John Barth, William W. Warner
Classic Chesapeake nature and ecology guide which won the Pulitzer Prize for nonfiction in 1977.

An Island Out of Time: A Memoir of Smith Island in the Chesapeake by Tom Horton
"This remarkable memoir gives readers an indelible picture of both the land and the people." — Booklist

Chesapeake Boyhood: Memoirs of a Farm Boy by William H. Turner
The author remembers his youth in Jamesville, Virginia following the Great Depression.

The Men All Singing: The Story of Menhaden Fishing by John Frye
The Cockrell Creek fishing industry that built 19th C. Reedville, VA.

East of the Chesapeake by William H. Turner
An exquisitely written continuation of Turner's memoirs, following his life on Virginia's Eastern hore.

This Was Chesapeake Bay by R.H. Burgess
A history of shipbuilding in the Chesapeake region.

The Workboats of Smith Island by Paula J. Johnson
An intense look at the boats that sustain the Smith Island watermen — the crab-scrapper, skiff and deadrise — and through that describes much of island life.

Green Shingles: At the Edge of Chesapeake Bay by Peter Svenson
His story begins at his green-shingled home on Maryland's Eastern Shore; he offers historical and ecological insights as he adventures through the rest of the Chesapeake.

From a Lighthouse Window: Recipes and Recollections from the Chesapeake Bay Maritime Museum
by Members of the Chesapeake Bay Maritime Museum
Recipes and memories of culture and life on the Eastern Shore.

Tobacco Coast: A Maritime History of the Chesapeake Bay in the Colonial Era (Maryland Paperback Bookshelf)
by Arthur Pierce Middleton
A book on the impact the Chesapeake Bay's ecology had on the economics of Colonial America.

Pirates on the Chesapeake: Being a True History of Pirates, Picaroons, and Raiders on Chesapeake Bay, 1610-1807
by Donald G. Shomette
Well-documented history of naval feats and piracy in the mid-atlantic region.

Colonial Chesapeake Society
by Lois Green Carr, Philip D. Morgan, Jean B. Russo
A history of Chesapeake settlers' culture from 1600-1775.

The Great Marsh: An Intimate Journey into a Chesapeake Wetland by David W. Harp, Tom Horton
A gripping portrayal of a trip in a captivating habitat in danger of extinction.

Turning the Tide: Saving the Chesapeake Bay by Tom Horton
An environmental columnist for The Baltimore Sun, Horton describes the ecosystem of the Chesapeake Bay and efforts to clean it up.

Chesapeake Bay Blues: Science, Politics, and the Struggle to Save the Bay (American Political Challenges) by Howard R. Ernst
This book combines both the ecological and political issues of the Bay and how different forces are at work to decide its fate.

Chesapeake: An Environmental Biography by John R. Wennersten
"Wennersten's careful research and obvious concern for the region show clearly in his reasoned discussions of the multitude of problems facing the area, as conservationists continue to battle with special-interest groups over how best to save the Bay" — ForeWord Magazine

Fishes of the Chesapeake Bay by Edward O. Murdy
This comprehensive treatise enables users to identify 267 species of fish found in Chesapeake Bay through a system of keys to the orders, to the families within orders, and to the species within families.

The Barrier Islands: A Photographic History of Life on Hog, Cobb, Smith, Cedar, Parramore, Metompkin and Assateague
by Curtis J. Badger, Rick Kellam
Badger and Kellam interviewed native islanders and arranged over 300 photos to tell the story of the Barrier Islands.

Chesapeake Bay: Nature of the Estuary: A Field Guide
by Christopher P. White
A natural history arranged into nine sections matching the major habitats of the area. Good brief descriptions and very attractive (and abundant) line drawings — Book News

Water's Way: Life Along the Chesapeake
by David W. Harp (Photographer), Tom Horton
A story of life along the Bay, with photographs and striking prose.

FICTION and FUN READS

Washed Up with a Broken Heart in Rock Hall by Peter Svenson
A series of vignettes divulging the story of a recently divorced novelist, who moves from New York to Rock Hall to start anew.

Course of the Waterman by Nancy Taylor Robson
A coming-of-age story of a teenage boy and his struggles with his inherited lifestyle as a Chesapeake Bay "waterman."

The Oysterback Tales by Helen Chappell
A collection of short stories parodying life on Maryland's eastern shore.

Oysterback Spoken Here by Helen Chappell
A second collection of humorous tales chronicling life and culture in a fictional Eastern Shore town.

The Waterman: A Novel of the Chesapeake Bay by Tim Junkin
The story of a college student who drops out of school when his father dies in a storm, and takes over his father's crabbing business on the Eastern Shore.

Secret Justice: A Novel by James W. Huston
A military thriller featuring Lt. Kent "Rat" Rathman as he fights terrorism, is put on trial, and works to prevent a hijacked nuclear-weapons tanker from destroying the Chesapeake Bay.

The Lord's Oysters by Gilbert Byron
A fictionalized story of the author's childhood in Chestertown, Maryland, featuring "Noah Marlin" as the protagonist. Often compared to Huckleberry Finn.

Done Crabbin': Noah Leaves the River by Gilbert Byron
A sequel to "The Lord's Oysters," Noah's adventures continue while coming-of-age on Maryland's Eastern Shore.

Run to the Lee by Kenneth Brooks, Jr.
Written in the 1960's, this novel tells the story of life on the Chesapeake at the turn of the century.

The Floating Opera and the End of the Road by John Barth
Two classic novels written in the mid 20th century which follow eccentric characters around the Chesapeake region.

The Tidewater Tales: A Novel by John Barth
A couple, the husband, a novelist, and the wife, a historian, travel on their boat in the Chesapeake Bay telling stories to break the husband's writer's block.

Sabbatical: A Romance by John Barth
A married couple try to make important decisions while taking a sabbatical on the Chesapeake.

The Sot-Weed Factor by John Barth
A humorous novel based on the life of the historical poet Ebenezer Cooke and his time in colonial Maryland.

Sea Swept: The Chesapeake Bay Saga #1 by Nora Roberts
Tells the story of three orphan brothers adopted by a Mr. Quinn and his wife.

Rising Tides: The Chesapeake Bay Saga #2 by Nora Roberts
This book continues the trilogy of the Quinn Brothers.

Inner Harbor: The Chesapeake Bay Saga #3 by Nora Roberts
This book is the conclusion to Robert's trilogy, as Philip has to care for his brother Seth.

Chesapeake Blue: The Chesapeake Bay Saga #4 by Nora Roberts
This is a sequel to the original trilogy, telling the story of Seth, the youngest Quinn brother.

CHILDREN'S BOOKS — Pre-School

Dancing on the Sand: A Story of an Atlantic Blue Crab
by Kathleen M. Hollenbeck
A blue crab travels through the bay on her journey and works to keep her unhatched eggs safe.

Boats for Bedtime by Ola Liwoinsky
A child imagines all kinds of boats in all kinds of places as he settles down to sleep.

Can You See What I See? Seymour and the Juice Box Boat
by Walter Wick
In this whimsical search-and-find story, readers join a little toy man as he gathers together an assortment of items, builds a boat out of a juice box, and sails away on a sea of blue.

Boats by Jan Pienkowski
This sturdy pop-up book features bright, colorful, expressive illustrations.

CHILDREN'S BOOKS — Ages 4 – 8

The Boat Alphabet Book by Jerry Pallotta
Covers a large variety of boats, from kayaks to aircraft carriers, presenting unusual facts and explaining basic nautical terms like hull, bow, and stern with wit and humor.

Awesome Chesapeake: A Kid's Guide to the Bay
by David Owen Bell, Marcy Dunn Ramsey (Illustrator)
A creative book detailing the flora and fauna of the Chesapeake region.

Chesapeake Bay Walk by David Owen Bell, Jennifer Heyd Wharton
An illustrated ecological "fieldtrip" for younger children.

Rambling Raft by Lynne N. Lockhart, Barbara M. Lockhart
This book tells the tale of an inflatable raft that falls from a truck. Indigenous animals, children, and nature all "play" with it before the raft returns to its owner.

The Reverend Thomas's False Teeth by Gayle Gillerlain
On the road to dinner with friends, a Reverend drops his false teeth in the Chesapeake Bay.

Sam: The Tale of a Chesapeake Bay Rockfish
by Kristina Henry, Jeff Dombek (Illustrator)
A charming story for young children including striped bass and the rescue of wildlife.

Chesapeake Rainbow by Priscilla Cummings, David Aiken (Illustrator)
A beautifully illustrated book displaying the range of color in the habitats of the Chesapeake Bay.

Chesapeake 1-2-3 by Priscilla Cummings, David Aiken (Illustrator)
A counting book for children to learn numbers and about the bay at the same time!

Chesapeake ABC by Priscilla Cummings, David Aiken (Illustrator)
Rhyming letters and delightful illustrations teach young children the alphabet as well as display the beauty of the Chesapeake region.

Meet Chadwick and His Chesapeake Bay Friends
by Priscilla Cummings, A. R. Cohen (Illustrator)
The story of a blue crab and his neighbors who live in the bay.

Chadwick the Crab by Priscilla Cummings, A. R. Cohen
Chadwick, an adventurous crab, is rescued by fellow marine wildlife.

Chadwick and the Garplegrungen
by Priscilla Cummings, A. R. Cohen (Illustrator)
A sequel to Cumming's other book on the adventures of a blue crab.

Chadwick's Wedding by Priscilla Cummings, A. R. Cohen
Yet another adventure for Chadwick the Crab.

Chesapeake Colors by Amelia Armoriell, Susan Lindbeck
A coloring book that looks at natural history, recipes, and "local color" of the Chesapeake Bay region.

CHILDREN'S BOOKS — Ages 9 – 12

Boat — An Eyewitness Book by Eric Kentley
A compelling and informative guide to the history and development of boats and ships worldwide. From fishermen on kayaks, to soldiers on galleys, to sailors on yachts, this book shows the importance and perils of a life at sea. Stunning photographs.

Into the Wind: Sailboats Then and Now by Steven Otfinoski
Examines the history of sailboats and describes different kinds that are used today.

Schooner by Pat Lowery Collins
Collins, who witnessed the building of the schooner, Thomas E. Lannon, in the shipyards of Essex, Massachusetts, a few years ago and took hundreds of photographs to study it, translates the story into an imaginary boy's diary; illustrated with Collins's evocative oils.

The Craft of Sail: A Primer of Sailing by Jan Adkins.
This beautifully illustrated young-adult book teaches sailing, knots, and other technical information in straightforward fashion.

Chesapeake Duke by Gilbert Byron
The story of two boys and their dog that go on adventures in a small Chesapeake town, during the early 20th century.

Where Did All the Water Go?
by Carolyn Stearns, David Aiken (Illustrator)
A book on the ecological rise and fall of saltwater bays.

Misty of Chincoteague
by Marguerite Henry (Author), Wesley Dennis (Illustrator)
Two siblings are resolute to buy a wild pony from Assateague Island. Misty's offspring are still living, and for sale, on Chincoteague.

Stormy, Misty's Foal by Marguerite Henry
Misty and her foal, Stormy, work to help the ponies on Assateague Island.

Sea Star: Orphan Of Chincoteague
by Marguerite Henry, Wesley Dennis (Illustrator)
A troubled mare raises a wild colt.

Misty's Twilight by Marguerite Henry
Fascinated by the story of "Misty of Chincoteague," a woman with an equine ranch in Florida raises a descendent of Misty to be a champion horse.

Jacob Have I Loved by Katherine Patterson
A girl who lives on the Chesapeake Bay struggles with feelings of jealousy regarding her twin sister and develops her own identity.

Sid and Sal's Famous Channel Marker Diner
by Priscilla Cummings, A. R. Cohen (Illustrator)
Ospreys have a diner in the Chesapeake Bay.

Stowaways to Smith Island by Michele Davidson
Two siblings sneak aboard a boat carrying nurses to Smith Island and discover all of the wonders of the island.

Waterman's Boy by Susan Sharpe
Two local boys aid a scientist in his efforts to preserve the Chesapeake Bay.

Meet Naiche: A Native Boy from the Chesapeake Bay Area (My World-Young Native Americans Today Series)
by Gabrielle Tayac, John Harrington (Photographer)
Tells the story of a Native American boy of Piscataway and Apache descent living out a normal day with indigenous customs and traditions.

Log onto www.AtlanticCruisingClub.com for more information and even more Suggested Readings.

Smith Family Crabcakes

1 lb. back fin (or lump) crab meat
1 1/2 tbs. low fat Hellmans' mayonnaise
1 egg, beaten
1 tbs. chopped parsley (or for a twist, fresh cilantro)
1 1/2 tsp. Old Bay seasoning
1/2 tsp. salt
1/4 tsp. freshly ground black pepper
Juice of 1/4 lemon
1 tsp. Worcestershire Sauce
1/4 C. cracker crumbs
2 tbs. extra virgin olive oil

Gently fold together all the ingredients, except for 1 tbs. of the cracker crumbs and the parsley. Take great care not to break up the crab meat. Form this into 6 cakes, pat reserved cracker crumbs around the outside and chill for an hour. Slide gently into hot extra virgin olive oil and sauté quickly.

Serves 6.

Wi-Fi: Wireless Broadband

Access Point

USB Antenna

PC Card

The ability to access both the web and email while cruising has become increasingly important to boaters. Marinas, and their surrounding communities, are providing a variety of solutions — some better than others. In each Marina Report, there is a brief description of the type and location of data ports (either at the marina or its environs) and also notes the availability of Wi-Fi — and details the terms of use for each.

Wi-Fi, or Wireless Fidelity, is the most useful of the currently available remote access technologies. It allows boaters to connect via their own laptop from their boat, a dock, the boaters' lounge, poolside, the coffee shop — or, if it is powerful enough, even the mooring field. It's wireless, provides broadband speed, doesn't require expensive equipment or a cumbersome installation, and can be used anywhere within the facility — as long as it is within range of a base station (the area covered by that range is called a "HotSpot").

How it works: The marina, the facility or the community contracts with a Wi-Fi provider, which sets up HotSpots that transmit and receive signals on the 802.11 specification. Some of these HotSpots provide open access and are paid for by the marina or community; others are installed by one of several Wi-Fi providers who then sell boaters a subscription for access. These subscriptions can range from an hour to a year with daily, weekly and monthly options as well. There are a small group of Wi-Fi subscription providers that focus on the maritime community, and the Marina Reports indicate which provider a marina has selected. That way one can choose a provider that services the greatest number of marinas that might be visited. (Currently, Beacon Wi-Fi appears to be the leading provider in the Chesapeake region.)

Pros and Cons: There are many advantages: 1. High-speed internet access - web and email — from a boater's own laptop. 2. Unlimited service — no waiting one's turn and no time limits, 3. Comfortable locations — anywhere within the signal's range — just open your laptop and log-on 4. Ease of use - once access is set up, the boater can use it at any marina with the same service — easily. 5. There is very little assistance required and most all services have 24/7 technical support. The disadvantages are not significant and, in our opinion, well worth it: 1. There are, generally, service charges — per diem or by subscription, 2. The boater's computer must either have a Wi-Fi card — internal or an external PC Card. (Many laptops built within the past few years are Wi-Fi ready and have internal cards.) Alternatively, basic 30 mW PC Cards ($30-60) are readily available and come (at press time) in three compatible types — "802.11b" (greater distance and less expensive), "g" (faster), or "a" (different bandwidth) — Linksys and D-Link are two popular brands. More powerful cards are also available: Lucent's 50 mW, Cisco's 100 mW or SMC's 200 mW — and for boaters a more powerful card may be a very worthwhile investment.

Technicalities: There are several infrastructure considerations that affect the quality of the Wi-Fi service. The HotSpot hardware both sends and receives. The sending antenna should be at the maximum FCC legal limit of 30 DBI — and most are. It is the receiving (or listening) antenna — the one in the computer — where there tend to be differences. High powered, high-gain antennas deliver better quality service. If the receiving antenna is at least as powerful as the sending antenna then the standard 30 mW Wi-Fi cards, that most people have, will work well. However, the more powerful the receiving card, the better the service.

Marina Options: In interviewing maritime Wi-Fi providers across the country, we found a variety of ways in which they work with marinas and, thus, with boaters: 1. The provider installs the infrastructure and delivers the broadband service to the marina free and then sells subscriptions to boaters to amortize the expense. 2. The marina pays for the installation of the infrastructure and the monthly broadband and then collects a subscription fee from boaters. 3. The provider installs the infrastructure, the marina pays for the broadband and they share the subscription fees. 4. Or, our favorite, the marina pays for the installation and then offers it to its boating guests as part of its complimentary amenities. There are also a number of large scale installations along the East coast that cover whole communities or harbors. These are perfect for outer docks, T-heads and mooring fields. and we hope to see this concept expanded.

Rates: At publication, per diem rates were comparable to those charged at hotels (about $9.95) and subscriptions ranged from $19.95 for three days to $79.99 for a single month to $29.99 per month based on an annual contract. As time goes on, these rates will likely drop. Also on the horizon is the concept that there will be shared services among Wi-Fi providers so that an annual subscription will offer more extensive coverage.

Wi-Fi Off the Boat: If the marina you've selected doesn't have a Wi-Fi system, check out the local coffee houses, libraries and hotels. A search on www.wi-fihotspotlist.com or www.wififreespot.com will tell you where the hot-spots are and the charges. Libraries are almost always free but have a firm limit on time. T-Mobile and AirPark are two of the biggest Hot-Spot providers to hotels, coffee shops (Starbucks), airports, libraries, etc. Boingo is a huge accumulator of Hot-Spots but doesn't actually install them.

Designated Clean Marina Program

Coastal areas host over 50% of the U.S. population squeezed into a mere 17% of its land mass — a situation rife with obvious environmental challenges, particularly to waterfront facilities. The National Coastal Management Program is a federal-state partnership dedicated to comprehensive management of the nation's coastal resources and, at the federal level, operates under the aegis of the NOAA's Coastal Programs Division. One of its major initiatives is the **Designated Clean Marina Program** which is interpreted and managed at the state level.

Keeping the waters in which we cruise clean, healthy and safe has become a significant priority for the states that border the Chesapeake Bay. In signing the Chesapeake 2000 Agreement, the Governors of Pennsylvania, Maryland, and Virginia; the Administrator of EPA; the Mayor of the District of Columbia; and the Chairman of the Chesapeake Bay Commission committed to removing the Bay from the EPA's "dirty waters" list by 2010. In each state, **Designated Clean Marinas** have been one way to fulfill that commitment. The maintenance, operation and storage of recreational vessels have the potential to pollute adjacent waters, impair air quality and lead to general environmental degradation. Contaminants include dust from hull scraping, solvents from engine repairs, petroleum from careless fueling, boat sewage discharge, and heavy metals from anti-fouling paints.

Maryland, Delaware and Virginia have each created its own version of a voluntary **Designated Clean Marina** program and developed "best practices" guidelines that it publishes in its "Clean Marina Guidebooks." The aim of these programs is to prevent pollution rather than to clean it up, and its linchpin is the Clean Marina Designation which marinas can earn by meeting stringent criteria and adhering to procedures that protect the environment. When a marina decides to participate in the program, it is provided assistance in complying with environmental laws and also becomes eligible for financial aid in the form of Incentive Grants. Marina owners and employees attend workshops to learn ecologically sound marina management. Educational materials are made available both to the marina's personnel and to its clientele. After performing a self-evaluation, the facility adopts simple, innovative approaches to those of their day-to-day operations which affect the environment. Areas covered include:

- site issues for new or expanding marinas
- vessel maintenance and repair
- marina management
- marina design and maintenance
- petroleum control
- laws and regulations
- storm water management
- sewage handling & waste containment
- boater education

After a successful review by a team of the home state's Clean Marina assessors, the facility is granted a Clean Marina Designation by the DEP and is awarded a state-specific flag that can be hoisted at the marina to advertise its accomplishments and status. When you see that flag (or read **"Designated Clean Marina"** or **DCM** in a guide such as this), you know that you're dealing with a marina which has gone the extra mile to keep fuel, sewage and hazardous chemicals out of the waters in which you cruise, fish and swim. Each marina in the Atlantic Cruising Club's Guide to Chesapeake Bay Marinas that has met this rigid standard is recognized in Marina Notes with a **DCM** notation. And, on the list on the following pages, each **Designated Clean Marina** is annotated with the local state Clean Marina symbol. We urge you to support the **DCM** facilities and their personnel who have worked so hard to ensure that they "do no harm." In fact, a number of marinas that ACC covers, York River Yacht Haven for one, have far exceeded the program requirements by instituting programs that actually improve the water quality around their facilities!

The Clean Vessel Program

Another program aimed at protecting U.S. waters, including the Chesapeake and its densely populated coastline, is the Clean Vessel Act Grant Program. Since October 1994, boaters have been prohibited from discharging raw sewage into fresh water or within coastal salt-water limits or 3 nautical miles off the Atlantic Ocean coast. The entire Bay is covered by the Clean Vessel Act. Additional No Discharge Areas have been designated, such as very fragile and sensitive regions like Herring Bay, where it is now illegal to dump even treated sewage. The Clean Vessel Grant Program provides reimbursement to a marina that installs pump-out facilities. The funds can support equipment purchases, operation and maintenance which, in turn, keep the waterways clean by reducing or eliminating discharge of black and gray water into the Chesapeake's waters. The Chesapeake Bay Watershed Partnership 2000 Agreement calls for a 50% increase in pump-out facilities by 2010.

Properly disposing of human sewage from boats is one measure that can make a big difference in the coastal environment, because sewage microorganisms have a threefold impact: they can be visually distasteful, they present a health hazard, and they lower oxygen levels necessary for aquatic life in water. Although aesthetic revulsion is the most visible of the three effects, it is the least important ecologically — the absence of floating waste does not mean that the surrounding waters are safe. Although invisible, microorganisms contained in human sewage, including E.Coli bacteria, can cause infectious hepatitis, diarrhea, bacillary dysentery, skin rashes and even typhoid and cholera. (Note that although onboard treatment facilities can reduce bacteria, they do nothing to control nutrients.) Oxygen depletion poses a serious threat to plant and animal sea life. In both air and water environments, the oxygen produced by plants is offset by the oxygen consumed by animals, and the reverse is true of carbon dioxide. The marine ecosystem goes out of balance as soon as an external source of oxygen demand is added, such as direct discharge of human waste.

Consider taking a more active role in the stewardship of the waters you ply. Install and use holding tanks, and look at other ways to keep your boat "green" and healthy: minimize oil discharge from the bilge, take care during oil changes and fueling, keep boat maintenance projects away from the water, rethink how you use and treat anti-fouling bottom paint, dispose of all wastes — hazardous and household — at designated shoreside recycling and trash centers, and consider pumping out gray water discharge as well as black. Guidelines and "Best Practices" pamphlets are available from many Designated Clean Marina facilities, county extension offices, www.AtlanticCruisingClub.com and Save the Bay.

Pump-Out Facilities and Designated Clean Marinas

LOCATION	MARINAS WITH PUMP-OUT FACILITIES	CLEAN MARINAS
DELAWARE		
Bear	Summit North Marina	
Delaware City	Delaware City Marina	
Lewes	City of Lewes Docks	
Rehoboth Beach	Indian River Inlet Marina	✓
MARYLAND		
Annapolis	Annapolis City Docks	
	Annapolis City Marina	
	Annapolis Landing Marina	
	Bert Jabin's Yacht Yard	✓
	Chesapeake Harbour Marina	✓
	Horn Point Harbor Marina	
	Mears Marina — Annapolis	✓
	Port Annapolis Marina	
	The Yacht Basin	✓
Baltimore	Anchorage Marina	✓
	Baltimore Marine Center	
	Harborview Marina	
	Hendersons Wharf Marina	
	Inner Harbor East Marina	
	Inner Harbor Marine Center	
	Porter's Seneca Marina	✓
	River Watch Marina Inc.	
Berlin	Ocean Pines Marina	✓
Cambridge	Cambridge Muni. Yacht Basin	
	Generation III Marina	
	Hyatt Regency River Marsh	
	Yacht Maintenance Co.	
Charlestown	Charlestown Marina	
	Lee's Marina	
Chesapeake Beach	Rod & Reel Docks	
	Fishing Creek Landings Marina	
Chesapeake City	Bohemia Bay Yacht Harbour	
	Bohemia Vista Yacht Basin	
	Chesapeake Inn & Marina	
	Schaefer's Marina	
	Two Rivers Yacht Basin	
Chester	Castle Harbor Marina	✓
	Island View Marina	
	Piney Narrows Yacht Haven	✓
	Skipjack Landing Marine Center	✓
Chestertown	Mears Great Oak Landing	✓
	Rolph's Wharf Marina	
	Tolchester Marina, Inc.	
	Worton Creek Marina	✓
Church Creek	Gootees Marine	
Church Hill	Kennersley Point Marina	
Cobb Island	Capt. John's Crabhouse	
	Pirate's Den Marina	
	Shymansky's River Restaurant	
Coltons Point	Coltons Point Marina	✓
Crisfield	Seamark Marine	
	Somers Cove Marina	✓
Deale	Rockhold Creek Marina	✓
	Shipwright Harbor Marina	✓
Dowell	Calvert Marina	
Drayden	Dennis Point Marina	
Dundalk	Anchor Bay East Marina	✓
Easton	Easton Point Marina	
Edgewater	Holiday Point Marina	
	Liberty Yacht Club & Marina	
	Oak Grove Marine Center	✓
	Pier 7 Marina	
	Selby Bay Yacht Basin	✓
	Turkey Point Marina	
Elkton	Cove Marina	
	Taylor's Island Marina	✓
	Triton Marina	
Essex	Essex Yacht Harbor	
	Norman Creek Marina	
Ewell	Smith Island Marina	
Fort Washington	Fort Washington Marina	✓
Friendship	Herrington Harbour South	✓
Galesville	Hartge Yacht Yard	✓
	Pirates Cove Mairna	
	West River Fuel Dock	
Georgetown	Duffy Creek Marina	✓
	Georgetwon Yacht Basin	
	Sailing Associates	
	Sassafras Harbor Marina	
	Skipjack Cove Yachting Resort	✓
Glen Burnie	Maurgale Marina	
Grasonville	Lippincott Marine	✓
	Mears Point Marina	✓
Havre de Grace	Havre de Grace City Yacht Basin	
	Havre de Grace Marina	
	Tidewater Marina	✓
Joppa	Gunpowder Cove Marina	
Lusb	Vera's White Sands Marina	
Middle River	Bowley's Marina	✓
	Long Beach Marine	
Newburg	Aqua-land Marina	
North East	Jackson Marine	
	McDaniel Yacht Basin Inc.	
	Bay Boat Works	✓
Ocean City	Bahia Marina	✓
	Harbor Island Marina	
	Ocean City Fishing Center	✓
	Sunset Harbour Marina	✓
Oxford	Campbell's Bachelor Pt.	✓
	Campbell's Boatyard at Jack's Pt.	
	Hinckley Yacht Services	✓
	Mears Yacht Haven	✓
	Oxford Boatyard	
Pasadena	Fairview Marina	✓
	Maryland Yacht Club	✓
	Oak Harbor Marina	✓
	Pleasure Cove Marina	
Perryville	Perryville Yacht Club	
Pocomoke City	Riverwalk Landing	
Ridge	Drury's Marina	
	Point Lookout Marina	✓
Rock Hall	Haven Harbour Marina	✓
	Lankford Bay Marina	
	Long Cove Marina	
	North Point Marina	

Pump-Out Facilities and Designated Clean Marinas, continued

LOCATION	MARINAS WITH PUMP-OUT FACILITIES	CLEAN MARINAS
Rock Hall, con't.	Osprey Point Marina	✓
	Rock Hall Landing Marina	
	Swan Creek Marina	
	The Sailing Emporium	✓
Salisbury	Port of Salisbury Marina	
Severna Park	Magothy Marina	✓
Sherwood	Lowes Wharf Marina	
Solomons	Beacon Marina	
	Harbor Island	
	Hospitality Harbor Marina	
	Solomon's Yachting Center	
	Spring Cove Marina	✓
	Zahniser's Yachting Center	✓
St. Leonard	Flag Harbor Yacht Haven	✓
St. Michaels	Chesapeake Bay Museum	
	Higgins Yacht Yard	
	St. Michaels Harbour Inn & Marina	
	St. Michaels Marina	✓
Stevensville	Bay Bridge Marina	✓
	Kentmorr Harbour Marine	
	Queen Anne Marina	
Tilghman	Harrison's Chesapeake House	
	Knapps Narrows Marina	✓
	Tilghman Island Inn	
	Tilghman Island Marina	
	Tilghman on Chesapeake	
Tracey's Landing	Herrington Harbour North Marina	✓
Trappe	Gateway Marina	✓
Welcome	Goose Bay Marina	
Westover	Goose Creek Marina	
Worton	Green Point Landing	
	The Wharf at Handy's Point	✓
VIRGINIA		
Alexandria	Washington Sailing Marina	
Belle Haven	Davis Wharf Marina	
Burgess	Great Wicomico Marina	
	Tiffany Yachts	
Callao	Olverson's Marina	
Cape Charles	Bay Creek Marina & Resort	
	Cape Charles Town Harbor	
Chincoteague	Chincoteague's Rob't Reed Park	
Coles Point	Coles Point Plantation	
Colonial Beach	Colonial Beach Yacht Center	
	Nightingale Marina & Motel	
Dahlgren	Dahlgren Marine Works	
Deltaville	Chesapeake Cove Marina	
	Deltaville Marina	
	Deltaville Yachting Center	✓
	Dozier's Regatta Point Y.C.	
	Fishing Bay Harbor Marina	✓
	Norton's Yacht Sales	
	Norview Marina	
	Ruark Marina	
Fort Monroe	Old Point Comfort Marina	✓
Gloucester Point	York River Yacht Haven	✓
Grimstead	Narrows Marina	

LOCATION	MARINAS WITH PUMP-OUT FACILITIES	CLEAN MARINAS
Hampton	Belle Isle Marina	
	Bluewater Yachting Center	✓
	Customs House marina	
	Downtown Hampton Public Piers	
	Salt Ponds Marina	✓
	Southall Landings	
	Sunset Boating Center	
Hayes	Severn River Marina	✓
	Crown Pointe Marina	
Heathsville	Ingram Bay Marina	
Irvington	Irvington Marina	
	The Tides Marinas	
Kilmarnock	Chesapeake Boat Basin	
Kinsale	Port Kinsale Marina	
	Kinsale Harbour Marina	
	White Point Marina	
Lancaster	Yankee Point Sailboat Marina	✓
Lottsburg	Coan River Marina	✓
	Lewisetta Marina	
	Olverson's Marina	
North	Mobjack Bay Marina	
Onancock	Onancock Wharf	
Poquoson	Poquoson Marina	
Port Haywood	Horn Harbor Marina	
Reedville	Buzzard Point Marina	
	Fairport Marina	
	Jennings Boat Yard	
	Reedville Marina	
Reedville	Smith Point Marina	✓
Seaford	Seaford Aqua Marina	
Smithfield	Smithfield Station	
Stafford	Aquia Bay Marina	
	Hope Springs Marina	
Topping	Locklies Marina	
	Regent Point Marina	
Williamsburg	Kingsmill Marina	
Urbanna	Burrell's Marine	
	Urbanna Town Marina	
	Urbanna Yachting Center	
Wachapreague	Captain Zed's	
White Stone	Windmill Pint Resort	
Williamsburg	Jamestown Yacht Basin	
Woodbridge	Belmont Bay Harbor	
	Hampton's Landing Marina	
	Occoquan Harbor Marina	
Yorktown	Dare Marina	
	Riverwalk Landing	
	Wormley Creek Marina	
DISTRICT OF COLUMBIA		
Washington	Capital Yacht Club	
	Gangplank Marina	
	James Creek Marina	
	Washington Marina	

Deciphering the Marine Industry Alphabets and Certifications

There are a number of trade organizations that assist the professional boating industry. They each serve a variety of purposes — some of greater interest to the boating services consumer than others. But knowledge is power, so we have listed the most prominent ones — preceded by the initials by which each is known.

In addition to the certifications provided by the manufacturers, there are several marine industry certifications. They are listed below as part of the description of their sponsoring organization. Facilities' memberships in these organizations, as well as the number of on-site employees which have been certified by each, is included under "Boatyard Services" in the Marina Reports — if ACC is aware of them. ABBRA and ABYC may be of most interest as these relate specifically to technicians who may work on your boat. It is quite possible that a facility may hold these, or other, certifications but did not, for a variety of reasons, relay that information to ACC. Exactly what is required to achieve each of these certifications is generally disclosed on the organization's website. In a number of cases, certification programs are offered jointly by two of these organizations. If such certifications are a deciding factor in choosing a marina or boatyard, it might be helpful to inquire.

- **ABBRA** is the American Boat Builders & Repairers Association located in Warren, Rhode Island — (401) 247-0318; www.abbra.org. ABBRA is a 250-member network of boatyards, repairers and associated industries that, among other functions, trains its members' management and employee craftsmen. It offers a series of Technician certificate programs (fiberglass, bottom paint, basic and advanced diesel repair) and management training programs.
- **ABYC** is the American Boat and Yacht Council in Edgewater, Maryland — (410) 956-1050; www.abycinc.org. ABYC develops the consensus safety standards for the design, construction, equipage, maintenance, and repair of small craft. It offers a variety of workshops, seminars and a Marine Technician Certification program.
- **IMI** is the International Marina Institute in Jupiter, Florida — (561) 741-0626; www.imimarina.org. IMI is a non-profit membership marine trade organization which offers management training, education and information about research, legislation and environmental issues affecting the marina industry. It offers a variety of workshops, training and certifications in marina management and equipment operations — particularly the Certified Marina Manager Program.
- **NMMA** is the National Marine Manufacturers' Association in Chicago, Illinois — (312) 946-6200; www.nmma.org. NMMA is the primary trade organization for producers of products used by recreational boaters. It devotes its resources to public policy advocacy, promoting boating as a lifestyle, enhancing the consumer experience, education and training, and building partnerships and strategic alliances. To serve the needs of its 1400 members, NMMA provides a variety of programs and services related to technical expertise (some include certification), standards monitoring, government relations avocation, and industry statistics. They also produce recreational boat shows in key North American markets and two trade shows, BoatBuilding and Marine Aftermarket Accessories. NMMA certifications that would be of most interest are the Yacht and Boat Certification Programs (based on ABYC guidelines) that help manufacturers comply with established standards and safety regulations. (To obtain a Yacht Certification, all components used must be on the NMMA "Type Accepted" list.)
- **MOAA** is the Marina Operators' Association of America in Washington, DC — (866) 367-6622; www.moaa.com. MOAA is the national trade association of the marina industry. It represents over 950 marinas, boatyards, yacht clubs, and public/private moorage basins across the United States. These companies provide slip space for over 240,000 recreational watercraft and employment for over 13,000 marine tradesmen and women. Suppliers of equipment and services to this industry complete MOAA's membership. Their mission is to provide critical legislative and regulatory support, serve as a communication base and to offer practical, money saving programs.
- **MITAs** are the Marine Industry Trade Associations, not-for-profit groups that represent the recreational boating and related marine industries in their particular states. Their collective mission is to promote the general welfare of the marine industry and advance the safe and proper use of boats, marine accessories, and facilities through means consistent with the public interest and welfare.
  - **MTAM — Marine Trades Association of Maryland:** Port Annapolis Marina; Annapolis, MD 21403
    Phone: (410) 269-0741, (301) 261-1021 • Fax: (410) 626-1940 • Email: director@mtam.org • www.mtam.org
  - **TMTA — Tidewater Marine Trade Association:** P.O. Box 566; Urbanna, VA 23175
    Phone: (800) 693-8682 • Email: info@tmtav.com • www.tmtav.com

Environmental Groups Dedicated to Improving the Bay

- **Alliance for the Chesapeake Bay** — www.acb-online.org
- **Chesapeake Bay Foundation** — www.cbf.org
- **Chesapeake Bay Trust** — www.chesapeakebaytrust.org
- **EPA's Region 3 – Mid-Atlantic** — www.epa.gov/region03
- **Bay Link** — www.baylink.org
- **Chesapeake Bay Program** — www.chesapeakebay.net
- **Chesapeake Bay Research Consortium** — www.chesapeake.org
- **NOAA Chesapeake Bay Program** — noaa.chesapeakebay.net
- **Interstate Commission on the Potomac River Basin** — www.potomacriver.org
- **Chesapeake Bay Environmental Effects Studies** — www.mdsg.umd.edu/CBEEC

Please go to www.AtlanticCruisingClub.com for links to all the marine associations and to the many environmental groups that are supporting and saving the Chesapeake Bay.

More than a bookstore...
...the world's leading marine navigational resource!

Worldwide Nautical Chart Agent
As the U.S. chart agent for hydrographic offices around the world, we offer the best selection of up-to-date charts for wherever your adventure takes you, from Fiji to Greece and back again.

Chart Plotter Cartridges Made Onsite...
...while you wait we can burn the latest chart cartridges for your **C-MAP, Navionics,** and **Garmin** chart plotters, in the store...in just a few minutes.

PC Software & Electronic Charts
The 21st century has changed the way we sail with the rise of electronic charts. Some are better than others for different parts of the world. We pride ourselves on being experts on the latest nautical software and electronic charts for **wherever** you cruise.

...and of course books!
We have nearly 35,000 titles available with the latest cruising guides, travel guides, flags, novels, government publications & more for you to browse. Visit our bigger, better Bluewater in our new Fort Lauderdale, Florida location. Can't make it to a store? Call or go online to www.BluewaterWeb.com.

Rhode Island
Armchair Sailor
543 Thames Street, Newport, Rhode Island
Toll Free Orders: 800-292-4278 | Tel: 401-847-4252

Florida [VISIT US AT OUR NEW LOCATION!]
Bluewater Books & Charts
1811 Cordova Road, Fort Lauderdale, Florida
Toll Free Orders: 800-942-2583 | Tel: 954-763-6533

help@bluewaterweb.com | www.BluewaterWeb.com

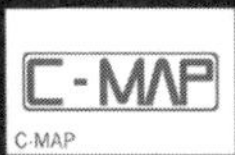

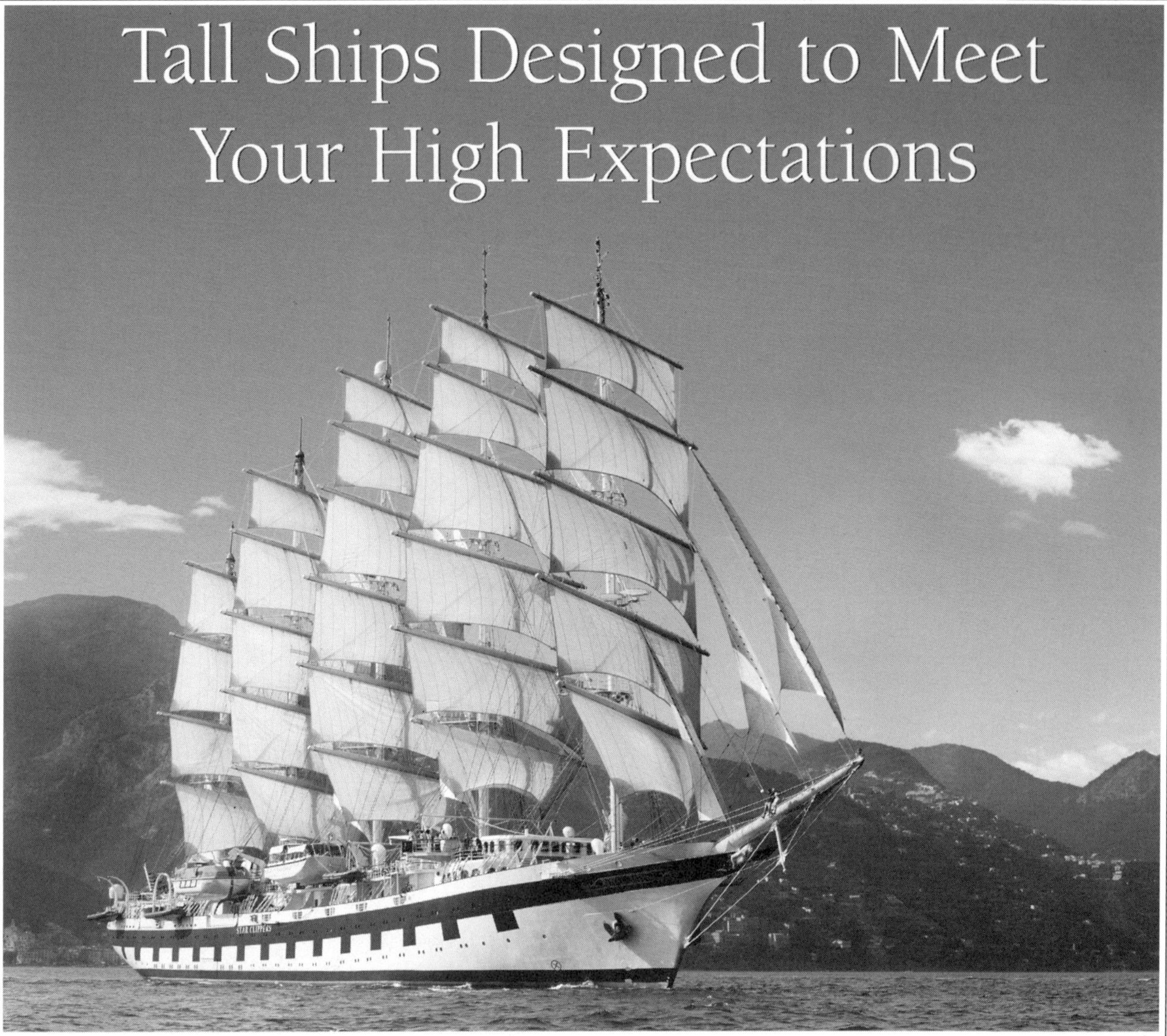

Save $8 on your order. Enter Code: ACCRNA. On Line Orders Only.

marinalife
Your Cruising Concierge
• Marina reservations
• Mega Yacht reservations
• Cruise planning assistance
• Discounts
• Maps/Charts
• The Fleet Captain
... and more
Simply visit www.marinalife.com or
call 1-800-RENT-A-SLIP (800-736-8275).

The Chesapeake Bay Foundation

Leaders in protecting a National Treasure

CBF needs your help to ***fight*** pollution and ***save*** the Bay for future generations.

Join Today.

Call 1-888-SAVEBAY—visit cbf.org.

CHESAPEAKE BAY FOUNDATION

Save the Bay

Supported by over 140,000 members, the Chesapeake Bay Foundation is dedicated to *saving the Bay* and its rivers and streams through education, restoration and protection.

Photo courtesy of David Owen Hawkhurst

Alphabetical Listing of Marinas, Harbors and Cities

The Data Gathering and Review Process

Collecting the data to create the Marina Reports is a multi-step process. A system of checks and balances keeps the information as accurate and as objective as possible. The intention is not to provide a promotional vehicle for marina and boatyard facilities — the intention is to provide a consumers' guide. Reasonable efforts have been made to confirm and corroborate the information. That does not mean that there won't be mistakes. The Marina Reports are a "snapshot in time" and things do change. It is also possible that, despite our best intentions, we just got it wrong. We hope that hasn't happened often, but a vehicle has been provided for you to tell us (and your fellow cruisers) if that is the case. Log-on to the ACC WebSite and add a Cruiser Note to the appropriate Marina Report (or send us an email). The data gathering and review process that ACC follows is outlined below:

- **Questionnaire:** A new marina, which has not been reviewed in an earlier edition, will be asked to fill out a very detailed four-page questionnaire — either before or after ACC's initial site visit and survey. The information provided is entered into ACC's proprietary database.

- **Site Visits:** Every facility included in the *Guide* is personally visited at least once (but, more likely, two to four times) by an ACC Reviewer who tours the marina or boatyard, walks the docks, pokes about the sheds, checks out the heads, showers and laundry, inspects the lounges, pool, beach, restaurants and hotel, and interviews the manager and/or dockmaster. The reviewer also takes photographs — one of which is included in each Marina Report in the Book and up to 16 more in full-color on the CD-ROM and also on the continually updated website. The information that has been provided by the marinas is reviewed, confirmed, corrected and/or supplemented. If the reviewers arrive by boat, their affiliation with the Atlantic Cruising Club is not disclosed until the end of their stay. If they arrive by car, they introduce themselves before touring the facility. Over time, marina managers and dockmasters have come to appreciate that ACC's goal is to provide objective, boater-biased in-depth reviews rather than "marina ads." Toward that end, ACC writers/editors have visited more than 2500 facilities ... at least once — in the most cases, several times.

- **Data Confirmation Report:** After the completion of the Questionnaire and the Site Visit, each facility receives a Data Confirmation Report (DCR) that includes all the information in our database for that facility — up to 300 data points — with a request for updates and corrections. If there are significant changes, a new visit is scheduled as early as is practical.

- **Independent Research:** Information that is included in the final Marina Report is derived from many sources. In addition to the Site Visit, the Questionnaire and the DCR, independent data is also collected. Local tourist offices, chambers of commerce and websites are surveyed and interviewed. Independent researchers are assigned to gather specific data for the "Mid Section" — the "what is where" material. Forty categories have been selected as the most important for cruisers; independent researchers seek out names, phone numbers, rates and distances (from the marinas) for each of these. This data is used to supplement and/or corroborate the information from all the other sources.

- **The Photographs:** About 98% of the photographs in the book and on the CD-ROM have been taken by ACC Reviewers at the time of their site visits (in some cases the photographs will be from more than one visit). In a few cases, marinas have contributed aerial shots which provide a very useful overview. The photographs are not travel or tourism photos or even photojournalistic images. They are "location shots" or "snapshots." The intention is to show you what is there — as accurately as possible. The old saw "a picture is worth a thousand words" certainly applies here. We shoot what you would have seen had you arrived at the same time we did. The quality varies — the weather was not always perfect — but the sense of the place is usually correct.

  We try to provide enough visual information so that you can both make an informed decision and recognize the place when you arrive. There's always a shot of the landside facility, of the view from the docks, and a close-up of a dock to show the quality of the slips and pedestals. And, finally, there are shots of the primary recreation facilities and restaurant, if they exist.

- **The Review and the Ratings:** As noted earlier, the ACC reviewers assign a three-part rating to each facility — A Bell Rating, a Boatyard Rating and a Sunset Rating. Then the Reviewers take all the material that has been gathered, including some subjective impressions, and write the bottom section's three-part Marina Review — "Setting," "Marina Notes" and "Notable."

- **The Draft Marina Report:** All of this material has been input into ACC's proprietary program called Datastract™, developed by the Atlantic Cruising Club's parent company, Jerawyn Publishing Inc. (JPI). The data is captured via a custom-designed multi-table input program which then collates, formats and outputs it as the single-page Marina Report. Every piece of data — including all the graphics and photographs — is placed in its precise position in the Marina Report by Datastract™. A Draft Report is sent to the marina facility for a final review for content accuracy before publication. Corrections are corroborated before the Marina Report is changed.

- **The Final Marina Report:** Datastract™ creates the final Marina Report, pulling all the corrected data and the photograph from the ACC database, and printing it to an Acrobat PDF file. Marina Reports are collated with the front and back ends and then sent to the printer. Datastract™ replaces traditional publishing software resulting in a product that is more accurate and more timely.

- **The CD-ROM and the WebSite:** A very user-friendly version of the marina database resides on the enclosed CD-ROM and also on the ACC WebSite. The Search Interface permits users to select up to 100 of the 300+ possible data points as search criteria for querying the database for suitable marinas. The search engine will return a list of the facilities that meet the requested criteria. A "double-click" on a marina name will generate a color two or three-page Marina Report — with up to 17 full-color photographs each. "Marina Reports" are created "on the fly" and can be viewed on the screen or printed out.

About the Authors

Richard and Beth have been "messing about in boats" at various times throughout their lives, individually and together, and for the last two decades have been "messing about" in "big boats." Coastal cruises have included numerous trips up and down the eastern seaboard, including the ICW, where they continue their efforts to perfect the art of "achievable cruising" — cruise for a week or two, leave the boat, go home, come back a month or two later and resume cruising. Other cruising adventures have taken them to Bermuda, the Bahamas, the Caribbean, the South Pacific and the Mediterranean. They have shared many of these experiences with three superb crew members — their now-grown children, Jason and Amanda, and their sea-dog, Molly. They are firm believers in "going" even if it means taking the office along. Technology has made that not only possible, but amazingly easy. They are also committed to wonderful food along the way — on board and ashore. Provisioning, they've discovered, may be the most entertaining and useful of all cruising skills (bested, perhaps, only by sail trim, engine mechanics and a clear understanding of navigation), and they seek out the best resources at every landfall. Along the way, they've also visited more than 2,000 marinas (most two, three or more times) on the east and west coasts as both cruisers and authors.

ELIZABETH ADAMS SMITH

Beth is editor-in-chief of Jerawyn Publishing Inc. and one of the primary writer/photographers of the Atlantic Cruising Club's Guides to Marinas — Books, CD-ROMs and Website. She is also a new media producer and has spearheaded the design and co-managed the development of Jerawyn's proprietary Datastract™ publishing technology and works with the programming team to continually enhance the quality of the user/boaters' print and online experiences.

In addition to nurturing the growth of the ACC Guides, Beth is incubating the Water Lovers imprint (land-based travel guides for people with a passion for the water), the Healthy Boat series (holistic approaches to crew lifestyle and vessel management), and The Art & Science of Achievable Cruising. As the "Wandering Mariner," she writes articles on cruising, destinations and waterborne and water-oriented travel. In addition, Beth has produced numerous documentaries and multiple media projects on holistic living, ecology, peacemaking, and food and health (including the award-winning "Children of War," the Mellon-funded "Students at Work," and "EarthFriends"). She developed the first and largest full-text and image database on complementary medicine, "Alt-HealthWatch," and is a consultant to firms focused on healthy living and integrative medicine.

Beth received a doctorate from Columbia University in Educational Technology and New Media, masters degrees in both Health Education (with a Nutrition focus) and Ed Tech from Columbia, and a B.S. in Broadcast Journalism from Boston University. She is a Certified Health Education Specialist, Reiki master, and a graduate of James Gordon's Advanced Mind-Body Professional Training Program. She is past president of the Board of Trustees, and currently Honorary Trustee, of Wainwright House, a U.N. NGO and spiritual and holistic educational institution. She is also a member of Boating Writers International and the Society of American Travel Writers.

RICHARD Y. SMITH

Richard is publisher of Jerawyn Publishing Inc. and president of Evergreen Capital Partners Inc. Jerawyn Publishing is an umbrella company for the Atlantic Cruising Club and other publishing imprints. In addition to marinas, JPI focuses on coastal lifestyles, maritime-oriented travel and holistic living. JPI's activities involve data collection and publication using Datastract™, a unique proprietary data input and publishing program, which Richard co-developed, that permits the creation, maintenance, and direct publication — in print, on CD & DVD-ROM and on the web — of extensive databases of both factual and editorial information — including a library of over 20,000 nautical images.

Evergreen Capital Partners Inc. undertakes merchant banking and private capital transactions both as an advisor and as a principal. Prior to establishing Evergreen Capital in 1993, Richard was a managing director of Chemical Bank (now JP Morgan Chase) and a senior vice president of Rothschild Inc., with responsibility for a broad range of investment banking and merchant banking activities.

Richard received a B. A. degree from Wesleyan University and an M.B.A. from Harvard Business School. He has also been awarded the Chartered Financial Analyst (CFA) designation. When not reviewing marinas, editing books, attempting to close private equity deals, or out sailing, Richard has been active in a number of not-for-profit activities including service as former Chair of the Rye Arts Center, Inc., past chair of the Wesleyan (University) Annual Fund, former Fleet Captain and current trustee of the American Yacht Club, and, perhaps most important, as the bass player in the venerable 60's rock 'n' roll band, "Gary and the Wombats."

Beth and Richard can be reached directly at:
Beth@AtlanticCrusingClub.com
Richard@AtlanticCrusingClub.com

www.AtlanticCrusingClub.com

Order Form

Please ask for the *Guides* at your local book store or chandlery or order directly.

☐ **Please register me as a member of the Atlantic Cruising Club so that I can benefit from even greater discounts and email specials.**

☐ **Please send me the following *Atlantic Cruising Club's Guides to Marinas — as soon as each is available.***

***Quantity Discounts Available** *(Titles may be mixed for maximum discount; Contact ACC for larger quantities)*
For orders of 2 books or more, deduct 10% — 4 books or more, deduct 17% — 6 books or more, deduct 25%.

_____ ***Atlantic Cruising Club's Guide to New England Marinas****; US $24.95* (CN $34.95*)*
Bar Harbor, ME to Block Island, RI *(Including Buzzards Bay, Narragansett Bay, Martha's Vineyard and Nantucket)*

_____ ***Atlantic Cruising Club's Guide to Long Island Sound Marinas****; US $24.95* (CN $34.95*)*
Block Island, RI to Cape May, NJ *(Including Connecticut River, New York Harbor and New Jersey Shore)*

_____ ***Atlantic Cruising Club's Guide to Florida's East Coast Marinas****; US $29.95* (CN $36.95*)*
Fernandina, FL to Key West, FL *(Including St. John's River, St. Lucie River and the Florida Keys)*

_____ ***Atlantic Cruising Club's Guide to Chesapeake Bay Marinas****; US $32.95* (CN $40.95*)*
C&D Canal to Hampton Roads *(Including Delmarva Atlantic Coast, Potomac, Rappahannock, Patapsco and James Rivers)*

_____ ***Atlantic Cruising Club's Guide to Pacific Northwest Marinas****; US $29.95* (CN $36.95*)*
Campbell River, BC to Brookings, OR *(Including the San Juan Islands, Puget Sound, Sunshine Coast and Strait of Juan de Fuca)*

_____ ***Atlantic Cruising Club's Guide to Mid-Atlantic & ICW Marinas*** *(late 2006); US $29.95* (CN $36.95*)*
Hampton Roads, VA to St. Mary's, GA *(Including the Virginia Coast, the ICW and the North Carolina Sounds)*

_____ ***Atlantic Cruising Club's Guide to Florida's West Coast Marinas*** *(late 2006); US $29.95* (CN $36.95*)*
Key Largo, FL to Pensacola, FL *(Including the Keys, Caloosahatchee River, Okeechobee Waterway and the Gulf Coast ICW)*

_____ ***Atlantic Cruising Club's Guide to Northern Gulf Coast Marinas*** *(2007); US $29.95* (CN $36.95*)*
Tarpon Springs, FL to Padre Island, TX *(Including Mobile Bay, the Tenn-Tom Waterway and the Gulf Coast ICW)*

__________ *Sub-Total*

__________ *Quantity Discount Percentage (see above)**

__________ *Tax (New York State Residents only add 6.75%)*

__________ *Shipping & Handling (USPS — add $4.00 for first book and $2.00 for each subsequent book)*

Final Total	*Note: Credit cards will not be charged until books are shipped.*

Please Charge the following Credit Card: Amex ☐ MasterCard ☐ Visa ☐ Discover ☐ Check Enclosed ☐

Number: __________ *Four-Digit Security Number:* __________

Expiration Date: __________ *Signature:* __________

Name: __________ *Email:* __________

Address: __________ *City:* __________ *State or Province:* __________ *Zip:* __________

Home Phone: __________ *Office Phone:* __________ *Fax:* __________

Boat Name: __________ *Length:* __________ *Manufacturer:* __________

Boat Type: Sail Mono-Hull ☐ Sail Multi-Hull ☐ Power ☐ Trawler ☐ Megayacht ☐

Home Port: __________ *Cruising Grounds:* __________

Please mail, fax. email, or call-in your order to: **Atlantic Cruising Club at Jerawyn Publishing, Inc.** PO Box 978; Rye, New York 10580
Tel: (914) 967-0994 or (888) 967-0994; Fax: (914) 967-5504; Email: Orders@AtlanticCruisingClub.com